THE YEAR'S WORK 1995

The Year's Work in English Studies 76

Edited by
PETER J. KITSON

and
MACDONALD DALY
MÁIRE NÍ FHLATHÚIN
ANGELA KEANE
LIONEL KELLY
R.E. PRITCHARD
ELAINE M. TREHARNE
(associate editors)

Published for
THE ENGLISH ASSOCIATION

© The English Association 1998
First published 1998

2   4   6   8   10   9   7   5   3   1

Blackwell Publishers Ltd
108 Cowley Road
Oxford OX4 1JF
UK

Blackwell Publishers Inc.
350 Main Street
Malden, Massachusetts 02148
USA

British Library Cataloguing in Publication Data

A CIP catalogue record for this book is available from the
British Library

ISBN 0–631–20897–6 (hbk.)

Typeset 9 on 10pt Times
by York House Typographic
Printed in Great Britain by
MPG Books Ltd, Bodmin, Cornwall

This book is printed on acid-free paper

Preface

The Year's Work in English Studies is a narrative bibliography that records and evaluates scholarly writing on English language and on literature written in English. It is published by Blackwell Publishers on behalf of the English Association.

The Editor and the English Association are pleased to announce that this year's Beatrice White Prize has been awarded to Christopher Baswell for his book *Virgil in Medieval England: Figuring The Aeneid From the Twelfth Century to Chaucer* published by Cambridge University Press in their series Cambridge Studies in Medieval Literature (ISBN 0 521 46294 0).

The authors of *YWES* attempt to cover all significant contributions to English studies. Writers of articles can assist this process by sending offprints to the journal, and editors of journals that are not readily available in the UK are urged to join the many who send us complete sets. These should be addressed to The Editor, *YWES*, The English Association, The University of Leicester, University Road, Leicester LE1 7RH.

Our coverage of articles and books is greatly assisted by the Modern Language Association of America, who supply proofs of their annual *International Bibliography* in advance of publication. We should like to record our gratitude for their generous co-operation.

The views expressed in *YWES* are those of its individual contributors and are not necessarily shared by the Editor, Associate Editors, or the English Association.

The Editor

The English Association

This bibliography is an English Association publication. It is available through membership of the Association; non-members can purchase it through any good bookshop.

The object of the English Association is to promote the knowledge and appreciation of the English language and its literatures.

The Association pursues these aims by creating opportunities of co-operation among all those interested in English; by furthering the recognition of English as essential in education; by discussing methods of English teaching; by holding lectures, conferences, and other meetings; by publishing a journal, books, and leaflets; and by forming local branches overseas and at home.

Publications

The Year's Work in English Studies. An annual evaluative bibliography. Published by Blackwell Publishers, Oxford and Malden, MA.

The Year's Work in Critical and Cultural Theory. The first issue of this new critical theory volume appeared in 1994. Published by Blackwell Publishers, Oxford and Malden, MA.

Essays and Studies. An annual volume of essays by various scholars assembled by the collector covering usually a wide range of subjects and authors from the medieval to the modern. Published by Boydell and Brewer, Woodbridge, Suffolk.

English. The journal of the Association, *English*, is published three times a year by the English Association.

Use of English. This journal is published three times a year by the English Association.

English 4–11. This journal is published three times a year.

Benefits of Membership

Institutional Membership

Full members receive copies of *The Year's Work in English Studies, Essays and Studies, English* (three issues), and three *News-Letters*.

Ordinary Membership covers *English* (three issues) and three *News-Letters*.

Schools Membership covers one copy of each issue of *English*, one copy of *The Use of English*, one copy of *Essays and Studies*, three *News-Letters*, and preferential booking for Sixth Form Conference places.

Individual Membership

Individuals take out basic membership, which entitles them to buy all regular publications of the English Association at a discounted price and three *News-Letters*.

For further details write to The Secretary, The English Association, The University of Leicester, University Road, Leicester LE1 7RH.

Contents

Abbreviations

1. Journals, Series, and Reference Works

1650–1850	*1650–1850: Ideas, Aesthetics, and Inquiries in the Early Modern Era*
A&D	*Art and Design*
A&E	*Anglistik und Englishunterricht*
AAR	*African American Review*
ABäG	*Amsterdamer Beiträge zur Älteren Germanistik*
ABC	*American Book Collector*
ABELL	*Annual Bibliography of English Language and Literature*
ABM	*Antiquarian Book Monthly Review*
ABQ	*American Baptist Quarterly*
ABR	*American Benedictine Review*
ABSt	*A/B: Auto/Biography Studies*
AC	*Archeologia Classica*
Academy Forum	*Academy Forum*
ACar	Analecta Cartusiana
ACH	*Australian Cultural History*
ACLALSB	*ACLALS Bulletin*
ACM	*The Aligarh Critical Miscellany*
ACS	*Australian-Canadian Studies: A Journal for the Humanities and Social Sciences*
Acta	Acta (Binghamton, N.Y.)
ADS	*Australasian Drama Studies*
AEB	*Analytical and Enumerative Bibliography*
Æstel	*Æstel*
AF	Anglistische Forschungen
AfricanA	*African Affairs*
AfrSR	*The African Studies Review*
AgeJ	*The Age of Johnson: A Scholarly Annual*
Agenda	*Agenda*
Agni	*Agni Review*
AH	*Art History*
AHR	*The American Historical Review*
AHS	*Australian Historical Studies*
AI	*American Imago*
AJ	*Art Journal*
AJL	*Australian Journal of Linguistics*
AJS	*American Journal of Semiotics*
AKML	Abhandlungen zur Kunst-, Musik- and Literaturwissenschaft

AL	*American Literature*
ALA	African Literature Association Annuals
ALASH	*Acta Linguistica Academiae Scientiarum Hungaricae*
AlexS	Alexander Shakespeare
ALH	*Acta Linguistica Hafniensia: International Journal of Linguistics*
ALitASH	*Acta Litteraria Academiae Scientiarum Hungaricae*
ALLCJ	*Association for Literary and Linguistic Computing Journal*
Allegorica	*Allegorica*
ALR	*American Literary Realism, 1870–1910*
ALS	*Australian Literary Studies*
ALT	*African Literature Today*
Alternatives	*Alternatives*
AmDram	*American Drama*
AmerP	*American Poetry*
AmerS	*American Studies*
AmLH	*American Literary History*
AmLS	*American Literary Scholarship: An Annual*
AMon	*The Atlantic Monthly*
AmRev	*The Americas Review: A Review of Hispanic Literature and Art of the USA*
Amst	*Amerikastudien/American Studies*
AmStScan	*American Studies in Scandinavia*
AN	*Acta Neophilologica*
Anais	*Anais*
AnBol	*Analecta Bollandiana*
ANF	*Arkiv för Nordisk Filologi*
Anglia	*Anglia: Zeitschrift für Englische Philologie*
Anglistica	*Anglistica*
AnH	*Analecta Husserliana*
AnL	*Anthropological Linguistics*
AnM	*Annuale Mediaevale*
Ann	*Annales: Economies, Sociétés, Civilisations*
ANQ	*ANQ: A Quarterly Journal of Short Articles, Notes, and Reviews* (formerly *American Notes and Queries*)
A-NSt	*Anglo-Norman Studies*
AntColl	*The Antique Collector*
AntigR	*Antigonish Review*
Antipodes	*Antipodes*
ANZSC	*Australian and New Zealand Studies in Canada*
ANZTR	*Australian and New Zealand Theatre Record*
APBR	*Atlantic Provinces Book Review*
APL	*Antwerp Papers in Linguistics*
AppLing	*Applied Linguistics*
APR	*The American Poetry Review*
AQ	*American Quarterly*
Aquarius	*Aquarius*
AR	*The Antioch Review*
ArAA	*Arbeiten aus Anglistik und Amerikanistik*

Arcadia	*Arcadia*
Archiv	*Archiv für das Studium der Neueren Sprachen und Literaturen*
ARCS	*The American Review of Canadian Studies*
ArdenS	Arden Shakespeare
ArielE	*Ariel: A Review of International English Literature*
ArkQ	*Arkansas Quarterly: A Journal of Criticism*
ArkR	*Arkansas Review: A Journal of Criticism*
ArQ	*Arizona Quarterly*
ARS	Augustan Reprint Society
ArtB	*Art Bulletin*
ArthI	*Arthurian Interpretations*
ArthL	*Arthurian Literature*
AS	*American Speech*
ASch	*The American Scholar*
ASE	*Anglo-Saxon England*
ASInt	*American Studies International*
ASoc	*Arts in Society*
Aspects	*Aspects: Journal of the Language Society of the University of Essex*
AspectsAF	*Aspects of Australian Fiction*
ASPR	*Anglo-Saxon Poetic Records*
ASSAH	*Anglo-Saxon Studies in Archaeology and History*
Assaph	*Assaph: Studies in the Arts (Theatre Studies)*
Assays	*Assays: Critical Approaches to Medieval and Renaissance Texts*
ASUI	*Analele Stiintifice ale Universitatii 'Al.I. Cuza' din Iasi (Serie Noua), e. Lingvistica*
ATQ	*American Transcendental Quarterly: A Journal of New England Writers*
AuBR	*Australian Book Review*
AuFolk	*Australian Folklore*
AuFS	*Australian Feminist Studies*
AuJL	*Australian Journal of Linguistics*
AUMLA	*Journal of the Australasian Universities Language and Literature Association*
AuS	*Australian Studies*
AuSA	*Australian Studies (Australia)*
AusCan	*Australian-Canadian Studies*
AusPl	Australian Playwrights
AuWBR	*Australian Women's Book Review*
AvC	*Avalon to Camelot*
AY	*Arthurian Yearbook*
BakhtinN	*Bakhtin Newsletter*
BALF	*Black American Literature Forum*
BARS Bulletin & Review	(British Association for Romantic Studies) *Bulletin & Review*
BASAM	*BASA Magazine*
BathH	*Bath History*
BB	*Bulletin of Bibliography*

BBCS	*The Bulletin of the Board of Celtic Studies*
BBCSh	BBC Shakespeare
BBN	*British Book News*
BBSIA	*Bulletin Bibliographique de la Société Internationale Arthurienne*
BC	*The Book Collector*
BCan	*Books in Canada*
BCMA	*Bulletin of Cleveland Museum of Art*
BCS	*B. C. Studies*
BDEC	*Bulletin of the Department of English (Calcutta)*
BDP	Beiträge zur Deutschen Philologie
Belfagor	*Belfagor: Rassegna di Varia Umanità*
BEPIF	*Bulletin des Études Portugaises et Brésiliennes*
BFLS	*Bulletin de la Faculté des Lettres de Strasbourg*
BGDSL	*Beiträge zur Geschichte der Deutschen Sprache und Literatur*
BHI	*British Humanities Index*
BHL	*Bibliotheca Hagiographica Latina Antiquae et Mediae Aetatis*
BHR	*Bibliothèque d'Humanisme et Renaissance*
BHS	*Bulletin of Hispanic Studies*
BI	*Books at Iowa*
Bibliotheck	*The Bibliotheck: A Scottish Journal of Bibliography and Allied Topics*
Biography	*Biography: An Interdisciplinary Quarterly*
BIS	*Browning Institute Studies: An Annual of Victorian Literary and Cultural History*
BJA	*British Journal of Aesthetics*
BJCS	*British Journal of Canadian Studies*
BJDC	*The British Journal of Disorders of Communication*
BJECS	*British Journal for Eighteenth-Century Studies*
BJHP	*British Journal for the History of Philosophy*
BJHS	*The British Journal for the History of Science*
BJJ	*Ben Jonson Journal*
BJL	*Belgian Journal of Linguistics*
BJPS	*The British Journal for the Philosophy of Science*
BJRL	*Bulletin of the John Rylands University Library of Manchester*
BJS	*British Journal of Sociology*
Blake	*Blake: An Illustrated Quarterly*
BLE	*Bulletin de Littérature Ecclésiastique*
BLJ	*The British Library Journal*
BLR	*The Bodleian Library Record*
BN	*Beiträge zur Namenforschung*
BNB	*British National Bibliography*
Boundary	*Boundary 2: A Journal of Postmodern Literature and Culture*
BP	*Banasthali Patrika*
BPMA	*Bulletin* (Philadelphia Museum of Art)
BPN	*The Barbara Pym Newsletter*

BQ	*Baptist Quarterly*
BRASE	Basic Readings in Anglo-Saxon England
BRH	*Bulletin of Research in the Humanities*
Brick	*Brick: A Journal of Reviews*
BRMMLA	*Bulletin of the Rocky Mountain Modern Language Association*
BSANZB	The Bibliographical Society of Australia and New Zealand Bulletin
BSE	*Brno Studies in English*
BSEAA	*Bulletin de la Société d'Etudes Anglo-Américaines des XVIIᵉ et XVIIIᵉ Siècles*
BSJ	*The Baker Street Journal: An Irregular Quarterly of Sherlockiana*
BSLP	*Bulletin de la Société de Linguistique de Paris*
BSNotes	*Browning Society Notes*
BSRS	*Bulletin of the Society for Renaissance Studies*
BSSA	*Bulletin de la Société de Stylistique Anglaise*
BST	*Brontë Society Transactions*
BSUF	*Ball State University Forum*
BTHGNewsl	*Book Trade History Group Newsletter*
BTLV	*Bijdragen tot de Taal-, Land- en Volkenhunde*
BunyanS	*Bunyan Studies*
BuR	*Bucknell Review*
BurlM	*The Burlington Magazine*
BurnsC	*Burns Chronicle*
BWPLL	*Belfast Working Papers in Language and Linguistics*
BWVACET	*The Bulletin of the West Virginia Association of College English Teachers*
ByronJ	*The Byron Journal*
CABS	Contemporary Authors Bibliographical Series
CahiersE	*Cahiers Élisabéthains*
CAIEF	*Cahiers de l'Association Internationale des Études Françaises*
Caliban	*Caliban (Toulouse, France)*
Callaloo	*Callaloo*
CalR	*Calcutta Review*
CamObsc	*Camera Obscura: A Journal of Feminism and Film Theory*
CamR	*The Cambridge Review*
CanD	*Canadian Drama/L'Art Dramatique Canadienne*
C&L	*Christianity and Literature*
C&Lang	*Communication and Languages*
C&M	*Classica et Medievalia*
CanL	*Canadian Literature*
CAnn	*The Carlyle Annual*
CanPo	*Canadian Poetry*
CapR	*Capilano Review*
CARA	Centre Aixois de Recherches Anglaises
Carib	*Carib*
Caribana	*Caribana*

CarR	*Caribbean Review*
Carrell	*The Carrell: Journal of the Friends of the University of Miami Library*
CaudaP	*Cauda Pavonis*
CBAA	*Current Bibliography on African Affairs*
CBEL	*Cambridge Bibliography of English Literature*
CCRev	*Comparative Civilizations Review*
CCrit	*Comparative Criticism: An Annual Journal*
CCTES	*Conference of College Teachers of English Studies*
CCV	*Centro de Cultura Valenciana*
CD	The Critics Debate
CDALB	Concise Dictionary of American Literary Biography
CDCP	Comparative Drama Conference Papers
CDIL	*Cahiers de l'Institut de Linguistique de Louvain*
CdL	*Cahiers de Lexicologie*
CE	*College English*
CEA	*CEA Critic*
CEAfr	*Cahiers d'Études Africaines*
CE&S	*Commonwealth Essays and Studies*
CentR	*The Centennial Review*
Cervantes	*Cervantes*
CFM	*Canadian Fiction Magazine*
CFS	*Cahiers Ferdinand de Saussure: Revue de Linguistique Générale*
Chapman	*Chapman*
Chasqui	*Chasqui*
ChauR	*The Chaucer Review*
ChH	*Church History*
ChildL	*Children's Literature*
ChiR	*Chicago Review*
ChLB	*Charles Lamb Bulletin*
CHLSSF	*Commentationes Humanarum Litterarum Societatis Scientiarum Fennicae*
CHR	*Camden History Review*
CHum	*Computers and the Humanities*
CI	*Critical Idiom*
CILT	Amsterdam Studies in the Theory and History of the Language Sciences IV: Current Issues in Linguistic Theory
CISh	Contemporary Interpretations of Shakespeare
Cithara	*Cithara: Essays in the Judaeo-Christian Tradition*
CJ	*Classical Journal*
CJE	*Cambridge Journal of Education*
CJH	*Canadian Journal of History*
CJIS	*Canadian Journal of Irish Studies*
CJL	*The Canadian Journal of Linguistics*
CJR	*Christian Jewish Relations*
CL	*Comparative Literature* (Eugene, Oreg.)
CLAJ	*CLA Journal*
CLAQ	*Children's Literature Association Quarterly*

ClarkN	*The Clark Newsletter: Bulletin of the UCLA Center for Seventeenth- and Eighteenth-Century Studies*
CLC	*Columbia Library Columns*
ClioI	*Clio: A Journal of Literature, History, and the Philosophy of History*
CLQ	*Colby Library Quarterly*
CLS	*Comparative Literature Studies*
Clues	*Clues: A Journal of Detection*
CMat	*Critical Matrix: The Princeton Journal of Women, Gender and Culture*
CMCS	*Cambridge Medieval Celtic Studies*
CML	*Classical and Modern Literature*
CN	*Chaucer Newsletter*
CNew	*The Carlyle Newsletter*
CNIE	*Commonwealth Novel in English*
CogLing	*Cognitive Linguistics*
ColF	*Columbia Forum*
Collections	*Collections*
CollG	*Colloquia Germanica*
CollL	*College Literature*
Comitatus	*Comitatus: A Journal of Medieval and Renaissance Studies*
Commentary	*Commentary*
Commonwealth	[see *CE&S*]
Comparatist	*The Comparatist: Journal of the Southern Comparative Literature Association*
CompD	*Comparative Drama*
ConL	*Contemporary Literature*
CompLing	*Contemporary Linguistics*
Connotations	*Connotations*
ConnR	*Connecticut Review*
Conradian	*The Conradian*
Conradiana	*Conradiana: A Journal of Joseph Conrad Studies*
ContempR	*Contemporary Review*
Cosmos	*Cosmos*
CP	*Concerning Poetry*
CQ	*The Cambridge Quarterly*
CR	*The Critical Review*
CRCL	*Canadian Review of Comparative Literature*
CRev	*The Chesterton Review*
CRevAS	*Canadian Review of American Studies*
Crit	*Critique: Studies in Modern Fiction*
CritI	*Critical Inquiry*
Criticism	*Criticism: A Quarterly for Literature and the Arts*
Critique	*Critique (Paris)*
CritQ	*Critical Quarterly*
CritT	*Critical Texts: A Review of Theory and Criticism*
CrM	*Critical Mass*
CRNLE	*The CRNLE Reviews Journal*
CRUX	*CRUX: A Journal on the Teaching of English*

CS	*Critical Survey*
CSASE	Cambridge Studies in Anglo-Saxon England
CSCC	Case Studies in Contemporary Criticism
CSLBull	*Bulletin of the New York C. S. Lewis Society*
CSPC	Cambridge Studies in Paleography and Codicology
CSR	*Christian Scholar's Review*
CTR	*Canadian Theatre Review*
CulC	*Cultural Critique*
CulS	*Cultural Studies*
CUNY	*CUNY English Forum*
Current Writing	*Current Writing: Text and Reception in Southern Africa*
CV2	*Contemporary Verse 2*
CVE	*Cahiers Victoriens et Edouardiens*
CW	*Current Writing: Text and Perception in Southern Africa*
CWAAS	*Transactions of the Cumberland and Westmorland Antiquarian and Archaeological Society*
CWS	*Canadian Woman Studies*
Cycnos	*Cycnos, Centre de Recherche sur les Ecritures de Langue Anglaise*, Université de Nice
DA	*Dictionary of Americanisms*
DAE	*Dictionary of American English*
DAEM	*Deutsches Archiv für Eforschung des Mittelalters*
DAI	*Dissertation Abstracts International*
DAL	*Descriptive and Applied Linguistics*
D&CN&Q	*Devon and Cornwall Notes and Queries*
D&S	*Discourse and Society*
DanT	*Dancing Times*
Daphnis	*Daphnis: Zeitschrift für Mittlere Deutsche Literatur*
DC	The Dickens Companions
DerbyM	*Derbyshire Miscellany*
Descant	*Descant*
DHLR	*The D. H. Lawrence Review*
DHS	*Dix-Huitième Siècle*
Diac	*Diacritics*
Diachronica	*Diachronica*
Dialogue	*Dialogue: Canadian Philosophical Review*
Dickensian	*The Dickensian*
DicS	*Dickinson Studies*
Dictionaries	*Dictionaries: Journal of the Dictionary Society of North America*
Dionysos	*Dionysos*
Discourse	*Discourse*
DLB	*Dictionary of Literary Biography*
DLN	*Doris Lessing Newsletter*
DM	*The Dublin Magazine*
DMT	Durham Medieval Texts
DNB	*Dictionary of National Biography*
DOE	*Dictionary of Old English*
Dolphin	*The Dolphin: Publications of the English Department,*

	University of Aarhus
DOST	*Dictionary of the Older Scottish Tongue*
DownR	*The Downside Review*
DPr	*Discourse Processes*
DQ	*Denver Quarterly*
DQR	*Dutch Quarterly Review of Anglo-American Letters*
DQu	*Dickens Quarterly*
DR	*Dalhousie Review*
Drama	*Drama: The Quarterly Theatre Review*
DrS	*Dreiser Studies*
DSA	*Dickens Studies Annual*
DU	*Der Deutschunterricht: Beiträge zu Seiner Praxis und Wissenschaftlichen Grundlegung*
DUJ	*Durham University Journal*
DVLG	*Deutsche Viertejahrsschrift für Literaturwissenschaft und Geistesgeschichte*
DWPELL	*Dutch Working Papers in English Language and Linguistics*
EA	*Études Anglaises*
EAL	*Early American Literature*
E&D	*Enlightenment and Dissent*
E&S	*Essays and Studies*
E&Soc	*Economy and Society*
EAS	*Essays in Arts and Sciences*
EASt	*Englisch Amerikanische Studien*
EC	*Études Celtiques*
ECan	*Études Canadiennes/Canadian Studies*
ECCB	*Eighteenth Century: A Current Bibliography*
ECent	*The Eighteenth Century: Theory and Interpretation*
ECF	*Eighteenth-Century Fiction*
ECI	*Eighteenth-Century Ireland*
ECLife	*Eighteenth Century Life*
ECon	*L'Epoque Conradienne*
ECr	*L'Esprit Créateur*
ECS	*Eighteenth-Century Studies*
ECW	*Essays on Canadian Writing*
EDAMN	*The EDAM Newsletter*
EDH	*Essays by Divers Hands*
EdL	*Études de Lettres*
EdN	*Editors' Notes: Bulletin of the Conference of Editors of Learned Journals*
EDSL	*Encyclopedic Dictionary of the Sciences of Language*
EEMF	Early English Manuscripts in Facsimile
EHR	*The English Historical Review*
EI	*Études Irlandaises* (Lille)
EIC	*Essays in Criticism*
EinA	*English in Africa*
EiP	*Essays in Poetics*
EIRC	*Explorations in Renaissance Culture*
Éire	*Éire-Ireland*

EiTET	Essays in Theatre/Etudes Théâtrales
EJ	English Journal
ELangT	ELT Journal: An International Journal for Teachers of English to Speakers of Other Languages
ELet	Esperienze Letterarie: Rivista Trimestrale di Critica e Cultura
ELH	Journal of English Literary History
ELN	English Language Notes
ELR	English Literary Renaissance
ELS	English Literary Studies
ELT	English Literature in Transition
ELWIU	Essays in Literature (Western Illinois Univ.)
EM	English Miscellany
Embl	Emblematica: An Interdisciplinary Journal of English Studies
EMLS	Early Modern Literary Studies (http://purl.cclc.org/emls/emlshome.html)
EMS	English Manuscript Studies, 1100–1700
EMu	Early Music
Encyclia	Encyclia
English	English: The Journal of the English Association
EnT	English Today: The International Review of the English Language
EONR	The Eugene O'Neill Review
EPD	English Pronouncing Dictionary
ER	English Review
ERR	European Romantic Review
ES	English Studies
ESA	English Studies in Africa
ESC	English Studies in Canada
ESQ	ESQ: A Journal of the American Renaissance
ESRS	Emporia State Research Studies
EssaysMedSt	Essays in Medieval Studies
ESTC	Eighteenth Century Short Title Catalogue
EWIP	Edinburgh University, Department of Linguistics, Work in Progress
EWN	Evelyn Waugh Newsletter
EWPAL	Edinburgh Working Papers in Applied Linguistics
EWW	English World-Wide
Exemplaria	Exemplaria
Expl	The Explicator
Extrapolation	Extrapolation: A Journal of Science Fiction and Fantasy
FAB	Frankfurter Afrikanistische Blätter
FCEMN	Mystics Quarterly (formerly Fourteenth-Century English Mystics Newsletter)
FCS	Fifteenth-Century Studies
FDT	Fountainwell Drama Texts
FemR	Feminist Review
FH	Die Neue Gesellschaft/Frankfurter Hefte

Fiction International	*Fiction International*
FJS	*Fu Jen Studies: Literature and Linguistics* (Taipei)
FLH	*Folia Linguistica Historica*
Florilegium	*Florilegium: Carleton University Annual Papers on Classical Antiquity and the Middle Ages*
FMLS	*Forum for Modern Language Studies*
FNS	*Frank Norris Studies*
Folklore	*Folklore*
FoLi	*Folia Linguistica*
Forum	*Forum*
FranS	*Franciscan Studies*
FreeA	*Free Associations*
FrontenacR	*Revue Frontenac*
Frontiers	*Frontiers: A Journal of Women Studies*
FS	*French Studies*
FSt	*Feminist Studies*
FuL	*Functions of Language*
Futures	*Futures*
GAG	Göppinger Arbeiten zur Germanistik
GaR	*Georgia Review*
GBB	*George Borrow Bulletin*
GEGHLS	*George Eliot–George Henry Lewes Studies*
GeM	*Genealogists' Magazine*
Genders	*Genders*
Genre	*Genre*
GER	*George Eliot Review*
Gestus	*Gestus: A Quarterly Journal of Brechtian Studies*
Gettysburg Review	*Gettysburg Review*
GHJ	*George Herbert Journal*
GissingJ	*The Gissing Journal*
GJ	*Gutenberg-Jahrbuch*
GL	*General Linguistics*
GL&L	*German Life and Letters*
GlasR	*The Glasgow Review*
Glossa	*Glossa: An International Journal of Linguistics*
GLQ	*GLQ: A Journal of Lesbian and Gay Studies* (New York)
GLS	*Grazer Linguistische Studien*
GR	*The Germanic Review*
Gramma	*Gramma: Journal of Theory and Criticism*
Gramma/TTT	*Tijdschrift voor Taalwetenschap*
GrandS	*Grand Street*
Granta	*Granta*
Greyfriar	*Greyfriar Siena Studies in Literature*
GRM	*Germanisch-Romanische Monatsschrift*
GSE	Gothenberg Studies in English
GSJ	*The Gaskell Society Journal*
GURT	*Georgetown University Round Table on Language and Linguistics*
H&T	*History and Theory*

Harvard Law Review	Harvard Law Review
HatcherR	Hatcher Review
HBS	Henry Bradshaw Society
HC	The Hollins Critic
HE	History of Education
Hecate	Hecate: An Interdisciplinary Journal of Women's Liberation
HEdQ	History of Education Quarterly
HEI	History of European Ideas
HeineJ	Heine Jahrbuch
HEL	Histoire Épistémologie Langage
Helios	Helios
Hermathena	Hermathena: A Trinity College Dublin Review
HeyJ	The Heythrop Journal
HFR	Hayden Ferry Review
HistJ	The Historical Journal
HistR	Historical Research
History	History: The Journal of the Historical Association
HJR	The Henry James Review (Baton Rouge, La.)
HL	Historiographia Linguistica
HLB	Harvard Library Bulletin
HLQ	The Huntington Library Quarterly
HNCIS	Harvester New Critical Introductions to Shakespeare
HNR	Harvester New Readings
HOPE	History of Political Economy
HPT	History of Political Thought
HQ	Hopkins Quarterly
HRB	Hopkins Research Bulletin
HSci	History of Science
HSE	Hungarian Studies in English
HSELL	Hiroshima Studies in English Language and Literature
HSJ	Housman Society Journal
HSL	University of Hartford Studies in Literature
HSN	Hawthorne Society Newsletter
HSSh	Hungarian Studies in Shakespeare
HSSN	The Henry Sweet Society Newsletter
HSt	Hamlet Studies
HT	History Today
HTR	Harvard Theological Review
HudR	Hudson Review
HumeS	Hume Studies
HumLov	Humanistica Lovaniensia: Journal of Neo-Latin Studies
HUSL	Hebrew University Studies in Literature and the Arts
HWJ	History Workshop
HWS	History Workshop Series
IAN	Izvestiia Akademii Nauk S.S.S.R. (Moscow)
I&C	Ideology and Consciousness
I&P	Ideas and Production
ICAME	ICAME Journal
ICS	Illinois Classical Studies

IEEETrans	*IEEE Transactions on Professional Communications*
IF	*Indogermanische Forschungen*
IFR	*The International Fiction Review*
IGK	*Irland: Gesellschaft und Kultur*
IJAL	*International Journal of Applied Linguistics*
IJECS	*Indian Journal for Eighteenth Century Studies*
IJES	*Indian Journal of English Studies*
IJL	*International Journal of Lexicography*
IJPR	*International Journal for the Philosophy of Religion*
IJSL	*International Journal of the Sociology of Language*
IJSS	*Indian Journal of Shakespeare Studies*
IJWS	*International Journal of Women's Studies*
ILR	*The Indian Literary Review*
ILS	*Irish Literary Supplement*
Imago	*Imago*
IMB	*International Medieval Bibliography*
Indexer	*Indexer*
IndH	*Indian Horizons*
IndL	*Indian Literature*
InG	*In Geardagum: Essays on Old and Middle English Language and Literature*
Inklings	*Inklings: Jahrbuch für Literatur und Ästhetik*
Inquiry	*Inquiry: An Interdisciplinary Journal of Philosophy*
Interlink	*Interlink*
Interpretation	*Interpretation*
IowaR	*The Iowa Review*
IRAL	*IRAL: International Review of Applied Linguistics in Language Teaching*
IS	*Italian Studies*
ISh	*The Independent Shavian*
ISJR	*Iowa State Journal of Research*
Island	*Island Magazine*
Islands	*Islands*
ISR	*Irish Studies Review*
IUR	*Irish University Review: A Journal of Irish Studies*
JAAC	*Journal of Aesthetics and Art Criticism*
JAAR	*Journal of the American Academy of Religion*
JAF	*The Journal of American Folklore*
JAfM	*Journal of African Marxists*
JAIS	*Journal of Anglo-Italian Studies*
JAL	*Journal of Australian Literature*
JAmC	*Journal of American Culture*
JAMS	*Journal of the American Musicological Society*
JAmS	*Journal of American Studies*
JArabL	*Journal of Arabic Literature*
JAS	*Journal of Australian Studies*
JBeckS	*Journal of Beckett Studies*
JBS	*Journal of British Studies*
JCAKSU	*Journal of the College of Arts, King Saud University*
JCanL	*Journal of Canadian Literature*

JCC	*Journal of Canadian Culture*
JCF	*Journal of Canadian Fiction*
JChL	*Journal of Child Language*
JCL	*The Journal of Commonwealth Literature*
JCP	*Journal of Canadian Poetry*
JCPCS	*Journal of Commonwealth and Postcolonial Studies*
JCSJ	*The John Clare Society Journal*
JCSR	*Journal of Canadian Studies/Revue d'Etudes Canadiennes*
JCSt	*Journal of Caribbean Studies*
JDECU	*Journal of the Department of English (University of Calcutta)*
JDHLS	*D. H. Lawrence: The Journal of the D. H. Lawrence Society*
JDJ	*John Donne Journal*
JDN	*James Dickey Newsletter*
JDTC	*Journal of Dramatic Theory and Criticism*
JEDRBU	*Journal of the English Department, Rabindra Bharati University*
JEGP	*Journal of English and Germanic Philology*
JEH	*The Journal of Ecclesiastical History*
JELL	*Journal of English Language and Literature*
JEn	*Journal of English* (Sana'a Univ.)
JEngL	*Journal of English Linguistics*
JENS	*Journal of the Eighteen Nineties Society*
JEP	*Journal of Evolutionary Psychology*
JEPNS	*Journal of the English Place-Name Society*
JES	*Journal of European Studies*
JETS	*Journal of the Evangelical Theological Society*
JFR	*Journal of Folklore Research*
JGE	*JGE: The Journal of General Education*
JGH	*Journal of Garden History*
JGN	*The John Gower Newsletter*
JH	*Journal of Homosexuality*
JHI	*Journal of the History of Ideas*
JHLP	*Journal of Historical Linguistics and Philology*
JHP	*Journal of the History of Philosophy*
JHSex	*Journal of the History of Sexuality*
JIES	*The Journal of Indo-European Studies*
JIL	*Journal of Irish Literature*
JIPA	*Journal of the International Phonetic Association*
JIWE	*Journal of Indian Writing in English*
JJ	*Jamaica Journal*
JJA	*James Joyce Annual*
JJB	*James Joyce Broadsheet*
JJLS	*James Joyce Literary Supplement*
JJQ	*James Joyce Quarterly*
JL	*Journal of Linguistics*
JLH	*The Journal of Library History, Philosophy and Comparative Librarianship*

JLP	*Journal of Linguistics and Politics*
JLS	*Journal of Literary Semantics*
JLSP	*Journal of Language and Social Psychology*
JLVSG	*Journal of the Loughborough Victorian Studies Group*
JMemL	*Journal of Memory and Language*
JMGS	*Journal of Modern Greek Studies*
JMH	*Journal of Medieval History*
JML	*Journal of Modern Literature*
JMMD	*Journal of Multilingual and Multicultural Development*
JMMLA	*Journal of the Midwest Modern Language Association*
JModH	*Journal of Modern History*
JMRS	*Journal of Medieval and Renaissance Studies*
JNLH	*Journal of Narrative and Life History*
JNPH	*Journal of Newspaper and Periodical History*
JNT	*Journal of Narrative Technique*
JNZL	*Journal of New Zealand Literature*
JoyceSA	*Joyce Studies Annual*
JP	*The Journal of Philosophy*
JPC	*Journal of Popular Culture*
JPCL	*Journal of Pidgin and Creole Languages*
JPhon	*Journal of Phonetics*
JPJ	*Journal of Psychology and Judaism*
JPrag	*Journal of Pragmatics*
JPRAS	*Journal of Pre-Raphaelite and Aesthetic Studies*
JPsyR	*Journal of Psycholinguistic Research*
JQ	*Journalism Quarterly*
JR	*Journal of Religion*
JRH	*The Journal of Religious History*
JRMMRA	*Journal of the Rocky Mountain Medieval and Renaissance Association*
JRSA	*Journal of the Royal Society of Arts*
JRUL	*Journal of the Rutgers University Libraries*
JSA	*Journal of the Society of Archivists*
JSaga	*Journal of the Faculty of Liberal Arts and Science, Saga University*
JSAS	*Journal of Southern African Studies*
JSSE	*Journal of the Short Story in English*
JTheoS	*The Journal of Theological Studies*
Judaism	*Judaism: A Quarterly Journal of Jewish Life and Thought*
JWCI	*Journal of the Warburg and Courtauld Institutes*
JWH	*Journal of Women's History*
JWIL	*Journal of West Indian Literature*
JWMS	*The Journal of the William Morris Society*
JWSL	*Journal of Women's Studies in Literature*
KanQ	*Kansas Quarterly*
KB	*Kavya Bharati*
KCLMS	King's College London Medieval Series
KJ	*The Kipling Journal*
KN	*Kwartalnik Neoflologiczny* (Warsaw)

KompH	Komparatistische Hefte
KPR	Kentucky Philological Review
KR	Kenyon Review
KSJ	Keats Shelley Journal
KSR	Keats Shelley Review
Kuka	Kuka: Journal of Creative and Critical Writing (Zaria, Nigeria)
Kunapipi	Kunapipi
KWS	Key-Word Studies in Chaucer
L&B	Literature and Belief
L&C	Language and Communication
Landfall	Landfall: A New Zealand Quarterly
L&H	Literature and History
L&L	Language and Literature
L&LC	Literary and Linguistic Computing
L&M	Literature and Medicine
L&P	Literature and Psychology
L&S	Language and Speech
L&T	Literature and Theology: An Interdisciplinary Journal of Theory and Criticism
L&U	The Lion and the Unicorn: A Critical Journal of Children's Literature
LangF	Language Forum
Language	Language: Journal of the Linguistic Society of America
Lang&S	Language and Style
LangQ	USF Language Quarterly
LangR	Language Research
LangS	Language Sciences
LanM	Les Langues Modernes
LATR	Latin American Theater Review, Center of Latin American Studies
LB	Leuvense Bijdragen
LBR	Luso-Brazilian Review
LCrit	The Literary Criterion (Mysore, India)
LCUT	The Library Chronicle of the University of Texas at Austin
LDOCE	Longman Dictionary of Contemporary English
LebS	Lebende Sprachen
LeedsSE	Leeds Studies in English
Legacy	Legacy: A Journal of Nineteenth-Century American Women Writers
LeS	Lingua e Stile
Lexicographica	Lexicographica: International Annual for Lexicography
Lexicography	Lexicography
LFQ	Literature/Film Quarterly
LH	Library History
LHY	The Literary Half-Yearly
Library	The Library
LibrQ	The Library Quarterly
LibT	Library Trends

LIN	*Linguistics in the Netherlands*
LingA	*Linguistic Analysis*
Ling&P	*Linguistics and Philosophy*
Ling&Philol	*Linguistics and Philology*
LingB	*Linguistische Berichte*
LingI	*Linguistic Inquiry*
LingInv	*Linvisticæ Investigationes*
LingP	*Linguistica Pragensia*
Lingua	*Lingua: International Review of General Linguistics*
Linguistics	*Linguistics*
Linguistique	*La Linguistique*
LiNQ	*Literature in Northern Queensland*
LIT	*LIT: Literature, Interpretation, Theory*
LitH	*Literary Horizons*
LitR	*The Literary Review: An International Journal of Contemporary Writing*
LittPrag	*Litteraria Pragensia: Studies in Literature and Culture*
LJGG	*Literaturwissenschaftliches Jahrbuch im Auftrage der Görres-Gesellschaft*
LJHum	*Lamar Journal of the Humanities*
LMag	*London Magazine*
LockeN	*The Locke Newsletter*
LongR	*Long Room: Bulletin of the Friends of the Library, Trinity College, Dublin*
Lore&L	*Lore and Language*
LP	*Lingua Posnaniensis*
LPLD	*Liverpool Papers in Language and Discourse*
LPLP	*Language Problems and Language Planning*
LR	*Les Lettres Romanes*
LRB	*London Review of Books*
LSE	Lund Studies in English
LSLD	*Liverpool Studies in Language and Discourse*
LSoc	*Language in Society*
LST	Longman Study Texts
LTM	Leeds Texts and Monographs
LTP	*LTP: Journal of Literature Teaching Politics*
LTR	*London Theatre Record*
LuK	*Literatur und Kritik*
LVC	*Language Variation and Change*
LWU	*Literatur in Wissenschaft und Unterricht*
MÆ	*Medium Ævum*
MAEL	Macmillan Anthologies of English Literature
Mana	*Mana*
M&H	*Medievalia et Humanistica*
M&L	*Music and Letters*
M&N	*Man and Nature/L'Homme et la Nature: Proceedings of the Canadian Society for Eighteenth-Century Studies*
Manoa	*Manoa*
Manuscripta	*Manuscripta*
MAR	*Mid-American Review*

MarkhamR	*Markham Review*
Matatu	*Matatu*
Matrix	*Matrix*
MBL	*Modern British Literature*
MC&S	*Media, Culture and Society*
MCI	Modern Critical Interpretations
MCJNews	*Milton Centre of Japan News*
McNR	*McNeese Review*
MCRel	*Mythes, Croyances et Religions dans le Monde Anglo-Saxon*
MCV	Modern Critical Views
MD	*Modern Drama*
Meanjin	*Meanjin*
MED	*Middle English Dictionary*
Mediaevalia	*Mediaevalia: A Journal of Mediaeval Studies*
MedPers	*Medieval Perspectives*
Melus	*MELUS: The Journal of the Society of Multi-Ethnic Literature of the United States*
Meridian	*Meridian*
MESN	*Mediaeval English Studies Newsletter*
MET	Middle English Texts
METh	*Medieval English Theatre*
MFN	*Medieval Feminist Newsletter*
MFS	*Modern Fiction Studies*
MHL	Macmillan History of Literature
MHLS	*Mid-Hudson Language Studies*
MHRev	*The Malahat Review*
MichA	*Michigan Academician*
MiltonQ	*Milton Quarterly*
MiltonS	*Milton Studies*
MinnR	*Minnesota Review*
MissQ	*Mississippi Quarterly*
MissR	*The Missouri Review*
MJLF	*Midwestern Journal of Language and Folklore*
MLAIB	*Modern Language Association International Bibliography*
MLJ	*The Modern Language Journal*
MLN	*Modern Language Notes*
MLRev	*Malcolm Lowry Review*
MLQ	*Modern Language Quarterly*
MLR	*The Modern Language Review*
MLS	*Modern Language Studies*
M/M	*Modernism/Modernity*
MMD	Macmillan Modern Dramatists
MMG	Macmillan Master Guides
MMisc	*Midwestern Miscellany*
MOCS	*Magazine of Cultural Studies*
ModA	*Modern Age: A Quarterly Review*
ModM	Modern Masters
ModSp	*Moderne Sprachen*

Monist	*The Monist*
MonSP	*Monash Swift Papers*
Month	*The Month: A Review Of Christian Thought and World Affairs*
MOR	*Mount Olive Review*
Moreana	*Moreana: Bulletin Thomas More* (Angers, France)
Mosaic	*Mosaic: A Journal for the Interdisciplinary Study of Literature*
MoyA	*Moyen Age*
MP	*Modern Philology*
MPHJ	*Middlesex Polytechnic History Journal*
MPR	*The Mervyn Peake Review*
MQ	*Midwest Quarterly*
MQR	*Michigan Quarterly Review*
MR	*Massachusetts Review*
MRDE	*Medieval and Renaissance Drama in England*
MRTS	Medieval and Renaissance Texts and Studies
MS	*Mediaeval Studies*
MSC	Malone Society Collections
MSE	*Massachusetts Studies in English*
MSEx	*Melville Society Extracts*
MSh	Macmillan Shakespeare
MSNH	*Mémoires de la Société Néophilologique de Helsinki*
MSpr	*Moderna Språk*
MSR	*Malone Society Reprints*
MSSN	*Medieval Sermon Studies Newsletter*
MT	*The Musical Times*
MTJ	*Mark Twain Journal*
MusR	*Music Review*
MW	*The Muslim World* (Hartford, Conn.)
MysticsQ	*Mystics Quarterly*
Mythlore	*Mythlore: A Journal of J. R. R. Tolkien, C. S. Lewis, Charles Williams, and the Genres of Myth and Fantasy Studies*
NA	*Nuova Antologia*
Names	*Names: Journal of the American Name Society*
N&F	*Notes & Furphies*
N&Q	*Notes and Queries*
Narrative	*Narrative*
Navasilu	*Navasilu*
NB	*Namn och Bygd*
NCaS	New Cambridge Shakespeare
NCBEL	*New Cambridge Bibliography of English Literature*
NCC	*Nineteenth-Century Contexts*
NCL	*Nineteenth-Century Literature*
NConL	*Notes on Contemporary Literature*
NCP	*Nineteenth-Century Prose*
NCS	New Clarendon Shakespeare
NCT	*Nineteenth-Century Theatre*
NDLR	*Notre Dame Law Review*

NDQ	*North Dakota Quarterly*
NegroD	*Negro Digest*
NELS	*North Eastern Linguistic Society*
Neoh	*Neohelicon*
Neophil	*Neophilologus*
NEQ	*The New England Quarterly*
NERMS	*New England Review*
NewA	*New African*
NewBR	*New Beacon Review*
NewC	*The New Criterion*
New Casebooks	New Casebooks: Contemporary Critical Essays
NewComp	*New Comparison: A Journal of Comparative and General Literary Studies*
NewF	*New Formations*
NewR	*New Republic*
NewSt	*Newfoundland Studies*
NewV	*New Voices*
NF	*Neophilologica Fennica*
NfN	*News from Nowhere*
NGC	*New German Critique*
NGS	*New German Studies*
NH	*Northern History*
NHR	*The Nathaniel Hawthorne Review*
NJL	*Nordic Journal of Linguistics*
NL	*Nouvelles Littéraires*
NL&LT	*Natural Language and Linguistic Theory*
NLH	*New Literary History: A Journal of Theory and Interpretation*
NLitsR	*New Literatures Review*
NLR	*New Left Review*
NLWJ	*The National Library of Wales Journal*
NM	*Neuphilologische Mitteilungen*
NMAL	*NMAL: Notes on Modern American Literature*
NMer	New Mermaids
NMIL	*Notes on Modern Irish Literature*
NMS	*Nottingham Medieval Studies*
NMW	*Notes on Mississippi Writers*
NN	*Nordiska Namenstudier*
NNER	*Northern New England Review*
Nomina	*Nomina: A Journal of Name Studies Relating to Great Britain and Ireland*
NoP	*Northern Perspective*
NOR	*New Orleans Review*
NortonCE	Norton Critical Edition
Novel	*Novel: A Forum on Fiction*
NOWELE	*North-Western European Language Evolution*
NPS	New Penguin Shakespeare
NR	*The Nassau Review*
NRF	*La Nouvelle Revue Française*
NRRS	*Notes and Records of the Royal Society of London*

NS	*Die Neueren Sprachen*
NSS	New Swan Shakespeare
NTQ	*New Theatre Quarterly*
NVSAWC	*Newsletter of the Victorian Studies Association of Western Canada*
NwJ	*Northward Journal*
NWR	*Northwest Review*
NWRev	*The New Welsh Review*
NYH	*New York History*
NYLF	New York Literary Forum
NYRB	*The New York Review of Books*
NYT	*New York Times*
NYTBR	*The New York Times Book Review*
NZListener	*New Zealand Listener*
OA	Oxford Authors
OAJ	*Oxford Art Journal*
OB	*Ord och Bild*
Obsidian	*Obsidian II: Black Literature in Review*
OBSP	Oxford Bibliographical Society Publications
OED	*Oxford English Dictionary*
OENews	*Old English Newsletter*
OET	Oxford English Texts
OH	*Over Here: An American Studies Journal*
OHEL	Oxford History of English Literature
OhR	*The Ohio Review*
OL	*Orbis Litterarum*
OLR	*Oxford Literary Review*
OPBS	Occasional Papers of the Bibliographical Society
OpenGL	Open Guides to Literature
OpL	*Open Letter*
OPL	Oxford Poetry Library
OPLiLL	*Occasional Papers in Linguistics and Language Learning*
OPSL	*Occasional Papers in Systemic Linguistics*
OralT	*Oral Tradition*
Orbis	*Orbis*
OS	Oxford Shakespeare
OSS	Oxford Shakespeare Studies
OT	*Oral Tradition*
Outrider	*The Outrider: A Publication of the Wyoming State Library*
Overland	*Overland*
PA	*Présence Africaine*
PAAS	*Proceedings of the American Antiquarian Society*
PacStud	*Pacific Studies*
Paideuma	*Paideuma: A Journal Devoted to Ezra Pound Scholarship*
PAJ	*Performing Art Journal*
P&C	*Pragmatics and Cognition*
P&CT	*Psychoanalysis and Contemporary Thought*

P&L	*Philosophy and Literature*
P&P	*Past and Present*
P&R	*Philosophy and Rhetoric*
P&SC	*Philosophy and Social Criticism*
PAPA	*Publications of the Arkansas Philological Association*
PAPS	*Proceedings of the American Philosophical Society*
PAR	*Performing Arts Resources*
Parabola	*Parabola: The Magazine of Myth and Tradition*
Paragraph	*Paragraph: The Journal of the Modern Critical Theory Group*
Parergon	*Parergon: Bulletin of the Australian and New Zealand Association for Medieval and Renaissance Studies*
ParisR	*The Paris Review*
Parnassus	*Parnassus: Poetry in Review*
PastM	Past Masters
PaterN	*Pater Newsletter*
PAus	*Poetry Australia*
PBA	*Proceedings of the British Academy*
PBerLS	*Proceedings of the Berkeley Linguistics Society*
PBSA	*Papers of the Bibliographical Society of America*
PBSC	*Papers of the Biographical Society of Canada*
PCL	*Perspectives on Contemporary Literature*
PCLAC	*Proceedings of the California Linguistics Association Conference*
PCLS	Proceedings of the Comparative Literature Symposium (Lubbock, Tex.)
PCP	*Pacific Coast Philology*
PCS	Penguin Critical Studies
PEAN	*Proceedings of the English Association North*
PE&W	*Philosophy East and West: A Quarterly of Asian and Comparative Thought*
PELL	*Papers on English Language and Literature* (Japan)
Pequod	*Pequod: A Journal of Contemporary Literature and Literary Criticism*
Performance	*Performance*
Peritia	*Peritia: Journal of the Medieval Academy of Ireland*
Persuasions	*Persuasions: Journal of the Jane Austen Society of North America*
Philosophy	*Philosophy*
PHist	Printing History
Phonetica	*Phonetica: International Journal of Speech Science*
PHOS	Publishing History Occasional Series
PhRA	*Philosophical Research Archives*
PhT	*Philosophy Today*
PIL	*Papers in Linguistics*
PIMA	*Proceedings of the Illinois Medieval Association*
PinterR	*Pinter Review*
PJCL	*The Prairie Journal of Canadian Literature*
PLL	*Papers on Language and Literature*
PLPLS	*Proceedings of the Leeds Philosophical and Literary*

	Society, Literary and Historical Section
PM	Penguin Masterstudies
PMHB	*Pennsylvania Magazine of History and Biography*
PMLA	*Publications of the Modern Language Association of America*
PNotes	*Pynchon Notes*
PNR	*Poetry and Nation Review*
PoeS	*Poe Studies*
Poetica	*Poetica: Zeitschrift für Sprach- und Literaturwissenschaft* (Amsterdam)
PoeticaJ	*Poetica: An International Journal of Linguistic-Literary Studies* (Tokyo)
Poetics	*Poetics: International Review for the Theory of Literature*
Poétique	*Poétique: Revue de Théorie et d'Analyse Littéraires*
PoetryCR	*Poetry Canada Review*
PoetryR	*Poetry Review*
PoetryW	*Poetry Wales*
PolR	*The Polish Review*
POMPA	*Publications of the Mississippi Philological Association*
PostS	*Post Script: Essays in Film and the Humanities*
PoT	*Poetics Today*
PP	Penguin Passnotes
PP	*Philologica Pragensia*
PPMRC	*Proceedings of the International Patristic, Mediaeval and Renaissance Conference*
PPR	*Philosophy and Phenomenological Research*
PQ	*Philological Quarterly*
PQM	*Pacific Quarterly* (Moana)
PR	*Partisan Review*
Pragmatics	*Pragmatics: Quarterly Publication of the International Pragmatics Association*
PrairieF	*Prairie Fire*
Praxis	*Praxis: A Journal of Cultural Criticism*
Prépub	*(Pré)publications*
PRev	*The Powys Review*
PRIA	*Proceedings of the Royal Irish Academy*
PRIAA	Publications of the Research Institute of the Abo Akademi Foundation
PRMCLS	*Papers from the Regional Meetings of the Chicago Linguistics Society*
Prospects	*Prospects: An Annual Journal of American Cultural Studies*
Prospero	*Prospero: Journal of New Thinking in Philosophy for Education*
Proteus	*Proteus: A Journal of Ideas*
Proverbium	*Proverbium*
PrS	*The Prairie Schooner*
PSt	*Prose Studies*
PsychR	*Psychological Reports*

PTBI	Publications of the Sir Thomas Browne Institute
PubH	*Publishing History*
PULC	*Princeton University Library Chronicle*
PURBA	*Panjab University Research Bulletin (Arts)*
PVR	*Platte Valley Review*
PWC	Pickering's Women's Classics
PY	*Phonology Yearbook*
QI	*Quaderni d'Italianistica*
QJS	*Quarterly Journal of Speech*
QLing	*Quantitative Linguistics*
QQ	*Queen's Quarterly*
Quadrant	*Quadrant (Sydney)*
Quarendo	*Quarendo*
Quarry	*Quarry*
QWERTY	*Q/W/E/R/T/Y: Arts, Littératures & Civilisations du Monde Anglophone*
RadP	*Radical Philosophy*
RAL	*Research in African Literatures*
RALS	*Resources for American Literary Study*
Ramus	*Ramus: Critical Studies in Greek and Roman Literature*
R&L	*Religion and Literature*
Raritan	*Raritan: A Quarterly Review*
Rask	*Rask: International tidsskrift for sprog og kommunikation*
RB	*Revue Bénédictine*
RBPH	*Revue Belge de Philologie et d'Histoire*
RCEI	*Revista Canaria de Estudios Ingleses*
RCF	*Review of Contemporary Fiction*
RDN	*Renaissance Drama Newsletter*
RE	*Revue d'Esthétique*
ReAL	*Re: Artes Liberales*
REALB	*REAL: The Yearbook of Research in English and American Literature* (Berlin)
RECTR	*Restoration and Eighteenth-Century Theatre Research*
RedL	*Red Letters: A Journal of Cultural Politics*
REED	Records of Early English Drama
REEDN	*Records of Early English Drama Newsletter*
Reinardus	*Reinardus*
REL	*Review of English Literature* (Kyoto)
Ren&R	*Renaissance and Reformation*
Renascence	*Renascence: Essays on Value in Literature*
RenD	*Renaissance Drama*
RenP	*Renaissance Papers*
RenQ	*Renaissance Quarterly*
Rep	*Representations*
RES	*The Review of English Studies*
Restoration	*Restoration: Studies in English Literary Culture, 1660–1700*
Rev	*Review* (Blacksburg, Va.)
RevAli	*Revista Alicantina de Estudios Ingleses*

Revels	Revels Plays
RevelsCL	Revels Plays Companion Library
RevR	Revolution and Romanticism, 1789–1834, ed. Jonathan Wordsworth
RFEA	*Revue Française d'Etudes Américaines*
RFR	*Robert Frost Review*
RH	*Recusant History*
Rhetorica	*Rhetorica: A Journal of the History of Rhetoric*
Rhetorik	*Rhetorik: Ein Internationales Jahrbuch*
RHist	*Rural History*
RHL	*Revue d'Histoire Littéraire de la France*
RHT	*Revue d'Histoire du Théâtre*
Ricardian	*The Ricardian: Journal of the Richard III Society*
RL	Rereading Literature
RLC	*Revue de Littérature Comparée*
RLM	*La Revue des Lettres Modernes: Histoire des Idées des Littératures*
RLMC	*Rivista di Letterature Moderne e Comparate*
RLT	*Russian Literature Triquarterly*
RM	*Rethinking Marxism*
RMR	*Rocky Mountain Review of Language and Literature*
RM	*Renaissance and Modern Studies*
RMSt	*Reading Medieval Studies*
Rom	*Romanticism*
RomN	*Romance Notes*
RomQ	*Romance Quarterly*
RomS	*Romance Studies*
ROO	*Room of One's Own: A Feminist Journal of Literature and Criticism*
RORD	*Research Opportunities in Renaissance Drama*
RPT	Russian Poetics in Translation
RQ	*Riverside Quarterly*
RR	*Romantic Review*
RRDS	Regents Renaissance Drama Series
RRestDS	Regents Restoration Drama Series
RS	*Renaissance Studies*
RSQ	*Rhetoric Society Quarterly*
Rubicon	*Rubicon*
RUO	*Revue de l'Université d'Ottawa*
RuskN	*Ruskin Newsletter*
RUUL	*Reports from the Uppsala University Department of Linguistics*
SAC	*Studies in the Age of Chaucer*
SAD	*Studies in American Drama, 1945–Present*
SAF	*Studies in American Fiction*
Saga-Book	*Saga-Book (Viking Society for Northern Research)*
Sagetrieb	*Sagetrieb: A Journal Devoted to Poets in the Pound–H.D.–Williams Tradition*
SAJL	*Studies in American Jewish Literature*
Sal	*Salmagundi: A Quarterly of the Humanities and Social*

	Sciences
S&S	*Sight and Sound*
SAntS	*Studia Anthroponymica Scandinavica*
SAP	*Studia Anglica Posnaniensia*
SAQ	*South Atlantic Quarterly*
SAR	*Studies in the American Renaissance*
SARB	*South African Review of Books*
SatR	*Saturday Review*
SB	*Studies in Bibliography*
SBHC	*Studies in Browning and His Circle*
SC	*The Seventeenth Century*
Scan	*Scandinavica. An International Journal of Scandinavian Studies*
ScanS	*Scandinavian Studies*
SCel	*Studia Celtica*
SCER	*Society for Critical Exchange Report*
SCJ	*The Sixteenth Century Journal*
SCL	*Studies in Canadian Literature*
ScLJ	*Scottish Literary Journal: A Review of Studies in Scottish Language and Literature*
SCLJ(S)	*Scottish Literary Journal Supplement*
SCN	*Seventeenth-Century News*
ScottN	*Scott Newsletter*
SCR	*The South Carolina Review*
Screen	*Screen* (London)
SCRev	*South Central Review*
Scriblerian	*The Scriblerian and the Kit Cats: A Newsjournal Devoted to Pope, Swift, and Their Circle*
Scripsi	*Scripsi*
Scriptorium	*Scriptorium: International Review of Manuscript Studies*
SD	*Social Dynamics*
SDR	*South Dakota Review*
SECC	*Studies in Eighteenth-Century Culture*
SECOLR	*The SECOL Review: Southeastern Conference on Linguistics*
SED	*Survey of English Dialects*
SEEJ	*Slavic and East European Journal*
SEL	*Studies in English Literature 1500–1900* (Rice Univ.)
SELing	*Studies in English Linguistics* (Tokyo)
SELit	*Studies in English Literature* (Tokyo)
SELL	*Studies in English Language and Literature*
Sem	*Semiotica: Journal of the International Association for Semiotic Studies*
Semiosis	*Semiosis: Internationale Zeitschrift für Semiotik und Ästhetik*
SER	*Studien zur Englischen Romantik*
Seven	*Seven: An Anglo-American Literary Review*
SF&R	Scholars' Facsimiles and Reprints
SFic	*Science Fiction: A Review of Speculative Literature*

SFNL	*Shakespeare on Film Newsletter*
SFQ	*Southern Folklore Quarterly*
SFR	*Stanford French Review*
SFS	*Science-Fiction Studies*
SH	*Studia Hibernica* (Dublin)
ShakB	*Shakespeare Bulletin*
ShakS	*Shakespeare Studies* (New York)
Shandean	*The Shandean*
Sh&Sch	*Shakespeare and Schools*
ShawR	*Shaw: The Annual of Bernard Shaw Studies*
Shenandoah	*Shenandoah*
SherHR	*Sherlock Holmes Review*
Shiron	*Shiron*
ShJE	*Shakespeare Jahrbuch* (Weimar)
ShJW	*Deutsche Shakespeare-Gesellschaft West Jahrbuch* (Bochum)
ShLR	*Shoin Literary Review*
ShN	*The Shakespeare Newsletter*
SHR	*Southern Humanities Review*
ShS	*Shakespeare Survey*
ShSA	*Shakespeare in Southern Africa*
ShStud	*Shakespeare Studies (Tokyo)*
SHW	*Studies in Hogg and his World*
ShY	*Shakespeare Yearbook*
SIcon	*Studies in Iconography*
Signs	*Signs: Journal of Women in Culture and Society*
SiHoLS	Studies in the History of the Language Sciences
SiM	*Studies in Medievalism*
SIM	*Studies in Music*
SiP	Shakespeare in Performance
SIR	*Studies in Romanticism*
SJS	*San José Studies*
SL	*Studia Linguistica*
SLang	*Studies in Language*
SLCS	Studies in Language Companion Series
SLitI	*Studies in the Literary Imagination*
SLJ	*Southern Literary Journal*
SLRev	*Stanford Literature Review*
SLSc	*Studies in the Linguistic Sciences*
SMC	Studies in Medieval Culture
SMed	*Studi Medievali*
SMELL	*Studies in Medieval English Language and Literature*
SMLit	*Studies in Mystical Literature* (Taiwan)
SMRH	*Studies in Medieval and Renaissance History*
SMS	*Studier i Modern Språkvetenskap*
SMy	*Studia Mystica*
SN	*Studia Neophilologica*
SNew	*Sidney Newsletter*
SNNTS	*Studies in the Novel* (North Texas State Univ.)
SOA	*Sydsvenska Ortnamnssällskapets Årsskrift*

SoAR	*South Atlantic Review*
Sociocrit	*Sociocriticism*
SocN	*Sociolinguistics*
SocT	*Social Text*
SohoB	Soho Bibliographies
SoQ	*The Southern Quarterly*
SoR	*The Southern Review* (Baton Rouge, La.)
SoRA	*Southern Review* (Adelaide)
SoSt	*Southern Studies: An Interdisciplinary Journal of the South*
Soundings	*Soundings: An Interdisciplinary Journal*
Southerly	*Southerly: A Review of Australian Literature*
SovL	*Soviet Literature*
SP	*Studies in Philology*
SPAN	*SPAN: Newsletter of the South Pacific Association for Commonwealth Literature and Language Studies*
SPAS	*Studies in Puritan American Spirituality*
SPC	*Studies in Popular Culture*
Spectrum	*Spectrum*
Speculum	*Speculum: A Journal of Medieval Studies*
SPELL	Swiss Papers in English Language and Literature
SphereHL	Sphere History of Literature
Sphinx	*The Sphinx: A Magazine of Literature and Society*
SpM	*Spicilegio Moderno*
SpNL	*Spenser Newsletter*
Sprachwiss	*Sprachwissenschaft*
SpringE	*Spring: The Journal of the E E Cummings Society*
SPub	*Studies in Publishing*
SPWVSRA	*Selected Papers from the West Virginia Shakespeare and Renaissance Association*
SQ	*Shakespeare Quarterly*
SR	*The Sewanee Review*
SRen	*Studies in the Renaissance*
SRSR	*Status Report on Speech Research (Haskins Laboratories)*
SSEL	Stockholm Studies in English
SSELER	Salzburg Studies in English Literature: Elizabethan and Renaissance
SSELJDS	Salzburg Studies in English Literature: Jacobean Drama Studies
SSELPDPT	Salzburg Studies in English Literature: Poetic Drama and Poetic Theory
SSELRR	Salzburg Studies in English Literature: Romantic Reassessment
SSEng	*Sydney Studies in English*
SSF	*Studies in Short Fiction*
SSL	*Studies in Scottish Literature*
SSt	*Spenser Studies*
SStud	*Swift Studies: The Annual of the Ehrenpreis Center*
Staffrider	*Staffrider*

STAH	*Strange Things Are Happening*
STC	*Short-Title Catalogue*
STGM	Studien und Texte zur Geistegeschichte des Mittelalters
StHum	*Studies in the Humanities*
StIn	*Studi Inglesi*
StLF	*Studi di Letteratura Francese*
StQ	*Steinbeck Quarterly*
StrR	*Structuralist Review*
StTCL	*Studies in Twentieth Century Literature*
Style	*Style* (De Kalb, Ill.)
SUAS	Stratford-upon-Avon Studies
SubStance	*SubStance: A Review of Theory and Literary Criticism*
SUS	*Susquehanna University Studies*
SussexAC	*Sussex Archaeological Collections*
SVEC	*Studies on Voltaire and the Eighteenth Century*
SWPLL	*Sheffield Working Papers in Language and Linguistics*
SWR	*Southwest Review*
SwR	*The Swansea Review: A Journal of Criticism*
TA	*Theatre Annual*
Tabu	*Bulletin voor Taalwetenschap, Groningen*
Talisman	*Talisman*
T&C	*Text and Context*
T&L	*Translation and Literature*
T&P	*Text and Performance*
TAPS	*Transactions of the American Philosophical Society*
TCBS	*Transactions of the Cambridge Bibliographical Society*
TCE	*Texas College English*
TCL	*Twentieth Century Literature*
TCS	*Theory, Culture and Society: Explorations in Critical Social Science*
TCWAAS	*Transactions of the Cumberland and Westmorland Antiquarian and Archæological Society*
TD	*Themes in Drama*
TDR	*The Drama Review*
TEAS	Twayne's English Authors Series
TEBS	*Edinburgh Bibliographical Society Transactions*
Telos	*Telos: A Quarterly Journal of Post-Critical Thought*
TenEJ	*Tennessee English Journal*
Te Reo	*Te Reo: Journal of the Linguistic Society of New Zealand*
TexasSLL	*Texas Studies in Language and Literature*
Text	*Text: Transactions of the Society for Textual Scholarship*
TH	*Texas Humanist*
THA	*Thomas Hardy Annual*
Thalia	*Thalia: Studies in Literary Humor*
ThC	*Theatre Crafts*
Theater	*Theater*
TheatreS	*Theatre Studies*

Theoria	*Theoria: A Journal of Studies in the Arts, Humanities and Social Sciences* (Natal)
THES	*The Times Higher Education Supplement*
Thesis	*Thesis Eleven*
THIC	*Theatre History in Canada*
THJ	*The Thomas Hardy Journal*
ThN	*Thackeray Newsletter*
ThoreauQ	*The Thoreau Quarterly: A Journal of Literary and Philosophical Studies*
Thought	*Thought: A Review of Culture and Ideas*
Thph	*Theatrephile*
ThreR	*The Threepenny Review*
ThS	*Theatre Survey: The American Journal of Theatre History*
THSLC	*Transactions of the Historic Society of Lancashire and Cheshire*
THStud	*Theatre History Studies*
THY	*The Thomas Hardy Yearbook*
TiLSM	Trends in Linguistics Studies and Monographs
TJ	*Theatre Journal*
TJS	Transactions (The Johnson Society)
TkR	*Tamkang Review*
TL	*Theoretical Linguistics*
TLR	*The Linguistic Review*
TLS	*TLS: The Times Literary Supplement*
TMLT	Toronto Medieval Latin Texts
TN	*Theatre Notebook*
TNWSECS	*Transactions of the North West Society for Eighteenth Century Studies*
TP	*Terzo Programma*
TPLL	*Tilbury Papers in Language and Literature*
TPr	*Textual Practice*
TPS	*Transactions of the Philological Society*
TR	*Theatre Record*
Traditio	*Traditio: Studies in Ancient and Medieval History, Thought, and Religion*
Transition	*Transition*
TRB	*The Tennyson Research Bulletin*
TRHS	*Transactions of the Royal Historical Society*
TRI	*Theatre Research International*
TriQ	*TriQuarterly*
Trivium	*Trivium*
Tropismes	*Tropismes*
TSAR	*The Toronto South Asian Review*
TSB	*Thoreau Society Bulletin*
TSL	*Tennessee Studies in Literature*
TSLang	Typological Studies in Language
TSLL	*Texas Studies in Literature and Language*
TSWL	*Tulsa Studies in Women's Literature*
TTR	*Trinidad and Tobago Review*

TUSAS	Twayne's United States Authors Series
TWAS	Twayne's World Authors Series
TWBR	*Third World Book Review*
TWeb	*Tangled Web*
TWQ	*Third World Quarterly*
TWR	*The Thomas Wolfe Review*
TYDS	*Transactions of the Yorkshire Dialect Society*
UCEPLL	*UCE Papers in Language and Literature*
UCrow	*The Upstart Crow*
UCTSE	*University of Cape Town Studies in English*
UCWPL	UCL Working Papers in Linguistics
UDR	*University of Dayton Review*
UE	*The Use of English*
UEAPL	*UEA Papers in Linguistics*
UES	*Unisa English Studies*
Ufahamu	*Ufahamu*
ULR	*University of Leeds Review*
UMSE	*University of Mississippi Studies in English*
Untold	*Untold*
UOQ	*University of Ottawa Quarterly*
URM	*Ultimate Reality and Meaning: Interdisciplinary Studies in the Philosophy of Understanding*
USSE	*University of Saga Studies in English*
UtopST	*Utopian Studies*
UTQ	*University of Toronto Quarterly*
UWR	*The University of Windsor Review*
VCT	Les Voies de la Création Théâtrale
VEAW	Varieties of English around the World
Verbatim	*Verbatim: The Language Quarterly*
VIA	*VIA: The Journal of the Graduate School of Fine Arts, University of Pennsylvania*
Viator	*Viator: Medieval and Renaissance Studies*
Views	*Viennese English Working Papers*
VIJ	*Victorians Institute Journal*
VLC	*Victorian Literature and Culture*
VN	*Victorian Newsletter*
Voices	*Voices*
VP	*Victorian Poetry*
VPR	*Victorian Periodicals Review*
VQR	*The Virginia Quarterly Review*
VR	*Victorian Review*
VS	*Victorian Studies*
VSB	*Victorian Studies Bulletin*
VWM	*Virginia Woolf Miscellany*
WAJ	*Women's Art Journal*
WAL	*Western American Literature*
W&I	*Word and Image*
W&L	*Women and Literature*
W&Lang	*Women and Language*
Wasafiri	*Wasafiri*

WascanaR	*Wascana Review*
WBEP	Wiener Beiträge zur Englischen Philologie
WC	World's Classics
WC	*The Wordsworth Circle*
WCR	*West Coast Review*
WCSJ	*Wilkie Collins Society Journal*
WCWR	*The William Carlos Williams Review*
Wellsian	*The Wellsian: The Journal of the H. G. Wells Society*
WEn	*World Englishes*
Westerly	*Westerly: A Quarterly Review*
WestHR	*West Hills Review: A Walt Whitman Journal*
WF	*Western Folklore*
WHASN	*W. H. Auden Society Newsletter*
WHR	*Western Humanities Review*
WLT	*World Literature Today*
WLWE	*World Literature Written in English*
WMQ	*The William and Mary Quarterly*
WoHR	*Women's History Review*
WolfenbütteleB	*Wolfenbüttele Beiträge: Aus den Schätzen der Herzog August Bibliothek*
Women	*Women: a Cultural Review*
WomW	*Women's Writing*
WorcesterR	*Worcester Review*
Word	*WORD: Journal of the International Linguistic Association*
WorldI	*The World and I*
WQ	*The Wilson Quarterly*
WRB	*Women's Review of Books*
WS	*Women's Studies: An Interdisciplinary Journal*
WSIF	*Women's Studies International Forum*
WSJ	*Women's Studies Journal*, Otago, New Zcaland
WSJour	*The Wallace Stevens Journal*
WTJ	*The Westminster Theological Journal*
WTW	Writers and Their Work
WVUPP	*West Virginia University Philological Papers*
WWR	*Walt Whitman Quarterly Review*
XUS	*Xavier Review*
YCC	*Yearbook of Comparative Criticism*
YCGL	*Yearbook of Comparative and General Literature*
YeA	*Yeats Annual*
YER	*Yeats Eliot Review*
YES	*The Yearbook of English Studies*
YEuS	*Yearbook of European Studies/Annuaire d'Etudes Européennes*
YFS	*Yale French Studies*
Yiddish	*Yiddish*
YJC	*The Yale Journal of Criticism: Interpretation in the Humanities*
YLS	*Yearbook of Langland Studies*
YM	*Yearbook of Morphology*

YNS	York Note Series
YPL	*York Papers in Linguistics*
YR	*The Yale Review*
YULG	*Yale University Library Gazette*
YWES	*The Year's Work in English Studies*
ZAA	*Zeitschrift für Anglistik und Amerikanistik*
ZCP	*Zeitschrift für Celtische Philologie*
ZDA	*Zeitschrift für Deutsches Altertum und Deutsche Literatur*
ZDL	*Zeitschrift für Dialektologie und Linguistik*
ZGKS	*Zeitschrift der Gesellschaft für Kanada-Studien*
ZGL	*Zeitschrift für Germanistische Linguistik*
ZPSK	*Zeitschrift für Phonetik, Sprachwissenschaft und Kommunikationsforschung*
ZSpr	*Zeitschrift für Sprachwissenschaft*
ZVS	*Zeitschrift für Vergleichende Sprachforschung*

Volume numbers are supplied in the text, as are individual issue numbers for journals that are not continuously paginated through the year.

2. Publishers

AAAH	Acta Academiae Åboensis Humaniora, Åbo, Finland
AAH	Australian Academy of Humanities
A&B	Allison & Busby, London
A&R	Angus & Robertson, North Ryde, N.S.W.
A&U	Allen & Unwin (now Unwin Hyman)
A&UA	Allen & Unwin, North Sydney, N.S.W.
A&W	Almqvist & Wiksell International, Stockholm
AarhusUP	Aarhus UP, Aarhus, Denmark
Abbeville	Abbeville Press, New York
ABC	ABC Enterprises
ABDO	Association Bourguignonne de Dialectologie et d'Onomastique, Dijon
AberdeenUP	Aberdeen UP, Aberdeen
Abhinav	Abhinav Pubns, New Delhi
Abingdon	Abingdon Press, Nashville, Tenn.
ABL	Armstrong Browning Library, Waco, Texas
Ablex	Ablex Pub, Norwood, N.J.
Åbo	Åbo Akademi, Åbo, Finland
Abrams	Harry N. Abrams, New York
Academia	Academia Press, Melbourne
Academic	Academic Press, London and Orlando, Fla.
Academy	The Academy Press, Dublin
AcademyC	Academy Chicago Pubs., Chicago
AcademyE	Academy Editions, London
Acadiensis	Acadiensis Press, Fredericton, New Brunswick, Canada
ACarS	Association for Caribbean Studies, Coral Gables, Fla.
ACC	Antique Collectors' Club, Woodbridge, Suffolk
ACCO	ACCO, Leuven, Belgium
ACP	Another Chicago Press, Chicago
ACS	Association for Canadian Studies, Ottawa
Adam Hart	Adam Hart Publishers Ltd, London
Addison-Wesley	Addison-Wesley, Wokingham, Berks.
Adosa	Adosa, Clermont-Ferrand, France
AEMS	American Early Medieval Studies
AF	Akademisk Forlag, Copenhagen
Affiliated	Affiliated East-West Press, New Delhi
AFP	Associated Faculty Press, New York
Africana	Africana Pub., New York
A-H	Arnold-Heinemann, New Delhi
Ahriman	Ahriman-Verlag, Freiburg im Breisgau, Germany
AIAS	Australian Institute of Aboriginal Studies, Canberra
Ajanta	Ajanta Pubns, Delhi
AK	Akadémiai Kiadó, Budapest
Al&Ba	Allyn & Bacon, Boston, Mass.
Albatross	Albatross
Albion	Albion, Appalachian State Univ., Boone, N.C.
Alderman	Alderman Press, London

AligarhMU	Aligarh Muslim Univ., Uttar Pradesh, India
Alioth	Alioth Press, Beaverton, Oreg.
Allen	W. H. Allen, London
Allied Publishers	Allied Indian Publishers, Lahore
Almond	Almond Press, Sheffield
AM	Aubier Montaigne, Paris
AMAES	Association des Médiévistes Angliciste de l'Enseignement Supérieur, Paris
Amate	The Amate Press, Oxford
AmberL	Amber Lane, Oxford
AMP	Aurora Metro Press, London
AMS	AMS Press, New York
Amsterdam	Amsterdam
AMU	Adam Mickiewicz Univ., Posnan
Anansi	Anansi Press, Toronto
Anma Libri	Anma Libri, Saratoga, Calif.
Antipodes	Antipodes Press, Plimmerton, New Zealand
Anvil	Anvil Press Poetry, London
APA	APA, Maarssen, Netherlands
APH	Associated Pub. House, New Delhi
APL	American Poetry and Literature Press, Philadelphia
APP	Australian Professional Pubns, Mosman, N.S.W.
Appletree	Appletree Press, Belfast
APS	American Philosophical Society, Philadelphia
Aquarian	The Aquarian Press, Wellingborough, Northants
ArborH	Arbor House Pub., New York
Archon	Archon Books, Hamden, Conn.
ArchP	Architectural Press Books, Guildford, Surrey
Ardis	Ardis Pubs., Ann Arbor, Mich.
Ariel	Ariel Press, London
Ark	Ark Paperbacks, London
Arkona	Arkona Forlaget, Aarhus, Denmark
Arlington	Arlington Books, London
Arnold	Edward Arnold, London
ArnoldEJ	E. J. Arnold & Son, Leeds
ARP	Australian Reference Pubns, N. Balwyn, Vic.
Arrow	Arrow Books, London
Artmoves	Artmoves, Parkdale, Victoria
ASB	Anglo-Saxon Books, Middlesex
ASECS	American Society for Eighteenth-Century Studies, c/o Ohio State Univ., Columbus
AshfieldP	Ashfield Press, London
Ashton	Ashton Scholastic
Aslib	Aslib, London
ASLS	Association for Scottish Literary Studies, Aberdeen
ASU	Arizona State Univ., Tempe
Atheneum	Atheneum Pubs., New York
Athlone	Athlone Press, London
Atlas	Atlas Press, London
Attic	Attic Press, Dublin

AucklandUP	Auckland UP, Auckland
AUG	Acta Universitatis Gothoburgensis, Sweden
AUP	Associated Univ. Presses, London and Toronto
AUPG	Academic & Univ. Pubs. Group, London
Aurum	Aurum Press, London
Auslib	Auslib Press, Adelaide
AustCU	Australia Catholic University
AUU	Acta Universitatis Umensis, Umeå, Sweden
AUUp	Acta Universitatis Upsaliensis, Uppsala
Avebury	Avebury Pub., Aldershot, Hampshire
Avero	Avero Pubns, Newcastle upon Tyne
A-V Verlag	A-V Verlag, Franz Fischer, Augsburg, Germany
AWP	Africa World Press, Trenton, N.J.
Axelrod	Axelrod Publishing Co., Tampa Bay, Fla.
BA	British Academy, London
BAAS	British Association for American Studies, c/o Univ. of Keele
Bagel	August Bagel Verlag, Düsseldorf
Bahri	Bahri Pubns, New Delhi
Bamberger	Bamberger Books, Flint, Mich.
B&B	Boydell & Brewer, Woodbridge, Suffolk
B&J	Barrie & Jenkins, London
B&N	Barnes & Noble, Totowa, N.J.
B&O	Burns & Oates, Tunbridge Wells, Kent
B&S	Michael Benskin and M. L. Samuels, Middle English Dialect Project, Univ. of Edinburgh
BAR	British Archaeological Reports, Oxford
Barn Owl	Barn Owl Books, Taunton, Somerset
Barnes	A. S. Barnes, San Diego, Calif.
BathUP	Bath UP, Bath
Batsford	B. T. Batsford, London
Bayreuth	Bayreuth African Studies
BBC	BBC Pubns, London
BClarkL	Bruccoli Clark Layman
BCP	Bristol Classical Press, Bristol
Beacon	Beacon Press, Boston, Mass.
Beck	C. H. Beck'sche Verlagsbuchhandlung, Munich
Becket	Becket Pubns, London
Belin	Editions Belin, Paris
Belknap	Belknap Press, Cambridge, Mass.
Belles Lettres	Société d'Edition les Belles Lettres, Paris
Bellew	Bellew Pub., London
Bellflower	Bellflower Press, Case Univ., Cleveland, Ohio
Benjamins	John Benjamins, Amsterdam
BenjaminsNA	John Benjamins North America, Philadelphia
BennC	Bennington College, Bennington, Vt.
Berg	Berg Pubs., Oxford
BFI	British Film Institute, London
BGUP	Bowling Green Univ. Popular Press, Bowling Green, Ohio

BibS	Bibliographical Society, London
Bilingual	Bilingual Press, Arizona State Univ., Tempe
Bingley	Clive Bingley, London
Binnacle	Binnacle Press, London
Biografia	Biografia Pubs., London
Birkbeck	Birkbeck College, University of London
Bishopsgate	Bishopsgate Press, Tonbridge, Kent
BL	British Library, London
Black	Adam & Charles Black, London
Black Cat	Black Cat Press, Blackrock, Eire
Blackie	Blackie & Son, Glasgow
Black Moss	Black Moss, Windsor, Ont.
Blackstaff	Blackstaff Press, Belfast
Black Swan	Black Swan, Curtin, Utah
Blackwell	Blackwell Publishers, Oxford
BlackwellR	Blackwell Reference, Oxford
Blackwood	Blackwood, Pillans & Wilson, Edinburgh
Bl&Br	Blond & Briggs, London
Blandford	Blandford Press, London
Blaue Eule	Verlag die Blaue Eule, Essen
Blizzard	Blizzard Publishing, Canada
Bloodaxe	Bloodaxe Books, Newcastle upon Tyne
Bloomsbury	Bloomsbury Pub., London
Blubber Head	Blubber Head Press, Hobart
BM	Bobbs-Merrill, New York
BMP	British Museum Pubns, London
Bodleian	The Bodleian Library, Oxford
Bodley	The Bodley Head, London
Bogle	Bogle L'Ouverture Pubns, London
BoiseSUP	Boise State UP, Boise, Idaho
Book Guild	The Book Guild, Lewes, E. Sussex
Borealis	Borealis Press, Ottawa
Borgo	Borgo Press, San Bernardino, Calif.
BostonAL	Boston Athenaeum Library, Boston, Mass.
Bouma	Bouma's Boekhuis, Groningen, Netherlands
Bowker	R. R. Bowker, New Providence, N.J.
Boyars	Marion Boyars, London and Boston, Mass.
Boydell	The Boydell Press, Woodbridge, Suffolk
Boyes	Megan Boyes, Allestree, Derbyshire
Bran's Head	Bran's Head Books, Frome, Somerset
Braumüller	Wilhelm Braumüller, Vienna
Breakwater	Breakwater Books, St John's, Newfoundland
Brentham	Brentham Press, St Albans, Herts.
Brepols	Brepols, Turnhout, Belgium
Brewer	D. S. Brewer, Woodbridge, Suffolk
Brewin	Brewin Books, Studley, War.
Bridge	Bridge Pub., S. Plainfield, N.J.
Brill	E. J. Brill, Leiden
Brilliance	Brilliance Books, London
Broadview	Broadview, London, Ont. and Lewiston, N.Y.

Brookside	Brookside Press, London
Browne	Sinclair Browne, London
Brownstone	Brownstone Books, Madison, Ind.
BrownUP	Brown UP, Providence, R.I.
Brynmill	Brynmill Press, Harleston, Norfolk
BSA	Bibliographical Society of America
BSB	Black Swan Books, Redding Ridge, Conn.
BSP	Black Sparrow Press, Santa Barbara, Calif.
BSU	Ball State Univ., Muncie, Ind.
BuckUP	Bucknell UP, Lewisburg, Pa.
Bulzoni	Bulzoni Editore, Rome
Burnett	Burnett Books, London
Buske	Helmut Buske, Hamburg
Butterfly	Butterfly
CA	Creative Arts Book Co., Berkeley, Calif.
CAAS	Connecticut Academy of Arts and Sciences, New Haven
Cadmus	Cadmus Editions, Tiburon, Calif.
Cairns	Francis Cairns, Univ. of Leeds
Calaloux	Calaloux Pubns, Ithaca, N.Y.
Calder	John Calder, London
CALLS	Centre for Australian Language and Literature Studies, English Department, UNewE, N.S.W.
Camden	Camden Press, London
C&G	Carroll & Graf, New York
C&W	Chatto & Windus, London
Canongate	Canongate Pub., Edinburgh
Canterbury	Canterbury Press, Norwich
Cape	Jonathan Cape, London
Capra	Capra Press, Santa Barbara, Calif.
Carcanet	The Carcanet New Press, Manchester, Lancs
Cardinal	Cardinal, London
CaribB	Caribbean Books, Parkersburg, Iowa
CarletonUP	Carleton UP, Ottawa
Carucci	Carucci, Rome
Cass	Frank Cass, London
Cassell	Cassell, London
Cavaliere Azzurro	Cavaliere Azzurro, Bologna
Cave	Godfrey Cave Associates, London
CBA	Council for British Archaeology, London
CBS	Cambridge Bibliographical Society, Cambridge
CBTS	Centre for Bibliographical and Textual Studies, Monash University
CCP	Canadian Children's Press, Guelph, Ont.
CCS	Centre for Canadian Studies, Mount Allison Univ., Sackville, N.B.
CDSH	Centre de Documentation Sciences Humaines, Paris
CENS	Centre for English Name Studies, University of Nottingham
Century	Century Pub., London

Ceolfrith	Ceolfrith Press, Sunderland, Tyne and Wear
CESR	Société des Amis du Centre d' Etudes Superieures de la Renaissance, Tours
CFA	Canadian Federation for the Humanities, Ottawa
CH	Croom Helm, London
C-H	Chadwyck-Healey, Cambridge
Chambers	W. & R. Chambers, Edinburgh
Champaign	Champaign Public Library and Information Center, Champaign, Ill.
Champion	Librairie Honoré Champion, Paris
Chand	S. Chand, Madras
ChelseaH	Chelsea House Pubs., New York, New Haven, and Philadelphia
Children's Lit. Association	Children's Literature Association
Christendom	Christendom Pubns, Front Royal, Va.
Chronicle	Chronicle Books, London
Chrysalis	Chrysalis Press
ChuoUL	Chuo Univ. Library, Tokyo
Churchman	Churchman Pub., Worthing, W. Sussex
Cistercian	Cistercian Pubns, Kalamazoo, Mich.
CL	City Lights Books, San Francisco
CLA	Canadian Library Association, Ottawa
Clarendon	Clarendon Press, Oxford
Claridge	Claridge, St Albans, Herts.
Clarion	Clarion State College, Clarion, Pa.
Clark	T. & T. Clark, Edinburgh
Clarke	James Clarke, Cambridge
Classical	Classical Pub., New Delhi
CLCS	Centre for Language and Communication Studies, Trinity College, Dublin
ClogherHS	Clogher Historical Society, Monaghan, Eire
Clunie	Clunie Press, Pitlochry, Tayside
CMAP	Caxton's Modern Arts Press, Dallas, Tx.
CMERS	Center for Medieval and Early Renaissance Studies, Binghamton, N.Y.
CML	William Andrews Clark Memorial Library, Los Angeles
CMST	Centre for Medieval Studies, Univ. of Toronto
Coach House	Coach House Press, Toronto
Cohen	Richard Cohen, London
Colleagues	Colleagues Press, East Lansing, Mich.
Collector	The Collector Ltd, London
College-Hill	College-Hill Press, San Diego, Calif.
Collins	William Collins Sons, London
CollinsA	William Collins (Australia), Sydney
Collins & Brown	Collins & Brown, London
ColUP	Columbia UP, New York
Comedia	Comedia Pub. Group, London
Comet	Comet Books, London

Compton	The Compton Press, Tisbury, Wilts.
Constable	Constable, London
Contemporary	Contemporary Books, Chicago
Continuum	Continuum Pub., New York
Copp	Copp Clark Pitman, Mississuaga, Ontario
Corgi	Corgi Books, London
CorkUP	Cork UP, Cork, Eire
Cormorant	Cormorant Press, Victoria, B.C.
CornUP	Cornell UP, Ithaca, N.Y.
Cornwallis	The Cornwallis Press, Hastings, E. Sussex
Coronado	Coronado Press, Lawrence, Kansas
Cosmo	Cosmo Pubns, New Delhi
Coteau	Coteau Books, Regina, Saskatchewan, Canada
Cowley	Cowley Pubns, Cambridge, Mass.
Cowper	Cowper House, Pacific Grove, Calif.
CPP	Canadian Poetry Press, London, Ont.
Crabtree	Crabtree Press, Sussex
Creag Darach	Creag Darach Publications, Stirling
CreightonUP	Creighton University Press, Omaha
Cresset	Cresset Library, London
CRNLE	Centre for Research in the New Literatures in English, Adelaide
Crossing	The Crossing Press, Freedom, Calif.
Crossroad	Crossroad Pub., New York
Crown	Crown Pubs., New York
Crowood	The Crowood Press, Marlborough, Wilts.
CSAL	Centre for Studies in Australian Literature, Univ. of Western Australia, Nedlands
CSLI	Center for the Study of Language and Information, Stanford Univ.
CSU	Cleveland State Univ., Cleveland, Ohio
CTHS	Éditions du Comité des Travaux Historiques et Scientifiques, Paris
CUAP	Catholic Univ. of America Press, Washington, D.C.
Cuff	Harry Cuff Pubns, St John's, Newfoundland
CULouvain	Catholic Univ. of Louvain, Louvain, Belgium
CULublin	Catholic Univ. of Lublin, Poland
CUP	Cambridge UP, Cambridge, New York, and Melbourne
Currency	Currency Press, Paddington, N.S.W.
Currey	James Currey, London
CV	Cherry Valley Editions, Rochester, N.Y.
CVK	Cornelson-Velhagen & Klasing, Berlin
CWU	Carl Winter Universitätsverlag, Heidelberg
Da Capo	Da Capo Press, New York
Dacorum	Dacorum College, Hemel Hempstead, Herts
Daisy	Daisy Books, Peterborough, Northants.
Dalkey	Dalkey Archive Press, Elmwood Park, Ill.
D&C	David & Charles, Newton Abbot, Devon
D&H	Duncker and Humblot, Berlin

D&M	Douglas & Mcintyre, Vancouver, B.C.
Dangaroo	Dangaroo Press, Mundelstrup, Denmark
Dawson	Dawson Publishing, Folkestone, Kent
DBAP	Daphne Brasell Associates Press
DBP	Drama Book Pubs., New York
De Boeck	De Boeck-Wesmael, Brussels
Dee	Dee
De Graaf	De Graaf, Nierwkoup, Netherlands
Denoël	Denoël S.A.R.L., Paris
Dent	J. M. Dent, London
DentA	Dent, Ferntree Gully, Vic., Australia
Depanee	Depanee Printers and Pubs., Nugegoda, Sri Lanka
Deutsch	André Deutsch, London
Didier	Didier Erudition, Paris
Diesterweg	Verlag Moritz Diesterweg, Frankfurt-on-Main
Dim Gray Bar Press	Dim Gray Bar Press
Doaba	Doaba House, Delhi
Dobby	Eric Dobby Publishing Ltd, St Albans
Dobson	Dobson Books, Durham
Dolmen	Dolmen Press, Portlaoise, Eire
Donald	John Donald, Edinburgh
Donker	Adriaan Donker, Johannesburg
Dorset	Dorset Publishing Company
Doubleday	Doubleday, London and New York
Dove	Dove, Sydney
Dovecote	Dovecote
Dovehouse	Dovehouse Editions, Canada
Dover	Dover Pubns, New York
Drew	Richard Drew, Edinburgh
Droste	Droste Verlag, Düsseldorf
Droz	Librairie Droz S.A., Geneva
DublinUP	Dublin UP, Dublin
Duckworth	Gerald Duckworth, London
Duculot	J. Duculot, Gembloux, Belgium
DukeUP	Duke UP, Durham, N.C.
Dundurn	Dundurn Press, Toronto and London, Ont.
Duquesne	Duquesne UP, Pittsburgh
Dutton	E. P. Dutton, New York
DWT	Dr Williams's Trust, London
EA	The English Association, London
Eason	Eason & Son, Dublin
East Bay	East Bay Books, Berkeley, Calif.
Ebony	Ebony Books, Melbourne
Ecco	Ecco Press, New York
ECNRS	Editions du Centre National de la Recherche Scientifique, Paris
ECW	ECW Press, Downsview, Ont.
Eden	Eden Press, Montreal and St Albans, Vt.
EdinUP	Edinburgh UP, Edinburgh
Edizioni	Edizioni del Grifo

Eerdmans	William Eerdmans, Grand Rapids, Mich.
EETS	Early English Text Society, c/o Exeter College, Oxford
Elephas	Elephas Books, Kewdale, Australia
Elm Tree	Elm Tree Books, London
ELS	English Literary Studies
Ember	Ember Press, Brixham, South Devon
EMSH	Editions de la Maison des Sciences de l'Homme, Paris
Enitharmon	Enitharmon Press, London
Enzyklopädie	Enzyklopädie, Leipzig
EONF	The Eugene O'Neill Foundation, Danville, Calif.
EPNS	English Place-Name Society, Beeston, Notts.
Epworth	The Epworth Press, Manchester
Eriksson	Paul Eriksson, Middlebury, Vt.
Erlbaum	Erlbaum Associates, N.J.
Erskine	Erskine Press, Harleston, Norfolk
ESI	Edizioni Scientifiche Italiane, Naples
ESL	Edizioni di Storia e Letteratura, Rome
EUFS	Editions Universitaires Fribourg Suisse
EUL	Edinburgh Univ. Library, Edinburgh
Europa	Europa Pubs, London
Evans	M. Evans, New York.
Exile	Exile Editions, Toronto, Ont.
Eyre	Eyre Methuen, London
FAB	Free Association Books, London
Faber	Faber & Faber, London
FAC	Fédération d'Activités Culturelles, Paris
FACP	Fremantle Arts Centre Press, Fremantle, W.A.
FALS	Foundation for Australian Literary Studies, James Cook Univ. of North Queensland, Townsville
F&F	Fels & Firn Press, San Anselmo, Calif.
F&S	Feffer & Simons, Amsterdam
Farrand	Farrand Press, London
Fay	Barbara Fay, Stuttgart
F-B	Ford-Brown, Houston, Texas
FDUP	Fairleigh Dickinson UP, Madison, N.J.
FE	Fourth Estate, London
Feminist	Feminist Press, New York
FictionColl	Fiction Collective, Brooklyn College, Brooklyn, N.Y.
Field Day	Field Day, Derry
Fifth House	Fifth House Publications, Saskatoon, Saskatchewan, Canada
FILEF	FILEF Italo-Australian Pubns, Leichhardt, N.S.W.
Fine	Donald Fine, New York
Fink	Fink Verlag, Munich
Flamingo	Flamingo
Flammarion	Flammarion, Paris
FlindersU	Flinders Univ. of South Australia, Bedford Park
FlorSU	Florida State Univ., Tallahassee, Fla.
FOF	Facts on File, New York
Folger	The Folger Shakespeare Library, Washington, D.C.

Folio	Folio Press, London
Fontana	Fontana Press, London
Footprint	Footprint Press, Colchester, Essex
FordUP	Fordham UP, New York
Foris	Foris Pubns, Dordrecht
Forsten	Egbert Forsten Pub., Groningen, Netherlands
Fortress	Fortress Press, Philadelphia
Francke	Francke Verlag, Berne
Franklin	Burt Franklin, New York
FreeP	Free Press, New York
FreeUP	Free UP, Amsterdam
Freundlich	Freundlich Books, New York
Frommann-Holzboog	Frommann-Holzboog, Stuttgart
FSP	Five Seasons Press, Madley, Hereford
FW	Fragments West/Valentine Press, Long Beach, Calif.
FWA	Fiji Writers' Association, Suva
FWP	Falling Wall Press, Bristol
Gale	Gale Research, Detroit, Mich.
Galilée	Galilée, Paris
Gallimard	Gallimard, Paris
G&G	Grevatt & Grevatt, Newcastle upon Tyne
G&M	Gill & Macmillan, Dublin
Garland	Garland Pub., New York
Gasson	Roy Gasson Associates, Wimborne, Dorset
Gateway	Gateway Editions, Washington, D.C.
Girasole	Edizioni del Girasole, Ravenna
GL	Goose Lane Editions, Fredericton, N.B.
GlasgowDL	Glasgow District Libraries, Glasgow
Gleerup	Gleerupska, Lund
Glenbridge	Glenbridge Publishing, USA
Gliddon	Gliddon Books Pubs., Norwich
Gloger	Gloger Family Books, Portland, Oregon
GMP	GMP Pub., London
GMSmith	Gibbs M. Smith, Layton, Utah
Golden Dog	The Golden Dog, Ottawa
Gollancz	Victor Gollancz, London
Gomer	Gomer Press, Llandysul, Dyfed
GothU	Gothenburg Univ., Gothenburg
Gower	Gower Pub., Aldershot, Hants.
Grafton	Grafton Books, London
Granta	Granta Publications, London
Granville	Granville Pub., London
Grasset	Grasset & Fasquelle, Paris
Grassroots	Grassroots, London
Graywolf	Graywolf Press, St Paul, Minn.
Greenhalgh	M. J. Greenhalgh, London
Greenhill	Greenhill Books, London
Greenwood	Greenwood Press, Westport, Conn.
Gregg	Gregg Publishing, Surrey

Greville	Greville Press, Warwick
Greymitre	Greymitre Books, London
Groos	Julius Groos Verlag, Heidelberg
Grove	Grove Press, New York
GRP	Greenfield Review Press, New York
Grüner	B. R. Grüner, Amsterdam
Gruyter	Walter de Gruyter, Berlin
Guernica	Guernica Editions, Montreal, Canada
Guilford	Guilford Press, New York
Gulmohar	Gulmohar Press, Islamabad, Pakistan
Haggerston	Haggerston
HakluytS	Hakluyt Society, c/o British Library, London
Hale	Robert Hale, London
Hall	G. K. Hall, Boston, Mass.
Hambledon	Hambledon Press, London
H&I	Hale & Iremonger, Sydney
H&M	Holmes & Meier, London and New York
H&S	Hodder & Stoughton, London
H&SNZ	Hodder & Stoughton, Auckland
H&W	Hill & Wang, New York
Hansib	Hansib Pub., London
Hans Zell	Hans Zell
Harbour	Harbour Pub., Madeira Park, B.C.
Harman	Harman Pub. House, New Delhi
Harper	Harper & Row, New York
Harrap	Harrap, Edinburgh
HarvardUP	Harvard UP, Cambridge, Mass.
Harwood	Harwood Academic Publishers, Langhorne, Pa.
Hatje	Verlag Gerd Hatje, Germany
HBJ	Harcourt Brace Jovanovich, New York and London
HC	HarperCollins, London
Headline	Headline Book Pub., London
Heath	D. C. Heath, Lexington, Mass.
Heinemann	William Heinemann, London
HeinemannA	William Heinemann, St Kilda, Vic.
HeinemannC	Heinemann Educational Books, Kingston, Jamaica
HeinemannNg	Heinemann Educational Books, Nigeria
HeinemannNZ	Heinemann Pubs., Auckland (now Heinemann Reed)
HeinemannR	Heinemann Reed, Auckland
Helm	Christopher Helm, London
Helm Information	Helm Information Ltd, Robertsbridge, UK
Herbert	Herbert Press, London
Hermitage	Hermitage Antiquarian Bookshop, Denver, Colorado
Hern	Nick Hern Books, London
Heyday	Heyday Books, Berkeley, Calif.
HH	Hamish Hamilton, London
Highsmith	Highsmith Press, USA
Hilger	Adam Hilger, Bristol
HM	Harvey Miller, London
HMB	Hodder Mon Beckett

HMSO	HMSO, London
Hodge	A. Hodge, Penzance, Cornwall
Hogarth	Hogarth Press, London
Hong KongUP	Hong Kong UP, Hong Kong
Horwood	Ellis Horwood, Hemel Hempstead, Herts.
HoughtonM	Houghton Mifflin, Boston, Mass.
Howard	Howard UP, Washington, D.C.
HRW	Holt, Rinehart & Winston, New York
Hudson	Hudson
Hueber	Max Hueber, Ismaning, Germany
HUL	Hutchinson Univ. Library, London
HullUP	Hull UP, Univ. of Hull
Humanities	Humanities Press, Atlantic Highlands, N.J.
Huntington	Huntington Library, San Marino, Calif.
Hutchinson	Hutchinson Books, London
HW	Harvester Wheatsheaf, Hemel Hempstead, Herts.
HWWilson	H. W. Wilson, New York
Hyland House	Hyland House Publishing, Victoria, Australia
Ian Henry	Ian Henry Pubns, Hornchurch, Essex
IAP	Irish Academic Press, Dublin
IBK	Innsbrucker Beiträge zur Kulturwissenschaft, Univ. of Innsbruck
ICA	Institute of Contemporary Arts, London
IHA	International Hopkins Association, Waterloo, Ont.
IJamaica	Institute of Jamaica Pubns, Kingston
Imago	Imago Imprint, New York
Imperial War Museum	Imperial War Museum Publications, London
IndUP	Indiana UP, Bloomington, Ind.
Inkblot	Inkblot Pubns, Berkeley, Calif.
IntUP	International Universities Press, New York
Inventions	Inventions Press, London
IonaC	Iona College, New Rochelle, N.Y.
IowaSUP	Iowa State UP, Ames, Iowa
IOWP	Isle of Wight County Press, Newport, Isle of Wight
IP	In Parenthesis, London
Ipswich	Ipswich Press, Ipswich, Mass.
ISCS	Indian Society for Commonwealth Studies
ISI	ISI Press, Philadelphia
Italica	Italica Press, New York
IULC	Indiana Univ. Linguistics Club, Bloomington, Ind.
IUP	Indiana Univ. of Pennsylvania Press, Indiana, Pa.
Ivon	Ivon Pub. House, Bombay
Jacaranda	Jacaranda Wiley, Milton, Queensland
JadavpurU	Jadavpur Univ., Calcutta
JAI	JAI Press, Covent Garden, London
James CookU	James Cook Univ. of North Queensland, Townsville
Janus	Janus Publishing Company, London
Jarrow	Parish of Jarrow, Tyne and Wear
Jesperson	Jesperson Press, St John's, Newfoundland

JHall	James Hall, Leamington Spa, Warwickshire
JHUP	Johns Hopkins UP, Baltimore, Md.
JIWE	JIWE Pubns, Univ. of Gulbarga, India
JLRC	Jack London Research Center, Glen Ellen, Calif.
Jonas	Jonas Verlag, Marburg, Germany
Joseph	Michael Joseph, London
Journeyman	The Journeyman Press, London
JT	James Thin, Edinburgh
Junction	Junction Books, London
Junius-Vaughan	The Junius-Vaughan Press, Fairview, N.J.
Jupiter	Jupiter Press, Lake Bluff, Ill.
JyväskyläU	Jyväskylä Univ., Jyväskylä, Finland
Kaibunsha	Kaibunsha, Tokyo
K&N	Königshausen & Neumann, Würzburg, Germany
K&W	Kaye & Ward, London
Kansai	Kansai Univ. of Foreign Studies, Osaka
Kardo	Kardo, Coatbridge, Scotland
Karia	Karia Press, London
Karnak	Karnak House, London
Karoma	Karoma Pubs., Ann Arbor, Mich.
KC	Kyle Cathie
KCL	King's College London
KeeleUP	Keele University Press
Kegan Paul	Kegan Paul International, London
Kenkyu	Kenkyu-Sha, Tokyo
Kennikat	Kennikat Press, Port Washington, N.Y.
Kcnsal	Kensal Press, Oxford
KenyaLB	Kenya Literature Bureau, Nairobi
Kerosina	Kerosina Pubns, Worcester Park, Surrey
Kerr	Charles H. Kerr, Chicago
Kestrel	Viking Kestrel, London
K/H	Kendall/Hunt Pub., Dubuque, Iowa
Kingsley	J. Kingsley Publishers, London
Kingston	Kingston Pubs., Kingston, Jamaica
Kinseido	Kinseido, Tokyo
Klostermann	Vittorio Klostermann, Frankfurt-on-Main
Kluwer	Kluwer Academic Publications, Dordrecht
Knopf	Alfred A. Knopf, New York
Knowledge	Knowledge Industry Pubns, White Plains, N.Y.
Kraft	Kraft Books Ltd, Ibadan
Kraus	Kraus International Pubns, White Plains, N.Y.
KSUP	Kent State UP, Kent, Ohio
LA	Library Association, London
Lake View	Lake View Press, Chicago
LAm	Library of America, New York
Lancelot	Lancelot Press, Hantsport, N.S.
Landesman	Jay Landesman, London
L&W	Lawrence & Wishart, London
Lane	Allen Lane, London
Lang	Peter D. Lang, Frankfurt-on-Main and Berne

LBQ	Library Board of Queensland, Australia
LC	Library of Congress, Washington, D.C.
LCP	Loras College Press, Dubuque, Iowa
LeedsUP	Leeds UP, Leeds
LehighUP	Lehigh University Press, Pennsylvania
LeicAE	University of Leicester, Dept of Adult Education
LeicsCC	Leicestershire County Council, Libraries and Information Service, Leicester
LeicUP	Leicester UP, Leicester
LeidenUP	Leiden UP, Leiden
Leopard's Head	Leopard's Head Press, Oxford
LeuvenUP	Leuven UP, Leuven, Belgium
Lexik	Lexik House, Cold Spring, N.Y.
LF	LiberFörlag, Stockholm
LH	Lund Humphries Pubs., London
Liberty	Liberty Classics, Indianapolis, Ind.
Libris	Libris, London
Liguori	Liguori, Naples
Limelight	Limelight Editions, New York
Lime Tree	Lime Tree Press, Octopus Publishing Group, London
LittleH	Little Hills Press, Burwood, N.S.W.
Liveright	Liveright Pub., New York
LiverUP	Liverpool UP, Liverpool
Livre de Poche	Le Livre de Poche, Paris
Llanerch	Llanerch Enterprises, Lampeter, Dyfed
Locust Hill	Locust Hill Press, West Cornwall, Conn.
Loewenthal	Loewenthal Press, New York
Longman	Longman Group, Harlow, Essex
LongmanC	Longman Caribbean, Harlow, Essex
LongmanF	Longman, France
LongmanNZ	Longman, Auckland
Longspoon	Longspoon Press, Univ. of Alberta, Edmonton
Lovell	David Lovell Publishing, Brunswick, Australia
Lowell	Lowell Press, Kansas City, Mo.
Lowry	Lowry Pubs., Johannesburg
LSUP	Louisiana State UP, Baton Rouge, La.
LundU	Lund Univ., Lund, Sweden
LUP	Loyola UP, Chicago
Lutterworth	Lutterworth Press, Cambridge
Lymes	Lymes Press, Newcastle, Staffs.
MAA	Medieval Academy of America, Cambridge, Mass.
Macmillan	Macmillan Pubs., London
MacmillanC	Macmillan Caribbean
Madison	Madison Books, Lanham, Md.
Madurai	Madurai Univ., Madurai, India
Maecenas	Maecenas Press, Iowa City, Iowa
Magabala	Magabala Books, Broome, W.A.
Mainstream	Mainstream Pub., Edinburgh
Maisonneuve	Maisonneuve Press, Washington, D.C.
Malone	Malone Society, c/o King's College, London

Mambo	Mambo Press, Gweru, Zimbabwe
ManCASS	Manchester Centre for Anglo-Saxon Studies, Univ. of Manchester
M&E	Macdonald & Evans, Estover, Plymouth, Devon
M&S	McClelland & Stewart, Toronto
Maney	W. S. Maney & Sons, Leeds
Mansell	Mansell Pub., London
Manufacture	La Manufacture, Lyons
ManUP	Manchester UP, Manchester
Mardaga	Mardaga
MarquetteUP	Marquette UP, Milwaukee, Wisc.
Marvell	The Marvell Press, Calstock, Cornwall
MB	Mitchell Beazley, London
McFarland	McFarland, Jefferson, N.C.
McG-QUP	McGill-Queen's UP, Montreal
McGraw-Hill	McGraw-Hill, New York
McIndoe	John McIndoe, Dunedin, New Zealand
McPheeG	McPhee Gribble Pubs., Fitzroy, Vic.
McPherson	McPherson, Kingston, N.Y.
ME	M. Evans, New York
Meany	P. D. Meany Pubs., Port Credit, Ont.
Meckler	Meckler Pub., Westport, Conn.
MelbourneUP	Melbourne UP, Carlton South, Vic.
Mellen	Edwin Mellen Press, Lewiston, N.Y.
MellenR	Mellen Research UP
MercerUP	Mercer UP, Macon, Ga.
Mercury	Mercury Press, Stratford, Ontario
Merlin	The Merlin Press, London
Methuen	Methuen, London
MethuenA	Methuen Australia, North Ryde, N.S.W.
MethuenC	Methuen, Toronto
Metro	Metro Pub., Auckland
Metzler	Metzler, Stuttgart
MGruyter	Mouton de Gruyter, Berlin, New York, and Amsterdam
MH	Michael Haag, London
MHRA	Modern Humanities Research Association, London
MI	Microforms International, Pergamon Press, Oxford
Micah	Micah Pubns, Marblehead, Mass.
MichSUP	Michigan State UP, East Lansing, Mich.
MidNAG	Mid Northumberland Arts Group, Ashington, Northumbria
Milestone	Milestone Pubns, Horndean, Hampshire
Millennium	Millennium Books, E. J. Dwyer Pty Ltd, Newtown, Australia
Millstream	Millstream Books, Bath
Milner	Milner, London
Minuit	Editions de Minuit, Paris
MIP	Medieval Institute Pubns, Western Michigan Univ., Kalamazoo

MITP	Massachusetts Institute of Technology Press, Cambridge, Mass.
MLA	Modern Language Association of America, New York
MlM	Multilingual Matters, Clevedon, Avon
MLP	Manchester Literary and Philosophical Society, Manchester
Monarch	Monarch Publications, Sussex
Moonraker	Moonraker Press, Bradford-on-Avon, Wilts.
Moorland	Moorland Pub., Ashbourne, Derbys.
Moreana	Moreana, Angers, France
MorganSU	Morgan State Univ., Baltimore, Md.
Morrow	William Morrow, New York
Mosaic	Mosaic Press, Oakville, Ont.
Motilal	Motilal Books, Oxford
Motley	Motley Press, Romsey, Hampshire
Mouton	Mouton Pubs., New York and Paris
Mowbray	A. R. Mowbray, Oxford
MR	Martin Robertson, Oxford
MRS	Medieval and Renaissance Society, North Texas State Univ., Denton
MRTS	MRTS, Binghamton, N.Y.
MSUP	Memphis State UP, Memphis, Tenn.
MtAllisonU	Mount Allison Univ., Sackville, N.B.
Mulini	Mulini Press, A.C.T.
Muller	Frederick Muller, London
MULP	McMaster University Library Press
Murray	John Murray, London
Mursia	Ugo Mursia, Milan
NAL	New American Library, New York
Narr	Gunter Narr Verlag, Tübingen
Nathan	Fernand Nathan, Paris
NBB	New Beacon Books, London
NBCAus	National Book Council of Australia, Melbourne
NCAS	National Centre for Australian Studies, Monash University
NCP	New Century Press, Durham
ND	New Directions, New York
NDT	Nottingham Drama Texts, c/o Univ. of Nottingham
NEL	New English Library, London
NELM	National English Literary Museum, Grahamstown, S. Africa
Nelson	Nelson Pubs., Melbourne
New Endeavour	New Endeavour Press
NeWest	NeWest Press, Edmonton, Alberta
New Horn	New Horn Press, Ibadan, Nigeria
New Island	New Island Press
New IssuesP	New Issues Press, Western Michigan University
NH	New Horizon Press, Far Hills, N.J.
N-H	Nelson-Hall, Chicago
NHPC	North-Holland Pub., Amsterdam and New York

NIE	La Nuova Italia Editrice, Florence
Niemeyer	Max Niemeyer, Tübingen, Germany
Nightwood	Nightwood Editions, Toronto
NIUP	Northern Illinois UP, De Kalb, Ill.
NLA	National Library of Australia
NLB	New Left Books, London
NLC	National Library of Canada, Ottawa
NLP	New London Press, Dallas, Texas
NLS	National Library of Scotland, Edinburgh
NLW	National Library of Wales, Aberystwyth, Dyfed
Nolishment	Nolishment Publications, Powis
Northcote	Northcote House Pubs., Plymouth
NortheasternU	Northeastern Univ., Boston, Mass.
NorthwesternUP	Northwestern UP, Evanston, Ill.
Norton	W. W. Norton, New York and London
NorUP	Norwegian University Press, Oslo
Novus	Novus Press, Oslo
NPF	National Poetry Foundation, Orono, Maine
NPG	National Portrait Gallery, London
NPP	North Point Press, Berkeley, Calif.
NSP	New Statesman Pub., New Delhi
NSU Press	Northern States Universities Press
NSWUP	New South Wales UP, Kensington, N.S.W.
NT	National Textbook, Lincolnwood, Ill.
NUC	Nipissing Univ. College, North Bay, Ont.
NUP	National Univ. Pubns, Millwood, N.Y.
NUU	New Univ. of Ulster, Coleraine
NWAP	North Waterloo Academic Press, Waterloo, Ont.
NWP	New World Perspectives, Montreal
NYPL	New York Public Library, New York
NYUP	New York UP, New York
Oak Knoll	Oak Knoll Press, New Castle, Detroit
O&B	Oliver & Boyd, Harlow, Essex
Oasis	Oasis Books, London
OBAC	Organization of Black American Culture, Chicago
Oberon	Oberon
O'Brien	The O'Brien Press, Dublin
OBS	Oxford Bibliographical Society, Bodleian Library, Oxford
Octopus	Octopus Books, London
OdenseUP	Odense UP, Odense
OE	Officina Edizioni, Rome
OEColl	Old English Colloquium, Berkeley, Calif.
Offord	John Offord Pubns, Eastbourne, E. Sussex
OhioUP	Ohio UP, Athens, Ohio
Oldcastle	Oldcastle Books, Harpenden, Herts.
Olms	Georg Olms, Hildesheim, Germany
Olschki	Leo S. Olschki, Florence
O'Mara	Michael O'Mara Books, London
Omnigraphics	Omnigraphics, Detroit, Mich.

Open Books	Open Books Pub., Wells, Somerset
OpenUP	Open UP, Buckingham and Philadelphia
OPP	Oxford Polytechnic Press, Oxford
Orbis	Orbis Books, London
Oriel	Oriel Press, Stocksfield, Northumb.
OrientUP	Oriental UP, London
Orwell	Orwell Press, Southwold, Suffolk
Oryx	Oryx Press, Phoenix, Ariz.
OSUP	Ohio State UP, Columbus, Ohio
OTP	Oak Tree Press, London
OUCA	Oxford University Committee for Archaeology, Oxford
OUP	Oxford UP, Oxford
OUPAm	Oxford UP Inc., New York
OUPAus	Oxford UP, Melbourne
OUPC	Oxford UP, Toronto
OUPI	Oxford UP, New Delhi
OUPNZ	Oxford UP, Auckland
OUPSA	Oxford UP Southern Africa, Cape Town
Outlet	Outlet Book Co., New York
Owen	Peter Owen, London
Owl	Owl
Pacifica	Press Pacifica, Kailua, Hawaii
Paget	Paget Press, Santa Barbara, Calif.
PAJ	PAJ Pubns, New York
Paladin	Paladin Books, London
Pan	Pan Books, London
PanAmU	Pan American Univ., Edinburgh, Texas
P&C	Pickering & Chatto, London
Pandion	Pandion Press, Capitola, Calif.
Pandora	Pandora Press, London
Pantheon	Pantheon Books, New York
ParagonH	Paragon House Pubs., New York
Parnassus	Parnassus Imprints, Hyannis, Mass.
Parousia	Parousia Pubns, London
Paternoster	Paternoster Press, Carlisle, Cumbria
Patten	Patten Press, Penzance
Paulist	Paulist Press, Ramsey, N.J.
Paupers	Paupers' Press, Nottingham
Pavilion	Pavilion Books, London
PBFA	Provincial Booksellers' Fairs Association, Cambridge
Peachtree	Peachtree Pubs., Atlanta, Ga.
Pearson	David Pearson, Huntingdon, Cambs.
Peepal Tree	Peepal Tree Books, Leeds
Peeters	Peeters Publishers and Booksellers, Leuven, Belgium
Pelham	Pelham Books, London
Pembridge	Pembridge Press, London
Pemmican	Pemmican Publications, Winnipeg, Canada
Penguin	Penguin Books, Harmondsworth, Middx.
PenguinA	Penguin Books, Ringwood, Vic.

PenguinNZ	Penguin Books, Auckland
Penkevill	The Penkevill Pub. Co., Greenwood, Fla.
Pentland	Pentland Press Ltd, Ely, Cambs.
Penumbra	Penumbra Press, Moonbeam, Ont.
People's	People's Pubns, London
Pergamon	Pergamon Press, Oxford
Permancnt	Permanent Press, Sag Harbor, N.Y.
Perpetua	Perpetua Press, Oxford
Peterloo Poets	Peterloo Poets, Cornwall, UK
Petton	Petton Books, Oxford
Pevensey	Pevensey Press, Newton Abbott, Devon
PH	Prentice-Hall, Englewood Cliffs, N.J.
Phaidon	Phaidon Press, London
PHI	Prentice-Hall International, Hemel Hempstead, Herts.
PhilL	Philosophical Library, New York
Phillimore	Phillimore, Chichester
Piatkus	Piatkus Books, London
Pickwick	Pickwick Pubns, Allison Park, Pa.
Pilgrim	Pilgrim Books, Norman, Okla.
PIMS	Pontifical Institute of Mediaeval Studies, Toronto
Pinter	Frances Pinter Pubs., London
Plains	Plains Books, Carlisle
Plenum	Plenum Pub., London and New York
Plexus	Plexus Pub., London
Pliegos	Editorial Pliegos, Madrid
Ploughshares	Ploughshares Books, Watertown, Mass.
Pluto	Pluto Press, London
PML	Pierpont Morgan Library, New York
Polity	Polity Press, Cambridge
Polygon	Polygon, Edinburgh
Poolbeg	Poolbeg Press, Swords, Co. Dublin
Porcepic	Press Porcepic, Victoria, B.C.
Porcupine	Porcupine's Quill, Canada
PortN	Port Nicholson Press, Wellington, N.Z.
Potter	Clarkson N. Potter, New York
Power	Power Pubns, Univ. of Sydney
PPUBarcelona	Promociones y Publicaciones Universitarias, Barcelona
PrestigeB	Prestige Books, New Delhi
Primavera	Edizioni Primavera, Giunti Publishing Group, Florence, Italy
Primrose	Primrose Press, Alhambra, Calif.
PrincetonUL	Princeton Univ. Library, Princeton, N.J.
PrincetonUP	Princeton UP, Princeton, N.J.
Printwell	Printwell Pubs., Jaipur, India
Prism	Prism Press, Bridport, Dorset
PRO	Public Record Office, London
Profile	Profile Books, Ascot, Berks
ProgP	Progressive Pubs., Calcutta
PSUP	Pennsylvania State UP, University Park, Pa.

Pucker	Puckerbrush Press, Orono, Maine
PUF	Presses Universitaires de France, Paris
PurdueUP	Purdue UP, Lafayette, Ind.
Pushcart	Pushcart Press, Wainscott, N.Y.
Pustet	Friedrich Pustet, Regensburg
Putnam	Putnam Pub. Group, New York
PWP	Poetry Wales Press, Ogmore by Sea, Mid Glam.
QED	Q.E.D. Press of Ann Arbor, Mich.
Quarry	Quarry Press, Kingston, Ontario
Quartet	Quartet Books, London
RA	Royal Academy of Arts, London
Rainforest	Rainforest
Rampant Lions	Rampant Lions Press, Cambridge
R&B	Rosenkilde & Bagger, Copenhagen
R&L	Rowman & Littlefield, Totowa, N.J.
RandomH	Random House, London and New York
RandomHAus	Random House Australia, Vic.
Ravan	Ravan Press, Johannesburg
Ravette	Ravette, London
Reaktion	Reaktion Books, London
Rebel	The Rebel Press, London
Red Kite	Red Kite Press, Guelph, Ont.
Reference	Reference Press, Toronto
Regents	Regents Press of Kansas, Lawrence, Kansas
Reichenberger	Roswitha Reichenberger, Kessel, Germany
Reinhardt	Max Reinhardt, London
Remak	Remak, Alblasserdam, Netherlands
RenI	Renaissance Institute, Sophia Univ., Tokyo
Research	Research Pubns, Reading
RETS	Renaissance English Text Society, Chicago
RH	Ramsay Head Press, Edinburgh
RHS	Royal Historical Society, London
RIA	Royal Irish Academy, Dublin
RiceUP	Rice UP, Houston, Texas
Richarz	Hans Richarz, St Augustin, Germany
RICL	Research Institute for Comparative Literature, Univ. of Alberta
Rizzoli	Rizzoli International Pubns., New York
RobartsCCS	Robarts Centre for Canadian Studies, York Univ., North York, Ont.
Robinson	Robinson Pub., London
Robson	Robson Books, London
Rodopi	Rodopi, Amsterdam
Roebuck	Stuart Roebuck, Suffolk
RoehamptonI	Roehampton Institute of Higher Education, London
Routledge	Routledge, London and New York
Royce	Robert Royce, London
RS	The Royal Society, London
RSC	Royal Shakespeare Co., London
RSL	Royal Society of Literature, London

RSVP	Research Society for Victorian Periodicals, Univ. of Leicester
RT	R.T. Pubns, London
Running	Running Press, Philadelphia
Russell	Michael Russell, Norwich
RutgersUP	Rutgers UP, New Brunswick, N.J.
Ryan	Ryan Pub., London
SA	Sahitya Akademi, New Delhi
SAI	Sociological Abstracts, San Diego, Calif.
Sage	Sage Pubns, London
Salamander	Salamander Books, London
Salem	Salem
S&A	Shukayr and Akasheh, Amman, Jordan
S&D	Stein & Day, Briarcliff Manor, N.Y.
S&J	Sidgwick & Jackson, London
S&M	Sun & Moon Press, Los Angeles
S&P	Simon & Pierre, Toronto
S&S	Simon & Schuster, New York and London
S&W	Secker & Warburg, London
Sangam	Sangam Books, London
Sangsters	Sangsters Book Stores, Kingston, Jamaica
SAP	Scottish Academic Press, Edinburgh
Saros	Saros International Publishers
SASSC	Sydney Association for Studies in Society and Culture, University of Sydney, N.S.W.
Saur	Bowker-Saur, Sevenoaks, Kent
Savacou	Savacou Pubns, Kingston, Jamaica
S-B	Schwann-Bagel, Düsseldorf
ScanUP	Scandinavian University Presses, Oslo
Scarecrow	Scarecrow Press, Metuchen, N.J.
Schäuble	Schäuble Verlag, Rheinfelden, Germany
Schneider	Lambert Schneider, Heidelberg
Schocken	Schocken Books, New York
Scholarly	Scholarly Press, St Clair Shores, Mich.
ScholarsG	Scholars Press, Georgia
Schöningh	Ferdinand Schöningh, Paderborn, Germany
Schwinn	Michael Schwinn, Neustadt, Germany
SCJP	Sixteenth Century Journal Publications
Scolar	Scolar Press, Aldershot, Hampshire
SCP	Second Chance Press, Sag Harbor, N.Y.
Scribe	Scribe Publishing, Colchester
Scribner	Charles Scribner's Sons, New York
Seafarer	Seafarer Books, London
Seaver	Seaver Books, New York
Segue	Segue, New York
Self-Publishing Association	Self-Publishing Association
Semiotext(e)	Semiotext(e), Columbia Univ., New York
Seren Books	Seren Books, Bridgend, Mid Glamorgan
Serpent's Tail	Serpent's Tail Pub., London

Sessions	William Sessions, York
Seuil	Editions du Seuil, Paris
7:84 Pubns	7:84 Pubns, Glasgow
Severn	Severn House, Wallington, Surrey
SF&R	Scholars' Facsimiles and Reprints, Delmar, N.Y.
SH	Somerset House, Teaneck, N.J.
Shalabh	Shalabh Book House, Meerut, India
ShaP	Sheffield Academic Press
Shearwater	Shearwater Press, Lenah Valley, Tasmania
Sheba	Sheba Feminist Pubs., London
Sheed&Ward	Sheed & Ward, London
Sheldon	Sheldon Press, London
SHESL	Société d'Histoire et d'Épistemologie des Sciences du Langage, Paris
Shinozaki	Shinozaki Shorin, Tokyo
Shinshindo	Shinshindo Pub., Tokyo
Shire	Shire Pubns, Princes Risborough, Bucks.
Shoe String	Shoe String Press, Hamden, Conn.
SIAS	Scandinavian Institute of African Studies, Uppsala
SIL	Summer Institute of Linguistics, Academic Pubns, Dallas, Texas
Simon King	Simon King Press, Milnthorpe, Cumbria
Sinclair-Stevenson	Sinclair-Stevenson, London
SingaporeUP	Singapore UP, Singapore
SIUP	Southern Illinois UP, Carbondale, Ill.
SJSU	San Jose State Univ., San Jose, Calif.
Skilton	Charles Skilton, London
Skoob	Skoob Books Pub., London
Slatkine	Editions Slatkine, Paris
Slavica	Slavica Pubs., Columbus, Ohio
Sleepy Hollow	Sleepy Hollow Press, Tarrytown, N.Y.
SLG	SLG Press, Oxford
Smith Settle	Smith Settle Ltd, W. Yorkshire
SMUP	Southern Methodist UP, Dallas, Texas
Smythe	Colin Smythe, Gerrards Cross, Bucks.
SNH	Société Néophilologique de Helsinki
SNLS	Society for New Language Study, Denver, Colo.
SOA	Society of Authors, London
Soho	Soho Book Co., London
SohoP	Soho Press, New York
Solaris	Solaris Press, Rochester, Mich.
SonoNis	Sono Nis Press, Victoria, B.C.
Sorbonne	Pubns de la Sorbonne, Paris
SorbonneN	Pubns du Conseil Scientifique de la Sorbonne Nouvelle, Paris
Souvenir	Souvenir Press, London
SPA	SPA Books Ltd
SPACLALS	South Pacific Association for Commonwealth Literature and Language Studies, Wollongong, N.S.W.
SPCK	SPCK, London

Spectrum	Spectrum Books, Ibadan, Nigeria
Split Pea	Split Pea Press, Edinburgh
Spokesman	Spokesman Books, Nottingham
Spoon River	Spoon River Poetry Press, Granite Falls, Minn.
SRC	Steinbeck Research Center, San Jose State Univ., San Jose, Calif.
SRI	Steinbeck Research Institute, Ball State Univ., Muncie, Ind.
SriA	Sri Aurobindo, Pondicherry, India
Sri Satguru	Sri Satguru Pubns, Delhi
SSA	John Steinbeck Society of America, Muncie, Ind.
SSAB	Sprakförlaget Skriptor AB, Stockholm
SSP	Swedish Science Press
StanfordUP	Stanford UP, Stanford, Calif.
Staple	Staple, Matlock, Derbyshire
Starmont	Starmont House, Mercer Island, Wash.
Starrhill	Starrhill Press, Washington, D.C.
Station Hill	Station Hill, Barrytown, N.Y.
Stauffenburg	Stauffenburg Verlag, Tübingen, Germany
StDL	St Deiniol's Library, Hawarden, Clwyd
Steel Rail	Steel Rail Pub., Ottawa
Steiner	Franz Steiner, Wiesbaden, Germany
Sterling	Sterling Pub., New York
SterlingND	Sterling Pubs., New Delhi
St James	St James Press, Andover, Hampshire
St Martin's	St Martin's Press, New York
St Mut	State Mutual Book and Periodical Source, New York
Stockwell	Arthur H. Stockwell, Ilfracombe, Devon
Stoddart	Stoddart Pub., Don Mills, Ont.
StPB	St Paul's Bibliographies, Winchester, Hampshire
STR	Society for Theatre Research, London
Strangers	Strangers Press, USA
Strauch	R. O. U. Strauch, Ludwigsburg
Studio	Studio Editions, London
Stump Cross	Stump Cross Books, Stump Cross, Essex
Sud	Sud, Marseilles
Suhrkamp	Suhrkamp Verlag, Frankfurt-on-Main
Sulis	Sulis Press, Bath
Summa	Summa Pubns, Birmingham, Ala.
SUNYP	State Univ. of New York Press, Albany, N.Y.
SUP	Sydney University Press
Surtees	R. S. Surtees Society, Frome, Somerset
SusquehannaUP	Susquehanna UP, Selinsgrove, Pa.
SussexUP	Sussex UP, Univ. of Sussex, Brighton
Sutton	Alan Sutton, Stroud, Gloucester
S-W	Shepheard-Walwyn Pubs., London
Swallow	Swallow Press, Athens, Ohio
SWG	Saskatchewan Writers Guild, Regina
Sybylla	Sybylla Feminist Press
SydneyUP	Sydney UP, Sydney

SyracuseUP	Syracuse UP, Syracuse, N.Y.
Tabb	Tabb House, Padstow, Cornwall
Taishukan	Taishukan Pub., Tokyo
Talonbooks	Talonbooks, Vancouver
TamilU	Tamil Univ., Thanjavur, India
T&H	Thames & Hudson, London
Tantivy	Tantivy Press, London
Tarcher	Jeremy P. Tarcher, Los Angeles
Tate	Tate Gallery Pubns, London
Tavistock	Tavistock Pubns, London
Taylor	Taylor Pub., Bellingham, Wash.
TaylorCo	Taylor Pub., Dallas, Texas
TCG	Theatre Communications Group, New York
TCP	Three Continents Press, Washington, D.C.
TCUP	Texas Christian UP, Fort Worth, Texas
TEC	Third Eye Centre, Glasgow
Tecumseh	Tecumseh Press, Ottawa
Telos	Telos Press, St Louis, Mo.
TempleUP	Temple UP, Philadelphia
TennS	Tennyson Society, Lincoln
TexA&MUP	Texas A & M UP, College Station, Texas
TextileB	Textile Bridge Press, Clarence Center, N.Y.
TexTULib	Friends of the Univ. Library, Texas Tech Univ., Lubbock
The Smith	The Smith, New York
Thimble	Thimble Press, Stroud, Glos.
Thoemmes	Thoemmes Press, Bristol
Thornes	Stanley Thornes, Cheltenham
Thorpe	D. W. Thorpe, Australia
Thorsons	Thorsons Pubs., London
Times	Times of Gloucester Press, Gloucester, Ont.
TMP	Thunder's Mouth Press, New York
Tombouctou	Tombouctou Books, Bolinas, Calif.
TorSVP	Sister Vision Press, Toronto
Totem	Totem Books, Don Mills, Ont.
Toucan	Toucan Press, St Peter Port, Guernsey
Touzot	Jean Touzot, Paris
TPF	Trianon Press Facsimiles, London
Tragara	Tragara Press, Edinburgh
Transaction	Transaction Pubs., New Brunswick, N.J.
Transcendental	Transcendental Books, Hartford, Conn.
Transworld	Transworld, London
TrinityUP	Trinity UP, San Antonio, Texas
TSAR	TSAR Publications, Canada
TTUP	Texas Technical University Press, Lubbock
Tuckwell	Tuckwell Press, East Lothian, UK
Tuduv	Tuduv, Munich
TulaneUP	Tulane UP, New Orleans, La.
TurkuU	Turku Univ., Turku, Finland
Turnstone	Turnstone Press, Winnipeg, Manitoba

Turtle Island	Turtle Island Foundation, Berkeley, Calif.
Twayne	Twayne Pubs., Boston, Mass.
UAB	Univ. of Aston, Birmingham
UAdelaide	Univ. of Adelaide, Adelaide
UAlaP	Univ. of Alabama Press, Tuscaloosa
UAlbertaP	Univ. of Alberta Press, Edmonton
UAntwerp	Univ. of Antwerp, Antwerp
UArizP	Univ. of Arizona Press, Tucson
UArkP	Univ. of Arkansas Press, Fayetteville
UAthens	Univ. of Athens, Athens, Greece
UBarcelona	Univ. of Barcelona, Barcelona
UBCP	Univ. of British Columbia Press, Vancouver
UBergen	Univ. of Bergen, Bergen
UBordeauxP	Université de Bordeaux Press
UBrno	J. E. Purkyne Univ. of Brno, Brno, Czechoslovakia
UBrussels	Univ. of Brussels, Brussels
UCalgaryP	Univ. of Calgary Press, Calgary
UCalP	Univ. of California Press, Berkeley
UCAP	Univ. of Central Arkansas Press, Conway
UChicP	Univ. of Chicago Press, Chicago
UCopenP	Univ. of Copenhagen Press, Copenhagen
UCordaP	Universidad de Cordoba Press
UdeG	Universidad de Granada
UDelP	Univ. of Delaware Press, Newark
UDijon	Univ. of Dijon, Dijon
UDur	Univ. of Durham, Durham
UEA	University of East Anglia, Norwich
UErlangen-N	Univ. of Erlangen-Nuremberg, Germany
UEssex	Univ. of Essex, Colchester
UExe	Univ. of Exeter, Exeter
UFlorence	Univ. of Florence, Florence
UFlorP	Univ. of Florida Press, Florida
UGal	Univ. College, Galway
UGeoP	Univ. of Georgia Press, Athens
UGhent	Univ. of Ghent, Ghent
UGlasP	Univ. of Glasgow Press, Glasgow
UHawaiiP	Univ. of Hawaii Press, Honolulu
UIfeP	Univ. of Ife Press, Ile-Ife, Nigeria
UIllP	Univ. of Illinois Press, Champaign
UInnsbruck	Univ. of Innsbruck, Innsbruck
UIowaP	Univ. of Iowa Press, Iowa City
UKanP	Univ. of Kansas Press, Lawrence
UKatowice	University of Katowice Press, Poland
UKL	Univ. of Kentucky Libraries, Lexington
ULavalP	Les Presses de l'Université Laval, Quebec
ULiège	Univ. of Liège, Liège, Belgium
ULilleP	Presses Universitaires de Lille, Lille
ULondon	Univ. of London, London
Ulster	Univ. of Ulster, Coleraine
U/M	Underwood/Miller, Los Angeles

UMalta	Univ. of Malta, Msida
UManitobaP	Univ. of Manitoba Press, Winnipeg
UMassP	Univ. of Massachusetts Press, Amherst
Umeå	Umeå Universitetsbibliotek, Umeå
UMel	Melbourne University Press, Victoria, Australia
UMichP	Univ. of Michigan Press, Ann Arbor
UMinnP	Univ. of Minnesota Press, Minneapolis
UMirail-ToulouseP	University of Mirail-Toulouse Press, France
UMIRes	UMI Research Press, Ann Arbor, Mich.
UMissP	Univ. of Missouri Press, Columbia
UMP	Univ. of Mississippi Press, Lafayette Co, Mississippi
UMysore	Univ. of Mysore, Mysore, India
UNancyP	Presses Universitaires de Nancy, France
UNCP	Univ. of North Carolina Press, Chapel Hill
Undena	Undena Pubns, Malibu, Calif.
UNDP	Univ. of Notre Dame Press, Notre Dame, Ind.
UNebP	Univ. of Nebraska Press, Lincoln
UNevP	Univ. of Nevada Press, Reno
UNewE	Univ. of New England, Armidale, N.S.W.
Ungar	Frederick Ungar, New York
Unicopli	Edizioni Unicopli, Milan
Unity	Unity Press Hull
Universa	Uilgeverij Universa, Wetteren, Belgium
UNMP	Univ. of New Mexico Press, Albuquerque
UNott	Univ. of Nottingham, Nottingham
UNSW	University of New South Wales
Unwin	Unwin Paperbacks, London
Unwin Hyman	Unwin Hyman, London
UOklaP	Univ. of Oklahoma Press, Norman
UOslo	Univ. of Oslo, Oslo
UOtagoP	Univ. of Otago Press, Dunedin, New Zealand
UOttawaP	Univ. of Ottawa Press, Ottawa
UPA	UP of America, Lanham, Md.
UParis	Univ. of Paris, Paris
UPColorado	UP of Colorado, Niwot
UPennP	Univ. of Pennsylvania Press, Philadelphia
UPFlor	Univ. Presses of Florida, Gainesville
UPittP	Univ. of Pittsburgh Press, Pittsburgh
UPKen	Univ. Press of Kentucky, Lexington
UPMissip	UP of Mississippi, Jackson
UPN	Université de Paris Nord, Paris
UPNE	UP of New England, Hanover, N.H.
Uppsala	Uppsala Univ., Uppsala
UProvence	Univ. of Provence, Aix-en-Provence
UPValery	Univ. Paul Valery, Montpellier
UPVirginia	UP of Virginia, Charlottesville
UQP	Univ. of Queensland Press, St Lucia
URouen	Univ. of Rouen, Mont St Aignan
URP	University of Rochester Press
USalz	Institut für Anglistik und Amerikanistik, Univ. of

	Salzburg
USantiago	University of Santiago, Spain
USCP	Univ. of South Carolina Press, Columbia
USFlorP	University of South Florida Press, Florida
USheff	Univ. of Sheffield, Sheffield
Usher	La Casa Usher, Florence
USPacific	Univ. of the South Pacific, Institute of Pacific Studies, Suva, Fiji
USydP	University of Sydney Press
USzeged	Univ. of Szeged, Hungary
UtahSUP	Utah State UP, Logan
UTampereP	University of Tampere Press, Finland
UTas	Univ. of Tasmania, Hobart
UTennP	Univ. of Tennessee Press, Knoxville
UTexP	Univ. of Texas Press, Austin
UTorP	Univ. of Toronto Press, Toronto
UTours	Université de Tours
UVerm	Univ. of Vermont, Burlington
UVict	Univ. of Victoria, Victoria, B.C.
UWalesP	Univ. of Wales Press, Cardiff
UWAP	Univ. of Western Australia Press, Nedlands
UWarwick	Univ. of Warwick, Coventry
UWashP	Univ. of Washington Press, Seattle
UWaterlooP	Univ. of Waterloo Press, Waterloo, Ont.
UWI	Univ. of the West Indies, St Augustine, Trinidad
UWiscM	Univ. of Wisconsin, Milwaukee
UWiscP	Univ. of Wisconsin Press, Madison
UYork	Univ. of York, York
Valentine	Valentine Pub. and Drama, Rhinebeck, N.Y.
V&A	Victoria and Albert Museum, London
VanderbiltUP	Vanderbilt UP, Nashville, Tenn.
V&R	Vandenhoeck & Ruprecht, Göttingen, Germany
Vantage	Vantage Press, New York
Variorum	Variorum, Ashgate Publishing Group, Hants.
Vehicule	Vehicule Press, Montreal
Verso	Verso Editions, London
VictUP	Victoria UP, Victoria Univ. of Wellington, New Zealand
Vieweg	Vieweg Braunschweig, Wiesbaden
Vikas	Vikas Pub. House, New Delhi
Viking	Viking Press, New York
VikingNZ	Viking, Auckland
Virago	Virago Press, London
Vision	Vision Press, London
VLB	VLB Editeur, Montreal
VR	Variorum Reprints, London
Vrin	J. Vrin, Paris
VUUP	Vrije Universiteit University Press
Wakefield	Wakefield Press
W&N	Weidenfeld & Nicolson, London

Water Row	Water Row Press, Sudbury, Mass.
Watkins	Paul Watkins, Stamford, Lincs.
WB	Wissenschaftliche Buchgesellschaft, Darmstadt
W/B	Woomer/Brotherson, Revere, Pa.
Webb&Bower	Webb & Bower, Exeter
Wedgestone	Wedgestone Press, Winfield, Kansas
Wedgetail	Wedgetail Press, Earlwood, N.S.W.
WesleyanUP	Wesleyan UP, Middletown, Conn.
West	West Pub., St Paul, Minn.
WHA	William Heinemann Australia, Port Melbourne, Vic.
Wheatsheaf	Wheatsheaf Books, Brighton
Whiteknights	Whiteknights Press, Univ. of Reading, Reading
White Lion	White Lion Books, Cambridge
Whitston	Whitston Pub., Troy, N.Y.
Whittington	Whittington Press, Herefordshire
WHP	Warren House Press, Sale, Cheshire
Wiener	Wiener Pub., New York
Wildwood	Wildwood House, Aldershot, Hampshire
Wiley	John Wiley & Sons, Chichester, New York, and Brisbane
Wilson	Philip Wilson, London
Winter	Carl Winter Universitätsverlag, Heidelberg, Germany
Winthrop	Winthrop Pubs., Cambridge, Mass.
WIU	Western Illinois Univ., Macomb, Ill.
WL	Ward Lock, London
WLUP	Wilfrid Laurier UP, Waterloo, Ont.
WMP	World Microfilms Pubns, London
WMU	Western Michigan Univ., Kalamazoo, Mich.
Woeli	Woeli Publishing Services
Wo-No	Wolters-Noordhoff, Groningen, Netherlands
Wolfhound	Wolfhound Press, Dublin
Wombat	The Wombat Press, Wolfville, N.S.
Woodstock	Woodstock Books, Oxford
Woolf	Cecil Woolf, London
Words	Words, Framfield, E. Sussex
WP	The Women's Press, London
WPC	The Women's Press of Canada, Toronto
WSUP	Wayne State UP, Detroit, Mich.
WVUP	West Virginia UP, Morgantown
W-W	Williams-Wallace, Toronto
WWU	Western Washington Univ., Bellingham
Xanadu	Xanadu Pubns, London
YaleUL	Yale Univ. Library Pubns, New Haven, Conn.
YaleUP	Yale UP, New Haven, Conn. and London
Yamaguchi	Yamaguchi Shoten, Kyoto
YorkP	York Press, Fredericton, N. B.
Younsmere	Younsmere Press, Brighton
Zed	Zed Books, London
Zena	Zena Pubns, Penrhyndeudraeth, Gwynedd
Zephyr	Zephyr Press, Somerville, Mass.

| Zomba | Zomba Books, London |
| Zwemmer | A. Zwemmer, London |

I

English Language

KATARZYNA JASZCZOLT, JULIE COLEMAN, NICOLA J.
WOODS, OLGA FISCHER, WIM VAN DER WURFF, CAROLE
HOUGH, ANDREAS H. JUCKER and CLARA CALVO

This chapter has the following sections: 1. General; 2. History of English Linguistics; 3. Sociolinguistics and Dialectology (including Creolistics); 4. Lexicology, Lexicography and Semantics; 5. Morphology; 6. Syntax; 7. Onomastics; 8. Pragmatics and Discourse Analysis; 9. Stylistics. Section 1 is by Katarzyna Jaszczolt; sections 2 and 4 are by Julie Coleman; section 3 is by Nicola Woods; sections 5 and 6 are by Olga Fischer and Wim van der Wurff; section 7 is by Carole Hough; section 8 is by Andreas H. Jucker; and section 9 is by Clara Calvo.

1. General

A number of enticing volumes on the linguistic history of humans appeared this year. They encompass such diverse areas as the origin of language, the nature of writing, the depiction of the reality in words, as well as gesture and the development of human language. Umberto Eco's *The Search for the Perfect Language* is a magnificent achievement in this group, as is the idea of the series it belongs to. The series, The Making of Europe, is devoted to aspects of the history of the European peoples, published in five languages. The work takes one influential idea and travels with it through 2,000 years of European thought: it is the idea that there once was an unambiguous, perfect language, spoken in the Garden of Eden, and that human wisdom should focus on the rediscovery of that language, or perhaps on a discovery of an artificial language that would be perfectly suited to serve all the required purposes. Eco discusses the rediscovery of old languages such as Hebrew, Egyptian or Chinese, the reconstruction of languages that are postulated as original, as well as the construction of artificial languages such as: (i) philosophical languages whose aim is a perfect expression of ideas; (ii) international languages for social and political purposes; (iii) practical but 'perfect' languages; and, perhaps most extraordinary, (iv) magic languages. The history of Europe is also seen as originating with a multitude of tongues, rather than nations: ' . . . Europe first appears as a Babel of new languages. Only afterwards was it a mosaic of nations' (p. 18). Eco sees the history of the pursuit of a perfect language as producing positive side-effects such as taxonomy in natural sciences, comparative linguistics, formal languages, artificial intelligence and cognitive sciences. He offers a clear and insightful analysis of texts supporting his ideas, which begin with St Augustine, Dante, Descartes, Rousseau, and cabalistic writings. He reviews popular arguments for the *Ursprache*, be it German, Hebrew, Indo-European, or any other language put forward by the nationalistic hypotheses of the seventeenth and eighteenth centuries, and also touches upon the contentious Nostratic hypothesis of Cavalli-Sforza, of the single origin of language based on the single origin of humans. Next follows Giordano Bruno and the mathematics of combination used for the perfect language, Vico's idea of a 'visual language' and 'speaking in hieroglyphs', the magic language of the brotherhood of the Rosicrucians, Leibniz's 'lingua generalis' and much more, including Solresol – a universal musical language, and Russell and Whitehead's syntax for a logical, unambiguous system. All in all, the advantages of the *confusio linguarum* of Babel are not to be missed: multiple languages are the prerequisite for a modern state, and the overall conjecture follows suit and makes the reader wonder what is next to come from this author. Adam's language is suggested to have been 'a complex of all languages' – whatever the reader wishes to read into it: English is not *perfect* after all! It is a magnificent, scholarly introduction to a fascinating topic. Although it will undoubtedly feel overly sketchy in places, references certainly remedy this shortcoming.

Writing is an independent mode of communication – or so the reader is consistently told in some of this year's works on the topic. Roy Harris can undoubtedly be credited with propagating this idea most successfully throughout many of his publications. *Signs of Writing* aims at demonstrating that signs of writing function differently from signs of speech. His new perspective on writing is best summed up in the claim that the written sign is explained by the reference to the activities of writing and reading; the standard approach would proceed in the opposite direction. The approach traced back to de Saussure's semiology results in a new idea of seeing sign as a product of communication: no system of signs is presupposed. The book exceeds in controversial statements of the type: if communication by gesture counts as writing, then writing precedes speech, and problems such as whether a gramophone record counts as writing, followed by a discussion of mathematical formulae, knitting patterns, dance notation and music scores. To sum up, this is a highly contentious book and unfortunately sometimes perfunctory in the treatment of discussed texts. Another aspect of language and humanity is presented in the claim that writing gives us models for thinking. David Olson in a book published late last year, *The World on Paper: The Conceptual and Cognitive Implications of Writing and Reading*, takes up the topic of the role of writing in understanding language and the world – an obvious paraphrase of Sapir and Whorf. The approach is divided between the history of ideas and developmental psychology. Like Harris, Olson reverses the traditional Aristotelian relation between language and speech: an ancient Sumerian clay tablet is analysed as a sample of script with a syntax but without presupposing speech. Generally, the book is a readable, brief history of writing that reaches beyond to cognitive science in drawing dependencies between literacy on the one hand, and the emergence of the theory of mind and theoretical knowledge on the other. It is original and witty, although the main strength seems to lie in the novelty of its contentious ideas rather than in their support.

Plato's *Cratylus* is in the forefront again with an English translation of Gérard Genette's *Mimologics*. Mimology says that the sounds, shapes, lengths and patterns of words imitate the world and language is the representation of reality. Genette shows how the belief in the relation of analogy between words and things is reflected in the literary achievements of various periods and genres. Saussurean arbitrariness of signs, Derrida's preoccupation with symbols are all applied to the French symbolists Rimbaud and Mallarmé, followed by a discussion of Condillac and Diderot on syntax and word order, Proust on names, and many other landmarks in human literary history. The book is defined as 'voyage en Cratylie' – a journey with Cratylus through époques, styles and ideas. Like most examples of French literary criticism that grew out of the structuralist tradition, it may appear somewhat exalted in style to an Anglo-American linguist but it is certainly worth the effort. *Gesture and the Nature of Language* is a deftly handled series of arguments to the effect that manual and vocal communication developed in parallel: the fundamental properties of syntax can be derived from the features of gesture. D. F. Armstrong, W. C. Stokoe and S. E. Wilcox offer an evolutionary approach to language in which life in social groups pushed early hominids to developing visual and vocal forms of communication such as gesture and speech. Language and its syntax are conjectured to have resulted from an analysis of gesture. *A fortiori*, language is not organized in the form of modules in the mind and language acquisition does not presuppose a language-specific device but rather is based on general principles. Corroboration from anthropology follows suit: the theory explains some puzzling facts such as (i) the large size of the brain in early humans prior to the appearance of *homo sapiens*, and (ii) the existence of Broca's (linguistic) area in the brain in *homo habilis* (and perhaps even in earlier australopithecines). The work also contains a sound discussion of modular and associationist theories of language in the light of recent findings. Finally, the climax of the book which cannot be rendered but by a direct quotation:

> Which is more in keeping with Occam's razor: having each brain contain S, NP, and VP; hence, S $\rightarrow$ NP + VP, and VP $\rightarrow$ V + NP (in other words, SVO); or having outside the brain, where any perceptive hominid can see in the same field of view, for example, a bird pecking at a berry and a thumb and forefinger plucking at a fingertip on the other hand? (p. 182)

The *richesse* of work on primates reported in my contribution to *YWES* 75 seems to continue and deliver excellent, thought-provoking theories like this one from CUP.

Reference books are slightly overshadowed this year by the magnificent achievement of David Crystal's *The Cambridge Encyclopedia of the English Language* from CUP which is a delight to browse through. It is an abundantly illustrated guide to: (1) the origins and history of English, embellished by the vividly presented history of invasions and examples from literary texts; (2) English as a world language; (3) English vocabulary; (4) discourse; (5) the writing system, and much more. In addition, it is overflowing with photographs, advertisements, cartoons, quotations, newspaper cuttings, poems, anecdotes, all benefiting from the latest technology of graphic design. Next, a batch of reference and textbooks from Routledge: Kirsten Malmkjaer's 1991 *The Linguistics Encyclopedia* appeared in an affordable paperback edition, Larry Trask published a 'pre-textbook introduction': *Language: The Basics*, a commendable coverage of the central topics of the study of language which also springs surprises on the reader: one can find out from it, for instance, what it means that 'grass smells purple' and a vowel is yellow. All this in the excellent chapter on Language, Mind and Brain. Much less praiseworthy is Ronald Carter's dictionary of linguistics-related terms, *Keywords in Language and Literacy*. It focuses on entries of the following type: 'proper English', 'accent', 'appropriate', 'correct' which are supposed to be of use in teaching literacy. The potentially ambitious aim is to show to what extent 'linguistics' and especially 'sociolinguistics' shed light on the debates as to how to teach language (NB. the definition of 'linguistics' is rather confounded there). Although the work is proudly announced as a challenge to modern linguistic pluralism of 'anything goes' in language, it turns out to be a rather selective and biased reference book, of dubious theoretical standard and practical value. Three new items from the Language Workbooks Series from Routledge seem to fulfil what the series promises: they are accessible to beginners, easy to use and almost saturated with exercises. All this applies to Patricia Ashby's *Speech Sounds*, Richard Hudson's *Word Meaning* and Raphael Salkie's *Text and Discourse Analysis*. The selection of topics in the series is at present far from being representative of the discipline; let us hope the series will expand to give a more balanced overview of current preoccupations in linguistics.

Deborah Cameron's *Verbal Hygiene* takes up the subject of literacy but avoids successfully the partiality and bias of Ronald Carter's approach discussed above. She states that attempts to regulate language use are a natural phenomenon; people not only use language but also typically comment on it and the benefit from this practice is that rules for language use impose order on social life. Generally, 'it is rare to find anyone rejecting altogether the idea that there is *some* legitimate authority in language. We are all of us closet prescriptivists – or, as I prefer to put it, verbal hygienists' (p. 9). So, the phenomenon of prescriptivism has to be studied because it is a pervasive feature of everyday life. Although the statement seems to be true, the whole reasoning looks rather dubious: it is possible, after all, that prescriptivism is a straw man that is highlighted by its former rejection and that the enterprise is highly theory-laden and potentially uninteresting from the outset. All in all, the work succeeds as a study of correlations between 'proper' speech on the one hand, and gender, ethnicity, or class on the other, supported by a discussion of case studies. As a eulogy of a 'new' prescriptivism, however, it is rather disappointing in offering the old story in a new disguise. John Edwards's *Multilingualism* appeared too late in last year to be included in *YWES* 75 but certainly should not be omitted. It traces the effects of multilingualism on individual speakers and society. Discussed topics include language and nationalism, language and identity, history, politics and education, as well as developmental and social consequences of multilingualism and language change, spread and decline – all permeated with a conviction that bilingualism and multilingualism are natural phenomena of modern life rather than departures from a norm. Edwards forestalls Cameron's concern with the gap between common interest in correctness and linguists' neglect of the topic and puts the problem in a historical (social and linguistic) perspective.

Another arrival from late last year is *Repetition*: a selection of symposium papers edited by Andreas Fischer. The phenomenon of repetition is discussed by contributors who take combinations of the following pairs of standpoints: (1) repetition is desirable or should be avoided; and (2) repetition is a linguistic or literary phenomenon. To mention three of the contributions, Jean Aitchison in 'Say, Say It Again Sam' finds the following senses of the title word: parroting, reinforcement, imitation, preservation, echolalia, stuttering, stammering, epizeuxis, ploce, anadiplosis, polyptoton, antimetabole, cohesion, alliteration, chiming, rhyme, parallelism, ritual, gemination, reduplication, copying, reiteration, and more, for instance repeated patterns in linguistics. In addition, repetition is divided into intentional and unintentional, and obligatory and optional. Andreas Jucker in 'Irrelevant Repetitions: A Challenge to Relevance Theory' concentrates on recycles and overlaps and tries to fit them into the relevance-theoretic claim of economy of processing effort in utterance interpretation. Derek Attridge in 'The Movement of Meaning: Phrasing and Repetition in English Poetry' claims that repetition is 'a crucial feature of all poetry' (p. 69) but argues that there is no *exact* repetition and no clear demarcation line between repetition and non-repetition. Ten remaining papers are likewise commendable. Derek Attridge is also the author of *Poetic Rhythm: An Introduction*. Attridge leads the reader from the rhythms of spoken English, through rhythms of nursery rhymes and popular music, to sophisticated rhythms of poetry. The book opens with an introduction to basic terms in reading poetry such as rhythm, metre, stress, metrical and free verse, and beat. The study of rhythms of spoken English follows suit and includes a study of English syntax, syllable structure and organization, stress and stress groups. In passing, one can also find there remarks on the sources of the popularity of rap and an analysis of rap's metric. A lucid and informative introduction, not to be missed by students of stylistics, prosody, conversation analysis or other related areas of linguistic and literary studies. To sum up, it has been a successful and prolific year for reference and textbooks, demonstrating the appearance of new areas and attitudes, as well as the high-quality continuation of established sub-fields.

Approaches to Language Typology edited by Masayoshi Shibatani and Theodora Bynon is a collection of nine articles presenting various ways of accounting for cross-linguistic variation. The contributions range from the Prague school approach to that of Principles and Parameters. The book begins with a thorough, informative introduction, written on historical principles and reaching as far back as Friedrich von Schlegel. Many of its contributions are highly commendable, including Joseph Greenberg's 'The Diachronic Typological Approach to Language' and William Croft's 'Modern Syntactic Typology'. On a related topic, Anthony Fox's *Linguistic Reconstruction: An Introduction to Theory and Method* is a praiseworthy achievement. It gives a lucid account of the application of the Comparative Method to phonology, morphology, syntax and lexicon, followed by an introduction to quantitative methods in reconstruction, including J. Nichols's 'population typology': a quantitative analysis of the distribution of certain relevant features across languages; Cavalli-Sforza's work on genetic and linguistic evidence for the spread of human populations, and much more. At a time when there is an abundance of books on language change, an account that focuses on reconstruction is certainly most welcome. It is possible, however, to add original ideas to the former topic: Rudi Keller's *On Language Change: The Invisible Hand in Language* is Brigitte Nerlich's translation of a 1990 German edition and is certainly an unusual book on historical linguistics. The book utilises ideas from various aspects of cognitive science to arrive at the claim that natural languages are neither natural phenomena nor artefacts – they are rather results of human action, but as 'phenomena of the third kind' (p. 57). Keller suggests the 'invisible-hand' explanation of language change: a group of speakers changes a language without any intentional behaviour aimed at this change, i.e. without an overall design for this change in mind. In effect, language change is likened to the life of social institutions such as money, taste, ghettos – the life of language is governed by the same principles. Keller uses a very simple metaphor to illustrate this idea: language changes just in the way a footpath appears: a footpath is a causal consequence of many individual intentional actions whose intentions need not be identical but merely partly similar: an effect of an 'invisible hand'. A natural question arises in this perspective as to whether language change is a socio-cultural process and, if so, then to what extent. This question also receives a fair treatment, with an appeal to philosophical ideas of the past. The author appeals to the ideas of Bernard Mandeville, Max Mueller, August Schleicher, W. D. Whitney, Noam Chomsky, Karl Popper, and many others. An unconventional and thought-provoking work.

Semantics and pragmatics benefited from many commendable texts this year. John Lyons's *Linguistic Semantics: An Introduction* encompasses word meaning, sentence meaning and utterance meaning and in a masterly fashion reconciles structuralism and atomism by pointing out the possibility of ultimate (and perhaps universal) atoms of meaning in componential analysis. Readers used to narrow-scope introductions to a particular semantic theory should be warned to be careful with adopting definitions of technical terms such as denotation, reference, sense, extension or intension: with the author's insight into the problems surrounding the use of these terms, their meaning can no longer be taken for granted. Lyons's *Introduction* was launched together with a Festschrift: *Grammar and Meaning: Essays in Honour of Sir John Lyons* (ed. F. R. Palmer) written by a number of contributors, all of whom should be listed here due to the outstanding quality of their papers: F. R. Palmer, A. Kilgariff and G. Gazdar, A. Lehrer and K. Lehrer, P. Matthews, R. M. Kempson, S. C. Levinson, J. Miller, P. Trudgill, B. Comrie, J. Anderson and R. M. W. Dixon. The final voice is granted to Sir John Lyons in 'Grammar and Meaning'. He uses it to advocate a wide, everyday view of the word 'meaning'; define linguistic semantics as dealing with both propositional and non-propositional meaning that is encoded in grammar and lexicon; explain the ingenious idea of bringing together Saussure's structuralism and Russellian relational treatment of abstract properties; and finally to observe that 'much of what linguists present as fact (in both semantics and grammar) can, and in my view should, be re-interpreted as fiction (i.e. as rough-justice model-construction)' (p. 235). This seems also to reflect the tone of Lyons's book. Each of the other contributions would be worth a review but, space permitting, I shall only mention Levinson's excellent defence of the theory of the 'Three Levels of Meaning' which includes utterance-type meaning between sentence-meaning and speaker-meaning: 'The theory of utterance-type meaning should be a theory of default interpretation' (pp. 109–10). To sum up, the volume is an intellectual feast and offers a chance to compare various dominant standpoints in current semantic-pragmatic debates. Finally, Timothy C. Potts's *Structures and Categories for the Representation of Meaning* is a survey of contributions made by linguistics, logic and computer science to the representation of meaning, followed by his own account inspired largely by the writings of Gottlob Frege. He offers there a new categorization of count nouns and proper names which are treated analogously, touching also upon the problems with generics and demonstratives, as well as providing a clear and informative exposition of Frege's views on these matters.

Two books on formal semantics from MIT require brief acknowledgement: Richard Larson and Gabriel Segal's *Knowledge of Meaning: An Introduction to Semantic Theory* follows Davidson in adopting the credo that Tarski's theory of truth is the formal basis of semantic theory. The results are formidable: all problematic areas of linguistic meaning are accounted for in a clear and intelligent manner, avoiding the dogmatism on points of philosophical interest which is so common for previous textbooks on the subject. The semantics remains truth-conditional but avoids the unnecessary formalism of Montague's approach and, what is especially admirable, offers a catholic approach to the boundary dispute between semantics and pragmatics: the absence of satisfactory solutions is openly stated where necessary (for instance in the case of definite descriptions) and the pragmatic option is left open. Sometimes, it seems perhaps to have been left too open when the authors ponder the possibility of providing a semantic theory for every particular speaker as an ultimate task: 'an important aspect of deciding when a semantic theory applies to a given speaker will lie in deciding whether an axiom may truly be associated with a concept in the speaker's mind (. . .) and when it may not' (p. 187). In spite of the authors' assurances to the contrary, it may not be an easy task for the hearer or discourse analyst. Next is Alice ter Meulen and *Representing Time in Natural Language: The Dynamic Interpretation of Tense and Aspect*. Based on Situation Semantics, Discourse Representation Theory and other approaches and methods in dynamic logic, the book sets off to provide a computational inference system of universal applicability to fragments of natural languages. Ter Meulen investigates how the temporal information from discourse or text is used by the hearer to establish the conveyed flow of time. The work is certainly commendable to formal semanticists. One more acknowledgement before passing to pragmatics: G. J. Huck and J. A. Goldsmith's *Ideology and Linguistic Theory: Noam Chomsky and the Deep Structure Debates* is essentially a dispute of Chomskyan school of Interpretive Semantics with Generative Semantics of the sixties and seventies, presented as a volume in the series History of Linguistic Thought. Although some of the presented details will only be of interest to a historian of ideas, the enterprise as a whole is historically significant in itself as one more tribute to Chomsky and one more favour by his followers: a debate which is relatively marginal from a scientific point of view has been brought to the fore due to the recognition given to the participants on one of its sides. According to Paul M. Postal, it was merely a dispute about 'the *right form* of transformational grammar'. And, as he explains, 'to me, there is no right form of that theory, any more than there is a right form of phlogiston theory. The bad thing is not that Generative Semantics disappeared but that the other branch of transformational theory didn't disappear' (p. 138). This is an extract from a conversation with Postal transcribed in the Appendix and presented along with interviews with Ray Jackendoff, George Lakoff and John Robert Ross. The book demonstrates that the history of this creative period in linguistics seems best told through the insight of the participants and survivors of the debate.

The long-promised presentation of pragmatics this year should be inaugurated by the *Handbook of Pragmatics: Manual*, a tremendous achievement of the editors J. Verschueren, J.-O. Östman and J. Blommaert. It is an encyclopaedic publication including lengthy entries on traditions and methods in pragmatics, preceded by Verschueren's introduction to the history and state-of-the-art of pragmatic research. The *Manual* is accompanied by a loose-leaf Handbook, to be updated every year, and a User's Guide. The scope is wide, from Analytical Philosophy to Creole Linguistics, all accompanied by extensive references. All this makes the work an invaluable reference guide, although probably not for beginners. The choice of entries suggests a historical perspective on theories and methods and expressions such as 'implicature', 'connectives', 'intentions' and other problematic phenomena have to be traced within the theory-oriented entries. Nevertheless, it fulfils its aim excellently as a reference on traditions and methods, which pleases the present author who had the pleasure of being one of the contributors. Next, Jenny Thomas's *Meaning in Interaction: An Introduction to Pragmatics* is a rather disappointing introduction to pragmatics, whose opening sentence sums up the perfunctory and sloppy presentation: 'People do not always or even usually say what they mean' (p. 1). The account is oversimplified to the extent of patronizing a beginner, and the muddled organization of the book is reminiscent of what Ron Scollon and Suzanne Wong Scollon (see below) call a 'medieval way of writing': counter-arguments are introduced and discussed before the real beginning appears on p. 22: 'In this book I shall be working towards a definition of pragmatics as meaning in interaction'. It is difficult to judge whether it is this dubious aim that makes Thomas compress the long and fascinating tradition of pragmatic research into a rather sketchy chapter confined to some aspects of Austin's views and summed up in what seems to be the style of the whole work: 'In this chapter we have seen how utterances perform actions, how speakers can mean considerably more than their words say' (p. 51). It will be difficult to find a novice student fascinated by pragmatics presented in this way: after all, what's new? If 'how' means theories, the text preceding the summary does not live up to the summary. What is particularly worrying is the lack of any account of post-Levinson-1993 pragmatics. No sense-generality and radical pragmatics, no Horn and Atlas, no Fodor and Sperber and Wilson, no implications of and for the cognitive science research. Longman generally offers accessible and simple textbooks, but even if one presents the tip of the iceberg, it must be at least the correct iceberg.

Ron and Suzanne Wong Scollon offer *Intercultural Communication: A Discourse Approach* – a wide-ranging introduction to pragmatics and the analysis of conversation. Throughout the book the main emphasis is placed on factors connected with intercultural differences. The discussed topics include Speech Act Theory, Brown and Levinson's Politeness Theory, corporate discourse (i.e. discourse in a multicultural environment), differences in discourse between generations and genders. The whole book is highly commendable but especially praiseworthy is the chapter on 'Ideologies of

Discourse' – it stresses the importance of the world-view, the philosophy of a group of people, for communication, but mainly introduces the utilitarian discourse system of Jeremy Bentham and J. S. Mill, characterized by clarity, brevity and sincerity (freedom of expression) as a model for discourse. The analysis of a particular historically and philosophically significant discourse system like this seems more illuminating than theories summarizing empirical data: it gives ideological foundations for what we say and how we say it. A very original contribution from Blackwell to the growing field of cross-linguistic pragmatics and a pleasure to read.

Gillian Brown's new book *Speakers, Listeners and Communication: Explorations in Discourse Analysis* aims at broadening the understanding of the cognitive basis of language use and showing the emerging patterns of behaviour of interlocutors. Using a cognitive-pragmatic approach, the Author demonstrates how speakers and listeners use language in a collaborative manner to talk about the common situation. The approach is data-driven. Groups of Scottish (Edinburgh) and English (Essex) children and students were exposed to various tasks focusing on the understanding of reference to persons and things, location in space and interaction in time. For instance, the listener had to identify spatial relationships on a map having heard the speaker's description of a route, or a group of students had to work out the sequence of events of watched and heard episodes. Understanding is presented as a matter of degree and it is concluded, among others, that 'misunderstandings frequently arise not directly from the linguistic form of the utterance but because of the listener's difficulty in relating what the speaker has said to the listener's own perception, or memory, of the nature of features or events in the world' (p. 235). The interdependence of theory and data works illustriously and one can only look forward to the promised sequel. A very different approach to discourse is on offer from Peter Fries and Michael Gregory, editors of *Discourse in Society: Systemic Functional Perspectives* which constitutes the second volume of the series Meaning and Choice in Language: Studies for Michael Halliday. The contributions focus on the relation of grammar to discourse – a systemic-functional idea, where 'grammar' means Halliday's functional grammar. Contributions are pleasingly open-minded, to mention only Barbara Horvath and Suzanne Eggins's 'Opinion Texts in Conversation' which puts together Labov's variationism and Halliday's systemic linguistics in the analysis of expressing attitudes. Hasan's text/context dialectics in his monograph 'The Conception of Context in Text' occupies all of the second part. All in all, clear and informative, although mainly of interest to systemic-functionalists.

On a cognitive note, Neil Smith and Ianthi-Maria Tsimpli's *The Mind of a Savant* sums up a four-year study of an impaired man, Christopher, and his extraordinary linguistic ability to read, write, translate and communicate in 15 to 20 languages. This case-study in cognitive science allows the authors to draw conclusions concerning the impact this research has on theories of cognition. Earlier findings of this project were reported in *YWES* 74.6. Christopher's linguistic competence was tested by using Chomsky's Principles and Parameters approach, which led to the conclusion that absolute syntactic principles of Universal Grammar underlie language learning of the savant but parameter resetting is absent: there are frequent instances of direct transfer from English into his second and further languages. Moreover, the savant is reported to cope with logical inference, but not with metalinguistic phenomena of irony or metaphor. He is unable to understand jokes as his 'extralinguistic aspects of language' located in the right hemisphere are impaired. The main achievement of Smith and Tsimpli is shedding some light on the 'central system': a largely unknown processor in the brain whose main function is, as the dominant story has it, to put the information from the modules together. By testing the savant on the so-called 'theory of mind tasks' Smith and Tsimpli concluded that the 'theory of mind' module, i.e. awareness of knowledge and beliefs, is placed in the central black box. Deficits in language use are attributed to the faulty interaction of the modular, linguistic faculty with the operations of this central system. The deficits are normally syntactic; lexicon is acquired with the close-to-native ability, which demonstrates the difference in learning of these two aspects of language. In conclusion, language module is proposed to intersect with the central system rather than being merely an input system as traditional Fodorian theory suggests. Leaving many open questions was ineluctable; one can only hope for an equally successful continuation of the project which would make the phrase 'black box' obsolete. D. Sperber and D. Wilson's immensely popular *Relevance: Communication and Cognition* reached its second edition, particularly interesting for its Postface: we are offered *two* principles of relevance: the first one says that human cognition tends to aim at the maximization of relevance, and the other remains as follows: 'Every act of ostensive communication communicates a presumption of its own optimal relevance', i.e. it contains a supposition that the utterance (or: 'ostensive stimulus') is relevant enough (and is the most relevant one) for the addressee to process. These revisions are claimed to be highly significant.

Finally, language acquisition: *The Lexicon in Acquisition* by Eve Clark appeared in paperback this year. It deals with the acquisition of words by children and some aspects of lexical semantics. The value of the study is significantly strengthened by the presentation of case-studies from many languages representing various language families, although the examples are not totally flawless. Kaj Sjöholm's *The Influence of Crosslinguistic, Semantic, and Input Factors on the Acquisition of English Phrasal Verbs* may not have a wide range of circulation (Abo) but it nevertheless deserves a brief mention. The study is a comparison between Finnish and Swedish learners of English, focusing on the acquisition of lexicon. Although the literature review is not quite up to date on the current theories of second language acquisition, the results are interesting even if predictable: Finns exhibit a poorer performance on phrasal verbs and this fact is attributed to language distance factors. It has been repeatedly observed in the literature that research on SLA suffers from being years if not decades behind the current developments in syntactic theory. Although it may be difficult to follow Chomsky closely and work on empirical and cognitive problems simultaneously, the sacrifices have to follow a sound methodological principle in order to avoid the effect of sloppiness. Sjöholm's work would certainly benefit from such a principle.

Journals do not offer many papers of general interest and the overall tendency seems to be a drive towards further and further specialization. Gregory Ward and Betty Birner in 'Definiteness and the English Existential' (*Language* 71.722–42) put forward some interesting ideas on definite noun phrases in *there*-constructions. Such phrases are permitted when the noun phrase represents an entity new to the hearer: formally definite, they are hearer-new. So, the constraint against definites in *there*-constructions should not be based on the formal definiteness of the noun phrase; sentences of this type are only infelicitous when there is 'a mismatch between the cognitive status to which definiteness is sensitive and that to which the postverbal position in *there*-sentences is sensitive. Postverbal position in *there*-sentences may felicitously be occupied by exactly those definite NPs that are construable as hearer-new in context' (p. 740). It is an original and insightful proposal for explaining a deficiency in syntactic generalization. A. J. Meier in 'Passages of Politeness' (*JPrag* 24.381–92) offers a re-examination of Brown and Levinson's theory of politeness, questioning its applicability to empirical data. First, she finds the notion of negative politeness (the desire to be unimpeded) subsumable under the notion of positive politeness (the desire to be approved of), which puts into question Brown and Levinson's distinction. Next, she argues, correctly, that the use of indirect speech act by a particular culture should not be automatically associated with a higher degree of politeness exhibited by this culture as compared with cultures exhibiting directness. She postulates a 'social interpretation of particular linguistic behavior within a particular speech community' (p. 387) instead of absolute 'directness' or 'politeness'. Politeness is for her relative to contexts and should be renamed as 'appropriateness'. A theoretical implication follows: speech acts cannot be assigned a degree of politeness. Marga Reimer in *Ling&P* (18.655–75) initiated an interesting discussion on the conventionality of performatives: in 'Performative Utterances: A Reply to Bach and Harnish' she argues against Bach and Harnish's idea that performative utterances are standardized indirect illocutionary acts, and, directly, constatives. She argues for a non-constative account: conventions are said to devoid performative utterances of their constative illocutionary force potential. Kent Bach's reply ('Standardization vs. Conventionalization', *Ling&P* 18.677–86) contains a convincing defence of his approach as a middle-ground between ambiguity and conventionalization. Finishing this presentation with a debate is symptomatic for general linguistics this year: many debates, controversies, unanswered questions, but open-minded approaches all seem promising for the years to come.

2. History of English Linguistics

The most important publication this year is *A Thesaurus of Old English* by Jane Roberts, Christian Kay and Lynne Grundy. The first volume consists of a brief introduction and the thesaurus, which is based upon the material to be found in Bosworth and Toller, and Clark-Hall, checked against the Toronto microfiche. Although the same material will also form part of the forthcoming Glasgow *Historical Thesaurus*, the advantage of the separate OE thesaurus is that the classification reflects the different concerns of that period. It is, therefore, in some senses 'a pilot study for the full thesaurus'. The second volume contains an index to the OE words in the thesaurus, so that words can be located, as in an ordinary thesaurus, either through synonyms or through the classification structure. This does mean that the work would be of little use to a reader unacquainted with OE, who will be better served by the full thesaurus. Cross-references within the classification provide extra help. Additional information about the frequency, distribution, and reliability of words is provided within the classifications, and the justifications for including this information are discussed in the introduction. Because of the finite nature of the OE corpus, the thesaurus, in combination with the Toronto microfiche, will enable scholars to locate all surviving vernacular references to the subject in which they are interested. Once users have become accustomed to its conventions, this work will become an indispensable tool for any linguist, literary critic, or historian of any kind who is interested in the Anglo-Saxon period.

Premyslaw Lozowski's 'Semantic Vagueness: A Split or Double Identity' (in Henryk Kardela and Gunnar Persson, eds, *New Trends in Semantics and Lexicography*) discusses ambiguities arising from OE translations of Latin *somnus* and *somnium* apparently indiscriminately, as *slæp* and *swefn*. He demonstrates that the failure to distinguish clearly between the two Latin forms reflects conceptual vagueness at the borderline between 'sleep' and 'dream'. Nancy Helen Goldsmith-Rose's 'Languages at the Norman Court of England' (in Françoise Le Saux, ed., *The Formation of Culture in Medieval Britain*) takes issue with the notion that a twelfth-century English court would contain speakers only of Anglo-Norman, Latin and 'Anglo-Saxon English'. She lists other languages which may also have been present, such as Welsh and other Celtic languages, Old Norse and Occitanian.

In 'Nuns and Midwives, Slaves and Adulteresses: OE Terms Denoting Women', Bengt Odenstedt (in Kardela and Persson, eds, *New Trends*) compares the OE lexis for women with Modern English and with Swedish, but fails to reach any convincing conclusion about the loss of 80 per cent of OE nouns for 'woman'. Along with Gunnar Persson and Mats Rydén's 'The Project "Male" and "Female" Terms in English. A Diachronic Study of a Semantic Field' in the same volume, the paper could have benefited from reference to the OE and Glasgow Historical Thesaurus projects, but at least Persson and Rydén right the imbalance of earlier sociolinguistic studies, which tended to concentrate on terms for women and to demonstrate limited diachronic awareness.

Stanley Hussey's *The English Language. Structure and Development* covers much of the material to be expected in an introductory text on the history of English, but in a rather unpredictable way. Instead of taking a chronological approach and dealing with aspects of the language period by period, Hussey has chapters on grammar, semantics, phonetics and orthography, and so on, and picks his illustrations from whichever period seems most appropriate, usually beginning with a discussion of PDE usage or contemporary attitudes. In the section on standard and non-standard English, for instance, he looks at the dialects of the Middle English period, the rise of Chancery English, and at attempts to establish an Academy. The chapter on vocabulary begins by comparing descriptions of hell by David Lodge and John Bunyan, and then talks about how and when terms were borrowed, moving from a discussion of the alternatives to borrowing, looking at compounding in OE, and then on to a consideration of contemporary neologism. He explains his terms as he goes along, but the linguistic glossary facilitates later reference. It defines terms such as *verb phrase, subject* and *relative clause*, but assumes an understanding of parts of speech. The volume concludes with a brief introduction to onomastics. Each section is followed by exercises to encourage the readers, presumably first-year undergraduates, to learn more for themselves.

Thorlac Turville-Petre's *England the Nation. Language, Literature, and National Identity, 1290–1340* also uses an interesting approach to the history of English. As the title suggests, the language of England is not the only focus of his study, with the text focusing largely on the position of the language in defining national identity. He shows that a growing sense of national identity was accompanied by a feeling that English was the most appropriate language for its expression, and demonstrates that, although the act of writing history is fundamental to a sense of nationhood, the choice of language in which to do this was by no means as straightforward as might appear. Among those concerned to stress the unity of the nation were churchmen, who wished to stress the community of the Christian family instead of the division between Church and laity. Turville-Petre selects his texts to explore the question of national identity, looking at, for instance, the *Liber Regum Anglie*, which emphasizes national unity by brushing aside inconvenient differences between the English and the British. The regional distinctiveness of Lincolnshire and Ireland, emphasized in the texts selected for the purpose, are studied alongside the express wish of, for instance, the English in Ireland, to be part of the image constructed as the nation as a whole. The question of national literature in a culture which had no standardized form of the language is also explored, and Turville-Petre concludes that none of the literature of this period considers itself to be national, but that the Harley Lyrics point the way ahead.

Julie Coleman's 'The Chronology of French and Latin Loan Words in English' (*TPS* 93.ii.95–124) updates Jespersen's seminal study of French loans based on material found in the OED. The OED's uneven coverage is taken into account, and the rate of acquisition is compared with obsolescence and with assimilation in the form of semantic development, affixation and naturalization. Tatsuo Miyajima's 'A Contrastive Study of Vocabulary Growth in Different Languages' (in Urs Egli et al., ed., *Lexical Knowledge in the Organization of the Lexicon*) suggests that although Chinese is set apart by its longer written history, the age of present-day vocabulary in Japanese, French and English, can be related to periods of intensive change in the languages.

Manfred Görlach's *New Studies in the History of English* is a collection of papers presented at conferences or given as guest lectures between 1986 and last year. Most were printed in conference proceedings, but it is useful to have them gathered together in this way, although there is no overall coherence to the volume. Some papers are discussed under Lexicology, Lexicography and Semantics. The introduction discusses developments in historical linguistics since it was pronounced dead in the 1960s and 1970s. Gaps in the standard works used and areas in need of revision are identified. The next paper discusses language death in general and with reference to English in particular. It is clear that the notion of language death is used to group together a variety of situations with many different causes. A few examples are given of cases where English or an English-related pidgin or creole died, but many more can be found where English is the successful competitor. Görlach suggests that official language-planning policies may have little effect on language vitality. 'Morphological Standardization: The Strong Verbs in Scots' compares 273 surviving strong verbs in OE and OHG, then compares the English and Scots forms. Next, a consideration of cookery books and dedications is taken as the starting point for an exploration of the problems of describing the correlation between socio-stylistic conditions and linguistic variation. The use of text types in descriptive linguistics is also proposed in 'English in nineteenth-century England'. 'Fifteenth Century English – Middle English or Early Modern English' concludes that although such boundaries are arbitrary, 1430/50 is as good a cut-off point as any.

Lynda Mugglestone's '*Talking Proper*'. *The Rise of Accent as Social Symbol* looks at changing attitudes to English speech in the late eighteenth and nineteenth centuries, and at how those attitudes were reflected in literature of the period as well as in prescriptive linguistic texts. She notes that the social disadvantage connected with local accents is necessarily associated with the development of Received Pronunciation, even though the earliest proponents of a national non-localized standard for speech, such as Sheridan, emphasized its use in promoting equality. Once the notion of 'correct' speech was codified, however, largely on the basis of the written language, the notion of 'literate speech' emerged, and it became possible to identify 'incorrect' speech as the result of lack of education, sloppiness of thought and lack of self-control. Schools and Sunday schools exerted themselves to standardize speech, equating RP with good behaviour. From being a source of shame, then, local accents and dialects thus developed into a perversion. Mugglestone traces the shifting fortunes of the long and short vowels in words such as *fast* and *bath* as markers of vulgarity, and the declining prestige of rhoticism in Britain since the nineteenth century, when r-dropping was considered to be a Cockney vulgarism. Spelling pronunciations, intrusive r, h-dropping and other variants are also considered in some detail. She discusses the tradition of depicting women as the guardians of language from the nineteenth century onwards, providing the link between her own study and the findings of sociolinguistics.

Rachelle Watson notes in 'She's a mensch and he's a bitch: neutralizing gender in the 90s' (*EnT* 11.ii.3–6), that the deliberate gender revolution of the 1970s led to an avoidance of gender-marked terms in the 1980s, but that originally marked terms such as *guy* and *dude* are now used unmarked.

3. Sociolinguistics and Dialectology (including Creolistics)

Starting this year's review with research on the use of English in America, Raymond Tatalovich's 'Voting on official English language referenda in five states' (*LPLP* 19.47–59) provides an update on the English-only policy (and the consequent backlash against Hispanics) in the states of Alabama, Arizona, California, Colorado and Florida. Tatalovich aims to assess the external factors which correlate with efforts to gain the enactment of English-only statutes (e.g. racism, ethnic rivalry, cultural-nativist ideology and political allegiance), and finds that the main factor related to the English-only movement is politics: in all five states studied, legislative sponsors of official English laws were from Republican areas which represented mainly suburban counties with above-average levels of income and education and below-average numbers of 'Hispanics, blacks, and persons in poverty'. Also on the 'English-only' movement is Howard Giles, Angie Williams, Diane Mackie and Francine Rosselli's paper 'Reactions to Anglo- and Hispanic-American-accented speakers: affect, identity, persuasion, and the English-only controversy' (*L&C* 15.107–20). In this complex paper, the authors examine how such factors as mood and nationalist feeling are affected by listening to Anglo- and Hispanic-American-accented speakers making statements for and against the English-only movement. Results reveal that Anglo-accented speakers were persuasive when they proposed arguments *against* 'English-only', and Hispanic-accented speakers were persuasive when they argued *for* the movement. Giles et al. conclude that their results suggest that attitudes towards 'English-only' policies are 'malleable and susceptible to modification, at least in the short term, depending on the speech style of the persuasive party' (p. 117).

Abdallah Hady Al-Kahtany's 'Dialectal ethnographic "cleansing": ESL students' attitudes towards three varieties of English' (*L&C* 15.165–80) examines Saudi Arabian students' perceptions of Standard American English, Black English and Indian English. The judgements of two groups of students are assessed: undergraduates who had been studying in America for a period of two to three years, and graduate students who had been studying for a period of five to six years. Perhaps the most important findings of the study relate to perceptions of Black English: analysis reveals that in all attitudinal areas (including ratings of intelligence, friendliness and ambition), graduate students judged Black English significantly lower than did undergraduates. Results also show that, while both sets of students consider Black English to be an unacceptable medium of instruction, graduate students felt this more strongly than undergraduates. Al-Kahtany notes that the findings on Black English are 'disturbing' since they show that graduate students – who have spent a longer time in the US and who are further advanced in their education – show a greater degree of linguistic stereotyping than undergraduates. He concludes that 'there should be an investigation to determine if ESL training and university education in the United States are promoting linguistic stereotyping based on race' (p. 177).

Other papers on English in America are produced by Yolanda Russinovich Solé and Cuor-Avila and Bailey. The former paper – 'Language, nationalism, and ethnicity in the Americas' (*IJSL* 116.111–37) – examines the factors stated in the title in four contrasting language contact situations: Spanish in the United States versus English in Argentina, and Guarani-Spanish in Paraguay versus Quechua-Spanish in Peru. The latter paper by Patricia Cukor-Avila and Guy Bailey – 'An approach to sociolinguistic fieldwork: a site study of rural AAVE in a Texas community' (*EWW* 16.159–93) – proposes a new method of overcoming the age-old problem of the Observer's Paradox. This method involves focusing research on a strategic site of linguistic interaction in which speakers can be recorded speaking to each other, rather than to the researcher. Such an approach, the authors argue, allows researchers to become 'overhearers' rather than addressees, and, as a consequence, contexts are created in which speech outside of the interview situation becomes the norm rather than the exception.

IJSL 114 is devoted to papers reporting on 'Sociolinguistic trends on the U.S.–Mexican border'. A number of papers included in this volume examine the relationship between Spanish and English in this area: Garland Bills, Eduardo Hernández Chávez and Alan Hudson discuss 'The geography of language shift: distance from the Mexican border and Spanish language claiming in the South-western U.S.' (9–27); Honorine Donelly Nocon asks 'Is the word "Mexican" taboo? The impact of the border on Spanish students' integrative attitude and motivation' (47–66); and Richard V. Teschner reports on 'Beachheads, islands, and conduits: Spanish monolingualism and bilingualism in El Paso, Texas' (93–105). Finally, we should note the publication of Jelena M. Savic's 'Structural convergence and language change: evidence from Serbian/English code-switching' (*LSoc* 24.475–92) in which the author uses Carol Meyers-Scotton's Matrix Language Frame model to investigate and analyse code-switching and structural convergence in the language of Serbian-American college students.

Michael Aceto provides a detailed and illuminating discussion of the use of a Caribbean cryptolect in his article 'Variation in a secret creole language of Panama' (*LSoc* 24.537–60). Aceto describes the phonological, lexical and syntactic features of the secret language of 'Gypsy', and also explains its primary function of excluding conversational participants from specific speech events thereby creating linguistic and social distance between those who can use the dialect and those who cannot. Aceto concludes by highlighting patterns of variation in the English-derived creole spoken on the island of Bastimentos in Panama; he claims that this variation has always existed on the island and is not due to a process of contact and decreolization which is the usual explanation proffered to explain diversity in creole languages. Other papers on English-based creoles published this year include Hirokuni Masuda's analysis of 'TSR formation as a discourse substratum in Hawaii Creole English' (*JPCL* 10.ii.253–88), John McWhorter's 'Sisters under the skin: a case for genetic relationship between the Atlantic English-based creoles' (*JPCL* 10.ii.289–334); Magnus Huber's 'Ghanaian pidgin English: an overview' (*EWW* 16.215–50); Valerie Youssef's 'Tense-aspect in Tobagonian English: a dynamic transitional system' (*EWW* 16.195–213); Peter Muhlhausler's 'Attitudes to literacy in the pidgins and creoles of the Pacific area' (*EWW* 16.251–72); and Hiroki Masuda's 'Versification and reiteration in Hawaii Creole English: "if nomo paila mæn, awrai!"' (*WE* 14.317–42). It should be noted that *JPCL* 10.i. remains unseen at the time of the writing of this section.

This year's volumes of *LVC* (7) are not yet available for review just as 1994 volumes were unavailable last year. However, we have now seen 1994's volumes and should at least mention the titles of three papers which may be of particular interest: Natalie Schilling-Estes and Walt Wolfram's 'Convergent explanation and alternative regularization patterns: were/weren't levelling in a vernacular English variety' (6.273–302); Robert Bayley's 'Consonant cluster reduction in Tejano English' (6.303–26); and, on British English, James Milroy, Lesley Milroy, Sue Hartley, David Walshaw's 'Glottal stops and Tyneside glottalisation: competing patterns of variation and change in British English' (6.327–57).

Other papers on British English published this year include Pauline Barbé's study of 'Guernsey English: a syntax exile?' (*EWW* 16.1–36), in which the author reports on 'neglected' syntactic constructions which, she argues, provide evidence of the 'distinctive' nature of this variety. It is easy to be convinced by Barbé's argument since the work clearly emerges from a meticulous methodology which provides numerous illuminating examples of Guernsey English syntax. Particular constructions recorded by the author include the use of FAPs (First verb plus the conjunction 'And' plus the Plain infinitive): *we went and live there*; pre-nominal, adjectival 'plenty': *now I got plenty apples*; and a characteristic use of the third person singular auxiliary 'have': *but remember, she have studied it*. From Guernsey to Scotland, EWW *16* includes two papers relating to the use of English in this region: Ronald Macaulay's 'The adverbs of authority' (37–60); and Alisdair Allan's 'Scots spellin – ettlin efter the quantum lowp' (61–103). The former provides a qualitative sociolinguistic analysis of middle class and lower class (*sic*) speakers' use of derivative adverbs ending in *-ly* and the adjectives from which these are derived. Macaulay reports that middle-class speakers use these forms significantly more frequently, and he explains these results by suggesting that the use of adverbs and adjectives by middle-class speakers reflects their 'self-confident and authoritarian attitude' (p. 56). The paper by Alasdair Allan aims to identify principles in the standardization of Scots orthography, and is written in the variety which it discusses.

In the opening lines of Delyth Morris's paper 'Language and class fractioning in a peripheral economy' (*JMMD* 16.373–87), the author argues that 'Neither sociolinguistics nor the sociology of language have taken seriously the role of language in the labour market' (p. 373). Morris's paper attempts to fill this gap by examining the relationship between language, labour and class in a marginal economy in Wales. Results show that a new middle/managerial class fractions along a cleavage that conforms to language groups: non-Welsh managers orientating upwards and aligning themselves with the bourgeoisie, and Welsh-speaking managers orientating in the opposite direction – downwards towards the proletariat.

Turning to Canada, research on the relationship between English and French in this region continues this year with the publication of a paper by Shalom Endelman: 'The politics of language: the impact of language legislation on French- and English-speaking citizens of Quebec' (*IJSL* 116.81–98). In this article, Endelman traces the French–English conflict in Quebec from the British conquest of New France in 1795 to the present day, and concentrates on how patterns of urbanization in the 1960s led French-speaking Canadians to an awareness of their deprived status and to a consequent political and cultural renaissance of this group. The 'Quiet Revolution' which resulted from this, and the language laws and bills which went with it, led to out migration of English-owned businesses and corporations and of the highly educated middle and managerial class of Anglophones working within these corporations. Endelman argues that this exodus paved the way for a newly created middle and managerial class of French-speaking Québécois and a change in power of the province from one which was in the hands of the English to one which is now in the control of the French. However, the success of these French controlled industries in Western Canada and the United States has led to work-related English-language requirements being made on upwardly mobile Francophones. Endelman concludes that within two generations it is possible that Quebec will accommodate not a single Anglophone, but that all will be able to speak English. Finally, on language use in Canada, we should mention Monica Heller's 'Language choice, social institutions, and symbolic domination' published in *LSoc* 24.373–405.

While little seems to have been published on the use of English in Africa this year, one notable exception is Rajend Mesthrie and Paula West's 'Towards a grammar of proto South African English' (*EWW* 16.105–33). In this paper the authors discuss what they claim is an important and underappreciated aspect of the history of this variety: namely, the nature and impact of the input British English dialects. Mesthrie and West argue against the common assumption that the English spoken by early settlers was largely standard, and claim that the non-standard varieties of early settlers, rather than contact with Afrikaans, provided many of the characteristic forms of grammar found in South African English today. Analysis of various forms of letters written between 1820 and 1825 reveals grammatical constructions including: adjective with infinitive (e.g. *I am lazy to acquire these skills*); never + past tense verb used with the meaning of 'didn't' rather than 'not ever' (e.g. *but I never got any pass yet and my contract is never near out*). Also worthy of mention is Edmund Bamiro's 'Syntactic variation in West African English' (*WEn* 14.189–204) which provides an analysis of literary texts in respect of such syntactic variants as subjectless sentences, omission of function words and reduplication. Results reveal that many of the constructions characteristic of West African English are also found in many other non-native varieties. Bamiro takes this as evidence to show that, in contrast to Randolph Quirk's view of the instability of such English varieties, new Englishes have acquired some permanent linguistic characteristics.

Following on from last year's publications on language maintenance and ethnolinguistic vitality in Australia by Michael Currie and Michael Hogg (*YWES* 75.19), John Gibbons and Lyn Ashcroft examine this topic in their paper 'Multiculturalism and language shift: a subjective vitality questionnaire study of Sydney Italians' (*JMMD* 16.281–99). The authors aim to investigate whether the real differences between Italian and Greek vitality are reflected in the subjective vitality of speakers, and they find that, in general, there is a relationship between subjective vitality and objective maintenance. Perhaps the most significant findings of the study concern the different perceptions that Italian speakers have of Italian dialects: 'Italo-Australians tend to be far more sanguine about the survival of Standard Italian in Australia than they are about the vitality of dialects such as Sicilian' (p. 295). Gibbons and Ashcroft conclude that this finding highlights a problem with census data which do not distinguish standard Italian from other Italian dialects, and they conclude that it is possible that standard Italian is being maintained in Australia to a far greater degree than census data suggests, but that other Italian dialects are being lost more rapidly. *IJSL* 113 is devoted to publishing research on 'Australian Aborigines and Torres Strait Islanders: sociolinguistic and educational perspectives'. Papers of particular interest are Stephen Harris's 'Evolution of bilingual education theory in Northern Territory Aboriginal schools' (7– 22); Brian Devlin's 'The evaluation of bilingual programs in the Northern Territory, Australia, 1973–1993' (23–36); and Anna Shnukal's 'From monolingualism to multilingualism in Australia's Torres Strait island communities' (121–36). The last of these provides a detailed and illuminating account of the shift from the use of two indigenous languages (Kala Lagaw Ya and Meriam Mir) to a more complex post-contact situation in which two other languages have been added (Australian English and Torres Strait Creole – an indigenous development of nineteenth-century Pacific Pidgin English) making the Torres Strait islands a quadrilingual speech area. Shnukal comments on the decline of the indigenous languages and how these are being displaced by English through the transitional medium of Torres Strait Creole.

Maria Stubbe and Janet Holmes report on '*You know, eh*', and other 'exasperating expressions': an analysis of social and stylistic variation in the use of pragmatic devices in a sample of New Zealand English' (*L&C* 15.68–88). Stubbe and Holmes look specifically at the social distribution of these forms across social class, age, gender and stylistic boundaries and find, for example, that the use of speaker-orientated particles such as 'I think' are used more frequently by the middle classes, while addressee-orientated forms such as 'you know' and 'eh' are used by the working classes. The paper concentrates on examining distribution in the *forms* of discourse particles, although some information is given on their function – e.g. as markers of social solidarity in New Zealand. The authors conclude that although forms such as tags and hedges are negatively evaluated forms of speech, they perform an indispensable function in conveying epistemic and affective meanings in situated speech encounters.

Anthea Fraser Gupta and Siew Pui Yeok provide a fascinating, if somewhat disturbing, account of 'Language shift in a Singapore family' (*JMMD* 16.301–14). In this article, the authors discuss how government initiatives towards the use of English and Mandarin have led to language shift across three generations of one family: a shift so rapid and drastic that it has led to a breakdown in communication between grandparents and grandchildren. Gupta and Yeok analyse the language and speech of three generations of an extended family: grandparents (70 years), their children (38 to 63 years), and their grandchildren (2 to 28 years). They find that the middle generation plays a significant role in mediating between the grandparents and grandchildren: for example, by translating the Cantonese of the oldest generation into English, and by code-switching between languages to allow everyone to participate in the same conversation. However, although this middle generation attempt to keep communication channels open between the old and the young, they are apparently unwilling to speak Cantonese themselves, but rather leave responsibility for the transmission of this language to the grandparents. Gupta and Yeok find that grandparents do not perceive a problem in speaking to their grandchildren: they claim, for example, that their grandchildren can use Cantonese to converse about simple topics. However, the authors' results show that the youngest children do not spontaneously use this language and that there is a considerable discrepancy between reported and observed language use. They conclude that 'in this family, the switch to English has resulted in loss of contact of grandchildren with grandparents, surely to the personal loss of both groups' (p. 313).

WEn includes two papers on English in Singapore this year: Phyllis Ghim Lian Chew's 'Lectal power in Singapore English' (14.163–80); and Bao Zhiming's '*Already* in Singapore English' (14.181–8). The former examines the importance of 'lectal power' – the ability to use the right lect at the right time – in admission interviews to a tertiary institution specialising in training for teachers. Analysis of lectal power at the lexical, syntactic, discourse and pragmatic levels reveals that applicants who wish to gain admittance to a particular professional group need to be in command of the linguistic norms of that group. Chew concludes that this creates a paradox inasmuch as that applicants need to use linguistic forms which reveal their affiliation to a professional class before they are able to seek admittance to it. The second paper by Bao Zhiming examines the use of 'already' in Singapore English and finds that it is used to express two aspectual properties: the completion of an action (perfectivity), and the beginning of an action (inchoativity). While the former use is consistent with the lexical meaning of 'already' in English, Zhiming argues that the inchoative use of this form has its source in the Chinese particle 'le'.

Raja Ram Mehrotra's 'How to be polite in Indian English' (*IJSL* 116.99–110) considers politeness as it is realized in forms of address, the expression of gratitude and status distancing. Numerous significant differences are observed between Indian English and British and American English: in respect of forms of address, Mehrotra notes that, while in British English a woman may be addressed by a stranger as 'darling' or 'my love', a man addressing a strange woman in such a fashion in India may be subjected to 'a beating by both the addressee and the passer-by' (p. 104); regarding the verbalization of gratitude by Hindi-English bilinguals, Mehrotra finds that gratitude is more common in interaction which takes place in English than in Hindi, and in situations where both languages are used in a single conversation, speakers say 'thank you' more often than its Hindi equivalent 'dhanyavad'. Mehrotra provides many other illuminating examples of this type, and he examines variation between the English of the East and West in terms of differences in stylistic and semantic space which characterize language use in these regions. However, he does not look in any detail at the cultural constraints which are surely crucial in explaining such variation in politeness phenomena. A. Suresh Canagarajah provides a detailed and illuminating account of 'The political economy of code choice in a "revolutionary society"': Tamil–English bilingualism in Jaffna, Sri Lanka' (*LSoc* 24.187–212). Canagarajah describes the apparent decline in Tamil-English bilingualism which has resulted as a consequence of military imposition of a 'Tamil Only' policy (for both formal and informal interactions). However, while this policy has led to a decline in grammatical competence in English and to the demise of English dominant bilinguals, Canagarajah argues that English is nevertheless living a 'vibrant afterlife' in the form of code-switching linguistic activity: an activity which enables English to continue in a more widely distributed and pervasive form than ever before, with both 'monolinguals and bilinguals using English in conventional and unconventional contexts' (p. 209). Canagarajah predicts that the future is likely to see a gradual separation of Englishized Tamil as an independent code in parallel use with both unmixed Tamil and English. Canagarajah also has a paper – 'Functions of codeswitching in ESL classrooms: socializing bilingualism in Jaffna' (*JMMD* 16.173– 95).

The use of English in Japan seems to be becoming a focal point for research with a large number of papers being published on this area this year. Nobuyuki Honna presents an analysis of 'English in Japanese society: language within language' (*JMMD* 16.45–62) in which she examines the use of English loan words – e.g. *ofureko* – 'off record', *sekohan* – 'second hand', *shou ene* – 'save energy' – and explains their incorporation into Japanese by reference to structural, functional and sociolinguistic factors. Regarding the last of these, Honna identifies the English Teaching Programme, and specifically the unrealistic goals of this programme and its consequent limited success, as responsible for the influx of English loan words. Specifically, Honna argues that, since Japanese speakers have not found it possible to achieve the 'native' type fluency that was a primary aim of the Teaching Programme, they have not taken on English as an International Language but have rather taken advantage of it as part of Japanese. In her paper 'Bilingualism in international families' (*JMMD* 16.63–85), Masayo Yamamoto examines language use in families resident in Japan where one parent is Japanese and the other English. She looks particularly at patterns of use between family members (spouse–spouse, parents–children), and argues that, while children who achieve bilingual proficiency in English are envied by their monolingual peers, they nevertheless face the problem of being conspicuous in a society which discourages uniqueness. Kumiko Murata's 'Repetitions: a cross cultural study' (*WEn* 14.iii.343–56) examines the use of repetitions in three cultural groups: native speakers of British English, native speakers of Japanese, and Japanese speakers of English. Murata finds that these groups use repetitions for different functions: for example, Japanese speakers use repetitions to signal solidarity with conversational participants, while English speakers use repetitions to avoid silence. Murata concludes that the use of repetitions are related to the different patterns of turn-taking used in English and Japanese and to the social and cultural values which characterize the use of repeated forms. Finally, we should mention that *WEn* 14.i is a special issue on 'The English language in Japan: history, attitudes and functions'. Edited by Harumi Tanaka, Sachiko Tanaka and Minoru Ike, the volume includes Ikuo Koike and Harumi Tanaka's 'English in foreign language education policy in Japan: toward the twenty-first century' (13–26); Sen Nishi Yama's 'Speaking English with a Japanese mind' (27–36); and Gillian Kay's 'English loanwords in Japanese' (67–76).

Zhao Yong and Keith Campbell's 'English in China' (*WEn* 14.377–90), is the only paper we have come across on this region this year. The authors' aims are threefold: to present a demographic account of users of English in China; to assess the differing degrees of proficiency of these users; to provide a sociolinguistic profile of the different functions of English in Chinese society. The authors conclude that the main purpose of use of English in China is not one of international communication, but rather of social and economic mobility.

Muhammad Hasan Amara presents a detailed and sensitive account of the social differentiation of Hebrew and English lexical items in a variety of Palestinian Arabic spoken in an Arabic village in north Israel. Entitled 'Hebrew and English lexical reflections of socio-political changes in Palestinian Arabic' (*JMMD* 16.165–72), the paper examines the relationship between language use and social and political change, and posits the hypothesis that the proportion of Hebrew and English words used will relate to villagers' degree of acculturation and hence to such factors as their educational history, occupational status, religious observance, age and gender. In fact, analysis reveals that, while significant differences in the use of *Hebrew* words is found according to these social dimensions (e.g. males use three times as many Hebrew words as females), the use of *English* lexical items does *not* vary according to the social characteristics of speakers. The author explains these results by arguing that the domains influenced by English are well established and that, consequently, ongoing acculturation is slow. This leaves Hebrew as the main source of innovation which represents fast and dynamic acculturation to Israeli Jewish culture, and the process of ongoing modernization.

Moving on to textbooks, the most detailed and thorough volume published on Sociolinguistics this year is Jack Chambers's *Sociolinguistic Theory*. As well as including the usual topics of language and social class, gender and social networks, Chambers places sociolinguistic study in its historical context by considering this discipline as a departure from traditional approaches which took as axiomatic the categorical nature of linguistic units. His chapter on 'Accents in Time' provides new and illuminating insights into the relationship between age, language use and linguistic change. This volume is perhaps not best suited for the student beginning the study of Sociolinguistics, but will be most useful for more advanced students needing to develop a more critical perspective. Martin Montgommery's textbook on Sociolinguistics – *An Introduction to Language and Society* – is published in its second edition, and includes sections on The Development of Language, Linguistic Diversity and the Speech Community, Language and Social Interaction, and Language and Representation.

On the topic of language and gender, first mention should go to Janet Holmes's *Women, Men and Politeness*. The assumption that women are more polite than men has long been taken as a primary index of male–female linguistic differences. However, not until Holmes's book has there been a single text bringing together the evidence for this assumption. In the first paragraph Holmes states explicitly that she believes that 'women are more polite than men', and in the rest of the volume she cites various evidence to support this view. She looks specifically at politeness strategies in conversational organization, as well as characteristic politeness discourse types such as the use of hedges, compliments and apologies. Holmes was one of the first scholars of language and gender to identify the importance of looking behind the forms of language used by women to the function that these forms fulfil. Employing this approach in this volume allows Holmes to draw important conclusions about the politeness strategies used by men and women. Sara Mills's *Feminist Stylistics* is published by Routledge this year, as is a volume of papers edited by Mills entitled *Language and Gender: Interdisciplinary Perspectives*. This volume includes papers originally presented at the Loughborough University conference on Language and Gender (1992), and includes Jennifer Coates's 'Language, gender and career'; Joan Swann and David Graddol's 'Feminising classroom talk?'; and Barbara Crowther and Dick Leith's 'Feminism, language and the rhetoric of television wildlife programmes'. *Gender Articulated: Language and the Socially Constructed Self* is edited by Kira Hall and Mary Bucholtz, and includes papers by Robin Tolmach Lakoff on 'Cries and whispers: the shattering of the silence', Susan Gal on 'Language, gender and power: an anthropological review' and by Penelope Eckert and Sally McConnell-Ginet on 'Constructing meaning, constructing selves: snapshots of language, gender, and class from Belten High'.

On language and ethnicity, Ben Rampton's *Crossing: Language and Ethnicity among Adolescents* must be the book of the year. It is a work of immense detail examining the language use and interactional strategies of young people of South Asian, Afro-Caribbean and Anglo descent. Rampton analyses how the varieties characteristic of each of these groups is used by the others in various contexts, with various participants, and for various functions (not least of these being the use of crossing to show solidarity and to overcome racial difference within a broad construct of youth culture). As well as providing numerous examples of *crossing*, in early chapters of the work Rampton also assesses the attitudes of each group to 'out-group' members use of each variety: he finds, for example, that white and black use of Panjabi is perceived enthusiastically, while crossing to the use of creole and stylized Asian English is perceived in a more equivocal manner. Later chapters deal with such topics as 'Crossing and performance art' and the implications of crossing for 'Educational Discourses on Language'. Throughout the work Rampton provides examples from spontaneous speech data of adolescents in various social contexts. These bring the work to life and, as with the rest of the text, reveal not only examples of crossing itself, but attitudes towards the use and function of this linguistic behaviour by those who carry it out. Also worthy of mention here is Lesley Milroy and Pieter Muysken's (eds) *One Speaker, Two Languages: Cross-Disciplinary Perspectives on Code-Switching* which includes papers by Marilyn Martin-Jones on 'Code-switching in the classroom: two decades of research' (90–112), Monica Heller on 'Code-switching and the politics of language' (158–74), and Carol Myers-Scotton on 'A lexically based model of code-switching' (233–56).

Finally, it is worth noting a selection of the texts published on discourse and text analysis. First mention should go to Norman Fairclough's *Critical Discourse Analysis* (published in Longman's *Language in Social Life* series) which brings together in one volume papers written by the author between 1983 and 1992. The volume is divided into four sections dealing with: (i) Language, ideology and power; (ii) Discourse and sociocultural change; (iii) Textual analysis in social research; and (iv) Critical language awareness. Fairclough's *Media Discourse* (Arnold) remains unseen at the time of writing this section. *Language and Context: A Functional Linguistic Theory of Register* is the title of Helen Leckie-Tarry's work which, described in her own words, provides an exploration of ways in which the relationship between the 'how' and 'what' of textual meaning and variation can be theorized within an oral-literate dimension. The volume, edited by David Birch after the author's death, provides analysis of register and genre, through lexicalization to theme and information structure. Raphael Salkic's *Text and Discourse Analysis* is a workbook-style volume providing methods and techniques for the analysis of such registers as news stories, novels and adverts. Carmen Rosa Caldas-Coulthard and Malcolm Coulthard's (eds) *Texts and Practices: Readings in Critical Discourse* includes a similarly wide-ranging selection of texts, each of which addresses the question of whether powerful members of society use language to control the powerless. This is, of course, an old question, but the volume provides some new answers. On literacy, two volumes certainly deserve to be mentioned. The first is Brian Street's ethnographic account of *Social Literacies* and the other is Mike Baynham's *Literacy Practices: Investigating Literacy in Social Practice* which looks specifically at the functions of literacy in multilingual settings.

Last for this year, but by no means least, we should note the publication of Deborah Cameron's *Verbal Hygiene*. Cameron begins her work by telling the story of how a visit to an exhibition on *The Use and Abuse of Language* led to an encounter in which she was asked 'what are linguists doing to combat the abuse of language?'. Her book seeks to answer this question by examining the role of the linguist in relation to the concerns of the layman. Having defined verbal hygiene roughly in terms of the 'urge to meddle in matters of language',

Cameron considers this issue under such chapter headings as 'Restrictive Practices: the Politics of Style' where she asks and seeks answers to the question of 'What are the rules of writing and who makes them?'; 'Dr. Syntax and Mrs Grundy: the Great Grammar Crusade' where Cameron comments specifically on the hysteria of the late 1980s relating to the teaching of English; and 'The New Pygmalion: Verbal Hygiene for Women' where she traces the history of advice given to women on how, and how not, to speak. Cameron's book is intellectually engaging but also entertaining. As such, it will be of interest to linguists and laymen alike.

4. Lexicology, Lexicography and Semantics

Collins's *Today's English Dictionary*, whose editor in chief is John Sinclair, is based on the Cobuild 'Bank of English' corpus, from which all illustrative quotations are taken. It is written informally, uses a minimum of abbreviations, concentrates on the most commonly used words, and includes some encyclopaedic information. No etymological information is included, and guidance to stress and pronunciation, where given, is represented by respelling rather than presentation in IPA, e.g. *ferment* is pronounced 'fer-*ment*' or '*fer*-ment'. Parts of speech are indicated by definition rather than by giving labels. Sexual taboo words are omitted, as are most racist terms, although *nigger* is included, and labelled 'offensive'. Reliance upon a corpus appears to have given rise to some strange inconsistencies, for example, *shit* is included, but *piss* is not. The style of definition is best illustrated by quotation: 'A *hairbrush* is a brush for your hair.' '*Teddy boys* were young men of the 1950s who wore long jackets, tight "drainpipe" trousers, and soft thick-soled shoes. They brushed their hair back and had sideburns. Teddy boys were associated with early rock and roll music and were often thought of as violent and aggressive.' 'A *girl* is a young woman up to the age of about 30. This use of "girl" is very common, but some people object to it. A *girl* or *little girl* is a female child.' The dictionary is not, then, aimed at sophisticated dictionary-users, but the introductory material gives no indication of who its target audience is, other than that they are expected to be native speakers.

Linda and Roger Flavell's *Dictionary of Word Origins* is an accessible etymological dictionary aimed at the browser rather than the serious scholar, though its sources are, on the whole, reliable enough. The introduction discusses briefly Indo-European languages and the history of English, but does not attempt to give more than half a page to, for instance, a subject like Middle English. The book contains articles on about 300 commonly used words, with longer essays scattered throughout the otherwise alphabetically arranged text, on subjects such as words from Arabic, Malay or Chinese, the days of the week and months of the year and negative prefixes. Within each article citations are provided, but it is not always clear whether they are intended to be illustrative, explanatory or merely amusing. These articles usually cover related terms, sometimes only listed (as *flora*, *floral*, *florist*, *flourish*, and *florid* are after *flower*), but sometimes discussed in their own right. Following the article on *focus*, for example, its relationships to *foyer* and *fuel* are discussed at some length. The short essays often provide an interesting and accessible introduction to a subject which the reader might otherwise not become aware of, and I can see them being used as the basis for undergraduate essays on various aspects of the development of English.

Two dictionaries of contemporary slang were reissued in new editions by Macmillan this year: Robert L. Chapman's *The Macmillan Dictionary of American Slang* and Jonathon Green's *The Macmillan Dictionary of Contemporary Slang*. Chapman admits the problem that both, and probably all, slang dictionaries face: of determining where slang ends and colloquialism begins, a problem which Green does not address, listing terms such as *bloody-minded, loner* and *off the cuff*, which should probably be considered colloquial. Both consider the nature of slang in their prefaces, with Chapman taking the strangely defensive stance that the production of slang dictionaries is justified even though they might fall into the hands of the impressionable. He gives a brief history of slang lexicography and discusses 'the individual psychology of slang speakers', dividing slang usage into the primary, found among integrated members of a subculture, and the secondary, which is more a matter of stylistic choice or personal image. Green's preface discusses etymologies of the word *slang*, but does not commit itself to any one of them, and then presents definitions of the term since the mid-eighteenth century: the British emphasizing vulgarity and class-distinctions, and the American vitality and progressiveness. Each dictionary represents, to some extent, a compilation of its forebears, with Green acknowledging his particular debt to Partridge, and Chapman to Wentworth and Flexner.

The dictionaries are similar in the nature of their entries, in that they each sometimes indicate date of earliest citation, place of origin and special currency. The entry for *choirboy* demonstrates the unnecessarily restrictive nature of some of Green's definitions: '*choirboys* n. (US police use) innocent, novice policemen who work strictly by the rulebook: *Hill Street Blues, Thames TV, 1983*'. There is, on the other hand, no indication of geographical restriction or origin for the terms *play possum* 'to pretend to be dead', *chippy on* 'to cheat on one's wife or husband with a new sexual partner', or *Hershey highway* 'the anus'. Green occasionally cites a term on the authority of works such as Barry Humphries's strip cartoons, which probably represent humorous linguistic inventiveness rather than genuine slang. Chapman marks some terms and uses as vulgar 'to be used only when one is aware of and desires their strong effect', and taboo '*never* to be used'. Taboo terms are generally four-letter words, racist terms, or derivatives of the two. Terms labelled as vulgar are more numerous and refer mainly to sexual behaviour, sexuality, and defecation. This labelling could be seen as descriptive or prescriptive; representing either a brave attempt to give some indication of the varying acceptability of these terms or a continuation of the defensiveness of the preface. Such labelling is, as Chapman concedes, subjective. For instance, *bimbo, bitch* and *broad* as terms for women, are all marked as vulgar, but *bird* is not, with the note 'regarded by some women as offensive' implying that these women are unnecessarily sensitive, while *chick* and *filly* are not labelled at all. Although each dictionary is interesting as an example of popular lexicography, their contribution to serious lexicography is not enormous.

Leonhard Lipka's 'Lexicology and lexicography: Poor relations, competition, or co-operation?' (in René Dirven and Johan Vanparys, eds, *Current Approaches to the Lexicon*) considers the relationship between the two disciplines and their relationship with linguistics as a whole, and concludes that while lexicographical practice is largely unrelated to lexicological theory, developments in linguistic theory are usually reflected in the work of lexicographers after some delay. In 'Meaning: Remarks on Methodological Problems of Representing and Modelling in Semantics and Lexicography' (in Henry K. Kardela and Gunnar Persson, eds, *New Trends in Semantics and Lexicography*), Krzysztof Korzyk finds that semantic theories are often mutually dependent, and that semanticists and lexicographers are striving to pin down different types of meaning. Michael Lesk discusses the different approaches of dictionary and thesaurus-makers in 'Why Use Words to Label Ideas: The Uses of Dictionaries and Thesauri in Information Retrieval' (in Donald Walker et al., *Automating the Lexicon*). He suggests that it should be possible to combine the lexicographer's need to distinguish words from each other with the thesaurus-constructor's assemblage of synonyms.

N. E. Osselton's *Chosen Words. Past and Present Problems for Dictionary Makers* is a collection of 16 essays: 14 of them published across the last 30 years, and two of them new. They deal with monolingual and bilingual dictionaries, covering modern dictionary practice as well as that of early dictionaries, including an aborted manuscript attempt at a monolingual dictionary dating from *c.*1570 (Bodleian Library, Rawlinson Poet 108). Individual essays deal with the character of early English dictionaries, the treatment of figurative, common, dialect, old and literary words, alphabetization and spelling, the use of style markers, the inclusion of phrasal verbs, compilation methods, the use of other dictionaries as secondary source material, and dictionary criticism. Osselton demonstrates that the use of labels such as 'fig' or 'dialect' in dictionaries is inconsistent both within and among modern dictionaries, and can be seen as a result of the dictionary tradition from which they have developed. 'Dialect', for instance, 'is often as much a social/educational discriminator as a vague indicator of regional use'. The assertion that Johnson's dictionary was responsible for fixing the spelling of English is examined and disproved. Throughout the collection the close relationship between monolingual and bilingual dictionaries is demonstrated, with monolingual dictionaries often including phrases corresponding to single words in the other language of a bilingual source, and sometimes listing words created in English for the sole purpose of translation. In many respects, such as the inclusion of ordinary words as well as hard words, bilingual dictionaries often led the way in establishing modern lexicographical practices.

Dialect coverage in dictionaries of the nineteenth century is relatively thorough, but the question posed by Manfred Görlach, in 'Dialect Lexis in Early Modern English Dictionaries' (in M. Görlach, ed., *New Studies in the History of English*), based on eMnE dialect dictionaries and on terms labelled dialectal in more general works, is whether it is possible to study the dialect of the sixteenth to the eighteenth centuries. A 636 entry word-list is provided for the letters *a–c*, along with distribution maps for some of the terms. Igor Burkhanov's 'On the Theoretical Foundations of Ideography' (in Kardela and Persson, eds, *New Trends*), deals with the branch of lexicography which considers the theory and practice of compiling non-alphabetical lexicographical works, such as thesauruses and synonym or thematic dictionaries. He concludes that none of the existing ideographic dictionaries fulfil the requirements of modern theoretical semantics. L. V. Shcherba's 'Towards a General Theory of Lexicography' (*IJL* 8.iv.314–50) reviews dictionary-types based on six main oppositions: academic versus informative, encyclopaedic versus general, concordance versus ordinary, ordinary versus ideological, defining versus translating and historical versus non-historical. In 'Identifying the Linguistic Foundations for Lexical Research and Dictionary Design' (in Walker, et al., eds, *Automating the Lexicon*), Richard Hudson argues that, because they have been brought up as dictionary-users, it is difficult for linguists to evaluate and design dictionaries objectively. He suggests that the relationship between grammar and the lexicon is one area which needs to be reconsidered. In the same volume, Nicoletta Calzolari's 'Structure and Access in Automated Lexicon and Related Issues' argues that the possibilities of electronic dictionaries require a new type of lexicography that builds upon the achievements of traditional lexicographers.

Alain Rey's *Essays on Terminology* is a collection of translated and re-edited essays on the discipline of terminology, which would also be of interest to those concerned with terminology, lexicography, lexicology and the history of knowledge and ideas. A term is defined as a name which can be defined within a coherently structured system and, at its most simplistic, terminology is the study of systems of lexical items in specialized fields, such as science and technology, which is where the discipline originated. Rey is particularly interested, however, in its social and communicative aspects, defining *terminology* as 'the history of terms, not considered simply as linguistic forms, but as signs linked to a specialised conceptual content'. He considers the origins and development of the discipline of terminology, tracing its name, at least, to the 1830s and 1840s in France, and goes on to discuss the theoretical issues involved. The chapter on neologism considers how the label should be used, and whether collective perception of a term as neologistic should influence terminologers. In this chapter he distinguishes between formal, semantic, and pragmatic neology. Later chapters deal with applied terminology, and with the relationships between terminology and both lexicography and terminography. Rey also discusses the place of terminology in language planning and standardization, and makes a number of interesting comments on English influence on French. He closes with an account of the place of terminology in a general language dictionary.

Henning Bergenholtz and Sven Tarp (eds) explain the difference between terminology, terminography and specialized lexicography in their volume *Manual of Specialised Lexicography*. They emphasize the common ground between these areas, however, and say that each can learn from the others. Aimed mainly at those producing printed dictionaries, although obviously with some relevance to the production of electronic lexicons, the work is presented as a manual, either to be read through or used as a reference work. The introductory material indicates which chapters might be relevant to which purpose, but the detailed contents page and index allow for easy reference use. Basic issues in specialized lexicography are discussed, such as the relationship between language for special purposes and language for general purposes, and what the function of specialized dictionaries is. Problems specific to specialized dictionaries are considered next, ranging from the monolingual and bilingual to dictionaries of particular subjects such as law, economics or science and technology. Preliminary work and selection procedures are covered, along with consideration of what linguistic information ought to be included, and how. Encyclopaedic information is discussed separately, as are the contents page, user's guide, appendices, and so on. Alphabetic and systematic macrostructures are presented as possible organizational principles, along with frame, cross-reference and access structure. The volume closes with a consideration of layout, proof-reading and dictionary criticism.

Winfried Lange's 'The special lexicon and problems of EST/ESP – course design or the box of the Pandora' (in Dirven and Vanparys, eds, *Current Approaches*) considers the rapid development of English for Science and Technology, and the scope for imperfect communication between disciplines arising as a result of this. In 'The Identification and Selection of Collocations in Technical Dictionaries' (*Lexicographica* 11.60–73), Jette Pedersen argues that technical dictionaries ought to help users form correct word-combinations, and concludes that criteria for including word-combinations and collocations should be determined at the planning stage.

Jürgen Handke's *The Structure of the Lexicon: Human versus Machine* is an interesting account of the linguistic, psycholinguistic and computational approaches towards the lexicon, both separately and interdisciplinarily in cognitive science. Parallels and differences between human and machine lexicons are considered in an attempt to determine how computer lexicons can be most efficiently designed. His primary concern, though, is language comprehension rather than production, and he divides the process into three stages, which are common to both human and machine lexical processing: pre-lexical processing, word recognition and lexical retrieval. He begins by describing the various types of ambiguity that occur harmlessly in natural language but cannot be permitted in computer languages and tries, by an analysis of speech-errors, to determine what is contained in the mental lexicon and how it is organized. Lexical decision tasks indicate that the lexicon may be organized by frequency of occurrence, by length of word, by regularity, lexicality, homophony, word-superiority (the principle that words are recognized more quickly than individual letters) and by context. Handke then gives an account of the Cohort and TRACE models of spoken word recognition, and of the Activate and Check and Word Detector models of written word recognition. His chapter on machine readable lexicons deals with optical character recognition as well as automatic speech recognition, and explains what morphological, phonological, syntactic and semantic information is included in various formats. Chapter six discusses LexEcon, an on-line machine-readable English–German, German–English lexicon. The text is provided with numerous illustrations, and useful summaries conclude each section.

Robert J. P. Ingria's 'Lexical Information for Parsing Systems: Points of Convergence and Divergence' (in Walker et al., eds, *Automating the Lexicon*) discusses the different ways in which lexical information has been expressed in parsing systems, and suggests that, although systems handle grammatical information in different ways, it should be possible to share lexical information between systems. In the same volume, Roy J. Byrd's brief article, 'Dictionary Systems for Office Practice', distinguishes between dictionaries for people and dictionaries for programs. He discusses the practical problems of copyright and of deciding what type of information should be included. Branimir Boguraev's 'Machine-Readable Dictionaries and Computational Linguistics Research' concludes that the next level of machine-readable dictionary should take into account the needs of both people and programs, as well as applying current theories in lexicography, computational linguistics, language engineering, information structuring and database management systems. Susanna Cumming's contribution to the same volume, 'The Lexicon in Text Generation: Progress and Prospects', tries to identify which type of linguistic knowledge is lexical knowledge, and what kind of lexical knowledge is most relevant to text generation. Susan Armstrong-Warwick catalogues the existing computerized dictionaries as potential resources in large-scale research in 'Automated Lexical Resources in Europe: A Survey'. She provides short sample entries as illustrations of each.

Urs Egli et al., eds, *Lexical Knowledge in the Organization of the Lexicon* is a collection of papers from the International Conference on the Lexicon, at the University of Constance, in 1991. The papers deal with a wide variety of languages and approaches, and are grouped into four sections, the first of which contains papers treating the problem of whether grammatical regularities are syntactic or lexical by nature. Mark C. Baker's 'Lexical and Nonlexical Noun Incorporation' concentrates on Mohawk, while both Gereon Müller and Wolfgang Sternefeld's 'Extraction, Lexical Variation, and the Theory of Barriers' and Arnim von Stechow's 'Lexical Decomposition in Syntax' deal mainly with German. The second section is entitled 'Model-Theoretical Approaches to Text Semantics', and includes papers by Urs Egli and Klaus von Heusinger ('The Epsilon Operator and E-Type Pronouns'), Reinhard Muskens ('Tense and the Logic of Change'), and Aarne Ranta ('The Understanding and Interpretation of Text'). Bruce Mayo's 'Describing Verbs of Motion in Prolog' opens the third section, on 'Lexical Meanings and Concepts'. He argues, as do Christoph Schwarze and Marie-Theres Schepping ('Polysemy in Two-Level-Semantics'), that lexical and cognitive understanding operate on different levels of meaning. Peter E. Pause, Achim Botz, and Markus Egg discuss ways of representing lexical polysemy with reference to French. The final paper in the section is Götz Wienold's 'Lexical and Conceptual Structures for Movement and Space: With reference to Japanese, Korean, Thai, and Indonesian as compared to English and German'. The last section, called 'The Historical Dimension', contains only one paper, discussed under 'The History of English Linguistics'.

In 'Assessing semantic information in memory: the mental lexicon as semi-module' Monika Schwarz (in Dirven and Vanparys, eds, *Current Approaches*) looks at whether there are connections between semantic memory and other knowledge systems in the long-term memory. Clinical observations indicate that it is possible to access semantic memory through tactile, perceptual and motoric processing routes. Also in Dirven and Vanparys, Beate Seidel's 'The reflection of lexical meaning relations in textual meaning concepts – a sample analysis of an English text' looks at a passage from *The Economist*, focusing on lexical networks within the text, and hypothesizing about the influence of these textual relations on the structure of the lexicon. Cornelia Zelinsky-Wibbelt's 'Insights from categorization for a mental model of lexicalization' considers the failure of natural language processing systems to incorporate speakers' flexibility and tolerance of flexibility, and argues that predictable cognitive constraints mean that there is a system to linguistic flexibility, and that this can be recreated artificially. Jürgen Handke's 'Mental and machine-readable lexicons: What can machines learn from the mind?' argues that a simulation of human language processing strategies might not necessarily be the most efficient way of processing linguistic information in machines, although understanding of the human lexicon could give insights which would enhance speed and data management.

David Corson's *Using English Words* is an interdisciplinary approach to the acquisition of Graeco-Latin vocabulary in students of English as a first and as a second language. It is a revised version of his *The Lexical Bar*, now out of print. Corson argues that 'formal education is very largely a process of teaching the rules of use for words and then judging how well those rules have been acquired', and demonstrates that although the same type of lexical bar exists in all modern languages, in English it is reinforced by sociological factors stretching back to the Renaissance. He discusses why some words are seen as more difficult than others and examines the active and passive vocabularies of various groups of students in English-speaking countries around the world, concluding that learners of English as a second language are not necessarily at a disadvantage, even when their first language does not help them with Graeco-Latin vocabulary in English. He then considers whether exposure to different types of discourse creates different mental structures and processes in the brain, and concludes that it can. His recommendation for educators is a concentration on critical awareness of vocabulary: that pupils' own language should be valued in itself, but that they should also learn vocabulary which might be more appropriate in formal contexts. The book would probably be of relevance to sociolinguists, psycholinguists, education-theorists, and those interested in the history of English, particularly lexicologists.

Susan Ferraro's *Sweet Talk. The Language of Love* is included here to ensure that the price does not give the misleading impression that it is an academic work. Ferraro describes her work as 'a compendium and commentary on words of love', but despite the apparently structured approach, with chapters on modifiers, terms of endearment, baby-talk, use of animal and food imagery, and so on, the prose moves breathlessly wherever whim takes it. From the cutesy 'alphabet of love' at the beginning, to the rousing self-developmental conclusion, the text was, on the whole, unconvincing. Despite, or perhaps because of, the wide geographical and chronological range, Ferraro makes some rather basic mistakes. These are most glaring in the etymologies, which are often given as if to provide an insight into the 'real' meaning of a word. *Gam*, for instance, meaning 'to perform oral sex', is related to the slang word *gam* for 'leg' (as in *third leg*), instead of what might seem the more obvious *gamahuche* 'to perform oral sex'. We are informed that Chaucer used both *fuck* and *futter* for 'to copulate', when the first is not recorded in the OED until the sixteenth century, and the second until the nineteenth. The name *Gladys*, we are told, includes the word *lady*, while *Cordelia* 'is an anagram for "ideal heart" in two languages: the Latin *cor* for "heart," and *delia*, a rearrangement of the letters in "ideal" '. I suppose the book may have a place, somewhere, but it is not in an academic library.

Another accessible, but more reliable text, is Jesse Sheidlower's *The F-Word*, which is based on material from the *Random House Historical Dictionary of American Slang*. Sheidlower gives priority to American English usage, but lists British and Australian sources for supplementation and pre-datings. The dictionary section purports to contain every phrase and compound in which the word in question is currently in use in American English, supported by citations from books, magazines, films, television and conversation. The introduction considers current taboos in newspapers and on television, and looks at their history in American English and before. The disproportionate number of early occurrences that are found in Scottish texts is attributed to a weaker taboo rather than being considered to provide any etymological evidence. The profusion of senses appearing around the time of the First World War is also seen as the result of greater freedom of expression rather than spontaneous word-coinage.

Evelyn Hatch and Cheryl Brown's *Vocabulary, Semantics, and Language Education*, is an introductory textbook aimed at trainee teachers on an introductory linguistics course, but much of its material would also be useful for other students. References to the pedagogical implications of the material they discuss succeed in demonstrating the practical applications of semantic analysis and are, therefore, of interest to all. The section which concentrates on teaching and learning vocabulary makes up only about 60 pages of the total text, and the section on vocabulary choice, although necessarily brief, does indicate that sociolinguistic forces are also brought to bear on the lexis. A detailed table of contents, index and bibliography, along with exercises and suggestions for further research for each section, would make this a useful coursebook, and the statement of objectives in the introduction clearly implies that the student is not to be a passive participant in the process. Many of the exercises suggest useful ways of introducing basic concepts such as synonymity and prototypicality by building upon the students' own use of English. Judy Kegl's 'Machine-Readable Dictionaries and Education' (in Walker, et al., eds, *Automating the Lexicon*), also considers pedagogical approaches to language acquisition, and identifies inappropriate tasks for machine-readable dictionaries by reviewing the role of conventional dictionaries in education. She suggests that the flexibility of computer-based dictionaries is an advantage, but that they are not necessarily useful for all of the tasks to which they are applied.

Christine Fellbaum's 'Co-occurrence and Antonymy' (*IJL* 8.iv.281–303) uses the Brown Corpus to explore the hypothesis that antonymous adjectives will co-occur more frequently in sentences than would be determined by chance. She finds that this co-occurrence also extends to nouns and verbs, and that the semantically opposed terms are not necessarily syntactically substitutable. In 'Lexical Semantics and Lexicographic Sense Distinction' (*IJL* 8.i.1–27), Pim van der Eijk, Olga Alejandro and Maria Florenza discuss the use of ambiguity tests in determining whether semantic variants should be treated as two separate senses or as examples of ambiguity. Such tests should, they conclude, be applied with care. John R. Taylor's 'Approaches to word-meaning: The network model (Langacker) and the two-level model (Bierwisch) in comparison' (in Dirven and Vanparys, eds, *Current Approaches*) concludes that although both are cognitive linguistic approaches, the network model, which regards polysemy as normal and uses psychological considerations to constrain linguistic description, is preferable because of its flexibility. Beth Levin's 'Approaches to Lexical Semantic Representation' (in Walker, et al., eds, *Automating the Lexicon*) is a review of efforts to represent semantic information based on, for instance, evidence from introspection, linking regularities, generalizations and so on. A consideration of semantic role-centred and predicate decomposition approaches leads her to conclude that predicate decomposition approaches appear to be more successful. Alan D. Cruse's 'Between Polysemy and Monosemy: Senses, Facets and Qualia Roles' (in Kardela and Persson, eds, *New Trends*) investigates the discontinuities lying between polysemy and monosemy, and suggests that cross-linguistic research would be a useful area for future investigation.

Boguslaw Bierwiacsonek's 'Love in Frames and Scripts' (in Kardela and Persson, eds, *New Trends*), attempts to characterize the conceptual structure of the notion of LOVE. He criticizes earlier attempts for being too restrictive, but himself defines erotic love as 'the most neutral and inclusive term for the heterosexual LOVE relationship between two familiarially unrelated adult individuals'. Friedrich Ungerer's 'The linguistic and cognitive relevance of basic emotions (in Dirven and Vanparys, eds, *Current Approaches*) deals with the deficiencies of the structuralist approach, and tries to move away from personal intuition by collecting other people's. He considers evidence from emotional psychology and cognitive linguistics, and analyses the metaphors used to discuss emotions. The discussion of metaphors continues in Elzbieta Tabakowska's 'Polish translation of English technical terms: Metaphor in the language of computer science' (in Dirven and Vanparys), which observes that translators into Polish tend to render metaphors non-metaphorically or to put them in inverted commas as insufficiently serious for their subject. In 'The lexicon of metaphor models as a mental tool for analogical problem-solving in science', Wolf-Andreas Liebert argues, based on his work with virologists in AIDS research, that reflection on metaphors used, and the adoption of new metaphors can actually help in scientific problem-solving.

Sol Saporta's paper 'Expressions for Sexual Harassment: a Semantic Hole' (*Verbatim* 21.iii.3–4) argues that the language of sexual harassment reflects the ideological bias of 'the largely puritanical segment of the women's movement'. He claims, for instance, that one who makes *unwelcome sexual advances* cannot possibly be aware that the advances are unwelcome until they have been rejected. In 'Building on a Corpus: A linguistic and lexicographical look at some near synonyms' (*IJL* 8.ii.85– 114), B. T. S. Atkins and Beth Levin look at the treatment of the verbs *quake*, *quiver*, *shake*, *shiver*, *shudder*, *tremble* and *vibrate* in three dictionaries of English, and deduce, by reference to the Oxford Corpus, that there may be some system behind the syntactic differences between these verbs, but that there is little systematicity within or between accounts of them in dictionaries.

Manfred Görlach discusses reactions to borrowing into English and to English borrowings in other languages, particularly French and German in 'Euer Borrowing and Neuer Paying? Lexical Import/Export in the History of English' (in Görlach, ed., *New Studies*). Matti Vilpulli's 'The Sun and the Definition of Day' (*IJL* 8.i.29–38) identifies a weakness in definitions of *day* which refer to the period of daylight alone, without reference to the rhythm of human life. The flaws in such definitions are particularly apparent in regions far from the equator. In 'Possession Frame in Word Derivation: A Case of English Privative Adjectives' (in Kardela and Persson, eds, *New Trends*), Elzbieta Górska discusses the use of *-less* and *-free* in the formation of adjectives, and considers the different contexts in which pairs such as *sugarless* and *sugarfree* are employed. Henryk Kardela's 'Derivational or Compound-Specific Formations? Typological Aspects of Milos Dokulil's Theory of

Derivation' (also in Kardela and Persson) compares English and Polish, and concludes that Slavic languages make use of morphological and inflectional derivation, while Germanic languages are more inclined to resort to compounding.

Similarities between lists of 'beautiful' words are analysed by David Crystal in 'Phonaesthetically Speaking' (*EnT* 11.ii.8–12). He concludes that, although meaning obviously influences responses, 'beautiful' words are characteristically three syllables long, contain /m/ or /l/, have at least three types of consonant articulation, and contain short vowels moving from mid-high and front-back. Alan Major discusses terms of endearment, such as *sweetheart*, *baby*, *honey*, *darling*, *dear*, *popsy*, *precious*, *girlie*, *pet*, *duck* and *love* in 'Endearment Elucidation, or Love by Any Other Name' (*Verbatim* 21.iv.3–4). There is scope for only a brief, and not always convincing, account of their histories and geographical distribution.

5. Morphology

Dieter Wunderlich and Ray Fabri present in their 'Minimalist morphology: an approach to inflection' (*ZSpr* 14.236–94) a theoretical investigation of the place of inflection within generative theory: does it belong to syntax proper (see Anderson (*YWES* 73.24–5)), in which case it is difficult to deal with all kinds of subregularities, to the phonological domain, or does it constitute a component of its own? The authors advocate that both inflection and derivation belong to a separate morphological component because, among other things, they often undergo the same phonological rules, and because the former may feed the latter. They illustrate the working of their theory by means of data from German and classical Arabic. Dieter Wunderlich presents more detail on 'Minimalist morphology: the role of paradigms' in *YM* 1995.93–114. In this model (which is presented as an extension to morphology of the spirit of Chomsky's Minimalism), only a few general principles and constraints are accepted, but no arbitrary class features or abstract morphemes. Paradigms function as filtering and checking devices. In this paper too, illustration mainly comes from languages other than English. This is in fact true for all other papers in *YM* 1995, which has several interesting contributions on the volume's theme, 'Inflection and derivation'. In another general paper, Linda R. Waugh and Madeleine Newfield show that 'Iconicity in the lexicon [has] relevance for a theory of morphology' (in Marge E. Landsberg, ed., *Syntactic Iconicity and Linguistic Freezes*). They argue that morphemes are not the only elements that structure the lexicon and create patterns and networks, but that there are many other, iconically structured, cross-cutting connections that play a role in the make-up of the lexicon and in the changes that it undergoes. Thus, an important role is played by phonesthemes, submorphemes and word affinities which do not fit a more traditional morphological system.

In a book which we missed last year, John T. Stonham writes about *Combinatorial Morphology*. He argues that the only morphological operation that should be recognized is that of combination, and that there is therefore no need for very powerful, non-local string-dependent operations. Even though Stonham works with a rather enriched notion of affix (which may include autosegmental tiers, prosodic material, and constraint-based templates), there remain several types of phenomena that are problematic for a combination-based view of morphology. In separate chapters, he therefore addresses complex types of reduplications, subtractive morphology (all cases of which can be re-analysed), exchange rules (also re-analysable), ablaut (an unproductive process in English and even German, involving lexical specification; a productive but phonological process in Sanskrit, involving the linking of features), and metathesis (all purported cases of morphological conditioning actually being phonological).

Andrew Spencer writes about 'Morphological theory and English' in a new journal, *Links & Letters* (1 [1994].71–84), initiated by the University (Autònoma) of Barcelona and having as its main aim to provide easy access to all the different subfields that English Studies comprises so that its members can take cognisance of areas related to their own of which they have no specialist knowledge. In this linguistic issue, Spencer provides a review of recent issues in generative morphology concentrating on two aspects, i.e. the internal structuring of words (e.g. do they have constituent structure as in syntax, or would it be better to adopt a 'word-and-paradigm' model also for derivational processes?) and the relation between this and syntactic processes. Abdellatif Adouani also writes on the general question, 'La morphologie est-elle la syntaxe des mots?' (*LingInv* 19.1–13). His answer is, 'Non', since X-bar theory in particular is not obeyed by the internal make-up of many (French) words. A final general piece that we read this year is by Joan Bybee and Jean Newman; it investigates the question, 'Are stem changes as natural as affixes?' (*Linguistics* 33.633–54). Cross-linguistically, affixation is more common than stem change, but the authors found no clear preference for affixation in an experiment that they carried out with an artificial language: the two types of morphological operation were equally easy to learn, provided they were equally regular in the input. As the authors demonstrate, diachronic developments (in particular grammaticalization) will more often lead to regular affixation than regular stem changes, and they conclude that the cross-linguistic preference for affixation is a result of the nature of diachronic processes.

The article by Maarten Lemmers, 'De paradigmatische conditionering van het Engelse -er suffix' (*LB* 84.519–28), restricts itself to deverbal -er formation. His first aim is to show that the various -er morphemes are semantically related, which makes it possible to explain these derivations systematically (*pace* Levin and Rappaport [*YWES* 69.74]), and secondly he wishes to show that -er derivation is conditioned by transitive and ergative paradigms. All -er derivations are seen as prototypically 'agent'. The transitive agent-type is indeed the most frequent, as Lemmers's figures show. Only 2.6 per cent of -er words are ergative types, i.e. examples such as *choker*. In 'The importance of being *ernist*' (*LingA* 25.121–36), Probal Dasgupta also starts out from one pattern of word formation, i.e. that seen in *northern*, *southern*, *eastern*, and *western*. These look like easily segmentable forms, but Dasgupta shows that things get complicated as soon as related formations are taken into account (e.g. *northerly* etc.; *northerner* etc.; *islander*, *insider* etc.). He concludes that lexical integrity should be recognized, with paradigms mediating between related words.

The paradigm also plays an important role in the approach to syncretism that James Blevins proposes ('Syncretism and paradigmatic opposition', *Ling&P* 18.113–52). He argues that a form like present tense *walk* is simply unmarked for person and number. The ungrammaticality of **he walk* should be seen as a case of blocking, best expressed in terms of paradigmatic relatedness. Using the GPSG feature system, Blevins constructs a tree-like model of the paradigm of the verb *walk*, in which third person singular *walks* is dominated by present tense *walk*. A general principle then ensures that a non-terminal like present tense *walk* will be blocked by a descendant like *walks*. Further data illustrating the approach come from German.

In *Constraints on Suffixation: A Study in Generative Morphology of English and Polish*, Adam Wójcicki applies the theory of lexical phonology to data from English and Polish. His findings for English include the following: past tenses like *knelt* can be viewed as being due to attachment of a dental suffix at Stratum 1; genitive *'s* is attached outside the lexicon, yet it is blocked by the final sibilant of the plural and third person singular – this means that Bracket Erasure cannot have applied; the choice between [id], [d], and [t] can be handled post-lexically (forms like *priestdom* are no problem, since the relevant rule applies to tautosyllabic clusters); most suffixes do not attach to already suffixed forms; only three Stratum 2 affixes can be attached to any product of Stratum 1. These data, and others from Polish suffixes, are obviously problematic for the model of lexical phonology.

Adrienne Lehrer has looked at 'Prefixes in English word formation' (*FoLi* 29.133–48). She deals separately with Romance-derived prefixes (*meta-, anti-, pro-, counter-, mini-, maxi-, micro-, pre-, post-, ante-, pseudo-, arch-, semi-,* etc.) and Germanic ones (*in-, out-, up-, down-, under-, over-,* etc.). On the basis of a lot of data, she shows that prefixes can generally combine and iterate rather freely, as in *ex-pseudo-anti-intellectual*, and *supersubintelligent* (with two meanings). Moving on now to this year's few historical studies, we first come to Michiko Ogura's 'The interchangeability of Old English verbal prefixes' (*ASE* 24.67–93). This article contains, as we have come to expect from this author, a wealth of information about the way particle verbs were used in Old English. It deals with the following topics/questions: was the interchange of prefixes or particles confined to certain verbs; how freely could prefixes be added, changed, omitted; what meaning differences were expressed by the various possibilities; which prefixes were lost, which retained in later periods; how are prefixes used stylistically in poetry and rhythmical prose; what is the relation between prefixes and tense; what influence did Latin have on the use of prefixes; and finally, what is the relation between prefix-verb and verb-particle in Old English, and how can we account for the change to mainly verb-particle in Middle English?

Three papers deal with morphological issues in Early Modern English. Christiane Dalton-Puffer writes, 'Are Shakespeare's agent nouns different from Chaucer's? – On the dynamics of a derivational sub-system' (in Dieter Kastovsky, ed., *Studies in Early Modern English*). Using the Helsinki Corpus and Shakespeare's comedies for material, she shows that some native agent suffixes (*-ende, -ild*) had disappeared by Late Middle English, but others were kept (most notably *-er* and *-ster*). Late Middle English also had some marginal French elements (*-ant, -ary, -ess*), and these became better established in the Early Modern period. The various forms and their development from Early Middle English to Early Modern English are usefully presented within a hierarchy of meanings which recognizes that agent suffixes can also have meanings such as instrument, location or source. Helena Raumolin-Brunberg looks at 'The development of the compound pronouns in -*body* and -*one* in Early Modern English', i.e. forms like *anybody*, *everybody*, *some* and *no man* (also in Kastovsky). She reports that, in the Early Modern part of the Helsinki Corpus, the use of *man* is formal and gradually declines (perhaps due to semantic specialization of the noun *man*), the use of simple forms first peaks and then decreases, while forms in both -*body* (more oral) and -*one* become commoner (the latter receiving support from prop *one*, indefinite *one*, and expressions like *any one person*). Finally, in the same collection Terttu Nevalainen considers several 'Aspects of adverbial change in Early Modern English'. On the morphological side, she provides detailed data on the use of -*ly* in several types of adverbs. As for other adverbial developments, she notes that disjunct adverbs (and 'subjective' adverbs generally) become more common in this period, and she discusses changes in the use and meaning of several individual adverbs. These matters, however, come more properly under the heading of syntax, to which we therefore now proceed.

6. Syntax

(a) Modern English
Philip W. Davis, ed., *Alternative Linguistics*, aims to open up new perspectives on the study of language, and is of interest to anyone working in this field. All the articles in it are highly stimulating and refreshing, showing the limits and possible shortcomings of current formal approaches to language. The first two are both concerned with conversation analysis. The question in the title of Tsuyoshi Ono and Sandra Thompson's paper, 'What can conversation tell us about syntax?', is seen as a prolegomenon to a further aim, namely a syntax based on conversational data, because conversation is taken to be the most common and fundamental condition of language use. The authors outline a theory of dynamic syntax that arises purely out of the data without any preconceived notion of what syntax is; this will in fact be a model of how the cognitive routines (the always emerging but never fixed grammatical frames) work in everyday conversational encounters. The syntax will include as grammatical: (constraints on) repairs, reformulations and repetitions, and local and social constraints characteristically present in spoken language. What the authors are particularly interested in is how and why constructional schemas extend over the boundaries of so-called 'intonation units' (the basic clause unit of conversation-syntax), and how this affects the integrity of the sentence in traditional syntax. The overall aim is to find out how these conversation data yield clues about the nature of syntax. Barbara Fox and Robert Jasperson concentrate on one aspect of conversation-syntax in their 'A syntactic exploration of repair in English conversation'. The main and important point that this paper wishes to make is that self-repair (which is not limited to error-correction) is not chaotic, a pure performance feature that can safely be ignored. Rather, it is highly patterned, organized by syntax, and as such offers us valuable insight into the structure of the theory of grammar. Questions considered in this exploratory study are: what constitutes repair, what is its syntactic organization, and what is the interrelation between repair

and syntax? As a data base, transcripts of American English conversation and tutoring-sessions are used. One of the important findings of this study is that 'it appears that syntax is *created* during the course of a conversation, and one of the strategies for creating syntax is repair'. The third noteworthy paper from this volume is Ronald Langacker's 'Viewing in cognition and grammar', the hypothesis of which is that 'conception in general has various properties that are most evident and clearly discernable in perception, vision in particular'. Perception is seen as analogous to conception; this is important because the central claim of cognitive grammar is that it is the result of the symbolization of structured conceptualization. Langacker first discusses some of the basic notions of cognitive grammar; for example, how traditional grammatical categories and relations can be characterized in terms of symbolic assemblies, and how constituency is no more than simple symbolic structures progressively integrated into more elaborate ones, whereby the structure must be seen as a growth, not as an independent syntactic entity (as in generative grammar). Most important in the determination of a grammatical construct is not the conceptual content it invokes, but the way it is viewed. Thus, there are expressions that profile 'things' (nouns, articles etc.) and expressions that profile relationships (verbs, prepositions). Other 'viewing' factors, such as time, are also involved. Finally, there follows an extensive discussion of many 'expressions', how they can be analysed and understood from the point of view of viewing, such as tense and aspect, anaphora etc. In another paper, 'Raising and transparency' (*Language* 71.1–62), Langacker applies his model of cognitive grammar to what have been called raising constructions (subject-to-subject, as in *He is likely to be late*, subject-to-object, as in *We believe him to be honest*, and object-to-subject, as in *This was hard to understand*). After reviewing earlier analyses and the problems they face, and providing a compressed outline of cognitive grammar, he presents a detailed account of all three constructions in cognitive terms (which of course means they do not involve raising, but certain types of construal and profiling).

We should also mention here some other items that link up well with the articles from Davis's book reviewed above. Jim Miller asks: 'Does spoken language have sentences?' (in Frank R. Palmer, ed., *Grammar and Meaning*). He argues that intonation is not a reliable criterion for identifying sentences in speech, that intuitions about sentencehood in speech are shaky, and that even in writing the concept of the sentence varies from culture to culture. He concludes that the basic unit in speech is the clause, within which a lot of syntax takes place. Relations between clauses are determined by discourse rules. Sidney Greenbaum and Gerald Nelson study 'Clause relationships in spoken and written English' (in *FuL* 2.1–21), using the same classification (in terms of simple clauses, compound clauses, complex clauses, clause fragments, etc.) for both modes. They find that in the British part of the International Corpus of English, speech and writing overlap and also show great internal variability. Conversations, however, are special: they have less coordination and subordination than any other text type.

A great deal of emphasis is placed on the linear, incremental nature of speech (in particular, story-telling) in David Brazil's *A Grammar of Speech*. He does not believe in constituent structure for spoken sentences, since this suggests that we are dealing with a product, while spoken discourse is much more of a process. The basic idea of his grammar is that speakers move from an initial state, through the use of an increment, to a target state. The states are viewed as being determined by communicative need. In the body of the book, Brazil then presents a grammar of speech consisting of chaining rules, with extensions (the addition of further elements after a target state has been reached) and suspensions (the addition of elements before the target state has been reached, as in the placement of the adverbial in *He often says things like that*). In the absence of hierarchical structure, a great deal of interpretative work has to be done by what follows from the communicative needs at hand (these, for example, have to determine the interpretation of empty subjects in infinitive clauses).

Another general study that we would like to mention here is Talmy Givón's *Functionalism and Grammar*. This book, Givón confesses in his preface, was written out of a certain frustration with the lack of critical scrutiny that exists with respect to many functionalists' writings, and also with their tendency to reductionism, fed by their enmity towards the Chomskyan paradigm. As Givón himself puts it 'As the overripe Generative orthodoxy crumbles of its own weight of formal vacuity and methodological indifference, functionalists on their various stripes trumpet their reductive visions in a mounting cacophony of self-indulgence and parochialism'. The main aim of this book, therefore, is to put functionalism on a sound footing, and to view it critically. For this it is important to pay attention to what is happening in closely related fields, such as language-specific neurology, evolutionary biology, memory and attention (discussed in the last two chapters), and to provide a functional, rather than structural basis for universals and grammatical typology (chapters 3 and 4). Here, also the notion of markedness (related to iconicity) plays an important role because it describes what is natural about the grammatical code (chapter 2). Chapters 5 and 6 argue that functionalists should take structure seriously. Givón shows that grammatical structures must have cognitive and neurological reality, and goes on to discuss the constituents that play a role in structure and how they are (hierarchically) organized. William Croft also addresses the debate on 'Autonomy and functional linguistics' (*Language* 71.490–532). He makes two important distinctions (between arbitrariness of syntax and its self-containedness; between autonomy of syntax vis-à-vis semantics, phonology etc., and autonomy of the grammar as a whole vis-à-vis change, acquisition etc.) and uses these to good effect in his survey of the various positions in the debate that have been taken up by scholars in the past. He argues that these positions can be meaningfully compared and tested. Such testing shows, for example, that the more rabid forms of functionalism can safely be assigned to the dustbin of scholarly detritus, since there is overwhelming cross-linguistic evidence against them. On the other side, the facts of language variation argue against self-containedness of the grammar.

While on questions of general linguistic interest, Randolph Quirk's *Grammatical and Lexical Variance in English*, a rich collection of nineteen articles, some of them written versions of recent lectures, others (revised) versions of papers published earlier. The first five articles deal with broad issues of variation and varieties (e.g. questions of standards, good usage, types of variation, variation and education, etc.), chapter 6 is on Orwell's linguistic views (shown to be neither original nor consistent), while the remaining thirteen articles all deal with variation involving specific lexical or grammatical phenomena. Among this group we find the Lord of English Usage's papers on the Modern English genitive, on the verb *become*, on non-finite clauses in Chaucer, on the *have-a-look* construction, on adverbials in the SEU material, on elicitation and acceptability tests, on *tough*-movement, on *-ing* vs. *to*-complements, on 'latent' contrasts, and on the difference between forms like *leapt* and *leaped*.

Quirk's book provides a natural transition to detailed studies of specific, more limited topics. Turning to contributions on different aspects of the noun phrase, Paul Rastall looks at changes in the use of determiners in contemporary English in 'Definite article or no definite article' (*EnT* 11.ii.37–8). He comments on the tendency for the definite article to disappear in redundant positions, such as before words referring to illnesses (*He has (the) measles*), geographical names (*(the) Sudan*), in certain complements of copulative verbs (*John is (the) captain*), and in fixed phrases (*in (the) rush hour*). More analytic and semantic in nature is Barbara Abbott's 'Some remarks on specificity' (in *LingI* 26.341–7), which considers the proper analysis of specific NPs and the question whether NPs of the form *a certain N* and those in existentials are also specific.

Case forms continue to spark debate. In 'A new rule for the Queen and I?' (*EnT* 11.iv.3–8), John Honey considers the usage of coordinated pronouns. He is especially concerned with the need for prescriptive rules in foreign language teaching (for an opposite view see Wardhaugh, discussed below), taking as an example the way in which the case (form) of the pronoun has been used in combinations (*you and I/me, we/us professionals*, hypercorrect use of relative *whom*) for the last 15 years by 'authoritative' speakers. His data make clear that these speakers use a special rule in such contexts (i.e. the case of the pronoun is not the grammatically expected one), one which involves a kind of 'freezing', i.e. the elements in the phrase become an integrated unit, which does not change according to function. Richard Hudson probes deeper, and wonders, 'Does English really have case?' (in *JL* 31.375–92). He notes that most linguists assume that English has three cases, subjective, objective and genitive (in *he*, *him* and *his*, and hence also in *John*, *John* and *John's*). As he puts it, 'If one were to look for a matter on which linguists speak with almost one voice, this would be a good example'. However, Hudson can think of at least six objections to this view (the subjective/objective distinction is found in only five words in the entire language; some dialects have even further reduction; the existence of the type of data reviewed by Honey; the supposed genitives behave like determiners; the difference *my-mine* equals that in *none-no*; in other languages, forms corresponding to *my* are not pronouns). He also notes that it is incorrect to call the element *'s* a noun ending, since it combines with full NPs. His solution is to say that English has no case; selection of forms like *he* and *him* can be handled by minor lexical rules, and forms like *my/mine* are possessive pronouns.

Rachelle Waksler is interested in gender changes certain nouns have undergone in 'She's a mensch and he's a bitch: neutralising gender in the 90s' (*EnT* 11.ii.3–6). She shows that there has been a change in the way the 'gender revolution' has affected the use of gender-sensitive words. Whereas in the seventies, the fashion was to change the gender-specific constituent into a neutral term (e.g. *chairperson* for *chairman*), and in the eighties to replace both specific male and female forms by a different neutral term (e.g. *steward(ess)* became *flight attendant*), in the nineties it is becoming the rule to neutralize gender, i.e. gender-specific words like *bitch* or *guy* can now be used for any sex. In her article, Waksler discusses the typology of observed changes and the system of rules that operates here. D. J. Allerton discusses in his column of 'Problems of Modern English Grammar' (*ES* 76.81–9), ' "Headless" noun phrases: how to describe the exceptional'. The article looks briefly at the origin of this construction, but is mainly concerned with its present-day use. Concerning the use of the construction in the plural (now the only common type), it is noted that they especially occur as a reference to a distinct social group that is in some sense vulnerable and/or unfortunate; at the same time, these expressions also indicate a kind of permanence. Thus, *the handicapped, the unemployed, the innocent* all occur, while *the employed, the bored, the guilty* are much less likely to occur. Concerning the use of the nominalized adjective in the singular (with abstract meaning, for example, *the unreal* = 'unreality'), it is noted that this use is also restricted semantically. It usually concerns an aspect of something which would interest an observer intellectually (e.g. *the lovely, the foreign* is not found). Other points discussed are the analysis of headless NPs, the way in which they are used to refer to nationalities, and their restriction to particular styles.

As in earlier years, there are several contributions on relative clauses. Christine Johansson's published doctoral thesis, *The Relativizers whose and of which in Present-day English: Description and Theory*, looks at the way the genitive is relativised after non-personal antecedents. It describes the factors that condition the distribution of *whose* and *of which* (both of which are awkward, see also the article discussed immediately below) in different written and spoken texts (corpora used are LOB, Brown, London-Lund, and the spoken part of the Birmingham corpus). It also looks at the alternative ways in which the genitive may be expressed. Some findings are: (1) *Whose* is clearly less preferred when the relatival genitive is of an 'objective' kind (*slogans, whose repetitions* ...), where the genitive is further removed from the 'possessive' core meaning of the genitive; another reason for the lower frequency of *whose* here is that the antecedent has to be definite to allow *whose*. (2) There is a clear preference in written English for the pattern *the car the brakes of which* to the one with the relative immediately after the antecedent (except when the relative is a subject complement). (3) The main difference between written and spoken English is that *whose* and especially *of which* are much lower in frequency in the spoken language, not only absolutely (as is to be expected) but also in relation to other Wh-words. Alternatives used in spoken English are discussed in the last chapter (e.g. *cottages whose insides have been ripped off* becomes *cottages which have their insides* ... / *cottages with their insides* ... / *cottages in which/where their insides* ...). Also discussed are non-standard alternatives such as *that's, what his, as his, at his* etc. This brings us automatically to the contribution by Aimo Seppänen and Göran Kjellmer, entitled 'The dog that's leg was run over: on the genitive of the relative pronoun' (*ES* 76.389–400). The authors have looked at the use of this construction in present-day British and American English and have found that the construction (which fills a syntactic gap especially in those areas where *whose* is avoided, for example, in Scotland, Ireland, and parts of northern England) seems relatively recent in all varieties of the language. It is most strongly present in northern dialects and in colloquial non-written English, but shows signs of spreading even into the standard language after inanimate antecedents. They also note that *that's* is only acceptable when it is part of the subject of the relative clause, and that the *'s* (which comes from earlier *his*) has developed into a genitive inflection.

Gregory Guy and Robert Bayley write on 'The choice of relative pronouns in English' (*AS* 70.148–62). They have analysed data from The White House Transcripts (containing unmonitored white male speech) and from academic articles on language variation, paying attention to factors like animacy (human antecedents turn out to disfavour *that*), mode (writing favours Wh-forms), and position of the gap. The authors are careful to point out that, unlike what is sometimes suggested in similar studies, quantitative data of the type that they present cannot be used to decide questions in the theoretical (i.e. formal) analysis of relative clauses. There are, however, also theoretical issues more directly connected with frequencies, and some of these are addressed in 'Relative clauses, the Accessibility Hierarchy and the Contrastive Analysis Hypothesis', by Flor Aarts and Erik Schils (*IRAL* 33.47–63). The authors carried out an experiment in which some 100 Dutch students were tested twice on English relative clause formation, with teaching taking place during the intervening period. The results show an overall improvement, but it is not clear how far this is the effect of direct teaching or of continued exposure. Both before and after teaching, the Accessibility Hierarchy was obeyed (but subject and direct object showed little difference). 'Long' movement (as in *The book which he had told me that I should read*) was more difficult than short movement (*The books that I should read*), but few violations of the *that*-trace filter were found, even though these do occur in the students' first language.

Another book-length study of relatives is Christer Geisler's *Relative Infinitives in English*. Three main types of relative infinitives are distinguished: subject relatives (usually found in matrix object position, and containing a transitive verb, as in *they found somebody to fix the car*), object relatives (*the thing to consider*), and adverbial relatives (*two minutes to answer the question (in)*). A detailed description is given of the distribution of these types, and their subtypes, in the Brown, LOB and London-Lund corpora, with information about definiteness, form and function of the antecedent, the givenness or newness of material in the relative clause, the interpretation of the PRO subject, the occurrence of a *for*-phrase, the presence of premodifying adjectives, etc.

There are two further relative papers in *Ling&Philol* 15. The first, Kay Nakago's 'Conditions on relative pronoun deletion' (63–76), discusses the kind of conditions that license the absence of the object relative pronoun in restrictive relative clauses. Nakago argues (very briefly) that the traditional and generative accounts of this phenomenon are inadequate because they do not *explain* why deletion takes place and/or do not deal with all the phenomena involved, and that we therefore need a rule based on perceptual strategies dealing with surface linear order, to give a unified account of the different phenomena. This rule states that the relative pronoun can only be deleted if it immediately follows its antecedent and is itself immediately followed by an NP. Atsushi Takekoshi's 'Licensing condition on resumptive pronouns and free relatives' (99–114) is a highly technical discussion of types of clauses which are all on the borderline between grammaticality and ungrammaticality, but in which it is argued that resumptive pronouns are grammatical in relatives (*The automobile that the policeman who impounded it got a citation was a Buick*) and not in Wh-questions and free relatives (e.g. **What (automobile) did the policeman who impounded it get a citation*) because 'Wh-phrases can not enter into predication relation at D-structure because there are no heads [i.e. antecedents] at this level'. Finally, we mention here a paper by José Luis González Escribano, 'On the incompatibility of genitives and restrictive relative clauses: an explanation within the theory of principles and parameters' (*Linguistics* 33.711–40). This deals with the ungrammaticality of NPs such as *John's book that I borrowed*, the explanation of which crucially rests on the idea that the genitive occupies SpecDP. The author points out that earlier English allowed such NPs, and attributes their loss to a shift of the genitive from D to SpecDP at the time the group genitive arose.

We now turn to studies concerned with verbal patterns. Bas Aarts and Charles Meyer have edited an entire volume on this topic, entitled *The Verb in Contemporary English: Theory and Description*. In their 'Introduction: theoretical and descriptive approaches to the study of the verb in English', they provide a useful basic orientation to issues such as verb complements and adjuncts, government, subcategorisation, selection, grammatical functions, the status of auxiliaries, secondary predicates, the semantics and pragmatics of verbal constructions, and much more. We shall first consider the contributions (in Aarts and Meyer's volume and elsewhere) on verb forms, meanings and choices, and then move on to verbal complementation of various types. Jan Svartvik and Olof Ekedahl discuss 'Verbs in public and private speaking' (in Aarts and Meyer). They present data from the London-Lund Corpus and the Lancaster/IBM Spoken English Corpus on the frequency of verbs and other word classes, and also on the most frequent individual verbs. They find, for example, that the London-Lund Corpus has a few extremely frequent verbs (e.g. *know, think, get, go, say, mean*) and that the auxiliaries are even more frequent. They show that in these respects, and others, London-Lund differs from the Lancaster Corpus (and also written English). We also briefly mention here Anna-Brita Stenström's 'Some remarks on comment clauses' (in Aarts and Meyers), which looks at the grammar, prosody, textual distribution, and pragmatics of phrases like *I mean, I think, you know*, etc.

As for forms of the verb, Eva Grabowski and Dieter Mindt supply us with 'A corpus-based learning list of irregular verbs in English' (*ICAME Journal* 19.5–22). This paper provides a didactic tool to learn irregular verbs more efficiently. Rather than ordering them alphabetically (as is common practice in textbooks), it ranks the verbs according to their frequency in authentic English usage (based on the Brown and LOB corpus). It also shows the extent to which verbs use both regular and irregular forms. A rather special verbal form is the topic of Gerd Övergaard's *The Mandative Subjunctive in American and British English in the 20th Century*. He looks at the variant forms available to express futurity and/or volition after so-called mandative predicates. Three forms are used: the inflectional subjunctive, a modal (usually *should*) + V, and the indicative (the latter only in British English). Övergaard investigates the stylistic and affective meaning differences between the forms, and the changes that have occurred in this area in the last hundred years. Both the Brown and the LOB corpus are used, as well as a corpus of written texts spanning the whole century. The use of the indicative as a variant form is difficult to establish, because most of the time the form is ambiguous between subjunctive and indicative. The tables do not make clear how they are distinguished, i.e. in how far V and V-ed can be counted as subjunctive and indicative. Where unambiguous indicatives are used, the context is usually less mandative; it is especially frequent after verbs like *suggest* and *insist*. Diachronically, the study shows that the subjunctive has been gaining ground again in both American and British English, but at a different pace, at different times and for different reasons (in British English it really has only caught on dramatically in the 1990 corpus). An interesting development is the use of *not* without *do*-support, possibly on analogy with *never*. Concerning the periphrastic 'subjunctive', it is clear that the range of modals used here has been drastically reduced, *should* now being the only common one.

Modals usually attract a fair amount of attention in themselves, and this year is no exception. Paul Westney's book, *Modals and Periphrastics in English*, looks at a wide range of periphrastic constructions. This study explores the relationship between modal verbs and other periphrastic modal structures such as *will* vs *be going to*, *must* vs *have (got) to* etc. (these sets are established on the basis of compatibility tests), especially the extent to which they are used as semantic and/or pragmatic variants of one another. The following claims are investigated: are the core modals the semantically unmarked forms; and, connected with that, do the periphrastic forms have more autonomous (additive) meaning? Do the core modals involve the speaker's own consent or agreement, while the periphrastics are neutral in this regard? The first three chapters are general, discussing the syntactic, semantic and phonological criteria used in this area, and previous studies. In chapters 4 and 5, the different sets are discussed in detail with reference to the degree of equivalence, the nature of the relationship, the extent of application and in how far the use of items in each set is constrained by aspects of style, variety, discourse functioning etc. The account is primarily descriptive and mainly based on the *Corpus of* (British) *English Conversation*.

Another mainly descriptive study is John Myhill's 'Change and continuity in the functions of the American English modals' (*Linguistics* 33.157–211). On the basis of a collection of 5,000 modal tokens from speech-based writings from both before and after the Civil War, a detailed analysis of which is presented, Myhill identifies a trend away from the modal expression of absolute evaluations and universally valid principles grounded in a clear social order (as in *My daughter shall marry you*) to the use of modals for interactive purposes based on equal power relations (as in *You've got to help me*). He very tentatively suggests, after discussing other possibilities, that this shift may be related to a shift in world view. Jennifer Coates writes about 'The expression of root and epistemic possibility in English' (in Aarts and Meyer, eds, *The Verb in Contemporary English*). Using some of the diagnostics developed by Heine for German modals, Coates shows that the distinction is not particularly strong in English. Still, by and large *can* and *may* are used to express root and epistemic possibility respectively. *Can*, however, seems to be acquiring an epistemic possibility meaning (in *Can it be true?* and *We hope it can be useful*), a development that would fit in with Traugott's idea that deontic modals may become epistemic. More modality can be found in 'Modals and adverbs in English with reference to Romanian', by Leo Hoye and Mihai Zdrenghea (*Rask* 2.25–50), in which the authors show that, in both English and Romanian, there are several modal + adverb collocations that seem to operate as units (e.g. *might conceivably, will probably, must surely*) and that can be arranged to form a sort of continuum of, for example, epistemic certainty. We also mention here Stig Johansson's ' "This scheme is badly needed": some aspects of verb-adverb combinations' (in Aarts and Meyer, eds, *The Verb in Contemporary English*), which presents data on various adverb-verb collocations (with special attention being paid to the adverb *badly*). The final item in this group deals with the analysis of modals: Michael Menaugh writes on 'The English modals and established models of probability and possibility: a sign-based analysis' (*SL* 49.196–227). He interprets modal meaning in terms of the notions of Probability in limited outcome systems, Probability in unlimited outcome systems, and Possibility; he also proposes physical analogues for the modals, and deduces from these some of their grammatical properties (e.g. whether they have a past tense or not, and how they behave under negation).

A large number of articles deal with issues of tense and aspect. Two of them are concerned with the simple form of the present tense but from different theoretical viewpoints. Dick Leith reports on 'Tense variation as a performance feature in a Scottish folktale' (*LSoc* 24.53–77). The author compares the use of the 'historical present' as analysed for narratives involving personal experience with its use in a different kind of oral narrative, i.e. a folktale narrated on two separate occasions by the same story teller (the first a 'full' performance, the second more like an interview). He finds that usage is much more complex than earlier studies (by Wolfson and Schiffrin, for example) have suggested, and that the use of the present tense is strongly influenced by the 'fullness of the performance'. Thus, he links the use of tense with other performance features, and finds that, although Wolfson's and Schiffrin's ideas that the shift in tense highlights the significance of certain stretches of narrative works to some extent for the interviewed narrative, its use is much more generic in the full performance, and may indeed function as a generic marker of 'performance' to distinguish the narrative from the surrounding discourse.

The main point of Walter H. Hirtle's article 'The simple form again: an analysis of direction-giving and related uses' (*JPrag* 24.265–81) is to find out whether a rather specific usage of the simple form, i.e. that of direction-giving (as in *You take the first turning on the left*) is compatible with the 'central' meaning of the simple form. In previous studies many different interpretations were given of this usage, suggesting it expressed habit, iteration, futurity, command etc. Quite clearly there was no consensus and the usage was seen as difficult to classify. The framework adopted here is Guillaume's (1984) theory of the psychomechanics of language, which postulates that every grammatical form has one 'potential' meaning on the level of 'langue', which, however, can be diversely 'actualized' on the level of 'parole'. In this theory the potential meaning of the simple form is its representation of 'the event time required for all development involved in the event'. It is shown that the directive present is linked to the use of some other presents and that it fits this potential meaning when analysed as a 'prospective realization'.

Whether English has a future tense has long been a controversial question. Rodney Huddleston argues 'The case against a future tense in English' (*SLang* 19.399–446). He does so in the framework of a theory of tense and modals, which recognizes that the past in English often has modal meaning.

According to Huddleston, the pair *will-would* can be straightforwardly compared to the pair *can-could*. He presents formal and semantic/pragmatic arguments for regarding *will* as a modal (with *would* as its past tense), and also examines and rejects the idea that *will* can function both as a modal and as a future tense marker.

There are nine papers dealing with tense and aspect in this year's proceedings of the *Anglistentag*, held in Graz in 1994 (ed. Wolfgang Riehle and Hugo Keiper). It is interesting to observe that all the papers except one are based on corpus research and are focused on four basic issues, identified by Ekkehard König in his contribution 'On analysing the tense-aspect system of English: a state-of-the-art report'. The first issue concerns categorization: what exactly constitutes 'tense' and 'aspect', which of the English verbal forms belongs where, and on the basis of what criteria does one decide? The second issue concerns the meaning of the various tense and aspectual forms; here the question is especially whether to proceed onomasiologically (aspect as a semantic, language-independent category) or in the opposite direction, semasiologically. A third point concerns the distinction between semantic and pragmatic uses, and also in how far certain pragmatic uses in the course of time have become more centrally semantic. Finally, questions are asked about changes taking place within the tense-aspect system. Wolfgang Klein shows in his 'A simplest analysis of the English tense-aspect system' that the term 'current relevance' for the English perfect may be an important intuitive notion, but does not explain all the uses of the perfect. Instead, he proposes to analyse the perfect by means of three notions which are needed independently, i.e. the notions of 'temporal relations between time spans, assertion, and lexical meaning which is used to describe a situation'. The article is based on his book (*YWES* 75.43). Klein is not the only one to write about the perfect. Bernd Kortmann argues in 'Compositionality and the perfect' that a compositional, semantically parallel analysis of the perfect is still the best solution in spite of Comrie's (1985) rejection of this. Kortmann concentrates on the fact that the present perfect cannot collocate with a past time adverbial, while the past and future perfects can. He discusses a number of studies that have argued that the non-use of the time adverbial in the present perfect is not part of its semantics. Referring to Salkie (1989), Klein (1992) and Stump (1985), he shows that independent motivations can be given for the fact that the present perfect behaves differently. These relate to the similarity between the simple present and the present perfect (the present also being more restricted than the simple past), to pragmatic factors and to the fact that the present perfect is the only one of the perfect forms that has a direct semantic competitor, i.e. the simple past. He concludes that the present perfect, which is usually seen as the prototype perfect, in fact provides the least insight into the nature of the perfect. Matthias Meyer advocates in 'Past tense and present perfect in the *Brown* and the *LOB* corpora' a purely formal distinction of all verbal categories with no preconceived meaning, seeing only the past as a tense category. Each formal category has one core (-emic) meaning, which through contextualization can lead to individual readings (here adverbial modifications are seen as the most decisive factors). This also involves the belief (*contra* Kortmann) that verbal categories must be defined language-specifically (semasiologically). What follows is a statistical survey of the uses of the two categories in the corpora. As is to be expected, the study is mainly descriptive. Rodney Huddleston also investigates the past and the present perfect in 'The English perfect as a secondary past tense' (in Aarts and Meyer, eds, *The Verb in Contemporary English*). He focuses on the difference in meaning between the preterite (the primary past) and the present perfect (a secondary past), and provides a Reichenbachian characterization of the meanings of the two forms.

Part of Huddleston's characterization of the preterite is that it can be backshifted (as in *He said he was feeling ill*). Such a rule is also posited by Toshiyuki Ogihara, who writes on 'The semantics of tense in embedded clauses' (*LingI* 26.663–79). More precisely, Ogihara argues that there is a rule of tense deletion in such cases, making the embedded past interpretatively empty. This specific rule is set within a framework in which tense is viewed as involving existential quantification. Over the years, Renaat Declerck has several times expressed in print the view that there is no such rule as backshifting or sequence of tenses. In this year's 'Is there a relative past tense in English?' (*Lingua* 97.1–36) he lists ten empirical arguments for saying that an embedded past can function as a relative tense (i.e. it expresses simultaneity with a point which lies in the past). He also presents six tests that can be used to distinguish the relative past from the absolute past (which establishes a point in the past). We look forward to seeing further contributions on this topic.

The pluperfect is examined in Mimo Caenepeel's 'Aspect and text structure' (*Linguistics* 33.213–53). Caenepeel compares narrative fiction with newspaper reporting, and shows that characteristics of the text type influence the use of events and states. The pluperfect is prominent in fiction, since it is concerned with temporal ordering, but not in newspaper reports. Precise constraints are put forward spelling out the factors determining tense choice. A novel kind of pluperfect is described by Carole Chaski in 'The future pluperfect: double tenses in American English auxiliaries' (*AS* 70.3–20). In a survey, many of her students (both white and Afro–American, coming from various parts of the country) indicated that they were familiar with, and might also produce, sentences such as *John will have had run the race* and *John will had run the race*. Chaski also provides a formal analysis of such structures in terms of the clausal architecture of McCawley (1988).

We now turn to the use of the progressive. Peter Lucko's 'Between aspect, actionality and modality: the functions of the expanded form' (Wolfgang Riehle and Hugo Keiper, eds, *Anglistentag 1994 Graz. Proceedings.*) is especially interested in the more recent developments in the BE+ing form. He gives examples where the expanded form (EF) can hardly have any aspectual meaning. In such cases, the EF in fact expresses 'actional difference', as in *The neighbours are being friendly*, because the verb phrase does not just imply temporariness and duration, but 'triggers a complete reinterpretation of the situation'. Similar developments away from aspect seem to be taking place in expanded passives and progressives of the type *I am hoping that . . . .* This use of the EF leads, according to the author, to more and more verbs being used in it that from an aspectual point of view could not have been used in the progressive in the past. In other words the EF seems to be developing its own weight, thus enhancing the expressive power of utterances. Elizabeth Couper-Kuhlen ('On the foregrounded progressive in American conversational narrative: a new development' in the same volume reports on a new use of the progressive employed to foreground an activity rather than the usual role of the progressive, which is to provide narrative background. In all cases in her data the progressive can be replaced by a simple form: the verb is sequentially ordered with respect to prior and subsequent events and it does not serve as a frame for another event. A number of causes are suggested for this new development, such as a change in lexical class or 'aktionsart', a result of aspect neutralization, and a modification of the pragmatic conventions for narrative grounding. A similar question is asked in Christian Mair and Marianne Hundt's paper 'Why is the progressive becoming more frequent in English? A corpus-based investigation of language change in progress' also in Riehle and Keiper's volume (the same article also appeared in ZAA 43.111–22). It is based on a comparison of the Brown and LOB corpora with two new similar corpora compiled 30 years later, called F[reiburg]LOB and Frown. The existence of these new corpora makes it possible to test existing hypotheses on language change in progress, and to find out more about how 'synchronic regional and stylistic variation can be separared from [or result in?] true instances of diachronic change'. The comparison makes clear that the use of the progressive has increased (especially the use of is going to, discussed separately), but that the increase is not on the whole statistically significant. The increase is not found with stative verbs, so the authors conclude it must have been current usages that were extended. They believe that this extension is due to the closing of the gap between written and spoken English and to the affective-emotional use of the progressive becoming less and less marked.

Norbert Freckmann has written on 'The progressive and adverbial colloca-tions: corpus evidence' (in Riehle and Keiper, eds, Anglistentag). This is an empirical study that explores the interaction between adverbials and aspect/tense in British English (corpora used are LOB and London-Lund). Four major types of progressive-adverbial co-occurrences are distinguished: adver-bials that are obligatory, optional, excluded completely, or excluded only in certain denotations. The final progressive item to be discussed here is Karin Königs's 'Zur Übersetzung der Verlaufsform ins Deutsche' (Lebende Sprachen 40.153–8), where she shows the various possibilities of translating the English progressive into German. Such translation is problematic because German has no equivalent 'progressive' form, and therefore different transla-tions are needed for different semantic aspects of the progressive. Thus, the various functions that the progressive has are discussed (future intention, process, intensity etc.) and for each aspect various translation suggestions are given. It is noticeable that in German many aspects are expressed by such 'affective' adverbs as gleich, noch, aber, doch, etwa etc.

Aktionsart plays a prominent role in two papers. Yasuhiro Shirai and Roger Andersen's 'The acquisition of tense-aspect morphology: a prototype account' (Language 71.743–62) investigates data from CHILDES, focusing on two questions about the early acquisition of the past and the progressive: does it correlate with Aktionsart? and does it correlate with caretaker's speech? The answers turn out to be: yes, yes. The past is mainly associated with achievements (i.e. predicates like reach the mountain) and the progressive with activities (e.g. playing with a ball); the authors give a prototype account of these correlations. Ilse Depraetere writes 'On the necessity of distinguishing between (un)boundedness and (a)telicity' (Ling&P 18.1–19). After briefly surveying terminology used for Aktionsart, she proposes that a distinction should be made on the basis of potential endpoint (telicity) and a further one on the basis of actual temporal boundaries (boundedness). She then shows the interaction between these categories and tense, the nature of NPs and PPs in the clause. In the final tense-aspect item for this year, Hildegard Tristram is interested in 'Aspect in contact' (Riehle and Keiper, eds, *Anglistentag*). The approach in her comparison of aspect in English and the insular Celtic languages is synchronic and semasiological, i.e. it compares surface forms, that is, the Celtic equivalents of the English perfect and progressive. The article is a useful inventory of all the forms found, but is more descriptive than analytic. As for the similarities in usage, the author believes that substratum influence, both ways, is more likely than incidental parallel development.

We move on to verb complementation. There seems to be a real 'hype' about the indirect object, not surprising perhaps because it is a theoretically odd constituent in present-day English. Jennifer Herriman's published doctoral thesis of the University of Gothenburg is exclusively concerned with *The Indirect Object in Present-Day English*. It is in the first place a descriptive study of this phenomenon (based on the Brown and LOB corpora). The definition of the indirect object it provides is based on a combination of formal syntactic and functional criteria (position, deletability, possibility of conversion into a PP). Semantic criteria are not used, on the grounds that the recipient role, typical of indirect objects, can also be realized by subjects (with verbs meaning to possess) and direct objects (with verbs like *help*). The investigation starts off with a useful survey of earlier analyses. The indirect objects are divided into 11 different classes, among which there are four main ones. The first two show the alternation between a bare indirect object and one in a *to*-phrase, the difference being whether the verb in question allows the direct object to be omitted. The third class contains verbs that take a *for* phrase, while verbs in class 4 can take both *to* and *for*. For each class we are given a list of verbs belonging to it, and its main properties (including semantic roles). The remaining seven classes contain very few verbs and are distinguished mainly on the basis of the preposition that they take in the alternative PP; many of these expressions are idiomatic. The last two chapters deal with the requirements that discourse and style place on the way the indirect object is used. More description of the indirect object can be found in A. Kakouriotis's 'On the double object construction in English and Modern Greek' (*SLang* 19.1–35), which contains a detailed comparison of the two languages. Points paid attention to include case marking, the range of thematic roles of subject and indirect object, argument structure, form and meaning constraints on the verb, and the grammatical status of the indirect object.

Jaroslav Macháček's approach to the same topic is much less descriptive. In his 'Indirect object, dative, beneficiary, or recipient' (*LingP* [1995].92–100), he tries to find a more coherent, less fuzzy definition/structural description for the syntactic element variously described in his title, by showing that indirect objects take part in a HAVE relation in which they function as subject. He thus treats them as 'nominalized predications of the HAVE relation kind' (p.100). A description of the different kinds of HAVE relations possible ((im)material possession, perception) follows. Maya Arad is concerned with the way indirect objects must be generated, in her 'On the projection of ditransitive verbs' (*UCWPL* 7.215–33). The article starts off with a consideration of a lexical-entry-driven approach and a predicate-based approach to the projection of arguments, and next begins to explore the plausibility of Borer's syntactic predicate-based approach, which assumes no internal hierarchical structure in the VP, and makes no distinction between internal and external arguments for ditransitive verbs. It is shown that this approach can work provided the lexical entry contains semantic information about telicity. Masachiyo Amano's contribution is also concerned with the projection of the indirect object, but as part of a larger theoretical question. He proposes to change the adjacency condition on structural case marking into 'The sisterhood condition (on case marking in English)' (*Ling&Philol* 15.1–21), using as evidence the 'peculiar' behaviour of ditransitive verbs, where the direct object is not adjacent to the verb, and is therefore, somewhat ad-hoc-ly, assumed to have inherent rather than structural case. Amano argues that the 'sisterhood condition' is simple, less ad-hoc, and can be shown to work (in combination with Stowell's 'Case Resistance Principle') not only for direct objects of intransitive verbs, but also for ECM constructions, and in other constructions where an element intervenes between the verb and the direct object.

Sandra Thompson approaches indirect objects from a different point of view in 'The iconicity of "dative shift" in English: considerations from information flow in discourse' (in Marge E. Landsberg, ed., *Syntactic Iconicity*). She considers the alternation of the indirect object and the *to*-phrase from an iconic point of view, namely that there is a relationship between the position of the recipient in the clause with material in the previous discourse. This concerns both its position vis-à-vis the patient role, which it usually precedes, within the clause and its relation to discourse elements outside the clause. In both cases, it is shown that the degree of 'topicworthiness' of the recipient is responsible for its position. A somewhat similar line of attack is taken by Peter Collins in 'The indirect object construction in English: an informational approach' (*Linguistics* 33.35–49). Using a collection of 108 tokens from an Australian English corpus, he examines the accessibility (i.e. recoverability from preceding discourse or speech situation), end weight (i.e. length), pronounhood, and definiteness of both objects. In this way, he is able to show that, for example, the bare object construction usually has strong differentiation between the two objects (the indirect object conveying given information, being short, definite, and often pronominal), while the *to*-construction has less differentiation.

Yet another type of approach to indirect objects is found in Marcel den Dikken's *Particles: On the Syntax of Verb-Particle, Triadic, and Causative Constructions*, a detailed generative study. Although we review generative work below, we deal with this book here, since it proposes a novel analysis of ditransitives (and also phrasal verbs and related constructions in other languages), and contains a critical overview of earlier generative work on these topics. Den Dikken establishes on the basis of various types of data an analysis for (complex) particle constructions such as *They made John out a liar*, viewing particles as ergative, non-lexical, prepositional heads of small clauses. This analysis is then somewhat elaborated to take on board also ditransitives, which have the indirect object inside a PP with an empty P; this PP starts out as complement to a small clause headed by an empty particle, moves to the specifier position, and then has the empty preposition moving up further to be incorporated with an abstract copula above the particle phrase. Presenting the analysis in four or five lines like this may make it sound complicated, but it is the best we can do here. The rationale for the apparent complexity is that this analysis can account for most of the puzzling properties of indirect objects, and we would urge the interested reader to take a first-hand look at Den Dikken's own careful and crystal-clear exposition. A much more descriptive item on phrasal verbs is Samuel Ahulu's 'Variation in the use of complex verbs in international English' (*EnT* 11.ii.28–34). This is the third part (we have not seen the other two) of an investigation into particular usages in the standard English of West Africa and India, dealing with phrasal verbs. He examines two main types of international divergence, i.e. forms which do not occur in Standard British/American English (e.g. *to voice out an opinion*), and forms that have undergone a semantic shift (e.g. *the event will come on tomorrow*). He distinguishes five common patterns in the way changes are made; for instance, it is common for the particle to be dropped (*to pick* for *pick up*), to be added (*to cope up with*), or to be substituted (*congratulate for*).

There are not many items on direct objects. John Algeo's 'Having a look at the expanded predicate' (in Aarts and Meyer, eds, *The Verb in Contemporary English*) contains a description of various aspects of expressions such as *take a seat*, *make a comparison* and *do a somersault*. He attributes the increase in the number of such combinations to the loss of inflections (though without giving much evidence for this view), and describes the construction as a device to focus on an event rather than the participants, and as a way to avoid an unmodified subject-verb sequence. Several types are distinguished, and data on types and tokens in the Brown and LOB corpora are presented. Marjolein Groefsema's 'Understood arguments: a semantic/pragmatic approach' (*Lingua* 96.139–61) is about implicit or empty objects in sentences such as *John was eating* and *John followed*. She finds fault with Fillmore's (1986) analysis of this phenomenon; instead, she proposes that verbs like *eat* restrict their internal argument to a type of thing, while *follow*-verbs restrict it to an instance of a thing. She explains how Relevance Theory can be invoked for an account of when understood arguments are possible. In a paper 'On the semantics of the object' (also in Aarts and Meyer), I. M. Schlesinger proposes that the direct object is generally a 'defining participant' in the event. Sometimes, a defining participant is expressed in a PP (*put a book on the table*), but if the preposition is recoverable, expression as a direct object is possible (*swim (across) the Channel*, *ride (on) a horse*). In other cases, choice of a PP suggests lack of completion, while a direct object suggests completion (as in *push (at) the table*, *load the hay onto the wagon/load the wagon with hay*). Some verbs select a direct object when a 'feat' is expressed (as in *swim a lake/*?the pond*).

Middles have often been analysed as involving movement of the direct object to subject position. Such analyses are criticised by Peter Ackema and Maaike Schoorlemmer in their 'Middles and non-movement' (*LingI* 26.173–97). Their arguments against the movement analysis involve the use of reflexive pronouns, the impossibility of adding a *for*-phrase to most middles, the presence of uncontrolled PRO in adjunct clauses, and the oddity of the Affectedness Constraint on movement. Thomas Stroik, one of the proponents of a movement analysis, writes 'On middle formation: a reply to Zribi-Hertz' (*LingI* 26.165–71). He focuses on the occurrence of anaphors, as in *Books about oneself read poorly*, defending his earlier analysis, by which the anaphor is bound in its underlying object position by the external PRO argument which is in VP-adjoined position. Further support for his analysis comes from control facts and certain *donkey*-anaphora sentences. The meaning of middles is addressed in Andrew Rosta's ' "How does this sentence interpret?" The semantics of English mediopassives' (in Aarts and Meyer, eds, *The Verb in Contemporary English*). He notes that the agent can be specific (as in *The car handles smoothly when Sophie drives it*), that the subject need not be affected by the event (*The river fords easily*), and that the referent of the subject is always primarily responsible for the situation or event (cf. *The paint sprayed easily* with ??*The car sees easily*). The genericity and dynamicity of middles are also discussed. In the same volume are two further relevant articles. Charles Meyer's 'Grammatical relations in English' considers the notions of complement and complementation, and contrasts the latter with modification and disassimilation on the basis of criteria like optionality, latency, and constrainedness. Using the term complement for the final element in sentences like *he was an idiot* and *they called him stupid*, Geoffrey Leech and Lu Li investigate 'Indeterminacy between noun phrases and adjective phrases as complements of the English verb'. Data from various (mainly written) corpora show that NPs with complement function are quasi-adjectival, in that they are non-referential, often take the zero article, often have a gradable head noun, often consist of an adjective plus a dummy noun such as *one*, *thing*, or *people*, and sometimes fail to show concord (as in *They fell victim to ...*). Peter Lasersohn, in 'Sounds like *like*' (*LingA* 25.70–7), contrasts the two sentence types *The song sounded good* and *A beer sounds good*. He interprets the second type as a case of raising; the complement can also be clausal, but then the word *like* has to be inserted (as in *He sounds like he knows all about it*). The formal analysis of constructions with an object complement is investigated in Beom-Mo Kang's 'On the treatment of complex predicates in Categorial Grammar' (*Ling&P* 18.61–81). In a sentence like *John considers Mary intelligent*, the sequence *consider intelligent* is taken to form a discontinuous complex predicate, and a Categorial Grammar analysis is proposed which will derive the surface word order. Bas Aarts has looked at 'Secondary predicates in English' (also in Aarts and Meyer). Aarts makes a distinction between depictive predicates (*John ate the meat raw*) and resultative ones (*They elected her treasurer*), and discusses the forms they can take, the constraints they impose on the other clause elements, their syntactic position (inside the VP), and possible analyses (as a small clause, with or without PRO; as an element in a ternary-branching VP; or as a discontinuous complex predicate).

Three items focus on the complementation of specific verbs. Jan Aarts and Flor Aarts write about '*Find* and *want*: a corpus-based case study in verb complementation' (in Aarts and Meyer). They find that the specific form and meaning of *find* correlates with the type of complement it takes, and somewhat less clearly so in the case of *want*. Christian Mair considers 'Changing patterns of complementation, and concomitant grammaticalisation, of the verb *help* in present-day British English' (in Aarts and Meyer). After reviewing earlier work on *help*, Mair presents a comparison of the LOB corpus with material from 1991. This shows that *help* + bare infinitive has become more frequent, is no longer colloquial, and no longer shows consistent semantic differentiation from *help* + *to*-infinitive. Mair points out that the bare infinitive pattern meets some of the criteria associated with grammaticalization. Hiroyuki Nawata looks at 'The complement structures of causative *make* and *have*' (*Ling&Philol* 15.115–31). He discusses the problems that arise with the various proposed analyses of these constructions, such as the ternary branching, the complex predicate and the small clause analysis. The author opts for an explanation in terms of functional categories, coming to the conclusion that *make* has both Agr and T, when its complement is verbal, but that the complement of *have* never contains a T node.

These items have brought us to a discussion of clausal complementation. A study of gerundial complements is Juhani Rudanko's '*Balking at* and *working at*: on verbs governing *at -ing* in present-day English' (*ES* 76.264–81). Its main aims are to compile a list of verbs (based on the Brown and LOB corpora) that take this type of complement, and to describe the semantic and syntactic characteristics of such verbs. Thus, the difference between adverbial and complemental *at*-gerunds is described, the interchangeability of *at* + nominal NP and *at* + gerund (and the difference between *at* + gerund and *to*-infinitives). Semantically, all *at*-taking verbs select a [+ animate] subject. They are divided up into four different semantic classes, but most verbs have in common that they express some kind of emotion (unwillingness, anger, delight etc.) on the part of the matrix subject. Geart van der Meer's 'Verb complementation and the role of syntax' (*NOWELE* 25.89–106) deals with the proper analysis of sentences like *they want us to help*, *I hate the children quarrelling* and *I saw her leave the room*. He argues that the syntactic analysis of these constructions should not be based on semantics, but only take into account words, order and some markers. He then proposes that in the sentences at issue the postverbal NP is the object (defined as 'the first nominal modifier of the verb') while the rest is a second modifier. Interpretation will be guided by the meaning of the verb and the context.

Richard Hudson's 'Con PRO, or the virtues of sharing' (*UCPWL* 7.277–96) makes a plea for what he calls the 'sharing analysis' of EQUI verbs, i.e. the idea that in a clause like, *Mary persuaded Fred to help*, *Fred* is both object of the matrix verb, and subject of the infinitive, rather than the PRO analysis, in which *Fred* is not itself a syntactic subject, and where the link with *Fred* is made via coreference. He argues that syntactic theory should allow such a sharing-analysis for EQUI verbs. In support of sharing, he gives case evidence from languages other than English (e.g. Icelandic) and he also discusses a number of other constructions which would benefit from such an analysis, such as relative clauses (with support from Modern Greek relatives). The last paper in this section is by F. G. Droste, 'WH between knowledge and belief' (*LB* 84.159–63). It discusses the silent disappearance of the rule of Wh-raising with verbs such as *believe*, which was related to the rule of NEG-raising, which is also no longer heard of. This raising of Wh was one of the showpieces of early generative grammar, because of the special gap it left behind, not possible with other verbs that are not NEG-raisers, as in *Who do you know/believe Leif invited to his house?*. Droste makes clear that the unacceptability of this structure with *know* is not a syntactic matter (as the generative analysis assumed) but a pragmatic one, i.e. verbs like *know* do not allow insertion into a Wh-question because that would make the structure pleonastic. The difference between the behaviour of *know* and *believe* in this respect relates to the type of questioning (Wh-questions and truth or yes/no questions).

We now come to generative work, in the Principles and Parameters and/or Minimalist framework. Not all of it is strictly and directly on English, yet it must be of interest to anyone working on English within this theory. It is appropriate to start with Noam Chomsky's *The Minimalist Program*, in which his recent papers have been very conveniently collected. The first chapter, 'The theory of principles and parameters', written with Howard Lasnik, was first published in 1993 (*YWES* 74.25); it sketches what is more or less the classical GB model, though some modifications are introduced (for example, the idea that PRO can have Case). Chapter 2, 'Some notes on economy of derivation and representation' (1991) contains some more modifications (the functional projections AgrOP, NegP etc. are adopted, the idea of least effort is introduced, and the possibility of LF-adjunction to *there* is explored). Chapter 3, 'A minimalist program for linguistic theory' (*YWES* 74.27–28) goes further by abolishing S-Structure, introducing generalized transformations, the checking approach, and Spell-Out. Chapter 4, 'Categories and transformations' extends the minimalist approach by eliminating phrase structure theory, and restricting the occurrence of strong features and functional projections.

If anyone should want a detailed guide to the minimalist program, and also to its immediate predecessor, GB-theory, we would recommend the book *Government and Binding Theory and the Minimalist Program: Principles and Parameters in Syntactic Theory*, ed. Gert Webelhuth. It contains chapters on each of the main modules of the theory, written by practising specialists, who were asked to describe the history of the module, its core data, the major competing approaches and their literature. The result is a very rich work. In chapter 1, Gert Webelhuth discusses 'X-bar theory and Case theory'; chapter 2 is on 'Theta theory', by Edwin Williams; chapter 3, by James Huang, deals with 'Logical form'; in chapter 4, Wayne Harbert presents 'Binding theory, control, and *pro*'; chapter 5 is on 'The empty category principle', by Norbert Hornstein and Amy Weinberg; chapter 6, by Randall Hendrick, deals with 'Morphosyntax'; in chapter 7, Alec Marantz explains 'The minimalist program' (up to 1993); and in the final chapter, Noam Chomsky writes on 'Bare phrase structure' (a much revised version of which has become chapter 4 of his own work reviewed above). This book will be extremely useful and instructive not only for students that have gone through an introduction to generative grammar (e.g. the work by Haegeman) and want to continue, but also for researchers from other fields who want to keep up with the latest developments in generative work.

More of these developments can be found in Norbert Hornstein's *Logical Form: From GB to Minimalism*. After a brief sketch of what LF does in GB-theory and an outline of the minimalist program, it has four chapters on the minimalist interpretation of LF phenomena (antecedent-contained deletion; linking, binding and weak cross-over; superiority effects; quantifier scope). In each case, Hornstein tries to eliminate LF A-bar movement (QR, for example, is made to follow from the choice of deleting different trace-copies). A final chapter ponders further implications and problems for minimalism. Another book-length study, Michael Brody's *Lexico-Logical Form: A Radically Minimalist Theory*, goes completely minimal by denying the existence of Move α. LF is argued to be the only syntactic level; chains (which are needed

anyway) do the work of Move α, by containing a higher expletive corresponding to covert movement (i.e. instead of assuming a LF structure like *John
comes$_i$ often t$_i$ late*, the LF will be *John e$_x$ often comes$_x$ late*). An overall
conceptual advantage of this analysis is that the syntax does not produce large
numbers of ill-formed structures which need to be filtered out at LF. It also
immediately explains why intermediate structures do not obey any specific
constraints – this is because such intermediate structures do not exist. Further
chapters deal with potentially problematic issues such as multiple Wh-
questions, subjacency, parasitic gaps, the position in which elements are
spelled out at PF, and reconstruction effects. Ideas similar to Brody's are put
forward by M. Rita Manzini, who proposes that the theory should move away
'From Merge and Move to Form Dependency' (*UCWPL* 7.323–45). She
discusses a number of classical problems in movement and locality theory
(head movement constraint, strong island, head government), which remain
open or problematic under minimalism. She therefore suggests replacing
Chomsky's movement rule (we can see how fast we must move) with a rule of
Form Dependency.

The economy principle of Greed receives separate attention in two papers.
Howard Lasnik's 'Case and expletives revisited: on Greed and other human
failings' (in *LingI* 26.615–33) deals with constructions of the type *There is
someone in the room*. Chomsky's analysis would be to posit LF raising of
someone, to adjoin to *there*, for Case checking, but Lasnik proposes that
someone can get Case from the verb *be* (Lasnik [*YWES* 73.51]) and raises
because *there*, being an LF-affix, cannot remain unattached. This implies that
an element can move not because of requirements it has to meet itself, but
because of requirements that some other element has to meet, i.e. Greed has
to be replaced by the principle of 'enlightened self-interest'. In 'Case properties of clauses and the Greed principle' (*SL* 49.32–53), Zeljko Boškovic,
however, crucially appeals to Greed in its original form to explain the
distribution of clausal arguments. He shows that clauses do not need Case
except when they function as subject (**It was believed that John likes Mary to
be surprising*) or are topicalized (**That John will be late I'm afraid*). The
subject cases are ruled out because, if the clause has Case, this Case must be
checked, and if it does not have Case, the clause cannot move due to Greed
(satisfying the EPP is not a sufficient reason for movement). The topicalization cases are explained by the same reasoning, on the assumption that
A-bar movement of the object passes through AgrOP. A pre-minimalist
account of the distribution of both *that*-clauses and infinitive clauses is given in
Kunihiro Iwakura's 'The distribution of non-NP categories: a government
approach' (*LingA* 25.78–94). Here, it is the ECP that is invoked to explain
facts like the impossibility of movement across clausal subjects (**How easy is
to please John?*) and the ungrammaticality of clausal subjects of infinitives (**I
consider that he said it to be unfortunate*).

There is more on expletives in Erich Groat's 'English expletives: a minimalist account' (*LingI* 26.354–65). Groat argues against existential *there* being an
LF-affix. Rather, he proposes that *there* is inserted in SpecAgrS to check
AgrS's Case features, while the subject NP adjoins to *there* to check AgrS's ø-
features. So *there* is special in having Case features but not ø-features;
furthermore, it has a 'null' interpretation at LF. The subject NP too has a 'null'
interpretation, which disqualifies it as a binder in sentences like **There seem to

each other$_i$ to be some suitable candidates$_i$ for the job, even though it raises to a c-commanding position at LF. The unexpected ungrammaticality of this type of sentence is the starting point for Marcel den Dikken's 'Binding, expletives, and levels' (*LingI* 26.347–54). He proposes that, in fact, there is no LF-raising of the subject. Instead, what happens is that *there* is raised overtly from a small clause predicate position (the underlying structure being something like *e entered [$_{SC}$ a man there]*. This account, it seems to us, avoids a lot of stipulation and complication. Den Dikken also points out that the analysis makes it possible to have the binding theory apply at LF, as minimalism requires.

The Extension Requirement in the minimalist program is scrutinized by Hisatsugu Kitahara ('Target: deducing strict cyclicity from derivational economy', *LingI* 26.47–77). He notes that the requirement contains two stipulations (it does not hold for adjunction, or after Spell-Out), and proposes an alternative. Minimize the number of operations in a derivation. Assuming a particular way of counting the number of operations needed for building trees and also deleting trace-copies, this condition can derive the effects of the Extension Requirement, and may make it possible to eliminate the principle of Procrastinate. Island phenomena, cases of head movement, reconstruction phenomena, and object shift are adduced in support of this approach. In 'Generalized transformations and the theory of grammar' (*SL* 49.103–51), Robert Frank and Anthony Kroch also point at problems with the Extension Requirement, and several further troublesome aspects of minimalism. They argue that the model of Tree Adjoining Grammar (certain elements of which have in fact been incorporated in minimalism) can solve these problems. The data discussed include scope and connectivity effects.

In 'The syntactic function of auxiliaries of time' (*LIN* 1995.37–48), Hans Broekhuis and Kees van Dijk try to solve the puzzle posed by sentences such as *John has eaten the meat*. The problem is how to get the subject from its VP-internal position into SpecIP (or SpecAgrSP), while the verb does not seem to move overtly, which makes Equidistance difficult to achieve. Their solution is to posit two AgrOPs, the higher one for checking the object's Case, and the lower one for checking its ø-features, with the subject originating in the specifier position of the VP headed by the auxiliary. The authors show that this will make all the required movements licit. Annabel Cormack argues in 'The semantics of case' (*UCWPL* 7.235–76) that abstract case is not simply a syntactic matter but that it has reflexes in both lexical and compositional semantics. This analysis is shown to be motivated through a consideration of raising structures. There is more movement in Marcel den Dikken's squib 'Extrapositie als intrapositie en Engelse tag-vragen' (*Tabu* 25.128–32), which is concerned with the question of how to deal with extraposed elements if rightward movement (according to Kayne [*YWES* 75.41]) is no longer allowed. Den Dikken argues that heavy NP shift in fact involves leftward movement of the heavy NP to SpecAgrOP, which coincides with overt leftward movement of the rest of the VP across the landing place of the heavy NP. He suggests that this analysis is supported by the fact that sentences that show antecedent-contained deletion of the type, *John wanted to visit every city that Bill did*, need the same analysis. In addition, the behaviour of heavy NPs combined with tag-questions, when the heavy NP unlike the regular object follows the tag, suggests a leftward movement of the remainder of the VP.

There is more movement still in Sten Vikner's *Verb Movement and*

Expletive Subjects in the Germanic Languages. In the introductory chapter, Vikner first discusses the notion of 'relativised minimality', i.e. in what way empty categories should be analysed. He describes the different kinds of chains that exist between a trace and its governor/antecedent (A-chains, A-bar chains, X°-chains or Head movement) and how they are constrained. These are necessary preliminaries for his investigation of the differences in the way verb movement is employed in the various Germanic languages (he concentrates on English, German and Danish) and how this is connected with the use of expletive subjects. The two different types of verb movement (movement of the finite verb to C° via I°, traditionally called verb second, and the more general movement of V° to I°) are each discussed at great length in separate chapters. He also offers here alternative analyses for V2 movement in embedded clauses. The main point of the book is to show that the distribution of NPs which are linked to an expletive subject (by means of an A-chain) co-varies systematically with the way the verb movement rules function in each language. The expletive constructions discussed are: ergatives, active and passive transitives, and active and passive intransitives. Some of the general findings are that all languages have expletive ergatives and passive transitives, only V2 languages may have expletive passive and active intransitives, and only V2 languages that also have V° to I° movement may have expletive transitives.

Susan Rothstein's 'Pleonastics and the interpretation of pronouns' (*LingI* 26.499–529) is on English expletive or pleonastic *it* in sentences like *It seems he is a fool* and *I consider it obvious that* . . . . She argues that pleonastics can only occur in subject position of a syntactic predicate. Various purported cases of pleonastics are examined in detail, and several of them (e.g. sentences like *I regretted it that he was late*) are argued to contain the ordinary pronoun *it*. We also discuss here a non-generative paper by Aimo Seppänen, Solveig Granath and Jennifer Herriman, 'On so-called "formal" subjects/objects and "real" subjects/objects' (*SN* 67.11–19), since it deals with the syntactic status of 'expletive' or 'provisional' arguments. The authors first test in how far these 'formal' elements and their 'real' or 'logical' counterparts qualify grammatically as subject/object. It is found that in terms of position and concord, it is the formal elements that function truly as subjects and objects. In other words, the logical subject/object must be given another grammatical function. The proposal is to call them *chômeurs* ('unemployed'), the term used for them in Relational Grammar. Existential *there* is also discussed, and it is noted that both formal *there* and the logical subject have grammatical subject properties. This is a peculiar situation, and it is therefore seen as not surprising that this construction is in a state of fluctuation in present-day English.

An extended principles-and-parameters analysis of a non-standard variety is presented in Alison Henry's *Belfast English and Standard English: Dialect Variation and Parameter Setting.* After some background on Belfast English, the problems in studying it, and the principles and parameters model, Henry discusses and analyses in detail such non-standard Belfast features as lack of third person subject-verb agreement (in some cases), overt subject imperatives like *Read it you to me* (with a dialectal subdivision on which types of verbs allow this word order), *for-to* infinitives, inversion in embedded questions, and subject-contact relatives. Henry's careful analyses of all these constructions resist brief summary, but we can note that her general approach is to locate the parametric differences in functional heads. To make things work, she has to allow for features to be optionally strong, for specific instances of functional heads to be strong (e.g. C in imperatives, but not elsewhere, can be strong), and to deal with the subject-contact relatives, a phrase structure parameter has to be admitted.

Several articles focus on binding. Peter Culicover and Ray Jackendoff have 'Something else for the binding theory' (LingI 26.249–75). They analyse the expression something else as an implicit anaphor, which can be unpacked as [other than α], with α obeying binding principle A. They then go on to show that the antecedent of this anaphor need not be a syntactic constituent (e.g. in John patted the dog, and Sam did something else to it), which they take to mean that the binding of something else (and perhaps also other elements) takes place at the level of Conceptual Structure. Mary Dalrymple and Andrew Keller write 'On the constraints imposed by respectively' (LingI 26.531–6). Although they do not analyse the relevant constraints in terms of binding theory, they also come to the conclusion that the pairing effected by respectively need not involve syntactic constituents, but operates with semantic entities in the discourse (which Culicover and Jackendoff might regard as entities at Conceptual Structure). Also concerned with binding at (Lexical) Conceptual Structure is Patrick Farrell's 'Lexical binding' (Linguistics 33.939–80). Farrell decomposes verbs like eat into structures of the type [x CAUSE y GO INTO DIGESTIVE TRACT OF x], and investigates the properties and conditions of the binding relationship existing in them, arguing that these can also account for certain facts of control and verb reflexivization (i.e. se/si verbs in French, Italian and other languages).

Unbound reflexives are the topic of C. L. Baker's 'Contrast, discourse prominence, and intensification, with special reference to locally free reflexives in British English' (Language 71.63–101). Baker has collected (mainly British English) sentences such as His imprudence had made her miserable for a while; but it seemed to have deprived himself of all chance of ever being otherwise (from Sense and Sensibility), and proposes that reflexives of this type are not anaphors or logophors, but intensive NPs, which are used to mark a character as being more prominent or central in the discourse than others (other intensive NPs being genitive + own + N, and also N + X + self). Extensive illustration is provided (with many examples coming from Jane Austen's work), and a comparison with earlier analyses is made. Two non-generative papers also look at reflexive forms. Laurel Brinton writes on 'Non-anaphoric reflexives in free indirect style: expressing the subjectivity of the non-speaker' (Dieter Stein and Susan Wright, eds, Subjectivity and Subjectivisation: Linguistic Perspectives). The emphasis here is on the function of such elements as an expression of subjectivity, and on their occurrence in (free) indirect speech. Suzanne Kemmer's 'Emphatic and reflexive -self: expectation, viewpoint, and subjectivity' (in Stein and Wright, 55–82) considers both emphatic and reflexives self-forms, arguing that they are different, though related (one sign of their relatedness being their shared use to express unexpected reference, either to signal an unexpected shift back to an earlier topic, by emphatic -self, or unexpected coreference, by reflexive -self). Viewpoint uses of -self are also examined, and the degree of subjectivity of all the self-forms is investigated.

Karen van Hoek writes about 'Conceptual reference points: a cognitive grammar account of pronominal anaphora constraints' (*Language* 70.310–40). The constraints referred to in the title have to do with excluded coreference even in the absence of c-command (as in **I spoke to him_i about finances in Ben's_i office*, and *His_i fear is that John_i might have cancer*). The cognitive grammar solution proposed by van Hoek is to say that full NPs are used when a referent is not highly accessible (defined in terms of conceptual reference points), and that they can therefore not occur in the dominion of a coreferential reference point. Yuji Takano has examined 'Predicate fronting and internal subjects' (*LingI* 26.327–40), in response to Huang (*YWES* 74.36). The problem addressed is the ungrammaticality of sentences like **[_VP Criticise John_i] he_i did*. Huang had argued that the fronted predicate is not reconstructed, and that the sentence is ungrammatical because the trace of the VP-internal subject binds *John*. On the basis of further facts, Takano argues that there must be reconstruction, and he shows that this is in fact forced (since otherwise the VP-internal subject trace would not be bound).

Frontings and reconstructions of different types are further examined in several other papers. Caroline Heycock writes about 'Asymmetries in reconstruction' (*LingI* 26.547–70). She examines a wide range of fronted phrase types, and argues that non-referential phrases (so not just predicates) have to reconstruct, while referential phrases do not have to. Thomas Hukari and Robert Levine examine 'Adjunct extraction' (*JL* 31.195–226). They note that the *Barriers* account of adjunct extraction is costly, and wonder whether, instead of analysing it as a case of movement, it might not be better to base-generate fronted adjuncts in situ and provide an interpretive rule. However, they provide evidence from several languages which flag extraction that adjuncts are indeed extracted. English evidence for this conclusion comes from cross-over effects (which adjuncts obey). The interaction between 'Extraction and contraction' is investigated by Andrew Barss (*LingI* 26.681–94). The data are of the following types: *John seemsta be outside, I wanna be outside*, and *Who do you think's outside*. Earlier analyses are examined and rejected on empirical and theoretical grounds. Instead, Barss proposes that in the first two types, the matrix V governs *to* (which licenses contraction) since the complement clause is an AgrSP, and not CP. In the third type, the Wh-word raises from the VP-internal subject position straight to the embedded SpecCP, while *is* raises to C for Case reasons.

Dana McDaniel, Bonnie Chiu and Thomas Maxfield present 'Parameters for Wh-movement types: evidence from child English' (*NL&LT* 13.709–53). Data from children aged 2.11 to 5.7 shows that some children for a while allow not only regular Wh-movement, but also partial Wh-movement (*what do you think who Bert kissed?*), Wh-copying (*who do you think who Bert kissed?*), and multiple Wh-movement (*who thinks what Bert drank?*). The acceptance of such structures is accompanied by acceptance of *that*-trace violations. The authors provide a detailed analysis, according to which the children do not distinguish between C [+WH] and C [−WH]. The transition to the adult system would be triggered by the acquisition of *tough*-movement. Shichiro Tanaka provides arguments 'In defense of the Agr(P) analysis of *who/whom* alternations' (*LingA* 25.21–69). In earlier work, Tanaka had proposed that *who* is licensed by passing through AgrSP, and *whom* by passing through AgrOP. In this paper, Tanaka addresses systematically the objections that have been raised against such an analysis, showing that they do not in fact invalidate his claims. In addition, he provides some new support for his analysis (coming from the area of antecedent-contained deletion). Thomas Stroik offers 'Some remarks on superiority effects' (*Lingua* 95.239–58). He reviews earlier analyses of these phenomena and finds them wanting. His own proposal, supported by analysis of many data, is to leave the Wh-in-situ where it is, and to say that it will prevent the trace of the fronted Wh from being antecedent-governed by COMP (since it will count as a closer potential governor).

COMP also plays a crucial role in Richard Campbell's 'Inflectional domains and Comp features' (*Lingua* 96.119–38). Campbell argues that English and other languages have V-to-I for feature checking, but other languages have inflectional features spread from X to VP. These languages all allow serial verb constructions; the relevant difference concerns the relation between inflectional features and features of COMP. COMP is also central in Richard Hudson's 'Competence without Comp?' (Aarts and Meyers, eds. *The Verb in Contemporary English*) but for a different reason: Hudson suggests that COMP does not exist. He describes various kinds of problems and inconsistencies in standard accounts of COMP, and argues on the basis of further data that the word class of complementizer (with items such as *that, if, whether,* and *for*) is a chimera too. He thinks traditional grammarians were right not to recognize either complementizers or COMP, and considers these elements 'an invention rather than a discovery' (p. 50).

Next, two generative contributions that do not fit in well elsewhere. Mark Baltin has looked at 'Floating quantifiers, PRO, and predication' (*LingI* 26.199–248). He considers various types of (im)possible sentences with floating quantifiers, in particular, sentences featuring infinitive clauses, and explains the data by arguing that words like *all* must introduce a predicative constituent, and that PRO is not moved out of SpecVP. Rose-Marie Déchaine argues for 'One *be*' (*LIN* [1995].73–88), analysing copula, equative, passive, progressive, existential and main verb *be* as all being the same *be*. This one *be* is thematically inert, and is licensed only by c-selection.

Negation receives attention in one book and several articles. Liliane Haegeman's *The Syntax of Negation* analyses sentential negation within the principles and parameters model. An important role in her analysis is played by the Neg-criterion, which stipulates that a Neg-operator must be in the specifier position of X^0 [NEG], and vice versa. This criterion is assumed to hold at S-structure. In several of the many languages that Haegeman deals with, the criterion forces overt movement of negative constituents. With regard to English, Haegeman argues that the NegP in English can have empty Neg-elements in both head and specifier position. In a sentence such as *He said nothing*, for example, the verb and the direct object remain inside VP, but the Neg-criterion is satisfied by a Brody-chain consisting of an empty Neg-operator in SpecNegP and the coindexed object *nothing*. If a negative constituent is fronted, as in *At no time did he . . .* , the auxiliary also has to move to C, passing through the head of NegP on the way up, for the Neg-criterion to be satisfied. The negator *not* is taken to be in SpecNegP, but cliticized *-n't* is a negative head. A double issue of *LingA* 25 is entirely devoted to negative polarity items, but since the emphasis is on the semantics of these elements, we leave it at this brief mention. The syntax of negative polarity is discussed by Laurence Horn and Youn-Suk Lee in 'Progovac on polarity' (*JL* 31.401–24), a reaction to Progovac's book (*YWES* 75.36–7). The authors find much to commend in Progovac's proposals, and provide further supporting evidence for some of them (e.g. they point out that *He disliked any crumbs on the carpet* will normally be interpreted as something like *He disliked there being any crumbs on the carpet*, with the operator in embedded COMP that features so prominently in Progovac's analysis). However, they think that the semantic notion of downward entailment still seems necessary.

Renaat Declerck presents 'The problem of *not ... until*' (*Linguistics* 33.51–98), in sentences such as *John didn't wake up until nine*. The solution to the problem that Declerck advances, and compares with two earlier analyses on the basis of a wide range of data, is that the sequence *not ... until* is a discontinuous lexicalized unit, with the meaning 'only at x', where 'only' is a restrictive focusing adjunct and 'at x' has temporal meaning. In a final negative paper, Libuše Dušková offers 'A contrastive view of the rule of single and multiple negation with reference to English and Czech' (*LingP* [1995].63–75). This is indeed a purely contrastive investigation in that it shows which systemic differences there are between English and Czech due to the fact that in Czech in sentences like, *I haven't bought anything*, multiple negation is compulsory, so no distinction such as with English, *I have bought nothing* is possible.

Two items deal with comparative structures this year. Wolf Friederich discusses (*Lebende Sprachen* 40.57–8) '"As coolly as anything" – eine häufige, aber wenig beachtete schwierige Konstruktion'. He explores the use of this structure, *as* + Adj. + *any(thing)/ever*, in English, noting that it does not actually express a comparison, but rather functions as a superlative. It has not been paid much attention to in grammar books, and is only mentioned in a few dictionaries (where these structures are usually given as separate idioms). What follows is a list of them found in contemporary texts, which shows that they are more than just lexically idiomatic. A more philosophical approach is found in John Cantwell's 'Comparatives' (*TL* 21.145–58). He addresses the problems for traditional modal logic posed by sentences such as *John could have been taller than he is* (which involves comparison across different worlds) and *John is happier than he was* (which involves different times). Cantwell solves the problem by using temporal operators on sentences and terms.

Before moving on to discourse-oriented contributions, there remain to be discussed several more formally oriented papers. János Révai's paper 'Asserting identity' (in Davis, Philip W., ed., *Alternative Linguistics: Descriptive and Theoretical Modes*) was instigated by the question of how languages handle agreement and anaphora in equational sentences of the type *A is (not) B*. Two alternatives to simple subject-verb agreement are considered, 'unlicensed agreement', where B agrees with the verb rather than A, and 'agreement cop-outs', where the verb agrees with neither A nor B. Concerning the former, Révai argues that it is wrong (but usual in most formal accounts) to consider A to be a semantically empty or abstract element. This is the usual analysis because the theory is committed to subject-verb agreement. Révai's general point is that low-level grammatical machinery (like agreement) is generally totally automatic (which is indeed the way in which formal linguistics has tried to solve this problem), i.e. not sensitive to context or message-information, but that the phenomena under investigation are interesting precisely because they *are* sensitive to this. In other words, these facts show the fallaciousness of a rigid distinction between message and code. Beatrice Santorini and Shahrzad Mahootian have studied 'Codeswitching and the syntactic status of adnominal adjectives' (*Lingua* 96.1–27). Using a Tree Adjoining Grammar, and the principle that the language of a head determines the phrase structure position of its complements, the hierarchical position of adnominal adjectives is probed. The authors come to the conclusion that some adjectives behave like heads, while others are adjuncts (corresponding exactly to the two competing views in the literature).

Charles F. Meyer's 'Coordination ellipsis in spoken and written American English' (*LangS* 17.241– 69) builds on earlier work conducted by Greenbaum and Meyer (1982) concerning the greater acceptability and frequency of some kinds of elliptical coordinations over others in terms of psycholinguistic principles, such as the 'Suspense Effect' (the antecedent is known prior to ellipsis) and the 'Serial Position Effect' (the ellipsis at the beginning of the second conjunct is most favoured in English because its antecedent is more prominent). Meyer studies the actual usage of elliptic coordination in two corpora, the Brown corpus and the International Corpus of English. It is shown that the above two principles indeed explain general tendencies in the corpus, but that there are also numerous exceptions that are explained with the help of grammatical (i.e. the type of coordinator used) and pragmatic (concerning the communicative goal of clarity) factors that interact with the psycholinguistic principles. The question is also addressed to what extent genre influences the type of ellipsis used. The main point that Josef Hladky discusses in 'Frozen forms in Czech and English' (*LingP* [1995].86–91) is that frozen forms are the result of 'secondary processes', i.e. they do not follow conventional grammatical rules. This links up with a number of articles on 'freezes' which have appeared in Marge E. Landsberg, ed. *Syntactic Iconicity and Linguistic Freezes. The Human Dimension*, which try to show that iconicity plays an important role here. Iconicity is seen as a basic, primitive rule or principle in language, of a different order, more creative and less conventional than the regular rules of grammar. Indeed, Ivan Fónagy suggests in his contribution, 'Iconicity and expressive syntactic transformations', that there is a dual structuring of sentences, a linguistic and a paralinguistic code, the latter being an expressive transgression of the regular linguistic word order rules. He adds (and shows) that these expressive transgressions are necessarily motivated or iconic because otherwise we would not recognize them (since they are not part of the learned grammar). These iconic expressive rules may, however, in time become conventionalized and thus become part of grammar. (These secondary processes or transgressive rules are rather similar to what Lecercle has termed the 'remainder', see *YWES* 71.50–1).

We now change over to consider some questions of grammar from the point of view of discourse and pragmatics. Edoardo Lombardi Vallauri offers 'A simple test for theme and rheme in the clause complex' (*LangS* 17.257–78). He discusses the shortcomings of the well-known theme-rheme test, i.e. the Wh-question test. This test had been proposed to find out more about the distribution of categories in a functional sentence perspective, arguing that every clause can be perceived as an answer to one or more Wh-questions. The problem is, however, that: (1) not every clause is an 'answer', it can also be a simple assertion; (2) answers of the type *JIM went to Boston yesterday*, are in real discourse not in fact answers to a who-question, because the actual answer would simply be *Jim*; and (3) the test is not sensitive to other context-dependent functional distinctions. The author instead proposes what he terms an 'illocutionary-change test', which consists of projecting the utterance by means of a negating, interrogating or doubting predicate. In 'A pragmatic approach to echo-questions' (*UCWPL* 7.107–40), Eun-ju Noh seeks to approach and describe the properties of echo-questions of the type, *Columbus discovered America in 1492 – Columbus discovered America when?*, within the Relevance Theory framework. Echo-questions serve as a request to the speaker to repeat his remark or to express incredulity. They are called questions, but apart from the use of the Wh-word, they do not really behave like questions. It is argued here that they should be analysed as a variety of free indirect speech. It is also shown that echo-questions and metalinguistic negation are two varieties of echoic use expressing different attitudes.

'A[nother] relevance-based' paper is the 'analysis of Lakoffian hedges: *sort of*, *a typical* and *technically*' (*UCWPL* 7.87–105). This is a further study by Reiko Itani into the behaviour of hedges, which do not only serve to weaken the speakers' commitment to a proposition but also serve to intensify a speaker's commitment, to make an utterance 'less fuzzy' in Lakoff's words. The use of these hedges is here related to Rosch's ideas on prototypicality, because hedges may serve to make the membership of a less than prototypical element more 'true'. (E.g. *A robin is a bird* (true), *A robin is a sort of bird* (false, because a robin is prototypically a bird); *A penguin is a bird* (less than true), *A penguin is a sort of bird* (close to true).) Or, in the words of this author, hedges like *sort of* fall in 'with a range of other linguistic devices which contribute to relevance by reducing the processing effort required of a hearer in order to arrive at the intended interpretation'. Jim Miller and Regina Weinert look at 'The function of LIKE in dialogue' (*JPrag* 23.365–93). Two bodies of Scottish conversations are analysed with respect to the use of *like*. One of these is clause-final *like*, which is used in spontaneous conversation 'to (anticipate and) counter (possible) objections and assumptions', while the other *like*, which is found in all positions, is used as a highlighting device to elucidate previous comments. The paper shows that *like* has a clear discourse function and is not just a randomly occurring item devoid of any semantic or pragmatic importance, as had been suggested in some earlier studies. Francisca Snoeck Henkemans tries to establish the conditions under which 'But' is used 'as an indicator of counterarguments and concessions' (*LB* 84.281–94) after first analysing how these two types of *but* work in argumentative discourse.

Kathleen Ferrara and Barbara Bell discuss 'Sociolinguistic variation and discourse function of constructed dialogue introducers: the case of *be + like*' (*AS* 70.265–90). They have examined several corpora of speech, and have found that *be like* is gaining ground both linguistically (it is shifting from introducing 'internal thought' to ordinary direct speech, also with third person subjects), and in the population (it is more and more often used also by males, and non-whites, but is still predominantly associated with younger urban speakers). The authors attribute the spread of *be like* to its great versatility (it can introduce gestures, internal dialogue, and speech of second and third persons), which makes it an asset in on-line production.

There are two articles concerned with deixis. The more general one is Hardarik Blühdorn's 'Was ist Deixis?' (*LB* 84.109–42). The examples dicussed are from German, but anyone interested in deixis would be well advised to take note of this article. For a better understanding of what deixis is, Blühdorn has worked out twelve properties that deictic elements possess, seen especially from a semiotic and pragmatic point of view. One of these properties, 'the opposition of proximity and remoteness', is elaborated upon further, focusing again on German. More laterally connected with deixis is Regina Weinert's 'Focusing constructions in spoken language: clefts, Y-movement, thematization and deixis in English and German' (*LB* 84.341–96). In this article, the term Y-movement is used as a structural (not a functional) cover-term for all constructions where the subject is not found in initial position. The first position is called the theme, and the deictic elements looked at are indefinite deictics in Wh-clefts (*what* etc.), and definite demonstrative deictics in 'reverse' Wh-clefts of the type, *That's what I have done* and Y-movement constructions. The purpose of the paper is to compare the function of Wh- and reverse Wh-clefts in English and German within a discourse framework of focus, thematization and deixis. The data are taken from conversational corpora. The main conclusions are that German uses clefts much more sparingly than English; they have a similar function (they indicate major discourse boundaries or, like deixis, they have an important signposting function) but the focusing function is stronger. German has a variety of devices which fulfil the function that in English is covered by clefting.

Judy Delin and Jon Oberlander discuss 'Syntactic constraints on discourse structure: the case of *it*-clefts' (*Linguistics* 33.465–500). Different types of *it*-clefts are distinguished, depending on information structure and discourse effects; aspectual characteristics are shown to correlate with discourse function. Gregory Ward and Betty Birner provide oral corpus data on 'Definiteness and the English existential' (in *Language* 71.722–42). They show that the NP in English existentials is not always indefinite. However, it is always 'hearer-new', i.e. it is assumed by the speaker not to exist in the hearer's knowledge store. It can therefore be a new token of an old type, a member of a list, or a 'false definite' (*There was this huge sheet of ice in the street*). Betty Birner has investigated 'Pragmatic constraints on the verb in English inversion' (*Lingua* 97.233–56). She shows that in sentences of the type *Up in my room is ...* and *Arrested were ...* , the verb is not (pace claims by other scholars) always unaccusative, or presentational. The relevant constraint appears to be pragmatic, in that the verb may not present new information (i.e. it must convey evoked or inferable information).

A number of textbooks have appeared on grammar and linguistics. Ronald Wardhaugh's *Understanding English Grammar: A Linguistic Approach* is a pedagogical grammar of spoken English meant for students without any (necessary) prior knowledge of linguistics, which can be used both for native speakers and EFL learners. The main aim is to make readers understand how English 'works'. For that reason the book proceeds from the relatively known to the relatively unknown. It starts with the elements we are most conscious of, i.e. words and the classes they fall into, and then slowly moves towards larger constituents, more purely syntactic relationships, rules and principles, and the sound-shape of the words. Unlike Honey (see above), Wardhaugh advocates a descriptive approach because his first aim is understanding of usage, which in itself, he hopes, will provide a guide to usage. The emphasis on understanding also explains why his approach is eclectic: he wishes to explore the nature of linguistic elements by showing all their facets, functional as well as structural ones. Dennis Freeborn has produced a second edition of *A Course Book in English Grammar*. This new edition retains the same approach to grammar (functional, essentially corpus-based) but has been thoroughly revised and enlarged. There are three new chapters, and the last two chapters have each been separated out into two. The emphasis is on language in use, so that it also does not come as a surprise that the chapter on sentence grammar is followed by a discussion of how sentences are used in context in both written text and speech. The new chapters concern an introduction to the notion of 'correct' English: how this should be understood from both a purely linguistic and a sociolinguistic point of view. In connection with the author's liberal stance here, it is to be noted that all through the book references to other dialects have been added, which are treated as 'legitimate and fully grammatical in their context of use'. Another new chapter deals with vocabulary. This treats the core lexicon of English, its native and non-native sources, and how different vocabulary choices affect the meaning and style of the texts that we read.

We also include here Nigel Turton's *ABC of Common Grammatical Errors for Learners and Teachers of English*. This work is unabashedly prescriptive (the alphabetical arrangement is actually based on incorrect forms or usages), but then it is meant for second-language learners. It contains 895 entries, which tell the reader that, for example, *Despite he is much older* is wrong, and that the correct forms are *Although he is much older, Despite the fact that he is much older*, and *Despite (his) being much older*. This particular entry also contains a reference to another one, which lists more conjunctions and prepositions that are often confused. More structural errors, involving for example the tense-aspect system or relative clauses, also receive full treatment. This work as it were shows error analysis in reverse.

Jean Aitchison's *Linguistics: An Introduction* (now in its fourth edition) is meant as preliminary reading for anyone interested in language, but it can also be used as a first-year textbook for language students. New parts added reflect new interests in the field of linguistics, which is including more and more of language than merely its formal system of grammar. This is shown in the emphasis on speech and how it differs from writing. Thus, attention is being paid to conversational repairs and to more pragmatic aspects such as the effect of politeness on language use. We also find a section on language disorders and the use of language in advertising. A fuller work, and one definitely intended to be a textbook, is *Linguistics: An Introduction to Language and Communication* (4th edition), by Adrian Akmajian, Richard Demers, Ann Farmer and Robert Harnish. A wide range of topics is included (morphology, phonetics and phonemic transcription, phonology, syntax, semantics, variation, change, pragmatics, speech production and comprehension, acquisition, language and the brain), but the emphasis throughout is on methods and concepts rather than description. Each chapter includes useful study questions and exercises.

C. L. Baker's *English Syntax* has appeared in a second edition, but no great changes have been made. It is still a thorough construction-based survey of English syntax, which pays a great deal of attention to tree representations of structure. The many topics covered do not just include the basic introductory syntax fare of determiners, heads, NPs, (di)transitives, subclauses, etc., but also locatives and particles, free relatives, existentials, identificationals, clefts, conjunctions and ellipsis, and verbal modifiers (13 different types of these being distinguished). A new work in this field is Roderick Jacobs's *English Syntax: A Grammar for English Language Professionals*. The target audience of this book consists of language teachers, speech therapists and people working on natural language and computers. Twenty-five short chapters deal with such topics as thematic roles and levels of structure, properties of sentence structure, types of nouns, empty NPs and anaphors, tense, aspect, etc. Tree diagrams and exercises (with a key) are included, and a great deal of attention is paid to points of special importance for non-native learners of English.

More advanced students could profitably read Richard Hudson's 'A spectator's guide to syntactic theories' (*Links & Letters* 1 [1994].25–50), which provides – in an easy and pleasant manner – a bird's eye view of nine different, current syntactic theories (such as GB theory, Systemic, Functional, Cognitive, Relational Grammar etc.). Hudson begins with a description (using football as a metaphor) of what a theory should be able to do, how the space between the facts and the theory should be filled in, how the theories themselves and their practitioners sometimes lessen our insight into syntax by being too parochial and exclusive (exclusively formal/functional), and how widely the theories are applied elsewhere (in teaching, computer applications etc.). He compares the different theories by discussing the various solutions that have been offered for one particular problem, that of discontinuities produced by topicalization (see also *YWES* 75.61). He rounds off by showing, as a good salesman, that his own theory 'Word Grammar' might be better suited to deal with such discontinuities. Further specialization is provided by Paul A. Bennett's *A Course in Generalized Phrase Structure Grammar*. This provides a full introduction to GPSG, explaining the various formalization devices used in this theory and showing how they can be applied to constructions in English. Finally, Walter Meyers's 'Linguistics in textbooks: a forty-year comparison' (*AS* 70.30–68) examines the grammatical advice given in current composition handbooks. The author's conclusion is that what these books do is merely 'repeating their prescriptions ritualistically and ignoring what goes on all around them'.

(b) Early English

More and more work is being done on the methodology and theory of syntactic change. This year saw the appearance of Alice C. Harris and Lyle Campbell's *Historical Syntax in Cross-linguistic Perspective*. It is no exaggeration to say that this book is the most important contribution to (the methodology of) historical syntax since Lightfoot's (1979) controversial but seminal study in this area. The treatment of the subject is rigorous; in this it resembles Lightfoot, but the resemblance also ends there. Unlike Lightfoot this study acknowledges the importance of functional motivations, and unlike Lightfoot these authors start, not from the theory, but from a consideration of the actual changes themselves, which of course, as they recognize, will have relevance for the theory. They outline a fairly simple theory of syntactic change (but with more content than Lightfoot's), containing only three mechanisms of syntactic change (re-analysis, extension and borrowing); a set of general diachronic operations and principles which interact with the mechanisms; and, in addition, they recognize a set of universally available syntactic constructions, which any speaker may draw upon, which they call 'exploratory expressions'. These expressions may lead to change, to re-analysis, and thus become part of the grammar, but this is not necessary. They are optionally produced (for clarity, reinforcement etc.), and may also remain optional. In other words, the emergence of these 'new' structures does not need to be explained. It is emphasized again and again that we can only learn how change works by looking at the actual changes in the most minute detail. It is a strong feature of the book that it presents numerous cases of syntactic change, so that we feel that there is a good foundation for an understanding of how change is caused and implemented, but at the same time this wide scope is also one of the drawbacks of this study. Each single case is not (and cannot be) discussed in depth, so that it is not always evident that the case in question indeed illustrates a particular phenomenon. For instance, in the chapter on language contact and syntactic borrowing, the cases discussed did not convince us that borrowing in syntax regularly introduces structures which do not harmonize with the existing system. For each case more details would need to be available of the grammar itself as it undergoes the change, and of the exact nature of the contact (for a more rigorous approach to the latter see Coetsem, below).

It is instructive to compare the views set forth in *Historical Syntax* with those in David Lightfoot's 'Grammars for people' (*JL* 31.393–9). In this reaction to a negative review of his 1991 book, Lightfoot emphasizes that he takes a biological view of grammar, and that change in the grammar will generally be triggered by a prior change in primary linguistic data. To account for apparent cases of optionality in verb-movement in earlier English, Lightfoot suggests that there may be 'internalised diglossia' (or competing grammars), an idea due to Anthony Kroch. Further exposition of generative views on change can be found in the 'Introduction' to *Clause Structure and Language Change*, ed. Adrian Battye and Ian Roberts. They set diachronic change in the context of parameter setting, arguing that the opacity of the trigger experience may allow other principles (e.g. the subset principle) to determine part of the direction of change. This is followed by a section on verb movement and the structure of the clause.

Very welcome too to students of historical linguistics interested in processes of change is an annotated translation of Kurylowicz's well-known article 'La nature des procs dits analogiques' (1947) by Margaret Winters (*Diachronica* 12.113–45). It is preceded by an introduction that discusses the problems that exist with this influential article, how it has been misread due to a mistaken conception of the word *loi* and due to the fact that the article itself is not everywhere as clear as one would wish it to be. This translation provides some remedy and at least makes it available in its totality, rather than just the second part – dealing with the six 'laws' or formulae of analogy – which is most widely known. It also provides a brief summary of the main interpretations that have been made of this article, and other related studies of analogy, such as the statistically based one by Manczak. Frans van Coetsem is interested in another methodological aspect of language change, in which he 'Outlin[es] a model of the transmission phenomenon in language contact' (*LB* 84.63–85). This article is a compacted version of his 1988 study on the same phenomenon, outlining more clearly the theoretical framework of transfer phenomena. Van Coetsem shows how transfer is determined by two factors: (1) that of the agent of performance of the transfer action; and (2) the stability gradient of language. Concerning (1), it is important to determine whether the agent is a speaker of the source language or the receiving language. As far as (2) is concerned, one has to make a distinction between the various subcomponents of language, i.e. those that are more stable or cohesive (syntax, phonology), against those that are not (lexicon). Stability again is measured in terms of structuredness and consciousness, and can be influenced by factors such as the affinity between the two languages in contact and the attitudes of the speaker. Another important distinction that has to be made is that between borrowing and imposition. Laurel Brinton and Dieter Stein look at another aspect of the processes of change, which they have termed 'Functional renewal' (in Henning Andersen, ed., *Historical Linguistics 1993*). In this paper the authors contend two standard assumptions, i.e. the idea that linguistic change is unidirectional, and that the semantics of syntactic structures can be presumed to remain constant. They discuss a number of cases of what might be called 'syntactic exaptation' to prove their point: the development of the conclusive perfect (their most convincing case), developments taking place in inversion, aspects of the history of *do*, invariant *be* and quasi-modal *have to*. They show, for example, that the conclusive meaning of examples such as, *I had them trained*, was a renewal of one of the possible meanings (i.e. the stative one) that the perfect had in OE, which came about through the fixation in word order of the regular perfect construction, and was supported by other *have* constructions (the indirect causative, the indirect passive, and the passive of experience), which it resembled in a number of crucial respects. Also on exaptation, but more narrowly defined, is an article by Nigel Vincent in the same volume. Although his examples are all from the Romance languages, the author provides a discussion of great general interest on the notion of exaptation, its relation to grammaticalization, and the need for what he has termed 'matching' in processes of exaptation. A general paper of a rather different kind is Peter Richardson's 'The consolation of philology' (*MP* 92 [1994].1–13), which provides a plea for reinstating philology in literary studies on two grounds: to come to a linguistic analysis of texts, in order to achieve a better understanding of non-contemporary texts, and to end the traditional exclusion of literature from the domain of linguistic enquiry. For instance, a linguistic investigation into the use of 'tense' in Chaucer may enlighten us on the narrative structure of Chaucer's text, but may also tell us more about the different linguistic roles that tense fulfils in discourse.

There are a few more detailed studies dealing with the form and function of the noun phrase. Robert McColl Millar writes about the development of the determiner. His 'Ambiguity in ending and form: "reinterpretation" in the demonstrative systems of Laȝamon's "Brut" ' (*NM* 95.145–68) shows that the more or less traditional view, i.e. that *þe* as the undeclined form gradually replaced all the other forms of the demonstrative paradigm, is too simple. Rather, there was a general ambiguity of form (in which *þe* was, for instance, associated with *þa* and *þeo*), which led to constant re-interpretation, in which conservative desires tried to rescue as much of the inherited system as possible, but in which the desire to present information cohesively finally led to the replacement of the multiple paradigm by simple forms. A paper by Belén Mendéz Naya deals with the so-called provisional subject, ' "Hit" and "þæt" anticipating subject clauses in Old English', but this is not so much concerned with the function of this element (cf. Seppänen et al. discussed in section 6a above) but rather with the question whether they are 'True syntactic equivalents?' (*NM* 95.23–37). It is first of all noted, on the basis of a corpus of Alfredian and Ælfrician OE that, unlike in present-day English, the pronoun is not mandatory. It is found that the pronoun is usually absent when some other constituent is topicalized (especially when this is a 'heavy' element: so not *þa* or *þonne*) into first position. As far as the difference between *hit* and *þæt* is concerned, this is mainly one of reference, *þæt* being still more fully referential than *hit*. Secondly, when an oblique case is needed, *þæt* is the rule. Two other papers here concern the genitive. Roswitha Raab-Fischer asks herself 'Löst der Genitive die *of*-Phrase ab? Eine korpusgestützte Studie zum Sprachwandel im heutigen English' (*ZAA* 43.123–32). This is another study that makes use of the new FLOB corpus (see Mair and Hundt in the synchronic section). It examines the possible decline in the use of the *of*-phrase in favour of its synthetic counterpart. An interesting development is the much higher frequency of personal names (especially first names) with the genitive, but the relatively more frequent use of personal names itself is also significant in this respect. For instance, in newspapers the number of genitival instances has increased by 50 per cent, while the number of *of*-phrases with a genitive function has gone down by 13 per cent. Similar increases or decreases are also found in other genres. Other spectacular increases, of 30 to 40 per cent, are found with all lexemes except personal nouns. Hyeree Kim writes 'On the genitive of Anglo-Saxon poem *Deor*' (*NM* 96.351–9). The author addresses the status of the genitive case in the well-known *Deor*-line: *þæs ofereode, þisses swa mæg* in the light of the general use of the genitive in OE. The article classifies this genitive in the group of genitive verbal complements on a par with two other, similarly structured verbs, i.e. *ofercuman* and *oferstigan*, that are both found once with a genitive object, and on the basis of the Gothic synonymous verb *usleiþan*, which can also govern a genitive.

Infinitives are again arousing a lot of interest this year. Both Jairo Nunes and Olga Fischer offer a contribution on the form of the infinitive, the former from a formal, Principles and Parameters point of view, the latter more historical and cognitive-linguistically orientated. Nunes proposes in his 'The diachronic distribution of bare and prepositional infinitives in English' (in Andersen, ed., *Historical Linguistics 1993*) that the English *to*-infinitive was a null-infinitival head with the features [− V, + N], and that *to* before the infinitive is a dummy Case marker, necessary for the null-infinitival head to comply with the Case filter. He contends further that the replacement of the bare by the *to*-infinitive in ME is the result of the loss of verb movement. In his account, the presence of *to* in the complement of passive causative and perception verb constructions plays a crucial role. The analysis relies heavily on the generative theoretical apparatus, and seems circular at times: for instance, the way in which *to*-insertion is required after *expect*-type verbs in ECM constructions, but not after causatives and perception verbs, is said to 'account' for the fact that the latter take a TP complement, and the former an AGRP. Both of these are functional heads not visible on the surface. Fischer's article, 'The distribution between *to* and bare infinitival complements in late Middle English' (*Diachronica* 12.1–30) concentrates on the variation in form of the infinitive in verbal complementation, the distribution between *to* and zero being relatively clearcut in other syntactic positions. The author argues that the use of either *to* or zero (even with the same verb) is not arbitrary in this position (which is the usual claim) but creates a distinction in meaning, which may be related to an original (OE) case distinction, the bare infinitive being linked to the accusative, and the *to*-infinitive to other oblique cases. Like the accusative, the bare infinitive expresses a direct relation with the matrix verb, i.e. the verbal complement shares a tense domain with the matrix verb, it involves an entailment relation, and when causation or perception is involved, this is direct. For the *to*-infinitive the opposite is true. It is also suggested that the steep rise of the *to*-infinitive in ME is not so much the result of its replacing the bare infinitive; rather, the *to*-infinitive replaces OE *þæt*-clauses, with which it has much in common. In a short contribution, Stephen Nagle examines 'Infl in Early Modern English and the status of *to*' (in Kastovsky, 233–41). He points out that an analysis of *to* by which it becomes an Infl-element in late Middle English is problematic, since it cannot explain why split infinitives disappeared at that point, only to resurface again in the late eighteenth century. Nagle therefore suggests that perhaps *to* was in SpecVP, or adjoined to it, during this period.

Another cognitive-linguistic approach to the increase in the use of the infinitive is provided by Günter Rohdenburg in his, 'On the replacement of finite complement clauses by infinitives in English' (*ES* 76.367–88). He addresses a number of interesting questions. Two functional principles said to play a role in the replacement mentioned in the title are the iconic 'principle of clause integration' and the 'complexity principle'. Concerning the former Rohdenburg shows that those matrix verbs that first replace the finite clause by an infinitive are more highly manipulative, matching the semantics of the matrix verb with the greater degree of semantic dependence of the *to*-infinitive in comparison to the *that*-clause. This principle, however, interacts with the complexity principle, which demands that more complex clause structures in the main clause require a more explicit sentential status of the dependent clause, i.e. they prefer *that* to the infinitive. Rohdenburg's data indeed show that with the 'manipulative' verbs, the *that*-clause is used longest when the main clause contains certain complexities, such as a more complex object, an intervening adverbial clause, or negation in the complement. Developments in *that*-deletion form the topic of Edward Finegan and Douglas Biber's '*That* and zero complementisers in Late Modern English: exploring ARCHER from 1650–1990' (in Aarts and Meyer, eds, *The Verb in Contemporary English*). Earlier studies had shown that *that*-deletion had reached 70 per cent by 1700; in the categories Medicine and Sermons in ARCHER, however, *that* is consistently and strongly preferred, and in Letters it comes to be preferred after 1750.

Another article on clausal complementation is Mitsihiro Ohmura's 'On the historical developments of gerunds with special reference to their sentential aspect' (*Ling&Philol* 15.77–97). The author first lists the (familiar) stages the gerund has gone through from nominal to verbal status, and then proceeds to describe this development within a minimalist framework. Ohmura also links certain developments within the gerund with the development of the structural genitive in English (see also *YWES* 74.60), the relevance of which does not become entirely clear to us.

Word order is pretty strongly represented this year. Paul Kiparsky traces the 'Indo-European origins of Germanic syntax' (in Battye and Roberts, eds,

Clause Structure). He identifies as archaic features of Old English syntax the variation between IP and CP main clauses (the latter but not the former showing V2), the possibility of having a topic adjoined to CP, i.e. to the left of a Wh-phrase in SpecCP, the orders topic-clitic and Wh-V-clitic, the omission of SpecCP and C in non-initial conjuncts, V-final main clauses, and relative clauses with *þe*. There are two word order articles by Susan Pintzuk, both based on the author's important 1991 doctoral thesis in the area of Old English word order. In 'Variation and change in Old English clause structure' (*LVC* 7.229–60), her main point is that the syntax of main and subclauses is the same in OE, and that the differences in verb position (which are usually accounted for by accepting a rule of V2 for main clauses, absent in subclauses, and a number of other rules – such as Verb Raising etc. – which would account for the various positions of the finite verb in the subclause) can be explained by accepting that there is synchronic variation in underlying structure allowing both INFL-medial and INFL-final structures. Evidence for INFL-medial structures in subclauses is found in the postverbal position of particles, the distribution of negative constituents, and the relatively low frequency of Verb (Projection) Raising in other OE structures, making it more likely that they are low in frequency in subclauses too, thus favouring an INFL medial analysis of such cases. Pintzuk also shows that the use of the INFL-medial structure increases during the OE period at the same rate in both main and subclauses, thus providing further evidence for Kroch's 'Constant Rate Hypothesis'. In the other paper, 'Verb-seconding in Old English' (in Andersen, ed., *Historical Linguistics*), she addresses two unresolved questions with respect to V2 in OE: the landing site of the finite verb and the syntactic contexts in which V2 applies. Her proposal is that when the verb moves, it is generally to INFL in both main and subclauses, rejecting other theoretical possibilities, such as asymmetry in landing sites between main and subclauses, and a general movement to COMP in main clauses. The evidence for asymmetry involves the position of subjects (especially pronominal ones) with respect to the finite verb. The evidence for OE as a symmetrical V2 language involves cases of subordinate clauses, in which the finite verb has clearly moved leftwards (as can be seen from stranded particles).

Willem F. Koopman's 'Verb-final main clauses in Old English prose' (*SN* 67.129–44) looks at similar data but wishes to address the question how these verb-final clauses can be analysed without taking recourse to Pintzuk's double base hypothesis. The problem with Pintzuk's hypothesis is that it does not really explain the very low frequency of verb-final main clauses. Koopman presents us with a data-base of main clauses that do not show the expected verb fronting, first weeding out cases that may look verb-final but can still be interpreted as V2 (such as clauses with clitic pronouns, and structurally external PPs and adverbial phrases appearing between subject and verb) and next showing their frequency in relation to V2 clauses. Although the verb-final main clause is nowhere frequent (it hardly rises above the 5 per cent level), still there are too many to simply write them off as ungrammatical. A possible explanation for their occurrence may be stylistic variation; this would need further investigation. Latin influence seems a rather unlikely factor, and the possibility of a diachronic development has to be dismissed because no clear direction is visible. Kozo Kato investigates what looks like an insignificant element in OE syntax, but shows that interesting conclusions can be drawn from it ('The interjection *la* and subject pronouns in Old English' (*Ling&Philol* 15.23–39)). The author shows that the position of clause-internal *la* can tell us something about the status of subject pronouns in Old English. His data make clear that *la* can intervene between the finite verb and the inverted non-pronominal subject, but not between a finite verb and a personal pronoun subject. This provides evidence for the system proposed by van Kemenade (1987), which predicts that a personal pronoun subject is cliticized to C (into which the verb has been raised) predicting in turn that nothing can intervene between V_{fin} and the pronoun. In Pintzuk's system, however, pronouns are not cliticized to the fronted V_{fin}, but to IP, predicting that elements can occur in between, which the position of *la* suggests is not the case.

Masayuki Ohkado argues on the basis of 'AP [Auxiliary Predicate] constructions in *Apollonius of Tyre*' (*Ling&Philol* 15.41–61) that Verb (Projection) Raising is an available operation in Old English, which, although in line with previous suggestions (e.g. by van Kemenade and Koopman), had not really been shown conclusively so far, according to the author. What follows is a discussion of the earlier proposals and a rejection of their arguments. However, since most of the arguments used are theory-internal (i.e. no new data are brought forward), it is difficult for the general reader to decide whether they should indeed be rejected. The evidence that Ohkado brings forward is that AP constructions, when the predicate is verbal rather than adjectival (i.e. *was known* rather than *was poor*), show a higher frequency of Pred. Aux. order, that is, cases where movement must have taken place. Since it is unlikely that such rightward movement is more frequent with verbal predicates, the conclusion is drawn that another kind of movement must be co-responsible, i.e. Verb (Projection) Raising.

Eric Haeberli and Liliane Haegeman's 'Clause structure in Old English: evidence from negative concord' (*JL* 31.81–108) argues that several apparent cases of Verb Projection Raising in Old English are actually not what they seem to be. Such an apparent case would be *forþæmþe þa Iudeiscan noldon* [$_{VP}$ *næfre brucan nanes þinges*]. In a language like West-Flemish, however, a negative concord reading is impossible in structures of this type (**dan-ze da geld en-willen* [$_{VP}$ *an niemand geven]*), and the authors argue that the structure of the Old English example must therefore be different. They adopt the Pintzukian device of an INFL-medial structure.

Two papers investigate the further history of V2 in Late Middle English. Christer Platzack's 'The loss of verb second in English and French' (in Battye and Roberts, eds, *Clause Structure*) interprets the loss of V2 (if indeed it was lost, see below) as a shift of the feature [+ Finite], which attracts V, from C^0 to I^0. The reasons for this shift include the loss of clitic pronoun objects in the fourteenth century (also a disputable claim, see below), and the occurrence of sentences such as *Certis þei ben opyn foolis*, which earlier on might have been analysed as having a clitic subject, but later on were taken to instantiate V3 order. In 'Verb second, *pro*-drop, functional projections and language change' in the same volume, Aafke Hulk and Ans van Kemenade describe the difference between V2 and non-V2 somewhat differently, as involving the relative prominence of C and I. The reason for I becoming prominent after 1350 is seen to be a change in the position of nominal subjects. Prominent C and I can both license expletive *pro*-drop, so the loss of *pro*-drop in the fifteenth century must be attributed to other factors.

Tony Foster and Wim van der Wurff are interested in 'The survival of object-verb order in Late Middle English', for which they provide 'some data' (*Neophil* 79.309–27). In generative historical studies it has usually been taken for granted that the basic word order of English changed from SOV in OE to SVO in early ME. This study examines in detail, on the basis of a corpus of late ME texts, how consistent SVO in fact was in ME. Some of the conclusions drawn from the material are that the number of preverbal nominal and prenominal objects is almost equal (pronominal objects are more frequent though in subclauses); that the OV object is usually short and adjacent to the verb; and that the frequency of OV decreases at approximately the same rate in all subcategories, but faster in prose than in poetry. With the help of these data, further studies can now be carried out on the discourse function of the different word order patterns, and the path followed by the shift from OV to VO. Ian Roberts has investigated 'Object movement and verb movement in Early Modern English' (in Hubert Haider, Susan Olsen and Sten Vikner, eds, *Studies in Comparative Germanic Syntax*). He analyses word orders such as *She loves him not* (which are very common with pronominal objects, but non-existent with nominal objects) as being due to movement of the object to AgrO. The trigger for this movement is V-movement through AgrO; this activates AgrO's → -features, which can be checked by a pronoun but not a noun.

Leiv Egil Breivik and Toril Swan have looked at 'Initial adverbials and word order in English with special reference to the Early Modern English period' (in Kastovsky, ed., *Studies in Early Modern English*). They present detailed empirical data on the occurrence of V2 after initial adverbials from Old through Early Modern English, showing that there is certainly a decline in the frequency of V2, but that even in Early Modern English, initial adjuncts still trigger V2 in about 25 per cent of all cases. They conclude that the idea that V2 was lost around 1400 'is on the wrong track'. It is difficult to disagree with a statement as polite as this. The function of inversion in later stages of English is traced in Dieter Stein's 'Subjective meanings and the history of inversions in English' (in Stein and Wright, eds, *Subjectivity and Subjectivisation*). Stein examines the patterns *In came Chaucer* (without *do*; found from the eighteenth century) and *Bitterly did he regret his decision* (with *do*; found from the sixteenth century), explores the emotional/expressive meanings they have, and points out that such meanings could only develop after inversion had become a marked pattern.

As we saw above, Ian Roberts has looked at the relative order of object and *not*. The order of subject and *not* is investigated by Matti Rissanen in 'The position of *not* in Early Modern English questions' (Kastovsky, ed., *Studies in Early Modern English*). He shows that there is a difference between nominal and pronominal subjects: the former nearly always show the order as in *Did not your father warn you?*, while the latter in nearly 70 per cent of his cases show the order *Did he not warn you?*. Rissanen interestingly suggests that the occurrence of *Did not he warn you?* with pronominal subjects (which is virtually restricted to clauses with an auxiliary) can be seen as evidence of cliticization of *not*. Reduced spellings of *not* are only found from 1600 onwards, but the word order facts may give an early glimpse of what was happening. In 'Negation in English: a diachronic view' (*FLH* 16.123–35), Frits Beukema and Olga Tomic focus somewhat more widely; they describe the

Jespersen cycle that English negation has undergone, and analyse it in terms of the Neg-criterion, with *ne* acting as head and *not* as specifier of NegP. The pattern *I not doubt it* is somewhat problematic for such an analysis, and the authors suggest that it involves Neg raising to Agr, with *not* adjoining to it. We also discuss here Gunnel Tottie's *'Any* as an indefinite determiner in non-assertive clauses: evidence from present-day and Early Modern English' (in Kastovsky, ed., *Studies in Early Modern English*). Using the LOB, London-Lund and Helsinki corpora, she traces the variation between *any* + sing. N and *a* + sing. N over the last few centuries. It turns out that *any* is roughly as frequent in the earlier period as today. However, there may be a difference in meaning/function: in the Helsinki Corpus, *any* seems to have some stress in most cases, and it is particularly frequent in legal texts (which would require universal statements).

Cynthia Allen has written *Case Marking and Reanalysis: Grammatical Relations from Old to Early Modern English*, a detailed study of changes in impersonals and passives. She provides very full data on Old English impersonals (which show, amongst other things, that there is considerable lexical variation in the patterns attested) and uses these, in a LFG framework, to argue that some preposed dative experiences, but not those in passives of ditransitives, behave like subjects (since they allow coordinate subject deletion). She next describes the Middle English decline of the case system and the changes in impersonals, concluding that these were not directly caused by the case changes. The final part of the book deals with changes in passives: the rise of passives of verbs like *help*, which did not allow promotion of the object to subject in Old English, but start to do so in Middle English, and the rise of *He was given the book*, which Allen attributes to a re-analysis as direct object of *him* in the active clause *They gave him the book* (a re-analysis made possible by the fixing of word order of direct object and bare indirect object). Some of the data addressed by Allen are also discussed in Linda Roberts's wide-ranging paper 'Pivots, voice and macroroles: from Germanic to Universal Grammar' (*AJL* 15.157–214), which extends Van Valin's Role and Reference Grammar analysis of Icelandic to Old English and other languages. One of the points Roberts makes is that Old English did not allow passives of the type *Es wurde getanzt*, and she derives this from the requirement that all Old English clauses had to have a behavioural subject.

Lilo Moessner describes 'Early Modern English passive constructions' (in Kastovsky, ed., *Studies in Early Modern English*). She focuses on passives with 'empty' *it, there* or zero as a subject (as in *To the message might be added that* ...), *have*-passives (these had tended to be limited to ditransitives in Late Middle English), *get*-passives (not frequent), and the expression of the agent. More theoretical in outlook is Anthony Warner's 'Predicting the progressive passive: parametric change within a lexicalist framework' (*Language* 71.533–57). He explains the rise of combinations such as *is being carried* (in the second-half of the eighteenth century) as being due to the English auxiliaries becoming a separate category, with special statements for individual forms. The trigger for this change in turn was the completion of the changes affecting dummy *do*, and the loss of the second person singular ending *-st*, which led to loss of the inflectional categories for auxiliaries. Other changes triggered by the new status of the auxiliaries were the loss of VP-reductions like *(Is she angry?) It is possible she should*, the rise of *is being* (first with the passive participle), and the loss of *being V-ing*. Warner describes the change as one of parameter resetting (involving the question whether auxiliaries have inflectional categories just like V), and gives a formal account of it in HPSG, which easily allows the kind of statement needed.

Stanley Dubinsky and Kemp Williams have written on 'Recategorization of prepositions as complementizers: the case of temporal prepositions in English' (*LingI* 26.125–37). They note that temporal conjunctions such as *before*, *after* and *while* must be in C in present-day English, since they do not allow a following *that* (not even in dialects which allow clauses to be introduced by *without that* and *despite that*). Until *c.*1700, however, *before that* etc. were possible, so these words must have changed from being prepositions taking a CP complement to being in C themselves; another preposition that has undergone this change is *for*. The authors consider some further present-day data on temporal complementizers, postulating a Temporal Government Criterion to rule out cases like **He left after me telling him to*. Risto Hiltunen's 'On phrasal verbs in Early Modern English: notes on lexis and style' (in Kastovsky, ed., *Studies in Early Modern English*), describes the use of particles in the period 1500–1700 in the Helsinki Corpus. He shows that many of the collocations found are still common in present-day English (except those with *forth*), but that the Early Modern material has fewer metaphorical readings. Somewhat surprisingly, the Bible, fiction and handbooks (and not letters) have most phrasal verbs. The Bible probably shows the effects of a conscious preference for native idioms, and in the handbooks and fiction, the phrasal verbs usually have concrete meanings. In another item on the grammar (and lexis) of Early Modern English, Hans Peters deals with 'Degree adverbs in Early Modern English' also in the same volume. This is primarily a study of boosters and maximizers; the ways in which they develop from other word classes are discussed, and it is shown that many new boosters are attested around 1600 and also 1660.

A study of a rather different nature is Debra Ziegeler's 'Diachronic factors in the grammaticalization of counterfactual implicatures in Singaporean English' (*LangS* 17.305–28). This article is concerned with finding an explanation for the variation in past tense marking in 'Singlish'. Factors that were found to play a role are substratum influence and the lexical aspect of the verb (punctual or stative). Examining the use of the past tense in counterfactual clauses, Ziegeler discovered that the way in which the past tense has grammaticalized in L2 speakers (reflecting diachronic processes of the grammaticalization of the perfect), also influences the perception of counterfactual implicatures, occurring first with non-stative verbs and then slowly spreading to stative ones. Elizabeth Traugott examines 'Subjectification in grammaticalisation' (in Stein and Wright, eds, *Subjectivity and Subjectivisation*). She shows how various cases of grammaticalization (of *be going to*, *let us*, *let alone*, *I think*, *while*, etc.) show an increase in subjectification along several dimensions, and proposes that this is a unidirectional process. In 'Grammaticalisation and social structure: non-standard conjunction-formation in East Anglian English' (in Frank R. Palmer, ed., *Grammar and Meaning*), Peter Trudgill links grammaticalization to fast-speech phonetic reductions, which are particularly likely in small, tightly knit networks where a great deal of knowledge is shared. In the case of East Anglia, this has resulted in *yet* and *more* meaning 'nor' (from earlier *nor yet* and *no more*), *case* being used for *in case*, and *do* meaning 'otherwise' (perhaps through a development such as *Don't move because if you do, I'll hit you* > *Don't move do I'll hit you*, and subsequent generalization to the third person singular and other tenses).

Now that we are on to the subject of grammaticalization, we should also briefly mention a book that came out last year, *Perspectives on Grammaticalization*, ed. William Pagliuca, which contains two articles on the grammaticalization of the perfect in English. Dan Slobin looks at the 'Discourse origins of the present perfect' in 'Talking perfectly' and draws special attention to the ontogenetic and phylogenetic similarities in the development of the perfect, pointing out that the circumstances under which these developments take place are not at all similar. With children, the process of perfect usage is attributable to cognitive maturation, while historically the extended use of the perfect is due to the possibilities of grammatical extension and reanalysis. Kathleen Carey considers 'The grammaticalization of the perfect in Old English' providing 'An account based on pragmatics and metaphor'. The paper shows that, although the first OE uses of a perfect-like construction with *habban* probably occurred as conversational implicatures with verbs that have an external object, the new perfect meaning became first conventionalized (grammatical) in mental state verbs and verbs of reporting, the so-called *verba cognitandi et declarandi*. In another paper ('Subjectification and the development of the English perfect' (in Stein and Wright, eds, *Subjectivity and Subjectivisation*), Carey uses the same development to compare Traugott's and Langacker's views on subjectification.

The large amount of work on present-day modals this year has apparently meant that there was little time left for diachronic modal matters. We have seen two papers on this topic, the first one by Juan de la Cruz, who considers 'The geography and history of double modals in English: a new proposal' (*FLH* 16.75–96). De la Cruz provides an overview of the distribution of double modals and the types most widely used, and concludes that Scots-Irish origin seems plausible. In Scots itself, they are not likely to go back to Middle English, since there is a long gap in attested examples and the modern types are different from the medieval ones. The new proposal announced in de la Cruz's title is the suggestion that they could be due to influence from Gaelic, which has several expressions for modality that can be combined; bilinguals might well have constructed comparable modal-modal compounds in English. A second paper is by Dieter Stein, who looks at 'The expression of deontic and epistemic modality and the subjunctive' (in Kastovsky, ed., *Studies in Early Modern English*). Data are provided on the ways in which Early Modern English writers expressed subjunctive meaning (by means of the subjunctive form or modals). There seems to have been an increase in the use of the subjunctive in this period; Stein suggests that this may be because the use of the zero-ending (which is how the subjunctive was marked) enabled speakers to avoid the use of inflectional endings.

Some further work on the verb group has been done by Andrei Danchev and Merja Kytö, who have studied 'The construction *be going to + infinitive* in Early Modern English' (in Kastovsky, ed., *Studies in Early Modern English*). They discuss the meanings of the earliest fifteenth-century examples, point out that even these show little lexical or syntactic restriction, and suggest that the appearance of the construction may be due to a combination of French influence, functional need, and the general development of the progressive. Susan Wright contemplates 'The mystery of the modal progressive' (in the same volume), which concerns uses like *I am warning you*. This type of progressive is found in letters from the seventeenth century onwards, and appears to have been a conversational feature. A further examination of Restoration and Augustan prose drama reveals a quite consistent use of this feature (primarily in main clauses). In another paper on this type of progressive ('Subjectivity and experiential syntax', in Stein and Wright, eds, *Subjectivity and Subjectivisation*), Wright explores in more detail the expressive meaning of the construction, with reference to a great number of attested examples.

There are some further papers on the Early Modern English period (which is particularly well covered this year). Udo Fries considers 'Text deixis in Early Modern English' (in Kastovsky, ed., *Studies in Early Modern English*). He provides an inventory of the expressions in the Helsinki Corpus corresponding to present-day *here, above, below, in this section* etc. Gabriella Mazzon writes on 'Pronouns and terms of address in Shakespearean English: a socio-affective marking system in transition' (*Views* 4.20–42). Using data from three tragedies, she analyses the use of T and V in the different types of relationships and situations. She finds, among other things, that absent characters and non-human entities are addressed with T, and that the distinction is used for expressing distance vs. intimacy, power vs. solidarity, and for strategic switching. Jonathan Hope has looked at 'The use of *thou* and *you* in Early Modern spoken English: evidence from depositions in the Durham ecclesiastical court records' (in Kastovsky, ed., *Studies in Early Modern English*). He finds that the T/V distinction is used for social marking and for 'micropragmatics' (e.g. the expression of anger). Shifting is found especially in exchanges. In the data (which consist of conversations repeated for the benefit of the judges), *thou* and *you* are equally frequent; since the pronouns are used in the context of insults and arguments, this may mean that *thou* was already the marked option in speech (as opposed to, for example, drama). Helena Raumolin-Brunberg and Terttu Nevalainen cover a lot of material in their 'Social conditioning and diachronic language change' (in Kastovsky, ed., *Studies in Early Modern English*). They note that the period 1580–1660 saw a good deal of linguistic change (e.g. the introduction of new vocabulary, a peak in periphrastic affirmative *do*, changes in complementizers, relative clauses, the gerund, the third person singular ending, the genitive of *it* and so forth), and attribute this to various social and societal developments (conveniently summarized in a table) leading to weakened network ties and therefore weaker linguistic norm enforcement.

Since the Helsinki Corpus has become an essential tool in diachronic studies, we also include here Merja Kytö and Atro Voutilainen's 'Applying the Constraint Grammar Parser of English to the Helsinki corpus' (*ICAME Journal* 19.23–48). This paper considers the possibility of using a parser designed for analysing Modern English in the diachronic field and in other varieties of English. The main question is, to what extent is it possible to formalize the differences found in regional or older varieties of English so that the parser can cope with them? The article first explains how the parser works and then concentrates on the difficulties the parser had with the above texts, and how these can best be overcome.

Recent changes in (mainly) the verbal group are studied by John Myhill, in

'The use of features of present-day AAVE in the Ex-Slave Recordings' (*AS* 70.115–47). The Recordings (made around 1940, of speakers born in the period 1844–61) were searched for the occurrence of features characteristic of present-day AAVE (e.g. the tense-aspect features *be done*, *steady*, *come*, stressed *been*, *is*-deletion, invariant *be* and *ain't* for *didn't*). Myhill found that only two (rather exceptional) speakers used them. The other speakers all used a great many non-standard features, but *not* the specific AAVE features. Myhill discusses several possible explanations, among them the possibility that the ex-slaves were accustomed to extreme style-shifting in front of whites, the possibility that there was age-grading, and the possibility that there has been real-time change since the 1860s.

Even more recent is the phenomenon studied by John Rickford et al. in 'Syntactic variation and change in progress: loss of the verbal coda in topic-restricting *as far as* constructions' (*Language* 71.102–31). The authors have collected 1,200 contemporary tokens of the construction *As far as the question who must pay (is concerned), that is something we still have to decide*, a VARBRUL analysis of these data reveals that personal pronoun NPs are always followed by the coda *is/are concerned*, that NPs containing a clause are less likely to have the coda, that the coda becomes more frequent as we move from speech to e-mail and exam papers to printed texts, that younger speakers omit the coda more often than older ones, and that female speakers omit it slightly more often than men. The earlier historical development is also traced: the construction (with coda) is first found in the late eighteenth century, and the earliest (rare) examples without coda date from the early nineteenth century (they all feature very heavy NPs). It is only from the 1960s that coda omission becomes common.

There are two papers on the phenomenon of contraction, one dealing with its function and the other with normative usage. Yoko Iyeiri discusses 'Negative contraction and syntactic conditions in Middle English verse' (*ES* 76.424–33). Her study confirms the idea that negative contraction in ME is primarily conditioned dialectically (it is typical of southern texts), but it finds also some (slight) syntactic conditioning in those texts which have both contracted and uncontracted forms. Thus, contraction is more prevalent in existential clauses (but only with *is*, contracted past forms of *be* are rare in the mixed texts) and in fixed, idiomatic phrases, while uncontracted forms are preferred in relatively emphatic contexts, such as imperatives, when combined with *never* or *noght*, and also when the object of the negated verb is topicalized. Kari E. Haugland wonders about the acceptability of contracted forms in later English writings in, 'Is't allowed or ain't it? On contraction in early grammars and spellingbooks' (*SN* 67.165–84). The study deals with contraction of both bound and free morphemes, as the title illustrates, and it shows that these contractions were not always looked upon as colloquialisms, but had acquired a more formal status in the late seventeenth and early eighteenth centuries. Due, however, to Addison's and Swift's strictures on the phenomenon, the usage disappeared again. The evidence for this investigation comes from linguistic commentaries, but also from usage in the texts themselves.

Finally, a new textbook (by an old master), Bruce Mitchell's *An Invitation to Old English and Anglo-Saxon England*. This has been written with a view to attracting more students to Old English by presenting the facts of Old English in a socio-cultural context (thus, there is a lot of information – but in very condensed form – on such topics as archaeology, place-names, social life and literature). The author tries to interest the student by pointing out how relevant the content of Old English texts still is to present-day circumstances, and by illustrating the socio-cultural topics with appropriate Old English texts, some of which can also be used as translation exercises. Similarly, the grammatical facts are presented in such a way that it takes account of what first-year students already know (their knowledge of present-day English and some very basic grammar), so that the whole looks quite appetising. There is no painful confrontation with loads of paradigms (but some are given at the end 'For Those Who Would Like It'). The book also contains a good and very helpful glossary in which most declined forms are included as well.

7. Onomastics

Some good work on field-names has been published this year. Mary Hesse analyses thirteenth-century and later sources for the field-names of South Creake, Norfolk, and discusses their significance in revealing the location and extent of open fields and assarts ('Early Field-Names in a Norfolk Parish', *JEPNS* 27.30–42). John Titterton presents 'The perambulation of Purley-on-Thames, Berkshirc, 1786' (*Local Historian* 25.88–94), an interesting document containing the earliest recorded instances of a number of Purley field-names. John Field has compiled 'Indexes to the Field-Name Sections in *The Place-Names of Surrey* and *The Place-Names of Essex*' (*JEPNS* 27.50–5), which will be of assistance to all scholars working with these volumes. In the EPNS series, the second part of Margaret Gelling's *The Place-Names of Shropshire* provides detailed coverage of minor-names and field-names from the Hundreds of Ford and Condover. For major settlement-names, which were treated separately in Part 1 (*YWES* 71.161), the definition is briefly reiterated but no early spellings are given unless additional forms have more recently been identified, as for Amaston. The scholarship is exemplary, and although a text consisting largely of lists of early field-names is unlikely to attract a wide readership among the interested public, the book is a delight for the serious scholar. Where much is given, the human reaction is to want more, and it is slightly disappointing to find that the names of streets and buildings do not receive the detailed coverage afforded by previous EPNS volumes on Lincolnshire and Rutland. The potential interest of Shropshire street-names is amply illustrated by John Pryce-Jones' article on 'The Origins of the Name Willow Street, Oswestry' (*Shropshire History and Archaeology* 70.213–16), which explores the possibility of a link with the Welsh wool trade.

There are some small pieces on individual place-names and place-name elements. Carole Hough reviews a variety of proposed etymologies for 'Bonhunt: an Essex Place-Name', and concludes in favour of an original **Banan funta* 'Bana's spring' (*Anglia* 113.207–12). The same author identifies an unattested 'ON **hjarðar-bý(r)* "Herd Farm"' as the etymon of Harby in Leicestershire and Nottinghamshire and of the lost names *Herdebi* in Derbyshire and *Hertheby* in Nottinghamshire (*N&Q* 42.264– 5). In *Names*, Richard Coates makes a case for Pamlico Sound in Virginia as the source of the English place-name Pimlico ('The First American Placename in England: *Pimlico*',

43.213–27), and in *JEPNS*, he proposes an OE **cucu* 'cuckoo' as the first element of Coxwold in the North Riding of Yorkshire and of other place-names ('English Cuckoos, Dignity and Impudence', 27.43–9), and an ON **Gausli* '(at the) gushing spring' as the etymon of Goxhill in Lincolnshire and the North Riding of Yorkshire ('The Two Goxhills', 27.5–13). Also in *JEPNS*, Matthew Townend argues in favour of Ashingdon rather than Ashdon as the site of the battle of 1016, on the basis that the form *Assatún* preserved in Ótarr's *Knútsdrápa* (*c.*1026) represents a Scandinavianization of an OE *Assandūn*, not *Æscendūn* in '*Assandūn* and *Assatún*: The Value of Skaldic Evidence for English Place-Name Studies' (27.21–9). In a paper originally given to the 1993 Annual Conference of the Society for Name Studies in Britain and Ireland, Victor Watts presents a rigorous examination of 'The Place-Name Hexham: a Mainly Philological Approach', bringing a wide range of evidence to bear on this problematic formation (*Nomina* [1994] 17.119–36). A summary is printed in *Hexham Historian* ('The Place-Name Hexham', 5.4–5). 'The Place-Names *Bridford, Britford* and *Birdforth*' are analysed by Carole Hough, who challenges the established interpretation 'ford suitable for a bride' and puts forward a range of possible alternatives (*NMS* 39.12–18). R. W. McConchie's article on 'The Place-Name Icklingham' argues against the Icenian theory in favour of a derivation from an Old English personal-name **Ycel* (*NM* 96.113–22). Carole Hough discusses place-names attributed to OE *īsern* 'iron', suggesting that the alternative meaning 'kingfisher' also attested for this word is more plausible in at least some of the toponymic contexts ('OE *īsern* in Place-Names', *SN* 67.145–7). The same author examines the first element of 'The Place-Name Felderland' in Kent, proposing a derivation from OE *feldeware* 'field-fare, thrush', a bird-name recorded in an eleventh-century glossary, in preference to the traditional derivation from an unattested OE **feldware* 'dwellers in the open country' (*N&Q* 42.420–1). In the Swedish journal *Ortnamnssällskapets i Uppsala Årsskrift*, Zeth Alvered discusses the occurrence of ON *bekkr* in place-names in the British Isles and in Normandy ('*Bekkr*, ett Nordiskt Ortnamnselement Som Färdats i Västerled' ['*Bekkr*, a Scandinavian Place-Name Element Gone West'] 1995.63–8). An English summary is provided.

Coincidentally, three articles focus on place-name references to wolves in Anglo-Saxon England. C. Aybes and D. W. Yalden discuss 'Place-Name Evidence for the Former Distribution and Status of Wolves and Beavers in Britain', assembling an extensive corpus of material derived largely from the county volumes of the English Place-Name Society supplemented by other sources for Scotland, Ireland and Wales (*Mammal Review* 25.201–27). Surprisingly, they find little correlation between wolf place-names and woodland, although upland areas are well represented. Meanwhile, Carole Hough suggests that the substantive use of OE *grǣg* 'grey' evidenced in place-names refers not to the badger, as previously supposed, but to the wolf ('OE **Grǣg* in Place-Names', *NM* 96.361–5). She also makes a case for taking OE *wearg* in some place-names to mean 'wolf' rather than 'criminal', the meaning attested for the word in literary sources ('OE *Wearg* in Warnborough and Wreigh-burn', *JEPNS* 27.14–20).

Ann Cole provides some insights into the significance of Old English place-names for 'The Anglo-Saxon Traveller' (*Nomina* [1994] 17.7–18). Discussing formations such as *stān-weg, strǣt-ford, drǣg-tūn* and *strǣt-tūn*, she argues that place-names provided the traveller with an indication not only of the type of terrain which lay ahead, but of suitable crossing-places, places where assistance in dragging loads could be obtained, and places to halt for food, water and overnight accommodation.

There are two small pieces on Domesday Book identifications. G. F. Leake contributes 'Notes on the Correct Identification of "Rugutune", a Domesday Holding of Hugh de Montfort', demonstrating that it probably refers to Runton rather than to Roughton (*Norfolk Archaeology* 42.196–200). Paul Luscombe puts forward Oddicombe in Sherford as a more likely referent for *Wodicome* than either Widdicombe or Woodcombe in Stokenham ('A Domesday Identification in the South Hams', *D&CN&Q* 37.268–71). Also concerned with identification are Pamela Combs and Malcolm Lyne, who suggest that the early names *Haestingaceaster* and *Haestingaport* may refer to Pevensey Castle rather than to Hastings ('Hastings, *Haestingaceaster* and *Haestingaport*: a Question of Identity', *SussexAC* 133.213–24). Their case is well argued and deserves serious consideration.

Cyril Hart examines the mint–name *Sceldfor* on two coins from the Cuerdale hoard, and offers numismatic, historical and archaeological evidence in support of an identification with Shelford in Cambridgeshire ('The *Aldewerke* and Minster at Shelford, Cambridgeshire', *ASSAH* 8.43–68). In the same journal, John Blair's analysis of 'Anglo-Saxon Pagan Shrines and Their Prototypes' includes a section on place-name evidence in which he raises the possibility that some names in OE *bēam* may have a cultic significance (1–28), while Audrey Meaney contributes a wide-ranging discussion of 'Pagan English Sanctuaries, Place-Names and Hundred Meeting-Places' (29–42). Place-name scholars are likely to find some of her arguments difficult to accept, particularly as regards the proposed return to Bradley's interpretation of the 'animal's head' names in terms of pagan sacrificial rites; but the paper as a whole is both well-researched and stimulating, offering much food for thought.

The second publication from the Centre for English Name Studies is Carole Hough's *The English Place-Name Survey: A Finding-List to Addenda and Corrigenda*. It indexes all addenda to the county volumes of EPNS, as published in later EPNS volumes and in the *Journal of the English Place-Name Society*, and should prove to be a useful research tool. Also by Carole Hough, an article on 'Some Ghost Entries in Smith's *English Place-Name Elements*' discusses criteria for omitting doubtful headword entries from the forthcoming new edition of *EPNE* (*Nomina* [1994] 17.19–30).

Barbara E. Crawford has edited a fine collection of articles entitled *Scandinavian Settlement in Northern Britain: Thirteen Studies of Place-Names in Their Historical Context*. Nine of the papers deal with Scandinavian place-names in Scotland, presenting original research into small geographical areas based largely on unpublished materials. These differ in kind from the four papers relating to England, which are able to draw on a much longer tradition of place-name scholarship consolidated in the published volumes of the English Place-Name Survey. Thus Gillian Fellows-Jensen presents a review of work on Scandinavian place-names in Yorkshire over the last 23 years, analysing the significance of her own discoveries and those of other scholars such as Cameron and Gelling ('Scandinavian Settlement in Yorkshire –

Through the Rear-View Mirror'). She deals in turn with names in -*tūn*, -*bý*, -*thorp* and -*thveit*, identifying the first as mostly English settlements taken over by the Danes, the second as old estates split up into small independent units, the third as settlements named by the Danes or their successors but possibly previously occupied and the fourth as new land brought under cultivation through colonization. So too Margaret Gelling uses the lists of elements in the Cheshire volumes of the English Place-Name Survey as the starting-point for her study of 'Scandinavian Settlement in Cheshire: the Evidence of Place-Names'. Analysing the distribution of different types of place-name vocabulary, she argues that whereas the Scandinavian place-names of the Wirral area testify to Norse colonization during the early tenth century, those found elsewhere in the county may date from considerably later. Mary C. Higham also builds on earlier scholarship in her analysis of place-names relating to 'Scandinavian Settlement in North-West England, With a Special Study of *Ireby* Names'. Particularly interesting is her discussion of the three Irby/Ireby names in Cheshire, Cumberland and Lancashire, each representing land occupied by a minority racial group of Irishmen or Norwegians from Ireland. Higham draws attention both to the relatively poor quality of land allocated for these settlements, and to their remarkable longevity. Finally, Victor Watts demolishes the toponymic evidence for Scandinavian settlement in Northumberland. Discussing the place-names for which a Scandinavian origin has been posited, he demonstrates that none of the etymologies is secure, while in County Durham the only area to offer evidence of early Scandinavian settlement is the Tees valley ('Northumberland and Durham: the Place-Name Evidence').

Two articles by the Swedish scholar Karl Inge Sandred, both relating to his work as editor of the ongoing English Place-Name Survey for Norfolk, were overlooked last year. In 'Nordiskt i Norfolk. Ortnamn och Bebyggelsehistoria i en Del av Danelagen' ('Scandinavians in Norfolk. Place-Names and Settlement History in One Part of the Danelaw'), he discusses contact between English and Scandinavian in Norfolk place-names, focusing particularly on names in -*by*, -*thwaite* and -*thorp*, and including a detailed discussion of the place-name *Carl(e)ton* (*Kungl. Humanistiska Vetenskaps-Samfundet i Uppsala*, Årsbok 1994, 129–54, with English summary). There is some overlap with his other piece, 'Viking Administration in the Danelaw: A Look at Scandinavian and English Hundred-names in Norfolk' in *Developments Around the Baltic and the North Sea in the Viking Age* (ed. Bjorn Ambrosiani and Helen Clarke), in which Sandred uses a close analysis of individual hundred-names to argue persuasively that the hundredal system was already established in Norfolk before the coming of the Scandinavians.

Adrian Room has produced two more onomastic dictionaries for the popular market, one on personal-names and one on place-names. The title of the latter is either *Hutchinson Pocket Dictionary of Place Names* (according to the cover) or *British Place-Names* (according to the title page). This inconsistency is unfortunately symptomatic of the standard of presentation. The five-page introduction (divided into sections with twee sub-headings such as 'The -ing- thing' and 'Reading the rivers') has clearly not been proofread, since a section of 14 lines is displaced from p. vi to p. ix, and page numbers are cited as '000'. Misprints in the entries themselves, such as *rūt* for *rūh* as the first element of Rawtenstall, *tō* for *tōt* as the first element of Tow Law, and *tu* for *tūn* as the second element of Willington, are obvious to the name scholar but are unlikely to be intelligible to the target audience of interested non-specialists. The etymologies given agree in the main with those found in standard reference books, and the dictionary concludes with tables of 'Old English and Old Scandinavian place-name components', 'Welsh and Gaelic place-name components', 'American place-names exported from Britain', 'Literary place-names', 'Local fare', 'Fictional place-names' and 'Gypsy place-names', assembled in fairly random fashion. Considerably more care has gone into the production of Room's *Cassell Dictionary of First Names*, where a coherent 12-page introduction is followed by an alphabetical list of entries, mostly of substantial length, giving the origin and meaning of a wide range of names as well as a résumé of their main periods of popularity and examples of real and fictional bearers. Separate entries are given for name variants and diminutives used independently, and examples are drawn from contemporary television and sports personalities as well as historical and literary characters. There is some confusion between Old German and Old English, and other errors in the treatment of historical material – St Hild, for instance, was abbess of Whitby during the seventh century, not the sixth – but the main focus of the book is on popularity trends and famous name-bearers, and in that respect it provides a useful and handy source of information. The quality of binding is not high, so careful handling is required. One page had already detached itself from my copy within 24 hours of receipt, with several others starting to become loose.

Hard on the heels of the sixth edition of Leslie Dunkling's *The Guinness Book of Names* (*YWES* 74.64–5) is a seventh edition, offering some additional quotations from literature (expanded into a full chapter entitled 'First Names Appraised') but little other new material. Tables of the 50 most popular first names for girls and boys in England and Wales, the USA, and Australia have been updated from 1993 to the present year, and Chapter 1 has also gained an extra page of literary extracts, but the text is otherwise virtually unaltered, with errors pointed out in reviews of previous editions (*Nomina* 7.134–6; *YWES* 74.65) continuing to appear. As before, the book contains a rich and entertaining collection of material for the amateur enthusiast, presented in an accessible format which guides the reader through the names of people and of places to those of magazines, pop groups, flowers, ships, styles of beard and so on. Enjoyable though it is, however, more rigorous revision and updating is required to justify a new edition after only two years.

Emma Merry's *First Names: The Definitive Guide to Popular Names in England and Wales 1944–1994 and in the Regions 1994* is a book of statistics compiled from registers at the Office of Population Censuses and Surveys. It is divided into two main sections. In the first section, tables ranking the 100 most common girls' names and the 100 most common boys' names at ten-year intervals from 1944 to 1994 make it possible to monitor popularity trends at a national level over a 50-year period. In the second section, tables showing the top 50 names for 1994 subdivided by geographical area make it possible to extrapolate information on regional variation. This is valuable data which will no doubt be quarried by future editors of forename dictionaries. The tables are very clearly presented, with short commentaries drawing attention to features of particular interest, and the book deserves a place in all reference libraries. As with other statistical compilations, however, it needs to be used with some care. The practice of treating variant spellings as different names leads to a substantially lower rating for such names as Alan, Brian and Carol than if they had been grouped together with Allan, Bryan and Carole; and it would be interesting to know how the statistics would be affected by the inclusion of second, as well as of first, forenames.

On the local history front, Sylvia Laverton's *Exploring the Past Through Place-Names: Woolverstone* outlines the development of the Suffolk village of Woolverstone and assembles a collection of place-names from Glebe Terriers, Court Rolls, Tithe Maps and other sources. The book illustrates the contribution that can be made in this area of research by a self-described 'interested amateur'.

Angela G. Ray's 'Calling the Dog: the Sources of AKC Breed Names' (*Names* 43.3–28) is a well-researched article investigating the origins of the names of dog breeds recognized by the American Kennel Club. A computerized database is used to facilitate analysis, and the study draws attention to shifts in naming patterns over time, and to the significance of appearance, behaviour and geography as sources of breed names. Also in *Names*, Eric P. Hamp uses the French place-name Chorges as the starting-point for a short essay on 'The Linguistic Evidence of Placenames for History' (43.131–4), while Harold E. Gulley reports on a computer-assisted analysis of the distribution of 'British and Irish Toponyms in the South Atlantic States' and discusses the implications for settlement and migration patterns (43.85–102).

Computerized applications are the subject of a special issue of *Names* for December this year, entitled 'Computers and Onomastic Research'. With the exception of Carole Hough's article on 'A Database for English Placenames' (43.255–74), which describes a project currently in progress at the Centre for English Name Studies, University of Nottingham, most contributions are concerned with research into North American place- and personal-names. None the less, English name scholars will find much of interest, since the emphasis throughout is on methodology and many of the techniques described could equally be applied to the study of names outside America. Irina Ren Vasiliev, for instance, deals with software programs for 'Mapping Names', providing illustrations of the different types of maps that can be created using computers (43.294–306), and Herbert Barry III discusses the role of electronic databases and computer programs in analysing personal-names ('Computers and Research on Personal Names' 43.315–24).

Barrie M. Rhodes's 'Caution on Naming Names' (*TYDS* 18.35–40) is a slight and curiously naive discussion of place-names and surnames. It would have benefited from closer reference to recent scholarship on both topics.

Turning now to interdisciplinary studies, an outstanding book this year is Catherine Cubitt's *Anglo-Saxon Church Councils c.650–c.850*, which provides a thorough and perceptive analysis of the organization, attendance, location and significance of church synods during the period in question. The book is divided into two parts, the first comprising chapters on 'The Organization of Synods', 'Transactions and Business' and 'The Formalities of Anglo-Saxon Church Councils', while the second part deals with individual synods: the Council of *Clofesho* in 747, the legatine councils of 786, and the Council of Chelsea in 816. A separate chapter examines charter evidence relating to councils during the Mercian Supremacy, looking particularly at the relations between the Mercian kings and the Southumbrian bishops; and two appendices present exhaustive catalogues of evidence for the convocation of church councils and for all known sites, giving name-forms, etymologies and information on archaeological remains and other features of interest. Place-name evidence is handled more than competently throughout. The identification of several synod sites is uncertain, as most notably that of *Clofesho* itself, and Cubitt's treatment of problematic instances is based on sound philological criteria. Particularly interesting are her analyses of the elements recorded in the names of synod meeting-places, which, as she demonstrates, throw important light on the types of location chosen for church councils during the early Anglo-Saxon period. The evidence is clearly presented and lucidly discussed, and the book as a whole represents a very impressive achievement.

Barbara Yorke's *Wessex in the Early Middle Ages* presents a cogent and well-researched survey of the development of the six historic shires of Devon, Somerset, Dorset, Wiltshire, Berkshire and Hampshire from AD 400 to 1066. Like its companion volumes in the series 'Studies in the Early History of Britain', *The East Midlands in the Early Middle Ages* by Pauline Stafford and *The West Midlands in the Early Middle Ages* by Margaret Gelling (*YWES* 73.68–9), the study provides an up-to-date account of recent scholarship, bringing together evidence from a range of related disciplines, and is copiously illustrated with photographs and maps. The limitations of contemporary written sources are clearly set out, and form the background to a valuable synthesis of the strengths and weaknesses of other types of historical evidence. Good use is made of onomastic material, with close reference in particular to Margaret Gelling's work, although it is disconcerting to read on p. 68 that 'there have not been any recent detailed studies of place-names in Devon, Somerset or Dorset'. Since the first three volumes of A. D. Mills's *The Place-Names of Dorset* in the EPNS series had appeared by 1989, it is difficult to know what to make of this, other than to note the omission from Dr Yorke's otherwise extensive bibliography not only of Mills's work but also of the second volume of the early EPNS survey of *The Place-Names of Devon* by J. E. B. Gover et al.

Della Hooke and Simon Burnell edit a collection of six papers on the general theme of *Landscape and Settlement in Britain AD 400–1066*, mostly based on talks given at a conference in Exeter in 1990. The authors draw largely on archaeological evidence, but place-names and charter-bounds are also used to good effect, particularly in the paper by Peter Rose and Ann Preston-Jones on 'Changes in the Cornish Countryside AD 400–1100', and in Della Hooke's paper on 'The Mid-Late Anglo-Saxon Period: Settlement and Land Use'. It is somewhat surprising to find place-name etymologies presented by C. J. Bond in 'Settlement, Land Use and Estate Patterns on the Failand Ridge, North Somerset: a Preliminary Discussion' twice contradicted in editorial footnotes. Both corrections are pertinent, but the result is to draw attention to the fact that Bond has not consulted the most up-to-date toponymic sources. Editorial guidance at an earlier stage might have improved the situation.

Oswald: Northumbrian King to European Saint, ed. Clare Stancliffe and Eric Cambridge, comprises a collection of 11 papers arising from a conference held in Durham in 1992, and includes topics as diverse as 'The Making of Oswald's Northumbria' (Rosemary Cramp), 'St Oswald in Post-Conquest England' (David Rollason) and 'The Development of the St Oswald Legends on the Continent' (Annemiek Jansen). Several contributors make substantial use of onomastic evidence: notably Alison Binns, who compiles a gazetteer of 'Pre-Reformation Dedications to St Oswald in England and Scotland', and Eric Cambridge, who attempts to establish how many of these dedications may date to the Anglo-Saxon period ('Archaeology and the Cult of St Oswald in Pre-Conquest Northumbria'). Of particular interest is the discussion of the site of Oswald's death by Clare Stancliffe, who argues in favour of the traditional identification of *Maserfelth* with Oswestry in Shropshire ('Where Was Oswald Killed?').

S. E. Kelly's new edition of the *Charters of St Augustine's Abbey Canterbury and Minster-in-Thanet* contains much valuable material for name scholars. Many of the 53 charters in the St Augustine's archive purport to date from the early Anglo-Saxon period, and the study of Kentish place-names in particular will be facilitated by the availability of this corpus in a reliable and scholarly edition. The treatment of onomastic material is sensible and well-informed, and the volume includes indexes to personal-names and place-names as well as to words and personal-names used in boundary clauses.

Several articles examine individual Anglo-Saxon charter bounds, using local field-work to identify landmarks and improve on earlier 'solutions'. J. A. Barnard describes research undertaken by members of the West Dorset Local History Society on 'The Boundaries of Two Anglo-Saxon Charters Relating to Land at Corscombe: a Commentary on the Paper by Grundy (1935)', suggesting several revisions to the landmarks previously proposed by Grundy (*Dorset Natural History and Archaeological Society: Proceedings for 1994* 116.1–9). The article demonstrates the importance of local knowledge in order to supplement the written documentation on which Grundy's work was based; and the same point is made by Christopher K. Currie, who writes on 'Saxon Charters and Landscape Evolution in the South-Central Hampshire Basin', presenting a detailed analysis of several charter bounds dating from the tenth and eleventh centuries and discussing their implications in terms of land-use traditions (*Proceedings of the Hampshire Field Club and Archaeological Society* 50 [1994].103–25). Mary Hesse demonstrates that 'The Anglo-Saxon Bounds of Littlebury' recorded in a charter of King Æthelred correspond closely to the later parish boundary of Littlebury with Strethall (*Proceedings of the Cambridge Antiquarian Society* 83 [1994].129–39), while David A. Hinton examines three boundary lists in the Shaftesbury Cartulary and attempts a new reconstruction of some Purbeck estates ('Some Anglo-Saxon Charters and Estates in South-East Dorset', *Dorset Natural History and Archaeological Society: Proceedings for 1994* 116.11–20).

Gillian Fellows-Jensen asks, 'What do English, Frisian and Scandinavian Place-Names Tell Us About the Frisians in the Migration Period?' (*NOWELE* Suppl 12.97–117). As she acknowledges in the opening paragraph, the answer is 'not very much'. Arguing along traditional lines that the toponymic evidence points to a Frisian presence in England but is insufficient to prove Frisian involvement in the early Anglo-Saxon settlements, she makes a plea for international co-operation on research into the movement of population during the migration period.

Gillian Fellows-Jensen also contributes a paper on 'The Light Thrown by the Early Place-Names of Southern Scandinavia and England on Population Movement in the Migration Period' to the proceedings of a symposium held in

Kiel in 1992 and edited by Edith Marold and Christiane Zimmermann under the title *Nordwestgermanisch*. Hers is a substantial piece which begins by reviewing the place-name evidence for Scandinavian settlement in England during the Viking Age and goes on to examine name-types dating from the Migration Age, focusing particularly on Danish place-names in *-lev*, *-heimr* and *-ing(e)*, and on English names in *-hām*, *-ingas*, *-ing*, *-ingahām* and *-ingtūn*. In the same volume, Jürgen Udolph examines parallels between English and continental toponyms, dealing in turn with names from *Rip*, *fenn*, *-ithi*, *Strut-/Strod-*, *wik*, *skarn*, *Riede*, *mar-*, *hor*, *hude* and *Büttel* ('Die Landnahme Englands durch germanische Stämme im Lichte der Ortsnamen'). Also included although not read at the symposium is an essay by W. F. H. Nicolaisen entitled 'Is There a Northwest Germanic Toponymy? Some Thoughts and a Proposal', in which he argues that the presence of cognate terms of similar meaning and pronunciation in the place-name vocabulary of Old English and Old Norse testifies to the existence of an earlier Northwest Germanic toponymic dialect as distinct from the ordinary lexicon. Nicolaisen concludes with a stirring plea for a comprehensive survey of the early place-names of all areas with ancestral links with Northwest Germanic, in order to establish whether or not such a toponymic dialect can be identified and linked with the period of dialectal development of the Germanic languages in Europe. This is an exciting concept which is well worth pursuing.

The 1994 Dorothea Coke Memorial Lecture, Gillian Fellows-Jensen's *The Vikings and Their Victims: the Verdict of the Names*, is primarily concerned with Scandinavian personal-names and place-names in the Danelaw, but concludes with a brief discussion of other areas of Scandinavian settlement in the British Isles. It is an important paper which utilizes a wide range of evidence from both Britain and Scandinavia, and draws particular attention to the development of new Scandinavian personal-names in England.

C. P. Lewis uses personal-name evidence to build up a picture of the substantial presence of 'The French in England Before the Norman Conquest' (*Anglo-Norman Studies* 17.123–44). He also discusses criteria for identifying names of French origin, and provides an Appendix of 'Pre-Conquest Domesday Landowners with French Names'.

Personal-names are also the main focus of a collection of articles and reviews by the late Cecily Clark (ed. Peter Jackson) under the title *Words, Names and History: Selected Writings of Cecily Clark*. Twenty-six important studies are reproduced here, many of them representing Clark's pioneering work on onomastic evidence for social and cultural history in the immediate post-Conquest period. They include for instance her three articles on the *Liber Vitae* of Thorney Abbey, together with essays on 'Women's Names in Post-Conquest England', 'People and Languages in Post-Conquest Canterbury', 'Battle *c*.1100', and 'The Early Personal Names of King's Lynn'. In addition, a new article on 'Socio-Economic Status and Individual Identity: Essential Factors in the Analysis of Middle English Personal-Naming' has been included from a forthcoming book edited by David Postles. Smaller pieces such as 'The *Codretum* (Whatever That May Be) at Little Roborough' illustrate another aspect of Clark's prolific output, and the volume contains a complete bibliography of her published writings, as well as extensive indexes to names, words and manuscripts cited in the text.

Now available in paperback is the third edition of P. H. Reaney and R. M.

Wilson's *A Dictionary of English Surnames*, first published in hardback in 1991. Coverage is considerably fuller than in the second edition, with the inclusion of some 4,000 additional entries. The change of title from *A Dictionary of British Surnames* reflects, as explained in the Preface, 'a concentration on surnames of specifically English rather than Celtic origin', so that the book is of particular value to English name scholars. As before, early forms and dates are provided for each name as well as etymological and historical information, and the dictionary is deservedly regarded as a standard reference tool.

David Postles's *The Surnames of Devon* is No. 6 in the *English Surnames Series*, and maintains the high standards established by previous volumes on the surnames of Yorkshire, Norfolk and Suffolk, Oxfordshire, Lancashire and Sussex. Written in a lucid, scholarly style, it presents the results of extensive and meticulous research into surnaming patterns, demonstrating regional differences not only between Devon and other parts of the country, but within the county itself. Close attention is paid to chronological changes, as with the decline in the proportion of locative surnames during the later Middle Ages; to naming traditions represented by different social groups; and to differences between rural and urban communities. The often complex data is illustrated by tables and figures, while the problems presented by the sources – principally lay subsidies – are explained with admirable clarity both in the opening chapter on 'Methodological Questions' and throughout the book. Dialectal and local usages are discussed in Chapter 2, identifying not only those name-types characteristic of Devon, such as topographical surnames with the suffix *-ing*, but also those that were rare in comparison with other counties, such as topographical surnames with the suffix *-er* and patronymics in *-son*. Chapter 3 deals with the diffusion of surnames through the migration of fugitives, women, agricultural labourers, criminals, clergy, apprentices and others: again, the presentation of evidence is exemplary. A fascinating chapter by Richard McKinley on 'The Evolution of Hereditary Surnames in Devon', is followed by 'Some Further Reflections on the Heritability of Surnames Amongst the Free and Unfree Peasantry' by Postles, raising the possibility that bynames may have developed into hereditary surnames earlier in east Devon than in west Devon. A later section examines the incidence and causation of isonymy (the concentration of surnames within communities), and the book concludes with comprehensive indexes to places, names and subjects.

Postles has also produced a study of patronymic and metronymic bynames in the old counties of Leicestershire and Rutland, focusing particularly on compounds with *-son* ('At Sørensen's Request: The Formation and Development of Patronyms and Metronyms in Late Medieval Leicestershire and Rutland', *Nomina* 17 [1994].55–70). This is an important article which discusses the relationship between bynames and socio-legal status in an area on the border of Scandinavian influence. Further north, Constance Fraser presents an analysis of 'Tynedale Surnames' recorded in the Hearth Tax returns of Northumberland for 1664 (*Tyne and Tweed* 49.39–53).

For those wishing to undertake their own investigation of the history of individual surnames, *The Surname Detective: Investigating Surname Distribution in England, 1086–Present Day* by Colin D. Rogers, provides a practical and thorough guide to sources and methodology. Using a sample of

100 names, Rogers demonstrates the techniques and difficulties of tracing distribution patterns back through time, and discusses the relative merits of different ways of mapping the results. As its title suggests, the book is aimed at the popular market, and in particular at amateur genealogists. None the less, it contains much useful information for name scholars and others, illustrating for instance how geographical distribution may be used to identify the likely area of origin for surnames such as *Heath* and *Quick*, or to suggest a disparate origin for apparently related names such as *Blake* and *Black*. Particularly useful are the maps illustrating the distribution of selected surnames during the twentieth, seventeenth and fourteenth centuries, especially where different time-periods are shown on facing pages, as for *French* and *Baxter*.

In the Collins Pocket Reference series, David Dorward's *Scottish Surnames* offers information on the history and derivation of about 1,000 of the most common surnames in present-day Scotland, including many of English origin. Although aimed at the popular market, the book is based on sound philological principles, and is refreshingly reliable. Selection is on the basis of current prevalence rather than linguistic origin, so that there are entries for such names as Brough, a name whose presence in Scotland is mostly attributable to recent immigration, Burke, a name of English derivation and mainly Irish provenance, and the English name Parsons as well as its Gaelic equivalent MacPherson. The introduction will be partly repeated in the second volume of *Namenforschung: ein internationales Handbuck zur Onomastik*, an ambitious reference work in three languages (English, French and German) which this reviewer has not yet seen. The first volume was published this year, with contributions by such stalwarts as Ian A. Fraser ('Name Studies in the United Kingdom'), Margaret Gelling ('Place-Names in England'), W. F. H. Nicolaisen ('Name and Appellative', 'Names in English Literature') and Veronica Smart ('Personal Names in England'). The editors are Ernst Eichler, Gerold Hilty, Henrich Löffler, Hugo Steger, and Ladislav Zgusta, and two further volumes are projected for next year.

8. Pragmatics and Discourse Analysis

We shall start this section with a number of publications that are relevant not just for English but for the pragmatic or discourse analytic study of language in general. The most important publication this year for pragmatics and discourse analysis was without doubt the *Handbook of Pragmatics* (ed. Jef Verschueren, Jan-Ola Östman and Jan Blommaert). This handbook, which is prepared under the scientific auspices of the International Pragmatics Association (IPrA), is designed as an annually updated publication in loose-leaf format for which a ring-binder is provided with the first instalment. The editors plan to publish approximately 320 pages every year.

Prior to the publication of the first loose-leaf instalment a substantial manual has now been published. The manual starts with an introductory chapter by Jef Verschueren, in which he briefly sketches the history, the delimitational problems, and the definition of pragmatics. The main body of the manual contains over 100 survey articles written by leading scholars in their respective fields. Eighty-eight articles appear under the heading 'Traditions'. These include not only the core areas of pragmatics such as

'Conversation analysis', 'Ethnomethodology', 'Speech act theory', but also less expected entries such as 'Chomskyan linguistics' 'Generative semantics' or 'Tagmemics'. Part 3 entitled 'Methods' contains 16 papers on topics such as 'Corpus analysis', 'Fieldwork' and 'Statistics'. The two final papers constitute part 4 and are devoted to 'Notational systems'. There can be no doubt that the *Handbook Manual* even on its own will remain a standard work of reference for a very long time to come. Together with the main body of the handbook in loose-leaf format it will be indispensable for anyone working in the area of pragmatics and indeed the study of language as a whole.

The first instalment of the *Handbook*, dated 1995, contains three papers that update the *Manual* and 15 contributions to the alphabetical thematic main body of the loose-leaf part of the handbook. These include topics such as 'Codeswitching', 'Culture', 'Mass media' and 'Register'.

Three new textbooks that appeared this year testify to the unabated popularity of the field of pragmatics and discourse analysis: Jenny Thomas's *Meaning in Interaction. An Introduction to Pragmatics*; Peter Grundy's *Doing Pragmatics*; and Raphael Salkie's *Text and Discourse Analysis*. All three of them are designed for the beginner with very little previous knowledge of pragmatics or discourse analysis. Jenny Thomas presents a fairly traditional view of pragmatics. Her book is dominated by John R. Searle's speech act theory, H. Paul Grice's co-operative principle, Leech's politeness principle, and Penelope Brown and Stephen Levinson's theory of politeness. More recent approaches in cognitive pragmatics, as for instance relevance theory, are hardly mentioned at all. However, she draws from a vast reservoir of personal anecdotes, literary examples and newspaper clippings and other media extracts to illustrate and exemplify the various approaches and presents them quite generally in an entertaining and accessible style. This textbook may not claim comprehensiveness (a virtue that is in any case no longer achievable in pragmatics within the limits of a textbook that is affordable for students), but it could well be successful in the undergraduate classroom because of its detailed and accessible treatment of some of the key issues in pragmatics.

Grundy's book is even more pedagogically inclined. He covers a rather wider selection of topics than Thomas but occasionally at the cost of brevity. He includes short chapters on deixies, on relevance theory and on speech events in addition to the traditional core areas of pragmatics that are also treated by Thomas. The entire text is interspersed with study questions and exercises and described as an interactive coursebook (hence *Doing Pragmatics*). Indeed, this may be an ideal text for self-study since it contains a detailed key with suggested solutions to the study questions and exercises, and it gives very practical advice on project work in pragmatics, including data collection and transcription. Ironically, he relies much more on intuited examples than Thomas to illustrate the different approaches and problems. The interactive nature of the book tends to give it a somewhat breathless air. As soon as the exposition of some topic gets under way, it is interrupted by the next study questions.

Salkie's text appeared in Routledge's Language Workbooks series and follows its general pattern. The preface states the aim of the book very clearly: 'This is not a normal textbook but a workbook ... it tries to help you ask interesting questions about language – and work out some answers for yourself'. These questions are mainly concerned with cohesive devices. In fact, nine out of ten chapters are devoted to individual cohesive devices such as word repetition, synonyms, superordinates, opposites, substitutes, ellipsis, reference and connectives. The last chapter looks at 'larger patterns'. The exercises which form the backbone of the book are based on a wide variety of authentic English texts such as news stories, adverts, novels, forms, manuals and textbooks. The emphasis is very much on written texts but the implicit claim is that the cohesive devices work similarly in all types of text or discourse.

A second edition that appeared this year deserves a special mention here. One of the most influential books in pragmatics published in the 1980s was without any doubt Dan Sperber and Deirdre Wilson's *Relevance Theory* (1986). Its aim was no less than 'to lay the foundation for a unified theory of cognitive science'. It has now been published in a second edition. The second edition, *Relevance: Communication and Cognition*, preserves the text, and even the pagination of the first edition, except for the correction of misprints and a handful of new endnotes to the original text. This means that references to the first edition can easily be traced in the second edition. The main features that distinguish the second from the first edition are a postface of some 25 pages and a bibliography that has increased from eight to 20 pages and gives a good survey over the wealth of research that the first edition has engendered. The postface sketches very briefly the most important research trends within the framework, and it outlines some important modifications to the original framework. The most important modification concerns the introduction of a second principle of relevance. The principle of relevance, as outlined in *Relevance*, makes a claim about ostensive communication: 'Every act of ostensive communication communicates a presumption of its own optimal relevance'. This principle is the consequence of a more general claim about human cognition: 'Human cognition tends to be geared to the maximisation of relevance'. This more general claim is now called the First (or Cognitive) Principle, while the more specific claim is called the Second (or Communicative) Principle. In the text of the first edition, the term 'Principle of Relevance' always refers to the Second, Communicative Principle.

As always, there appeared several collections of articles in the area of pragmatics and discourse analysis. Franz Hundsnurscher and Edda Weigand published a collection of articles entitled *Future Perspectives of Dialogue Analysis*. The term 'dialogue analysis' is not intended as a mere notational variant of the more common designation 'discourse analysis'. Discourse analysis, according to Weigand, 'can constitute neither a discipline, because it has no clear object, nor a new methodology which would have to be based on an object'. However, in spite of this call for a unified field of dialogue analysis, the collection of eight papers comprises a variety of approaches. The contributors are Eddy Roulet, Kirsten Adamzik, Franz Hundsnurscher, Edda Weigand, Andreas H. Jucker, Alessandro Capone, Bernd Naumann and Henning Westheide. Two papers are in German, one in French and the rest in English.

Two books on critical discourse analysis deserve mentioning. Carmen Rosa Caldas-Coulthard and Malcolm Coulthard have edited a very useful collection of readings within this approach (*Texts and Practices. Readings in Critical Discourse Analysis*). Critical discourse analysis differs from other approaches in having an explicit political dimension. 'Discourse is a major instrument of power and control and Critical Discourse Analysts (...) feel that it is indeed part of their professional role to investigate, reveal and clarify how power and discriminatory value are inscribed in and mediated through the linguistic system'. The volume is split up into five more theoretical papers by Roger Fowler, Gunther Kress, Theo van Leeuwen, Norman Fairclough and Teun A. van Dijk, and nine more practical papers. These papers are devoted to a diverse range of data, but most of them use English language data. Michael Hoey, for instance, analyses gender bias in dictionary definitions of the lexemes 'man' and 'woman' ('On clause-relational analysis of selected diction-ary entries: Contrast and compatibility in the definitions of "man" and "woman" '). Several contributors use English newspapers or magazines for their analyses: Ramesh Krishnamurthy ('Ethnic, racial and tribal: The lan-guage of racism?'); Val Gough and Mary Talbot (' "Guilt over games boys play". Coherence as a focus for examining the constitution of heterosexual subjectivity on a problem page'); Andrew Morrison ('Barking up the wrong tree? Male hegemony, discrimination against women and the reporting of bestiality in the Zimbabwean press'); and Carmen Rosa Caldas-Coulthard (' "Women who pay for sex. And enjoy it". Transgression versus morality in women's magazines').

The other book on critical discourse contains ten papers, written between 1983 and 1992 by the most prominent proponent of this type of discourse analysis, Norman Fairclough (*Critical Discourse Analysis: The Critical Study of Language*). The papers are arranged into four groups. The first two groups represent Fairclough's earlier and more recent work respectively. The first group is devoted to the relationship between language, ideology and power, whereas the second is concerned with the relationship between discourse and sociocultural change. The remaining two groups are shorter, consisting of one and two papers respectively. They deal with the centrality of textual analysis to social research and with the principles and practice of critical language awareness. The data used by Fairclough includes such diverse texts as adver-tisements for academic posts, newspaper discourse and medical interviews.

In their Festschrift in honour of Charles J. Fillmore's 65th birthday, the editors Masayoshi Shibatani and Sandra Thompson present as vast an array of contributions as the title they have chosen – *Essays in Semantics and Pragmatics* – promises. Not only have they managed to include essays on semantics, pragmatics and on both semantic and pragmatic issues (even taking into consideration lexicographical as well as ethnographical approaches), but they have also introduced a special focus on Asian languages and cultures. These are not only presented by Asian researchers or researchers of Asian descent, but also in joint projects such as the one on 'Shifting face from Asia to Europe' by Susan Ervin-Tripp, Kei Nakamura and Jiansheng Guo. A very interesting aspect is that not only the importance of the influence of Charles Fillmore's work on the contributions is emphasized, but also Charles (or Chuck, as he is referred to by Shibatani and Thompson in their preface) Fillmore's personal impact on several of the researchers that have participated in the project.

In the following I want to mention a number of publications in specific subfields of pragmatics. The first field to be mentioned here is intercultural pragmatics. Ron Scollon and Suzanne Wong Scollon (*Intercultural*

Communication: A Discourse Approach) present a textbook in this field in the prestigious Blackwell series Language in Society. The emphasis is on intercultural communication in business situations between Asians and Americans, but their understanding of intercultural communication goes much further. It also refers to communication between men and women, between members of different professional groups, or between people of different generations. Every individual is a member of many overlapping communities. Communication between individuals of different discourse communities is described as interdiscourse communication. The basic tenet of this book is that most miscommunication does not arise through grammatical infelicities or mispronunciations but through differences in patterns of discourse. Much of the book is therefore taken up by outlining some of the relevant differences in patterns of discourse between different communities. Scollon and Scollon's book is a very useful antidote to such stereotyping. It provides a lot of useful information on discourse styles of various groups but, more importantly, it warns against turning such information into fail-safe expectations.

Anna Trosborg (*Interlanguage Pragmatics. Requests, Complaints and Apologies*) provides a case-study of Danish learners of English and the way in which they acquire the pragmatic functions of requests, apologies and complaints. Requests constitute a face-threat to the addressee while apologies constitute one for the speaker. They are therefore particularly interesting for a contrastive analysis. In the former case the speaker intrudes on the addressee's negative face, i.e. his or her claim to freedom from impositions, by asking him or her to do something that he or she might not have done otherwise. An apology is an admission of guilt on the part of the speaker and therefore constitutes a threat to the speaker's positive face, i.e. his or her wish to be approved of and appreciated by others. Complaints, finally, constitute a face threat to the positive face of the addressee because the speaker expresses some displeasure with something for which the addressee is held responsible. Trosborg's analysis of these speech acts, their seriousness and the mitigating strategies employed by the informants relies heavily on the methodology developed by Blum-Kulka and her associates (the Cross-cultural speech act realization project, CCSARP). However, Trosborg uses different data. Instead of written discourse completion tasks, she uses 400 videotaped and transcribed five-minute role play sequences. Each of the three speech acts (request, complaint and apology) was represented by 120 dialogues, half of them between two native speakers and half of them between a Danish learner of English and a native speaker. The remaining 40 dialogues were designed to elicit argumentation.

Another important and very active subfield of pragmatics is gender pragmatics. Janet Holmes (*Women, Men and Politeness*) presents a textbook in Longman's new sociolinguistic Real Language Series. It is explicitly aimed at 'second year undergraduate students following courses on sociolinguistics and language and gender' (cover text). But it will be of value far beyond this narrow target audience. Holmes tackles the very difficult question of whether women are more polite than men. Using evidence drawn mainly from data collected in New Zealand she compares a range of politeness strategies in the speech of men and women and discusses possible reasons for the differences. In particular, she discusses interactional strategies, 'hedges and boosters', and compliments as positive politeness strategies as well as apologies as negative politeness strategies. The last chapter of her book considers some of the implications of her findings for educational and professional contexts. Holmes's book is interdisciplinary in that it uses and introduces sociolinguistic, pragmatic and discourse analytic methods.

The last subfield of pragmatics to be mentioned here is a very recent addition to the field of pragmatics. Andreas H. Jucker has published a substantial volume of papers entitled *Historical Pragmatics. Pragmatic Developments in the History of English*. The volume, which contains 22 original articles, starts with an introduction by Andreas Jacobs and Andreas H. Jucker, which is both a state-of-the-art account of historical pragmatics and a programmatic statement of its future potential and its different subfields. Part I contains seven pragmaphilological papers by Heinz Bergner, Gert Ronberg, John Lennard, Werner Hüllen, Ulrich Bach, Richard J. Watts and M. Pilar Navarro-Errasti. These papers deal with historical texts and their interpretations by paying close attention to the communicative context of these texts. The second and third parts comprise papers in diachronic pragmatics. The ten papers of part II take a linguistic form as their starting point, e.g. particular lexical items or syntactic constructions, and study their pragmatic functions at different times (diachronic form-to-function mappings). The contributors are José Pinto de Lima, Enrique Bernárdez and Paloma Tejada, Scott A. Schwenter and Elizabeth Closs Traugott, Cynthia L. Allen, Katie Wales, Barbara Kryk-Kastovsky, Brita Wårvik, Monika Fludernik, Noriko Okada Onodera and Irma Taavitsainen. The four papers of part III take a particular pragmatic function as their starting point, e.g. discourse strategies or politeness, and study their linguistic realization at different times (diachronic function-to-form mappings). The contributors of this part are Gerd Fritz, Tuija Virtanen, Roman Kopytko, and Terttu Nevalainen and Helena Raumolin-Brunberg.

9. Stylistics

Amongst the stylistic publications this year, Sara Mills's *Feminist Stylistics* is to be particularly welcomed because it covers a great deal of new ground: although feminist literary theory and feminist linguistic analysis are areas which have received considerable attention in recent years, there was no single volume which offered an introduction into how stylistic analysis could account for gender issues. *Feminist Stylistics* fills the gap rather nicely: it is geared towards the practical analysis of texts without ignoring theoretical issues and, although it has students and teachers in mind like many of the titles published by the Interface series, its scope is far from elementary. Mills points out how gender differences are manifested in language at all linguistic levels: gender is present in the choice of single words, in the way words combine to form phrases and sentences, and in larger discoursal structures. A separate chapter is dedicated to each of these three linguistic levels and in each of them the reader can find analyses of both literary and non-literary texts. Mills's analyses rest on an awareness of what texts *do*: some texts interpellate the reader, some construe readers as gendered and some ignore or exclude women readers altogether. Mills shows very convincingly how readers can have an active role – and resist or negotiate the meanings of texts: the practice of feminist stylistics alerts the reader to the means texts have of displaying gender difference and trains the eye to read texts suspiciously. This book will surely turn out to be first-rate teaching material but it is to be hoped that it will also become instrumental in encouraging stylistic analyses from a feminist perspective.

Two other books which help to make this year good for pedagogical stylistics are John Haynes's *Style* and Rob Pope's *Textual Intervention: Critical and Creative Strategies for Literary Studies*. Both are designed for the class-room and teachers in need of course material will be grateful for what they have to offer. In the Introduction to *Style*, Haynes claims that the book aims to give the reader a taste of what the analysis of style can do and indeed, the book remains slightly sketchy throughout. Its usefulness lies in its potential as a simple, compact tool for introducing students to the basic skills of stylistic analysis. It is organized into units which address a particular aspect of style, ranging from metaphor and patterns of grammar to ideology and point of view, and it offers activities, a reading list and suggestions for project-work. Since it is part of the Language Workbooks series, its concern with literary texts is minimal and the range of texts discussed is perhaps one of the most disappointing aspects of this book.

Rob Pope cannot be accused of having settled on a narrow selection of texts for *Textual Intervention*, a textbook in which all sorts of texts (literary and non-literary, canonical and non-canonical, naturally occurring and elicited) blend without difficulty. The reader is often asked to intervene and create or modify the texts under analysis: this is one of the basic tenets of the book, that interpretation can be successfully achieved through rewriting: producing parallel or alternative texts enhances our understanding of the departure text. It is therefore a book to be used rather than merely to be read. Some of the issues addressed by the different chapters are the construction of subjectivity and agency in texts (Chapter 2); the articulation of narrative both at the level of micro-structures such as the clause or the sentence and at the level of macro-structures such as mythologies and ideologies (Chapter 3); the explora-tion of different 'voices' and 'discourses' in dramatic dialogue from a 'Brechtian/Bakhtinian' perspective and the conflict of cultural discourses in colonial and post-colonial texts (Chapter 4). Read one after the other, these chapters are likely to produce a slight sensation of dizziness, as they force the reader to jump from one critical realm to another at speed. However, taken separately, they can prove to be rather painless introductions to difficult critical concepts. Chapter 5 is a bicephalous final chapter which can be read either before or after the rest of the book: it can be used as either an annotated 'Further Reading' list or as an introduction to the key theoretical positions used in the preceding chapters.

Peter Barry's *Beginning Theory* also deserves to be warmly welcomed here, partly because it contains a chapter on stylistics which is a sensible, if succinct, introduction to the field for students with no previous background in linguis-tics, but mostly because it grants stylistics the place it deserves in contemporary critical theory. Its opening gambit is to lament that introduc-tions to literary theory seem unaware of the existence of linguistic approaches to literature and ignore the ground shared by critical theory and recent developments in stylistics. Most of the usual readers of this section will perhaps find it *too* introductory and might feel the need to take issue with some of the judgements that Barry makes on stylistics. For example, he asserts that contemporary stylistics aims to be *objective*, when he probably means *replicable*; he seems to suggest that stylistics makes no distinction between literary language and everyday speech, when he might have introduced the concept of *literariness* as a quality which can be equally present in literary and non-literary texts. However, its purpose – to work as an eye-opener for students of literary/critical theory – is amply fulfilled, and the reading list accompanying the chapter allows adventurous students the ability to explore further in the right direction.

Non-literary stylistics is a territory which is difficult to chart because both linguistics and stylistics seem to have a competing claim on it, but articles such as Linda Waugh's 'Reported Speech in Journalistic Discourse: The Relation of Function and Text' (*Text* 15.129–73) – which looks at the use of direct and indirect speech in newspaper reporting and explores the ways in which it differs from novels or conversation – or Per Van Der Wijst's 'The Perception of Politeness in Dutch and French Indirect Requests' (*Text* 15.477–501) – which uses Brown and Levinson's politeness model to compare perception of politeness in request by speakers of French and speakers of Dutch – have a great deal in common with contemporary approaches to stylistics. Matters of linguistic politeness and verbal 'correctness' can very often turn into matters of style, and Deborah Cameron's *Verbal Hygiene* addresses issues which will interest, amuse or enrage many of those who practise stylistics today. For Cameron, 'verbal hygiene' includes not only prescriptive practices, whether conservative and restrictive attempts at regulating or at unifying, but also those language practices which stem from democratic and egalitarian principles, such as political correctness, campaigns to promote language rights of minority groups, preservation of 'endangered' language and dialects, etc. Even those who claim that language should be 'let alone' are practising a verbal hygiene of their own. Since verbal hygiene is related to issues of value and linguistic choice, it is inevitably related to style and overlaps with stylistics. Cameron's view of style as a commodity in the modern marketplace will be of interest to those who practise stylistic analysis: a text is often 'packaged' in a particular style having in mind a type of potential customer; some newspapers, however, have to adopt a style which will appeal to a variety of possible customers. Style then becomes that which enables one to sell a product.

New Essays in Deixis: Discourse, Narrative, Literature (ed. Keith Green) is a collection of articles which share an interest in the relation between deixis and literary texts. Some of the contributions are concerned with theoretical discussions of deixis whereas others are orientated towards the analysis of texts in narrative or poetry. Keith Green's 'Deixis: A Revaluation of Concepts and Categories' is an introductory chapter which opens the discussion, charts a new typology of deictic categories and stresses the link between deixis and genre. Peter Jones, in 'Philosophical and Theoretical Issues in the Study of Deixis: A Critique of the Standard Account' offers a critique of the most widespread approach to deixis and proposes an alternative framework based on Voloshinov/Bahktin and on Bühler's concept of 'harmonious orientation within an order'. Paul Werth, in 'How to Build a World (in a Lot Less than Six Days, Using Only What's In Your Head)' develops his exciting theory of discourse worlds and text worlds and explores the role played by deixis in the construction of narrative worlds whereas Catherine Emmott, in 'Consciousness and Context-Building: Narrative Inferences and Anaphoric Theory', takes issue with existing accounts of anaphora, claiming that much anaphoric theory fails because it rests on elicited texts which do not reflect naturally occurring language. Monika Fludernik's 'Pronouns of Address and "Odd" Third Person Forms: The Mechanics of Involvement in Fiction' opens the second part of the collection and examines the deictic role of pronouns in fiction. Her analysis shows how writers of fiction, particularly experimental fiction, can exploit 'odd' pronominal choices to achieve referential ambiguity, gender indeterminacy and involvement on the part of the reader. In the remaining chapters, the focus of attention rests on the importance of deixis in poetic texts. Alison Tate's 'Deictic Markers and the Disruption of Voice in Modernist Poetry' explores deictic markers in Ezra Pound's *Cantos* and in the opening lines of Eliot's *The Waste Land*, relating deictic elements in modernist poetry to modernist preoccupations with identity and the presentation of self. Taking as her departure a view of poetic voice as dynamic rather than static, Elena Semino studies the link between deixis and poetic *persona* in 'Deixis and the Dynamics of Poetic Voice', where she provides very lucid analyses of Ted Hughes's 'Wind', Philip Larkin's 'Talking in Bed' and Elizabeth Bartlett's 'Charlotte, Her Book', and shows how deixis plays a role in signalling the presence of multiple voices. In a thought-provoking final chapter, 'Keats and the Disappearing Self: Aspects of Deixis in the Odes', Tony Bex examines the use of deictic elements in Keats's *Odes* (particularly in 'Ode to Psyche', 'Ode to a Nightingale', 'Ode on Melancholy', 'Ode on a Grecian Urn' and 'To Autumn') and regards them as a sequence in which Keats made consecutive attempts to break free from the limitations of person and place imposed by the unavoidable presence of deixis in language. Bex concludes that it was in 'To Autumn' that Keats came closer to achieving his liberation from the pressure of deixis and this accounts for the interpretive difficulties posed by this poem.

Fiction, and particularly twentieth-century fiction, continues to attract a good deal of attention in the area of stylistic studies. Miguel Angel Martínez-Cabeza's *Lengua y Estilo en las Novelas de E. M. Forster* is a monographic study of Forster's style which combines the analytical techniques of speech and thought presentation, discourse and conversation analysis, politeness phenomena and functional grammar in a model which the author, following Leech, calls *pragmalinguistic*. The conclusions to this study confirm Forster's ambivalent status as a writer who blends modernist and traditional elements: his fiction lacks some of the characteristic stylistic features of modernism (experimentation, formal complexity, ellipsis, etc.) but it heavily displays the use of free indirect discourse, a stylistic trait which is frequently found in the novels of other modernist writers. *Twentieth-Century Fiction: From Text to Context* (ed. Peter Verdonk and Jean Jacques Weber) is a sequel to the editors' *Twentieth-Century Poetry: From Text to Context*. Each chapter is preceded by a useful introduction from one of the editors and is followed by a substantial amount of suggestions for further work. As the editors' introduction helpfully points out, chapters have been arranged into three groups dedicated to explore the textual level, the narrative level and the contextual level. Chapters 1 to 4 single out a particular textual feature: lexical repetition, cognitive metaphor, fictional dialogue and politeness. Chapters 5 to 9 deal with point of view in narrative and address issues such as shift of point of view, free indirect discourse and the ideological dimension of point of view. Chapters 10 to 13, without ignoring textual features, pay attention to the importance of contextual factors in enabling the reader to reconstruct the fictional world: the conventions of narrative genres, the theory of text worlds, the interplay between narrative schemata and gender issues, and the political dimension of narrative discourse are all shown to play a part in the process of assigning meaning to narrative texts.

The articles in *Twentieth-Century Fiction* offer a very fruitful exploration of a wide array of contemporary narrative texts with a varied set of analytic frameworks. Peter Verdonk's 'Words, Words, Words: A Pragmatic and Socio-Cognitive View of Lexical Repetition', draws on Susan Hill's *The Mist in the Mirror* – a novel which echoes Dickens's opening of *Bleak House* – and Virginia Woolf's *Mrs Dalloway* to discuss different types of lexical repetition with a pragmatic model of meaning. The analysis is enriched by a socio-cognitive view of lexical repetition as based in our desire for symmetry in the world and by an exploration of the relation between lexical repetition and imitation/parody. Cognitive linguistics also plays an important role in Jean Jacques Weber's 'How Metaphor Leads Susan Rawlings into Suicide: A Cognitive-Linguistic Analysis of Doris Lessing's "To Room Nineteen"' which shows that neurosis is conceptually described in Lessing's short story as military invasion and as a take-over bid. Weber studies the different linguistic realizations of these metaphors in 'To Room Nineteen' and explores the role played by conceptual metaphor in Susan Rawling's career to self-destruction. 'Character talk' as opposed to 'narrator's talk' is the object of analysis in Mick Short's 'Understanding Conversational Undercurrents in "The Ebony Tower" by John Fowles' which makes use of discourse analysis (turn-taking, speech-acts, politeness, inferred meanings) to prove that stylistic analysis can tell us how interpretation is achieved (i.e. how we reach an understanding of a text). Short's study also reveals that the analysis of a brief piece of dialogue can return the attention we invest in it at compound interest: it can procure for us a surprising amount of information about character and character-relations. The only other chapter in the collection which deals with fictional dialogue is Rosemary Buck and Timothy Austin's 'Dialogue and Power in E. M. Forster's *Howards End*', which applies Brown and Levinson's politeness model to the conversation Margaret Schlegel and Henry Wilcox have at Simpson's restaurant. Buck and Austin reach the conclusion that social power is not stable; it is, like *face*, potentially under threat in each new conversational turn and it has to be negotiated again and again by those taking part in a conversation.

Twentieth-Century Fiction dedicates a good deal of room – five chapters – to the analysis of narrative point of view and related issues such as focalization, perspective and reported discourse. Susan Ehrlich's 'Narrative Iconicity and Repetition in Oral and Literary Narratives' points out that the repetition of a narrative event in a story can be responsible for a particular stylistic effect: in the novels of Virginia Woolf, the second mention of an event is not a mere flashback but an indication of a shift in point of view. Helen Dry's 'Free Indirect Discourse in Doris Lessing's "One Off the Short List": A Case of Designed Ambiguity' offers a brief, concise introduction to reported discourse which can be used with students as introductory reading to the classic formulation in Geoffrey N. Leech and Michael N. Short's *Style in Fiction* (*YWES* 62.83) but its interest lies in its discussion of narrative ambiguity and Free Indirect Discourse (FID). FID can be manipulated by a writer wanting the reader to remain uncertain whether to attribute a particular utterance to the narrator or to a character and this is illustrated with Lessing's ambiguous presentation of the main character in 'One Off the Short List', inducing the reader both to remain distant from the character's world-view and to empathize with the character's sense of failure. David Lee, in 'Language and Perspective in Katherine Mansfield's "Prelude" ', offers a very shrewd study of the relation of point of view to interpretation. Taking narrative point of view to be either visual perspective or ideological colouring, Lee shows that both are inextricably bound together since the act of perception involves interpretation. Mansfield's 'Prelude' enables Lee to exemplify how certain choices of word, phrase or sentence in a narrative disclose a character's visual and ideological perspective. Michael Toolan's 'Discourse Style Makes Viewpoint: The Example of Carver's Narrator in "Cathedral" ' shows how the style of a text (i.e. the linguistic choices made by a text) can be responsible for conveying the narrator's point of view, his beliefs and attitudes to others. Apparently 'inoffensive' linguistic features such as deictics, connectors and the repeated avoidance of first names are meaningful linguistic choices which convey the narrator's feelings, and so do more elusive linguistic elements such as presupposition or implicature. Paul Simpson and Martin Montgomery's 'Language, Literature and Film: The Stylistics of Bernard MacLaverty's *Cal*' show how issues of characterization can very often be interwoven with focalization and point of view, even in third person narratives such as MacLaverty's *Cal*. This is one of the most thrilling chapters because it not only offers an interesting analysis of *Cal*, both the novel and its filmed version, but it also delineates a six-category model for the analysis of narrative: based on the fundamental distinction between *plot* and *discourse*, this model identifies six different elements which help to make up a narrative: *textual structure*, *cultural context and linguistic code*, *intertext(s)*, *characterisation 1: actions and events*, *characterisation 2: focalization* and, finally, *textual medium*. These categories, according to the authors, illuminate each other and the result is that, rather than ending with a fragmentary vision of the work analysed, we can obtain a better understanding of the text as a whole through an awareness of the parts from which it is made. The model seems promising but it requires testing on other narrative texts, as Simpson and Montgomery anticipate, particularly to see if it is, as they claim, both 'holistic and particular'.

The last four chapters address issues as different as literary genre, text worlds, sexism or the political dimension of communication, but they all share a preoccupation with the context a narrative is steeped in. Irene Fairley, in 'Virginia Woolf's "Old Mrs Grey": Issues of Genre', after a close analysis of Woolf's essay, explores the relation between the literary essay and other genres, such as fictional narrative and autobiography. Paul Werth, in ' "World Enough, and Time": Deictic Space and the Interpretation of Prose', applies his theory of text-worlds to the fictional worlds of novels and short-stories and provides a description of the text-world of Chandrapore in E. M. Forster's *A Passage to India*. Sara Mills's, 'Working with Sexism: What Can Feminist Text Analysis Do?' offers a close analysis of agency in the opening passage of Martin Amis's *London Fields* and very convincingly argues for the need to resort to an intermediate structure if we want to expose the link between words and sexism: individual linguistic features and ideological structures are mediated by narrative schemata and these narrative patterns or 'narrative pathways' explain how we assign a particular meaning to linguistic elements which are in themselves polyvalent and potentially have multiple meanings. In the final chapter, cryptically entitled 'Strategy and Contingency', David Birch uses a passage from Bruce Chatwin's *The Songlines* to raise several questions about the nature of communication (which is seen as an 'interested activity'), the ways in which ideologies are hidden in texts, and the different political positions a text can be read from. Birch's questions point to the reader, not the author, as the ultimate builder of the meaning of a text and they foreground an idea which permeates most of the articles in *Twentieth-Century Fiction*, that stylistic analysis is not simply concerned with *what* a text means but also, and more importantly, with *how* discourse means. Most chapters transcend purely pedagogical stylistics and point out many paths future research could venture into, such that anyone interested in the stylistics of fiction will find it a very rewarding companion.

There are very few book-length studies of dramatic dialogue from a stylistic perspective and Vimala Herman's *Dramatic Discourse: Dialogue as Interaction in Plays* is no doubt a considerable step to redress the balance. Drama has been for a long time the Cinderella of stylistics, for historical reasons which are not difficult to understand: this century has seen the evolution of linguistics from the sign to syntax and only then to pragmatics and discourse and this has been paralleled within stylistics with an evolution from the analysis of lexis in poetry, to the analysis of sentence structure in narrative, and only since the late 1970s and early 1980s to an interest in discoursal structures in drama. Even today, though, the bulk of stylistic analyses deal with texts taken from either poems or novels: out of a total of 39 articles published so far by *L&L*, a journal dedicated to stylistic analysis, only five deal with texts taken from plays. Seen from this perspective, Herman's work is an attempt to fill a gap, mostly with the help of concepts taken from the ethnography of communication and conversation analysis. The first three chapters ('The Ethnography of Speaking', 'Ethnomethodology and Conversation Analysis' and 'Turn Sequencing') constitute the core of the book and its most interesting contribution to the linguistic analysis of drama: the system of turn-taking is successfully applied to several dramatic passages whose authors range from Shakespeare and Chekhov to Wesker and Bond. The remaining chapters are less rewarding. In the chapter entitled 'Pragmatics', the reader finds a discussion of Brown and Levinson's politeness model: the model is summarized but it is not then systematically used to analyse any texts, so the reference to politeness sounds more perfunctory than really convincing, casting a very inexact image of what this model can do for dramatic texts. The chapter on 'Gender and Language' is also unsatisfactory: too much space is taken by a review of research in this area and by theoretical considerations on the linguistic study of gender, with the inevitable effect that too little space is left for the analysis of gender in the language of plays; when the reader finally sees some textual analysis, the texts which actually get analysed are the two most canonical texts by the most canonical writer, Shakespeare's *Hamlet* and *King Lear*. The discourse analysis model developed in Birmingham by Sinclair and Coulthard and applied to dramatic texts by Deirdre Burton is conspicuously almost absent: it is heavy-handedly dismissed in less than a page. Herman's book, however, is an important foundation, even if further discussions of dramatic discourse are necessary to bring stylistic analysis of drama on a level with the stylistics of poetry and fiction.

This year's volume of *L&L* does not contain one single article on dramatic texts, but it is full of interesting work, mostly on poetry. In one of the best articles published in 1995, 'Schema Theory and the Analysis of Text Worlds in Poetry' (*L&L* 4.79–108), Elena Semino successfully applies to poems analytical techniques frequently associated with fiction: schema theory and the theory of text worlds are put to use in the analysis of two poems by Seamus Heaney and Sylvia Plath. Semino redefines the notion of schema refreshment and opens it up to accommodate more subtle cases which the traditional notion could not cope with, such as the connections of apparently unrelated schemata or the role of a poem in forcing the reader to become aware of, analyse and re-appraise schemata which are usually taken for granted. With impeccable methodology, Semino successfully shows how a poem can either reinforce the reader's schemata (Heaney's 'A Pillowed Head') or question them (Plath's 'The Applicant'). Her analysis proves how Plath's poem, a schema refreshing poem, can be more challenging as a text than Heaney's, because it questions the reader's schemata and it projects less conventional and more problematic views of reality. The analysis of Plath's poem is particularly interesting because it relates the conflict between clashing text-worlds and competing schemata, via the notion of heteroglossia, to the presence of multiple voices in the poem. 'Transitivity and Ergativity in "The Lotos-Eaters" ' (*L&L* 4.31–48) by James D. Benson, William S. Greaves and Glenn Stillar, also rests on the belief that the concepts of dialogism and heteroglossia (*pace* Bakhtin) can be applied to poetry and provides an analysis of Tennyson's poem from the perspective of Halliday's systemic-functional linguistics, with particular attention to transitivity and ergativity. The systemic-functional system of transitivity is perhaps an acquired taste but this article shows how successful it can be: Benson, Greaves and Stillar unveil the three worlds or voices ensconced in the poem and this leads to an understanding of the mariners' dilemma. Pétur Knútsson's 'Intertextual quanta in formula and translation' (*L&L* 4.109–25) discusses Halldóra B. Björnsson's translation of *Beowulf* into Icelandic in the light of cognate and non-cognate terms and formulaic links between Anglo-Saxon and Old Norse poems and concludes that intertextuality has to be invoked to explain some of the phenomena taking place between Björnsson's translation and its source. In 'Lewis Carroll's "Jabberwocky": Non-Sense not Nonsense' (*L&L* 4.1–15), Adam Rose takes issue with Martin Gardner's view of Carroll's poem as 'nonsense' and argues that even if the poem is a 'non-sense' poem it 'makes sense' if we reject an approach based on semantics and look instead at it in the light of semiotics and pragmatics. Alice herself – who after reading the poem states that the one thing she gets out of it is that *someone* killed *something* – would probably agree with Rose's claim that the poem has both a 'denotational' and an 'interactional' meaning.

There are only two articles dealing with the stylistics of fiction in *L&L* 4. Pamela Faber and Celia Wallhead's 'The Lexical Field of Visual Perception in *The French Lieutenant's Woman* by John Fowles' (127–44) and Cris Yelland's 'Hardy's Allusions and the Problem of "Pedantry" ' (17–30). The first of these finds that the lexical field of vision is foregrounded in Fowles's novel and that the superordinate terms 'see' and 'look' together with their hyponyms 'stare', 'sight', 'view', etc. are linked to the main characters at crucial points in the narrative. The second is a very illuminating study which explores the syntactical realizations of generics and specific allusion in *Far From the Madding Crowd*. Yelland shows how these two features play a role in the 'pedantic' tone which both Victorian and modern critics associate with Hardy's style and concludes that the hostility Victorian critics displayed against Hardy's pedantry is understandable in the context of Late Victorian anxiety about 'culture' and the place of classical learning.

In an article which will no doubt prove to be polemical, 'Discourse Analysis: A Critical View' (*L&L* 4.157–72), H. G. Widdowson dissects the confusion surrounding the use of the terms 'discourse' and 'analysis' in 'discourse analysis' (DA). 'Analysis' is often used with the meaning of 'interpretation' and 'discourse' is used interchangeably with 'text'. The article, however, seems to be a frontal attack on those who understand discourse analysis as the study of linguistic units above the clause or the sentence (the Birmingham school of DA) and on those who practise *critical* discourse analysis (CDA). Widdowson thinks CDA is unable to provide a real *analysis* of a text and can only provide a partial *interpretation* of it. He offers his own vision of what discourse analysis ought to be: based on a distinction between *text* and *discourse* as totally different concepts, he sees DA as a tool to uncover and explain all the possible discourses which can be derived from a given text. It is to be hoped that practitioners of critical linguistics feel tempted to reply, because Widdowson's views could kindle an interesting debate on the aims and purposes of discourse analysis. Critical discourse analysis, preoccupation with the study of language in its social context and interest in the relation between ideology and language is, nevertheless, at the base of two articles which keep Widdowson's essay company in the same issue of *Language and Literature*. Joe Foley's 'Form Criticism and Genre Theory' (*L&L* 4.173–91) sees in the *Formgeschichte* School (or Form Criticism School) of biblical exegesis a conception of literary genres which has much in common with the social theory of language developed by Halliday, Martin, Kress, Threadgold and Fairclough. Nicole Geslin's 'Ideology in Crisis on a South African Campus' (*L&L* 4.193–207) uses Halliday's functional-systemic linguistics and his concept of 'antilanguage' to analyse two texts concerning the expulsion of a student from a South African university.

Ideology and the ideological dimension of texts is also the topic of a special issue of the *RBPH* which was conceived, according to its editors, Jean-Pierre Van Noppen and Richard Tuffs, with a view to show how language both reflects and constructs ideology. The issue contains some articles which may be of interest to readers of this section, such as Gunther Kress, 'Moving Beyond a Critical Paradigm: on the Requirements of a Social Theory of Language' (*RBPH* 73.621–34), Philippe De Brabanter, '*Long Walk to Freedom* or How *Time Magazine* Manipulates Nelson Mandela into Unwittingly Forging his Own Image' (*RBPH* 73.725–40), and John Stephens, '*Writing By* Children, *Writing For* Children: Schema Theory, Narrative Discourse and Ideology' (*RBPH* 73.853–64). This issue also includes Jean-Pierre Van Noppen's interesting study of religious discourse, 'Methodist Discourse and Industrial Work Ethic: A Critical Theolinguistic Approach' (*RBPH*

73.693–714) which discusses Methodist tracts and Wesleyan hymns from the perspective of critical linguistics and concludes that the favourable reception granted to Methodism by miners and industrial workers can be accounted for in terms of certain linguistic features present in Methodist discourse.

Metaphor has received a good deal of attention this year. G. J. Finch's 'Metaphor and poetic discourse' (*English* 44.56–70), first argues in favour of considering metaphor not as deviation from a grammatical norm but as an integral part of the linguistic system and then applies the theory of conceptual metaphor developed by Lakoff, Johnson and Turner to Wordsworth's 'Tintern Abbey'. In a special issue of *JPrag* (24) which bears the title 'Literary Pragmatics: Cognitive Metaphor and the Structure of the Poetic Text', the same theory of metaphor is applied to texts from Shakespeare by Antonio Barcelona in 'Metaphorical Models of Romantic Love in *Romeo and Juliet*' (667–88), and by Donald Freeman, in ' "Catch[ing] the Nearest Way": *Macbeth* and Cognitive Metaphor' (689–708). Barcelona studies the models of romantic love in *Romeo and Juliet* and finds that the dominant metaphors in the construction of these models are light-darkness or part-whole metaphors. Donald Freeman shows that the CONTAINER and PATH schemata lie behind most of the metaphors in *Macbeth*, as well as behind most of the critical language which has been used to discuss the play. Conceptual metaphor in poetry is discussed by P. D. Deane in 'Metaphors of Center and Periphery in Yeats' *The Second Coming*' (627–42) and by Margaret Freeman in 'Metaphor Making Meaning: Dickinson's Conceptual Universe', (643–66), which shows how in her poems Dickinson replaced the metaphor prevailing in the religious environment of her time, LIFE IS A JOURNEY THROUGH TIME, with another metaphor from contemporary scientific discoveries, LIFE IS A VOYAGE IN SPACE.

Finally, although there is no room to review them here, the following articles published this year may be of interest to those working at the interface of language and literature: Akosua Anyidoho, 'Stylistic Features of Nnwonkoro, and Akan Female Song Tradition' (*Text* 15.317–36); Clara Calvo and Ronald Geluykens, 'Politeness Strategies and Sequential Organization in Crime Fiction Telephone Conversations' (*Interface* 9.49–66); James Fitzmaurice, 'The Language of Gender and a Textual Problem in Aphra Behn's *The Rover*' (*NM* 96.283–93); Anthony J. Gilbert, 'Shakespearean Self-Talk, the Gricean Maxims and the Unconscious' (*ES* 76.221–37); Neal R. Norrick and William Baker, 'Metalingual Humor in Pinter's Early Plays' (*ES* 76.253–63); Stefan Oltean, 'Free Indirect Discourse: Some Referential Aspects' (*JLS* 24.21–41); and Rosanna Vallarelli, 'Babel in Manhattan: The Linguistic Worlds of Henry Roth's *Call it Sleep*' (*LeS* 30.605–17).

Books Reviewed

Aarts, Bas, and Charles F. Meyer, eds. *The Verb in Contemporary English: Theory and Description*. CUP. pp. 313. hb £37.50. ISBN 0 521 46039 5.

Aitchison, Jean. *Linguistics: An Introduction*. H&S. pp. 232. pb £5.99. ISBN 0 340 64397 8.

Akmajian, Adrian, Richard A. Demers, Ann K. Farmer, and Robert M. Harnish. *Linguistics: An Introduction to Language and Communication*. 4th edn. MITP. pp. 577. pb £18.95. ISBN 0 262 51086 3.

Allen, Cynthia L. *Case Marking and Reanalysis: Grammatical Relations from Old to Early Modern English*. OUP. pp. 528. hb £60. ISBN 0 19 824096 1.

Ambrosiani, Bjorn, and Helen Clarke, eds. *Development Around the Baltic and the North Sea in the Viking Age* (1994). Birka Studies 3. Stockholm.

Andersen, Henning, ed. *Historical Linguistics 1993: Selected Papers from the 11th International Conference on Historical Linguistics, Los Angeles, 16–20 August 1993*. Current Issues in Linguistic Theory 124. Benjamins. pp. 460. hb Dfl 190. ISBN 90 272 3627 5.

Armstrong, D. F., W. C. Stokoe, and S. E. Wilcox. *Gesture and the Nature of Language*. CUP. pp. ix + 260. hb £37.50, pb £12.95. ISBN 0 521 46213 4, 0 521 46772 1.

Ashby, P. *Speech Sounds*. Routledge. pp. xi + 104. pb £7.99. ISBN 0 415 08571 3.

Attridge, Derek. *Poetic Rhythm: An Introduction*. CUP. pp. xx + 274. hb £32.50, pb £10.95. ISBN 0 521 41302 8, 0 521 42369 4.

Baker, C. L. *English Syntax*. 2nd edn. MITP. pp. 647. hb £42.50, pb £18.95. ISBN 0 262 02385 7, 0 262 52198 9.

Barry, Peter. *Beginning Theory: An Introduction to Literary and Critical Theory*. ManUP. pp. 239. ISBN 0 7190 4325 5.

Battye, Adrian, and Ian Roberts, eds. *Clause Structure and Language Change*. Oxford Studies in Comparative Syntax. OUP. pp. 369. pb £27.50. ISBN 0 19 508633 3.

Baynham, Mike. *Literary Practices: Investigating Literacy in Social Practice*. Longman. 1994. hb £42, pb £15.99. ISBN 0 582 087090, 0 582 08708 2.

Bennett, Paul. *A Course in Generalized Phrase Structure Grammar*. Studies in Computational Linguistics. ULondon. pp. 227. ISBN 1 85728 217 5.

Bergenholtz, Henning, and Sven Tarp, eds. *Manual of Specialised Lexicography. The Preparation of Special Dictionaries*. Benjamins. pp. 254. 90 Hfl/$50. ISBN 9 027 21612 6, 1 556 19693 8.

Brazil, David. *A Grammar of Speech*. Describing English Language. OUP. pp. 264. pb £15.05. ISBN 0 19 437193 X.

Brody, Michael. *Lexico-Logical Form: A Radically Minimalist Theory*. Linguistic Inquiry Monographs 27. MITP. pp. 155. hb £33.95, pb £16.95. ISBN 0 262 02390 3, 0 262 52203 9.

Brown, Gillian. *Speakers, Listeners and Communication: Explorations in Discourse Analysis*. CUP. pp. xii + 251. £35.00. ISBN 0 521 48157 0.

Caldas-Coulthard, Carmen Rosa, and Malcolm Coulthard, eds. *Texts and Practices. Readings in Critical Discourse Analysis*. Routledge. pp. 294. pb £15.99. ISBN 0 415 12143 4.

Cameron, Deborah. *Verbal Hygiene*. Routledge. pp. xvi + 264. hb £40, pb £11.99. ISBN 0 415 10354 1, 0 415 10355 X.

Carter, Ronald. *Keywords in Language and Literacy*. Routledge. pp. xii + 172. hb £30, pb £9.99. ISBN 0 415 11928 6, 0 415 11929 4.

Chambers, Jack. *Sociolinguistic Theory*. Chambers. pp. 284. pb £14.99. ISBN 0 631 183264.

Chapman, Robert L. *The Macmillan Dictionary of American Slang*. Macmillan. pp. 499. pb £8.99. ISBN 0 333 63405 5.

Chomsky, Noam. *The Minimalist Program*. Current Studies in Linguistics 28. MITP. pp. 420. hb £33.95, pb £18.95. ISBN 0 262 03229 5, 0 262 53128 3.

Clark, Eve. V. *The Lexicon in Acquisition*. CUP. pp. xii + 306. pb £12.95. ISBN 0 521 48464 2.

Corson, David. *Using English Words*. Kluwer. pp. 226. £77. ISBN 0 792 33710 7.

Crawford, Barbara E., ed. *Scandinavian Settlement in Northern Britain: Thirteen Studies of Place-Names in Their Historical Context*. LeicUP. pp. 248. £45. ISBN 0 7185 1923 X.

Crystal, David. *The Cambridge Encyclopedia of the English Language*. CUP. pp. vii + 489. £29.95. ISBN 0 521 401798.

Cubitt, Catherine. *Anglo-Saxon Church Councils c.650–c.850*. LeicUP. pp. 363. £45. ISBN 0 7185 1436 X.

Davis, Philip W., ed. *Alternative Linguistics: Descriptive and Theoretical Modes*. Amsterdam Studies in the Theory and History of Linguistic Science 102. Benjamins. pp. 325. hb Dfl 125. ISBN 90 272 3635 6.

Dikken, Marcel den. *Particles: On the Syntax of Verb-Particle, Triadic, and Causative Constructions*. Oxford Studies in Comparative Syntax. OUP. pp. 288. hb £35, pb £19.50. ISBN 0 19 509134 5, 0 19 509135 3.

Dirven, René, and Johan Vanparys, eds. *Current Approaches to the Lexicon*. Lang. pp. 517. pb 50 DM. ISBN 3 631 48756 8.

Dorward, David. *Scottish Surnames*. HC. pp. 365. pb £4.99. ISBN 0 00 470463 0.

Dunkling, Leslie. *The Guinness Book of Names*, 7th edn. Guinness. pp. 272. pb £11.99. ISBN 0 85112 669 3.

Eco, Umberto. *The Search for the Perfect Language*. Blackwell. pp. x + 385. £20.00. ISBN 0 631 17465 6.

Edwards, John. *Multilingualism*. Routledge. 1994. pp. xiv + 256. £19.99. ISBN 0 415 12011 X.

Egli, Urs, et al. *Lexical Knowledge in the Organization of the Lexicon*. Benjamins. pp. 367. 160 Hfl/$89. ISBN 9 027 23617 8, 1 556 19568 0.

Eichler, Ernst, Gerold Hilty, Henrich Löffler, Hugo Steger, and Ladislav Zgusta, eds. *Namenforschung: ein internationales Handbuck zur Onomastik*. Vol. 1. Handbooks of Linguistics and Communication Science. Gruyter. pp. 977. DM 780. ISBN 3 11 011426 7.

Fairclough, Norman. *Critical Discourse Analysis. The Critical Study of Language*. Longman. pp. 265. pb £16.99. ISBN 0 582 219841.

Fellows-Jensen, Gillian. *The Vikings and Their Victims: The Verdict of the Names*. Viking Society for Northern Research. pp. 34. n.p.

Ferraro, Susan. *Sweet Talk: The Language of Love*. S&S. pp. 219. £11.99. ISBN 0 671 79234 2.

Fischer, Andeas, ed. *Repetition*. Narr. 1994. pp. 268. pb DM 68. ISBN 3 8233 4682 2.

Fisiak, Jacek, ed. *Linguistic Change under Contact Conditions*. Trends in Linguistics 81. Mouton. pp. 438. DM 198. ISBN 3 11 013950 2.

Flavell, Linda, and Roger Flavell, eds. *Dictionary of Word Origins*. KC. pp. 277. pb £6.99. ISBN 1 85626 214 6.

Fox, Anthony. *Linguistic Reconstruction: An Introduction to Theory and Method*. OUP. pp. xvii + 372. hb £35, pb £11.99. ISBN 0 19 870000 8, 0 19 870001 6.

Freeborn, Dennis. *A Course Book in English Grammar: Standard English and the Dialects*. 2nd edn. Studies in English Language. Macmillan. pp. 338. pb £12.99. ISBN 0 333 62493 9.

Fries, Peter H., and Michael Gregory, eds. *Discourse in Society: Systemic*

Functional Perspectives. Ablex. pp. xiv + 305. pb £26.95. ISBN 1 56750 043 9.

Geisler, Christer. *Relative Infinitives in English*. Studia Anglistica Upsaliensia 91. Uppsala. pp. 269. ISBN 91 554 3502 5.

Gelling, Margaret, in collaboration with H. D. G. Foxall. *The Place-Names of Shropshire, part two*. EPNS. pp. 212. £30. ISBN 0 904889 43 2.

Genette, Gérard. *Mimologics*. Transl. T. E. Morgan. UNebP. pp. lxvi + 446. hb £62, pb £23.95. ISBN 0 8032 2129 0, 0 8032 7044 5.

Givón, Talmy. *Functionalism and Grammar*. Benjamins. pp. 486. hb Dfl 150, pb Dfl 70. ISBN 90 272 2147 2, 90 272 2148 0.

Görlach, Manfred. *New Studies in the History of English*. Winter. pp. 264. DM 58. ISBN 3 825 30314 4.

Green, Jonathon. *The Macmillan Dictionary of Contemporary Slang*. 3rd edn. Macmillan. pp. 374. pb £6.99. ISBN 0 333 63407 1.

Green, Keith, ed. *New Essays in Deixis: Discourse, Narrative, Literature*. Rodopi. pp. 189. $40. ISBN 90 5183 831 X.

Grundy, Peter. *Doing Pragmatics*. Arnold. pp. 216. hb £35, pb £13.99. ISBN 0 340 62514 7, 0 340 58965 5.

Haegeman, Liliane. *The Syntax of Negation*. Cambridge Studies in Linguistics 75. CUP. pp. 335. £40. ISBN 0 521 46492 7.

Haider, Hubert, Susan Olsen, and Sten Vikner, eds. *Studies in Comparative Germanic Syntax*. Studies in Natural Language and Linguistic Theory 31. Kluwer. pp. 340. Dfl 180. ISBN 0 7923 3280 6.

Hall, Kira, and Mary Bucholtz, eds. *Gender Articulated: Language and the Socially Constructed Self*. Routledge. pp. 512. hb £50, pb £16.99. ISBN 0 415 913985, 0 415 913993.

Handke, Jürgen. *The Structure of the Lexicon: Human versus Machine*. Mouton. pp. 388. pb DM 68. ISBN 3 110 14786 6.

Harris, Alice C., and Lyle Campbell. *Historical Syntax in Cross-linguistic Perspective*. Cambridge Studies in Linguistics 74. CUP. pp. 488. hb £50, pb £19.95. ISBN 0 521 47294 6, 0 521 47881 2.

Harris, Roy. *Signs of Writing*. Routledge. pp. viii + 185. £40. ISBN 0 415 10088 7.

Hatch, Evelyn, and Cheryl Brown. *Vocabulary, Semantics, and Language Education*. CUP. pp. 468. £30. ISBN 0 521 47409 4.

Haynes, John. *Style*. Routledge. pp. 89. pb £7.99. ISBN 0 415 10396 7.

Henry, Alison. *Belfast English and Standard English: Dialect Variation and Parameter Setting*. Oxford Studies in Comparative Syntax. OUP. pp. 148. hb £37.50, pb £17.50. ISBN 0 19 508291 5, 0 19 508292 3.

Herman, Vimala. *Dramatic Discourse: Dialogue as Interaction in Plays*. Routledge. pp. 331. £45. ISBN 0 415 08241 2.

Herriman, Jennifer. *The Indirect Object in Present-Day English*. Gothenburg Studies in English 66. GothU. pp. 292. ISBN 91 7346 277 2.

Holmes, Janet. *Women, Men and Politeness*. Longman. Real Language Series. pp. 254. hb £39, pb £12.99. ISBN 0 582 06362 0, 0 582 06361 2.

Hooke, Della, and Simon Burnell, eds. *Landscape and Settlement in Britain AD 400–1066*. UExe. pp. 156. pb £12.95. ISBN 0 85989 386 3.

Hornstein, Norbert. *Logical Form: From GB to Minimalism*. Generative Syntax 2. Blackwell. pp. 267. hb £45, pb £16.99. ISBN 0 631 17912 7, 0 631 18942 4.

Hough, Carole. *The English Place-Name Survey: A Finding-List to Addenda and Corrigenda*. CENS. pp. 125. pb £3.50. ISBN 0 9525343 1 2.

Huck, G. J., and J. A. Goldsmith. *Ideology and Linguistic Theory: Noam Chomsky and the Deep Structure Debates*. Routledge. pp. x + 186. £19.99. ISBN 0 415 11735 6.

Hudson, Richard. *Word Meaning*. Routledge. pp. xii + 86. pb £7.99. ISBN 0 415 08565 9.

Hundsnurscher, Franz, and Edda Weigand, eds. *Future Perspectives of Dialogue Analysis*. Niemeyer. pp. 199. DM 124. ISBN 3 484 75008 1.

Hussey, Stanley. *The English Language. Structure and Development*. Longman. pp. 188. £38. ISBN 0 582 21762 8.

Jackson, Peter, ed. *Words, Names and History: Selected Papers of Cecily Clark*. Brewer. pp. 448. £65. ISBN 0 85991 402 X.

Jacobs, Roderick A. *English Syntax: A Grammar for English Language Professionals*. OUP. pp. 378. pb £13.70. ISBN 0 19 434277 8.

Johansson, Christine. *The Relativizers* whose *and* of which *in Present-day English: Description and Theory*. Studia Anglistica Upsaliensia 90. Uppsala. pp. 274. ISBN 91 554 3501 7.

Jucker, Andreas H., ed. *Historical Pragmatics. Pragmatic Developments in the History of English*. Benjamins. pp. 623. Hfl 119. ISBN 90 272 5047 2 (Eur.), 1 55619 328 9 (US).

Kardela, Henryk, and Gunnar Persson, eds. *New Trends in Semantics and Lexicography*. Swedish Science Press. pp. 231. 212 SEK. ISBN 9 171 74981 0.

Kastovsky, Dieter, ed. *Studies in Early Modern English*. Topics in English Linguistics 13. Mouton. pp. 507. DM 248. ISBN 3 11 014127 2.

Keller, Rudi. *On Language Change: The Invisible Hand in Language*. Transl. B. Nerlich. Routledge. 1994. pp. xi + 182. hb £35, pb £11.99. ISBN 0 415 07671 4, 0 415 0 7672 2.

Kelly, S. E., ed. *Charters of St Augustine's Abbey Canterbury and Minster-in-Thanet*. OUP. British Academy. pp. 233. £45. ISBN 0 19 726143 4.

Landsberg, Marge E., ed. *Syntactic Iconicity and Linguistic Freezes: The Human Dimension*. Studies in Anthropological Linguistics 9. Mouton. pp. 453. DM 238. ISBN 3 11 014227 9.

Larson, Richard, and Gabriel Segal. *Knowledge of Meaning: An Introduction to Semantic Theory*. MITP. pp. xvii + 639. hb £67.95, pb £19.99. ISBN 0 262 12193 X, 0 262 62100 2.

Laverton, Sylvia. *Exploring the Past Through Place-Names: Woolverstone*. Watkins. pp. 116 + 24 plates. £17.95. ISBN 1 871615 78 X.

Leckie-Tarry, Helen. *Language and Context: A Functional Linguistic Theory of Register*, ed. David Birch. Pinter. pp. 178. hb £45, pb £16.99. ISBN 1 85567 271 5, 1 85567 272 3.

Le Saux, Françoise, ed. *The Formation of Culture in Medieval Britain*. Mellen. pp. 197. $89.95. ISBN 0 773 49119 8.

Lyons, John. *Linguistic Semantics: An Introduction*. CUP. pp. xvi + 376. hb £35, pb £12.95. ISBN 0 521 43302 9, 0 521 43877 2.

Malmkjaer, Kirsten, ed. *The Linguistics Encyclopedia*. Routledge. 1991. (reprinted) pp. xx + 575. pb £16.99. ISBN 0 415 12566 9.

Marold, Edith, and Christiane Zimmermann, eds. *Nordwestgermanisch*. Gruyter. pp. 299. $126.15. ISBN 3 11 014818 8.

Martínez-Cabeza, Miguel Angel. *Lengua y Estilo en las Novelas de E. M. Forster*. Universidad de Granada. pp. 237. ISBN 84 338 2072 9.

Merry, Emma. *First Names: The Definitive Guide to Popular Names in England and Wales 1944–1994 and in the Regions 1994*. HMSO. pp. 97. pb £4.95. ISBN 0 11 691633 8.

Mills, Sara, ed. *Language and Gender: Interdisciplinary Perspectives*. Longman. pp. 282. pb £14.99. ISBN 0 582 226317.

Mills, Sara. *Feminist Stylistics*. Routledge. £12.99. ISBN 0 415 05028 6.

Milroy, Lesley, and Pieter Muysken, eds. *One Speaker, Two Languages: Cross-Disciplinary Perspectives on Code-Switching*. CUP. pp. 365. hb $59.95, pb £16.95. ISBN 0 521 473500, 0 521 479126.

Mitchell, Bruce. *An Invitation to Old English and Anglo-Saxon England*. Blackwell. pp. 424. hb £45, pb £12.99. ISBN 0 631 17435 4, 0 631 17436 2.

Montgomery, Martin. *An Introduction to Language and Society*. Routledge, 2nd edn. pp. 272. pb £9.99. ISBN 0 415 072387.

Mugglestone, Lynda. *'Talking Proper'. The Rise of Accent as Social Symbol*. Clarendon. pp. 353. £40. ISBN 0 198 23948 3.

Olson, David R. *The World on Paper: The Conceptual and Cognitive Implications of Writing and Reading*. CUP (1994). pp. xix + 318. £17.95. ISBN 0 521 44311 3.

Osselton, N. E. *Chosen Words. Past and Present Problems for Dictionary Makers*. UExe. pp. 188. £27.50. ISBN 0 859 89419 3.

Övergaard, Gerd. *The Mandative Subjunctive in American and British English in the 20th Century*. Studia Anglistica Upsaliensia 94. pp. 139. np. ISBN 91 554 3676 5.

Pagliuca, William, ed. *Perspectives on Grammaticalization*. Amsterdam Studies in the Theory and History of Linguistic Science 109. Benjamins (1994). pp. 306. hb Dfl 150. ISBN 90 272 3612 7.

Palmer, Frank R., ed. *Grammar and Meaning: Essays in Honour of Sir John Lyons*. CUP. pp. 265. hb £37.50. ISBN 0 521 46221 5.

Pope, Rob. *Textual Intervention: Critical and Creative Strategies for Literary Studies*. Routledge. pp. 213. £12.99. ISBN 0 415 05437 0.

Postles, David. *The Surnames of Devon*. Leopard's Head. pp. 332. £19. ISBN 0 904920 25 9.

Potts, Timothy C. *Structures and Categories for the Representation of Meaning*. CUP (1994). pp. xiv + 308. £40. ISBN 0 521 43481 5.

Quirk, Randolph. *Grammatical and Lexical Variance in English*. Longman. pp. 220. hb £39, pb £15.99. ISBN 0 582 25359 4, 0 582 25358 6.

Rampton, Ben. *Crossing: Language and Ethnicity Among Adolescents*. Longman. Real Language Series. pp. 384. hb £47, pb £17.99. ISBN 0 582 217903, 0 582 217911.

Reaney, P. H. *A Dictionary of English Surnames*, 3rd edn with corrections and additions by R. M. Wilson. OUP. pp. 509. pb £9.99. ISBN 0 19 863146 4.

Rey, Alain, trans. and ed. Juan C. Sager. *Essays on Terminology*. Benjamins. pp. 223. Hfl 120. ISBN 9 027 21607 X.

Riehle, Wolfgang, and Hugo Keiper, eds. *Anglistentag 1994 Graz. Proceedings*. Niemeyer. pp. 616. pb DM 74. ISBN 3 484 40017 X.

Roberts, Jane, and Christian Kay, with Lynne Grundy. *A Thesaurus of Old English*. KCLMS. 2 Vols. pp. 1555. £55. ISBN 0 952 21190 4 (both vols). 0 952 21192 0 (vol. I), 0 952 21193 9 (vol. II).

Rogers, Colin D. *The Surname Detective: Investigating Surname Distribution in England, 1086–Present Day*. ManUP. pp. 260. hb £35, pb £10.99. ISBN 0 7190 4047 7, 0 7190 4048 5.

Room, Adrian. *Cassell Dictionary of First Names*. Cassell. pp. 335. £14.99. ISBN 0 304 34398 6.

——. *Hutchinson Pocket Dictionary of Place Names*. Helicon. pp. 246. pb £4.99. ISBN 1 85986 105 9.

Salkie, Raphael. *Text and Discourse Analysis*. Language Workbooks. Routledge. pp. 115. pb £6.99. ISBN 0 415 09278 7.

Scollon, Ron, and Suzanne Wong Scollon. *Intercultural Communication: A Discourse Approach*. Blackwell. pp. xiii + 271. hb £40, pb £13.99. ISBN 0 631 19488 6, 0 631 19489 4.

Sheidlower, Jesse. *The F-Word*. Random. pp. 232. £7.99. ISBN 0 099 62891 0.

Shibatani, Masayoshi, and Theodora Bynon, eds. *Approaches to Language Typology*. OUP. pp. ix + 381. £42.50. ISBN 0 19 824271 9.

Shibatani, Masayoshi, and Sandra Thompson, eds. *Essays in Semantics and Pragmatics. In Honor of Charles J. Fillmore*. Pragmatics & Beyond New Series 32. Benjamins. pp. 330. Hfl 165. ISBN 90 272 5044 8 (Eur.), 1 55619 325 4 (US).

Sinclair, John, ed. *Today's English Dictionary*. Collins. pp. 966. pb £9.99. ISBN 0 003 70949 3.

Sjöholm, Kaj. *The Influence of Crosslinguistic, Semantic, and Input Factors on the Acquisition of English Phrasal Verbs: A Comparison between Finnish and Swedish Learners at an Intermediate and Advanced Level*. Åbo. pp. vi + 290. pb FIM 150. ISBN 952 9616 56 2.

Smith, Neil, and Ianthi-Maria Tsimpli. *The Mind of a Savant*. Blackwell. pp. xviii + 243. hb £40, pb £14.99. ISBN 0 631 19016 3, 0 631 19017 1.

Sperber, Dan, and Deirdre Wilson. *Relevance: Communication and Cognition*. 2nd edn. Blackwell. pp. viii + 326. pb £15.99. ISBN 0 631 19878 4.

Stancliffe, Clare, and Eric Cambridge, eds. *Oswald: Northumbrian King to European Saint*. Watkins. pp. 299 + 24 plates. hb £24, pb £14.95. ISBN 1 871615 46 1, 1 871615 51 8.

Stein, Dieter, and Susan Wright, eds. *Subjectivity and Subjectivisation: Linguistic Perspectives*. CUP. pp. 230. £35. ISBN 0 521 47039 0.

Stonham, John T. *Combinatorial Morphology*. Current Issues in Linguistic Theory 120. Benjamins. 1994. pp. 206. hb Dfl 90. ISBN 90 272 3623 2.

Street, Brian. *Social Literacies*. Longman. Real Language Series. pp. 184. hb £35, pb £10.99. ISBN 0 582 102200, 0 582 102219.

ter Meulen, Alice G. B. *Representing Time in Natural Language: The Dynamic Interpretation of Tense and Aspect*. MITP. pp. xii + 144. £15. ISBN 0 262 20099 6.

Thomas, Jenny. *Meaning in Interaction: An Introduction to Pragmatics*. Longman. pp. xiv + 224. pb £12.99. ISBN 0 582 29151 8.

Trask, Larry. *Language: The Basics*. Routledge. pp. xv + 197. hb £30, pb £7.99. ISBN 0 415 12540 5, 0 415 12541 3.

Trosborg, Anna. *Interlanguage Pragmatics. Requests, Complaints and Apologies*. de Gruyter. pp. 581. £101. ISBN 3 11 014468 9.

Turton, Nigel D. *ABC of Common Grammatical Errors, for Learners and Teachers of English*. Macmillan. pp. 408. pb £6.95. ISBN 0 333 56734 X.

Turville-Petre, Thorlac. *England the Nation. Language, Literature, and*

National Identity, 1290–1340. Clarendon. pp. 256. £32.50. ISBN 0 198 12279 9.

Verdonk, Peter, and Jean Jacques Weber. *Twentieth-Century Fiction: From Text to Context*. Interface. Routledge. pp. 269. £12.99. ISBN 0 415 10590 0.

Verschueren, Jef, Jan-Ola Östman, and Jan Blommaert, eds. *Handbook of Pragmatics: Manual*. Benjamins. pp. xiv + 658. Hfl 275. ISBN 90 272 5081 2 (Eur.), 1 55619 503 6 (US).

Vikner, Sten. *Verb Movement and Expletive Subjects in the Germanic Languages*. Oxford Studies in Comparative Syntax. OUP. pp. 294. hb £50, pb £25. ISBN 0 19 508393 8, 0 19 508394 6.

Walker, Donald E., Antonio Zampolli, and Nicoletta Calzolari, eds. *Automating the Lexicon. Research and Practice in a Multilingual Environment*. OUP. pp. 413. £50. ISBN 0 198 23950 5.

Wardhaugh, Ronald. *Understanding English Grammar: A Linguistic Approach*. Blackwell. pp. 279. pb £12.99. ISBN 0 631 19641 2.

Webelhuth, Gert, ed. *Government and Binding Theory and the Minimalist Program: Principles and Parameters in Syntactic Theory*. Generative Syntax 1. Blackwell. pp. 483. hb £60, pb £17.99. ISBN 0 631 18059 1, 0 631 18061 3.

Westney, Paul. *Modals and Periphrastics in English: An Investigation into the Semantic Correspondence between Certain English Modal Verbs and their Periphrastic Equivalents*. Niemeyer. pp. 225. pb DM 118. ISBN 3 484 30339 5.

Wójcicki, Adam. *Constraints on Suffixation: A Study in Generative Morphology of English and Polish*. Linguistische Arbeiten 340. Niemeyer. pp. 100. pb DM 74. ISBN 3 484 30340 9.

Yorke, Barbara. *Wessex in the Early Middle Ages*. LeicUP. pp. 367. hb £49.50, pb £16.99. ISBN 0 7185 1314 2, 0 7185 1856 X.

II

Old English Literature

E. M. TREHARNE

This chapter contains the following sections: 1. Bibliography; 2. Manuscript Studies, Palaeography and Facsimiles; 3. Social, Cultural and Intellectual Background; 4. Literature: General; 5. The Exeter Book; 6. The Poems of the Vercelli Book; 7. The Junius Manuscript; 8. The *Beowulf* Manuscript; 9. Other Poems; 10. Prose.

1. Bibliography

The *OENews* 28.ii reviews the work in Old English studies for 1993; 28.iii includes a report on *Fontes Anglo-Saxonici* (9), and on 'Old English Studies in Germany *ca.* 1965–95' by Hans Sauer (11–22), and abstracts of conference papers (A.1–A.66). Appendix B ('Insular, Anglo-Saxon and Early Anglo-Norman Illuminated Manuscripts: Survey of Research Past, Present and Future, Part II', B.1–B.34) offers a survey of manuscript codicology and art, edited by Thomas H. Ohlgren, which is divided into four sections: Kathleen Openshaw outlines 'Liturgical Miscellanea' (B.1–B.15) where she raises issues for the categorizing of liturgical manuscripts, and provides suggestions for publishing descriptions of such manuscripts which include full reference to the manuscripts' illustrations. A useful list of these manuscripts is included at the end of the discussion; Gernot Wieland provides an overview of '*Psychomachia* Manuscripts' (B.16–B.19); Herbert R. Broderick speaks of 'Old Testament Manuscript Art' (B.20–B.22); and Richard Gameson looks at 'Early Anglo-Norman Illuminated Manuscripts, *c.*1066–1125' (B.23–B.34). Volume 28.iv contains the Bibliography for 1994 while 29.i includes reports on the *Dictionary of Old English* (9–10), 'Anglo-Saxon Studies in Spain' by Antonio Bravo and Maria José Mora (23–7), an article detailing the 'Rebuilding [of] Bede's World' by Helen Damico and George H. Brown (28–31), and an interesting study by Catherine Brown Tkacz, 'Unlocking the Word Hoard: Conducting Word Studies Using *MCOE*' (32–9). Catherine E. Karkov proposes, among other things, that Mercian coins produced *c.*910–18 had the function of linking Mercia with the glory of Rome in 'Æðelflæd's Exceptional Coinage' (41), and Paul E. Szarmach's 'Æðelflæd in the *Chronicle*' (42–4) demonstrates that the chronicler of the 920s 'offers a most de-gendered picture of Alfred's daughter', disinterested as the account otherwise appears to be in her personal life.

2. Manuscript Studies, Palaeography and Facsimiles

Robert Deshman's magnificent volume, *The Benedictional of Æthelwold* contains 248 plates, 35 of them in full colour and a lengthy, meticulous introduction which discusses the history and methods of production of this famous manuscript. Eight chapters give a detailed account of the illustrations in the Benedictional, their sources, historical, liturgical and art historical context: 'The Miniatures of the Infancy and Baptism of Christ'; 'The Miniatures of the Later Life of Christ'; 'The Miniatures of the Saints'; 'The Sources and Structure of the Cycle'; 'The Monastic Program'; 'The Royal Program'; 'The Benedictional and the Winchester Style'; 'Conclusions'. Three Appendixes discuss the 'Description, Reconstruction, and Date of the Benedictional of Æthelwold', 'The Copy Relationship to the Brunswick Casket'; and 'The Copy Relationship to the Benedictional of Archbishop Robert'. This is a splendid and lavishly produced work of the first importance to Anglo-Saxon art historians and manuscript scholars.

This year's addition to *The Anglo-Saxon Chronicle: A Collaborative Edition* is the *Facsimile of MS F: The Domitian Bilingual* (ed. David N. Dumville). This reproduction is published because of the delay in bringing out the edition and aims 'to encourage a wider awareness of and debate about this version of the *Anglo-Saxon Chronicle*'. Dumville provides introductory matter which details the manuscript's contents, history and previous editorial work. He rejects Ker's theory that the manuscript once belonged with Cambridge, University Library, Hh.1.10 before being separated once it had reached Parker. The facsimile itself is good and will be especially useful to codicologists and palaeographers working in the later period. Historians and literary scholars will also find it valuable, especially when Peter Baker's critical edition is published and the two volumes can be used together.

OENews has published the noteworthy and very useful *Subsidia* 23 this year: *The Liturgical Books of Anglo-Saxon England* (ed. and intro. Richard W. Pfaff) includes the following contributions: Richard W. Pfaff, 'Massbooks' (7–34); K. D. Hartzell, 'Graduals' (35–8); E. C. Teviotdale, 'Tropers' (39–44); Alicia Corrêa, 'Daily Office Books: Collectars and Breviaries' (45–60); Phillip Pulsiano, 'Psalters' (61–85); Janet L. Nelson and Richard W. Pfaff, 'Pontificals and Benedictionals' (87–98); and Sarah Larratt Keefer, 'Manuals' (99–109).

Patrick McGurk's and Jane Rosenthal's excellent article 'The Anglo-Saxon gospelbooks of Judith, countess of Flanders: their text, make-up and function' details the historical, codicological and literary contexts of its subject (*ASE* 24.251–308). The four eleventh-century manuscripts, written in English Caroline minuscule, are probably representatives of a commission patronized by Judith, countess of Flanders. The gospels of three of the manuscripts are 'almost inexplicably selective', but all of them share certain textual characteristics with gospelbooks copied by Alan Bishop's scribe B. An examination of the manuscripts concerned demonstrates their points and raises issues about the function of the gospelbooks, especially since omission in the texts require some explanation: one suggestion is that 'the books may have been made essentially for symbolic or ceremonial use for members of a household', leading to a less than meticulous copying process. The four codices are carefully described in the Appendix with a fifth manuscript proposed, in Appendix B, as belonging to Judith. In sum, this is a scholarly and thorough discussion revealing numerous fascinating aspects of these gospelbooks and their importance to eleventh-century manuscript studies.

Else Fausbøll reports and edits seven fragments of Ælfric material found in a discarded binding in 'More Ælfric Fragments' (*ES* 76.302–6). These small, eleventh-century fragments, six of which are from one, original leaf are part of the end of Ælfric's *In Die Sancto Pentecosten* and beginning of *Sermo ad Populum in Octavis Pentecosten Dicendus*. The textual order of these fragments parallels that of the homilies in Cambridge, Corpus Christi College, 188. In a very detailed study, 'Two Fragments of an Old English Manuscript in the Library of Corpus Christi College, Cambridge' (*Speculum* 70.502–29), R. I. Page, Mildred Budny and Nicholas Hadgraft discuss the possible provenance and conservation of two fragments in CCCC 557 of *The Legend of the Holy Cross* which may be from the same manuscript as the fragment, University of Kansas, Pryce MS C2:1. These two fragments in Corpus can be dated to the first-half of the eleventh century, and probably attributed to Worcester. The Worcester 'Tremulous' scribe's hand is evident in these fragments, and the glosses are here provided alongside an edition of the Old English text and a selection of variants from the only full extant version in Oxford, Bodleian Library, Bodley 343.

3. Social, Cultural and Intellectual Background

An excellent edition of a neglected text is Jane Stevenson's *The 'Laterculus Malalianus' and the School of Archbishop Theodore*, the fourteenth volume in the CSASE series. The text is an historical exegesis of the life of Christ, possibly by Theodore himself. Stevenson provides an edition of the seventh-century text, composed at Canterbury, stating that the work is representative of the school at Canterbury – an often underestimated centre of learning and literacy functioning at the same time as Bede. Bede's achievements and those of the north-eastern monastic centres often tend to overshadow the south-eastern counterparts. The *Laterculus* is thus of great importance and particularly so since it shows that Greek texts were used in early Anglo-Saxon England. Stevenson outlines the contents of the 25 chapters which include two versions of the life of Christ. The text's date and origin are assessed using internal and circumstantial evidence, and the eastern Mediterranean influences are demonstrated. In examining the nature of the *Laterculus*, its pedagogic tone is emphasized, its chronography contextualized, and its theological and exegetical methodology appraised. Stevenson looks at the sources and language of the text to complete her introductory matter. Detailed manuscript analyses of the two versions are very well done, and, as a whole, this is an important addition to the CSASE series, introducing a little-known text which challenges many assumptions made by scholars about Christian, pre-Alfredian England.

CSASE 15 is *The Text of the Old Testament in Anglo-Saxon England*, the result of sustained and focused research by Richard Marsden. This is an immensely detailed work reflecting meticulous study on the transmission of the Vulgate Old Testament and its uses in the Anglo-Saxon period and in the wider context of the Vulgate history on the Continent. The complexity of the subject is complicated further by the existence of an Old Latin tradition of Old Testament text which sometimes became mixed with the Vulgate version. But Marsden handles the material with clarity and erudition making this volume, to date, the seminal work on these manuscripts. An historical and textual overview of the origin and dissemination of the Vulgate Old Testament opens the volume and this is followed by a wide examination of the use of the biblical books in Anglo-Saxon England. The books of the Old Testament, according to Marsden, circulated as 'handy part-Bibles' throughout the earlier Anglo-Saxon period, and many of these were based on continental exemplars. Later in the period, whole Bibles were more commonly made for practical use. All the surviving manuscripts, 17 of them, dating from the second-half of the sixth century to the middle of the eleventh, and representing between them at least 13 original codices, are closely analysed. The 11 central chapters of the book follow an essentially chronological structure, beginning with 'Early South-umbrian scholars and writers' and ending with 'The late period: Bible fragments' and 'Vernacular evidence for the Old Testament'. Within this broad perspective, Marsden gives close accounts of individual witnesses to the text, such as 'The Ceolfrithian Text', 'The Egerton Codex' and 'The Royal Bible'. Methodologically, this is an in-depth scrutiny of the format of surviving manuscripts and their textual traditions. The manuscripts are evaluated by close reading to determine relationships between the extant texts and the Vulgate versions and the influence on the texts in Anglo-Saxon England from scholars such as Alcuin and Theodulf. Marsden also looks at vernacular versions of the Old Testament and at scriptural citations which appear in Alfredian and Ælfric texts. The *Heptateuch*, for example, is examined for the evidence it might provide about the Latin text(s) from which it derives. The authorship of Ælfric is confirmed, but the existence of two anonymous translators also at work on this text complicate the issue of textual tradition. The majority of the text appears to be faithful to the Vulgate version of the Old Testament, but there are portions where the Latin has been translated idiomatically or with syntactic alteration, or where Old Latin or patristic sources might have been preferred. Specific analyses of Ælfric's text of Genesis and the variants of the Vulgate point primarily to the Theodulfian manuscripts of the latter as the influence; for Ælfric's text of Numbers, it is Alcuinian influence that is determined in the few variants that exist, quite contrary to the text of the anonymous portions of Genesis. In this way and with numerous case-studies, Marsden builds up a detailed picture of the many variant Vulgate traditions used by those translating the *Heptateuch*. Through this work on the vernacular, and through the meticulous work on the Latin texts, Marsden has presented an excellent insight into the transmission and function of the Old Testament in Anglo-Saxon England. He rightly concludes that 'The history of the Old Testament text in Anglo-Saxon England not only reflects the intellectual history of the period but is part of it', a fact that can now be duly recognized.

Marsden continues his important work in his essay, 'Theodore's Bible: The Pentateuch' (236–54) in *Archbishop Theodore: Commemorative Studies on his Life and Influence* (ed. Michael Lapidge) as volume 11 in the CSASE series.

This substantial book, with contributions by leading scholars in their respective fields, contains the following essays: 'The Career of Archbishop Theodore' by Michael Lapidge; Sebastian P. Brock, 'The Syriac Background'; G. Cavallo, 'Theodore of Tarsus and the Greek Culture of His Time'; Thomas F. X. Noble, 'Rome in the Seventh Century'; Henry Chadwick, 'Theodore, the English Church and the Monothelete Controversy'; David N. Dumville, 'The Importation of Mediterranean Manuscripts into Theodore's England'; Martin Brett, 'Theodore and the Latin Canon Law'; T. Charles-Edwards, 'The Penitential of Theodore and the *Iudicia Theodori*'; Carmela Vircillo Franklin, 'Theodore and the *Passio S. Anastasii*'; Jane Stevenson, 'Theodore and the *Laterculus Malalianus*'; C. E. Hohler, 'Theodore and the Liturgy'; Patrick McGurk, 'Theodore's Bible: the Gospels'; Michael Lapidge, 'Theodore and Anglo-Latin Octo-syllabic Verse'; and J. D. Pheifer, 'The Canterbury Bible Glosses: Facts and Problems'.

Eleven papers are contained in *Oswald: Northumbrian King to European Saint* (ed. Clare Stancliffe and Eric Cambridge). These papers were read at or commissioned following the 1992 conference marking the 1350th year of Oswald's death. The introduction by the editors highlights the main areas of Oswald's importance: as a royal saint; as a popular focus of veneration; as a founder of the Northumbrian church; and as the subject of numerous pictorial and iconographical forms. Rosemary Cramp offers a study of 'The Making of Oswald's Northumbria', examining the seventh-century cultural background to Oswald's life. She comments that Oswald's own contribution – by turning to Iona to re-establish Christianity in Northumbria – was perhaps the most crucial, creating a cultural situation, in particular, that led to the later developments of Insular art which was of such outstanding importance. Clare Stancliffe's 'Oswald, "Most Holy and Most Victorious King of the Northumbrians" ' looks at various aspects of Oswald's life and reputation, including Bede's account of the king, Oswald's political achievements, his role as a religious figure, and his legacy. In a second paper, Stancliffe asks 'Where was Oswald killed?'. The usual response is that the king died at Oswestry in Shropshire. Stancliffe re-examines the evidence for such an assumption, concluding that the place – *Maserfelth* – could indeed be Oswestry. Alan Thacker's '*Membra Disjecta*: the Division of the Body and the Diffusion of the Cult', discusses the origins of Oswald's cult focusing on centres where the king was venerated, such as Lindisfarne, Hexham and Echternach. Thacker traces the evolution of the cult into the later Anglo-Saxon period at places such as Winwick and Malpas when Oswald was firmly established as a popular saint. This popularity was due, in part, to his adoption by the Benedictine reformers in the later tenth century. Eric Cambridge writes a lengthy and erudite account of 'Archaeology and the Cult of St Oswald in pre-Conquest Northumbria' providing a useful Appendix of dedications and local archaeological features. David Rollason writes on 'St Oswald in Post-Conquest England' attributing a renewed eleventh- and twelfth-century interest in the saint to the re-discovery of the importance of Bede's *Historia* at that time. Continuing the post-Conquest emphasis, Victoria Tudor studies 'Reginald's *Life of St Oswald*' written at Durham in the second-half of the twelfth century. Richard N. Bailey provides an interesting discussion on the saint's relics, 'St Oswald's Heads', where he traces the various institutions' claims to hold the head of the saint. A skull found at Durham may well have been that of Oswald, making spurious the others' claims. Dagmar Ó Riain-Raedel analyses the question of patronage in the dissemination of the saint's cult on the Continent in 'Edith, Judith, Matilda: The Role of Royal Ladies in the Propagation of the Continental Cult', while Annemiek Jansen looks at 'The Development of the St Oswald Legends on the Continent'. Finally in the volume, Alison Binns gives a detailed list of 'Pre-Reformation Dedications to St Oswald in England and Scotland: A Gazetteer' noting that dedications are to be primarily found in the north of England and the north Midlands. Also on Oswald is Nicholas Orchard's 'The English and German Masses in Honour of St Oswald of Northumbria' (*Archiv für Liturgiewissenschaft* 37.347–58).

For the very late Anglo-Saxon period and the transition into the twelfth century, a valuable scholarly contribution has been made this year with the publication of *Canterbury and the Norman Conquest: Churches, Saints and Scholars 1066–1109* (ed. Richard Eales and Richard Sharpe). This volume contains nine essays offering a reappraisal of this fulcral period in history from a number of different perspectives: ecclesiastical, archaeological, liturgical, art historical, palaeographical and historical. The introduction by Richard Sharpe provides the context and outlines the essays. Sharpe's contribution discusses 'The Setting of St Augustine's Translation, 1091' in which Goscelin's account of the events of the translation are compared with the archaeological evidence yielded by the remains of the tombs of the first six archbishops of Canterbury in the original porticus. Martin Brett examines the events and central characters in Canterbury and Rochester in the 25 years after the Conquest in 'Gundulf and the Cathedral Communities of Canterbury and Rochester'. In 'The Life and Writings of Osbern of Canterbury', Jay Rubenstein discusses the career of Osbern, precentor of Christ Church, who wrote the *Life and Translation of St Elphege* and *Life and Miracles of St Dunstan*, and who allows us insight into the status of Anglo-Saxon saints at Canterbury following the Conquest. Tim Tatton-Brown reports on the excavations of two of Lanfranc's foundations in 'The Beginnings of St Gregory's Priory and St John's Hospital in Canterbury', remarking that St John's is the oldest hospital in Britain. T. A. Heslop, in 'The Canterbury Calendars and the Norman Conquest', analyses the text of Bodleian Library, MS Add. C. 260, the earliest post-Conquest calendar from Christ Church, dated to the 1120s. Heslop scrutinizes the litanies of both Canterbury houses to provide a firmer context for the calendar surviving in Add. C. 260. 'The Bosworth Psalter and St Augustine's Missal' by Nicholas Orchard attributes the psalter, London, British Library, MS Add. 37517 to pre-Conquest St Augustine's; the Missal, CCCC 270, is the earliest of Lanfranc's texts of the Bec sacramentary which also preserves masses for St Augustine's saints. Richard Gameson's 'English Manuscript Art in the Late Eleventh Century: Canterbury and its Context', is a lengthy and trenchant account of decoration in Canterbury manuscripts. In an important essay, Teresa Webber questions whether a housestyle really existed in 'Script and Manuscript Production at Christ Church, Canterbury, after the Norman Conquest', focusing on Eadmer and his writings, and scribes who wrote at approximately the same period as him. The final essay, 'The Historical Tradition of St Augustine's Abbey, Canterbury', by Richard Emms centres on diplomatic material and on notable historians such as Goscelin, Sprott and William Thorne, showing their importance for recreating post-Conquest history in Canterbury.

In an extensive and detailed study with wide-reaching implications for scholars' views of Anglo-Saxon legal practices, Alan Kennedy examines 'Law and litigation in the *Libellus Æthelwoldi episcopi*' (*ASE* 24.131–83). Although the *Libellus* is a twelfth-century product, Kennedy demonstrates through a careful analysis how rich a source for revealing Anglo-Saxon legal practices the work is. He considers the Old English sources (*c.*990) used in the compilation of the *Libellus*, in particular, in its 18 out of 25 chapters which concern monastic legislation. Commenting on the neglect of this important text, Kennedy raised issues about the 'Courts and Court-Holders' of late tenth-century England with their 'fluid and intermeshed administrative structures', of the centrality of Ealdorman Byrhtnoth in Cambridgeshire's legislative system, and of the relationship between the secular and ecclesiastical judiciary. He shows in 'Issues and Procedures' that the primary focus of the *Libellus* is land and disputes about land ownership which he details with case evidence. In his section on 'Judgement', current views on who made the laws in Anglo-Saxon England are analysed in the light of the *Libellus* where 'one looks in vain ... for much sense of a legal order defined by principles and rules'. The amount of perceptive reading and wide knowledge shown throughout this essay makes it a rich source of information for Anglo-Saxon historians and legal scholars; its lucid style also makes it accessible to a more general audience. The twelfth-century Rochester compilation, the *Textus Roffensis*, is the focus of Patrick Wormald's '*Laga Edwardi*: The *Textus Roffensis* and Its Context' (*Anglo-Norman Studies* 17.243–66). Catherine Cubitt's *Anglo-Saxon Church Councils c.650–c.850* is reviewed in Chapter 1, section 7 above.

Nicholas Orchard's 'An Anglo-Saxon mass for St Willibrord and its later liturgical uses' (*ASE* 24.1–10) traces the manuscript occurrences of this saint's mass from the original Echternach manuscript to the text adapted for St Birinus contained in the 'Missal of Robert of Jumièges' created in either Peterborough or Ely in the first-quarter of the eleventh century, and in the 'New Minster Missal' written at the beginning of the eleventh century at Winchester. In Anglo-Saxon England and Northern France, this mass was also adapted for numerous other saints. It is similar in style to the prayers composed by Alcuin for St Martin, and Orchard proposes that the mass for Willibrord was actually written by Alcuin to accompany his *vita* of the saint, and was subsequently disseminated and re-used by religious houses on the continent and in Anglo-Saxon England.

Later missionary activity is the focus of two studies by Lesley Abrams. In the first, Abrams painstakingly traces the available evidence of 'The Anglo-Saxons and the Christianization of Scandinavia' (*ASE* 24.213–44) though there is not a substantial amount of documentation surviving; thus it is difficult for a clear picture of how the English church was involved in the conversion of the Scandinavians to emerge. This well-researched essay nevertheless shows how important the Anglo-Saxon church was in its activity in Europe and Scandinavia and includes a great deal of information on the relationship between England and Northern Europe in the period. Abrams continues her research on missionary activity in this late period in 'Eleventh-Century Missions and the Early Stages of Ecclesiastical Organisation in Scandinavia' (*Anglo-Norman Studies* 17.21–40).

4. Literature: General

The Cambridge Studies in Anglo-Saxon England series goes from strength to strength. This year sees the publication of two important volumes for Old English poetry: Peter Clemoes's *Interactions of Thought and Language in Old English Poetry* which will be reviewed in *YWES* 77, and Carole Braun Pasternack's *The Textuality of Old English Poetry*. This volume is billed in the jacket blurb as a 'groundbreaking study [which] theorizes how Old English poetry functioned for readers of tenth-century manuscripts' and it is a work which combines (perhaps paradoxically) formalist and post-Structuralist analyses, together with an intertextual examination. While this sounds rather daunting, Pasternack treats her subject with great clarity of expression and with insight. It is a thought-provoking study which develops the work of scholars such as Katherine O'Brien O'Keeffe and John Miles Foley. The first chapter essentially sets the scene, providing a sound intellectual background for the rest of the book: the reappraisal of the poetic corpus by investigating fully the manuscript context of the texts, the formulaic nature of the poetic vocabulary and its aural structure. Such texts when considered in these ways are 'inscribed'. Each performance, copying or reading of the poetic texts becomes, in essence, its own poem – an individual response working through conventions and traditions. Based on this premise, that Old English poems are appropriated by each teller, scribe or reader, Pasternack shows that Old English verse is based not on the notion of the author, but rather of tradition. The reader's act in reading aloud effectively makes them a poet by proxy. The detail of this act of re-composition is via aural patterns determining syntactic, thematic or verbal parallels, which create the poem's structure and coherence. These methods of analysis are developed by practical example in the subsequent four chapters: 'The Polyphony of *The Wanderer*'; 'Rhythm, repetition, and traditional expression'; 'The designs of syntax, modes of thought, and the author question'; and 'Borders and time'. Among the poems discussed in chapters three to five are *Beowulf*, *The Ascension*, *Elene*, *Phoenix*, *Widsith*, *Andreas*, *Exodus*, *Christ and Satan*, *The Seafarer*, *Genesis* and others. The final chapter, 'Conditions of coherence' concentrates on the physical aspects of the texts in their codicological settings, stressing the need for the reader to recognize conventional structures in order to form discrete units.

While, then, this is a broad and interesting survey of the poetic texts and their reception by readers, it has to be wondered who these readers were in the Anglo-Saxon period. The processes of readerly composition described by Pasternack seem complex, and while they may be somewhere near to the ways in which these poems were read, there appears too little substantial evidence to be sure. In particular, it appears that here Pasternack has in mind not a transcendental, general reader, but very much an historically constructed one (one, who at that, seems more late twentieth century than tenth). Quite who this might be is left unsaid, while this issue is surely of the most fundamental importance.

Also on literacy, is this year's Toller Memorial Lecture, 'The Dynamics of Literacy in Anglo-Saxon England (*BJRL* 77.i.109–42) by George Hardin Brown. This is a sound summary of the current state of scholarship focusing on literacy. Brown explores the meaning and practices of literacy by analysing how the skills of reading and writing were acquired by the minority. Brown treats monastic education first: in order to access the word of God, monks would have had to learn Latin in the earliest centuries; this would be achieved by use of glossed manuscripts in the classroom. Alfred's educational reforms herald a second stage: that of vernacular literacy; and the Benedictine Reform, a third, the co-existence of Latin and vernacular literacy among the few. The second part of Brown's study focuses on the texts used for education, namely, the Psalter, manuscripts of which and the uses of which are detailed; grammars; the prose texts of Ælfric and Wulfstan; and various Latin pedagogic texts.

Bruce Mitchell's *An Invitation to Old English and Anglo-Saxon England* is a splendid textbook aimed at the student and the non-specialist. The friendly tone of the book amply justifies the 'Invitation' of the title: Mitchell compares his volume to a meal with a wide and varied menu and numerous courses, or a garden rich in literary flowers. An introduction places Old English in its historical linguistic context offering areas of comparison with Present-day English to ease the readers into the language. This is followed by a useful section on spelling, pronunciation and punctuation where the importance of editorial procedures are highlighted, and light editorial intervention in the manuscript text advocated. A large section on Old English grammar and syntax is disguised under the relatively friendly title 'Other differences: Old and Modern English'. This is no fierce and daunting Mitchell and Robinson language introduction, but is much more accessible, though basic terms such as 'dative', when provided as here with the alternative 'indirect object', will still baffle British undergraduates whose general level of language analysis in their first year extends to 'noun: a naming word'. The bulk of this volume is taken up with the subsequent 'An Introduction to Anglo-Saxon England' and 'The Garden of Old English Literature'. The first of these is subdivided into literature, history, archaeology, place-names, life in the Heroic Society and the impact of Christianity. These are thematically arranged discussions with relevant extracts from texts: 'Archaeology', for example, includes an introduction to the importance of weapons and provides snippets of *Beowulf* to reinforce the discursive detail and to show how literature and society are closely inter-related. In 'The Impact of Christianity', the history of the period is exemplified with excerpts from Ælfric, Alfred's bequest to Shaftesbury, and *Solomon and Saturn*. In this way, Mitchell integrates the literature into the history in a way which will make the implications of the literature the greater and provide an immediacy to it which is not usual in an independently edited text. Such an arrangement will also permit traditional Old English courses to be taught thematically giving a more rounded view than can be gained from translating any text word by word from start to finish. 'The Garden of Literature' gives more extensive extracts from texts, divided into prose and poetry sections. Here, we see the familiar selections from Alfred's programme of translation, from Bede, and from Ælfric, but Mitchell also includes less common texts: medical, prognosticatory, diplomatic and epistolary. These selections are more representational of Old English literature than the usual textbooks tend to be. The same is also true of the poetry which includes portions of *Beowulf*, *The Seafarer* and riddles, but also *Exodus*, *Genesis*, charms and *Solomon and Saturn*. Again, as tasters, these give a good overview of the extant literature. The major disadvantage to the inclusion of so many texts is the short length of some of the extracts: *The Wife's Lament*, for example, is only partially included, and lines 92–110 of *The Wanderer* provide the excerpt. Constraints of space will always be a problem for a publisher wishing to maintain an affordable price, and these texts are an appropriate compromise. Paradigms ('for those who wish them'!), a bibliography, chronology, and glossary complete this book which will make an excellent introductory coursebook for undergraduate modules, as well as a good read for the generalist.

BJRL 77.iii contains the proceedings of the second G. L. Brook Symposium held at the University of Manchester in 1993, *The Bible and Early English Literature from the Beginnings to 1500*. This excellent volume (ed. A. R. Rumble, S. C. Weinberg, J. J. Anderson and G. R. Owen-Crocker) contains seven essays of relevance to this chapter, the majority of which are dealt with in the appropriate sections. Here, M. R. Godden's essay, 'The Trouble with Sodom: literary responses to biblical sexuality' (97–119) can be covered. Godden looks at the reception of the story of Lot, the angels and Lot's daughters from Genesis 19, in the Anglo-Saxon period and later. Alcuin, for example, compared the illicit sex of the English in the eighth century to that illustrated by the Sodomites; Ælfric, in his translation of the *Heptateuch*, skips over what happened at Sodom in his horror at explicating the Old Testament narrative, while he nevertheless factually recounts Lot's incest with his daughters. In *Genesis A*, Sodom is partially conceived of as a male and female homosexual society, and the incest episode is relatively emphasized by the poet with little sense of outrage or embarrassment. Godden thus links these literary references to the biblical story to what they can tell us about authorial concerns at particular times in the period.

In a fascinating study, Hugh Magennis shows how the theme of treachery incorporated into many Anglo-Saxon texts sometimes 'reflects the interests of the real world' in 'Treatments of treachery and betrayal in Anglo-Saxon texts' (*ES* 76.1–19). He has also found that the emphasis and treatment of betrayal within texts is, among other things, dependent on the text's period of composition. In Bede's *Historia* and the earlier portions of the *Chronicle*, for instance, treachery is not so much an issue relevant to contemporary society; rather, it is depicted as a characteristic of pagans and enemies of the Anglo-Saxons in general. In literature, treachery derives in part from a sense of the Germanic past and is superimposed on biblical texts such as *Genesis A*, *Exodus* and *The Dream of the Rood*. In later texts of the second-half of the tenth century and eleventh century, 'treachery is seen not primarily as something to be associated with "other people" but is perceived as infecting Anglo-Saxon society and institutions'. Magennis demonstrates this with examples from Wulfstan, Ælfric, *The Battle of Maldon*, the later law-codes and various saints' lives. Interestingly, his discussion of the theme in *Beowulf* suggests that the poem fits appropriately into the category of later rather than earlier treatments of betrayal. Magennis also writes on issues of sexuality in ' "No Sex Please, We're Anglo-Saxons?": Attitudes to Sexuality in Old English Prose and Poetry' (*LeedsSE* 26.127).

Anita Riedinger looks at the concept of ' "Home" in Old English Poetry' (*NM* 96.51–9) focusing particularly on *Exodus*, *The Battle of Maldon*, *Beowulf*, *The Fates of the Apostles*, *Genesis A*, Riddle 29, *The Wife's Lament*, *Andreas*, *Guthlac* and other poems. She examines the various terms for 'home' to show that some refer to a homeland (e.g. *eðel*), some an actual building (*reced*), and others, the family (*cnost*). The use of these words in their poetic contexts helps to provide definitions of momentous aspects in life such as birth, death and victory.

Maria Josè Mora, in 'The Invention of the Old English Elegy' (*ES* 76.129–39), trenchantly questions the generic classification of the elegies, particularly on the grounds of 'feeling' that the poems belong together, attributing such modern notions of generic grouping to scholars in the nineteenth century, perpetuated by twentieth-century Anglo-Saxonists.

E. G. Stanley's 'Old English = "Anglo Saxon": the modern sense for the language ... together with notes on how the OED treats such terms' (*N&Q* 42.168–73) traces the use of the term 'Old English' from its earliest occurrence, to Matthew Parker's usage and that of William Camden. John Strype used the term to refer to the language of the Anglo-Saxons in 1711 in his *Life and Acts of Matthew Parker*. The term's use in the *OED* is also discussed. In 'Old English = "Anglo-Saxon": William Lambarde's Use in 1576' (*N&Q* 42.437), Stanley notes the appearance of a marginal note, 'the olde Englishe tongue' for 'the Saxon speach' in *Lambarde's Perambulation of Kent* (1576).

Mark Atherton is concerned with 'Grasping Sentences as Wholes in Henry Sweet's Idea of Language Study in the Early Middle Ages' (*NM* 96.177–85). Atherton examines Sweet's principle of 'synthesis' in acquiring language skills: the spoken sentence as opposed to the unit of the word. Sweet, it appears, gained his knowledge of this method of language learning from his perception of the way in which medieval scholars worked. It seems that the latter part of Alfred's translation of the *Pastoral Care* as 'sometimes word for word and sometimes sentence for sentence' influenced Sweet, who as Atherton points out, can be regarded as a pioneer of education like his regal predecessor.

C. P. Biggam's 'Sociolinguistic aspects of Old English colour lexemes' (*ASE* 24.51–65) looks specifically at the use of colour vocabulary in a number of different Old English texts to determine whether diction reflects a particular audience and authorial intention. Biggam divides colour into 'basic, learned, poetic, specialized, and popular', and investigates examples of each in their contexts and immediate collocations, in order to show that social information can be gleaned from the use of particular colour lexemes within particular texts.

5. The Exeter Book

Phillip Pulsiano's 'Spiritual Despair in *Resignation* B' (*Neophil* 79.155–61) argues that the penitential psalms (particularly Psalms 142 and 141) are more influential for a reading of the text than has previously been recognized. Instead of seeking to find a univocal theme, Pulsiano demonstrates that the two sections of *Resignation*, *A* and *B* (lines 1–69 and 70–118 respectively), might more appropriately be individually entitled 'The Penitent's Prayer' and 'The Penitent's Lament'. The influence of the Psalms, presumably well known to the poem's audience, would have facilitated their interpretation of the text in this light: *Resignation B* shows an 'anti-type of the penitent, one who is an unwitting exile from spiritual understanding', edifying thereby by means of negative example.

In 'A Woman's Loss and Lamentation: Heledd's Song and *The Wife's Lament*' (*Neophil* 79.147–54), Dorothy Ann Bray offers a comparative analysis of these examples of early Welsh and Old English monologues which show 'the expression of women's lamentation in those societies which both valorized heroic ideals'. The two poems, Bray suggests, may be women's utterances of personal despair spoken within the background of some political conflict, and within the context of a larger, non-extant, cycle of works.

Peter Orton analyses the syntax and accidence of '*Juliana* 719: þe þis gied wræce' (*N&Q* 42.421–3). His main concern is to determine the possible meanings of *wræce*. He suggests that the antecedent of *þe þis gied wræce* is *ic* and not *gehwone* so that the translation would read 'I, who am uttering this story, pray ... '.

Paul Cavill, in 'Biblical realignment of a maxim in the Old English *Phoenix*, (lines 355b–60) (*BJRL* 77.iii.193–8), analyses lines 355b–60 of the text within the context of the maxim's conventional modes of expression: here, '*x ana x*' (as in 'God ana wat' in line 355b of *The Phoenix*). The poet uses this maxim for a number of purposes: to bring 'a sense of wonder' to the poem; to refer to eschatalogical issues; to attribute all knowledge of mortality to God; and to create a link between the phoenix, Christ and the Christian. As such, the maxim is particularly appropriate in this context, enhancing 'the spiritual message and effectiveness of the poem'. Mark Griffith's 'Old English *bræd*, 'flesh': a ghost form' (*N&Q* 42.7–8) queries the unique form of *bræd* in *The Phoenix*, lincs 240–2, which has previously been translated as 'burnt' or 'incinerated flesh'. He suggests it may be the past participle of *brædan*: thus, 'grown'.

Convincingly, Collete Stévanovitch suggests that the solution to riddle 70A, offered previously as 'shepherd's pipe', 'shuttle', 'harp' and 'lyre', may be 'nose' in 'Exeter Book Riddle 70A: Nose?' (*N&Q* 42.8–10). Andrew Breeze, in 'Old English *Gop* "Servant" in Riddle 49: Old Irish *Gop* "Snout" ' (*Neophil* 79.671–3), regards that Old English use of *gop* as a loan from Irish. This may therefore provide evidence for the localization of the origin of riddle 49 to Northumbria. Keith P. Taylor looks at riddle 55 in 'Mazers, Mead and the Wolf's-head Tree: a Reconsideration of Old English Riddle 55' (*JEGP* 94.497– 512), and Roberta Dewa considers 'The Runic Riddles of the Exeter Book: Language Games and Anglo-Saxon Scholarship', *Nottingham Medieval Studies* 39.26–36.

Hyeree Kim focuses on the textual refrain 'þæs ofereode, þisses swa mæg' in 'On the Genitive of the Anglo-Saxon Poem *Deor*' (*NM* 96.351–9) to propose, using comparative evidence, that the genitive is used as an object of *ofergan*.

6. The Poems of the Vercelli Book

There are a small number of articles on the poems of the Vercelli Book this year (but see also section 4 above): on the *The Dream of the Rood*, Emma B. Hawkins discusses 'Gender, Language, and Power in *The Dream of the Rood*' (*W&Lang* 18.2.33–6); and on *Andreas*, John Miles Foley writes on 'The Poet's Self-Interruption in *Andreas*' while Brian Shaw examines 'Translation and Transformation in *Andreas*'. These two papers are included in M. J. Toswell, ed., *Prosody and Poetics in the Early Middle Ages: Essays in Honour of C. B.*

Hieatt (UTorP), but not made available for review in time for inclusion this year.

7. The Junius Manuscript

J.-A. George examines 'Repentance and Retribution: The use of the book of Daniel in Old and Middle English Texts' (*BJRL* 77.iii.177–92). George analyses the use of the Daniel story in the Old English *Daniel* and Middle English *Susannah* to show certain shared characteristics in treatment: those of sin and repentance and the relationship between them. Daniel's speech at lines 585–92 in the Old English poem can be placed in the context of penitential literature, focusing as it does on the need to make amends for sin and live in charity. Likewise, Nebuchadnezzar's preaching at lines 645–51 can be seen in the light of one who has sinned and publicly confessed. George offers an interesting comparison of this role of the king by looking at similar aspects in the Old English poetic saints' lives.

Also in *BJRL* 77.iii. (141–64), is Richard Marsden's 'The Death of the Messenger: the "spelboda" in the Old English *Exodus*'. Marsden examines line 14a of the poem, 'spelbodan [eac]', an expansion on the Vulgate narration which states that not one of the Egyptians survived alive after the closing of the Red Sea. Citing evidence from Judith, Marsden suggests that *spelbodan* ought to be treated as a singular noun ('messenger'). This same noun is used in Psalm 105:11 in the Paris Psalter: 'and heora feondas flod adrencte, þæt þæra æfre ne com an spelboda', and Marsden goes on to analyse in some detail knowledge of the Old English psalms in Anglo-Saxon England, the influence of them on *Exodus*, and the significance of *spelboda* to the contemporary audience; that is, as one who would recite notable deeds. Thus, the Old English poet celebrates the living warrior nation he is part of, consigning the Egyptians firmly to hell since their regenerative *spelboda* has perished along with their army.

In '*Exodus* 362–446 and the Book of Wisdom' (*N&Q* 42.4–7), Hugh Fogarty discusses the interpretative difficulties of the Noah/Abraham digression and the fruitfulness of examining this portion of the text in the light of the book of Wisdom. Fogarty proposes that the typology linking this digression to the rest of the poem is that of judgement and eschatology as a whole, as influenced by chapters nine and ten of Wisdom.

8. The *Beowulf* Manuscript

Andy Orchard's *Pride and Prodigies: Studies in the Monsters of the Beowulf-Manuscript* is the most significant volume on this manuscript to be published in a very long time. It covers an extensive amount of related material from classical and patristic literature, to heroic texts. It is both detailed and readable, and, perhaps most importantly, it reminds *Beowulf* scholars about the manuscript context in which that poem belongs. The work consists of six studies which 'seek to consider the motivation and background to the compilation of the *Beowulf*-manuscript' with particular reference to the monsters who form a central part of each of the texts (*Beowulf*, *Judith*, *The*

Passion of St Christopher, The Wonders of the East and *The Letter of Alexander to Aristotle*) and to the literary tradition informing them. The introductory chapter, 'The *Beowulf*-manuscript', is a methodical overview of the manuscript and its Anglo-Saxon texts: *Judith*, for example, represents the polarization of the heroine and her victim; *St Christopher* is about similar polarizations and is seen to parallel some of *Judith*'s themes and contrasts. These concerns with 'monsters, and with the activities of mighty pagan men' are further seen in *The Wonders of the East* where conflict between the worlds of monsters and men is stressed. These links between the central aspects of the texts are investigated in relation to *Beowulf* and *The Letter of Alexander to Aristotle* in Chapter 2, 'Psychology and Physicality: The Monsters of *Beowulf*'. Here, Orchard looks at specific features of both texts that reflect their concern with the conflict of monstrous and human worlds: *Beowulf* shows a type of liminality in the description of the scene where the hero and monster meet: neither character is clearly visible or defined. In *Alexander to Aristotle*, certain types of monsters (water-monsters, for example) are paralleled. Both Alexander and Beowulf are 'monster-slaying heroes', a characterization that casts them in the mould of classical and biblical predecessors. Biblical and patristic sources are thus considered in Chapter 3, 'The Kin of Cain', while Chapter 4 considers the importance of the *Liber Monstrorum* in the transmission of legends of monsters. Parallels are distinguished between the *Liber* and the Old English texts of the *Beowulf*-manuscript (e.g. the shining eyes of Grendel and those of the monstrous men in the *Liber*). This detailed and thought-provoking study leads directly into a discussion of monster-slaying men, focusing on Alexander in Chapter 5, 'The Alexander-Legend in Anglo-Saxon England'. The two main traditions of the Alexander legend, highlighting either the 'pride' or the 'prodigies' of the subject, were evident in Anglo-Saxon England as well as in other literatures. The Old English text emphasizes the negative aspects of Alexander, his pride and cruelty, and translates its source with freedom sometimes 'surpassing the original in style and effect' to produce an immediate narrative. The depiction of Alexander is at once that of powerful hero, seeking glory, and a negative example of pride and mortality for a Christian audience. Orchard points out that this depiction is immediately followed by the opening lines of *Beowulf* on the succeeding page and must surely have provided a telling manuscript context (and scholars will surely be thankful to Orchard for putting *Beowulf* back into its manuscript context). This theme of the monster-slayer is continued in Chapter 6, 'Grettir and Grendel Again', which compares the *Grettis saga Asmundarsonar* and *Beowulf*, focusing on the shared episodes, the 'common narrative paradigm'. A 'Postscript' summarizes the essays emphasizing that all the texts, while stressing battles with monsters and the dangers of pride, 'are concerned with the relationship between pagan past and Christian present, and with the tension between an age which extolled heroic glory and an age in which vainglory was condemned'. This is a valuable reminder to scholars of the importance of seeing texts where they properly belong – within their manuscript contexts – and it develops an argument that shows remarkable breadth and knowledge. The book's uses are varied, and made the more so by the inclusion in an Appendix of the Latin, Old English and modern translations of *The Wonders of the East* and *The Letter of Alexander to Aristotle*. A Latin text of the *Liber Monstrorum* is also provided.

Francelia Mason Clark's book, *Theme in Oral Epic and in Beowulf*, focuses on theme as it is employed by scholars of oral literature to show how traditional narratives extend across literatures. She compares *The Song of Bagdad* and *Beowulf* in five chapters, 'Approaching Comparison', 'The Basic Contrasts', 'Scenes Comparable in Theory', 'Aesthetics and the Recurring Subject', and 'Conclusions: Theme in Oral Epic and in *Beowulf*'. She concurs with Lord's view that 'the *Beowulf* poet hypothesized an oral-traditional poet who in later years lives in a monastery', adding that 'However he did it, the *Beowulf* poet composed within a poetic narrative tradition that all descendant signs suggest was itself variable. It is in either medium [oral or written] that the *Beowulf* poet stands in the Old English literature remaining to us as an individual master, poet of rich language in our only heroic, reflective, Christian, pagan-honoring narrative'. An Appendix tabulates characteristics of the themes of Funeral Pyres, Beowulf's Use of Swords, and Monarch's Rewards in *Beowulf*. A second volume published this year on oral literature is John Miles Foley's *The Singer of Tales in Performance* (IndUP) (which was not seen for review).

Garland continues its useful series on Basic Readings in Anglo-Saxon England with the publication of volume 1 in paperback, *'Beowulf': Basic Readings* (ed. Peter S. Baker). Included in this are previously printed and newly commissioned essays covering a wide range of perspectives from the metrical to gender studies, and the dating issue. Those new or revised essays included in this invaluable book are: Fred C. Robinson, 'Elements of the Marvellous in the Characterization of Beowulf: a Reconsideration of the Textual Evidence'; Kevin S. Kiernan's revised essay, 'The Legacy of Wiglaf: Saving a Wounded *Beowulf*'; Mary Blockley and Thomas Cable on 'Kuhn's Laws: Old English Poetry, and the New Philology'; Roy Michael Liuzza, 'On the Dating of *Beowulf*'; and Gillian R. Overing's revised 'The Women of *Beowulf*: a Context for Interpretation'.

Michael Alexander has published *Beowulf* for the Penguin Classics series, but this is not, as one might expect, a translation. Instead, it is an edition of the poem with a brief scholarly introduction, glossary of proper names and notes on manuscript readings, and *The Tale of Finnsburh*. The edition is presented with an *en-face* glossary and translation or explanatory notes at the foot of the page. The price of this volume makes it readily purchasable but one wonders at whom it is aimed. Alexander's statement of perceived audience 'presupposes a reader with some sense of grammar, and with access to an Old English grammar. Such a reader, a persistent person, will become familiar with common accidence . . . [the glosses] should enable a student to make out the sense, and to begin to make a translation'. This would suggest that the edition is intended for students studying *Beowulf* having already completed an introductory course in Old English. The cheap price certainly makes it welcome from that viewpoint, but this edition is in competition with a number of other, recently published, affordable editions (*YWES* 75.111–12). What makes this edition both easy and difficult to use from a student viewpoint, is that the glossary only includes headwords in, for example, the nominative or inflectional form. One example of this policy is lines 694–5: 'ac hie hæfdon gefrunen, þæt hie ær to fela micles / in þæm win-sele wæl-deað fornam' glossed *ac* 'but', *gefrignan* 'learn', *ær* 'previously', *to* 'too', *fela* 'many', *micles* 'far', *win-sele* 'wine-hall', *wæl-deað* 'sudden death', *forniman* 'take away'. This works for a literal translation as long as the students can recognize tense but a literal translation obviously requires further modification to make good, modern English. It is also so completely glossed that it virtually becomes a translation in its own right.

Johann Köberl, in 'Referential Ambiguity as a Structuring Principle in *Beowulf*' (*Neophil* 79.481–95), argues that ambivalences abound in *Beowulf* often as a result of the use of particular pronouns or nominal structures. By use of textual examples – such as lines 113–15 and 166b–70 – Köberl illustrates that recognition of referential ambiguity which links important textual aspects and creates analogies between referents provides an extra dimension to a reading of the text.

David Gould proposes 'A new approach to Old English meter based on an analysis of formulaic language' (*Neophil* 79.653–9) with reference to *Beowulf*. He discovers, through a practical analysis, that the meter depends on syncopation: 'the imposition of one rhythm upon another'. He deduces that Old English meter is accentual and concentrates his discussion on formulaic language and relative stress patterns to show this. The latter can be demonstrated through examination of the *Beowulf*-poet's use of compound words. Focusing on numerous lines, Gould claims that 'Many of the half-lines in Old English poetry are synthesized out of two elements, one which fulfils the metrical and alliterative requirements of the half-line, and the other, consisting mostly of unstressed monosyllables, which may be considered extrametrical' causing the effect of syncopation. Mary Blockley, meanwhile, considers B-type and A3 verses and the stress placed on the final syllable of these verse types, as well as the differences between the off-verses in 'Klaeber's Relineations of *Beowulf* and verses ending in words without categorical stress' (*RES* 46.321–32). In her discussion of A3 off-verses followed by B-type on-verses, Blockley proposes and illustrates that: 'When the first three syllables of an on-verse are not categorically stressed, and when the stressed syllable of a finite verb falls on the fourth or subsequent syllable, that verse will be an A3 and will end with that verb'. It is in this light that Blockley examines and criticises some of Klaeber's relineations of *Beowulf* in the third edition of his work. Seiichi Suzuki's 'In defense of resolution as a metrical principle in the meter of *Beowulf*' (*ES* 76.2–33) provides a reappraisal of the assumptions upon which discussions of resolution such as Hoover's, Keyser's and Obst's are based. By using examples from *Beowulf*, Suzuki rejects the proposition of obligatory resolution, and instead suggests that 'resolution constitutes a significant metrical principle' and that on 'applicability of resolution crucially depends the particular metrical contexts involved'. Suzuki has also written on 'Anacrusis in the Meter of *Beowulf*' in *SP* 92.141–63.

Alfred Bammesberger discusses the editorial decision to transfer *ond* from its manuscript reading before *þes* in line 432a to the beginning of 431b in *Beowulf*. ('A textual note on *Beowulf* 431–432', *ES* 76.297–301.) This transference, Bammesberger argues, alters Beowulf's claim to cleanse Heorot alone to one where he will do the job with others. The various emendations offered by editors are explored, but Bammesberger holds firm in favour of the manuscript reading and justifies his case with a syntactic and semantic explanation. Bammesberger has also written on 'Beowulf's Descent into Grendel's Mere' (*NM* 96.225–7) in which he questions the clausal interpretation of lines 1494b–96 where Beowulf is usually regarded as having stayed under water for an incredible length of time. In his reading, Bammesberger regards line 1496 as dependent on 1494b–95a which thus obviates the superhuman element of Beowulf's feat; the translation would thus be 'the surging water received the warrior – then it was daytime –, before he could make out the bottom of the mere'.

Close reading is also M. S. Griffith's method in 'Some difficulties in *Beowulf*, lines 874–902: Sigemund reconsidered' (*ASE* 24.11–41). Here, Griffith reassesses the relationship between Beowulf and Sigemund in these lines. Commenting on the interpretative difficulties of the passage for the modern reader, Griffith questions how easily *Beowulf*'s contemporary audience would have understood the Sigemund allusions: particular descriptive phrases (such as 'uncuþes fela' at line 876b and 'eam his nefan' at line 881a) are closely examined within the poetic, and in a wider literary, context. The results of this analysis are important, showing that the Sigemund digression is more complex and opaque than is generally recognized. It appears to be a deliberate attempt by the Christian poet to make ambivalent and 'blurred' the depiction of Sigemund and his relationship with Beowulf.

I have not seen the following: Alan Bliss, *The Scansion of Beowulf* (ed. Peter J. Lucas) and published as *Old English Newsletter*, Subsidia 22 by Kalamazoo: Medieval Institute, Western Michigan University.

On *Judith*, Hugh Magennis looks at 'Contrasting narrative emphases in the Old English poem *Judith* and Ælfric's paraphrase of the book of Judith' (*NM* 69.61–6). He hypothesizes about the authorial interest behind the composition of each text, and the different audience receptions. *Judith*, for example, operates through oppositions celebrating the heroine's defeat of hostile forces, while Ælfric highlights Judith's chastity and focuses in the main on Holofernes's evil nature rather than Judith's behaviour. The homiletic passage in Ælfric's version of the narrative is clearly aimed at a specific audience: nuns. The different interpretations thus reveal the varied uses to which such received texts could be put in Anglo-Saxon England.

9. Other Poems

L. C. Weston situates the metrical charms concerning childbirth within the context of the female voice which shows knowledge of healing practices in 'Women's Medicine, Women's Magic: The Old English Metrical Childbirth Charms' (*MP* 92.279–93). In terms of the texts of the *Leechbook* and *Lacnunga*, Weston views the codices as essentially products of a male textual tradition with the exception of these childbirth charms. She examines, in a somewhat disjointed argument, the role of women in magical practice and ritual, and discusses, in some detail, the charms themselves to show how they represent the self-healing of the female speaker.

Peter J. Lucas discusses 'The *Metrical Epilogue* to *the Alfredian Pastoral Care*: a postscript from Junius' (*ASE* 24.43–50). Lucas examines the manuscripts of this text and the sixteenth- and seventeenth-century versions of it. Junius's version in Oxford, Bodleian Library, Junius 53, using as its base text, London, British Library, Cotton Tiberius B.xi, is an important witness to the *Metrical Epilogue*, and is an aspect of the Old English text not previously investigated. Lucas carefully scrutinizes the extant manuscript texts and their page layouts along with Junius's transcription methods to demonstrate that Junius paid particular attention to verse lineation when copying from the Anglo-Saxon manuscripts.

Charles Abbott Conway's 'Structure and Idea in *Cædmon's Hymn*' (*NM* 69.39–50) concerns itself with the 'architecture' of the poem to show its tripartite revelation of the creation. This reflects, within the context of Bede's work, 'a grounding in theological and philosophical ideas' demonstrable through the use of the temporal adverbs in the Old English, *ærist*, *þa*, and *æfter*, which exemplify the logical progression of God's creation, and the dynamic of the poem itself.

Two articles on *The Battle of Maldon* have come to my attention: Paul Cavill's 'Interpretation of *The Battle of Maldon*, lines 84–90: A Review and Reassessment' (*SN* 67.149–64) and Margaret A. L. Locherbie-Cameron's 'Some things the *Maldon* poet did not say' (*Parergon* 13.1.69–80).

10. Prose

Peter S. Baker and Michael Lapidge's comprehensive and definitive new edition of *Byrhtferth's Enchiridion* in the EETS series is to be warmly welcomed. It has a detailed introduction, an accessible editing policy (with, unusually for EETS, an *en-face* translation), and a thorough and very helpful commentary. The introduction includes a wealth of information about the ecclesiastical and cultural background in which Byrhtferth operated: Ramsey in the time of Abbo of Fleury's visit in the years 985–7, and in the succeeding decades. Byrhtferth's works are outlined and discussed: his Computus, the *Enchiridion* (of *c*.1010–12), the *Vitae S. Oswaldi* and *Ecgwini*, early portions of the *Historia regum* and other Latin texts. A very full examination of the workings and history of Computus gives an excellent insight into the text and its complex workings; and manuscripts of Byrhtferth's Computus and related texts are scrutinized to place Byrhtferth's in context. Sources of the *Enchiridion* focus on the monastic, pedagogic, computistical and patristic. The language of the text is late West Saxon, though the lexis is particularly interesting since it shows a proclivity for gloss-type words. An Appendix includes a reconstructed Computus to allow for close comparison with Byrhtferth's text, and, as a whole, this is a useful, scholarly and very thorough edition.

A number of essays in the *BJRL* special volume on 'The Bible and Early English Literature from the Beginnings to 1500' (see above, section 4) concern themselves with prose texts. Barbara Raw writes on 'Verbal icons in late Old English' (121–39) where she looks at the typological interpretation of Old Testament figures and what they prefigured in the New Testament to show how important such types were to Ælfric in his emphasis on biblical unity, and man's unity with God. Raw comments upon *De fide Catholica*, the Feast of the Holy Innocents, and a number of other homilies and treatises of Ælfric drawing out Ælfric's repeated emphasis on Christ's unifying of the Old and New law, and of the importance of Old Testament prophecy and signs to Christian belief. Stuart Lee reappraises the evidence for sourcing Ælfric's Maccabees in 'Ælfric's treatment of source material in his homily on the books of the Maccabees' (165–76). Lee shows that the Vulgate and the 'Cotton-

Corpus Legendary' versions were probably not behind Ælfric's considerable expansions in his homily, but since no other source has been identified, it has to be considered that the Vulgate itself may have formed a main source with material supplied from other works such as Isidore's *Etymologiarum*. Commenting on Ælfric's translation methods, Lee notes the skilful episodic structure of the Maccabees homily which, among other things, presents 'stories of the righteous keeping their faith in the face of cruel torment', a fitting example for the troubled Anglo-Saxons in the late tenth and early eleventh centuries.

Christopher A. Jones's 'Ælfric's Pastoral Letters and the Episcopal *Capitula* of Radulf of Bourges' (*N&Q* 42.149–55) is an important article which addresses the difficulties of interpreting the lists of liturgical books advocated by Ælfric as reading for priests, in particular, if the lists are sourced to Egbert's Penitential. While the Penitential might provide a source for the first of Ælfric's pastoral letters, Jones suggests that the *Capitula* of Radulf, Bishop of Bourge (incorporated in an expanded version with an interpolated book list into CCCC 265) may well have been the intermediate source for some of the details in others of the pastoral letters.

Also in *N&Q* 42 (423–6), Stephanie Hollis provides a careful study of a portion of 'Napier's XLII and Wulfstan's homily V' to show that the translation into Old English of part of Adso's *De Antichristo* in Napier XLII (198.5–18) preceded its use in Wulfstan's homily V (88–96). Stephen Morrison writes about 'A Reminiscence of Wulfstan in the Twelfth Century' (*NM* 69.229–34) detecting a close parallel to Wulfstan's *Secundum Marcum* in the *Ormulum: Luc* III.14. His argument, however, as he readily admits, raises more questions than it can answer, particularly concerning the accessibility of Old English preaching materials in the twelfth century. In 'Ælfric's *truð* "buffoon": Old Irish *druth* "buffoon"' (*N&Q* 42.155–7), Andrew Breeze suggests that *truð* is derived from Old Irish *druth*.

In 'The hypocorism *Bata* – Old English or Latin?' (*NM* 69.345–9), David W. Porter traces the origin of the name of Ælfric Bata to Isidore's *Etymologiae*, Book 16.26.12, where it is traced to Hebrew 'beth' meaning an oil press which holds 50 pints. Porter allies this nomenclature of Ælfric Bata to drinking practices in monastic houses.

Lucia Kornexl continues her excellent work on the Regularis Concordia in 'The *Regularis Concordia* and its Old English gloss', partially a summary of her edition published in 1993 (*ASE* 24.95–130). Following a discussion of the historical context and the issue of authorship of the *Regularis Concordia* (generally attributed to Æthelwold), Kornexl outlines the structure, contents, sources and related texts of the work. She shows that the criticisms by some scholars of the text's seeming lack of structure is probably due to the rapidity of its compilation and dissemination. The continental influences on the work are often noted, but of particular importance in informing the structure and liturgy of the English work are Theoderic's *Consuetudines*. A detailed discussion of the manuscripts' history with the implications of Cotton's activities with the manuscripts demonstrates how complex the reconstruction of the original version has become. Careful analysis shows that the Faustina version is the 'more explicit' and may have been used for instruction, but the difficulties of reconstructing the *Regularis Concordia's* history have made for a complicated editorial task, outlined here. The Old English interlinear gloss to the Tiberius version of the text, although not the original gloss, may have been a 'library copy' rather than a classbook. Kornexl provides a linguistic examination of the gloss to illustrate that late Old English, most West Saxon, forms are dominant with some Kenticisms evident. Phonological and morphological changes in English are seen to be underway by the time the gloss was composed. Her concluding sections looking at the lexis of the gloss are scholarly and interesting, and emphasize the importance of further scholarship into Old English glossing as a whole.

In *BJRL* 77.iii., D. G. Scragg's 'The Bible in *Fontes Anglo-Saxonici*' (199–203) explains the operation of the project and the complexities involved in providing data on the Bible's use as a source. He gives the example of a biblical tag in Vercelli homily V to show that a variant spelling in the Vercelli book version of *omnes* (elsewhere seen as the Vulgate *omnis*) may indicate a particular biblical tradition at the time of the homiliary's composition. Alterations and corrections by later copyists of earlier texts help provide evidence for a knowledge of the version of the Bible in use in the relevant period.

In 'A unique Old English formula for excommunication from Cambridge, Corpus Christi College, 303' (*ASE* 24.185–211), E. M. Treharne edits the Latin and Old English forms for excommunication added as a quire-filler to the mid-twelfth century Rochester manuscript, CCCC 3030. Placing the texts within the context of legal and ecclesiastical literature, Treharne shows that the practice of excommunication became formalized in the eleventh and twelfth centuries, perhaps resulting in the copying of this unique vernacular witness to the ceremony of excommunication.

Andrew Breeze has two notes on diplomatic material. His 'Old English *þeru* "loaves" in a Westbury charter on 793–796' (*N&Q* 42.13–14) compares the form *þeru* with the Welsh legal terms to suggest that it means 'loaves' and that, as such, its use illustrates the practice of giving food as rent. 'Cardinal Berard of Palestrina and a Shropshire Writ of 1060–1061' (*N&Q* 42.14–16) focuses on the writ's reference to 'Begard Biscop' who Breeze here identifies as Berard, possibly a papal legate in 1061. If this is the case, knowledge of the operations of the Papacy in England is extended.

Books Reviewed

Alexander, Michael. *Beowulf*. Penguin Classics. Penguin. pp. 237. pb £5.99. ISBN 0 14 043377 5.

Baker, Peter S., ed. *'Beowulf': Basic Readings*. Basic Readings in Anglo-Saxon England 1. Garland. pp. 306. hb $45, pb $19.95. ISBN 0 8153 0098 0, 0 8153 0491 9.

——, and Michael Lapidge, eds. *Byrhtferth's Enchiridion*. EETS 15. OUP. pp. 480. £45. ISBN 0 19 722416 4.

Clark, Francelia Mason. *Theme in Oral Epic and in Beowulf*. Milman Parry Studies in Oral Tradition. Garland. pp. 252. $50. ISBN 0 8153 1874 X.

Clemoes, Peter S. *Interactions of Thought and Language in Old English Poetry*. CSASE 12. CUP. pp. 547. £50. ISBN 0 521 30711 2.

Deshman, Robert. *The Benedictional of Æthelwold*. Studies in Manuscript Illumination 9. PrincetonUP. pp. 287 + 248 plates. $90. ISBN 0 6910 4386 8.

Dumville, David, N., ed. *The Anglo-Saxon Chronicle: A Collaborative Edition* is the *Facsimile of MS F: The Domitian Bilingual*. Brewer. pp. 110. £75. ISBN 0 85591 125 X.

Eales, Richard, and Richard Sharpe, eds. *Canterbury and the Norman Conquest: Churches, Saints and Scholars 1066–1109*. Hambledon. pp. 182. £34. ISBN 1 85285 068 X.

Lapidge, Michael, ed. *Archbishop Theodore: Commemorative Studies on his Life and Influence*. CSASE 11. CUP. pp. 343. £45. ISBN 0 521 48077 9.

Marsden, Richard. *The Text of the Old Testament in Anglo-Saxon England*. CSASE 15. CUP. pp. 506. £60. ISBN 0 521 46477 3.

Mitchell, Bruce. *An Invitation to Old English and Anglo-Saxon England*. Blackwell. pp. 424. pb £12.99. ISBN 0 631 17436 2.

Orchard, Andy. *Pride and Prodigies: Studies in the Monsters of the Beowulf-Manuscript*. B&B. pp. 352. £39.50. ISBN 0 85991 456 9.

Pasternack, Carole Braun. *The Textuality of Old English Poetry*. CSASE 13. CUP. pp. 219. £35. ISBN 0 521 46549 4.

Stancliffe, Clare, and Eric Cambridge, eds. *Oswald: Northumbrian King to European Saint*. Watkins. pp. 299. ISBN 1 871615 461.

Stevenson, Jane, ed. *The 'Laterculus Malalianus' and the School of Archbishop Theodore*. CSASE 14. CUP. pp. 254. £45. ISBN 0 521 37461 8.

III

Middle English: Excluding Chaucer

GREG WALKER, DAVID J. SALTER and ALAN J. FLETCHER

This chapter has the following sections: 1. General and Miscellaneous; 2. Alliterative Poetry; 3. The *Gawain*-Poet; 4. *Piers Plowman*; 5. Romances; 6. Gower, Lydgate, Hoccleve; 7. Middle Scots Poetry; 8. Lyrics and Miscellaneous Verse; 9. Malory and Caxton; 10. Other Prose; 11. Drama. Sections 1, 3, 4, 6, 7, and 9 are by Greg Walker; sections 2, 5, and 8 are by David J. Salter; and sections 10 and 11 are by Alan J. Fletcher.

1. General and Miscellaneous

The breadth and variety of the activities conducted under the banner of medieval studies is well reflected in this year's publications. Approaches from the most traditional forms of textual scholarship to the most modish of theoretical analyses are all exemplified in the work considered below. Most noteworthy, perhaps, is the continuing strength of interdisciplinary work, which grounds the subject under consideration, whether it be a literary text, an artefact, or an idea, in the broader historical, intellectual and cultural context which produced it. Medievalists have always been favourably inclined towards a broadly based, historically informed approach to their subject, but movements towards 'historicism' in other periods have, perhaps, helped to remind us of the virtues of that broad cultural methodology.

New Science Out of Old Books: Studies in Manuscripts and Early Printed Books in Honour of A. I. Doyle, edited by Richard Beadle and A. J. Piper, contains, in addition to a bibliography of Doyle's printed writings, a helpful index of manuscripts and printed books cited, and 69 monochrome plates, 15 stimulating and scholarly essays reflecting the wide ranging interests and expertise of its dedicatee. Mary Rouse and Richard H. Rouse revisit, in 'From Flax to Parchment: A Monastic Sermon from Twelfth-Century Durham', the early or mid-twelfth century Latin sermon somewhat misleadingly titled '*De Scriptibus bonis et malis*' in Durham Cathedral MS B.IV.12. They place the better known section which interprets the tools of the scribe symbolically as aids to Christian faith in the context of the hitherto unpublished middle section of the sermon which allegorizes the process of turning flax into linen. Drawing out the link between the scribal tools and the nature of linen (traceable to Ezekiel 9.2–3 and the reference to 'the man dressed in linen' who carries a scribe's inkhorn) the essay argues that the connection between the two sections of the sermon was a natural – indeed inevitable – consequence of the choice of allegorical theme: Everyman as scribe.

Two of the essays concentrate on manuscripts in Cambridge. Margaret Laing and Angus McIntosh offer a detailed analysis of 'Cambridge Trinity College, MS 335: its Texts and Transmission'. Taking up Neil Ker's suggestion that a careful study of the hands of the three scribes involved in producing the text would throw light upon its history and upon the *Poema Morale* which, *inter alia*, it contains, Laing and McIntosh subject the text to 'computer tagging' analysis of the linguistic evidence. They conclude that the *Poema Morale* may have a northern Essex provenance, while the contributions of Scribe A to the Trinity Homilies may well place him on the borders of Essex, Suffolk and Cambridgeshire, and the contributions of Scribe B might be placed in south Suffolk or south Cambridgeshire. Anne Hudson's account of 'Trial and Error: Wyclif's Works in Cambridge, Trinity College MS B.16.2' provides a detailed analytical description of 'the most extensive manuscript of Wyclif's Latin writings now surviving in England', which contains 12 early scholarly tracts, four sets of sermons and the four books of the *Opus Evangelicum*. Despite the attractive appearance of the manuscript, Hudson concurs with earlier unfavourable opinions of the accuracy of its texts, judging it to be frequently faulty and markedly inferior to other analogous manuscripts.

Other essays deal with the business of scribal production. Kathleen L. Scott's 'Limning and Book-Producing Terms and Signs *in situ* in Late-Medieval English Manuscripts: A First Listing', provides insights into the techniques and mental processes of the producers of manuscripts, explaining terms such as 'champ', 'demi venet' and 'endented letter' with exemplary illustrations. In 'Serving the Needs of Readers: Textual Division in some Late Medieval English Texts', George R. Keiser shows how such editorial practices as the division into chapters, the addition of headings, etc., addressed texts such as Lydgate's *Lyf of Our Lady* and a range of remedy books and other more pragmatic works, to the needs and reading habits of lay purchasers. One such lay book-owner was Roger Marchall, who provides the subject of Linda Ehrsam Voigts's 'A Doctor and His Books'. Voigts describes and comments upon the sizeable manuscript collection owned or used by this doctor of medicine, one of the few identifiable large-scale lay owners and donors of books. Her article, the longest in the collection by a considerable margin, provides biographical information on Marchall and his relatives, suggests corrections to earlier attempts to identify manuscripts as part of his library, and in a series of appendices provides descriptions of the manuscripts associated with him, those with potential Marchall connections, lost manuscripts known to have been in his hands and codices erroneously attributed to him. The essay is rounded off with lists of texts donated by Marchall, chiefly to Peterhouse and King's College Cambridge, and illustrations of the various manuscripts themselves. Another manuscript collector, albeit on a more modest scale, was the monk Thomas Hyngham. Richard Beadle's 'Monk Thomas Hyngham's Hand in the Macro Manuscript' examines afresh his ownership and use of those texts known to have passed through his hands. Beadle confirms Ian Doyle's identification of the 'Monk Hyngham' who owned the Macro manuscripts with Thomas Hyngham, monk of Bury St Edmunds, who once owned a copy of John Walton's Middle English verse translation of Boethius's *De Consolatione Philosophiae*, now in private hands in Oslo. Through an analysis of the hands in the Macro *Wisdom* and *Mankind* texts, Beadle makes a powerful case for their being the work of a single scribe (a claim previously made by Mark Eccles but denied by David Bevington), and – although the evidence is less conclusive – for that scribe being Hyngham himself. Peter J. Lucas takes a similar theme in his essay 'An Author as Copyist of His Own Work: John Capgrave OSA (1393–1464)'. Lucas subjects the notion of authorial 'original' manuscripts to critical scrutiny. Examining the errors and corrections in autograph and holograph copies of Capgrave's works, he distinguishes between 'working copies', 'superior copies' and 'luxury copies', all of which have different levels and frequency of authorial alterations and correction. Focusing upon a rather later period, Lotte Hellinga's 'Wynkyn de Worde's Native Land' examines the geographical origins of Caxton's successor. On the basis of the evidence of his woodcut and type stock, and from variations in the spelling of his surname, Hellinga argues that de Worde may as plausibly have hailed from Woerden in Holland as from Wörth in Alsace-Lorraine. Mary C. Erler focuses upon the 'Exchange of Books Between Nuns and Laywomen: Three Surviving Examples', providing further details of the traffic in books between nuns and the laity, chiefly in the fifteenth and sixteenth centuries.

Studies of the experience(s) of medieval women, their reading and writing continue to form a substantial proportion of the work published this year. In *Women, The Book, and The Godly: Selected Proceedings of the St. Hilda's Conference, 1993*, vol. I, Lesley Smith and Jane H. M. Taylor bring together a number of short contributions to the field. Female learning is the subject for a number of the papers. In ' "Sharpen Your Mind With The Whetstone of Books": The female recluse as reader in Goscelin's *Liber Confortatorius*, Aelred of Rievaulx's *De Institutione Inclusarum* and the *Ancrene Wisse*', Gopa Roy charts a marked decline in the learning of the female religious in the period from the late eleventh century to the early thirteenth century, accompanied by, and perhaps consequent upon, increasing male intervention in and regulation of the nature and structure of the life of the female recluse. A more positive note is struck in Catherine Innes-Parker's '*Ancrene Wisse* and *The Wohunge of Ure Lauerd*: The Thirteenth Century Female Reader and The Lover-Knight'. Innes-Parker re-examines the parable of the Lover-Knight in the *Ancrene Wisse* in the light of the version in the *Wohunge*, arguing, contrary to much recent criticism, that the model it employs does not condemn the anchoress to the passivity of the lady of romances, wooed and won by Christ, but offers support for a more active female spirituality.

Differing views on the extent of female reading are offered in Anne M. Dutton's 'Passing The Book: Testamentary Transmission of Religious Literature to and by Women In England, 1350–1500' and Shannon McSheffrey's 'Literacy and the Gender Gap in the Late Middle Ages: Women and Reading in Lollard Communities'. The latter, while perhaps erring on the side of generosity in claiming to locate 270 women Lollards in the period 1420–1530, offers the sobering observation that only seven of them can be positively identified as literate, and five of those were part of the same conventicle in Coventry. Women were, McSheffrey argues, far more likely to be reliant upon passages of texts read to them by their male co-religionists and memorized than to have access to entire texts to which they could refer. Their influence in conventicles was thus likely to be highly circumscribed. Dutton, considering the traffic in more orthodox communities, argues for increased penetration of book-ownership down the social scale in the later medieval period, with 'women of merchant families' beginning to leave books (generally in the vernacular) in their Wills by the first quarter of the fifteenth century. She also argues that there was essentially no difference in the kinds of books owned by religious and secular women in this period.

Women's writing is the focus of Helen Phillips's essay 'Re-Writing the Fall: Julian of Norwich and the *Chevalier Des Dames*'. Phillips compares and contrasts the parable of the lord and the servant in Julian's *Revelation of Divine Love* and the allegory of the Tree of Men and Women in the *Chevalier* (*c.*1460–77), as rewritings of the Fall from a female perspective. Men's writing about women is the centre of attention in Jacqueline Murray's essay 'The Absent Penitent: The Cure of Souls and Confessors' Manuals in Thirteenth-Century England'. Murray uses examples from confessors' manuals from across the century to claim that confession was an 'androcentric' phenomenon, in which women were seen as only secondary to male-centred models of sin and salvation.

The collection of essays on *The Cultural Patronage of Medieval Women* edited by June H. Cash, offers further exposition of medieval female cultural experience. Cash's introduction, 'The Cultural Patronage of Medieval Women: An Overview' provides precisely that, spanning western Europe in its examples of female patrons and dedicatees of written, sculpted and painted works. Much of the work represented here is in the 'documenting and celebrating' mode of historical scholarship, marking with approval the contributions of eminent women to a field, and describing the forces and practices which they had to overcome in order to make them. Thus John C. Parsons's 'Of Queens, Courts, and Books: Reflections on the Literary Patronage of Thirteenth Century Plantagenet Queens' surveys the evidence for the literary patronage and interests of Eleanor of Provence (d.1291) and Eleanor of Castile (d.1290), successive queens of England. Lois L. Huneycutt's ' "Proclaiming Her Dignity Abroad": The Literary and Artistic Network of Matilda of Scotland, Queen of England, 1100–1118' argues for Matilda, first Queen of Henry I of England, as 'a true partner in the administration of his realms', rather than 'a wealthy dilettante trying to fill the empty hours' through artistic patronage. Frances A. Underhill focuses upon 'Elizabeth de Burgh: Connoisseur and Patron' and uses surviving account books and other documents to exemplify the material culture of her household and her patronage of education, most notably her foundation of Clare College, Cambridge. Karen J. Jambeck in 'Patterns of Women's Literary Patronage: England, 1200–*ca.*1475' provides an account of female patronage in her chosen period. She offers a list of texts and female dedicatees which partially substantiates the claim that many female patrons enjoyed a more hands-on role in commissioning works than is often assumed.

A number of essays in the collection take a wider view. In a trenchant and provocative analysis, Madeline H. Caviness's 'Anchoress, Abbess, and Queen: Donors and Patrons or Intercessors and Matrons?' brings the insights and assumptions of Marxist feminist analysis to bear upon the question of women's artistic patronage, exploring both those images created 'for' women and those which (like those in modern, so-called, women's magazines) are perhaps better described as created 'against' them. She revisits, among other issues, the debate over the nature and provenance of the Albani-Salter, offering reasons for renaming it, despite its predominantly male-to-male discourse and probable monastic origins, 'Christina of Markyate's Psalter'. In 'Some Norfolk Women and Their Books, ca.1390–1440', Ralph Hanna III reflects upon the class-based nature of most, if not all, cultural patronage, and its restriction to the sphere of the privileged and powerful. He directs his attention lower down the social scale at the 'activities with books' (not strictly patronage *per se*) of two Norfolk peasant women, Margery Baxter of Martham and Avis Mone of Loddon, whose heterodox religious activities brought them to the attention of Bishop Alnwick of Norwich in 1428–31. Both women, although probably illiterate, formed part of a network of 'reading communities', the investigation of which would add depth to our appreciation and understanding of the ways in which both men and women used books in this period. Hanna also looks at the better known cases of Julian of Norwich and Margery Kempe, charting how each was absorbed within male reading communities and patriarchal textualization, Kempe's testimony being recorded in the (male) records of the ecclesiastical court which 'corrected' her, and Julian's surviving only in the manuscripts of the male clerical communities which read and annotated her work.

Readers interested in issues of gender, sex and sexuality in the medieval period will benefit greatly from Joan Cadden's lucidly argued and copiously documented *Meanings of Sex Difference in the Middle Ages*, first published in 1993 but now issued in paperback. Addressing, *inter alia*, a number of the biases and lacunae in Foucault's hugely influential *History of Sexuality*, Cadden offers a stimulating account of the development of medical and scientific attitudes to sex difference from the classical period to the fourteenth century, setting these ideas in the wider context of social and religious mores about reproduction, sexual orientation and carnality. The result is a subtle and open-minded study which gives due weight to the full range of opinions and agenda addressed by scholars in the period when they talked about men and women, their bodies and the sexual dimension to their natures and appetites.

A number of monographs address individual texts, authors, or themes. Christopher Baswell's *Virgil in Medieval England: Figuring the Aeneid from the Twelfth Century to Chaucer* traces not a single tradition but a number of distinct ways in which Virgil was understood, glossed and annotated in the medieval period. Twelfth-century English manuscripts formed the basis of one tradition as they were read and re-read by generations of scholars in the monastic schools, another was created by the spiritual exegetes who used the author as a source of allegorical exempla, a third was generated among courtly readers (frequently female) of the Norman *Roman d'Eneas*, who were interested in the social and cultural dimensions to the text. Baswell's final chapter considers Chaucer's handling of this complex interweaving of traditions in his *House of Fame* and *Legend of Good Women*. For Chaucer, Baswell claims, a creative re-reading of Virgil was the means by which he negotiated his own social and poetic position. The book is completed by a series of appendices providing an annotated index of manuscripts of the *Eclogues*, *Georgics* and the *Aeneid* copied or owned in England up to 1542, including an indication of the contents of the manuscripts, brief descriptions of any marginalia and cross-reference to fuller descriptions in print elsewhere.

In *The Devil's Rights and The Redemption in the Literature of Medieval England*, C. W. Marx seeks to clarify the role of the, so-called, Devil's rights and their relationship to the Redemption, as portrayed in such works as *Piers Plowman*, *The N-Town Play*, *The Gospel of Nicodemus*, Robert Grosseteste's *Chateau D'Amour*, the Cornish *Ordinalia* and *The Devil's Parliament*. The idea is based upon the notion that God was obliged to respect the Devil's right to possess humanity unless or until the Devil abused his powers, which he did when he allowed the killing of the sinless Christ. R. W. Southern and others had argued that this idea held good only until St Anselm's *Cur Deus Homo*, which replaced it with the idea of Christ, not as the bait 'hidden' in human form which lured Satan into abusing his powers, but as a sacrifice sufficient to repay humanity's debt to God. As a result, critics have tended to see the use of the idea of the Devil's rights in such works as *Piers Plowman* and *The N-Town Play* as evidence of the archaic, backward-looking nature of much English vernacular literature in its treatment of the Redemption in particular and theology in general. Marx demonstrates that this model of 'progress' in treatments of the Redemption is too simple, and offers instead a more nuanced account of the way in which authors might utilize the Devil's Rights as one of a number of different approaches towards literalizing or dramatizing the Redemption, without necessary consequences for their overall theological position. Appendices reprint, with translations, relevant portions of Hugh of St Cher's *Postilla Super Totam Bibliam*, Robert de Melun's *Sentences* and Grosseteste's *Sermo 44/ Dictum 10*. A study with similar scope and ambitions is Michael P. Kuczynski's *Prophetic Song: The Psalms as Moral Discourse in Late Medieval England*, which seeks to trace the influence of the Psalms upon the language of ethical instruction in late medieval England, focusing in particular upon the writings of Richard Rolle and early Lollard interpolations in his Psalter, the work of Langland, Lydgate and others. The chapters on individual authors will be discussed in the relevant sections below.

Also intent upon illuminating the relationship of individual texts to broader theological traditions is Denys Turner's *The Darkness of God: Negativity in Christian Mysticism*. Centred on an analysis of theological metaphors (of interiority, ascent and light and darkness in the progress of the soul towards God) central to Christianity in general but most directly to what we now (in Turner's view too loosely) think of as the 'mystical' tradition, this monograph provides a challenging but richly rewarding exploration of the nature of mysticism and the language and concepts through which it was expressed by authors such as St John of the Cross, Denys the Areopagite (pseudo-Denys), Meister Eckhart and the author of *The Cloud of Unknowing*. Turner argues powerfully that mysticism, far from privileging experience, was based upon a scepticism of notions of spirituality founded upon the possibility of obtaining knowledge of God in experiential terms. In his chapter on *The Cloud*, he develops this line further, stressing the ways in which the text advocates a spirituality beyond cognition itself, a discipline in which 'unknowing' 'is an apophatic strategy, not a mere ignorance ... a routine of progressive simplification and attenuation of the imagination and reason. To "unknow" is, for the *Cloud* Author, an active verb-form.'

Also deconstructing accepted notions of mysticism, this time from a feminist, philosophical perspective, is Grace M. Jantzen's *Power, Gender, and Christian Mysticism*. An avowed 'non-medievalist', Jantzen offers a polemical account of what she claims is the systematic misrepresentation of mystical experience – especially female mystical experience – by both contemporary male authors and modern academics. For the author this study is part of a quest for justice in the modern world as well as an attempt to be faithful to the voices of medieval mystics. We must, she warns, 'become aware of the ways in which the language of the mystical has been appropriated by philosophers and theologians, whose discourses of power work, often unwittingly, against women and oppressed groups; and we must reclaim the dangerous memories of mystical writers, especially women, which enable our discourses of resistance'. This is heady stuff, and at times the overt political agenda can conceal the subtleties of what is being said, but the book presents, none the less a powerful and persuasive case for a major re-evaluation of medieval mysticism and the models with which modern scholarship approaches it. What emerges is a more fragmented picture, and perhaps a less coherent one, than is often presented. There is not one mystical tradition, but many, and mysticism itself is always and everywhere not just mediated through but actively constructed by social and political pressures and agents. It is the latter, whether medieval monks and bishops or modern academics, who determine what is to be accepted as legitimate mystical activity at any given moment and which criteria are to be considered relevant to that decision. Jantzen has her own agenda, of course, but it is an enabling one. Rejecting the notion that mystical experience is an essentially private affair, she offers an ambitious rewriting of mystical thinking from Plato onwards, refocusing upon the public and political aspects and implications of mystical experience. If, as she claims, there is no hidden 'essence' uniting all forms of mysticism, then scholars must dispense with general assumptions and return to first principles and primary texts afresh. The result can only revitalize study of the subject.

In *Three Studies in Medieval Religious and Social Thought*, a companion piece to his forthcoming monograph on the Reformation of the twelfth century, Giles Constable examines changes in religious life and thought from antiquity to the Renaissance. He focuses on three key themes, each of which opens up wider issues and questions: the differing interpretations of the figures of Martha and Mary which reflect the different emphases given to the active and contemplative Christian lives, the ideal of the imitation of Christ, with its growing recognition of and emphasis upon the physical humanity of Christ and his suffering, and the example they offer for Christian conduct in the world, and finally the stresses and strains placed upon the notion of a society divided into distinct orders by social change and the recognition of the 'rise of the middle class'. Over 30 years in the writing, these three copiously documented and lavishly footnoted studies are free-standing essays in their own right. But, taken together, they form a satisfying and coherent exploration of aspects of the development of medieval spirituality from one of the major figures in historical studies.

In a shrewd and thought-provoking article, Malcolm Andrew turns his attention to 'The Realizing Imagination in Late Medieval English Literature' (*ES* 76.113–28). Andrew contends that 'alongside the ubiquitous medieval tendency to generalize, a countervailing fascination with particulars may be observed in the literature written in England during the late Middle Ages'.

This might appear uncontentious, but in exemplifying the potentially sub-versive effects of this 'realizing imagination', 'by which the ... creative writer gets to work on a received story – developing, elaborating, and bringing to imagined life; particularizing general issues, realizing the abstract, and draw-ing out potential implications', the essay has much to suggest about the way in which medieval poets suggest 'the complexity and elusiveness of moral choice'. True to his subject, Andrew grounds his general analysis firmly in the particular, selecting four key passages from different late medieval authors: the coming of the Flood in *Cleanness* and *Noah's Flood* from the Chester Cycle, Jonah's experience in the whale's belly in *Patience* and *Joseph's Doubt* from *The N-Town Play*, revealing how in each episode moral judgement is rendered problematic by the focus upon the victim or transgressor's experi-ence.

In 'The Female Body Politic and the Miscarriage of Justice in *Athelston*' (*SAC* 17.79–98), Elizabeth Ashman Rowe offers a reading of the late fourteenth-/early fifteenth-century political romance *Athelston* as 'Lancas-trian propaganda'. Dating the poem to the end of the reign of Richard II, Rowe reads it as 'anti-Ricardian without being anti-royalist'. Although rather naive in its treatment of Ricardian politics and over-reliant upon some highly questionable readings (most notably on the central issue of the role of Athelston's queen in the political crisis which his conduct provokes), the article none the less reopens the debate about this intriguing and enigmatic romance.

The Owl and The Nightingale is the subject of two contrasting pieces of work. In '*The Owl and the Nightingale* and the Perils of Criticism' (*NM* 96.367– 80), Ivana Djordjevic reviews recent scholarship on the poem, taking its various authors to task for sins of omission and commission, over and under-literalism, self-contradiction and plain bad writing. She finishes, some-what anti-climactically, with an uncontentious call to focus 'on what the text does say instead of what we wish it would say', advocating an approach which is 'the product of careful reading combined with scrupulous attention to context, both historical and manuscriptal'. Already practising such an approach, albeit on a small scale, Claire Catalini suggests, in 'A Note on *The Owl and The Nightingale*, lines 427–8' (*N&Q* 42.267– 9), that the Nightingale's taunt to her adversary that the latter would like to see everyone miserable, like one who 'Ne roȝte he theȝ flockes were / Imeind bi toppes and bi here' might best be read as a reference to flocks of animals rather than snowflakes, and be best translated as 'He could not care less if flocks got mixed up together, by their heads and their hair', an allusion to the anti-social consequences of the accidental mixing of swine from different herds during pannaging.

In the same issue of *N&Q*, Tamarah Kohanski's 'Two Manuscripts of Mandeville's *Travels*' (*N&Q* 42.269–70) seeks to correct two entries in M. C. Seymour's 'English Manuscripts of Mandeville's *Travels*' (*Edinburgh Bibliographic Society Transactions* IV (1966).169–210). The reference to BM MS Royal 17.B.xliii (item 1 in Seymour), Kohanski states, actually under-estimates the amount of text missing from the final section, while BM MS Harley 2386 (item 13) should be considered a complete variant text rather than an 'imperfect' text with two folios of material missing. Bengt Lindström's 'Notes on the Middle English *Genesis and Exodus*' (*NM* 96.67–80) offers some suggested corrections on points of detail to the edition of the text edited by

Olof Arngart (Lund Studies in English, 36, 1968), an edition which the author otherwise commends as commanding the field.

On a more general theme, Heinz Bergner's essay 'The Openness of Medieval Texts', contained in *Historical Pragmatics: Pragmatic Developments in the History of English* edited by Andreas H. Jucker, offers a formal analysis of the factors which render a text 'open', that is amenable to different interpretations. Citing examples from Caedmon to Lydgate and Dunbar, Bergner seeks to demonstrate how culture, language and often uncertain textual transmission combine to make medieval texts especially prone to openness. Joel Fredell's article 'The Three Clerks and St. Nicholas in Medieval England' (*SP* 92.181–202) examines 'The exclusion of his best-known miracle from virtually all vernacular lives of this universal saint'. The story, in which Nicholas resurrects three young scholars who have been murdered by an innkeeper or butcher and turned into meat for sale in his establishment, is frequently depicted in the visual arts, but only rarely related in literary hagiography. Fredell conjectures that the story may have had its origins in a now largely lost tradition of dramatic representations of the saint's life associated with the Boy Bishop celebrations, and that its association with such 'slightly disreputable, sophomoric' events may have led to its lack of appeal for clerkly hagiographers.

In ' "A Good Remedie Aȝens Spirituel Temptacions": A Conflated Middle English Version of William Flete's *De Remediis Contra Temptationes* and Pseudo-Hugh of St Victor's *De Pusillanimate* in London BL MS Royal 18.A.X' (*ES* 76.307–54), F. N. M. Diekstra prints the text of the *Good Remedie* (a letter of spiritual instruction addressed to a 'dere sister') in parallel with the Latin sections of Flete and St Victor, with variant readings and a detailed commentary. Also in *ES* 76 is Yoko Iyeiri's linguistic analysis of medieval poetic practice 'Negative Contraction and Syntactic Conditions in Middle English Verse' (424–33), which investigates the process of 'agglutinating the adverb *ne* with the verb that follows', whereby, for example, *ne wolde* becomes *nolde* and *ne wot* becomes *not*, etc. Based upon a preliminary survey of some 20 Middle English texts, Iyeiri's thesis concludes that dialectic rather than syntactic conditions have the greater influence on the choice of either contracted or uncontracted forms in a given text. Also examining issues of influence, this time textual and intellectual, Colin Wilcockson's short article '*Mum and the Sothsegger, Richard II*, and *Henry V*' (*RES* 46.219–24) speculates that Shakespeare's use of the political allegories of the gardeners in *Richard II* and the beehive in *Henry V* may have been prompted by a passage in *Mum and the Sothsegger* which combines politicized allusions to the same motifs. Omitted from *YWES* 75 was Edward Wilson's '*The Testament of The Buck* and the Sociology of The Text' (*RES* 45.157–84), in which Wilson sets *The Testament* in its literary context, offering a list of literary testaments down to *c.*1565, and in the context of its *mis-en-page* in the surviving manuscript and printed versions.

Of considerable interest in terms of the cultural historical background is the copiously illustrated and affordably priced volume of essays which comprise *A History of Canterbury Cathedral*, edited by Patrick Collinson, Nigel Ramsey and Margaret Sparks. After chapters on 'The Anglo-Saxon Cathedral Community, 597–1070' and 'Normans and Angevins, 1070–1220', by Nicholas Brooks and Margaret Gibson respectively, there is a comprehensive overview by Barrie Dobson of 'The Monks of Canterbury in the Later Middle Ages, 1220–1540'. In a wide-ranging and stimulating summary, Dobson charts the history of the cathedral from the disputatious years of the first half of the thirteenth century, when conflict between the Christ Church chapter and their archbishop was endemic, through years of prosperity to the depredations of the Reformation. Taken in on the way are expositions of the role of the prior in the cathedral community, the establishment of Canterbury College, Oxford and the intellectual accomplishments of the chapter, the social and regional origins of the monks, and the fortunes of the shrine and cult of St Thomas. A further valuable chapter, written by Nigel Ramsey on 'The Cathedral Archives and Library' discusses Canterbury's manuscript holdings, donations and acquisitions from the Anglo-Saxon period onwards. Particularly interesting in the present context are the sections on the long priorate of Henry of Eastry (1284–1331) and 'The Later Middle Ages, c.1340–1540'. Roger Bowers's chapter on 'The Liturgy of the Cathedral and Its Music, c.1075–1642' takes a similarly long view of its subject, detailing cathedral practice from the *Constitutions* of Archbishop Lanfranc through the development of plainsong, polyphony and organ-music, to the replacement of the Benedictine Use by that of Salisbury and the foundation of the cathedral choir at the Dissolution. Finally, an essay by Christopher Wilson on 'The Medieval Monuments' also offers much of interest to later medievalists from all disciplines, not least in its detailed accounts of the plethora of ecclesiastical and lay tombs and monuments which would have greeted Chaucer's pilgrims on their arrival at the shrine of 'the hooly blisful martir'.

On a far broader canvas, R. N. Swanson's *Religion and Devotion in Europe, c.1215–c.1515* provides an overview of religious belief and practice in western Europe between the Fourth and Fifth Lateran Councils. Drawing frequently upon English examples and experience, Swanson portrays the medieval church in terms which will be familiar to scholars of the period as far from the monolithic institution in terminal decline once beloved of historians of the Reformation. Rather, Roman Christendom was the proverbial broad church, whose doctrines were not rigidly defined beyond the injunctions contained in the Creed, but which despite (or perhaps because of) this was a vibrant, vital organism capable of satisfying and absorbing the demands and energies of its adherents through time. With chapters outlining the central tenets of Catholic faith and practice, the institutional machinery of the church, 'The religious life', 'the pilgrimage of life and death', and 'inclusion and exclusion' (dealing with orthodoxy and its discontents), and a substantial biography of selected further reading, this study provides a reliable guide to late medieval religious culture to those with little or no background knowledge of the subject and a lively consolidation and development of work in the field for those better informed. Teachers will be able to direct their students to its pages with some confidence.

Equally illuminating in its analysis of cultural history is Malcolm Barber's *The New Knighthood: A History of the Order of the Temple*, first published in 1994 but now reissued in a Canto paperback edition which brings it within the price range of most undergraduates. Students of Romance and chivalry will welcome Barber's sober and scholarly treatment of the origins and development of the Order, its ideals and culture from its inception in 1119 to its dramatic suppression in 1312. And conspiracy theorists of all ages will benefit from the final chapter 'From Molay's Curse to Foucault's Pendulum' charting the origins of some of the many fictional and mythical 'after-histories' which have become seemingly inextricably linked to the Order since the fourteenth century, associating it with every *cause celebre* from the preservation of the Turin Shroud to the crimes of Jack the Ripper (Barber's curious omission of any reference to this last case may itself fuel further conspiracy theories of its own).

Literary patronage remains a rich seam for scholarly study, but it is important to recall that not every medieval aristocrat was equally zealous in his or her reward and encouragement of writers. As David Head's detailed political biography *The Ebbs and Flows of Fortune*, reveals, Thomas Howard, third Duke of Norfolk, the son of the patrons of Skelton and Barclay and the father of the ill-fated poet Earl of Surrey, sought books during his imprisonment, not for spiritual comfort or aesthetic pleasure, but because he could not fall asleep satisfactorily without reading in bed.

Arthur Stephen McGrade and John Kilcullen have edited a collection of the political works of the English Franciscan theologian William of Ockham, *William of Ockham: A Letter to the Friars Minor and Other Writings*. According to McGrade and Kilcullen, Ockham is probably best remembered as the figure who was 'largely responsible for the widely held modern conviction that religious institutions and secular government should normally operate independently of one another'. However, as the editors also note, because Ockham acted as the Franciscans' leading propagandist in their quarrel with Pope John XXII on the subject of the poverty of Christ, he holds the distinction of being 'the first major western theologian to enter into protracted dispute with the papacy on matters of Christian doctrine'. *A Letter to the Friars Minor* is Ockham's justification to his fellow Franciscans for his opposition to John XXII, a stance that he defended in more detail in the passages from the other works that are also included in the collection (*The Work of Ninety Days, A Dialogue on the Power of the Pope and Clergy, A Dialogue on the Rights of the Roman Empire* and *Eight Questions on the Power of the Pope*). This volume is therefore useful both as an introduction to William of Ockham's life and thought, and as a detailed and authoritative statement of the Franciscan position in its extremely bitter dispute with the papacy.

Vox Mystica: Essays on Medieval Mysticism in Honor of Professor Valerie M. Lagorio, edited by Anne Clark Bartlett, Thomas Bestul, Janet Goebel and William F. Pollard, is a collection of articles covering the diverse range of topics that come under the heading of 'mystical studies'. As well as general essays on such issues as the use of mystical language in secular literature and the influence of the Church fathers on the mystical writers of the fourteenth century, there are also articles on individual authors such as Richard Rolle, Thomas à Kempis, St Teresa of Avila and Julian of Norwich. A broad range of theoretical approaches are applied to the study of mystical experience, and the concluding section of the volume contains an edition of a previously unpublished mystical text (*Of Three Workings in Man's Soul*) and a translation of a short passage from Mechthild of Hackeborn's *The Book of Special Grace*.

Finally, Debra Hassig's *Medieval Bestiaries: Text, Image, Ideology*, is a painstakingly detailed study of 28 bestiary manuscripts dating from the twelfth, thirteenth and fourteenth centuries. Focusing on 12 creatures, and giving equal weight to both text and image, Hassig places the bestiary within the context of medieval animal lore, noting not only its debt to works from the medieval Christian tradition such as *The Physiologus* and *The Etymoligiae* of Isidore, but also the influence of such classical authors as Pliny and Solinus. In addition, Hassig explores some of the many ways in which bestiaries reflected the central concerns and preoccupations of medieval life, concentrating in particular on what they are able to tell us about medieval attitudes towards women and the Jews. [The last three reviews are by D.J.S.]

2. Alliterative Poetry

This year saw the publication of W. R. J. Barron and S. C. Weinberg's edition of the complete text of Laȝamon's *Brut*. (Their earlier edition of the Arthurian section of the *Brut* was reviewed in *YWES* 70.183.) In their preface, Barron and Weinberg argue that critical appreciation of the *Brut*, both in relation to its literary qualities, and in terms of its enormous cultural significance, has been hampered by the absence of a complete and accessible modern edition. To remedy this situation, Barron and Weinberg have produced a clear and readable text of the British Library, Cotton Caligula A.ix, along with a parallel modern English translation to assist the student reader in understanding the *Brut*'s difficult language and diction. Their introduction, which also seems to be aimed at the student reader, not only discusses the poem's debt to Wace's *Roman de Brut* and Geoffrey of Monmouth's *Historia Regum Britanniae*, but also examines its relationship with Old English literature and Anglo-Saxon culture. In addition, the editors speculate upon the possible reasons for the poem's popularity, suggesting that Laȝamon may have consciously tried to encourage his English compatriots to identify themselves with their ancient British predecessors, thus making his text a 'focus for a wider patriotism in which all races could associate themselves with the victorious British and identify the foreign invader, whatever his nationality, as the perennial enemy'.

Also on the subject of Laȝamon's *Brut*, 'The Wolf Doesn't Care: The Proverbial and Traditional Context of Laȝamon's *Brut* Lines 10624–10636' (*RES* 46.41–8), by Susan E. Deskis and Thomas D. Hill, examines the possible sources – both Latin and Old Norse – for King Arthur's speech before his final assault on Colgrim, the Saxon leader, in which he compares himself to a wolf, and his adversary to a goat.

There has been a further contribution this year to the debate about anti-Semitism in *The Siege of Jerusalem*. In '*The Siege of Jerusalem* and Augustinian Historians: Writing about Jews in Fourteenth-Century England' (*ChauR* 29.227–48), Elisa Narin van Court disagrees with those readings of the poem which see the Jews simply as representatives of marginal or heretical groups such as the Lollards. Rather, Narin van Court argues that the poem testifies to the continuing interest in late-medieval England in the 'Jews *qua* Jew', claiming that the poem depicts the Jews in a complex and nuanced way, so that in addition to the text's overtly anti-Semitic narrative, there is also 'a competing sympathetic narrative strand that complicates what has been considered a straightforward and brutal poem'.

3. The *Gawain*-Poet

In *Sir Gawain and The Green Knight and French Arthurian Romance*, Ad Putter illuminates the shared conventions employed by the *Gawain*-Poet and his French precursors in the description of landscapes, matters of courtesy, hospitality and explorations of the nature of honour. He reveals the poet's intimate and detailed knowledge of the French Arthurian romances, yet curiously omits any detailed study of the prose romances. M. Victoria Guerin seeks, in *The Fall of Kings and Princes: Structure and Destruction In Arthurian Tragedy*, to provide an overarching analysis of the Matter of Britain in which Mordred takes centre stage. The chapter on *Sir Gawain and The Green Knight*, following others focusing on the Vulgate cycle, Chrétien de Troyes' *Le Chevalier de la Charrete* and *Le Conte du Graal*, summarizes the main elements of the narrative and suggests possible connections, some more strained than others, with later events in the history of the Round Table. The significance of Mordred to the poem remains at best tangential, however, although the author's concentration upon themes of sexual transgression highlights important aspects of the text. In 'Communicative Clues in *Sir Gawain and The Green Knight*' (in Jucker, ed., *Historical Pragmatics*), Mª Pilar Navarro-Errasti offers a rather baffling attempt to apply 'the relevance-theoretic framework' devised by Dan Sperber and Deidre Wilson (in *Relevance: Communication and Cognition* [*YWES* 67.66]) to the works of the *Gawain*-Poet. Neither framework nor text seems to benefit greatly from the application. On a more particular level, Arthur Lindley suggests in 'Lady Bertilak's Cors: *Sir Gawain and The Green Knight*, 1237' (*N&Q* 42.23–4) that Lady Bertilak's contentious remark 'Ye ar welcum to my cors' should be read as an allusion to the green girdle (*MED*: Cors: (a) Silk ... [or] a length of silk used as a ceinture or belt), adding a further level of ironic interest to the dilemma in which it places Gawain. J. Stephen Russell's essay 'The Universal Soldier: Idealism and Conceptualism in *Sir Gawain and The Green Knight*' (in Richard J. Utz, ed., *Literary Nominalism and the Theory of Rereading Late Medieval Texts*) offers a reading of the key confrontations in the poem (the Green Knight's challenge to Camelot, the attempted seductions of Gawain and the encounter at the Green Chapel) as moments in which a realist standpoint (exemplified by Arthur and Gawain) is tested and confounded by a nominalist one (represented by the Knight, Lady Bertilak and her husband in his mortal guise).

Pearl is the subject of a new edition by William Vantuono which seeks to fill a gap in the market for texts. Whereas previous volumes have offered either scholarly treatments of the Middle English text or more or less readable modern translation, this book provides both. The poem is presented in its original form with a modern verse translation on facing pages and footnotes explicating textual cruces and seeking to clarify questions of interpretation at the foot of the page. This material is supported by a generous amount of critical apparatus: an introduction dealing with previous scholarship and questions of date, authorship and genre, 71 pages of commentary and appendices dealing with language, metre and prosody, the poet's sources (including a useful table of Biblical references and allusions), a generous bibliography, glossary and index of proper names cited in the text. The result is a volume which will be a valuable aid to teachers and students at all levels of higher education. Inevitably, there are quibbles and objections which one might offer. Translation is always fraught with perils, and the attempt to provide a text which not only stays as close to the original sense as possible but also reproduces an approximation of its metrical form, alliteration and rhyme-scheme seems designed to maximize the potential pitfalls. The edition seems to acknowledge the difficulties when it frequently has to gloss its own moder-nized text in the footnotes, not only to convey the sense of what is lost in the translation, but at times simply to clarify the sense of the new version. And there are moments when the modern text obfuscates as much as it illuminates. The narrator's lament that 'I dewyne, fordolked of luf-daungere' (line 11), with its disorienting connotations of *fin amour*, is rendered as the more anodyne 'I bear within love's pangs severe', while the description of his spirit passing 'In aventure [th]er mervayleȝ meven' (line 64) emerges almost unrec-ognizable from the modernizing process as 'moving swiftly in miraculous sweep'. One might also question the value of translating 'such a burre myȝt make myn herte blunt' (line 176) as 'The shock sped forth confusion's phase', when the relevant footnote provides a reading ('But bewilderment struck my heart a blow') which captures the sense and spirit of the original far more capably. If the desire to produce an alliterating verse translation forces the editor so far from the original, one wonders whether he would have not been better advised to produce a literal prose translation instead. As an exercise in reproducing the poetic qualities of the original text, then, the translation is only a very limited success. But as a means of providing students with rapid access to the general sense of the original text it is effective enough. And the critical apparatus which goes with it is more than sufficient to recommend the edition to teachers.

In '*Pearl* in its Royal Setting: Ricardian Poetry Revisited' (*SAC* 17.111–55), John M. Bowers argues for a date of 1395 for the poem, and places it in the court of Richard II. The poet's allusions to John the Baptist, his stress upon the image of the Lamb of God, his focus upon the pearl insignia of Christ's *familia* (seen by Bowers as analogous to Richard's use of white hart badges), the very circular nature of the pearl and the poem itself ('simulating in its form the most important piece of royal jewellery, the King's crown'), are all cited as evidence of the poet's origins in or around the royal household. It may well have been, Bowers argues, the close association of the poet, and all things hailing from Cheshire, with the Ricardian cause that led to the poem's lack of popularity after the accession of Henry IV, hence its survival in only one manuscript copy. In search of textual sources rather than political contexts, Santha Bhattacharji's '*Pearl* and the "Common of Virgins"' (*MÆ* 64.74–84) identifies the Common of Virgins – the office shared by virgin saints – as a possible point of origination for the pearl imagery around which the poem is structured. In particular, the office's joining the pearl of great price with the wise and foolish virgins in its choice of readings is seen as influencing the presentation of the Pearl-maiden herself. Andrew Breeze, in 'A Celtic Etym-ology for Glaverez "Deceives" at *Pearl* 688' (*N&Q* 42.160–2), suggests that the verb *glaver*, to flatter, in *Pearl*'s description of the righteous who 'ne glaverez her neighbor wyth no gyle', might derive from the Welsh *glafoerio* 'to drivel'.

'The least popular of the *Gawain*-poet's works' is the subject of Michael Calabrese and Eric Eliason's attentions in 'The Rhetorics of Sexual Pleasure and Intolerance in the Middle English *Cleanness*' (*MLQ* 56.247–75). Taking as their starting point the generally favourable response which critics have afforded the passage in which God states his approval of the 'play of para-mourez', the authors explore the ways in which the text balances (if that is the word) the approval of heterosexual acts with the violent denunciation of homosexual ones. Critical responses to the text, they argue, need to examine those elements of his source narratives which the poet omits from the poem (Lot's 'rape' by his daughters for example) as well as those which he includes and embellishes if they are to make sense of the full implications of his sexual politics. Monica Brzezinski Potkay, in '*Cleanness*'s Fecund and Barren Speech Acts' (*SAC* 17.99–109) draws out the connections between the multivalent senses of cleanness exemplified in the text and the eloquence of its exponents. The poem's exemplary figures: Christ, Noah, Abraham, Lot and Daniel are, like the poet himself, exponents of powerful, civilized discourse, whereas the sinners, from the hapless guest at the wedding feast to the inebriated tyrant Belshazzar, are either incapable of effective speech or reduced to dysfunctional or filthy utterances. Drawing on the links drawn by, *inter alia*, Gregory the Great and John Bromyard, between effective preaching and sexual fecundity, Potkay then, with less success, argues that the exemplary figures are also all fertile, whether literally, like Noah and Abraham, or symbolically, like Daniel.

4. Piers Plowman

The major event of the year in Langland studies is clearly the publication of the first volume of A. V. C. Schmidt's mammoth two-volume *William Langland, Piers Plowman: A Parallel-Text Edition of the A, B, C, and Z Versions*. Revising Skeat's 1886 edition in the light of subsequent scholarship and adding the disputed Bodleian Library Z-Text, Schmidt provides an invaluable new research tool for students of Langland, and of Middle English literature more generally. The volume contains a list of manuscripts consulted, a table of symbols and abbreviations, and a short note on the texts and apparatus. The texts themselves are printed in parallel, with textual apparatus at the foot of the page. The base texts for the four versions are Oxford, Bodleian Library, Bodley 851 (Z-Text), Cambridge, Trinity College MS R.3.14 (A-Text), Cambridge, Trinity College MS B.15.17 (B-Text), and San Marino, Huntington Library, 143 (C-Text), and these are presented as clearly and readably as the tangle of variant readings and major alterations will allow. A judgement on the principles lying behind Schmidt's editorial decisions and his 'correction' of a number of important readings in the base texts must, however, await the publication of the second volume which promises a full discussion of the aims and procedures of this edition as well as detailed textual notes, an extensive interpretative commentary, and a complete glossary. But in the interim, scholars in the field will surely welcome the availability of so comprehensive and accessible an edition of the texts. It is only regrettable that, at £145 per copy, it is unlikely to find a wider market.

Volume 9 of *The Yearbook of Langland Studies*, edited by J. A. Alford and J. Simpson, like volume 8 before it (reviewed in *YWES* 75), is largely devoted to the proceedings of the first International Langland Conference, publishing the discussion papers and responses delivered at the conference to complement the plenary addresses printed in the previous issue. Among these, John A. Alford's 'Langland's Learning' reviews the scholarly debate over the extent of the poet's 'clerkly' credentials, ultimately siding with those who favour a highly learned Langland. 'To understand *Piers Plowman*', he argues, 'we must go to school not only with medieval grammarians ... but also with medieval logicians, lawyers, theologians, philosophers, [and] political thinkers'. In their responses to Alford's paper, Stephen A. Barney adds to the range of the poet's potential reading matter with the suggestion that he may also have been using Ovid's *Metamorphoses*, the *Southern Passion* and *Cursor Mundi*. Conversely, Andrew Galloway, prompted by later polemical uses of the plowman figure as an exemplary anti-intellectual voice, seeks to recuperate the *un*learned dimension to *Piers Plowman* in order to illuminate the dialogic treatment of education – and all forms of 'knowing' – which the text offers. Richard Barnes's 'Langland's Stance and Style' bravely attempts to compare the text to the dramaturgy of Samuel Beckett, identifying common ground in their shared capacity for righteous 'hilarious anger' and their ability thereby to give human compassion new and startling expression. In response, Mary Clemente Davlin and M. E. J. Hughes offer a cautious welcome to the piece, the former discretely side-stepping the comparison to Beckett and concentrating on Barnes's appreciation of Langland's stylistic sensibilities, the latter politely denying the analogy and rejecting Barnes's reading of the entry into Jerusalem passage as a burlesque.

Following the work of Thorlac Turville-Petre and Derek Pearsall (see *YWES* 75.147–8, 153, 172), Helen Barr's 'Poetic Tradition' argues for the existence of 'a poetic tradition inspired by *Piers Plowman*', encompassing *Mum and The Sothsegger*, *Pierce the Plowman's Creed*, *Richard the Redeless* and *The Crowned King*, works of political truth-telling which adopt and reproduce the 'distinctly social poetic temper' evident in Langland's work. Ronald Waldron and Joseph Wittig, in responding, variously seek to qualify the notion of a single poetic tradition, arguing for a greater variety within the alliterative tradition(s) than Barr allows, and questioning her conception of the institutional discourses available to medieval poets. In '*Piers Plowman*'s William Langland: Editing the Text, Writing the Author's Life', John M. Bowers explores the ways in which the editing of the poetic text and the creation of an assumed authorial biography have informed each other in circular and often misleadingly reductive ways. He considers the evolution of the text in the light of the possibility that the A-Text may well be the latest rather than the earliest authorial redaction. Charlotte Brewer responds pragmatically that such circular arguments and the notions of authorial intention which underpin them, may be theoretically unreliable, but are almost inevitable if the task of editing the text is to proceed. Countering Bowers's textual claims, Traugott Lawler argues for the retention of the accepted order of redactions, A, B, C. In 'Imaginatif, *Memoria*, and the Need for Critical Theory in *Piers Plowman* Studies', Mary Carruthers rebels against her brief to 'evaluate the usefulness of "theory" to Langland Studies' and offers instead an exposition of the treatment of memory and cognition in *Piers Plowman*, focusing on Langland's use of visual metaphors and imagery. Jeremy Tambling and Stephany Trigg, in responding, further explore the issues raised, focusing respectively upon the poet's uses of allegory and images of imperfect reading in the Lady Mede episodes. Langland's learning is revisited in the penultimate section of the collection, led by Wendy Scase's 'Writing and the Plowman: Langland and Literacy'. Scase examines approaches to literacy and to writing itself in the tearing of the Pardon and other key moments in the text. Her implied suggestion that the brevity of the text of the pardon is in itself a disappointment is denied by Gerald Morgan, who argues in a response that in the simplicity and clarity of its utterance it represents the realization of a scholarly ideal. In a final 'forum', Lawrence M. Clopper and Samuel A. Overstreet offer brief responses to articles by Robert Adams ('Langland's *Ordinatio*') and D. Vance Smith ('The Labours of Reward') published in *YLS* 8. Vincent Di Marco completes the volume with a helpful annotated bibliography of Langland studies published during 1994.

In 'Langland's Tree of Charity and Usk's Wexing Tree' (*N&Q* 42.429–33), Lucy Lewis argues that Usk's borrowings in *The Testament of Love* were not from the Tree of Charity in Passus XVIII of the C-Text of *Piers Plowman*, but from Anselm's *De Concordia Praedestinationis Nec Non Gratiae Dei Cum Libero Arbitrio*. Thus the execution of Usk in 1388 is not significant for the dating of the C-Text. Another article to focus on the same episode is Andrew W. Cole's 'Trifunctionality and the Tree of Charity: Literacy and Social Practice in *Piers Plowman*' (*ELH* 62.1–27). Bringing together literary and social history, Cole reads Langland's poem through analogous material in Septuagesima Sunday sermons and the 'three estates' model of society, claiming that the Half-Acre episode addresses 'the problems that pertain to the peasant search for economic autonomy from lords' and that the Tree of Charity can be read as a further exemplification of the tensions inherent in the tripartite model of society.

Andrew Galloway's 'The Rhetoric of Riddling in Late-Medieval England: The "Oxford Riddles", the *Secretum Philosophorum* and the Riddles in *Piers Plowman*' (*Speculum* 70.68–105) ingeniously interprets Patience's cryptic words to the Doctor of Divinity at the end of the banquet in Passus XIII of the B-Text in the light of analogous late medieval riddles as an allusion to the heart given to God. Also in this year's *Speculum* is Elizabeth Fowler's 'Civil Death and the Maiden: Agency and the Conditions of Contract in *Piers Plowman*' (*Speculum* 70.760–92). This remarkably wide-ranging and sophisticated analysis reveals how Langland's texts draw into their complex examination of subjectivity and agency the discourses of marital law, concepts of just price and constitutional theory. Also concerned with marriage is M. Teresa Tavormina's *Kindly Similitude: Marriage and Family in Piers Plowman*, which explores Langland's treatment of marriage and family life through an explication of key sections of the text (the debate over Mede's marriage, Wit's homiletic analysis of marriage and *kynde*, the Tree of Charity episode, etc.). Ranging across all three major redactions of the poem, Tavormina charts the poet's increasingly spiritualized conception of family relations, demonstrating the importance to his thinking of the family unit, both as an enabling metaphor for and a concrete example of the relationships (both good and bad) which govern his society and illuminate the doctrinal mysteries of the Trinity, Incarnation and Redemption.

In *Prophetic Song: The Psalms as Moral Discourse in Late Medieval England*, Michael P. Kuczynski argues that Langland found in the Psalms precisely the fraught negotiation between the public and private spheres to which he was striving to give voice in *Piers Plowman*. Kuczynski examines the substratum of Psalmic language and citation which underpins Langland's text, and which is most evident in Passus V and XVIII. He also revisits the vexed tearing of the Pardon in Passus VII, reading the incident as a test or exercise, in which Piers's response reveals his spiritual and poetic identification with the Psalmist and exposes the hapless priest's merely literal engagement with the text. Another work which deals with *Piers Plowman* as part of a more general analysis is C. W. Marx's *The Devil's Rights and The Redemption in the Literature of Medieval England*. In a reading of Passus XX of the C-Text (Passus XVIII in the B-Text), Marx argues that Langland does not base his account of the Redemption on a legalistic conception of the Devil's Rights (see section 1 above for an account of the central theme of Marx's study), but follows the post-Anselmian tradition. Marx suggests that attempts to present the poet's theological position on this issue as either consistently old-fashioned or consistently innovative are mistaken. The episodes of the joust with Lucifer and the dispute in Hell remain simply episodes, not part of an over-arching theological argument.

5. Romances

Some of the less well-known Middle English romances have been well served this year with the publication of three anthologies from the Medieval Institute at Kalamazoo. *The Middle English Breton Lays*, edited by Anne Laskaya and Eve Salisbury, brings together in one collection all of the non-Chaucerian Middle English Breton Lays (*Sir Orfeo, Lay le Freine, Sir Degaré, Emaré, Sir Launfal, Sir Gowther* and *The Erle of Tolous*), along with an edition of *Sir Cleges*, and translations of Marie de France's *Lay of the Ash Tree* and *Lay of Sir Launfal*. The volume contains clear introductions to each of the texts, as well as to the genre as a whole, and the bibliography, notes and glossary are ideally suited to meet the needs of the student reader. Thomas Hahn's *Sir Gawain: Eleven Romances and Tales* is equally good. Hahn gathers together all of the so-called 'popular' Gawain romances of the fourteenth and fifteenth centuries, four of which have not been edited for over 100 years (*The Greene Knight, The Carle of Carlisle, The Jeaste of Sir Gawain* and *King Arthur and King Cornwall*). The critical apparatus is excellent, and the volume benefits considerably from the thematic unity that the figure of Gawain brings to it. Finally, Mary Flowers Braswell's edition of *Sir Perceval of Galles* and *Ywain and Gawain* offers the same high standards of clarity and scholarship that are to be found in the other two collections, although this volume will probably excite slightly less attention, coming so soon after the appearance of Maldwyn Mill's Everyman edition of the same two texts. Also of related interest is Patricia Terry's *The Honeysuckle and the Hazel Tree: Medieval Stories of Men and Women*, an anthology of eight verse translations of Old French narrative poems, including Chrétien de Troyes's non-Arthurian romance *Philomena*, and five of Marie de France's lays, *The Nightingale, The Two Lovers, Honeysuckle, Lanval* and *Elidus*.

The Formation of Culture in Medieval Britain: Celtic, Latin and Norman Influences on English Music, Literature, History and Art, edited by Françoise H. M. Le Saux, contains an article by the editor on the Middle English romance *Amys and Amiloun* ('From Ami to Amys: Translation and Adaptation in the Middle English *Amys and Amiloun*'). In her article, Le Saux describes how the Middle English *Amys and Amiloun* differs from the various French and Latin versions of the romance. In particular, she concentrates upon the unique way in which the Middle English text depicts the relationship between the two eponymous heroes, arguing that simply by altering this one aspect of the narrative, the Middle English adapter was able to produce a recognizably distinct version of the romance.

The various pictures and picture cycles which depict the story of Ywain form the subject of James A. Rushing Jr's study, *Images of Adventure: Ywain in the Visual Arts*. Covering a period from the thirteenth through to the fifteenth century, and obtaining his material from wall paintings, manuscript illuminations, misericord wood carvings and an embroidered tapestry, Rushing has sought to understand the part played by visual images in the production, transmission and reception of medieval narrative. Taking as his starting point the dictum of Gregory the Great that pictures are the literature of the laity, Rushing argues that many more people must have encountered the story of Ywain in pictorial form than through knowledge of the various literary versions of the romance (Chrétien's *Le Chevalier au Lion*, Hartmann von Aue's *Iwein*, and the anonymous Middle English *Ywain and Gawain*). As a result, Rushing rejects what he considers to be the standard scholarly view which sees the role of the illustrator as one of simply recreating the literary text in visual form. Rather, he treats the various pictures and picture cycles as autonomous works of narrative art, and employs a structuralist methodology derived from Roland Barthes's analysis of narrative to present a series of close readings of the stories they depict.

There are two articles on the subject of romance in *Medium Ævum*. In 'The Literary Use of Religious Formulae in Certain Middle English Romances' (*MÆ* 64.250–63), Roger Dalrymple notes the common occurrence of prayers and invocations in the romance canon, arguing that such verbal formulae should not be viewed simply as tags which have little or no semantic weight, but as 'stylistic devices which carry with them a strong aesthetic charge'. Mark Balfour's 'Moses and the Princess: Josephus' *Antiquitates Judaicae* and the *Chansons de Geste*' (*MÆ* 64.1–16) suggests that Josephus's account in the *Jewish Antiquities* of Moses's marriage to Thabis, the Ethiopian princess, was a possible source for the motif – often found in the French *Chansons de Geste* – of the Saracen princess who renounces her heathen ways by converting to Christianity, and marrying the Christian hero.

Finally, two articles appeared in 1995 which attempted in different ways to apply theoretical insights to the study of romance themes. In 'Middle English Romance: The Structure of Genre' (*ChauR* 30.1–14), Robert B. Burlin argues that most scholars who have tried to define the characteristics of the romance genre have tended to minimize the importance of ideology. To correct this apparent oversight, Burlin proposes a generic model which he claims is able to take account of both the ideological and narrative elements of Middle English romance. Meanwhile, Ellie Ragland's 'Psychoanalysis and Courtly Love' (*Arthuriana* 5.1–20) asks whether contemporary Lacanian Psychoanalysis can contribute to an understanding of Medieval Studies, a question which she answers by elaborating upon some of Jacques Lacan's comments on the subject of courtly love. Unfortunately, Ragland makes no concessions to those who are unfamiliar with Lacanian theory, which means that her article will only be comprehensible to a few specialist readers.

6. Gower, Lydgate, Hoccleve

Two books deal with Gower in some detail. In Michael P. Kuczynski's *Prophetic Song*, the author offers an analysis of Lydgate's imitations of the Psalms, notably his use of Psalm 136. He examines the psalmic symbolism of the poet's *Defence of The Holy Church*, and argues for an earlier dating than has generally been accepted, reading it in tandem with British Library, Harley 1245 as a response to the Oldcastle rising of 1413 addressed to Henry V. In *Sciences and The Self in Medieval Poetry: Alan of Lille's Anticlaudianus and John Gower's Confessio Amantis*, James Simpson argues that the structure of the *Confessio* is 'informed by, and [is] itself a commentary on the structure of the sciences, and in particular the relations between ethics, politics and cosmology'. For Simpson, Genius and Amans represent faculties of the same soul, whose *bildungsroman* the poem is. Yet the text is not a seamless developmental narrative. There are 'deeply planted structural incongruences' within it. Using his reading of Ovid, Gower has created a text which, unlike his other works, has no reliable authority figure within it. 'Far from being coherently, consistently and persuasively didactic, the poem involves its reader as an active participant in the construction of its meaning'. This challenging and provocative study is more than simply a reading of its two chosen texts, however. It sets out to identify and categorize two distinct traditions within medieval humanism which are exemplified by Alan of Lille and Gower respectively. Alan, Simpson argues, is rooted firmly in 'humanism's absolutist strain', writing for a small elite, in 'difficult and highly mannered' Latin, his psychology is rooted in the Intellect, the supreme power of the soul, and he treats the body as marginal. His sympathies lie with Plato and Virgil, and his politics are absolutist, investing all power in the philosopher king. Gower, on the other hand, like Chaucer and Jean de Meun, belongs in the liberal humanist tendency. He writes 'for Englandes sake', in the vernacular, in a 'plain and limpid' style, for a wide audience. His psychology is rooted in the Imagination which 'mediates between the sensual desires and the reason'. His politics are constitutionalist, 'recognizing at every point the necessity for mediation between the king and the rest of the body politic', and his sympathies lie with Aristotle and Ovid.

　　Frank Grady's article 'The Lancastrian Gower and the Limits of Exemplarity' (*Speculum* 70.552–75) gives us Gower the politically engaged poet, and re-examines his 'In Praise of Peace' as a carefully modulated text, negotiating the political conditions of the years immediately after Henry IV's ascendancy. M. B. Parkes's 'Patterns of Scribal Activity and Revisions of the Text of Early Copies of Works by John Gower' (in Beadle and Piper, eds., *New Science Out of Old Books*) subjects the poet's work to careful palaeographical study. From a close analysis of three scribal hands in early Gower manuscripts, Parkes argues that, contrary to earlier accounts, the texts were not produced under the close supervision of the author in a scriptorium, whether at the Priory of St Mary Overeys or elsewhere. Rather, the evidence suggests that they were the work of 'neighbourhood scribes' in the London area, working independently or on ad hoc commissions.

Lydgate receives scant critical attention this year. In 'A Fragment of John Lydgate's *Life of Our Lady* in Gonville and Caius College, Cambridge', Stephen R. Reimer identifies 'a slip of vellum, presumably rescued from bookbinding' (Gonville and Caius MS 804/808 [1]) as part of a lost manuscript of Lydgate's *Life of Our Lady* from which two other fragments also survive elsewhere. He prints the text, parts of six rhyme-royal stanzas, and speculates about the nature of the manuscript as a whole. John Finlayson's 'Guido De Columnis' *Historia Destructionis Troiæ*, the *"Gest Hystorial" of The Destruction of Troy*, and Lydgate's *Troy Book*: Translation and the Design of History' (*Anglia* 113.141–62) touches on the poet, considering the late fourteenth- or early fifteenth-century alliterative romance, the *Gest Hystorial* in the light of its source, Guido de Columnis's *Historia*, and another translation of the same text, Lydgate's *Troy Book*. Rejecting the older view that both later texts are simply faithful translations of their source and so merit little literary attention, Finlayson argues that the *Gest*-poet, like Lydgate, is 'as concerned to interpret and shape his narrative material at the macro-level as he is at the micro-level; [and] that, while setting himself the restricting task of being faithful to his source-text, he gives it a clearer literary shape which amounts to an interpretation of the *sensus* of the story. Thus both texts ' "emplot" their revisioning of the Troy story as heroic tragedy'.

Hoccleve scholarship is even less well represented numerically speaking this year. Charity Scott Stokes's short article, 'Thomas Hoccleve's *Mother of God* and *Balade to the Virgin and Christ*: Latin and Anglo-Norman Sources' (*MÆ* 64.37–50) carries the field by default. Stokes finds sources for the *Mother of God* and *Balade* in the well-known prayer *O intermerata et in aeternum benedicta, specialis et incomparabilis virgo* and the Anglo-Norman poem *Pastourelle* respectively. Sections of Hoccleve's texts are printed in parallel with the relevant sections of the source texts to make good the claim.

7. Middle Scots Poetry

Teachers of Scottish Literature survey courses will be grateful for the publication of Roderick Watson's comprehensive anthology *The Poetry of Scotland: Gaelic, Scots, and English*, which seeks to make available in one volume 'the full canon of poetry from Scotland'. A brief but thought-provoking introductory essay sets the volume in the context of attempts to map out both a literary canon and a definition of Scottish national identity. There then follows a conventional table of contents and a further 'Table of Contents by Theme' which groups the poems under sub-headings such as 'The Common Folk', 'Political Life', 'Religion and Metaphysics', 'The Life of Women', 'Landscape and the Seasons' and 'Lament and Exile'. This arrangement creates an interesting and illuminating series of cross-references and inter-textual resonances, but readers will surely miss the opportunity to create such effects for themselves through the sort of browsing or pursuit of individual lines or ideas which a proper index and an index of first lines would have enabled. Sadly, neither is provided in this volume. The chosen works are lightly footnoted with a marginal glossary, with the Gaelic verse translated into modern English on the facing page. The texts themselves range from extracts from Barbour's *Bruce* and *The Kingis Quair* through Holland's *The Buke of the Howlat*, the anonymous *Taill of Rauf Coilyear* and Blind Harry's *William Wallace*, to the work of contemporary authors such as Tom Leonard and Liz Lockhead. From the Middle Scots period Dunbar's poetry is well represented, as are Henryson (in the form of extracts from *The Moral Fables* and the full text of *The Testament of Cresseid*) and Lindsay (extracts from *The Dreme* and *The Historie of Squyer Meldrum*) and a number of the anonymous contributors to the Asloan, Bannatyne and Maitland manuscripts. Gaelic poetry is represented by Giolla Críost Brúilingeach's 'The Poet asks an Irish Patron for a Harp', Aithbhreac Inghean Corcadail's '*A phaidrin do dhúisg mo dhéar*' and the anonymous '*Ar sliocht Gaodhal*', each with facing modern English verse translation by Derick Thomson.

Rather outside the scope of the current section, but of considerable interest to medievalists is Thomas Owen Clancy and Gilbert Márkus's *Iona: The Earliest Poetry of a Celtic Monastery*, which collects together eight poems in Latin and Gaelic written in the Irish monastery on the Hebridean island of Iona between AD 563 and 704. The texts are printed in the original languages with what the editors describe as 'fairly literal' translations into English on facing pages. The book is divided into four sections. Part One provides chapters on Iona's early history, the life and work of the Monastery, and Iona as a literary centre. Part Two prints the poems themselves with the translations, along with brief introductions and a commentary illuminating theological and literary themes and references. The texts printed are two abecedarian texts: the Hiberno-Latin hymn *Altus Prosator* and the *Adiutor Laborantium*; the brief Latin hymn *Noli Pater*, the Gaelic elegy for St Columba *Amra Choluimb Chille*; and the two Columban poems of Beccán mac Luigdech *To-fed andes/ Tiughraind Beccáin* and *Fo réir Choluimb*; Adomnán's *Colum Cille co Día domm eráil* and Cú Chuimne's hymn to the Virgin, *Cantemus in Omni Die*. Taken together these texts give a unique insight into the creation and consolidation of the cult of St Columba in the seventh century and the forms and cadences of 'Celtic Christianity' as practised and contemplated in this remote, but hugely significant monastic community. The volume is completed by two further sections, the first, 'The Alphabet of devotion', printing a translation of the *Apgitir Chrábaid* attributed to 'Colmán Elo' and the second, 'Iona's Library', identifying the texts probably known to the monks and used in their writings.

Henryson is the subject of Sabine Volk-Birke's 'Sickness unto Death: Crime and Punishment in Henryson's *The Testament of Cresseid*' (*Anglia* 113.163–84). After surveying previous treatments of Cresseid from Benoît de Sainte-Maure onwards, and late medieval literary and theological attitudes towards leprosy, the essay focuses upon a recuperative analysis of Henryson's protagonist. For Volk-Birke, the poem offers not a narrative of transgression and punishment intended to discipline unfaithful women, but the story of a heroine who finally learns to accept responsibility for her own sin and thereby gains self-knowledge and the freedom to act independently.

In 'The Entry of Wealth in the Middle Scots "Crying of ane Playe"' (*MP* 93.23–36), David Parkinson reads the early sixteenth-century poem 'The Manere of the Crying of ane Playe' (a grotesque cornucopia acting as prologue to the May Day celebrations in Edinburgh) in the context of both its literary heritage and its social consequences. The text, for Parkinson, is a Janus-faced cultural document, speaking for both social cohesion and demarcation, for mastery and liberty, husbandry and excess.

In '*Pamphilus De Amore* "In Inglish Toung" ' (*MÆ* 64.264–72), Priscilla Bawcutt draws attention to an extremely obscure Middle Scots translation of *Pamphilus* which was made at the end of the sixteenth century by James Burel, an Edinburgh goldsmith, and whose existence has been entirely overlooked by modern scholars. Bawcutt argues that the rediscovery of Burel's poem should be of interest not only to Scottish literary historians of the reign of James VI, but also to medievalists, as it provides further evidence of the enduring popularity of this important but neglected work. [David Salter]

8. Lyrics and Miscellaneous Verse

There are only two articles on lyrics this year. In 'The Troubadour's Lady Reconsidered Again' (*Speculum* 70.256–74), Don A. Monson takes issue with those critics, inspired by such figures as D. W. Robertson, E. Talbot Donaldson and John F. Benton, who dismiss the concept of courtly love as a modern myth. While accepting that the notion of courtly love needs to be refined, Monson argues that one can observe in troubadour poetry 'what must have been a considerable tolerance ... for love that transgresses the bounds of marriage and social class'. Meanwhile, Bella Millett's 'The Songs of the Entertainers and the Song of the Angels: Vernacular Lyric Fragments in Odo of Cheriton's *Sermones de Festis*' (*MÆ* 64.17–36), draws upon Siegfried Wenzel's discussion of sacred and profane love in *Preachers, Poets, and the Early English Lyric*, to examine Odo of Cheriton's use of secular lyrics in the *Sermones de Festis*.

9. Malory and Caxton

Two of the essays in *The Formation of Culture in Medieval Britain: Celtic, Latin, and Norman Influences on English Music, Literature, History, and Art*, edited by Françoise H. M. Le Saux, discuss Malory and the *Morte*. Barbara Belyea's 'Malory as Translator' traces the author's development as a translator, demonstrating his capacity for judicious amplification and abbreviation of his vulgate sources. P. J. C. Field's 'Fifteenth Century History in Malory's *Morte Darthur*' reviews previous historical readings of the *Morte*, identifies a number of possible contemporary allusions in the text, and ultimately rejects the notion that the author was investing the work with either a Lancastrian or a Yorkist slant. Elsewhere, Field offers a more particular interpretation of the text. In ' "Above Rubies": Malory and *Morte Arthure* 2559–61' (*N&Q* 42.29–30), he plausibly suggests that the Winchester manuscript reading that Gawain sundered 'the rubyes that were ryche' of the stranger knight might more plausibly be read as a scribal mistranscription of 'rybbys', removing the awkward implication that the knight carried precious stones beneath his hauberk.

Arthuriana also proves a useful source of work on Malory this year. In 'The Prose *Lancelot*'s Galehot, Malory's Lavain, and the Queering of Late Medieval Literature' (*Arthuriana* 5.21–51), Gretchen Mieszkowski applies 'queer theory' to medieval romances, drawing out potentially positive representations of homoerotic feelings and the men who experience them in the texts. In addition to a lengthy exposition of the homoerotic aspects of the treatment of Galehot in the Old French prose *Lancelot*, Mieszkowski attempts, perhaps with less success, to bring Sir Lavain, the brother of Elaine, the Fair Maid of Astolat, out of the closet as a conscious evocation on Malory's part of Galehot's devotion to Lancelot. In 'The Saint's Life of Sir Lancelot: Hagiography and the Conclusion of Malory's *Morte Darthur*' (*Arthuriana* 5.62–78), Karen Cherewatuk shows how Malory adopted and adapted the hagiographic tone and procedures of his sources in depicting Lancelot's final years.

Werner Hüllen's essay 'A Close Reading of William Caxton's *Dialogues*: ' . . . To Lerne Shortly Frenssh and Englysh' in the curate's egg of a collection *Historical Pragmatics*, ed. Andreas H. Jucker, subjects the printer's pedagogic dialogue to a modified form of the framework devised by John Sinclair and R. Malcolm Coulthard (*Towards an Analysis of Discourse* [OUP, 1975]) for the analysis of classroom discourse. Hüllen concludes that the *Dialogues* display a 'scholastic realism', a lively reflection of actual schoolroom practice, albeit the performance recorded is more likely to be a monologue performed by a teacher, possibly in the Mercers' schools in Bruges and London, than a true dialogue between tutor and pupil.

10. Other Prose

One of the most impressive achievements this year has been Linne R. Mooney's contribution to *The Index of Middle English Prose Handlist XII*. Her handlist of Middle English prose contained in the library of Trinity College, Cambridge, is bulky, and reflects the size of the library's holdings in this area. Prominent is theological prose, some orthodox and some heterodox, and also well-represented are scientific interests. Mooney's handlist has brought to light a large quantity of new or previously unascribed texts and translations, and is to be thoroughly recommended for the evident care of its preparation and its usefulness as a research tool.

The Middle English Texts series, under the general editorship of Manfred Görlach and Oliver Pickering, can always be relied on to deliver editions of quality, and volume 27, missed for review last year, is no exception. Görlach has edited *The Kalendre of the Newe Legende of Englande*, first published by Pynson in 1516. *The Kalendre* is based on de Worde's *Nova Legenda Angliae*, published also in 1516. In the introduction, Görlach shows how *The Kalendre* relates to the *Nova Legenda*, and suggests that *The Kalendre* may be aiming at 'a bourgeois readership eager for information but incapable of getting it from Latin texts'. The edition comes with a standard (and copious) apparatus.

James M. Girsch provides a very useful commentary on 'An Elizabethan Manuscript of Mirk's *Festial* Sermon on St Winnifred and Observations on the "Shrewsbury Manuscript" ' (*NM* 96.265–9). His textual findings will be indispensable to the new projected edition of the *Festial* currently being prepared by Susan Powell and Alan J. Fletcher. In 'William Taylor's 1406 Sermon: A Postscript' (*MÆ* 64.100–6), Anne Hudson is able to add a Latin version of William Taylor's sermon, preserved in Prague, National Library, III.G.11, alongside the Middle English one witnessed in Oxford, Bodleian Library, Douce 53. George A. Keiser is able to make good a gap at the end of the Early English Text Society edition of the *Secreta Secretorum*, which was based on British Library, Royal 18.A.7, from a version in British Library, Cotton Vespasian E. XVI, in 'Filling in a Lacuna in a Middle English *Secreta Secretorum*' (*NM* 96.381–8).

As might be currently expected, Margery Kempe is enjoying a new lease of life. Michael J. Wright argues in his sensitively tuned piece, 'What they said to Margery Kempe: Narrative Reliability in her *Book*' (*Neophil* 79.497–508), that it may indeed be possible to discern moments of historical transparency in her narrative, and that moments that seem irrelevant, or apparently contradictory, to the main thrust of the narrative may be the most productive in this regard. In 'Cobham's Daughter: *The Book of Margery Kempe* and the Power of Heterodox Thinking' (*MLQ* 56.277–304), Ruth Shklar presents Margery as a rock upon which popular notions of heresy and dissent, exposed as incoherent, perish. Though occasionally overstated, this article provides much thoughtful reflection on the terms in which orthodox ideology constructed itself, and on Margery's stance vis-à-vis both the orthodox and heterodox parties inhabiting early fifteenth-century England. Janette Dillon persuasively endorses the maxim that identity is socially constructed in 'The Making of Desire in *The Book of Margery Kempe*' (*LeedsSE* 26.113–44). In an analysis of Margery's desire in the *Book*, she makes the interesting suggestion, among others, that Lollardy was a cultural force instrumental in clearing a space in which Margery's own struggle for control and identity could be played out.

F. N. M. Diekstra's substantial and careful article ' "A Good Remedie aȝens Spirituel Temptacions": A Conflated Middle English Version of William Flete's *De Remediis contra Temptationes* and Pseudo-Hugh of St Victor's *De Pusillanimate* in London BL MS Royal 18.A.X' (*ES* 76.307–54) edits *A Good Remedie* in parallel with its immediate sources. The whole is furnished with invaluable apparatus. Tamarah Kohanski proposes two adjustments to M. C. Seymour's 'English Manuscripts of *Mandeville's Travels*' in 'Two Manuscripts of *Mandeville's Travels*' (*N&Q* 42.269–70).

11. Drama

This section is divided into the following subsections: (a) Editions and General Studies; (b) Chester; (c) N-Town; (d) Moralities.

(a) Editions and General Studies

This year there is relatively little to report, but what there is is of good quality. Janet Burton throws 'New Light on the "Summergame" ' (*N&Q* 42.428–9), a term scantily attested in early English sources. Her additional evidence suggests that the summergame was a significant event in the life of English parishes; that part of the game's proceeds went to church funds; and that a king and queen of the game were elected from among the children present. In 'Plays as Play: A Medieval Ethical Theory of Performance and the Intellectual Context of *The Tretise of Miraclis Pleyinge*' (*Viator* 26.195– 221), Glending Olson surveys a group of texts from which he usefully distils many medieval concepts of performance. In particular, he isolates the concept of which many medievals seem to have been possessed that plays were a variety of play. Some of his sources are familiar, others refreshingly less so.

(b) Chester
In 'The Rainbow as Archer's Bow in the Chester Cycle's *Noah's Flood*' (*N&Q* 42.27–9), Kathryn Wells demonstrates an analogue to the Chester play of *Noah's Flood*, lines 321–4, in Guillaume de Deguileville's *Pèlerinage de la Vie humaine*.

(c) N-Town
An interesting study of 'Mary's Obedience and Power in *The Trial of Mary and Joseph*' (*CompD* 29.348–62) by Cindy L. Carlson takes as her point of departure the theories of the fifteenth-century lawyer Sir John Fortescue in order to understand the legal framework within which *The N-Town play* of Mary and Joseph's trial has been constructed. She finds Mary's trial to subject not only her but also the legal system in which she is located to judgement.

(d) Moralities
Denise Ryan complicates the significance of the word 'chered' in the admonition of Good Deeds to *Everyman* in ' "If ye had parfytely chered me": The Nurturing of Good Deeds in *Everyman*' (*N&Q* 42.165–8). She convincingly illustrates resonances in the word beyond those detected by *Everyman*'s editors.

Books Reviewed

Barber, Malcolm. *The New Knighthood: A History of the Order of the Temple.* Canto, CUP. pp. 419. pb £8.95. ISBN 0 521 55872 7.
Barron, W. R. J., and S. C. Weinberg, ed. and trans. *Laʒamon's Brut.* Longman. pp. 896. ISBN 0 582 24651 2.
Bartlett, Anne Clark, Thomas Bestul, Janet Goebel, and William F. Pollard, eds. *Vox Mystica: Essays on Medieval Mysticism in Honor of Professor Valerie M. Lagorio.* Brewer. pp. 235. £39.50. ISBN 0 85991439 9.
Baswell, Christopher. *Virgil in Medieval England: Figuring the Aeneid from the Twelfth Century to Chaucer.* Cambridge Studies in Medieval Literature, 24. CUP. pp. 422. £40. ISBN 0 521 46294 0.
Beadle, Richard, and A. J. Piper, eds. *New Science Out of Old Books: Studies in Manuscripts and Early Printed Books in Honour of A. I. Doyle.* Scolar. pp. 440. £65. ISBN 1 85928 003.
Braswell, Mary Flowers, ed. *Sir Perceval of Galles and Ywain and Gawain.* WMU. pp. 212. $16. ISBN 1 879288 60 5.
Cadden, Joan. *Meanings of Sex Difference in the Middle Ages.* CUP. pp. 303. hb £40, pb £14.95. ISBN 0 521 34363 1, 0 521 48378 6.
Cash, June H., ed. *The Cultural Patronage of Medieval Women.* UGeoP. pp. 372. hb £47.95, pb £19.95. ISBN 0 8203 1701 2, 0 8203 1702 0.
Clancy, Thomas Owen, and Gilbert Márkus, eds. *Iona: The Earliest Poetry of a Celtic Monastery.* EdinUP. pp. 268. £12.95. ISBN 0 7486 0531 2.
Collinson, Patrick, N. Ramsey, and M. Sparks, eds. *A History of Canterbury Cathedral.* OUP. pp. 570. £25. ISBN 0 19 820051 X.

Constable, Giles. *Three Studies in Medieval Religious and Social Thought: The Interpretation of Mary and Martha, the Ideal of the Imitation of Christ, the Orders of Society*. CUP. pp. 403. £40. ISBN 0 521 30515 2.

Görlach, Manfred, ed. *The Kalendre of the Newe Legende of Englande*. MET. CWU. pp. 253. pb DM 128. ISBN 3 8253 0217 2.

Guerin, M. Victoria. *The Fall of Kings and Princes: Structure and Destruction in Arthurian Tragedy*. StanfordUP. pp. 321. £27.95. ISBN 08047 2290 0.

Hahn, Thomas, ed. *Sir Gawain: Eleven Romances and Tales*. WMU. pp. 439. $16. ISBN 1 879288 59 1.

Hassig, Debra. *Medieval Bestiaries: Text, Image, Ideology*. CUP. pp. 300. £55. ISBN 0 521 47026 9.

Head, David M. *The Ebbs and Flows of Fortune: The Life of Thomas Howard, Third Duke of Norfolk*. UGeoP. pp. 370. £43.95. ISBN 0 8283 1683 0.

Jantzen, Grace M. *Power, Gender, and Christian Mysticism*. CUP. pp. 379. hb £40, pb £14.95. ISBN 0 521 47376 4, 0 521 47926 6.

Jucker, Andreas J., ed. *Historical Pragmatics: Pragmatic Developments in the History of English*. Benjamins. pp. 601. US$97. ISBN 1 55619 3289.

Kuczynski, Michael P. *Prophetic Song: The Psalms as Moral Discourse in Late Medieval England*. UPennP. pp. 283. £34.95. ISBN 0 8122 3271 2.

Laskaya, Anne, and Eve Salisbury, eds. *The Middle English Breton Lays*. WMU. pp. 444. $10. ISBN 1 879288 62 1.

Le Saux, Françoise H. M. *The Formation of Culture in Medieval Britain: Celtic, Latin, and Norman Influences on English Music, Literature, History, and Art*. Mellen. pp. 197. £49.95. ISBN 0 7734 9119 8.

Marx, C. W. *The Devil's Rights and The Redemption in the Literature of Medieval England*. Brewer. pp. 178. £29.50. ISBN 0 8599 1455 0.

McGrade, Arthur Stephen, and John Killcullen, eds. *William of Ockham: A Letter to the Friars Minor and Other Writings*, trans. John Killcullen. CUP. pp. 390. £16.95.

Mooney, Linne R., ed. *The Index of Middle English Prose Handlist XII: Manuscripts in the Library of Trinity College, Cambridge*. Brewer. pp. 251. £45. ISSN 0267 2472.

Putter, Ad. *Sir Gawain and The Green Knight and French Arthurian Romance*. Clarendon. pp. 279. £30. ISBN 0 19 818253 8.

Rushing, James A. *Images of Adventure: Ywain in the Visual Arts*. UPennP. pp. 300. £38. ISBN 0 8122 3293 3.

Schmidt, A. V. C., ed. *William Langland, Piers Plowman: A Parallel-Text Edition of the A, B, C, and Z Versions*. Longman. pp. 762. £145. ISBN 0 582 00325 3.

Simpson, James. *Sciences and The Self in Medieval Poetry: Alan of Lille's Anticlaudianus and John Gower's Confessio Amantis*. CUP. pp. 314. £40. ISBN 0 521 47181 8.

Smith, Lesley, and Jane M. H. Taylor, eds. *Women, The Book, and The Godly: Selected Proceedings of the St. Hilda's Conference, 1993*, volume I. Brewer. pp. 184. £35. ISBN 0 85991 420 8.

Swanson, R. N. *Religion and Devotion in Europe, c.1215– c.1515*. Cambridge Medieval Textbooks. CUP. pp. 538. hb £40, pb £14.95. ISBN 0 521 37076 0, 0 521 37950 4.

Tavormina, Teresa M. *Kindly Similitude: Marriage and Family in Piers Plowman*. B&B. pp. 248. £39.50. ISBN 0 85991 454 2.

Terry, Patricia, trans. *The Honeysuckle and the Hazel Tree: Medieval Stories of Men and Women*. UCalP. pp. 218. ISBN 0 500 08379 2.

Turner, Denys. *The Darkness of God: Negativity in Christian Mysticism*. CUP. pp. 275. £35. ISBN 0 521 45317 8.

Utz, Richard J., ed. *Literary Nominalism and the Theory of Rereading Late Medieval Texts: A New Research Paradigm*. Mellen. pp. 251. US$89.95. ISBN 0 7734 8882 0.

Vantuono, William, ed. *Pearl: An Edition with Verse Translation*. UNDP. pp. 255. hb £23.95, pb £12.95. ISBN 0 268 03810 4, 0 268 03811 2.

Watson, Roderick. *The Poetry of Scotland: Gaelic, Scots, and English*. EdinUP. pp. 714. £19.95. ISBN 0 7486 0607 6.

IV

Middle English: Chaucer

VALERIE ALLEN and MARGARET CONNOLLY

This chapter is divided into four sections: 1. General, 2. *Canterbury Tales*; 3. *Troilus and Criseyde*; 4. Other Works. The ordering of individual tales and poems within the sections follows that of the *Riverside Chaucer* edition.

1. General

Once again Mark Allen and Bege K. Bowers have compiled 'An Annotated Chaucer Bibliography, 1993' (*SAC* 17.287–362). Francis X. Ryan evaluates 'Sir Thomas More's Use of Chaucer' (*SEL* 35.1–17), gathering together a number of Chaucerian citations in More's work. Even though his approach is conservative rather than comprehensive, his tally includes 15 references to the *Canterbury Tales*, as well as less frequent allusions to *Troilus and Criseyde*, *An ABC* and the *Parliament of Fowls*. Ryan pays particular attention to More's use of the Griselde figure in the depiction of the two central female characters in the *History of Richard III*, and also identifies a number of More's works in which no Chaucerian influence has been traced. D. E. Wickham sheds some possible light and local colour upon Thomas Speght in 'An Early Editor of Chaucer Reidentified?' (*N&Q* 42.428). In 1612, Ralph Treswell drew up a survey of the estates of the London Clothworkers' Company, in which he notes that the house and chapel of St James in the Wall was leased, at the time of survey, by one Thomas Speght (whom the *DNB* describes as a schoolmaster) and that the second storey contained a 'Schoolhowse'.

In 'A Chaucerian "Courtly Love Aunter" by Henry Howard, Earl of Surrey' (*Neophil* 79.675–87), Martine Braekman looks at a little-known poem by Surrey as an example of the continuity rather than disjunction between the late medieval and sixteenth-century English love lyric. The courtly love aunter is a narrative frame that gives rise to a lyric such as a lover's complaint or a debate contained within itself; as a form, the aunter is highly stylized, with topoi such as the opening description of a spring morning or a walk into a *locus amoenus*. Surrey's poem, which is written in this aunter convention, *Complaint of a diyng louer refused vpon his ladies iniust mistaking of his writyng*, is shown to have echoes of the *House of Fame*, *Troilus and Criseyde* and, most closely, the *Book of the Duchess*, as well as a number of post-

Chaucerian poems, imitative of Chaucer's style. Michael Watson notes stylistic similarities, albeit modified by their respective cultural and literary contexts, between Chaucer's work and the *Tale of the Heike* in 'Genre, Convention, Parody, and the "Middle Flight": *Heike Monogatari* and Chaucer' (*Poetica* 44.23–40). In the same journal (13–22), Bonnie Wheeler contends that what Chaucer did for the English language, the earlier female writer, Murasaki Shikibu, did for Japanese: 'Grammar, Genre, and Gender in Geoffrey Chaucer and Murasaki Shikibu'. The grammatical openness of both writers, notably in their paratactic style, enables a fluid movement between and blending of narrative voices; and for both writers, the preoccupation with womanly nature and female subjectivity is paramount.

Michael Seymour has published the first volume of *A Catalogue of Chaucer Manuscripts* which covers the works before the *Canterbury Tales*. This extremely useful little book covers 88 manuscripts and fragments, bringing together descriptions of manuscripts, some published by Seymour himself, from separate contexts. The works are treated in the assumed order of Chaucer's composition, each entry beginning with a headnote which records information about the work's date, the circumstances of its composition, and its early readership. Seymour takes account of recent textual and linguistic scholarship, and offers a fresh assessment of the bibliography of each work. His description of each manuscript provides details of its collation, decoration and layout; a list of its contents and any marginalia; some information about the scribal hand; and some details of the manuscript's subsequent history, where this is known. He does not include the *Equatorie of the Planetis*, and, regrettably, all of the shorter poems, with the exception of *Anelida and Arcite*, are grouped as apocrypha and consigned to an appendix, where their manuscript witnesses are not indexed, nor even individually identified. It is a pity too that considerations of cost have precluded the inclusion of facsimile pages, but the volume's format is easy to use, and its size will make it a handy companion on research trips; this will be a welcome reference tool for manuscript scholars. A. S. G. Edwards charts 'Chaucer from Manuscript to Print' (*Mosaic* 28.iv.1–12), seeking to theorize some of the historical factors involved in the transition. Whereas medieval readers were content merely to have a text, the development of a print culture created different expectations; the onus on the early printers was to produce a text which was complete (a particular problem in the light of Chaucer's many unfinished works), and then to provide more works by the same authors, leading to canonical confusion and a steady process of textual corruption. Edwards contrasts the previous focus on the preservation of text with the current insistence on its recovery, achieved through the production of critical editions; though he claims not to be arguing against this mode of scholarship, he does contend that contextual forms of editorial activity may be equally valid.

Sae-gon Park writes about 'The Transition from the Impersonal to the Personal Construction in English – with Reference to Data Analysis of the Sentences which Contain the Infinitives' (*JELL* 41.827–43) (in Korean, with an abstract in English). Various classes of construction are identified: for example, the A-type impersonal construction in which the logical subject of the infinitive is a dative or accusative ('me were levere dye'); or the S-type impersonal construction in which the bare infinitive becomes the '(for) to' infinitive with the appearance of a dummy 'it' ('it happed hym to ryde'). In this latter case, the dummy 'it' no longer permits the feeling of the impersonal. Taking *Beowulf* and the *Canterbury Tales* as representative Old and Middle English texts, Park finds that Old English constructions are exclusively of the A-type while Middle English constructions are various, showing the verb construction to be in transition in this period. Andrew Breeze elaborates on 'Chaucer's "Malkin" and Dafydd ap Gwilym's "Mald y Cwd" ' (*N&Q* 42.159–60), noting the general associations, borne out by the Man of Law's 'Malkyn' and the Reeve's 'Malin', of a low born, perhaps also wanton, woman. The association is also there in the Welsh equivalent 'Mald'. Breeze disputes the authorities that trace the name from 'Mary' and shows that it derives from 'Matilda' or 'Maud'. Norman Blake discusses the relationship between 'Speaking and Writing: An Historical Overview' in a special issue of *YES*, entitled 'Non-standard Englishes and the New Media' (25.6–21). Blake brings Chaucer into the discussion in observing how difficult it is to establish whether apparently spoken elements of a text have been introduced deliberately to create an oral effect, or whether they are simply variants of the written. A quote from the Hengwrt text of the *Knight's Tale* that shows some confusion in subject/verb agreement illustrates the uncertainty of division between the spoken and written. On the other hand, the northernisms of the *Reeve's Tale* do demonstrate an attempt to make the written mimic speech, which implies that the written conventions have to have been stable enough to make the dialectical variation noticeable.

In 'Chaucer, Humanism, and Printing: Conditions of Authorship in Fifteenth-Century England' (*UTQ* 64.ii.274–88), David R. Carlson considers the growing professionalization of writing in the fifteenth century. Although Chaucer himself was not a professional writer, those who imitated and eulogized him after his death did so for monetary gain. The early printers were similarly motivated, as Carlson notes (without irony): 'Printing Chaucer was not risky. Chaucer's name, even attached to things he did not write, made books saleable'. He also charts, briefly, the impact of the humanists on literary history, and prints and translates Surigone's eulogy of Chaucer, but his article leaves the impression that too many large topics have been crammed into too small a space. Derek Pearsall offers a well-researched discussion of 'Chaucer's Tomb: The Politics of Reburial' (*MÆ* 64.51–73). Providing a nice plan of Westminster Abbey, Pearsall describes how Chaucer achieved his objective of being buried within the church, but unfortunately ended up in 'a fairly modest place'. The translation of his remains, and their reburial in the south transept (a much worthier resting place), in 1556, constituted an act of Catholic readoption typical of the brief reign of Mary Tudor. And in a complicated article, 'On "Correctness": A Note on Some Press Variants in Thynne's 1532 Edition of Chaucer' (*Library* 17.156–67), Joseph A. Dane criticizes the indiscriminate use of the terms 'corrected' and 'uncorrected' in the description of early press variants. His particular concern is with the 1974 Scolar Press facsimile, now the most accessible and best-known copy of William Thynne's edition, because its unsigned 'Publisher's Postscript' implies, wrongly, that the facsimile offers a 'corrected state' of the 1532 edition. The details of Dane's argument are hard to follow, but his conclusion is clear.

André Crépin introduces a selection of French translations of Chaucer's works, done by a number of French scholars, in 'Geoffrey Chaucer' in *Premières mutations de Petrarque à Chaucer 1304–1400*, edited by Jean-

Claude Polet. The introduction contains biographical detail and description of his major works and adopts a cautious attitude towards less well attested assumptions such as Chaucer's visit to Spain and his authorship of *Equatorie of the Planetis*. The excerpts themselves are from *Anelida and Arcite*, *Troilus and Criseyde*, *Truth*, *General Prologue* and the *Wife of Bath's Prologue*, the last being the only prose translation in this collection of the original verse.

Music in the Age of Chaucer is the second edition of Nigel Wilkins's study of Chaucer's music which first appeared in 1979 (*YWES* 60.104); the reissue is different only in that it also incorporates Wilkins's other volume, *Chaucer Songs*, first published in 1980 (*YWES* 61.103). Joyce Coleman challenges the theoretical assumptions that have erased aurality from the modern conception of the past in 'Interactive Parchment: The Theory and Practice of Medieval English Aurality' (*YES* 25.63–79). She cites the evidence of contemporary medieval records to show that literate book-owners nevertheless continued to listen to their books, rather than read them silently and privately, throughout the late Middle Ages, and concludes that Chaucer wrote with an audience of literate listeners in mind. Problems connected with reading are also Jill Mann's concern. At the beginning of her presidential address to the New Chaucer Society on 'Chaucer and Atheism' (*SAC* 17.5–19), she asks how an atheist reads Chaucer, working round some time later to the not very surprising answer 'as an atheist', but before she reaches this conclusion she explores historicism, presentism and humanism, and takes some side-swipes at those who have criticized aspects of her feminism.

Jane Chance has a densely packed study entitled *The Mythographic Chaucer: The Fabulation of Sexual Poetics*. Where earlier mythographic study has tended to focus on questions of individual sources, or on single lines, Chance's method is more systematic and comprehensive, grounded, as it is, in the belief that Chaucer's use of myth is not piecemeal and that his earlier and later work is more unified in design than has been usually acknowledged. Where medieval mythography is associated most with allegory, Chaucer's use of mythography to ironize, localize, and characterize is so singular that Chance calls it 'antimythography'. The ambivalent status of mythography as simultaneously authoritative and yet marginalized through its paganness leads, not unsurprisingly, to its feminization as 'other'. Chance contends that the classical gods and heroes, ironically depicted by Chaucer, disclose feminizing and subversive attitudes. The Macrobian and received view of mythography – that it is a narrative or allegorical *integumentum* hiding often unsavoury truths – is only half the story for Chaucer; alongside it is the Parson's injunction to declare the truth plainly; the two exist at least in tension with each other, yet both must constitute art. The book is divided into three parts and ranges across the whole Chaucerian corpus. The first part examines feminine authority in the dream visions. Thus, by her virtue of *praesumptio* (boldess, courage), Alceste in the Prologue to the *Legend of Good Women* is mythographically linked not to Cupid but to Hercules, who rescued her from the underworld, which signifies irrationality, and is the prototype of *fortitudo* and *sapientia*. And Venus in the *Parliament of Fowls* gets a very positive reading, the negative implications of unchaste lust being largely displaced onto the mythographical significance of her companions and surroundings. Part Two constitutes one long chapter on the topos of 'cross-gendering' in *Troilus*. Where courtly love effeminizes Troilus, the exchange of Criseyde for

Antenor, ironically an event that underscores the feminine vulnerability of her situation, masculinizes her, forcing her to rationalize her emotion. In the final section, the emergence of a feminine subjectivity is explored in the *Canterbury Tales*. Here, the veiling of political reference is more pointed. The figure of Zephirus is mythographically read by Chance as analogous to St Thomas à Becket, whose feminization is seen in a martyrdom that amounts to political rape. Theseus in the *Knight's Tale* acts in the beginning with more martian boldness than with minervan wisdom, but progresses through the poem to a 'feminine side' enabled by the female characters in the story. And the Wife of Bath brings new meaning to feminine subjectivity when she upends the traditional, exegetic and patristic relation between tale and interpretation by making the fictional tale she tells act not as that which is to be glossed but as the gloss itself upon her own autobiography. The book is a long read but well rewards perseverance with its erudite scholarship. Another difficult but thoughtful book comes from last year: James J. Paxson's *The Poetics of Personification*, in which Paxson rescues the device of prosopopeia from its status of poor cousin to allegory and considers its philosophical significance in the light of contemporary postmodern theory. In his schema, he distinguishes between various ontological levels of personified being: the speaking aspect of a figure is central to a proper taxonomy of personification poetics. In the *House of Fame, Parliament of Fowls* and *Nun's Priest's Tale*, Chaucer is seen to complicate the personification trope into an elaborate act of self-reflexivity. Particularly striking is Chaucer's contrast between aphasic 'real' characters (such as the historical poets mentioned in *House*, or Africanus and the narrator in *Parliament*) and the voluble prosopopoetic characters of Fame etc. or of Nature and the birds in *Parliament*. Even in the *Nun's Priest's Tale*, the human characters only utter broken exclamations and noises. The boundaries between the exclusive ontological and phenomenal worlds of the human and the prosopopoetic are thus called by Chaucer into question.

Last year saw Susan Crane's *Gender and Romance in Chaucer's Canterbury Tales* (*YWES* 75.176–7); this year sees a continuation of the theme, though with broader application to the Chaucerian corpus, with Angela Jane Weisl's *Conquering the Reign of Femeny: Gender and Genre in Chaucer's Romance*. Throughout the discussion, the spatial topos is employed as a metaphor for gender: the feminine is represented by closed, interior spaces, the masculine by open; indeed, in romance, gender difference is what sustains the very extension of narrative itself. In *Troilus and Criseyde*, the play between public and private space is most pronounced; the discourse of the public sphere is marked by martial masculinity; that of the private, by amorous femininity. Just as the private space of Criseyde's widowed subjectivity, in which she attains at least a degree of autonomy, must be invaded by masculine presence, so the enclosure that is Troy inevitably must relinquish its internal dominion to the sacking Greeks. Criseyde's banishment spells out the death of Troy, suggesting that the apparently public and male world of Trojan history and politics defines itself by means and in terms of the possession of the feminine. The point also stands for romance in its entirety: it is a genre that paradoxically requires woman as the narrative's sustaining telos and marginalizes woman by reducing her to object, rather than subject, of the narrative. In the *Knight's Tale*, 'Femynye' – a dark unexplored continent of the sexual Other, in true Hélène Cixous fashion – poses a threat to Theseus's chivalric order. The denial of Emelye's wish to remain chaste represents the conquest of Femynye necessary to maintain that chivalric order. The Squire, on the other hand, grants Canacee a degree of self-determination, thereby creating a tale that threatens the very notion of romance and that must be attenuated. The feminization of Thopas only highlights the total absence of female presence in the poem and shows Chaucer parodying the gender assumptions of romance in order to critique them. The Breton *lai* offers more liberating possibilities for female agency which Chaucer avails of in the tales of the Wife of Bath and Franklin. However, the Wife's 'maistrye' and Franklin's egalitarian marriage between Dorigen and Arveragus offer only momentary possibilities of such liberation, for the Loathly Lady transforms herself to romance heroine and Arveragus abandons his 'servage' in favour of traditional marital dominion. Robert Burlin also considers the genre in terms of a Saussurean analysis of a paradigmatic axis of chivalric and courtly codes and a syntagmatic axis of the quest and the text: 'Middle English Romance: The Structure of Genre' (*ChauR* 30.1–14). By plotting the *Knight's Tale* onto this graph, we find that Chaucer develops a tension between the chivalric and courtly codes and exposes the contingent nature of their supposedly abstract systems of behaviour. In the analysis of *Troilus*, it is too simple to say that Criseyde is tested and fails the courtly code; Chaucer rather calls into question the code itself.

Norman Klassen's *Chaucer on Love, Knowledge and Sight* is a comparative examination of a number of discourses all of which converge on the issue of sight and its significance for the relationship between love and knowledge. The doctrine of illumination, physical representation in aesthetics, optical theory, epistemology, as well as love poetry, are all informing influences upon Chaucer's visual metaphors. In the first chapter, the metaphysical background (provided by Plato, Augustine, Pseudo-Dionysius etc.) is considered; although it is from here that we can trace the opposition between inner and outer vision (that is, between sight and belief), it is also from here that the connection can be drawn between epistemological and aesthetic vision (that is, between truth and beauty). This eliding of knowledge and love is nicely brought into focus in a quote from Leon Battista Alberti, where the analogy is drawn between achieving optimal visual perspective and shooting an arrow through the eye. Klassen's own dominating metaphor is that of the *parasitisme*, which maintains a 'relationship of hostility and symbiosis between love and knowledge'. This parasitic relation is demonstrated in how, on the one hand, thinkers such as Grosseteste argue that human sense perception had remained intact after the fall and was actually capable of aiding the rehabilitation of the higher faculties – in other words, that natural light and the light of revealed truth have a common source; yet on the other hand, there persist representations of love as a sickness (with all the sensory corruption it entails), and an entrenched poetic opposition between passion and reason (as in Amant's dismissal of Raison in *Roman de la Rose*). The corruptive power of love at first sight upon reason is traced by Klassen in Arcite's love malady and in both Troilus's and Criseyde's first visual encounters with each other (Chapter Three). The amphitheatre expresses the equivocation between love and knowledge; although built on account of love, it represents Theseus's opposition to the lovers' enterprise. The tempering of passion and its concomitant reconciliation between love and knowledge is represented in the transmuting of Palamon's desire into marriage and in Troilus's ascent to the eighth sphere, with which Klassen contrasts its source in the *Commedia*. Where Dante prefers to look upwards and finds the vision of earth a mere curiosity, Troilus's attention is focused upon looking downwards. Some of the technicalities of optical theory have interesting implications. Opinion was divided upon whether light emanates from the eyes to illuminate the object (extramission) or emanates from objects to penetrate the eyes (intromission); the debate raises the question of the relation of subject to object in a manner analagous to how the Chaucerian narrator exhibits an increasing self-awareness in his position of viewing subject (e.g. the repetition of 'sawgh I' in the *House of Fame*).

Jeffrey L. Singman's and Will McLean's *Daily Life in Chaucer's England* is the latest in the growing collection of books on rituals of the quotidian in fourteenth-century England. Its focus, however, is less exclusively on the scholarly audience than is, for example, Derek Brewer's *Chaucer and his World* (*YWES* 59.104–5). The authors prefer to describe their project as 'living history' with a 'hands-on approach to the past'. This difference of perspective is apparent from the book's ample directions for contemporary re-enactment of medieval mores: patterns for making men's and women's clothes, food recipes, musical scores and lyrics (including *Angelus ad virginem*), rules for card, board and ball games and many more, steps for dances, calligraphic characters and so on. Certainly, the book is directly useful for those involved in medieval festivals and events, but it may also provoke the imaginations of school and university teachers as well as costume designers for theatre. Although explicit allusion to and explanation of Chaucer's text is rarely made, the chapters are full of details that bear upon it. From the chapter on clothing and accessories, we learn that black was a particularly expensive dye (think of Alison's clothes), that fustian was a cotton/linen mix used particularly for military undergarments (think of the Knight), and we are taken through the complete toilette of both sexes in a way that brings Alison's, Absolom's and the Wife's portraits to life. A passage on privies is most instructive, down to the 'arsewisps' made of cloth or straw. Since the subject has been raised and especially in view of the book's emphasis upon history from the bottom up, as it were, one looks in vain for any discussion of the logistics of female sanitary protection, given that women did not wear breeches. Accessible and informative, the book is well worth recommending to students, although, as background reading goes, it is not cheap.

In the same vein, though with more specific attention to Chaucer, is Margaret Hallissy's *Canterbury Tales: A Companion to Chaucer's Canterbury Tales*. This book is for the student who is entirely new to Chaucer. Using the text of the Riverside edition, Hallissy provides all quotations from the original with her own paraphrases and each chapter ends with a list of suggested further reading. The introductory chapter, on Chaucer's world, presents a medieval world characterized as 'strikingly homogeneous' by modern comparisons, with its inhabitants sharing a common belief in the afterlife and an 'all-pervasive concept of order'. Apart from the fact that this quietist picture has long since been called into question by contemporary critical opinion (in which the moments of dissent and marginalization in medieval culture are emphasized instead), one could make similar claims anyway for late twentieth-century beliefs as all sharing, for example, a common acceptance of basic psychoanalytic truths, such as the power of the unconscious and the relation between dreams and waking life. A chapter on Chaucer's language delineates the tri-lingual culture of England with its Latin, French and English, but gives no grammatical instruction as such. One chapter is devoted to each of the main tales although the interrupted tales (*Cook's, Squire's, Monk's* and *Tale of Sir Thopas*) and the prose tales (*Parson's* and *Tale of Melibee*) are placed in appendixes. Some connections between the tales are drawn: the *Franklin's* and *Physician's Tales* both concern themselves with the preservation of female chastity; the tales of Fragment A are associated by the motif of *quyting* and by the image of Fortune's wheel; indeed, the turning of the wheel of Fortune becomes the touchstone of the entire study. An appendix on the links also elaborates the relations between tales. Critical positions on individual tales tend, as one might expect with a propaedeutic work such as this, towards the conservative, and usually take the relation between the pilgrims and their narratives as the point of departure for exegesis of any tale. Focus is also very much on the Canterbury text and so references to extrinsics such as statutes, sumptuary law or rules of ecclesiastical orders are not usually cited directly. By far the longest chapter is on the *Wife of Bath's Tale*, reflecting Hallissy's interests continued from her recent book on Chaucer's women: *Clean Maids, True Wives, Steadfast Widows* (*YWES* 74.147). These interests are evident in the analysis of the *Clerk's Tale* also, where Griselde's sorry story is read entirely within the context of medieval books on marriage and conduct for women; allegorical interpretations are not addressed; nor are their possibilities explored, for example, in reading the *Friar's Tale* as a parody of Pentecost. Exposing the novice student to a variety of interpretative approaches could surely have been accommodated without compromising the integrity of Hallissy's own analysis. Like Singman's book, *A Companion* comes in hardback and is not cheap.

The aim of Carol Falvo Heffernan's book, *The Melancholy Muse: Chaucer, Shakespeare, and Early Medicine*, is to show that these poets and their contemporary physicians viewed melancholy in a parallel way. She begins by exploring what the poets could have known, placing their texts against a background of medical prose writing, as well as offering a definition of melancholy; this first chapter also includes discussion of Chaucer's 'verray parfit praktisour', the Physician. In the second chapter, she moves on to examine how sleeping, reading, and talking were used by contemporary doctors to treat the symptoms of mental disease, and then considers how the narrator-dreamer in the *Book of the Duchess* employs these same three 'cures'. The third chapter, which has already appeared in print (*YWES* 71.249), focuses on *Troilus and Criseyde* and draws parallels between the literary portrayal of love and medieval medical thinking on *amor hereos*; the latter, she argues, is an integral part of the imaginative structure of Chaucer's long poem. The remaining chapters deal with Shakespeare and need not concern us here; with regard to Chaucer, Heffernan concludes that his grasp of medieval medicine was technically sound, and that he probably had direct knowledge of some medical texts.

Subjects on the World's Stage, edited by David G. Allen and Robert A. White, is a collection of 18 papers on medieval and Renaissance literature which were originally presented at the Seventh Citadel Conference on Literature in 1991. Three of the essays deal with Chaucer. In the first, A. C. Spearing attempts an overview of 'The Poetic Subject from Chaucer to

Spenser', arguing that during this period English poets moved away from a stylized, allegorical mode towards one which was more personal, appearing in their own poems not as stable selves but as unstable subjects. His discussion focuses more on medieval than Renaissance poets, and he includes reference to most of Chaucer's major works. The other two essays in the collection, on the Pardoner and *Troilus and Criseyde*, are considered in the relevant sections below. *By Word of Mouth: Metaphor, Metonymy, and Linguistic Action in a Cognitive Perspective* is a collection of seven essays edited by the contributors themselves (Louis Goossens et al.), which investigate the expression and conceptualization of the domain of linguistic action in English. Though most of the studies concern contemporary English, two adopt a diachronic approach, and one of the latter has some relevance to Chaucer studies. In 'From Three Respectable Horses' Mouths: Metonymy and Conventionalization in a Diachronically Differentiated Data Base', Goossens examines the word 'mouth' as used by Aelfric, Chaucer and Shakespeare, demonstrating a gradual shift in the term's use from metonymic to metaphoric; additionally, he identifies some of the factors involved in its conventionalization.

A number of Festschrifts have appeared this year. The volume presented to Siegfried Wenzel, *Literature and Religion in the Later Middle Ages*, edited by Richard G. Newhauser and John A. Alford, contains 17 essays which span a wide range of medieval literature; its different sections are devoted to *Piers Plowman*, pastoral literature, scripture and homiletics, and lyric poetry, as well as Chaucer. Each of the four Chaucerian pieces offers literary analysis with a strong historical perspective. In the first, 'Chaucer's Ballade "To Rosemounde" – a Parody?', Theo Stemmler surveys the critical history of this poem and concludes, against majority opinion, that Chaucer intended it as a serious courtly love lyric. The other three essays deal with the *Canterbury Tales*. In the first, ' "My Tale is of a Cock" ', Piero Boitani discusses the *Nun's Priest's Tale*, considering not just Chaucer's original text but also Dryden's translation. He focuses on the problems of literal interpretation, queries the distinction between the fruit and the chaff, and argues that this is not after all a tale which is just about a cock. In the second, Edward B. Irving Jr compares two 'Heroic Worlds: "The Knight's Tale" and "Beowulf" ', in an attempt to reveal what he terms a 'dark traditional dimension' in Chaucer. His aim is to place the *Knight's Tale* within a broad context of epic atmosphere and epic themes, but whilst he succeeds in drawing many parallels between the two works, he also ignores many aspects of Chaucer's poem, as he himself is aware. And finally, Albert E. Hartung draws a picture of Chaucer the sinner in ' "The Parson's Tale" and Chaucer's Penance'. He rejects current critical viewpoints in favour of the earlier belief that the tale had its origin as a separate composition, and, using the evidence of five specific passages, he argues that the work is a personal statement of penance which relates to a specific time in Chaucer's life (though, disappointingly, he is not able to point to any specific events). Another Festschrift, this time for Ladislav Zgusta, entitled *Cultures, Ideologies, and the Dictionary*, edited by Braj B. Kachru and Henry Kahane, contains one item which may interest Chaucerians: 'Chaucer and Lydgate in Palsgrave's *Lesclarcissement*'. In this short paper, Gabriele Stein demonstrates that Palsgrave's English-French dictionary (produced in 1530 as the third part of his *Lesclarcissement de la langue francoyse*), took note of the linguistic usage of these authors. They are the only English writers to be included, and it seems that Palsgrave was better acquainted with Lydgate (more than 100 references), than with Chaucer (only three references).

The Festschrift for Marie Borroff, *The Endless Knot*, edited by M. Teresa Tavormina and R. F. Yeager contains 16 essays, seven of which deal with Chaucer. In the first, 'Elvish Chaucer', J. A. Burrow considers suitable glosses for 'elvyssh', a term used in the *Canterbury Tales* to describe Chaucer himself. In the next, Anne Higgins draws a portrait of 'Alceste the Washerwoman', compiling evidence from royal household records to suggest that one Alice Chester, laundress, may have been the model for Alceste in the *Legend of Good Women*. Biographical speculation also colours Tavormina's own contribution to the collection ' "Lo, swilk a complyn": Musical Topicality in the Reeve's and Miller's Tales', in which she suggests that the names of Chaucer's northern clerks may have been chosen to recall the English composer, John Aleyn, who was associated with the chapel royal in the 1360s and early 1370s. The topic of Warren Ginsberg's essay, in which he discusses the pilgrim portraits of the Wife, the Miller and the Franklin, is 'Chaucer's Disposition', though he never really achieves a satisfactory definition of the term. H. Marsall Leicester Jr struggles to define 'piety' and reviews previous attempts to identify the 'religious tales' in 'Piety and Resistance: A Note on the Representation of Religious Feeling in the *Canterbury Tales*'. The two remaining papers range more widely. In 'Contextualizing Chaucer's Constance: Romance Modes and Family Values', E. Archibald surveys a number of Middle English family romances in order to decide what features the *Man of Law's Tale* shares with this genre, and in 'Artistry, Decorum, and Purpose in Three Middle English Retellings of the Cecilia Legend', Sherry L. Reames contests the view that all saints' legends are very much alike, arguing instead that their differences are crucially important.

Contradictions: From Beowulf to Chaucer, edited by Theodore M. Andersson and Stephen A. Barney, is not a Festschrift but a collection of the essays of Larry D. Benson. It comprises 13 papers on medieval literature, six of which deal with Chaucer; all except one of these have been previously published, and in terms of his Chaucerian criticism this selection spans Benson's scholarship over 14 years. All of the essays are characterized by lucidity, impeccable organization, and a gentle humour. The first two are of a technical nature and involve laborious methodology. 'Chaucer's Spelling Reconsidered' was published in 1992, though thus far it has escaped review in these pages. Here Benson challenges Michael Samuels's opinion that a set of spellings may be confidently identified as Chaucer's own. Whilst deferring to Samuels as a 'man of gret auctorite', Benson is doubtful of such conclusions, and his reexamination of the evidence, involving a comparison of manuscript readings and an assessment of contemporary usage, only leads him into further scepticism. The *Equatorie of the Planetis*, he contends (in a somewhat self-contradictory fashion), is not in Chaucer's own spelling, and therefore cannot be written by Chaucer's own hand; further, if it is indeed an author's working draft, then that author cannot have been Chaucer. In 'The Order of The Canterbury Tales' (*YWES* 62.133), he argues that the manuscripts of the *Canterbury Tales* show only two methods of ordering the tales, that both of these orders can be assigned to Chaucer, and that the order in the Ellesmere manuscript represents Chaucer's own final arrangement. In reaching these conclusions Benson reviews the manuscript evidence at some length, relying upon Manly and Rickert's analyses of manuscript contents, and also reproducing five charts from their work in an appendix. In discussing 'The Occasion of *The Parliament of Fowls*' (*YWES* 63.110), Benson returns to the once-popular theory that the poem's subject concerns the marriage negotiations of Richard II and Anne of Bohemia. His lucid and succinct review of the evidence for this link demonstrates that the work is a unified whole, and not, as has often been claimed, 'a puzzle whose parts do not quite fit'. He uses a similar approach to identify the man of great authority and 'The "Love-Tydynges" in Chaucer's *House of Fame*' (*YWES* 67.190), arguing again that matrimonial negotiations (this time for a match between Richard and Caterina Visconti of Milan) provide the occasion for the poem. He believes that the poem was deliberately left unfinished, and that the much-vaunted love tidings did not need to be articulated because Chaucer's audience already knew what they were: the marriage negotiations had failed. Both of these essays are firmly grounded in the hard work of historical interpretation, though they avoid the equally hard work of literary criticism; their conclusions, if accepted, should prompt a critical reassessment of these poems. Benson returns to a close examination of language in 'The "Queynte" Punnings of Chaucer's Critics' (*YWES* 68.179), where he argues that Chaucer's so-called favourite obscene pun is more the favourite of critics, who have fundamentally mistaken the word's meaning, and therefore its suitability for use in punning. Undeterred by his own assessment that we live in an age where 'a vial of pun is worth a bucket of philology', Benson argues that the word *queynte* is not the forerunner of the modern obscenity, that it was not the normal word for 'vagina' in Chaucer's time, and that it was considered neither vulgar nor obscene by Chaucer and his contemporaries. However, despite his criticism that others have attributed far too many puns to Chaucer, he manages to discover an unnoticed one himself during the course of this discussion. And finally, in discussing 'The Beginnings of Chaucer's English Style', Benson limits himself to the period before 1370, since its comparative lack of documentation allows him more freedom in devising theories. In trying to explain why Chaucer chose to write in English, and how he did this so well, Benson speculates on the poetry that Chaucer read whilst 'growing up', and shows how he used the native lyric and popular romance traditions in his writings, as well as emulating the courtly French style. This paper derives from a talk given in 1992 and is on its first outing in print here, though it is also forthcoming in another collection of essays.

In a collection containing essays that too often offer reductive syntheses and overviews rather than new research as such, Richard Utz's introduction to his *Literary Nominalism and the Theory of Rereading Late Medieval Texts: A New Research Paradigm* is much the best of the essays that deal with Chaucer. We deal here with the introduction and one other essay, the rest being discussed below according to the relevant texts. Utz introduces the collection by remarking upon how lately nominalism has come to be deemed important to late medieval English studies; hitherto, this area of study was dominated by a conception of a Middle Ages fundamentally united in its celebration of hierarchy and of sacred abstraction over secular concreteness, a conception, that is, fundamentally realist in philosophical outlook. This shift towards a serious reconsideration of the influence of nominalist thought is nowhere more evident than in Chaucer studies, where, for example, Utz shows that there is suggestive evidence to identify Ralph Strode (to whom *Troilus and*

Criseyde is dedicated) with nominalism despite the received assumption that Strode was a Thomist and hence a realist. Developing his thoughts on *Troilus and Criseyde*, Utz explains the abrupt turn of its epilogue towards a conventional and other-worldly piety in terms of the nominalist emphasis upon fideism. Nominalist epistemology increasingly represented a universe separated, on the one hand, into a world of contingent individuals, knowable empirically and rationally and, on the other hand, a world of religious truth apprehended only by the eyes of faith. Antinomical rupture thus structures both nominalist thought and what Utz terms the 'literary nominalism' of Chaucer's poetry. John Michael Crafton, in the same collection, provides a survey of Chaucer's writing career, in 'Emptying the Vessel: Chaucer's Humanistic Critique of Nominalism'. Seeing Chaucer suffering, in the wake of Boccaccio and Dante, from an attack of Harold Bloomian 'anxiety of influence', Crafton suggests that the poetic result is a certain reluctance in Chaucer to commit to any philosophical schema and that Chaucer's position towards both realism and nominalism is radically inconclusive. Crafton sketches out a scenario according to which Chaucer's attitude towards language develops away from a sensibility represented by Vinsauf's *ars poetria*, to one represented by the *ars dictaminis* of Hugh of Bologna, and eventually to a humanistic eloquence inspired by Cicero and anticipatory of Renaissance rhetoric. This movement correlates to the chronology of his poetry: from the early *ABC* and *Book of the Duchess*, through the *Parliament of Fowls* and *House of Fame*, to *Troilus and Criseyde* and finally the *Canterbury Tales*, his most mature (i.e. most 'inconclusive') work. The *ABC* and *Book of the Duchess* exhibit a realist confidence in the power of the sign to denote reality; in the *Parliament*, Chaucer is seen to move away from realism and towards nominalism, but to critique that also, for the poem ends in a cacophony of empty signifiers. *Troilus* exhibits a 'minor obsession' with the two poles of thought while the *Tales* demonstrate a mature dialectic between the two. Thomas J. Farrell's edition on *Bakhtin and Medieval Voices* brings together a selection of essays that elaborate the connections between literary theory of Mikhail Bakhtin and medieval texts, noting especially the usefulness of the concepts of heteroglossia and, of course, carnivalesque. Essays on individual texts are reviewed below and certainly the collection is to be praised for avoiding the obvious Bakhtin-Chaucer routes, such as carnivalesque and the fabliaux. Steve Guthrie's 'Dialogics and Prosody in Chaucer' constitutes a statistical prosodic analysis of lines from Chaucer, Gower, Hoccleve and Lydgate, with special emphasis on the contrast between Gower and Chaucer. Polyglossia, Bakhtin's term for the co-existence of two national languages within one culture, applies insofar as Guthrie's purpose is to examine the 'interanimation' of French and English in the poets' language (the term 'dialogics' here is used interchangeably). Guthrie finds Gower's French verse inflexibly monologic: French words squeezed to fit and subordinated to an English prosodic template. By contrast, Chaucer's lines inhabit the two linguistic worlds dialogically. The *Book of the Duchess* is the test case for these conclusions: the final 'she ys ded' of the poem captures the register of the English tongue in its concrete directness, yet the means by which that knowledge is achieved belongs to a different linguistic register – that of French. Willi Erzgräber discusses Chaucer's medievalism and modernity in 'Chaucer zwischen Mittelalter und Neuzeit' (*LJGG* 36.27–46). Chaucer is seen very much as a writer of his time, in tune with his contemporaries, 'moral Gower' and 'philosophical Strode'; yet he also anticipates the 'bourgeois narrative' ('die bürgerliche Erzählkunst') of Fielding, Sterne and, most especially, Joyce. Indeed, for vitality of detail and characterization, the Wife of Bath can be matched only by Molly Bloom and the concerns with language in the *House of Fame* register the prescience of Chaucer's scepticism.

'A steady ironic focus on the contradictions and blind spots inherent in the chivalric outlook' is noted by Winthrop Wetherbee in 'Chivalry under Siege in Ricardian Romance' (in Ivy A. Corfis and Michael Wolfe, eds, *The Medieval City under Siege*). Distinguishing between interests in chivalry and in battle proper, Wetherbee observes that, in a century historically dominated by warfare, Ricardian poetry tends to be concerned with the former and at a distance from the latter. The scene at Deiphobus's house in *Troilus* sums up for Wetherbee the blindness of the Trojan aristocracy to their situation and its concomitant preoccupation with private matters, here, the plight of Criseyde. In the *Knight's Tale*, the chivalric code is seen to be incapable of incorporating the feminine unless in terms of an occasion for violence. Again, one scene tells all: the description of the temple of Mars contains moments of realistic description of battle scenes, but these moments undercut the poem's ideological commitment to a representation of chivalry as a code that contains and transcends violence.

Carolyn Dinshaw, in 'Chaucer's Queer Touches/A Queer Touches Chaucer' (*Exemplaria* 7.75–92), is not out to 'out' the Middle Ages in the cause of queerdom, for she wishes to resist such essentializing of (homosexual) identity. Rather, the 'essence', if one may use the term, of being queer lies in its constructedness, in the play-acting of genders, and the defamiliarization of heteronormative representations of body and sexual role. Queer identity, that is, is not essential but relational. The effect of these alienation effects is not so much to create a dialectic between constructedness and naturalness, the artificial and the authentic, but to problematize the very distinction between them and ultimately to expose the constructedness of heterosexual identity. Dinshaw's discussion is located in the exchange between the Wife of Bath and the Pardoner. The queerness, or otherwise, of the Pardoner is not really addressed in any detail, but the reader should consult Dinshaw's previous work on the Pardoner's eunuchry and ambiguous sexuality (*YWES* 69.190). Her intention in this essay is to examine the ways in which a queer Pardoner can demonstrate to us the local, history-specific constructions of 'natural', red-blooded heterosexuality. From the very outset of the pilgrimage, this construction of naturalness is in place through the opening lines of the *General Prologue* where human nature is linked to the generative cycles of earth and animals. Yet even within the domain of the heterosexual, this procreative telos must be reaffirmed as dominant discourse. The Wife's discussion of the purpose of her 'membres … of generacion', whether for pleasure or for procreation, shows the body to be a contested site of meaning rather than any unified, natural given. In a move that has by now become the accepted characteristic position of Chaucer on all such contentious issues, the momentary if explicit articulation of queer or of feminist identity is silenced back into orthodoxy through the Pardoner's kiss of peace and, in the Wife's case, through the Loathly Lady's transformation into a submissive and beautiful wife. *Le corps dans tous ses états*, edited by Marie-Claire Rouyer, contains one essay on Chaucer: 'Corpus Chaucérien et corporéite [*sic*] des vertus. Le MS Cambridge GG 4.27 (1)', by Florence Bourgne. Containing, as it does, a miscellany of minor poems, *Troilus and Criseyde*, the *Parliament of Fowls* and the *Canterbury Tales*, Gg.4.27 dates from between 1415 at the earliest estimation and 1440 at the latest. We can speak about the 'body' of the manuscript not only because it clearly represents an attempt to construct a Chaucerian 'corpus' (*compilatio*) but also because, through its punctual use of majuscules and obliques, the manuscript internally differentiates its various parts or members (*ordinatio*). The illustrations also help create the sense of organic unity; for example, the Canterbury portraits of Gg.4.27 (such that remain) are integrated into the body of the text in a way that they are not in Ellesmere, where the portraits remain detached and marginal. Bourgne also links the illuminations to a broader tendency in the late Middle Ages to personify virtue visually and hence to endow abstraction with a more concrete sense of corporeality. Although Bourgne's arguments pertain to the entire manuscript, her examples are drawn mostly from the *Parson's Tale*.

The *Chaucer: Life and Times CD-ROM* is a snazzy multi-media application aimed at a broad market of historians, researchers, university students and lecturers. Its marketing blurb makes the bold claim that it is 'the complete Chaucer resource on one CD-rom', but in reality it is a marriage of the *Riverside Chaucer* and Coghill's modern translations, teamed with some attractive extras and presented in a glossy packaging, and as such it reinforces the textual dominance which the *Riverside Chaucer* has gained in Chaucer studies. The application comes alive to the sound of lyre-like music, revealing the main menu which is designed to resemble a scholar's desk (more like a Victorian bureau than a medieval desk). Positioned on the desktop ready to be opened are several books, a folder and an hourglass; selecting these icons allows access to Chaucer's texts in Middle English or in translation; to information about his life and times, and, separately, about his life within its historical context; and to a number of critical overviews of Chaucer's style and of specific works. There are some anomalies. The folder of overviews contains a short essay entitled 'Missing Poems and Shorter Poems', in which the poem *Gentilesse* is mentioned, though its text is not included amongst the volume of Chaucer's 'Other Poems', and in general the shorter poems are very badly represented. When one pulls open the reference drawer one discovers mostly maps and pictures, including a map of the Canterbury pilgrims' route which, improbably, incorporates Winchester. Selecting any of the places mentioned brings up explanations and the possibility of further pictures. Though the maps tend to be rather small, for the most part the illustrations (more than 200 in all), are good photographs of actual places and high-quality reproductions of manuscript images; unsurprisingly, the package draws on the Ellesmere illuminations and the usual woodcut images of the Canterbury pilgrims. The advice on 'how to read a medieval manuscript' is simply an essay, and not perhaps as exciting as one might have expected, though picture pop-ups are available in this section too. The reference drawer also offers information on predefined thematic routes, such as, for example, on authority or marriage, which could prove distressingly useful for undergraduate essay preparation! Other useful tools in this regard are the guides to further reading, the fairly basic glossary of Middle English, and the 17 critical essays. There is no obvious rationale governing the selection of the latter, though one suspects that copyright restrictions may have been the guiding principle; certainly Norman Davis would be surprised to see one of his essays reappearing in this medium! Finally, across the top of the desk runs what is inelegantly described as the 'top cubby hole bar'. This contains various menu functions such as searching and highlighting, and a general help facility; it also offers access to readings of the Middle English texts recorded by John Burrow. A further possibility is that the user is allowed to record personal comments or notes. However, such interactive aspects are obviously inappropriate to communal library use, which, given the pricing policy, is how most people are going to be able to access the package, if at all.

For some years now, the Chaucer Studio, under the directorship of Paul Thomas, has been producing cassettes of Chaucer's individual tales and poems, as well as some other Middle English material. The quality of narration is high and the tapes make for excellent teaching aids. It would help, however, if the length of time of recording were noted on the outside. A number of tales were published this year and they, along with a couple from 1994, are reviewed individually below. With one of the productions, *Specimens of Middle English Pronunciation*, a complementary guide by Alex Jones, *How to Pronounce Middle English*, accompanies his tape, three of whose five excerpts are Chaucerian and based on the Riverside edition: from the *General Prologue, House of Fame* and *Franklin's Tale*. The booklet is short and clear without being over-simplified; it not only gives the phonetic value and notation of Middle English vowels and consonants but also explains the phonetic height and frontness of the vowels as well as the vocal variations between Modern British, American and Australian English. At such a reasonable price, the tape and booklet create the real possibility of teaching students how to stop mispronouncing Middle English poetry when asked to read it aloud.

2. *Canterbury Tales*

The appearance of *The Canterbury Tales by Geoffrey Chaucer: The New Ellesmere Facsimile* edited by Daniel Woodward and Martin Stevens and co-published by the Huntington Library and Yushodo, makes this a red-letter year in Chaucer studies. This precious production, full-colour, full-size, is a limited run of 250 copies and in three different editions. These are packaged in three different ways, with the differences reflected in the tripartite price structure: the first edition (1–50) is characterized by an early fifteenth-century-type binding, oak boards covered with tawed calf, and a full leather presentation box; the second (51–150) comes with a slightly different style of binding, cover and box; and the third edition (151–250), the version principally aimed at scholars, comes in the unusual form of unsewn gatherings.

The copy which this reviewer was able to consult (courtesy of the library of Trinity College Dublin) was one of the first 50 copies. It must be said at once that, without a doubt, the facsimile is very fine, and has been crafted into an object of beauty to rival the original. A striking feature not revealed by previous reproductions is the manuscript's lavish use of gold, not just in the most elaborate borders but also for paraph markers in the main text and running headers. It is possible to spot where bits of paint are starting to flake in the original, and to perceive differences in ink tone; the degree of 'show-through' from the verso of the page is also well-produced, almost irritatingly well at times! In general, the experience of using the facsimile mimics very closely the experience of handling a real medieval manuscript; the only real differences are in the volume's smell (which is too 'new-book-like'), and in the feel of the pages, which are too uniformly flat and even, a homogeneity which is maintained because whilst creases and prickings are marked on the page, they are not marked into it. The facsimile's price and comparative rarity will also ensure that libraries will treat it as a manuscript, restricting its availability to those admitted to rare books rooms, or perhaps putting it on public display.

It is useful to compare *The New Ellesmere Facsimile* with the previous facsimile produced by ManUP in 1911 which was itself subsequently repro-duced by Brewer in 1989 (*YWES* 70.219). Each is a product of its own age: the 1995 version shows not just the glories of the text but also its stains and flaws in a 'warts and all' reproduction, an approach which would have appalled the producers of the earlier version, who strove instead to 'enhance' their results by touching-up and washing. The current desire in facsimile production to obtain the fullest possible picture may be linked to the fashionable trend for editions which are inclusive of all possible textual readings. Ironically, neither method can recover the realities of medieval reception: the Ellesmere facsim-ile cannot recapture the exact way the manuscript would have appeared in the Middle Ages (at one stage it must have been cleaner); instead the intention is to reproduce the manuscript as nearly as possible in its current state. This publication will obviously be helpful to those interested in manuscripts, to textual scholars and art historians, and it will no doubt save many a trip to California; an additional benefit of its production is that it will now be possible to publish detailed accounts of the appearance of the Ellesmere manuscript without having also to provide illustrations. The facsimile is also a potentially valuable teaching resource, but one wonders how many of the 250 copies will actually be used in this way; one also wonders how much more difficult it will now become to obtain permission to handle the original manuscript at the Huntington Library.

The facsimile is accompanied by a volume of 14 interpretative studies, *The Ellesmere Chaucer: Essays in Interpretation*, compiled by Daniel Woodward and Martin Stevens. This companion volume is itself lavishly illustrated with black and white photographs and diagrams, and is prefaced by a splendid, if slightly fragile, fold-out section showing the pilgrim portraits in colour. The book is divided into three parts: the introductions, the essays and the appen-dixes. Woodward's introduction is aimed at the student and the 'common reader'; in it, he helpfully glosses technical terms, and gives an informative account of the process of making a facsimile. Indeed, his description of how the 'project became a venture in international technical, crafts, commercial, and scholarly co-operations' serves to increase one's awe at the skill of the medieval craftsmen. Stevens, by contrast, is writing for the scholar, and his introduction follows the usual format of a preface to a volume of this kind. Following this is a summary of Anthony G. Cains's report of the disbinding of the manuscript; this is designed with the non-technically minded medievalist in mind, and offers a fascinating insight into the whole process of conservation and repair.

The 14 essays which follow comprise a series of tales by different tellers, though, unlike the *Canterbury Tales*, all are very firmly focused on the same subject. The first speakers in this debate are the palaeographers, M. B. Parkes and A. I. Doyle. Parkes's meticulous explanation of 'The Planning and Construction of the Ellesmere Manuscript' must constitute the best factual account of the manuscript on record. Doyle then concentrates on one aspect of the manuscript's composition, its scribal hand, giving in typically measured and authoritative fashion a minutely detailed description of the hand's characteristics. This reaffirms his (and Parkes's) already-stated view that 'The Copyist of the Ellesmere *Canterbury Tales*' was also the scribe of the Hengwrt manuscript, and Jeremy J. Smith's discussion of 'The Language of the Ellesmere Manuscript' serves to reinforce this. Smith does not assume much prior knowledge of historical linguistics amongst his readers, and so takes a longer run up to the wicket than most of the other contributors; an analysis of the linguistic forms of the *Pardoner's Prologue* and *Tale* in both manuscripts is given as an appendix to his essay.

The next four contributors concentrate on visual aspects of the codex. Kathleen L. Scott has been searching for other work by the Ellesmere illuminators, managing to turn up 'An Hours and Psalter by Two Ellesmere Illuminators' in MS Bodley Hatton 4. Her article is generously illustrated, and she ingeniously uses the ownership evidence of the Hatton manuscript to push back the supposed date of composition for Ellesmere to around 1400–5. Alan T. Gaylord considers the ideas governing the production of medieval portraits, arguing in 'Portrait of a Poet' that the intention behind Chaucer's iconic portrait was not to reproduce his physical appearance but to convey an idea of his importance. Richard K. Emmerson complains that the other pilgrim portraits have been comparatively neglected, but the presence of two papers concerning them in this collection will redress the balance somewhat. Emmerson's contribution, 'Text and Image in the Ellesmere Portraits of the Tale-Tellers', gives a detailed catalogue of the portraits, and also attempts to classify (not very conclusively, and not without qualification) their 'discursive' and 'figural' features. Betsy Bowden then attempts a more wide-ranging perspective in the 'Visual Portraits of the Canterbury Pilgrims 1484(?) to 1809', trying to determine whether any of the later artists were influenced by the Ellesmere portraits. Unfortunately, her discussion leads her quite far away from the manuscript itself, and she never really provides an answer to her own question.

In what is otherwise a paean to the Ellesmere manuscript, N. F. Blake's voice strikes a discordant note. His discussion of 'The Ellesmere Text in the Light of the Hengwrt Manuscript' reinforces the view for which he is now famous, namely that the Hengwrt version of the *Canterbury Tales* is the closest to Chaucer's original. He also claims a growing acceptance of this view amongst scholars, and challenges them to carry its implications through into editorial practice. The next speaker in the textual debate is Ralph Hanna III, who takes '(The) Editing (of) the Ellesmere Text' as his theme. Using eclectic methods of analysis, he surveys the complete variant corpus for the first quarter of the *Canterbury Tales*, showing that even amongst the compilers of Ellesmere itself there were attempts to remove deviant readings. Both Blake and Hanna touch on the arrangement of the tales, but it is Helen Cooper who takes up this difficult topic in 'The Order of the Tales in the Ellesmere

Manuscript'. She is seemingly undismayed by her own observation that 'the first problem we encounter in reconstructing a "correct" order of the tales is that we do not know if there is one'. Instead, she contends that order does matter, suggests that there should be eight rather than ten fragments and judges the ordering of tales in the Ellesmere manuscript as 'arguably the best' even if it may not be fully authorial.

The next three contributions widen the focus to discuss the development and history of the English book. Derek Pearsall's essay, 'The Ellesmere Chaucer and Contemporary English Literary Manuscripts', is characteristically urbane. He considers the growth and character of the fifteenth-century London book trade, and the range of factors which might have affected textual stability, as well as making careful observations as to the type of person who might have commissioned such a sumptuous manuscript; however, he offers no concrete suggestions as to the volume's origins, and ends by leaving such questions open. Alfred David takes up this theme and charts 'The Ownership and Use of the Ellesmere Manuscript', following the trail of marginal notations and inscriptions left in its pages, and thus tracing the volume's progress through various noble families and into the Bridgewater library. He also concludes that 'a definitive authorial version of the *Canterbury Tales* is bound to elude us because it never existed'. Laura Kendrick is interested in placing 'The *Canterbury Tales* in the Context of Contemporary Vernacular Translations and Compilations'. She examines the steps that continental poets took to authorize their works, arguing that Chaucer had to devise alternative means to achieve the same ends because of an absence of princely patronage for such activities in England. To substantiate her point she ranges more widely amongst Chaucer's works, citing the dream visions as well as the *Canterbury Tales*.

The final essay, 'Chaucer Studies in Japan: A Personal View' by Toshiyuki Takamiya, sits somewhat incongruously at the end of the collection. However, since Japanese interest and finance have underpinned the production of the facsimile, it may be thought appropriate to try to determine why Chaucer studies should be so popular in Japan. And finally there are two brief appendixes. The first is intriguingly entitled 'An Ellesmere Chaucer Almanac', but seems to be a random inclusion of useful bits of information which just didn't fit anywhere else in the volume; the second gives 'A Note on Identifying Pages in Versions of the Facsimile Lacking Margins', and is followed by a complete key of the pagination. This book is more than just the sum of its parts; it is a gathering of the great and the good, identifying those deemed to be experts on Chaucer in this year, and as such it will serve in the future as an index of late twentieth-century Chaucer scholarship.

Some references to the *Tales* not spotted by Caroline Spurgeon are supplied by Jackson Campbell Boswell and Sylvia Wallace Holton in 'References to the *Canterbury Tales*' (*ChauR* 29.311–36). The citations are taken from a work in progress that notes all references to Chaucer and his work between 1475–1640; an update of Spurgeon is much needed, especially in light of the fact that some 20 per cent of the authors' total references are entirely new. There are 54 references in all (listed alphabetically and then chronologically within the group of entries for each character), the most numerous of which, as might perhaps be expected, are to 'Patient Grizelda' and the lusty Wife of Bath.

Jesús L. Serrano Reyes looks at the possible influences upon Chaucer's work resulting from the poet's visit to Spain in 1366 in *Didactismo y Moralismo en Geoffrey Chaucer y Don Juan Manuel: Un Estudio Comparativo Textual*. As his title suggests, Serrano Reyes looks to the evidence of common proverbs, *exempla*, and *sententiae* to base his argument for a connection between Chaucer's *Canterbury Tales* and *El Conde Lucanor*, by Don Juan Manuel, who was, incidentally, related to the House of Lancaster, thereby establishing a political as well as a possible literary connection with the English poet. The historical evidence, argues Serrano Reyes, makes it possible for Chaucer to have read the work during the 90 days or so that he spent in Spain. 'Didactismo', suggesting a general didactic intent, and 'moralismo', bearing more upon the specific regulation of habitual acts, cannot always be meaningfully distinguished and both are clearly implied in paired oppositions such as *fruyt/chaf* and *sentence/solaas*, where the distinction has more to do with that between instruction and delight. Although Serrano Reyes argues more for *El Conde* as an analogue rather than as source for the Tales, he none the less makes some close textual comparisons between the texts, noting parallels of syntax and grammatical construction; in particular, he notes the close relations between the *Franklin's Tale* and *Exemplo L* (compare 'trouthe is the hyeste thyng that man may kepe' with 'la vergüença es la meior cosa que omne puede aver en sí') and between the *Canon's Yeoman's Tale, Pars Secunda* and *Examplo XX*; Serrano Reyes suggests that, for these sections anyway, *El Conde* may well have been one of Chaucer's sources. This is a welcome consideration of a little-acknowledged literary connection, although it is a pity that there is no index and that there are a number of typos in the text.

Bonnie D. Irwin discusses the genre of frame tales in 'What's in a Frame? The Medieval Textualization of Traditional Storytelling' (*OT* 10.i.27–53). She offers a definition of the frame tale and lists its particular characteristics, drawing on a wide range of examples which includes the *Canterbury Tales*; in particular, she is concerned to show how this written genre reuses features of oral performance. *Oral Tradition in the Middle Ages*, a volume of conference papers edited by W. F. H. Nicolaisen, contains one item which will be of interest to Chaucerians. Carl Lindahl's essay explores 'The Oral Undertones of Late Medieval Romance', arguing that the structure of the *Canterbury Tales* was based not on the models of an élite culture but on those of fourteenth-century folk entertainment. The discussion then focuses on the *Wife of Bath's Tale*, succinctly summarizing the differences between this text, Gower's version, and the *Wedding of Sir Gawain and Dame Ragnell*. Not surprisingly, Lindahl finds the latter to be the most popular in idiom, and Gower's the most élite; the *Wife of Bath's Tale*, on the other hand, is judged to be an oral performance which follows the oral mode of presenting unglossed actions, and accordingly Lindahl concludes that it must have been written for an audience thoroughly familiar with oral romance. The frequency of markers of affect, such as interjections and exclamations, are analysed in Irma Taavitsainen's 'Narrative Patterns of Affect in Four Genres of the *Canterbury Tales*' (*ChauR* 30.191–210). Sermons are the first generic category treated and in them, 'Allas', 'Lo' (which frequently signals a didactic message), and 'O' feature most commonly. The same interjections are found in saints' lives, though their presence is very restricted. In courtly romance, the range of interjections is wider, although the same three exclamations feature prominently; 'Hoo', however, appears to be genre-specific. It is in the fabliaux that the interjections come into their own; they constitute an index of surprise or relief at the resolution of suspense, which are essential narrative effects of the genre; 'Harrow' is the only genre-specific fabliaux interjection.

In *To Be Continued*, Peter Conrad examines four stories and their survival, wondering in his first chapter, 'Arrival at Canterbury', what happened to Chaucer's pilgrims after the poet deserted them halfway through their pilgrimage. He finds that twentieth-century continuations of Chaucer have wars as their context, but his definition of what constitutes a continuation is extremely broad, allowing him to cover poetry by T. S. Eliot and Les Murray, novels by William Burroughs and Margaret Atwood, criticism by G. K. Chesterton, and films by Powell, Pasolini and Jarmusch. Long before the discussion reaches Elvis Presley one realizes that the works' connections with Chaucer are tenuous, a difficulty which Conrad himself acknowledges on occasion. Furthermore, most medievalists would take issue with his opening assertion that the *Canterbury Tales* is the inevitable starting point for English literature.

In *Chaucer and the Mystics*, Robert Boenig seeks to situate the *Canterbury Tales* within the context of contemporary devotional prose, arguing that Chaucer's work shares imagery and ideas with the writings of the Middle English mystics, and focusing specifically on three themes: control, silence and fragmentation. The book, which is not a source study, begins by surveying the vast body of medieval mystical prose treatises, though thankfully it stops short of trying to provide a history of medieval mysticism, concentrating instead on outlining the ideas of Pseudo-Dionysius and the mystics' attitude towards language. Having thus filled in the background, the discussion then turns to the *Canterbury Tales*, but does not confine itself to the religious tales. Boenig begins by exploring the similarities between the Wife of Bath and Margery Kempe, before moving on to the *Parson's Tale*, and those comic tales which 'tend towards sin'. His approach is informed by an understanding that our reception of Middle English texts has become too compartmentalized. He points to manuscript contexts where works which are now divided into 'literary' and 'non-literary' co-exist happily, and uses this lack of generic distinction to argue that the influence of mystical prose may be discerned even where Chaucer did not intend it, in tales such as those of the Nun's Priest and the Reeve. Whilst recognizing the dangers of intentionality: 'critics must guard themselves from reading their own intentions into those of dead authors', this does not always stop him from doing just that, though he later remarks, sensibly, that it is better to speak 'of Chaucer's tendency than of his intentions'. The tendency of the discussion itself is to focus on women: in Chapter Four, the Prioress comes under detailed scrutiny, and Chapters Five and Six deal respectively with 'good women', that is, those portrayed by the Man of Law, the Clerk and the Second Nun, and the 'other women' depicted by the Merchant, Franklin, Shipman and Manciple. Boenig posits a strong connection between the Prioress's use of language (especially her metaphorical use of food terms), and the language theories outlined by Pseudo-Dionysius, and draws some interesting associations between virgin martyrs, food and text, using manuscript illustrations to support his argument (though, sadly, they might have been better reproduced). He argues that the Pseudo-Dionysian themes of control, silence and fragmentation, take on a more metaphysical light in the tales which deal with good women. One wonders why Dorigen was excluded from this set, not least because her presence in the second group frustrates the urge to label its members simply as 'bad'. Nevertheless, we are offered an interesting perspective on her activities, which are viewed as attempts to gain control using the only means available to religious women (fasting, sleep-deprivation), but whilst the points made about her are compelling, the suggestion that the frequent references to Saint-Denis in the 'Shipman's Tale' are an indication of Pseudo-Dionysian influence is less than convincing. The final chapter examines the *Tales of Sir Thopas* and *Melibee*, and the *Retraction*, which Boenig classifies as another of Chaucer's own tales. Drawing links with the work of the *Cloud*-author, Boenig argues that the disturbing type of closure offered by the *Retraction* may be regarded, in mystical terms, as success rather than failure; he similarly manages to present fragmentation as a virtue, rather than as a lack. All too easily this final section turns into an act of Chaucer worship, for having identified a critical weakness for the image of the all-controlling arch-poet, Boenig asserts his own adherence to this creed: 'He is that, and I affirm it with all my strength', and then concludes: 'In Chaucer's fragmentation and failure and silence paradoxically is his genius'. There is no separate conclusion, as Boenig prefers to fall into silence in a Chaucerian fashion. The notes which accompany the text are for the most part brief and avoid self-indulgence, but in contrast the bibliography extends to almost 20 pages.

Beverly Boyd is also interested in Chaucer's mysticism, charting his Marian devotion in 'Chaucer's Moments in the "Kneeling World"' (in Anne C. Bartlett et al., *Vox Mystica*); she begins with an examination of the 'profoundly spiritual' *ABC* before discussing the tales of the Prioress and the Second Nun. Katherine Heinrichs writes on 'Tropological Woman in Chaucer: Literary Elaborations of an Exegetical Tradition' (*ES* 76.iii.215–20), considering Chaucer's allusions to allegories of the Fall in several of the *Canterbury Tales*, and his fullest exposition of it in the *Parson's Tale*.

That masculinity is constructed around and out of competition and control and that femininity around and out of obedience and submission is the recurring theme of Anne Laskaya's *Chaucer's Approach to Gender in the Canterbury Tales*. If the question of proper male behaviour involves how to govern, that of proper female behaviour involves how to obey. Contest, indeed, constitutes the very raison d'être and structure of the *Tales* and even the image of the artist participates in a discourse of control: the artist, inevitably male, is the one who can exercise mastery over his materials; creativity and control, then, are intimately involved with one another. Laskaya organizes her treatment of masculine identity around four basic categories: heroic or chivalric; courtly; emergent humanist; and Christian. In the first, the Knight is presented as a control freak whose concerns are projected upon Theseus, who himself matures throughout the tale from his early attempts to master by violence to mastery by diplomacy. In the second, the *Miller's* and *Merchant's Tales* are examined more as anti-courtly narratives which disclose a recurring structure of love triangles; feminine identity is here inscribed within and a cause of male competition. What Laskaya notes in the narratives of courtly love, funny or serious, is that Chaucer finds the lover's loss of control ultimately comic. The *Clerk's Tale* provides the context for Laskaya's consideration of scholasticism, with its own brand of combative *disputatio*, and the intellectual climate of Chaucer's day which was critical of scholasticism and marked by a refusal of certainty. What distinguishes the truly Christian Parson of the *Tales* and makes him in an ironic sense the 'winner' of the contest is precisely his refusal to escalate the *quyting* match. The rationale for the chapter divisions was not always clear in the light of the four-fold distinction elaborated in Chapter Two. A smaller section of the book is devoted to the 'second sex' under their categorizations of obedience or rebellion. In the former, Custance, Virginia and Griselde are the avatars of submissiveness, but Laskaya argues that their suffering is gender-specific, that they are not Everyperson figures representing the human condition, but victims of their own gendered bodiliness; Prudence, however, provides a more positive model. The next group of females, if not all rebels, are at least seen to possess a more fleshed-out feminine perspective by themselves being narrators: the Second Nun, Prioress and Wife of Bath. Laskaya's critical method is based on close reading of the tales she discusses along with a self-confessed theoretical eclecticism she finds appropriate to feminism. She reads Chaucer's own perspective upon gender to be ambivalent, a pronouncement appropriate enough to her positioning of him 'on the margin' (as the phrase, now a commonplace, goes) of the bourgeois, clerical and noble classes.

Kathryn Jacobs sees Chaucer spelling out some adulterous implications of medieval marital legislation in 'Rewriting the Marital Contract: Adultery in the *Canterbury Tales*' (*ChauR* 29.337–47). The ecclesiastical courts required every spouse to pay his or her marital debt as a sacred obligation. Jacobs argues that a colourable case for adultery in the event of a spouse's marital bankruptcy can be made but that medieval law shrank from spelling out such an implication; Chaucer, however, did not. In the *Shipman's Tale*, adultery is presented as legitimate compensation for the merchant's niggardliness; in the *Franklin's Tale*, Arveragus gives Dorigen leave to go with Aurelius because she would never have got into the scrape she did had he not been neglecting his own marital obligations and spending too much time abroad in the first place.

Paul Beekman Taylor writes about 'Time in the Canterbury Tales' (*Exemplaria* 7.371–93). Establishing a general intellectual context for the *Tales*, Taylor traces two kinds of time: one that locates dates and measures within physical, perdurable time; another that looks to the metaphysical pattern of all things and ultimately, paradoxically, becomes timeless. The two are not, of course, independent, the origin of creaturely time and its *terminus ad quem* both being inscribed within God's infinity. The *Tales*, for Taylor, is all about the play of physical and metaphysical time and the way in which Chaucer 'deconstructs' historical time in order to reveal its supra-temporal origins (a strange effect of a deconstructive reading, one might think). Despite a good synthesis of ancient thought on temporality and some interesting observations – for example, the idea that the regulation of time in the *Tales* is predominantly a male activity and that the female figures tend to embody a principle of timelessness – the reading of the text too often seemed forced, as in the argument that Harry Bailly's 'demand for obedience at the beginning of the pilgrimage, accompanied by an oath on his own food and drink, recalls God's command to Adam, whose disobedience is paid for by Christ's flesh and blood'. The ubiquitous and unnecessarily gendered language didn't help matters either and, by now, sounds tendentious. Abdul R. Yesufu, in 'The Spring Motif and the Subversion of Guaranteed Meaning in Chaucer's *The Canterbury Tales*' (*ESA* 38.1–15), considers how Chaucer, traditionally praised for working within the conventions of narrative poetry, can rather be seen to subvert those conventions. In the spring motif which opens the *General Prologue*, the heightened sexuality of the imagery is at odds with the ostensible occasion of the poem – a pilgrimage – thus belying the pilgrims' pious intentions. So also the narrative process exists merely as a way to keep boredom at bay rather than elaborating any consolatory theory of art. Paule Mertens-Fonck, in '*The Canterbury Tales*: New Proposals of Interpretation', in *Atti della Accademia Peloritana dei Pericolanti* (69.5–29), considers some differences between Boccaccio's *Decameron* and Chaucer's *Tales* which, although at first sight slight, reveal important philosophical differences in outlook. Where Boccaccio names all of his ten narrators, Chaucer names only two, preferring to introduce them by descriptive representation. Read against the medieval debates between realists and nominalists, Chaucer's eschewing of names as mere abstract notions that offer no information about things themselves (*res*), aligns the English poet more with nominalist preference for experience over authority and concrete particulars over abstractions. The numbering of the pilgrims in the *General Prologue* as 29 (a number which, any way we count up, doesn't tally with the list of portraits) similarly exhibits Chaucer's refusal of authority: readers must rely on counting for themselves. Noting another reference to the number 29 in the *Parson's Prologue*, Mertens-Fonck suggests that the number, in resisting reduction to any numerological symbolism, appealed to Chaucer precisely because it renders it impossible to allegorize away the significance of the pilgrimage experience. These, and other instances, suggest Chaucer's affinity with a theory of knowledge in which, as Ockham puts it, 'the real is always individual, not universal'. Eyvind C. Ronquist further debates the uncertain status of authority in 'Rhetoric and Early Modern Skepticism and Pragmatism' (*CJRS* 5.49–74) when he argues that, in key moments such as the Wife's preference for experience over authority and the pilgrim-narrator's legitimation of his descriptive strategy through the authority of Plato and Christ, Chaucer undoes the idea of tradition as a fixed entity, turning it instead into a discursive, intertextual web. Consensus becomes rhetorical and negotiable in a manner that anticipates both the scepticism of Montaigne and the twentieth-century pragmatism of C. S. Peirce and William James. Ronquist finds a similar discourse of uncertainty in Langland and suggests that its origins may possibly be located in Cicero's pragmatic rhetoric rather than in Ockham's epistemological scepticism. So close are the affinities between these fourteenth-century writers and the later Montaigne that Ronquist finds it more helpful to describe the period as early modern rather than as late medieval. In a well-researched article, Laura F. Hodges considers 'Costume Rhetoric in the Knight's Portrait: Chaucer's Every-Knight and his Bismotered Gypon' (*ChauR* 29.274–302) and finds the Knight's soiled clothes unusual for literary representations of worthy knights, where they are inevitably clean and their armour shining. Moreover, the 'gypon' and 'habergeon' are not usual sartorial items inventoried in romance description; Chaucer's Knight clearly lacks the trappings of chivalry as depicted in literature – the coat of arms, shield, spear, etc.; he is altogether a realistic figure, looking like what knights then looked like; For Hodges, this 'bismotered gypon' both points to the Knight's secular estate and allegorizes his spiritual condition. The great medieval unwashed tend more to appear as Everyman figures in pilgrim narratives and thus Hodges moralizes the Knight's soiled appearance as an Everyknight figure, stained with the grime of the Active Life. The combination of realism and allegoresis is offered in preference to the conventional choice critics pose between the Knight as thug or chivalric hero. The Riverside's gloss on the Summoner's Latin – 'The question is, what point of the law (applies)?' – is queried by Leofranc Holford-Strevens in '*Quid Iuris Questio*' (*N&Q* 42.164–5). Showing that the phrase *quid iuris questio* occurs in a manuscript of French and Latin poems, he glosses it as: 'The question arises of what the law is upon these facts'. *Iuris* thus means not 'right' but 'law' and is not partitive with *quid* but predicative with an implied *sit*.

Alan Gaylord reads the *Knight's Tale* in the Chaucer Studio tapes. Longer than most, this recording runs for over two hours, although it is paced well so that each of the four parts occupies one side of tape. The diction, however, although usually very good, does at times sound slightly adenoidal. Jesse M. Gellrich continues his work on the textual interface between book and voice in his *Discourse and Dominion in the Fourteenth Century: Oral Contexts of Writing in Philosophy, Politics, and Poetry*, in which he devotes a chapter to the *Knight's Tale*. Gellrich's thesis is that literacy, far from sounding the death knell for orality in the fourteenth century, symbiotically cohabits with it. The two discourses imitate each other and their metaphors displace themselves upon one another. Despite the received linguistic wisdom of the times that writing is the sign of speech, Chaucer presents writing, through its self-reflexivity, as something other than the shadow of voice, bestowing upon it an immanence and independence of its referent, *res*. Taken against the political events of the 1380s, 'voice' was something much contested, with *parlement* frequently overriding the sovereign decree of Richard II, then still a minor. Chaucer's tale engages with the problem of sovereign voice through the conflict between the written, a self-reflexive discourse, and the oral, a referential discourse. The gap between the sovereign voice of Theseus and the self-reflexivity of his utterance calls into question the sovereignty of political voice; the massive use of the trope of *occultatio* in the tale shows the occlusions, gaps, suppressions and silences within political discourse. Edgar Laird writes on 'Cosmic Law and Literary Character in Chaucer's *Knight's Tale*' in Utz, *Literary Nominalism*. Here Laird takes issue with an over-easy dismissal of Theseus's concluding speech as so much 'aristocratic ideology', defending it rather as a metaphysical expression of hierarchy that none the less recognizes its intrinsic limitations. Laird finds such an expression antagonistic to the new nominalism and locates its tradition in the thought of Albumascar, Grosseteste and Wycliff. These thinkers develop a hierarchy of knowledge by which one progresses (in Albumascar's particular case) from the bald sensory knowledge of individuals (which is not in itself scientific knowledge) to a higher, scientific knowledge of species, and finally of astrological type. In this context, what has hitherto been seen as a flaw in design of the *Knight's Tale*, namely, the lack of character differentiation between Palamon and Arcite, is rather an attempt to rise above the lowest order of knowledge, that is, non-scientific apprehension of mere individual traits, for the two are already carefully distinguished as astrological types, and are thus intelligible on a superior cognitive plane. Susannah Mary Chewning draws upon feminist semiotics in ' "Wommen ... folwen alle the favour of Fortune": A Semiotic Reading of Chaucer's *Knight's Tale*' , in Robert S. Corrington and John Deely, eds, *Semiotics*. The essay reviews contemporary French and Anglo-American feminist semiotics and interprets Emelye as an inherently empty sign, whose semiotic valence is bestowed upon her by the male guarantors of the word, in this case, Theseus, Palamon and Arcite. Chewning finds the tale to be one of Chaucer's darkest statements about feminine signification in matters of courtly love. Pamela Farvolden, in ' "Love Can No Frenship": Erotic Triangles in Chaucer's "Knight's Tale" ', in Whitaker, *Sovereign Lady*, compares Chaucer's and Lydgate's poems, finding that, despite differences in the resolution of the narrative, they both are ordered around a primary homosocial bond that simultaneously opposes itself to yet depends upon the marital bond of love.

The Oxford Student Texts series adds to its Chaucer collection with Peter Mack and Chris Walton's *Geoffrey Chaucer: The Miller's Tale*. This edition, drawing from the combined experiences of teaching Chaucer at secondary and tertiary levels, offers a detailed and affordable study guide of the text, which itself is excerpted from the Riverside edition. These virtues of detail and affordability are the edition's main strengths, as the bibliographical material does not provide much of an update on the scholarship of the Riverside edition. None the less, there are some welcome ad hoc references, such as that to The Tallis Scholars' recording of the song *Angelus ad virginem*. The textual commentary is full, although it is a shame that, with the exception of the noted repetition of the line 'allone, withouten any compaignye', no attention is paid to the structural parallels and inversions between the *Miller's* and *Knight's Tales*. Topics for discussion and analysis follow the text and its succeeding commentary. These topics for the most part observe well-trodden paths – character studies, realism, sources, etc. – but they also address less obvious aspects of the tale, such as proverbs, concealment and association. Useful illustrations include a diagram of the layout of John's house, complete with the lovers in bed, Absolom at the window, and the carpenter snoring in the roof, as well as a reproduction from the *Queen Mary Psalter*, depicting Noah's wife hindering the progress of his building of the ark. The section on Chaucer's language though inevitably brief, none the less manages to illustrate effectively both the changes in meaning between much of Chaucer's vocabulary and its modern descendant, and the less formalized grammatical condition of his English. The omission, however, of any comment on infinitives in the section dealing with verbs is regrettable. The Miller's famous maxim warning against prying into the secrets of God or wife is reconsidered by Katheryn Walls in 'The Significance of *Arca* and *Goddes Pryvetee* in *The Miller's Tale*' (*N&Q* 42.24–6). She links it to an entry on 'archa' in the *De Proprietabus rerum* of Bartholomaeus Anglicus, which glosses it as a vessel that keeps things hidden. Certainly, there is a link here between 'archa' and the Ark of the Covenant but it is less obvious how Noah's ark and 'archa' could be connected, although, in popular lore, Noah did counsel his wife to keep the building of the ark a secret. James H. Morey suggests a link between trial by ordeal and 'The "Cultour" in the *Miller's Tale*: Alison as Iseult' (*ChauR* 29.373– 81). Trials by cultour and ploughshare were primarily used in cases of sexual crimes committed by women. Absolom thus selects the instrument most appropriate for an adulteress. The use of the cultour for this purpose also establishes a connection with Iseult in *Tristan and Iseult*, who undergoes just such a trial by ordeal. (The cultour was, of course, initially intended for Alison.) That Iseult miraculously passes the trial further strengthens the parallel with Alison. Linda Lomperis, in 'Bodies that Matter in the Court of Late Medieval England and in Chaucer's *Miller's Tale*' (*RR* 86.ii.243–64), moves away from essential identities fixed by gender and class towards a more performative notion of agency in the *Miller's Tale*, for the characters are all theatrically invested, and playing parts throughout the action. Gender is so uncertain in the tale (think of Absolom's effeminacy) that the routine playing of female parts by men on the stage provides the link to Lomperis's argument for Alison's 'somatic masculinity', i.e., that 'she' is a man in woman's clothing. Although all the obvious objections that spring to mind are addressed (*queynte* means simply a 'pleasing thing', John is too old to have sex with Alison and thus discover 'her' secret, and so on), persuasion, in this case anyway, did not occur. The argument is broadened outside the tale to discuss a culture of male erotics in the sartorial celebration of the male anatomy in contemporary fashion, and in a possible preference of Richard II for male sexual companions; the non-productivity of homoeroticism signals the aristocracy's inability to reproduce itself. And along the same lines, Wolfgang Rudat's 'Gender-Crossing in the *Miller's Tale* – and a new Chaucerian Crux' (*JEP* 16.i–ii.134–46) continues in much the same vein as his *Ernest Exuberance in Chaucer's Poetics* (*YWES* 74.149–50). Indeed, his earlier representation of Alison's buttocks and thighs extending out the window as a huge pair of scissors cutting off Absolom's hair makes a return appearance here and is further elaborated into the following gems: it is Alison's vagina, and not anus, that is kissed by Absolom; Absolom's 'allas, I ne hadde ybleynt' (the philological 'crux' of the title) means that he regrets involuntarily jumping back from this act of near-cunnilingus because he wanted to revenge himself by biting into Alison's labia and shearing her pubic hair off with his teeth (hence the 'gender-crossing' of the title by Absolom playing the castrating female role of *vagina dentata*); Nicholas's decision to take part in the kissing game suggests an intention for Absolom to perform fellatio on him. After reading this, one begins to wonder whether Tourette syndrome might be emerging as a new kind of literary theory. In one of two articles published this year, Howell Chickering offers a close reading of Chaucer's metrics: 'Comic Meter and Rhyme in the *Miller's Tale*', in Michael N. Salda and Jean E. Jost, *Chaucer Yearbook*. His approach is motivated by the perceived lack of critical attention that Chaucer's prosody now receives and the article begins with an extended review of such attention as has been received. His line-by-line analysis of the tale's metrics, which involves some repunctuation of the Variorum edition of Hengwrt, results in the to-be-expected conclusion that the tale is funnier for having been written in verse rather than prose. While Chickering's observation of an imbalance in prosodic criticism is certainly just, his redress makes for an overly detailed discussion of metrical minutiae that, in its turn, tends to neglect a general argument.

If unpublished verse be permissible evidence, then E. G. Stanley displaces Dryden from the throne of being the first to modernize Chaucer's tales: 'Francis Burton: Old Chaucer's *Reeve's Tale* "Put Into Better Englishe"' (*N&Q* 42.271–8). Burton, in the early seventeenth century, made a verse modernization of the Reeve's tale. Stanley proceeds to describe the manuscript, which is owned by the Bodleian, then to describe his own editorial procedures, and finally follows with his transcription of Burton's text. The rhyme structure groups the verses into quatrains, with an *abab* rhyme scheme. Burton's verse makes no attempt to elevate Chaucer's language while modernizing it, as is made clear by the following (ll. 177-80): 'Shee thought to sleepe, but mought not there/ for John would needes bee duckinge./ She wondred much, for this manye a yeare/ shee had not such a –'. The text is generously annotated by Stanley but the essay would have been made an even better read than it already is had he added some general thoughts about the implications of the text for seventeenth-century reception of Chaucer's bawdy. Charles R. Smith, in 'Chaucer's Reeve and St. Paul's Old Man' (*ChauR* 30.101–6), connects the Reeve's disquisition upon the 'foure gleedes' of old age in his prologue with St Paul's characterization of the spiritually dead *vetus homo* (Ephesians 4.22–8). The Reeve himself, Symkyn, John and Aleyn are all spiritually old men; together, they exhibit the 'four gleedes' of lying, anger, covetousness or stealing and pride (which is Smith's gloss on 'avauntyng'). 'The Logic of Deprivation in the *Reeve's Tale*' (*ChauR* 30.150–63), by William F. Woods, inverts the logic of plenty that motivates the *Miller's Tale*, which claims that there is plenty (of Alisoun?) to go around. Symkyn is a predator upon the economic resources of the countryside and seeks to displace his superiors. Woods thus takes issue with Lee Patterson's reading which presents the *Reeve's Tale* as a characteristic Chaucerian retreat from the class conflict instigated by the poet between the Knight and the Miller. It is a shame, however, that Woods does not support his reading with the same range of historical evidence as Patterson does. Stuart Justman writes about '*The Reeve's Tale* and the Honor of Men' (*SSF* 32.i.21–7). Here cuckoldry is linked to the ritual of ridicule, frequently enacted as some kind of 'rough music', that is known in popular culture as 'charivari'. Justman finds this tradition of ridicule ambivalent in its simultaneous sanctioning of patriarchal values (submissive wives, authoritative husbands) and carnivalesque interrogation of the very notion of authority itself. The *Miller's Tale* similarly both affirms the stereotype of the adulterous wife and overthrows the authority of the *Knight's Tale*. The *Reeve's Tale*, shown in contrast to its known sources and analogues, is preoccupied with the satirizing of pretension to honour and with the moral that honour is better left to those who are worthy of it; in this it aligns itself with the conventional side of the charivari ethic. However, it also exposes the violence and sexual politics of that honour by showing its foundation to be the reduction of women to mere pawns of men.

Tom Burton reads Chaucer's *Man of Law's Tale* for the Chaucer Studio Occasional Readings. Robert M. Jordan investigates 'Heteroglossia and Chaucer's Man of Law's Tale' (in Farrell, *Bakhtin and Medieval Voices*) and finds that the concept helps explain the tale's notorious problems of characterization and narrative voice, including its many apostrophes, abrupt shifts in style, digressions, etc. Jordan finds that criticism of the tale, even feminist criticism, has assumed too much the presence of an autonomous narrating subject. Heteroglossia, with its assumption of multiple perspective within narrative, allows Jordan to appreciate the stylistically discontinuous narrative as sheer rhetorical virtuosity without resort to ironic readings of the Man of Law's 'character'. Peter G. Beidler also challenges the resort to pilgrim characterization in 'Chaucer's Request for Money in the Man of Law's Prologue', in Salda and Jost, *Chaucer Yearbook*. He argues that what constitute interpretative problems and inconsistencies in the prologue could be resolved were we to entertain the possibility that the prologue represents an earlier 'begging' poem – much in the spirit of 'Complaint of Chaucer to His Purse' – recited by Chaucer before a company of merchants and was only later assigned to the Man of Law. This would explain Chaucer's adaptation of his source to single out poverty as the ultimate misery, not to mention the apostrophe to 'O riche marchauntz'; the only problem is that Beidler can adduce no hard historical evidence to support the thesis and this inevitably keeps his argument tentative. Hagiographical motifs in this tale, along with other Middle English romances, are analysed by Karen A. Winstead in 'Saints, Wives, and Other "Hooly Thynges": Pious Laywomen in Middle English Romance', in Salda and Jost, *Chaucer Yearbook*. Winstead resists the tendency to collapse the distinction between romances which clearly contain hagiographical elements and hagiography proper, arguing rather for a discrete sub-category of 'pious romance'. Constance is thus a pious romance heroine whose difference from an actual saint is established by contrast with Chaucer's own Cecilia legend. The latter celebrates a 'resourceful virgin martyr' who proves herself beyond the laws of the material conditions imposed by being boiled and having her throat cut while Constance, on the other hand, is obliged to suffer patiently the afflictions of female thraldom in a patriarchal world.

The tape of *The Wife of Bath's Tale*, produced by the Chaucer Studio, offers us a frolicsome Wife, narrated by Mary Hamel, along with a range of colourful characters from a Pardoner afflicted by a 'smal', goaty voice to a crabbed Loathly Lady. Distinctive to Hamel's pronunciation is the south-German-sounding [ɣ] rather than [x] in words such as *nyght*. Some textual concerns are addressed by John Eadie in 'The Wife of Bath's Non-Hengwrt Lines: Chaucerian Revision or Editorial Meddling?' (*NM* 96.ii.169–76). He identifies four groups of lines from the Wife's *Prologue* which, although occurring in Ellesmere, are in none of the other earliest and most authoritative manuscripts including, of course, Hengwrt. These lines, almost unique to Ellesmere, are usually printed in modern editions with, at most, the passing assumption that the lines are the result of authorial revision. Eadie's dispute is with the very notion of revision itself as presupposing a single, finished text and proposes instead that the lines should at best be considered as a variant version, always supposing that Chaucer himself included them. Eadie argues that the passages in question (ll. 575–84, 609–12, 619–26, 717–20 of the Riverside edition) all carry anti-feminist overtones and shift the emphasis away from the Wife's unorthodox individuality to more conventional anti-feminist characterization. Although not discounting the possibility that Chaucer did introduce the material, Eadie suggests that the lines are rather the result of later anti-feminist, editorial 'meddling'. In her study of 'The Variant Passages in the Wife of Bath's Prologue and the Textual Transmission of *The Canterbury Tales*: The "Great Tradition" Revisited' (in Smith and Taylor, *Women, the Book and the Worldly*), Beverly Kennedy examines why the authenticity of these six passages continues to go unchallenged. She looks at their hermeneutic impact, noting their blatant misogyny, and argues that they fundamentally alter the representation of the Wife's moral character. Skipping quickly through the history of the textual transmission of the *Canterbury Tales* from Caxton to the present day, she concludes that the current inclusion of these passages in the canonical text is mostly the result of a conservative adherence to tradition. For her part, she finds it hard to believe in Chaucer's authorship of these passages, citing not just their limited manuscript attestation and stylistic clumsiness, but also their disambiguating function, which, she claims, contradicts Chaucer's normal practice in the *Canterbury Tales*. In 'The Marital Dilemma in the Wife of Bath's Tale: An Unnoticed Analogue and its Chaucerian Court Context' (*ELN* 33.i.1–7), Glending Olson argues for a comparison between the knight's choice, namely, whether to have his wife ugly and faithful or beautiful and of more doubtful virtue, and a *demande d'amour* that occurs in a balade by Deschamps, in which the choice for an absentee husband is whether to take a young and pretty wife or one who is middle-aged. The court circle with which Deschamps's balade is connected most probably includes Lewis Clifford, thereby both establishing a connection with Chaucer's own court circle and gesturing towards an aristocratic discourse associated with *luf-talkyng*. The beauty versus fidelity topos, then, would appear to be associated less with a learned tradition of anti-feminism, with which the Wife's question has been associated, and more with an aristocratic *demande d'amour*. Cynthia Ho finds Japanese analogues to the middle-aged, amorous Wife and her prototype, La Vieille, in 'Old "Wives" and their Sources: The Wife of Bath, *The Romance of the Rose*, *Genji Monogatari*, and *Ise Monogatari*' (*Poetica* 44.1–11); she contends that the sexuality of the Japanese older women betrays a more 'benign objectification' and 'acquiescence to difference' than do their Western counterparts. Edward Vasta studies 'Chaucer, Gower, and the Unknown Minstrel: The Literary Liberation of the Loathly Lady' (*Exemplaria* 7.395–418) in the light of Mikhail Bakhtin's comments on the grotesque carnivalesque. In comparison with the Loathly Lady type in other cultures, for example, Greek and Celtic, Vasta finds the Loathly Lady of the English romances to be both lacking in personal sovereignty and an outsider in the official culture of the court. However, he argues for distinctions between the individual authors, finding Gower the most conservative in his treatment of the Loathly Lady's transformation. Although Chaucer, like Gower, assimilates her into official culture, he simultaneously grants the woman greater stature by her sovereignty over her husband and by placing her story in the mouth of a proto-Loathly Lady, the Wife of Bath. However, in order to find a narrative in which the transformation of the Loathly Lady goes beyond individual liberation to entail a transformation of official culture, Vasta argues that we have to turn to the *Weddynge of Sir Gawen and Dame Ragnell*. Dame Ragnell's grotesqueness ultimately renews and perpetuates official culture in a way that is more faithful to Bakhtin's criteria of carnivalesque energy than is either Gower's or Chaucer's heroines. In 'Exploitation and Excommunication in *The Wife of Bath's Tale*' (*PQ* 74.i.17–35), Brian S. Lee comments upon the trivialization of rape in both the Wife's tale and medieval practice, despite the formal gravity of the act in the eyes of the law. Rape is understood in terms of excommunication: in order to be raped in the first place, the virgin is already in a sense excommunicate; and the knight's punishment is a type of excommunication from the court. For Lee, the tale is organized around a symbolic exchange of bodies, at odds with contemporary notions of justice: the woman's body disappears from the tale and the knight's body is bestowed in exchange – through excommunication and then through marriage. The tale then is about an ethic of rehabilitation rather than revenge. Susanne Weil, in 'Freedom Through Association? Chaucer's Psychology of Argumentation in *The Wife of Bath's Prologue*' (*PCP* 30.i.27–41), contends that the Wife's diction reveals not the working of a deliberative, rational memory but a spontaneous recall, what Weil terms 'associative thinking'. The distinction is based upon Aristotelian faculty psychology, a summary of which opens the essay. Considerable lengths are gone to in order to establish Chaucer's acquaintance with the philosopher's thought through his early education; a rather easier route would have surely been to establish links with Aristotle through Dante. Seeing Chaucer as a self-taught sceptic, Weil identifies his stance with that of the Wife, whose sex prevents her from the benefits of the logically sharp mind that a proper education (reserved for males) would have bestowed upon her. The footnotes, it must be said, are a mess, being badly out of sequence, frequently disorganized in material, and with Aristotle not cited by the standard Bekker notation.

In 'The Devil's Bow and Arrows: Another Clue to the Identity of the Yeoman in Chaucer's *Friar's Tale*' (*ChauR* 30.211–14), Clarence H. Miller adds to reasons already attested why the yeoman in the tale is a devil. That the devil goes about well supplied with arrows and a bow to hunt unwary souls is a commonplace in patristic and later medieval commentary, as well as medieval hymns and iconography, and so the significance of the yeoman's 'bowe' and 'arwes brights and kene' should not have been lost on the Friar's slow-witted summoner.

John F. Plummer III continues the Variorum series with his fine edition of the *Summoner's Tale*. The introduction provides a survey of critical opinions about the tale from 1635–1986, of which much the most memorable is Theodore Roosevelt's complaint that Chaucer is 'altogether needlessly filthy' and that the *Summoner's Tale* is 'unpardonable, and indeed unreadable'. The section on the textual tradition of the tale bases its scholarship largely upon the comments of Manly and Rickert's 1940 edition and some of the main points of the argument can be summarized as follows: the prologue and tale appear together, there being no separate textual history for them; the concluding episode of the tale, in which the friar visits the lord of the manor, does not appear in a number of manuscripts; Hengwrt, which forms the base manuscript for the Variorum series, and Ellesmere diverge in the course of the friar's sermon (l. 1991), at which juncture the variants in Ellesmere increase dramatically, suggesting that at this point in the text, the Ellesmere scribe shifted exemplars. The text of the tale follows Hengwrt closely, with few and minor exceptions; for that matter, the discrepancies between Hengwrt and Ellesmere are also very minor in nature, mostly amounting to changes of prepositions. Plummer also notes that the metre of the Hengwrt text suggests a supple and varied use of the pentameter line – further reason to adhere to this early manuscript. A detailed description of the base-group manuscripts constitutes a large part of the textual commentary, from which the following points are of note: on the evidence of the *Summoner's Prologue and Tale* alone, Plummer cannot find any conclusive evidence to support Manly and Rickert's argument that Ellesmere is a heavily edited text, although, from line 1991 onwards, he cannot dismiss that possibility; MS Cambridge Gg.4.27 is of some interest because, in modern editions of the prologue and tale, its readings have often taken precedence over Hengwrt and Ellesmere, although it tends to bear out Manly and Rickert's thinking that the scribe did not well understand his exemplar; MS Harley 7334 has a far higher number of unique variants than is recognized by Manly and Rickert. In the description of the printed editions, Plummer notes the cautious and conservative nature of Caxton's emendations in his second edition; that evidence would suggest that Thynne did indeed consult manuscripts as well as earlier printed editions for the tale in his first edition; but that on the other hand, there is little evidence to suggest that Speght used manuscripts to emend his second edition. However, for those who cannot face these 100 pages of detailed, valuable commentary, the salient details of the textual and critical comments are recorded beneath the actual text of the tale, which makes, as one might expect, for a very heavily annotated page. Catherine S. Cox, in ' "Grope wel bihynde": The Subversive Erotics of Chaucer's Summoner' (*Exemplaria* 7.145–77) gives a detailed and thought-provoking reading of the textual/sexual play in the *Summoner's Tale*. Its humour is not usually thought of as sexual, rather as scatological, but Cox sexualizes the relationship between the Friar John and Thomas through an alignment between the Summoner and Pardoner. Her identification of the Summoner with Friar John is rather at odds with the Summoner's anti-fraternal motives against the Friar-pilgrim; and her gloss on *grope* as 'indecent touch' does emphasize the sexual at the expense of the confessional sense (since the word is frequently used to refer to the confessor's questioning of the penitent's conscience) which also is appropriate to the context. Elaborating the rhetorical associations of the sodomy trope with (the abuse of) language and, in particular, with Friar John's glossing, Cox argues that gender and sexual identity are blurred and made contingent in the tale. The Summoner's fartwheel gets reconsidered in Phillip Pulsiano's 'The Twelve-Spoked Wheel of the *Summoner's Tale*' (*ChauR* 29.382–9). Alongside the more familiar interpretations of the wheel as a parody of Pentecost or as the Wheel of False Religion, Pulsiano posits an association between the wheel and the problem in the natural sciences of the division of the winds; the association was first made by Wentersdorf (*YWES* 61.109). Some confusion is shown to have existed over the division and naming of the lesser winds, but there are commonly 12 of them and, in some illuminated manuscripts, they are arranged in the shape of a 12-spoked wheel, with the division of the winds placed in the centre as a thirteenth figure.

In another clear, leisurely recording, Tom Burton narrates *The Clerk's Tale* for the Chaucer Studio Occasional Readings series. An interesting essay by Linda Georgianna features the bleak message of 'The Clerk's Tale and the Grammar of Assent' (*Speculum* 70.793–821), concluding that the story is not meant to offer any rationalization of or consolation in suffering, but to remind Christians of the radically absolute demands of faith. Examining the tale's lexicon of forethought and choice, Georgianna notes an unusual opposition between them, as in Walter's 'wol ye assente or elles yow avyse?'. Griselda's instantaneous assent goes beyond mere absence of dissent to an active willing that, by definition, does not premeditate or take counsel. Such terms, then, as 'patience' or 'passivity' fall short of capturing the extremity of Griselda's obedience. Thomas J. Farrell's 'The Chronotopes of Monology in Chaucer's Clerk's Tale', in Farrell, *Bakhtin*, brings some welcome specificity to the overused terminology associated with Bakhtin: heteroglossic, monologic, et al. For Farrell, the *Clerk's Tale* is monologic in conception, for its voice is single and continuous. The *Envoy*, on the other hand, with its de-authorization of the tale, is heteroglossic, but not, Farrell argues, dialogic. That is, although different voices speak both in the *Envoy* and throughout the *Tales*, each voice is allocated its own separate space: with a few important exceptions, the voices tend not to be depicted in conflict, dialogically. One can also apply this discreteness to the generic markers in the *Clerk's Tale*, to what Bakhtin calls 'chronotopes'. The tale, often critiqued for being neither alleg-ory nor folk story proper, participates in what Farrell calls 'Ecclesiastes time', a principle based on there being a separate, appropriate time to reap, to sow, to kill, to heal, etc. Thus, the *Clerk's Tale* is an assembly of generic gestures that do not come together into dialogic tension. Howell Chickering writes about 'Form and Interpretation in the *Envoy* to the *Clerk's Tale*' (*ChauR* 29.252–72). Noting that the manuscript evidence is unclear about the status of the *Envoy*, whether it is part of the tale or separate from it, Chickering draws indirectly upon Bakhtin in arguing that the successive frames established by the alternative narrative termini reveal the dialogic nature of discourse. The form of the *Envoy* is thought to be unique, not having any exact counterpart in Middle French or English poetry; Chickering combs through the language of the *Envoy*, 'listening to its astounding texture of repeating sounds' (p. 369) and argues that its uniqueness of form and ironic content renders it impossible to assign the passage exclusively to the Clerk. Natalie Grinnell, in 'Griselde Speaks: The Scriptural Challenge to Patriarchal Authority in "The Clerk's Tale"' (*CMat* 9.i.79–94), notes that received critical wisdom has argued that the unpalatable anti-feminism of the tale is resolved, whether successfully or not, through reading the literal story of marital affliction as an allegory of the spiritual sufferings of Christ or Job. Grinnell argues that the association between Griselde and Christ and Job, well established in the text, does not transcend the difficulties so much as it provides feminist critique of the relationship between God and his suffering servants. The volte-face of Walt-er's behaviour at the end of the tale conflates the behaviour of God and of Satan towards Job, suggesting that God and Satan are merely two parts of the same personality. Joseph Grossi discusses 'The Clerk vs. the Wife of Bath: Nominalism, Carnival, and Chaucer's Last Laugh' in Utz, *Literary Nominalism*. The Clerk's response to the extreme nominalism of the Wife (apparent, presumably, from her emphasis upon individual experience as opposed to authoritative givens) is to offer a realist counterblast. The Clerk's philosophical proclivities are demonstrated in the manner in which he alle-gorizes the story of Griselde, turning it from Petrarchan *exemplum* to abstraction. This is not to say, however, that the tale is lacking in particulariz-ing detail; rather the Clerk particularizes his characters badly, quite intentionally, in order to caricature nominalist individualism. Walter, in his capricious and selfish testing of Griselde, is not an allegory of providence but instead incarnates the worst excesses of nominalist voluntarism. Neither is Griselde any ideal of patience, for her love of Walter goes beyond reason, demonstrating thereby the wilful irrationality of fideism under a nominalist dispensation. These flawed characterizations are intended by the Clerk, but Grossi finds unintended rhetorical flaws in the Clerk's diction that enable him to argue for an ironic separation between the narrator-Clerk and Chaucer the poet. In the *Envoy*, the Clerk's academic, ironic and monoglossic joking is set apart from carnivalesque, polyglossic laughter. Although Chaucer is aligned with neither of the extremes of realism or nominalism, Grossi suggests that Chaucer's sympathies are on the side of plurality and inconclusiveness, and thus latently nominalist: 'the Clerk's univocal Realism must yield, at least to some extent, to Nominalist multivocality' (p. 178). In '"If it youre wille be"': Coercion and Compliance in Chaucer's Clerk's Tale', by Andrew Sprung (*Exemplaria* 7.345–69), an antinomy is identified between the Clerk's criticism of Walter's tyranny and his celebration of Griselde's patience. Sprung draws upon D. W. Winnicott's account of the process by which a child's perception of external reality is formed; according to which the child's emergent recognition of the mother's otherness arouses aggressive impulses released by playing out the destruction of the mother in the fantasy; the mother's 'survival' of this destruction and non-retaliatory love empower the child to recognize the external world outside the self. Tracing an infantile imagery in Walter's depiction and the representation of Griselde as nurturing, Sprung draws Winnicott's and Chaucer's narratives together. However, so total is Griselde's and the populace's submissiveness that Walter does not progress to the necessary recognition of the independence of the external other but remains fixed in his drive to dominate. Chaucer's narrative becomes a study of the psychodynamics and politics of, as well as the distinction between, true and false dominion. The Clerk himself, in his dealings with the Host, with the Wife and ultimately with Petrarch, displays exemplary submission coupled with critical authority. Muriel Whitaker's 'The Artists' Ideal Griselda' in Whitaker, *Sovereign Lady* is for the most part a study of visual representations of Griselde from the eighteenth century onwards, there being no extant pictures of her from before this point. The earliest picture of her, Angelica Kauffman's 'Gualtherius and Griselda' makes no attempt at historical accuracy and reflects neo-classical rather than medieval aesthetic concerns. Whitaker does also discuss the iconographic significance of the depiction of Griselde in Chaucer's tale, where the aesthetic theory that beauty, goodness and light are all identified with each other informs her imagery: Griselde is depicted in scenes of spinning and drawing water from the well, in imitation of Marian iconography; her multiple changing of clothes in the tale signals the changing circumstances of her *historia*, while her unchanging visage reflects her constancy.

Carol Everest concludes, from her consideration of medieval medicine and its general acceptance of the two-seed-doctrine of conception, that May's impregnation by Januarie was impossible: '"Paradys or Helle": Pleasure and Procreation', in Muriel Whitaker, ed., *Sovereign Lady*. Because female orgasm was generally thought to be either downright necessary or at least desirable for conception to occur, May's evident lack of pleasure in her husband had to make her claim to pregnancy false. Damien's ascent into the tree 'that charged was with fruyt' assumes an added significance once we consider the physical effects of his lovesickness and sexual frustration. His potent fertility, opposed to Januarie's decrepit sterility, introduces the possibility that May is indeed made pregnant from her encounter in the pear tree, although critical opinion is divided as to whether or not Januarie's restored vision interrupted events at the decisive moment. Carol Falvo Heffernan neatly provides the *sed contra* to Everest's position in 'Contraception and the

Pear Tree Episode of Chaucer's *Merchant's Tale'* (*JEGP* 94.v.31–41). Heffernan draws attention to a traditional assumption of the pear's contraceptive
properties. Although Chaucer's use of a pear tree can be explained by its
presence in his sources, there is also every possibility that he would also have
been acquainted with the *De vegetalibus* of Albertus Magnus, in which such
reference is made. The *Merchant's* and *Franklin's Tales* are treated by Robert
R. Edwards in 'Some Pious Talk about Marriage: Two Speeches from the
Canterbury Tales', in Eibert R. Edwards and Vickie Ziegler, *Matrons and
Marginal Women in Medieval Society*. Edwards compares the long encomium
on marriage (ll. 1267–392), which is placed, it is generally thought, in a free-
standing discourse registering Januarie's thoughts, with its various sources,
and he finds that its apparently approbatory intention is shadowed by subtle
shifts of emphasis from the originals and by the literary contexts from which
they have been borrowed. The uncertainty of narrative voice, however
(namely, who exactly is uttering these lines), keeps the meaning of the speech
open-ended. The Franklin also utters a speech, in this instance, in praise of
friendship within marriage and in rejection of *maistrye* (ll. 761–91); but once
again, the contexts from which the allusions are borrowed ironize the apparent meaning, for it reveals friendship to be essentially homosocial rather than
heterosexual. Mary Dove considers the tale briefly in ' "Swiche Olde Lewed
Wordes": Books about Medieval Love, Medieval Books about Love and the
Medieval Book of Love', in Andrew Lynch and Philippa Maddern, eds, *Venus
and Mars: Engendering Love and War in Medieval and Early Modern Europe*,
arguing that the literal, carnal level of meaning is contained and subsumed
within, rather than opposed to, the allegorical levels. Thus, Januarie's carnal
gloss on his quote from the Song of Songs is not strictly a wrong interpretation
of the text.

The *Squire's Tale* is coupled, unusually, with the *Man of Law's Tale* in
Elizabeth Scala's 'Canacee and the Chaucer Canon: Incest and Other Unnar-
ratables' (*ChauR* 30.15–39). The Man of Law's concern not to tell Canacee's
story with its allusion to her imputed brotherly incest – his concern, that is,
with what he isn't going to relate – 'signifies along a particularly Derridean
chain that links incest to storytelling'. Incest becomes present in the tale by its
conspicuous absence. This kind of proof-by-denial logic undermines the Man
of Law's control of meaning and ultimately the intentionality of Chaucer
himself (the demolition of the Man of Law as fictional 'character' whose
narrative inconsistencies can be explained by recourse to irony is insistently
under attack in the criticism this year). In the *Squire's Tale*, the reference to
Cambalo is taken by Scala to signal the brother and sister's incestuous
relationship, yet the tale fails to narrate any story of such a union, implying, for
Scala, another conspicuous absence. While the claim to metanarrativity in
Chaucer's narrative may not be new, its implications, says Scala, are; inasmuch
as the *Squire's Tale* has a theme, it is how narrative is founded upon exclusions, in this case, incestuous. In an essay coupling the tale with that of the
Franklin, Kathryn L. Lynch addresses geographical concerns in 'East Meets
West in Chaucer's *Squire's* and *Franklin's Tales'* (*Speculum* 70.530–51) and
finds that both tales are linked by an excess of female sexual power connoted
by the fabulous East. The Orient functions in the *Squire's Tale* as a figure of
exotic alterity. Applying Edward Said's work on orientalism to Chaucer,
Lynch argues that these two tales attempt to control cultural difference by first

depicting the East as strange and dehumanized and then proceeding to incorporate and domesticize its alterity. Suggesting a distant acquaintance by Chaucer of the *Thousand and One Arabian Nights*, Lynch reads storytelling as a space for feminine resistance to masculine power. The *Squire's Tale*, with its rhetoric of excess, 'out-Easts the East' in taking the *Nights'* loose dilatory structure to the degree almost of caricature and thus the Squire is seen to be 'exogamous' in marrying, however unhappily, East and West. The Franklin's interruption of the Squire's narrative can be read not so much as a meditation upon *gentilesse* but as a counter to this Oriental excess, for the Franklin tells a British, 'endogamous' tale that restrains and controls the momentary threat posed by Dorigen's 'Oriental' play.

In '"Considerynge the Beste on Every Syde": Ethics, Empathy, and Epistemology in the *Franklin's Tale*' (*ChauR* 29.390–415), Anne Scott applies Mary Belenky's work on gender-specific epistemologies to Chaucer's tale. Arveragus's epistemological world exhibits a 'blind adherence to abstract universals' while Dorigen's functions at the other end of the spectrum, by intuition, subjectivism, and oral traditionalism. The 'constructivist' Aurelius turns out to be the unlikely epistemological hero by his imaginative ability to move between the dual worlds of (masculine) abstract universals and of (feminine) sensory particulars: quite the new age man.

The Clerk is further discussed in relation to the Franklin in Carolynn Van Dyke's 'The Clerk's and Franklin's Subjected Subject' (*SAC* 17.45–68). For Van Dyke, the longstanding critical controversies about the tales inevitably mark in part the intrinsic irresolution of the tales themselves on the subject of female agency, notwithstanding the extent to which the two tales do in fact exhibit a marked interest in structure, order and thematic unity at the allegorical or moral level. It is precisely this interest in order and synthesis that appears to include woman in their notion of humanity, but Van Dyke suggests that the position of woman in the morals of the tales remains deeply enigmatic, for the Clerk's narrative shifts from distinguishing woman from 'us' to the direct address to a female audience, and the Franklin, having given Dorigen a developed subject-position in the tale, finally reduces her to the 'functional equivalent of one thousand pounds'. The facts that Griselde is a wife who exemplifies mankind but not wives and that Dorigen is the cause of yet excluded from male *fredom* expose the doubleness of Chaucer's narratives and simultaneously undermine the implied conclusions of the tales, namely, that only men are subjects. Derek Pearsall considers '*The Franklin's Tale*, Line 1469: Forms of Address in Chaucer' (*SAC* 17.69–78). The line in question contains the only occasion in the tale in which Dorigen is addressed by name (here, by Arveragus). Comparing this instance with other occurrences of direct address by name in Chaucer, most particularly, in *Troilus and Criseyde*, Pearsall argues that the use of personal names occurs less in courtly speech than in more formal exchanges. The formality of Arveragus's vocative here suggests a tone of authority no longer consistent with his avowed lack of *maistrye*, but perhaps assumed in response to Dorigen's desperation. Pearsall further notes that the occurrences of the direct address by name tend to correspond to the use of the second person singular (*T* forms) rather than the use of the second person plural (*V* forms) and, sure enough, Arveragus follows his use of Dorigen's name shortly after with a *T* form of address. Barbara Stevenson, in 'West Meets East: Geoffrey Chaucer's "Franklin's Tale" and the Japanese "Captain of Naruto" ' (*Poetica* 44.41–52) argues for the value of cross-cultural perspectives and offers this Japanese tale as another analogue to the *Franklin's Tale*. Stevenson points to ideological consonances between the disparate cultures that have produced these tales: the emergent notion of individual rights in late medieval England that undermined the late feudal structure and the erosions of privilege resulting from the late feudalization of Japan in the thirteenth century; and a common retrospective attitude towards the preservation of tradition. One difference between them, however, is that while the Franklin's equality is ultimately anti-feudal in conception, the Japanese author insists on peaceful co-existence between the differing feudal classes. See also Edwards's essay above in the *Merchant's Tale* section.

In an interesting discussion about 'John of Arderne and Chaucer's Physician' (*ANQ* 8.i.3–8), Elaine E. Whitaker outlines the clear parallels between the portrait of the Physician in the *General Prologue* and John of Arderne's description of the ideal medical practitioner in *Fistula in Ano*. Whilst initial comparisons suggest that Chaucer's Physician is an excellent doctor, his tale itself reveals that he lacks the skill of storytelling – one of the means by which the medieval physician was supposed to promote healing. Indeed, his tale provokes the opposite response of near-sickness in the Host, an outcome which leads Whitaker to condemn the Physician as guilty of malpractice. Carlyn P. Collette examines the references to images in Virginia's portrait in the context of Wycliffite debates: '"Peyntyng with Greet Cost": Virginia as Image in the *Physician's Tale*', in Salda and Jost, *Chaucer Yearbook*. Wycliffite objections to images centre upon the profit motive behind their production and the danger of them leading those of 'rude wittis' into a confusion between the likeness and the reality; the image itself, however, is perceived to be neutral. The word *countrefete*, so emphasized in Virginia's portrait, itself is a neutral term without the necessary pejorative connotation it carries today and can imply either a false or a true likeness; Virginia of course is the perfect image. Collette's assertion that Chaucer's audience would have been attuned to the contemporary discourse on images stands upon its own merits and hardly needs the ratification of her opening discussion of Michael Riffaterre's 'intertext'.

Joseph Gallagher's taped rendition of *The Pardoner's Tale* is delightfully done, featuring a swaggering, bombastic Pardoner; Gallagher reads all the different parts. In 'The Moral Landscape of the Pardoner's Tale' (in Allen and White, *Subjects*), Bruce A. Johnson finds 28 geographic references in the tale and argues that Chaucer's addition of these was a conscious attempt to intensify the story's moral impact. Paul Strohm's article 'Chaucer's Lollard Joke: History and the Textual Unconscious' (*SAC* 17.23–42) began life as the Biennial Chaucer Lecture, but in fact, as he himself comments, it constitutes not one address but 'six short lectures'. These take a joke from the *Pardoner's Tale* as their common theme, and explore it from a multiplicity of perspectives, allowing Strohm to fulfil the promise he gives at the outset which is that he will 'eventually suggest' that the fullest understanding of a text must include attention to what it omits as well as what it includes. In 'Trade Secrets: Chaucer, the Pardoner, the Critics' (*MLS* 25.iv.1–36), Gregory W. Gross looks to the recent readings of the Pardoner as 'gay' and asks by what rhetorical strategies the correlations between the contemporary and the late medieval have been constructed. A certain rhetoric of secrecy is seen to inform critical readings of the Pardoner which originates in Kittredge's unhappiness with the dramatic inconsistency between the prologue uttered by a corrupt Pardoner and the moral tale he tells and which culminates in the assumption that the pilgrim bears a dark 'secret'. Finding the critical tradition of reading the Pardoner as a eunuch to be ultimately essentialist in its need to establish sexual identity, albeit by its privation, Gross argues that the Pardoner's sodomitical allusions are to be understood in terms of their contemporary associations with the idolatrous worship of false relics and simony. More specifically, Gross connects the 'ful *vicious*' Pardoner with *uicium* in the *Planctus naturae* (a word that for Alan of Lille denotes both pseudography and sodomy) and thereby draws out the connection between the Pardoner's sodomy and fraudulent rhetoric. In Rita Copeland's 'The Pardoner's body and the disciplining of rhetoric', appearing in *Framing Medieval Bodies*, edited by Sarah Kay and Miri Rubin and published last year, a connection is drawn between the Pardoner's sexually transgressive body which is 'disciplined' verbally by the Host at the end of the tale and the unruly corpus of rhetoric, itself carefully regulated by theorists from antiquity to the Middle Ages, eventually emerging into the biddable discipline we encounter in the trivium. The article begins with a most proficient synthesis of opinion upon the status of rhetoric, *viz* whether it really is a valid subject matter in its own right or rather a tool, or *organon*, of thought. Either way, the result is the same: the regulation of rhetoric and putting of it to civic and moral use, in order to produce a disciplined body of thought. Copeland notes that the word *disciplina*, under Christian thought, acquires the association of corporal punishment, thereby conflating the ideas of intellectual regulation and physical correction. Moreover, in writers such as Quintilian, Matthew of Vendôme, and Alan of Lille, we see this unruly body sexualized, with 'unnatural' practices being invoked as a dominant metaphor for rhetorical excess. Characterization of rhetoric presents it as a lewd behaviour that cannot resist exposing itself, thereby implicitly inviting correction and in turn thereby constituting itself as discipline. The analogy with the Pardoner here begins to emerge clearly. With the Host's kiss, bestowed of course at the Knight's insistence, the Pardoner and his rhetoric become inscribed into a system of discursive control. Jay Ruud returns to the question of the identity of the Old Man in '*The Pardoner's Tale* and the Parody of the Resurrection', in *Proceedings of the Third Dakotas Conference on Earlier British Literature*, edited by Bruce E. Brandt. Instead of the conventional typological or allegorical interpretations offered of this figure, Ruud prefers to read him as an instance of 'figural parody', in this case, of the resurrection; as an interpretative paradigm, Ruud finds figural parody more flexible and discontinuous than the allegorical method of one-to-one correspondence. Chaucer's access to resurrection narratives is located in the mystery cycles and the parallels between the accounts duly noted: the quest in both to vanquish death; the presence of a directing guide, be it Mary or the Old Man; the key question in both of 'whom do you seek?'. The Old Man is read as a parodic figure of the resurrected Christ who is sometimes iconographically depicted with a spade in his hand, gesturing to his mistaken identity by Mary as a gardener; the spade is parodied in the Old Man's staff. The 'phallic' tree is a similar parody of the tomb/womb. Where Christ, the new Adam, gardens the earth by digging it, the Old Man can only tap its surface impotently. Ruud's argument is that the

Pardoner's narrative is a sterile parody of the biblical by its avoidance of female, regenerative power. Mary Flowers Braswell speaks of the relation between the tale of the Pardoner and Christ's betrayer in 'Chaucer's Palimpsest: Judas Iscariot and the *Pardoner's Tale*' (*ChauR* 29.303–10). Judas's betrayal for money popularly links him to the Pardoner's theme – 'radix malorum est cupiditas'. And in his association with Oedipus, for he supposedly also killed his father and married his mother, Judas echoes the Old Man, who desires death but cannot attain it. Although Biblical authority has Judas hang himself, medieval commentary has Judas remain alive until after the resurrection, lest the disciple plead forgiveness in Christ's harrowing of hell. A further correspondence is established in the oak tree that appears in the tale and in accounts of Judas's (attempted) hanging. The manner in which Chaucer recycles the stuff of old legends suggests to Braswell the metaphor of the palimpsest. Finally, in a rather opaque article from last year, 'Church Office, Routine, and Self-Exile in Chaucer's Pardoner' (*SAC* 16[1994].69–98), Fred Hoerner applies to the Pardoner Max Weber's construct of 'charisma', according to which the special personal powers possessed by certain individuals, whether religious or political figures, constitute a type of legitimate authority; charisma is opposed to and yet usually degenerates into a permanent routine structure that itself constitutes a different type of bureaucratic authority. Hence the 'charisma' of early radical Christianity stagnates into the routine of church bureaucracy, of which the Pardoner's abuse of his office is a sure sign. Except for the caveat that the Pardoner is 'no bourgeois', the essay makes no attempt to distinguish between the historical conditions out of which Weber conducts his analysis of charismatic leadership, *viz* a mass culture of high capitalism, and those of Chaucer's England; rather the Pardoner's performance 'inverts charisma to commodity and takes the greedy veer from sentiment to slogan'. The Pardoner enacts his own type of demonic charisma as an embodiment of Augustinian concupiscence. He both longs for and cuts himself off from a social whole, displaying a 'doubleness of allegiance' (Lee Patterson's phrase) that echoes our own postmodernity.

R. H. Winnick draws 'Luke 12 and Chaucer's *Shipman's Tale*' into relation with each other (*ChauR* 30.164– 90). The biblical chapter delivers a stinging critique of false piety and materialism and Winnick finds the correspondences between it and the tale too numerous to be coincidental although at the same time claims the reference to the gospel to be only 'oblique'. Winnick posits the chapter not so much as a source proper for the tale but, in a phrase borrowed from Chauncey Wood, as a 'biblical quark'. The similarities found between the two texts are mainly structural and thematic and include that between the counting house scene in Chaucer's tale and the Parable of the Rich Fool, as well as the wife's excessive concern with fine clothing; the main textual connection made is in Chaucer's phrase 'eat and drynke and pleye', which echoes the Latin 'comede bibe epulare'.

Richard Rex's book '*The Sins of Madame Eglentyne' and Other Essays on Chaucer* is a collection of nine papers, four of which have previously appeared in print. Most of the essays are concerned with the Prioress and her tale. In 'Pastiche as Irony in the Prioress's Prologue and Tale', Rex contends that both tale and prologue are intended as pastiche; he then considers 'Wild Horses, Justice, and Charity in the Prioress's Tale', focusing on the particular type of punishment meted out to the Jews in order to highlight the Prioress's lack of charity, and to argue that the tale's implication is its teller's damnation. Some details of the Prioress's appearance are his next concern. In ' "Grey" Eyes and the Medieval Ideal of Feminine Beauty' (an essay which really deals only tangentially with the Prioress), he puzzles over the exact colour intended by this description, eventually declaring that 'grey' in this context implies 'clear', and that colour is not an issue here at all. But colour most definitely is the issue in the following essay as he ponders 'Why the Prioress's Gauds are Green', suggesting that their hue is a conspicuous sign of hypocrisy. Moving on to behaviour, he then explains 'Why the Prioress Sings through her Nose', collecting evidence to show that such a manner of singing was regarded as a sign of weak faith and was therefore proscribed. Some of these points are aired again in the titular essay where Rex argues against the view that the Prioress's shortcomings are pretensions rather than sins; instead he finds her guilty of false piety and little different from the sinful Monk. The point of the rather elaborate argument in 'Madame Eglentyne and the Bankside Brothels' depends upon a double entendre in the name 'Eglentyne'. Rex suggests that Chaucer chose this appellation not just because of its popularity amongst romance heroines, but because the nuns of Stratford-at-Bow owned property at Bankside which may have included a brothel named the Rose. The first essay in the collection takes a broader approach to 'Chaucer and the Jews' by reviewing contemporary attitudes towards the Jews in relation to Christian charity; this leads Rex to suggest that although the Prioress's Tale may be said to mirror contemporary bigotry, 'the bigotry is not Chaucer's'. The only paper which has nothing to do with the Prioress is 'Chaucer's Censured Ballads'. Here a lack of open-mindedness amongst modern editors is Rex's target as he discusses two poems (one of which is obscene), which are indistinctly attributed to Chaucer by John Shirley, and which were brought to the attention of Chaucerians in the late nineteenth century by Furnivall, only to be resolutely ignored ever since. This is an interesting essay, and the poems in question do merit further attention, but the paper is misplaced here, and the volume would have benefited from its omission; the collection as a whole would have been stronger and more coherent if its author had provided a general introduction and conclusion instead.

In 'Heeding the Counsel of Prudence: A Context for the *Melibee*' (*ChauR* 29.416–33), Carolyn P. Collette places the tale in the context of books of instruction for women, such as those by the Ménagier de Paris and Christine de Pizan. Usually identified as a manly and princely virtue, prudence assumes a specifically feminine aspect in becoming a 'science of actions within human relations, particularly marriage' and its practice, in short, means keeping the domestic peace at all times and enduring your husband's intolerable behaviour until he repents. The connection between this ideal wifely behaviour and Prudence's deportment in *Melibee* is recognized by the Host when he makes a jaundiced comparison between Prudence and his own wife, Goodelief. The emphasis Collette claims for wifely prudence in *Melibee*, where the wife must both be patient and give wise counsel, has consequences for the rest of the tales, in particular, for the questionable passivity of Griselde. Judith H. Anderson compares Spenser and Chaucer in 'Prudence and her Silence: Spenser's Use of Chaucer's *Melibee*' (*ELH* 62.29–46). The focus is primarily upon Spenser's character in Book Six of *The Faerie Queene* and Anderson alludes to Chaucer's tale as a partial influence in Spenser's Melibee, usually

associated with more pastoral figures. Both characters can be read allegorically; both stories about Melibee are preoccupied with prudence, by
definition, a virtue concerned with time and memory, and hence with history.
Through *Melibee's* preoccupation with the 'costs of historical engagement',
Spenser's own history of colonial endeavour in Ireland is linked with the
concerns of Book Six.

The tape of *The Nun's Priest's Tale*, narrated by Paul R. Thomas and others,
is great fun and embellishes the text with impressively authentic chicken
noises. Arthur Chapin's article 'Morality Ovidized: Sententiousness and the
Aphoristic Moment in the *Nun's Priest's Tale* (*YJC* 8.i.7–33) reads the tale as
'a primal scene of Menippean laughter in the Renaissance'. The tale parodies
the sententious tendencies of fourteenth-century thought, exemplified even in
manuscripts by the *guillemet* or finger pointing from the margin of the page to
the edifying message. The *sententiae* in the tale are ubiquitous – so much so that
'looking for the "moral" becomes as sexy as the sexy parts of Ovid'; hence the
title. We read as much to spot *sententiae* as to find out what happens next. The
animality of the setting materializes the abstraction of *sententiae* constituting,
for Chapin, a clear case of 'mennipulating' the moral. The essay is full of such
bons mots but is making the basic point that Chaucer's renunciation of
(sententious) authority is a precursor of modern aphoristic writing. Grover
Furr's 'Nominalism in the *Nun's Priest's Tale*: A Preliminary Study' (in Utz,
Literary Nominalism), examines the significance of the discussion of free will
and determinism between Pertelote and Chauntecleer. In his fatalist acceptance of the dream as ill omen, Chauntecleer represents a determinist, and thus
anti-nominalist, position, while Pertelote, in her refusal of all meaning beyond
the material cause of bodily digestion, exhibits an extreme nominalism.
Although the narrating Nun's Priest appears to come down on the side of
determinism in his allusion to Augustine, Boethius, and Bradwardine, Furr
suggests that Chauntecleer's decision to 'diffye bothe sweven and dream' is
reminiscent of the fideism elaborated by Ockham in his arguments against
Augustinian and Boethian intellectual determinism. For a similar consideration of voluntarist thought in Chaucer, see Utz's essay above. Michael Vander
Weele with Deb Powell consider ' "Fruyt" and "Chaf" Revisited, or What's
Cooking in Chaucer's Kitchen?' (*CEA* 57.iii.39–50). They propose an ethical
interpretation of the terms 'fruyt' and 'chaf' (as distinct from the conventional
allegorical interpretation), whose purpose is ultimately to consider the relation
between rhetoric and justice. Thus, 'fruyt' suggests true and 'chaf' false
counsel. Without claims for any historical textual connection between the two
works, Plato's *Gorgias* and the *Nun's Priest's Tale* are associated for their
common interest in the connection between rhetoric and justice; the *Gorgias*
provides the backdrop for a '*performative*' (= conjectural?) reading of Chaucer's tale. Thus Pertelote is read in terms of Socrates's criticism of the
apothecary and hence as a figure of false persuasion (flattery).

Marc Pelen considers 'Idleness and Alchemy in Fragment VIII (G) of
Chaucer's Canterbury Tales: Oppositions in Themes and Images from the
Roman de la Rose' (*FMLS* 31.193– 214), and argues that Chaucer's dramatic
mode of composition in Fragment VIII owes much to the structure of the
Roman de la Rose where the theme of contradictions and contraries plays a
major role. Whilst acknowledging that specific similarities in image, character,
and subject have long been noted between this section of the *Canterbury Tales*

and the French poem, Pelen asserts that the correspondence he perceives goes far beyond these. Elaine Filax attempts to cut across the too-polarized Mary/Eve dichotomy in 'A Female I-deal: Chaucer's Second Nun', in Whitaker, *Sovereign Lady*. The antithesis between the two, mirrored in the concomitant opposition between spirit and body, is complicated by the treatment of the female body in the *Second Nun's Tale* which, instead of erasing the body carnal, glorifies the body virginal. Female corporeality is never, in a sense, left behind and thus the absence of bodily detail given by Chaucer about the Second Nun continues, paradoxically, to signal its presence. Connection between the Second Nun and the Virgin Mary is also considered. Marian theology emphasized two particular points: the intact, unpenetrated boundaries of the virginal body; and the role of mediatrix played by Mary. The latter quality is indicated by the Marian allusion in the prologue, which itself mediates between the narrative of the pilgrimage and that of the tale; the former by the emphasis in the tale upon virginity. The essay also contains some useful historical context of nuns in late medieval England. The shadowy personality of the Second Nun is discussed by Daniel F. Pigg in 'Constructing a Voice for Chaucer's Second Nun: Martyrdom as Institutional Discourse' (*Æestel* 3.81–95). Pigg's contention is that criticism is still locked into an expectation of a teller/tale correspondence that draws upon assumptions of individual agency; this expectation is frustrated by the Second Nun, whose voice we can identify only by turning to more societal and institutional notions of subjectivity dispersed within the tale. Her reference to herself as an 'unworthy sone of Eve' hints at the denial and suppression of the feminine in church discourse; while the physical martyrdom of St Cecilia invokes the spiritual martyrdom that the Second Nun, in taking orders, must embrace. Bruce Kent Cowgill, in 'Sweetness And Sweat: The Extraordinary Emanations in Fragment Eight of the *Canterbury Tales*' (*PQ* 74.343–57), notes the copious reference to sweat in the *Canon's Yeoman's Prologue* and, contrasting it to the Second Nun's reference to St Cecilia who never sweated during her bath of flames, argues for an opposition between a human or carnal and a divine alchemy. The abundant sweating in the Canon's Yeoman's narrative functions as an ironic antithesis to the purifying baptisms in the *Second Nun's Tale*. On the strength of the homonymic association between *sweten* (to sweat) and *sweten* (to sweeten), Cowgill elaborates the opposition between the two tales by counterpointing the hagiographical commonplace of saints' bodies exuding only sweet odours (rather than bodily fluids) with the sweaty carnality of the characters in the *Canon's Yeoman's Prologue* and *Tale*.

Peter G. Beidler draws attention to an allusion, at two removes, to the *Canon's Yeoman's Tale* in 'William Cartwright, Washington Irving, and the "Truth": A Shadow Allusion to Chaucer's *Canon's Yeoman's Tale*' (*ChauR* 29.434–9). The epigraph of Irving's story 'Rip Van Winkle' is a quotation from Robert Moth, a character in Cartwright's play *The Ordinary*, whose lines are a direct citation from Chaucer's tale. The term 'shadow allusion' is invoked because Beidler doubts that Irving was aware of the provenance of the lines. Beidler notes, however, a play upon notions of truth in all three texts.

Seeta Chaganti notices 'A Thai Analogue for *The Manciple's Tale*' (*N&Q* 42.26–7). Uniquely amongst the tale's recorded analogues, the Thai story of the tell-tale *sao* bird includes no mention of adultery, but it reaches the same conclusion nevertheless as to the destructive power of words.

Missed from last year is Jameela Lares's 'Chaucer's *Retractions*: A "Verray Parfit Penitence"' (*Cithara* 34[1994].i.18–33) which returns to the art versus religion dilemma seeking not to resolve it but to accept the *Retraction* for what it is, *viz*, an act of penitence. Such a position entails a rejection of interpretations that see the *Retraction* as literary topos or as ironic. The ending of *Troilus* is, however, deemed by Lares to be a literary topos for Chaucer absents himself from any personal act of penitence; the *Retraction*, usually connected with the *Troilus* ending, is wholly different in its absolute and personal quality of repentance.

3. *Troilus and Criseyde*

One of the more substantial items which deals with Troilus and Criseyde this year is Laura D. Kellogg's study of *Boccaccio's and Chaucer's Cressida*. The book is divided into three main parts, and discusses both Cressida's general literary history, and the way her character is represented by Boccaccio and Chaucer. In the first section, Kellogg outlines the derivation of the story, showing how Benoît de Sainte-Maure uses classical sources in the *Roman de Troie*, and how Cressida's bad name is blackened still further by Guido delle Colonne. She follows the interesting idea that Cressida's heritage stems from the legends of Dido, and examines medieval representations of the latter, but in effect this means that she discusses Chaucer, as the subject of Boccaccio's Dido is relegated to an appendix, a decision which seems mistaken. In the second and third sections, Kellogg concentrates on the relationship between Cressida and her narrator, as depicted by Boccaccio and Chaucer respectively. This involves a detailed appraisal of both texts, though her comments are more extensive when she comes to deal with Chaucer. Her view is that Chaucer's narrator fears his own subject, and is torn between 'a desired fiction for a true Criseyde and the historical truth of a false Cressida'; only by prolonging the story can the narrator avoid confirming the truth of Criseyde's inconstancy. Kellogg demonstrates the effects of this in the poem's structure and narrative patterns, and pays special attention to Chaucer's use of imagery. Her discussion is clear and perceptive, and the book will be a useful addition to student reading lists. The text is accompanied by informative notes and an extensive bibliography which is particularly strong on primary sources.

Diane Vanner Steinberg contributes a very interesting article which takes as its starting point the words of Hector in Book IV: ' "We do usen here no wommen for to selle": Embodiment of Social Practices in *Troilus and Criseyde*' (*ChauR* 29.259–73). She begins by defining the poem's social spaces in gendered terms: the walled city of Troy is feminine, the Greek camp is masculine. Her argument is that by the end of the poem, Trojan practices which allow women value and status, have been overtaken by Greek attitudes which allow women to be commodified. Thus she views Criseyde's succumbing to Diomede as the first successful masculine/Greek penetration of feminine/Trojan space; as such, it is a prefiguration of Troy's fall, but lest we should be tempted to blame Criseyde for precipitating the city's doom, Steinberg also points out that it was the Trojans' action in turning Criseyde into an object of exchange which sealed their fate, since this commodification represents Troy's initial capitulation before the force of Greek ideas and cultural practices. Steinberg's well-structured essay is cogent and persuasive, though she does fail to assimilate one aspect of the legend: Helen's previous abduction by the Trojans, an event which somewhat undermines her insistence that the Trojan mentality is one which respects and supports women's freedom and choices. A. S. G. Edwards offers a note on Pandarus's urging of Troilus to kidnap Criseyde in 'Chaucer's *Troilus and Criseyde* IV.588' (*Expl* 53.66). The 'nyne nyght' wonder the line refers to is an intended variant of the more usual 'nine days' wonder', ironically foreshadowing the length of time it will take for Criseyde to abandon her lover.

In 'The Metamorphosis of *Musorno*: A Note on Chaucer's Translation of Filostrato I, 54 in *Troilus I*, 526–32' (*ChauR* 29.348–51), Paul Spillenger suggests that Chaucer's apparent reference to a particular fool may have arisen from a misreading of Boccaccio's text. Conversely, in 'Chaucer's Articulation of the Narrative in *Troilus*: The Manuscript Evidence' (*ChauR* 30.111–33), Phillipa Hardman argues that Chaucer's narrative practices may be closer to Boccaccio's than has usually been thought. Although the manuscripts of Troilus show great variation in terms of the amount of annotation that they contain, in a number of cases these annotations (broadly defined) correspond to Boccaccio's placing of prose rubrics. Her detailed analysis of this correspondence leads her to conclude that Chaucer took both the substance and the formal structure of his narrative from his Italian source. Hardman quotes the related work of Julia Boffey, 'Annotation in Some Manuscripts of Troilus and Criseyde' (*EMS* 5.1–17), which catalogues the poem's range of scribal headings and marginal glosses, concentrating in particular on two manuscripts, Bodley Rawlinson poet.163 and Selden B.24. Boffey notes that later manuscripts of the text have more extensive marginalia, and suggests that this apparatus might have been assembled accidentally and cumulatively as subsequent copyists and readers added their own comments.

Roberta Milliken, in 'Neither "Clere Laude" Nor "Sklaundre": Chaucer's Translation of Criseyde' (*WS* 24.iii.191–204) acknowledges the protracted debate concerning Chaucer's status as 'wommanis frend' and returns to it in relation to the 'delightfully controversial' Criseyde. Familiar ground is retrodden: the changes wrought from Boccaccio's source, *Il Filostrato*, making Chaucer's heroine more vulnerable, less calculating; C. S. Lewis's characterization of her as fearful; her precarious position in a male-dominated society. The article does not seem to add much that is new to the debate and the conclusion that Criseyde is 'an individual rather than the traditional abstraction or type' scarcely takes account of more recent readings of feminine subjectivity. Thomas J. Farrell's essay, 'The Fyn of the Troilus' (in Allen and White, *Subjects*), considers not the poem's ending, but its use and meaning of the word 'fyn'. He notes that in Troilus the word occurs most frequently as a noun, whereas elsewhere in Chaucer's poetry it is usually found as an adjective. Farrell argues that the narrator's use of the word 'fyn' in Troilus is illustrative of his difficulty in reconciling the opposing perspectives of his main characters, and that the text as a whole resists closure, not wanting to limit itself to a single resolution. In refusing to provide any definition of the term under discussion he imitates what he finds in the poem, but this only obscures his argument, and when he speaks of 'defyning' the poem it is hard not to see his prose as too self-consciously clever.

4. Other Works

The publication of *The Shorter Poems* completes the trilogy of volumes in the 'Oxford Guides to Chaucer' series, and constitutes the most important publication in this area of Chaucer studies during 1995. A. J. Minnis is the main author of this work, but he deals only with the major shorter poems (if they may be so described), leaving the minor shorter poems (complaints, lyrics etc.) to V. J. Scattergood; J. J. Smith contributes a lucid appendix on Chaucer's language, but its brevity gives the impression of only a token interest in linguistic issues on the part of the publishers. In the main part of the volume Minnis begins by setting the poems within their social and cultural contexts, and examining the form of the love-vision; he then discusses each of the dream visions in turn, devoting most attention, by some way, to the *Legend of Good Women*, and least to the *Parliament of Fowls*. His approach is more theoretical than that adopted in the previous two volumes, and students will be glad of the introductory notes on terminology. The intended audience of this book includes first-time readers of Chaucer, and so clarity and synthesis are high amongst its aims; it achieves these objectives admirably, and there can be no doubt that it will quickly become a staple of secondary reading lists.

The *House of Fame* and the *Legend of Good Women* receive special attention as examples of a medieval English Virgilian tradition in Christopher Baswell's *Virgil in Medieval England: Figuring the Aeneid from the Twelfth Century to Chaucer*. As a brief background to the chapter on Chaucer, Baswell traces three dominant but overlapping categories of Virgilian exegesis: first, an allegorizing trend, stretching from Fulgentius to the Renaissance, sophisticated and absorbing the thought of twelfth-century platonism; secondly, a romance trend that renders the antique past contemporary, focuses on the Dido-Æneas story, is primarily vernacular and demonstrates a strong secular audience of Virgil readers; and thirdly, a pedagogical trend, arising from the schools and scriptoria and the most widespread of the three, that analyses the poem in terms of its grammatical and rhetorical aspect. By the fourteenth century, these trends were well mingled. Baswell's method merges thematic and textual organization in such a way that each chapter contains a reading of specific manuscripts. Valuable insights are gained by these readings, such as is given by the marginalia in MS London BL Add. 27304 where, against a reference in the *Æneid* to the seditious crowd (*Æneid* I.123), specific reference to peasant insurrection in Norwich and London is made. Out of the complex tangle of transcription, mythography, illustration, contradictory annotations and annotations of annotations, Chaucer claims to deliver a 'naked text' of Virgil's poem first in the *House* and then in the *Legend*. In Book One of the former, Baswell identifies the Chaucerian reading of Virgil as belonging to the category of 'romance'; he also sees Geoffrey the narrator and Æneas to be parodically aligned as hermeneutic figures, 'reading' the events of literature and of history and destined for an arduous journey. The subsequent books of the *House* reveal an increasingly perplexed narrator-reader embroiled in the complexities of grammatical nicety (the 'pedagogical' category) and symbolic import ('the allegorical' category). Through this confusion of interpretation, the incompleteness of the text, and the ultimate silence of *auctoritas*, Baswell suggests that Chaucer, whether consciously or not, registers the hopelessly conflicted condition of Virgilian exegesis. In this way Virgil is both cited and ignored and the whole edifice of tradition usurped by the 'figure of the margins', Geoffrey the narrator-reader. The situation is somewhat different in the later *Legend*. Here both Dido and the narrator are active and empowered. The narrator, no longer befuddled by tradition, synthesizes tradition by bringing together a Virgilian text (from *Æneid* II and IV) and an Ovidian plot (from the *Heroides* VII). Similarly, Dido, no longer abandoning public duty for private and sensual indulgence, is repeatedly called by her title of 'queen' and retrieves her initial role of city-builder and law-giver. Baswell's book is a fine piece of scholarship that both revivifies and redefines by its historicism that much-abused critical practice of source comparison.

In ' "I wot myself best how y stonde": Literary Nominalism, Open Textual Form and the Enfranchizement of Individual Perspective in Chaucer's Dream Visions' (another essay in Utz, *Literary Nominalism*) Hugo Keiper offers the bumptious assertion that to read Chaucer's dream visions as 'open texts' requires an open mind found more in 'the younger generation of readers and critics, brought up on postmodernist fictions' than in 'adepts of the Robertsonian school'. The medieval open text is the text informed by nominalist thought (the closed text presumably being that informed by realist thought), and is characterized by inconclusiveness, plurality, metafictionality, self-reflexivity and intertextuality. The *Parliament of Fowls*, with its voluble birds and undecided heroine, demonstrates the indeterminacy of the open text; the *Book of the Duchess*, with its elaborate chess metaphors clarified into the stark admission of physical death, demonstrates the profound distrust of abstractions and absolutes; and the *House of Fame*, with its narrator's assertion that 'I wot myself best how y stonde', demonstrates the enfranchisement of individual perspective associated with nominalist contingency and openness of meaning.

In 'The Death of the *Book of the Duchess*' (*ChauR* 29.249–58), Steve Ellis argues that the poem is a reenactment of Blanche's death, and that its main theme is a statement of death's power over youth and happiness. Working from Chaucer's own references, Ellis contends that the poem's proper title is the 'Death of Blanche the Duchess'; he prefers this title because it puts the theme of death, rather than that of consolation, into a central position. He also traces the history of the poem's titles from its earliest manuscripts to the twentieth century.

J. Stephen Russell asks 'Is London Burning?' (*ChauR* 30.107–9), arguing that Book II of the House of Fame contains geographical allusions to the events of June 1381; if accepted, his conclusions will have implications for the dating of the poem. Huriye Reis discusses 'Writing and Dido in *The House of Fame*' (*JELL* 39.7–20), concentrating on Dido's position and function in the narrative, and finding her powerlessness all too typical of the textual representation of women. Kathryn L. Lynch, in 'The Logic of the Dream Vision in Chaucer's *House of Fame*' (in Utz, *Literary Nominalism*), turns from the more usual understanding of the poem as literary parody, with its consequent emphasis upon the Dreamer's failure to achieve knowledge, and towards a consideration of the failure of knowledge itself, 'from epistemology to ontology, from knowing to the knowable' (p. 187). She develops the previous work of William Wilson (*YWES* 45.95; 48.100) and of Martin Irvine (*YWES* 66.183) who argued, respectively, that the *House* was a satire of the trivium and, more particularly, of grammar. Lynch finds the discipline of logic at the centre of the poem's interests and she continues to point out the fallacious logic of the Eagle's disquisition in Book II. The visual and textual nature of communication in Book I, the oral nature in Book II, and the more conceptual nature in Book III together follow the three kinds of *oratio* expounded in medieval logic. Fame herself appears not so much as a figure of anti-logic as of parodic logic, for her arguments are not entirely illogical; she is as logical, that is, as is a world full of fragmentary individuals, resistant to any final principle of unifying order.

Janet Cowen and George Kane describe their critical edition of *Geoffrey Chaucer: The Legend of Good Women* as an experiment. It is an open edition which aims to present the manuscript evidence as fully as possible, and in it they apply the principles used by Kane and Donaldson in their editions of *Piers Plowman*. Cowen and Kane begin their long introduction by describing the 12 manuscripts and the early printed edition of the poem, classifying these according to the methods previously applied to the A and B versions of *Piers Plowman*. This done, the editors offer a minute and lengthy analysis of the poem's textual variants, attempting to identify originality from the quality, rather than quantity, of variant readings; they finally select their copy-text on the grounds of completeness and language. They also discuss the grammar of Chaucer's final 'e' in relation to editorial problems of metre, and pay particular attention to the text of the poem preserved in Cambridge University Library, MS Gg.4.27. The edition is aimed at textual scholars rather than literary critics. A more literary appraisal of the poem is offered by Helen Phillips in 'Literary Allusion in Chaucer's ballade, "Hyd, Absalon, thy gilte tresses clere" ' (*ChauR* 30.134–49). She finds that Chaucer's use of the familiar device of a catalogue of names and attributes in the Prologue is there divided into two distinct parts: the first concentrates on the praise of the perfect woman, whilst the second takes up the themes (central to the whole poem) of fidelity and suffering in love. With particular reference to the *Legend*, Judith Laird writes about 'Good Women and Bonnes Dames: Virtuous Females in Chaucer and Christine de Pizan' (*ChauR* 30.58–70) and finds that where Pizan's aim is to deconstruct the patriarchal narratives, Chaucer's is to 'reherce' the tradition he inherits. In Laird's eyes, the fact that the *Legend* narrator is male automatically restricts the scope of his defence of the feminine. The goodness of women is further limited in the *Legend* by their paganness. Five figures are portrayed in both works: Hypsipyle, Medea, Dido, Thisbe and Lucrece. In *Le Livre de la cité des dames*, Pizan presents her women as independent, proactive subjects; but Chaucer misogynistically curtails the very possibility of feminine goodness.

A number of Chaucer's shorter poems are included in Thomas G. Duncan's edition of *Medieval English Lyrics 1200–1400*. Most of the lyrics in this volume have an unfamiliar appearance, since, in an effort to present these poems in a readily readable form, Duncan has normalized their language in accordance with the grammar and spelling of late fourteenth-century London. As this is of course Chaucer's own language, the Chaucerian items are the least changed; a dozen are selected in all, most belonging to the category of love lyrics, including four described as 'probably, but not certainly, by Chaucer': *Against Women Unconstant, Complaynt D'Amours, Merciles Beaute, A Balade of Complaynte*. The Boethian poems appear under the heading 'Penitential and Moral Lyrics', and *The Complaint of Chaucer to his Purse* under

'Miscellaneous'. The introduction offers some comments about the nature of Chaucer's lyrics and their place in the tradition, but the most notable features of this volume are its radical editorial technique and its devoted attention to metre, an essential element of lyric poetry which is too often ignored by editors.

Books Reviewed

Allen, David G., and Robert A. White, eds. *Subjects on the World's Stage: Essays on British Literature of the Middle Ages and the Renaissance*. UDelP. pp. 319. $43.50. ISBN 0 87413 544 3.

Andersson, Theodore M., and Stephen A. Barney, eds. *Contradictions: From Beowulf to Chaucer*. Scolar. pp. 322. $84.95. ISBN 1 85928 173 7.

Bartlett, Anne C., et al, eds. *Vox Mystica: Essays on Medieval Mysticism in Honor of Professor Valerie M. Lagorio*. Brewer. pp. 235. £39.50. ISBN 0 85991 439 9

Baswell, Christopher. *Virgil in Medieval England: Figuring the Aeneid from the Twelfth Century to Chaucer*. CSML 24. CUP. pp. 438. $59.95. ISBN 0 521 46294 0.

Boenig, Robert. *Chaucer and the Mystics: The Canterbury Tales and the Genre of Devotional Prose*. AUP/BuckUP. pp. 231. £28.50. ISBN 0 8387 5288 8.

Brandt, Bruce E., ed. *Proceedings of the Third Dakotas Conference on Earlier British Literature*. English Department, South Dakota State University. pp. 125. $12. ISBN 1 883120 004.

Burton, Tom, narr. *The Clerk's Tale*. Chaucer Studio. Chaucer Studio Occasional Readings 15. 71 mins. $10 (institution), $5 (individual).

Burton, Tom, narr. *The Man of Law's Tale*. Chaucer Studio. Chaucer Studio Occasional Readings 14. 75 mins. $10 (institution), $5 (individual).

Chance, Jane. *The Mythographic Chaucer: The Fabulation of Sexual Politics*. UMinnP. pp. 378. hb $44.95, pb $18.95. ISBN 0 8166 2276 0, 0 8166 2277 9.

Chaucer: Life and Times CD-ROM. Primary Source Media Ltd. £395 (universities, colleges of higher education, public libraries), £150 (schools, colleges of further education). ISBN 0 86257 175 8.

Conrad, Peter. *To Be Continued*. OUP. pp. 207. £15. ISBN 0 19 818291 0.

Corfis, Ivy A., and Michael Wolfe, eds. *The Medieval City under Siege*. Boydell. pp. 292. $63. ISBN 0 85115 561 8.

Corrington, Robert S., and John Deely, eds. *Semiotics 1993: Proceedings of the Eighteenth Annual Meeting of the Semiotic Society of America Series*. Lang. pp. 612. $74.95. ISBN 0 61408 642 6.

Cowen, Janet, and George Kane, eds. *Geoffrey Chaucer: The Legend of Good Women*. Colleagues. pp. 344. £55. ISBN 0 937191 34 5.

Duncan, Thomas G., ed. *Medieval English Lyrics 1200–1400*. Penguin. pp. 314. pb £7.99. ISBN 0 14 043443 7.

Edwards, Robert R., and Vickie Ziegler, eds. *Matrons and Marginal Women in Medieval Society*. Boydell. pp. 127. £29.50. ISBN 0 85115 380 1.

Farrell, Thomas J., ed. *Bakhtin and Medieval Voices*. UFlorP. pp. 240. $49.95. ISBN 0 8130 1447 6.

Gallagher, Joseph, narr. *The Pardoner's Tale*. Chaucer Studio (1994). Chaucer Studio Occasional Readings 12. 52 mins. $10 (institution), $5 (individual).

Gaylord, Alan, narr. *The Knight's Tale*. Chaucer Studio. Chaucer Studio Occasional Readings 13. 134 mins. $20 (institution), $10 (individual).

Gellrich, Jesse M. *Discourse and Dominion in the Fourteenth Century: Oral Contexts of Writing in Philosophy, Politics, and Poetry*. PrincetonUP. pp. 304. $42.50. ISBN 0 691 03749 3.

Goossens, Louis, Paul Pauwels, Brygida Rudzka-Ostyn, Anne-Marie Simon-Vandenbergen, and Johan Vanparys, eds. *By Word of Mouth: Metaphor, Metonymy, and Linguistic Action in a Cognitive Perspective*. Benjamins. pp. 264. $63. ISBN 90 272 5045 6.

Hallissy, Margaret. *A Companion to Chaucer's* Canterbury Tales. Greenwood. pp. 333. $49.95. ISBN 0 313 29189 6.

Hamel, Mary, et al., narrs. *The Wife of Bath's Tale*. Chaucer Studio. New Chaucer Society Occasional Readings 9. 75 mins. $10 (institution), $5 (individual).

Heffernan, Carol Falvo. *The Melancholy Muse: Chaucer, Shakespeare and Early Medicine*. Duquesne Studies: Language and Literature 19. Duquesne. pp. 185. $48. ISBN 0 8207 0262 5.

Jones, Alex. *How to Pronounce Middle English*. Chaucer Studio (1994). pp. 18. ISBN 0646 20501 3.

—, narr. *Specimens of Middle English Pronunciation*. Chaucer Studio (1994). Chaucer Studio Occasional Readings 11. 58 mins. $10 (institution), $5 (individual).

Kachru, Braj B., and Henry Kahane, eds. *Cultures, Ideologies, and the Dictionary: Studies in Honor of Ladislav Zgusta*. Niemeyer. pp. 458. DM 242. ISBN 3 484 30964 4.

Kay, Sarah, and Miri Rubin, eds. *Framing Medieval Bodies*. ManUP (1994). pp. 287. $79.95. ISBN 0 7190 3615 1.

Kellogg, Laura D. *Boccaccio's and Chaucer's Cressida*. Studies in the Humanities 16. Lang. pp. 144. $42.95. ISBN 0 8204 2559 1.

Klassen, Norman. *Chaucer on Love, Knowledge and Sight*. Chaucer Studies 21. Brewer. pp. 225. $53. ISBN 0 85991 464 X.

Laskaya, Anne. *Chaucer's Approach to Gender in the* Canterbury Tales. Chaucer Studies 23. Brewer. pp. 224. £35. ISBN 0 85991 481 X.

Lynch, Andrew, and Philippa Maddern, eds. *Venus and Mars: Engendering Love and War in Medieval and Early Modern Europe*. UWAP. pp. 214. pb $24.95. ISBN 1 875560 45 9.

Mack, Peter, and Chris Walton, eds. *Geoffrey Chaucer: The Miller's Tale*. Oxford Students Texts. OUP. pp. 167. pb £7.50. ISBN 0 19 831988 6.

Minnis, A. J., with V. J. Scattergood and J. J. Smith. *The Shorter Poems*. Oxford Guides to Chaucer. Clarendon. pp. 592. £45. ISBN 0 19 811193 2.

Newhauser, Richard G., and John A. Alford, eds. *Literature and Religion in the Later Middle Ages: Philological Studies in Honor of Siegfried Wenzel*. MRTS 118. MRTS. pp. 414. $25. ISBN 0 86698 172 1.

Nicolaisen, W. F. H. *Oral Tradition in the Middle Ages*. MRTS 112. MRTS. pp. 231. $24. ISBN 0 86698 165 9.

Paxson, James J. *The Poetics of Personification*. Literature, Culture, Theory 6. CUP (1994). pp. 210. $52.95. ISBN 0 521 44539 6.

Plummer, John F. III, ed. *A Variorum Edition of the Works of Geoffrey Chaucer: Volume II, The Canterbury Tales: Part Seven, The Summoner's Tale*. UOklaP. pp. 242. $49.95. ISBN 0 8061 2744 9.

Polet, Jean-Claude, ed. *Premières mutations de Petrarque à Chaucer 1304–1400: Anthologie en langue française*. Patrimoine littéraire européen 5. De Boeck. pp. 827. ISBN 2 8041 2077 5.

Rex, Richard. *'The Sins of Madame Eglentyne' and Other Essays on Chaucer*. UDelP. pp. 201. £27. ISBN 0 87413 567 2.

Rouyer, Marie-Claire, ed. *Le Corps dans tous ses états*. UBordeauxP. pp. 266. pb F140. ISBN 2 86781 167 8.

Salda, Michael N., and Jean E. Jost, eds. *Chaucer Yearbook: A Journal of Late Medieval Studies: Volume 2*. Brewer. pp. 218. $49.95. ISBN 0 85991 465 8.

Serrano Reyes, Jesús L. *Didactismo y Moralismo en Geoffrey Chaucer y Don Juan Manuel: Un Estudio Comparativo Textual*. UCordobaP. pp. 385. np. ISBN 84 7801 340 7.

Seymour, M. C. *A Catalogue of Chaucer Manuscripts, Volume I: Works Before the Canterbury Tales*. Scolar. pp. 181. £39.50. ISBN 1 85928 056 0.

Singman, Jeffrey L., and Will McLean. *Daily Life in Chaucer's England*. Greenwood. pp. 252. $45. ISBN 0 313 29375 9.

Smith, Lesley, and Jane H. M. Taylor, eds. *Women, the Book and the Worldly*. Brewer. pp. 208. £29.50. ISBN 0 85991 479 8.

Tavormina, M. Teresa, and R. F. Yeager, eds. *The Endless Knot: Essays on Old and Middle English in Honor of Marie Borroff*. Brewer. pp. 262. £45. ISBN 0 85991 480 1.

Thomas, Paul R., et al., narrs. *The Nun's Priest's Tale*. Chaucer Studio. New Chaucer Society Occasional Readings 10. 37 mins. $10 (institution), $5 (individual).

Utz, Richard J., ed. *Literary Nominalism and the Theory of Rereading Late Medieval Texts: A New Research Paradigm*. Medieval Studies 5. Mellen. pp. 256. $89.95. ISBN 0 7734 8882 0.

Weisl, Angela Jane. *Conquering the Reign of Femeny: Gender and Genre in Chaucer's Romance*. Brewer. Chaucer Studies 22. pp. 133. £29.50. ISBN 0 85991 460 7.

Whitaker, Muriel, ed. *Sovereign Lady: Essays on Women in Middle English Literature*. Garland Medieval Casebooks 11. Garland. pp. 220. $40. ISBN 0 8153 1888 X.

Wilkins, Nigel. *Music in the Age of Chaucer* with *Chaucer Songs*. 2nd edn (with *Chaucer Songs*). Brewer. pp. 210. £39.50. ISBN 0 85991 461 5.

Woodward, Daniel, and Martin Stevens, eds. *The Canterbury Tales by Geoffrey Chaucer: The New Ellesmere Facsimile*. Yushodo Co. Ltd and Huntington. 1st edn $18,000, 2nd edn $15,500, 3rd edn $8,000. ISBN 0 87328 151 9.

——, and ——, eds. *The Ellesmere Chaucer: Essays in Interpretation*. Huntington and Yushodo Co. Ltd. pp. 363. $75. ISBN 0 87328 150 0.

V

The Sixteenth Century: Excluding Drama after 1550

CERI SULLIVAN and STEPHANIE J. WRIGHT

This chapter has four sections: 1. General; 2. Prose; 3. Drama before 1550; 4. Poetry. Section 4 is divided into three sections: (a) General; (b) Sidney; (c) Spenser. Sections 4 (b) and (c) are by Stephanie J. Wright. Apart from two reviews by Susan Bruce, sections 1, 2, 3 and 4 (a) are by Ceri Sullivan.

1. General

English is in crisis again, according to a special issue of *ELR* (25.iii) which looks at 'The State of Renaissance Studies'. It concentrates on the new challenges – in particular that of new historicism – to traditional historical scholarship. A number of defensive positions are taken up: Jonathan Crewe muses grimly on the disciplinary status of English among the humanities; Stanley Fish believes that academic work no longer now reaches an audience which might convert it into effective political action; Katharine E. Maus reflects on how the last 15 years have eroded the ability to read the 'manifest content' of Renaissance texts. More cheerfully, in separate essays, A. C. Hamilton, Annabel Patterson, Anne Lake Prescott and Kathleen E. McLuskie all praise the exploration of areas of interest common to literature and history; Lisa Jardine uses Holbein's 'Ambassadors' to look at how social and political readings have changed; Leah Marcus examines the interaction between early modern studies and computing; and Raymond Waddington reviews the leading schools of criticism dealing with the Renaissance (new historicism, gender studies, intellectual history, textual scholarship). These essays provide a shrewd review of how to place oneself as a scholar in the Renaissance today. They are also very funny to read: leading academics enormously enjoying their lugubrious prophecies. To actually see what has been produced, there is a wickedly crisp survey of 'Recent Studies in the English Renaissance' (*SEL* 35.159–92) by Richard Strier, which focuses primarily on collections of essays around historicist criticism in 1994.

He is in a good position to comment, then, in his *Resistant Structures. Particularity, Radicalism, and Renaissance Texts*, which argues that recent dogmatic criticism on the early modern period refuses to look at texts as they are, using instead the 'surely it was' formula to construct what they want to see. Asserting that not all founding principles are dogmas, he challenges pre-emptive appeals to traditional scholarship (examining among others the work of Rosamond Tuve), to general schemes of how literature works (self-consumption and the work of Stanley Fish, and deconstruction in the work of Jonathan Goldberg, Terence Hawkes and Terry Eagleton), and to political approaches (new historicism, with Stephen Greenblatt as the example). The second half of the book attempts to read certain texts out of their usual contexts: de Sales and Herbert read literally, through a social rather than devotional filter; Donne as a proponent of freedom of conscience; *Lear* as pre-empting notions of political radicalism. Strier provides a witty discussion of how literary theory can as easily impoverish texts, by filtering them, as enrich them with new meanings. I was less convinced by his claim to be reading without dogma himself – the book's description by Paul Alpers, suggesting Strier is writing within 'an emerging genre of corrective studies', effectively co-opts him into a new school of criticism.

In *Manuscript, Print, and the English Renaissance Lyric* Arthur F. Marotti considers Renaissance writing as a material textual practice, arguing that print gives a distorted picture of lyric production and consumption. Marotti starts with a general description of manuscript transmission and the types of collections made, for instance, at Court, by Catholics, by young lawyers and by women, one copy answering another and each being remoulded to suit the new conditions of reading. Marotti suggests that the manuscript collections were not superseded by print. Instead, both media participated in a project to attract support from old-style personal patrons and new-style commercial patrons. Marotti focuses specifically on political, parodic, obscene and lyric verse, as modes giving most scope for demonstrating the flexibility and historical specificity inherent in manuscript verse. The interaction between print and the collection of lyrics is studied using *Tottel's Miscellany*, Sidney's works, Jonson's 1616 folio, and posthumous editions of poems by Donne and Herbert. This is a clear, zestful and detailed application of those ideas which are usually discussed in lofty abstraction, set aside from the very examples which critics purport to be examining. In 'Writing without leisure: proof-reading as work in the Renaissance' (*JMRS* 25.17–31) George Hoffman uses the example of the difference between Montaigne's self-proclaimed amateur status and his actual, humanist anxiety over publishing a correct text, to examine attitudes towards proof-correction and textual production as manual work. In *Renaissance Essays for Kitty Scoular Datta* (ed. Sukanta Chaudhuri), Peter Mack sketches the habit of reading useful moral or practical lessons out of, or into, a text, using pedagogues ranging from Guarini to Brinsley. In the same collection Sukanta Chaudhuri understands Renaissance views of time as dynamic, reshaping material from the past, and Shyamal Kumar Sarkar looks at secular elements in some early drama. On the topic of reading, William Sherman's *John Dee. The Politics of Reading and Writing in the English Renaissance* tries to extend the view of Dee from cranky astrologer to intellectual and political intelligencer. Sherman reviews Dee's library at Mortlake and his reading practices, evidenced by his marginalia and other written responses, and provides a brief survey of his manuscript writings on politics; Dee's *Brytannicae Reipublicae Synopsis*, a survey of British govern-ment; his work on navigation and expansion overseas, *General and Rare Memorials, Of Famous and Rich Discoveries, Brytanici Imperii Limites* and

Thalattokratia Brettaniki. Sherman argues that Dee provided the 'first English think tank'. This description seems appropriate given the number and type of political topics Dee dealt with and the range of people who consulted him.

Robin Kirkpatrick has produced a useful undergraduate primer on the influence of the Italian Renaissance on English literature. *English and Italian Literature from Dante to Shakespeare. A Study of Source, Analogue, and Divergence* provides a brief introduction to Italian theorists on the state, education and culture. Detailed chapters follow, on the history of Britain's initial fascination with the style and confidence of Italian literature, which developed in the late sixteenth century into an appreciation of a specifically English way of writing. Kirkpatrick divides the period by representative genres: a chapter on early English humanism is followed by a discussion of the sonnet, the pastoral, the epic romance, the novella, the Italian comedy of *contaminatio*, and the theory of mixed forms. Sensibly, since the text deals with complex issues of genre, examples of English authors are paired with an Italian progenitor of the form and limited to a few representative authors.

Kate Aughterson's *Renaissance Woman: A Sourcebook. Constructions of Femininity in England* will prove an invaluable teaching aid for Renaissance courses. Her collection of texts either written or read in the sixteenth century delineates the enormous effort that went into the project of creating the feminine, under the broad headings of theology, physiology, conduct, sexuality and motherhood, politics and the law, education, work, writing and speaking and 'proto-feminisms'. The latter collections include texts which invert or escape the previous selections' agenda on women, though Aughterson works an example of resistant reading, Philip Stubbes's *A Crystal Glass for Christian Women*, to indicate how trace voices of protest can be heard in many of the texts she deals with. Old favourites in gynocriticism, such as John Knox, are also represented. The value of such inclusions lies in providing ease of access by undergraduates to their texts. For researchers, there are other unexpected items: the midwives' oath from Garnet's *Book of Oaths* of 1649, Thomas Tusser on housewifery, legal texts on women's property rights, petitions by gentlewomen and tradesmen's wives. Each extract covers three to five pages, spelling has been modernized, and a sentence or two before each item gives contextual information where necessary.

In *The Tears of Narcissus: Melancholia and Masculinity in Early Modern Writing*, Lynn Enterline produces an extraordinarily subtle and dense reading of how figures of grief in early modern texts are marked as moments of literary self-awareness. A long introduction on sixteenth-century poetic theory notes that these do not affirm the self; instead, the melancholic loses 'a sense of personal agency in language, a loss of "voice", a loss of reference, a loss of the capacity to distinguish between literal and figural senses, and, overall, a loss of a sense of authority over one's own discourse'. Enterline then focuses on Tasso's poetic theory and practice in an epic on the loss of the social site of meaning, *Jerusalem*, seen as accounting for the 'orphaned' condition of his autobiographical work. Shorter chapters then deal with losses in Marvell, *The Comedy of Errors* and *The Duchess of Malfi*.

In *Virgin Mother, Maiden Queen. Elizabeth I and the Cult of the Virgin Mary*, Helen Hackett develops work done by Frances Yates, Roy Strong and Margaret Aston on the iconography of Elizabeth. Rather than supplanting one Virgin with another, Marian comparisons operate to reinforce the sanctity of Mary in order to provide endorsement for Elizabeth's rule. Hackett is concerned to provide a detailed political context for the cult, not to describe a 'uniform national psychological need', discussing *The Faerie Queene*, courtly panegyric such as Puttenham's *Partheniades* or John Davies's *Hymnes of Astraea*, ballads, sermons, the rhetorical features of theological tracts, and reports of progresses and civic pageants.

Lawrence Manley's hefty, erudite study of *Literature and Culture in Early Modern London* covers the rise of the city from 1501 to 1670, discussing texts (such as *Utopia, The Faerie Queene*, early modern prose, city comedies and *Paradise Lost*) in three interlocking 'conceptual frameworks'. The first of these is the historical transition from feudalism to capitalism. The second, informed by sociological and geographical theory, is what Manley calls 'behavioural urbanization': the role of culture and its artefacts in the disciplining of populations for urban cohabitation, and the strategies by which the population of early modern London adapted to the challenges of its rapidly transforming urban environment. The third underlying theme of the book is the 'conceptual conflict between order and reform', which Manley sees as correlative with the 'paradoxical tendency of cities to enslave and liberate their populations'. Through all this Manley aims to trace the story of London in the period, from its literary emergence to the eventual ' "dissemination" of new forms of urbanity' in the writers of the Revolutionary period. This is a complex and wide-ranging study, an important contribution to our understanding of the history of the early modern city [SJB].

On art, the first volume on the Tudors of Roy Strong's *The Tudor and Stuart Monarchy. Pageantry, Painting, Iconography* makes use of literary analogues to explain Holbein's work as royal propagandist. The volume, a collection of Strong's previous essays, is extensively illustrated. An intriguing article by Leonard Barkan, 'Making Pictures Speak: Renaissance Art, Elizabethan Literature, Modern Scholarship' (*RenQ* 48.326–51), discusses the relationship in Elizabethan poetics between mimesis, reality and the metaphor of the speaking picture used by Sidney's *Defence of Poetry*. Barkan suggests that there is a utopian desire in Elizabethan and current poetics to theorize form across the media – a sort of critical synaesthesia. In particular, work on the icon has helped understand the actual point of contact between the word and the image, one being intended to provoke a reaction in terms of another, as when Michelangelo composes poems about sculpture. Barkan is particularly concerned with the process by which interest in an object is replaced by interest in its re-ordering, which he describes as an absence reinvented as a formal presence.

2. Prose

William Barker has produced a generous edition of Richard Mulcaster's *Positions Concerning the Training Up of Children* of 1581. The text is supplemented by a detailed critical apparatus; the laconically expressed annotation eschews literary interpretation for a dense involvement with social and cultural life in Britain at the time. Mulcaster influenced educational reform by his views and practice as First Master of the Merchant Taylors' School and High Master at St Paul's. Barker points out the modish aspects of Mulcaster's professionalism: education as a public art of character formation which includes advice on body and soul, schooling as a method of giving social mobility, and the necessity of training women. Ringler and Flachmann's edition of William Baldwin's *Beware the Cat* has been published in paperback. The edition provides a modern-spelling text, its printed marginalia, a contextual introduction claiming this as the first English novel, summaries of the plots of early prose fictions in English and a history of the genre.

There were several editions of religious texts. Roger A. Mason's edition of John Knox's writings *On Rebellion* includes five 1558 tracts (including *The First Blast of the Trumpet*) and extracts from *The History of the Reformation*. Each is preceded by a brief paragraph of contextualizing commentary; the edition also includes a (broadly biographical) introduction, a bibliography, a glossary and an index of names [SJB].

UTorP continues its densely annotated edition of Erasmus's works, with his 1524 *Paraphrase on the Acts of the Apostles* edited by John J. Bateman. A convoluted editorial process has produced a new translation of Thomas More's *Utopia* by George Logan, Robert Adams and Clarence Miller. Based on the Logan/Adams translation of 1989 using the Froben edition of March 1518, this revises the annotation, adds a redaction of the Latin text using modern conventions for Latin spelling, divides the text into paragraphs, and repunctuates it.

Five essays on *More's Utopia and the Utopian Inheritance* (ed. A. D. Cousins and Damian Grace) attempt to contextualize the paradoxes of the text. Damian Grace lays out More's methods of argument, in which he distinguishes an academic scepticism, by reference to Valla's *Dialecticae Disputationes*, Erasmus's *Praise of Folly* and Dorp's response. Less convincingly, Aleksandar Pavkovic argues that there is a conflict between the two aims of the Utopian economy: leisure to pursue intellectual interests, and prosperity. Dominic Baker-Smith and Miguel Martinez Lopez discuss the fallen nature of property. The importance of the common possession of things in *Utopia* corresponds to the values espoused by the Franciscan order and by Jewish Essenes. Fred Standley describes Utopia as an 'exemplary countermyth', where freedom and individualism are restricted. Other essays deal with later utopias, such as Biosphere 2 and those in Voltaire's writings, Caribbean missionary hopes and the colonization of the New World. Some of the facts about the parerga of More's *Utopia* are discussed in Karl Schroeder's 'Jerome de Busleyden and Thomas More' and Dale B. Billingsley's 'Halfhearted Busleyden' (*Moreana* 121.3–10; 122.499–55). They concentrate on the degree of support which More's correspondent gave to the project. Francis X. Ryan investigates 'Sir Thomas More's Use of Chaucer' (*SEL* 35.1–17), especially on the theme of authority. *The Dialogue Concerning Heresies, The Supplication of Souls* and *Richard III* are among the texts which Ryan sees as bearing traces of More using the proverbial and popular authority of Chaucer. The discussion centres on interpretative authority, ranging between More's notion of the commonweal to the *consensus fidelium* of the Catholic Church.

Studies of English recusant writers continue to appear. Ceri Sullivan's *Dismembered Rhetoric. English Recusant Writing, 1580 to 1603* argues that Catholic writers used secret press texts in a sacerdotal role, to supplement the efforts of missionaries attempting to reconvert Britain to Rome. Meditations are described as types of deliberative rhetoric, relying on amplification, and catechisms and hagiographies feature as exemplary witnesses proving and clarifying the faith. She ends by suggesting that a reliance on rhetoric was as important to recusant devotions, as is usually ascribed to the more frequently studied Protestant groups. There is a description of Robert Persons's techniques of disputation by Victor Houliston, in 'The Polemical *Gravitas* of Robert Persons' (*RH* 22.291–305). The discovery in the Beinecke Collection of 58 poems celebrating Church feasts is sketched by Michael F. Suarez in 'A New Collection of English Recusant Manuscript Poetry from the Late Sixteenth Century: Extraordinary Devotion in the Liturgical Season of "Ordinary Time" ' (*RH* 22.306–18).

Serene Jones's *Calvin and the Rhetoric of Piety* concentrates on the formal rhetoric of the first three books of Calvin's *Institutes*. She points to the Ciceronian emphasis on the audience. An introductory chapter looks in detail at the three chapters of the Institutes which deal with knowledge of God, the concept of piety and an awareness of divinity in each person. She aims to provide an analysis of how 'aesthetics, social praxis, and propositional truth claims cohere in the production of theological discourse'.

Several articles deal with Protestant polemic. In 'John Foxe as Hagiographer: the Question Revisited' (*SCJ* 26.771–89), I. Ross Bartlett suggests that while *Actes and Monuments* appears to sprawl wildly it actually follows the traditional aims and forms of early hagiography. Bartlett evaluates Foxe's account on the basis of a six-part *schema* of descriptions of saints' lives and deaths of descending probability, from official written reports to imaginative romances and forgeries, each with a different devotional import and set of *topoi*. Susan M. Felch replaces the dichotomy of male/female with godly/ungodly in John Knox's writings, in 'The Rhetoric of Biblical Authority: John Knox and the Question of Women' (*SCJ* 26.805–22), thus reclaiming Knox in the name of spiritual equality. John Bale's formulation of the difference between the Protestant and Catholic Churches as a difference between readings is examined by Claire McEachern in ' "A whore at the first blush seemeth only a woman": John Bale's *Image of Both Churches* and the terms of religious difference in the early English Reformation' (*JMRS* 25.245–69). Both the godly and the false church may put forward indecipherable signs: the seven-horned lamb, the pregnant woman clothed with brightness, the blushing woman. McEachern shrewdly delineates the dilemma facing interpreters of Bale: is he a hapless reader of Revelation, yearning for an impossibly pure signification, or is he the 'bilious' Bale, secure in his own polemic? In 'Satan and the Presbyterians: an Unnoticed *STC* Reprint' (*N&Q* 42.289–90) Joseph Black notes how a standard anti-Catholic polemic of 1557 is rewritten as a reformist attack on the foundations of the established Church, in *A Commission Sente ... by ... the Devil of Hell* of 1586. Donna Spivey Ellington's 'Impassioned Mother or Passive Icon: the Virgin's Role in Late Medieval and Early Modern Passion Sermons' (*RenQ* 48.227–61) surveys the shifts in the portrayal of Mary at the Crucifixion, which reveal an increasing concentration on the divine rather than the human body.

In *The Emperor of Men's Minds. Literature and the Renaissance Discourse of Rhetoric*, Wayne A. Rebhorn contends that certain works of literature expose the contradictions in sixteenth-century rhetoric. Orators picture themselves as able to guide the will of an audience through their words, but also as interlopers, unjustly getting power for themselves through verbal skill, not inborn right. Rhetoric, then, both subverts and conserves notions of rank and power. Its indirect link with action and public status leads it to be labelled as feminine, forcing its practitioners to prove their power by emphasizing those classical tropes which describe it as a violent invasion. The art is accused of being ethically and socially suspect, associated with the body, the passions and the people. Texts chosen by Rebhorn on which to conduct a brisk discussion include: *Lazarillo de Tormes*; Carew's elegy on Donne; *The Alchemist*; Erasmus's *Praise of Folly*; and Machiavelli's *The Mandrake Root*.

In *Place and Displacement in the Renaissance* (ed. Alvin Vos), Annabel Patterson discusses the editorial and commercial principles behind the representation of the popular voice in Holinshed's *Chronicles*. In particular, Patterson values the edition's commitment to verbatim reporting rather than editorial narrative, thus allowing diverse opinions to be voiced. At the other end of the social scale, Vos's collection also includes an essay by Evelyn B. Tribble on the political implications of representing a monarch speaking to her subjects, in Thomas Deloney's *Jacke of Newberie*.

Commentary on political writings including a concise guide to disputed topics is provided by *Niccolo Machiavelli's 'The Prince'. New Interdisciplinary Essays*, edited by Martin Coyle. Contributors discuss the original reception of its understanding of politics, the relationship it creates between political science and economics, ethics, history and rhetoric and the dialogue form. The collection is largely aimed at provoking responses to concepts behind *The Prince*, not at providing detailed historical readings. In *Voyages in Print. English Travel to America, 1576–1624*, Mary Fuller eschews the fashionable investigation of nationhood, for an intriguing view of discovery texts as commercial assets owned by the financiers of a voyage. Fuller points to the responsibility taken by texts in Hakluyt's *Principal Navigations*, Raleigh's *Discoverie ... of Guiana* and the pamphlets on the Virginia Company's settlements, for establishing realities, making it possible to think both about the new lands and the old world's intentions towards them. This was a more tentative project than either of the two current views of the process, of glorious expansion or topographical rape, would allow. 'In text after apologetic text, discovery of the self substitutes for discovery of America, Guiana, a new passage to Cathay'. The ethos, the hidden interior, of the author becomes the guarantee that these voyages did produce glorious results.

In *Scholars' Bedlam. Menippean Satire in the Renaissance*, W. Scott Blanchard defines this mode as one which challenges the categorization of knowledge. This popular Renaissance form refuses essentialist understandings, praising a refracted reading of texts by 'wise fools'. 'The Menippean satirist in the Renaissance was brave enough to critique the humanist claim that ancient sources could be recovered in their pristine state as paradigms for an authoritative understanding of the world.' Blanchard traces this mode of satire in multiple genres: in continental mock encomia, in parodies of learned treatises, concentrating on Rabelais and Burton's *Anatomy*, and in mock epics, in the shape of Nashe's *Lenten Stuff*. Each is seen to debunk a particular academic pretension, such as the fashion for allegorical poetics. Blanchard's is a learned study, with a firm grip on the classical and European analogues it uses. Two more items on Nashe: an essay by Calhoun Winton in a collection edited by Carmen Benito-Vessels and Michael Zappala, *The Picaresque. A Symposium on the Rogue's Tale*, argues against the usual citation of *The*

Unfortunate Traveller as the foundational text for the English picaresque. Other essays in the collection discuss the mode in relation to Spanish Golden Age literature. In a collection edited by Elizabeth Maslen, *Comedy: Essays in Honour of Peter Dixon by Friends and Colleagues*, Geoffrey Harlow identifies borrowings by Nashe from a hitherto unidentified source, a 1566 redaction of the first 16 books of Pliny's *Naturalis Historia, The Secrets and Wonders of the World*.

Deconstruction meets the occult, in Gary Tomlinson's *Music in Renaissance Magic*. A rebarbative opening registers the importance of the occasion, envisaging 'an intersubjective, dialogical interpretation that has emerged from the discussions of Heidegger, Gadamer, Ricoeur, Bakhtin, and others'. Behind Tomlinson's invocation of these powerful architects of thought stands his master-magus, Foucault. However, a more independent and historically sensitive reading follows, of Agrippa's *De occulta philosophia*, of Ficino's ideas on musical, magical and poetic furor or possession, contained especially in his *De vita*, and of works by Monteverdi. Tomlinson is sharp-eyed about the idealizing nature of that criticism which attempts to discuss the two arts together, as harmonizing influences which embody timeless values.

Some occasional articles included Sara Warneke's 'A Taste for New-fangledness: the Destructive Potential of Novelty in Early Modern England' (*SCJ* 26.881–96). This draws widely on denunciations – serious and ironic – of popular enthusiasms, such as those by Stubbes, Gosson and Greene, where novelty is seen as destructive to society and a peculiar addiction of the English people ascribed to personal degeneracy rather than to economic or demographic causes. E. G. Stanley notes the use of the term 'Old English' by Archbishop Matthew Parker in 1567 and by William Lambard in 1576 (*N&Q* 42.168–71, 437). 'The Structural Plan of Camden's *Britannia*' (*SCJ* 26.829–41) is examined by William Rockett. Camden's work is read not as a history of Roman Britain but rather as an attempt to disclose the origins of the ancient English peoples. In 'The Uses of Conversation: Moderata Fonte and Edmund Tilney' (*CLS* 32.1–25), Janet Levarie Smarr looks at how two texts on friendship use the same genre of the dialogue to open up and close down serious debate. A monologue was as likely to emerge as a discussion, despite the dialogue's formal flexibility. Both *Il merito delle donne* of 1592 and *The Flower of Friendshippe* of 1568 focus on a liberal interpretation of the relations between the sexes, but the radicalism of Tilney's position is compromised by inserting himself into the dialogue and by proclaiming a correct solution to the differences at the end of the work.

Finally, Reid A. Barbour provides a review of recent studies in Elizabethan fiction (*ELR* 25.248–76).

3. Drama before 1550

The major work on early drama this year is Howard B. Norland's *Drama in Early Tudor Britain 1485–1558*. Norland's interest is in transition, as medieval, local and religious traditions gave way to an renewed interest in classical models and the development of new genres of secular and political drama. Norland outlines theories on the subject discussed by humanist commentators, before moving on to the bulk of his study, an examination of the generic features of three groups of plays. Secularized morality plays examined are those on the theme of the prodigal (such as R. Wever's *Lusty Juventus*), John Redford's *Wit and Science*, John Skelton's *Magnificence*, John Bale's *King John*, *Respublica* and David Lindsay's *Satire of the Three Estates*, which are all seen as adapting moral allegory to political and educational concerns. Comedies are viewed as experiments in form: Henry Medwall's *Fulgens and Lucres*, *Calisto and Melebea*, *Johan Johan*, Nicholas Udall's *Roister Doister* and *Gammer Gurton's Needle*. Tragedy is also dealt with formally, in three academic dramas: Thomas Watson's *Absalom*, John Christopherson's *Jephthah* and Grimald's *Archipropheta*. It is enjoyable to see plays which are rarely dealt with being examined in detail. In *From Page to Performance* (ed. John A. Alford), Alford discusses Henry Medwall's use in *Nature* of the figure of a Vice masquerading as a Virtue, and challenges the view of critics who suggest that this is symptomatic of an emerging moral confusion; rather, he suggests, it is the sign of an evolving dramatic technique.

Alan Clarke Shephard's ' "Female Perversity", Male Entitlement: the Agency of Gender in More's *The History of Richard III*' (*SCJ* 26.311–28) considers how the three female protagonists of the play are represented. Shephard argues that a greater degree of political, sexual and rhetorical agency is given to these women than is usually granted, particularly in the figure of Elizabeth Woodville. More than one-third of the play is given over to Elizabeth's persuasion; Shephard suggests our reading of More's views on gender as being conservative may have to be revised.

On actual production, there were three essays. In 'The Revels Accounts: This Insubstantial Pageant Leaves not a Wrack Behind' (*RS* 9.1–17), Sybil M. Jack looks at the formal accounting processes for fifteenth- and sixteenth-century revels accounts, and warns against accepting these as complete. With Sir Thomas Carwarden's appointment as Master in 1545, accounting for the Revels Office was separated from that for household expenditure, making the accounts into more reliable documents for our assessment of the festivities. In 'Politics, Topical Meaning, and English Theater Audiences 1485–1575' (*RORD* 34.41–54), Paul Whitfield White briefly sketches two examples of how studies of audience reaction to pre-playhouse popular theatre might run. In 'Commentary as cover-up: Criticizing illiberal patronage in Thomas Nashe's *Summer's Last Will and Testament*' (*ELR* 25.148–78) Sherri Geller examines the work's pseudo-extempore commentary by Will Summer which she suggests provides a model of a subordinate mocking his patron/author.

4. Poetry

(a) General
A small collection of neo-Latin verse has been translated and edited by Dana Sutton, in *Oxford Poetry by Richard Eedes and George Peele*. *Iter Boreale* of 1583 comprises 668 lines on Eedes's journey to the north; the editor exaggerates in calling it a social history of the order of Camden's, but skilfully points out its social comedy, with the northerners' disdain for the Oxford newcomers and the latter's superciliousness towards the regions they travel through. George Peele's *Pareus* of 1585 is a mini-epic of 460 lines on the Parry conspiracy to murder Elizabeth. As Peele cheerfully admits, he inserts epi-

sodes for 'elegance and delight', for instance by creating a mastermind behind the plot in the shape of Cardinal Como, and linking this to demonic ambition (an outraged Satan rails against Britain's good fortune in possessing so great a Queen). Sutton's translation is clear and close, and her annotation detailed, though idiosyncratic in expression.

Once again, gender studies appear to have produced some of the best commentary on poetry this year. In 'The Early Modern Closet Discovered' (*Rep* 50.76–100), Alan Stewart argues that the closet, as a place where people meet socially, sexually and politically, is depicted as both a common and physical place in early modern literature. Our interest in the closet lies in our view of it as a marginal space of emergent subjectivity. Paradoxically, however, early modern accounts of the closet publicly mark the areas of activity which lie hidden from public inspection. Stewart's brilliant account of the functions of the Secretary, as a body personal and archival, retrieves the closet as a political and social space where men transact business. The public/private boundary of the self is constructed by this area in early modern writings and in their later, idealized evaluation by us. Jonathan Sawday's *The Body Emblazoned. Dissection and the Human Body in Renaissance Culture* is an eloquent delineation of the early modern image of interiority. A culture of enquiry, of dissection, was applied to the intellectual as much as to the physical arts. The divorce between the blazon and the self-dissected anatomy diagram is less absolute than subsequent criticism has made it. Feminist critics have theorized the erotic dismembering by the former as a practice of organized violence. Sawday puts flesh on these bones with a dense description of the historical moment when the interior was opened to view. He ranges over the physical rituals of the early modern anatomy theatres and the representation of the anatomized body in literature and art (including such unexpected texts as microcosmographies, Fletcher's *The Purple Island* and casuistry manuals, as well as the more standard loci such as Donne's lyrics, Spenser's house of Alma and Rembrandt's paintings of dissections). He ends by examining Cartesian epistemology. Sawday's is a sumptuous book. There is a fascinating examination by Clive Hart and Kay Gilliland Stevenson of the conflation of sexuality and ascensional imagery, in *Heaven and the Flesh: Imagery of Desire from the Renaissance to the Rococo*. Hart and Stevenson argue that the direct representation of a physical state is not merely, in this case, injudicious but as impossible as the representation of the divine: 'when the erotic arts attempt to express desire rather than the consequences of desire, they have recourse to a seemingly endless series of transformations, and the same is true when they attempt to represent the experience of the divine'. These works are mainly concerned to create images of bliss from a male point of view, even when they are written by women. An original examination of the Petrarchan ideal succeeds this discussion, which manages to avoid repeating previous work on its formal characteristics, the gaze or the ideal. Examples worked on in detail to argue this proposition include French and Italian easel painting, ornamentation in baroque and rococo churches in Germany and Austria and poetry by Spenser, Crashaw, Milton, John Hall, John Gore and Aphra Behn. The book is beautifully produced and illustrated.

An unusual cross-genre contribution is made by Diana E. Henderson in *Passion Made Public. Elizabethan Lyric, Gender, and Performance*. Henderson points to the extensive use of lyric poetry in Elizabethan drama, specifically in contexts of female power which is set against the rhetorical authority claimed by the poet. She sets out to answer three questions: how gender is seen in the stage lyrics, how this has been affected by previous associations between gender and the genre, and what interpretative strategies are needed to view this lyric poetry within a stage performance. George Peele's *Arraignment of Paris*, Marlowe's *Dido, Queen of Carthage* and Shakespeare's *Love's Labour's Lost* are analysed. Henderson's initial rather conventional attention to the gendering of these lyrics gives way to an original understanding of the implications of performing them, in her detailed readings of the three plays. Patricia Berrahou Phillippy discusses the contradiction between the Petrarchan ideal which resists the influence of the world in the service of love, and the professional necessity to regret having written youthful trifles, in *Love's Remedies: Recantation and Renaissance Lyric Poetry*. Moments of recantation in Petrarch's *Rime sparse*, Gaspara Stampa's *Rime d'amore*, Sidney's *Astrophil and Stella* and Spenser's *Shepheardes Calender* are compared with the original instance, Stesichorus of Himera's palinode to his *Helen*. The dialogic form of the palinode is crucial in considering the self-interpretation of the poet's career. In a complex argument, Phillippy suggests that this leads to an interrogation of the Petrarchan tradition of solipsistic ethics, of a mode of obsessive consideration, and of the gendering of the lyric form. Judith Haber's *Pastoral and the Poetics of Self-Contradiction: Theocritus to Marvell* also details a contradictory genre, where the formal recreation of an idyllic past can be read as a criticism of contemporary situations. This is not, as Haber admits, a new approach. Her argument aims to redefine readings of the contradictions in Theocritus, Virgil, Sidney and Marvell. Haber wants a recognition of the frequent moves made in the genre between play and political meaning, between a recognition of pastoral as a social commentary and as a self-consciously limited literary tradition.

In *History and Warfare in Renaissance Epic*, Michael Murrin focuses on how developments in military practice and technology were represented in the epic. A heroic narrative evolved which was not founded upon outright fighting. This, Murrin feels, provoked experiments in form, though it was doomed to fail: the peaceful epic was an anomaly. After an introductory section dealing with classical and medieval precedents Murrin concentrates on continental Renaissance epic. Sidney's *Arcadia*, Drayton's *Barons Warres* and Daniel's *Civile Wars* are examined as poems of peace which refuse to celebrate military prowess.

Some minor poets are considered: Zara Bruzzi deals with the conflict between idealism and eroticism in Petrarchan courtship, in a rather thin essay, ' "I find myself unparadis'd": the integrity of Daniel's *Delia*' (*CahiersE* 48.1–15). 'The Complaint of Rosamond' appended to the sonnets is seen by her to reflect on the excess and self-deception of the sonnet lover himself. In 'A Precursor of Nonsense: John Taylor, the Water Poet (c. 1580–1653)' (*CahiersE* 48.37–43), Emma Renaud convincingly extends the theory of competitive game-playing usually noted in courtly verse to the caricature and puns of a lower-ranked poet. However, her arguments are less full when dealing with Taylor's nonsense verse as evidence of the grotesque. In an essay in *Fins de Siècle: English Poetry in 1590, 1690, 1790, 1890, 1990* (ed. Elaine Scarry), Margreta de Grazia discusses periodization in the 1590s. Enveloped within a series of rather tendentious meditations on how turn-of-the-century writers see themselves as standing outside history are interesting discussions on an early modern understanding of the century as a general unit of account, not of time, the awareness of time in the sonnet and the sonnet sequence as a form without closure, an exhausted form. In 'A new golden age? More, Skelton, and the accession verses of 1509' (*RS* 9.58–76), David Rundle compares the presentation poems which these poets wrote to celebrate Henry's coronation. Standard *topoi* are noted: Ovidian references, comparisons with the previous reign, seemingly naive flattery from poets momentarily overcome by the occasion. Rundle, however, argues that More's 'Carmen gratulatorium' and Skelton's 'Lawde and prayse' provide ambiguous praise in their choice of classical parallel and phrasing. Finally, Simon Cauchi reviews recent studies on John Harrington (*ELR* 25.112–25).

(b) Sidney

Katrina Bachinger's *Male Pretense: A Gender Study of Sir Philip Sidney's Life and Texts* offers a reading of Sidney's life and texts which concerns itself with Sidney's gender problems and the detection of Sidney's illicit sexual desires. The introduction reads in the dedication to *The Old Arcadia*, Sidney's incestuous desire for his sister. Chapter 2 detects mutual homoerotic desire in Sidney's correspondence with Hubert Languet and Chapter 3 initially departs into a historical background to Elizabeth I's succession and reign before viewing *The Lady of May* as 'highly likely to be a depository of his quandaries over the pleomorphism of gender difference'. In Chapter 4, Bachinger points to the gender significance of suspended royal judgement upon Prince Pyrocles in *The Old Arcadia* before a consideration of Philisides 'to see what it can add to an analysis of Sidney's gender in particular'. Chapter 5 re-addresses the critical problem of Astrophil's and Stella's historical identities, and proposes Hubert Languet as the real object of the poet's affections. The brevity of Bachinger's bibliography is emphasized by the appearance of *Sir Philip Sidney: An Annotated Bibliography of Texts and Criticism (1554–1984)*, edited by Donald V. Stump et al. The stated aim is to provide the Sidney scholar with a single, comprehensive work which will eliminate the need to consult the numerous, but individually limited, bibliographies published so far.

Astrophil and Stella is the central text in 'Fair Texts/Dark Ladies: Renaissance Lyric and the Poetics of Color', Chapter 2 of Kim F. Hall's *Things of Darkness: Economies of Race and Gender in Early Modern England*. Hall's reading of various sonnet sequences is based upon the premise that the dark ladies 'are at least in part the literary cousins of the foreign women encountered in travel narratives' who serve to demonstrate the poet's power to 'lighten' them. She identifies references to foreign difference and wealth in the supposedly insulated language of the love lyric, seeing sites of contestation between the old and new world in Sidney's sonnets. When he looks inward for inspiration, in sonnets 1 and 3, Hall claims this constitutes a 'rejection of strangeness and "foraging abroad" [which] seems to be an integral part of Sidney's project for English poetry'. Maria Teresa Micaela Prendergast's 'The Unauthorized Orpheus of *Astrophil and Stella*' (*SEL* 35.19–34) eschews the conventional Sidney/Astrophil and Penelope Rich/Stella identification. Drawing on Sidney's use of the Orphic myth, she argues for a reading of the text as 'a dramatic enactment of the popular Renaissance debates on the nature of fiction' in which Stella represents conventional poetics and Astrophil stands for an aesthetics of originality. Clare R. Kinney's 'Chivalry Unmasked: Courtly Spectacle and the Abuses of Romance in Sidney's *New Arcadia*' (*SEL* 35.35–52) focuses on the substantially revised Book 3, in which the original narrative of small-scale intrigues is displaced by civil war. The series of one-to-one engagements is dealt with in detail, particular attention being paid to the destruction of the chivalric exemplars, Argalus and Parthenia. Kinney concludes that Sidney has 'purged his narrative of the beguiling masks of chivalry' and offered a 'critique of the "kidnapping" of the protocols of knightly romance for ... politically self-serving purposes'.

A brief section of Helen Hackett's *Virgin Mother, Maiden Queen: Elizabeth I and the Cult of the Virgin Mary* uses the *Defence of Poesy* to help explain Sidney's ambiguous role 'as a participant in the panegyric of Elizabeth'. She points to Sidney's comment that when an idealized poetic image bears the name of a real person, it does not necessarily claim to be an accurate description of that person. Therefore, the idealized poetic images of Elizabeth can be seen as an ideal of virtue to be emulated by the reader even, Hackett argues, if the reader is Elizabeth herself. Robert Matz's 'Sidney's *Defence of Poesie*: The Politics of Pleasure' (*ELR* 25.2.131–47) argues against recent studies of Sidney which claim that the text proposes 'the use of literature for the profit of a Protestant ideology', valuing service over pleasure. Matz offers a sustained comparison with Gosson's *Schoole of Abuse*, to which Sidney responded with hostility because 'it drew too close to the tensions in Sidney's position as courtier and Protestant activist', and concludes that the unresolved conflicts in the *Defence* are deflected onto poetry itself, the ambiguity of the text arising from Sidney's position as a member of the courtly élite and an impoverished gentleman. Ty F. Buckman focuses on Sidney's response to Queen Elizabeth's proposed match with Alençon in 'The Perils of Marriage Counselling: John Stubbs, Philip Sidney, and the Virgin Queen' (*RenP* [1995].125–41). By way of a comparison of these two writers, Buckman demonstrates that Sidney recognized, whereas Stubbs did not, the need to account for the royal gaze: 'writing *about* the Queen was inseparable from writing *to* the Queen'. George Gömöri's 'Sir Philip Sidney's Polish Friend: an Amendment' (*PolR* 40.1.69–72) shows that the man Sidney met was in fact a Polish aristocrat, Martin de Obory Lésniowolski, who, despite being a Catholic, was actively involved in the Protestant Henry Valois's election to the Polish throne. R. E. Pritchard analyses Mary 'Sidney's Dedicatory Poem' (*Expl* 54.i.2–4) preceding her continuation of Philip's Psalms, to bring out the poem's central metaphor of a quasi-sexual union of 'angel sprite' Philip and human Mary producing a joint 'brain-child'.

(c) Spenser
This year, a high proportion of the critical work on Spenser focused upon *The Faerie Queene*. In *Rereading Allegory: A Narrative Approach to Genre*, Deborah L. Madsen identifies and explores the problems raised by post-structuralism for the field of genre theory. In an examination of the emergence of Protestant allegory, she argues that the Protestant 'shift away from the objective means of grace towards individual subjectivity' is reflected in Book I of *The Faerie Queene*. Linda Gregerson's *The Reformation of the Subject: Spenser, Milton, and the English Protestant Epic* opens by referring to the iconoclastic controversy over the distinction between a sign and an idol.

Gregerson aims to analyse the features 'adopted to distinguish a poem from an idol, while preserving for the poem those suasive powers that iconoclasts have long and rightly attributed to icons of every sort'. She identifies three such strategies, the double-edged disclaimer, the conspicuous announcement of artefactual status and 'the formal and thematic rendering of a subject in exile from its authorizing ground'. Gregerson also points to the specular aspect of the epic poem, placing it in the same tradition as Early Modern cautionary literature, concluding that Spenser 'exploits and mitigates the iconic status of his poem, soliciting an idolatrous response from the reader – the "enjoyment" of signs for their own sake – and reforming this impulse by breaking the surface of illusion'. John M. Steadman's *Moral Fiction in Milton and Spenser* takes a rather more traditional line, its stated aim being to focus upon the diverse ways in which both poets utilize the epic genre as a vehicle for ethical and historical truth. There is a great emphasis upon contextual and comparative material at the expense of Spenser's and Milton's works, with a survey of the development of the epic and romance genres in Renaissance literature, linking this to Spenser's use of the two forms in *The Faerie Queene*. Steadman then considers Spenser's debt to Classical and Renaissance writers, goes on to explore the lack of determinate geography or history in the poem, and explores Spenser's use of the past, identifying in his poetry an equivocal attitude to analogies between past and present, partly because antiquity offers patterns of virtue, while the present offers a superior model in the shape of Elizabeth I. Steadman emphasizes the variety of works upon which Spenser drew, but ultimately identifies a missing element, the heroic ethos of the classical epic.

Chapter 2 of Qingyun Wu's *Female Rule in Chinese and English Literary Utopias* offers a comparison between Spenser's poem and Luo Maodeng's *Sanbao's Expedition to the Western Ocean* (1597) and debates the representation of female rule. Mary Villeponteaux's 'Displacing Feminine Authority in *The Faerie Queene*' (*SEL* 35.53–67) focuses upon the character of Britomart, who 'best exemplifies Spenser's ambivalent depiction of woman's authority' and examines the way in which the poem is careful to delineate the difference between Britomart and Elizabeth I. Villeponteaux also explores the moments in the poem, such as the scene in Merlin's cave, which reveal 'anxiety about feminine power and its threat to masculinity'. Mark J. Bruhn's 'Approaching Busyrane: Episodic Patterning in *The Faerie Queene*' (*SP* 92.275–90) proposes that Book III is constructed out of discontinuous episodes which are nevertheless linked by patterns of action, character and imagery, providing the reader with an interpretative context. Therefore, we can read Amoret and Hellenore with the same approval as we have read Florimell, and Scudamour with the same disapproval as we have read Malbecco and Marinell. This, concludes Bruhn, leaves only Britomart to represent chaste male love, 'the one force that can resolve the central conflict variously manifest in all three episodes'.

Lauren Silberman's *Transforming Desire: Erotic Knowledge in Books III and IV of The Faerie Queene*, offers a particularly exciting and well-conceived reading of the poem. She begins by stating her view that Books III and IV are intellectual projects in which a beautiful progressive ideal is constructed and then unsentimentally subjected to a less attractive reality. Silberman identifies the specular function and imagery of Book III whereby the reader is 'fashioned' alongside the heroine, Britomart, and argues that 'Spenser emphasizes improvisation as a principle both of individual self-fashioning and of narrative'. The later chapters deal with Book IV, in which, Silberman argues, Spenser moves on 'to examining how a discursive construct conveys meaning' and concludes that 'Spenser exposes fictions of total understanding and total control as just that: fictions, seductive and empowering ones, but fictions nonetheless'. In the introduction to *Spenser's Allegory of Love: Social Vision in Books III, IV, and V of The Faerie Queene*, James W. Broaddus claims that his critical approach is somewhat mixed, citing New Criticism and historicisms old and new as influences. The traditional historicist influence would appear to be the strongest. Broaddus reads Britomart's initiation in terms of Renaissance science, understanding her psychology and physiology 'as parts of her larger psyche', whereby, Broaddus argues, 'she provides the entrée to Spenser's allegory of love'. He then offers largely descriptive discussions of the major events of Books III, IV and V, which suffer somewhat from over-quotation. As a piece of criticism, this is an untidily written book which lacks a discernible argument and offers little conclusion beyond a re-affirmation of the poem's moral as seen by Broaddus: 'we are not to devote our lives to our selves; we are to subordinate those selves to a greater good'.

Maria R. Rohr Philmus's '*The Faerie Queene* and Renaissance Poetics: Another Look at Book VI as "Conclusion" to the Poem' (*ES* 6. 497–519) proposes a revision of the view that Book VI is about the power of poetry. Philmus argues that, instead, Spenser denies the morally improving effect of poetry, strongly suggesting 'that the virtue of courtesy belongs in a realm apart, the realm of poetic imaginings', thereby taking issue with, rather than subscribing to, Sidney's theories in the *Defence of Poesy*. Philmus suggests that Spenser takes leave of the original conceit of *The Faerie Queene* and, citing sonnet 80 of *Amoretti*, concludes that any work on faeryland beyond Book VI was seen by the poet as both a new work and a continuation of the old. Judith H. Anderson, in 'Prudence and her Silence: Spenser's use of Chaucer's Melibee' (*ELH* 62.29–46), also views Book VI as a debate about poetry. She builds on the identification of Vergil's Meliboeus and Tityrus as the ancestors of Spenser's Melibee and Colin by tracing their English ancestry. Anderson points out that unlike Spenser's character, Chaucer's Melibee is morally culpable, yet both suffer destruction. Acknowledging the temptation to read the fate of Spenser's shepherd as deserved, Anderson suggests that Melibee is representative of a careless pastoral idyll which is 'sacrificed on the altar of prudence, in this case mainly a blind for realism, in order to enable and implicitly to delimit Colin's still greater liberty'. Anne D. Hall's 'The Actaeon Myth and Allegorical Reading in Spenser's "Two Cantos of Mutabilitie"' (*SCJ* 26.561–75) investigates the central paradox of the cantos, that Christians should be vigilant but that God will provide, through an examination of the character of Faunus. Carefully tracing the influence of Ovid, Hall highlights the complex and multiple allegorical function of Faunus, demonstrating that at one point Spenser 'wavers uncertainly between Actaeon-Faunus-Satan and Actaeon-Faunus-Christ'. Richard J. Berleth in 'Fraile Woman, Foolish Gerle: Misogyny in Spenser's *Mutabilitie Cantos*' (*MP* 93.37–53) makes a fresh identification of Mutabilitie as a mortal woman, yet argues against the identification of Mutabilitie with Eve, suggesting that 'Spenser surely knew that the dire aspects of Mutabilitie were consequences of mankind's sin'. Berleth reads the Jove-Mutabilitie encounter as a debate between the sexes to be judged by a Nature of significantly indeterminate sex, in which Mutabilitie stands up 'for the triumph of feminine realism in the face of over-arching schemes of male superiority'.

Four articles dealt with Spenser's relationship with Ireland. In 'The Failure of Moral Philosophy in the Work of Edmund Spenser' (*Rep* 51.47–76), Elizabeth Fowler reads *The Faerie Queene* in its colonial context and identifies the issue of lawful 'dominion' as the central problem for moral philosophy in the poem *via* a close examination of two exemplary moments in the second half – the rape of Amoret and the debate between Artegall and the Giant. Fowler then goes on to examine the presentation of Jurisprudence in the *Mutabilitie Cantos*, concluding that Spenser's work dramatizes the 'competing claims of moral philosophy and its elaboration of ethical virtues ... and the claims of an emerging political theory based on natural law and possessory rights'. Walter S. H. Lim, in 'Figuring Justice: Imperial Ideology and the Discourse of Colonialism in Book V of *The Faerie Queene* and *A View of the Present State of Ireland*' (*Ren&R* 19.45–70) claims that 'Spenser's conception of justice expressed in Book V can be read as a poeticization of the vision of justice given in *A View of the Present State of Ireland*'. Drawing upon biographical and historical details, Lim argues that Spenser's own attempt to 'produce a powerfully coherent blueprint for the colonization of Ireland' is disrupted by the lack of an Elizabethan consensual ideology on the matter. Identifying Spenser with Irenius from the *View*, Lim's article offers a reading of Spenser as a harsh and ambitious colonist for whom '*justice* functions as a synonym for *power*'. Paul Stevens's 'Spenser and Milton on Ireland: Civility, Exclusion, and the Politics of Wisdom' (*ArielE* 26.4.151–67) offers a similar view of Spenser, by different means. He argues for 'the crucial importance of the Bible's Wisdom literature' to Spenser's understanding of his colonial role, proposing that Spenser's colonial rhetoric seems to be little more than arrogation of Yahweh's absolute authority. Thereby, Stevens argues for the political power of Scripture as 'the master code of emergent Western colonialism'. Donald Bruce's 'Edmund Spenser and the Irish Wars' (*ContempR* 266.129–38) begins by asserting that Spenser's poetry 'is poignant with regret for the impermanence of all worldly things'. Bruce focuses upon Spenser's role as Lord Grey's secretary, describing in detail Lord Grey's campaigns in Ireland, and drawing parallels between events, places and people in Spenser's life and those depicted in his literary works. A further article by Bruce, 'Spenser's Birth and Birthplace' (*N&Q* 42.283–5) traces the likely dates of composition of sonnets 4, 60, 62 and 68 of *Amoretti* to calculate that Spenser's birthday could be placed on or near 12 March 1553. Bruce also cites the burial of John Spenser, recorded in the register of St Botolph, as evidence to support the seventeenth-century view that Spenser was born in East Smithfield and to suggest that Spenser's mother returned to her native Lancashire after her husband's death, and that Spenser may have joined her there in 1577, after gaining his MA.

Louise Schleiner's densely theoretical *Cultural Semiotics, Spenser, and the Captive Woman* selects *The Shepheardes Calender* as the text for a Greimassian discourse analysis in the quest to identify a Renaissance English ideologeme. She proposes to discover a reading that treats the three central themes of *The Shepheardes Calender*, the poetic, the political/ecclesiastical and the erotic, in an integrative way. After subjecting the poem to a close analysis using the Greimas model, she explores the images of plant growth, excrescence, production and reproduction which function as metaphors of sexual, artistic and prophetic expression, before proposing a new ideologeme, the 'captive woman', in *The Faerie Queene* and other texts. She then returns to *The Shepheardes Calender* to investigate the text's layers of framing 'in the functioning of some of their utterances as paratexts, namely texts constructed to define, condition, and shape an ideologically desired readership' that allowed Spenser to 'open his publishing career with a culturally definitive book'. Ted Brown's 'Pride and Pastoral in *The Shepheardes Calender*' (in David G. Allen and Robert A. White, eds, *Subjects on the World's Stage: Essays on British Literature of the Middle Ages and Renaissance*) alerts the reader to the often overlooked fact that the Colin of 'January' is not the Colin of 'December', and that his pipe-breaking in January is the petulant response of a frustrated adolescent rather than a conscious repudiation of the pastoral, and asks that we take the poem on its own terms, as a pastoral delineation of life and death, rather than as a statement that 'pastoral poetry is an inadequate medium for great art'. A section on the April Eclogue appears in Hackett's *Virgin Mother, Maiden Queen: Elizabeth I and the Cult of the Virgin Mary*. Here, Hackett argues that Spenser presents 'one of the most notable and influential encomiastic icons of Elizabeth ... as "Queene of shepheardes all"', which was to be imitated by future writers. The April Eclogue established the convention whereby fertility and virginity were seen as complementary qualities in the figure of the Queen and, Hackett goes on to suggest, Spenser hereby re-appropriates the myth of the holy virgin-bride-mother for Protestantism.

James A. Riddell and Stanley Stewart's *Jonson's Spenser: Evidence and Historical Criticism* emerges from the fortuitous discovery of a 1617 first folio edition of Spenser's works which was owned by Ben Jonson. The book attempts to evaluate Jonson's opinion of and debt to Spenser, before examining Jonson's reading of Spenser's shorter poems and *The Faerie Queene* via the annotations and markings on Jonson's first folio edition. Riddell and Stewart then compare Jonson's markings on the description of the House of Alma with the comments made by Sir Kenelm Digby, previously regarded as the earliest commentator on Spenser. Taking care to avoid the accusation that they are attempting to privilege Jonson's reading in any way, the authors justify the value of their work by pointing out that 'Jonson's views are instances of a reading contemporaneous with authorial usage, and so, potentially relevant to an understanding of that contemporary usage'. The authors have usefully appended several photographs from Jonson's 1617 Folio together with two lists of Jonson's markings and annotations.

Books Reviewed

Alford, John A., ed. *From Page to Performance. Essays in Early English Drama*. MichSUP. pp. 266. £24.50. ISBN 0 870 13379 9.
Allen, David G., and Robert A. White, eds. *Subjects on the World's Stage. Essays on British Literature of the Middle Ages and Renaissance*. AUP. pp. 319. £34.50. ISBN 0 874 13544 3.

Aughterson, Kate. *Renaissance Woman: A Sourcebook. Constructions of Femininity in England.* Routledge. pp. xxiv + 316. hb £45, pb £14.99. ISBN 0 415 12045 4, 0 415 12046 2.

Bachinger, Katrina. *Male Pretense: A Gender Study of Sir Philip Sidney's Life and Texts.* SSELER. Mellen. pp. 156. £39.95. ISBN 0 773 41270 0.

Barker, William, ed. *Richard Mulcaster: Positions Concerning the Training Up of Children.* UTorP (1993). pp. lxxxvi + 521. $80. ISBN 0 802 02987 6.

Bateman, John J., ed., and Robert D. Sider, trans., annotation. *Desiderius Erasmus: Paraphrase on the Acts of the Apostles. Collected Works of Erasmus,* vol 50. UTorP. pp. xix +389. C$125. ISBN 0 803 00664 7.

Benito-Vessels, Carmen, and Michael Zappala, eds. *The Picaresque. A Symposium on the Rogue's Tale.* AUP (1994). pp. 191. £26.95. ISBN 0 874 13458 7.

Blanchard, W. Scott. *Scholars' Bedlam. Menippean Satire in the Renaissance.* AUP. pp. 205. £27. ISBN 0 838 75281 0.

Broaddus, James W. *Spenser's Allegory of Love: Social Vision in Books III, IV and V of The Faerie Queene.* AUP. pp. 185. £25. ISBN 0 838 63632 2.

Chaudhuri, Sukanta. *Renaissance Essays for Kitty Scoular Datta.* OUPI. pp. 287. £16.99. ISBN 0 195 63702 X.

Cousins, A. D., and Damian Grace, eds. *More's Utopia and the Utopian Inheritance.* UPA. pp. 159. £26.95. ISBN 0 819 19915 X.

Coyle, Martin, ed. *Niccolo Machiavelli's 'The Prince'. New Interdisciplinary Essays.* ManUP. pp. 211. hb £35, pb £12.99. ISBN 0 719 04195 3, 0 719 04196 1.

Enterline, Lynn. *The Tears of Narcissus: Melancholia and Masculinity in Early Modern Writing.* StanfordUP. pp. x + 429. £40. ISBN 0 804 72397 4.

Fuller, Mary C. *Voyages in Print. English Travel to America, 1576–1624.* CUP. pp. xiii + 210. £30. ISBN 0 521 48161 9.

Gregerson, Linda. *The Reformation of the Subject: Spenser, Milton, and the English Protestant Epic.* CUP. pp. 281. £35, $49.95. ISBN 0 521 46277 0.

Haber, Judith. *Pastoral and the Poetics of Self-Contradiction: Theocritus to Marvell.* CUP. pp. xiv + 218. £35. ISBN 0 521 44206 0.

Hackett, Helen. *Virgin Mother, Maiden Queen. Elizabeth I and the Cult of the Virgin Mary.* Macmillan. pp. xii + 303. hb £40, pb £14.99. ISBN 0 333 56664 5, 0 333 66863 4.

Hall, Kim F. *Things of Darkness: Economies of Race and Gender in Early Modern England.* CornUP. pp. 319. hb £35.50, pb £13.95. ISBN 0 801 43117 4, 0 801 48249 6.

Hart, Clive, and Kay Gilliland Stevenson. *Heaven and the Flesh. Imagery of Desire from the Renaissance to the Rococo.* CUP. pp. xiv + 237. £30. ISBN 0 521 49571 7.

Henderson, Diana E. *Passion Made Public: Elizabethan Lyric, Gender, and Performance.* UIllP. pp. x + 279. hb $44.95, pb $17.95. ISBN 0 252 02162 2, 0 252 06460 7.

Jones, Serene. *Calvin and the Rhetoric of Piety.* Westminster John Knox Press. pp. 240. £13.50. ISBN 0 664 22070 3.

Kirkpatrick, Robin. *English and Italian Literature from Dante to Shakespeare. A Study of Source, Analogue, and Divergence.* Longman Medieval and Renaissance Library. Longman. pp. ix + 328. hb £45, pb £16.99. ISBN 0 582 06559 3, 0 582 06558 5.

Logan, George M., Robert M. Adams, and Clarence H. Miller, eds. *Thomas More, Utopia. Latin Text and English Translation*. CUP. pp. xlvi + 290. £55. ISBN 0 521 40318 9.

Madsen, Deborah L. *Rereading Allegory: A Narrative Approach to Genre*. Macmillan. pp. 177. £26.50. ISBN 0 333 63443 8.

Manley, Lawrence. *Literature and Culture in Early Modern London*. CUP. pp. xvi + 603. £40. ISBN 0 521 46161 8.

Marotti, Arthur. *Manuscript, Print, and the English Renaissance Lyric*. CornUP. pp. xx + 348. hb £35.50, pb £15.50. ISBN 0 801 42291 4, 0 801 48238 0.

Maslen, Elizabeth, ed. *Comedy: Essays in Honour of Peter Dixon by Friends and Colleagues* (1993). Queen Mary and Westfield College Department of English. pp. xx + 343. £22.50. ISBN 0 9521577 0 5.

Mason, Roger A., ed. *John Knox. On Rebellion*. Cambridge Texts in the History of Political Thought. CUP. pp. 219. hb £35, pb £12.95. ISBN 0 521 39089 3, 0 521 39988 2.

Murrin, Michael. *History and Warfare in Renaissance Epic*. UChicP. pp. xvi + 371. £25.95. ISBN 0 226 55403 1.

Norland, Howard B. *Drama in Early Tudor Britain 1485–1558*. UNebP. pp. xxix + 394. £42.75. ISBN 0 803 23337 X.

Phillippy, Patricia Berrahou. *Love's Remedies. Recantation and Renaissance Lyric Poetry*. AUP. pp. 261. £29.50. ISBN 0 838 75263 2.

Rebhorn, Wayne A. *The Emperor of Men's Minds. Literature and the Renaissance Discourse of Rhetoric*. CornUP. pp. xix + 276. £27.50. ISBN 0 801 42562 X.

Riddell, James A., and Stanley Stewart. *Jonson's Spenser: Evidence and Historical Criticism*. Duquesne. pp. 218. £45. ISBN 0 820 70263 3.

Ringler, William A., and Michael Flachmann, eds. *William Baldwin: Beware the Cat: The First English Novel*. Huntington. pp. 126. pb $44.50. ISBN 0 873 28154 3.

Sawday, Jonathan. *The Body Emblazoned. Dissection and the Human Body in Renaissance Culture*. Routledge. pp. xii + 327. hb £35, pb £12.99. ISBN 0 415 04444 8, 0 415 15719 6.

Scarry, Elaine, ed. *Fins de Siècle: English Poetry in 1590, 1690, 1790, 1890, 1990*. JHUP. pp. xiii + 142. hb £32, pb £11.50. ISBN 0 801 84928 4, 0 801 84929 2.

Schleiner, Louise. *Cultural Semiotics, Spenser, and the Captive Woman*. AUP. pp. 278. £32.50. ISBN 0 934 22336 X.

Sherman, William H. *John Dee. The Politics of Reading and Writing in the English Renaissance*. UMassP. pp. xiv + 291. £31.50. ISBN 0 870 23940 6.

Silberman, Lauren. *Transforming Desire: Erotic Knowledge in Books III and IV of The Faerie Queene*. UCalP. pp.189. £34. ISBN 0 520 08486 1.

Steadman, John M. *Moral Fiction in Milton and Spenser*. UMissP. pp. 200. £34.50. ISBN 0 826 21017 1.

Strier, Richard. *Resistant Structures: Particularity, Radicalism, and Renaissance Texts*. UCalP. pp. xiii + 239. £30. ISBN 0 520 08915 4.

Strong, Roy. *The Tudor and Stuart Monarchy. Pageantry, Painting, Iconography. Vol. 1: Tudor*. Boydell. pp. 277. £60. ISBN 0 85115400 X.

Stump, Donald V., Jerome S. Dees, and C. Stuart Hunter. *Sir Philip Sidney: An Annotated Bibliography of Texts and Criticism (1554–1984)*. Hall (1994). pp. 834. £58.95. ISBN 0 816 18238 8.

Sullivan, Ceri. *Dismembered Rhetoric. English Recusant Writing, 1580 to 1603*. AUP. pp. 184. £26. ISBN 0 838 63577 6.

Sutton, Dana, ed. *Oxford Poetry by Richard Eedes and George Peele*. Garland. pp. ix + 249. $67. ISBN 0 815 32161 9.

Tomlinson, Gary. *Music in Renaissance Magic. Toward a Historiography of Others*. UChicP (1993). pp. xvi + 291. £30.75. ISBN 0 226 80791 6.

Vos, Alvin, ed. *Place and Displacement in the Renaissance* (1994). MRTS. SUNYP. pp. xxii + 291. $25. ISBN 0 866 98139 X.

Wu, Qingyun. *Female Rule in Chinese and English Literary Utopias*. LiverUP. pp. 225. hb £25, pb £15. ISBN 0 853 23570 8, 0 853 23580 5.

VI

Shakespeare

JILL BARKER, PETER J. SMITH, PAULINE KIERNAN, SUSAN
BRUCE and LISA HOPKINS

This chapter has three sections: 1. Editions and Textual Matters; 2. Shakespeare in the Theatre; 3. Criticism. Section 1 is by Jill Barker; section 2 is by Peter J. Smith; sections 3 (a) and (e) are by Pauline Kiernan, sections 3 (b) and (c) are by Susan Bruce and section 3 (d) is by Lisa Hopkins.

1. Editions and Textual Matters

This year sees the publication of the first three titles in the new third edition of ArdenS, following a thoroughly revamped editorial policy. This takes account of current debates about editorial practices by offering a diplomatic text re-edited from the 'best' early text, with emendations and collations flagged in the notes. Where the divergences between an early edition and the conflated Arden edition are very great, a reduced photographic facsimile of the early edition is given as an appendix, thus saving a great deal of space and complexity in the notes, while giving the reader an opportunity to see the structure of the early quarto. Such a method of course places considerable responsibility on readers to do their own collation. The textual apparatus (in some cases) indicates the presence of insertions and alterations by means of various typefaces and bracketing conventions. Thus Arden 3 attempts to display both a conservative text and an eclectic 'ideal' text which incorporates the current editor's opinions. Given the inherent contradictions of the project, it succeeds in supplying an information resource from which sophisticated users may construct the text they require. Paradoxically, if understandably, this transfer of authority to the reader takes place within a context of modernized or conventionalized spelling and punctuation. Perhaps the most important change in approach is the redesigned format of the introduction, which now (with the exception of T. W. Craik's *King Henry V*) places textual analyses and argument last and foregrounds the critical discussion, including a response to the growing preference for seeing plays as 'plays in performance'. An expansive attitude to appendixes continues the tradition of allowing editors scope to display source material. On the page, Arden 3 looks reassuringly little different from Arden 2. Collations have moved to below the footnotes, while headers giving act and scene numbers make the task of locating text easier. The bracketing conventions can make a page look complex and technical, but this seems a small price to pay for the information contained. In a highly self-conscious way, Arden 3 inserts itself within the historical stream of Shakespearean editions and attempts with considerable success to satisfy a wide variety of sometimes conflicting scholarly and practical demands.

Of the editions reviewed here, John Wilders's workmanlike edition of *Antony and Cleopatra* is perhaps the most like the old Arden. In general, Wilders adjusts F1 in line with that scholarly tendency which seeks to 'make sense' of puzzling words, phrases or lines. When F1 prose lines appear as verse, the original versions are listed in an appendix. This system involves constant checking between text and appendix, as the lines that have been treated in this way are annoyingly not indicated in the text.

In a comprehensive introduction to *Henry V* which treats textual matters extensively, T. W. Craik argues that F1 is effectively the original text of 1599, of which Q1 is 'an inaccurately reconstructed version'. Q1 is so divergent from the text as presented here, that a reduced facsimile appears as Appendix One. The volume contains other immensely useful appendixes: maps, a genealogical table and a doubling chart. Act and scene divisions are conventionally re-sorted, and lines perceived as 'imperfect' tidied up with the addition of conjectural words or phrases. There is no typographical indication of such emendations. A discussion of plot and its value as performance is followed by a sceptically presented, though thorough, summary of critical opinions, including the most contemporary. The introduction concludes with a lucid account of the familiar evidence from the quartos suggesting that Q1 is a memorial reconstruction dictated by actors. Acknowledging the current high profile of textual debate, Craik puts the case for editorial intervention concisely and moderately; whether one agrees with his editorial judgements or not, he has thus done both the general reader and the student a great service by making accessible the scholarly principles and arguments which the current textual controversy contests so hotly.

Jonathan Bate's edition of *Titus Andronicus* supersedes J. C. Maxwell's 1953 ArdenS edition (revised 1961), against which it defines itself. Bate bases his text on Q1 with the addition of the fly-killing scene from F1 (indicated with a change of typeface). He also makes corrections from Q2 and Q3, and emendations based on those of later editors, ending with himself. His approach to stage directions, clear but complex, is to insert F1 on the grounds that this gives valuable information about Jacobean staging practices. Other suggested stage directions, including his own, are given within square brackets. Numerous emendations adjust line length and distribution, though Bate is on the whole more conservative than earlier editors. Punctuation has been completely, though lightly, modernized.

Bate believes the play to be wholly by Shakespeare, arguing that it is a coherent work, prepared specifically for the 1594 season, and that Q1 was set directly from exceptionally clean 'foul papers'. Bate's introduction integrates performative and textual analyses and relates the play, without quite using the word 'intertext', to works by Kyd, Greene and Peele, offering informative samples of the relevant sections in the Appendix as evidence. The critical introduction is a *tour de force*, presenting the text of *Titus Andronicus* as a polymorphous object variously realized through history, from eighteenth and nineteenth centuries to Peter Brook's production and Deborah Warner's 1988 RSC production. Bate's edition is clearly one more 'performance' in that long inheritance of re-workings. Among its many virtues, the greatest strength of his interpretation lies in his use of editorial control over doubtful lines to argue for complex readings and absolute clarity about the choices he is making and why he is making them, which is in itself an education in this particular version of editorial practice.

Six further volumes appeared in the PH (previously Harvester Wheatsheaf) series 'Shakespearean Originals: First Editions' (henceforward SO) the first four of which appeared in 1993 (*YWES* 74.195), and which were the subject of a spirited controversy in the letters pages of the *TLS*. The volumes for this year are: *The Tragedie of Anthonie, and Cleopatra* ed. John Turner; *M. William Shak-Speare: His True Chronicle Historie of the Life and Death of King Lear and his Three Daughters* ed. Graham Holderness; *The Most Excellent Historie of The Merchant of Venice* ed. Annabel Patterson; *The Tragedy of Othello, The Moore of Venice* ed. Andrew Murphy; *An Excellent Conceited Tragedie of Romeo and Juliet* ed. Cedric Watts; and *Twelfe Night; or, What You Will* ed. Laurie E. Osborne.

John Turner edits a single copy of *Antony and Cleopatra* F1, in a manner exemplary for this kind of project. In returning to an unmediated text without act or scene divisions and without the accustomed geographical interpolations, we are offered an even stronger sense than usual of the fluidity of the play in performance. Turner conducts a discussion on new historicist lines, reading the comma in the title as an indicator that the play is about Antony, rather than about a composite entity called 'Antony and Cleopatra', and demonstrating the strengths of basing a critical analysis on an unedited original text. Turner's interpretation of the text as a site of editorial rivalry illuminates many of the current debates about textual editing. The endnotes are excellent, glossing where necessary, indicating earlier emendations and finding good reasons why editors should allow F1 to stand.

Graham Holderness introduces Q1 of *King Lear* at length, taking the opportunity to expand on the general introduction and to re-enter the debate begun in the *TLS* (*YWES* 74.195) about the purposes of the series. This clarification was needed. He is especially concerned about the terms on which texts historically described as 'Bad Quartos', 'memorial reconstructions' and so on are now accepted as authentically Shakespearian, rightly noticing that this involves a critically conservative resurrection of the author as 'father' of the text. (PH themselves are scarcely squeaky-clean on this issue, marketing the series as 'Shakespearean Originals: First Editions', and so implying undisputed Shakespearean authorship of the whole series.) Holderness also points to the 'specious integrity' generated by parallel-text versions, as they offer themselves to the reader as symmetrical, comparable and so stable in opposition to each other. By contrast, this old-spelling text is put forward to focus on textual volatility, and a destabilization of previously accepted versions of *King Lear*. The strength of Holderness's reading appears in the section regarding the generic emphases of the variant texts of *King Lear*, where insight into the position of Cordelia as an exemplary figure derives from analysing the various texts' relationships with the genres of romance, tragedy, comedy and history. Footnotes, though sparse and apparently arbitrary, are generally useful. Through the practice of citing (and recommending) variant readings without quoting them, the notes assume that the reader has simultaneous access to F1. It is hard to see how this expectation can be aligned with Holderness's attack on parallel texts, so here perhaps is a demonstration that differences in editorial theory are not as great as editors themselves might wish.

Introducing the 1600 Quarto of *The Merchant of Venice*, Annabel Patterson notes that this is 'the version ... that records indisputably Shakespeare's intentions', and is thus authoritative. It also contains 'signs of historical contingency and fossilized evidence of the materiality of printing'. Patterson is a self-conscious and highly competent editor, who is very aware of the problems raised by the SO project: when 'i' is routinely modernized to 'j', one needs special finesse to discuss the significance of the 'disconcerting spray of capital italic I's and sometimes J's', but Patterson manages this with clarity and grace.

Andrew Murphy, editing *Othello*, appears torn between the overt task of the series to present Q1 in its own right as a bare text, and his wish to consider it in comparison with F1. He thus loses the opportunity to conduct a critical discussion of the text before us, but also refrains from offering a state-of-the-art summary of current thinking by textual scholars, though he does supply sufficient references for the interested student to follow up these issues. Murphy appears to be unsure of his readership: the text is lightly, inconsistently and sometimes incompetently annotated. He defines 'cuckold' for us, using the noun form to relate to a passage in which the word occurs as a verb; he quotes Arden Shakespeare annotations, but is not in general stimulated to add to scholarship regarding the play.

Introducing his edition of Q1 of *Romeo and Juliet*, Cedric Watts adopts a briskly affable tone to summarize accessibly, though without discussion, the complex relationships amongst the early editions of the play. He questions the long-standing notion that a line that sounds 'better' to us is more likely to be by Shakespeare than one that sounds 'worse'. This play has suffered from the consequent inflation of style rather more than most, and an uncluttered Q1 gives a very different view of its performance possibilities. Watts does not compromise with scholarship: a prefatory Editorial Note lists the readings which are most obviously misprints, while the endnotes collate portions of this text against Q2. The latter exercise is perhaps conducted in a rather more minimalist spirit than one might wish. The explanatory notes are well-judged.

Laurie E. Osborne, introducing F1 of *Twelfth Night*, draws attention with great precision to the implications for understanding carried by an early text. Both 'Ay' written as 'I' and 'myself' as 'my selfe' focus the reader on issues of identity, for example. Early modern punctuation gives rise to 'multiple possibilities for meaning' even when, as here, there is no earlier quarto with which to compare it. A satisfyingly detailed section on variants in performance history is convincingly related to an originary multiplicity in this text, whose 1623 first printing post-dates numerous (lost) versions both written and performed. 'The Folio *Twelfe Night* ... offers in its typographical and theatrical materiality as many alternatives and multiple versions as any of the more obviously doubled or trebled Shakespearean originals.' Once again, the endnotes are unsatisfying: too brief to help the innocent, too basic to help the sophisticate and too casually sparse to convince the reviewer that they are uttered with serious intent. Some inaccuracy creeps in: the character who wields a 'dagger of lath' is not the Devil, but the Vice.

It should be noted that, in spite of the practice of retaining the text as printed, including manifest misprints, SO volumes are not precisely facsimile reprints but editions, in that numerous contractions and other typographical conventions have been modernized, and catchwords omitted. Watts is the only editor to point this out. In general, the laudable project of the series is still patchy in realization: it remains supplementary (in every sense of the word) to the major scholarly editions.

Much of Eric Sams's *The Real Shakespeare: Retrieving the Early Years, 1564–1594* consists of history-cum-biography of a fairly speculative kind, and falls outside the scope of this review. Sams develops the theory that several plays from the Shakespeare apocrypha are early works. The texts in question are: the lost *Hamlet* (1589); *Hamlet* (1603); *The Taming of A Shrew* (1594); *The Troublesome Reign of King John* (1594); *The First Part of the Contention betwixt the two famous houses of Yorke and Lancaster* (1594); *The True Tragedy of Richard, Duke of Yorke* (1595); *Faire Em* (*c*.1587); and *Locrine* (*c*.1594). Sams's contention is that modern scholarship has been handicapped by the twin theories of memorial reconstruction by actors and of Bad Quartos. The biographical material with which he opposes these is suggestive rather than convincing, but in either case irrelevant to the textual concerns which surface in the latter part of the book. There the approach is not so much textual as critical of the methods of earlier textual scholars, while committing the very intellectual sins which Sams locates in his opponents: namely, confusing possibility with fact and inference with evidence. One cannot refute the textual analyses of decades with simple assertion and brief lists of verbal parallels. While it is reasonable to perceive that much early twentieth-century scholarship was based on tendentious evaluative assumptions, Sams does not then move to suggest that these would bear re-thinking. Within an oblique engagement with textual scholarship, however, the discussion of stylometry and its potential is lucid and even-handed.

Inviting comparison with Sams, John Jones subscribes to the 'plausible fantasy' school of textual analysis. His project in *Shakespeare at Work* is to guess what MS might lie behind the printed text, and from that to discuss the process of composition. Jones assembles palaeographic information about *The Booke of Sir Thomas More*, from which he moves more widely into numerous thoughtful insights regarding the history plays, *Troilus and Cressida* and *Hamlet*. He struggles, however, to make his idea that only Shakespeare could achieve a particular kind of effect cohere with the appearance of such effects in 'bad texts', by seeing him as a revising playwright. Regarding *Hamlet*, Jones argues that Q1 is memorial reconstruction, and that the cuts between Q2 and F are authorial improvements which should be respected in a modern edition. Like Sams, Jones deals in probabilities founded in unprovable beliefs about Shakespeare's creative behaviour, and although his goal is textual rather than biographical reconstruction, only the quality of his more sceptical scholarship makes his book preferable. Simon Jarvis, in *Scholars and Gentlemen: Shakespearian Textual Criticism and Representations of Scholarly Labour 1725–1765*, analyses the editorial procedures of eighteenth-century scholars including Pope, Samuel Johnson, Rowe, Theobald and Warburton. This takes place in relation to a discussion of the position and purpose of scholarly textual research within the wider cultural context. Keying in to a growing interest in the implications for interpretation and performance that can be drawn from the vagaries of early modern punctuation is Anthony

Graham-White's *Punctuation and its Dramatic Value in Shakespearean Drama*. Graham-White usefully explains how punctuation marks functioned, relating this to *Richard III*, among other plays.

Several articles address matters common to the *oeuvre*, and to the practice of textual study. A. J. West provides a comprehensive finding list in the 'Provisional New Census of the Shakespeare First Folio' (*Library* 6.xvii. 60–73), including notes on copies which may still exist, but have yet to be traced. H. R. Woudhuysen (*ShS* 48. 268–87) offers an admirable summary of the debate generated by the SO series, which he describes as representing 'the beginnings of a movement proclaiming the death of the editor and the arrival of the New Textualism'. Responses drew wide-ranging discussion between the proponents not only of the '"bad quartos" are first versions' school but also from the 'editors are agents of textual oppression' faction. The article includes a detailed resumé of Janette Dillon's article in *ShQ* 45 (*YWES* 74.198). Graham Holderness, Brian Loughrey and Andrew Murphy contribute a substantial and closely argued article to this debate: '"What's the Matter?" Shakespeare and Textual Theory' (*TP* 9.93–119). A witty and contentious resumé of the changing face of editing, and of the belief-structures motivating different approaches, is presented through a systematic analysis, from a historical perspective, of the ways in which scholars, from the New Bibliographers onwards, have interpreted the 'material' nature of early printed texts. Holderness et al. re-state the view that the attempted reconstruction of a presumed earlier Text is 'idealism', against 'New Textualists' such as the editors of the OS project, *William Shakespeare: A Textual Companion* (*YWES* 68.216–17). From this, the argument moves to consider those purportedly cultural materialist readings which constitute another kind of idealist position, because reading text as 'an element in a more general process of cultural production' commonly focuses on the early modern printing trade, which thus becomes a 'greater object' to be reached through the text. The article refers at length to a key article by Peter Stallybrass and Margreta de Grazia (*YWES* 74.198). Using the recent multiple editions of *King Lear* as examples, Holderness identifies a school of 'Textual Revisionists', who accommodate the multiplicity of texts by referring all versions back to a single authentic revising author, and 'New Textualists' who feel that, since each textualization has equal value, a modern conflated text is as useful as any, and carries its own virtues. Holderness et al. are not happy with this, calling for any text, whatever its various manifestations, to be seen in relation to the 'historical contingencies of its production'.

Howard Marchitello carries the radicalization of textual studies further in '(Dis)embodied Letters and *The Merchant of Venice*: Writing, Editing, History' (*ELH* 62.237– 65). He faces traditional modes of reconstruction with the problems that follow logically from a recognition that language does not embody authorial intention, and associates the desire to discover the 'true' text with a belief in causality, and in a teleological view of history. He argues that the letters and Portia's father's will, set apart from the text, claim to embody their senders. In this they replicate the assumptions of traditional editors. Marchitello argues further that accidents in a text are significant, and any editorial attempt to adjust these into a more coherent framework involves a falsification of the text as an event (as opposed to the text as an object). Such attempts are often justified by a reconstructed narrative of causality which recuperates the 'accident' as presumed authorial intention. Here on a small scale we have a riveting discussion of the bases of a new kind of textual criticism, which now needs to move beyond conflict with traditional modes and demonstrate what it can offer in its own right. Also on *The Merchant of Venice*, from a textual revision standpoint, is R. J. C. Watt, 'Commendable Silence: A Crux in *The Merchant of Venice*', *NQ* 42.316–17.

Eric Sams in ' "My name's Hamlet, revenge": Why two Dutchmen have the answer to the riddle of Shakespeare's early *Hamlet*'(*TLS* 4829.18), bases his argument on the de Witt drawing of the Swan playhouse of 1596, and on tax records, to claim that the drawing represents the closet scene from *Hamlet*, and that Shakespeare and the Lord Chamberlain's Men were performing at the Swan in that year. A result of this is a challenge to the idea that the text of *Hamlet* published in 1603 is based on memorial reconstruction of a 1599 play. In 'A *Hamlet* Crux', *N&Q* 42.319–20, David Farley-Hills considers the treatment of the hobby-horse.

Also interested in the dating of texts is E. A. J. Honigmann, in 'The First Quarto of *Hamlet* and the date of *Othello*' (*RES* 44.211–19). Honigmann revises Hart's (1935) case for echoes of Q1 *Hamlet* in *Othello*, finding different evidence, but the same conclusion, and thus strengthening the case for dating *Othello* before mid-1602. Within a substantial address to the Bibliographical Society, Peter Davison discusses Q1 of Richard III ('Bibliography: Teaching, Research and Publication. Reflections on Editing the First Quarto of *Richard III*', *Library* 17.1–33). (Davison's edition for CUP is due to be published next year.) Davison argues through a comparison of the roles of Richard, Hastings, Richmond and Buckingham in Q1 and F1 that Q1 is the product of memorial reconstruction and modification for use by a small touring company. A doubling chart and material about theatrical conventions support this argument, showing that ten men and two boys could perform the shortened version. Revision by Shakespeare may also be found. Joan Ozark Holmer's 'Nashe as "Monarch of Witt" and Shakespeare's *Romeo and Juliet*' (*TSLL* 37.314–43) is an extensive essay locating echoes of Nashe's *Have With You to Saffron Walden* in *Romeo and Juliet*. While some of the arguments are suggestive rather than persuasive, and some assertions tendentious, the accumulation of fragments and indications builds a strong case. Pointing out that textual conclusions are inevitably interpretative, Phebe Jensen in 'The Textual Politics of *Troilus and Cressida*', *SQ* 46.414–23, criticizes Gary Taylor's (1982) view of *Troilus and Cressida*, which elevated the status of F over Q. She argues that Taylor's conclusions are driven by a wish to categorize *Troilus and Cressida* as a tragedy rather than a satiric comedy. Jensen sees *Troilus and Cressida* as generically unsettled.

Several articles address very specific textual matters. Gary Taylor, in 'Shakespeare and Others: The Authorship of *Henry VI, Part 1*' (*MRDE* 7.145–205) argues, against Cairncross and others, that the spelling and stage direction habits of four different writers can be detected in the play. One of these is certainly Thomas Nashe, while Shakespeare contributed relatively small sections. Sidney Thomas, in 'The Integrity of *King Lear*' (*MLR* 90.572–84), opposes the current orthodoxy established by Michael Warren (1978) and Gary Taylor (1983) that Q and F are separate plays, or at least that F is a revised version of Q. Thomas considers changes in the final scene of F, where he feels that we are dealing, not with revisions, but with the replacement of omissions and mishearings committed in Q. In many places, Q's errors are attributable to mishearings by a compositor. Thomas thus argues that *Lear*

was 'conceived and written … as an integral work, and left untouched …
except for minor changes made *currente calamo*, or in the course of rehearsal
and initial staging'. This view then becomes part of a more general vision of
Shakespeare as a non-revising author. Robert Clare in ' "Who is it that can tell
me who I am?" ': The Theory of Authorial revision between Quarto and Folio
Texts of *King Lear*' (*Library* 6.xvii.34–59) disagrees with those such as Wells
and Taylor (1986) who believe F to be the result of authorial revision,
demonstrating the theatrical importance of the cut scenes designed to enhance
Edgar's role. He therefore argues for the widespread use of a conflated text.
Richard Knowles in 'Revision Awry in Folio *Lear* 3, i' (*ShQ* 46.32–46),
similarly considers variants between *King Lear*, Act III, scene i, in Q and F, to
involve revisions by one or more people other than Shakespeare. He, like
Clare, disagrees with Gary Taylor and Stephen Urkowitz's view that the
changes in F are improvements, and suggests a clarifying re-sorting of the F
and Q lines to take account of the possibility that some lines are missing from
both. Also on specific points from the texts of *King Lear* are Joseph A. Dance,
' "Which Is the Iustice, which is the Theefe": Variants of Transposition in the
Text(s) of *King Lear*' (*N&Q* 42.322–7) and Penelope Hicks in 'Did Goneril
look "black", "back", or "blank" upon her Father?' (*N&Q* 42.322). T. G.
Bishop in 'Reconsidering a Folio Reading in *Macbeth* 5.1' (*ShQ* 46.78–80) re-
reads 'What need we fear who knows it?' as two questions: 'what need we
fear? who knows it?', on the basis of F1 punctuation, and Davenant's 1663–4
version. Such a reading invites examination of the nature of knowledge.

2. Shakespeare in the Theatre

Anthony B. Dawson's *Hamlet* joins the Shakespeare in Performance series.
The volume is not merely an engaging account of salient productions from
Garrick to Branagh (Adrian Noble's 1992 Barbican production, not the 1997
film) but it assiduously contends that the play is a barometer of various
cultural attitudes to the idea of self: when leading actors 'take on Hamlet', he
writes, 'they help to reveal an era's understanding of subjectivity'. Thus
Dawson demonstrates how Garrick's rational and controlled Hamlet was
fired up by the electrical performances of Kean: 'During the nineteenth
century, Hamlet became a Romantic'. In contrast, Edwin Booth's portrayal
'was generated by, and implicated in, the very capitalist processes to which it
seemed to stand in opposition'. Henry Irving's version, conditioned by the
'cultivation of the private self' which, for Dawson, typifies Victorian culture,
has, he argues, become the dominant way of performing the role (at least in
the Anglo-American tradition). Thus, 'The shifts from Garrick to Kean to
Irving can … be used to trace the fitful trajectory of the human subject … over
almost two centuries'.

Dawson has a good eye for production details. His chapter contrasting an
urbane and intelligent Gielgud with a reckless, unruly Olivier, is especially
stimulating and his reading of Franco Zeffirelli's cinematic version especially
acute as he traces the motif of the glance and the film's Oedipal intricacies.
Dawson notes the inclination of Anglo-American productions towards being
politically disengaged, the emphasis being instead on the 'domestic and
psychological' and demonstrates that nothing could be further from the truth
in the case of continental Europe. Dawson has written an interesting and

worthwhile study though occasionally its cultural contextualization is a little perfunctory.

Rosalyn L. Knutson has a systematic and persuasive piece on the dating of *Hamlet*: 'Falconer to the Little Eyases: A New Date and Commercial Agenda for the "Little Eyases" Passage in *Hamlet*' (*ShQ* 46.1–31), using evidence about the companies' financial structures to argue that Burbage and the Chamberlain's Men had a vested interest in the success of the children of the chapel. Q1 on 'the humor of children' reflects the positive attitude of the Chamberlain's Men towards boy actors in 1599–1600; F's 'little eyases' does not refer to a theatre 'war' in 1599 but was an attempt to limit damage in the form of official sanctions that tactless political remarks in children's plays of 1606–8 threatened to bring down on the King's Men in particular, and the theatre business generally [JB].

Leslie Thomson, in '"With patient ears attend": *Romeo and Juliet* on the Elizabethan Stage' (*SP* 92.230–47), mines the play for the clues it offers as to its staging, though it must be said that his inferences are, at best, tentative. He speculates, for example, that the bed may have remained curtained on stage and later have become the bier. He adduces some verbal evidence – various instances of the sustained parallel between death and sleep – to support this possibility but then adds in a footnote that there is 'no evidence that [this staging] was used here – or in any other play of the period, for that matter'. Too often, Thomson gropes for details of staging by literalizing the text's metaphors. Thus as Juliet descends from the balcony following the departure of Romeo, Thomson notes that the action moves down 'and so it should as the downward movement of Fortune's wheel begins'. His assertion that 'At certain points in *Romeo and Juliet*, perhaps what the characters say was determined as much by the circumstances and conventions of staging as by the themes' is hardly a revelation and, anyway, it is true of any and every other play as well.

In 'Shakespeare in Ashland: 1994' (*ShakB* 13.22–7), Alan Armstrong provides a full and detailed review of the Oregon Shakespeare Festival's fifty-ninth season. The review is usefully descriptive rather than merely judgemental and so will be of use to those theatre historians who were unable to attend. Occasionally, Armstrong is over-colloquial, such as when he notes Ophelia's 'diffident spunkiness'. He draws our attention to several of the season's novel readings such as the playing of Rosencrantz and Guildenstern in Henry Woronicz's *Hamlet* as a heterosexual couple; the way in which Jerry Turner's *The Tempest* 'dignifies Caliban ... in stark contrast to most of the European conspirators'; and the 'especially passive' capture of Conrade and Borachio in *Much Ado* directed by Kirk Boyd, resulting from the way in which 'the conspirators have been reduced to helpless laughter by the ludicrous ineffectuality of the watch'.

3. Criticism

(a) General
Alan C. Dessen's *Rediscovering Shakespeare's Theatrical Vocabulary* is an important addition to the study of Shakespearean staging, which concentrates on stage effects and images that original playgoers would have seen, and which

today tend to get overlooked. For example, Dessen re-examines the entrance of a smiling Malvolio in yellow stockings and cross-gartered, which most modern editions place before Olivia's 'How now, Malvolio?' so that she and the audience see the figure entering at the same time. Dessen points out that in the Folio Malvolio is directed to enter two lines earlier, so the steward overhears Olivia talking about her own madness. This is an example of what Dessen terms 'early entrances' in which 'the original printed text brings in a figure one or two or ten lines before he or she actually speaks or is noticed by those already on the stage'. This is one of the roughly 600 stage directions from English professional plays performed before 1642 which the book explores, and Dessen makes a persuasive case for recovering such signals that have been 'lost in translation'. Aspects of Elizabethan staging practices, such as the symbolic use of 'sick chairs' or thrones, the use of the two or three stage doors in a given playhouse, the practice of conceptual casting and the shared vocabulary among playwrights of theatrical terms, take on a new life. It is to be hoped that such recovered significances will be field-tested at the new Globe on Bankside.

In *Shakespearean Narrative*, Rawdon Wilson states that the pattern of Shakespearean narrative in the plays is 'playful, disruptive and anachronous', and argues that the embedded narratives vary the dramatic action, 'deepen it and paradoxically call attention to the nature of drama itself'. The book explores Shakespeare's narrative procedures in the context of Renaissance narrative theory and practice. A chapter on 'Character' offers a helpful consideration of the subject in relation to classical interior monologue, particularly Ovid, and in another on 'Boundaries', which I found the most suggestive part of the book, Wilson argues that embedded narrative 'interrupts that action, shifts all attention to another fictional world with its distinct time scheme, its own space and its internal characters'. I was disappointed at the absence of analysis of one of the most intriguing instances of Shakespearian narrative: in *The Tempest*, the narrative of the marriage of Claribel to the King of Tunisia.

Eric Sams sets out to recover the first 30 years of the playwright's life in *The Real Shakespeare: Retrieving the Early Years 1564–1594*, and comes up with a Shakespeare born into an illiterate Catholic family 'whose father took him away from school' at 'about thirteen to help out on the family farm', whose experience in the butcher's trade explains much of the imagery of blood in the plays, and was, we are also told, 'clearly named and identified in the Parnassus plays'. There is a good deal of simplistic equation between biographical fact or, more usually, dubious belated record, and textual meaning in the plays. For all the emphasis on 'documentary evidence', Sams relies a great deal on biographical speculation. When, in a chapter entitled 'Butchery and By-Products' Sams reads in *Hamlet* 'When Brutus killed Caesar in the Capitol "it was a brute part of him to kill a calf there"' he pictures the 'young Shakespeare constrained to kill a calf'. But the book does prompt the reader to think about issues which are currently occupying Shakespearean criticism, questions of canonicity, and what constitutes the 'real' Shakespeare or an 'authentic' text, for example.

For examples of less certain statements, John J. Burke Jr provides a useful survey in 'Filling the Blanks of Shakespeare's Biography: A Review Essay' (*SoAR* 60.iii.103–12). There are two notes by David Chandler: in one, he reconsiders eighteenth- and nineteenth-century theories on whether Shakespeare had visited Italy and on speculation about his homosexuality, in 'William Taylor and Some Traditions of Shakespeare Biography' (N&Q 42.338–40); and in 'Upstart Crow: Provenance and Meaning', he suggests that the *Groatsworth* reference to an 'upstart Crow' may 'allude to the clash between Shakespeare and Greene in rather more dramatic terms than has yet been recognized' (N&Q 42.291–4).

Mary A. Blackstone and Cameron Louis offer a suggestive essay, 'Towards "A Full and Understanding Auditory": New Evidence of Playgoers at the Globe' (*ELH.* 556–72) by examining recently discovered contemporary documents connected to a Star Chamber case concerning a group of Globe playgoers in 1612 to question the value of the simple categories of 'privileged' or 'plebeian', 'or even the relative concept of social class in understanding the success and complexity' of a performance text. They suggest that although factors such as birth, title, land holdings and public office could be expected to 'unify the "privileged" perspective, they are equally causes for difference' within the group involved in the incidents recorded in the document – 'the public climax of a private drama'. Other factors, they say, relating to gender, education, wealth and religion also apply: 'We need to talk about the differences between individual playgoers within specific theatres before we can talk with any confidence about the distinctions between collective audiences across different theatres.' An important essay on a topic that merits more of this kind of rigorous examination.

Deborah Barker and Ivo Kamps's (eds) *Shakespeare and Gender: A History* is an anthology of influential essays in Shakespeare feminist criticism. It is a good time to bring out such a volume, and in their introduction to the book the editors offer a survey of the trajectory of feminist criticism, and an assessment of its developments. The essays anthologized here include Coppélia Kahn's 'On the Rape of Shakespeare's Lucrece'; Phyllis Rackin's 'Engendering the Tragic Audience: The Case of *Richard III*'; William Van Watson's 'Shakespeare, Zeffirelli, and the Homosexual Gaze'; Gayle Greene's 'Sexual and Social Tragedy in *Othello*'; Marianne Novy's 'Shakespeare and Emotional Distance in the Elizabethan Family'; Jacqueline Rose's '*Hamlet*, the Mona Lisa of Literature', and an 'Afterword' by Lisa Jardine in which she assesses the significance and progress of feminist criticism, and re-examines the treatment and culpability of Gertrude in *Hamlet* in the light of the significance of surveillance in the closet scene.

Peter J. Smith, in *Social Shakespeare: Aspects of Renaissance Dramaturgy and Contemporary Society*, 'aims at a distinct refocusing of political criticism upon the Shakespearean text as realised in a performance'. Smith discusses the difficulty of defining Shakespearean comedy, and rejects the idea of the 'fatal flaw' because, he says, it is 'essentialist and ahistorical in its assumptions and reactionary and deterministic in its politics' and also because 'there is no need for abstract critical machinery' when Shakespeare 'sites his drama in the physicality of his scripts and the actors speaking them'. The book examines Shakespeare's 'subversive' exploration of the Renaissance idea of gendered geography, sexuality in *Cymbeline*, and linguistic ambiguity and the subversion of patriarchy in *Romeo and Juliet* and *The Two Gentlemen of Verona*. In the final section, Smith offers a thoughtful essay on the specific controversies that *The Merchant of Venice* and *The Jew of Malta* raise in the post-Holocaust period. A chapter on all-male companies in Shakespearean drama insists that 'Shakespeare wanted deliberately to expose the boy beneath the gown', and a final chapter calls for the reform of politically neutral treatment of Shakespeare in the theatre and in education.

Edward Pechter's response to recent conflicts in Shakespearean criticism (what Brian Vickers has famously termed 'contemporary critical quarrels' [*YWES* 74.202–3]) is to urge us to recognize the provisional nature of all critical positions. In *What was Shakespeare? Renaissance Plays and Changing Critical Practice*, Pechter argues against the view of alternative criticism as a triumphant innovation and to the question he himself poses, 'Is the New Historicism "emergent", "dominant" or "residual"?', answers that it is all three. He argues that 'new historicist criticism is a criticism of recognition, of knowing again what one knew before. It is criticism that systematically deprives the text of its capacity to surprise'; and although he goes on to 'acknowledge the enormous interest and energy this kind of criticism has generated', he insists that putting the text back into history is 'far too important to leave to the new historicists'.

Essays I have been unable to see include John S. Hunt's examination of Shakespeare's treatments of the physicality of the human body, 'Embodied Consciousness in Shakespeare' (in Donald E. Morse, ed., *The Delegated Intellect: Emersonian Essays on Literature, Science and Art in Honor of Don Gifford* [Lang]); and Robert Ornstein's 'Shakespeare's Art of Characterization: An Unambiguous Perspective' (in David C. Allen and Robert A. White, eds, *Subjects on the World's Stage: Essays on British Literature of the Middle Ages and the Renaissance*). General pieces that can be mentioned briefly are Edward J. Milowicki and R. Rawdon Wilson's comparative examination of treatments of identity in 'Ovid Through Shakespeare: The Divided Self' (*PoT* 16.ii.217–52). Notes covering general topics are Robert A. Peters's 'Shakespeare's Speech' (*JEngL* 23.245–55), a linguistic approach to the role of pronunciation; Naseeb Shaheen considers whether Shakespeare owned an edition of the Geneva New Testament which ran to 36 editions between 1576–1612 ('Shakespeare and the Tomson New Testament', *N&Q* 42.290–1); Graham Holderness and Andrew Murphy visit ' "Shakespeare Country": The National Curriculum and Literary Heritage' (*CS* 7.110–15); and Louis Marder offers 'Not as Visionary as It Sounds: A Proposal for Co-ordinating Computer Studies of Shakespeare' (*ShN* 45.21–2). Three comparative studies this year are: Haydn Mason on the treatment of Shakespeare in Voltaire (*BJECS* 18.173–84); Thomas F. Van Laan on Shakespeare's influence on Ibsen (*SSEng* 67.287–305); and William Flesch on 'Keats Reading Shakespeare' (*ELH* 62.149–69).

SQ (46.ii) offers a special teaching issue five years after its previous one (*YWES* 71.276–7). In the first section, Peggy O'Brien provides a bibliography on the teaching of Shakespeare up to the present year in ' "And Godly Teach": Books, Articles and a Bibliography on the Teaching of Shakespeare' (165–72). In 'Pedagogy, *Hamlet* and the Manufacture of Wonder' (125–34), Niels Herold examines the critical debate between performance and political criticism in recent years. His point that 'Shakespeare can be more political in the academic press and the classroom than in the traditional theatre of *auteur* directors' is, sadly, demonstrated with every passing RSC season. Edward L. Rocklin examines the effects of the 'performance approach to drama' on the work of Shakespeare teachers in 'Shakespeare Script as a Cue for Pedagogic Invention' (135–44); Russ McDonald provides a platform for four teachers to discuss some current practices in the American High School Classroom in

'Shakespeare goes to High-School'(146–56); and Michael Yogev writes on his teaching experience in the English Department at the University of Haifa and is particularly interesting on the resonances students found in their Shakespeare texts with Israel's current debate on its own 'true' history in '"How shall we find the Concord of the Discord' (157–64). In the second section, Charles A. Hallett provides valuable practical advice on how to train students to 'read' action in 'Scene versus Sequence: Distinguishing Action from Narrative in Shakespeare's Multipartite Scenes' (183–95). David Kennedy Sauer also writes helpfully on ways in which performance-based techniques can be used to explore theoretical questions in '"Speak the speech I pray you", or Suiting the Method to the Moment:A Theory of Classroom Performance of Shakespeare' (173–82). In 'The Universal Is the Specific: Deviance and Cultural Identity in the Shakespeare Classroom', Milla C. Riggio writes about a seminar on *Othello* with a class of 24 students, ten of whom were African-American and Caribbean students of colour (169–209). Hanna Scolnicov writes on 'progressive' or 'radical' intertexuality which 'reverses the traditional perception that a text can be said to be influenced only by its antecedents: the older text can now be filtered through a later text'. In the third section, Martha Tuck Rozett offers ways of 'Creating a Context for Shakespeare with Historical Fiction' (220–7) which she suggests can help students to come to terms with Shakespeare's 'otherness'; Michael J. Collins writes on 'Using Films to Teach Shakespeare' (228–35); and Stephen M. Buhler in 'Texts, Eyes and Videotape: Screening Shakespeare Scripts' writes on his experience of using videotaped excerpts from film and television versions of the plays (236–44).

(b) Comedies and Late Plays
Jonathan Hall's *Anxious Pleasures: Shakespearean Comedy and the Nation State* includes chapters on most of Shakespeare's comedies as well as on *The Jew of Malta* and *Henry IV Parts 1 and 2*. Hall attempts to fuse 'psycho-social' and 'historical' theoretical perspectives to explain how comic drama participates in the formation of the subject of the modern nation state. The joke, he claims, 'is the privileged ... moment of the breakdown of the unifying hold of a discourse within the laughing subject', and Shakespeare's comedies can be read as a critique of the 'unifying perspective' of the imagined community. Hall's very densely theoretical preface and opening chapter is sometimes impenetrable, and beneath the jargon lies some dubiously slippery thinking, even about the very conception of nationhood. On p. 8 the 'narrative of state formation on the basis of nationhood' is described as the 'very antithesis' of the 'power of mercantile capitalism'. Can a narrative be the antithesis of power? or of mercantile capitalism? or does Hall mean that 'nationhood' is the antithesis of mercantile capitalism? If he means the latter, what are we to make of the claim that 'the modern nation state' is the 'political formation' of the 'radically schizophrenic subject of bourgeois culture' for which Shakespearean comedy is 'foundational and constitutive'?

More straightforward is Michael Shapiro's *Gender in Play on the Shakespearean Stage: Boy Heroines and Female Pages*, which argues, against those who would see the cross-dressed figure as an 'emblem of idealised androgyny', that the female page is a 'figure of unfused, discretely layered gender identities ... any one of which could be highlighted at any given moment'. Accordingly, Shapiro is concerned to counter readings which propose uniformity in Shakespeare's treatment of the cross-dressed heroine with an account that claims that in each of the plays discussed in the book (*Two Gentlemen, The Merchant of Venice, As You Like It, Twelfth Night* and *Cymbeline*) Shakespeare invests the figure with different meanings. An introduction to the book reviews different theoretical accounts of cross-dressing in the period; Shapiro's own discussions are situated in a legal as well as a theatrical context: appendixes recount legal records of the punishments meted out to real cross-dressers in the period, as well as literary instances of transvestism.

Both Ivo Kamps's *Materialist Shakespeare* and its companion volume, *Shakespeare and Gender* (the latter edited with Deborah E. Barker) aim to chart changes within the theoretical traditions they respectively cover, reprinting significant essays from the mid-1970s to the mid-1990s and including introductions offering an overview of developments in materialist and in gender criticism, situating interventions on Shakespeare within a broader theoretical context. Both are good anthologies (*Materialist Shakespeare* perhaps a little top-heavy on American critics, and thinner on British ones), and will be useful teaching tools. Essays reprinted with general relevance to the comedies and/or romances are: Marianne Novy's 'Shakespeare and Emotional Distance in the Elizabethan Family' and William C. Carroll's 'The Virgin Not: Language and Sexuality in Shakespeare' (both in *Shakespeare and Gender*), and (in *Materialist Shakespeare*) Stephen Greenblatt's 'Martial Law in the Land of Cockaigne' and Lynda E. Boose's 'Scolding Brides and Bridling Scolds'. Essays on individual plays are mentioned below. The second edition of Kiernan Ryan's *Shakespeare* includes some new material (on *King Lear, Romeo and Juliet* and the histories) as well as a considerably updated bibliography and notes. Peter J. Smith's 'Ajax By Any Other Name Would Smell as Sweet: Shakespeare, Harrington, and Onomastic Scatology' (in André Lascombes, ed., *Tudor Theatre: Emotion in the Theatre*), which offers significations for a number of characters' names, maintaining that scatological naming is not necessarily a sign of Shakespeare's contemptuous attitude to the lower orders, since early modern attitudes to 'faecal language' differed substantially from our own.

Only one essay treated *The Two Gentlemen of Verona* this year. This was Michael D. Friedman's 'To be slow in words is a woman's only virtue' which examined 'Silence and Satire in *The Two Gentlemen of Verona*' (*SPWVSRA* 17[1994].1–9). Friedman proposes that a feminist production of the text might preserve the play's comic element whilst making a political point about the subordination of women in the text by gagging Silvia in the play's final act, Valentine kissing her without noticing that she has a gag over her mouth. *Much Ado About Nothing* was also neglected this year: apart from Carol Cook's ' "The Sign and Semblance of Her Honor": Reading Gender Difference in *Much Ado About Nothing*' (reprinted in *Shakespeare and Gender*), and another essay by Friedman discussed below, the play was treated only by Martin Mueller, who proposes that attention to Shakespeare's use of Bandello offers an alternative reading to feminist claims about the text's containment of female erotic power. Mueller also argues that an examination of Shakespeare's use of various sources across several plays can show how 'stories and ... plays are related [by Shakespeare] as a web of "internal" and "external" sources' ('Shakespeare's Sleeping Beauties: The Sources of *Much Ado About Nothing* and the Play of their Repetitions', *MP* 91.288–311).

Five essays on *The Taming of the Shrew* offer different assessments of the degree to which the play endorses Renaissance patriarchal attitudes. Carolyn E. Brown's is the most liberal interpretation: Kate and Petruchio's lack of conformity to the stereotypes of shrew and shrew tamer results, she claims, from Shakespeare's merging of the shrew tradition with that of the patient Griselda, stories of whom draw attention not to the desirability of female submission, but rather to male cruelty. This allows her to posit a subversive subtext in *The Taming* wherein Shakespeare 'makes his audience feel uncertain ... about Katherine's future safety' ('Katherine of *The Taming of the Shrew*: "A Second Grissel"', *TSLL* 37.285–313). Wayne A. Rebhorn's discussion of 'Petruchio's "Rope Tricks": *The Taming of the Shrew* and the Renaissance Discourse of Rhetoric' proposes that the play 'critiques the very discourse of rhetoric which it evokes', rejecting the claims of Renaissance rhetoricians, and enabling Katherine 'to subvert ... the male authority which otherwise threatens to possess her'; in *The Taming* 'qualities [elsewhere] imagined as distinguishing men and women do not inhere in either sex, since both sexes are capable of manifesting them' (*MP* 92.294–327). Two essays which compare later plays both end up pointing to the more conservative aspects of the earlier play. Molly Easo Smith uses *The Taming* to examine the politics of Fletcher's *The Woman's Prize*, concluding that the later play revises the argument of the earlier one, recognizing that 'male tyranny and female silence do not constitute universally desirable social norms' ('John Fletcher's Response to the Gender Debate': *PLL* 31.38–60), whilst Sid Ray looks at 'Containment Metaphors in Renaissance Marriage Tracts, *The Taming of the Shrew*, and *The Maid's Tragedy*' to conclude that Shakespeare's play replicates the marriage tract insistence on the literal and figurative containment of the unruly female body which *The Maid's Tragedy* wants to critique ('Holy Knots', *SPWVSRA* 18.1–27). Dennis S. Brooks also sees the play as endorsing the desirability of governing threats to social order, examining 'The Varieties of Education in *The Taming of the Shrew*' to argue that Shakespeare rejects two Renaissance pedagogies (rote learning and private tutorials) in favour of an 'eikastic education' where the the theatre operates as a model classroom, taming 'humanity's asocial passions in the interests of civility'. In his view, Petruchio really is taking 'reverend care' of Katherine when he prevents her from eating and sleeping ('"To Show Scorn Her Own Image"', *RMR* 48 [1994].7–32). Lynda E. Boose's 'Scolding Brides and Bridling Scolds' and Leah Marcus's 'The Shakespearean Editor as Shrew Tamer' are reprinted, respectively, in *Materialist Shakespeare* and in *Shakespeare and Gender*.

The general aim of the Macmillan's New Casebooks is to offer students a selection of essays embodying 'new critical approaches ... [and illuminating] the rich interchange between critical theory and critical practice that characterises so much current writing about literature'. Richard Dutton's New Casebook *A Midsummer Night's Dream* begins with David Bevington's account of love and magic in the play, offered to us here as implicit critique of Jan Kott, and as exemplary of the voice of the 'traditional reader' against whose assumptions of consensus the more theoretical pieces which follow are to pit themselves. Theoretical approaches covered in this volume are: Marxism (Elliot Krieger), psychoanalysis (Norman N. Holland), feminism (Shirley Nelson Garner), new historicism (Louis Adrian Montrose), the play in performance (Philip C. McGuire), textual/ editorial criticism (Barbara Hodgdon), class and the carnivalesque (Annabel Patterson), cultural materialism (Richard Wilson, whose piece is described, rather depressingly, as 'post-Marxist') and deconstruction (Terence Hawkes). Dutton's introduction attempts to specify the points of agreement and disagreement between these critical positions, and also to explain some of the theoretical underpinnings of the various arguments, as do the brief notes which follow each essay. An annotated bibliography lists material both specifically on the play and more generally on Shakespeare.

SunHee Kim Gertz's densely written, and highly theoretical, discussion of 'Authorial Audiences in Shakespeare's *A Midsummer Night's Dream*' (*Sem* 106.153–70) claims that in the play 'Shakespeare presents ... tensions between ... dramatic and performance texts as critical, [exploring], from the perspective of authorship, how such tensions may generate meaning'; Shakespeare realizes, Gertz argues, that theatrical audiences use 'shared conventions to refashion what is before their very eyes': 'how audiences read', she concludes, 'determines how the literary system and drama are re-envisioned and transformed'. Rather more traditionally, Barbara Baruzzo discusses 'Ovidian Tales of Love and Metamorphosis' in the play, arguing that Shakespeare adopts a metamorphic method in *A Midsummer Night's Dream*, condensing into eight lines a whole series of Ovidian tales concerning romantic metamorphoses ('Ten Little Fabulae' *CahiersE* 45 [1994].21–31), whilst Anthony Brian Taylor resumes an interest in Shakespeare's use of early translators of the classics in 'Bottom's "Hopping" Heart and Thomas Phaer' (*N&Q* 42.309–15); in the same volume, W. L. Godshalk proposes that 'Bottom's "Hold or Cut Bow-Strings" (*A Midsummer Night's Dream* I.II.106)' is a comically pretentious use of a military metaphor (*N&Q* 42.315–16). Another note by Michael Ray Taylor offers a brief commentary on Theseus's 'airy nothing' speech ('Shakespeare's *A Midsummer Night's Dream*', *Expl* 54.4–5). William H. L. Godsalve's *Britten's A Midsummer Night's Dream: Making an Opera from Shakespeare's Comedy* focuses almost entirely on the opera, and is little concerned with Shakespeare's play. Also appearing in *CompD* (29.91–107) was Frederick Kiefer's speculation that the identity of the singers of the songs of 'Spring and Winter in *Love's Labour's Lost*' derives from early modern iconographic art, in particular, woodcuts, etchings and engravings. David Chandler argues that the source for the 'text' to which Nathaniel refers in Act 4 of the play is an Epicurean maxim ('The "Text" at *Love's Labour's Lost* IV.ii.160', *N&Q* 42.307–9).

Last year, I neglected Grace Tiffany's excellent essay ' "That Reason Wonder May Diminish": *As You Like It*, Androgyny, and the Theatre Wars' (*HLQ* 57 [1994].213–39). This essay offers a well-argued case for adding *As You Like It* to the list of Shakespeare's interventions in the 'theatre wars', claiming that in 'dismissing both the anti-comic impulses of romantic idealization and satiric misogyny, Shakespeare dismisses ... Jonson', embracing instead, the irrational erotic sensibility which connects the members of the audience as an antidote to human suffering. Rather weaker was Gene Fendt's 'Resolution, Catharsis, Culture' (*P&L* 19.248–60), which posits, unconvincingly, the operation of different kinds of catharsis in the text, and whose odd conclusions are matched by its odd phrasing: Emily Dickinson finds her way into a footnote of this article, where she is described as 'that poor mild virgin'. In a somewhat unfocused piece, Juliet Dusinberre asks what the women in Shakespeare's audience really wanted ('As *Who* Liked It?' *ShS* 46.9–21), positing intertextual links between the play, *The Shepheardes Calender*,

Rabelais, and the writings of Sir John Harington to claim that the play 'rewrite[s] the record of female desire so that women want to read it ... releasing into the auditorium an eroticism constantly open to revision by women'. David Chandler notes some similarities between 'An Incident from Greene's *Alphonsus* [and] *As You Like It*' (*N&Q* 42.317–19), and finally, Louis Montrose's essay on 'The Place of a Brother in *As You Like It*' is reprinted in *Materialist Shakespeare*.

Like Dutton's *A Midsummer Night's Dream* (see above), R. S. White's New Casebook on *Twelfth Night* also begins with an outline of contemporary issues in critical theory. White's introduction, however, is considerably weaker than Dutton's. I found it difficult to make sense of sentences like this: 'it might be superficially concluded that there are violent quarrels between critics who are even ostensibly of the same persuasion, but I would argue that each approach, in a sense, could not exist without the other, since the fundamental concentration on underlying ideologies, and the rejection of traditional habits, such as seeking unity and claiming the existence of universals, are swept away'. In an introduction of merely 15 pages this kind of confusion should have been eradicated; similarly, a theoretically informed introduction might surely be expected to adopt a more nuanced usage of the theoretical terminology it employs (such as 'ideology': here, as throughout, used as it would be in the *Sunday Times*). Perhaps most confusing of all to a student would be White's claim that 'all of the ... writers in this collection [are] ... reader response critics'. Those writers are, incidentally, Geoffrey Hartman, Elliot Krieger, Michael D. Bristol, Leonard Tennenhouse, Stephen Greenblatt, Dympna Callaghan, Cristina Malcolmson and Barbara Everett. Notes on individual articles are shorter than Dutton's; the bibliography is sometimes (very briefly) annotated (*Rabelais and His World* 'became very influential in the West because it complements Barber and Frye') but more often not.

Therese Steffen, in 'Modes of Iteration in Shakespeare's Plays: The "Hanging-Love" Cluster' (*ShJ* 131.128–37) uses linguistic analysis based on translation theory, identifying a word-cluster in which 'love'-related words (such as 'marry', 'cuckoldry' and 'whoredom') are associated with words related to 'hanging', and tracing it through *Twelfth Night* I.v.16 and 14 other plays [JB].

In 'Filming Shakespeare in a cultural thaw' (*TPr* 9.325–47), Laurie E. Osborne examines Russian films of *Twelfth Night* and *Othello* produced immediately subsequent to Stalin's death. Both productions, Osborne argues, 'place more emphasis on the loyalty and betrayal of male bonds than of other motivations', using such bonds to thematize and ultimately to contain the response to Stalin's betrayal. Film is also, in part, the concern of Jonathan Crewe's essay, 'In the Field of Dreams', which uses *Twelfth Night* as a touchstone for a consideration of the transvestite politics of *The Crying Game* (*Rep* 50.101–21). The figure of the transvestite, Crewe argues, is central to the way in which both texts reconfigure the sex-gender field in male universal terms: in *Twelfth Night* the apparent threat to the hegemonic marriage plot represented in the complex of desires surrounding Viola/Cesario is in fact 'the preliminary condition for any reconstruction ... of the marriage plot'. Joseph Pequigney's 'The Two Antonios and Same-Sex Love in *Twelfth Night* and *The Merchant of Venice*' is reprinted in *Shakespeare and Gender*. Finally, in 'Malvolio and the Eunuchs' (*ShS* 46[1994].23–34) John Astington reads Malvolio as a parodic festival figure, and juxtaposes his letter with Matthew 19 to argue that in the 'some are born great' sentence, Malvolio is being warned of the futility of his desires for marriage.

Avraham Oz's *The Yoke of Love: Prophetic Riddles in The Merchant of Venice* argues that in the play 'the traffic of subjectivity is channelled along the signifying chain informed by the ideological signifiers of semantic representation' and that 'the major rhetorical instrument whereby such dramatic moves are channelled is the prophetic riddle, constantly challenging the dramatic subjects to transgress their accepted identities through acts of symbolic interpretations'. The prophetic riddle, according to Shapiro, is a subversive rhetorical device, particularly useful in countering the authority of the Law of the Father. The best article on *The Merchant of Venice* this year was Howard Marchitello's '(Dis)Embodied Letters and *The Merchant of Venice*: Writing, Editing, History' (*ELH* 62.237–65), which constructs a provocative argument concerning the status of the accident in the text. Centring his article around the problem of the characters Solanio, Salerio and Salarino, Marchitello concludes with a plea for 'unediting'; along the way he offers some spectacular insights on various 'letters' in the play. Also good was Stephen A. Cohen's '"The Quality of Mercy": Law, Equity and Ideology in *The Merchant of Venice*' (*Mosaic* 27[1994].35–54). Reading the text as staging a contest between competing claims of equity and common law, he argues that this reflects a battle between the large landowners, epitomized in the Crown and in the play's Christians, and the 'rising class' of merchants, represented in the text by Shylock (these terms are, not entirely successfully, distinguished in Cohen's argument from aristocracy and bourgeoisie). Walter Cohen's earlier Marxist account of the play, '*The Merchant of Venice* and the Possibilities of Historical Criticism' is reprinted in *Materialist Shakespeare*.

Several other pieces appeared this year on *The Merchant*, but none of these was anywhere near as strong as the two articles just discussed. Robert Zaslavsky's ' "Which is the Merchant here? and which the Jew?": Keeping the Book and Keeping the Books in *The Merchant of Venice*' (*Judaism* 44.181–92) is aimed mainly at a non-academic audience, but includes some interesting comments on the derivation of the names in the play. Lisa Burrell discusses the links between 'Wealth and Desire' in the play (*SPWVSRA* 18.75–89), arguing that women and money are both 'slippery objects of desire' in the text, and offering a liberal reading of the relationship between Portia and Bassanio, claiming that Portia 'maintains a balance by exercising ownership only over the self, and in that way, protecting it'. Michel Jay Willson claims to focus on 'A View of Justice in Shakespeare's *The Merchant of Venice* and *Measure for Measure*' (*NDLR* 70.695–726) but might usefully have condensed his argument and eradicated the plot summary in it. He concludes that both plays are allegorical, *The Merchant* representing the triumph of Christian mercy over Judaic justice, *Measure* showing, through the 'Heavenly ideal' represented by the Duke, how justice can only be achieved when the law is applied with mercy. R. J. C. Watt proposes emending Antonio's apparently corrupt 'It is that any thing now' at 1.i.113 to 'It is that in anything now' ('Commendable Silence: A Crux in *The Merchant of Venice*', *N&Q* 42.316–17).

Two pieces from last year focused on the dialogue between Jessica and Lorenzo in Act 5. Paul Gaudet asks what the 'alternative stories' of romantic tragedy referred to by the lovers have to do with them and with the play as a whole, and argues that the lovers are engaging in a status competition with each other, Lorenzo seeking to affirm patriarchal norms of possession whilst

Jessica tries to subvert them (' "A Little Night Music": Intertextuality and Status in the Nocturnal Exchange of Jessica and Lorenzo', *EiTET* 13[1994] 3–14). Matthew Fike argues that the tragic allusions denote disappointment's ascendancy in the 'universe of the play', disappointment being 'the burden of mortality', 'full enjoyment [abiding] only ... in the realization of divine love' ('Disappointment in *The Merchant of Venice*' *ANQ* 7 [1994] 7.13–17). Olivia Delgado de Torres offers some 'Reflections on Patriarchy and the Rebellion of Daughters in Shakespeare's *Merchant of Venice* and *Othello*' (*Interpretation* 21[1994].333–51) observing that Brabantio sees Desdemona as his property, that there may be 'a similarity between the relationships of father and daughter and of husband and wife', and that Jessica is mean to Shylock. In 'Shylock and the Struggle for Closure' John Picker defends the politics of Shakespeare's representation of Shylock by positing an analogous relationship in the play between 'Jewish usurers ... and the place of marginal figures in the model of Shakespearean comedy as expressed by C. L. Barber' (*Judaism* 43[1994].173–89). Finally, *ShS* 48 included a couple of articles addressing the ways in which the play has functioned in times of especially strong anti-Semitism. In 'Wilhelm S and Shylock', Laurence Lerner looks at Nazi appropriations of the play in pre-war Germany to ask how writing an anti-Semitic play differs from offering an anti-Semitic interpretation of one, concluding that since 'a play is a representation of social behaviour, not an explanation of it' its politics will ultimately rest in audiences' various responses to it (*ShS* 48.61–8). And in 'Shakespur and the Jewbill' James Shapiro argues that the play became 'a powerful weapon in the arsenal of those opposed to the naturalization of Jews in England', and that the Jewish Naturalization Act of 1753 'was instrumental in the creation of a Shakespeare who ... [is] bound up with fantasies of social exclusion and cultural longing' (*ShS* 48.51–60).

The single article on *The Merry Wives of Windsor* this year was Leslie S. Katz's '*The Merry Wives of Windsor*: Sharing the Queen's Holiday' (*Rep* 51.77–93), which reads the play, in the context of *Henry IV 1 and 2*, as 'Shakespeare's meditation on the afterlife of dramatic characters', examining the way in which the 'local drama' of *Merry Wives* figures, or is figured in, the national drama of the history play, and claiming that the 'usurpation ... of one history by the other happens at the level of poetic image or device'.

Michael D. Friedman published two articles on *All's Well That Ends Well* this year. In 'Male Bonds and Marriage in *All's Well* and *Much Ado*' (*SEL* 35.231–49) he invokes *Much Ado* as a 'shadow text' to demonstrate the significance of performance choices made in modern productions of *All's Well*, in particular, the problem of the play's (and its audiences') final attitude to Bertram. In underplaying the preservation of male bonds and exaggerating the influence of Parolles, modern productions attempt to shore up a romantic vision of the marriage between Bertram and Helena, whereas the text, Friedman claims, subordinates those romantic interests to the importance of homosocial and political ties. In ' "Service is no heritage": Bertram and the Ideology of Procreation' (*SP* 92.80–101) he pursues a similar argument, claiming that performances of the play have tended to minimize the conflictual elements which inhabit the written text (such as that between the desire for illicit sexual encounters and the 'social obligation to father male heirs'). Willem Schrick (*All's Well That Ends Well* in its Historical Context', *ShJ* 131.106–15) locates echoes from contemporary letters, including a newly discovered letter from James I to Archduke Albert of Austria, to argue that the play can be related significantly to the peace negotiations and the Somerset House conference of 19 August 1604 [JB]. *All's Well* was also the subject of one of the chapters of Sally B. Porterfield's *Jung's Advice to the Players*. In 'The Anima as Trickster in *All's Well*' she reads Helena as the trickster/ healer/ saviour in the play, and Bertram as the *puer aeternus*, acting out his dead father's unrealized desire. The argument unfortunately, gets profoundly silly at the end of the chapter, when Porterfield suggests that a modern production of the play might costume Helena in 'early-twentieth-century safari gear' (including pith helmet) and have her 'give birth onstage, not to an infant, but to a pillow, which she hands to the astounded Bertram before running offstage toward freedom'.

Porterfield also includes a chapter on *Measure for Measure*; once again, she reads each of the play's characters as corresponding to a different Jungian archetype (Angelo, false virtue; Claudio, natural man; Pompey, trickster and so forth). Jungian readings often seem to approach literary texts as if they were packs of tarot cards; Porterfield's is no exception to this rule. *Measure*, Porterfield argues, 'shows the effect of complete shadow suppression and the ways in which such unrealistic expectations can result in possession by those qualities we most want to avoid'. Also reappearing with an article on *Measure for Measure* was Michael D. Friedman, whose '"O, let him marry her"' (*SQ* 46.454–64) discussed 'Matrimony and Recompense in *Measure for Measure*', arguing that the explanation for Vincentio's proposal to Isabella lies in his desire to atone for the sexual offence he has caused her, that offence being to insist that she makes the false declaration of having slept with Angelo, a declaration which, Friedman claims, taints her socially. Another aspect of the Duke's motivation was treated by David Thatcher, whose 'Questionable Purpose in *Measure for Measure: A Test of Seeming or a Seeming Test*' (*ELR* 25.26–44) argued (I thought unconvincingly) that Vincentio does not intend to test Angelo, and that the word 'seemers' in the Duke's crucial lines ('Hence we shall see/ If power change purpose, what our seemers be') refers not to Angelo but to other Viennese hypocrites, or to the Duke himself. Thatcher's other contribution this year, a discussion of 'natural guiltiness' in the play, was somewhat more convincing. Here he aims to expose what he sees as the 'moral, logical, and legal absurdities inherent in the "natural guiltiness" theme' (i.e. the phenomenon of a judge condemning someone for a crime he himself is guilty of), drawing a distinction between the exhibition of forgiveness (a legitimate consequence of natural guiltiness) and of mercy (an inappropriate response to the recognition of one's own culpability) ('Mercy and "Natural Guiltiness" in *Measure for Measure*', *TSLL* 37.264–84).

The relation between judging another and judging oneself is also taken up by Louis Burkhardt's thoughtful, and thought-provoking, discussion of 'Spectator Seduction' in the play (*TSLL* 37.236–63). Using Girardian theories of mimetic desire and monstrous doubling, Burkhardt analyses relations between different characters in *Measure for Measure* to justify his claim that 'the ... doubling that occurs among the characters is mirrored by the emotional doubling that occurs between the characters and *Measure*'s spectators' who are 'contaminat[ed] with fear and ... pitilessness'. This was one of the best articles I read this year: intelligent, original and challenging. Of the other essays on the play, two treated it in terms of other, comparable texts. A. D. Harvey looked at Davenant's rewriting of the play to argue that modern audiences are not the only ones to have had problems with Isabella's extreme aversion to sex ('Virginity and Honour in *Measure for Measure* and Davenant's *The Law Against Lovers*', *ES* 75[1994].123–32) and Ivo Kamps juxtaposes the play with Thomas Middleton's *The Phoenix* to attack cultural-materialist views of the Duke as sinister and controlling; for early modern audiences, he claims, 'the basic premise of a ruler who [operates] ... by means of guile ... was not nearly so distasteful' as it might be to us, but rather, comforted in its fulfilment of a fantasy of political security ('Ruling Fantasies and the Fantasies of Rule: *The Phoenix* and *Measure for Measure*', *SP* 92.248–73). In 'Mortality and Mercy in Vienna' (*ESC* 21.375–92), Mark Fortier uses the play to defend the applicability of Foucauldian theory to the reading of early modern literary texts, claiming that the play manifests the movement Foucault has posited from the 'right of death' to the 'power over life'.

'On the first day of class, I tell my Shakespeare students that experiencing Shakespearean drama is like having sex: none of it's bad, just some of it's better.' Jayne Carducci and Vicki Boynton's account of a pedagogical exercise (the mock trial) they have found useful in the teaching of the play is not as bad as its opening sentences would lead one to expect, although I never did warm to its casual tone (' "Let My Trial Be Mine Own Confession": Angelo and the Mock Trial Experience in the College Classroom', *SPWVSRA* 17[1994].104–11). David Chandler suggests 'Robertoes Tale', from Greene and/or Chettle's *Groats-worth of Witte* as a source for the play's bed-trick (*N&Q* 42.320–1).

Two somewhat different accounts of *The Winter's Tale* read the play in a political context. C. B. Hardman argues for an analogy between the play's harmonious conclusion and early seventeenth-century beliefs in the restoration of an Apollonian Golden Age ('Shakespeare's *The Winter's Tale* and the Stuart Golden Age', *RES* 45[1994].69–79); Daryl W. Palmer, in an interesting essay, pursues a strategy of 'attenuated reading' to defend his claim that within the play's treatment of discursive fields such as winter, tyranny and knowledge lie identifications with Muscovy, invoked as an 'imperfect analogue' to England ('Jacobean Muscovites: Winter, Tyranny and Knowledge in *The Winter's Tale*', *SQ* 46.323–39). Ian MacKillop applies Byron's 'only-child-as-orphan' idea to characterize Leontes in his '*The Winter's Tale* and Orphans of the Heart' (*UCEPLL* 2.25–8); Verna A. Foster argues that through his manipulation of 'Tragicomic Dramaturgy in *The Winter's Tale*' Shakespeare allows his audience to anticipate, emotionally, the resurrection of Hermione, since the audience's desires for that resurrection are fostered and encouraged throughout the text ('The "Death" of Hermione', *CahiersE* 48.43–56).

Two articles on *The Winter's Tale* appeared in *ShS* 46 (1994). In his rather commonsensical 'Reconstructing *The Winter's Tale*' Kenneth C. Bennett uses the play to attack deconstructive notions of 'a limbo of undecideability' embodied, for him, in articles on the play by Howard Felperin and Joyce Wexler; 'deconstructing unity,' he concludes, 'is like cutting off the Hydra's head: more unities will spring into being to take its place' (81–90). Whilst Valerie Traub's earlier essay on male anxiety about female erotic power, 'Jewels, Statues and Corpses' is reprinted in *Shakespeare and Gender*, Lawrence Danson examines jealous husbands in *Othello*, *The Winter's Tale* and *Cymbeline* to argue that the representation of self and other in these plays moves from an earlier figuration 'as an economic and social phenomenon toward an interiorized correlative which yields the repertoire of the modern psychological subject': such subjectivity itself a function of masculinist constructions of the 'threateningly foreign country of women' (69–79).

Also on *Cymbeline* was Jodi Mikalachki's discussion of 'Early Modern English Nationalism' in the play, a complex essay which focused on the masculine embraces which often conclude Jacobean dramas set in Roman Britain. Such embraces, Mikalachki claims, are contingent on the exorcism of a savage female figure who has in the text led British resistance to Rome, and who thus articulates (despite her expulsion) British patriotism ('The Masculine Romance of Roman Britain', *SQ* 46.301–22). Danielle Clarke is also interested in the play's connections with nation; in her note on the play, she proposes that North's Plutarch serves as a common source for *Cymbeline* II.iv and *Antony and Cleopatra* II.ii, and for similarities between Cleopatra and Cymbeline's Queen (*N&Q* 42.329–31). In the same volume, John Boe argues that Ezekiel 17 is the source for the 'lofty cedar' of the play's riddle (*N&Q* 42.331–4). In a note on *Pericles*, L. M. Anderson proposes that Edmund Dudley's *Tree of Commonwealth* is the source for Cerimon's words on 'Virtue and Cunning' (*N&Q* 42.327–9).

The Tempest once again garnered a great deal of interest, although more than one critic expressed a challenge to the now hegemonic new historicist account of the play represented by articles such as Stephen Greenblatt's 'Martial Law in the Land of Cockaigne' reprinted in *Materialist Shakespeare*. Donald Bruster, for instance, argues that the most salient sources of the play lie in the dramatist's experience of working in the Globe and the Blackfriars playhouses, and that the inspiration for the figure of Caliban came from the tensions between Shakespeare and Will Kemp; an interpretation of the text which emphasizes such local aspects, he claims, qualifies (if not negates) a thoroughly colonialist reading of it ('Local *Tempest*: Shakespeare and the work of the early modern playhouse', *JMRS* 25.33–53). In a much less focused piece, Peter Holland reiterates the need to attend to 'the play's form, its dramatic structure, its scenic method, to work, that is, unfashionably close to the play as a theatrical object' in his 'The Shapeliness of *The Tempest*' (*EIC* 45.208–29).

Interest in the colonial discourses of the play, however, continued to dominate discussion of this text. Arthur F. Kinney, in the context of a wider discussion of matters such as the relation between texts and events, raises some questions about the status of the Strachey letter as source for *The Tempest*, and proposes some other possible sources: a letter written by James Rosier, Henry Smith's *First Sermon on the punishment of Jonah*, and the display, in London, of captive Native Americans brought back by the explorers ('Revisiting *The Tempest*', *MP* 93.161–77). A weaker (and inadequately focused) essay by Jean-Marie Maguin looks at '*The Tempest* and Cultural Exchange'; unlike Kinney, Maguin accepts the status of the Strachey letter, whose substance he takes 'as defining a new type of cultural exchange' different from commercial negotiation (*ShS* 48.147–54). In the same volume, Jonathan Bate examines Caribbean appropriations of the play, especially that by Edward Braithwaite, and argues that Ariel's voice has been silenced by critical concentration on Caliban ('Caliban and Ariel Write Back', *ShS* 48.155–62). Bate's claim that 'the Caribbean appropriation of *The Tempest* still remains unknown to many' is rather starkly at odds with Thomas Cartelli's contention that 'the practice of postcolonial writers to "write back" to the centre has … been exhaustively documented, especially with respect to *The Tempest*'; Cartelli examines the appropriation of the play by Michelle Cliff in her novel, *No Telephone to Heaven* ('After *The Tempest*: Shakespeare, Postcoloniality, and Michelle Cliff's New, New World Miranda', *ConL* 36.82–102). And in what I thought was one of the two best articles on the play this year, Jonathan Baldo offers a wide-ranging account of the way that the play's interest in memory is linked to its colonial contexts, and 'how the numerous forms of vanishing in the play reinforce its status as English literature's urtext about colonization'. Baldo's is a rich and consistently intelligent reading of the play, and, well written, a pleasure to read ('Exporting Oblivion in *The Tempest*', *MLQ* 56.111–44).

Also extremely good was Howard Felperin's 'Political Criticism at the Crossroads: The Utopian Historicism of *The Tempest*', which appeared in Nigel's Wood's volume for the OU 'Theory in Practice' series. Felperin's essay uses *The Tempest* to defend his contention that apparent irreconcilabilities between, on the one hand, idealist/ formalist approaches to texts and, on the other, historicist/ materialist perspectives on them can be bridged through the invocation of Jameson's theory of the 'political unconscious' of literature; two key terms in his own analysis of the play are 'ideological' and 'utopian'. I found this an elucidating reading of the play in its own right, and also, for students, a very good introduction to the Marxist theory Felperin discusses. The book is worth ordering for your library for this essay alone, but also strong was Richard P. Wheeler's 'Fantasy and History in *The Tempest*' which uses psychoanalytic theory to examine the ways in which the play 'remembers its own past, with how *The Tempest* looks back on, and takes its place within, Shakespearean history'. Like Felperin, John Turner also focuses his essay on the tension between idealist and materialist readings of the play, using Bruno Bettelheim's *The Uses of Enchantment* and Malinowski's 'Myth in Primitive Psychology' to argue that the play is at once healing (and wish-fulfilling) dream, and, in 'the intractability of its conflicts and the implausibility of its conclusion, dream interpretation ('Reading by Contraries: *The Tempest* as Romance' in *The Tempest*). The other essay in the book is Charles H. Frey's 'Embodying the Play', which describes his own methodology in *Experiencing Shakespeare*, and attacks all his other fellow contributors on the grounds that none of them 'goes beyond practice of theory to a genuine theory of student readerly practice'.

Although the general conception of the 'Theory in Practice' series – which aims to introduce students to particular theoretical issues through the explicit application of such theories to the same text – is one which most of us would welcome as a valuable teaching aid, I am not sure this objective was as well fulfilled as it might have been. Felperin's essay in particular might serve as an exemplar for how one ought to go about fulfilling this function, but the apparatus of the book as a whole was not successful. Each essay is preceded by a foreword by Wood, and followed by the transcription of a dialogue between Wood and the author; Wood also provides an introduction and an 'endpiece' to the book as a whole. All this could have been very useful, but in none of these pieces were the issues at stake clearly enough signposted for a student reader. Most of my own students would feel quite lost in these sections, and would also be intimidated by the numerous references to both primary and theoretical texts they could not be expected to have read.

Two articles this year treated music in *The Tempest*. Pierre Iselin's '"My Music For Nothing": Musical Negotiations in *The Tempest*' offered some observations of the way in which the play's music 'may be said to articulate several discursive voices: those of myth and praise, that of *furor*, but also that of disruption and scepticism' (*ShS* 48.135–45) whilst Peggy Muñoz Simonds, in a more developed piece, claims that in the play Shakespeare wants to illustrate 'those aspects of Renaissance kingship that must be corrected if the monarchy is to survive'; she focuses her argument around the play's adoption of the images of Orpheus and of the ideal commonwealth as melodious garden ('"Sweet Power of Music": The Political Magic of "the Miraculous Harp" in Shakespeare's *The Tempest*', *CompD* 29.61–90). Brian Gibbons argues that interruption is the 'key to Shakespeare's dramatic originality in *The Tempest*', being also an expression of power, since all interruption in the play is effected by Prospero ('*The Tempest* and Interruptions', *CahiersE* 45[1994].47–58). In a note on 'The Costumes of Caliban and Ariel Qua Sea-Nymph' Michael Baird Saenger proposes that two costumes used in a pageant celebrating Prince Henry's investiture as Prince of Wales, were, in part, the inspirational seeds for the figures of Caliban and Ariel (*N&Q* 42.334–6). Ann Thompson's ' "Miranda, Where's Your Sister?": Reading Shakespeare's *The Tempest*' is reprinted in *Shakespeare and Gender*.

(c) Poems
The best article on the *Sonnets* was Margreta De Grazia's 'The Scandal of Shakespeare's Sonnets' (*ShS* 46[1994].35–49), the most successful aspect of this essay being its attempt to introduce categories of class and race into the reading of a sequence usually read principally in terms of a binary, gendered, division. This is pursued in defence of De Grazia's claim that 'the love of the youth ... which tradition has deemed scandalous promotes a social pro-gramme while the love for the mistress ... which tradition has allowed threatens to annihilate it'. In 'Truth and Decay in Shakespeare's Sonnets' (*CahiersE* 47.43–53), James Dawes reads the young man as a figure for 'the very possibility of belief', whose fallibility thus generates the speaker's fasci-nation with death in the first section of the sequence. Katherine Duncan-Jones examines the implications of the words 'fild' and 'mynuits' in 1609 *Sonnets* to criticize editorial modernization, and, implicitly, to defend her contention that the copy-text for the edition was Shakespeare's own manuscript ('Filling the Unforgiving Minute: Modernizing SHAKE-SPEARES SONNETS (1609)', *EIC* 45.199–207) whilst Barry Nass notes an 'Etymological Wordplay in Shakespeare's Sonnet 68' between 'robbery' and 'robe' ('Robbing No Old To Dress His Beauty New', *ANQ* 8.8–11). Rather longer a contribution was A. D. Wraight's *The Story that the Sonnets Tell*, at over 585 pages. Wraight is quite unabashed about his conviction that the only way to read the Sonnets is to take them entirely literally; he thinks Marlowe is the poet of the sonnets and of everything else Shakespearean.

In 'Death By Rhetorical Trope: Poetry Metamorphosed in *Venus and Adonis* and the Sonnets' Pauline Kiernan examines Shakespeare's treatment of his Ovidian source material to argue that Shakespeare invokes these sources in order to conduct a 'self-conscious exploration of the nature of poetic identity, and of his own role as a dramatist in literary history' (*RES* 46.475–501). Catherine Belsey reads *Venus and Adonis* as a 'literary *trompe-l'oeil*' which 'promises a definitive account of love but ... withholds the finality that such a promise might lead us to expect' ('Love as *Trompe-l'oeil*: Taxonomies of Desire in *Venus and Adonis*', *ShQ* 46.257–76);

Belsey's argument here involves, amongst other things, an account of the way in which critics have traditionally reproduced the values ascribed to Adonis in the text, whilst the text itself does not. Like Kiernan, Jennifer Laws is interested in Shakespeare's relation with his Ovidian sources: in combining the genres of the Ovidian narrative and the woman's complaint, she argues, Shakespeare allows a subversive feminist voice to undercut the more patriarchal framework of *The Rape of Lucrece* ('Paradoxes of Possession in Shakespeare's *Lucrece*', *Parergon* 13.53–68). Coppélia Kahn's 'The Rape in Shakespeare's *Lucrece*' is reprinted in *Shakespeare and Gender*.

(d) Histories

Falstaff in particular, and the *Henry IV* plays in general, were the subject of much comment this year, with a notable emphasis on praising Hal, often at the expense of his former companions. In 'The Sentimentalizing of *Communitas* in Kenneth Branagh's *Henry* V' (*SB* 13.i.35–6), Patricia P. Salomon argues that, while Henry V 'takes great pains ... to establish the closest possible rapport with his troops at Agincourt', the Branagh film, 'both minimizes and sentimentalizes the anti-social behaviour of the Boar's Head Tavern characters', thus 'problematizing Henry's already demonstrated maturity, discipline, and social responsibility'. Finally, she hints that some at least of the 'egalitarian' filmic choices may be attributable to Branagh's own working-class Irish background. If anyone still doubts that cultural materialism has a point about the ways in which Shakespeare has been used to hegemonic purpose, they should read this article and take note of some of its palpable anxieties.

Tom McAlindon also defends Hal in his important essay 'Testing the New Historicism: "Invisible Bullets" Reconsidered' (*SP* 92.411–38), a companion piece to his 'Cultural Materialism and the Ethics of Reading: or, the Radicalizing of Jacobean Tragedy' (*MLR* 90.830–46). That, however, is not his primary purpose; he aims mainly to critique Stephen Greenblatt's seminal essay 'Invisible Bullets', which argues that the Shakespearean text is a symptom of hegemony's production of apparent subversion in order to achieve more effective containment. McAlindon, however, argues that the Elizabethan regime felt itself too precarious to encourage even mock-subversion. Most tellingly, McAlindon shows that Greenblatt has deplorably misrepresented Machiavelli, Harriot and Harman and fallen victim to the old trap of taking individuals' speeches, out of context, as representing authorial opinion. However, McAlindon's hostility to Greenblatt and all his works leads him to become rather reductive when it comes to discussing the complexities which will necessarily be produced by discussing the notion of 'testing' if one is hesitant about intentionality. Greenblatt's Hal is seen as 'founding the modern state', and McAlindon relates Greenblatt's views on that state to the failure of protests against the Vietnam war, which has led him to stress disproportionately the cynicism of all government, and thus of Hal. McAlindon himself is sensitive and illuminating on the subject of Francis, as he is when, contrasting Hal with his brother John, he astutely points out that 'in Shakespeare's design likeness frequently emphasizes difference'. Equally well taken is his point that theatricality on the Renaissance stage was not simply to be identified with deception and manipulation. Ultimately, McAlindon is stronger in his demolition of Greenblatt than in his unargued, unasserted canonization of Hal; nevertheless, this is a very significant contribution to contemporary criticism of the plays.

In 'Pilgrims of Grace: *Henry IV* Historicized' (*ShS* 48.69–84), McAlindon begins by again taking issue with Greenblatt's reading of the plays in relation to the Virginia colony, and Graham Holderness's view of it as concerned solely with the feudal past. The 1536 Pilgrimage of Grace and the 1569–70 Northern Rebellion are what McAlindon sees as the major contexts for the play, and grace as a particularly important concept for the two parts of *Henry IV*, 'a play whose seemingly reprobate and much censured hero was fixed in history as one of the elect', and in which the figure of Falstaff was originally overtly based on the Lollard Sir John Oldcastle. Shakespeare 'the demystifier' homes in on hypocrisy wherever, or in whatever religious denomination, he detects it, though McAlindon still has an axe to grind about the graciousness of Hal himself. Nevertheless, McAlindon's eloquence, erudition, and attention to detail make this an original and important contribution to the study of *Henry IV* Parts One and Two.

Nigel Wood's collection of essays, *Henry IV, Parts One and Two*, is part of the Theory in Practice series, of which the *Hamlet* volume attracted so much opprobrium in D.S.'s *TLS* column (4861.16). D.S. would probably feel much the same about this volume. Wood's introduction is not really introductory, and Kiernan Ryan's post-Jamesonian reading spends so much time expounding its theoretical background that he doesn't really get much beyond the well-established view that the plays are ironic and ambiguous, while Peter Womack's reading of them produces the conclusion that they should be seen not as great art but as a great potboiler. Jonathan Goldberg's comparison of Hal with the young man of the sonnets, in the light of Gus van Sant's film *My Own Private Idaho*, engages more closely with the plays and offers some illuminating close readings, and Ronald Macdonald is lucid and informative on the plays' heteroglossia, though again the texts themselves are sketchily dealt with. A distinguishing feature of the volume as a whole is the concluding section to each essay in which Nigel Wood questions the contributors (to be regularly told that he has misunderstood their arguments). Overall, the actual practice of producing readings of the plays suffers by comparison with the time and energy devoted to the theory. Jonathan Hall's *Anxious Pleasures* (on the Comedies) includes an interesting discussion of the carnivalesque in the *Henry IV* plays.

To some extent, Hal retains his halo in Steven Marx's 'Holy War in *Henry V*' (*ShS* 48.85–97), which aims to trace 'some of the relationships between war, religion and politics that connect Shakespeare's play to the depiction of holy war in the Bible'. The approach is rather blinkered – to see 'war as the scourge of God' as an essentially biblical idea, and to invoke this as justification of Henry's threats at Harfleur, for instance, seems quite remarkably blind to the distinctly non-biblical Tamburlainean resonances of both phrase and episode. Marx does modify his overall concentration on the biblical by an emphasis on those aspects of Henry's approach which tally with Machiavelli's; however, he shows that even for deceptiveness, biblical precedents can be found.

In sharp contrast to this general admiration for Hal is Peter C. Herman's '"O, 'tis a gallant king": Shakespeare's *Henry V* and the crisis of the 1690s' (in Dale Hoak, ed., *Tudor Political Culture*). Herman starts from the gap between the idealized portraits of Elizabeth I painted *c*.1600 and the raddled looks of the real queen, which he takes as emblematic of wider fractures in the social and political order. Analogously, Herman argues, '*Henry V* strongly implies that Henry's golden reputation shares about the same relation to reality as do

Elizabeth's late portraits to her actual physical appearance', in ways which '[reflect] the generalized crisis of authority in late Elizabethan England'.

The prize for the catchiest title when writing on the Henriad must certainly go to Kristen Poole's 'Saints Alive! Falstaff, Martin Marprelate, and the Staging of Puritanism' (*SQ* 46.47–75). Poole's essay starts, in typical New Historicist style, with an anecdote, recounting the death of Sir John Oldcastle as told by John Bale and aims to recover the reasons for Shakespeare's apparently inappropriate choice of Oldcastle, seen variously as martyr or as aggressive heretic, by 'examining the Henriad in the context of Elizabethan polemical religious discourse'. This leads her to conclude that Shakespeare's representation of puritanism as Falstaffian is in fact in tune with most anti-Puritan literature, particularly the anti-Marprelate tracts, 'which frequently depicted puritans as grotesque individuals living in carnivalesque communities'. This is a Falstaff who is a direct ancestor of Jonson's Zeal-of-the-Land Busy and Middleton's Plumporridge.

Scott E. Goins seeks for parallels at a rather greater historical distance in his 'Pain and Authority in the *Aeneid* and *Henry V*' (*CML* 3.67–74). Goins sees recent downplayings of Aeneas's *pietas* in favour of concentration on his flaws and insecurities as parallel to emphasis on the negative side of Hal. He traces the parallels between Hal's rejection of Falstaff and Aeneas's desertion of Dido, and the path between cruelty and leniency that both heroes must negotiate. It is puzzling, though, that Goins never really suggests that these echoes may have arisen because Shakespeare *knew* Virgil.

T. W. Craik's *Henry V* was one of the three plays with which the third series of Arden editions was launched. The approach is unashamedly traditionalist. Preferring the Folio and largely discounting the Quarto, Craik also feels that the text is less ambiguous than some critics have argued: '*Henry V* is a celebratory play, commemorating a famous victory', without any of the 'politically inspired irony' of, say, the Southey poem of which he expects his readers instantly to think. Craik's readings, indeed, are relentlessly recuperative, other perspectives are referred to only obliquely and the curious reader could never make his or her way from this cursory comment to any alternative voices.

There were also some notes and shorter essays on the Henriad. James H. Forse wonders if he has detected 'An Echo of *Henry IV, Part 2* in a Work by King James I?' (*ANQ* 8.ii.3–6). It is Falstaff, though, who takes centre stage in Clayton Mackenzie's 'Falstaff's Monster' (*AUMLA* 83.83–6). Showing that Falstaff's version of the Gadshill affair seems to draw on the imagery of the Hydra, Mackenzie points up the irony of Falstaff as a parodic Hercules and reminds us of the link to the overt use of the Hydra metaphor at Shrewsbury. Finally, in another short piece, 'Shakespeare's *Henry IV, Part 2*' (*Expl* 53.iii.131–3), Gary Harrington argues that Hal's rejection of Falstaff has a metatheatrical force, permanently defining the knight's role and securing his own unchallenged pre-eminence in *Henry V*. However, Harrington suggests that the old knight's voice is heard once more, in the tones of the Epilogue. Falstaff, it seems, is not so easily silenced, and indeed James R. Simmons Jr, in 'Scrooge, Falstaff, and the Rhetoric of Indigence' (*ELN* 32.iii.43–6) shows that his distinctive tones are still being heard in a speech of Ebenezer Scrooge's.

It is on the first rather than the second tetralogy that Ellen C. Caldwell focuses in 'Jack Cade and Shakespeare's *Henry VI, Part 2*' (*SP* 92.18–79).

Caldwell offers a long and detailed examination of the actual rebellion of 1450 in order to argue that its focus on two specific grievances, government corruption and the French wars, had telling resonances for late Elizabethan England, and that, although Shakespeare was discreet, we can still see his handling of the rebellion as less negative than has generally been suggested. Caldwell is quite interesting on why, when the real enemy was Spain, it is France that is so insistently focused on in history plays, but in general the impact of this essay's ideas seemed to me inversely proportional to its length, and I remain unconvinced that conventional readings of Cade are all radically flawed.

Richard II, by contrast with the Henry plays, has figured little this year. Lister M. Matheson's 'English Chronicle Contexts for Shakespeare's Death of *Richard II*' (in John A. Alford, ed., *From Page to Performance*) regards Richard's death as showing him finally as 'a man of action', and shows that Shakespeare's dramatization of it 'represents a choice among conflicting current accounts and that the language has been carefully constructed' in order to emphasize the status of *Richard II* as a tragedy rather than a chronicle – a politically astute move in view of the dangerous potential parallels between the king's reign and that of Elizabeth I. Matheson's scholarship has produced a judicious illumination of some of the politically charged meanings which Shakespeare's representation of the death of Richard II might have held for its original audience.

Colin Wilcockson also addresses *Richard II*, and in similarly detailed manner, in '*Mum and the Sothsegger, Richard II*, and *Henry V*' (*RES* 46.219–24). Linking the garden scene of *Richard II* to the emblem of the beehive in *Henry V*, he relates both back to the medieval alliterative poem *Mum and the Sothsegger*. Wilcockson cannot prove that Shakespeare read this, but he does make a clear and suggestive case for these images having an ancestry which is traceable back to the *Georgics*.

King John featured in two essays this year. Brian Boyd's '*King John* and *The Troublesome Raigne*: Sources, Structure, Sequence' (*PQ* 74.37–56) addresses the question of whether Shakespeare's *King John* came before or after the anonymous *Troublesome Raigne*. Received wisdom used to be that *King John* used *Troublesome Raigne* as a source, and one reason why this seemed the better idea is that it is hard to imagine anyone who already had *King John* to work from producing something so much worse. It has, though, been suggested that the author of *Troublesome Raigne* did not have access to the whole of *King John*, but only to a summary. Focusing particularly on comparison of the two plays' treatments of Arthur and of the Bastard, Boyd argues lucidly and energetically that *Troublesome Raigne* does indeed follow *King John*.

In '"The sequence of posterity": Shakespeare's *King John* and the Succession Controversy' (*SP* 92.460–81), Robert Lane relates *King John* to the issues and speculations surrounding the question of who would succeed Elizabeth I. Lane argues that Shakespeare deliberately played down the religious controversies of John's reign to emphasize the parallel importance of monarchs' wills, succession of foreigners and popular opinion in the two situations, and that he also creates divided sympathies which force the audience to assess the relative merits of each of these considerations – which, in turn, 'constitutes the theater as a deliberative forum where ... judgment can be stimulated and nurtured'. These are interesting arguments, and Lane's essay supports them well.

Richard III received some rare attention in Steve Larocco's 'Contentious Intimations: John Donne, Richard III, and the Transgressive Structures of Seduction' (*Exemplaria* 7.237–67). Beginning, improbably enough, with Simone de Beauvoir, Larocco's Lacanian reading, with its emphasis on transhistorical psychic and linguistic structures, does tend to schematize the text, and also to respond to it in terms which may well seem to many readers to be inappropriate: to say 'as Anne notices, the dead flesh itself of Henry traverses the finality and silence of death' is a strange way of referring to an event which must surely strike the spectators with rather more force than simple 'noticing'. However, despite this, and despite too his rather thin reading in existing Shakespeare scholarship, when Larocco actually turns his attention to close analysis of the dialogue he has some sharp points to make.

Jo Eldridge Carney discusses the last of the history plays in 'Queenship in Shakespeare's *Henry VIII*: The Issue of Issue' (in Carole Levin and Patricia A. Sullivan, eds, *Political Rhetoric, Power, and Renaissance Women*). Carney argues that Shakespeare is concerned in this play not only with kingship, but also with queenship, as embodied in the three queens of the play, Katherine, Anne and the infant Elizabeth herself. Their common characteristics as queens are association with spectacle, superiority to other women, and the pressure to produce an heir. Carney's essay offers some interesting commentary on the question of fertility, but does not develop into a reading of the play as a whole.

The canon of Shakespeare's history plays is showing signs of expansion: *Edward III*, or parts of it at least, is beating at the gate. E. Pearlman, in '*Edward III* in *Henry V*' (*Criticism* 37.519–36), takes the possibility of Shakespeare's authorship as one potential reason amongst many why Shakespeare might have been familiar with the play, but his main point is the existence of that familiarity, which, he argues, is demonstrated most clearly in *Henry V*: Shakespeare had no choice but to come somehow to terms with the earlier play. He did this, Pearlman suggests, either by incorporation or by an attempt 'to overwhelm and obliterate the memory of *Edward III* with far fuller treatments of matters that appear in both plays', as in his explication of the Salic law. Ultimately, Pearlman argues, memories of the earlier hero help Hal construct his own new heroic identity, and *Edward III*'s glorification of royalty even serves as a counterweight to *Henry V*'s Essex reference. Pearlman is less interested in the question of Shakespeare's possible authorship of *Edward III* than in the ways in which the earlier play 'lay in his landscape', and of these he offers an acute and persuasive mapping.

(e) Tragedies

In *Shakespeare's Festive Tragedy: The Ritual Foundations of Genre*, Naomi Conn Liebler examines Shakespearean tragedy as a celebration of what is lost, as 'a celebration of a community's survival', and argues that 'focussing on the "flaw" of the protagonist effaces the tragedy's relation to its audience, excludes the audience completely from its implications, and makes the drama itself irrelevant'. She examines the problem of interpretation of *hamartia*, which, as a result of a misunderstanding of Aristotle, has 'generally been read as an error or a moral failing'. As Liebler states, *hamartia* is a deed, an action, and she is right to say that the 'emphasis on morality has clouded tragic exegesis for at least the last century and a half'. An examination of *Richard II* in relation to the Foucauldian theory of 'subjugated knowledges' to trace the play's roots to the Cain-and-Abel cycle play, is followed by a reading of *Julius Caesar* drawing on Lévi-Strauss's principle of *bricolage* to examine why of all the festivals referred to in Shakespearean drama, the Lupercal is given such remarkably detailed attention. There is an interesting discussion of *Titus Andronicus* as a play in which 'all cultural definitions are nullified' by 'the confusion or neglect of cultural markers'; a suggestive piece using Derrida's discussion of *pharmakon* as the embodiment of the binary oppositions of poison and remedy, on liminality and adolescence in *Romeo and Juliet*; and another on the complex treatment of the scapegoat in *Coriolanus*. A final chapter examines the origins of the significances of the hobby-horse figure in relation to *Hamlet* and the Aristotelian definition of tragic action as a violation of specific social bonds in *King Lear* and *Macbeth*.

In *The Shapes of Revenge*, Harry Keyishian states that 'while revenge is frequently condemned in Renaissance thought and literature, it is also recognized as having potentially affirmative and even heroic functions', and the book goes on to examine the ways in which Shakespeare distinguishes between 'authentic revenge' (Titus), vindictiveness (Iago) and the 'mixed types' (Othello and Hamlet). Some of the conclusions made give little insight into how and why audiences respond in the ways they do. We are told that 'in moving to resolve *Hamlet* and the Gloucester subplot of *King Lear*, Shakespeare has *tried to deproblematize* the revenges of Hamlet and Edgar by casting them as servants of higher authorities' (my emphasis). Keyishian concludes: 'I think he has not quite succeeded', and, demonstrating a reluctance (or incapacity) to distinguish artistic failure and artistic meaning, describes the playwright's 'efforts' failing to bring 'the issues raised by the revenge ... to closure'. There are sections on *King Lear*, *Julius Caesar*, *Othello*, the first History plays, Leontes and Timon. I was surprised to find so little attention paid to one of the most complex treatments of revenge in the canon, *The Merchant of Venice*.

One of the best essays on the tragedies is Antony Gilbert's 'Shakespearean Self-Talk. The Gricean Maxims and the Unconscious' (*ES* 76.221-37) which applies the theories of Paul Grice to the use of soliloquy in *Hamlet*, *Macbeth* and *Othello* to demonstrate how the audience is 'engaged in a silent dialogue with the speaker on stage'. Hamlet's 'How all occasions ... ' speech is examined as a masterpiece of the ways in which the Gricean maxims of relevance, quantity, quality and manner are employed: the technique of 'undercutting assertions by implicit ambiguity is the main pragmatic device in this speech'. Similarly, Gilbert's analysis of Macbeth's 'If it were done ... ' is perceptive. Macbeth, he says, 'is always lucid and honest with himself, but this lucidity only heightens the dramatic tension between the opposed mental stances in his self-talk'. I also found suggestive the examination of the patterns of thought and feeling in Othello's 'It is the cause ... ' speech as revealing a long litany of 'false reason and genuine emotion creating a structural ambiguity in the language he speaks'.

In studies of individual tragedies this year there was very little on *Romeo and Juliet*. Susanna Fein's 'Verona's Summer Flower: The "Virtues" of Herb Paris in *Romeo and Juliet*' (*ANQ* 8.iv.5-8) examines herb imagery in the play, and David Lucking's 'That Which We Call a Name: The Balcony Scene in *Romeo and Juliet*' (*English* 44.1-16) considers the darker implications of the scene, particularly how Romeo's 'subjugation to the world of language in all its manifestations is called into question by Juliet'. Lucking argues that 'despite its predominantly lyrical tone' the scene 'mirrors within its own reduced compass the tensions operating throughout the entire work'.

In great contrast, reviewing *Hamlet* criticism has begun to feel like a full-time job. In an interesting if uneven collection of essays, *Hamlet and Japan* (ed. Yoshiko Uéno), the work of different generations of Japanese Shakespeare scholars shows a wide range of topics. The volume is divided thematically into three parts, the first concerned with the history and ideas of the period, the second with reconsiderations of the representations of Ophelia and Gertrude and the third with Japanese adaptations, translations, and productions of the play. The women in the play receive special attention in this volume. The editor offers an essay on 'Three Gertrudes: Text and Subtext' in which he examines the Gertrude self-image, Gertrude as she is seen from Hamlet's perspective, and the Gertrude the original audience would have seen. Akiko Kusunoki in '"Oh most pernicious Woman . . . "' considers the representation of Gertrude within the socio-cultural context of early seventeenth-century England, particularly in the light of its ideas on remarriage. Takashi Sasayama's 'The Night Wanderer and The Fantasy of Dawn: Notes on the Psycho-Aesthetic Meaning of the Ophelia Scenes in *Hamlet*' offers a scene-by-scene commentary on the role of the 'over-submissive' Ophelia in the audience's theatrical experience of the play; and Emi Hamana argues in 'Whose Body is it anyway? – A Re-Reading of Ophelia' that 'Ophelia's body presents itself as a site of discourses which define, control and contain it' and that through madness, she escapes containment and achieves autonomy as a subject. In 'Ophelia: Experience into Song', Toshiko Oshio argues that in the first half of the play Ophelia cannot express herself in words, but that she later finds power in song, though at the cost of her sanity.

Shoichiro Kawai's essay discusses the relationship between Hamlet's imagination and Elizabethan philosophy, particularly Thomas Wright's study of perception. In 'Hamlet's "Method in Madness" in Search of Private and Public Justice', Toyoko Shimizu focuses on the play's treatment of justice. Soji Iwasaki ('*Hamlet* and Melancholy: An Iconographical Approach') examines the play in the context of 'the unity of meditation and action' which was 'the ideal striven for in Renaissance education'. There is an essay by Tetsuya Motohashi on writing and 'the Liberty' in *Hamlet*. Hidekatsu Nojima examines mirror imagery in the play in relation to Alberti's theory of perspective, and sees Hamlet as 'a prisoner of the curious perspective' in which 'everything seems double'. Hiroshi Ozawa examines apocalyptic imagery in the play with a new historicist perspective; and Yasunari Takahashi looks at 'Speech, Deceit and Catharsis', analysing the pluralistic and metatheatrical qualities of the play in terms of semiotics and the theory of speech acts. Hiroshi Izubuchi examines Japanese language adaptations of the play, including Odashima's Noh version and the influence on contemporary Japanese productions of Ingmar Bergman's 1988 production. The last chapter provides a chronological overview of the history of Shakespeare's reception against the backdrop of the modernization of Japan.

Of the journal output on the play this year, one of the best pieces is a closely argued essay entitled 'Falconer to the Little Eyases: A New Date and Commercial Agenda for the "Little Eyases" Passage in *Hamlet*' (*SQ* 46.1–31), in which Rosalyn L. Knutson challenges the view of textual studies and theatre history which still govern the interpretation of the lines in *Hamlet* known as the 'little eyases' passage by examining the stage runs of the play with events current in the commercial and political environment, and the critical assumptions that have been made about the relationship between the Quartos' 'humour of children' and the Folio's 'little eyases' passages, to suggest that in 1606–8 'in response to the behaviour of the boys' company at Blackfriars, the King's Men added the "little eyases" passage in the place that had been occupied by the humour of children passage in their *Hamlet* of 1600'. Knutson argues that the War of the Theatres to which the 'little eyases' passage alludes is not that between men's and boy's companies, but relates to the potential threat to the King's Men posed by the demise of the Children of St Paul's in 1606–7 – 'boys that were soon to be men' – after which 'there might be only adult companies, and one of them might be making trouble at Burbage's own Blackfriars', and assigning the passage to a new date, 1606–8. The essay, by attending to the shifting commercial agenda in the life of Shakespeare's company, discovers political and commercial reasons for the revision, particularly Burbage's resumption of the lease of Blackfriars in 1608.

In his book-length study, *Hamlet and Narcissus*, John Russell argues that Hamlet's delay is a result of his parents' narcissism. Revising Freud's formulation, using the work of Margaret Mahler and Heinz Kohut, Russell's study reflects his belief that 'the deep action of Shakespearean tragedy resonates with the great themes of psycho-analytic science'.

Jonathan Baldo's essay on the relationship between synecdoche and Ophelia's rhetoric provides some valuable insights on a fascinating topic (*Criticism* 37.1–35). 'Ophelia's Rhetoric, or Partial to Synecdoche' examines the figure's importance both in characterization in drama and the politics of the period. In a carefully argued essay, '*Hamlet* and "A Matter Tender and Dangerous"' (*SQ* 46.383–97), Mark Matheson examines the question of the relation of the play to early modern religious discourse, and argues that 'the play's inconsistent repression of religion is interesting in itself', and substantiates his interesting conclusion: 'That predestination and its worldly consequences were tender political matters may be an important reason for Shakespeare's rather oblique and suggestive handling of Hamlet's transformation'.

Of the articles in *HSt* 17 relevant to this section, Francesca Bugliani (10–42) argues that there are many points of similarity including verbal parallels between the 'To be' soliloquy and Cicero's *Tusculan Disputations*, particularly in John Dolman's English translation. Hamlet is 'pondering Socrates' famous speech as recorded in the first book of Cicero's *Disputations* on whether life is preferable to death'. In '*The Woman Hater* as Beaumont and Fletcher's reading of *Hamlet*' (63–77), Ruth Vanita suggests that Hamlet is parodied in the persons of Gondarino and Lazarello and that the parody is critical rather than merely imitative. In '*Hamlet* and Friendship' (54–62), Keith Doubt examines Hamlet's friendship with Horatio in the light of Max Weber's interpretive sociological theories, to argue that Hamlet's adult relationships are seen as conditioned on an unconscious level by his early relationships with his parents. Political journalist William Rees-Mogg writes on 'The politics of *Hamlet*' (43–53), focusing on 'the tragedy of Claudius' and the limitations of his 'politician's perspective' in the context of earlier and contemporary power struggles. In the 'Critical Forum' section, Sikander Lal ('A Note on Halverson's Horatio', 109–11) discusses 'the socialization/secularization' of the play's four scholars and takes issue with John Halverson's 'The Importance of Horatio' in *HSt* 16 (*YWES* 75.253) to argue that Horatio 'has affinity more with the world of Claudius than of Hamlet'. Rani Drew gives an account of her feminist view of the play using Lacanian elements in '*The III-Act Hamlet*; a feminist Extension/Reconstruction of Shakespeare's *Hamlet*' (122–33). Among the notes, R. F. Fleissner examines '*Hamlet*, T. S. Eliot and the final Pagan Rites' (101–8) to argue that the 'overall effect of vindictiveness and thus paganism' is the quality which 'basically disturbed Eliot, not merely the issue of Hamlet's having to make up his mind in time'. In 'Hamnet or *Hamlet*? That is the Question' (94–8), Eric Sams takes Shakespeare scholars to task for not arriving at the 'commonsense conclusion' that 'of course the name bestowed by Shakespeare on his son in 1585 was Hamlet, not "Hamnet"'. John K. Hale suggests an interesting parallel between the openings of *Hamlet* and *Agamemnon*, in 'Watchmen on the Ramparts: *Hamlet*'s Opening Image' (98–101), focusing on the function of watchmen as connoting 'ambiguity and its potential for dread'; and Barbara Hardy offers a solution to the 'hawk and handsaw' crux (94).

Hamlet has received more than its usual disproportion of criticism in relation to the rest of the canon this year, so there is space to do little more than briefly mention the following. Dorothea Kehler provides helpful contributions to the increasing discussion of the character of Gertrude in recent years, in 'The First Quarto of *Hamlet*: Reforming Widow Gertred' (*SQ* 46.398–413), and, in an article I missed last year, her examination of the treatment of Gertrude in study guides, 'The Outline Industry and the Processing of Gertrude' (*UCrow* 14[1994].47–66). Philip C. McGuire, in 'Bearing "A Wary Eye"': Ludic Vengeance and Doubtful Suicide in *Hamlet*' (in Alford, ed., *From Page to Performance*) examines the play's treatment of revenge, suicide and playfulness. James Schiffer, in 'Mnemonic Cues to Passion in *Hamlet*' (*RenP* 65–79), writes on the relationship between the use of mnemonics and passion in the play. I have not been able to see Jacquelyn Fox-Good's essay 'Ophelia's Mad Songs: Music, Gender, Power' in Allen and White, eds, *Subjects on the World's Stage* or John S. Pendergast's essay on the play's influence on *Star Trek VI: The Undiscovered Country*, in 'A Nation of Hamlets: Shakespeare and Cultural Politics' (*Extrapolation* 36.10–17).

One of the best notes on *Hamlet* this year is Mark Thornton Burnett's examination of the multiple contexts of the 'baffling reference' to the 'False Steward', in Biblical allusions, the sharp business practice references in sermons and moral guides of the time, metrical romances in which stewards courted women above them on the social scale, and a balladic reference, the 1580 'The Lord of Lorn and the False Steward' (*RES* 46.148–56). Other notes on the play are provided by Ricks Carson ('Shakespeare's *Hamlet*', *Expl.* 53.iii.130) who examines sources in Ecclesiasticus; Thomas Aksteens in '"Country Matters": Hamlet's Pornographic Imagination and the Postfeminist Audience' (*ShakB* 13.ii.5–8); and in a suggestive short piece, Kerri Lynne Thomsen ('Ovidian References in Hamlet's First Soliloquy', *ELN* 33.19–24) argues that Hamlet, in an allusion to the 'melting' and 'thawing' metamorphosis of Cyane in Book V of Ovid's poem, 'asks for an Ovidian alternative to both life and death'. Charles Edelman considers 'Another Bawdy Allusion in *Hamlet*?' (*ELN* 32.22–4), in Osric's 'rather unfortunate testimonial to Laertes's "weapon"' at 5.ii.136–46 (to add to his note on Osric's indecent reference to testicles at line 147–53, *YWES* 75.252); David Farley-Hills examines the reference to the hobbyhorse in *Eastward Ho*'s *Hamlet* parody in 'A Hamlet

Crux', and provides a note on Betterton's acting version of the play in *N&Q* 42.319–20, 59–61.

Othello received much less attention than last year. Hyungji Park examines the play's treatment of race and sexual violence in 'The Traffic in Desdemona: Race and Sexual Transgression in *Othello*' (*JELL* 41.1061–82). Mark Gauntlett writes on 'The Perishable Poetry of the Unpoetical: A. C. Bradley Performs *Othello*' (*ShS* 47.71–80). Two essays focusing on Iago are John Crawford's 'Iago as Villain' (*PAPA* 21.21–7); and a suggestive piece by Hugh Grady on 'Iago and the Dialectic of Enlightenment: Reason, Will, and Desire in *Othello*' (*Criticism* 37.537–58). Robert Fleissner provides an analogy for Othello's 'base Indian' allusion in *Love's Labour's Lost* (*ES* 76.140–2); and an essay I have not seen is Peggy Anne Russo's 'Othello goes to Washington: Cultural Politics and the Thomas/Hill Affair' (*JAmC* 17.iv.15–22).

The *King Lear* volume in the new 'Writers and Their Works' series appears this year. Terence Hawkes devotes one chapter of the slim volume to explaining cultural materialism and new historicism, and another to reiterating his well-rehearsed argument that Shakespearean texts and their author exist only in the meanings that we mean by them. Hawkes offers readings of the play's treatments of unemployment, language, madness and gender. The book's intended readers are not allowed to historicize criticism of the play for themselves, nor are they directed towards studies which are deemed traditional or humanist in their approaches.

In ' "The Name and All th'Addition": *King Lear's* Opening Scene and the Common Law Use' (*ShakS* 23.146–86), Charles Spinosa productively restricts his essay to the first scene of *King Lear* to examine the play's treatment of property, law and personal identity. Spinosa shows why the first scene of the play 'does not show us a puerile, senile or nursery-tale Lear', and calls for 'certain presuppositions regarding early modern social stability' in essays such as Dollimore's and Greenblatt's to be 'revised'. The essay demonstrates the importance the play places on 'the legal, political, personal and ontological consequences of Lear's putting his kingdom in a "proto-use" '. Ronald J. Boling examines characterization in the play with reference to the death of Cordelia and Edmund's identity in 'Edmond and Cordelia: Self- and Selfless-Fashioning in *King Lear*' (*PAPA* 21.1–20). Janet M. Green writes on the play's exploration of the relationship between judgement, God and the law in 'Earthly Doom and Heavenly Thunder: Judgment in *King Lear*' (*UDR* 23.ii.63–73).

A new electronic journal, *Early Modern Literary Studies*, has come on line this year. Ben Ross Schneider's essay in the first issue, '*King Lear* in its own time' (*EMLS* 1.1.95) examines the play in the context of Stoic attitudes to death in a way that could have been more structured in its argument. Philip Armstrong contributes to Shakespeare criticism's interest in matters geographical with his 'Spheres of Influence: Cartography and the Gaze in Shakespearean Tragedy and History' (*ShakS* 23.39–70) in which he uses the theories of Lacan to examine the treatment of maps in *King Lear*, *Coriolanus* and *1HIV*.

Macbeth was noticeably under-represented this year. Apart from the section on the play's use of soliloquy in Anthony Gilbert's essay on 'Shakespearean Self-Talk' (see above), Michael Baird Saenger suggests sources from *Dr Faustus* in *Macbeth* (*Expl.* 53.iii.133–5), and there was a brief note by E. O. Williams (*N&Q* 42.327).

Criticism of the classical tragedies is patchy this year. In a rather strained argument, Barbara L. Parker ('The Whore of Babylon and Shakespeare's *Julius Caesar*', *SEL* 35.251–69), examines the play in relation to the Protestant identification of Rome with sexual perversion. In this reading, Brutus is 'purger of Rome', and the flames of burning Rome are 'emblematic of sexual frenzy'. Finding a considerable number of sexual puns to contend that Antony's speech in 3.2. 'waxes progressively more erotic', Parker says he 'transmutes the corpse into a phallus, and the crowd into the receiving agent': Antony's curing of 'Caesar's heirlessness occurs, ironically, at the funeral, the play's sexual climax and one of the most ingenious seduction scenes in literature. The action subtextually replicates all the stages of the sex act, from arousal to coitus to orgasm.' Lloyd Davis examines body language in the play (*LiNQ* 22910.104–13). Matthew H. Wikander has written an essay on the play in a volume which I have not been able to see – 'The Clock in Brutus' Orchard Strikes Again: Anachronism and Achronism in Historical Drama' (in Donald E. Morse, ed., *The Delegated Intellect* [Lang]).

Among the Roman plays *Coriolanus* and *Antony and Cleopatra* are the most strongly represented. David Wheeler has edited *Critical Essays: Coriolanus* in the Garland series. The collection of criticism of the play is taken from studies published from the seventeenth century to the present; there is a considerable number of theatre reviews, and the volume concludes with three new essays, one of which is relevant to this section: Karen Aubrey argues that *Coriolanus* has to be seen as a satire, rather than a tragedy, or at least, as a satire as well as a tragedy. (The editor's new essay on Restoration and eighteenth-century treatments of the play and an examination by S. K. Bedford of Peter Hall's 1984 production with Ian McKellen in the title role are the two other new pieces). Overall, this is a collection that could have been a little more inspiring.

Christopher Wortham attempts 'to identify a Jacobean mentality that operates through a discourse of ideological expression' in 'Temperance and the End of Time: Emblematic *Antony and Cleopatra*' (*CompD* 29.1–37). He examines the emblematic traditions of Mars and Hercules to suggest 'a relationship between mental constructs exemplified in emblematic imagery and a persistent theme' in the play – temperance. Donald Cheney writes on antonomasia in '"A Very Antony": Patterns of Antonomasia in Shakespeare' (*Connotations* 4.8–24). In 'At "The Very Heart of Loss": Shakespeare's Enobarbus and the Rhetoric of Remembering' (*RenP* 81–91). Allyson P. Newton examines the play's treatment of loss, the rhetoric of memory and the relationship between Shakespeare's character and Cneius Domitius Ahenobarbus. A. S. Weber looks at the play in relation to Stoic and Hermetic traditions in 'New Physics for the Nonce: A Stoic and Hermetic Reading of Shakespeare's *Antony and Cleopatra*' (*RenP* 93–107). In a note on the play, Rick Bowers argues that Octavia does not speak the 'Good Night sir' line at 2.iii.8 (*ELN* 33.8–11).

Titus Andronicus continues to receive more attention than it used to. Philip C. Kolin's *Critical Essays: Titus Andronicus* is another collection of mostly reprinted essays. The editor's introduction provides a helpful survey of the play's vexed critical history from Edward Ravenscroft's denouncing it as a 'heap of rubblish' in 1687 to recent theoretical criticism. It is particularly strong on assessing the critical and theatrical history of the chief characters and has an extremely valuable bibliography, with studies printed up to 1995. Eugene M.

Waith's 1957 influential essay 'The Metamorphosis of Violence' in the play is here, but I regret the absence of Albert Tricomo's article on the aesthetics of mutilation (1974) and S. Clark Hulse's on rhetoric and violence (1979) which might have been included in a book which has the declared aim of providing 'the most influential historical criticism'. Also included is Alan Sommers's 'Wilderness of Tigers' on structure and symbolism and the studies of Aaron by Eldred Jones and Leslie Fielder and Bernard Spivak. More recent studies which are included in the volume include Emily Bartels's essay on Aaron and Othello; Heather James's discussion of the play's relationship to Virgil and Ovid; and Kolin's piece on the play's emphasis on the performance of writing/reading. Original essays written for the volume are Dorothea Kehler's '"That Ravenous Tiger Tamora": *Titus Andronicus*' Lusty Widow, Wife, and M/other', which argues that Tamora is portrayed as 'a particularly vicious representation of a stereotype soon to be a major presence in Jacobean drama – the lusty widow'. In '"O Cruel, Irreligious Piety!"': Stage Images of Civil Conflict in *Titus Andronicus*' David Bevington argues that the dramatic structuring and stagecraft in the play can be illuminated by the plays Shakespeare 'might well have seen (or possibly even acted in)' in the 1580s and early 1590s. Scilla's return to Rome 'in *triumph in his chair triumphant of gold*', and '*drawn by four Moors before the chariot*' with his prisoners manacled, is, Bevington says, 'a transparent borrowing from *Tamburlaine*'. The essay also considers the use of the pit or trap in relationship to the hellmouth of the Corpus Christi plays, and to the beginning and end of *The Spanish Tragedy*, and shows how the currency and emblematic character of onstage thrones are used in *Titus*. This is an important and thought-provoking essay; by focusing on the stagecraft and theatrical language of the time, the essay demonstrates a need to reassess our definition of 'source material' in Shakespeare's plays.

In '*Titus Andronicus* and the Canons of Contemporary Violence' Kolin argues that the atrocities acted out in the play 'correspond to many of the horrors that shock America today'. In 'Upon Her Wit Doth Earthly Honour Wait': Female Agency in *Titus Andronicus*' Carolyn Asp examines 'the representation, signification and function' of Lavinia and Tamora, with a reading of the play's contests between 'Rome' and 'Goths' by using a theoretical approach based on Freud and Lacan. In 'Common Words in *Titus Andronicus*: The Presence of Peele' (*N&Q* 42.300–7), Brian Boyd argues that there is 'little doubt' that Peele was responsible for I.i, II.i, and IV, identifying 'the lazy repetition' of certain words such as 'honour' with 'Peele's preferred verbal putty to fill any gap' as found in *The Battle of Alcazar*. Edward Washington examines racial stereotypes in relationship to evil in 'Tragic Resolution in Shakespeare's *Titus Andronicus*' (*CLAJ* 38.461–79).

Books Reviewed

Alford, John A., ed. *From Page to Performance*. MichSUP. pp. 265. £24.50 ($32.95). ISBN 0 87013 379 9.

Allen, David, and Robert White, eds. *Subjects on the World's Stage: Essays on British Literature of the Middle Ages and the Renaissance*. AUP. UDelP. £34.50. ISBN 0 87 413 544 3.

Barker, Deborah E., and Ivo Kamps, eds. *Shakespeare and Gender: A History*. Verso. pp. ix + 342. hb £39.95, pb £14.95 ISBN 0 86091 458 5, 0 86091 669 3.

Bate, Jonathan, ed. *Titus Andronicus*. ArdenS. Routledge. pp. 308. hb£30, pb£5.99. ISBN 0 415 04867 2, 0 415 04868 0.

Craik, T. W., ed. *King Henry V*. ArdenS. Routledge. pp. 419. hb £30, pb £5.99. ISBN 0 415 01413 1, 0 415 01414 X.

Dawson, Anthony B. *Hamlet*. SiP. ManUP. pp. ix + 261. 12 plates. £40. ISBN 0 7190 3933 9.

Dessen, Alan C. *Rediscovering Shakespeare's Theatrical Vocabulary*. CUP. pp. 283. £30. ISBN 0 5214 7080 3.

Dutton, Richard, ed. *New Casebooks: A Midsummer Night's Dream*. Macmillan. pp. ix + 270. hb £37.50, pb £14.95 . ISBN 0 333 60196 3, 0 333 60197 1.

Godsalve, William H. L. *Britten's A Midsummer Night's Dream: Making an Opera from Shakespeare's Comedy*. FDUP. pp. 237. £30 ($39.50). ISBN 0 8386 3551 2.

Graham-White, Anthony. *Punctuation and its Dramatic Value in Shakespearean Drama*. AUP. UDelP. pp. 192. £29.50. ISBN 0 874 13542 7.

Hall, Jonathan. *Anxious Pleasures: Shakespearean Comedy and the Nation State*. AUP. pp. 291. £32 ($42.50). ISBN 0 8386 3569 5.

Hawkes, Terence. *King Lear*. WTW. Northcote/British Council. pp. 79. pb £5.99. ISBN 0 7463 0746 2.

Hoak, Dale, ed. *Tudor Political Culture*. CUP. pp. 326. £45. ISBN 0 521 40494 0.

Holderness, Graham, ed. *M. William Shak-Speare: His True Chronicle Historie of the Life and Death of King Lear and his Three Daughters*. SO. PH. pp. 164. pb £6.95. ISBN 0 13 355363 9.

Jarvis, Simon. *Scholars and Gentlemen: Shakespearian Textual Criticism and Representations of Scholarly Labour 1725–1765*. Clarendon. pp. 240. £32.50. ISBN 0 19 818295 3.

Jones, John. *Shakespeare at Work*. Clarendon. pp. 289. £35. ISBN 0 19 811966 6.

Kamps, Ivo, ed. *Materialist Shakespeare: A History*. Verso. pp. ix + 342. hb £39.95, pb £14.95. ISBN 0 86091 463 1, 0 86091 674 X.

Keyishian, Harry. *The Shapes of Revenge*. Humanities. £27.50. pp. 182. ISBN 0 3910 3828 1.

Kolin, Philip. *Critical Essays: Titus Andronicus*. Garland. pp. 518. $45. ISBN 0 8153 1159 1.

Lascombes, André, ed. *Tudor Theatre: Emotion in the Theatre* vol. 3, Table Ronde V. Lang. pp. 212. £23. ISBN 3 906754 49 9.

Levin, Carole, and Patricia A. Sullivan, eds. *Political Rhetoric, Power, and Renaissance Women*. SUNYP. pp. 293. £44.75 ($57.50). ISBN 0 7914 2546 0.

Liebler, Naomi Conn. *Shakespeare's Festive Tragedy: The Ritual Foundations of Genre*. Routledge. pp. 266. hb £45, pb £14.99. ISBN 0 4150 8657 4, 0 4151 3183 9.

Murphy, Andrew, ed. *The Tragedie of Othello, the Moore of Venice*. SO. PH. pp. 153. £6.95. ISBN 0 13 355488 0.

Osborne, Laurie E. *Twelfe Night; or, What You Will*. SO. PH. pp. 116. pb £6.95. ISBN 013 355504 6.

Oz, Avraham. *The Yoke of Love: Prophetic Riddles in The Merchant of Venice*. AUP. pp. x + 253. £27. ISBN 0 87413 490 0.

Patterson, Annabel. *The Most Excellent Historie of The Merchant of Venice*. SO. PH. pp. 136. pb £6.95. ISBN 0 13 355520 8.

Pechter, Edward. *What was Shakespeare? Renaissance Plays and Changing Critical Practice.* CornUP. pp. 200. hb £23.50, pb £9.95. ISBN 0 8014 3065 8, 0 8014 8229 1.

Porterfield, Sally B. *Jung's Advice to the Players: A Jungian Reading of Shakespeare's Problem Plays.* Greenwood. pp. 119. £31.95. ISBN 0 313 29305 8.

Russell, John. *Hamlet and Narcissus.* AUP. UDelP. pp. 246. £30. ISBN 0 8741 3533 8.

Ryan, Kiernan. *Shakespeare.* HW. pp. x + 165. £13.95 ($16.95). ISBN 0 13 355546 1.

Sams, Eric. *The Real Shakespeare: Retrieving the Early Years, 1564–1594.* YaleUP. pp. 256. £19.95. ISBN 0 300 06129 3.

Shapiro, Michael. *Gender in Play on the Shakespearean Stage: Boy Heroines and Female Pages.* UMichP. pp. viii + 282. hb £28.95, pb £14.50. ISBN 0 472 10567 1, 0 472 08405 4.

Smith, Peter J. *Social Shakespeare: Aspects of Renaissance Dramaturgy and Contemporary Society.* Macmillan. pp. xi + 246, 16 plates. hb £37.50, pb £15.99. ISBN 0 333 63216 8, 0 333 63217 6.

Turner, John, ed. *The Tragedie of Anthonie, and Cleopatra.* SO. PH. pp. 178. pb £6.95. ISBN 0 13 355595 X.

Uéno, Yoshiko, ed. *Hamlet and Japan.* AMS. pp. 313. $57.50. ISBN 0 4044 6231 2.

Watts, Cedric, ed. *An Excellent Conceited Tragedie of Romeo and Juliet.* SO. PH. pp. 128. pb £6.95. ISBN 0 13 355629 8.

Wheeler, David. *Critical Essays: Coriolanus.* Garland. pp. 434. $45. ISBN 0 8153 1057 9.

White, R. S., ed. *Twelfth Night.* New Casebooks. Macmillan. pp. ix + 221. hb £37.50, pb £10.99. ISBN 0 333 60676 0, 0 333 60677 9.

Wilders, John, ed. *Antony and Cleopatra.* ArdenS. Routledge. pp. 308. hb £30, pb £5.99 . ISBN 0 415 01102 7, 0 415 01103 5.

Wilson, Rawdon. *Shakespearean Narrative.* AUP. UDelP. pp. 313. $46.50. ISBN 0 8741 3525 7.

Wood, Nigel, ed. *Henry IV, Parts One and Two.* OpenUP. pp. 194. pb £12.99. ISBN 0 395 35690 8.

——, ed. *The Tempest.* Theory in Practice Series. OpenUP. pp. xvi + 197. pb £12.99. ISBN 0 335 15688 6.

Wraight, A. D. *The Story That the Sonnets Tell.* Adam Hart . 1994. pp. vi + 585. hb £25, pb £9.95. ISBN 1 897763 01 8, 1 897763 05 0.

VII

Renaissance Drama: Excluding Shakespeare

SARAH POYNTING, PETER J. SMITH, EMMA SMITH, DARRYLL
GRANTLEY and JULIE SANDERS

This chapter has three sections: 1. Editions and Textual Scholarship; 2. Theatre History; 3. Criticism. Section 1 is by Sarah Poynting; section 2 is by Peter J. Smith; section 3(a) is by Emma Smith; section 3(b) is by Darryll Grantley; and section 3(c) is by Julie Sanders.

1. Editions and Textual Scholarship

This was a remarkably productive year for the publication of Renaissance plays, with major new critical editions of works by Webster, Jonson and Marlowe, as well as useful collections of dramatic texts both by single authors and in generic or thematic combinations.

After an appropriately long gestation period, *The Works of John Webster*, ed. David Gunby, David Carnegie and Antony Hammond, have begun to appear from CUP, in an old-spelling edition intended to replace F. L. Lucas's standard *Complete Works* of 1927; this beautifully produced first volume contains *The White Devil* and *The Duchess of Malfi*. Hammond (assisted by Doreen DelVecchio) sets out the principles governing the editing of the text itself with admirable clarity in the textual introductions, combining a recognition of recent concern with 'un-editing' with a refusal to abdicate the editor's duty to make choices, in particular in distinguishing between what he describes as 'signals' and 'noise'. The logic of his decisions in this respect, while carefully argued, is not always wholly persuasive, some of the contributors to the collaborative process of the production of the original quartos being seen as more equal than others. For example, the punctuation of the 'naive' Compositor N of *The White Devil* is defined as 'noise', to be adjusted to the standards of Compositors A and B: a perfectly justifiable editorial policy, but not one entirely consistent with the general textual principles. Of greater concern is the decision, on the grounds that 'the external circumstances of censorship are not quite part of the collaborative process we had in mind', to disregard the effects on *The Duchess of Malfi* of the statute forbidding profanity in plays, and to replace 'Heaven' with 'God' at those places in the text where it seems appropriate in an attempt 'to restore Webster's words'.

The apparatus itself is brief and clear, without a full historical collation, any variants of interest from earlier editions being pointed out in the critical commentary (printed at the end of each play), which also includes useful suggestions and comments on staging as well as the more conventional notes on sources and textual cruxes. The concern with the plays as texts for the stage is indeed one of the strengths of the edition: David Carnegie's theatrical introductions go beyond a discussion of Jacobean staging and a descriptive cataloguing of past productions to consider the implications of possible different approaches in performance. In his critical introductions, David Gunby also examines the thematic significance of stage action, but concentrates on analyses of Webster's use of paralleling and repetition as support for his argument that both plays contain evidence of an underlying providential order. Final sections of the edition document sources and press variants, and the volume concludes with a short and interesting discussion by Peter Walls of the music in *The Duchess of Malfi*.

The publication of OUP's *Complete Works of Christopher Marlowe* continued this year with Roma Gill's old-spelling edition of *The Jew of Malta*, which, in keeping with earlier volumes, is critically concise and textually conservative. The very brief introduction, which focuses on the question 'Why Malta?', raises interesting questions, but is finally rather disappointing, while the more satisfying commentary which follows the play is particularly strong on Biblical references. Use of the commentary, however, can be frustratingly slow, with no heading to indicate the act and scene referred to on each page. The textual introduction contains a short discussion of the problems posed by the inconsistencies of the 1633 quarto and appears to favour T. W. Craik's argument for its being based on a playhouse manuscript possibly copied, according to D. J. Lake, by Thomas Dekker; Gill does not consider the suggestion that the second part of the play may have been reworked by another hand, perhaps Heywood's. The latter's dedicatory epistle, prologues and epilogues are gathered together at the end of the play, as are the lists of accidental emendations and corrected mislineations. The on-page collation contains only major substantive variations from the copy-text, and it is fortunate that these are rare, as only too often the line-numbering of the apparatus is incorrect, mostly by one line, occasionally by two, and once by five.

ManUP have followed up last year's publication of Jonson's *The Devil is an Ass* with Tom Cain's welcome Revels edition of *Poetaster*, using the 1616 Folio for his copy-text, but re-inserting satirical references to knighthoods from the 1602 Quarto and four lines cut from Act IV of F because of their non-literary nature, which 'should at least be available for a modern director'. Cain's commentary is thorough and interesting, drawing where possible on the scholarship available to Jonson in clarifying classical references, while in his introduction he offers a balanced assessment of its topical ones, arguing that 'Far from the two readings of the play, as personal lampoon or as "meaningful work of art", being mutually exclusive, the two are interdependent': Cain's Jonson is both high-minded and rancorous. The introduction suffers a little from attempting to cover so much ground, including sections on the place of *Poetaster* in relation to (amongst others) concepts of government, satire and language, classical imitation, the boys' companies, the War of the Theatres, *Twelfth Night*, the Essex rebellion and the Middle Temple. The result is that Cain's discussion is both dense and fragmented, but always thought-provoking.

The three texts included in the Revels Plays Companion Library publication, *Three Renaissance Travel Plays* (ed. Anthony Parr), are even further from the beaten track: *The Travels of the Three English Brothers* by Day, Rowley and Wilkins (acted 1607), *The Sea Voyage* by Fletcher and Massinger (1622) and *The Antipodes* by Richard Brome (1638). Of these, only the latter has ever been available in a modern critical edition, so this collection is especially timely in responding to the current upsurge of interest in Early Modern travel-writing of all kinds. The plays cannot, of course, be dealt with as comprehensively as in single volumes and the light collation is not particularly informative, but there is still a reasonably detailed commentary and Parr's introduction helpfully places the plays within the context both of contemporary travel and attitudes towards it, while his discussion of them individually is perceptive and to the point. One might quibble with some of the details of the editorial modernization, but not with the value of the enterprise.

Six volumes in the Oxford Drama Library series were published by OUP, both in rather fine hardbacks, and, much more usefully, in cheap WC editions: Marlowe's *Dr Faustus and Other Plays* (ed. David Bevington and Eric Rasmussen, also responsible for the 1993 Revels edition of *Dr Faustus*), Jonson's *The Alchemist and Other Plays* (ed. Gordon Campbell), Middleton's *A Mad World My Masters and Other Plays* (ed. Michael Taylor), Ford's *'Tis Pity She's a Whore and Other Plays* (ed. Marion Lomax), *Four Revenge Tragedies* (ed. Katharine Eisaman Maus) and *Court Masques* (ed. David Lindley). These follow a common format, with a brief critical introduction and bibliography preceding the texts and explanatory notes and a glossary following them, though there are some variations within that format. Campbell, for example, is a more vigorous modernizer than other editors (if it were not for the fact that the word 'volpone' still exists in modern Italian, we would apparently have had to learn to call Jonson's play *Volpe*), and less generous in his provision of a bibliography; Lomax and Lindley alone give frequent text references in their glossaries. All the editors, though, have provided useful student editions, with some minimal textual information and notes which on the whole are restricted to clarifying meaning and sometimes historical context. Where they may have an advantage over similar paperback collections is in their selection of plays, at least one less common text being printed in each volume. The Marlowe volume contains both the A- and B-texts of *Dr Faustus*, as well as both parts of *Tamburlaine*, *The Jew of Malta* and *Edward II*, the generosity on *Faustus* presumably (and unfortunately) leaving no space for Marlowe's remaining plays. The collection of Jonson plays includes *Epicene*, as well as *Volpone*, *The Alchemist* and *Bartholomew Fair*; the Ford plays are *'Tis Pity*, *The Lover's Melancholy*, *The Broken Heart* and *Perkin Warbeck*. *Four Revenge Tragedies* contains *The Spanish Tragedy* and *The Revenger's Tragedy* together with the rather less familiar (at undergraduate level) *The Revenge of Bussy d'Ambois* and *The Atheist's Tragedy*, while *Court Masques* makes available 18 Stuart masque texts, which are mostly not in print at all – it is only to be regretted that more could not be included. The Middleton edition should perhaps have been titled *A Mad World My Masters and Other City Comedies*: the three other plays are *Michaelmas Term*, *A Trick to Catch the Old One* and *No Wit, No Help Like a Woman's*. The omission of *A Chaste Maid in Cheapside* is surprising in an anthology such as this, but it is,

I suppose, more easily available. Finally, John Butcher has produced an edition of *Dr Faustus*, based on the B-text, specifically for schools, in the Longman Literature series. With a brief historical introduction and notes, it provides a study programme for students, making use of both analysis and performance.

By contrast with the number of new editions, there were few articles of textual interest. In a piece too late for the editors of the new Webster edition, 'Notes on Editing Webster', Martin Wiggins draws attention to problematic readings in *The White Devil, The Duchess of Malfi, The Devil's Law-Case* and *A Cure for A Cuckold*, and suggests solutions and possible emendations of particular interest to those preparing modernized texts (*N&Q* 42.369–77). In 'The Concluding Pages of the Jonson Folio of 1616' (*SB* 47[1994].147–54), James A. Riddell discusses the evidence concerning the printing of the Folio's last two pages and the proper order of the final speeches of *The Golden Age Restored*, and argues that, contrary to the conclusions of Herford and Simpson and subsequent critics, the detailed bibliographical evidence of press correction, supported by literary evidence, shows that the corrected version is that which has Astraea's final speech preceding that of Pallas. Since influential interpretations of the masque, and of Jonson's relationship with James I, have been put forward by Stephen Orgel, Jonathan Goldberg and Joseph Loewenstein based on the reverse order, Riddell's argument has considerable significance; he will, no doubt, be pleased that Lindley's *Court Masques* prints the speeches in the order he proposes. Robert R. Fleissner considers the arguments concerning the intended spelling of Faustus's university in '"Wittenberg," not "Wertenberg": A Nominal Discrepancy in The A-text of *Doctor Faustus*', and some of the implications of preferring one to the other (*PBSA* 89.ii.189–92). Stephen Tabor's 'Additions to STC' includes an entry giving details of the printing of the two 1605 editions of *The Case is Altered* (*Library* 16[1994].190–207). Extracts from George Walton Williams's 1986 address at the Folger Shakespeare Library, 'On Editing Beaumont and Fletcher', have been printed (*ShN* 44[1994].63, 66, 68; 45.3, 6, 20) in recognition of the final volume of the Cambridge edition. In the first part Williams traces the printing and publishing history of the plays up to the initiation of that edition, and in the second surveys its progress, briefly discussing its strengths and weaknesses, and ends by addressing the question of whether Beaumont and Fletcher are worth the effort involved in the preparation of a new edition. His answer that 'they did the best they could; they are entitled to the best we can do', is one with which all editors, of any author, must concur. Finally, James P. Saeger and Christopher J. Fassler have produced 'The London Professional Theater, 1576–1642: A Catalogue and Analysis of the Extant Printed Plays' (*RORD* 34.63–109), which 'lists by author all known extant printed plays associated with the theater of the period and provides for those plays information on author and play-company attributions and on the printed editions of each'. The catalogue, which includes only plays written for the professional theatre, draws together information from Greg's *Bibliography of the English Printed Drama to the Restoration*, Harbage's *Annals of English Drama* and the *STC*. The amount of original input is minimal, any 'imperfections' in the *Annals* apparently having been transferred to the catalogue as 'acceptable', and for a listing which claims to provide a 'summary of the universe of extant printed plays', it seems extraordinary to omit details of the printer. Following the catalogue are tables showing (rather roughly) the changes in the pattern of publication on a yearly basis and by decade, including the percentage of new plays, and of plays printed with attributions of author and company. Again, these comparisons are based only on extant plays. The information provided in the article might prove useful as a starting-point, but most students are more likely to find their way to the reference works on which it is based, and would probably be best advised to do so. I was, though, rather taken with the concept which appears in one of the footnotes, of the printing of a 'discreet play'.

2. Theatre History

In *The Stage Designs of Inigo Jones: The European Context*, John Peacock seeks to correct a misapprehension promulgated by Orgel and Strong's edition of the masque designs. Rather than read the ubiquity of foreign art in Jones's work as a lack of originality (as Orgel and Strong suggest) Jones is a conduit through which the civilizing influences of ancient and contemporary continental art find their way to the English court, and his extensive quotation of the work of others, such as Palladio, Alberti and Jacques Callot, a symptom of his own aesthetic sophistication. Jones is seen to be responding not only to shifts in European artistic sensibilities but also to political pressures closer to home. *The Masque of Oberon* (1611) blends primitive, neo-Gothic elements with a harmonious classicism intended to reflect 'the duality of Oberon's [Prince Henry's] virtue, at once chivalric and antique'. Again, the classicism of the masques for James can be read as an index of the monarch's aspiration to be perceived as an imperial Caesar ruling over the United Kingdom. Peacock is a sophisticated and learned art historian but he also rightly insists on the influence that material and technical aspects have on masque design, as in his commentary on the proscenium arch. While most of this handsome book is engaging and subtle, Peacock is occasionally guilty of making too little concession to the non-specialist which, given the interest of the subject matter to those in literature and theatre, as well as the trained art-historian, is unfortunate.

In their engaging article, 'Towards "a full and understanding auditory"': New Evidence of Playgoers at the First Globe Theatre' (*MLR* 90.556–71), Mary A. Blackstone and Cameron Lewis explicate a series of legal documents presented before Star Chamber which relate to a Jacobean punch-up at the Globe Theatre in 1612, and use the occasion to demonstrate the complexity of societal structures which govern the construction of the playhouse audience, based on the interaction of such features as 'birth, title, land holdings and public office' as well as 'education, wealth and religion'. In so doing, they call into question the tendency to homogenize theatrical audiences and to label them 'plebeian' or 'privileged'. The authors share Andrew Gurr's aspiration to analyse audience members not merely by social class but by 'mental composition' though this nebulous criterion is never sufficiently particularized. The article's attempt to draw together the characters involved in the altercation with those of *The Duchess of Malfi* never really gets off the ground.

Two articles focus on *The Knight of the Burning Pestle*. Richard Madelaine in 'Apprentice Interventions: Boy Actors, the Burning Pestle and the Privy Mark of Irony' (*QWERTY* 5.73–7) demonstrates the various ways in which the play is an apprentice-piece. It contrasts the obedient and the independent, 'risk-taking' apprentices, Rafe and Jasper, while each role offers a 'suitably testing private theatre apprentice-piece'. Madelaine suggests that the play itself 'might be considered to be Beaumont's apprentice-piece' and accounts for its hostile reception in terms of his inexperience with private theatre audiences whose gallants would have found themselves victims of the play's withering satire. This conviction is shared by Roy J. Booth in ' "Down with your title, Boy!": Beaumont's *The Knight of the Burning Pestle* and its Insurgent Audience' (*QWERTY* 5.51–8). Booth concentrates particularly on the syphilitic knights whom Rafe rescues from Barbaroso and contends that the 'pox-ridden gallantry' watching the play would have recognized an image of themselves, so that Beaumont's irascible attack constitutes a 'way of accounting for the failure of this brilliant comedy to please its first audiences'. Beaumont, he concludes, under the influence of Jonson, presents an 'uneasily supercilious version of carnival'.

3. Criticism

(a) General
Book-length works dedicated to Renaissance drama are thin on the ground this year. Rowland Wymer's *Webster and Ford* would, however, stand out in any year as a model of stimulating and concise dramatic criticism. Wymer is sensitive to historical context and the qualities of the plays in performance, and his introductory chapter on 'Revivals, reputations, and the question of value' is particularly interesting in its engagement with the frequent charges of sensationalism and moral decadence levelled at both authors over the centuries. Further chapters consider Webster and then Ford play by play, and this chronological approach has a kind of logic sometimes missing from other pairings of dramatists in this Macmillan series. Wymer's detailed readings reveal plays of uneven but considerable emotive power and intensity, and his attention to performance means that he is able to refute certain dismissive critical orthodoxies about plays such as *The White Devil*. The study of Webster and Ford, particularly at undergraduate level, is immeasurably aided by this highly recommended work. Other articles on Ford and Webster this year include several short pieces in the conference proceedings edited by James Hogg, *Jacobean Drama as Social Criticism*. Dimiter Daphinoff asks 'How Conservative was John Ford?' and concludes that 'undecided' is a more accurate epithet, given that while the tragi-comedies may show a nostalgic yearning for the past, the chronicle play *Perkin Warbeck* dramatizes an interrogation of the Stuart ideal of divine authority. Thomas Sorge discusses 'Baroque Theatricality and Anxiety in the Drama of John Ford', and concentrates on baroque signification in Ford's theatricalized world with particular reference to *'Tis Pity She's a Whore*. The relationship of this play to *Othello* is discussed by Raymond Powell in 'The Adaptation of a Shakespearean Genre: *Othello* and Ford's *'Tis Pity She's a Whore*' (*RenQ* 48.582–92), which traces echoes in characterization, plot and language. On a similar theme is Lisa Hopkins's 'John Ford's *Perkin Warbeck* and *Henry IV Part One*' (*N&Q*

42.380–1). The same volume also has two other notes by Hopkins, both of which relate Ford to earlier drama: '*Perkin Warbeck* and *Fulgens and Lucres*', and 'John Ford's Annabella and the Virgin Mary' claims an element of parody in '*Tis Pity* in relation to the mystery play *Joseph*. On Webster, James Hogg's 'Court Satire in John Webster's *The White Devil*' (in Hogg, *Jacobean Drama*) is remarkable for its proliferation of footnotes which offer a running commentary on the play in performance. The main body of the article reads the play as satire on the perceived decadence and excess of the Jacobean court, and sees the play's Giovanni as a type for Prince Henry, in whom the hopes for the reinstatement of justice and order are located. Martin Wiggins offers extensive advice on preparing a modernized annotated edition in his 'Notes on Editing Webster' (*N&Q* 42.369–77).

Jeffrey Masten's essay 'Family values: euthanasia, editing, and *The Old Law*' (*TPr* 9.445–58) is also, but very differently, concerned with editing. His article engagingly combines an analysis of the play, which he is editing for OUP's forthcoming collected works of Middleton, a recognition of the peculiar freedoms of editing and writing about an almost unknown text, and the suggestion that editing should be concerned with reception as well as production. This Masten addresses through his work on the unidentified seventeenth-century annotations on one copy of the play, which, while they cannot be used to stabilize the text's meaning, can indicate what meanings might be imaginable at certain historical points. In an essay in the Festschrift for the historian David Underdown, Lisa Jardine uses *The Changeling* as a basis for a discussion of 'Companionate marriage versus male friendship: anxiety for the lineal family in Jacobean drama' (in Susan D. Amussen and Mark A. Kishlinsky, eds, *Political Culture and Cultural Politics in Early Modern Europe*). The play illustrates the dynastic anxiety prompted by a friction between new models of companionate marriage and traditional patterns of social organization. Jardine analyses its treatment of male friendship, and the strategies by which it shifts the blame for the disruption of family and the violation of male/male intimacy onto woman, arguing that it captures contemporary collisions between domestic and public interests. The play is the subject of James Hogg's 'William Hayley's *Marcella* and Thomas Middleton and William Rowley's *The Changeling*: A Watered-Down Jacobean Masterpiece' (in Hogg, *Jacobean Drama*) which discusses *Marcella* as an eighteenth-century adaptation. Also on Middleton are two pieces on *A Game at Chess*, a note by Jeanne Shami tracing an analogue in a sermon by Robert Harris at the funeral of Sir Anthony Cope in 1614 ('Thomas Middleton's *A Game at Chess*: A Sermon Analogue', *N&Q* 42.367–9) and Hogg's 'An Ephemeral Hit: Thomas Middleton's *A Game at Chess*', again in his collection. As with other of his essays surveyed here, Hogg provides a useful and well-annotated account of critical opinions rather than a new reading, but the article is clear and helpful to students of this difficult play. A final Middleton piece is found in a collection of essays dedicated to the memory of Margot Heinemann, *Heart of the Heartless World* (ed. David Margolies and Maroula Joannou). Inga-Stina Ewbank's article, '"O Cunning Texture to Enclose Adultery": Sexuality and Intertextuality in Middleton's *Hengist, King of Kent*' examines Middleton's intertextuality, his use of other dramatists, and his characters' use of each others' sexuality. The intertextual references are particularly interesting, and Ewbank reads the scene of Castiza's rape in the context of the conventional dramatic bed-trick and its configurations of gender and power. Traces of the influence of the contemporaneous *Duchess of Malfi*, and the suggestion that the same actor might play Bosola and Horsus, are fruitful, as is an unexpected comparison with Ridley Scott's 1991 film, *Thelma and Louise*.

The question of the theatrical representation of women has, deservedly, received much critical attention in recent years. Carol Hansen's re-issued work *Woman as Individual in English Renaissance Drama: A Defiance of the Masculine Code* adds to the number of works on this subject, but little to our understanding. She argues that in 'Elizabethan drama we find women characters caught in a maze of the masculine code, a psychological mind-set based upon anti-feminist stereotyping', and these generalizations abound. Hansen makes use of contemporary material about the question of woman, but is disappointingly blurred about this social context, tending to homogenize opinions from the mid-sixteenth to the mid-seventeenth centuries without demur. As the book's subtitle suggests, it argues that dramatists did not accept the stereotype of women but instead produced female characters who struggle for their own individuality against 'the masculine code'. Through readings of Shakespeare's plays, Heywood's *A Woman Killed with Kindness*, Webster's *The Duchess of Malfi* and Middleton and Rowley's *The Changeling* the book traces the emergence of strong women characters, constructing an over-simplified narrative of progress from submission through defiance to a 'partial resolution' in the figure of the disguised woman as equal or friend.

Ilse Born-Lechleitner's study *The Motif of Adultery in Elizabethan, Jacobean, and Caroline Tragedy* offers a more successful historical reading of a play theme, drawing extensively on contemporary commentary to provide 'legal background' and 'moral background'. Born-Lechleitner sees adultery as a symbolic device signifying 'the dramatists' sense [. . .] of a disintegration of political, social and moral ideals through the pursuit of individualistic pleasures'. Her readings of domestic tragedy, and the plays of, among others, Heywood, Marston, Chapman and Webster give her book a wider chronological and dramatic basis than that offered by Hansen.

Jacobean tragedy gets further attention in Hogg's collection. Andreas Mahler's 'A Lost World, No New-Found Land – Disorientation and Immobility as Social Criticism in Early Seventeenth-Century Tragedy' emphasizes the idea of a society in crisis. Masculine order, Mahler argues with reference to *The Duchess of Malfi*, tries to 'reassert itself through a strategy of subordination by confinement'. Rowland Wymer asks 'Jacobean Pageant or Elizabethan Fin de Siècle? The Political Context of Early Seventeenth-Century Tragedy' and gives a lucid and measured account of recent critical attempts to historicize the drama. He argues against over-identification of playworlds with the contemporary court, with the exception of *The Revenger's Tragedy* which does articulate 'a radical alienation from [James's] court'. Peter Corbin's article, 'A Dog's Obeyed in Office: Kingship and Authority in Jacobean Tragedy' agrees with this account of Middleton's play, discussing it in the context of the intervention of the Master of the Revels. Corbin argues for the political significance of plays by Beaumont and Fletcher, Chapman, and others, not so much in their themes but in the 'dramatic dynamics by which they organise audience response'. Uwe Baumann considers 'The Presentation of the Roman Imperial Court in Jacobean Tragedy' as a figure for dissatisfaction nearer home, with reference to plays by Jonson, Massinger and Fletcher. In 'Abjection and Power: The Semiotics of Violence in Jacobean Tragedy', Attila Kiss presents a more theorized inquiry into the 'representation of identity-shaping discursive practices'. This essay has a disjointed quality and readers may find its use of italics over-emphatic, but it offers an interesting perspective on language, metatheatricality and violence. Overall, this collection is uneven and curiously under-edited. Other articles include Michael Scott on 'Confrontational Comedy', a likeably digressive piece (partly) on Marston, Gotz Schmitz's work on 'Satirical Elements in Latin Comedies Acted on the Occasion of Royal Visits to Cambridge University', Stanley Hussey's 'Social Stratification by Language' which considers different registers in a number of plays and Edward Burns's 'The Sharp Spectator' which raises some interesting questions about spectatorship and audience response. Also concerned with audiences are David Farley-Hills's 'The Audience Implications of some Paul's and Blackfriars' Plays', and, in *RORD* 34, Paul Whitfield White on 'Politics, Topical Meaning and English Theater Audiences 1485–1575'. Farley-Hills tries to reconstruct the audiences of a play like *Westward Ho* from internal evidence. Whitfield White argues that in order to understand the topicality of plays performed prior to the opening of professional playhouses, detailed localizing work needs to be done. Ilse Born-Lechleitner discusses 'Implicit Social Criticism in *The Witch of Edmonton*' (in Hogg, *Jacobean Drama*), finding in the play both 'a realistic representation of Jacobean society' and a typology of moral degeneration. Simon Dorangeon's 'Beaumont and Fletcher, or a Self-Subverting Praise of Virtue in an Impure Society' reads a rhetorical complicity with the audience which compromises moral clarity.

The collection of essays edited by David L.Smith, Richard Strier and David Bevington as *The Theatrical City: Culture, Theatre and Politics in London 1576–1649* presents a different relationship between disciplines which might be called 'history' and 'literature'. The book proceeds through paired essays, one by a historian and the other by a literary critic, on different aspects of London's theatricality. Dekker's *The Shoemaker's Holiday* is addressed by Paul Seaver and David Bevington, Marston's *The Fawn* by Linda Levy Peck and Frank Whigham, and Massinger's *A New Way to Pay Old Debts* by Keith Lindley and Martin Butler, among other texts which define theatricality more broadly. The results are stimulating: sometimes a dialogue between the two essays is clear and at other times their coupling is puzzling, sometimes the sense of disciplinary boundaries is blurred and at other times firmly asserted. This makes for an interesting intervention into the question of the intellectual validity of inter-disciplinarity and its possible format in an institutional context, as well as offering new perspectives on these plays as part of their historical and literary world. Dekker and Massinger also appear elsewhere in this year's work. Joost Dalder and Antony Telford Moore present 'New Variants in the First Part of Dekker's *The Honest Whore*' (*N&Q* 42.342–4). There are two essays on Massinger, 'Giving and Taking in Massinger's Tragicomedies' by Robert Y. Turner (*SEL* 35.361–82) and D. M. De Silva's 'Society, Politics and the Aesthetic Life of Massinger's Plays' (in Hogg, ed., *Jacobean Drama*). Turner addresses Massinger's interest in an alternative economy of patronage and mutuality rather than the city market of earlier playwrights' focus. He finds that the plays attempt to speak up on behalf of 'the subject, the female, and the servant', and that those who shirk the responsibilities of this community of interdependence are demonized. De Silva discusses Massinger's moral and political stances in a number of plays, and finds them not incompatible.

Political readings of the drama have produced some stimulating work. Michel Bitot's ' "Alteration in a Commonwealth": Disturbing Voices in Caroline Drama' (*CahiersE* 47.79–86) argues that Caroline forms of drama 'reflect in their variety the political turbulence of [their] age', and, in readings of plays from 1638–41, he finds a theatricalized attempt to preserve social harmony through the representation of benevolent monarch or of an ideal commonwealth. Generic mixtures and varieties in this period are a displaced effort to bring forth a form of social and political reconciliation, a kind of dramatic oil on politically troubled waters. In the same journal issue, Faith M. Nosbakken's 'Rowley's *When You See Me You Know Me*: Political Drama in Transition' (71–8) sees Rowley's play of 1604 at a turning point, both political and dramatic. She discusses its yoking of two distinct traditions, the earlier chronicle history plays and the political mythology of masques, arguing ultimately that the play's discrepancies result from this generic and political disjunction, rather than from any 'deliberate effort to expose, challenge, or subvert political complexities'. Nosbakken sees Prince Edward as intended to honour James's heir, Henry and Susan E. Krantz, in her article 'Thomas Dekker's Political Commentary in *The Whore of Babylon*' (*SEL* 35.271–92), also discovers a pro-Henrician stance. Her reading of Dekker's play in the social and thematic context of militant Protestant texts reacting to the Gunpowder Plot reveals how its author manipulated his sources in order to consolidate the powerful dramatic cocktail of anti-Spanish, anti-Catholic, pro-Essex, pro-Elizabeth, pro-Henrician sympathies. Also concerned with national/religious xenophobia in the drama is A. J. Hoenselaars's 'The Elizabethans and the Turk at Constantinople' (*CahiersE* 47.29–42), which argues for an early modern pre-history to the narrative of western constructions of the Orient which Edward Said's book *Orientalism* charts for the eighteenth century. Hoenselaars traces the phrase about taking the Turk by the beard in Constantinople from Shakespeare's *Henry V*, through Brome's *The Antipodes* and Thomas Nabbes's *Tottenham Court* to show its association with virility, procreation, and comic self-fictions. He argues that the phrase becomes self-consciously theatrical, showing an awareness of its wish-fulfilment mastery of the Turk as a fiction.

Karen L. Raber's essay on Elizabeth Cary, 'Gender and the Political Subject in *The Tragedy of Mariam*' (*SEL* 35.321–44), discusses the ideology of closet drama as a form duplicitously public and private, and allies this to her overall theme of the disjunction between domestic ideology and political philosophy in the play. In a wide-ranging essay on 'Staging Modernity: Chapman, Jonson, and the Decline from the Golden Age' (*CahiersE* 47.9–28), Peter K. Ayers discusses the contradictions in the dramatic representation of this decline. Chapman offers a distinctively urban reworking of the myth as liberation from past values, linked to the licence of linguistic self-creation. These references offer a new perspective on *The Alchemist*. Janette Dillon is also concerned with dramatic languages in '*The Spanish Tragedy* and Staging Languages in Renaissance Drama' (*RORD* 34.15–40), in which she discusses the theatrical effect of the 'sundry languages' in Hieronimo's play 'Soliman and Perseda'. Her analysis of the use of Latin is cogent and her conclusion, that the confusion of languages emphasizes the inexplicable emptiness of the play's conclusion, is a compelling one. Kyd's language in the play is used as the basis of a principal component analysis of authorship for 'Possible Light on a Kyd Canon' (*N&Q* 42.340–1). Thomas Merriam suggests that Kyd is the author of *Soliman and Perseda*, and also notes that his analysis divorces *The Jew of Malta* from Marlowe's other works. Source studies such as that presented by Richard Rowland in '*The Captives*: Thomas Heywood's "Whole Monopoly off Mischeiff"' (*MLR* 90.585–602) and Hilary Gatti in 'Giordano Bruno and the Stuart Court Masques' (*RenQ* 48.809–42), offer interesting insights. Rowland discusses Heywood's reworking of Plautus's *Rudens* and his use of Masuccio di Salerno's fifteenth-century novella for the subplot, in arguing for the play as more interesting and more accomplished than has previously been allowed. Gatti traces Bruno's influence on the political language of the masque, beginning with an analysis of Samuel Daniel's *Tethys' Festival* and including Thomas Carew's use of Bruno's fourth Italian dialogue, *Lo spaccio della bestia trionfante* in his *Coelum Britannicum*. Others offer smaller-scale elucidations of particular sources: Swapan Chakravorty elaborates '"Upon a Sudden Wit": On the Sources of an Unnoticed Pun in *The Revenger's Tragedy*' (*N&Q* 42.352), and Martin Wiggins discusses 'A Nightingale in Poplar: The Sub-plot of *A Cure for a Cuckold*' (378–80). Other notes include Wiggins's on 'The Date of *A Cure for a Cuckold*' (377–8), Hans Werner's 'A Vindication of A. H. Bullen's Dating of *The Costlie Whore*' (352–7), and T. W. Craik's 'Notes on the Text of Marston's *Antonia and Mellida*: A Postscript' (342).

(b) Marlowe

Though the year has produced no book-length studies of Marlowe, the essays that have appeared range over almost the full range of his dramatic texts, as well as *Hero and Leander*. In addition, there is the appearance of a paperback edition of the plays in *Doctor Faustus and Other Plays* by David Bevington and Eric Rasmussen which includes *Tamburlaine I and II*, *Doctor Faustus* (A- and B-texts), *The Jew of Malta* and *Edward II*. The introduction attempts to make some connection between the plays and what is supposed or known of Marlowe's life and ideas, albeit in a relatively conservative light, with little or no reference to more recent critical readings which have explored the oppositional and subversive potential of Marlowe's work. However, the plays are presented in a clear and uncluttered format, the explanatory notes being relegated to the end of the volume. This makes them a little less accessible during reading, though words and expressions which get a note are marked. Spelling and punctuation are modernized, though original words are kept if historically separate from their modern cognates, and archaic forms are preserved when the metre demands it. All plays are edited in five acts. A glossary and a limited bibliography are provided. This volume joins the OUP WC collection as a useful edition for teaching and the general reader.

Undoubtedly the most significant critical piece on Marlowe to appear this year is Richard Wilson's '*Tamburlaine the Great* and Ivan the Terrible' (*ELH* 62.47–68). Wilson examines Marlowe's Tamburlaine in relation to the reports of the English emissary to Russia, Sir Jerome Horsey, regarding the ruthless Tsar Ivan IV. Wilson draws various parallels between the virulent qualities of

Tamburlaine and the Russian emperor on the one hand, and on the other the empire-building activities of Marlowe's tyrannical hero and the aggressive trading ventures of the Muscovy Company. Perceived analogies between the two would have struck a chord with London investors, providing the play with a historical context which was curiously relevant and favourable. The essay points to Tamburlaine's subversion of the binary division between western and oriental through his conquests which encompass a wide geographical area, and compares this to the dealings of the trading companies that cut across cultures.

The two most interesting essays on *Doctor Faustus* examine, in somewhat complementary ways, the text's position in cultural history. George Geckle contributes to the debate about the contesting authority of the A- and B-texts of *Doctor Faustus* in 'The 1604 and 1616 Versions of *Dr. Faustus*: Text and Performance' in *Subjects on the World's Stage: Essays on British Literature of the Middle Ages and the Renaissance* (ed. David Allen and Robert White). He argues for the authority of the A-text on the basis of a comparison between the professional productions of both texts, which appeared close in time to each other: the 1988 Young Vic production using John Jump's B-text edition, and a 1989 Royal Shakespeare Company production using the A-text edition by David Ormerod and Christopher Wortham. He sees a comparison between these productions as revealing that the A-text gives Faustus full responsibility for his choices. Geckle does not contest the view of Marlowe as an atheist, but rather re-asserts it, while perhaps somewhat paradoxically arguing for a version of the play which has at its basis a strong medieval theological consistency, insisting that this conflict creates a powerful and complex Renaissance play. In the same volume is Sallye Sheppeard's 'Marlowe's Icarus: Culture and Myth in *Doctor Faustus*', which has the play illustrating the Renaissance origins of modern humanity in a cultural crisis resulting from, on the one hand Christian orthodoxy's failure to loosen its mythology from dogma and accommodate its vision to changing circumstances, and, on the other modern humanity's resultant move into the unknown, without the support of cultural myths. Faustus is seen as representing simultaneously Renaissance humanism in its ideas of man as perfectible through knowledge, and the Protestant reformist doctrine of man as inherently corrupt and incapable of change except through divine intervention, the Icarus myth symbolizing the destructive consequences that result when imagination proceeds without regard for wisdom.

The theology of the play is the subject of two other studies, Thomas McAlindon's '*Doctor Faustus*: The Predestination Theory' (*ES* 76.215–20) and Frédéric Peyré's '*Lines, Circles, Letters and Characters*: The Conjuration of Tragedy in Marlowe's *Doctor Faustus*' (*CahiersE* 47.1–8). McAlindon examines the play in the light of the Calvinist dogma of reprobation and suggests that the predestination theory is reductive and simplifies unacceptably the tragic complexity of the work and that if Marlowe was attacking anything it was the harshness of Christian theology itself. If McAlindon's thesis is rooted in contemporary religious issues, it is hard to see what theological or other basis informs the argument of Peyré's impenetrably written piece, which constitutes what can only be regarded as a modern example of scholasticism. Peyré contends that the renunciation of God causes Faustus to drift into the paradoxical status of a performing object engrossed in shaping an illusory omnipotent identity; he is a character doomed to time-marking incantations of fundamentally undifferentiated ritual. The character's performance turns him into his own prop, and the performance of the magic ritual solemnizes the subordination of the initiate to the tragic space of illusion created by the devil.

Both Marlowe's history plays are addressed by Marie-Noelle Zeender in 'De l'influence de Machiavel sur le théâtre de Christopher Marlowe' (*Cycnos* 12.i.1–9) who argues that the key figures in *The Massacre at Paris* and *Edward II* are conceived in machiavellian terms, and under the influence of the writings of the philosopher. The argument is less than convincing, particularly in respect of the latter play, which is given more attention. Marlowe's historiography in *The Massacre at Paris* is examined in two essays, Penny Roberts's 'Marlowe's *The Massacre at Paris*: a historical perspective' (*RS* 9.430–41), and Andrew M. Kirk's 'Marlowe and the Disordered Face of French History' (*SEL* 35.193–213). Remarking that Paul Kocher has argued that Marlowe's source for his depiction of the massacre comes from an English version of a text attributed to François Hotman, a Huguenot propagandist who presents a narrative of unscrupulous Catholic murderers and pious Protestant martyrs, but that Julia Briggs has argued for more direct sources for accounts of the assassination of Duke and Cardinal of Guise and Henry III (1588 and 1589), resulting in a stance different from the earlier part of the play, Roberts sets out as part of the purpose of her essay to see if these standpoints can be reconciled, so that Marlowe's play takes a firmly pro-Protestant line, though it incorporates elements of differing versions of events into its narrative. Among the issues which she identifies the play as presenting are the dangers of weak monarchy, the reliance on favourites, allowing nobles too much influence, and an insecure succession, all of which had resonance during Elizabeth's last years. Roberts concludes that Marlowe's version is surprisingly close to historical record and also acts as a warning to monarchs of the consequences of their actions. Andrew Kirk resists the idea that *The Massacre at Paris* is a thinly veiled appeal to English Protestants who supported the Queen, and that the text can be read simply as a code. Instead, he suggests that what produces the impression of chaos in the play is that the French history it dramatizes is perceived through the lens of English historiography. Flawed French kings are at the centre of the explanation of historical events, an idea which proceeds from English perceptions of French inconstancy.

In their examination of Marlowe's other history play, it is cultural history rather than historiography that is the subject of the two essays on *Edward II*, Elisabeth Angel-Pérez's '*Edouard II* de Christopher Marlowe ou les prémices de l'Absurde: la naissance de l'espace tragique' (*RHT* 47.7–14) and Ian McAdam's '*Edward II* and the Illusion of Integrity' (*SP* 112.203–29). Angel-Pérez argues that the work of Marlowe, despite just having emerged from the Middle Ages, resonates with modernity and that as a transitional dramatist, Marlowe creates theatre which still has the imprint of medieval drama. The article sets out to provide an anachronous reading to reveal, in Derridean terms, more the *intentio operis* than the *intentio auctoris* and to defend the idea that Marlowe in *Edward II* (and in *The Jew of Malta*) conceals his modernity with a cover of prudent conservatism. *Edward II* is presented as demolishing thematic and dramatic mechanisms, and Angel-Pérez argues that the play abandons the Aristotelian concept of tragedy in favour of a Nietzschean idea of human existence as inevitably tragic. She concludes that the affirmation of the contradictory is one of the proofs of Marlowe's modernity. McAdam's discussion of the play proceeds from a perspective that is much more directly social than philosophical, advancing the idea that *Edward II* is about a failure in self-fashioning. He reviews the debate about Marlowe's handling of Edward's homosexuality, and sets out to locate the argument about the meaning of Edward's death in something other than a critique of homophobia or the social control of sexuality. He emphasizes instead the question of responsibility and identifies the significant issue as being the fact that Edward has chosen to 'play the boy'. McAdam argues that imagination in the play is used as an *escape* from the world, rather than a means of coming to terms with it, and in doing so he offers some sideswipes at new-historicist notions of power.

If the issue of sexuality is largely sidestepped in these two essays, it is squarely addressed by M. Morgan Holmes in 'Identity and the Dissidence it Makes: Homoerotic Nonsense in Kit Marlowe's *Hero and Leander*' (*ESC* 21.151–69). Holmes argues that Marlovian homoeroticism is very unsettling, and stands in opposition to the definition of individual identity through the discourse of exclusive and immutable sexual desire. The essay challenges Bruce Smith's idea (in *Homosexual Desire in Shakespeare's England* [*YWES* 73.222]) that Marlowe's art expresses beginnings of a specifically homosexual subjectivity, and maintains instead that the poem's strategic deployment of homoerotic discourse challenges the increasing tendency of early modern society to establish 'sexuality' as a primary basis of subjective identity. It sees *Hero and Leander* as embodying a carnivalesque refusal of identity through the transgression of signs and symbols, which disrupts the production of reified identities that are both the cause and effect of homophobia. He suggests that the poem undermines any notion of absolutes in desire and emphasizes the relatedness of a variety of sexual identifications and attachments.

One final offering is Lloyd Edward Kermode's ' "Marlowe's Second City": The Jew as Critic at the Rose in 1592' (*SEL* 35.215–29). In a somewhat tortuous and over-ingenious argument, the essay argues that the location of the 'second city' (the theatre) could potentially inflict damage on the city of London, while also cushioning it from the power of the drama. Kermode advances the notion that, as an outsider, the Jew became a critic of the state, of the city and of the ruling class, and sets out to examine how this figure came to be a 'hero'. He contends that an identification with the Jew is encouraged by the fact that Malta is Spanish-Catholic governed, making the undermining of it not an unattractive prospect to Londoners. However, the homogeneity of their response discourages individualistic response, and thus does not create an anti-authoritarian united force.

(c) Jonson

This has been a reasonably strong year for Jonson publications, with a cluster of monographs coming into print. A new literary biography of Jonson was published: W. David Kay's *Ben Jonson: A Literary Life*. Kay covers all the expected (indeed required) areas – fathers (of natural, adopted and literary varieties), Jonson's classical education and forebears, his somewhat contentious engagement with matters of state, the complex patronage network in which he operated – and offers brief 'readings' of plays, poems and masques *en route*. Yet there are still notable absences, not least a questioning of some of the 'givens' of Jonsonian criticism of recent decades: his anti-theatricalism, his absolutist politics, his misogyny. Women are perhaps the most notable absence of all, with Jonson's significant female patrons or subject matter discussed only briefly if at all, and the feminocentric accommodations of the later plays, and indeed the much earlier masques, subsumed within arguments about male power. If Kay resists some of the more theoretical and psycho-analytical readings of Jonson's work (not least those of Jonson's most recent previous biographer, David Riggs [*YWES* 70.300–1]), he nevertheless provides a generously exhaustive account of the Jonsonian canon. The localism and the 'politically volatile' nature of much of his material is responsibly acknowledged, as are Jonson's influences, ancient and contemporary. The aristocentrism and androcentrism of the whole, however, offers what is a very particular version of Ben Jonson's 'literary life'.

This year also saw the publication of another monograph by the enviably productive Robert C. Evans: *Habits of Mind: Evidence and Effects of Ben Jonson's Reading*. This is a dense and scholarly account of the significance of Jonson's markings and marginalia in those books from his extensive personal collection which remain extant. Evans elects to concentrate on Jonson's engagement with literary sources and precursors. Each chapter provides an account of the relevance of the chosen texts to Jonson's own compositions, as well as providing a detailed and thorough appendix cataloguing Jonson's annotations, marginal and otherwise. If Chapter 2 confirms in some respects Jonson's reputation as a 'Senecan writer', Chapter 3 more unusually stresses the influence of medieval English literature on Jonson's work, in particular that of Chaucer who provided Jonson with a careerist precursor as the self-fashioned laureate. Evans thus acknowledges Jonsonian investment in the classical tradition but also indicates his identification with his native literature. Evans has also provided an extensive topical index to the book.

William W. Slights's *Ben Jonson and the Art of Secrecy* investigates the various forms and operations of secrecy and encodement in Jonsonian drama. Whilst in a number of ways this book reinforces certain stereotypical stances and interpretations from mainstream Jonsonian criticism – the concentration is, for example, on the 'middle' dramas with the inevitable focusing on *Volpone*, *The Alchemist* and *Bartholomew Fair* (the presence of the tragedies in this context, with their plot intrigues accorded equal status by Slights, is, however, welcome), whilst texts such as the masques or the later plays with their complex encodements and subtexts are dismissed in a matter of lines – there are nevertheless some important contributions to the discussion of the more familiar Jonsonian playtexts to be found here. The book is as a whole admirably alert to issues of genre, emphasizing from the beginning the paradox involved in theatrical displays of secrecy and concealment, and offering subtle accounts of the operations of public and private space within Jonsonian drama as a result.

Elsewhere, central chapters in several books have focused on Jonson. Chapter 5 in Katharine Eisaman Maus's *Inwardness and Theater in the English Renaissance* on 'Prosecution and Sexual Secrecy' investigates the dramatist's particular investment in the impotence trials of early modern England and the questions about inwardness to which they relate. In an illuminating reading of

Epicoene, which employs current gender theory by those such as Judith Butler, Maus acutely interprets the play as being one about social constructions of masculinity and femininity, rather than the misogynist diatribe much criticism has presented it as.

Kim F. Hall's *Things of Darkness: Economies of Race and Gender in Early Modern England* treats *The Masque of Blackness* and *The Masque of Beauty* in its third chapter on ' "Commerce and Intercourse": Dramas of Alliance and Trade'. Hall examines the meeting of economic, social, and sexual concerns at the site of 'blackness' in the two masques, suggesting the potential subversive and feminocentric qualities of these texts under performance conditions. She also offers a persuasive reading of Richard Brome's Caroline play *The English Moor* as a conscious inversion of *Blackness*. Katherine Schwarz's article 'Amazon Reflections in the Jacobean Queen's Masque' (*SEL* 35.293–319) also covers the well-rehearsed material on the staging of female power in the masques for Queen Anne, focusing in particular on the figure of the Amazon and its potential subversiveness in a Jacobean context. Masques also concern Peter Holland's 'The Shapeliness of *The Tempest*' (*EIC* 45.208–29) which considers pattern and parallel in Shakespeare's late play and suggests Jonson's 1609 *Masque of Queens* with its 'first great antimasque' is a source-text for the 1611 play's composition and design.

Two essays in dialogue with each other in *The Theatrical City* (ed. David L. Smith, Richard Strier and David Bevington) discuss *Bartholomew Fair*. Patrick Collinson's 'The Theatre Constructs Puritanism' carries an understanding of theatrical agency to a logical extreme in suggesting that the stereotypical stage Puritan in plays by Jonson, Marston, Middleton and others was a dramatic 'construct', created by playtexts, as well as by the circulation of the inherently theatrical Marprelate pamphlets. Leah Marcus's 'Of Mire and Authorship' rewrites her own 'contained' reading of the play in the 1970s, suggesting instead a positively low-culture, carnivalesque focus for its dramatic events, although she fights shy of aligning Jonson himself directly with this popular cultural energy, discussing it rather in terms of authorial displacement and ambivalences.

Bartholomew Fair is also the focus for G. M. Pinciss's '*Bartholomew Fair* and Jonsonian Tolerance' (*SEL* 35.345–59) which advances an intriguingly liberal humanist version of Jonsonian politics, suggesting that encoded within the hectic action of *Bartholomew Fair* lies a plea for religious tolerance. Pinciss rightly stresses that this is no direct allegory, but finds indirect clues in Cokes's and Wasp's geographical origins and the St Bartholomew Day setting. In *Expl* (54.i.7–8), John King analyses the subtly ironic use of 'stiff-necked' (from Exodus) in 'Jonson's *Bartholomew Fair*'.

BJJ 2 provides another group of articles. Martin Butler's 'Sir Francis Stewart: Jonson's Overlooked Patron' (*BJJ* 2.101–27) explores the history of the dedicatee of Jonson's *Epicoene* in the 1616 Folio version, revealing him as a significant Scottish courtier at the court of King James as well as a significant player (social and intellectual) in the town society which the play of *Epicoene* so adeptly explores, as well as suggesting the significance of the 1616 publication date for both Stewart and Jonson. David M. Whalen's ' "Composing the Imperfect": Ridicule and the Rhetoric of Generosity in Jonson's *Every Man In His Humour*' (129–41) is, as its title suggests, a rhetorical study of this early play, which investigates in particular the operations of satirical comedy within the playtext, arguing for a generous treatment of his subjects by the dramatist. Thomas L. Martin's 'Enormity and *Aurea Mediocritas* in *Bartholomew Fayre*: The Ideas of Classical Comedy' (143–56) also looks at the 'rules' of comic drama and dramatic design, examining Jonson's satirical focus on the 'enormities' of his age and his interest in restoring the 'golden mean' via the medium of drama. Dennis Quinn's 'Polypragmosyne in the Renaissance: Ben Jonson' (157–69) is another rhetoric-invested article which considers the existence of curious or 'polypragmatic' men in Jonsonian and Shakespearean drama. The article explores 'gullible' Jonsonian creations such as Sir Politic Would-Be and Fabian Fitzdottrel, suggesting that the dramatist regularly lampooned curiosity as a cultural activity.

Two notes this year touch on Jonson: Peter R. Moore's 'The Date of F. B.'s Verse Letter to Jonson' which identifies the subject of F.B.'s (presumed to be Francis Beaumont's) letter to Jonson of 1613 as Robert Devereux, Earl of Essex and subject of one of those impotence trials Maus focuses on in her essay, and Neil P. Probst and Robert C. Evans's 'Bishop Duppa and Jonson's "Epick Poem"' (*N&Q* 42.361–3). Duppa collected and edited the book of elegies on Jonson – *Jonsonus Virbius*; Probst and Evans suggest that Duppa knew Jonson during his lifetime, even encouraging his writing in 1619.

BJJ 2 also includes Ian Donaldson's account of the projected OUP New Complete Works of Jonson (223–31), Ton Hoenselaars's report on this year's University of Leeds conference relating to that same project (233–7) and Peter Happé's review of the Royal Shakespeare Company's performance, also this year, of *The Devil is an Ass* (239–46) which are all of considerable interest to Jonson scholars.

Elsewhere, Michael Shapiro's 'The Casting of Flute: Planes of Illusion in *A Midsummer Night's Dream* and *Bartholomew Fair*' (*ET* 13 [1993].147–52) treads familiar ground, comparing Shakespeare's and Jonson's plays in terms of their metatheatricality and their treatments of illusion. *Bartholomew Fair* is presented as an ironic "green world" comedy which distrusts illusion as much as its Shakespearean counterpart celebrates it. In a dense and difficult study, Victoria Silver's 'Totem and Taboo in the Tribe of Ben: The Duplicity of Gender and Jonson's Satires' (*ELH* 62.29–57) considers the duplicitous representations of totemic patriarchy, including kingship, in Jonsonian poetic satire: themes such as modesty and effeminacy are seen both to transcend and to complicate our understandings of gender.

Questions of sexuality rather than gender concern Mario DiGangi's 'Asses and Wits: The Homoerotics of Mastery in Satiric Comedy' (*ELR* 25.179–208). DiGangi subjects the work of Jonson and Chapman to the scrutiny of queer theory, concluding, persuasively, that it is by considering the 'homoerotics of mastery' and of personal service, in *Volpone* and *Epicoene* in particular, that we can begin to comprehend Jonson's dealings in matters 'sodomitical'. This article suggests genuinely new routes for Jonsonian criticism in forthcoming years.

Books Reviewed

Allen, David, and Robert White, eds. *Subjects on the World's Stage: Essays on British Literature of the Middle Ages and the Renaissance*. AUP. UDelP. pp. 161. £34.50. ISBN 0 87413 544 3.

Amussen, Susan D., and Mark A. Kishlinsky, eds. *Political Culture and Cultural Politics in Early Modern Europe: Essays Presented to David Underdown*. ManUP. pp. 369. £50. ISBN 0 7190 4695 5.

Bevington, David, and Eric Rasmussen, eds. *Christopher Marlowe: Doctor Faustus and Other Plays*. OUP. pp. 503. hb £35, pb £6.99. ISBN 0 19 812159 8, 0 19 282737 5.

Born-Lechleitner, Ilse. *The Motif of Adultery in Elizabethan, Jacobean and Caroline Tragedy*. Mellen. pp. 413. $109.95. ISBN 0 7734 1284 0.

Butcher, John, ed. *Doctor Faustus*. Longman. pb £4.99. ISBN 0 582 25409 4.

Cain, Tom, ed. *Poetaster, by Ben Jonson*. Revels. ManUP. pp. 304. hb £40, pb £12.99. ISBN 0 7190 1549 9, 0 7190 1637 1.

Campbell, Gordon, ed. *Ben Jonson: The Alchemist and Other Plays*. OUP. pp. 530. hb £40, pb £6.99. ISBN 0 19 812150 4, 0 19 282252 7.

Evans, Robert C. *Habits of Mind: Evidence and Effects of Ben Jonson's Reading*. BuckUP. pp. 296. £34.50. ISBN 0 8387 5301 9.

Gill, Roma, ed. *The Jew of Malta. The Complete Works of Christopher Marlowe*, vol. IV. OUP. pp. 127. £35. ISBN 0 19 812770 7.

Gunby, David, David Carnegie, and Antony Hammond, eds. *The Works of John Webster*. vol. I, *The White Devil* and *The Duchess of Malfi*. CUP. pp. 713. £90. ISBN 0 521 26059 0.

Hall, Kim F. *Things of Darkness. Economies of Race and Gender in Early Modern England*. CornUP. pp. 312. £32.50. ISBN 0 8014 3117 4.

Hansen, Carol. *Women as Individual in English Renaissance Drama: A Defiance of the Masculine Code*. Lang. pp. 217. pb £12.95. ISBN 0 8204 2009 3.

Hogg, James, ed. *Jacobean Drama as Social Criticism*. Mellen. pp. 361. $99.95. ISBN 0 7734 4186 7.

Kay, W. David. *Ben Jonson: A Literary Life*. Macmillan. pp. 256. hb £37.50, pb £10.99. ISBN 0 333 45446 X, 0 333 46447 8.

Lindley, David, ed. *Court Masques*. OUP. pp. 286. hb £40, pb £6.99. ISBN 0 19 812164 4, 0 19 282569 0.

Lomax, Marion, ed. *John Ford: 'Tis Pity She's a Whore and Other Plays*. OUP. pp. 378. hb £40, pb £6.99. ISBN 0 19 812151 2, 0 19 282253 5.

Margolies, David, and Maroula Joannou, eds. *Heart of the Heartless World: Essays in Cultural Resistance in Memory of Margot Heinemann*. Pluto. pp. 239. pb £14.99. ISBN 0 7453 0981 X.

Maus, Katharine Eisaman, ed. *Four Revenge Tragedies*. OUP. pp. 426. hb £35, pb £6.99. ISBN 0 19 812170 9, 0 19 282633 6.

——, *Inwardness and Theater in the English Renaissance*. UChicP. pp. 232. hb £29.95, pb £11.95. ISBN 0 226 51123 5, 0 226 51124 3.

Parr, Antony, ed. *Three Renaissance Travel Plays*. RevelsCL. ManUP. pp. 330. £45. ISBN 0 7190 3746 8.

Peacock, John. *The Stage Designs of Inigo Jones: The European Context*. CUP. pp. xxii + 387. 195 plates. £80. ISBN 0 521 41812 7.

Slights, William W. *Ben Jonson and the Art of Secrecy*. UTorP. 1994. pp. 242. £32.50. ISBN 0 8020 0462 8.

Smith, David L., Richard Strier, and David Bevington, eds. *The Theatrical City: Culture, Theatre and Politics in London: 1576–1649*. CUP. pp. 288. £35. ISBN 0 521 44126 9.

Taylor, Michael, ed. *Thomas Middleton: A Mad World My Masters and Other Plays*. OUP. pp. 389. pb £6.99. ISBN 0 19 282255 1.

Wymer, Rowland. *Webster and Ford*. Macmillan. pp. 174. pb £10.99. ISBN 0 333 56738 2.

VIII

The Earlier Seventeenth Century: Excluding Drama

MELANIE OSBORNE

This chapter has three sections: 1. General; 2. Poetry; 3. Prose.

1. General

The collection of essays edited by Paola Bottalla and Michela Calderaro, *Counting and Recounting: Measuring Inner and Outer Space in the Renaissance*, addresses the act of counting – the creating of a spatial collocation – and recounting – the establishing of temporal continuity – which is central to the new exploration and description of the world during the English Renaissance. The first essays, by Stephen Greenblatt, Gianfranco Battisti and William Boelhower, focus on the two-way relationship between time and space, inner and outer reality, and more specifically on the inscription in the new continent of the history, law, religion and myths of the old continents. Loretta Innocenti, Paola Bottalla and Bilberto Sacerdoti concentrate upon the intertwinings and conflicts of the cognitive modes of moral and literary codes in Elizabethan and Jacobean culture. Finally, Loretta Innocenti and Valerio de Scarpis focus upon aspects of the counterpoint between poetry and painting, music and poetry. In *The Rest is Silence: Death as Annihilation in the English Renaissance*, Robert N. Watson argues that the fear of death as annihilation produced a crisis in English Renaissance culture, a crisis discernible in both Shakespearean drama, which criticizes and parodies traditional promises of immortality, and Metaphysical poetry, which experiments with new versions of those promises. Throughout this densely written text, Watson traces in a variety of funeral sermons, in the drama of the period and in the work of Donne and Herbert, a blasphemous protest against mortality. This protest or crisis, it is argued, articulates the psychological roots and political consequences of denying that death permanently erases sensation and consciousness, so that these Renaissance texts consistently expose the origins of our continuing struggle to reconcile a materialist view of the universe with a narcissistic valuation of the self. Also on the subject of death in the Renaissance, Bettie Anne Doebler's *'Rooted Sorrow': Dying in Early Modern England* concerns the multiple expressions of death as a rite of passage and what the rite meant between 1590 and 1631. The first section of the book concentrates upon some of the major images that exemplify the tradition and, in particular, upon the death of Essex which, for Doebler, illustrates the impact of social and historical context upon theological, literary and philosophical convention. The second section of the book deals with the temptation to despair within the tradition of preparation for death and primarily in terms of a frame of attitudes from Spenser and Milton and their more mimetic expression in Shakespeare. The final section argues that in Donne's poetry and sermons there is an articulation of a life – the articulation of a process by which people came to a faith in the relationship between life and death – which is embedded in the expressive forms of his work.

The entire edition of *ELR* 25.iii is dedicated to a reflection on the state of Renaissance Studies. In 'Strains of Renaissance Reading' (289–306), Lisa Jardine explores the way in which Greenblatt's work has shaped current possibilities for Renaissance historicized textual studies. Focusing on Greenblatt's opening 'self-fashioning' image – that of Holbein's painting of 'The Ambassadors' – she re-examines that image in the light of what we have subsequently learned about the political and social complexity of the period. David Bevington's 'Two Households, Both Alike In Dignity: The Uneasy Alliance between New Historicists and Feminists' (307–19) surveys several debates between New Historicists and Feminists, outlines the theoretical issues at stake and considers them from a multidisciplinary vantage-point. In 'The Priest, the Slanderer, the Historian and the Feminist' (320–40), Lynda Boose negotiates the crossroads at which feminist historical and literary scholars meet. She argues for the construction of a 'new new historicism', one that is able to investigate within an analysis of difference, the cultural narrative that literary texts and historical documents transmit and argues that despite differences, feminist scholars in the two disciplines at least share a crucial common ground in the recognition that early modern men and women had two different histories. Jonathan Crewe's 'The State of Renaissance Studies; Or, a Future for *ELR*?' (341–53) grounds a discussion of the state of Renaissance studies by means of a focus upon the history and present anniversary of *ELR*, and argues that threats to the scholarly professional status quo demand a renewed support and commitment from academics willing to redefine goals and priorities. In 'What it Means to do a Job of Work' (354–71), Stanley Fish explores recent debates that focus upon the wider influence that literary and cultural studies might exact within the social and political context with which it interpretatively engages. In 'The Renaissance of the Study of the English Literary Renaissance' (372–87), A. C. Hamilton posits that a renaissance of Renaissance studies in the 1980s was achieved at the cost of turning from literary form to content. For Hamilton, it is only an interest in history which merges with an interest in literature that can bring about a genuine renaissance of the study of the English literary Renaissance, an argument which is explained through his analysis of the role of the Reformation and Elizabeth I in literary production of the 1580s. Leah S. Marcus's 'Cyberspace Renaissance' (388–401) argues that one of the great transformations wrought in our discipline with the assimilation of computerized technologies is a general abandonment of violence as a focal point for interpretation. For Marcus, as a discipline, we are coming to generate meaning less in terms of agonistic models – of confrontation, class warfare, crises of distinction within hierarchical structures – and more in terms of networks –

horizontal systems of relationship – in which violence can still be conceptualized but has lost its originary force. In 'Renaissance Studies Today' (402–14), Katharine Eisaman Maus presents an overview of the state of English Renaissance literary criticism in the mid-1990s and focuses particularly upon the lack of consensus about how seriously to take the 'manifest content' of Renaissance texts. Kathleen E. McLuskie's 'Old Mouse-Eaten Records: The Anxiety of History' (415–31) examines the continued debate on the relationship between literature and history, and suggests that rather than abandoning the historical project, cultural analysis must pay attention to the intersections between literary and theatrical traditions and the cultural institutions in which they are enacted in the early modern period. Following an exploration of the significance of the changing terminology of 'Renaissance' and 'Early Modern', Annabel Patterson's 'Still Reading Spenser After All These Years' (432–44) addresses two central questions: 'If the premises of the inquiry and the focus of attention have shifted somewhat, are there matching changes in the "methods" of inquiry, in the rules of evidence? Has the practice of reading changed since *ELR* came into existence?'. Patterson engages with these questions by offering an historical close reading of Spenser's *Mother Hubberd's Tale* and *The Shepheardes Calender* that also considers Spenser's wider cultural agenda, the English Reformation and Elizabeth I's ecclesiastical polity. Anne Lake Prescott's 'Divided State' (445–57) reflects on the divisiveness provoked by current Renaissance criticism, articulating that divisiveness by means of a dialogue between two speakers. Finally, Raymond B. Waddington's 'What's Past is Prologue' (458–68) selectively reviews Renaissance studies in the past 25 years.

Michael Neill's 'Putting History to the Question: An Episode of Torture at Bantam in Java, 1604' (*ELR* 25.45–75) questions the new historicist deployment of the suggestive anecdote, as it is articulated by its arch exponent, Stephen Greenblatt, by analysing Edmund Scott's *Exact Discourse of the Subtilties, Fashions, Religion and Ceremonies of the East Indians*, from which one of Greenblatt's more celebrated anecdotes in *Learning to Curse* derives. Far from it being an anecdote that evokes 'wonder' and a sense of 'estrangement' that 'opens up' historical narrative, Neill contends that Greenblatt's readings seriously distort the historical significance of Scott's narrative.

Michael Bath's 'Applied Emblematics in Scotland: Painted Ceilings, 1550–1650' (*Embl* 7.259–305) explores the distinct Scottish tradition of applied emblematics in the painted ceilings which became a feature of domestic and ecclesiastical buildings in Scotland and examines their importance for continuing research into the place of applied emblematics in the visual culture of sixteenth- and seventeenth-century Britain. In 'Childhood Education in Emblem Books of the Sixteenth and Seventeenth Centuries' (*Embl* 7.321–44), Ayers Bagley shows how these childhood texts manifest a variety of thematic clusters and motifs expressing ideas about child development, learning, motivation, nature versus nurture, and methods, content and purposes of instruction.

2. Poetry

In 'The Daily Muse: Or, Seventeenth-Century Poets Read the News' (*SC* 10.189–218), Joad Raymond explores both how occasional poetry from the 1640s and 1650s was influenced by newsbooks and how poets did not turn to newsbooks only as a source of information: they also took images and ideas from them, and recognized in their practice that these ways of writing were interdependent. Esther Gilman Richey's ' "Small Rent": Seventeenth-Century Parable and the Politics of Redemption' (*SP* 92.102–17) illustrates that English Churchmen often employed tenant parables to legitimize their ecclesiastical power and sanction their spiritual control, both before the Civil War and during the Interregnum. To recover the nature of their intertextual transformations, Richey looks at the tenant parables and marginalia of *The Geneva Bible*, a sermon of Joseph Hall, the reflections of Barnabas Oley, and the tenant parables in Herbert and Vaughan to reveal that social and political intentions operate even within texts long considered devotional in emphasis.

Barbara Smith's somewhat pedestrian *The Women of Ben Jonson's Poetry* seeks to reconsider Jonson's representations of women from an historicized and contextualized point of view. Smith points out that his political satires castigate both sexes and that he was to some extent constrained by the cultural values of his time, but fails to deal adequately with the subtler nuances of Jonson's treatment of women. The book effectively constitutes a series of close readings, focusing on such matters as poetic praise, the patronage network and Jonson's classical forebears, but rarely goes beyond the highly localized or obvious, with little attention paid to his network of female contemporaries [JS]. *Selected Poems of Ben Jonson* (ed. Ted-Larry Pebworth and Claude J. Summers) presents selections from Jonson's *Epigrammes*, all the poems of *The Forest*, selections from *The Underwood* and 'To the memory of . . . William Shakespeare'. Retaining the original spelling and punctuation throughout, the editors have provided concise notes and glosses, critical and textual introductions to Jonson's poetry, a short chronology of Jonson's life, a selected bibliography, and notes on the text. In 'Totem and Taboo in the Tribe of Ben: The Duplicity of Gender and Jonson's Satires' (*ELH* 62.729–58), Victoria Silver discusses the way in which Jonson 'ironically extends the patriarchal scheme of feminine values, making the self-abnegating traits of feminine modesty into his tribe's totemic good, in order to inculcate a degree of docility or tractableness in the great men and women he eulogizes'. For Silver, this strategy enables Jonson to deflect attention from the poet's criticisms of the very class comprised by his patrons, a strategy that culminates in the ambivalent depiction of patriarchy even as it implicates the poet in the very disorder that he satirizes.

There are two editions of Donne this year. The first is *The Variorum Edition of the Poetry of John Donne: The Anniversaries and the Epicedes and Obsequies*, commentary by Paul A. Parish, Donald R. Dickson and Dennis Flynn, and edited by Ted-Larry Pebworth et al. The ordering of the *Anniversaries* follows the generically ordered editions of 1635–69, positioning them immediately before the *Epicedes and Obsequies*, the ordering which appears in this edition. The texts of the poems are followed by commentary arranged in sequence with the texts and to reflect the critical histories attending the poems, so that this edition includes an organized digest of all criticism and scholarship on Donne's poetry, from the sixteenth century to the present day. This mammoth scholarly undertaking, facilitated by the Donne Variorum Collation Programme, will undoubtedly become a central teaching and research resource. The second edition published this year is *John Donne: Poems and Devotions*, edited by Robert van de Weyer, which provides selections from Donne's *Songs and Sonnets*, Divine Poems, Sermons and Devotions. Whilst it is certainly helpful to students to have a cheap one-volume edition of this poetry and prose, it is far from useful to have such an edition that contains no indexing, no textual commentary, no bibliography and no glosses to the poetry at all. Furthermore, the brief introduction is essentially biographical and rather reductive in its claims for the context in which Donne's poetry was produced. In 'Comparing Sappho to Philaenis: John Donne's "Homopoetics"' (*PMLA* 110.358–68), Paula Blank emphasizes that the rhetorical homogenization of Renaissance lovers poses a challenge to historical discriminations between heterosexuality and homosexuality, thus providing support for the idea that the study of Renaissance sexuality in general needs 'queering'. Blank shows how Donne's lesbian lyric exposes sameness as rhetorical rather than material, as the product of a comparative procedure she calls 'homopoetics' – the cultural making of likeness; and she goes on to argue that Donne presents Sappho's version of homosexuality as humanly impossible to achieve, no matter who attempts to achieve it, as a figure of language that can never materialize in any other form. Barbara Correll's 'Symbolic Economies and Zero-Sum Erotics: Donne's "Sapho to Philaenis"' (*ELH* 62.487–507) suggests a link between the crisis of significa-tion Donne presents in his 'lesbian' poem and the masculinist crisis that structures his heteroerotic poems, a crisis that is not unique to Donne. Correll interprets the poem as both utterly characteristic and thus continuous with the other Elegies and as a different way of addressing the kind of failure that marks the success of the heteroerotic poems. For Correll, the 'failure' that Donne sees paralyzing women's same-sex love and the undermining significa-tion in this poem is also the failure of difference that haunts other poetic works in the Donne canon.

Kate Gartner Frost's 'The Lothian Portrait: A New Description' (*JDJ* 13.i–ii.1–11) offers a detailed description, with accompanying photographs, of the second of the five extant portraits of Donne. For Gartner Frost, her revision has numerous implications, including the relationship between this portrait and the poem 'His Picture', the issue of artist and provenance, the dating and identification of the artist and the portrait's possible connection with the Marshall engraving. Donne's rather neglected poem 'Image of her whom I love' is the subject of discussion in R. E. Pritchard's 'Donne's Image and Dream' (*JDJ* 13.i–ii.13–27). Through establishing direct links to Sidney's sonnets, particularly in the use of devices, and in making use of Lacanian analysis, Pritchard argues that this poem 'is a notably subtle and searching poem, exploiting and exceeding the conventional expectations, both formal and thematic, of late Elizabethan Petrarchist verse' and reflects 'a critical stage in Donne's career'. In 'Political Play and Theological Uncertainty in the *Anniversaries*' (*JDJ* 13.i–ii.29–49), Jill Peláez Baumgaertner considers the evocation of Elizabeth in these poems, arguing that it enabled Donne to invoke images and myths of monarchy which had recently been introduced in Prince Henry's honour. With regard to the theology of these poems,

Baumgaertner shows how Donne's outlook seems similar to that of the English Church at that time. For this writer, the 'Anniversaries' reveal Donne's 'astute awareness of the acceptable political metaphors of the time, metaphors which would do two things at once: lavishly memorialize the dead child, and compliment the Prince of Wales'. Roger B. Rollin's 'John Donne's "Holy Sonnets": The Sequel: "Devotions upon Emergent Occasions" ' (*JDJ* 13.i–ii.51–9) argues that 'new light can be shed upon Donne's 1624 *tour d'force* [*sic*] in metaphysical prose when it is viewed as a kind of sequel to his miscellany of sacred sonnets'; for Rollin, the 'Devotions' become Dean Donne's valedictory to Sonneteer Donne. Helen Wilcox's 'Squaring the Circle: Metaphors of the Divine in the Work of Donne and his Contemporaries' (*JDJ* 13.i–ii.61–79) succinctly addresses and questions the sources, functions and limitations of metaphor in the work of Donne, Mary Sidney, Herbert, Anne Southwell, Richard Hooker, Aemilia Lanyer, Anne Ley and 'Eliza'. She explores the way in which these religious writers attempt to render God linguistically, the kinds of metaphor available to them and their limits, and the functions for which these metaphors of the divine are intended. Wilcox concludes by questioning the impact of gender upon usage of metaphor and the relationship of individuality to linguistic creation. In 'John Donne's "Nocturnal Upon S. Lucies Day": Punctuation and the Editor' (*JDJ* 13.i–ii.81–99), Emma L. Roth-Schwartz examines this poem in the light of Renaissance and contemporary editing practices, noting the inconsistencies of transmission that are synonymous with Donne's work. She concludes that although the usefulness of modern-spelling editions cannot be doubted, 'what should probably be avoided is an eclectic jumble of modern and baroque punctuation techniques that sometimes preserve the worst features of both'. Robert Parker Sorlien's 'Apostasy Reversed: Donne and Tobie Matthew' (*JDJ* 13.i–ii.101–12) explores Donne's friendship with Matthew, the rebellious son of an Anglican prelate, whose conversion to Catholicism marked him as the most famous or notorious recusant in Jacobean and Caroline England. In 'More Early Allusions to Donne and Herbert' (*JDJ* 13.i–ii.113–23), John T. Shawcross emphasizes the continuing importance of collating references to these poets that illustrate their audience and enable contemporary critics to 'analyse more fully the world of the later seventeenth and eighteenth centuries that they define' and catalogues 30 additional items. Diana Treviño Benet introduces three essays in 'Introduction to Cluster on "A Valediction forbidding Mourning" ' (*JDJ* 13.i– ii.125–6), the first of which is Janice Whittington's 'The Text of Donne's "A Valediction forbidding Mourning" ' (*JDJ* 13.i–ii.127–36) which studies various manuscripts and seventeenth-century editions of *Poems* to determine the families of textual transmission for this poem. In 'Reading [out] Biography in "A Valediction forbidding Mourning" ' (*JDJ* 13.i–ii.137–42), Judith Scherer Herz warns against 'the perils of biographical criticism'. The third essay in this group, Graham Roebuck's ' "A Valediction forbidding Mourning": Traditions and Problems of the Imagery' (*JDJ* 13.i– ii.143–9) offers a detailed stanza-by-stanza exploration of the imagery of this poem. In '*Paronomasia celata* in Donne's "A Valediction: forbidding mourning" ' (*ELR* 25.97–111), Matthias Bauer suggests that paronomasia serves to connect the very different and seemingly unrelated images of the poem and like the conceit of the compasses, thus illuminates its own function as well as the subject of the poem. Gregory Machacek's 'Donne's "The Indifferent"'

(*Expl* 53.iv.192–4) reconsiders the poem's implied audience, arguing that the reader can imagine the poem being spoken to an audience of precisely two women who have discovered that they are both lovers of the speaker and have confronted him concerning his infidelity. In this interpretation, the point of the poem is to portray a speaker in the process of extemporaneously constructing a tendentious and self-serving (but rhetorically dazzling) argument. In 'Donne through contemporary eyes: New light on his participation in the Convocation of 1626' (*N&Q* 42.441–4), N. W. Bawcutt and Hilton Kelliher examine anew Donne's presence at this occasion by referring to two new pieces of evidence.

There are also two editions of Herbert's poetry this year, the first being *George Herbert 'The Temple': A Diplomatic Edition of the Bodleian Manuscript (Tanner 307)*, edited and introduced by Mario A. Di Cesare. This impressive piece of editing is an exact transcription, page by page, of the text proper, rendering precisely the orthography and punctuation. This edition represents the graphic and visual characteristics of this version of Herbert's work and includes five sets of textual notes. Di Cesare also presents a full critical introduction to the text, discussing in detail the textual history of *The Temple*. *The Works of George Herbert* (ed. Tim Cook) presents poems of *The Temple*, 'The Church Militant', additional sacred poems, psalms and secular poems and six suggested critical texts for further reading. The poetry is briefly introduced, the introduction providing a short biographical and critical commentary. The celebration of Herbert's quatercentenary in 1993 has given rise to the conference, collected in *George Herbert: Sacred and Profane*, edited by Helen Wilcox and Richard Todd. The essays all address a central concern in Herbert's work, that of the interplay of the spiritual and the secular, from a whole variety of perspectives: from overview, whether liturgical or analogical, to such captivating details as the lyrics' titles; from the contemporary seventeenth-century context to our own present; and from verbal rhetoric to visual and musical impact. This collection represents some of the most engaging work currently being carried out on Herbert and by some of Herbert's most well-known scholars. In 'Herbert's "The Pulley"' (*Expl* 53.ii.70–2), Wilfred L. Guerin argues that although the reader accepts the possibility that the myth of Pandora aids appreciation of the narrative of this poem, much more important for a considered explication are the Augustinian mentality and the Augustinian contrast of rest and restlessness.

Renaissance Women: The Plays of Elizabeth Cary, The Poems of Aemilia Lanyer, edited by Diane Purkiss, is an important new edition of two of the most significant seventeenth-century women poets, presenting Cary's *The Tragedy of Mariam, The Fair* and *The History of the Life, Reign, and Death of Edward II*, and Lanyer's *Salve Deus Rex Judaeorum*. Its extensive and engaging introduction offers both biographical and contextual criticism that enables new readers to gain access to this writing and adds to the criticism already available. Despite claims made by Margaret Ezell and Germaine Greer et al. for the status of Elizabeth Middleton as an early modern woman writer, Elizabeth Clarke points out in 'Elizabeth Middleton: Early Modern Copyist' (*N&Q* 42.444–5) that, in fact, Middleton was much more of a plagiarist than has previously been acknowledged. Bernard Capp's 'The Poet and the Bawdy Court: Michael Drayton and the Lodging-House World in Early Stuart London' (*SC* 10.27–37) explores the biographical import of the

discovery that on 8 March 1627, Drayton appeared before the London
Consistory Court in St Paul's charged with 'suspicion of incontinency with
Mary Peters, wife of John Peters, as ye fame goeth' and attempts a 'micro-
history that throws light on several aspects of social life in early Stuart
London'. 'English Responses to the Death of Moritz the Learned: John Dury,
Sir Thomas Roe, and an Unnoticed Epicede by William Cartwright' (*ELR*
25.235–47) by Timothy Raylor, and with a text and translation by J. W. Binns,
reprints with a translation a hitherto unnoticed Latin poem by William
Cartwright, in a volume published to commemorate Moritz the Learned,
Landraf of Hesse. This article also considers the manner in which the English
contributions were collected and how the collection itself is a significant body
of English Renaissance funerary verse that provides new information about
occasional poetry produced at the universities as well as the literary relations
between England and continental Europe during the early seventeenth century. In 'A Precursor of Nonsense: John Taylor, the Water Poet (*c.*
1580–1653)' (*CE* 48.37–44), Emma Renaud identifies a 'technique of nonsense' in the political and religious work of this royalist poet. She comments
upon the grotesque, farcical and Rabelaisian aspects of that work, which looks
forward to the technique of nonsense that will reach its apotheosis in the
nineteenth century.

Alan Rudrum's edition of *Henry Vaughan: The Complete Poems* presents
the poetry in the order in which it was published and subjects it to only partial
modernization – spelling has been modernized, contractions expanded, capitals reduced whilst Vaughan's italics have been preserved. There are detailed
annotations and notes to the poetry and a wide-ranging bibliography and a
table of dates. Stevie Davies's *Henry Vaughan* offers a biographical and
literary analysis of the poet, taking as her vantage-point her own work as a
novelist and critic. This is a lively and thoughtful reading of Vaughan's poetry,
sensitive to both the poetry and the political and religious context. Dafydd
Roberts's 'An Allusion to Henry More's Poetry by Thomas Vaughan' (*N&Q*
42.446) claims that Vaughan's use of the phrase 'pin-dust and egg-shells' in
Magia Adamica probably derives from More's *Infinitie of Worlds* and thus
confirms his opposition to More.

3. Prose

King James's Bible: A Selection, edited by W. H. Stevenson, contains comprehensive extracts from the AV and includes brief explanatory footnotes to the
text. Stevenson has introduced this selection with clear and informative
textual chapters, with sections on a range of thematic issues, the source texts,
a brief history of the Bible and biblical translation from Tyndale to James as
well as a useful commentary on the language of the AV. This edition includes
a chronology that charts the Histories, a bibliography, maps and an index.
Stevenson has produced a welcome edition that should encourage students of
this period to become much more familiar with this central text, although at
£21 this edition might be used only in library reference.

Female Replies to Swetnam the Woman-Hater (ed. Charles Butler) reproduces both the original Swetnam text as well as four replies: Rachel Speght, *A
Mouzell of Melastomus*; Ester Sowernam, *Ester hath hang'd Haman*; Con-

stantia Munda, *The Worming of a Mad Dogge*; and the anonymous *Swetnam, the Woman-hater, Arraigned by Women*. This reproduction, which reprints original copies of each book together with the useful introduction to these texts, will provide an invaluable source text for students and scholars alike. Jennifer Richards's 'Anna Weamys's "Continuation of Sir Philip Sidney's Arcadia"' (*BSRS* 12.ii.20–40) discusses how Weamys's *Continuation* is a reworking of the *Arcadia* rather than a derivative story and that the characters of her text, though recognizably those of Sidney's, bear the stamp of her own influence. Richards throws light on the appropriation of Sidney's text by its female readership in the seventeenth century and how it constitutes an entertaining precursor to the novels written by women in the eighteenth century. In 'Eroticizing the Subject, or Royals in Drag: Reading the Memoirs of Anne, Lady Halkett' (*PSt* 18.134–49), Donna Landry illustrates how by inscribing herself in her narrative of Stuart loyalist intrigue as an independent agent and heroine of romance, Halkett illuminates the fundamental inter-connectedness of private and public spheres. For Landry, Halkett's text should be read as, at once, a document of protest against women's subordination, a document of political resistance to the English Revolution and the Interregnum governments, and an attempt to reconcile herself to both histories as they played themselves out and found some closure in her marriage to James Halkett.

Bacon's analysis of the 'delicate learning' or 'vain affectations' of the Ciceronians, who 'began to hunt more after words than matter' is the subject of Judith Rice Henderson's '"Vain Affectations": Bacon on Ciceronianism in *The Advancement of Learning*' (*ELR* 25.209–34). In this densely argued article, Henderson studies Bacon's rejection of the Protestant rector Johanne Sturm's influence on the Cambridge humanists, where he complained that they had reduced the humanist curriculum to a narrow reading list, chosen to teach the forms of classical literature more than its rich and varied content. Willy Maley's '"Another Britain"?: Bacon's *Certain Considerations Touching the Plantation in Ireland* (1609)' (*PSt* 18.1–18) argues that Bacon's short treatise 'captures some of the complexities of the Irish problem in a British context, or, perhaps more accurately, the British problem in an Irish context'. Maley illustrates Bacon's belief in progress and the possibility of change, and the frequent analogies he draws in his writing between the acquisition of knowledge and the politics of empire, conquest and discovery, which make his pronouncements on Ireland sharply relevant. In 'A Source for the "Aethiop" in Francis Bacon's *New Atlantis*' (*N&Q* 42.366–7), Craig M. Rustici identifies Bacon's source for Joebin in Jacobus de Voragine's *The Golden Legend*.

Sir Thomas Browne: Selected Writings, edited by Claire Preston, provides a selection of Browne's work that includes extracts from *Religio Medici*, *The Garden of Cyrus*, *Pseudodoxia*, *Commonplace Books*, *Notebooks*, *Miscellany Tracts*, *Christian Morals* and the complete *Urn-Burial*. Organized themat-ically, the spelling modernized only as 'consistent with Browne's rhythm and pronunciation', this edition is briefly introduced with biographical and textual notes and a bibliography. In the densely written 'A Strategy for Writing the "Impossibilium: Aporia" in Sir Thomas Browne's The Garden of Cyrus' (*PSt* 18.19–35), Frank D. Walters considers that for Browne, writing began with the onset of epistemological doubt whilst, simultaneously, writing was the very cause of that doubt. Walters suggests a paradox in Browne's writing – on the one hand, these writings are expressions of epistemological conflict and, on the other, they are infused with a discursive logic that stimulates the object and renders its ontological status knowable.

In '"Man is the Woman"': Levelling and the Gendered Body Politic in Enthusiastic Rhetoric' (*PSt* 18.36–58), Clement Hawes examines the ambiguous effect of the recent inclusion of the 'Ranter' Abezer Coppe in the sixth edition of the *Norton Anthology of English Literature*. For Hawes, this inclusion in an 'ambivalent mode of canonization' invites a certain degree of misreading. This article argues that to understand Coppe as other than mad, or ignorant, or both, entails a rethinking of anti-enthusiastic history. Hawes demonstrates that Coppe's project of enthusiastic levelling remains of particular interest precisely in its utopian re-invention of the 'body politic' and that it is, above all, through its revisions of the gendered body politic, that enthusiastic rhetoric seeks to point towards new subjectives and an alternative order. In 'Richard Overton and the Secularism of the Interregnum Radicals' (*SC* 10.63–75), B. J. Gibbons traverses the critical minefield that surrounds our knowledge of Overton's biography, arguing that it is possible that Overton underwent a severe religious crisis in 1643, 'veering into sectarian enthusiasm before arriving at a sceptical deism'. Michele Valerie Ronnick's 'The title "Lord Protector" and the Vulgate Bible' (*N&Q* 42.446–7) claims that a number of passages from the Vulgate might well have influenced John Lambert's drafting of Cromwell's title.

Robert E. Stillman's 'Hobbes's *Leviathan*: Monsters, Metaphors, and Magic' (*ELH* 62.791–820) argues that there is a peculiar doubleness in Hobbes's philosophy, the creation of the *Leviathan* as a monster text to do battle against the monster of history – as a text whose doubleness consists in its reliance upon metaphor to constitute its crucial arguments, and in its warfare against metaphor as an abuse of language and thought. For Stillman, this battle exemplifies Hobbes's concern with a 'dream' of a positive science to discover a discourse that is objective, neutral and uncontaminated by monstrous desires, and in the 'design' of a pious magic to create a discourse in which words have the power to become incarnate as things, as the very fulfilment of desire. As Hobbes's text makes manifest, the dream of discovering a positive 'science' is linked historically to magical designs. Stephen Clucas's ' "Noble virtue in extremes": Henry Percy, ninth Earl of Northumberland, patronage and the politics of stoic consolation' (*RS* 9.267–91) discusses the way in which the Earl of Northumberland's reading betrays an intense interest in the doctrines of consolation, and concludes that the Earl's reading of stoic texts armed him well for his prison career and together with the stoic sentiments expressed in his clients' dedicated texts are an excellent example of the way in which humanistic reading practices could help to shape both aristocratic self-image and political conduct in the Jacobean period. In ' "To Speak Truth": Blackloism, Scepticism, and Language' (*SC* 10.237–54), B. C. Southgate focuses on the English Catholic priest Thomas White (1593–1676) who published some 40 theological and philosophical works in the middle decades of the century, and examines the significance of White and Blackloism in relation to contemporary debates about language.

Books Reviewed

Bottalla, Paola, and Michela Calderaro, eds. *Counting and Recounting: Measuring Inner and Outer Space in the Renaissance.* UTrieste. pp. 231. np.

Butler, Charles, ed. *Female Replies to Swetnam the Woman-Hater.* Thoemmes. pp. xli + unpaginated. pb £15.75. ISBN 1 85506 379 4.

Cook, Tim, ed. *The Works of George Herbert.* Wordsworth Classics, Penguin (1994) pp. 223. pb £2. ISBN 1 85326 421 0.

Davies, Stevie. *Henry Vaughan.* PWP. pp. 213. pb £6.95. ISBN 1 85411 143 4.

Di Cesare, Mario, ed. *George Herbert 'The Temple': A Diplomatic Edition of the Bodleian Manuscript (Tanner 307).* MRTS 54. MRTS. pp. lxxx + 313 + 107. $56. ISBN 0 86698 038 5.

Doebler, Bettie Anne. *'Rooted Sorrow': Dying in Early Modern England.* AUP (1994). pp. 296. £32.50. ISBN 0 8386 3543 1.

Pebworth, Ted-Larry, John T. Shawcross, Gary A. Stringer, and Ernest W. Sullivan II, eds. *The Variorum Edition of the Poetry of John Donne: The Anniversaries and the Epicedes and Obsequies.* IndUP. pp. 689. £42.50. ISBN 0 253 31811 4.

Pebworth, Ted-Larry, and Claude J. Summers, eds. *Selected Poems of Ben Jonson.* MRTS. SUNYP. pp. xix + 89. pb $7.95. ISBN 0 86698 178 0.

Preston, Claire, ed. *Sir Thomas Browne: Selected Writings.* Carcanet. pp. 168. pb £9.95. ISBN 1 85754 052 2.

Purkiss, Diane, ed. *Renaissance Women: The Plays of Elizabeth Cary, The Poems of Aemilia Lanyer.* P&C (1994). pp. 338. £24.95. ISBN 1 85196 029 5.

Rudrum, Alan, ed. *Henry Vaughan: The Complete Poems.* Penguin. pp. 718. pb £9.99. ISBN 0 14 042208 0.

Smith, Barbara. *The Women of Ben Jonson's Poetry: Female Representations in the Non-Dramatic Verse.* Scolar. pp. 132. £30. ISBN 1 85928 228 8.

Stevenson, W. H., ed. *King James's Bible: A Selection.* Longman (1994). pp. 537. pb £21. ISBN 0 582 06619 0.

van de Weyer, Robert, ed. *John Donne: Poems and Devotions.* HC. pp. 165. pb £2.99. ISBN 0 00 627923 6.

Watson, Robert N. *The Rest is Silence: Death as Annihilation in the English Renaissance.* UCalP (1994). pp. 416. £40. ISBN 0 520 08494 2.

Wilcox, Helen, and Richard Todd, eds. *George Herbert: Sacred and Profane.* VUUP. pp. 211. pb £20. ISBN 90 5383 368 4.

IX

Milton

JOAD RAYMOND

> Enervate critic! – cease thy fruitless rage,
> Nor touch with impious hands the hallow'd page! ...
> Truth shall preserve great *Milton*'s honour'd page
> From Time's encroachment, and from Envy's rage.
> *Gentleman's Magazine* (1747)

These impatient lines, spurred by the mid-eighteenth-century controversy over Milton's alleged plagiarism, appear in volume 2 of John T. Shawcross's *John Milton: The Critical Heritage, 1732–1801*. The two Critical Heritage volumes (the first covering the period 1628–1732), originally published in 1970 and 1972, have been reprinted; they cover Milton's first notices, the burgeoning acknowledgement of *Paradise Lost* as a modern classic, and the periods of textual and religious criticism and of analysis and discomforted detraction. The two volumes show just how many twentieth-century themes were anticipated and explored prior to the invention of literature and literary criticism. The reprints have not been re-edited: the ample selections are accompanied by Shawcross's original introductions, succinct and highly informative. These volumes remain essential library purchases, though it is a shame that there appears to have been no opportunity for revision to incorporate recent developments.

Such revisions might include Nicholas von Maltzahn's recent work on Milton's early reception. In 'Samuel Butler's Milton' (*SP* 92.482–95) von Maltzahn forcefully (re-)attributes to the satirist Samuel Butler *The Censure of the Rota* (1660), and thus by association *The Character of the Rump* (1660) and *The Transproser Rehears'd* (1673). *Censure*, one of the most interesting Restoration attacks on Milton and other republicans, is usually accepted as the work of Richard Leigh; one clinching piece of evidence is a manuscript ascription to Butler by the army secretary William Clarke. John Toland's attribution to the royalist Samuel Barrow of the early response to Milton, '*In Paradisum Amissam*', (the *other* prefatory poem to *Paradise Lost*, 1674 [hereafter *PL*]), has recently been doubted. Von Maltzahn, in '"I admired Thee": Samuel Barrow, Doctor and Poet' (*MiltonQ* 29.25–8), challenges this scepticism, assisted by transcripts of other writings by Barrow in the Clarke MSS; this enables him to consider the distinctive focus of the poem, and to underscore the social dimension to late seventeenth-century literary publication.

This year sees the publication of three large collections of essays. Some of the most penetrating and original studies appear in David Armitage, Armand Himy and Quentin Skinner, eds, *Milton and Republicanism*, including two very distinguished articles by Martin Dzelzainis. In 'Milton's classical republicanism', Dzelzainis traces the trajectory of Milton's republicanism from *Of Education* through the 1649 tracts, argues that its roots lie in Cicero, Aristotle and Sallust rather than Polybius and suggests that the doubts which have been cast upon the fact of Milton's republicanism stem partly from its extremism. He finds an echo of these 1650s debates in *PL* II. In 'Milton and the Protectorate in 1658', Dzelzainis explores Milton's two largely neglected publications of 1658: his edition of *The Cabinet Council*, and a new edition of the *Defensio*, and suggests that they articulate, through irony and implication, a critique of the retrogressive tendencies of the Cromwellian Protectorate even before its collapse and the confusion of 1658–60. Thomas N. Corns, in 'Milton and the characteristics of a free commonwealth', argues that Milton's writings reflect the reactiveness of English republicanism, always lagging behind political events. Yet while arguing that there is no concrete republican agenda in Milton's prose (before *The Readie & Easie Way*), Corns finds radical sentiments and a subversive idiom, and rightly argues that the heart of English republicanism consists in its language. In 'Great senates and godly education: politics and cultural renewal in some pre- and post-revolutionary texts of Milton', Cedric C. Brown explores the continuing concern with the education of public men into godly virtues in Milton's writings from the 1634 *Maske* through the 1659–60 tracts to *PL*, suggesting that the continuity reflects the way Milton subordinates political issues, both in theory and in focus, to religious concerns. By contrast, in 'Biblical reference in the political pamphlets of the Levellers and Milton, 1638–1654', Elizabeth Tuttle compares the developing use of biblical references in the prose of Milton and the Levellers, suggesting not only the flexibility they offered for political argument but their limitation, particularly as a classical vocabulary for natural rights grew into fashion. In 'The metaphorical contract in Milton's *The Tenure of Kings and Magistrates*', Victoria Kahn analyses the exegesis of scriptural covenants in the arguments of Hobbes and Milton concerning political contracts, focusing particularly on *The Tenure* which she sees as a key to Milton's republicanism. In 'Milton, Satan, Salmasius and Abdiel', Roger Lejosne suggests that there are parallels between Satan and Abdiel and Salmasius and Milton, in their debates concerning the legitimacy of monarchy. The conclusion that *PL* is not implicitly monarchist is persuasive. In '*Paradise Lost* as a republican "tractatus theologico-politicus"', Armand Himy explores some of the theological contexts for Milton's ideal of government. In 'Popular republicanism in the 1650s: John Streater's "heroick mechanicks"', Nigel Smith persuasively argues that the 1650s writings of printer and soldier John Streater represents a bridge between the political arguments and gestures of the Levellers in the 1640s and the concerns of the classical republicans of the 1660s. The relationship between Milton and pamphleteers, especially Marchamont Nedham, is becoming a hot topic in Milton studies, owing partly to Blair Worden's work on the history of republicanism. In the present volume, Blair Worden's 'Milton and Marchamont Nedham' outlines in broad strokes the literary and

political analogies between the two writers, focusing mainly on the early
1650s. David Armitage's 'John Milton: poet against empire' discusses republican thought, most often expressed through Machiavelli and Sallust, on the
important though sometimes destructive relations between policies on internal and external affairs: the recurring dilemma of stability versus expansion.
Armitage suggests that *The Readie & Easie Way* and *PL* contain criticisms of
the expansionist policy, mainly the 'Western Design', of the Protectorate. This
rejection of empire represents a Restoration modulation of classical republican political theory. Picking up on this last theme, in 'The Whig Milton,
1667–1700', Nicholas von Maltzahn describes Milton's gradual and uneasy
transformation into a Whig in Restoration England. Initially avoided by the
Whigs for his notorious beliefs, Milton served as a convenient fiction in Tory
propaganda; the reign of James II saw his acclamation as a national poet by an
Anglican consensus, which paved the way for his acceptance after the Revolution of 1688 as a Protestant champion of liberty. Tony Davies, in 'Borrowed
Language: Milton, Jefferson, Mirabeau', looks at the uses of Milton in
revolutionary America and France as a means of presenting or justifying the
need for political change.

Contesting precisely the insights offered by *Milton and Republicanism* is
Robert Thomas Fallon's *Divided Empire: Milton's Political Imagery*, an
account of the impact of Milton's political life on *PL* (with a chapter on
Paradise Regained [hereafter *PR*] and *Samson Agonistes* [hereafter *SA*]).
Fallon proposes to discover not what the poetry says about historical events,
but what the events say about the poetry. Fallon is in a good position to discuss
such material, and makes interesting points about the role of ambassadors in
the epic in relation to Milton's experience of writing letters of state in the
1650s. Those readers who, like myself, admire Fallon's earlier work, and
particularly his excellent *Milton in Government* (PSUP, 1993) may face disappointment. A great deal of this book is spent inveighing against recent
criticism which imputes Milton's political beliefs to a poem which, Fallon
argues, is a product of the 'creative imagination'. Prose is rational, and can be
interpreted as reflecting reasoned beliefs; poetry is imaginative, and therefore
while it is informed by experience, it cannot be taken to reflect the author's
value systems. The first three chapters issue polemical statements without
detailed analysis. The parallels Fallon notes are very general, and in contrast to
his earlier work he offers a homogenous account of the 1650s, using few
primary sources. The better chapters are on the parallels between Heaven and
Hell and the representation of love and hate, and on diplomatic missions. Yet
here we find lapses: an interesting passage on subordination is followed by the
absurd statement that the only political counterpart of love lies in images of
absolute monarchy. In the same way, Fallon uses 'king' and 'rebel' as simple
nominal definitions, happily branding commonwealthsmen with the latter, in
order to impute loose connections between them and Satan. Fallon seems to be
of the king's party. In 1942, Arthur Barker dismissed the eighteenth-century
assumption that poetry and prose 'expressed two strangely incompatible sides
of Milton's personality', a prejudice 'which prevented a fully satisfactory
estimate of his genius' (*Milton and the Puritan Dilemma, 1641–1660*, UTorP),
a verdict resonant today.

The nature of the relationship between Milton's writings and the political
world is also the subject of Laura Lunger Knoppers's *Historicizing Milton:*

Spectacle, Power, and Poetry in Restoration England (1994), a reading of the longer poems which situates them in their Restoration context. Knoppers shows how *PR* rewrites the Restoration appropriation of martyrdom in anti-monarchical terms; how *SA* exposes displays of power; how *PL* defines joy as an internal, spiritual quality, incompatible with public celebration; and she explores the imaging of Roman triumphs and conquests, which Milton uses to reflect his disillusionment with Cromwell as well as Charles II. Her point that Milton's 'emotional investments lie in the Restoration' is certainly well made, and some of her readings of the 1671 poems are particularly insightful and judicious. The study is excellently and usefully illustrated.

There are several other interesting interventions on the argument of *SA*. Harold Skulsky's *Justice in the Dock: Milton's Experimental Tragedy* mixes approachableness with sheer difficulty. The Book of Judges, argues Skulsky, makes unpromising material for tragedy, through both its unpleasantness and its fundamentalist approach to morality: witness the deliberations of George Buchanan's *Iephthes* (*c.*1539). Skulsky treats us to a reading of Joost van den Vondel's *Holy Revenge*, a tragedy based on the Samson story, which, like Milton's, seems implicitly to make a case for the Philistines by drawing attention to their grievances, and marking the anti-rational zeal which drives Samson's revenge. Skulsky highlights those areas where Milton allows us to look askance at God. Reformation theology, and especially predestination, can lead the humanist Christian into panic and pettifogging, suggests Skulsky, and Samson can make his God seem capricious and manipulative. Skulsky fashions himself not unlike a polite version of William Empson. If the genocide is holy, if reason is opposed to zeal, then why fashion an argument at all? The premise of the drama, for him, is scandal. Milton offers the case against Samson and his God by hinting that God is guilty of entrapment. The righteousness of Samson's last act is brought into the dock. The playwright is its advocate, but he wants it vindicated by correct judicial and juridical procedures: he never claims that God's justice is beyond question. This is a brisk and welcome book, all the more to be admired for its brevity.

In '"True Religion" and Tragedy: Milton's Insights in *Samson Agonistes*' (*Mosaic* 28.1–29), George H. McLoone interprets Samson as neither saint nor sinner, but as heroic and flawed. What passes in him for tragic insight and revelation is undermined by the trappings and rhetoric of criticism and establishment religiosity. His 'Holy Revenge' is a mythology which obscures some of the demands of the reformed religion, a gung-ho blind strength which overrides the imperatives of self-questioning. In '"In Place": *Kairos* in *Samson Agonistes*' (*SC* 10.219–35), Andre Furlani suggests the importance to *SA* of *kairos*, loosely translated as '"opportune" or "decisive moment"', but equally having a spatial dimension. Drawing on parallels with Sophocles's *Philoctetes*, Furlani suggests that the drama entirely vindicates Samson's action by showing him moving towards a fitting *kairos*.

There are two pieces on Milton in a very good collection of essays, *Culture and Society in the Stuart Restoration* (ed. Gerald MacLean), both of which emphasize the Restoration context of Milton's later writings. In 'Milton, Dryden, and the politics of literary controversy', Steven N. Zwicker suggests that a Whig orthodoxy has taken over our view of the direction of literary influence in the seventeenth century, not least between John Dryden and Milton. Zwicker counterbalances this by considering Dryden's possible influence on Milton, and reads *PR* as a response to heroic drama of the 1660s. Finally, he suggests a further symmetry in Dryden's greater sympathy with Milton after the 1688 revolution. Blair Worden's, 'Milton, *Samson Agonistes*, and the Restoration', draws parallels between the position Samson finds himself in and that experienced by the republicans Sir Henry Vane, Algernon Sidney and Edmund Ludlow after 1660. This suggests that the drama was written some time after the trials of 1662, and that Samson is to some extent Milton's self-representation, his final iconoclastic gesture perhaps being the publication of *PL*.

The second of this year's collections of essays also focuses on Milton's politics, though in a much more diffuse sense than *Milton and Republicanism*, covering the more familiar themes of the poetic vocation and questions of gender. In *Of Poetry and Politics: New Essays on Milton and His World*, P. G. Stanwood collects papers from the Fourth International Milton Symposium, held at the University of British Columbia. The festivities begin with Louis L. Martz's 'Milton's Prophetic Voice: Moving Towards Paradise', which connects the curious placement of the autobiographical passage in *Reason of Church Government* with a pattern established by Old Testament prophets, in which the self-revelation of the prophet follows denunciation and is followed by a vision of redemption. Martz adds that this is also, to some extent, the pattern of *PL* Books I–IV and that the experience of writing the prose tracts with his left hand was perhaps a vital training for the poetry of the right. The same has been said of the Latin, and essays on Latin themes include John K. Hale's 'The Pre-Criticism of Milton's Latin Verse, Illustrated from the Ode "Ad Joannem Rousium"'. This discusses the methodological principles of 'recovering' Milton's Latin poetry in preparation for literary understanding and interpretation, using as an example the ode to John Rouse. In 'Alpheus, Arethusa, and the Pindaric Pursuit in *Lycidas*', Stella P. Revard looks at the Pindaric structure implied in the digressive passages of 'Lycidas' that creates a level of allusion beyond the poem's immediate frame of reference; an interesting and perhaps neglected source, though briefly considered here. Essays on the big poems include Lee M. Johnson's 'Language and the Illusion of Innocence in *Paradise Lost*', which suggests that innocence in Eden is not merely presented by its linguistic distance – through familiar ironies – but through presence. Focusing on Eve's love-lyric and the Edenic hymn, Johnson claims that the speech patterns evoke a sense of circumscription and enclosure, partly through the symbolic structural order underlying what appears as spontaneous irregularity. David Robertson, in 'Soliloquy and Self in Milton's Major Poems', looks at the soliloquies in *PL*, *PR* and *SA* and concludes that while John Broadbent's claim that only fallen characters soliloquize is strictly wrong, it contains a germ of truth, in that these speeches reflect some sense of self-division and the potential for change. In '"Improv'd By Tract of Time": Art's Synopticon in *Paradise Lost* Book 12', Douglas Chambers discusses Milton's debt to visual presentations of synoptic views of history, especially in tapestries; the piece is suggestive but impressionistic. In his brief 'Directing the Audience in *Samson Agonistes*', Michael R. G. Spiller notes the critical dissent over the form and meaning of *SA*, and he claims that a metapoetic turn at the end of the drama guides the audience to a very classical catharsis: the poem becomes a tomb.

Among the more scholarly and detailed general essays is 'Milton and "The

Rounded Theatre's Pomp"', in which T. H. Howard-Hill suggests that the early twentieth-century fiction of Milton's childhood love of the stage and of Shakespeare misrepresents not only the author but the place of the theatre in seventeenth-century culture. Mary Ann Radzinowicz's 'Milton and the Tragic Women of Genesis' looks at Milton's use of women in his numerous plans for a Biblical drama based on *Genesis* (supported by allusions in his polemical writings), and finds in Milton's historical relativism, and his marked emphasis on the multivalency of Biblical interpretation, a proto-feminist stance, only occasionally clouded by polemical deployment. Though tenuous at points, this is a challenging essay, which underscores the complex Judaic element in Milton's historical and theological thought. Dayton Haskin, in 'Choosing the Better Part with Mary and with Ruth', unpacks the complexities of the allusion to Mary and Ruth in Sonnet 9, suggesting that it carries autobiographical connotations, which Haskin places in Milton's patterns of Biblical interpretation (as in his previous monograph: *YWES* 75.300).

On sex and gender: in '"Thir Sex Not Equal Seem'd": Equality in *Paradise Lost*', Michael Wilding takes us through the gender difficulties of *PL*. His argument is not unfamiliar: there is a patriarchal, anti-egalitarian reading of Eden, but it is Satan's, while in the propriety before the Fall there is no male rule or hierarchy of gender. Instead, these oppressions follow sin. Wilding's exposition is simple and lucid, its reason to be commended. Contrarily, Donald M. Friedman, 'Divisions on a Ground: "Sex" in *PL*', discusses the nature of sexual difference, and the meaning of the word 'sex' in *PL*: pre-Lapsarian spiritual essences bear no simple dependencies on external signifiers, but solidify through the Fall into the familiar markers of physical difference. Friedman questions the extent to which our first sight of Adam and Eve in *PL* IV can simply be written off as Satan's misperception. John Leonard's 'Milton's Vow of Celibacy: A Reconsideration of the Evidence' deals with the old shibboleth by looking at Milton's uses (actual and supposed) of the 144,000 virgins of Revelation 14. Leonard concludes that there is no substantial evidence that the young poet expressed a commitment to anything other than chastity. On questions of empire: in 'Banyan Trees and Fig Leaves: Some Thoughts on Milton's India', an essay rich with historical and interpretative detail, Balachandra Rajan considers the presentation of India in the similes of *PL*. He finds Milton self-divided, associating India with infernality but also with the victimization of created nature. Milton's academic and exact poetic imagination uses orientalist thought even as it advocates spiritual liberty and derogates empire. J. Martin Evans, in 'Milton's Imperial Epic', considers the motifs of empire in *PL*, not only in Satan's colonial expedition, but also in relation to God's emissaries and to Adam's place in Eden as settler, native or labourer. Evans points not to a political critique so much as the presence in the epic of the interest and confusion these issues provoked in the seventeenth century. On church discipline: in '*Paradise Regained* and the Private Houses', a stimulating and too brief essay, Gary D. Hamilton situates the brief epic in the context of the Conventicle Acts, suggesting that Milton's presentation of the Son as a private man is a careful rejection of Erastianism in favour of a Quaker-like nonconformism. Achsah Guibbory, in 'Charles's Prayers, Idolatrous Images, and True Creation in Milton's *Eikonoklastes*', suggests that the attacks on iconography and plagiarism outline a model of creativity, in which a legitimate literary imagination would be modelled on the spontaneity and originality of individual prayer. According to Ken Simpson in '"That Sovran Book": The Discipline of the Word in Milton's Anti-Episcopal Tracts', the emphasis on scripture as the basis of church discipline in the antiprelatical tracts divides Milton from the Presbyterian grouping he is defending (not then defined by solidified party lines anyway): while advocating a Presbyterian settlement as preferable to episcopacy, Milton simultaneously advocates a more radical, individualist form of worship.

Janel Mueller also identifies early radical manoeuvres. In 'Contextualizing Milton's Nascent Republicanism', she offers an important revisionary reading of a passage in *Of Reformation* in which Milton proposes and discusses an analogy between civil and ecclesiastical government. Mueller suggests that in his account of the three estates, Milton implicitly invests political sovereignty in parliament. In doing so, he draws upon a Presbyterian version of the separation between church and state that suggests the Scottish contribution to the origins of English republicanism. This early republicanism, defined as parliamentary sovereignty, continues with his addressing parliament in *Areopagitica*. Wyman H. Herenden, in 'Milton's *Accidence Commenc't Grammar* and the Deconstruction of "Grammatical Tyranny"', also finds early traces of republicanism or proto-republicanism in Milton's grammar, accepting the usual composition date of 1640–6. In his more-Ramist-than-Ramus compression of William Lily's *Shorte Introduction*, Milton apparently deleted numerous *exempla* which observe hierarchical political structures and idioms and added much Cicero, thus removing language from associations of political controversy. Finally, in 'The Poet in the Marketplace: Milton and Samuel Simmons', Peter Lindenbaum looks at the printer-publisher responsible for the first three editions of *PL*, the skilful craftsman though unsuccessful entrepreneur Simmons. Far from exploiting Milton in the notorious contract, Simmons acknowledged Milton's property rights in his text, contrasting with the publisher of the 1645 poems, Humphrey Moseley, who exerted greater control over presentation. This is a useful contribution to our understanding of Milton's status, and the status of the literary author in the mid-seventeenth century.

Elsewhere, Lindenbaum offers more evidence on the early publication of Milton's works, in 'Authors and Publishers in the Late Seventeenth Century: New Evidence on Their Relations' (*Library* 17.250–69). He suggests that Joseph Watts and Awnsham Churchill were co-operating on the projected 1698 edition of the prose, and the fact that Watts contacted Elizabeth Milton suggests an implicit recognition of the author's (or his widow's) residual rights in a text. Lindenbaum also suggests that while publishers were first and foremost businessmen, recognition of scholarly and creative merit was not unknown to them. Also rescuing printers from the aggregation of historical disparagement is Sally P. Power. In 'Assessing the Textual Accuracy of John Baskerville's Editions of *Paradise Lost*' (*N&Q* 42.34–7), she compares the texts of the printer Baskerville's 1758 and 1759 edition of *PL* with Thomas Newton's edition of 1749 and suggests that, contrary to Baskerville's reputation, the texts were prepared with diligence and accuracy.

Historicism is certainly the main path in Milton studies these days, but there are also attempts to combine historicism with more theoretical concerns. The winner of this year's James Holly Hanford Prize of the Milton Society of

America is Lana Cable's *Carnal Rhetoric: Milton's Iconoclasm and the Poetics of Desire*. By 'carnal rhetoric' Cable means language intended to produce affect in readers over and above – sometimes in opposition to – rational argument. Milton would dismiss this persuasive dimension in *De Doctrina Christiana* (as *'fiducia carnalis'*: Columbia *Works*, 17.56–7); yet it is fundamental to his argumentative techniques. Cable reassembles Milton as a Nietzschean, breaking images to prove the unattainable truth. She offers some stimulating and inventive close readings of the prose. Reading the anti-prelatical tracts she examines the moral intensity that resides in the affective language of spiritual truth rather than the language of example and reason. In the divorce tracts, by contrast, she suggests that the rhetorics of affect and reason are perfectly aligned, notably in the use of syntactic parallels; she also traces the image of perfect (sexual) union, which may reflect a monistic vision wrestling with dualistic language. The chapter on *Areopagitica* argues that Milton depicts a path to truth that uses images as stepping stones without assimilating them to the unattainable truth itself, a dialectical process necessary to produce a desire for truth. *Eikonoklastes* she reads as an attempt imaginatively to transform the idolatrous minds of the readers of *Eikon Basilike*. Milton's assault on Clarke's rhetoric endeavours to shatter the tendency to treat words as idols. In the final chapter, on *SA*, Cable outlines the protagonist's path to rejuvenation by breaking his own idols and coming to recognize the nature of true witnessing that the champion bears witness to God and not the other way around. This is a dense and intelligent book, frequently well-crafted, though in it history creaks under the weight of metaphor.

Other theoretically oriented readings include the post-structuralist approach of Douglas Lanier, in '"Unmark't Unknown"': *Paradise Regained* and the Return of the Expressed' (*Criticism* 37.187–212). Lanier discusses the anxiety over authorship expressed in Milton's pamphlets. Milton's emergent bourgeois subjectivity fears the fixing and consequent exposing to assault involved in publication, but in *PR* the Son successfully negotiates a hero's defence of private integrity through words that are none the less partly public, thus becoming a model of an ideal author. *PL* and Jacques Derrida are two authorities that remain as yet conspicuously undeconstructed, according to Thomas L. Martin; so in 'On the Margin of God: Deconstruction and the Language of Satan in *Paradise Lost*' (*MiltonQ* 29.41–7) he sets about remedying this. He begins by comparing the rhetorical moves of Derrida and *PL* (mainly Satan, in fact), and some of the analysis of Satan's word-play will be familiar from other rhetorical criticism. He concludes by querying Derrida's framework, suggesting that the supposedly irreconcilable actions of play and centring cohabit the drama of *PL*. In '"Fire to Use": A Practice-Theory Approach to *Paradise Lost*' (*Rep* 51.94–117), Fred Hoerner draws (in sometimes opaque language) parallels between Milton's theory of agency and authority and the social theories of Pierre Bourdieu and Anthony Giddens. Milton is seen to undermine and account for the failings in the 'structuralist' fictions of him as an authoritarian prohibitor: his emphasis is on praxis rather than laws, creation rather than constraint.

A very different interest in theory emerges in John Rumrich's controversial 'Milton's God and the Matter of Chaos' (*PMLA* 110.1035–46), which trenchantly rejects the view that Chaos is represented as innately evil in *PL*.

Looking at Books II and X, Rumrich suggests that it is Satan who tries to reduce the potential otherness within Chaos. In fact, he concludes, Chaos seems to be God's feminine and creative aspect: it is his womb, essential to his being. With chaos theory behind him, Rumrich locates an "indeterminate otherness", though it may just be a particular dialectical resolution to a contradiction.

The third substantial collection of essays devoted to Milton this year returns to rather more traditional approaches. The essays collected in Margo Swiss and David A. Kent, eds, *Heirs of Fame: Milton and Writers of the English Renaissance*, link Milton with near-contemporary writers, though against the current of Milton studies the contributors focus on canonical parallels. Swiss and Kent's introduction claims that the volume affirms traditional 'presences' in literature, and links an aestheticist approach with historicism. Thomas P. Roche's 'Spenser, Milton, and the Representation of Evil' explores Milton's interpretation of Spenser, as implied by the Sin and Death allegory, suggesting that the influence reaches beyond mere verbal echoes to a moral reading, and that the gendering in the passage partly derives from (and reacts against) the matrilineal genealogy of evil in *The Faerie Queene*. John Steadman's comparative study of these two authors, *Moral Fiction in Milton and Spenser* is reviewed elsewhere in this volume (221). The premise of M. J. Doherty's 'Beyond Androgyny: Sidney, Milton, and the Phoenix' seems to be that Sidney was seen as a Phoenix, so when Milton alludes to the Phoenix, or something that looks like one, he is acknowledging Sidney as a poetic forebear to his own, Phoenix-like creation. P. G. Stanwood, in 'Of Prelacy and Polity in Milton and Hooker' suggests that there are some similarities to be found in the ecclesiological writings of Milton and Hooker: namely in their arguments from reason and natural law. Hooker, Stanwood suggests, anticipates the impracticality of Milton's perfectionism, and offers a critique of Milton's as much as vice versa. Maren-Sofie Røstvig, in 'The Craftsmanship of God: Some Structural Contexts for the *Poems of Mr. John Milton* (1645)', continues her recent work on Christian numerology and explores symmetries within and between the poems of the 1645 volume. The implications for the volume are certainly intriguing, though some suggestions are rarified: such as that Milton included the two Greek poems in order to create a quaternion of languages, embodying fullness and perfection. 'Myth, Masque, and Marriage: *Paradise Lost* and Shakespeare's Romances', by Stella P. Revard, proposes the influence of the romances on *PL* in the heavenly masque blessing Edenic marriage and the spousal reconciliation. Margo Swiss, in '*Lachrymae Christi*: The Theology of Tears in Milton's *Lycidas* and Donne's Sermon "Jesus Wept"', discusses sixteenth- and seventeenth-century interpretations of Christ's tears, with particular emphasis on Donne's sermon, and suggests that it is within this context that 'Lycidas' was conceived. In 'Milton: The Truest of the Sons of Ben', John Creaser argues for the Jonsonian character of Milton's early poems, after the 1629 ode, and suggests that the poets parted thereafter owing to religious and political differences, and Milton's greater confidence in his vocation. Charles Cantalupo, in '"By Art Is Created That Great ... State": Milton's *Paradise Lost* and Hobbes's *Leviathan*' juxtaposes the masterpieces of Milton and Hobbes in order to suggest that the latter is also an epic, and should be read as a literary text as much as the former. The argument is overshadowed by recent writings by Quentin Skinner. Paul A. Parrish, 'Milton and Crashaw: The Cambridge and Italian Years', compares the respective experiences in Cambridge and Italy of the two poets, suggesting the very different effects of these experiences. Parrish does not look closely at the poetry, but provides some useful and detailed contexts.

Accepting earlier suggestions that 'Upon Appleton House' alludes to 'Il Penseroso', Diana Treviño Benet, in 'The Genius of the Wood and the Prelate of the Grove: Milton and Marvell', suggests that this gentle ridicule of Milton's vatic self-presentation turns to acceptance in 'On Mr. Milton's *Paradise Lost*', where Marvell publicly praises the bard for a prophetic voice exceeding the bounds of poetry. After a brief introductory outline of Reformation doctrine and church discipline, Dennis Danielson, in 'Milton, Bunyan, and the Clothing of Truth and Righteousness', discusses the theme of nakedness and clothing in *PL* and *Pilgrim's Progress*, then uses this metaphor to suggest that literary clothing, far from being damaging to the word, can make good Christian practice. The volume concludes with a shorter version of Steven N. Zwicker's 'Milton, Dryden, and the Politics of Literary Controversy', discussed above.

One of the more interesting articles on *PL* this year is John K Hale's '*Paradise Lost*: A Poem in Twelve Books, or Ten?' (*PQ* 74.131–49), which explores Milton's possible intentions in revising his ten-book epic to the canonical 12-book version. Surveying the existing (largely numerological) arguments, Hale suggests that the strong interpretation would involve the reception of the poem, which encouraged Milton, already impelled to revise it, to heighten its Virgilian appearance. This is a most useful and detailed argument, with much in its favour; but Hale's brief justification of the original ten-book form (the delayed circumstances of its composition, and its origins in dramatic form, resulted in an imperfect, effectively provisional structure) is unpersuasive. So half of the story remains untold. Louis L. Martz's '"Hail holy light": Milton, Rembrandt, and the Protestant Baroque' (in Scaglione Aldo and Viola Gianni Eugenio, eds, *The Image of the Baroque*) discusses Milton's baroque use of light, comparing it with Rembrandt's; he suggests that the symmetry of the theme of light and darkness is weakened in the 12-book edition of *PL*.

There's a *recherché* feel to Teresa Michals's claim, in '"Sweet gardening labour": Merit and hierarchy in *Paradise Lost*' (*Exemplaria* 7.499–514), that *PL*, in its representation of labour and of the relations between hierarchy and meritocracy, reflects the transition from feudalism to capitalism. Drawing conspicuously on the work of Maureen Quilligan and Andrew Milner, she suggests that the Fall is precipitated by a breakdown in fealty relations, in which Eve furthers an individualistic, capitalist ethic (perhaps that of an improving landlord), which overthrows the fragments of feudal ideology that Adam represents. The broad point is not entirely improbable, but Michals sees the literary reflection of history as profoundly unmediated.

In 'With Mortal Voice: Milton Defends Against the Muse' (*ELH* 62.509–27), a lively article which pursues his broader thesis of Milton's contradictory attitude to God, Stanley Fish analyses the invocation beginning *PL* VII. He suggests that the ambiguously gendered muse of the epic, the aggressive women and impotent fathers, figure Milton's unease at singing God's song rather than his own. His 'jockeying for verbal power' reflects discontent and resentment at being incorporated under God. In '"The Copious Matter of My Song": A Study of Theology and Rhetoric in Milton's

Paradise Lost and 23rd Sonnet' (*PCP* 30.42–58), Nicholas Wallerstein endeavours to persuade that the angelic Hymn in *PL* III.372–415 takes the form of a eucharistic prayer into which the reader is drawn to participate. The same formal focus on the reader's response can be found, according to Wallerstein, in 'Methought I saw', where the turn at line 13 ('But O') requires the reader, through form, to participate in the author's distressed surprise: form does not merely transmit meaning, says Wallerstein, but creates it. A related piece of interest is Gert Ronberg's 'They Had Their Points: Punctuation and Interpretation in English Renaissance Literature' (in Andreas H. Jucker, ed., *Historical Pragmatics: Pragmatic Developments in the History of English*), which discusses some differences between Renaissance punctuation (rhetorical and elocutionary) and modern (logical and grammatical). Ronberg takes *PL* V.86–92 as one example where the lighter, original punctuation is a better guide to original meanings, and should be kept for modern editions.

The essays in the two issues of *Milton Quarterly* that have appeared this year include 'A Note on *Paradise Lost* 2' (*MiltonQ* 29.28–9), in which John T. Shawcross, furthering a point made by Diana Treviño Benet last year (*YWES* 75.302), identifies some suggestively close parallels between the Great Consult in Pandaemonium and a 1647 pamphlet, *The Devil in His Dumps*. The question of what to do with Milton's undoubted familiarity with the world of popular political pamphlets persists. According to Philip Hardie in 'The Presence of Lucretius in *Paradise Lost*' (*MiltonQ* 29.13–24), Lucretius has been underrated as an influence on Milton, not only at the level of allusion, but in the didactic strategies of *PL*, which, Hardie suggests, directly reflect those of *De Rerum Natura*. Marvell's prefatory poem, he concludes, recognizes this Lucretian subtext. In '"The middling temper of nourishment": Biblical Exegesis and the Art of Indeterminate Balance in *Tetrachordon*' (*MiltonQ* 29.1–12), Reuben Sanchez argues that the dense schematic parallels and antitheses in the syntax of *Tetrachordon* correspond to Milton's strategy, which is rhetorically to dissolve the extreme position on divorce and create an "indeterminate middle ground". Sanchez concludes that this conspicuous change in style (from the antiprelatical tracts) stems from Milton's personal crisis in the mid-1640s, his sense of fallen human imperfection emerging from his own failed marriage. David Norbrook, in 'Euripides, Milton, and *Christian Doctrine*' (*MiltonQ* 29.37–41) draws attention to the nuanced allusions to Euripides in *De Doctrina Christiana*, their similarities with Milton's other, undoubted writings, and affinities with the annotations on Milton's copy of Euripides. If the treatise is not Milton's, then its author had a comparable interest in Greek drama.

Two articles consider the sonnet 'Avenge O Lord thy slaughtered Saints'. George Bellis's, 'Fish and Milton – Briefly' (*ELN* 32.23–34) is an anti-pluralist reading of the sonnet, attacking Fish's account, which suggests that its contradictions embrace criticism of God. Bellis's trumpet blows loudly on behalf of a New Critical reading, ironically Fish's point of departure. In my own 'The Daily Muse; Or, Seventeenth-Century Poets Read the News' (*SC* 10.189–218), I explore the origins of the same sonnet in reports on the massacre from Switzerland, and compare Milton's presentation of this material with its treatment by Nedham in the government newsbook *Mercurius Politicus*. Kurt Schlueter, in 'Milton's Heroical Sonnets' (*SEL* 35.123–36), argues that the Fairfax, Cromwell and Vane sonnets form a distinctive group, which could be defined by the genre 'heroical sonnets', a critical term which critics have inopportunely missed, which derives from the 'prayer hymn of classical antiquity'.

Looking at some of the less overburdened works: Paul Stevens, in 'Spenser and Milton on Ireland: Civility, Exclusion, and the Politics of Wisdom' (*ArielE* 26.151–67), touches on Milton's *Observations upon the Articles of Peace*, discussing the involvement of notions of civility and of politicized biblical thought in writings on colonialism in Ireland. Peter C. Herman, in 'Milton and the Muse-Haters: *Ad patrem, L'Allegro/Il Penseroso*, and the Ambivalences of Poetry' (*Criticism* 37.37–56), suggests that Milton's representation of his father's depreciation of a poetic vocation draws on the Protestant critique of poetry as an ungodly pastime; and that a similar voice creeps into 'L'Allegro' and 'Il Penseroso', implicating both figures in this potential misuse of the imagination.

Cedric C. Brown's *John Milton: A Literary Life* is a biographically organized introductory survey of Milton's works, evidently designed for undergraduates. It has plenty of virtues to recommend it: lucidity and the broad range of texts it considers. The elegies, though not the prolusions, many sonnets, the early poems, most of the prose works and the 'major poems' are explicated, with a focus on Milton's self-presentation, and his intended audience. Most of the chapters will help students understand and historically place the texts: that on *PL* is a little more narrowly focused (on the issue of the poem as a public speech act).

Prominent among the shorter notes which discuss Milton's sources is Michelle Valerie Ronnick's 'Forty Source Notes to Milton's *Pro Populo Anglicano Defensio Prima*' (*MiltonQ* 29.48–52), which identifies an impressive list of mainly classical borrowings that contribute to the rhetorical verve of the *Defensio*. Ronnick's 'On the verb *Aegyptizo* in Milton's *Pro Populo Anglicano Defensio Prima* 5.290.18' (*N&Q* 42.31–2) identifies Milton's creation of his own Greek loan-word in Latin (meaning to play the Egyptian, to act deceitfully). In 'Salmacis and Salmasius: *Pro Populo Anglicano Defensio Secunda*' (*N&Q* 42.32–4), Ronnick outlines Milton's use of 'salmacis' and 'hermaphroditus' in his representation of Salmasius and More, and suggests that Milton is more faithful to Ovid than the Yale editors imply. Philip Rollinson's 'The Homoerotic Aspect of Temptation in *Paradise Regained*' (*ELN* 32.31–5) rejects Gregory W. Bredbeck's suggestion (*YWES* 72.229) that Milton innovated the homoerotic dimension of Christ's temptation (in the banquet scene in *PR* I), and identifies precedents in Cicero and Tasso. John K. Hale in '*Paradise Lost*, X.783' (*N&Q* 42.450) suggests that Adam's words 'lest all I cannot die' allude not to Milton's mortalism but to Horace's *Odes* III.xxx.6. M. J. Edwards, in 'Chrysostom, Prudentius, and the Fiends of *Paradise Lost*' (*N&Q* 42.448–50), identifies some debts to Prudentius's *Hamartigenia* in Milton's representation of Satan; and, interestingly, to John Chrysostom in the depiction of Sin. Other notes of interest include Gene Michael Anderson's 'Milton's *Paradise Lost*' (*Expl* 53.iii.135–7), which claims that the 'most important' – and overlooked – word-play in Milton's epic is where Satan, whose mission is to create a false theology, invents the cannon: a pun on canon law, which undermines the Word of God. Frances Malpezzi's 'Milton's *Comus*, lines 743–4' (*Expl* 53.iii.194–6) looks at the multivalent, scripturally tinged meanings implicit in the rose simile, spoken by Comus. Martin K. Doudna, in

'"Nay Lady, Sit": The Dramatic and Human Dimensions of *Comus*' (*ANQ* 8.38–44), argues that the philosophical and abstract interpretation of *A Maske* as a discussion of the virtues of chastity has eclipsed its real attention to the dramatic situation of a young woman threatened by an external force which she is not able to repel with mere reason. The argument is reinforced by a modernized screenplay treatment. Todd Nelson, in 'Death Hath Broke His Girt': Printing Imagery in Milton's Hobson Epitaphs' (*ANQ* 8.6–8) considers printing terminology in the poems on the University carrier.

Among the notes and studies which consider questions of influence is Eleanor Cook's '"Methought" as dream formula in Shakespeare, Milton, Wordsworth, Keats, and others' (*ELN* 32.34–46), which suggests that 'methought' in *PL* indicates more than the past tense of 'methinks' (generally describing conscious judgement) and carries strong associations with dreams or visions. This Milton inherits from Shakespeare, and his usage proceeds to influence the Romantics and others. In 'Keats's "Mawkish Fame"' (*N&Q* 42.185–6), discussing Keats's influence on John Brown's *Psyche* (1818), Nicholas Roe mentions their mutual allusions to Milton's imaginative flight; Stanley Jones's 'More Hazlitt Quotations and Allusions: Shakespeare, the Bible, Milton, Quintillian/Steele, Pope, Burke' (*N&Q* 42.186–7) notes Hazlitt's use of 'at whose sight all the stars/Hide their diminished heads'; John K. Hale, in 'The Title of *Great Expectations*' (*N&Q* 42.193), notes that 'our great expectation' is Milton's honorific for Christ in *PL*, prompting Dickens's irony.

Other studies which look at Milton's influence (reviewed in their respective sections) include Patrick Colm Hogan's *Joyce, Milton and the Theory of Influence*; Raymond Powell, 'Wordsworth, Dorothy Wordsworth, Tintern Abbey and *Samson Agonistes*' (*Neophil* 79.689–93); and Daniel Clay, 'Pope, Milton, and Dunces' (*UDR* 23.75–86).

Finally, as bedside reading there is *Paradise Lost: The Novel*, an adaptation by Joseph Lanzara. Lanzara paraphrases the original text very closely; this novel version seeks to overcome the anxieties of those intimidated by complex language, or by lines that do not reach the edge of the page. Some of the phrases appear strangely defamiliarized in their new context: for instance, 'His gentle hand seized hers, and she yielded' evokes the bodice-ripper more than the epic. The volume includes Gustav Doré's illustrations, and is very nicely printed. It is strange to think that language could be an obstacle to reading *PL*.

Books Reviewed

Aldo, Scaglione, and Viola Gianni Eugenio, eds. *The Image of the Baroque*. Lang. pp. 240. $59.95. ISBN 0 8204 2473 0.

Armitage, David, Armand Himy, and Quentin Skinner, eds. *Milton and Republicanism*. CUP. pp. xii + 281. £35. ISBN 0 521 55178 1.

Brown, Cedric C. *John Milton: A Literary Life*. Macmillan. pp. xviii + 212. hb £37.50, pb £9.99. ISBN 0 333 42515 4, 0 333 42516 2.

Cable, Lana. *Carnal Rhetoric: Milton's Iconoclasm and the Poetics of Desire*. DukeUP. pp. x + 231. hb £42.75, pb £16.95. ISBN 0 8223 1560 2, 0 8223 1573 4.

Fallon, Robert Thomas. *Divided Empire: Milton's Political Imagery*. PSUP. pp. xviii + 190. $40, £35.95. ISBN 0 271 01460 1.

Jucker, Andreas H., ed. *Historical Pragmatics: Pragmatic Developments in the History of English*. Pragmatics and Beyond New Series 35. Benjamins, BenjaminsNA. pp. xvi + 624. £62, $97. ISBN 90 272 5047 (Eur), 1 55619 328 9 (US).

Knoppers, Laura Lunger. *Historicizing Milton: Spectacle, Power, and Poetry in Restoration England*. UGeoP (1994). pp. xi + 209. £35.50. ISBN 0 8203 1594 X.

Lanzara, Joseph. *Paradise Lost: The Novel*. New Arts Library (1994). pp. 255. $24.95. ISBN 0 9639621 4 0.

MacLean, Gerald. *Culture and Society in the Stuart Restoration*. CUP. pp. xvi + 292. hb £37.50, pb £13.95. ISBN 0 521 41605 1, 0 521 47566 X.

Shawcross, John T., ed. *John Milton: The Critical Heritage*, 2 vols. Vol. 1: *1628–1731*; vol. 2: *1732–1801*. Routledge. pp. xi + 276, xi + 439. £75 and £85. Boxed set £150. ISBN 0 514 13420 X, 0 415 13421 8.

Skulsky, Harold. *Justice in the Dock: Milton's Experimental Tragedy*. UDelP. pp. 133. £22. ISBN 0 87413 555 9.

Stanwood, P. G., ed. *Of Poetry and Politics: New Essays on Milton and His World*. MRTS, vol. 126. pp. xxi + 323. $39. ISBN 0 86698 131 4.

Swiss, Margo, and David A. Kent, eds. *Heirs of Fame: Milton and Writers of the English Renaissance*. AUP. BuckUP. pp. viii + 317. £34.50. ISBN 0 8387 5276 4.

X

The Later Seventeenth Century

STUART GILLESPIE, MARION LOMAX, JAMES OGDEN and
ROGER POOLEY

This chapter has three sections: 1. General; 2. Dryden; 3. Other Authors. Sections 1(b) and 3(b) are by Marion Lomax; section 2(b) is by James Ogden; sections 1(c) and 3(c) are by Roger Pooley; and the rest is by Stuart Gillespie.

1. General

As usual, two scholars compiled the listings of 'Some Current Publications' in *Restoration* this year: Stephen M. Adams (19.55–71) and Maja-Lisa von Sneidern (19.103–14). But there was also an unexpected supplement by Gary Layne Hatch, under the subtly different title 'Some Recent Publications' (19.115–29). This is an attempt to catch up on items omitted from these *Restoration* listings over the last few years, and so constitutes a courageous admission of failure on the journal's part – but no bibliography is perfect, as even readers of *YWES* may occasionally find themselves reflecting. John Sitter sat in judgement on 'Recent Studies in the Restoration and Eighteenth Century' for *SEL* (35.598–639), but attended to notably little material on the seventeenth century.

A number of studies, mostly of book length, fall into this general section this year. The reasons are partly practical (publishers currently find it easier to sell periods and topics than most individual authors) and partly ideological (academics currently find Cultural Studies more exciting than literature). *Culture and Society in the Stuart Restoration: Literature, Drama, History* (ed. Gerald MacLean) is not just a case in point: its entire rationale as a volume lies in overlapping the areas indicated by the nouns in the title. One of the essays, Blair Worden's 'Milton, *Samson Agonistes*, and the Restoration', is reviewed above (299). The rest could all be discussed in this chapter if I were convinced by MacLean's somewhat laboured attempt in his introduction to suggest that there is no difference between literature and history. Since I am not convinced, I shall confine my remarks to the contributions based on written texts, and among these simply register the presence of Elaine Hobby on Hannah Woolley (the well-known Restoration cookery writer), N. H. Keeble on various Royalist women's memoirs and Robert Iliffe on Isaac Newton's 'self-fashioning'. James Grantham Turner is fascinating on Pepys's attitudes to the sexuality of the king and Lady Castlemaine. In the two pieces on drama, Andrew R. Walkling and Nancy Klein Macguire document supposed political allusions in, respectively, Tate and Purcell's *Dido and Aeneas* and John Crowne's *Henry VI*. Oddly, there is no reference here to Walkling's other essay this year on the same subject ('Political Allegory in Purcell's "Dido and Aeneas" ', *M&L* 76.540–71) or vice versa: they are distinct pieces but cover almost the same ground. In the one belonging to MacLean's collection, Walkling is unusually explicit about the assumptions on which this now popular form of allusion-hunting is based. He also provides a perfect example of the hedging of bets it always seems to involve, when he makes the 'indeterminacy' he discovers in his text's allusions evidence in itself of 'strategies of concealment'. There can be few non-comic Restoration plays left now which have not been found to contain copious concealed comment on contemporary politics. Finally in this volume, Steven N. Zwicker meditates on Dryden's response to Milton and, more surprisingly, Milton's to Dryden. The whole becomes a disappointingly reductive tale of 'influence and anxiety', at the centre of which is Dryden's postulated 'hostility' to *Paradise Lost* because of its politics. Unhappy at his inability to demonstrate conclusively that Dryden was deliberately 'trivializing' the poem in *The State of Innocence*, Zwicker goes on to claim that Dryden's *Dedication* to James and Mary 'subjugate[s] Milton's Protestant poetry and politics in a most humiliating way'. According to Zwicker, Dryden was later able to 'make his peace' with Milton through the 'sympathy for the marginal' he acquired once he occupied a 'minority position in his own culture'. This essay says more about the current concerns of American academics than about Dryden's or Milton's writing. Zwicker is unaware that Paul Hammond has shown Dryden and Milton worked in the same office in the 1650s (*YWES* 62.246), and so thinks they might not have met until much later; he seems unaware of J. R. Mason's unpublished doctoral dissertation 'To Milton through Dryden and Pope' (University of Cambridge, 1986).

Two further 'general' studies might end up in the history rather than the literature section of many libraries. Raymond A. Anselment's *The Realms of Apollo: Literature and Healing in Seventeenth-Century England* is less about 'healing' than sickness (specifically venereal disease, smallpox and plague) and other phenomena treated by medicine (such as childbirth), and 'literature', even on a broad definition, is secondary in a survey along traditional historical lines. Medical writings and personal narratives are supposed by Anselment to provide the 'context for poetic works', but his accounts of the contexts are much more extensive than his accounts of the poetry. There are discussions of poems by Dryden, Katherine Philips and some much less well-known Restoration writers, but only one or two poems in each case, and only small-scale discussions. This book is actually reminiscent of the social history of Lawrence Stone. There are just scattered signs of its author's literary expertise, and it is readable for the same reasons Stone is readable. Harold M. Weber's *Paper Bullets: Print and Kingship under Charles II* seeks to explain 'the way in which printed texts functioned as both author and effect' in the process of 'shaping Charles's monarchical identity'. Weber's world is that of pamphlets, tracts and poems on affairs of state. The issues are those of propaganda, censorship, licensing, ultimately power and the manipulation of the reading public, specifically vis-à-vis the monarch; the section headings are 'The Incognito King and Providential History', 'The Monarch's Sacred Body', and so on. Weber's book, then, is a further example of how, in this year's work on the later seventeenth century, the common ground shared by those areas traditionally designated 'history' and 'literature' has seen something of a population explosion.

More specifically literary in orientation is Warren Chernaik's *Sexual Freedom in Restoration Literature*. Again the title presumably reflects marketing priorities, for the book is very largely about just two writers, Aphra Behn and Rochester, as cases of literary Restoration libertinism. Contexts in Hobbes are discussed, and something is made of Restoration comedy and of other women writers, but two of the five chapters are devoted to each of these two principal figures and this is scarcely a comprehensive treatment of the subject. Some other reviewers have found Chernaik too conventional on Rochester and more exciting on Behn. For me, the more subtle and convincing material is on Rochester, especially on materialist aspects of his libertinism, whereas the Behn chapters tend merely to position her work on currently fashionable axes – most often those connected with gender, as in discussion of 'passages of cross-dressing in Behn's writings' and 'Behn's myth of the androgyne'.

Moving finally to essay-length work, two pieces in the Myers and Harris volume are on publishing in the Restoration period, and both are useful. Germaine Greer's 'Honest Sam. Briscoe' is a straightforward scholarly account of this publisher's career, gathering plenty of scattered information together. There could have been more detail, but what we have is helpful. Some emphasis is given to Briscoe's connections with Aphra Behn, and Greer ends by suggesting that Behn's genuine remains should be 'rescued by scrupulous editing from the suffocating mass of spurious attribution in which Briscoe buried them'; but see the next section, below, for Greer's own substantial proposed addition to the Behn *oeuvre*. The second essay here, Giles Mandelbrote's 'From the warehouse to the counting-house: booksellers and bookshops in late 17th-century London' is, one gathers, part of a longer work in progress. This instalment is an informative discussion of practical aspects of the trade, with resourceful use of documentary evidence on numerous points. How did booksellers attract customers to their shops? How wealthy could booksellers expect to become? Were literary works more important to the average bookseller's livelihood than bibles and psalters? The short answer to the last question is 'on the contrary'.

(a) Poetry

Leo Braudy's 'Unturning the Century: The Missing Decade of the 1690s' will not detain us long. It is in the paradoxically entitled volume *Fins de Siècle: English Poetry in 1590, 1690, 1790, 1890, 1990* (ed. Elaine Scarry). The essay parodies the project quite well enough on its own account: 'as decades go', Braudy muses, 'the 1690s haven't gotten much of a good press. In the ranks of concluding decades, the 1590s, the 1790s, and the 1890s stand out much more vividly'. Michael Brennan and Paul Hammond describe 'The Badminton Manuscript: A New Miscellany of Restoration Verse' (*EMS* 5.171–207) which can be found at Badminton House, Avon. This hitherto unexamined scribal miscellany has many poems in common with four others of its period, including the Gyldenstolpe, indicating that 'small anthologies of contemporary poems on particular themes were available to scribes'; all five may even have derived from the same scriptorium. The poet most strongly represented is Rochester, but all the major Restoration wits and several minor ones are here. The article also provides a description of contents, finding list and first-line index for the Badminton miscellany.

Germaine Greer's *Slip-Shod Sibyls: Recognition, Rejection and the Woman Poet* has one chapter on Katherine Philips, two on Aphra Behn and one on Anne Wharton. The work of Philips – considered by Greer 'a major poet of the Restoration' – is said to demonstrate the difficulties of establishing 'what women wrote and the way they wrote it', which are created by the way other people revised it for page and stage. In fact, there is nothing gender-determined about the kinds of revision she finds Philips's printers and friends in London practising. Greer's overall statement of the textual problems is along the right lines, but her examples of Philips being misrepresented (the verse is never improved by these alterations, apparently) are sometimes wrongly described in their details. One of Greer's two essays on Behn explains the extensive similarities between Thomas Killigrew's *Thomaso* and Behn's *The Rover* by suggesting that Behn was acting as Killigrew's amanuensis at the time his play was put together, and in effect wrote it by turning 'Killigrew's spoken word into the text of "Thomaso" '. Many of the links in this reasoning are extremely tenuous, and Greer's fancy is also on the wing in her other discussion of Behn, a wide-ranging biographical piece in which she suggests, for example, that Behn might have been American, or Creole, or Jewish, or have been George Villiers's mistress, or have committed suicide. This is a shame, because Greer is capable of robust common sense elsewhere in this essay, as when she rounds on *bienpensant* feminist biographers – 'Restoration actresses did not embark upon a theatrical career to avoid prostitution, but to attract a better class of protector'. Greer sets out to supply a general account of the life and poetic work of Anne Wharton, Rochester's half-niece, in a further chapter which is again vitiated by speculation, mostly about connections with Rochester. She ends by complaining that the *DNB* got Wharton's birthdate wrong by nearly 30 years, so perhaps it is not unfair to point out that the same wrong date is given in the caption to the portrait of Wharton reproduced in this volume.

(b) Drama

The Drama Series in OUP's World's Classics was successfully launched in this year under the General Editorship of Michael Cordner and his team. 'Marriage in crisis' is the subject of a fine collection of plays from the 1680s and 1690s which comprises Otway's *The Soldiers' Fortune*, Nathaniel Lee's *The Princess of Cleves*, Dryden's *Amphitryon; or The Two Sosias* and Southerne's *The Wives' Excuse; or Cuckolds Make Themselves*. Imaginatively edited by Michael Cordner (with Ronald Clayton), *Four Restoration Marriage Plays* challenges some of the many generalizations which have been applied to Restoration drama – particularly the view of L. C. Knights, that 'In the matter of sexual relations Restoration comedy is entirely dominated by a narrow set of conventions'. Cordner emphasizes the variety of approaches and the skilfulness of these dramatists in a modernized and thoroughly annotated collection which succeeds in its aim 'to provide as stylistically and tonally various a selection as possible'. He demonstrates the topicality of the plays well, particularly in relation to contemporary politics. There are also careful analyses of Lee's invocations of John Wilmot, Earl of Rochester, in *The Princess of Cleves*, and of *The Wives' Excuse*'s initial reception in the theatre. Throughout, knowledge of the plays' stage histories is used to good effect. There is a useful bibliographical summary of both general and specific texts, and a helpful glossary.

The conduct of sexual relations inside and outside marriage is examined by Warren Chernaik in his very readable *Sexual Freedom in Restoration Literature*. Chernaik argues that Restoration drama, like Rochester's poetry, took ideas of libertinism seriously, and that the ideological stance of plays such as *The Man of Mode*, *The Way of the World* or *The Provok'd Wife* is much more complex than has been previously recognized. As well as his poetry, Rochester's rarely discussed attempts at drama are considered – *Sodom* (if the attribution is accepted), his adaptation of Fletcher's *Valentinian*, and the fragmentary *Conquest of China*. The chapters on Aphra Behn tackle issues of female libertinism and Behn's plays are usefully compared with those of male contemporaries. There are less differences than one might expect and the roles of the androgyne, Amazon and virago, attitudes to cuckoldry, and the effects of cross-dressing on the stage are considered carefully.

More explorations of ideologies occur in two collections of essays of particular interest: *Culture and Society in the Stuart Restoration: Literature, Drama, History* and *Cultural Readings of Restoration and Eighteenth-century English Theater*. The former is edited by Gerald MacLean and the latter by J. Douglas Canfield and Deborah C. Payne. Three essays in MacLean's volume cover, between them, a diverse range of material. John Patrick Montaño, in 'The Quest for Consensus: the Lord Mayor's Day Shows in the 1670s', demonstrates the way these pageants were used 'to bring an oral and emblematic version of government policy onto the streets for the ideological consumption of the London populace'. This detailed study of the political use of civic pageantry is complemented by Andrew R. Walkling's examination of Tate and Purcell's *Dido and Aeneas*, and Nancy Klein Maguire analyses John Crowne's adaptation of Shakespeare's *Henry VI* plays. MacLean's collection is firmly placed in the popular arena of cultural studies – considering drama in relation to national identity – but Canfield and Payne, in *Cultural Readings of Restoration and Eighteenth-century English Theater*, argue that their field has, hitherto, resisted critical methods such as semiotics, deconstruction, feminism, Marxism, new historicism and cultural studies. James Ogden's review of the previous year would seem to suggest that this was certainly no longer the case in 1994 (*YWES* 74.313–18, 325–9): perhaps Canfield and Payne's project was in preparation when the tide was on the turn. As a showcase for 'consciously theoretical readings of Restoration and Eighteenth-century Drama and Theater' the volume is effective. Helen Burke takes issue with the traditional critical reception of Wycherley's *The Plain Dealer*, particularly 'the tendency to treat the text almost exclusively in terms of character analysis and the habit of overlooking one of the play's two plots'. The former, she argues, through a privileging of the male subject has led to 'a preoccupation with the character of Manly' and disregard for the Blackacre plot indicates, she notes, a denial of the drama's wider cultural dimension. After a careful, detailed analysis of the play, Burke concludes: 'To disengage the complexity of *The Plain Dealer*, an

"Other" kind of criticism is required': her feminist historicist application of
Cixous and Lacan provides a plausible challenge to the traditional approach.
Deborah C. Payne's essay, 'Reified Object or Emergent Professional?
Retheorizing the Restoration Actress' surveys contemporary and critical
attitudes to Restoration actresses to show 'how professional regard and sexual
objectification coexisted during the Restoration'. While, for Payne, display
'amplified' actresses, Kristina Straub, in 'Actors and Homophobia', cites
William Prynne's *Histrio-Mastix* (1633) and notes the view that the stage
display of a male body 'made it somehow not-male'. Focusing finally on Colley
Cibber and David Garrick, Straub charts the ways actors were sexually
defined (from the late seventeenth to the late eighteenth centuries) in an
attempt to examine the role they played 'in marking the limits of what
masculinity could be'. There is a great deal of intriguing information here. I
had no difficulty following the clear line taken by Harold Weber in his essay,
'Carolinean Sexuality and the Restoration Stage: Reconstructing the Royal
Phallus in *Sodom*'. Courageous in his attempt to tackle such a notoriously
obscene text for convincingly critical reasons, Weber shifts the focus from
obscenity to politically directed misogyny and shows how a play which opens
as a sexual fantasy intended to arouse general desires, soon takes on more
serious satirical overtones as pleasure is set above state power. '*Sodom*
represents a monstrous inversion of the royal masque, for in it the king
becomes a symbol not of order's triumph but of its defeat in a climactic sexual
apocalypse. The king becomes the antimasque, his erotic obsessions responsible for the nation's destruction.'

Aphra Behn's politics, both feminist and state, were the subject of several
articles last year (*YWES* 74.327) and the scrutiny continues in Robert Markley's essay, ' "Be impudent, be saucy, forward, bold, touzing, and leud": The
Politics of Masculine Sexuality and Feminine Desire in Behn's Tory Comedies'. Markley focuses on *The Rover, Part II*, *The Roundheads*, and *The City
Heiress* – all popular in their day, but less popular with recent critics. For him,
'Behn's comedies savage the Puritan ideology of self-denial that both historically and conceptually underlies the construction of the gendered self' and
her 'political attacks on the Whigs in the 1680s and the Commonwealthsmen
of the 1650s are efforts to demystify what we might call the masculinizing of
desire – the creation of women as other and as object'.

Following the lead of Michael Neill and Nicholas Jose, Richard Braverman's 'The Rake's Progress Revisited: Politics and Comedy in the
Restoration' exposes the political dimension of the theatrical libertine, tracing
his career and transformations from the 1660s to the 1690s beginning with
Etherege's *The Comical Revenge; or, Love in a Tub*. The essay considers
Etherege's *She Would if She Could*, Sedley's *The Mulberry Garden*, Wycherley's *The Country Wife* and *The Plain Dealer* and finishes by tracing 'the
development of the *honnête homme* from Congreve's early comedies to *The
Way of the World* ... ', proving that there are more possibilities for political
readings of these plays than has previously been supposed.

J. Douglas Canfield's interest, in 'Shifting Tropes of Ideology in English
Serious Drama, Late Stuart to Early Georgian', concerns tropic analysis,
particularly in relation to class and gender; his essay traces 'tropes that shift
from *emergent* status in the aristocratic to *dominant* status in the bourgeois
era'. Among Canfield's representative texts, chosen to chart the shifts from

Restoration to post-Revolutionary drama, are: Dryden's *Conquest of Granada*, Rowe's *Tamerlane*, Delarivier Manley's *Lucius, the First Christian King of Britain*, Addison's *Cato*, Rowe's *Lady Jane Gray*, Catherine Trotter's *The Fatal Friendship*, Lillo's *The London Merchant* and Shadwell's *The Lancashire Witches, and Tegue o Divelly the Irish-Priest*. His view is 'that, despite their democratic, meritocratic political rhetoric, the plays are exclusionary: they portray the consolidation of power in the hands of a new (male) elite – a power based ostensibly on law but really on the sword and the gun'. This is a useful contribution to a neglected area of criticism.

From tropes, or ideologemes, to metaphors: in 'The Novelty; or, Print, Money, Fashion, Getting, Spending, and Glut', J. S. Peters examines the way the theatre's metaphors reflected 'the general cultural interest in novelty (and the accompanying suspicion of it) in the late seventeenth century' and shows how theatre interacted with 'the expansion of commodity circulation and consumerism'. On a related theme, Charles H. Hinnant's article 'Pleasure and the Political Economy of Consumption in Restoration Comedy' (*Restoration* 19.77–87) argues that, despite the centrality of gentry and the aristocracy in the drama – and although those involved in trade or the professions are marginalized and often portrayed as stock figures of fun – 'mercantilism and its values began to permeate the more established idioms of Restoration comedy' through the language used by major characters. This is a stimulating article which places 'conspicuous consumption' at the heart of everything: clearly there are alternative responses – e.g. to the double standards applied to male and female libertinism – but Hinnant makes a persuasive case for allowing his topic a recognized place in the cultural frame.

There was a lack of articles on Restoration drama in *SEL* during the year but one piece, of interest to stage historians, is Deborah Kaplan's 'Representing the Nation: Restoration Comedies on the Early-Twentieth-Century London Stage' (*ThS* 36.37–61), covering productions in the capital between 1900 and 1930.

(c) Prose

A test: what were Richard Verstegan, John Weever, William Burton, Aylett Sammes and Edward Lhwyd? Answer: seventeenth-century antiquarians. Graham Parry's informative, enthusiastic and important book *The Trophies of Time: English Antiquarians of the Seventeenth Century* discusses them all alongside Camden, Selden, Aubrey and other more familiar figures. As a compendium it is, like its subject, curious and fascinating; as a contribution to seventeenth-century historiography it restores an important line of development to our attention. For some readers, it may seem under-theorized, an intellectual world away from newer historicizers, but in fact it has a lot to say to new historicist concerns, such as nationalism, the construction of the past, ideas of the primitive and iconoclasm.

The Margins of Orthodoxy: Heterodox Writing and Cultural Response 1660–1750 (ed. Roger D. Lund) has a number of chapters of direct relevance to the period. The two introductory pieces by J. G. A. Pocock and Christopher Hill extend their familiar positions into new areas – Pocock into the historiography of Christian doctrine, Hill into the eighteenth century. There are two interesting essays on Locke by established authorities, Richard Ashcraft on his anticlericalism, and G. A. J. Rogers on his conservatism and radicalism, based on a discussion of certainty in knowledge. Gordon Schochet discusses Samuel Parker without simply focusing on him as a target for Marvell; and Joseph M. Levine, in a study of Deists and Anglicans which must surely be only the start of a larger project, deals with Temple, Wotton, Lord Herbert and Bentley, amongst others, and suggests that it was the Christian moderns, rather than the radical deists, who did more in the long term to undermine the universalist claims of Christian belief.

Gary S. de Koey investigates Restoration radicalism, using a model owing more to Richard Ashcraft than Christopher Hill, in 'Rethinking the Restoration: Dissenting cases for conscience, 1667–1672' (*HistJ* 38.53–84). He sees the period 1667–72 as a crisis in the Restoration settlement, and provides some interesting re-contextualization for Marvell, Milton, Bunyan and Locke.

2. Dryden

(a) Poetry
The first two volumes of Paul Hammond's *The Poems of John Dryden* appeared this year, covering the period up to 1685. They are the result of a complete independent re-editing, perfectly capable of correcting the California Dryden on substantive textual and interpretative matters, and considerably more up to date in their scholarship. The format is, roughly speaking, the familiar Longman Annotated English Poets: headnotes to each text; textual and explanatory footnotes reaching typically a third of the way up the page; references provided for secondary works of 'scholarship' but not of 'criticism'. Accidentals are modernized and the texts presented in the form (and in the order) not in which they were first printed but in which they first entered the public domain. The editor's work is as meticulous as one would expect; indeed, Hammond does everything he sets out to do so well that it would be churlish to complain about details of editorial policy. The major remaining questions concern the form the edition will take in future: it is fervently to be hoped that the publishers will allow two extra volumes for the *Aeneis* in addition to the four covering the rest of the poetic corpus, and that the whole will eventually make its way into paperback.

An article in the *TLS* sparked an exchange over four subsequent contributions. Steven N. Zwicker started it with his piece 'What Scribling Slave . . . : A New Poem for the Dryden Canon?' (*TLS* 4795.13), in which he argued with more energy than conviction for the attribution to Dryden of a short (and most undistinguished) commendatory verse for one of Henry Higden's plays signed 'J.D.' Two replies were attracted (*TLS* 4807.12–13): David Hopkins thought the poem certainly not Dryden's, while D. N. DeLuna thought it an imitation of Dryden's style by Tom Brown. Zwicker then replied to both in a piece headed 'Dryden restored?' (*TLS* 4814.16), easily seeing off DeLuna. Hopkins had the last word by pointing out in a letter (*TLS* 4815.17) that Zwicker had not answered his case. A related note by Hopkins, 'Dryden, John Harvey, and the Tenth Satire of Juvenal' (*N&Q* 42.54–6), sets out the textual evidence to show that Dryden used Harvey's 1683 MS translation of Juvenal X in composing his version of 1692. This note should be used in conjunction with Hopkins's much more substantial *T&L* article, 'Dryden and the Tenth Satire of Juvenal' (*T&L* 4.31–60), which sets out the implications of these findings for our understanding of Dryden's translation. Commencing with a survey of previous commentary, working through the text with fresh and illuminating interpretative detail, and concluding with suggestions as to the place the Tenth Satire occupies in Dryden's *oeuvre*, it is, in fact, the authoritative reading of this most elusive of Dryden's poetic translations.

Two further articles concern Dryden's use of the classics. Nanette C. Tamer's ' "These are the Joys": Poetic Effects and the Idea of Poetry in Dryden's Translations from Horace' (*CML* 15.215–22) begins oddly by casting doubt on the attribution to Dryden of two Horatian translations in *Sylvae* which have been universally ascribed to him since 1685. She deals only with Dryden's Odes I.3 and I.9, pointing out a little pedantically how the translations approach the Latin from line to line – 'Dryden treats the mythological references inconsistently and, hence, detracts from the effectiveness of his poem'. Dryden's renderings are said to be 'philosophically reflective' where Horace's poems are 'particularizing and individualizing', a contrast which cannot entirely be sustained. In his very brief 'Dryden's "Epigram on Tonson" and Martial' (*N&Q* 42.454), Keith Walker suggests that Dryden may have had in mind Martial XII.54 when composing his epigram.

Two essays treated *Absalom and Achitophel*, the first by *YWES*'s own James Ogden: 'Dryden's Satirical Tendency' (*FMLS* 31.215–22). Noting that the portraits of Shaftesbury, Buckingham and the rest 'are by common consent the best things in the poem', and the 'assertion of the Tory arguments is not wholly convincing', Ogden wonders whether Dryden is not drawn so naturally to satirical effects that he is prone to create them accidentally, hence for example sometimes undercutting his own presentation of Charles II in the poem. If so (and so it would seem), this is not entirely a weakness: for one thing, it shows that Dryden can 'see the funny side of his own party' and thus works against any impression of a 'partisan satirist lampooning his enemies'. Susan C. Greenfield is long-winded and much less illuminating on the same poem in 'Aborting the "Mother Plot": Politics and Generation in *Absalom and Achitophel*' (*ELH* 62.267–93). This would be so even if Greenfield were a competent reader of the text (she grossly misinterprets some of her key passages), because her whole purpose is to discuss notions the poem does not engage with. By the end she has proved to her own satisfaction that 'by insisting on the mother's role in conception', the poem rejects the idea that 'David (or Charles) was sexually responsible for making his own chaos'. Surely there must be more likely texts in which to look for 'patriarchal theory' or 'attacks on maternity'?

There are four other items to report. Katherine M. Quinsey's '*Religio Laici*? Dryden's Men of Wit and the Printed Word' is to be found in *The Wit of Seventeenth-Century Poetry*, ed. Claude J. Summers and Ted-Larry Pebworth. This essay knowledgeably discusses the poem's presentation of notions of truth – ultimately separated by Dryden from poetic language or wit – and hence what Quinsey takes to be its 'inconsistencies and its collapsing contrarieties'. Quinsey expounds rather than seeking to resolve these divisions. There is a careful consideration of some hitherto unpublicized seventeenth-century notes on *The Hind and the Panther* by Howard Erskine-Hill in his essay 'On Historical Commentary: The Example of Milton and Dryden' in *Presenting Poetry* (ed. Howard Erskine-Hill and Richard A. McCabe). The commentary is found in a MS transcription of the poem at Traquair House,

Peebles, with identifications for the figures which have considerable evidential value, and call into question some important decisions made by recent editors of the poem. Kirk Combe's main subject is Dryden, and the main text *Mac Flecknoe*, in ' "But Loads of Sh– almost Choked the Way": Shadwell, Dryden, Rochester, and the Summer of 1676' (*TSLL* 37.127–64). This sprawling article, with nine pages of notes, invites us to reconsider the roles played by Dryden and these two antagonists. Thomas Shadwell, Combe asserts, is a much more important figure both in his own right and in terms of Dryden's development than we are predisposed to imagine: 'with every uninformed judgement about Shadwell, we remain the real victims of Dryden's satire'. Combe's work should be read in conjunction with Brean Hammond's essay ' "An Allusion to Horace", Jonson's Ghost, and the Second Poets' War' in *Reading Rochester* (ed. Edward Burns) which is reviewed below. Finally for this section, Bruce Lawson's note 'Fortuna as Political Image in Three Poems on Cromwell' (*ANQ* 7.ii[1994].68–71) sees Dryden's reference to Fortune in line 29 of *Heroique Stanzas* as implicitly anti-Cromwell because it raises doubts about the role of Providence in his career. Dryden seems to have had especially strong personal feelings about Fortune and this rather than any subtle tactical manoeuvre might explain the line. Lawson briefly compares the Dryden passage with others in the work of Thomas Sprat, Cowley and Milton.

(b) Plays

Amphitryon appeared for the first time as a 'World's Classic' in the collection *Four Restoration Marriage Plays* (ed. Michael Cordner and Ronald Clayton). The text is reliably modernized and fully annotated. In his introduction, Cordner considers the play Dryden's 'greatest comedy' and 'a masterpiece well worthy of a place on the world's stage beside the versions of Plautus and Molière'. Such claims are neither new nor excessive, but better sustained when Cordner emphasizes the dramatist's psychological insight than when he explores his political implications: was the world ever interested in Dryden's reactions to William III? More striking on the stage today would be the mixture of farce and cynicism, which leads to the conclusion that 'the man who weighs the matter fully/Would rather be the cuckold than the cully'.

To be fair to Cordner, Dryden's politics detain many of his critics. In her lively if long-winded account of ' "Profuse, proud Cleopatra": "Barbarism" and Female Rule in Early Modern English Republicanism' (*WS* 24[1994].85–130), Mary Nyquist focuses on the figure of the allegedly barbaric female ruler in Shakespeare's *Antony and Cleopatra*, Charles Sedley's play of the same title, Dryden's *All for Love*, and the works of Milton, especially *Samson Agonistes*. Sedley's play is seen as a republican attack on Charles I, and Dryden's as a conservative reply, in which Antony's nobility depends on Cleopatra's submissiveness, so that patriarchy is upheld. In his *Incest, Drama and Nature's Law* Richard A. McCabe maintains that incest was a major dramatic theme from Elizabethan to Restoration times because it questioned what might be thought 'natural' in the family and the patriarchy. Dryden develops the theme, at times with great skill and subtlety, in *Aureng-Zebe*, *Oedipus*, *The Spanish Friar*, *Don Sebastian*, *Love Triumphant* and the translation of Ovid's tale of Cinyras and Myrrha for the *Fables*. In the plays, 'incest as a political metaphor takes precedence over incest as sexual plight' but both political and moral censorship thwarted further developments 'until the Gothic and Romantic periods'. A more predictable conclusion is reached by Richard Kroll in 'Instituting Empiricism: Hobbes's *Leviathan* and *Marriage à la Mode*' (in J. Douglas Canfield and Deborah C. Payne, eds, *Cultural Readings of Restoration and Eighteenth-Century English Theater*): even as defenders of the status quo, Hobbes and Dryden 'denaturize its imagery: their double rhetoric shows that it may be inevitable, but it is not to be treated as transparent'. Perish the thought!

Political considerations are secondary in two essays by Hugh MacCallum. In 'The State of Innocence: Epic to Opera' (*MiltonS* 31[1994].109–31) he sees Dryden's opera as a critique of Milton's epic, bringing the myth of the Fall into more direct relationship with the life of the time and hence perhaps human life generally. This is a comprehensive and helpful discussion of what are undoubtedly great arguments: 'comparison of the two versions illuminates the revolution in sensibility that is taking place as Dryden writes'. In 'Dryden's *Don Sebastian* and the Tragedy of Heroic Leadership' (*Restoration* 19.43–54), MacCallum contends that this play 'can be seen not only as a response to the historical moment of change in which it was written, but also as a depiction of the failure of heroic virtue to achieve epic dimension and expression', ending as it does in 'withdrawal, loss, and silence'. After *Don Sebastian* and *Cleomenes* self-centredness came to signify for Dryden not so much tragic egoism as balanced virtue.

Two essays considered Dryden's operas: what he thought they were, and what we think they should be. In a useful survey of 'Augustan Criticism and Changing Conceptions of English Opera' (*ThS* 36.ii.1–36), Todd S. Gilman shows that the conceptions were extremely volatile. Dryden called *The State of Innocence* an opera, perhaps meaning no more than that it included supernatural personages. Later he implied that opera should all be sung, after the Italian manner, a point disputed by those who wanted spoken parts, after the English manner. Later still he apparently accepted the Betterton-Purcell *Diocletian* as an opera, and apparently described *King Arthur* as a 'dramatic opera' because it combines drama and musical interludes; but then, so does *Diocletian*. In 'Our Fairest Isle Revived' (*MT* 136.368–9), Richard Langham Smith reviews this year's *King Arthur* at Covent Garden. He emphasizes that while this production aimed at 'jolly good fun' rather than authenticity, it did show that the opera gains enormously from a theatre rather than a concert performance. Other reviews suggested that the year's *Indian Queen* at the Queen Elizabeth Hall could have suffered by comparison.

In ' "Is This the Faith?" ': An Allusion to Spenser in Dryden's *Indian Emperor*' (*N&Q* 42.37–8), Gillian Manning reports that Cydaria, thinking she has been betrayed by Cortez (IV.iv.31), echoes Belphoebe, thinking she has been betrayed by Timias (*Faerie Queene*, IV.vii.36). The allusion is the earliest sign of Spenser's influence on Dryden, and the implied parallel accords with Dryden's later statements on the resemblance of heroic drama to heroic poetry.

3. Other Authors

(a) Poets

Rochester is the subject or principal subject of one volume and three articles this year. *Reading Rochester*, Edward Burns (ed.), is a collection of 11 essays almost all contributed by past or present members of Liverpool University English Department and published in the 'Liverpool English Texts and Studies' series. Their considerable diversity of approach and quality makes them hard to characterize collectively. Several relate Rochester to his poetic contemporaries, including probably the best contribution, Bernard Beatty's suggestive comparative essay on Rochester and Dryden ('Dryden's imagination takes us up into its own exaltation [...] Rochester shares his exasperation with us but remains apart'). Beatty plainly writes from a strong idea – whether or not identical with his reader's – of Rochester's poetic personality in general. Other contributors write, alas, about their own interests (transvestism and Freud, for example), or content themselves with in-depth discussion of one or two poems. Helen Wilcox, for instance, writes on 'Song of a Young Lady to her Ancient Lover'; but the usefully sharp focus here narrows too far when Jim McGhee meditates on the expurgations in a textually insignificant edition of 'The Imperfect Enjoyment'. Tony Barley seems to be using the wrong lens altogether when he quotes Stephen Hawking, Carl Sagan and R. D. Laing to elucidate 'Upon Nothing'. The fact that this poem has three times as much space devoted to it as any other in this book is an extreme example of the imbalances which the collection suffers from, but which of course are to a degree inevitable in such a volume.

Harold Love's unusual short paper 'Hamilton's *Mémoires de la vie du comte de Grammont* and the Reading of Rochester' (*Restoration* 19.95–102) sets out from the references in Hamilton's celebrated memoirs to several Rochesterian texts which have never been identified. The likely explanation is that they never existed, because the stories Hamilton attaches to them are clearly distorted or elaborated to a degree that makes them wholly untrustworthy. What interests Love, however, is the evidential value of the Memoirs not for individual Rochester works but for the circumstances in which Rochester's poems were composed and read. They 'give us a vivid sense of the way he operated as a writer within the confines of the court of Whitehall and of the social use made of his poetry'; yet information of this kind is precious in proportion to its rarity, and so evanescent a culture as the Restoration court's has left few relevant records behind.

The last two Rochester items this year could be called precious in a different sense. So much might be guessed of Leo Braudy's paper from its title: 'Remembering Masculinity: Premature Ejaculation Poetry of the Seventeenth Century' (*MQR* 33[1994].177–201). Within a framework of huge and unanswerable questions about the historicity of constructions of the body, Braudy analyses both Rochester's and Etherege's poems called 'The Imperfect Enjoyment', making Etherege's 'pretty amorous discourse' the foil to Rochester's 'assertion of equality in desire'. The discussion veers disconcertingly from the straightforward and lucid – 'Etherege's lines comfortably rein in his feelings with language, while Rochester's test the boundary between them' – to the hopelessly silly. Etherege's Phillis is 'the displaced phallus – his own lost possession, now recaptured through language'; both poems 'are in couplets, a ready counterpart to the theme of coupling they include'. Braudy's main idea is that Rochester's poem 'arises from a male body that is the site of an elusive, fallible sexuality', and that there was something new about this at the time. Pat Gill's ' "Filth of All Hues and Odors": Public Parks, City Showers, and Promiscuous Acquaintance in Rochester and Swift' (*Genre* 27[1994].333–50) starts out from a comparison between *A Ramble in St James's Park* and *A Description of a City Shower*. Gill's show of modish sophistication ('the category of woman operates anaclitically') cannot conceal the real level of the discussion, which is undergraduate. Gill informs us that 'a cavalier attitude toward the opinion of the world characterizes Rochester', summarizes the life-story ('apparently, he engaged in a good number of drunken debauches'), and describes *A Ramble* as Rochester's 'poetic exploration of his philosophy'.

Elizabeth H. Hageman and Andrea Sununu proceeded with their studies of Katherine Philips-related MSS (*YWES* 74.272) in ' "More Copies of it abroad than I could have imagin'd": Further Manuscript Texts of Katherine Philips' (*EMS* 5.127–69). Often by closer investigation of items to which Patrick Thomas (*YWES* 71.351) and Peter Beal (*YWES* 74.261) have already drawn attention, they discuss substantial examples of little-known texts by Philips; texts in which other writers respond to Philips or to which Philips is responding in her poems; and uninvestigated MS transcriptions, especially collections, of Philips's work. The title alludes to Hageman and Sununu's overall view that these materials do not show the restricted circulation for Philips's poems they have hitherto imagined: 'in fact, we now see that Philips provides a near-perfect case study of a mid-seventeenth-century coterie poet whose work suited, or was made to suit, a wide range of literary tastes'. Like the previous instalment, this article shows the kind of thoroughness that makes it obvious the forthcoming Hageman-Sununu edition of Philips's verse will be author-itative. Hageman goes it alone in a smaller-scale paper, 'The "false printed" Broadside of Katherine Philips's "To the Queens Majesty on her Happy Arrival" ' (*Library* 17.321–6). This shows why a 1662 broadside on the arrival in England of Catherine of Braganza (Wing T 1598A) should be ascribed to Philips rather than 'Anon'.

The only item on Aphra Behn's verse this year, Elizabeth V. Young's 'Aphra Behn's Elegies' (*Genre* 28.211–36), discovers in four Behn poems precisely what its writer wants to discover: a 'radical revisioning of the woman writer', a questioning of 'the very nature of poetic language', and a conversion of 'oppressive masculine desire into inclusive love'. But this gushing Cali-fornian kind of feminism is more likeable than the sour northern variety found in 'Elizabeth Thomas and the Two Corinnas: Giving the Woman Writer a Bad Name' (*ELH* 62.105–19). Here, Anne McWhir tries to show first that Dry-den's apparent epistolary compliment to Thomas in calling her 'Corinna' is 'merely condescending', 'an ambiguously flattering name that served to con-trol her' because Dryden refers to Ovid's Corinna as well as the poetess. But on this point McWhir temporizes: admittedly Dryden says he 'means not' the Ovidian Corinna; even so, he can be said thus to 'complicate the spirit of the compliment'. There follow efforts to get the mud to stick to Pope and practically every other male writer who mentions Thomas subsequently, 'effectively silenc[ing]' her over the years up to the triumphant ungagging achieved by Roger Lonsdale in his Oxford Anthology (*YWES* 70.365–6), which allows us to appreciate 'the strength of her poetry'.

Maureen E. Mulvihill's 'Butterfly on the Wheel of Scholarship' (*Restoration* 19.132) is a note of such brevity (a paragraph) that it certainly should not have been published in this form. But its content is extraordinary: Mulvihill claims to have 'discovered' that the enigmatic author of the *Female Poems on Several Occasions*, 1679, which Mulvihill edited in 1992, was none other than its dedicatee, Mary Stuart, Duchess of Richmond and Lennox. This is the 'clever dodge' that has 'kept researchers fumbling for centuries'. Now that Mulvihill has seen through it, we must await the promised elaboration of the case. Warren Chernaik plays the judicious Sherlock Holmes to Mulvihill's impulsive Watson in 'Ephelia's Voice: The Authorship of *Female Poems* (1679)' (*PQ* 74.151–72). Chernaik argues first that there is no worthwhile evidence, internal or external, to show either that the poems are autobiographical, or that they are by a woman. Stressing their place in the genre of Ovidian epistle used regularly by Restoration poets, Chernaik goes on to show that the collection could equally well have been written by George Etherege, who is certainly the author of one of the items. He concludes, 'the author and the character "Ephelia" are both fictions. *Female Poems* achieves coherence by the construction of a persona', and so 'the attempt to penetrate the disguise [...] is in some ways misconceived'. Chernaik, then, has no solution partly because he thinks the problem has been misstated. But this is much the most clear-headed account of the position now available.

Butler attracts two commentators this year. Nicholas von Maltzahn seeks in 'Samuel Butler's Milton' (*SP* 92.482–95) to revive the attribution to him (never strongly contested but never widely approved) of the two anti-Milton pamphlets of 1660, *The Censure of the Rota* and *The Character of the Rump*. To older stylistic arguments, von Maltzahn adds an apparent contemporary attribution, then proceeds to illustrate what knowledge of Milton's writings Butler must have had if he wrote these works. The article concludes with a rather unusual attempt to compare *Paradise Lost* and *Hudibras*. Alok Yadav's 'Fractured Meanings: *Hudibras* and the Historicity of the Literary Text' (*ELH* 62.529–49) says that we nowadays have assumptions which necessarily make our interpretation of *Hudibras* differ from that of Butler's contemporaries. We approach it as a 'unitary text' of 'discrete singleness', and we assume it is straightforwardly a satire on the Puritans. But these points have to be severely qualified, as Yadav partly admits: most people's experience of the poem today (if any) is probably through anthologized excerpts, and seventeenth-century readers thought its purpose was to mock the Puritans too. There is something significant in all this, but it is complicated, and Yadav's theoretical sophistication may have impeded clear analysis and expression of it.

Finally, Paul Hartle's '"Quaint Epigrammatist": Martial in Late Seventeenth-Century England' (*Neophil* 79.329–51) offers a general account of Martial's *Rezeptionsgeschichte* in the period 1650–1700. Though Hartle says his 'main concern' is to examine the translations of Martial, it turns out this is 'not the place to discuss in detail the quality of Cowley's versions' (which are surely the best). The essay is sufficiently wide-ranging to take in some French as well as English responses, but not comprehensive enough to deal with William Dingley's many translations of 1694, which Hartle seems not to know.

(b) Dramatists

Carole Levin and Patricia A. Sullivan's *Political Rhetoric, Power, and Renaissance Women* contains one item relevant to this section. In a clearly argued essay, 'Wits, Whigs, and Women: Domestic Politics as Anti-Whig Rhetoric in Aphra Behn's Town Comedies', Arlen Feldwick offers a possible solution to the apparent contradictions in, on the one hand, Behn's championing of her female characters in the face of patriarchal oppression and, on the other, her support for a Royalist monarchy which operated on strongly patriarchal lines. Tyrannical fathers and husbands are identified as Whigs and the essay demonstrates how Behn usually characterizes them as old, materialistic, brutal, vulgar inadequates – often impotent and finally defeated when their women shake off oppression and take up with young cavaliers. Feldwick proposes that Behn's women are strong in order to reveal Whig stupidity and suggest that Whigs were incapable of governing their women, their money, or the country during the Commonwealth. Three other pieces make Behn's *The Rover* a popular subject for the year. In 'The Language of Gender and a Textual Problem in Aphra Behn's *The Rover*' (*NM* 96.283–93), James Fitzmaurice focuses on Behn's use of the word 'whe' in *The Rover Part II* and *The Feigned Courtesans* as well as in the named text. Apart from cursory attention to a few oaths, 'whe' is the only example of 'the language of gender' analyzed. Although the range of his argument is narrow and there are minor details over which to cavil, Fitzmaurice does provide an interesting and detailed analysis of Behn's application of a word associated with cursing and male sexual appetite, even, sometimes, with sexual violence when it issues from a male mouth, but a word also used by certain women to express defiance in the face of male authority, or sexual desire.

In 'Shadow and Substance in Aphra Behn's *The Rover*: the Semiotics of Restoration Performance' (*Restoration* 19.29–42), John Franceschina deals with the ways 'Both audience and character are asked to differentiate between the sign vehicle, or *signifier*, and its referent' throughout the play. Beginning with the song, 'Stay gentle Shadow of my Dove' in Act IV, he works his way through a wide range of associations to demonstrate Behn's skilful manipulation of theatrical devices. This study grows more fascinating as it progresses, and is an energetic and exciting piece.

Adapting *The Rover* for performance is the subject of Susan Carlson's lively article, 'Cannibalizing and Carnivalizing: Reviving Aphra Behn's *The Rover*' (*TJ* 47.517–39). Her study pays due attention to Behn's use of the material she found in Killigrew's *Thomaso*, and to John Barton's adaptation (which drew on both texts and added to them) in 1986. JoAnne Akalaitis's 1994 version also made its own changes – and adopted some of Barton's – but, because she avoided the stereotyping of female characters and did not sacrifice ambiguities as Barton did, Carlson is 'much more sanguine' about its impact on possibilities for future productions, dwelling on the centrality of carnival and the way Akalaitis 'seems cognizant of the gendered dimensions of carnival's foundation in cultural and ideological conflict'. As well as providing a modernized, annotated text based on the 1677 Quarto, and the usual biographical and bibliographical introductory material, the New Mermaids edition of *The Rover* (ed. Marion Lomax) also contains sections on carnival and the play in performance.

Paying much more attention to modern productions and stage history is a fairly recent and useful innovation in the New Mermaids series and, since

1989, almost a third of the list has been newly edited. *The Rover* was the series' only new Restoration edition of this year, but at the beginning of the year, a welcome second edition of Congreve's *The Way of the World* appeared with a substantially revised, illustrated introduction by Brian Gibbons, the General Editor, which provided material on a recent Chichester production. Another edition of Behn appeared from World's Classics in 1995, but Jane Spencer's *The Rover and Other Plays* does not make a great deal of recent productions. The volume is useful because it includes *The Feigned Courtesans*, *The Lucky Chance* and *The Emperor of the Moon* as well as *The Rover* and, as with all WC texts, there are full notes, a bibliography, chronology and a glossary, but the introductory material on all but *The Rover* is less than two pages per play: the latter fares better at two-and-a-half.

George Farquhar's brief career (he died aged 29) is celebrated in *The Recruiting Officer and Other Plays* (ed. William Myers). Farquhar's 'linguistic openness', his 'passionate allegiances' and 'honest and intelligent response' lead Myers to consider him 'a great playwright' – and one concerned, above all, with realities – money, marriage and the situation of the soldier. The selection comprises: *The Constant Couple*, *The Twin Rivals*, *The Recruiting Officer* and *The Beaux' Stratagem*.

In 'Facing the Void in *The Wives' Excuse*; or, Characters Make Themselves' (*PLL* 31.78–98), Peggy J. Thompson begins by noting the play's largely unsuccessful record with audiences and critics. Believing it to be 'a powerful work', she joins defenders like Harold Love, Judith Milhous and Robert Hume. Her line is, initially, to 'place the play's widely recognized attack on libertine comedy in the context of a second, heretofore unrecognized repudiation, that of heroic drama' and to focus on the characters' 'desperate struggles for control of their own and others' identities in a world where they can conceive of those identities as little more than public patchworks of antiquated cultural and literary conventions'. Above all, Thompson champions Southerne for showing 'visionary courage in portraying human beings who must define themselves in a void' and invites us to re-assess him as an early example of a playwright fascinated by existentialist dilemmas. Finally, political dilemmas are at the heart of Odai Johnson's article 'Empty Houses: The Suppression of Tate's *Richard II*' (*TJ* 47.503–16). The appearance of a comet, two banned plays and a treason trial are some of the ingredients in this fascinating exploration of the treatment and impact of Tate's supposedly 'loyal' play.

(c) Prose

David E. Hoegberg has extended our appreciation of the classical allusions in Behn's *Oroonoko* in 'Caesar's Toils: Allusion and Rebellion in *Oroonoko*' (*ECF* 7.239–58). He argues that naming Oroonoko 'Caesar' and likening him to Achilles is both ennobling and confining, making him act in other's scripts, Plutarch's as well as the colonists'.

Robert Boyle's ambivalent attitude to romances is explored in Lawrence M. Principe in 'Virtuous Romance and Romantic Virtuoso: The Shaping of Robert Boyle's Literary Style' (*JHI* 56.377–97), which shows how he adapted the style of French heroic romance into religious romance, moral discussion and even some scientific narrative. There are useful references to his brother Roger's *Parthenissa*.

Thomas H. Luxon's *Literal Figures: Puritan Allegory and the Reformation Crisis in Representation* is fascinating and essential reading for Bunyanists and others joining in the current reappraisal of the impact of the Reformation on thinking and writing about the self. He begins with the question about why a Puritan should write in the apparently discredited mode of allegory – not a new question in Spenser studies, say, but it comes out differently as a result of Luxon's knowledge of the Commonwealth sectaries and recent work on Paul. Students in a hurry may skip to the last two chapters, which extend out of a revaluation of Stanley Fish's seminal work on *The Pilgrim's Progress* into a discussion of the usefulness of allegory as 'a mode peculiarly suited to finessing the issue of the real'. Armand Himy also joins the debate about the meaning of pilgrimage and progress which began with Stanley Fish in 'Errance et Election dans *The Pilgrim's Progress*' (*BSEAA* 35[1992].57–68). There are some interesting and suggestive remarks about interiority and the status of time in religious narrative, particularly when it is Calvinist like Bunyan's.

Peter Walmsley, in 'Prince Maurice's Rational Parrot: Civil Discourse in Locke's *Essay*' (*ECS* 28.413–25) discusses the passages where Locke seems aware of the distinction between the philosophical and the civil use of words, language as a medium of thought and language as having a public provenance.

Dan Jaeckle revises his earlier view of the text [*YWES* 70.348] in 'De-Authorizing in Marvell's *The Rehearsal Tranpros'd*' (*JDJ* 10[1991].129–42). He details a number of Marvell's strategies for 'finding and widening cracks within the dominant discursive regime', though without locating himself as a centre of authority either. Jaeckle is also helpfully alive to the (limited) success of Parker and to Marvell's own, often overlooked, compromises.

James Grantham Turner discusses *The Whores Rhetorick* (1683) and its Italian prototype *La Retorica delle Puttane* by Ferrante Pallavicino in a wide-ranging exploration of the relation between sexual morality, rhetoric and the 'Rise of the Novel'. '*The Whores Rhetorick*: Narrative, Pornography, and the Origins of the Novel' (*SECC* 24.297–306) is particularly interesting on the way that pornography 'rehearses' narrative realism. Finally, John H. O'Neill, in 'Samuel Pepys: The War of Will and Pleasure' (*Restoration* 19.88–94) discusses 'his struggle to become the person the dominant ideology of his time seemed to require him to be', and thus places Pepys's private life in the same context of the battle for control as his public service.

Books Reviewed

Anselment, Raymond A. *The Realms of Apollo: Literature and Healing in Seventeenth-Century England*. UDelP. pp. 316. £32.50. ISBN 0 87413 553 2.

Burns, Edward, ed. *Reading Rochester*. LiverUP. pp. 232. hb £30, pb £11.75. ISBN 0 85323 038 2, 085232 309 8.

Canfield, J. Douglas, and Deborah C. Payne, eds. *Cultural Readings of Restoration and Eighteenth-century English Theater*. UGeoP. pp. 320. pb £23.95. ISBN 0 8203 1751 9.

Chernaik, Warren. *Sexual Freedom in Restoration Literature*. CUP. pp. 268. £35. ISBN 0 521 46497 8.

Cordner, Michael, and Ronald Clayton, eds. *Four Restoration Marriage Plays.* WC. OUP. pp. 439. hb £40, pb £6.99. ISBN 0 198 12163 6, 0 192 82570 4.

Erskine-Hill, Howard, and Richard A. McCabe, eds. *Presenting Poetry: Composition, Publication, Reception.* CUP. pp. 272. £37.50. ISBN 0 521 47360 8.

Gibbons, Brian, ed. *The Way of the World by William Congreve.* 2nd edn. NMer. Black. pp.170. pb £4.99. ISBN 0 7136 3943 1.

Greer, Germaine. *Slip-Shod Sibyls: Recognition, Rejection and the Woman Poet.* Viking. pp. 517. £20. ISBN 0 670 84914 6.

Hammond, Paul, ed. *The Poems of John Dryden.* Longman. Vol. I: *1649–1681.* pp. 551. £75. ISBN 0 582 49213 0; Vol. II: *1682–1685.* pp. 447. £70. ISBN 0 582 23944 3.

Levin, Carole, and Patricia A. Sullivan, eds. *Political Rhetoric, Power, and Renaissance Women.* SUNYP. pp. 293. hb $57.50, pb $18.95. ISBN 0 7914 2545 2, 0 7914 2546 0.

Lomax, Marion, ed. *The Rover by Aphra Behn.* NMer. Black. pp160. pb £5.99. ISBN 0 7136 3941 5.

Lund, Roger D, ed. *The Margins of Orthodoxy: Heterodox Writing and Cultural Response 1660–1750.* CUP. pp. xiv + 298. £35. ISBN 0 521 47177 X.

Luxon, Thomas H. *Literal Figures: Puritan Allegory and the Reformation Crisis in Representation.* UChicP. pp. xii + 256. £22.50. ISBN 0 226 49785 2.

MacLean, Gerald. *Culture and Society in the Stuart Restoration: Literature, Drama, History.* CUP. pp. 292. hb £37.50, pb £13.95. ISBN 0 521 41605 1, 0 521 47566 X.

McCabe, Richard A. *Incest, Drama and Nature's Law 1550– 1700.* CUP. 1993. pp. 362. £35. ISBN 0 521 43173 5.

Myers, Robin, and Michael Harris, eds. *A Genius for Letters: Booksellers and Bookselling from the 16th to the 20th Century.* StPB. pp. 188. £27.50. ISBN 1 873040 24 5.

Myers, William, ed. *The Recruiting Officer and Other Plays by George Farquhar.* WC. OUP. pp. 429. hb £40, pb £7.99. ISBN 0 1981 2153 9, 0 1928 2249 7.

Parry, Graham. *The Trophies of Time: English Antiquarians of the Seventeenth Century.* OUP. pp. viii + 382. £45. ISBN 0 19 812962 9.

Scarry, Elaine, ed. *Fins de Siècle: English Poetry in 1590, 1690, 1790, 1890, 1990.* JHUP. pp. 142. £32. ISBN 0 8018 4929 2.

Spencer, Jane, ed. *The Rover and Other Plays by Aphra Behn.* WC. OUP. pp. 430. hb £40, pb £6.99. ISBN 0 1981 2154 7, 0 1928 2248 9.

Summers, Claude J., and Ted-Larry Pebworth, eds. *The Wit of Seventeenth-Century Poetry.* UMissP. pp. 222. £35.95. ISBN 0 8262 0985 8.

Weber, Harold M. *Paper Bullets: Print and Kingship under Charles II.* UPKen. pp. 292. $39.95. ISBN 0 8131 1929 4.

XI

The Eighteenth Century

STEPHEN COPLEY, EMMA MAJOR, KAREN O'BRIEN and
GEORGE JUSTICE

This chapter has five sections: 1. General; 2. Poetry; 3. Prose; 4. Novel; 5. Drama. Sections 1, 3 and 5 are by Stephen Copley and Emma Major. Section 2 is by Karen O'Brien and section 4 is by George Justice.

1. General

There have been some interesting re-issues of important studies this year, some of which were not listed on their first publication, and we have tried to include these where possible. This year has also seen the publication of some very useful eighteenth-century texts, among which should be noted Mary Wollstonecraft's *Thoughts on the Education of Daughters*, which has been issued as a facsimile reprint, using the 1787 first edition. Wollstonecraft's undeservedly neglected first book, generally left out of popular collections of her work, helps to set her ideas on women in context. Janet Todd introduces this educational work, reissued as part of Thoemmes Press's series of conduct books. Another very welcome and extremely useful edition, also produced by Thoemmes, is *The Young Lady's Pocket Library, or Parental Monitor* (intro. Vivien Jones). This 1790 compilation of conduct books comprises of texts ranging across half a century, and was published until at least 1808. The texts included are: Marchioness de Lambert, *Advice of a Mother to her Daughter* (1727); Edward Moore, *Fables for the Female Sex* (1744); Sarah Pennington, *An Unfortunate Mother's Advice to her Absent Daughters* (1761); and John Gregory's *A Father's Legacy to his Daughters* (1774). Gregory's text gained notoriety through Wollstonecraft's discussion of it in her *Vindication*; it was also discussed by other women writers of the 1790s, including Hannah More in her *Strictures*, and is a useful compendium of attributes of a certain type of femininity. Jones's suggestive introduction and helpful bibliography help to set this facsimile reprint of the *Parental Monitor* in context. The less well-known author, the Quaker educationalist and writer Priscilla Wakefield (1751–1832), has also had a work re-issued this year, this time by Colleagues. They have chosen to bring out one of her educational works: *Mental Improvement: or the Beauties and Wonders of Nature and Art, Conveyed in a Series of Instructive Conversations* (1794), ed. Ann B. Shteir. This consists of conversations between various members of the well-educated, open-minded Harcourt family, with the less well-educated and prejudiced visitor, Augusta, acting as a foil for the Harcourt children. This edition, which comes with some, but not enough, footnoted notes, an introductory essay and a bibliography, is based on the 1794 text, but it is unclear whether alterations have been made to the original text. Shteir's edition of this book should be warmly welcomed as a timely reminder of Wakefield's powerful and intriguing contributions to eighteenth- and early nineteenth-century debates about education and femininity.

Last year's *The Crisis of Courtesy: Studies in the Conduct-Book in Britain 1600–1900* (ed. Jacques Carré), concentrates (unsurprisingly) on the late seventeenth and eighteenth centuries. Alongside essays specifically on conduct books some contributors discuss the treatment of conduct in more general terms in the period. Remy Saisselin suggests that Shaftesbury's *Characteristicks* can be seen as a form of conduct book; Dieter Berger compares Swift's *Polite Conversation* with his other writings on similar topics; Tim McLoughlin reads Fielding's *Joseph Andrews* in the light of his 'Essay on Conversation'; Georges Lamoine discusses Chesterfield's *Letters*; Niels Haastrup writes on phrasebooks and Gilles Duval on chapbooks; Peter Wagner looks at Hogarth; and Michael Baridon treats Pope, Shenstone and Mason as gentlemen gardeners. The volume contains a bibliography of conduct books published in the period. In a related area, in *BJECS* (18.63–77) Stephen Copley discusses the relation between 'Commerce, Conversation and Politeness in the Early Eighteenth-Century Periodical'; and *Rhetorical Traditions and British Romantic Literature* (ed. Don H. Bialostosky and Lawrence D. Needham) includes an essay by Nancy S. Struever entitled 'The Conversable World: Eighteenth-Century Transformations of the Relation of Rhetoric and Truth' which traces the legacy of debates about politeness and conversability from Shaftesbury and Hume to Jane Austen.

The Consumption of Culture 1600–1800: Image, Object, Text (ed. John Brewer and Ann Bermingham) is an important collection offering a generous selection of essays which range from portraiture in the eighteenth century to female reading practices. The book is divided into five parts: (I) The formation of a public for art and literature; (II) Engendering the literary canon; (III) Consumption and the modern state; (IV) The social order: culture high and low; and (V) What women want. These five parts are introduced by Ann Bermingham's useful and thought-provoking introductory essay, 'The consumption of culture: image, object, text'. In the first section, Terry Lovell writes on women as consumers of texts in 'Subjective powers? Consumption, the reading public, and domestic woman in early eighteenth-century England', and Peter H. Pawlowicz looks at the construction of the woman reader in 'Reading women. Text and image in eighteenth-century England', while Frank Donoghue shifts the focus to a more masculine sphere in his 'Colonizing readers. Review criticism and the formation of a reading public'. Louise Lippincott's excellent essay 'Expanding on portraiture. The market, the public, and the hierarchy of genres in eighteenth-century Britain' is followed by Thomas Crow's 'The abandoned hero. The decline of state authority in the direction of French painting as seen in the career of one exemplary theme, 1777–89', which traces the decline of stoic classicism in this period. In 'Gombrich and the rise of landscape' W. J. T. Mitchell looks at the global theorizing of landscape in art-historical discourse. The second section, on the history of canon formation, opens with Anne K. Mellor's consideration of Angelica Kauffman, Maria Cosway and Mary Moser in relation to British Romanticism and somewhat disturbingly concludes that these women painters shared a 'feminine romanticism' with women writers of the period 1780–1830. There follow two essays on the marketplace: Don E. Wayne's study of the effect on Ben Jonson of the way in which Shakespeare was marketed and Robert Iliffe's essay on the role of the editor in literary production, in which he focuses on the construction of a marketable Newton. This section is rounded off by Mitzi Myers's thought-provoking piece on Maria Edgeworth, 'Shot from canons; or, Maria Edgeworth and the cultural production and consumption of the eighteenth-century woman writer'. In this section, though, as with the collection of essays as a whole, one is left wondering why the inclusion of the issue of gender so often means only looking at women in separate studies, as though men had no gender worth speaking of, and femininity and masculinity had nothing to do with each other. Part III, 'Consumption and the modern state', has a nicely eclectic range of chapters that radiate out from the central questions of the relationship between politics and government and the creation and consumption of culture. Felicity A. Nussbaum looks at the connections between racism and sexism in notions of marriage, while Kathleen Wilson considers representations of the state and empire in popular theatre. Richard Sorrenson explores links between scientific measuring instruments and the commercial world views of the British Empire, and connections between state and science are also the subject of Jay Tribby's study of the experiments in the Medici court. The other two essays in this section consider the signifying uses of the body: Anne M. Wagner looks at the statues of kings in 'Outrages. Sculpture and kingship in France after 1789', and Nicholas Mirzoeff traces the implications of the development of sign language for the deaf in 'Signs and Citizens. Sign language and visual sign in the French Revolution'. John Brewer's useful '"The most polite age and the most vicious". Attitudes towards culture as a commodity, 1660–1800' opens the penultimate section, followed by Lawrence E. Klein's disappointing 'Politeness for plebes. Consumption and social identity in early eighteenth-century England', which does little with the very interesting politeness manuals it looks at. Ronald Paulson contributes 'Emulative consumption and literacy. The Harlot, Moll Flanders, and Mrs Slipslop', and Paula Rea Radisich analyses Hubert Robert's landscape murals in '"La chose publique." Hubert Robert's decorations for the "petit salon" at Mereville'. The final section, 'What Women Want', focuses on the role of women as consumers and producers of culture. The first two essays, by James Grantham Turner and Elizabeth Bennett Kubek, look at representations of women's participation in urban, commercial culture, while the last three consider painting, music and accomplishment: Mary D. Sheriff writes on Elisabeth Vigee-Lebrun, Ann Bermingham on 'Elegant females and gentlemen connoisseurs' and the sexual division of knowledge and Richard Leppert concludes the volume with his piece on 'Social order and the domestic consumption of music. The politics of sound in the policing of gender construction in eighteenth-century England'. There are some excellent essays in this huge volume, and the collection forms an exciting landmark in eighteenth-century cultural studies. We have not seen *Early Modern Conceptions of Property* (Routledge), part of this Routledge series, but hope that it maintains the high standard set by the *Consumption* volume.

R. O. Bucholz's *The Augustan Court: Queen Anne and the Decline of Court Culture* attempts to depict the gathering secular trappings of the last Stuart court. Decline is a relative term, as Bucholz also shows how the actual court population showed no great reduction since 1660, yet he is clear in his thesis that the destruction of the emblems associated with monarchy did not start with the Hanoverians. Christine Gerrard's *Walpole and the Patriots: Politics, Poetry and Myth, 1725–1742* takes the reader into the thorny brakes of rhetorical self-consciousness. Gerrard invests Whiggism with more variety of tone and audience than is allowed for in a focus just on the periodical press. The care with which Gerrard has assembled her evidence shows in the detail of her re-definition of 'Cultural Patriotism' and its links with a 'Patriot Gothic' and revival of Elizabethan allusion. The chapter on 'Ideas of a Patriot King' is illuminating, and genuinely contributes to our knowledge of Bolingbroke's real agenda, yet there is also a circumspection here where non-mythical or literary documents are concerned. There has been much recent basic research on the journalism and ever-changing emphases of the latter years of the 1720s and beyond, and to skip this seems a rather abbreviated way to deal with a complex cultural struggle [review of Bucholz and Gerrard by Nigel Wood].

The Past as Prologue (ed. Carla Hay and Syndy M. Conger), is published as a celebration of 25 years of the American Society for Eighteenth-Century Studies. It contains 19 essays, nine of which are reprinted from *ECS*. The other, newly commissioned, essays reflect the range of interdisciplinary interests of the society. Among these are essays by Paula R. Backscheider on the relation between Defoe's *Religious Courtship* and Richardson's *Clarissa*; Kevin L. Cope on Locke, Mandeville and empiricism; Patricia Craddock on 'History's Stories, Historians' Accounts: or, Why Take Edward Gibbon's Word?'; and Thomas McGeary on 'Opera, Satire and Politics in the Walpole Era'. Donald Greene surveys the history of the society and Barbara Maria Stafford considers the relation between the Enlightenment and 'Late Modernism'. Two useful guides have appeared: John H. Middendorf covers 'Eighteenth-Century English Literature' in *Scholarly Editing: A Guide to Research* (ed. D. C. Greetham), and *Eighteenth-Century British Literary Biographers* (ed. Steven Serafin).

Writers, Books, and Trade: An Eighteenth-Century Miscellany for William B. Todd (ed. O M Brack Jr) contains a range of essays on issues relating to books and the book trade in the period. In 'Selling One's Life', James Raven examines the published autobiographies of three book-trade figures – James Lackington, William Hutton and George Miller; C. J. Mitchell considers the place of 'Women in the Eighteenth-Century Book Trade'; Patricia Hernlund offers a study of three trade bankruptcies; Beverley Schneller concentrates on the role of advertisements as evidence of the publishing activities of Mary Cooper in one year, 1753; K. I. D. Maslen discusses the relation between London printers and booksellers; Jan Fergus and Ruth Portner survey the book purchasing habits of provincial subscribers to the *Monthly* and *Critical Reviews*; and B. J. McMullin and G. Thomas Tanselle discuss press figures. Literary case studies are offered by David L. Vander Meulin, who comments on unauthorized editions of Pope's *Dunciad*; Hugh Amory on the relation between author, editor and compositor in Fielding's *Amelia*; O M Brack Jr on

Smollett's promotion of his history by Nicolas Barker on William Strahan and Laurence Sterne; John Horden on John Freeth; Betty Rizzo on Bonnell Thornton; and J. D. Fleeman on the construction of the subscription list for Johnson's *Shakespeare*. The volume also contains a supplement to the 1972 bibliography of John Brown, by Donald D. Eddy, and a list of mount and page imprints, by Thomas B. Adams. In *PBSA* (89.61–71), Edward Jacobs discusses 'John Roson and the role of circulating-library proprietors as publishers in eighteenth-century Britain' under the title 'A Previously Unremarked Circulating Library'. *N&Q* 42 offers notes on 'Bishop Gibson's Codex and the Reform of the Oxford University Press in the Eighteenth Century', by William Gibson (42.47–52), and 'An Eighteenth-Century Concordance of *Piers Plowman*', by C. J. Grindley (42.162–4).

A new scholarly annual, *1650–1850: Ideas, Aesthetics, and Inquiries in the Early Modern Era*, appeared last year. Its first issue includes a foreword in which the editor, Kevin L. Cope, announces its interdisciplinarity and its intention to 'showcase new responses to the ever-revising picture of modernization' in the long eighteenth century. The first issues contain a wide range of multidisciplinary essays. General articles include Barbara M. Benedict's 'The "Beauties" of Literature 1750–1820' (1[1994].317–46), in which the author suggests that the terms on which commentators recommend the 'beauties' of literature in the period reveal 'a general shift in the eighteenth-century location of literary value from craftsmanship to moral application that endorsed individual responses to art'. Other articles are noted in the relevant sections of this review.

Les Ages de la Vie en Grande-Bretagne au XVIIIe Siècle, a collection of papers in French and English from a seminar organized by Serge Soupel, is rather arbitrarily divided, with a first section supposedly covering theoretical, philosophical, historical, artistic, cultural and religious aspects of the topic, and a second section dealing with literary topics. Among the essays in the first section Franck Lessay writes on Locke; Pierre Carboni considers Kames's *The Culture of the Heart*, Myles W. Jackson compares ideas of genius and the stages of life in England and Germany; Peter De Voogd considers 'generation' in Hogarth's *Marriage-a-la-Mode*; Messad Dequeker discusses medical treatises; Georges Lamoine the law; Marie-Cécile Révauger British freemasonry; and Patrick Menneteau discusses Blake. In the literary section, Fritz-Wilhelm Neumann comments on 'Computing the Semantic Network of Age in Early Eighteenth-Century Political Writing'; Josette Hérou discusses the comic and dramatic function of age in eighteenth-century English drama; Denise Bulckaen writes on *Robinson Crusoe*; Gerald J. Butler examines Fielding's representation of female sexual desire at various ages; James Basker comments on adolescence in *The Rambler*; Madeleine Descargues looks at Sterne and Alain Lauzanne at Ann Radcliffe. In two essays Norman Simms writes on eighteenth-century imaginary visions of coming of age in Madagascar, and generally on the discourse of childhood in the period.

A wide-ranging volume, *Theorizing Satire: Essays in Literary Criticism* (ed. Brian A. Connery and Kirk Combe), contains a general survey of Augustan satire by Richard Nash, and essays by Erin Macie on 'Swift and the Progress of Desire', Fredric Bogel, also on Swift and Jon Rowland on Swift and Churchill. *Transatlantic Crossings: Eighteenth-Century Explorations* (ed. Donald W. Nichol) contains an eclectic range of contributions. Under the title 'Wilkes &

Editorial Liberty' Nichol and Jacob Larkin discuss 'Attacks on Warburton as Pope's Editor'. Yvonne Hann contributes an essay entitled 'Rediscovering Laetitia: A Text of The Statues', and Iona Bulgin writes on 'Anne Finch's Defence of a Woman's Right to Be a Poet'. Vincent McB. Tobin considers 'The Mythical World of Handelian Opera', and Stanley Tweyman asks what Hume is telling us in the 'Appendix' about his account of personal identity. A 'Film Forum' in *ECLife* 19 on Kubrick's underrated and gratifyingly bleak *Barry Lyndon* (1975) covers some of the interesting questions raised when a twentieth-century director films a nineteenth-century novelist's representation of the eighteenth century. John Engell considers irony (83–8), Elise F. Knapp and James Pegolotti music (92–7), Frank Cossa life and art (79–82), and Jeffrey L. L. Johnson 'Darwinian pessimism' in the film (89–91).

General studies not noted last year include Catherine Gallagher's *Nobody's Story: The Vanishing Acts of Women Writers in the Literary Marketplace, 1670–1820*, which is mainly concerned with fiction by women writers from Aphra Behn to Maria Edgeworth, but which includes some discussion of their other literary productions. Stephanie Barbé Hammer's *The Sublime Crime: Fascination, Failure, and Form in Literature of the Enlightenment*, which treats literary texts from Lillo's *The London Merchant* to Godwin's *Caleb Williams* and Kleist's *Michael Kolhaas*; and Elizabeth Wanning Harries' *The Unfinished Manner: Essays on the Fragment in the Later Eighteenth Century*, which covers a wide range of British, French and German writers, including Richardson, Sterne and Mackenzie, and takes in the architectural fragment of the ruin as well as the literary fragment.

There have been some thought-provoking historical studies this year. Murray J. Pittock's *The Myth of the Jacobite Clans* claims to steer a course between the sentimental mythologizers of Jacobitism and its debunkers, who are seen as actually remythologizing it in different terms. For Pittock both these groups effectively marginalize the influence of Jacobitism, whereas he seeks to present it as culturally central right across Scotland – an argument which is sometimes pursued in terms which are hard to distinguish from the forms of mythologization that he rejects. None the less he surveys a range of interesting material, sometimes sharply. In *HT* (45.vii.24–39), Jeremy Black asks 'Could the Jacobites have won?', while in 'Seditious Anger: Achilles, James Stuart, and Jacobite Politics in Pope's *Iliad* Translation' (*ECLife* 19.38–58), John Murillo looks at Pope's possible Jacobitism in the years 1710–1720, connecting his translation of Homer's *Iliad* with the political turmoil of 1710–15 and the subsequent failure of the attempted restoration of the Old Pretender. In '"Give us our eleven days!"': Calendar reform in eighteenth-century England', Robert Poole focuses on the English calendar riots of 1752 to consider the importance and growth of time-awareness during the eighteenth century, tracing its wider effects in the division of elite culture from the plebeian festive calendar (*P&P* 149.95–139). Susan Dwyer Amussen explores notions of power through violence by taking a range of examples from the sixteenth to early eighteenth centuries that extend from domestic violence and witchcraft to village brawls and state trials in order to gain a sense not just of the frequency of social violence but also its causes and significance in *Punishment, Discipline and Power: The Social Meanings of Violence in Early Modern England* (*JBS* 34.i.1–34). Also in *JBS* (34.ii.165–95), John Sainsbury argues that Wilkes's personality is central to an understanding of the movement he started. Considering the significance of his debts and his support from London tradesmen, he focuses on two events: Wilkes's argument with the King's Bench debtors during his term as Sheriff of London, and responses to his candidature for Chamberlain of London in the late 1770s. Michael Sanderson's *Education, Economic Change and Society in England 1780–1830* provides a solid introduction to the subject, and has a useful bibliography. Going further afield, in *P&P* Sumit Guha looks at 'An Indian penal regime: Maharashtra in the eighteenth century'(147.101–26), contrasting the Marathan regime with that of the Hanoverian state.

Stella Tillyard's *Aristocrats: Caroline, Emily, Louisa and Sarah Lennox 1740–1832* has also been reissued by Vintage. First published by C&W last year, Tillyard's beguiling history of a family has been issued in paperback. Vivid prose and fascinating primary material make this stimulating reading for anyone interested in the second half of the eighteenth century. Olwen Hufton's project in *The Prospect Before Her: A History of Women in Western Europe, Volume I, 1500–1800* of examining a history of Western European women over three centuries in topic-based chapters whilst still maintaining cultural and temporal differences in the histories she presents is perhaps over ambitious; yet her immaculate research and lively, informative prose are extremely persuasive. Though inevitably tantalizing and occasionally frustrating in its breadth, this is an important contribution to the cultural history of the period. The book's chapters do not follow a strict chronology; rather, several threads of history are carried through the sections, forming a multi-layered narrative under headings which include 'Constructing Woman', 'Marriage as Goal', 'On Being a Wife', 'Motherhood', 'Widowhood', 'Kept Mistresses and Common Strumpets' and 'Women and the Devil'. Illustrations, copious notes and a rich bibliography add to the magisterial feel of Hufton's book. A possible companion volume, though very thin in comparison, is *Women and History: Voices of Early Modern England* (ed. Valerie Frith), which offers a collection of extracts and prefatory essays that aim to provide access to seventeenth- and eighteenth-century women's voices. Divided into two sections, 'The Female Community' and 'The Real and the Ideal', it uses court records, diaries, letters and memoirs to provide insights into a range of female experience of crime inside and outside the home, gambling and the difficulties of matching behaviour as a wife and widow with contemporary ideal models. The collection would have benefited from more space, as both excerpts and introductions are frustratingly short, but it still could serve as a useful introduction or supplement to those interested in the lives of women in this period.

The back cover of Amy Louise Erickson's impressive *Women and Property in Early Modern England* claims to cover the period from the late sixteenth to the early eighteenth centuries; although it does include information about the beginning and end of this period, in fact it focuses mainly on the seventeenth century. Erickson's approach is one so concerned with detail that it is inevitable, for reasons of space, that she should not cover the whole period in equal depth. Drawing on a wide range of sources, she explores the difference between the theory of women's legal rights and their social practice, and gives a more positivist account than previous studies of the property powers of maids, wives and widows (the three main headings of the book). She also emphasizes regional variations in her conclusions. There is some detailed information here for those studying the first 15 or 20 years of the eighteenth century, but it is also stimulating and important background reading for anyone interested in gender and property in the later eighteenth century. Deborah Valenze also offers a thought-provoking study this year, *The First Industrial Woman*.

Felicity A. Nussbaum's *The Autobiographical Subject: Gender and Ideology in Eighteenth-Century England* has appeared in paperback, a welcome re-issue of her important study of the emergence of autobiography in the eighteenth century. Looking at texts ranging from the scandalous memoirs of Laetitia Pilkington to John Wesley's journals and diaries, she discusses the importance of class, gender, genre (e.g. the spiritual autobiography) and religion in the construction of representations of the self. In '"Above oecon-omy"': Elizabeth Griffith's *The History of Lady Barton* and Henry Mackenzie's *The Man of Feeling' ECLife* (19.1–17), Gillian Skinner considers eighteenth-century notions of economy in relation to the construction of the heroes and heroines of the sentimental novel with regard to gender and class, suggesting that there are differences in the time of decline between male and female authored sentimental novels. Michael McKeon provides a broad survey of 'the emergence of gender difference in England, 1660–1760' (*ECS* 28.295–322), under the title 'Historicizing Patriarchy'; Antoinette Emch-Deriaz offers 'An Eighteenth-Century Case-Study' of 'Health and Gender Oriented Education' (*WS* 24.521–30); and Katharine M. Rogers comments briefly on 'Eighteenth-Century Women' in *Belles-Lettres* (10.27–9). Eleanor Ty considers 'Jane West's Feminine Ideals in the 1790s' (*1650–1850* 1.137–56). In *ECS* (29.97–109), Lawrence E. Klein raises useful questions about 'evidence and analytic procedure' in a discussion of 'Gender and the Public/Private Distinction in the Eighteenth Century'. Beth Kowaleski-Wallace writes on 'Women, China, and Consumer Culture in Eighteenth-Century England' in *ECS* (29.153–67). In 'On the Town: Women in Augustan England' (*HT* 45.12.20–7), Joyce Ellis looks at the increasing numbers of women who migrated to towns in the long eighteenth century, the resulting female bias in urban populations, and the attractions that led them there, from work to pleasure gardens. In 'The Pleasure of Business and the Business of Pleasure' (*SECC* 24.191–210), Catherine Ingrassia argues that 'representations of the South Sea Bubble placed women symbolically and materially at the center of the crisis, as they warn of speculative investment's feminizing influence on culture as a whole'. Daniel A. Rabuzzi considers 'Eighteenth-Century Commercial Mentalities as Reflected and Projected in Business Handbooks' (*ECS* 29.169–89), while Sandra Sherman writes on 'Credit, Simulation, and the Ideology of Contract' in the period (*ECLife* 19.86–102), considering the development of the discourse of early modern finance and the inadequacy of its terminology when faced with the financial crises of the early eighteenth century, and its consequent dependence on the rationalistic vocabulary of the law. We have not seen Martin Daunton's *Progress and Poverty: An Economic and Social History of Britain 1700–1850* (OUP).

In *The Emergence of Civil Society in the Eighteenth Century* Marvin Becker continues his project of mapping what he describes as 'the transition from civility to civil society' in the modern world. Eighteenth-century England and Scotland are seen as offering historical examples of the development of civil society within 'a privileged society existing at a privileged historical moment'. The book is sometimes clumsily written, and Becker's generalizations can at times demand tighter definition. None the less, the study makes some useful contributions to current debates about the historical emergence of civil societies, and about their place in the modern world. Gibbon has also received some attention: Myron C. Noonkester discusses 'Memoranda, Memories and Gibbon's *Memories*' (*ELN* 32.iv.65–70), while Rodney Stenning Edgecombe comments briefly on his *History of the Decline and Fall of the Roman Empire* (*Expl* 53.ii.79–81).

The lesser-known American historian Mercy Otis Warren is the subject of a new study by Jeffery H. Richards. Warren (1728–1814) was an historian, political activist and playwright who corresponded with George Washington, Thomas Jefferson, Marquis de Lafayette, Francisco de Miranda, Alexander Hamilton and John and Abigail Adams and wrote the magisterial three-volume *History of the Rise, Progress and Termination of the American Revolution*. Her plays were deeply political, promoting the Revolutionary cause in dramas such as *The Adulateur* and *The Defeat*, and she saw herself as a patriot historian in all aspects of her work and correspondence. In *Mercy Otis Warren*, Richards provides a solid and sympathetic commentary on her writing and includes new biographical and bibliographical information.

We have not seen the magisterial eight-volume edition *Political Writings of the 1790s: The French Revolution Debate in Britain* (ed. Gregory Claeys), published by P&C. The influence of the French Revolution on British culture is considered in 'The Politics of Literary Production' (*SECC* 24.279–95), where Zeynep Tenger and Paul Trolander suggest that the changes in 'discourse formation' which resulted in the movement from comprehensive to specialized coverage in late-century literary periodicals depended crucially on the English reaction against the French Revolution. The French Revolution is also important in Dohr Wahrman's *Imagining the Middle Class: The Political Representation of Class in Britain, c.1780–1840*, in which he emphasizes the importance of politics in the identification of British national identity with the middle class. The influence of the French Revolution is considered in depth, and comparative studies of France and America are used to substantiate his thesis. In 'Liberty Caps and Liberty Trees', J. David Harden considers the origins of the French symbols of liberty in the 1790s (*P&P* 146.66–102).

The general thesis of Elizabeth Bohls's *Women Travel Writers and the Language of Aesthetics 1716–1818* is that the eighteenth century sees a wide range of male aesthetic theorists setting out to establish the domain of the aesthetic as an area of disinterested observation – a posture which can be seen to be the projection of a very specific social and gender identity on the part of the theorists, and which is challenged in a variety of ways by contemporary women writers in the course of their own characteristic productions – tour journals or narrative fiction. As Bohls writes, 'Writings by male aesthetic theorists of the period pervasively construct the aesthetic subject or perceiver as not just a man, but a gentleman. Women's aesthetic writing, as it tampers with the gender of the perceiver, tends to expose the interests that inform supposedly disinterested acts of aesthetic appreciation'. This thesis is pursued determinedly and sometimes rather relentlessly through readings of works by Mary Wortley Montagu, Janet Schaw, Helen Maria Williams, Mary Wollstonecraft, Dorothy Wordsworth, Ann Radcliffe and Mary Shelley. Bohls makes striking points about the gendered implications of aesthetic categories of the period, and about the relation between those categories and the discourses of colonialism, orientalism and revolutionary politics. Sometimes her arguments edge towards the predictable or the schematic. Usually, however, this danger is at least acknowledged in this stimulating study.

The second edition of Billie Melman's *Women's Orients* includes a new preface in which the author surveys recent work on the relation of gender and colonialism and places the project of her own book in relation to that work. Melman's fascinatingly documented discussion is concerned mainly with nineteenth- and early twentieth-century material, but it inevitably includes consideration of the writings of influential figures from the start of the period she surveys, such as Mary Wortley Montagu. *Objects of Enquiry: The Life, Contributions, and Influences of Sir William Jones (1746–1794)* (ed. Garland Cannon and Kevin R. Brine), contains some interesting essays on this major figure – called by some the father of orientalism in Europe – including useful pieces such as that by R. H. Robins on 'Jones as a General Linguist in the Eighteenth-Century Context'.

Felicity Nussbaum's *Torrid Zones: Maternity, Sexuality and Empire in Eighteenth-Century English Narratives* offers exciting readings of eighteenth-century culture through its focus on the relationship between femininity, sexuality, the exotic, commerce and empire. Novels considered include *Roxana, Pamela, Memoirs of a Woman of Pleasure, Life of Savage, The Female Quixote* and *Millenium Hall*, all of which are examined alongside other cultural texts such as medical and legal documents, letters and travel narratives. Jonathan Lamb considers 'The Representation of South Pacific discovery' in *ECS* (28.281–94), while Kathleen Wilson discusses 'Citizenship, Empire, and Modernity in the English Provinces' between the 1720s and the 1790s in *ECS* (29.69–96). Philip Edwards's *The Story of the Voyage*, not noted last year, offers an extensively documented survey of the narratives arising from different types of voluntary and involuntary 'voyages' in the period, whether they were produced by explorers or slaves. Edwards's resistance to theory ultimately limits the scope of his arguments, but he introduces a fascinating range of material in the course of his discussions. The curious *Peter Wilkins* is the focus of two essays in *Anticipations: Essays on Early Science Fiction and Its Precursors* (ed. David Seed). Paul Baines writes on '*The Life and Adventures of Peter Wilkins* and the Eighteenth-Century Fantastic Voyage' under the title ' "Able Mechanik" ', while Paul Baines discusses '*Peter Wilkins* and the Eighteenth-Century Fantastic Voyage'.

A useful anthology, *Black Atlantic Writers of the Eighteenth Century*, edited by Adam Potkay and Sandra Burr, offers complete texts of narratives and a sermon by Ukawsaw Gronniosaw and John Marrant, substantial extracts from Quobna Ottabah Cugoano's *Thoughts and Sentiments* on slavery and an abridgement of Olaudah Equiano's *Life*. In his brief introduction Potkay considers the form of the writings and their historical contexts in the period, and compares them with nineteenth-century slave narratives. In *ECS* (28.379–96), Eve W. Stoddard examines 'A Serious Proposal for Slavery Reform' in Sarah Scott's *Sir George Ellison*, while in *P&P* (148.149–86), Shane White and Graham White examine the importance of dress as a form of cultural expression for slaves. In 'Slave Clothing and African-American Culture in the 18th and 19th Centuries' they look at the significance of the adoption by slaves of parts of elite dress and the importance of African-American aesthetics in the textile industry. Clare Midgley's thorough and extremely useful *Women Against Slavery: The British Campaigns 1780–1870* has been re-issued in paperback, and J. R. Oldfield's *Popular Politics and British Anti-Slavery: The Mobilisation of Public Opinion Against the Slave Trade, 1787–1807* also appeared this year.

This has been a good year for the Gothic, with the publication of three thought-provoking studies. Fred Botting's *The Gothic*, part of the Routledge Critical Idioms series, is a rigorous study of the category, and offers some subtly theoretical readings. *Exhibited by Candlelight: Sources and Developments in the Gothic Tradition* (ed. Villani Valeria Tinkler, Peter Davidson and Jane Stevenson), contains an interesting range of general and specific essays. Michel Baridon discusses 'The Gothic Revival and the Theory of Knowledge in the First Phase of the Enlightenment', and the volume also contains an article by Emma Clery entitled 'Laying the Ground for Gothic: The Passage of the Supernatural from Truth to Spectacle', which surveys eighteenth-century attitudes to the representation of the supernatural, including those of Johnson. Peter Sabor has collected a judicious and interesting selection of critical commentaries on *Horace Walpole* and his various literary, aesthetic and political preoccupations for a new Critical Heritage volume from Routledge.

Religion still seems a rather neglected area of eighteenth-century studies. However, some studies have appeared this year, and Joanna Southcott's intriguing *A Dispute Between Woman and the Powers of Darkness* has been re-issued by Woodstock. In *HT*, Penelope Corfield emphasizes the pluralism of religion and its problematic relation to statehood in the long eighteenth century in 'Georgian England: One State, Many Faiths' (45.iv.14–21). In *The Rhetoric of Suffering: Reading the Book of Job in the Eighteenth Century*, Jonathan Lamb looks at the importance of the notion of complaint in eighteenth-century culture, and the reasons for the failure of traditional consolations in this period. William Warbuton's interpretation of Job is discussed at length, but Lamb also looks at a whole range of thinkers, from Richardson to Blackstone, rather self-consciously avoiding limitations of discipline and genre. This rejection of formal boundaries is supposed to communicate the widespread urgency of the debate, but ends up being only an over-ambitious attempt to offer new interpretations of – among others – the sublime, *Clarissa*, Pope, sympathy, travel-writing and the law in the eighteenth century, in a series of readings which though thought-provoking, lack discursive coherence and remain ultimately unsatisfying. In *The Flesh Made Word: The Failure and Redemption of Metaphor in Edward Taylor's 'Christographia'*, David G. Miller produces the first book-length study of this Puritan preacher and poet. Miller sets Taylor's writing in historical and discursive context and looks at the problems faced by Taylor in the verbal representation of the divine. Mark Bence-Jones's *The Catholic Families* has been re-issued in paperback. Taking as his starting-point the Relief Act of 1778, Bence-Jones traces the history of the aristocratic Catholic families to the present day. We have not seen S. J. Connelly's *Religion, Law and Power: The Making of Protestant Ireland 1660–1760* (Clarendon).

Eighteenth-century writings about the body and science have inspired some interesting if curious articles this year. Anita Guerrini's 'Case History as

Spiritual Autobiography' considers 'George Cheyne's "Case of the Author"'
(*ECLife* 19.18–27). She sees the last case study of Cheyne's *The English
Malady* (1733), 'The Case of the Author', as an 'autopathography', analysing
its presentation of both patient's and physician's perspectives, and situating it
in the seventeenth-century tradition of spiritual autobiography. The extraordinary gestatory powers claimed by Mary Toft, who apparently mothered
many rabbits, forms the centre-piece of Alan Shepard's 'The Literature of a
Medical Hoax: The Case of Mary Toft, "The Pretended Rabbet-Breeder"'
(*ECLife* 19.59–77), a study of the impact of an expanding print culture on
eighteenth-century definitions of monstrosity. In *ECLife*, Clive Hart and Kay
Gilliland Stevenson offer a critical edition of John Armstrong's sex manual of
1736, *The Oeconomy of Love*, with a brief introduction contextualizing the
work (19.38–69). We have not seen Roy Porter's *Disease, Medicine and
Society in England, 1550–1860* (CUP).

In an intriguing essay in *ECS* Greg Laugero examines the relation between
'road-making, the public sphere, and the emergence of literature' under the
title 'Infrastructures of Enlightenment' (29.45–67); while in *ECLife*, James G.
Buickerood considers the difficulties involved in understanding 'eighteenth-
century maps of the mind', under the title 'Pursuing the Science of Man'
(19.1–17). *BJHS* contains useful discussions of eighteenth-century scientific
interests by Alan Q. Morton, who writes on 'Concepts of power' and 'the uses
of machines in mid-eighteenth-century London' (28.63–78); and by Simon
Schaffer, who discusses perpetual motion in the early eighteenth century
under the title 'The Show that Never Ends' (28.157–89). In *HSci* (33.127–77),
Patricia Fara discusses animal magnetism in eighteenth-century England. In
'Immovable Objects, Irresistible Forces: The Sublime and the Technological
in the Eighteenth Century' (*ECLife* 19.18–38), Kevin L. Nevers considers the
relationship between the aesthetic of the sublime and the emergent discourse
of modern science, and the relationship of both to colonialist agendas, while
Ted Underwood discusses 'Productivism and the Vogue for "Energy" in Late
Eighteenth-Century Britain' (*SIR* 34.103–25). The sublime is also discussed in
' "I have before me the idea of a dove" ', where Alan T. McKenzie considers
Burke's *Sublime and Beautiful* (*1650–1850* 1.267–94).

In *The Sleep of Reason*, Frances S. Connelly offers to 'reconstruct the
framework of ideas through which Europeans of the eighteenth and nineteenth centuries understood those arts they described as "primitive"'.
Surveying a wide range of treatises and other writings from the time of Vico
onwards, the author argues persuasively that 'the classical tradition was the
shaping force of primitivism', casting it as a category which represented 'a
dark mirror image of itself' through the development of a terminology of the
grotesque and the ornamental to describe its characteristics – qualities toler-
able only insofar as they define the marginal opposites of the classical ideals of
rational order and abstraction. The study makes telling links between a central
discourse of the Enlightenment and the vocabulary of twentieth-century art.

In *BJECS*, David E. Shuttleton examines the relation between John
Arbuthnot and the Scottish Newtonians under the title ' "A Modest Examina-
tion" ' (18.47–62). In 'History and the Primitive: Homer, Blackwell, and the
Scottish Enlightenment' (*ECLife* 19.57–69), Duane Coltharp looks at Thomas
Blackwell's *An Enquiry into the Life and Writings of Homer* (1735) as a
foundational text of the Scottish Enlightenment which, in its consideration of

the relationship between the savage and civilization, 'reveals the epistemological and social foundations that make such writing possible'. In 'The
"Failing Soul"': Macpherson's Response to Locke" (*ECLife* 19.39–56), Stephen L. Clark questions the general tendency of studies on James Macpherson
to consider his work as being in opposition to Enlightenment rationalism, and
traces Lockean ideas and imagery in his work.

In 'The Idea of Life as a Work of Art in Scottish Enlightenment Discourse'
(*SECC* 24.51–67), Leslie Ellen Brown considers the 'life/art paradigm' – the
association in Scottish writings of 'moral excellence' with 'scholarly and
artistic excellence'. Joel Weisheimer examines 'The Philosophy of Rhetoric in
Campbell's *Philosophy of Rhetoric*' (*1650–1850* 1.227–46) and M. A. Box asks
'How Disturbed was Hume by his own Skepticism?' (*1650–1850* 1.295–316). In
'Arguing by Analogy', David Marshall discusses Hume's account of the
standard of taste (*ECS* 28.323–43).

Giancarlo Carabelli's *On Hume and Eighteenth-Century Aesthetics: The
Philosopher on a Swing* has been published in English, translated by Joan
Krakover-Hall. *Chance, Culture and the Literary Text* (ed. Thomas M. Kava-
nagh), includes an article entitled 'Fortuna and the Passions' by Lorraine
Daston, covering writers such as Hume. We have not seen Robert E. Norton's
The Beautiful Soul: Aesthetic Morality in the Eighteenth Century (CornUP) or
the collection of essays on *Thomas Reid on the Animate Creation*, ed. Paul
Wood (EdinUP). In *The British Moralists and the Internal 'Ought', 1640-1740*,
Stephen Darwall considers the different ways in which the two traditions of
early modern ethics sought to deal with the notion of internalism, looking at
the empiricist line through Hobbes, Locke, Cumberland, Hutcheson and
Hume, and on the other side, Cudworth, Shaftesbury and Butler. A fresh and
stimulating handling of an important debate.

A very welcome edition of an important standard Enlightenment history
has appeared: Adam Ferguson's *An Essay on the History of Civil Society*. It is
based on the first edition text of 1767 and includes major alterations and
additions from the third and fourth editions of 1768 and 1773 in footnotes.
Fania Oz-Salzberger also provides a useful introduction, chronology and
bibliography. The edition is admirably complemented by Vincenzo Merolle's
edition of the copious *The Correspondence of Adam Ferguson* with the other
leading lights of the Scottish Enlightenment.

Adam Smith's life is hardly the stuff of romantic biography, but, as Ian
Simpson Ross amply demonstrates in *The Life of Adam Smith* his personal
position at the centre of the intellectual and social life of the Scottish
Enlightenment repays close scholarly attention as a key to the range of his
interests and preoccupations, and his career has attracted biographical studies
from Dugald Stuart to John Rae and Jacob Viner. Ross's lucid and attractively
presented new biography is a valuable complement to the Glasgow edition of
Smith's works, for which Ross previously edited Smith's letters, and will
replace Rae's as the standard scholarly biography for the foreseeable future.
Adam Smith's 'Wealth of Nations': New Interdisciplinary Essays (ed. Stephen
Copley and Kathryn Sutherland) is one of the first volumes in a series aimed
at offering interdisciplinary approaches to culturally significant texts. Essays
by Keith Tribe, Heinz Lubasz, Andrew Skinner, Noel Parker, Ted Benton
fulfil this remit from the disciplines of economics, history and sociology.
Amongst the essays contributed by literary scholars, Kathryn Sutherland

writes on 'Women and the *Wealth of Nations*' and Kurt Heinzelman considers the book as 'The Last Georgic'. In 'Smith's *The Theory of Moral Sentiments*: Sympathy, Women and Emulation' (*SECC*, 24.175–90), Maureen Harkin argues that Smith's account of sympathy as a 'socially useful bond' is problematized in ways not recognized by commentators because of his acknowledgement of the 'feminine and disruptive response' to that bonding. We have not seen Athol Fitzgibbon's *Adam Smith's System of Liberty, Wealth and Virtue* (Clarendon).

Oxford Art Journal 18.i contains an interesting selection of essays which consider eighteenth-century art and its larger cultural context. In ' "Squabby cupids and clumsy graces": Garden Sculpture and Luxury in Eighteenth-Century England' (18.i.3–13), Malcolm Baker looks at the connections between upwardly-mobile middle-rank garden sculpture, anxieties about luxury and consumption, and the discrepancies between evidence about the consumption of lead sculptures and eighteenth-century associations of leads with cits; while in 'Nakedness and Tourism: Classical Sculpture and the Imaginative Geography of the Grand Tour' (18.i.14–28), Chloe Chard considers the discourses surrounding classical sculpture in the eighteenth century and looks at some of the strategies employed to appropriate classical sculpture for a notion of the familiar that removed them from a foreign topography. Robert W. Jones contributes a fascinating essay entitled ' "Such Strange Unwonted Softness to Excuse": Judgement and Indulgence in Sir Joshua Reynolds's *Portrait of Elizabeth Gunning, Duchess of Hamilton and Argyll*' (18.i.29–43). Taking Reynolds's portrait of Elizabeth Gunning as a focus for his discussion, Jones considers the problems of the public representation of women in the period, and looks at the wide range of debates mobilized by such a picture. In ' "The British Sappho": Borrowed Identities and the Representation of Women Artists in late Eighteenth-Century British Art' (18.i.44–57), Gill Perry considers the plurality of readings available in the many disguises used by the conventions of feminine portraiture, taking Mary Robinson ('Perdita') and Angelica Kauffman as her main examples. Fintan Cullen considers 'Visual Politics in 1780s Ireland: The Roles of History Painting' (18.i.58–73), tracing the dynamics of national politics in Wheatley's 1780s Irish contemporary history paintings. Under the title 'Rule Britannia?', Brian Allen considers problems of inspiration and tradition in 'History Painting in Eighteenth-Century Britain' (*HT* 45.vi.12–28). An 'Art Forum' in *ECS* 29 includes short pieces by Wendy Wassyng Roworth, entitled 'Painting for Profit and Pleasure', which covers 'Angelica Kauffman and the art business in Rome' (225–8), and by Paula Rea Radisich on 'Deconstructing Dissipation' (222–5). Under the title 'Re-dressing Classical Statuary', Arline Meyer looks at the nationalistic significance of the eighteenth-century ' "hand-in-waistcoat" portrait' (*ArtB* 77.45–64), suggesting that in withdrawing the 'speaking hand' England constructed a type of public virtue that opposed the excesses of French rhetoric with a natural gesture that involved and was validated by classical precedents. In 'Writing the Picture' (*SECC* 24.69–89), Pamella Cantrell argues that there is 'a more fruitful correspondence' between the work of Hogarth and Smollett than that of Hogarth and Fielding; in *BJECS* (18.125-37), Anthony Strugnell discusses 'Diderot, Hogarth and the Ideal Model'; and in 'Judicial Wigs and the Majesty of the Law' (*L&H* 4.1–26), Stephen Copley discusses 'Hogarth's *The Bench* and the Representation of

English Legal Costume' over an extended historical period. Vincent Caretta offers a substantial illustrated survey of 'Catherine the Great in British Political Cartoons' in *1650–1850* (1.23–82). In ' "The family piece" ' (*ECS* 29.127–52), Christopher Flint writes on Oliver Goldsmith and the politics of the everyday in eighteenth-century domestic portraiture.

Reynolds is the subject of Martin Postle's *Sir Joshua Reynolds: The Subject Pictures*. His scholarship is combined with lavish production (85 black and white illustrations and 16 colour plates). However, his book is disappointing in its lack of contextualization, and is thus less useful and stimulating than it might have been. Clive Hart and Kay Gilliland Stevenson's *Heaven and the Flesh: Imagery of Desire from the Renaissance to the Rococo* is a self-confessedly old-school study of representations of desire and the overlap of the visual and verbal vocabulary used to depict the erotic and the heavenly; the authors disassociate themselves from 'recent explorations of the history of sexuality', despite the dangerous hints of interdisciplinarity in their juxtaposition of text and image. Katie Scott's *The Rococo Interior: Decoration and Social Spaces in Early Eighteenth-Century Paris* has been criticized for being overly theoretical in its handling of connoisseur material, but Scott's use of theory is sophisticated and it provides a stimulating reading of architecture and decoration in this period in Paris.

This year and last have been very good for those interested in landscape and gardening, with the publication of several extremely useful anthologies and some major studies. Simon Schama's *Landscape and Memory* is a lavishly produced and illustrated book. Although it covers a huge timespan and geographical range, there is much here to interest and stimulate anyone interested in eighteenth-century notions of nature and gardening. There is a lack of direction and sharpness of argument, however, that mean that the reader is not so much presented with a coherent argument about, say, nationalism and landscape in the eighteenth century as much as an overflow of detail on a bewildering range of periods and places. The opening chapters of the book, the prologue on Schama's trip to Poland in vague search of family roots, and the first two chapters on the importance of landscape to the construction of national identities in Germany, Poland and Lithuania, suggest themes that are frustratingly unexplored later in the book. Schama's rich layering of anecdotes is ultimately negative, as it seems to smother the discussion of fundamental issues such as competing definitions of landscape and memory; however, his eloquence and attention to fascinating detail are as always extremely beguiling.

In the introduction to *Polite Landscapes: Gardens and Society in Eighteenth-Century England*, Tom Williamson surveys the terms in which recent commentators have sought to explain developments in garden design in the period, comparing them with the assumption of 'an earlier and perhaps more fortunate generation of garden historians' that 'Gardens just changed'. The volume is particularly useful for the qualifications that it offers to conventionally accepted accounts of the lineage of garden designs, and for Williamson's insistence on distinguishing between the programmes expounded in garden theory and the much more complex and less homogeneous actuality that developed on the ground. Williamson thus counters the view that all forms of landscaping in the period were informed by a steadily emerging 'naturalism', insisting instead on the discontinuities that marked its development. At the same time he suggests that 'the "key sites" which loom large in the literature are often a poor guide to the gardens created by the majority of landowners'; and that the owners of gardens played a larger and more distinctive role in their design than has usually been acknowledged. The study is lucidly presented and attractively illustrated, and it concludes with a useful discussion of the landscaped park, developed by great landowners and local gentry as a sign of 'polite' social distinction which effectively excluded 'the broad mass of the middle class' on the grounds that 'Parks could only be created by those who owned land in abundance'. In 'Blenheim Park on the Eve of "Mr Brown's Improvements"' (*JGH* 15.107– 25), David W. Booth looks at the gardeners who worked on this garden before Brown, referring extensively to the records Brown had made of the garden as it was before he began his labours. Booth shows that these records demonstrate that Brown was not responsible for many of the changes attributed to him, in particular the destruction of the Military Gardens, and he calls for new research on the identity of the designer who worked on Blenheim Park before Brown, sometime between 1748 and 1758. In 'The Duke of Kent's Garden at Wrest Park' (*JGH* 15.149–178), Linda Cabe Halpern argues that the formality of the gardens at Wrest Park and their importance in the eyes of contemporary commentators in the first half of the eighteenth century point to a less rigidly linear trend towards the picturesque than has recently been suggested.

Two volumes in a useful series from Helm Information, not noted last year, collect generous selections of primary material on landscape history from a wide range of literary and documentary sources. *The Picturesque* (ed. Malcolm Andrews), and *The English Garden* (ed. Michael Charlesworth), have substantial introductions, helpful head-notes to sections and passages, chronologies and bibliographies. Both editors manage to include lengthy complete texts as well as extracts. Malcolm Andrews thus includes works such as Burke's *Sublime and Beautiful* and Gilpin's *Observations on the Wye* in his first volume. He understandably devotes almost the whole of his second volume to the 1790s, and his third volume surveys the continuing debate in the nineteenth century. His general introduction defines the Picturesque as a 'peculiarly complex' term, which he suggests has also been 'inordinately problematised' in academic publications in recent years. Unfortunately, the collection has not been very carefully proofread. Michael Charlesworth includes material from 1550–1914 in his collection, with a particular emphasis on the period between 1700 and 1830. He choses 'works that assert or demonstrate the position and value of the garden as a cultural and artistic product', supported by an interesting account of the importance of semiotics in writing garden history, and of the values traditionally inscribed in garden design. Inevitably, perhaps, the material he includes is more fragmentary than that in the volumes on the Picturesque, but he does include some substantial individual texts, such as Thomas Whately's *Observations on Modern Gardening*. A third set in the series, which we have not seen, covers *The American Landscape*. It includes a large amount of eighteenth- and nineteenth-century material. *The Picturesque Landscape: Visions of Georgian Hertfordshire* (ed. Stephen Daniels and Charles Watkins), is the attractive catalogue of an exhibition celebrating the bicentenary of Uvedale Price's *Essay on the Picturesque* and Richard Payne Knight's *The Landscape*. Not noted last year was a beautifully presented and illustrated exhibition catalogue by John Harris, *The Palladian Revival: Lord Burlington, His Villa and Garden at Chiswick.*

Two volumes from 1993 have related concerns. Gina Crandell's *Nature Pictorialized* covers a broad swathe of 'the history of seeing' from ancient Greece to the present in its account of the evolution of pictorial conceptions of 'nature' in the modern world. The limitations of the book's approach are clear in the section on the eighteenth century. Christopher Hussey provides the central reference point in the discussion of picturesque vision in this period, and Crandell follows a familiar route through aesthetic theory, tours and landscaping projects, in pursuit of the claim that in the period 'a comprehensive set of expectations ... developed: nature should be scenic'. Unfortunately, she does not draw to any great extent on the extensive recent discussions of landscape, the spectator, the gaze and the ideology of the picturesque. Instead her argument, reinforced with brief discussions of sites such as Castle Howard, Painshill, Stourhead and Stowe, tends to emerge as a series of summaries of well-established positions, couched in unexceptionable but unexciting terms. A stimulating collection, *Landscape, Natural Beauty and the Arts* (ed. Salim Kemal and Ivan Gaskell), includes essays on the aesthetics and to a lesser extent the politics of landscape from the eighteenth century to the present day. Discussions draw substantially on the aesthetic debates of the eighteenth century, as do a number of the case studies in the volume. Amongst these, Don Gifford outlines the transformation of European aesthetics of landscape in the new context of America, while Stephanie Ross traces the aesthetic links between the eighteenth-century landscape garden and recent environmental works. Yi-Fu Tuan considers the landscape attractions of regions of 'desert and ice' and the volume includes John Barrell's reprinted piece on 'The Public Prospect and the Private View'.

In the brief introduction to his edition of *Richard Pococke's Irish Tours*, John McVeagh suggests that Pococke's travels between the 1740s and the 1760s represent 'explorations rather than tours'. The journals are fascinating, offering a wealth of information from the perspective of 'a favoured son of the English clerical caste which ruled Irish life after the Williamite wars', whose habitual adherence to the 'ideology of domination' is qualified by intelligent and sympathetic observation of contemporary social reality. McVeagh does not try to regularize Pocoke's sometimes wayward prose. The volume is attractively illustrated with contemporary prints of some of the better known sites that he visited.

2. Poetry

This year saw the arrival, after an interval of 15 years, of the second and third volumes of John D. Baird and Charles Ryscamp's Clarendon edition of the poems of William Cowper. These volumes include *The Task* and many of Cowper's best known shorter poems, all presented with detailed annotation, textual and general introductions and a variety of appendices. Along with James Sambrook's Longman selected edition of his poetry (*YWES* 75.356), the Clarendon edition has rendered Cowper one of the eighteenth century's most accessible and fully edited poets. Scholars are still without a modern edition of Cowper's blank verse translations of Homer (briefly excerpted in

Sambrook's edition but excluded from the Clarendon), but this should not impede a revival of interest in his work. Baird and Ryscamp have restored to view a poet of infinite variety, his subtle palette undimmed by unwarranted typographical or textual intervention. Volume II contains *The Task* alongside the other poems which accompanied the work in its first edition (including 'The Diverting History of John Gilpin'). There is no extant manuscript of Cowper's longest work, and the editors' detailed commentary gives us, instead, not the delicate domestic saint of Victorian mythology, but a poet deeply engaged with contemporary affairs. Literary allusions are not neglected, however, and new sources and resonances are identified for many of the purple passages. Cowper's verse translations occupy space in this and the following volume, including his renditions of Mme Guyon's poetry and Milton's Latin and Italian poems. The remainder of the third volume contains Cowper's shorter poems reprinted in broadly chronological order from manuscript sources. Most have appeared before, but important manuscript variants surface, including one in 'On the Receipt of my Mother's Picture out of Norfolk'.

The completion of this excellent edition of Cowper's poetry coincided this year with the collection, in a single volume, of a number of Vincent Newey's more important essays, *Centring the Self: Subjectivity, Society and Reading from Thomas Gray to Thomas Hardy*. One, on 'Cowper and the Condition of England' makes a detailed case, and no doubt provided some of the impetus, for the politically minded Cowper of the Clarendon edition. Further essays, on Gray and other poets, place Cowper in the broader context of an evolving poetic understanding of selfhood. These essays are, in turn, complemented by Deborah Heller's fine essay on 'Cowper's *Task* and the Writing of a Poet's Salvation' which examines Cowper's typological transfiguration of his private self into a poetic servant of God (*SEL* 35.575–98). *The Task*, she argues, was designed to effect Cowper's poetic salvation in the absence of any sense of divine election. The poem is, therefore, something other than spiritual autobiography, and literary typologies, as her reading of the stricken deer passage shows, establish their own modes of signification.

The Task approximates in parts to the tradition of British formal georgic which was waning by this late point in the century but which had enjoyed considerable popularity throughout the period. This tradition receives its first book-length treatment in some years in John Goodridge's *Rural Life in Eighteenth-Century Poetry*. The book examines the native British strain of georgic and, what it calls, proletarian anti-pastoral in the eighteenth century, and focuses in detail on the process by which agricultural labour was made visible and intelligible to a non-labouring readership. The first section of the book discusses the representations of various types of rural work in the poetry of Thomson, Duck and Collier. Goodridge contrasts the communal sense labour in Collier with Thomson's philosophical idea of work, and writes sensitively about Collier and Duck's attempts to represent and dignify the most arduous and menial of rural tasks such as threshing and gleaning. A second section of the book gives detailed consideration to the neglected poem, Dyer's *The Fleece*. Dyer's poem has always seemed indigestibly technical, even in its own time, but Goodridge grasps the generic nettle by reading the poem on its own georgic terms and evaluating it according to its agricultural accuracy and practical value. Goodridge's research into mid-eighteenth-century agricultural practices pays dividends, and he is able to vindicate the technical precision of material which had hitherto appeared to be only inflated, polysyllabic verbiage. Dyer, it seems, was one of the first writers to give a description of 'New Leicester' sheep (no doubt, the alert eye of a Welshman in the Midlands), and his understanding of the new mutton-orientated sheep husbandry was second to none. Overall, Goodridge's approach tends to be a little schematic, though this, too, is in the spirit of georgic, and the book, despite its lively style, sometimes lacks a sense of the ridiculous (the phrase 'Duckian decorum' appears on one occasion). The strength of the book, in addition to its significant quantity of background research, is the way in which it succeeds in retaining its literary focus; the stated objective, to explore the fusion of socio-economic particularities with inherited and adapted literary conventions, is rarely far from view. What is needed now is an edition of Dyer's *The Fleece* with annotations based upon the second half of this interesting book.

One general book which includes essays on eighteenth-century poetry deserves special mention for providing some genuinely new and valuable perspectives on theoretical questions of satire. Brian Connery and Kirk Combe's, eds, *Theorizing Satire* brings together a broad range of essays on classical and modern understandings of this mode of writing. These include Frederic Bogel's lucid essay on 'The Difference Satire Makes' which examines the way in which satire, rather than simply affirming norms, creates differences out of ambiguous relationships of identification. Richard North's 'Satyrs and Satire in Augustan England' looks at hidden and explicit anxieties about the limits of the human in satire, and Jon Rowland discusses Swift and Churchill in the light of satire's membership of the rhetorical mode of epideictic. Also under the heading of general studies should be mentioned Richard Arnold's study *The English Hymn* which continues and expands Donald Davie's work on the century's most popular kind of poetry, and Nathaniel Paradise's useful 'Interpolated Poetry and Female Accomplishment' on the poetry interpolated by women writers into their novels, which prompts reflections on generic hierarchies and narrative structure (*PQ* 74. 57–76).

Pope was better served by articles than by books this year. On *The Dunciad*, there is Richard Braverman's ambitious and rather broad-brushed article on 'The Gothic Bequest in the *Dunciad*' which argues that Pope reopens the classical/gothic faultlines of the Renaissance debate about nationhood, and identifies Dullness and the Hanoverians with the gothic strand. Bolingbroke's oppositional reappropriation of gothic ancestries is then linked to an alleged critique, in *The Dunciad*, of George II's failure to be properly gothic, and to Pope's poetic rejection of the classical symbolism of Jacobitism (*ELH* 62.863–82). As a case for Pope's purely 'emotional Jacobitism', this does not convince, nor does it do justice to the complexities of eighteenth-century notions of the gothic. Thomas Jemielity provides a scholarly and persuasive article on 'Sir Richard Blackmore in the *Dunciad*' which explains that the reason why Pope continued to flog the old horse even after he died was because he held Blackmore responsible for charges of blasphemy levelled against him (*PQ* 74.249–77). Shef Rogers's 'Pope, Publishing, and Popular Interpretations of the *Dunciad Variorum*' gives details of Pope's legal negotiations and business (rather than simply malicious) motivations prior to the publication of this work (*PQ* 74.274–95). Anne Bailey's ' "How Much for Just the Muse?'": Alexander Pope's *Dunciad, Book IV and the Literary Market*' unhelpfully suggests that 'Pope recognises that language is a symbolic construct whose signs are arbitrary' (of what poet might this *not* be said?), and serves to demonstrate that, after Laura Brown and many others, there is little left to be said on the subject of this poem and literary capitalism (*ECent* 36.99–118). In 'Women, China, and Consumer Culture', Beth Kowaleski-Wallace takes a similarly familiar theme – the historical construction of woman as consumer in *The Rape of the Lock* – but breathes new life into it by focusing in detail upon one particular imported commodity (*ECS* 29.153–67). Also on the subject of Pope and women, Chris-Anne Stumpf, in an essay on Pope's 'Epistle to Miss Blount. With the Works of Voiture', gives an elegant account of the way in which Pope subverts the *galant* style of epistolary address in order to criticize the social mores which defined and constrained his female friend. This last essay can be found in Donald W. Nichol's (ed.) *Transatlantic Crossings*, a worthwhile volume privately printed by the Memorial University of Newfoundland in order to showcase the work of very young scholars, and readily available in the British Library. Pope's translations received some attention this year, with a general, somewhat belletristic defence of the *Odyssey* from Robin Sowerby ('The Augustan Odyssey', *T&L* 4.157–82). There is also a fascinating and plausible article by John Morillo entitled 'Seditious Anger: Achilles, James Stuart and Jacobite Politics in Pope's *Iliad*' which finds parallels between Achilles' encounter with Agamemnon and the failures of English diplomacy which lead to the Jacobite rising of 1715 (*ECLife* 19.38–58).

A range of other poets received article-length attention. On the early part of the century, Faith Gildenhuys ruminates, to no obvious purpose but with critical sensitivity, on Prior's enduringly popular love lyrics in 'Convention and Consciousness in Prior's Love Lyrics', and, in the same journal, D. N. DeLuna's '*Modern Panegyric* and Defoe's *Dunciad*' reassesses Defoe's *Modern Panegyrist* (*SEL* 35.437–55; 419–35). The much neglected William Diaper is briefly discussed by William Kupersmith in the cumbersomely titled 'William Diaper and two others imitate Swift imitating Horace' (*SStud* 10.26–36). Brean Hammond gives sophisticated theoretical consideration to 'A Beautiful Young Nymph', exploring the ways in which Swift's radical imagination forces the reader to confront prostitution as the reduction of a person to a set of economic relations. As a reading, this is both historically and critically more productive than those which simply engage in a demystification of capitalist or patriarchal ideologies at work in the poem. On a quite different note, two publications draw attention to the persistence of neo-Latin traditions of poetry in the eighteenth century. Barry Baldwin's edition of *The Latin and Greek Poems of Samuel Jonson* is definitive, correcting and surpassing the standard of textual editing and commentary in the Yale Johnson. Johnson's Latin poetry is varied and stems from all phases of his career from undergraduate exercises to poems on Skye and Inchkenneth. This edition will do much to round out our picture of Johnson's literary life, as will W. B. Hutching's detailed 'Conversations with a Shadow: Thomas Gray's Latin Poems to Richard West' (*SP* 92.118–39). Unlike Johnson, Gray associated writing in Latin with a single subject; almost all his Latin poetry is either addressed to his friend or acts as the medium of private reflection upon West after he died.

Lorna Clymer sheds a quite different kind of light on the same poet in her impressive article on the 'Figural Logic of Epitaphs and Elegies in Blair, Gray, Cowper, and Wordsworth' (*ELH* 62.347–86). Applying and developing De Man's work on 'Autobiography as De-Facement', Clymer tries to identify the precise rhetorical logic of address in elegy, its collective, rather than individual, epitaphic charge, and its creative conflation of the figures of prosopopoeia and apostrophe. She establishes connections between Blair's *The Grave* and Gray's 'Elegy' in a line of what she describes as *vanitas* elegy (a composite of elegy and epitaph); this line helps to explain the enigmatic final epitaph in Gray's poem, but also enables her to understand a public mode of 'epitaphic intersubjectivity' in Wordsworth's *The Excursion* which is now little understood by Romantic critics. This is a demanding article, but, along with Heller's considered piece on Cowper, represents the critical highlight of the year. The comic highlight belongs to Alexander Lindsay's short edition of 'A Lost Ballad by Thomas Warton the Elder' on the subject of turnips: 'Of all the roots the Hannover Turnip is best' (the Regency *Blackadder*'s turnip-obsessed servant Baldrick would certainly agree) (*Scriblerian* 28.1–5). There is also much comic and intriguing material in John ('The Art of Preserving Health') Armstrong's manual of sex education in verse, *The Oeconomy of Love* (ed. Clive Hart and Kay Gilliland Stevenson for *ECLife* 19.38–69). The message seems to be that the young, and, in particular, young women, should be as oeconomical as possible.

3. Prose

A very useful reissue has been brought out by Thoemmes this year: Jonathan Swift's *A Collection of Genteel and Ingenious Conversation*, in which Swift, writing as Simon Wagstaff, presents a lively satire of polite manners and conversation in the guise of a conduct book. This facsimile reprint of the 1755 edition is introduced by Michael Foot. In addition to this reprint, some astute critical pieces have been published. *Jonathan Swift's Gulliver's Travels: Complete, Authoritative Text with Biographical and Historical Contexts, Critical History, and Essays from Five Contemporary Critical Perspectives* (ed. Christopher Fox and Ross C. Murfin), contains an unusually interesting set of commentaries on the book and its contexts. Carol Barash writes on 'Swift, Psychoanalysis, and the 1720's', Michael J. Conlon on 'Performance as Response' in the book, Carole Fabricant on 'History, Narrativity, and Swift's Project to ' "Mend the World" ', and Felicity Nussbaum on 'Gulliver's Malice: Gender and the Satiric Stance', while Terry Castle asks 'Why the Houyhnhnms Don't Write'.

An interestingly varied volume, *Walking Naboth's Vineyard: New Studies of Swift* (ed. Christopher Fox and Brenda Tooley), contains essays by Michael DuPorte on 'Swift, God and Power', Margaret Anne Doody on 'Swift and Romance' and Seamus Deane on 'Swift: Virtue, Travel and the Enlightenment'. Carole Fabricant deals with Swift as an Irish historian, Robert Mahony discusses his relation to Catholic Ireland, Joseph McMinn writes on his relation to Thomas Sheridan and County Cavan, Heinz J. Vienken surveys his library and reading, James Woolley considers the role of Sarah Harding as his printer and A. C . Elias Jr. asks how reliable Laetitia Pilkington's comments on him really are. We have not seen An-chi Wang's *'Gulliver's Travels'* and *'Ching-hua yuan' Revisited: A Menippean Approach* (Lang). Marie Mulvey Roberts writes on 'Science, Magic and Masonry: Swift's Secret Texts' in *Secret Texts: The Literature of Secret Societies*, edited by herself and Hugh Ormsby-Lennon.

This year's *SStud* (10) contains essays by Michael Treadwell on 'The Text of *Gulliver's Travels*, Again' (62–79); William Kupersmith on William Diaper and other contemporaries who imitated Swift in producing imitations of Horace (26–36); Margaret Weedon on 'A Post-Reformation Wall-Painting in Swift' (37–42); Mary Margaret Stewart on William Collins's transcript of his *On the Day of Judgement* (43–7); Stephen Wood on the possible authenticity of a fragment of his writing (48–56); and Clive T. Probyn on 'A New Letter' by him (57–61). Daniel Traister surveys the Herman Teerink Swift Collection at the University of Pennsylvania (80–8); Michael Düring continues his annotated bibliography of Swift in Russia (89–101); and the journal prints an appreciation of Arthur H. Scouten by Ann Cline Kelly (5–13), and the text of an inauguration lecture given by Herbert Davis at Smith College in 1940 (14–25). A note by Gene Washington deals with 'Swift's Menière's Syndrome and *Gulliver's Travels*' (104–8).

In 'Swift's Struldbruggs, Progress, and the Analogy of History' (*SEL* 35.457–72), William Freedman argues that the episode is 'the culmination of the attack on the doctrine of progress that dominates the Third Voyage'. In *ModA* (37.170–5), A. Owen Aldridge discusses 'Jonathan Swift's Message for Moderns'. In *PQ* (74.415–41), Richard C. Frushell considers 'Swift's 6 August 1735 letter to Mary Pendarves Delany', picking up on the phrase ' "all other days I eat my chicken alone like a king" '. 'Cadenus and Vanessa' is examined by Thomas E. Maresca in an essay entitled 'Men Imagining Women Imagining Men' (*SECC* 24.243–57), while in *ECent*, Brean S. Hammond writes on 'Corinna's Dream' (36.99–118). Kelly Anspaugh writes on 'Reading the Intertext in Jonathan Swift's A Panegyrick on the Dean' in *ELWIU* (22.17–30). A special issue of *Clio Medica* devoted to health and illness in the eighteenth century, contains an article by Jean-Paul Forster entitled 'Santé et maladie: Instruments de la satire de Jonathan Swift' (*Clio Medica* 31.69–78). In *CHum* 29.339–61, Julius Laffal offers 'A Concept Analysis of Jonathan Swift's *A Tale of a Tub* and *Gulliver's Travels*'. We have not seen Philip Sicker's 'Leopold's Travels: Swiftian Optics in Joyce's "Cyclops"' (*JoyceSA* 6.59–78) or Mary R. Ryder's 'The Houyhnhnms – A Breed of Benevolent Projectors' in *Proceedings of the Third Dakotas Conference on Earlier British Literature* 1995, 109–16. In *ANQ*, Richard Levin finds 'A Possible Source for Swift's Laputians' (1995 8.ii.8–9) and John R. Clark comments on 'The 'Different Sects' in Swift's 'Day of Judgement' (8.i.11–13). *N&Q* includes comments by Geoffrey M. Sill on 'Swift's "As Sure as God's in Gloc'ster" and the Assurance of the Moderns' (42.458–9), by Arthur Sherbo on 'A Forgotten Poem by Swift (?)' (42.61–3), and by Cyndy Hendershot on 'A Contemporary Annotated Manuscript of Swift's Poem "A Character, Panegyric, and Description of the Legion Club" (42.455–8). In *Expl* (53.ii.73–5) William Chad Stanley comments on 'Swift's "The Day of Judgement"'. Robert Mahony's *Jonathan Swift: The Irish Identity* also appeared this year.

There has also been much good work published on Johnson and Boswell. In *Samuel Johnson's Critical Opinions: A Reexamination*, Arthur Sherbo builds on Joseph Epes Brown's collection of the author's marginal critical comments, originally published in 1926 as *The Critical Opinions of Samuel Johnson*. Sherbo rightly suggests that the range of new sources of information about Johnson now available reveals the incompleteness of Brown's anthology, and he accordingly adds around 400 notes of Johnson's critical opinions of 130 authors and works to Brown's original tally. These are culled from a wide range of direct and indirect sources. The vast majority, of course, are concerned with Shakespeare, but they also cover historical and contemporary writers, and general literary topics such as 'Language', 'Composition' and 'Translation'. Sherbo does not try to present his collection as definitive, and indeed it is not: in fact it seems eccentric in various ways.

Two books approach Johnson's politics from a wider contextual angle than is usually the case. J. C. D. Clark's *Samuel Johnson: Literature, Religion and English Cultural Politics from the Restoration to Romanticism* is not only about the great man, but rather about how Johnson can illuminate larger and wider systems of belief in the whole century. Whether this quite helps the cause of Johnson studies in isolation is still in doubt, I would venture, as this History of Ideas format, whilst informative according to its own lights, still makes a virtue of a certain narrowing of focus, here, the determination to place Johnson firmly within the Anglo-Latin tradition that motivated the period's Humanism. For a wider, and less polemical, account, I would still prescribe consulting Nicholas Hudson's recent work as well. In origin, this study shares some of the basic assumptions of De Maria's biography noted above: namely, that Johnson prized the accolade of being a successor to the great minds of classical humanism most of all, and that this involved the assumption of certain political identities throughout his writing career. Clark is surely correct in his chapter five to identify Johnson with non-juring ideas, and he writes a valuable and lucid section on their theology, prefacing a chapter on 'Johnson's Political Conduct, 1737–1760' that illuminates London, the pamphlets of 1739 and then his later political opinions post-1760 that create a consistent frame of reference for many apparently disconnected literary and non-literary acts. Clark then supplies an excellently judged account of 'The Denigration of Samuel Johnson, 1775–1832' to help advance the notion that Boswell's lionization was not a summation of how the culture at large viewed him. The writing is vivid and clear, and furthers Clark's anti-Namierite views about the age's secular ideas. For a reliable synthesis of how Johnson's contemporaries valued literature, then a glance at chapter one, 'Politics, Literature and the Culture of Humanism', would be all that would be necessary. In John Cannon's *Samuel Johnson and the Politics of Hanoverian England* there would seem to be the same ground covered, as he staunchly proclaims his project to be one of rescuing Johnson from 'liberals and Americans', and re-instituting him as 'one of the founding fathers of mainstream conservative thought'. This is fighting talk, yet from a *YWES* perspective, it can be seen to be something of a truism to feel it necessary to locate the politics of the Right in Johnson studies at the moment. Nevertheless, this is a useful overview of the subject. A series of 'Johnson-and' chapters (Religion, Jacobitism, Politics, the Constitution, Aristocracy, Enlightenment and Nationalism) is followed by a concluding 'The Nature of Hanoverian Politics', which summarizes the volume but still leaves the reader needing a little more than bald statements that Johnson was no Wilkite. The most cursory glance at Johnson's early reputation (see Clark above), however, provides us with the disconcerting fact that he was distrusted as much by political conservatives as by radicals. Maybe Johnson is not as clearly aligned as Cannon would like [review of Clark and Cannon by Nigel Wood].

Beth Carole Rosenberg's *Virginia Woolf and Samuel Johnson: Common Readers* (Macmillan) was not seen. Mark Pedreira considers 'Johnsonian Figures: *Copia* and Lockean Observation in Samuel Johnson's Critical Writings' (*1650–1850* 1.157–96). In *MP* 92, Helen Deutsch discusses 'moral economics in Johnson's *Life of Savage*' under the title '"The name of an author"' (328–45). In *PQ*, Gwin J. Kolb and Robert DeMaria Jr ask if there is evidence of 'Reciprocal Indebtedness' in 'Thomas Warton's *Observations on the "Faerie Queene" of Spenser*, Samuel Johnson's "History of the English Language" and Warton's *History of English Poetry*' (74.327–35). In 'Radical Letters and Male Genealogies in Johnson's *Dictionary*' (*SEL* 35.493–518), Dennis Dean Kezar Jr suggests that 'stereotypical notions of gender prevalent in the eighteenth century helped Johnson to articulate ideas peculiar to his own conception of language'. In 'The Insufficiency, Success, and Significance of Natural History' (*SEL* 35.519–34), Eric Miller charts 'the place of natural history for the private individual' in *Rasselas*, Sterne and Smart. Chester Chapin writes interestingly on 'Samuel Johnson, Anthropologist' (*ECLife* 19.22–37), considering the relationship between Christianity, civilization and savagery in the writer's thought. In *ELN* (33.ii.36–48), Thomas G. Kass writes on 'Holy Fear and Samuel Johnson's Sermons' while in *Renascence* (47.89–101), Thomas G. Kass discusses 'The Mixed Blessings of the Imagination in Johnson's *Sermons*'. Under the title ' "The Sinking Land"' (*PLL* 31.i.61–77), Charles LaChance discusses 'Pessimism in Johnson's *London*'. *N&Q* contains notes on 'A Deathbed Anecdote of Dr. Johnson' by G. M. Ditchfield (42.468–9), the dating of Johnson's Reply to impromptu verses by Baretti, by R. J. Dingley (42.468) and 'A Classical Source for Johnson on Augustus and Lord Bute' by Barry Baldwin (42.67–8). In *ANQ*, Neill R. Joy explains 'A Samuel Johnson Allusion in a Letter to Benjamin Franklin' (8.i.13–16).

Johnson and Boswell: The Transit of Caledonia by Pat Rogers offers a collection of complementary essays on various aspects of the tour to the Highlands of 1773. Rogers takes the writings generated by the tour as an index of the place of the two participants 'within the wider world' of contemporary intellectual and cultural life. Johnson's project in undertaking the tour is addressed in the two opening essays, in which Rogers asks 'Why 1773?' and 'Why Scotland?' The timing of the tour is convincingly read as Johnson's response to his own ageing, represented specifically in terms of his approach to the 'climacteric': the decision to travel to Scotland is seen as offering him the chance to construct an inverted version of the European Grand Tour, in which he can reverse all the expectations which informed participation in that event. Further individual essays on Johnson cover the writer's interest in 'Omai, and other primitives', the relation between his tour and the literature generated by contemporary 'voyages of discovery', and the links between his letters to Hester Thrale and his published *Journey*. Boswell's hero-worshipping tendencies are traced in the accounts of Prince Charles Edward which run through his *Journal*, and his complicated feelings about his own Scottish identity, revealed in his concern over 'Scotticisms', are compared with what Rogers sees as

Johnson's unearned reputation for hostility to the Scots. The essays are full of useful information and offer illuminating insights into the topics they consider. In *N&Q*, David Chandler comments on 'John Henry Colls and the Remarks on the Journal of a Tour to the Hebrides' (42.469–71).

The Yale edition of *The Private Papers of James Boswell* continues its magisterial progress with the appearance of the research edition of the first volume of Boswell's *Life of Johnson*, edited from the original manuscript by Marshall Waingrow. Waingrow deploys a range of useful editorial devices to allow the edition to fulfil what he takes to be its main purpose, displaying 'the *process* of composition' of the *Life*, in the main text rather than in the apparatus. With a copy text as complex and as heavily revised as this there is clearly a danger that such an approach will produce an impossibly cluttered reading page, but Waingrow avoids this pitfall admirably. This volume covers the years 1709–65: three more volumes will complete the edition. *Boswell: Citizen of the World: Man of Letters* (ed. Irma S. Lustig), contains essays by 11 prominent scholars, commemorating the bicentenary of Boswell's death in 1795. The first six essays form a section entitled 'Boswell and the Enlightenment', surveying various aspects of his intellectual, emotional and social life, and his contacts with his Scottish, English and European contemporaries, from Rousseau and Voltaire to Lord Kames and Henry Dundas. The second section concentrates on the *Life of Johnson*. Hitoshi Suwabe counts 'Boswell's Meetings with Johnson'; John B. Radner surveys the visit to Ashbourne; Isobel Grundy considers the place of 'Uncertainty' in the *Life* and Lustig the role of Margaret Montgomerie Boswell; Carey McIntosh writes on Boswell's prose style, and William Yarrow on his use of metaphor. Thomas Crawford considers his relations with Temple, Michael Fry those with Henry Dundas and Richard B. Sher those with Lord Kames. John Strawhorn writes on 'Boswell as Enlightened Laird'; Peter F. Perreten on 'Boswell's Response to the European Landscape'; and Marlies K. Danziger on 'Boswell's Travels through the German, Swiss, and French Enlightenment'. *James Boswell: Psychological Interpretations* (ed. Donald J. Newman), contains an interesting range of essays. Newman himself writes on 'James Boswell, Joseph Addison, and the Spectator in the Mirror' and on Boswell's poetry; Sanford Radner tackles the subject of 'James Boswell's Silence'; Brian Evenson writes on 'Boswell's Grand Tour of Selves', Elaine Perez Zickler on the *London Journal*, Greg Clingham on 'The Erotics of Narrative in the *Life of Johnson*' and George E. Haggerty on Boswell as a hypochondriac, under the title 'Boswell's Symptoms'. Erin F. Labbie offers 'A Psycholinguistic Reflection' on 'Identification and Identity in James Boswell's Journals'. Philip E. Baruth's 'Mushroom Votes and "Staged" Subjects' links Boswell's 'simulations of consciousness' to the novel and voting practices in the period. Under the title 'From Paralysis to Power', John B. Radner examines Boswell's relation to Johnson between 1775 and 1778. In 'Appreciating Gall: Boswell's Frank Wit' (*1650–1850* 1.369–80), Colby H. Kullman considers the attractions (and otherwise) of the author's 'incredible gall'.

An excellent anthology of women's criticism, *Women Critics 1660–1820*, has been edited by the Folger Collective on Early Women Critics; it provides short introductions to the women included. Writers represented in this collection include Jane Barker, Elizabeth Elstob, Sarah Fielding, Clara Reeve, Anna Laetitia Barbauld, Elizabeth Inchbald and Hannah More. Although the pieces chosen are sometimes frustratingly short, and not very representative, the collection as a whole is a pleasure to read, as it includes not only less well-known writers, but less well-known pieces by those who are more famous. Other writers of prose who have received attention in 1995 include Bishop Hurd, Lord Forbes and Bernard Mandeville. *The Early Letters of Bishop Richard Hurd 1739–1762* (ed. Sarah Brewer), offers 276 private letters or sections of letters, which the editor divides into six distinct groups in her introductory notes, in which she offers commentary on Hurd's correspondence with John Potter, the Macro family, Edward Littleton, William Mason, Thomas Balguy and William Warburton. The letters themselves are lucidly presented, with a helpful editorial apparatus in this substantial volume. In 'Lord Forbes of Pitsligo and the Maxims of La Rochefoucauld' (*1650–1850* 1.347–368), Irwin Primer narrows the focus of a broad survey of the reputation of La Rochefoucauld to concentrate on one neglected commentator, the Jacobite Lord Forbes. In *JHI*, E. J. Hundert considers 'Bernard Mandeville and the Enlightenment's Maxims of Modernity' (56.577–93).

4. Novel

If we take the continued propagation, enjoyment and explanation of eighteenth-century fiction as the main task of our scholarship in the field, this year should be judged successful. The last decade has witnessed an outpouring of valuable work in eighteenth-century studies, and if even a few of the excellent articles written this year are followed up by book-length studies, the continued vitality of our field should be assured. Much of the recent work on the eighteenth-century novel has been fuelled by new paperback editions, most notably by OUP, Penguin, and Broadview. This year saw, in particular, an important edition of Frances Sheridan's *The Memoirs of Miss Sidney Bidulph* (ed. Patricia Köster and Jean Coates Cleary). As Cleary writes in the introduction, the novel's ultimate punishment of its perhaps too scrupulously virtuous narrator gives it an intriguing presence in late eighteenth-century debates over 'poetic justice'. Cleary's introductory essay discusses the novel in terms of simultaneous support for and 'deconstruction' of codes of propriety soon to be codified in female conduct literature. The novel itself will be a revelation for readers who are new to it. Sheridan, like Frances Burney after her, is ultimately ambivalent about the worldly aspect of the virtues her novel seems to uphold. As Köster points out in the Notes to the Text, Miss Sidney Bidulph is yet another Job figure in eighteenth-century culture. Unlike Job's, however, the narrator's suffering serves no material purpose. Her virtue is never rewarded, but neither is any of the novel's major characters revealed to be responsible for her undoing. The novel's main candidate for villain would seem to be the 'female rake' Miss Burchell, who seduced and then bore the child of Orlando Faulkland, thus preventing his marriage to Sidney Bidulph. Without her and her conniving aunt, Mrs Gerrarde, Sidney's life would presumably have worked out. Cleary's introduction argues for Miss Burchell as a kind of 'other' to Sidney Bidulph – Miss Burchell is in touch with the dictates of the heart while Sidney continually represses her impulses. Indeed, as this edition's introduction implies, our ultimate interest in *The Memoirs of*

Miss Sidney Bidulph lies in its complex rendering of human psychology in dialogue with social ideology. In a move that bodes well for competing editions of novels already in print and for the revival of underappreciated works, *SNNTS* devoted a special issue to 'Editing Novels and Novelists, Now'. The eighteenth century was well represented in the issue. O M Brack Jr writes about 'Smollett's *Peregrine Pickle* Revisited' (*SNNTS* 27.260–72). Among the difficulties faced by Brack, who is editing the text of the novel for the Smollett edition being published by UGeoP, is whether to reproduce the first or the revised edition of the novel of 1758. Smollett both fixed stylistic problems and deleted text in his revision. Peregrine's character is 'darkened', but some of his practical jokes are eliminated. Smollett's revision also excised the novel's satirical portraits of Fielding and Garrick. (This edition was customarily reprinted until James Clifford decided upon the first edition for his 1964 edition for OUP.) Postmodern theories are appealing to Brack – he wants to produce both editions for a public and spends some time ruminating over the possibilities offered by electronic technology. He concludes that, practically speaking, one must 'privilege' the first edition for its comprehensiveness and historical significance. He will record the changes of 1758 in a textual apparatus. A more limited editorial decision is explored by Irving N. Rothman in 'Coleridge on the Semi-Colon in *Robinson Crusoe*: Problems in Editing Defoe' (*SNNTS* 27.320–40). Rothman considers the difficulties facing an editor of Defoe through an examination of the 'O Drug!' scene in the novel. Obviously, Coleridge's beloved semi-colon was not in any edition that appeared in Defoe's lifetime. Following Paula Backscheider, Rothman suggests that the attention Defoe paid to his texts may have caused compositors to follow the manuscript, even when punctuation was used inconsistently or illogically. Therefore, Coleridge's commentary is revealing about Coleridge but not about Defoe. The word 'use' in *Crusoe* is another problem: for no apparent reason, it is sometimes capitalized and sometimes in lower case. The diligent editor must nevertheless reproduce the eighteenth-century text, but Rothman suggests a way in which both an edition's accuracy and Coleridge's enthusiasm can be reconciled: the comma in the eighteenth-century editions later supplanted by the semi-colon had the effect of making the limited stop in the passage that Coleridge so admired, and so, argues Rothman, there really is no controversy. Jim Springer Borck's article in the same issue of *SNNTS*, 'Composed in Tears: The *Clarissa* Project' (*SNNTS* 2.341–50), looks at the economics and politics behind publishing decisions. Despite its melancholy title, Borck's essay is rather cheerful, even triumphant, in its explanation of the necessity of reproducing the complete third edition of the novel. Borck uses the opportunity to promote this edition and argue for the essentially typographical nature of Richardson's novel.

J. Paul Hunter and Marilyn Butler offer two more general approaches to opportunities created by new editions of eighteenth-century novelists. Hunter, in 'Editing for the Classroom: Texts in Context' (*SNNTS* 27.284–94), discusses the new series of undergraduate texts he is preparing for Bedford Books. Hunter sees great potential in an expanded format for reprints, including a basic amount of historical context and snippets from other literary works of the time, in order to illuminate if not explain away the 'strangeness' of a text like *Moll Flanders*. This is lucidly written and argued, and we should welcome Hunter's focus on the needs of undergraduate students and instructors. We should also thank Marilyn Butler for working hard to produce various editions of women writers. In 'Editing Women' (*SNNTS* 27.273–83), she argues passionately and intelligently in favour of the format adopted by Penguin of presenting well-edited texts with introductions by prominent scholars at an affordable price. However, she wants 'the whole loaf': cheap paperback editions *and* complete editions of important women novelists. In the case of Edgeworth, in particular, Butler wants to be sure that all of the major works – and not just those deemed economically feasible by Penguin and others – will be available to students and scholars.

Politically inflected criticism of one stripe or another continues to dominate scholarship and criticism in the field of eighteenth-century fiction. The categories of race, gender and empire continue to influence much of the most compelling work. Usually these categories are considered separately, as if the category under consideration determined by itself the world and its production of culture. However, Felicity A. Nussbaum's *Torrid Zones: Maternity, Sexuality, and Empire* ambitiously attempts to see all of these categories in complex relation. Nussbaum yokes together domestic narratives dealing with the lives of English women to British colonial narratives that make use of images of 'Other' women: Arabs, Africans, Indians. Her ultimate project, she explains, is the creation of an understanding of a 'postglobal feminist collectivity' that would function for women's interests without either participating in or abandoning the paradigms for 'freedom' and 'woman' set up by the texts of the Enlightenment that she discusses in the book. The results of her endeavours are mixed but always interesting, as she brings together fictional texts and purportedly non-fictional narratives in chapters that combine a historical approach with literary interpretations. Nussbaum argues that the 'torrid zones' of the colonies both open up British women to sexual freedom (to this end she looks at Lady Mary Wortley Montagu's letters from Turkey) *and* allow British women to define themselves against the colonial 'Other', thus bolstering an ideology of domesticity which is dependent upon hierarchies of class, race, gender, sexuality and disability. For example, Nussbaum analyses Phebe Gibbs's novel *Hartly House, Calcutta* in light of various narratives concering *sati*, the act in which Hindu women immolated themselves after the death of their husbands. Nussbaum is able to discuss the form and the meaning of *Hartly House* as a novel that 'uses' a colonial setting to play with notions of women's freedom in a context very different from the strictures back home while succumbing to the narrative demands of the form of the novel and the domestic ideology of safe marriage. And, of course, Nussbaum places her analysis in the controversy over the role of the East India Company and the trials of Warren Hastings. A chapter on 'feminotopias' is also interesting. Nussbaum does a critical reading of *Millenium Hall* that sees the community of women the novel sets up not only as liberating but also as complicitous in creating unfortunate differences: 'The invention of the "Other" woman of empire enabled the consolidation of the cult of domesticity in England and, at the same time, the association of the sexually transgressive woman at home – the prostitute, the lesbian, the asexual being – with the Orientalized exotic woman' (160). To this end she compares the novel to verses that celebrate 'lesbian' desire in eighteenth-century Britain. The most startling aspect of the chapter concerns the novel's treatment of people with 'deformities'. Nussbaum links the novel to William Hay's *Deformity: An Essay* (1754) and treatises on the sublime that deal with deformity, arguing that the novel is able to redefine deformity as beauty.

Not all of the chapters are so successful. The pairing of Johnson's *Life of Savage* with Mungo Park's account of African mothers, for example, seems forced, and does not tell us much new about biographies, the travel narratives, or eighteenth-century motherhood. Nussbaum spends so much time setting up her arguments that her critical readings seem aborted at times. An otherwise interesting account of *Fanny Hill* is marred by some unfortunate phrasemaking: 'Though her clitoris is through most of the novel a lower-class one . . . by the conclusion of the novel it has been raised to bourgeois status and fully domesticated' (105). Nussbaum's argument reaches its culmination in an epilogue beginning with Mary Wollstonecraft and ending with Trinh T. Minh-ha. It seems to me that Nussbaum and some of the more recent poststructuralist feminists she quotes are unduly harsh in their treatment of Wollstonecraft – but that is an argument perhaps outside of the boundaries of this essay.

Also discussing 'deformity' is one of the most interesting and original works produced in eighteenth-century scholarship this year, Dennis Todd's *Imagining Monsters: Miscreations of the Self in Eighteenth-Century England*. Beginning with the case of Mary Toft, Todd examines in more scrupulous detail than does Nussbaum the importance of monsters to the eighteenth-century imagination. While the book focuses more on Swift and Pope than on the period's fiction, the book will be interesting to scholars working on novels precisely because as Todd argues monstrosity is central to the more lurid aspects of literature; and just as Nussbaum focused on deformity in her study, so, too, does E. J. Clery in her study on the rise of the Gothic in the eighteenth century (see below). Whoever typeset Todd's book did so incompetently, however. UChicP should be ashamed.

Sarah Scott received further scholarly attention. Broadview, which has done an admirable job of printing long-ignored eighteenth-century novels, published an edition of Sarah Scott's novel, finely edited by Gary Kelly. Felicity Nussbaum's argument on *Millenium Hall* finds its echoes in articles published this year. First, Dorrice Williams Elliott offers 'Sarah Scott's *Millenium Hall* and Female Philanthropy' (*SEL* 35.535–53) in order to describe the form of philanthropy practised by Scott's female characters. Elliott offers a perfectly convincing, if not spectacularly novel, reading that argues against lesbian analyses. Elliott suggests that since conventional philanthropy always sexualized women, Scott's particular form of good work creates independence out of a negation of sexuality. In making her argument, Elliott relies upon a reading of the 'monstrous' women of *Millenium Hall*. Along similar lines is James Cruise's 'A House Divided: Sarah Scott's *Millenium Hall*' (*SEL* 35.555–73), which places the novel in the context of conduct literature. Cruise's article is well-written but does not take many interpretive risks. He argues that Sir George Ellison, the narrator of the novel, is the subject of this reversed conduct writing. The novel, argues Cruise, leaves suspended whether Ellison will learn properly from his experience among the women. Johanna M. Smith's 'Philanthropic Community in *Millenium Hall* and the York Ladies Committee' (*ECent* 36.266–82) appears in a special edition of *ECent* devoted to ideas of 'community'. Smith's somewhat pedestrian article compares Scott's novel to Catherine Cappe's report of her *Observations on*

Charity Schools, Female Friendly Societies, and other subjects (1805). Women, in Smith's view, are 'agents of change' in both, but Smith wishes to 'interrogate' this agency. Both communities evidently rely upon a distressing form of surveillance. Eve W. Stoddard rounds out the year's work on Sarah Scott with 'A Serious Proposal for Slavery Reform: Sarah Scott's *Sir George Ellison*' (*ECS* 28.379–96). Stoddard argues that despite appearance, and despite Moira Ferguson's recent work to the contrary, Scott's later novel can be considered anti-slavery in its intents and effects. The novel, Stoddard writes, uses precept rather than sentiment in order to argue fundamentally for human equality and for 'a reform of plantation management with an eye toward the eventual education and manumission of slaves' (383). One can sympathize with Stoddard's intentions and appreciate the historical context she brings to bear without being completely convinced.

Women's writing in general received a great deal of attention this year. Claudia L. Johnson's *Equivocal Beings: Politics, Gender, and Sentimentality in the 1790s* is the most important work on these issues that appeared. It is a witty and enjoyable analysis of some of the writings of Wollstonecraft, Radcliffe, Burney and Austen. Johnson argues that the cultural crisis in Britain caused by the French Revolution engendered a crisis over the forms and meanings of masculinity. Burke's appropriation of a traditionally feminine 'feeling' for a masculinity that would reject the cruelties of the French Revolution left little space for women, whose sentiment was disvalued insofar as it remained 'feminine'. (Johnson points to a history of male sentimentality prior to Burke's *Reflections on the Revolution in France*, but has space to discuss only Sterne, in her chapter on Burney's *Camilla*.) The writers Johnson studies reject traditional femininity and construct women characters who are 'equivocal beings', who either passively or actively occupy cultural space defined by rationality even as they must avoid being 'masculine' in the old-fashioned sense. Ultimately, the only psychologically or politically successful relationships these characters can have is with other women in a kind of proto-homoerotic social space. Johnson's readings of novels – she looks at Wollstonecraft's *Mary* and *The Wrongs of Woman*, Radcliffe's *The Romance of the Forest*, *The Mysteries of Udolpho* and *The Italian* and Burney's *Camilla* and *The Wanderer* after an analysis of Wollstonecraft's *Vindications* – are ingenious and illuminating, even if her insistence on forcing them into her scheme occasionally seems awkward. The analysis of *Camilla*, in particular, is the best I have seen; but when Johnson accuses *The Wanderer* of 'incoherence', I am not sure if it is Frances Burney's novel or Claudia Johnson's scheme that fails. Johnson ends her book with an 'afterword' on Austen's *Emma*, which most readers will wish were expanded. Johnson makes sense of the novel's new vision of masculinity, which Johnson argues harks back to a period before sentimental excess and the 1790s even as it embraces the new modes of economic production championed by Mr Knightley. Johnson is able to shed light upon twentieth-century critical controversies over the novel even as she remains sensitive to its literary structure. Johnson's book is essential reading for anyone interested in the novels of the last part of the eighteenth century.

Frances Burney continued to arouse interest this year. George E. Haggerty's 'A Friend, a Fop, and a Feminist: The Failure of Community in Burney' (*ECent* 36.248–65), also part of *ECent*'s special issue on 'community', argues

that Burney finds female autonomy and community mutually exclusive. Haggerty's reading of Burney's heroines' relationships with Monckton in *Cecilia*,
Sir Sedley Clarendel in *Camilla* and Elinor Joddrel in *The Wanderer* make his
point adequately, although he is a bit hard on Sir Sedley. In any case,
Haggerty's argument is a welcome relief from a strand of criticism that has
tended automatically to associate 'women' with 'community' in an unre-
flectively positive sense. Mary Severance argues in 'An Unerring Rule: The
Reformation of the Father in Frances Burney's *Evelina*' (*ECent* 36.119–38)
that 'in its epistolary relationship between a "more-than-father" and his
"more-than-daughter", *Evelina* participates in the symbolic mutation which
resulted in England's emergence as a modern nation' (120). Severance never
makes clear what she means by 'participates in' and this article exemplifies the
weakness of some 'theoretical' approaches that use ambiguous language and
jargon to make connections that are forced at best and irrelevant at worst.

Burney and economics has been an important issue, especially after Edward
Copeland's recent work on the subject of women and money. Two articles
take complementary views. In 'Courting Ruin: The Economic Romances of
Frances Burney' (*Novel* 28.131–53), Miranda J. Burgess attempts to tie
together the Donaldson v. Becket decision on copyright, the consumer explosion (or lack thereof) of the eighteenth century, and the form of Burney's
novels, which the author sees as eschewing both the sentimental and the Whig
in favour of a stern Toryism. In particular, Burgess discusses the 'market' for
sensibility, and the ability of some to 'put on' tears or other sentimental traits
for a market that consumed them. Burgess disagrees with Claudia Johnson,
Kristina Straub and others who have seen Burney's novels as 'divided fictions'. Instead, she sees them as 'coherent wholes', insofar as they protest the
intrusion of commerce into private relations. Timothy Dykstal's '*Evelina* and
the Culture Industry' (*Criticism* 37.559–81) puts forward the notion that
Burney's first novel fits more into Adorno's scheme of the 'culture industry'
than Habermas's 'public sphere'. Dykstal argues in a perceptive reading that
the novel rejects a public sphere based on 'spectacle' and supports instead a
private culture of reading that avoids coercion. Rounding out work on
Burney, E. W. Pilcher points out in 'Frances Burney's *Cecilia* and the "Q in
the Corner"' (*N&Q* 42.71– 2) that there might be a real critic lurking behind
a piece of criticism brought to attention by the character Gosport. Pilcher
suggests, plausibly I suppose, that Gosport could be modelled on this critic
unidentifed but for his penname.

Ann Radcliffe receives updated and common-sense treatment in Robert
Miles's *Ann Radcliffe: The Great Enchantress*. Miles's book is pitched at the
upper level undergraduate or postgraduate student in literature, and the work
admirably fulfils its aims of being both comprehensive and useful and of
making its own strong argument. Occasionally the writing lacks polish, and
Miles's attempt to make all twentieth-century theory tie together neatly in
Radcliffe's 'female Gothic' becomes too pat. Yet his argument that Radcliffe's
works are both culturally significant and aesthetically interesting works. Miles
attributes Radcliffe's success not only to the historical and literary historical
movements of the 1790s but to Radcliffe's internal conflict forced by 'stresses
between the proper lady and the woman writer' (176). Anne Williams's *Art of
Darkness*, on the other hand, is an overwrought attempt to dehistoricize the
'cognitive structure' (17) of the Gothic and draw links between formally

diverse texts based on their relationship to this 'complex' (23). Outdated words like 'mode' and 'genre' are not expansive enough to contain the Gothic, which 'systematically represents "otherness"' (18). Here is an example of Williams's technique, this from a passage in an interesting, if unconvincing, chapter on *Bluebeard*: 'And so he forbids her the room in order to be sure that she will open the door, for the contents of the room represent patriarchy's secret, founding "truth" about the female: women as mortal, expendable matter/*mater*. Sexual "difference" is indeed the "key" to the secrets of the patriarchal power structure' (43). Eighteenth-century novels Williams treats include *The Mysteries of Udolpho* and *The Monk*. Interest in the Gothic might stem both from the women writers who practised the genre and from its literary oddities. The best book to appear on the Gothic this year was E. J. Clery's *The Rise of Supernatural Fiction, 1762–1800*. The book ties the vogue for supernatural fictions to the consumer revolution of the second half of the eighteenth century. Clery thus traces a shift in the fundamental cultural meaning of narratives that treat of supernatural events. In the beginning of the period under discussion, Clery argues, the primary issues raised by the supernatural involved belief and disbelief: Dr Johnson's investigation of the Cock Lane Ghost serves as the crucial moment in which serious discussion of philosophical, social and religious implications of the existence and representation of the supernatural give way to an economically driven vogue of supernaturalism. Clery spends most of the rest of the book discussing the cultural mechanisms of the spread of the consumption of supernatural fictions and providing tentative reasons *why* an increasingly consumer-driven economy would turn to the Gothic.

The literary thread of the book leads from a prehistory of the literary supernatural to an extensive and interesting discussion of competing Gothic fictions of the 1790s. The most interesting portion of the book discusses the mass production of the Gothic by the Minerva Press in the 1790s. Clery is able to tie together aesthetic conceptions of the sublime, the material workings of the literary marketplace, and political implications of both the consumer economy and the representations of supernatural powers. Thus she looks at the debate between Radcliffean 'explained Gothic' and the straightforward presentation of the supernatural world in, for example, Lewis's *The Monk* in terms of the literary market. She ends her study with an analysis of the similarity between both of these traditions of the Gothic and the political philosophy of Godwin in *Caleb Williams*. Enlightenment, which Clery had associated with early resistance to supernatural fictions, has come to use its conventions to represent aspects of political power. CUP's new series on Romanticism, of which Clery's book is a part, includes a number of books more properly on eighteenth-century topics. One wonders about the logic of discontinuing their series on eighteenth-century culture when the field remains so energetic.

One of the best pieces of scholarship this year focuses on issues raised by Clery's book. Edward Jacobs's 'Anonymous Signatures: Circulating Libraries, Conventionality, and the Production of Gothic Romances' (*ELH* 65.603–29) talks of circulating libraries as active publishers of books in the last quarter of the eighteenth century. Jacobs wishes to avoid old conceptions that associated circulating libraries with the lower literary classes of both readers and writers. Instead he associates novelistic conventions with the marketplace for popular books. He draws on the catalogues of the circulating libraries of Lowndes (1766) and M. Heavisides (1790) to establish a field of fiction produced and distributed in this novel fashion. This essay offers a better account than does Clery's book of the relationship between Gothic fiction and the literary marketplace. In his argument about Frances Burney and Ann Radcliffe, Jacobs contends that Burney imitated Richardson while Radcliffe was a 'novel' kind of novel writer. The article discusses reviews in the 1790s of the two novelists' writings, concluding that attacks on Radcliffe were 'paradoxical' in that they attacked her both for novelty and conventionality (622).

Other work on the Gothic trod more conventional critical ground. Emily Jane Cohen's 'Museums of the Mind: The Gothic and the Art of Memory' (*ELH* 62.883–905) argues cleverly that the Gothic creates in the eighteenth century especially 'memorable' images that serve to construct identity. It thus corresponds to the 'art of artificial memory'. Cohen discusses tourism and interest in the English past from 1770–1830. She ends with a defence of sorts of the genre: 'If the Gothic novel seems repetitive, it is simply performing its duty by attempting to combat the corrosive effects of time' (901). In 'Interpolated Poetry, the Novel, and Female Accomplishment' (*PQ* 74.57–76), Nathaniel Paradise looks at the poetry included in women's novels of the eighteenth century arguing that it 'should be seen in the context of the century's ongoing debate about female education and abilities. Novelists used poetry to claim status, challenging their culture's gendering of both genre and intellect as they incorporated verse in a public and self-conscious display of female learning and accomplishment' (57). Paradise discusses Radcliffe, Charlotte Smith and others in order to talk both about the representation of female characters and the form of the novel.

Frances Brooke's novels are beginning to receive greater attention, especially in the light of her transatlantic career and her contemporary popularity. Julie Ellison discusses both Brooke and fellow bi-continental Charlotte Lennox in 'There and Back: Transatlantic Novels and Anglo-American Careers' as a contribution to *The Past as Prologue: Essays to Celebrate the Twenty-Fifth Anniversary of ASECS* (ed. Carla H. Hay and Syndy M. Conger). Ellison suggests that 'intellectual workers' who plied their trade in two continents 'understood [their] careers, and the whole process of emigration (and possible return), as propelled by the economic insecurity of the relatively genteel'. The article discusses Brooke's *Emily Montague*, Lennox's *Euphemia* and Gilbert Imlay's *The Emigrants*, noting that all three rely upon a 'there and back' plot.

Kate Levin's excellent ' "The Cure of Arabella's Mind": Charlotte Lennox and the Disciplining of the Female Reader' (*WomW* 2.271–90) adds to the substantial body of work recently appearing on Lennox. Levin places the seemingly harsh 'cure' of Lennox's heroine in the context of Lennox's literary career, which had been characterized by contemporary critical attacks upon the alleged immorality of her poems and early novels. In effect, Levin argues, the move to '"regulate" rather than "suppress," "restrain" rather than "subdue"' (285) marks a marketing strategy through which Lennox could become critically accepted and commercially successful. Levin's analysis is both historically informed and critically perceptive and provides a welcome respite from simplistic debates over Lennox's feminism. Cynthia Richards reaches back earlier in the century in ' "The Pleasures of Complicity": Sympathetic Identification and the Female Reader in Early Eighteenth-Century Women's Amatory Fiction' (*ECent* 36.220–33). This article, yet another essay in *ECent*'s special issue on 'community', argues that moments of female identification in novels by Behn, Haywood and others, create bonds that supersede the stories actually told from one woman to another. 'Desire' is deflected from men to the women telling scandalous stories.

Sarah Fielding, too, received some attention this year. Stewart J. Cooke's ' "Good Heads and Good Hearts": Sarah Fielding's Moral Romance' (*ESC* 21.268–82) is a fairly straightforward reading of *David Simple* with a good deal of historical background of Sarah Fielding. Cooke calls the novel a 'moral romance' to differentiate it from both her brother Henry Fielding's and Samuel Richardson's novels, and he discusses the novel's unhappy ending as, in a sense, realistic. Arlene Fish Wilner offers 'Education and Ideology in Sarah Fielding's *The Governess*' (*SECC* 24.307– 27), which argues the uncontroversial thesis that Fielding's novel was relatively conservative. The more interesting aspect of Wilner's article focuses on *The Governess* as a children's novel in the context of the inculcation of 'middle class values' in eighteenth-century children's literature. The refreshing moment in the article occurs when Wilner suggests that to Fielding, 'female friendship and community become yet another aspect of enforced passivity and submission' (314). Terri Nickel gave us a clever cultural reading in ' "Ingenious Torment": Incest, Family, and the Structure of Community in the Work of Sarah Fielding' (*ECent* 36.234–247). This article suggests that the only kind of community Fielding can create is through shared suffering, and since this suffering comes from violations to or even the dismantling of communities, 'community can only reproduce itself as the object of an impossible desire' (246).

Of course, scholars still write about Fielding's brother Henry. Jill Campbell's *Natural Masques: Gender and Identity in Fielding's Plays and Novels* marks, one hopes, a renewed viability for book-length studies on Fielding. Campbell's work functions in the high-powered tradition of Michael McKeon, John Bender and Nancy Armstrong's recent analyses of the eighteenth-century novel. Campbell is interested in charting a development in Fielding's career, from an early period in which gender distinctions were natural and easy, to a struggle with the 'constructedness' of gender that affects the very form of the novel. The strongest chapters in this work discuss Fielding's creation of a novel from the parodic form used in *Shamela*. The close reading of *Joseph Andrews*, in particular, is noteworthy. Later chapters discuss Fielding's handling of gender in *Tom Jones* and the *Jacobite's Journal* and then 'Female Heroism in *Amelia*'. Campbell draws useful attention to Fielding's self-conscious deployment of gender for literary and political effect, even if she occasionally seems insensitive to Fielding's pervasive irony. (In this Campbell is not alone among recent prominent critics – when critics are more concerned with the 'issues' underlying Fielding's fiction they sometimes forget to emphasize the comic aspect of his writing.)

Fielding also received general treatment in articles by Gary Gautier and Bertrand A. Goldgar. Goldgar's 'Fielding on Fiction and History' (*ECF* 7.279–92) attacks recent critics who say that Fielding disputes the possibility of 'history' in his fictional career. Goldgar's article places Fielding in the context of a historiographical tradition that he knew well. Fielding's attacks on history and historians, suggests Goldgar, are 'playful'. Instead of being sceptical about a difference between fiction and history, Fielding enjoyed history and tried to keep the two fields separate. Goldgar's edgy writing and knowledge are much appreciated. Gautier's 'Marriage and Family in Fielding's Fiction' (*SNNTS* 27.111–28) is a useful survey of the representations of marriage in Fielding's career, arguing that Fielding's views should be understood as basically conservative, but flexible.

Raymond D. Tumbleson's 'The Novel's Progress: Faction, Fiction, and Fielding' (*SNNTS* 27.12–25) makes an ambitious argument primarily about *Tom Jones* and the history of the novel. Tumbleson argues that the 'extreme skepticism' associated by Michael McKeon with Fielding works only until *Tom Jones*, at which point Fielding expresses wholehearted approval for British values (thus forgetting the brutal history leading up to the modern British state). Much of Tumbleson's argument is made by a contrast between *Tom Jones* and Fielding's anti-Jacobite pamphlets; the novel, suggests Tumbleson, erases the past rather than engaging with it. All 'literature itself as an ideological system is heir to a methodical forgetting' (21). Well, maybe. Betty Rizzo's 'The Gendering of Divinity in *Tom Jones*' (*SECC* 24.259–77) makes a perceptive argument on the contrast between 'Fortune' and 'Providence' in the novel. By the end, Tom develops morally while Sophia learns how to 'lie, flatter, and manipulate' (273). These skills are desirable for women, and in Sophia's case align her more with the attributes assigned to Fortune. Fielding 'constructed a universe of which the deity itself provided a blueprint for male-female relations and justified masculine privilege' (275). Some excellent work on the law and *Tom Jones* was produced by William G. Sayres. 'A Loophole in the Law: The Case of Black George and the Purse in *Tom Jones*' (*JEPG* 94.207–19) examines an analogy between Black George's unpunishable crime of taking Tom's purse with its £500 and the treatment of Sophia Western as property by her domineering father. Sayres's piece successfully combines literary analysis and legal history in order to conclude that 'Since the Black George case ultimately fails to provide Fielding with the legal paradigm he needs to support Allworthy's call for legal restraint on Western's authority over Sophia, the case appears to be dismissed, despite Allworthy's moralizing, when the defendant "runs away", as the novel's closure also seems to run away from the author' (219). The ending of the novel, Sayres suggests, resists interpretation as Sophia has escaped the grasp of her creator.

Amelia was particularly interesting to scholars and critics this year. Alison Conway's 'Fielding's *Amelia* and the Aesthetics of Virtue' (*ECF* 8.35–50) is an intelligent and elegant analysis of Fielding's characterization of Amelia. Conway focuses on two elements: Amelia's nose (which in its defect becomes an emblem of perfect moral beauty) and the portrait miniature, which is a 'precious object' both for the diamonds and gold in the frame and for the representation of Amelia's beauty. George E. Haggerty also honed in on Amelia's nose. His 'Amelia's Nose: Or, Sensibility and its Symptoms' (*ECent* 36.139–56) discusses the political valences of developing ideas of sensibility in the eighteenth century. First, Haggerty discusses Sterne and Mackenzie, who link sensibility to new forms of sexuality – to androgyny. Then Haggerty speaks of Amelia, whose nose 'gives the lie to sentimental feeling' (152). The article is amusing, if not wholly illuminating. Elizabeth Kraft takes a more literary historical tack in 'The Two Amelias: Henry Fielding and Elizabeth

Justice' (*ELH* 62.313–28), which discusses the publication histories and contents of the identically titled novels by both writers. Kraft relies on 'postmodern thought' (313) to suggest that the novels are of similar quality, and that both novels reveal the power imbalances of eighteenth-century marriage. A complex history of the eighteenth-century novel, Kraft rightly suggests, would take into account a balance between market conditions and literary form, just as Justice and Fielding's novels both concern a relationship between 'aestheticism' and 'commodification'.

Of note here as well is a book not exactly on Fielding's fiction, even if both 'Fielding' and the 'novel' are partly its subjects. Judith Moore's *The Appearance of Truth: The Story of Elizabeth Canning and Eighteenth-Century Narrative* (published in 1994 but not mentioned in *YWES* 75) is part scholarly detective work and part fluid interpretation. Moore makes a persuasive argument that the kind of narrative exemplified by, for example, the *Genuine and Impartial Memoirs of Elizabeth Canning* resists the theoretical frameworks laid out for eighteenth-century writing by Lennard Davis or Michael McKeon. To that effect, Moore begins to develop a theory of eighteenth-century narrative informed by rhetoric – but the book is more than worthwhile as well for its compelling unpacking of the case's legal and cultural history.

Richardson has recently garnered more critical attention than his rival. Richard Gooding treats both writers in his compelling article, '*Pamela, Shamela* and the Politics of the *Pamela* Vogue' (*ECF* 7.109–30). Gooding argues that the political aspects of the post-publication debate over the meaning of Richardson's novel were as important as the oft-discussed moral aspects. Gooding discusses both the pro-Pamela and anti-Pamela responses to the initial publication and concludes that even some of the pro-Pamela writings, especially John Kelly's *Pamela's Conduct in High Life*, do not understand the point of the novel, which was to erase class lines by creating a complex psychology for Pamela. The article goes on to discuss *Shamela*, crediting it with taking strong shots at Richardson but criticizing it for ultimately failing to understand what Richardson was up to. In 'Pamela's Textual Authority' (*ECF* 7.131–46), John B. Pierce discusses Richardson's heroine's use of language. Since Pamela has no social authority she must rely upon her textual authority. Thus there are echoes of the psalms and of fables that lend credibility – authority – to what Pamela writes. This becomes authoritative 'objective evidence' in a world that is moving to print culture from oral culture. As with Gooding's article, this is interesting and well-written, if not startlingly original. Toni Bowers discusses Pamela, but in her later adventures, in her article, '"A Point of Conscience": Breastfeeding and Maternal Authority in *Pamela 2*' (*ECF* 7.259–278). Bowers discusses the quality of the debate between Pamela and her surly spouse and concludes that even though the novel has Mr B. prevail, and the couple hire a wetnurse, Pamela's arguments are persuasive in favour of breastfeeding. The debate, though, is really over who controls a woman's body. Mr B. wins, but his patriarchal authority is undercut by Pamela's arguments. Bowers ties this to the form of the novel – critics have not liked *Pamela 2*, but Bowers reads this aesthetic judgement politically. She concludes that Richardson's continuation contributes to a patriarchal structure still at work today. In 'The Dialectic of Love in *Sir Charles Grandison*' (*ECF* 8.15–34), Wendy Jones puts Richardson's hero through an invasive analysis. Sir Charles, says Jones, is stuck in a 'dialectic' between companionate and sentimental love, thus accounting for his own divided attentions. The reading of the novel is competent, but suffers from the all-too-common desire of some critics to 'explain away' features of fiction by assigning them rigidly to features apparently possessed by 'culture' writ large.

Spurred on perhaps by the aforementioned *Clarissa Project*, critics continued to turn their attention to Richardson's great novel. The best work was done by Murray L. Brown in '*Emblemata Rhetorica*: Glossing Emblematic Discourse in Richardson's *Clarissa*' (*SNNTS* 27.455–76). Brown's argument is both traditional in its attention to literary history and contemporary in its aggressive stance towards much of the recent writing on *Clarissa*, by critics such as Terry Eagleton and Terry Castle (although William Warner's absence from the bulk of Brown's argument is conspicuous). Brown analyses the 'dialogic struggle' between Clarissa and Lovelace over the meaning of emblems that were popular in the eighteenth century. Richardson ultimately wants to see the emblems as 'unitary and sacrosanct' (455), thus endorsing Clarissa's view of her situation. The emblems comprise a 'metalanguage' which fixes the meaning of the novel and definitively refutes Lovelace's epistolary voice. Brown discusses hearts, avian symbols and the lily. This is an interesting article with important implications for interpretation; it brings to the attention of the modern reader a literary structure that affects our understanding of the novel's situation and makes us see the dense literary texture of the novel. Modern readers less familiar with the tradition Brown relies on might remain unconvinced, as would many of the novel's eighteenth-century readers, but the article is well worth a reading. In 'Deconstructing Richardson. Terry Castle and *Clarissa*'s Ciphers' (*ES* 76.520–31), D. C. Rain joins in the attack upon contemporary readings whose methods deny *Clarissa* the coherence one might wish for. As his piece's title would indicate, Rain engages in a direct attack upon Terry Castle's book on Richardson, taking issue with an 'anything goes' attitude he associates with deconstructive readings. He succeeds at ridiculing Castle, but his attack seems oddly timed. Unlike Brown, Rain has little positive to add to our knowledge of *Clarissa*, and this argument would have made more sense as a review of her book than as an independent article. Two other articles focused on *Clarissa*. Joy Kyunghae Lee gave us 'The Commodification of Virtue: Chastity and the Virginal Body in Richardson's *Clarissa*' (*ECent* 36.38–54) and Leila S. May 'The Violence of the Letter: *Clarissa* and Familial Bo(u)nds' (*ELN* 32.24–32). Lee takes a densely theoretical approach, using Irigaray and Lukacs to argue that Richardson creates Clarissa as an oxymoronically embodied abstraction of virtue; she goes on to situate this notion of virtue in the historical terms set out by Michael McKeon. May's article is also based in various kinds of theory, in this case Lévi-Strauss, Saussure and Lacan. She argues, quite startlingly, that Clarissa hungrily collects kin, creating bonds wherever she goes, and that her death represents in linguistic/psychoanalytic terms 'the anarchial wish for the destruction of civilization' (30). Finally, Paula Backscheider writes in '"The Woman's Part": Richardson, Defoe, and the Horrors of Marriage' (part of *The Past as Prologue: Essays to Celebrate the Twenty-Fifth Anniversary of ASECS*) about a thematic and material connection between the two early novelists. She argues that Richardson used Defoe's *Religious Courtship*, which he helped print, in the construction of *Clarissa*. Backscheider notes the similarities between the two texts, and then argues through some of the implications of Richardson's basing his novel on such conduct literature. The reading of the literature here is probing and sympathetic.

Defoe, as always, was the subject of strong work. Sandra Sherman in particular wrote a few important articles, two of which discuss Defoe's fiction: 'Lady Credit No Lady; or, The Case of Defoe's "Coy Mistress," Truly Stat'd' (*TSLL* 37.185–214) and 'Commercial Paper, Commercial Fiction: "The Compleat English Tradesman" and Defoe's Reluctant Novels' (*Criticism* 37.391–411). Both are ingenious and thought provoking, if of similar content and procedure. The first spends most of its space discussing the figure 'Lady Credit' in Defoe's *Review* and other tracts, before turning to Roxana, who, like Lady Credit, inserts herself fictionally into the marketplace. Even the form of the novel is affected by the pervasive influence of the economic model: it aspires towards nonresolution, although in its affecting ending the novel 'is romance abruptly closed' (202). The other, even more significant piece lays out a broad framework of analysis relating Defoe's fiction to his writings on economic matters. The truth-claims Defoe gives us in the novels are related to his defences of credit and his attacks upon straightforward accounting, which do not mirror reality as faithfully as is assumed. The characters, too, are not liars in a conventional sense. Rather they illustrate that, in Sherman's term, reading is 'perilous'. It was a big year for Defoe's fiction and economics. Ann Louise Kibbie's 'Monstrous Generation: The Birth of Capital in Defoe's *Moll Flanders* and *Roxana*' (*PMLA* 110.1023–34) covers some of the same ground. In the two novels, 'usury' is transformed to 'capital' through the means of the woman's body. Kibbie reads the 'Amy' episode as indicative of Roxana's 'incipient monstrosity, predicated on and signaled by barrenness – the monstrosity of capital' (1030). Kibbie writes, 'For Defoe, both capital and fiction are forms of an imaginary increase that consumes the self' (1031). This is interesting stuff, but not as persuasive as Sherman's similar arguments.

Robinson Crusoe was discussed by several critics. In '"My Savage," "My Man"': Racial Multiplicity in *Robinson Crusoe*' (*ELH* 62.821–61), Roxanne Wheeler discusses the range of racial identifications in Defoe's novel, arguing that a simple black/white distinction is historically inaccurate and insensitive, too, to the fictional representations. The article meanders a bit, but when it focuses on the moments when Defoe's narrative downplays the evils of slavery by individualizing the plights of Xury, Friday and so forth, it achieves its aims. Frank Donoghue's 'Inevitable Politics: Rulership and Identity in *Robinson Crusoe*' (*SNNTS* 27.1–11) is an intelligent, if not groundbreaking, close reading of Crusoe's identities as a ruler. Donoghue focuses on unsuccessful moments of public and private self-construction, arguing that they are forced by historical circumstances including geographical and political pressures. Cameron McFarlane's 'Reading Crusoe Reading Providence' (*ESC* 21.257–67) is a very clever reading of Defoe's novel that suggests that at many key moments *Robinson Crusoe* becomes about reading, about interpretation, rather than remaining an opaque representation of events. The novel is 'anxious' about how to read Providence into the occurrences of life. This can be seen, for example, at the crucial moment in which Friday asks Crusoe why God does not kill the Devil. David Fausett's *The Strange Surprizing Sources of Robinson Crusoe*, argues that the ultimate source for Defoe's novel was an obscure Dutch work, *The Mighty Kingdom of Krinke Kesmes* by Hendrik

Smeets. Within a conventional political allegory, Smeets included the story of a character named El-ho, who is stranded while taking part in a voyage to Australia. Fausett relies upon literary analysis of the form of the novel as well as on the continental traditions he cites to impress upon his readers Defoe's debt to predecessors. Fausett argues that Defoe's rendering of the story indicates a shift from political allegory to 'realistic fiction'. One does not have to agree with Fausett's ends to appreciate the work he has done here, although the book reminds me occasionally of the overemotional tracts upon Shakespeare's authorship that periodically appear than of the best work that has been done on Defoe in the previous 30 years.

The most important piece of work on Defoe, though, and perhaps the most enjoyable and useful thing published in scholarship on the eighteenth-century novel this year, is David Blewett's *The Illustration of 'Robinson Crusoe',
1719–1820*. The book does more than survey, with copious reproductions, the variety of illustrations of Defoe's novel in its first two centuries. The history of the illustrations has an intrinsic interest, which Blewett's selection and explanation heighten. But, in addition, this book provides a cultural history of the reception of the novel. Blewett sets out his purpose concisely: 'The illustrations of *Robinson Crusoe* record several tales. First, the critical esteem in which the novel was held; then, the way in which each generation saw a reflection of itself in the strange, surprising adventures of Defoe's hero; and, finally, the development of a pictorial tradition in which artists and engravers responded both to new techniques and to changing views of the nature and function of illustration itself' (11). The history of the illustrations reveals that the French perceived the merit of the novel before the English – and, as Blewett argues, that the French used illustrations to emphasize a Rousseauean state-of-nature in the novel. In nineteenth-century France, Crusoe became a monumental figure, as the remarkable frontispieces by Grandville (1840) and Fesquet (1877) show. The former depicts a colossal statue of Crusoe 'on a plinth decorated with the head of Friday, while below parents bring their children to wonder at the sight' (79). The Fesquet frontispiece depicts a godlike Crusoe with sword in one hand, orb in the other and his foot placed firmly on the head of a supine native. The French illustrations are much more interesting than the English, which tend to emphasize in turn the social, the religious and the contemplative natures of our hero. By the end of the nineteenth century *Robinson Crusoe* in English was a book for boys, and the illustrations turn the novel (generally printed as what we know as parts I and II of the novel) into an innocent adventure story. What emerges from Blewett's fascinating account most strongly is the inadequacy of nearly all the illustrations. As interpretations or amplifications, most of them are weak or 'inaccurate' even. Blewett makes the case successfully that the classic status of the novel in part derives from the endless ambition of illustrators to capture or interpret the novel, and their inevitable failure. The novel both exceeds the grasp of the illustrators and presents a palimpsest for them to record their view of their nations' literature and culture. I do love, though, the N. C. Wyeth painting that the publishers reproduce on the back cover of the book's jacket: 'All this while I sat upon the ground, very much terrified and dejected'. Superb.

Tobias Smollett also received book-length treatment this year. Aileen Douglas's *Uneasy Sensations: Smollett and the Body* is a very welcome analysis of its subject. The book, however, is uneven. The chapters that focus on politics are more successful in general than those that focus on gender, although Douglas's look at Lady Vane's Memoirs in *Peregrine Pickle* is excellent. The most interesting parts of the book are on lesser-known works of Smollett, *Sir Launcelot Greaves* and *The History and Adventures of an Atom*. In both cases, Douglas is able to account for aspects of Smollett's writing that seem unaccountable to present tastes by focusing on their political dimensions. Along the way, Douglas is able to express clearly how Smollett's disgust with those who mistreat the body can combat those who might view Foucault's *Discipline and Punish*, for example, as a kind of nostalgia for the bad old days. Douglas's book will not only make us understand Smollett better, but also the physical tradition which he is a part of. For example, we will be able to see Frances Burney's Smollettian moments not as an aberration but as an intensification of her compassionate social satire in a novel like *Evelina*. One article stands out in its look at Smollett. Pamela Cantrell's 'Writing the Picture: Fielding, Smollett, and Hogarthian Pictorialism' (*SECC* 24.69–89) persuasively argues that despite both historical associations and scholarly commentary, Smollett more successfully than Fielding adapts Hogarthian clements in his prose. Through an excellent close comparison of scenes in Smollett's novels and engravings by Hogarth, Cantrell suggests that Smollett and Hogarth both 'meant to break from tradition in order to create a composite modern form' (70).

Smollett's rival Laurence Sterne was the subject of a greater amount of study in this year. Michael Rosenblum's 'Why What Happens in Shandy Hall Is Not "A Matter for the Police"' (*ECF* 7.147–64) is an ambitious theoretical look at the association of 'narrative' with 'law', focusing on the minute particulars of eighteenth-century novelistic narrative, specifically *Tristram Shandy* and its elaborated time scheme. Rosenblum believes critics have become overeager to assimilate all narrative within the eighteenth century to a forensic model. Through a comparison of Sterne to Fielding (the writer most often associated with such a model, particularly in the analysis of John Bender in *Imagining the Penitentiary*), Rosenblum argues that 'Sterne's circumstantially dense representational space' argues against theories of narrative in which details considered 'relevant' point merely to guilt or innocence. This article is well worth a read. In '"weavers, gardeners, and gladiators": Labyrinths in *Tristram Shandy*' (*ECS* 28.397–411), Stephen Soud examines the uses of the 'labyrinth' and the 'maze' in Sterne's novel. The piece is careful and well-presented though it covers familiar territory. *The Shandean* as usual offers a number of interesting articles on Sterne. The lead article this year is by Duncan Large. '"The Freest Writer": Nietzsche on Sterne' (*Shandean* 7.9–29) is a careful analysis of the German philosopher's references to Sterne and, more significantly, an exploration of Sterne's influence on his thinking and prose. Also in this volume, W. G. Day gives us 'Michael Angelo Rooker's Illustrations to *Tristram Shandy*' (*Shandean* 7.30–42), which reproduces the art as well as correcting the *DNB*'s account of Rooker. Day argues that Rooker was interested in Sterne beyond financial considerations. Martha Bowden's 'The Liturgical Shape of Life at Shandy Hall' (*Shandean* 7.43–60) argues that Sterne relies upon the Book of Common Prayer in moments when the practical theology of Trim and Toby are given precedence in the text over Walter's pedantic obsession with Slawkenbergius. Bowden focuses on particular rites to make her claims, which are interesting if a touch humourless. Fred C. Pinnegar argues from medical evidence in 'The Groin Wounds of Tristram and Uncle Toby' (*Shandean* 7.87–100) that Toby is not physically impotent and that Tristram's own physical status in the book is not resolved. Pinnegar musters impressive evidence from medical tracts of the time and a close reading of the text for his assertions, but his conclusions are a tad less convincing. For Pinnegar, sexuality and creativity in the novel are in alignment, and therefore Toby's failure with the widow Wadman stems from an overwhelming fear: death overcomes life. In addition, the cartoonist Martin Rowson in 'Hyperboling Gravity's Ravelin: A Comic Book Version of Tristram Shandy' (*Shandean* 7.62–86) presents the material circumstances, personal motivations and a generous sampling of frames for his forthcoming version of *Tristram Shandy*.

Sterne's fellow sentimentalists received a fair portion of attention this year. Barbara M. Benedict's book *Framing Feeling: Sentiment and Style in English Prose Fiction, 1745–1800* is an ambitious look at the device of framing in many eighteenth-century sentimental novels. Benedict suggests that this particular device contains the radical potential of sentiment and turns novels into conservative documents. Private feeling is communicated only through self-conscious devices that enforce perspective upon an observing public. Benedict examines a wide range of eighteenth-century texts, including *The Female Spectator* and *Amelia*; *The Vicar of Wakefield* and *The Fool of Quality*; *Tristram Shandy* and *A Sentimental Journey*; Frances Brooke's *History of Julia Mandeville* and *History of Emily Montague*; *The Man of Feeling*; and *The Romance of the Forest* and *The Mysteries of Udolpho*. She concludes with a look at *Sense and Sensibility*. The strengths of this study are also its weaknesses. Benedict covers so much ground that the analyses of the fictional works seem scattered, and apart from the attention paid to 'framing', one is not sure how the book fits together. Nevertheless, it will find an audience in those interested in the relationship between sentiment and the novel in eighteenth-century English literature.

Benedict speaks more directly upon the topic of physiognomy in relation to sentimentality in 'Reading Faces: Physiognomy and Epistemology in Late Eighteenth-Century Sentimental Novels' (*SP* 92.311–28). She looks at some of the novels discussed in her book to explain the re-emergence of physiognomy late in the century as well as its change in meaning. In the cases she describes, physiognomy appropriated sentimentally causes an observer to turn inward, to reflect and feel. In ' "Above oeconomy": Elizabeth Griffin's *The History of Lady Barton* and Henry Mackenzie's *The Man of Feeling*' (*ECLife* 19.1–17), Gillian Skinner ponders the possibility presented in the phrase quoted in her title by sentimental fiction. Can women ever exist 'above' their oeconomic (in the eighteenth-century term) cares? Alas, the answer seems to be 'no'. Jayne Lewis's ' "Every Lost Relation": Historical Fictions and Sentimental Incidents in Sophia Lee's *The Recess*' (*ECF* 7.165–84) is a very interesting analysis not only of *The Recess* but of the development of the genres of 'novel' and 'history' at the end of the eighteenth century. The piece may overstate the importance of Lee's novel, but it makes persuasive claims for the effects of a late eighteenth-century understanding of history 'in affective terms'. Timothy Dykstal's 'The Story of O: Politics and Pleasure in *The Vicar of Wakefield*' (*ELH* 62.329–46) approaches its topic with gusto.

Dykstal discusses the relationship between the Vicar of Wakefield's 'house' (in its many senses) and his belief in political patriarchy. Dykstal seeks to consider the 'wishes' of Olivia as opposed to the positions of Squire Thornhill and the Vicar, who see her as 'property'. Female sexuality cannot be contained by systems of alliance. Olivia, indeed, only possesses subjectivity as an expression of her sexuality; the end of the novel brings her back into the system of exchange. Dykstal writes, 'The weakness in the Vicar's political theory, then, is its failure to account for the power of sexuality (specifically of woman's sexuality) – in a word, of pleasure' (343). Following up on Dykstal's title, if not his argument, are one article on John Cleland and one more generally on eighteenth-century pornography. In 'Fanny Hill's Mapping of Sexuality, Female Identity, and Maternity' (*SEL* 35.473–91), Gary Gautier relates Cleland's 'remapping' of categories of sexuality, female identity and maternity to a supposed anti-bourgeois political position. Cleland's satire, Gautier suggests, puts forward the bourgeois reifying of the sexual organs but attacks it. (The return of Nussbaum's 'bourgeois, domesticated clitoris'?) This essay seems to assume that a reading of *Fanny Hill* can reveal many hidden secrets of eighteenth-century culture, but it fails to put Cleland's work in sufficient literary historical perspective. James Grantham Turner's '*The Whores Rhetorick*: Narrative, Pornography, and Origins of the Novel' (*SECC* 24.297-306), on the other hand, reads pornography as integral to the development of the novel in the eighteenth century. Pornography (literally, Turner reminds us, writing about prostitutes) meets rhetoric in a few seventeenth-century texts. Both, Turner suggests, are based in 'arousal', although it is difficult to imagine that the same parts of a person are affected. The essay discusses the particularized character going through a wrenching crisis as a hallmark of the novel, suggesting that this device first appeared as a 'whore's trick'. This is a useful corrective for those who wish to talk about pornography but refuse to talk about its material effects upon the reader – but, still, this reader was not entirely convinced. Laura L. Runge also talks about the construction of the genre of the novel. 'Gendered Strategies in the Criticism of Early Fiction' (*ECS* 28.363–78) looks at eighteenth-century criticism of the novel, discussing the gendered terms used by critics to denigrate the novel as peculiarly female while making space for 'serious' male writers. Runge's analysis is indebted to Nancy Armstrong's association of the novel with domestic space, but Runge's attention to the rhetoric of criticism makes this an interesting complement to recent work in the field done by Joseph Bartolomeo and Antonia Forster.

Among review essays on eighteenth-century scholarship published this year, two stand out. Jerry C. Beasley's 'The History of the Novel Writ Large – and New' (*ECF* 8.73– 80) is an appreciative, yet probing long review of *The Columbia History of the British Novel* (ed. John Richetti and others; *YWES* 75.415). Beasley focuses on the many interesting chapters Richetti's book includes on eighteenth-century novelists. Beasley compares the 'sprawl' of the book to novels by Smollett or Dickens. What he means by this is that the collection of essays Richetti assembled move in different directions while covering the chronological literary history of the novel fully. He singles out for dispraise chapters on eighteenth-century novelists by Richard Kroll (Defoe) and Jill Campbell (Fielding). John Sitter's review of 'Recent Studies in the Restoration and Eighteenth Century' (*SEL* 35.599–639) is a model of intelligent and sensitive criticism. I particularly want to mention a book that was published too late last year to be covered in *YWES* 75, Catherine Gallagher's *Nobody's Story*. Gallagher's book won a prize for the best book published in English studies of its year, but at the same time has come under fire from many specialists in eighteenth-century literature. Gallagher's book looks at five writers, Aphra Behn, Delarivier Manley, Charlotte Lennox, Frances Burney and Maria Edgeworth, in order to discuss the relationship among the self-effacement of these women, the representation of certain economic issues in their novels, and the genres themselves in which they wrote. (A strength of the book consists of its refusal to insist too strongly on the unity of the genre of the novel.) The book is valuable primarily for its attentive close readings – in particular, the chapters on Manley and Lennox are excellent – but *Nobody's Story* can be criticized for a lack of depth in its examination of such a broad period in literary history. John Sitter wonders why Gallagher neglected male writers, and his review expresses frustration at the clever, possibly *primarily* clever, readings that Gallagher provides. He quotes from a passage comparing the blackness of Behn's hero Oroonoko with the blackness of ink, and then writes: 'The book has many stretches of this sort, chains of equivalence in which it seems anything can be bound to anything. Such passages are undeniably ingenious, but they also have the unmistakable note of the academic soliloquy' (613). It would be well if fewer of us were guilty of such soliloquizing.

5. Drama

An inspiring biography of John Gay has appeared from OUP. David Nokes's *John Gay: A Profession of Friendship. A Critical Biography*. A substantial biography, both in length and research, in which the complex figure of Gay is explored through court, theatre and Grub Street in compelling detail. His friendships and connections with other literary figures, such as Swift, Arbuthnot, Pope and Addison, render the biography to some extent a constellation of Scriblerian lives, and the insights gained into their lives, and those of lesser figures, like Aaron Hill, make fascinating reading. Yet it is the enigmatic Gay who tantalizes through the paradoxes in which he is presented: childish sophisticate, bawdy innocent, he eludes categorization, not least on the matter of his sexuality. His connections with the rumouredly gay Lord Burlington suggest that it is possible, and Nokes, after considering the tenuous evidence, cannot give a definite answer, although he suggests that Gay probably was gay. Nokes's enthusiasm is infectious, his knowledge of Gay and the period deep, and this timely biography of the unjustly neglected Gay should be of interest to anyone studying the period.

   Cultural Readings of Restoration and Eighteenth-Century English Theater (ed. J. Douglas Canfield and Deborah C. Payne) offers a range of essays by 'scholars committed to consciously theoretical readings of Restoration and eighteenth-century drama and theater'. The editors rightly regret the general dearth of such theorized studies of drama in the period, in comparison to the work that has appeared on other literary genres. They do not attempt to suggest that their contributors have any degree of common theoretical ground, beyond an interest in cultural studies, defined as an awareness of 'those societal codes that constitute meaning and value', leavened by an awareness of the need to see culture as 'material social process' rather than simply product. They also comment on the tendency of commentators on the period to concentrate on comedy – a tendency that is reflected in this collection and justified in terms of the malleability of the material and (with whatever qualifications), the directness of its reflection of material social reality. Essays on the Restoration by Payne, Richard Kroll, Harold Weber, Helen Burke, Robert Markley, Richard Braverman and J. S. Peters cover topics such as gender politics, property, fashion and novelty in relation to a wide range of canonical and non-canonical plays. Essays covering the later period include pieces by Canfield on the changing tropes of aristocratic and bourgeois ideology in late Stuart and early Georgian serious drama and sentimental comedy; Susan Green on Charlotte Lennox's *Shakespear Illustrated*, models of cultural authority and female abjection; Kristina Straub on homophobia, the figure of the actor and representations of masculine stereotypes such as the fop between the time of William Prynne and David Garrick; and James Thompson, who offers an interesting analysis of the relation between representations of value in drama and political economy, under the title '"Sure I Have Seen that Face Before"'. *Coriolanus: Critical Essays* (ed. David Wheeler) includes an essay by the editor entitled 'To Their Own Purpose: The Treatment of Coriolanus in the Restoration and Eighteenth Century'.We have not seen Jean I. Marsden's *The Re-Imagined Text: Shakespeare, Adaptation, & Eighteenth-Century Literary Theory* (Kentucky University Press).

Last year's *Time, Literature and the Arts: Essays in Honor of Samuel L. Macey* (ed. Thomas R. Cleary), includes an essay by Donald Greene entitled 'Gay and Brecht: *The Beggar's Opera* and *Die Dreigroschenoper*', while Aparna Dharwadker writes on 'John Gay, Bertolt Brecht, and Postcolonial Antinationalisms' (*MD* 38.4–21). In *RECTR*, Kevin J. Gardiner writes on 'Cultural Anxiety in Richard Steele's *The Tender Husband*' (10.i. 44–58), while in *EA* (47[1994].312-16), Paul D. Cannan considers the relation between 'An Unrecovered Epilogue for *The Recruiting Officer* and Steele's Loss of the Gazetteership in 1710'. Alexander Pettit discusses 'Anxiety, Political Rhetoric and Historical Drama under Walpole' in *1650– 1850* (1.109–137). In *Criticism* (37.57–84), Lucinda Cole writes on Lillo's '*The London Merchant* and the Institution of Apprenticeship': among last year's essays, Helen Burke discusses '*The London Merchant* and Eighteenth-Century British Law' in *PQ* (73[1994].347-66). *TJ* contains two interesting articles on the period. In 'Gazing at his Seraglio' Mita Choudhury discusses 'late eighteenth-century women playwrights as Orientalists' (47.481–502); while Beth H. Friedman-Romell offers suggestions towards the formation of 'a reception theory of theatrical cross-dressing in eighteenth-century London' under the title 'Breaking the Code' (47.459–79).

In *Getting Into the Act*, Ellen Donkin surveys the careers of seven female playwrights in London between 1776 and 1829. An introductory chapter outlines the constraints on women as playwrights in the Restoration and eighteenth century in fairly predictable terms: expectations about female conduct and education and the difficulties of negotiating with male theatre managers are seen as providing the main reasons for the dearth of productions of plays by women. The latter area provides the main focus in the subsequent chapters, which offer narrative accounts of the attempts of the women dramatists who are Donkin's concern to survive as professionals, and of the positive and negative aspects of the relation between them and their patrons in theatre management. Donkin broaches some interesting problems, but the analysis she offers is generally couched in disappointingly unsophisticated terms. Garrick is praised as a mentor of women writers, but his limitations in this role are demonstrated in his treatment of Frances Brookes. The paper war between Hannah More and Hannah Cowley is read in the light of the ending of Garrick's mentorship with his death; and the careers of Sophia Lee, Mrs Inchbald, Frances Burney and Joanna Baillie are surveyed in their own right and in relation to the managements of Sheridan, Coleman and Harris. A more ambitious theoretical framework, and sustained attention to the plays produced by the women whose work is discussed, might have resulted in a more substantial study of the fascinating relation between gender politics and the conditions of production of drama in the period, but the present volume at least offers a useful introduction to the careers of the figures it surveys, and an encouragement to further work in the area.

Sheridan figures large in work on the drama of the period this year. *Sheridan Studies* (ed. James Morwood and David Crane) not only aims to re-establish Sheridan's reputation as a great dramatist, but further, to establish him 'as the outstanding playwright between Congreve and Wilde'. The essays included examine Sheridan, his work and context, from an exciting variety of perspectives – the collection concludes with a piece by Peter Wood 'On producing Sheridan' – offering insights into theatre in general in this period as well as fresh studies of Sheridan himself. Mark S. Auburn's 'Theatre in the age of Garrick and Sheridan' provides some useful information on the practices of the theatrical world in this period, from play-going to debt-contracting. Richard C. Taylor considers Sheridan's critical reception in ' "Future retrospection": rereading Sheridan's reviewers', while Eric Rump and James Morwood both focus on the context of *The School for Scandal* in their respective 'Sheridan, Congreve and *The School for Scandal*' and 'Sheridan, Molière and the idea of the school in *The School for Scandal*'. David Crane contributes 'Satire and Celebration in *The Critic*', and Jack Durant considers Sheridan's theory of language in 'Sheridan and Language', an area further explored by Christopher Reid in 'Foiling the rival: argument and identity in Sheridan's speeches'. Sheridan's political career is covered by Christopher Clayton's 'The political career of Richard Brinsley Sheridan' and Marc Baer's 'The ruin of a public man: the rise and fall of Richard Brinsley Sheridan as political reformer'. *Sheridan Studies* provides a lively collection of essays and is a timely and welcome reminder of Sheridan's complexity, interest and lasting importance.

QWERTY: Arts, Littératures et Civilisations du Monde Anglophone contains three short commentaries on *The Critic*. Doris Feldman writes on 'The Modern "Art of Puffing": Theatrical and Political Discourses in Richard Brinsley Sheridan's *The Critic*' (*QWERTY* 5.87–97); Louise M. Miller on 'Invasion as Theatrical Appropriation in *The Critic*' (*QWERTY* 5.99–104); Susan Blattes on '*The Critic* ou les jeux de l'illusion' (*QWERTY* 5.79–85); and David Crane on 'The Limits of the Theatrical' in Beaumont's *Knight of the Burning Pestle*, Buckingham's *Rehearsal* and Sheridan's *Critic* (*QWERTY* 5.59–64). In *BSEAA*, Jean Dulck also writes on the play under the title '*The*

Critic: Ou, vous n'avez pas fini de rire' (41.27–36). In *TJ* (46[1994].303–21), Mita Choudhury writes on 'Sheridan, Garrick, and a Colonial Gesture: *The School for Scandal* on the Calcutta Stage'. *RECTR* has some interesting pieces this year: Arthur Sherbo writes on 'John Duncombe and the 1782 *Biographia Dramatica*' (10.1.59–65), focusing on Duncombe's criticism of the *Biographia* in the *Gentleman's Magazine*, while Kevin J. Gardner looks at 'Cultural Anxiety in Richard Steele's *The Tender Husband*' (10.1.44–58) and considers problems of national identity, gender roles and the idea of nature. Leslie Radford contributes ' "Alas! I fear I've been too hasty!" and other reconsiderations of Addison's *Cato*' (10.2.32–41), while Paola Polesso examines the implications of the transfer of Pamela from book to stage in 'The Character of Pamela from Richardson's Novel to Goldoni's Comedy' (10.2.42–51).

Gillian Russell's study of the cultural context of the Revolutionary and Napoleonic Wars in *The Theatres of War: Performance, Politics and Society 1793–1815* focuses on the ways in which the theatre mediated and helped shape patriotism and national self-images, both for the domestic public and the forces abroad. A lively use of anecdote and tantalizing footnotes render this study a pleasurable read, but the book would have benefited from a more theoretical approach, which might have sharpened and focused the arguments, and done more with the material. However, Russell's book is well researched, and there is a wealth of interesting material here for anyone interested in the theatre, the army or cultural life in general in this period.

The first edition of Frances Burney's *Complete Plays* comes in two volumes from P&C edited with an introduction by Peter Sabor, for a hefty £120. The comedies and tragedies are collected in separate volumes. Burney wrote these dramas between 1778 and 1802; they are by no means rediscovered masterpieces, but Burney's talent for light and witty dialogue is turned to good effect in the comedies, and the collection as a whole is to be welcomed as providing unique access to a neglected aspect of the writer's work. Anthony Amberg's edition of Edward Moore's popular sentimental comedy *The Foundling* and tragedy *The Gamester* offers a very full and informative chronology and narrative account of Moore's career and literary output, and an elaborately well supported editorial apparatus to the texts of the plays. The volume provides a very welcome addition to current scholarly documentation of the theatrical literature of the mid eighteenth century, in relation to which Amberg on the one hand traces the links between Moore's plays and earlier English drama, and on the other argues convincingly for his importance as a precursor of writers such as Cumberland.

Curtis Price, Judith Milhous and Robert D. Hume have collaborated most fruitfully to produce *Italian Opera in Late Eighteenth-Century London: The King's Theatre, Haymarket, 1778–1791, Volume I*. The authors shift the traditional focus on opera in Vienna in the 1780s to look at the lively situation in London, following through the seasons chronologically and leaving us with the tantalizing beginnings of Mozart's celebrity status in London in the early 1790s. The first three chapters are taken up with contextualization, and provide a diverse range of sources to build up a sense of background. Librettos, newspapers, periodicals, scores, lawsuits, letters and diaries are skilfully used to remind us of the foreignness of those performances. We look forward to the next volume. Ruth Smith's *Handel's Oratorios and Eighteenth-Century Thought* provides another refreshing perspective on the place of music in eighteenth-century culture. Smith argues against the traditional dismissal of the libretti of Handel's oratorios, emphasizing the importance for Handel's audiences of the relationship between the text and the music, and the cultural resonances of the textual content. Arguing against the Handel scholar Winton Dean's abstraction of the composer from contemporary debates, she analyses the Old Testament oratorios in the light of eighteenth-century notions of allegorical history and produces fruitful readings of the libretti as disguised comments on political issues of the day. Her persuasive argument and sound grasp of the intellectual context of the libretti make this a stimulating read, even if the music seems almost forgotten in the enthusiastic reclamation of the libretti. We have not seen the collection edited by Thomas Bauman, *Opera and the Enlightenment*, or that *On Mozart* (ed. James M. Morris), both published by CUP.

Books Reviewed

Amberg, Anthony, ed. *Edwin Moore. The Foundling and The Gamester.* UDelP. pp. 448. £45. ISBN 0 87413 530 3.

Andrews, Malcolm. *The Picturesque: Literary Sources and Documents.* 3 vols. Helm Information Ltd (1994). Vol. 1: pp. xiii + 497. Vol. 2: pp. vii + 351. Vol. 3: pp. viii + 359. £200. ISBN 1 873403 10 0.

Arnold, Richard. *The English Hymn. Studies in a Genre.* Lang. pp. 272. $35.95. ISBN 0 8204 2485 4.

Baird, John D., and Charles Ryscamp, eds. *The Poems of William Cowper.* OUP. Volume II (1782–85). pp. 454. £60. ISBN 0 19 812339. Volume III (1785–1800). pp.413. £55. ISBN 0 19 818296 1.

Baldwin, Barry. *The Latin and Greek Poems of Samuel Johnson: Text, Translation and Commentary.* Duckworth. pp. 300. £55. ISBN 0 715 626558.

Becker, Marvin B. *The Emergence of Civil Society in the Eighteenth Century: A Privileged Moment in the History of England, Scotland, and France.* IndUP. 1994. pp. xxiii + 164. £22.50. ISBN 0 253 31129 2.

Bence-Jones, Mark. *The Catholic Families.* Constable. pp. 341. pb. £12.95. ISBN 0 09 474350 9.

Benedict, Barbara M. *Framing Feeling: Sentiment and Style in English Prose Fiction, 1745–1800.* AMS. pp. 261. $45. ISBN 0 404 63526 1.

Bialostosky, Don H., and Lawrence D. Needham, eds. *Rhetorical Traditions and British Romantic Literature.* IndUP. pp. vii + 312. £35. ISBN 0 253 31180 2.

Blewett, David. *The Illustration of 'Robinson Crusoe', 1719–1920.* Smythe. pp. 235. £35. ISBN 0 901072 67 2.

Bohls, Elizabeth A. *Women Travel Writers and the Language of Aesthetics 1716–1818.* CUP. pp. x + 309. £35. ISBN 0 521 47458 2.

Botting, Fred. *The Gothic.* Routledge. pp. 240. hb £30, pb £7.99. ISBN 0 415 12266 X, 0 415 09219 1.

Brack Jr, O M, ed. *Writers, Books, and Trade: An Eighteenth-Century Miscellany for William B. Todd.* AMSP. pp. xi + 412. $57.50. ISBN 0 404 63519 9.

Brewer, John, and Ann Bermingham, eds. *The Culture of Culture 1600–1800: Image, Object, Text.* Routledge. pp. xv + 548. £120. ISBN 0 415 121353 3.

Brewer, Sarah, ed. *The Early Letters of Bishop Richard Hurd 1739–1762*. BoydellP/Church of England Records Society 3. pp. lxxx + 466. £65. ISBN 0 85115 653 3, ISSN 1351 3087.

Bucholz, R. O. *The Augustan Court: Queen Anne and the Decline of Court Culture*. StanfordUP (1993). pp. 356. $49.50. ISBN 0 8047 2080 0.

Campbell, Jill. *Natural Masques: Gender and Identity in Fielding's Plays and Novels*. StanfordUP. pp. 324. hb $45.00, pb $16.95. ISBN 0 8047 2391 5, 0 8047 2520 9.

Canfield, J. Douglas, and Deborah C. Payne, eds. *Cultural Readings of Restoration and Eighteenth-Century English Theater*. UGeoP. pp. 328. hb £47.95, pb £23.95. ISBN 0 8203 1681 4, 0 8203 1751 9.

Cannon, Garland, and Kevin R. Brine, eds. *Objects of Enquiry: The Life, Contributions, and Influences of Sir William Jones (1746–1794)*. NYUP. pp. ix +185. $40. ISBN 0 8147 1517 6.

Cannon, John. *Samuel Johnson and the Politics of Hanoverian England*. Clarendon (1994) pp. vii + 326. £35. ISBN 0 19 820452 3.

Carabelli, Giancarlo, trans. Joan Krakover-Hall. *On Hume and Eighteenth-Century Aesthetics: The Philosopher on a Swing*. Lang. pp. ix + 222. $49.95. ISBN 0 8204 2528 1.

Carré, Jacques. *The Crisis of Courtesy: Studies in the Conduct-Book in Britain 1600–1900*. Brill (1994). pp. 250. $83.50. ISBN 90 04 10005 9, ISSN 0920 8607.

Charlesworth, Michael. *The English Garden: Literary Sources and Documents*. 3 vols. Helm Information Ltd (1994). Volume 1: pp. xv + 428. Volume 2: pp. ix + 590. Volume 3: pp. vii + 514. £200. ISBN 1 873403 11 9 (set).

Clark, J. C. D. *Samuel Johnson: Literature, Religion and English Politics from the Restoration to Romanticism*. CUP. pp. 272. £35. ISBN 0 521 47304 7.

Clery, E. J. *The Rise of Supernatural Fiction, 1762–1800*. CUP. pp. 240. $49.95. ISBN 0 521 45316 X.

Connelly, Frances S. *The Sleep of Reason: Primitivism in Modern European Art and Aesthetics*. PSUP. pp. 176. hb £29.50, pb £19.95. ISBN 0271 013052, 0271 01105X.

Connery, Brian A., and Kirke Combe, eds. *Theorizing Satire: Essays in Literary Criticism*. Macmillan. pp. xi + 212. £28.50 ($39.95). ISBN 0 312 12302 7.

Copley, Stephen, and Kathryn Sutherland, eds. *Adam Smith's 'Wealth of Nations': New Interdisciplinary Essays*. ManUP. pp. xiii + 205. hb £35, pb £12.99. ISBN 0 7190 3942 8, 0 7190 3943 6.

Crandell, Gina. *Nature Pictorialized: 'The View' in Landscape History*. JHUP (1993). pp. 240. £30. ISBN 0 8018 4397 9.

Daniels, Stephen, and Charles Watkins, eds. *The Picturesque Landscape: Visions of Georgian Hertfordshire*. no details.

Darwall, Stephen. *The British Moralists and the Internal 'Ought', 1640–1760*. CUP. pp. xii + 352. £40. ISBN 0 521 45167 1.

Donkin, Ellen. *Getting Into the Act: Women Playwrights in London 1776–1829*. Routledge. pp. 256. hb £40, pb £12.99. ISBN 0 415 08249 8, 0 415 08250 1.

Douglas, Aileen. *Uneasy Sensations: Smollett and the Body*. UChicP. pp. 232. $29.95. ISBN 0 226 16051 3.

Edwards, Philip. *The Story of the Voyage: Sea-Narratives in Eighteenth-Century England*. CUP (1994). pp. x + 244. £37.50. ISBN 0 521 41301 X.

Erickson, Amy Louise. *Women and Property in Early Modern England*. Routledge (1993). pp. xiii + 306. pb £14.99. ISBN 0 415 13340 8.

Fabricant, Carole. *Swift's Landscape*. UNDP. pp. xxxv + 307. £13.95. ISBN 0 268 01754 9.

Fausett, David. *The Strange Surprizing Sources of Robinson Crusoe*. Studies in Comparative Literature 3. Rodopi (1994). pp. 299. £28. ISBN 90 5183 705 4.

Ferguson, Adam. *An Essay on the History of Civil Society*. CUP. pp. xxxv + 283. pb. £13.95. ISBN 0 521 44736 4.

Folger Collective. *Women Critics, 1660–1820: An Anthology*. IndUP. pp. xxv + 410. £14.99. ISBN 0 253 20963 3.

Fox, Christopher, and Ross C. Murfin, eds. *Jonathan Swift's Gulliver's Travels: Complete, Authoritative Text with Biographical and Historical Contexts, Critical History, and Essays from Five Contemporary Critical Perspectives*. St Martin's. pp. x + 480. $9.33. ISBN 0 312 06665 1.

Fox, Christopher, and Brenda Tooley, eds. *Walking Naboth's Vineyard: New Studies of Swift*. UNDP. pp. 224. £26.50. ISBN 0 268 01950 9.

Frith, Valerie, ed. *Women and History: Voices of Early Modern England*. Coach House. pp. xxiii + 262. pb £9.99. ISBN 0 88910 500 6.

Gallagher, Catherine. *Nobody's Story: The Vanishing Acts of Women Writers in the Literary Marketplace, 1760–1820*. UCalP (1994). pp. 339. hb $38, pb $14.95. ISBN 0 520 08510 8, 0 520 20338 0.

Gerrard, Christine. *Walpole and the Patriots: Politics, Poetry and Myth, 1725–1742*. OUP. pp. 350. £40. ISBN 0 19 812982 3.

Goodridge, John. *Rural Life in Eighteenth-Century Poetry*. CUP. pp. 245. £35. ISBN 0 521 43381 9.

Greetham, D. C., ed. *Scholarly Editing: A Guide to Research*. MLA. pp. vii + 740. $45. ISBN 0 87352 560 4.

Hammer, Stephanie Barbé. *The Sublime Crime: Fascination, Failure, and Form in Literature of the Enlightenment*. SIUP (1994). pp. xi + 224. $24.95. ISBN 0 8093 1831 8.

Harries, Elizabeth Wanning. *The Unfinished Manner: Essays on the Fragment in the Later Eighteenth Century*. UPVirginia (1994). pp. xi + 226. $29.50. ISBN 0 8139 1502 3.

Harris, John. *The Palladian Revival: Lord Burlington, His Villa and Garden at Chiswick*. YaleUP (1994). pp. ix + 280. $50. ISBN 0 300 05983 3.

Hart, Clive, and Kay Gilliland Stevenson, eds. *Heaven and the Flesh: Imagery of Desire from the Renaissance to the Rococo*. CUP. pp. xiv + 237. £35. ISBN 0 521 49571 7.

Hay, Carla, and Syndy M. Conger, eds. *The Past as Prologue: Essays to Celebrate the Twenty-Fifth Anniversary of ASECS*. AMS Studies in the Eighteenth Century No. 28. AMS. pp. xvi + 436. $52.50. ISBN 0 404 63528 8.

Hufton, Olwen. *The Prospect Before Her: A History of Women in Western Europe, Volume I, 1500–1800*. HC. pp. xi + 654. £25. ISBN 0 00 255120 9.

Johnson, Claudia L. *Equivocal Beings: Politics, Gender, and Sentimentality in the 1790s*. UChicP. pp. 239. hb $30, pb $14.95. ISBN 0 226 40183 9, 0 226 40184 7.

Jones, Vivien, intro. *The Young Lady's Pocket Library: or, The Parental Monitor.* Thoemmes. pp. xlix + 311. pb. £15.75. ISBN 1 855 06382 4.

Kavanagh, Thomas M., ed. *Chance, Culture and the Literary Text.* Michigan Romance Studies 14. UMichP (1994). pp. 245. pb $10. ISBN 0 939739 8.

Kelly, Gary, ed. *Sarah Scott. A Description of Millenium Hall.* Broadview. pp. 260. $15.95. ISBN 1 55111 015 6.

Kemal, Salim, and Ivan Gaskell, eds. *Landscape, Natural Beauty and the Arts.* CUP (1993). pp ix + 278. hb £37.50, pb £13.95. ISBN 0 521 43279 0, 0 521 55854 9.

Köster, Patricia, and Jean Coates Cleary, eds. *Sheridan, Frances. Memoirs of Miss Sidney Bidulph.* OUP. pp. 478. £6.99. ISBN 0 19 282308 6.

Lamb, Jonathan. *The Rhetoric of Suffering: Reading the Book of Job in the Eighteenth Century.* Clarendon. pp. 342. £40. ISBN 0 19 818264 3.

Lustig, Irma S., ed. *Boswell: Citizen of the World: Man of Letters.* UPKen. pp. xviii + 270. $37.50. ISBN 0 8131 1910 3.

Mahony, Robert. *Jonathan Swift: The Irish Identity.* YaleUP. pp. xvii + 222. £25. ISBN 0300 06374 1.

Marsden, Jean I. *The Re-Imagined Text: Shakespeare, Adaptation, & Eighteenth-Century Literary Theory.* UPKen. pp. x + 193. $30. ISBN 0 8131 1901 4.

McVeagh, John, ed. *Richard Pococke's Irish Tours.* IAP. pp. 245. £27.50. ISBN 0 7165 2539 9.

Melman, Billie. *Women's Orients: English Women and the Middle East, 1718–1918.* 2nd edn. Macmillan. pp. xxix + 417. £17.99. ISBN 0 333 64144 2.

Merolle, Vincenzo, ed. *The Correspondence of Adam Ferguson.* 2 vols. P&C. pp. 608. £135. ISBN 1 85196 140 2 (set).

Midgley, Clare. *Women Against Slavery: The British Campaigns 1780–1870.* Routledge. pp. xii + 281. £12.99. ISBN 0 415 12708 4.

Miles, Robert. *Ann Radcliffe: The Great Enchantress.* ManUP. pp. 201. hb £35, pb £12.99. ISBN 0 7190 3828 6, 0 7190 3829 4.

Miller, David G. *The Flesh Made Word: The Failure and Redemption of Metaphor in Edward Taylor's 'Christographia'.* SusquehannaUP. pp. 149. £23. ISBN 0 945 63685 7.

Moore, Judith. *The Appearance of Truth: The Story of Elizabeth Canning and Eighteenth-Century Narrative.* UDelP (1994). pp. 278. $38.50. ISBN 0 87413 494 3.

Morwood, James, and David Crane, eds. *Sheridan Studies.* CUP. pp. xiv + 203. £30. ISBN 0 521 46466 8.

Newey, Vincent. *Centring the Self: Subjectivity, Society and Reading from Thomas Gray to Thomas Hardy.* Scolar Press. pp. 291. £45. ISBN 1 85928 151 6.

Newman, Donald J., ed. *James Boswell: Psychological Interpretations.* St. Martin's. pp. xviii + 222. $39.95. ISBN 0 312 12142 3.

Nichol, Donald W., ed. *Transatlantic Crossings: Eighteenth-Century Explorations.* Department of English Language and Literature, Memorial University of Newfoundland. pp. 117. np. nd.

Nokes, David. *John Gay: A Profession of Friendship. A Critical Biography.* OUP. pp. 578. £25. ISBN 0 19 812971 8.

Norton, Robert E. *The Beautiful Soul: Aesthetic Morality in the Eighteenth Century.* CornUP. pp. xi + 314. $35. ISBN 0 8014 3050 X.

Nussbaum, Felicity A. *The Autobiographical Subject: Gender and Ideology in Eighteenth-Century England*. JHUP. pp. xxii + 264. £14. ISBN 0 8018 5237 4.

——, *Torrid Zones: Maternity, Sexuality, and Empire in Eighteenth-Century English Narratives*. JHUP. pp. 248. hb £37, pb £12.50. ISBN 0 8018 5074 6, 0 8018 5075 4.

Oldfield, J. R. *Popular Politics and British Anti-Slavery: The Mobilisation of Public Opinion against the Slave Trade, 1787–1807*. MUP. pp. x + 197. £35. ISBN 0 7190 3856 1.

Pittock, Murray J. *The Myth of the Jacobite Clans*. EdinUP. pp. 240. pb £12.95. ISBN 0 7486 0715 3.

Postle, Martin. *Sir Joshua Reynolds: The Subject Pictures*. CUP. pp. 396. £50. ISBN 0 521 42066 0.

Potkay, Adam, and Sandra Burr, eds, intro. Adam Potkay. *Black Atlantic Writers of the Eighteenth Century: Living the New Exodus in England and the Americas*. St. Martin's. pp. xii + 268. hb $39.95, pb $16.95. ISBN 0 312 12133 4, 0 312 12518 6.

Price, Curtis, et al. *Italian Opera in late Eighteenth-Century London: The King's Theatre, Haymarket, 1778–1791, Volume I*. Clarendon. pp. 736. £60. ISBN 0 19 816166 2.

Richards, Jeffrey H. *Mercy Otis Warren*. Twayne. pp. xvii + 195. £17.50. ISBN 0 8057 4003 1.

Roberts, Marie Mulvey, and Hugh Ormsby-Lennon, eds. *Secret Texts: The Literature of Secret Societies*. AMSP. pp. xv + 349. $60.50. ISBN 0 404 64251 9.

Rogers, Pat. *Johnson and Boswell: The Transit of Caledonia*. Clarendon. pp. x + 245. £30. ISBN 0 19 818259 7.

Rosenberg, Beth Carole. *Virginia Woolf and Samuel Johnson: Common Readers*. St. Martin's. pp. 300. £29. ISBN 0 333 62090 9.

Ross, Ian Simpson. *The Life of Adam Smith*. Clarendon. pp. 448. £25. ISBN 0 198 28821 2.

Russell, Gillian. *The Theatres of War: Performance, Politics and Society 1793–1815*. OUP. pp. 224. £35. ISBN 0 198 12263 2.

Sabor, Peter, ed. *Complete Plays of Frances Burney*. 2 vols. P&C. pp. 800. £120. ISBN 1 851 96073 2 (set).

Sanderson, Michael. *Education, Economic Change and Society in England 1780–1830*. CUP. pp. 92. pb £6.95. ISBN 0 521 55779 8.

Schama, Simon. *Landscape and Memory*. HC. pp. 624. £25. ISBN 0 00 215897 3.

Scott, Katie. *The Rococo Interior: Decoration and Social Spaces in Early Eighteenth-Century Paris*. YaleUP. pp. 352. £45. ISBN 0 300 04582 4.

Seed, David, ed. *Anticipations: Essays on Early Science Fiction and Its Precursors*. LivUP. pp xvi + 225. hb £27.50, pb £12.25. ISBN 0 85323 348 9, 0 85323 418 3.

Serafin, Steven. *Eighteenth-Century British Literary Biographers*. Dictionary of Literary Biography 142. Gale (1994). pp. ix + 370. $140. ISBN 0 8103 5556 6.

Sherbo, Arthur. *Samuel Johnson's Critical Opinions: A Reexamination*. AUP. pp. 230. £27. ISBN 0 87413 547 8.

Shteir, Ann B., ed. *Priscilla Wakefield. Mental Improvement: or the Beauties and Wonders of Nature and Art, Conveyed in a Series of Instructive Conversations.* Colleagues. pp. xxi + 171. £29.50. ISBN 0 937191 51 5.

Smith, Ruth. *Handel's Oratorios and Eighteenth-Century Thought.* CUP. pp. 498. £45. ISBN 0 521 40265 4.

Soupel, Serge, ed. *Les Ages de la Vie en Grande-Bretagne au XVIIIe Siècle: Actes de colloques decembre 1990 et decembre 1991 sous la direction de Serge Soupel.* Presses de la Sorbonne Nouvelle. pp. 233. 160 FF. ISBN 2 87854 074 3.

Southcott, Joanna. *A Dispute Between Woman and the Powers of Darkness.* RevR. Woodstock. pp. 128. £25. ISBN 1 85 477194 9.

Swift, Jonathan, ed. Marie M. Roberts, intro. M. Foot. *A Collection of Genteel and Ingenious Conversation.* Thoemmes. pp. xiii + 296. £13.75. ISBN 1 855 06380 8.

Tillyard, Stella. *Aristocrats: Caroline, Emily and Sarah Lennox 1740–1832.* C&W. pp. xiv + 462. pb £8.99. ISBN 0 09 947711 4.

Tinkler, Villani Valeria, Peter Davidson, and Jane Stevenson, eds. *Exhibited by Candlelight: Sources and Developments in the Gothic Tradition.* Rodopi. pp. 298. $42. ISBN 9 05183 832 8.

Todd, Dennis. *Imagining Monsters: Miscreations of the Self in Eighteenth-Century England.* UChicP. pp. 339. hb $52, pb $17.95. ISBN 0 226 80555 7, 0 226 80556 5.

Valenze, Deborah. *The First Industrial Woman.* OUP. pp. 262. hb £25, pb £13.99. ISBN 0 19 508981 2, 0 19 508982 0.

Wagner, Peter. *Reading Icontexts: From Swift to the French Revolution.* Reaktion. pp. 211. £19.95. ISBN 0 948462 71 X.

Wahrman, Dvor. *Imagining the Middle Class: The Political Representation of Class in Britain, 1780–1840.* CUP. pp. xiv + 428. £45. ISBN 0 521 47127 3.

Waingrow, Marshall, ed. *James Boswell's 'Life of Johnson': An Edition of the Original Manuscript: In Four Volumes: Volume I: 1709–1765.* The Yale edition of The Private Papers of James Boswell. EdinUP/YaleUP (1994). pp. xxxix + 518. £75. ISBN 0 7486 0471 5.

Wheeler, David, ed. *Coriolanus: Critical Essays.* Garland. pp. xxii + 434. $75. ISBN 08153 10579.

Williams, Anne. *Art of Darkness: A Poetics of Gothic.* UChicP. pp. 324. hb $39, pb $14.95. ISBN 0 226 89906 3, 0 226 89907 1.

Williamson, Tom. *Polite Landscapes: Gardens and Society in Eighteenth-Century England.* JHUP/Sutton. pp. ix + 182. $35. ISBN 0 8018 5205 6.

Wollstonecraft, Mary. *Thoughts on the Education of Daughters.* Thoemmes. pp. xiv + 160. pb £13.75. ISBN 1 85506 381 6.

XII

The Nineteenth Century: Romantic Period

DUNCAN WU, DAVID WORRALL, PETER J. KITSON, ROBERT MILES and E. J. CLERY

This chapter has three sections: 1. Poetry and Drama; 2. Non-Fictional Prose; 3. Fictional Prose. Section 1 is by Duncan Wu and David Worrall (Blake material); section 2 is by Peter J. Kitson; and section 3 is by Robert Miles and E. J. Clery.

1. Poetry and Drama

This section has two categories: (a) Bibliographies, Editions and General Studies; (b) Works on Individual Poets. A number of books and articles were not available to me for review this year and where this is the case they are mentioned without evaluative comment. The primary journals and newsletters relevant to British Romantic poetry and drama are: *BARS: Bulletin and Review* 7/8; *Blake* 30/31; *ByronJ* 23; *ChLB* 89–92; *ERR* 6; *KSJ* 44; *JCSJ* 14; *NCL* 50; *SHW* 6; *SIR* 34; *WC* 26. Besides these, an important new journal appeared this year entitled *Romanticism* (ed. J. Drummond Bone, Nicholas Roe and Timothy Webb). It appears twice yearly and is published by EdinUP.

(a) Bibliographies, Editions and General Studies
The most important bibliographical work on a single writer to appear this year was *An Annotated Critical Bibliography of William Wordsworth* by Keith Hanley, assisted by David Barron. Unlike earlier bibliographies of Wordsworth criticism it is selective, not comprehensive; the grounds on which it selects are that it aims to offer 'a detailed scholarly guide to the major contributions in the textual history, history of reception and critical discussion of Wordsworth'. It does this very well; its summaries of seminal critical works are accurate and useful, and the evaluative comment is invariably shrewd – though the volume could have done with more. My only complaint is that, given only 300-odd pages, Hanley is compelled to omit many books and articles from his listing not because of their quality, but simply because there is not sufficient space to include them. A comprehensive bibliography is still needed, especially for the years since 1984, when the last such work came to an end.

This year Penguin Classics published an important new edition of Words-worth's most famous long poem: *The Prelude: The Four Texts (1798, 1799, 1805, 1850)*, edited by Jonathan Wordsworth. Professor Wordsworth has of course been along this road before; his editions of the 1799, 1805 and 1850 *Prelude*s for Norton (1979) is probably the most widely used. For the Penguin edition he has substantially augmented his annotations which, however, are collected at the back of the volume. The tendency to ghettoize annotations rather than place them on the same page as the text to which they refer is a disincentive to consult them, as the unfortunate reader is compelled to keep two bookmarks in place at any one time, wearily turning back and forth from one part of the volume to another. It is a convention which has come into being largely for economic reasons, and publishers would be well advised to reconsider it. But the main distinction between Professor Wordsworth's new Penguin *Prelude* and earlier editions is that he has added another version of the poem. In fact, *Was it for this*, as he entitles the 1798 text, has been published a number of times, most recently in the Norton edition, as a transcription from MS JJ. Its appearance here as 'a self-contained poem of 150 lines', as Professor Wordsworth describes it, begs the question: At what point does a draft, hitherto published as such, become a self-contained poem? The answer, of course, is that it all depends on what the editor decides to call it; in 1979 Professor Wordsworth regarded the draft as a draft and it was nothing more. This year he regards it as a self-contained poem and in doing so generated a new version of *The Prelude*. More surprisingly, perhaps, he has chosen not to include in this edition a rather more intriguing version of the poem, the contents of which his pioneering work established as long ago as 1977, but which still remains unpublished – *The Five-Book Prelude* (which is, none the less, mentioned in his introduction and chronology). It seems a shame that instead of finally bringing that still unseen work to light, he has chosen to promote a fragmentary and not very interesting early draft, already widely available and well known.

More puzzlingly, Professor Wordsworth's text of the 14-Book poem derives not from the poet's manuscripts, like that produced by W. J. B. Owen for the Cornell Wordsworth Series a decade ago; his copy-text, in the face of the numerous objections which he himself adduces in his note on the texts, is the first edition of 1850. This seems to me the most controversial decision of the entire edition. The 1850 text is riddled with errors and revisions introduced by Wordsworth's relatives and executors. Owen's strategy successfully produced, for the first time, a version in which every substantive could be traced back to the poet. While no one would seek to deny the importance of the 1850 edition, it cannot now be viewed as an authoritative copy-text in its own right. To have any value to the modern reader, any text of the 14-Book poem must derive principally from the poet's manuscripts; the work simply cannot and should not be taken solely from the various printed sources. All the same, the Penguin Classics edition boasts a useful chronology, a brief introduction, and a short essay on Wordsworth as reviser. At £9.99 it will no doubt enjoy a steady sale among students, particularly as it undercuts the Norton by several pounds.

It would be interesting, in years to come, to see how well the Penguin Classics *Prelude* fares as compared with, say, Andrew Ashfield's new anthol-ogy, *Romantic Women Poets 1770–1838*. Interest in women Romantics continues to boom, and at the time of writing I am aware of at least five other anthologies of this kind in preparation. This is an extraordinary situation – all the more so, when you consider that most editors of these anthologies are selecting from writers whose published work has been long out of print and for whom, in most cases, there are no modern, and certainly no scholarly, editions. When, one wonders, has the anthologist ever been so powerful, so instrumental in the formation of a canon? Only in 1993 did J. R. de J. Jackson publish his exemplary *Romantic Poetry by Women: A Bibliography 1770–1835* (*YWES* 74.305–6); in other words, it is only in the last three years that we have been in a position to sample the full range of published poetry from which to make a selection. This would account, at least in part, for the rather eccentric impression made by Jennifer Breen's *Women Romantic Poets 1785–1832* appearing the year before Jackson (*YWES* 73.340). Even now, there is no listing either of manuscripts, or of women's poetry in ephemeral sources; all the same, that has not stopped the anthologists from exploiting what they take to be a gap in a growing market. One wonders what the chances are of Breen or Ashfield, or any of their future competitors in the marketplace, being selected as classroom texts. The question is not one of quality – the poetry is very good indeed, as Ashfield's volume demonstrates – but are teachers prescribing women's writing alongside the 'big six' male poets for their undergraduate classes? Will they do so in future?

At any rate, Ashfield must be right in selecting from a broad range of writers (40), and extracting from some of their longer works. For the first time, readers can enjoy, in a single volume, passages from Barbauld's *Eighteen Hundred and Eleven*, More's *The Search After Happiness*, Smith's *The Emigrants*, Robinson's *The Progress of Liberty* and Tighe's *Psyche*. And Ashfield's selection shows the benefits of having Jackson's bibliography at his disposal. He has ranged widely through the period, and comes up with some interesting finds. Not everyone will be aware of the poems of Mary Knipe, Mary Hunt and Mary O'Brien, all of whom can be found here. Like Roger Lonsdale in his anthology, *Eighteenth-Century Women Poets* (*YWES* 71.368) – a volume that, like Jackson, does a good deal of bibliographical spade-work within the period – Ashfield provides biographical headnotes for each writer. It is, perhaps, a shame that the headnotes say little or nothing about the poems he has selected, or the critical reception they received, and it is hard not to resent the fact that all his annotations are corralled at the end of the volume, but then such privations are the result very largely, I suspect, of economic restrictions imposed by the publisher. And that, perhaps, is typical of the feeling one has as one reads this book – that at just over 300 pages it hints at a wealth of literature that Ashfield presents only in snatches. Many of the longer works either not included, or published here only in part, deserve to be reprinted in complete form once again, so that modern readers can experience them as they were meant to be read. But that is the task for an editor backed up by a richer – or more adventurous – publisher.

Other editions published this year include two further titles in Everyman's revamped list: Keats's *Selected Poems* (ed. Nicholas Roe) and Shelley's *Poems and Prose* (ed. Timothy Webb). Curiously enough, the market for reasonably priced paperback selections has become extremely competitive in recent years. A key factor must be the appearance of Wordsworth Classics, which reprints out of copyright editions of complete works for a few pounds. Most students will be unaware of the textual inadequacies of such editions, and as a result they have sold very well. For the publisher, overheads are low, as there are no royalties to be paid. With the new Everymans, Roe and Webb certainly prove their worth. Besides authoritative texts (important in the case of both poets, but particularly so in that of Shelley), they offer copious annotation, extracts from important criticism, and suggestions for further reading. In other words, each volume, like all those in the new Everyman series, is designed specifically for the needs of students in the mid-1990s. Once again, it is a shame, given the excellence of so much of this work, that the annotations are collected at the end of each volume. All the same, the volume of notage is excellent: both editors provide over 100 pages. And Webb has no fewer than eight appendices containing valuable materials such as Horace Smith's 'Ozymandias', extracts from Peacock's *Nightmare Abbey* and letters by Shelley.

The question of selection and text is worth examining for a moment, particularly in the case of Webb's volume. It must be said that, given the parameters within which he is working (a volume of just over 550 pages), the contents are admirably chosen. Besides complete texts of *Alastor, Julian and Maddalo, The Mask of Anarchy, Epipsychidion, Adonais, A Defence of Poetry* and *The Triumph of Life*, there are extracts from *Queen Mab, Laon and Cythna, Prometheus Unbound, Peter Bell the Third* and *Hellas*. All the major lyrics are included here. And, as one would expect from an edition that sets out to bring the canon up to date, there are two versions each of *Mont Blanc* and *Hymn to Intellectual Beauty*. Webb has taken extraordinary care in the editing, and it would be hard to imagine a better choice for the undergraduate reader.

Alongside these, the relative shortcomings of the Routledge English Texts series are immediately evident. There are far fewer notes, no chronology and virtually nothing on critical reception. This is strikingly clear in the case of Donald Low's Routledge *Byron: Selected Poetry and Prose*, though it does have a critical essay at the back, which provides an excellent account of the poet's work. The selection provided by Low highlights the difficulties facing the editor of a relatively inexpensive volume of 400 pages. This selection contains some of the lyrics and shorter poems, with complete texts of *Childe Harold's Pilgrimage* Canto III, *Beppo, Mazeppa, Don Juan* Cantos I–II and *The Vision of Judgment*. The fact that they are complete texts is significant, but Low is unable to include even extracts from *Manfred* and *Cain*. Compelled to remain within strict economies of space, the editor needs to decide whether to offer complete works or extracts. In this case, Low has chosen to present complete works, and the price to be paid is a tight limit on the selection offered. It is worth noting that the paper used by Routledge is of noticeably higher quality than that of the Everyman volumes, and production standards may have some bearing on their respective prices: the Everymans are priced at £6.99, the Routledge at £10.99. Given increasing student poverty, that, as much as any other factor, may well influence which edition teachers choose to prescribe.

After a year of vigorous activity in commemoration of Clare's bicentenary in 1994, Clare studies slowed drastically this year. None the less the year sees the appearance of Clare's *Northborough Sonnets*, edited by Eric Robinson, David Powell and P. M. S. Dawson. These poems show Clare at his energetic best, writing with intensity and passion about the world around him, never completely obedient to the formal demands of the sonnet form. For this impressive work of scholarship, the editors are to be commended. And yet, as is often the case in recent editions of Clare's work, their procedures go unexplained. Anyone who has read one of these editions will be aware that, as if in reaction to John Taylor's 'intrusive' editing of Clare's poetry, modern editors have tended to produce reading texts that appear to preserve every detail of the text as it appears in the manuscripts – orthography, punctuation, slang, however inconsistent, however eccentric. But there is no indication in the introduction to this edition as to whether this is indeed the case. And, more to the point, no attempt is made to justify such a procedure. This is worth mentioning because the preservation of Clare's ampersands and his complete lack of punctuation in these sonnets does make the texts difficult to read, despite editorial insistence that the reader will 'get used to it'. What is the argument against simply expanding Clare's ampersands to the word he meant them to represent? Had he supervised publication of these poems in 1995, he would surely have done so himself. And, one imagines, he would have wished the poems to be punctuated for ease of reading. As it is, the reader is compelled to punctuate each text in the imagination – but isn't this the editor's job? The situation is most peculiar. It is as if Clare scholarship has taken a completely different path from that in any other area of romantic studies, choosing, for an author marginalized and ignored in his own time, an editorial methodology guaranteed to consolidate his melancholy isolation by high-lighting his idiosyncrasies. The three editors of this edition have performed a great service to the poet and his admirers, but it is disappointing to find them so unforthcoming on their methodology and its implications. The lack of information about the manuscripts themselves, and their relation to the reading texts, makes their labours almost impossible to assess. It is worth adding that, as with all Clare's recently edited texts, this edition is far too lightly annotated: for over 100 pages of poetry there are only eight pages of notes. Clare is not an easy poet to read, favouring words, phrases and comments that demand annotation, and it does him no credit if we deny him the same privilege granted to other poets.

This could not be said of the latest addition to the Collected Coleridge Series, *Shorter Works and Fragments* (ed. H. J. and J. R. de J. Jackson). In producing this volume, the Jacksons have performed a truly breathtaking act of literary scholarship. In two volumes amounting to 1,762 pages they have gathered together, in many cases for the first time, all the shorter works by Coleridge known to exist at present. Much of this material has not previously appeared in print, and it is scattered throughout the world, either in libraries or in private collections. Each text is preceded by a headnote providing precise location details and references, datings and brief comments linking it to other works of a similar nature. The annotations reflect the editors' formidable erudition, and provide much necessary and recondite information; the index, too, is excellent – over 200 pages long, as it needs to be. This edition will be of unquestionable value to scholars for years to come; it is also fun to read, from the school exercises Coleridge composed for Boyer, to the prayers of 1833. This is a worthy addition to the Collected Works, and stands as an essential reference work for all Coleridgeans.

This year saw the commencement of *The Stirling/South Carolina Research Edition of the Collected Works of James Hogg*, under the general editorship of

Douglas S. Mack. One of the three volumes to initiate the series was *The Queer Book*, edited by P. D. Garside. With these beautifully produced volumes, Hogg has finally found the editors and publishers he deserves. As with the Collected Coleridge, the reading texts are printed in bold, clear type, rigorously edited using a methodology described in detail by Garside in his introduction. This edition is proof, were it needed, that Hogg scholarship has now reached a very sophisticated level. Garside has not only taken into account the various editions of *The Queer Book*, but has also surveyed the relevant manuscripts in America, Scotland and New Zealand. It is hard to imagine a more thorough treatment of the textual sources. Garside's annotations do the poems full justice. Each is provided with a headnote outlining its textual history and describing the area in which it is set. He lists textual emendations and sources for allusions and borrowings, as well as dialect words, proverbial phrases and the like. For the first time, it is possible to enjoy such poems as 'The Wyffe of Ezdel-more', 'Robyn Reidde', 'The Goode Manne of Allowa', 'Love's Jubilee' and 'The Origin of the Fairies' in consistently edited texts.

It must be said that not everyone will agree with all of Garside's editorial decisions. I remain unconvinced, for instance, that anything is gained by refusing to augment the very light punctuation provided in works edited from manuscript. Hogg himself would not have wanted his poems to go into print in this form, and it only forces readers to punctuate for themselves. If there is an argument against what Jack Stillinger has called 'textual primitivism', it is strongest in this context – where editorial fidelity to textual sources actually hinders the reader's understanding. In the case of such poems as 'The Wyffe of Ezdel-more', as Garside himself admits, the reader has the added challenge of Hogg's 'ancient stile'. This deliberately archaic and stilted manner is one of the glories of the poem, but in combination with the virtually non-existent punctuation the work as a whole could hardly be described as an easy read. None the less, it would be churlish to deny that this edition represents a valuable and enduring addition to Hogg studies, and it should put this hitherto neglected work back on the map.

There was a time when Sir William Jones was known only as a translator. However, he is now fast becoming appreciated as a pre-romantic writer of considerable quality, and anyone wishing to sample his work at its best could not do better than to turn to Michael J. Franklin's edition of Jones's *Selected Poetical and Prose Works*. Nearly half the volume is given over to poetry, most of it hitherto unobtainable except in early printed editions. Franklin has designed his work for 'a university audience', and in this context it works very well. Each poem is preceded by a headnote informing the reader of its significance, occasion and bibliographical history, and the footnotes, which appear on the same page as the text to which they refer, are good. They are full of useful pieces of information, specific comments on the poetry, scholarly observations and the like. It has to be said that Franklin is not forthcoming enough about the influence on Jones of contemporary writers; occasionally one hears echoes of Collins and Gray, for instance, but little space is given to the literary context.

All the same, this selection establishes Jones's importance to the romantic writers beyond doubt; his original poems and translations helped create the climate in which Coleridge wrote *Kubla Khan*, Southey *Thalaba* and Byron

The Giaour. Is he a Romantic? Well, in spite of all the claims to the contrary, I'm not convinced that he is; you could hardly doubt that he is a very significant pre-Romantic force, whose work foreshadows what was to come, but he remains a writer of his own time – the last three decades of the eighteenth century – and for that reason it is a shame that Franklin does so little to document the literary world in which he lived and breathed (although this is a task taken up in his monograph, reviewed below).

Woodstock Books continues to publish invaluable reprints of Romantic texts: most of this year's volumes were either novels or non-fictional prose, but poetry titles included Mary Robinson's *Poems 1791*, Felicia Hemans's *The Domestic Affections 1812* and Anna Laetitia Barbauld's *Eighteen Hundred and Eleven: A Poem 1812*. Robinson's early volume stands very usefully alongside her *Lyrical Tales 1800*, which Woodstock published in 1989 (now out of print). Together they reveal just how rapidly her talents developed beyond the Della Cruscan manner that characterizes the early work into the much more accomplished later mode influenced by *Lyrical Ballads*. Hemans's *The Domestic Affections* is perhaps her next most important single volume after *Records of Woman 1828*, reprinted by Woodstock in 1991. In her case, too, comparison of the earlier and later work provides us with the chance to witness the maturing of Hemans's craft. It is possible also to see how, in the case of both volumes, she worked their contents around the elaboration of a theme. Barbauld's *Eighteen Hundred and Eleven* is probably her most accomplished single poem; it shows her addressing the world around her and writing about it in terms that would provoke her sternest critics. It has for too long been neglected, and with the appearance of it in facsimile and in William McCarthy and Elizabeth Kraft's edition of her collected poems (reviewed in these pages last year), there can be no excuse for the neglect it has suffered since its first appearance.

Two exhibition catalogues have come to my attention, both deserving mention here. The shorter comes from a display at the Albin O. Kuhn Library and Gallery, University of Maryland, in July this year, entitled *Romantic Archaeologies: Comprising Some Images of the Age and Selected Women Writers*. As the title indicates, the exhibition was in two parts, comprising, first, a collection of silhouettes, engravings and paintings from the Romantic period and, secondly, one of manuscripts by Romantic women writers. The extraordinary thing about it was that all of the items come from the much larger collection of Paul F. Betz, the author of the catalogue. This is a beautifully produced publication, containing detailed accounts of the various items, full of interest for the scholar. Among other things, Professor Betz lists manuscripts of Joanna Southcott, Mary Robinson, Helen Maria Williams, Joanna Baillie, Mary Wordsworth, Dorothy Wordsworth, Caroline Bowles, Felicia Hemans, Maria Jane Jewsbury, Letitia Landon and many others. Some are transcribed, some reproduced in facsimile, some are merely described. The catalogue is, in other words, a mine of useful information about these writers not available from any other source. No one with a serious interest in romantic women writers can be afford to be without it. It has no ISBN, but can be obtained from the Albin O. Kuhn Library and Gallery, The University of Maryland, Baltimore County, Baltimore, Maryland, USA.

Anyone who saw the Keats exhibition at Dove Cottage in Grasmere during the year will be aware of the value of its catalogue: *John Keats*, by Robert

Woof and Stephen Hebron. This lavish production is a good deal more than a mere listing; it is, rather, an encyclopaedia of Keats's life and works. It is divided into nine sections, following the course of Keats's life, beginning with his childhood in Enfield and concluding with a section called 'Afterlife', about his posthumous reputation. Each section has a short introduction, followed by short essays on each of the exhibits, many of which are illustrated here. The volume as a whole boasts a chronology, a general introduction, a bibliography and an index. It comprises a remarkably full and detailed account of the exhibition and contains a vast amount of scholarly material not available elsewhere. In what other publication on this author can one find facsimile reprints of Keats's poems in the *Examiner*, alongside pictures of his teachers at Guy's, paintings of Keats's London haunts as he knew them, facsimiles of the first published texts of his Odes, numerous manuscript letters and verses, and all the major portraits? It is a unique record of this important exhibition, and will remain an essential reference tool for all serious students of the poet.

Given how embattled the concept of Romanticism is these days, it is intriguing to find how many general studies of the period were published this year. Aidan Day's *Romanticism* provides an erudite and lucid account of the concept, from its origins in the eighteenth century to the critical debates of the 1990s. Day is an excellent guide. For those daunted by the intricate manoeuvrings of deconstructionists, poststructuralists, new historicists and feminists, his book is a godsend. He navigates his way sure-footedly through the critical undergrowth, mapping out the critical and cultural terrain in a lucid and compelling fashion. It has to be said that, by the end of this book, one feels a certain amazement at what heavy weather some critics have made of deconstructing a concept that they themselves invented, but then that, perhaps, is the story of all literary criticism. It may not be brilliantly written, nor is it wildly exciting, but this volume will be of use to graduate and undergraduate readers wishing to understand the evolution of one of the most important literary movements over the last two centuries.

Anthony Harding produced one of the most demanding – and rewarding – general studies of Romanticism this year. *The Reception of Myth in English Romanticism* focuses on the reception and reinterpretation of myth by the Romantics. Some may quibble with the book's range; there are two chapters on Coleridge, three on Wordsworth, two on Shelley, one on Keats and on Coleridge and Shelley, but nothing on Blake or Byron. However, Harding's grasp of the existing criticism on the subject is inclusive and faultless, and only a pedant would attack him for lack of breadth. The first chapter, on *The Ancient Mariner*, arrives at the conclusion that the poem is 'about the making of myth', rather than a coherent exemplification of one. The significant point for Harding is that the poem's mediations of myth are best seen contextually and historically, in Coleridge's relations to two opposing schools of mythography – the orthodox comparatist view that pagan myths are 'fallen' versions of revealed truth and the heterodox thesis that all religious beliefs are to be traced to a primitive religion of nature. This preoccupation with interpretive structures extends into the chapter on *Christabel*, in which gothicism is seen in terms of poetic and 'mythopoeic' logic. Once again, Harding's argument is detailed and meticulous, and it is not easy to resist his conclusion that Coleridge's poem is about the destruction of the kind of 'inward stillness' that is necessary for poetic utterance. The chapters on Wordsworth must rank among some of the most intelligent and perceptive writing on the poet in recent years. Discussing the two-Part *Prelude*, Harding finds it to be very much of its time – '"mythological" in the sense that its landscape is peopled with spirits and genii in the manner of Thomson, Akenside, Collins, and Burns'. If he is right – and he surely must be – he is also correct in asserting the need to understand subsequent versions of Wordsworth's poem as reinterpretations of an interpretation. Harding's discussion foregrounds rival language-myths; in the essay on Keats, he is preoccupied with the tensions between human language – frail and ephemeral – and 'the language of stable terms', which the mythopoeic imagination attributes to the gods. This opposition is one that resurfaces in various contexts throughout. Harding is a fine critic, and this volume presents the reader with some compelling readings. *The Reception of Myth in English Romanticism* must rank as one of the best general studies of the decade.

The contributors to *Rhetorical Traditions and British Romantic Literature* (ed. Don H. Bialostosky and Lawrence D. Needham) are also interested in language. They take as their starting-point the critical misconception that as Romanticism rose rhetoric went into decline. Some of these essays will be familiar: those by Bialostosky, Jerome Christensen, James Engell, J. Douglas Kneale, John R. Nabholtz, Nancy S. Struever, Leslie Tannenbaum and Susan Wolfson, have appeared in print elsewhere, in other forms. They are augmented, however, by a number of essays commissioned for the volume, by Lawrence D. Needham, Richard W. Clancey, Bruce E. Graver, David Ginsberg, Theresa M. Kelley, Stephen C. Behrendt, Scott Harshbarger and Marie Secor. As an appendix this volume carries an English translation of Klaus Dockhorn's seminal essay, 'Wordsworth and the Rhetorical Tradition in England' (1941). By this point it will be clear that the value of this important book lies partly in the calibre of its contributors. Nearly all the essays are, in their various ways, essential reading for anyone interested in the use of language and rhetoric by Romantic writers. The translation of Dockhorn – amazingly, the first undertaken of this work – is priceless. And unlike many essay collections, this is coherent and focused on its subject. It is in four parts. Part I, 'Sophistic Rhetoric', examines the affinities of Coleridge and De Quincey to the sophistical rhetorical tradition that has informed some recent deconstructive versions of rhetoric. In the opening essay Jerome Christensen examines Coleridge's attack on sophistry and its implications; Susan Wolfson goes on to discuss Coleridge's mediation of 'figural language' in his poetry; and, pursuing lines opened up by these essayists, Lawrence Needham shows how De Quincey draws on sophistical rhetorical techniques. Part II, 'Classical Rhetoric', begins with John Nabholtz's survey of classical rhetorical educations received by major Romantic writers. The next essays concentrate on Wordsworth. In one of the most important, Richard W. Clancey describes Wordsworth's classical education, and its effects on his *Convention of Cintra*; Bruce Graver then finds classical echoes in *The Excursion*; and David Ginsberg traces the influence of epideictic verse on *Poems, in Two Volumes*. The next three essays go on to trace the value of the three principal offices of classical rhetoric – invention, disposition and style – for our understanding of Romantic poetry. Theresa M. Kelley considers Romantic discussions of originality in the light of Wordsworth's use of the classical topics of invention; Don H. Bialostosky shows how disposition informs *The Prelude*; J. Douglas

Kneale investigates the rhetoric of apostrophe in relation to Wordsworth; and in the final essay of this section Stephen C. Behrendt provides a compelling analysis of classical influences on Shelley. In Part III, Leslie Tannenbaum and Scott Harshbarger, in two important essays, investigate the use of Biblical rhetoric by Romantic writers. And in Part IV, James Engell, Nancy S. Struever and Marie Secor discuss the secular strain of eighteenth-century rhetoric as it informed the work of such writers as Scott and Austen. The contributors are all impressively learned on the subject, and their essays herald a welcome return to consideration of textual and stylistic concerns in relation to Romantic poetry and prose.

Simon Bainbridge's *Napoleon and English Romanticism* is one of those books that ought to have been written a long time ago, so crucial is its subject to Romanticism itself. Napoleon was more than a politician and soldier who conquered most of Europe and was then brought down by an unlikely coalition. He was, as has been long known, a powerful force on his contemporaries; or, as Bainbridge puts it, he became 'an imaginary figure for them, a fabrication created to embody their political and personal hopes and fears'. The hold he had on their imaginations is indicated by the list of luminaries with whom he was compared: Alexander the Great, Augustus, Tiberius and Julius Caesar, the Emperor Nepos, Lucius Sulla, Diocletian, Amurath, Dionysius the Younger, Charles V of Spain, Timur and Genghis Khan, Milo of Crotona, Sesostris, Cambyses, Hannibal, Tamburlaine, Bazajeth, Alva of Belgium, Frederick the Great, Cesare Borgia, Catiline, Charlemagne, Emperor Julian, Charles XII, Attila, Callicles, Ali Pasha, Oliver Cromwell, Marat, George Washington, William Pitt, Spencer Perceval, Wellington, Rob Roy, Macbeth, Richard III, Ulysses, Sir Calidore, Prometheus, Argus, Jupiter, Saturn, Mars, Deucalion, Pisistratus, Goliath, Irus, Gog, Magog, Moloch, Belshazzar, Nebuchadnezzar, Nimrod and Byron.

Bainbridge ranges widely, focusing on Wordsworth, Coleridge and Southey, with additional chapters on Byron and Hazlitt. The first generation was capable of sustained hostility towards Napoleon; the second, of much admiration. Bainbridge is a good critic – there is much informed comment here on such topics as Landor's *Gebir*, Byron's *Childe Harold* and Hazlitt's writings on Napoleon – but not all of his arguments are persuasive. I remain unconvinced that Kubla Khan was intended to be Napoleon, and as for the argument that he is a powerful presence in the one great Romantic poem in which he is not mentioned, *The Prelude*, the jury remains out. All the same, this remains a valuable addition to the somewhat variable Cambridge Studies in Romanticism Series, and one of the few that will remain essential reading for years to come. An early version of chapter 5 also appeared this year in the first number of the new periodical, *Romanticism*, as 'To "Sing it Rather Better"': Byron, the Bards, and Waterloo' (68–81). A related article in the same journal by Philip Shaw, 'Commemorating Waterloo', discusses Wordsworth's response to the famous battle (50–67).

Romantic Visions and Revisions of a New World: The Relevance of Romanticism for Teaching and Studying English Literature (ed. Michael Gassenmeier, Katrin Kamolz and Kirsten Sarna) brings together a number of the papers delivered at the Symposium of the 'Gesellschaft fur englische Romantik' held at Charles University, Prague, in October 1992. In a disarmingly frank preface the editors admit that in planning the conference, 'We had aimed high', and go on to hope that 'we may have been successful in some respects'. At any rate, don't allow the title to get your hopes up: there is nothing here about teaching, or indeed studying English Literature. Nor are the essays all concerned with visions of new worlds. Some are impressive, others are out of touch with current critical thought, and one or two seem surprisingly elementary. It is, in short, the sort of very mixed bag you would expect if you were to publish virtually the entire proceedings of a fairly small conference held in central Europe six years ago. It is essential reading for three first-rate essays: J. Drummond Bone, ' "Secular Criticism" and Byron's Ottava Rima Poems', Horst Höhne, 'The Concept of Energy in Keats's Poetry' and Horst Meller, 'Saving Poetry: Percy Bysshe Shelley as Legislator for the New World Order?'. Other contributions by Hermann Fischer, Martin Prochazka, Joseph Swann, Isabelle Famchon, Kirsten Sarna, Hans Ulrich-Möhr and Eberhard Schneider deal with such topics as *Peter Bell the Third*, the picturesque and Mozart. This book would have been improved considerably had it been less sloppily produced. It is packed with typos and spelling errors that ought to have been picked up at proof stage, to say nothing of countless formatting errors made on the word-processor on which it was typeset.

As this discussion indicates, this was the year in which Romanticism itself, as an intellectual construct, came under much sustained examination. The most obvious line of attack was to examine the ideology underlying it. This, in large part, is the strategy of Forest Pyle in *The Ideology of Imagination: Subject and Society in the Discourse of Romanticism*. By ideology, Pyle refers not to Wordsworth's early radicalism, for instance, but to 'the fundamental necessity of a representation of the social'. At the same time, he is interested in the articulations between Marxism and deconstruction, and therefore in the ruptures, the 'break' between, say, Shelley's version of imagination, and what he actually says. We are locked, in other words, in the same padded cell as Althusser, Marx, Benjamin and the rest. Pyle's central thrust is to explicate the means by which Romantic works present their relationships to language, subjectivity and society. He explores this subject in some very detailed, and quite scholarly, chapters on Coleridge's criticism, the Arab dream in *Prelude* Book V, *The Triumph of Life*, Keats's poetry and George Eliot's novels. There are some shrewd observations here – on such matters as Wordsworth and Coleridge's perception of English nationhood and on De Man's reading of Shelley, for instance – but they emerge within the context of the various reservations about this school of criticism. There are also some wilful misreadings, for instance, imposed on the reader so as to justify the claim of 'ruptures' within the text – as for instance the confusion of the term 'enshrinement' as used by Wordsworth in *The Prelude*, and 'entombment' (which Pyle would like him to have meant). More worryingly, one is struck by the determination inherent in an essentially historicist approach to literature to marginalize the political and social context in which literature is made. Coleridge and Wordsworth's interest in 'England' positively demands to be understood as the result of their early radicalism and the disappointment that followed. Deconstructionists long ago decided that *The Triumph of Life* is one of those texts that need not relate to anything much in the outside world, and that is one of the things that has succeeded in relegating it to the status of some kind of grotesque – detached from reality, fragmentary and susceptible to whatever reading critics may impose. The fact that it is an incomplete work that exists in a draft notebook containing many interesting deletions, false starts, alternative readings and the like – the kind of information that could actually make for a highly interesting deconstructionist analysis – continues to go unrecognized.

The problematizing of Romanticism is debated more compellingly in *Questioning Romanticism*, a collection of 11 essays edited by John Beer, which tackles the issue head-on by proposing that the term be considered 'as a site of fragmentation'. As a means of unifying a diverse collection of essays, this strategy works well. The very question is, of course, one way of requiring contributors to write manifestos of their ideological and critical prejudices, and this most of them proceed to do. Beer's choice of contributor was therefore crucial, and most of these essays give the debate a thorough working-over from every conceivable perspective. A. C. Goodson provides a brilliant account of Romantic 'language' and its 'failure'; Martin Aske discusses the way in which envy and resentment form a 'context of antagonism' in Romantic criticism; Philip W. Martin writes on Byron and Clare's articulation of 'self-identity'; Nigel Leask on De Quincey's aesthetics of murder; J. Drummond Bone on the existence of a European Romanticism; Susan J. Wolfson on poetic form; Tilottama Rajan on phenomenology and Romantic theory; Frederick Burwick on Romantic notions of mimesis; Lucy Newlyn on the aesthetics of indeterminacy; and Beer concludes the proceedings with a refreshingly anti-Caledonian discourse (in the Elian sense) on fragmentation itself. The only weak link in an otherwise impressive line-up is Anne K. Mellor, who proposes, as in her *Romanticism and Gender* (*YWES* 74.316–7), a 'male' and 'female' version of the subject. It's not that gender is not pertinent to an understanding of the literature – it most assuredly is; nor can it be the case that there are not experiences peculiar to female writers of the time that do not have a determining effect on what they wrote. But this is not of itself proof either that gender is the dominant factor in the aesthetics of the literary work, nor that, even if it were, it would have such an effect on all, or even most, male and female writers of any historical period. But Mellor is more interested in special pleading than in critical analysis. Wild generalizations, selective readings, wilful misinterpretation – any tactic will do. 'Romantic women literary critics used their writings not only to advocate new roles and more egalitarian marriages for women but also to condemn the abuses of patriarchy and the traditional construction of masculinity', she writes. You can make this kind of claim only if you misrepresent what was actually written, and how the writers saw themselves. Mellor's contribution is a sadly botched job in an otherwise distinguished volume.

Jeffrey C. Robinson's *Romantic Presences: Living Images from the Age of Wordsworth and Shelley* is one of those rare volumes that uses the indefinability of the concept of Romanticism not as the excuse for deconstruction or, indeed, the insistence and relentless questioning typical of the spirit of the present age, but as the springboard for inspired musings on a range of images of the period. It is both a critical volume and a piece of creative writing, combining critical disquisition with poetry. Only a cynic could resist the impulsiveness and charm with which Robinson flits from subject to subject – from Lucy, to Rosamund Gray, to Juana, in the second chapter, and from Virgil to Coleridge to Wordsworth to Whitman, in that on the reclining poet.

This is a volume full of energy and enthusiasm and provides a valuable reminder of what so much contemporary criticism seems determined either to forget or to ridicule: that literature begins with an act of pleasure – that of reading. It is out of that pleasure that all criticism springs.

Vincent Newey's *Centring the Self: Subjectivity, Society and Reading from Thomas Gray to Thomas Hardy* is a distinguished exception. In 11 essays on Gray, Cowper, Wordsworth, Coleridge, Keats, Byron, Shelley, George Eliot and Hardy (all of which have been previously published), Newey addresses the theme of selfhood. The construction of the self, he argues, took place within the context of each writer's retreat from the social and political environment in which they flourished. This is, if you like, Newey's response to the new historicist arguments of recent years, and is most explicitly dealt with in the chapters on Keats and Shelley. Other chapters develop this theme through unusual subjects – that on Wordsworth explores the influence of Bunyan, and that on *The Ancient Mariner* engages with readers' responses to the poem throughout its history.

This is not just another incoherent collection of essays; given the length of time over which they were written (nearly 20 years) they are surprisingly consistent, and do add up, I think, to an argument. In the preface, Newey declares himself an existentialist, and claims a sympathy with the view that language 'is no simple prison or subterfuge but a site of endless labour in fashioning the self and fashioning reality'. It is a view that is itself refashioned, with endless artfulness, in the course of the volume. One reason why it succeeds in making so many observations that, in retrospect, seem exemplary (particularly in the chapters on Keats, Byron and Shelley), is that it provides a valuable and much-needed foil to the obsessive (and apparently ubiquitous) need to make the Romantics politically acceptable – the necessary passport to continued critical acceptance. For Newey is content to read 'To Autumn' as 'a contemplative poem of sustained forgetting' (rather than Keats's outrage at the contemporary political situation); *Adonais* as about 'Imagination and the Poets [as] the agency and enabling source, the *sine qua non*, of all improvement and advance in human affairs'; and *Childe Harold's Pilgrimage* as 'vividly referential, impressive in its realizations of history, civilization, or nature'. It is, in that sense, an invaluable tome, characterized by good sense and sound erudition.

Willard Spiegelman's *Majestic Indolence* examines the theme of indolence, in both positive and negative forms, as it appears in the work of Wordsworth ('wise passiveness'), Coleridge (the numbing torpor of dejection), Shelley and Keats, tracing the notion back to its origins in the economic, medical, philosophical, psychological, religious and literary discourses from the middle ages onwards. Much erudition has been invested in the intellectual history of indolence, supplied in the book's opening chapter. Spiegelman follows its twists and turns, out of the medieval church and into the eighteenth-century coffee-house, taking in comments by Foucault and Coco Chanel on the way. The remainder of the book is preoccupied with the subject as it bears on the Romantics. Spiegelman ranges widely through Wordsworth's poetry, finding indolence in the least expected places. For him, Wordsworth is aware of the origins of poetry in play, which is transformed in adulthood into the tranquillity from which emotion is recollected. The chapter on Coleridge is more focused, homing in on dejection as it is reworked in his poetry, particularly the famous ode, 'Limbo' and 'Ne Plus Ultra'. That of Keats is particularly fine, in which Spiegelman works backwards in time from 'To Autumn' to the rest of the Odes, concluding with an ingenious interpretation of these difficult poems. The concluding chapter provides much useful discussion of the work of American inheritors of the Romantic tradition – primarily Whitman and Frost.

Interest in women Romantics continues to burgeon; one of this year's most useful collections of essays was *Romantic Women Writers: Voices and Countervoices* (ed. Paula R. Feldman and Theresa M. Kelley). As with so many collections of this kind, this is a very diverse group. But the editors have given the volume structure by dividing it up under four headings. 'Reimagining Romantic Canons' assesses the case for reformulating the canon. One of the most impressive of the essays appears first – Isobel Armstrong's 'The Gush of the Feminine: How Can We Read Women's Poetry of the Romantic Period?' Armstrong's argument is that, for the moment, women's writing should be read in isolation from that of their male contemporaries. This is an important point; after all, the debate over a gendered Romanticism must stand or fall on whether it is possible to detach women's writing and examine it separately from that of men. In another essay, 'Gendering the Soul', Susan Wolfson takes a different tack; she believes that the poetry of men and women needs to be compared if we are to trace the different ways in which sex and the soul are discussed in verse. Other essays in Part One are Stephen C. Behrendt's 'Mary Shelley, *Frankenstein*, and the Woman Writer's Fate', and Mitzi Myers, 'De-Romanticizing the Subject: Maria Edgeworth's "The Bracelets", Mythologies of Origin, and the Daughter's Coming to Writing'. In Part Two, 'Textual Strategies', three contributors examine the rhetoric with which women writers specify the role of gender in their work. As the editor of the recent scholarly edition of Anna Laetitia Barbauld's collected poems, William McCarthy is well placed to discuss her preoccupations, and in a valuable essay, ' "We Hoped the *Woman* Was Going to Appear": Repression, Desire, and Gender in Anna Laetitia Barbauld's Early Poems', he places her within the evolving feminist tradition. He finds her to be 'emotionally conflicted, struggling against strong parental and cultural repressions of her energies'. In 'Felicia Hemans and the Effacement of Woman', Anthony John Harding observes that although Hemans records woman's experience without seeming to challenge the cultural paradigms by which it was defined in the nineteenth century, the experiences she records register the price of compliance, as female personae and voices were obliterated. Perhaps, as he argues, Hemans's poetry does valorize domesticity, but I wonder whether this might be to minimize the importance of her writing about such issues as Welsh nationalism, and to take a somewhat one-sided view of her comments on relations between the sexes. The final essay in this section of the book is Judith Pike's 'Resurrection of the Fetish in *Gradiva*, *Frankenstein*, and *Wuthering Heights*'. Two essays about Sydney Owenson, Lady Morgan, begin Part Three, 'Nationalism, Patriotism, and Authorship': Jeanne Moskal's 'Gender, Nationality, and Textual Authority in Lady Morgan's Travel Books', and Richard C. Sha's 'Expanding the Limits of Feminine Writing: The Prose Sketches of Sydney Owenson (Lady Morgan) and Helen Maria Williams'. The section concludes with a fine essay by Moira Ferguson, 'Janet Little and Robert Burns: The Politics of the Heart'. In this welcome analysis of that largely unknown

Scottish working-class woman writer, Janet Little, Ferguson analyses the way in which she criticized her social superiors through her attacks on Burns, and identifies the contours of her distinctive Romanticism. 'Performance and the Marketplace', Part Four, measures the impact of different kinds of performance on individual careers. Catherine Burroughs, in ' "Out of the Pale of Social Kindred Cast": Conflicted Performance Styles in Joanna Baillie's *De Monfort*', identifies a fundamental Romantic conflict in Baillie's dramatic theory and practice between a desire for the privacy of closet drama and a recognition that drama, particularly tragedy, requires public performance. She finds this conflict in *De Monfort*, where the heterosexual male protagonist is, Burroughs argues, a closeted homosexual. Susan Levin's 'The Gipsy is a Jewess: Harriett Abrams and Theatrical Romanticism' traces the career of one of the most successful theatrical performers of the time, to show how Abrams used her Jewishness and feminity as marketable qualities. Judith Pascoe's edition of Mary Robinson's poems is much awaited; in the meantime, her essay, 'Mary Robinson and the Literary Marketplace', provides a fascinating discussion of Robinson's contributions to the *Morning Post*. In the variety of her literary representations, Robinson dazzled her readership with her virtuosity, transcending the reputation of 'fallen woman' which had dogged her since the Prince Regent had so ignominiously and publicly abandoned her.

The word 'conflicted' is the one most frequently used in this collection, and the tracing of inner conflicts within women writers becomes almost axiomatic as a guiding principle. Could this be, perhaps, because the authors feel torn between the lure of traditional ways of thinking about women's writing, and those which have more recently been formulated? In any case, this is one of the most ambitious and successful collections of its kind to appear thus far, and many of its component parts will continue to be used by those interested in women's writing of the period.

Another book on this subject, Moira Ferguson's *Eighteenth-Century Women Poets: Nation, Class, and Gender*, is equally valuable. Ferguson examines the work of three women poets of the eighteenth century – Mary Collier, Ann Yearsley and Janet Little – exploring the ways in which national identity influenced gender and class affiliations, and how gender determined a nationalist impulse, particularly as played out during the revolutionary period (1770–1800) in which most of the texts were written. Parts of this book have appeared elsewhere, and the chapter on Little is very largely a reprise of Ferguson's contribution to *Romantic Women Writers*. But the volume as a whole is tremendously useful for the insights it has to offer on each of these important writers. One of the most useful chapters is that on the unpublished poems (in manuscript in Bristol) of Ann Yearsley; one regrets only that Ferguson did not see fit to publish these unknown works in an appendix to her volume. As it is, she asks that we obtain the relevant number of *TSWL* in which she first presented these fugitive works. But this is only a minor quibble; the volume is exceedingly valuable, and will provide the basis for much useful work in the future along similar lines. One yearns for a similar study of nationalism in the work of Lady Caroline Lamb, Sydney Owenson (Lady Morgan) and Felicia Hemans. The ever-useful *WC* provided a number of articles on Romantic women poets this year, including an overview of their work by Jonathan Wordsworth, 'Ann Yearsley to Caroline Norton: Women

Poets of the Romantic Period' (26.114–24); Pamela Woof's detailed analysis of Dorothy Wordsworth's Alfoxden journal, 'The Alfoxden Journal and its Mysteries' (26.125–33); Lisa Vargo on Coleridge and Mary Robinson (26.134–37); and Duncan Wu's lucid exposition of Lady Caroline Lamb's most impressive poem, 'Appropriating Byron: Lady Caroline Lamb's *A New Canto*' (26.140–6). That little-known, and largely neglected journal, *The Hatcher Review*, published what may be the first article about 'Emmeline Fisher, A Forgotten Wiltshire Poet: Her Links with William Wordsworth and the National Anthem', by Neville Hinxman (4.16–30). This welcome piece contains texts of three of Fisher's poems, otherwise extremely difficult to obtain.

Duncan Wu's *Romanticism: A Critical Reader* was published as a companion and a supplement to his *Romanticism: An Anthology* (*YWES* 75.383–4). It contains 18 essays which deal for the most part with works included in the anthology, while affording coverage to key elements, including fiction, beyond the anthologist's scope. Most of the movements and schools of thought active over the last 15 years are represented, including feminism, new historicism, genre theory, psychoanalysis and deconstructionism. The contributors are Marilyn Butler, James K. Chandler, V. A. De Luca, James A. W. Heffernan, Nelson Hilton, Margaret Homans, Alan Liu, Jerome J. McGann, Peter J. Manning, Anne K. Mellor, Tom Paulin, Balachandra Rajan, Tilottama Rajan, Edward Said, Karen Swann, Eve Kosofsky Sedgwick, Leon Waldoff and Kathleen M. Wheeler. No other anthology of modern criticism has such scope, either in terms of methodology, or of content. Its abiding impression is of the richness and variety of contemporary criticism, and it contains essays that will in years to come be regarded as canonical. It is an indispensable companion to any university course in Romantic studies. In addition, important articles published this year on the subject of Romanticism include Elinor S. Shaffer, 'Ideologies of Imagination: Remote Readings of Romanticism', *Proceedings of the XIIIth Congress of the International Comparative Literature Association*, and David Bromwich, 'A Note on the Romantic Self', *Raritan* 14.66–74. Theoretical disquisitions on the subject of considerable importance include Giuseppe Nori, 'The Problematics of Sympathy and Romantic Historicism' (*SIR* 34.3–28) and Steven E. Cole, 'Evading Politics: The Poverty of Historicizing Romanticism' (*SIR* 34.29–49).

It is worth mentioning a couple of extraordinary auction catalogues this year, which contain otherwise unobtainable bibliographical materials and other data of scholarly interest. Both auctions concerned date from December, the first from 6 December, when Bonhams of Knightsbridge held an auction of volumes of 'Provincial Poetry 1789–1839' (sale number 26829). This was, in fact, the sale of volumes collected by C. R. Johnson and described in his *Provincial Poetry 1789–1839, British Verse Printed in the Provinces: The Romantic Background*, which contained an introduction by Robert Woof (London, 1992). The sale thus included many significant and rare volumes of the period, including first editions of Joseph Cottle's *Alfred*, Mary Robinson's *Lyrical Tales*, Isabella Lickbarrow's *Poetical Effusions*, Frank Sayers's *Poems*, William Lisle Bowles's *Sonnets, Written Chiefly on Picturesque Spots* (1789), Ebenezer Elliot's *Corn Law Rhymes* and Barbara Hoole's *Poems*. It is regrettable that the collection could not have been kept together and acquired intact by a university library. The other catalogue of considerable interest dates from 18 December, when Sotheby's in London held a large sale of English Literature and History items. This included, among other things, some important Byron manuscripts. But by far the most intriguing items were from the Margaret Goalby collection of Wordsworthiana. Goalby's collection is legendary among scholars, and until this sale was completely inaccessible. Besides other things it contained (lot 279) a copy of Joseph Wilkinson's *Select Views in Cumberland, Westmorland, and Lancashire* bearing manuscript alterations in Wordsworth's hand. This important item is now at the Wordsworth Library, Grasmere.

Finally, this year saw the long-awaited publication of the Charles Lamb Society's *Handlist to the Charles Lamb Society Collection at Guildhall Library* by Deborah Hedgecock, which appeared as a Supplement to *ChLB* 89. It has long been known that the Society owns a number of Romantic manuscripts, and this catalogue, which documents the most significant, describes them in lavish detail. The kernel of the collection are letters by George Dyer, written to various correspondents including Southey and Mary Mathilda Betham. Others include items by Hazlitt, Lamb, Croker, Cottle, Sara Coleridge and J. G. Lockhart. The collection also includes some rare books and a number of unique portraits of various literary figures of the day [D.Wu].

(b) Works on Individual Poets
There are several significant publications to report, including a substantial Blake bibliography, a new biography and the last two volumes in the William Blake Trust facsimile series.

G. E. Bentley, Jr's *Blake Books Supplement* is a vast bibliographic compendium of the Blake original texts plus an exhaustive listing of secondary materials updating his earlier *Blake Books* (Clarendon, 1977). Bentley's indefatigable efforts over many years have produced this encyclopaedic and indispensable book. Most scholars will turn to it for its comprehensive listing of critical works published since the mid-1970s, in several major languages, which goes far beyond any of the IT-based databases known to the present writer. It lists some ten or 15 new textual works (interpreting a newly located copy of an illuminated book, as a 'new work') by Blake and provides a full technical analysis and account of these works and their movements around both private and public collections. It gathers together much of the consequence of Robert Essick's researches into the art and takes account of Joc Viscomi's technical discoveries announced in *Blake and the Idea of the Book* (*YWES* 74.321–2). With so many of Blake's illuminated texts having been split up or supplemented by the artist's own 'odd-jobbing' of separate plates from the illuminated books, keeping track of the vast amount of material is a gigantic and intricate task. Bentley's book and its format reflects the growing empiricism which abounds these days in Blake scholarship. It illustrates the complexities and paradoxes of working in an area where, while new discoveries of Blake's own writing do not much increase, the problems in understanding the materiality of Blake's text expands remorselessly as old scholarship is found technically wanting or inadequate and standard interpretations are proven, objectively, to have been chimeras. Considerations of provenance, watermarking, process, technique and dating cannot be avoided today. Bentley's book will be the first point of consultation for this purpose, but surely *Blake Books Supplement* will also be one of the last bibliographic enterprises on this scale to have eschewed publication in cd-rom format. Although Bentley's index is as comprehensive as his scholarship, a searchable electronic text would make more efficient use of the sheer wealth of information he has accumulated by good, 'old fashioned' labour, tenacity and skill.

Hot on the heels of *Blake Books Supplement* is Bentley's now annual 'William Blake and His Circle: A Checklist of Publications and Discoveries in 1995' in *Blake* (*Blake* 29[1996].131–67). Much new information, especially on original Blakes, which Bentley collates here makes it an essential supplement to the *Supplement*. Practically speaking, using these two works, year on year, will largely eliminate the need for searching anything but the current year's studies on the electronic databases. With a nice sense of self-deprecating comedy, Bentley's 'Checklist' for this year also provides a photograph of Blake's spectacles, courtesy of the Fitzwilliam Museum, plus the visionary's exact prescription requirements. For a stunningly collated, world-wide textual sampling of extant copies, Bentley's separate essay in the journal *Blake*, 'The Physiognomy of Lavater's *Essays*: False Imprints "1792" and "1789" ' (*Blake* 29.16–23) gives a marvellously detective tale of bibliographic sleuthery wonderfully revealing of the skill, dexterity and resourcefulness of the contemporary pressmen who were not above mixing and matching paper, resetting type to elide differences between 'editions' and generally indulging in a generation of mystifying publishing skulduggery. Not least, this *Blake* essay is also a *tour-de-force* of Bentley's painstaking researches and irrepressible humour.

Robert N. Essick's 'Blake in the Marketplace, 1995, Including a Survey of Blakes in Private Ownership' (*Blake* 29[1996].108–30) provides a complementary annual service which should be used in conjunction with Bentley's 'Checklist'. Notable photographs in this year's survey are a picture of a *Book of Urizen* pl. 3 headpiece, from a recently re-located colour printed separate plate, showing unique androgyny in the figure plus a photograph of the 'Leviathan' picture from *The Marriage*, another colour printed separate plate, with what looks to be a highly significant new caption (' "O revolving serpent"/ "O the Ocean of Time & Space" '). This is inscribed by Blake but the legend does not appear to be recorded in Erdman's Anchor/Doubleday standard edition.

The off-prints from the illuminated books which Blake had to hand more or less throughout his life are fairly representatively sampled amongst the several other introductory services provided by the two final volumes for the William Blake Trust, volume 4, *The Continental Prophecies*, edited by D. W. Dörrbecker and volume 6, *The Urizen Books*, edited by the present writer. I quote here from Bentley's notice in his *Blake* 'Checklist': 'One of the virtues of the series is that the copies reproduced have sometimes not been reproduced at all or adequately before. *America* (H) has not previously been reproduced, *Europe* (B) was reproduced in 1978 only in black-and-white and in 1990 in reduced size and *Song of Los* (A) was only somewhat approximately reproduced in 1890 and in black-and-white in 1978. *The Continental Prophecies* thus exhibits forms of Blake's works scarcely accessible otherwise save in the originals. Similarly, for *The First Book of Urizen* (D), *The Book of Ahania* (A), and *The Book of Los* (A) in *The Urizen Books*, *Urizen* (D) was previously reproduced in 1876 only in black-and-white, *Ahania* (A) in 1892, 1973, 1974 (in black-and-white). (*Ahania* and *The Book of Los* survive in one copy each.) *The Urizen Books* reproduced here are all color-printed, a medium notoriously difficult to reproduce, and these new reproductions are notably satisfactory in this respect. Equally impressive is the quality of the scholarship which accompanies the reproductions.'

Peter Ackroyd's new biography, *Blake*, is aimed at a broader market than academe but is none the worse for it. Ackroyd's strength lies not so much in making new discoveries about Blake's life, but rather in reading widely and synthesizing in his highly individual way much of the most interesting Blake scholarship of the last 20 years. Broadly speaking, Ackroyd's Blake is still recognizably Gilchrist's – perhaps too much so for my tastes – but there are some new angles on the visionary/mystic approach. For example, Ackroyd's detailed knowledge of eighteenth-century London topography is highly illuminating, and his thumb-nail sketches of contemporary popular culture or notable metropolitan incidents provide a vivid context for Ackroyd's careful assemblage of the narrative from his highly eclectic sources. Stylistically, Blake's life is told, as far as possible, through the direct quotation of Blake's own words from his letters, poetry, marginalia, inscriptions and other locations, but skilfully snipped and fragmented by Ackroyd out of their original context with, actually, great fidelity. Of course, Ackroyd's *Blake* won't suit everyone, and it is certainly not as definitive as some press reviews have suggested, but it is an important book because it will receive a wider readership than might ordinarily be expected. Blake studies are blessed by Ackroyd's imprint and enthusiasm. A more fully empirical biography of Blake has yet to be written but this one is a substantial advance in how to tell the story of Blake's life accurately and interestingly.

Meanwhile, the slow accumulation of new information continues to advance. Important amongst recent work is Aileen Ward's 'Who was Robert Blake?' (*Blake* 28[1994–5].84–9), which gives a new date for the birth of Blake's short-lived brother (June 1762) and Joe Viscomi's 'Blake in the Marketplace 1852: Thomas Butts, Jr. and Other Unknown Nineteenth-Century Blake Collectors' (*Blake* 29.40–68) which gives extensive and extremely detailed new information about the Butts family and the first sales, dispersal and general provenance of some major Blake pictures. Although difficult to summarize, Viscomi's work once again necessitates that we reassess the reputation and standing of Blake's art even before Gilchrist's biography. Viscomi is also the author of 'William Blake's "The Phoenix / to Mrs Butts" ' (*Blake* 29.12–15) which details the implications of new evidence (found by Keri Davies and Ted Ryan) that Blake's most significant patron, Thomas Butts, was *twice* married. The essay is a signal example of the perils of dating texts (in this case Blake's recently discovered 'Phoenix' poem) on purely stylistic grounds. Interpreter beware!

An unusual subtext of Ackroyd's *Blake*, but one which is revealing of the biographer's own interests, is that he appears to have picked up on the significance of the recent work of Marsha Keith Schuchard in Freemasonry and European *illuminati* studies. Schuchard is a notable influence on Ackroyd. Her richly researched 'William Blake and the promiscuous baboons: a Cagliostroan séance gone awry' (*BJECS* 18.185–200) actually takes as its starting point a few incidental details from one of the 'Memorable Fancies' in *The Marriage of Heaven and Hell*, but we are then led on an extraordinary, but exhaustively referenced, journey into Swedenborgian and *illuminati* subcultures at the end of the 1780s. Richard Cosway, Blake, Fuseli, Lord George Gordon and even the Prince of Wales, are brought together in the sort of chaotic blend of political radicalism, extreme religious dissent, shadowy international collaboration, theatrical spectacle and espionage which, more and more we now realize, was not uncommon in late eighteenth-century London. Unusually, Schuchard finds that these alternative ideologies transliterated themselves fluidly and extensively between both the artisan and the aristocratic classes. Highly researched (in this case with 85 footnotes to mainly primary sources), Schuchard's work is extremely important in helping us grasp this incredible picture of late eighteenth-century European mentalities.

As it happens, and this assists both Schuchard and Christopher Heppner's work discussed below, Jacqueline E. M. Latham's short note entitled 'The Arlington Court Picture' (*Blake* 29.24) suggests that the possible first purchaser of this important painting, Sophia Chichester, was a country house owning nobleman's daughter who moved in circles associated with Swedenborgianism, the millennial prophet Joanna Southcott and who funded freethinking radicals such as the much imprisoned *Republican* editor Richard Carlile.

A fine book on a still largely uncharted area of Blake studies is Andrew Lincoln's *Spiritual History: A Reading of William Blake's Vala or The Four Zoas*. There are formidable complexities in the chronology of the evolution of this manuscript poem, not to mention a legion of misconceptions about its meaning and status within Blake's output. Lincoln offers a lucid and comprehensive account of the poem which allows for, as he puts it, a 'staged reading' of the poem which remains faithful to the constraints of the text. There are helpful subheadings within chapters, much needed introductory textual comments at the beginnings of chapters and several appendices, all of which contribute to making *Spiritual History* an approachable and highly useful study. Specifically, Lincoln's modestly subtitled study charts developments in how *The Four Zoas* treated broad themes of human history, usually as explicitly relevant to Christianity but also maturing into Blake's understanding of how patterns of human development are capable of commenting critically on contemporary nationalism, radicalism and religion. A particular strength lies in the sure-footed way Lincoln traces Blake's critique in *The Four Zoas* of mainstream Enlightenment thinkers while at the same time being able to glance illuminatingly towards the breadth and sheer quirkiness of Blake's mythology which make it such an individual response to eighteenth-century thought. Everywhere in *Spiritual History* is evidence of much careful deliberation and sophisticated critical judgement applied to one of Blake's most truly daunting works.

Even as Blake fiddled interminably, if positively, with *The Four Zoas* manuscript, he was also turning out his vast contracted series of illustrations for Edward Young's *Night Thoughts*. Irene H. Chayes's '*Night Thoughts* 273 and "Mercury at the Crossroads": Constructing Blake's Quarrels with Young' (*CLQ* 31.123–41) draws on largely forgotten depictions of Mercury across nearly two centuries of emblem books in order to make a convincing case for Blake's knowledgeable critiquing of a visual trope which helped Blake distance himself from Young's non-visionary, surprisingly pessimistic understanding of faith, life and death.

Turning to studies which, on balance, are more interpretative than contextual, Dennis M. Welch's 'Blake's *Songs of Experience*: The Word Lost and Found' (ES 3.238–52) provides sensitively nuanced readings of major *Experience* poems in order to trace Blake's idea of the dissemination and reception of the Divine Word. In a valuable close reading of 'The Tyger', Welch picks up, unusually, on the Divine *comic* vision contained within many of these *Songs*. Also concerned with Blake's critique of religious values is David Goldweber's 'The Style and Structure of William Blake's "Bible of Hell" ' (*ELN* 32.51–65). The essay largely continues studies begun by Jerome McGann and Robert Essick. There are several nice individual observations on metrical matters in *Urizen*, *Ahania* and *The Book of Los* but the essay is done somewhat simplistically: 'Subject matter that should be exacting and invigorating (that is, Biblical) is actually frightening and upsetting (that is, Hellish).' Continuing the study of Blake and the Bible is Kerry Ellen McKeever's 'Naming the Name of the Prophet: William Blake's Reading of Byron's *Cain: A Mystery*' (*SIR* 34.615–36) which reminds us that Blake's still neglected *Ghost of Abel* is the only place where he acknowledges a contemporary poet. Incorporating a close examination of the Biblical texts, McKeever argues for a complex intertexuality between Blake and Byron in which 'Blake confers upon Byron's text the power of divine authority' before creating his own '(re)visionary' text (*The Ghost of Abel*) which then helps us understand both *Jerusalem* and Byron.

James Hogg's *William Blake's Recreation of Gnostic Myth: Resolving the Apparent Incongruities* is a book about which it is difficult to be positive. It is baldly stated that 'Blake was a Christian gnostic first and foremost' but, after disarmingly admitting the possibility of intuitive or supernatural gnostic sources available to Blake, Hogg settles on the argument that 'Blake's poetry was produced in the same revelatory fashion as the codices of Nag Hammadi [a major gnostic source], with which Blake could *not* have been familiar' (my emphasis). In other words, don't expect any transmission routes for knowledge but do expect that gnosticism will be, willy nilly, mapped onto Blake. It's all fairly ramshackle. For example, Paul Youngquist's *Madness and Blake's Myth* (PSUP, 1989) is cited but not listed in 'Works Cited', neither does the extensively referenced Nag Hammadi appear in the Index. As far as this reviewer can tell, Hogg's argument is quite simply that Blake was an intuitive gnostic or else that gnosticism was a revealed presence to him. If that's a valuable insight, and some might think it is, then other scholars might wish to proceed further, but hopefully using a more empirically based foundation than the one offered here.

Fortunately for Blake studies, there are plenty of good scholars willing to risk advanced theoretical and interpretative insights which are more substantially based. Gerda S. Norvig has written a challenging essay on 'Female Subjectivity and the Desire of Reading In(to) Blake's *Book of Thel*' (*SIR* 34.255–71) in which she reminds us of the Greek roots of Thel's name in 'desire' before the study takes off into a theoretically sophisticated (mainly Lacanian) examination of how Thel 'comes to stand *for* and stand *in*, a liminal position between theory and resistance to theory' which is 'radically gendered'. The gendered nature of Thel's resistive strategies against incarceration in Har have been noticed before, but Norvig's approach is a strong one, firmly grounded in relevant literary history. The essay notably extends the recent inauguration of Blake's *Thel* as an important site in which several cultural and theoretical issues contend. Not least, as Norvig recognizes, we must get used to thinking that Thel's natural next neighbours might be Wollstonecraft's heroines.

Another theoretically informed study is David Punter's 'Legends of the Animated Body: Blake's Albion and the Body and Soul of the Nation' (*Romanticism* 1.161–76). Despite its essay length, Punter's article has more of the feel of a mini-monograph in that it compasses a rich and widely ranging argument which strikingly enlists considerations of nationalism within a psychoanalytical theoretical framework. Punter discusses Blake's 'rhetoric of animation', the separateness and autonomy of the nation's minute particulars, variously figured in Blake as animal, county, city and zoa. Works such as *The Four Zoas* or *Jerusalem* prompt us to inquire whether we should (or can) make these (Kleinian) parts whole, perhaps to resolve them into Albion, Jerusalem or else their negations. This is a bold and original essay which has much to do with the purpose of myth as both constituting and being constituted by nation.

Concepts of nation and race also underpin Lauren Henry's fascinating article 'Sunshine and Shady Groves: What Blake's "Little Black Boy" Learned from African Writers' (*Blake* 29.4–11). In particular, Henry provides a consideration of several contemporary texts written by blacks which may have informed Blake's understanding of the black condition. Notable texts are Phillis Wheatley's 'An Hymn to the Morning' (reproduced in full here) whose tropes are closely read and which Henry argues reveal that Blake enclosed in his poem a critique of Christianity contrasted to African sun worship as recollected by American slaves such as Wheatley. The essay also usefully provides a full bibliography of contemporary and modern essays on these issues.

Christopher Heppner's *Reading Blake's Designs* is a careful and cautiously powerful monograph on Blake's pictures. It is also one of the most witty (viz. his chapter 'Humpty Dumpty Blake'). Heppner studies Blake's images (mainly his art rather than the illuminated books or engravings) and traces their evolution, both in relationship to their specific sources and how successfully they embody Blake's genius for allegorizing. Additionally, Heppner also considers how Blake's practice fitted in with such theoretical statements as he occasionally made about art. The result, as others have found in relationship to Blake's text, is that Blake was ever the visual *bricoleur*, someone continually evolving, fudging, adapting, rejecting, developing, experimenting. In particular, Heppner traces the complex stages of how Blake's visual imagination was mediated by the conceptual emphasis his art necessitated. This problem of the parameters of expressivity in Blake (especially given that the human body is virtually Blake's sole semiotic), is given a fascinating discussion throughout the book. However, it will probably be Heppner's striking new interpretation of the so-called 'Arlington Court Picture' which will become the first port of call for many Blakeans. This magnificently enigmatic late watercolour has long defeated and defied interpretation – much critical ink has been spilt, reputations have been lost and won, etc. Within one substantial chapter, Heppner identifies half of its complex subject as originating in Sandys's translation of Ovid's *Metamorphoses*, strongly relating it to a picture Samuel Palmer saw in Blake's room in Fountain Court. In short, on the basis of cognate Blake pictures and the presence of hitherto unnoticed Hebrew script on the cloak of the main male figure in the painting (crucially now identified as Isaiah), Heppner argues that the picture is an invitation to the viewer to choose between the Christian and Classical world pictures. Without wishing us to literally take him at his word, Heppner suggests that a good alternative descriptive title for this picture (since Blake supplied none himself) would be 'Isaiah's Prophecy of the Messiah's Coming to Redeem the Pythagorean Sea of Time and Space'. At last.

Of internet resources, these are still under development, but several came on-line this year. Chief amongst them is 'The William Blake Archive' edited by Morris Eaves, Robert Essick and Joseph Viscomi (http://jefferson. village.virginia.edu/blake/blake.wip-1.html). The facilities offered include, 'Search the Blake Archive', 'Works in the Archive', 'Public and Private Collections in the Archive', 'The contents of the Archive, organized by the collections from which they are drawn', '*The Complete Poetry and Prose of William Blake* Edited by David V. Erdman (The text and textual notes of Erdman's edition as revised in 1988)', 'Selected Bibliography and Reference Works. A list of useful critical articles and books about Blake's work, with a list of widely used editions and reference books', 'Plan of the Archive', 'The conception of the Archive and a schedule of the execution', 'Archive Update', 'Related Sites: A list of other Internet sites of interest to users of the Blake Archive'. This is a considerable and rapidly expanding facility by three of the best known scholars in Blake studies, complemented by wonderful facilities, including the human, at the University of Virginia. I have notified this one now because it is likely to prove the most stable and expansionist Blake site and so, as a matter of course, a site advisedly to be visited for archival information on Blake studies [D.Worrall].

Michael J. Franklin's monograph in the UWalesP's Writers of Wales series, *Sir William Jones*, is the essential companion to his edition of Jones's *Selected Poetical and Prose Works* (reviewed above). With these books behind you, it's impossible not to read Jones in the light of what was to come – particularly the poetry of Wordsworth and Byron – and yet I wonder whether that really qualifies him as a romantic. The fact is, few men can have been more thoroughly a product of enlightenment preoccupations than Jones; true, the study of language was to feed straight into Wordsworth's Preface, but Jones's interest had the same academic streak to be found in Blair and Monboddo, and resulted in what, despite their haunting lyrical beauty, are essentially on a par with the writings of Ossian. His contemporaries were Collins and the bluestockings, and it would be more accurate to read his work in that context. Franklin has performed a great service for Jones in writing this monograph, which documents Jones's life and work with care and wit. It will remain the standard introduction to this intriguing writer for a long time to come. R. K. Kaul's *Studies in William Jones: An Interpreter of Oriental Literature* is a collection of essays on diverse aspects of Jones's thought. The best of them is probably the first, a discussion of orientalism, although there are some good essays here on the impact of India on Jones's work, Persian poetry, and Jones's translation of Kalidasa's *Sakuntala*. Further critical work on Jones appeared this year in *N&Q* 42.75–6, in the form of a note by Peter Knox-Shaw, '*Vathek* and "The Seven Fountains" by Sir William Jones', which argued for his influence on Beckford's great novel.

After a quiet year in Wordsworth studies last year, 1995 has produced a bumper crop of monographs. Brennan O'Donnell's *The Passion of Meter: A Study of Wordsworth's Metrical Art* was among the most distinguished, the fruit of many years' sustained research into Wordsworth's metrical theory and practice. O'Donnell begins by observing how misunderstood, and misrepresented, Wordsworth's comments on the subject have been; placing them in context, he demonstrates that they are both more complex, and more innovatory, than has been understood. The romantic period, he argues, is 'a watershed in the history of versification'. On the basis of his study, it is clear also that the nuts and bolts of the poetry – its metre and rhythms – are indispensable to a full appreciation of its originality. The scope of the book is broad; O'Donnell begins with the early poetry – *An Evening Walk* and *Descriptive Sketches* – moves into *Lyrical Ballads*, the mature blank verse, and concludes with a discussion of *On the Power of Sound*. In each case, O'Donnell's argument is that, if Wordsworth refers back to his predecessors, he also reinvented poetic language with each phase of his career. This is a useful corrective to an age obsessed with theorizing; it grounds Wordsworth in the very issue that preoccupied him as a poet – the renewal of craft. Some may feel that this is carried to an extreme: few readers will pass by his table showing the distribution of pauses after syllables and percentage of occurrence in various texts without alarm. And, very occasionally, the prose can sound a little clogged by technicalities. But these are minor cavils. This is a triumph of scholarly criticism, and should be required reading for all Wordsworthians.

Mark Jones's *The 'Lucy Poems': A Case Study in Literary Knowledge* provides an exhaustive examination of that elusive group of lyrics, from their first appearance in print to their treatment by modern critics. It is not, as Jones admits, a study of the poet; it is concerned instead with reading, editing and criticism amid the rise of the institutional study of literature since Wordsworth. For this reason the Lucy poems are the ideal subject; their grouping is, after all, the invention of critics. Indeterminacy is a chief preoccupation here; that of the initial textual moment, and that of the published works in critical hands. What is a 'Lucy poem'? Jones answers that question with clarity: it 'is an untitled lyrical ballad that either mentions Lucy or is always placed with another poem that does, that either explicitly mentions her death or is susceptible of such a reading, and that is spoken by Lucy's lover'.

The substance of the volume is its analysis in chapters 2 to 5 of the critical history of these works. Chapter 2 deals with 'the nineteenth century's grouping and narratization of the "Lucy poems" as an effort to objectify and fix literary meanings and judgements'. In chapter 3, Jones proposes that parody is 'the bad conscience of nineteenth-century criticism', and that it is an alternative vehicle of interpretation and comment. In many ways, this chapter is the most surprising, and impressive. Besides offering a highly persuasive critical analysis of the function and nature of parody, it also contains some astute, and belated, discussion of parodies themselves. Chapters 4 and 5 deal with twentieth-century criticism from Hirsch to De Man, including useful comment on the limitations of deconstructionist criticism. A helpful appendix (a rarity these days) provides scholarly texts of the Lucy poems, including variants, manuscript sources, and so forth.

This is really a book about the limitations of literary criticism, and represents a timely admonition to those who would claim divinely inspired understanding of what goes on inside a poet's head to stand back for a moment, and pay heed to their own interpretive methods. Its subtext is that the critic is not a prophet, and that all too often a critic's utterances are no more than a form of creative utterance. Whatever one thinks of this line of thought, this is a well-written volume, intellectually adept, and completely sound in its scholarship. It should be read by everyone with a serious interest in romantic writers.

Wordsworth's Pope is neither a study of Wordsworth's use of Popean diction nor a history of Romanticism. Robert J. Griffin's central preoccupation is with the widely accepted 'narrative of literary history' by which Romanticism emerged in reaction to Pope – a development anticipated, and to some extent prepared for, by Thomas and Joseph Warton, and Edward Young. He goes on to show how this 'narrative' became established early in the nineteenth century, particularly through the agency of Francis Jeffrey. This is not a redundant historiographical exercise, because his thesis is that the values inherent in these judgements continue to determine our understanding of the period. Specifically, the critical work of M. H. Abrams is cited as responsible for having propagated assumptions about the chronological and conceptual boundaries of Romanticism; these, he argues, are no more than 'constructs'.

In some ways the most interesting chapter is that on Wordsworth and Pope, which argues that Wordsworth's construction of the 'Pope' which he had used to define his own objectives in poetry has prevented us from perceiving the numerous ways in which he is indebted to the earlier writer. There is a good deal of shrewd observation here, as Griffin analyses Wordsworth's criticisms of Pope in the 1800 Preface and the Essay, Supplementary to the Preface, 1815, and goes on to examine Pope's presence in the poetry. At the same time, I have doubts about the uneasy, somewhat undigested presence of various psychiatric notions in this chapter. For instance, Griffin regards Pope as a kind of 'father' to Wordsworth because he wants to prove that an 'oedipal' relation existed between them. In order for that to be true he invokes Murray Bowen, in whose terms ' "Pope represents for Wordsworth a literary 'family of origin' " '. In elaborating this notion in the context of *Tintern Abbey* Griffin suggests that 'the "father" (Pope) was transformed by repression first into a "mother" (Nature), and then into a younger sister'. This may or may not be true, but as so often when critics say such things, one wants to reply, 'so what?'. What does it add to one's appreciation of either the poet or his work?

The examination of Pope's literary influence on Wordsworth is probably the best piece of writing here, but it really belongs in another book. The question of any such influence is only marginally relevant to Griffin's argument: that the opposition between 'classicism' on the one hand and 'Romanticism' on the other is a kind of fiction initiated by eighteenth-century writers to whose judgements Wordsworth deferred in later years. The problem with all this is that it demands the reader's acceptance that 'Pope' equals 'classic', and Wordsworth means 'Romantic'. But can this element of Griffin's 'narrative' ever have been true? He would have us believe so, and for this reason the volume culminates with a critique of M. H. Abrams's *The Mirror and the Lamp*, illustrating its failure to question such simplistic judgements. None of which quite does Abrams justice; indeed, it is as harsh on him to say that his only permanent contribution is his learning, as it is on his readers to suggest that his 'identifiable misreadings ... have been accepted as useful truths by an astounding number of [them] over the past forty years'. Only by setting up the Wartons, or Wordsworth, or in this case Abrams, as a straw man, whose inevitable fall demonstrates the unviability of the Romantic/ Classic divide, can Griffin make his case.

G. Kim Blank, *Wordsworth and Feeling: The Poetry of an Adult Child*, is one of the few studies on Wordsworth in recent years to profess scepticism in most theoretically derived assessments of the poet; it is also distinguished by the refreshingly direct and straightforward manner in which it is written. It is immensely learned, and full of a passionate interest in its subject.

Blank argues that Wordsworth's inability fully to grieve for his parents led to depression in later life. Despite the fact that he is discussing someone who lived two centuries ago, you would think, given his language, that he was discussing a contemporary. It was in Wordsworth's poetry that one finds him 're-enacting' early trauma and, eventually, 'working it through'. My reservations stem from the way in which late twentieth-century concepts are used to assess the dynamics of Wordsworth's inner life: the Cooksons (the poet's grandparents) 'certainly emotionally abused' Wordsworth; John Wordsworth Sr was unwilling 'to assume a hands-on role as a single parent'; Wordsworth's 'relationship' with Annette Vallon was not 'a one-night stand'; and so forth. The fact is that the names we have devised to describe phenomena that predate them cannot help but change and even distort. It cannot be accurate to say that Annette and Wordsworth did not have a 'one-night stand' when neither would have used, or thought, in those terms – terms which, it must be said, are loaded in a way that would have been meaningless to them. More crucially, the charge of emotional abuse seems harsh; it is correct, as Blank observes, that the Cooksons treated the Wordsworth children unsympathetically – particularly in 1787, when Dorothy detailed their 'petty tyrannies' to her friend Jane Pollard. But to describe this as emotional abuse is to superimpose on the events described by Dorothy a distinctively twentieth-century set of value-judgements hardly warranted by the evidence.

The problem with much psychoanalytic criticism is the way in which everything done or said by the 'subject' is enlisted as evidence of a pathological state. On page 72 Blank announces that he will list all instances of the poet's bad health 'in order to open the case file on Wordsworth's condition'. This catalogue leads to the assertion that he was suffering from a 'chronic' illness, 'depression' and 'post-traumatic stress disorder'. Similarly, the poet's works represent 'the remarkable self-examination of a suffering, sole survivor'. It is not that all these claims are necessarily untrue – after all, most of us would admit that writing is a neurotic activity – but that the enrolment of an artist's life and work as part of some disease can only trivialize the artistic project. It is trivializing to argue that, in Margaret of *The Ruined Cottage*, Wordsworth 'reenacted his own grief', and does not, I think, bring us any closer to the sources of his very considerable power. Much as one must admire Blank's study for its eclecticism and directness, it leaves one yearning for another kind of study – one that refrains from pre-judgements formulated in late twentieth-century terms, preferring to let psychoanalytical insights emerge from a thorough examination of the poet's life and works in their own historical context.

Elizabeth A. Fay's *Becoming Wordsworthian: A Performative Aesthetic* also deals with the life and work of the poet. She wishes to 'resituate Dorothy

Wordsworth within the exclusionary terrain of High Romanticism as a partner in her brother's poetic project'. Wordsworth, she argues, is 'a consensual being composed of William and Dorothy', who are engaged in an act of collusion by which William constructs for himself a personality that 'is completed by his sibling companion ... always – through his ties to the sister-maiden – within safety'. This construction is 'performed', Fay suggests, through different kinds of poem, most explicitly a genre called the 'address-to-women', in which William directs his attentions to a maiden who is 'unquestioningly sympathetic, existing to fulfil both functions of listener and interlocutor. She is summoned as *the* ally against the weight of solitude and silence'. All of which is held to be a response to the Revolution – a kind of withdrawal governed by the 'feminine' values of the private and domestic. Bernardin de St Pierre's *Paul et Virginie* and Charlotte Smith's *Ethelinde; or the Recluse of the Lake*, are the models for this feminized retreat into domesticity and the pastoral. Along the way, Fay provides a shrewd intertexual analysis of poems by both Wordsworths, and some fine discussion of the canonical verse.

Becoming Wordsworthian is one of the most intelligent and ingenious gendered readings of Wordsworth yet published. It is not reductive or trivializing, and succeeds in pursuing gender-specific readings while acknowledging the power of the verse. All the same, it is not without occasional moments of tendentiousness. Can it really be, as Fay claims, that 'Dorothy leaves the sublime terrain to William, avoiding a competition that could threaten her dependent status in her brother's family'? It is hard to imagine her being kicked out of Dove Cottage on attempting to write her own version of the climbing of Snowdon. And although Fay is a sympathetic and astute reader of Dorothy's poetry, her line of argument occasionally overextends itself, as when she suggests that the sorrows of Dorothy's journals conceal 'the self-negation of abjection – not the masculine grotesque which is the maternal body but an abjecting of the bodily self, a disgust for one's own body'. Whether or not this bow to a current critical totem is a mere reflex, there is nothing in the journals or poetry to justify it. It is good, though, to find a critic willing to reclaim the sublime for the 'female' (it was an idiocy ever to have argued that the sublime was the domain only of male writers – what, after all, of the Duchess of Devonshire's *The Passage of the Mountain of St Gothard*?), and refreshing to encounter someone with a serious interest in Dorothy's function as collaborator and partner in the larger Wordsworthian project. A useful article this year on the relationship between the Wordsworths is Raymond Powell, 'Wordsworth, Dorothy Wordsworth, *Tintern Abbey*, and *Samson Agonistes* (*Neophil* 79.689–93).

Celeste Langan's *Romantic Vagrancy: Wordsworth and the Simulation of Freedom*, another volume in the Cambridge Studies in Romanticism series, comes with a dust-jacket endorsement from Alan Liu: 'This is an extraordinarily important, exhilarating and brilliant piece of work on Wordsworth, and one of the most interesting pieces of critical inquiry on any subject I have read in some time.' It offers an account of Wordsworth's representation of walking as the exercise of imagination, tracing the analogy between the poet in search of materials and the literally dispossessed beggars and vagrants he encounters. Langan suggests that literature and vagrancy are crucial images of the 'negative freedom' at the heart of liberalism, and goes on to show how the formal structure of the romantic poem (the excursion) mirrors its themes, usually narratives of impoverishment or abandonment. The encounter between the poet and the beggar reveals the advent of the liberal subject, its identity stretched between origin and destination, between economic and political forces, and the workings of desire. All of which depends on whether or not you accept Langan's definition of such terms as 'vagrancy', 'liberal', 'romantic' and so forth. So long as you do, the whole thing is perfectly consistent within itself. But its meticulously patterned construct relates to little beyond. If Langan aims to 'revise current views both of Wordsworth's poetry and of the relation of literature to its social and political context', her argument is so utterly hermetic in its endless internal debates, that one is hard put to see how it could relate to anyone else's view of literature, let alone the poetry of Wordsworth. No indication of its origins are given, but this book looks suspiciously like a thesis. Despite appearances, the blitz of critical authorities invoked to establish its veracity – Baudrillard, Nancy, Althusser, Marx, Guattari, and the rest – are not so much a means of intimidating the reader into numbed acquiescence as evidence of the author's lurking insecurity. And not without cause. Obsessed with her critical credentials, Langan is less scrupulous about her scholarship. It is surprising, to say the least, that a well-respected academic press like Cambridge should publish a monograph on Wordsworth that quotes the letters and poetry, and Dorothy's journals, from editions long superseded. Langan quotes frequently from *The Excursion* but without making the distinction (sometimes of critical importance) between different versions of the poem; nor, at any point, are we told from which text she quotes. Scholarly expertise, however, is not what this book is about; it is a display of undoubted theoretical ability, suffocating in its intricacy.

The other major contribution to the vagrancy school of criticism this year, Gary Harrison's *Wordsworth's Vagrant Muse: Poetry, Poverty and Power*, is a more confident and persuasive one, and also comes with endorsements – this time from Herbert Lindenberger, Clifford Siskin and Kurt Heinzelman. Harrison's method is to analyse a few 'key poems' which, he shows, are Wordsworth's attempts to engage with the debate that raged over poverty during the 1790s. He goes on to argue that such works as 'Salisbury Plain', 'The Old Cumberland Beggar', and 'Resolution and Independence' are implicated in an ideology that idealizes rural poverty, at the same time investing the image of the poor with a 'certain, if ambiguously realized, power'. While the vagrants, peddlers, and paupers that inhabit Wordsworth's poetry function as symbols of conventional moral value, the early poems challenge the complacency of middle-class readers by constructing a mirror in which they confront the possibility of their own impoverishment (both economic and moral) and by investing the marginal poor with a sense of dignity and morality otherwise denied them.

As Clifford Siskin observes in his endorsement of the book, Harrison's achievement here is to historicize the politics of Wordsworth's poetry, drawing on the paintings, poetry, treatises and stories of contemporaries such as Francis Wheatley, William Cowper, George Crabbe, Thomas Malthus and Hannah More. Harrison is no less engaged with critical matters than Langan, but his approach is a good deal less hermetic. In particular, his study is admirable for its concern with Wordsworth as a utopian – an aspect of his work that is seldom addressed by contemporary critics. Harrison does this in the context, quite properly, of *The Excursion*, but it is regrettable that he does not mention *The Recluse* and its remains, which are more properly the focus of Wordsworth's aspirations. This is, none the less, a careful, scrupulous analysis, which all Wordsworthians will find illuminating.

John Wyatt's *Wordsworth and the Geologists*, another volume in the Cambridge Studies in Romanticism series, is a study of the hitherto unexamined relationship between Wordsworth and early geologists. In his later work, Wordsworth shows considerable knowledge of contemporary geology, and an interest in many related philosophical issues. Wyatt's examination of the letters and diaries of leading geologists of the Victorian age reveal that they knew him, and discussed their subject with him. One of Wyatt's main arguments is that radical politics was closely connected with radical scientific research; the point is that Wordsworth did not retreat from radical science as he did from radical politics. In fact, his interest in science deepened with age. Wyatt guides the reader through *The Prelude*, offering some shrewd observations on its geological content, and goes on to speculate on how Wordsworth gained his education in this fledgling science. But perhaps the most valuable section of this volume is its findings as to Wordsworth's friendships with William Whewell and Adam Sedgwick. Wyatt shows that their excursions to the Lakes and connections with Trinity College Cambridge (where the poet's brother was Master) were instrumental in bringing them into contact with Wordsworth. The influence of their conversations with him are to be found throughout the later poetry. This excellent volume provides the Cambridge Series with a much-needed boost; it is also, by far, one of the more considered and less tendentious additions to ecological criticism of the poet. In a brief, related study, *Twentieth Century Wordsworth*, Margaret G. Barnes shows how the poet was influenced by the philosophical scientists of his day; her useful volume contains a number of her own verses, and concludes with a list of fauna and flora mentioned in Wordsworth's poetry.

For Michael Baron, in *Language and Relationship in Wordsworth's Writing*, Wordsworth is a poet of relationships – relationships formed, he argues, by language. In pursuit of various aspects of this notion, Baron examines a range of poetry, including most of the *Lyrical Ballads*, *Home at Grasmere* and *The White Doe of Rylstone*. Intriguingly too, he examines possible connections with the likes of Thomas Bewick, Robert Anderson, Herder and many others. This is no ordinary critical monograph; published in Longman's Studies in 18th and 19th Century Literature, it is 'aimed at the student and general reader', and is published in both hardback and paperback. The objective of the series is to steer the student away from any one critical identity or ideological approach, 'allowing the authors to explore their subject in their own way, taking account of recent changes in critical perspective'. This is no bad thing, and Baron manages it well enough; Bakhtin, Foucault, Levinson, McGann and the rest are introduced with a due combination of respect and scepticism. But Baron is at his best when unencumbered by the need to acknowledge the observations of others (intelligent or otherwise), as in his illuminating discussion of the poet's relationship with Sir George Beaumont.

In *An Experimental Reading of Wordsworth's Prelude: The Poetics of Bimodal Consciousness*, James P. Davis pursues what must be one of the most unusual studies of the poet yet published, aiming to assess the degree to which some of the paradigms from cognitive neuroscience might fruitfully inform one's reading of *The Prelude*. He finds that the poem describes such a paradigm for bimodal consciousness some 150 years earlier than has been recognized in the literature of neuroscience. On the surface, this sounds like an unconventional line of enquiry, as indeed it is. It is also scrupulous in its scholarship, both Wordsworthian and psychological. Davis begins with a clear and persuasive account of the failure of *The Recluse*, before launching into a careful discussion of various aspects of experimentation in *The Prelude*, including the use of discontinuities and the Wordsworthian conception of time. It provides what is finally an original and intriguing approach to the poetry. There is one major omission in this otherwise well-informed study; Davis has nothing to say about David Hartley, who was first and foremost a psychologist – the one whose work Wordsworth knew best. If Wordsworth was capable of anticipating some of the central tenets of modern neuroscience it must be due in part to the insights of the foremost associationist of the eighteenth century.

Duncan Wu's *Wordsworth's Reading 1800–1815* is the second and concluding volume in his study of the poet's reading. Like its predecessor, which dealt with the years 1770–1799, it lists all authors and titles read by Wordsworth during some of the most important years in his creative life – years which saw the composition of *Poems in Two Volumes*, *The Thirteen-Book Prelude*, *The White Doe of Rylstone* and *The Excursion*. The information is presented in an easy-to-use form, showing dates of reading and a summary of the available evidence at a glance. The scale and effort that has gone into this work is barely imaginable. Wu has scoured newspaper archives, manuscript collections, and has travelled the world in search of the books actually used by the poet. In several cases he has reconstructed the catalogues of libraries no longer in existence. Appendices contain corrections and additions to the first volume in the series; a collection of queried entries to the present one; a presentation of the accounts of Thomas Norton Longman, Wordsworth's publisher; a discussion of the various libraries used by Wordsworth; and, most useful of all, fugitive and unpublished works read by the poet. The final appendix contains a hitherto unavailable text of the 'Tale Imitated from Gower' in *Prelude* MS W, possibly by Mary Lamb.

Literature in the Marketplace: Nineteenth-Century British Publishing and Reading Practices, a collection of essays edited by John O. Jordan and Robert L. Patten, contains two important contributions on Wordsworth: 'Wordsworth in the *Keepsake*, 1829', by Peter Manning, and 'Copyright and the Publishing of Wordsworth', by Stephen Gill. Manning is concerned with the conflict between the 'dignity of literature' and entrepreneurial opportunism, and explores the surprising complicity between romantic idealism and the commercial world to which those ideals were apparently opposed. In doing so, he analyses the broader cultural significance of that curious, early nineteenth-century form of commodity publication, the fashionable literary annual. He shows how publishers bid for 'big names' by offering generous fees, inducing them to contribute new works. The 'annuals' themselves were luxury consumer items purchased by a predominantly female readership. Stephen Gill asks in his essay *which* Wordsworth was promoted and read during the nineteenth century. Drawing on much unpublished material, he shows how the poet's sons and publishers retained copyright control after Wordsworth's death, and how textual complexities arose as a direct result of the progressive lapsing of the poet's works from copyright. Paradoxically, the 1842 Copyright Act led directly to the deterioration of textual authenticity and to multiplication of unrepresentative and misleading editions. These two articles fill important gaps in our scholarly knowledge of Wordsworth and are well worth the price of the entire volume alone. Numerous periodical articles appeared on Wordsworth this year. In *ChLB*, Thomas Pearson discussed Wordsworth's relations with his patron, Sir George Beaumont, in 'Coleorton's "Classic Ground": Wordsworth, the Beaumonts, and the Politics of Place' (89.9–14); Susan A. W. Abbotson, 'Intimations by Moonlight: The Drive Towards Immortality in Wordsworth's "Great Ode" ', interpreted the poem as being about the poet's 'inner child' (90.85–93); and in two papers from the Wordsworth Winter School Mary Wedd discussed 'The Lucy Poems' (92.178–92) and Gordon Thomas *The Brothers* (92.193–207). Elsewhere, in 'Community and Mourning in William Wordsworth's *The Ruined Cottage*, 1797–1798' (*SP* 92.329–45), Kurt Fosso finds that Wordsworth's poem 'articulates a basis for community in the errant instabilities of mortal experience and memorial representation, representing community as an uncommonly unfinished product of acts of mourning whose incompleteness and interminability necessitate the ongoing mourning of mourning'. Michele Turner Sharp, in 'The Churchyard Among the Wordsworthian Mountains: Mapping the Common Ground of Death and the Reconfiguring of Romantic Community', wants to 'draw specific conclusions about how the notion of community functions in Wordsworth's thought, about where it ought to be located and what its defining traits should be'. She concludes that: 'The community centered around the graves of the dead, around the gesture of burial, is thus a community centered around its own mortality, centered by the inscription of singularity, and hence of difference, at its heart' (*ELH* 62.387–407). Lorna Clymer, 'Graved in Tropes: The Figural Logic of Epitaphs and Elegies in Blair, Gray, Cowper, and Wordsworth', provides a deconstructive analysis of how *The Excursion* 'attempts to employ simultaneously two competing poetic modes, that is, expressive and didactic/rhetorical' (*ELH* 62.347–86). In 'Consuming Nature: Wordsworth and the Kendal and Windermere Railway Controversy' (*MLQ* 56.305–26), James Mulvihill provides a fascinating discussion of the poet's opposition to the railway in 1847, showing how it related to his detestation of mass culture. Mulvihill is especially good on the ecological argument put forward by Wordsworth against the railway. On a related theme, Bruce Graver's ' "Honorable Toil": The Georgic Ethic of *Prelude* I' (*SP* 92.346–60) responds to the materialist tendencies of recent criticism, insisting on the ethical content of Wordsworth's writings about nature. 'Wordsworth and the Interpretation of Dreams', by Robert M. Philmus (*PLL* 31.184–205), provides a psychological analysis of the poetry. Against the tendency of new historicist readings to emphasize nostalgia, Fred Hoerner, 'Nostalgia's Freight in Wordsworth's *Intimations Ode*', returns to a more materialistic approach, exhorting us to 'internalize and be touched by power structures, challenging our self-protective and, so we learn from the *Ode*, self-incarcerating premises about the deep origins of structure and disposition' (*ELH* 62.631–61). Burrowing away, as he so often does, at scholarly niceties, Duncan Wu discussed Wordsworthian juvenilia in 'Navigated by Magic: Wordsworth's Cambridge Sonnets' (*RES* 46.352–65). W. J. B. Owen provided a typically forthright and hard-headed analysis of one of the most important passages in *The Prelude* in 'Imagination, How Impaired' (*WC* 26.51–8). Other important articles include Stephen C. Behrendt, 'Placing the Places in Wordsworth's 1802 Sonnets' (*SEL* 35.641–67), and Raymond Southall, 'Botany into Poetry: Erasmus Darwin, Coleridge and Wordsworth' (*ELN* 33.20–2).

The advent of poststructuralist theories of language and subjectivity provide the starting-point for Sheila M. Kearns's *Coleridge, Wordsworth, and Romantic Autobiography: Reading Strategies of Self-Representation*. For Kearns, poststructuralism has the advantage of destabilizing the general notion of the recoverability of the past through language. Her aim is to use this development as a means of defining a new way of reading, 'or perhaps negotiating with, the process of autobiographical representation'. But the more important objective in this study is to show that Wordsworth and Coleridge faced challenges to traditional notions of selfhood and self-representation that closely parallel the challenge to traditional strategies of self-representation by poststructuralism. Although an advocate of poststructuralist criticism, Kearns does not disavow historicist elements completely. But it is strange to read a book about Romantic autobiography with not a mention of Rousseau. Nor, for that matter, is any consideration given to a comparison of the ideas of 'confession' and 'autobiography'. But that would, perhaps, be going too far down a road Kearns has no intention of taking. In the chapters on Wordsworth, she is more concerned with exploring how he inscribed his own act of reading in the writing of his text; in those on Coleridge, she shows how he re-appropriates texts already in circulation, subject to the reading of others. This is a well-informed and perceptive volume, and no one concerned with poststructuralist approaches to the romantics can afford to ignore it.

The only full-length monograph dedicated solely to Coleridge this year, Ronald C. Wendling's *Coleridge's Progress to Christianity: Experience and Authority in Religious Faith* shows the poet progressing towards a total acceptance of Church of England orthodoxy. Wendling argues that, for Coleridge, the Logos provided the ground for a knowledge of God; it could be found in all beings. Coleridge aimed to prove that this philosophical idea was historically fulfilled in Jesus, the human and divine Word at the centre of Christian faith.

Coleridge's failed *magnum opus* indicates how far he remained from achieving that philosophical goal. Still, as the only major Romantic to look to historical Christianity for vindication for his peculiarly empirical form of transcendentalism, Coleridge remains significant for believer and non-believer alike. This erudite and helpful study will stand as a valuable contribution to Coleridge studies for many years to come. It is particularly useful for its account of the influence on Coleridge's thought of numerous thinkers including Hartley, Berkeley, Spinoza and Bruno. Wendling provides a sensitive account of Coleridge's early years, some excellent pages on 'Dejection: An Ode', and a fine account of Coleridge on love and imagination, but by far the larger part of the volume is preoccupied with Coleridgean orthodoxy (1809–20) – of which this is one of the most comprehensive discussions yet published. It should be read alongside Mary Anne Perkins's *Coleridge's Philosophy: The Logos as Unifying Principle*, which I failed to include in last year's review, and which I am pleased to discuss now, though belatedly. We have been waiting many years for Perkins's excellent study, which stands as probably the best available guide to Coleridge's religious and philosophical system of the London years. She is concerned less with criticism, or with her own theories, than with simply presenting Coleridge's ideas, such as they are. In doing so, she has gained access to all the relevant unpublished manuscripts, and shows how Coleridge diverges and develops the preoccupations of his predecessors. This is an utterly indispensable guide to late Coleridge, and ranks as one of the most important volumes on him in recent years. Further work on him this year includes a clutch of articles in *N&Q* 42: Valerie Grosvenor Myer, 'Sacred River from Switzerland' (176–7), suggesting a source for *Kubla Khan* in Saussure's *Voyage dans les Alpes*; Adam Roberts, 'Coleridge's *Ancient Mariner* and Mrs Radcliffe's *Mariner*' (177–8), suggesting the influence of Radcliffe's 'The Mariner' on Coleridge's poem; Bjørn Tysdahl, 'Edward Young in Coleridge's "Dejection: An Ode"' (178–9), arguing for Young's influence on Coleridge; David Chandler, 'Coleridge's "Address to a Young Jack-Ass": A Note on the Poetic and Political Context' (179– 80), finding the inspiration for Coleridge's poem in an issue of the *Norfolk Chronicle*; Robert Morrison, ' "Reviewers and Frenchmen" in Coleridge's *Biographia Literaria*' (180–1), identifying Coleridge's reference to 'reviewers and Frenchmen' in *Biographia* as an attack on the Scottish common-sense school; and Tomoya Oda, 'Coleridge's Quotation from Bowles' 'On Mr Howard's Account of Lazarettos in the Fifth Issue of *The Watchman*' (181–3). This year's *ChLB* also contained a number of articles: Carla Maria Gnappi offered a useful parallel to the story of the ancient mariner in that of St Brendan, in 'Two Old Navigators: St Brendan and the Ancient Mariner' (*ChLB* 89.15–26); Berta Lawrence commented on the postman at Nether Stowey in 'Coleridge's Carrier' (*ChLB* 89.27–30); Nicholas Reid published an exemplary account of the conversation poems, 'Coleridge: The Conversation Poems' (*ChLB* 91.143–56); and Seamus Perry's 'The Ancient Mariner Controversy' discussed some of the larger critical issues in recent accounts of the poem (*ChLB* 92.208–23). There was more source-hunting in Raymond Powell, 'Coleridge's Debt to Defoe: *The Ancient Mariner* and *The Farther Adventures of Robinson Crusoe*' (*ELN* 33.48–52) – a line of thought already traced in exhaustive detail by Patrick Keane (*YWES* 75.398). More theoretically inclined, Thomas M. Greene, 'Coleridge and the Energy of Asking', examined Coleridge's theory of symbolism through his notebooks, concluding that he saw the imagination as a means of releasing us from 'need' (*ELH* 62.907–31). Robert Woodall, 'Coleridge in the Cavalry' (*ContempR* 266.91–6), provided a new perspective on a much-mythologized episode in the poet's life. It is always good to find journals willing to devote whole issues to the proceedings of various conferences, for the benefit of those delegates who want a record of the proceedings, and those unable to attend. *WC* this year devoted an issue to the papers of the Coleridge Conference 1994, held at Cannington in Somerset, not far from Nether Stowey. All the papers are of interest, in particular James Engell, 'A Yet Deeper Well: "Kubla Khan", Wookey Hole, Cain' (26.3); Daniel Robinson, 'From "Mingled Measure" to "Ecstatic Measures": Mary Robinson's Poetic Reading of "Kubla Khan" ', which provides a shrewd reading of the poetic dialogue between Coleridge and Robinson (26.4–7); Douglas B. Wilson, 'Coleridge and the Endangered Self', a psychological reading of the poet (26.18–23); Michael John Kooy, 'The

End of Poetry: Aesthetic and Ethical Investigations in Coleridge and Schiller'
(26.23–6); and James McKusick, 'From Coleridge to John Muir: The Romantic Origins of Environmentalism', a brilliant examination of the influence of
Coleridge on John Muir (26.36–40). In a subsequent issue, Morton D. Paley
provided a useful reading of one of Coleridge's most important poems in
' "To William Wordsworth" and Coleridge's Later Poetry' (*WC* 26.45–50).
The Coleridge Bulletin, a comparatively new publication published by the
Friends of Coleridge at Nether Stowey, continued its excellent work with a
number of essential articles: Graham Davidson, 'Coleridge, Poetic Form and
Nationhood' (5.2–24); Reggie Watters, 'Coleridge, Family, and the West
Country' (5.25–49); Mary Wedd, 'What is the Lasting Appeal of *The Ancient
Mariner*?' (6.2–19), and Seamus Perry, 'Attempts at Sublimity: Young Cole-
ridge and *The Ancient Mariner*' (6.20–49).

Frank Whitehead's *George Crabbe: A Reappraisal* is centred on the belief
that Crabbe is an important, even a major poet, whose work remains undervalued. Describing itself as a 'straightforward account', the first five chapters
trace the changes in Crabbe's poetry up to what Whitehead sees as its pinnacle
with the *Tales* of 1812. Part II of the volume takes a different tack, forsaking
the chronological approach for one which explores Crabbe's response to the
work of Wordsworth and Coleridge, the question of realism in his work, genre,
deconstruction and ideology. This is not just special pleading; despite the
publication of a new edition of the works, and occasional essays by the likes of
Jerome J. McGann, Crabbe remains largely neglected by modern critics.
Whitehead has done a considerable service for his poet, not just in mapping
out his creative development, but in applying modern critical methods to the
works. What makes this so pleasurable is the honesty and scepticism with
which he does it. Deconstruction fails to convincingly 'explode into dissemination both the integrity and the significance' of these poems, just as new
historical approaches fail to prove Hazlitt's jibe that Crabbe was 'too much of
the parish beadle, an overseer of the country poor'. This is an exceedingly
enjoyable volume, and a long-overdue account of the work of a neglected
figure. If Crabbe is neglected, what does one say of Thomas Lovell Beddoes?
This year saw the publication of a small but valuable pamphlet, Alan Halsey's
A Skeleton Key to Death's Jest-Book, published by the Thomas Lovell Beddoes Society. Beddoes began writing *Death's Jest-Book* in 1825, had
completed a draft by 1829, but was discouraged from publishing it at the time.
During the 1830s he revised it, continued to work on it in the 1840s, and it was
eventually published posthumously in 1850. It was edited in a variorum
edition in 1935 and is now regarded as Beddoes's masterpiece. Halsey has
performed the useful task of setting this peculiar work in the context of its
author's life and thought, and provides many shrewd insights along the way.

Curiously, Keats's bicentenary year saw no monographs and only one book
dedicated to the poet: *Keats and History*, edited by Nicholas Roe. The aim of
this fine collection, which includes work by its editor, Susan J. Wolfson, Martin
Aske, John Barnard, Daniel P. Watkins, Kelvin Everest, Terence Allan
Hoagwood, Michael O'Neill, Vincent Newey, Theresa M. Kelley, Greg
Kucich, Nicola Trott and John Kerrigan, is to 'respond to recent interest in the
historical dimensions of Keats's poems and letters, and open fresh perspectives on his achievement'. Politics, social history, feminism, economics,
historiography, stylistics, aesthetics, and mathematical theory all play their

part in the opening up of these 'fresh perspectives'. This is less of a mixed bag than most collections, and the standard is consistently high. The essays by Susan Wolfson, John Barnard, Daniel P. Watkins, Michael O'Neill, Vincent Newey, Nicholas Roe and John Kerrigan, are especially useful. A number of journals devoted special issues to Keats this year, including the *ACM* and *ERR*. *SIR* 34 was a bicentenary issue commemorating Keats, featuring a range of articles, including Michael LaGory, 'Wormy Circumstance: Symbolism in Keats's *Isabella*' (321–42), Jeffrey N. Cox, 'Keats, Shelley, and the Wealth of the Imagination' (365–400), Gary Farnell, ' "Unfit for Ladies": Keats's *The Eve of St Agnes*' (401–12) and Jeffrey C. Robinson, ' "My Ended Poet": Poetic Tributes to Keats, 1821–1994' (441–69). The bicentenary issue of *KSR* is not to be published until next year, but this year's edition carried a useful article by Adam Roberts, 'Keats's "Attic Shape": "Ode on a Grecian Urn" and Non-Euclidean Geometry' (9.1–14). A scholarly article by Laura E. Campbell, 'Unnecessary Compromise: Publisher Changes to "Ode to Psyche" ', provides some important insights on one of Keats's best-known works (*ELN* 33.53–8). The new journal, *Romanticism*, carried an excellent piece by John Barnard, 'Keats's Belle Dame and the Sexual Politics of Leigh Hunt's *Indicator*' (1.34–49).

After a good year in 1994, this year produced few monographs on Shelley. Timothy Morton's *Shelley and the Revolution in Taste* is a study that brings together the themes of diet, consumption, the body and human relationships with the natural world. It is a quest that takes in eighteenth-century social and political thought concerning nature, culture and society. Morton skilfully combines a formidable scholarly range with much critical dexterity, embracing current theoretical issues, and anthropological and sociological approaches. Shelley's vegetarianism has too often been ignored by critics of his work, and this volume brilliantly redresses the imbalance. This is a thorough, intelligent and exemplary study, and is essential reading for all Shelleyans. By coincidence, this year saw the publication of an article (written without knowledge of Morton's book), 'Shelley's Ideal Body: Vegetarianism and Nature', in which Onno Oerlemans discussed Shelley's well-known dietary habits (*SIR* 34.531–52). The only other monograph on Shelley to be published this year, K. D. Verma's *The Vision of 'Love's Rare Universe': A Study of Shelley's Epipsychidion* (UPA), was not available for review. Alan Halsey's *The Text of Shelley's Death* is not, strictly speaking, a critical work, but will be of interest to Shelleyans. It collates the various manuscript accounts of Shelley's death using the techniques of the scholarly variorum, drawing on the 'voices' of Shelley himself, Mary Shelley, Edward and Jane Williams, Byron, Trelawny, Hunt, Roberts, the Tuscan authorities, the spy Torelli, and later biographers and embellishers. Halsey describes the result as a 'collage prose poem, a biographical and critical study, a mystery'. Whatever else it may be, it makes for a compelling read, and it is recommended to anyone interested in Shelley's life and work.

A number of good articles appeared on Shelley this year. In 'The Seashore's Path: Shelley and the Allegorical Imperative', Deborah Elise White explored didacticism in Shelley (*SIR* 34.51–79); Barry Magarian discussed 'The Indeterminacy of Shelley's *Adonais*: Liberation and Destruction' (*KSR* 9.15–36), and Ya-Feng Wu analysed *The Assassins* (*KSR* 9.51–62). Kyle Grimes offered a useful discussion of legal issues and *Queen Mab* in '*Queen Mab*, the Law of

Libel, and the Forms of Shelley's Politics' (*JEGP* 94.1–18). *Romanticism* carried some fine articles, including Jennifer Wallace, 'Tyranny and Translation: Shelley's Unbinding of Prometheus' (1.15–33), and a brilliant scholarly discussion of *Adonais* and *The Vision of Judgement* by Peter Cochran (1.193–205).

One major monograph on Byron appeared this year: Andrew Elfenbein's *Byron and the Victorians* is reviewed elsewhere in *YWES*. There was also a good deal of critical activity in journals. Drummond Bone provided a learned and informative account of Byron's technique in 'The Art of *Don Juan*: Byron's Metrics' (*WC* 26.97–103); David Punter wrote on 'The Transvaluation of *Don Juan*' in *Proceedings of the XIIIth Congress of the International Comparative Literature Association*; and James Soderholm on 'Teresa Guiccioli's Transubstantiation of Byron' (*NCC* 19.205–20). Paul Elledge produced two articles, one on 'Byron's Separation and the Endings of Pilgrimage' (*TSLL* 37.16–53), the other entitled 'Chasms in Connections: Byron Ending (in) *Childe Harold's Pilgrimage* 1 and 2' (*ELH* 62.121–48). The latter is particularly good; Elledge remarks that his subject, 'broadly, is Byron ending: suffering, evading, disguising, denying, performing, and surviving terminations'. Elsewhere, G. A. Wilkes provided a useful exposition of '*Don Juan*, IV.52–53' (*N&Q* 42.184–5), and Alastair W. Thomson offered a discussion of *Beppo*, in ' "A Nameless Sort of Person": Byron's *Beppo*' (*EA* 48.50–60). Readers of *Romanticism* were treated to some fine articles on the noble Lord, including one on 'Darkness', by Morton Paley (1.1–14), and Jane Stabler's 'Pit-bull Poetics: One Battle in Byron's "War in Words" ' (1.82–9).

Clare criticism continued only in journals, most notably in the indispensable *JCSJ*, which this year featured a number of articles with an ecological bent. The issue begins with Jonathan Bate on 'The Rights of Nature', a powerful exposition of the meaning of place in Clare's poetry (14.7– 15), and continues with W. John Coletta, 'Ecological Aesthetics and the Natural History Poetry of John Clare' (14.29–46) and Tim Fulford, 'Cowper, Wordsworth, Clare: The Politics of Trees' (14.47–59). Fulford's article is a particularly sharp piece of writing, laden with insights into the respective approaches of each of the writers whose work he discusses. It should be read alongside his other article this year, 'Wordsworth's "Yew-Trees": Politics, Ecology, and Imagination' (*Rom* 1.272–88).

2. Non-Fictional Prose

Highlights from this year's work include three new editions of prose writing from the period, a major study of William Cobbett's radical prose style and several excellent and substantial articles. Beginning with the three editions, Marion Kingston Stocking has edited *The Clairmont Correspondence: Letters of Claire Clairmont, Charles Clairmont and Fanny Imlay Godwin, Vol I: 1808–1834*. I have not been able to see this edition. Gregory Claeys has produced a substantial and important collection *Political Writings of the 1790s: The French Revolution Debate* for P&C. The collection consists of eight volumes and is divided as follows. Volumes One and Two cover responses to the arguments of Edmund Burke from 1790–1, including familiar works by Wollstonecraft, James Mackintosh and Joseph Priestley as well as less well-known pamphlets. Volumes Three and Four deal with radical and reformist works from 1790–1800, including works by Richard Price, Joel Barlow, Christopher Wyvill, William Frend, Henry Yorke, Joseph Gerrald and John Thelwall. The second half of the set is given to works of loyalism in the period, specifically responses to Paine (1791–93: Volumes Five and Six) and generally (1791–1800: Volumes Seven and Eight). This dual focus on radicalism and reform as set against loyalism makes Claeys's collection especially rewarding. With very few exceptions (Hannah More, William Paley and John Reeve) loyalist writing of the period is seldom studied, scarcely written on, and rarely anthologized. Claeys's collection will do much to restore the balance. The edition contains a substantial and very useful introduction which sets out the context of the writings, and also light annotations to the body of the text and basic index in the eighth volume. The texts collected stay closely to the political and eschew the more popular religio-political writings also current at the time. This is a very useful collection to have, and academic libraries will want to purchase it for undergraduate and postgraduate courses relating to the literary and historical concerns of the Romantic period. Claeys also produced a timely and major edition of the writings of the most significant of the English Jacobin leaders of the period: *The Politics of English Jacobinism: Writings of John Thelwall*. For a long time, Thelwall's political writings, so important to students of Romantic politics and poetry, have been accessible only in research collections or in short extracts. Claeys reprints Thelwall's best pamplets: his *The Natural and Constitutional Rights of Britons to Annual Parliaments* (1795), *Sober Reflections on the Seditious and Inflammatory Letter of the Rt. Hon. Edmund Burke to a Noble Lord* (1796), and *The Rights of Nature, Against the Usurpations of Establishments* (1796). Additionally, most of the volume is taken up with extracts from Thelwall's collection of political lectures *The Tribune* (1795–96). Claeys provides a good introduction and useful annotations to the text. Obviously, it would be good to have a complete facsimile of *The Tribune* but in its absence this is an excellent introduction to Thelwall's writings and an accessible scholarly edition. The shame is that Thelwall's literary writings, which he regarded as part of his radical endeavour, have not yet been reprinted in editions as good as this.

John R. Nabholtz's persuasive and informative essay 'Romantic Prose and Classical Rhetoric' (in Bialostosky and Needham, eds, *Rhetorical Traditions and British Romantic Literature*) discusses argumentative prose in the period, which he argues is actually more prevalent than the more Romantic 'impassioned prose' of De Quincey and Lamb. Nabholtz further divides this body of argumentative prose into the modes of '*deliberative, forensic*, and *epideictic*' modes of classical rhetoric: 'It is not surprising, therefore, that when the Romantics came to write works of persuasive prose, the mark of classic rhetoric should be evident in their productions.' Most of the essay focuses on Coleridge's social and political writings demonstrating how the mark of James Penn's *Latin Grammar for the Use of Christ's Hospital* (1761) remains visible in Coleridge's use of figures and tropes. Zeynep Tenger's and Paul Trolander's 'The Politics of Literary Production: The Reaction to the French Revolution and the Transformation of the English Literary Periodical' (*SECC* 24.279–95) discusses the treatment of the Revolution in the periodicals of the day.

Turning to individual authors. The anonymous work *The Autobiography of a Flea* (1789) is discussed by Robert Druce's 'Pulex Deixus, or, The Spell-bound Flea: An Excursion into Porno Gothic' (in Tinkler-Villani, ed., *Exhibited by Candlelight*). A few articles on Edmund Burke came to my attention. C. Dentandt's 'Invoking the Abyss – The Ideologies of the Post-modern Sublime' (*RBPH* 73.803–21) discusses Burke's treatise *Of the Sublime and Beautiful* along with Kant's *Critique of Judgement* as sources for Lyotard and Frederic Jameson. N. Ravitich discusses Burke's ideas about Church and State in 'Far Short of Bigotry: Edmund Burke on Church Establishments' (*Journal of Church and State* 37.365–83). Perhaps more current to the direc-tion of Burke studies is J. D. Bass's discussion of 'The Perversion of Empire: Edmund Burke and the Nature of Imperial Responsibility' (*QJS* 81.208–27). Two notes complete the complement of Burke studies for this year: Stanley Jones comments on Hazlitt's allusions to Burke in 'More Hazlitt Quotations and Allusions: Shakespeare, the Bible, Milton, Quintillian, Steele, Pope and Burke' (*N&Q* 42.182–7) and P.K. Tompkins provides 'A Note on Burke, Goethe and the Jews' (*QJS* 81.507–10). Only two articles on the work of Thomas Paine which might be of interest to literary scholars were noticed this year. Bernard Vincent discusses Paine's treatment of universal suffrage in 'Thomas Paine and the Issue of Universal Suffrage' (*QWERTY* 5.397–400) and Steven Blakemore contributes an important and interesting discussion 'Revisionist Parricide: Thomas Paine's "Letter to George Washington" ' (*Clio* 24.269–89).

This was a very good year for Cobbett studies with the publication of Leonora Nattrass's major study *William Cobbett: The Politics of Style* appear-ing in the Cambridge Studies in Romanticism series. Kevin Gilmartin's ' "This Is Very Material": William Cobbett and the Rhetoric of Radical Opposition' (*SIR* 34.81–102) provides a fascinating account of how Cobbett made a point of using physical materials rather than reason or argument to find an 'unambiguous and incontrovertible language for radical parliamentary reform and its many subsidiary agendas', distrusting even the most rudimen-tary of mimetic procedures, thus earning the scorn of subsequent Romanticists. More than this, Cobbett and other propangandists organized their work along the concrete axis of production and distribution, rather than the Romantic one of inspiration and authorship. Gilmartin's account of Cobbett's attempt to efface the difference between words and things is very relevant to the whole Burke-Paine controversy about political language in the period.

A handful of articles and two monographs appeared on the works of Thomas De Quincey this year. Alina Clej's *A Genealogy of the Modern Self: Thomas De Quincey and the Intoxication of Writing* adopts a biographical approach in discussing the role of drug addiction in his work. Matthew Schneider's *Original Ambivalence: Autobiography and Violence in Thomas De Quincey* discusses the treatment of violence in De Quincey's autobio-graphical prose. This subject was also tackled this year in N. Pireddu's 'Portable Ecstasies: The Rhetoric of Opuim in De Quincey's Autobiography' (*EA* 48.268–76). Grevel Lindop provides a fascinating account of the recur-rence of the crocodile in De Quincey's oeuvre in 'De Quincey and the Cursed Crocodile' (*EIC* 45.121–40). Lindop also discussed De Quincey's debts to the *Edinburgh Magazine* in 'English Reviewers and Scotch Professors' (*TLS* 4839.9–10). Claire B. May discusses aesthetics, dreams and the unconscious in

De Quincey's work in the light of the theories of Jung in 'From Dream, to Text: The Collective Unconscious in the Aesthetic Theory of Thomas De Quincey' (*JEP* 16.i–ii.75–83). De Quincey's pseudo-Germanic novel was commented on by R. J. Dingley in 'De Quincey and the Translation of *Walladmor*' in *N&Q* (42.188). *WC* 22.ii. contains three substantial pieces on aspects of De Quincey's work: Grevel Lindop discusses 'De Quincey's Wordsworthian Quotations' (58–67), finding that although Wordsworth is seldom mentioned in the *Confessions* he is nevertheless 'an ill-concealed figure behind the arras'; Fredrick Burwick's 'Motion and Paralysis in *The English Mail-Coach*' (66–77) discusses notions of temporality and *ekphrasis* in De Quincey's writing; and Laura E. Roman's 'Delving into De Quincey's Palimpsests: Myth-making Digressions and an Unpublished Text' (107–112) describes changes made to the manuscript for the essay 'Introduction to the World of Strife', especially relating to his editor James Hogg's emendations. Lawrence D. Needham discusses 'De Quincey's Rhetoric of Display' in the *Confessions of an English Opium-Eater* (in Bialostosky and Needham, eds, *Rhetorical Traditions and British Romantic Literature*), illustrating De Quincey's debt to classical rhetoric and his ingenious and innovative use of it in the *Confessions*.

Not noted last year was Morris R. Brownell's 'William Gilpin's "Unfinished Business": The Thames Tour' (1764)' (*The Walpole Society* 57.[1993–4] 52–78). Two articles relevant to William Godwin's prose were notable. Jon Klancher discusses Godwin's notions of republicanism in his essay 'Of History and Romance' in 'Godwin and the Republican Romance: Genre, Politics, and Contingency in Cultural History' (*MLQ* 56.142–65) and R. Helfield covers Godwin's involvement in the 1794 treason trials in 'Constructive Treason and Godwin's Treasonous Constructions' (*Mosaic* 28.ii.43–62).

A steady stream of articles on Hazlitt flowed this year. Arthur Freeman and Janet Ing Freeman reported on a manuscript fragment of the author in ' "The Report of the Illustrious Obscure": Hazlitt, Rackest and the Coronation' (*BC* 44.i.27–36). Stanley Jones identified 'More Hazlitt Quotations and Allusions: Shakespeare, The Bible, Milton, Quintillian, Steele, Pope, Burke' (*N&Q* 42.186–7). Jonathan Gross contributes an interesting discussion of 'Hazlitt's Worshipping Practice in *Liber Amoris*' (*SEL* 35.707–21), arguing that *Liber Amoris* reveals the growth of Hazlitt's 'fetishistic imagination'. Raymond Martin and John Barresi discussed 'Hazlitt on the Future Self' in *JHI* (56.463–81). M. Garnett discussed Hazlitt's critique of Hobbes in 'Self-Love and Misanthropy: William Hazlitt on Thomas Hobbes' (*HPT* 16.558–75) and Stephen Bann wrote on ' "A Language of the Body?" – The Art Criticism of William Hazlitt' in Marie-Claire Rouyer and Michcl Jouve, eds, *Le Corps dans tous ses état* (PU de Bordeaux) which was not seen.

The work of Sir William Jones continues to attract more and more attention, as Duncan Wu points out in his review of the year's work in Romantic poetry. Besides Michael Franklin's edition of the poetry and prose, his monograph on Jones's life and work, and R. K. Kaul's collection, *Studies in William Jones: An Interpreter of Oriental Literature*, a further collection of articles appeared this year. Garland Cannon and Kevin R. Brine, eds, *Objects of Enquiry: The Life, Contributions, and Influences of Sir William Jones (1746–1794)* contains articles by Kenneth A. R. Kennedy, David Kopf, Winfred P. Lehman, James Oldham, R. H. Robins and Rocher Rose on aspects of Jones's life and works. Garland Cannon's 'Oriental Jones: Scholarship, Literature, Multiculturalism and Humankind' and O. P. Kejariwal's 'William Jones: The Copernicus of History' in this collection are concerned with Jones's prose writings.

The gender implications of philanthropy in the case of Hannah More's are discussed in Dorice Williams Elliott, ' "The Care of the Poor Is Her Profession": Hannah More and Women's Philanthropic Work' (*NCC* 19.179–204). Antonia Forster considers the correspondence of Bishop Thomas Percy to and from Ralph Griffiths in 'The Griffiths Correspondence' (*N&Q* 42.173–4). Four substantial articles appeared this year on the work of Mary Wollstonecraft. Janet Todd's 'Aphra Behn – Whom Mary Wollstonecraft Did Not Read' (*WC* 26.152–8) provides an interesting discussion of the two very disparate feminist thinkers, contrasting their attitudes to sex and power. B. Hill considers 'The Links Between Mary Wollstonecraft and Catherine Macaulay – New Evidence' in *WoHR* (4.177–92). Also in comparative mode is Harriet Guest's 'The Dream of Common Language: Hannah More and Mary Wollstonecraft' in *TPr* (9.303–23). Finally, Corinne Field's 'Breast-Feeding, Sexual Pleasure, and Women's Rights: Mary Wollstonecraft's *Vindication*' was printed in *Critical Matrix: The Princeton Journal of Women, Gender, and Culture* 9.ii.25–44.

Only two articles on Southey's prose were noticed by me this year, these were H. R. Woudhuysen's discussion of Southey's discouraging correspondence with Charlotte Brontë, 'Advice from a Poet-Laureate' (*TLS* 4813.36) and Carolyn Misenheimer's 'Southey's Letter to Children' (*ChLB* 91.130–42). Finally, four articles on Dorothy Wordsworth's prose writing appeared this year. Berta Lawrence comments on Dorothy's presentation of Kilve in 'Kilve by the Green Sea' (*ChLB* 91.157–8). Two articles on Dorothy feature in *ABSt* 10.i.: Kay K. Cook writes on the treatment of immediacy of experience in the journals in 'Immersion' (66–80) and Robert A. Fothergill writes on the journal as autobiography in 'One Day at a Time: The Diary as Lifewriting' (81–91). Lisa Tyler also discussed the treatment of the self in 'Big Brother Is Watching You: Dorothy Wordsworth's Alfoxden and Grasmere Journals' (*UDR* 23.ii.87–98).

3. Fictional Prose

Jane Austen, Mary Shelley and the Gothic novel were once again the three main *foci* of the year's work. There is a degree of overlap between the *foci*, although it remains the case that study of Romantic fictional prose oscillates between the two main poles of Austen/Shelley, or novel/romance. Given this fact, it is somewhat surprising that the 'polarity' is not itself more often an object of study. Happily, among the year's work there are several exceptions to this general observation.

Interest in Jane Austen remains vigorous. *Jane Austen and Discourses of Feminism* directly tackles the vexed question of Jane Austen and feminism, as promised by the title. Devoney Looser, who edits and introduces the volume, helpfully identifies the different strands of approach taken by critics in linking Austen to feminist debates. Rather than arguing about whether Austen was a feminist, and, if she was, what kind she was, the contributors set about historicizing the issue, generally by asking what it meant to be a feminist in Austen's time. The overall answer is that the period's politics of gender and genre make for a complex picture, one critics are only now beginning to reconstruct. In other words, the emphasis has shifted from reclaiming Austen for a feminist tradition to a concern with how issues of gender, mediated through genre, condition Austen's concerns, themes and reception. The volume is divided into three sections, each successively more particular. The first, on 'Changing Histories', has contributions on Romantic Feminism and Civil Society (Gary Kelly); Austen's 'remaking of "English" history', in her *History* (Antoinette Burton); and Austen and the 'engendering' of disciplinarity (Clifford Siskin). The next section, 'Critical Re-examinations', revisits earlier feminist debates with regards to Austen (essays by Laura Mooneyham White, Jocelyn Harris and Glenda A. Hudson) while the last section focuses on *Northanger Abbey* (Diane Hoeveler and Maria Jerinic) and *Mansfield Park* (Ellen Gardiner and Misty G. Anderson).

One of the year's more interesting essays, Arthur E. Walzer's 'Rhetoric and Gender in Jane Austen's *Persuasion*' (*CE* 57.688-707) could easily slip into Looser's volume. Walzer situates *Persuasion* in the context of eighteenth-century theories of rhetoric, most notably, Hugh Blair's and George Campbell's. The crux is the difference between conviction and persuasion, of acting upon language that appeals to our understanding and reason, versus language acting upon the will and the affections. Walzer points out that this difference was also implicitly gendered: conviction belonged to a discourse of manly ethics whereas persuasion was a sign of the pleasing infirmity of women (and a sure sign of effeminacy in men). According to Walzer, Austen complicates the picture in two principal ways. First, she employs the countervailing duality of wilful obstinacy versus affectionate heart to disturb the moral picture, and, second, she participates in the process of female empowerment analysed by Nancy Armstrong whereby domesticity is positively revised as a means of enlarging the feminine sphere. In this reading, eighteenth-century rhetoric becomes the ground of early nineteenth-century sexual politics.

Tara Ghosal Wallace's *Jane Austen and Narrative Authority* is an acute, subtle, extended essay on the topic of Jane Austen's irony, and in various ways it dovetails with Walzer's argument. Wallace takes as given that Austen's complex attitude towards narrative authority is the principal source of Austen's irony. As Wallace points out, critics readily accept that Austen's narrators are not as authoritative as they seem, being neither fully in possession of the facts themselves, nor entirely disinterested in proceedings. However, rather than approaching the matter stylistically, through an analysis of Austen's complex way with free indirect speech, Wallace adopts a thematic perspective. That is, she investigates the way narrative authority is itself thematized in Austen's texts. In particular, Wallace notes how, for Austen, being articulate and being sincere are problematically related. Generally, the greater a character's linguistic facility, the greater their capacity for deception (including self-deception). For Austen's female characters, the situation is particularly tricky. Being too plausible risks moral compromise, while the alternative is scarcely better. Austen's reticent characters may have more depth, but reticence means surrendering the field of talk and knowing, and therefore power. In this way gender politics is interwoven into the thematization of narrative authority, where the same reservations and suspicions that hover over linguistically dextrous characters haunt overly facile narrators. Wallace carefully shows how Austen's narrative career is less a smooth arc than a series of thrusts and revisions as Austen works through the over-determined complexities of narration and authority. Overdetermined, because sincerity, gender, genre and family politics all coalesce around the act of female knowing.

A noteworthy feature of the year's work on Austen has been the number of paperback editions with new, critically significant introductions, Marilyn Butler's *Northanger Abbey* being an example. Butler comes down decisively in favour of a text largely unrevised after 1803 when Austen sent the manu-script to a London publisher. Butler regards the text as bearing the unchanged marks of the young author's experimental energy: 'It is, in fact, time to acknowledge *Northanger Abbey* for what it is: an ambitious, innovative piece of work, quizzically intellectual about fiction itself' (xv). In defending her innovative reading, Butler quickly and efficiently dispatches the disputes that have characterized much of the criticism to date: whether the text is an uneasy marriage of novel and burlesque; whether General Tilney is really a Montoni; and whether the text was subsequently re-worked. Above all else, Butler sees Austen's text revolving around reading, including the enlarged senses of decoding and interpretation, where these are bound by genres and games. *Northanger Abbey*'s concern with genre encompasses the Socratic conversa-tion piece (such as Clara Reeve's *The Progress of Romance*) as well as romance and novel, including Austen's three ghostly collaborators, Frances Burney, Maria Edgeworth and Ann Radcliffe. But genres are also games, and Butler extends this self-referential element to include Henry's games-playing, itself echoing the conflicting rules and contracts of common versus statute law (a reference that finds its relevance in the General's trampling over customary rights in the garish, capitalistic, modish improvements he inflicts upon his estate). For Butler, Austen's position is never stated; it is, rather, an ever shifting point that changes as yet other frames of reference are brought into play by the narrative. A principal frame she introduces is the new social adeptness of reading the signs of consumerism, particularly important in Bath, but also relevant to General Tilney. She argues that if we read these signs correctly, the General stands revealed before us, not as a Montoni, but as an ultra-modern, entrepreneurial Whig grandee despotically imposing anti-communitarian values. In her introduction, Ros Ballaster argues that *Sense and Sensibility* is also a novel of the 1790s, a text shaped by the decade's debates and concerns. Sensibility, inevitably, is at the heart of it. Despite her very different approach, Ballaster effectively concludes with Butler that Austen proceeds by subtly shifting the frames of reference, so that apparent dichotomies expand into something like an inclusive consciousness. Sense and sensibility emerge, not as opposites, but as linked states that reverse and double back upon each other. Thus, where earlier critics argued whether Austen sided with radical or conservative sensibility, Ballaster portrays a more complex picture where the narrative destabilizes any temporary cate-gorization it may have arrived at. There is a difference between Ballaster and Butler, which turns on the debate between Humphry Repton, on the one side, and Uvedale Price and Richard Payne Knight on the other. For Butler, the debate creates a series of contrasts: modernization/rural nostalgia; improvement/the picturesque; capitalism/community. In the unequal contrast between the General's improved Abbey and Woodston's ecologically integrated parsonage, Butler sees Austen coming down firmly on the Price/Knight side of the argument. By way of contrast, Ballaster reads 'improvement' (Repton) and the 'picturesque' (Price and Knight) as both being anticommunity in their own way, and therefore the butt of Austen's pointed irony. Patricia Meyer Spacks's edition of *Persuasion* follows the usual Norton format of contemporary contextual material and reviews followed by a selection of recent criticism.

Edward W. Said's *Culture and Imperialism* (*YWES* 74.685) continues to cause reverberations among Austen's critics. In 'The Ethics of *Mansfield Park*: Macintyre, Said, and Social Contract' (*Soundings* 78.483-500), Allen Dunn argues against both Said's and Alasdair Mcintyre's positions (as represented in *After Virtue*). Macintyre and Said both agree that morality is intimately linked to its social basis, but then markedly differ. Whereas for Macintyre the social basis is the ground of ethics, for Said the social basis compromises ethics through ideological entrapment. In Austen's case, the same 'political unconscious' that underpins and shapes the imperial adventure also shapes and underpins her moral outlook. Dunn doesn't so much settle for a place in between as shrewdly point out that morality in *Mansfield Park* is more complex than either his adversaries allow. That said, his secret strategy appears to be to grant the case against Mcintyre the more effectively to undermine Said's. Susan Fraiman also takes issue with Said's simplification of Mansfield Park's 'moral complexity' in 'Jane Austen and Edward Said: Gender, Culture, and Imperialism' (*CritI* 21.805–21). Fraiman argues that Said overlooks Austen's irony 'towards reigning constructions of citizenship'; or rather, given that his argument requires complicity, the traditional construction of Austen as a myopic woman writer unconcerned with big issues comes suspiciously easy to Said. Fraiman's argument is not that Austen is a sharp-eyed critic of English imperialism; but that as a woman writer she was marginalized within her own culture, and that as a result the placidly depicted scenes of patriarchal culture embraced by Said are in fact too ironically inflected in *Mansfield Park* to do the work Said needs them to do.

Brooke Allen's 'Jane Austen for the Nineties' (*NewC* 14.i.15–22) is a well written, belletristic essay focusing on aspects of Austen's character and art as they arise from Deirdre Le Faye's new edition of the Letters. Readers looking for a serious discussion of the nineties' Austen boom will be disappointed. Those interested in an account of Jane Austen's place within 'the culture' will find D. A. Miller's 'Austen's Attitude' (*YJC* 8.1–5) more pertinent. In this short, bravura essay, Miller argues that Austen's impregnable, epigrammatic style is not a defence against her spinsterhood, her exclusion from an omnipresent cult of marriage, but a means of gaining mastery over it. 'A central meaning of Austen's highly peculiar cultural destiny cannot be grasped unless her will to style is linked to the felt unrepresentability of her situation' (4). Miller's very dense piece is almost impossible to précis; suffice to say that Miller ends by linking Austen's example of 'absolute style' to the style wars of her progeny, a '*salon des refuses*'. Finally, Athlone have reissued Warren Roberts's classic study *Jane Austen and the French Revolution*, first published in 1979.

As already mentioned, the Gothic novel was another major focus of the year's work. Like last year, there were several monographs, of which the most substantial is probably Ann Williams's *Art of Darkness: A Poetics of Gothic*. Williams starts by observing the confused multiplicity of the Gothic. Williams seems nonplussed by this hybridity. The Gothic begins (insofar as it can be said to begin) as pastiche, with Walpole's *The Castle of Otranto*. This act of over-determined iconographical bricolage was succeeded by a situation where the Gothic coalesced into formulaic fiction while simultaneously following a path of multiplication and division. The Gothic novel mutated into new sub-genres (the Victorian ghost story, vampire fiction, the sensation novel, modern horror) or alternatively embedded itself in other, more stable, genres (for instance, in disruptive moments within 'realist' fiction). Given that the Gothic is most interesting when it isn't simply formulaic, the obvious critical strategy would seem to be to accept, and focus on, its hybridity, its unstable, cross-generic life. Williams adopts a different approach: she searches for a unified-field theory, a key myth. Although she prefers 'complex' to 'genre', what the Gothic complex points to is really a singularity: a confrontation with otherness, where 'the *mythos* or structure informing this Gothic category of "otherness," is the patriarchal family' (22). Readers will not have been holding their breath waiting for this news. 'Like all dreams ... Gothic narratives enabled their audiences to confront and explore, and simultaneously to deny, a theme that marks the birth of the Romantic (and modern) sensibility: that "the law of the father" is a tyrannical *paterfamilias* and that we dwell in his ruins' (24). This reformulation of David Punter's *The Literature of Terror* (Longman, 1980), reconstituted through Kristeva and spiced with Lacan, is the basis of Williams's conception of the Gothic. Through the Semiotic and the abject the maternal intrudes into the patriarchal Symbolic. 'Thus Gothic may indeed be aligned with the "poetic" in Kristeva's sense of the term. It permits the return of the repressed – the maternal principle, the "female", in all the modes in which it may be recognised: in heroines, in feelings, in the landscape, in death, in *l'ecriture*' (96).

Williams divides the Gothic poetic into two traditions, the male and female, distinguished by three main differences. Narratologically, the female Gothic employs representative perception in such a way that we are left guessing with the heroine at the meaning of the various mysteries unfolding around her, whereas the male Gothic creates dramatic irony through multiple points of view. Secondly, the female Gothic explains the supernatural, whereas the male accepts the supernatural as real. Thirdly, the female Gothic plot is comic (it ends in marriage) whereas the male is tragic (it always remains on poor terms with the Symbolic). 'Male Gothic is a dark mirror reflecting patriarchy's nightmare, recalling a perilous, violent, and early separation from the mother/ mater denigrated as "female". "Female Gothic" creates a Looking-Glass World where ancient assumptions about the "male" and "female," the "line of Good" and the "line of Evil," are suspended or so transformed as to reveal an entirely different world, exposing the perils lurking in the father's corridor of power' (107). The male Gothic is akin to pornography insofar as it colludes with the patriarchal by stigmatizing the female as other and implicitly dangerous. The female Gothic, by contrast, challenges patriarchal culture. The female Gothic plot offers the reader a moment of potential self-fashioning where the comic plot and the 'insistence on the possibilities of female "reason"' promise control, as well as the opportunity to fashion a female self outside the confines of the customary patriarchal one where the female self is 'archetypal', 'stereotypical', and 'other'. Williams takes feminist critics to task for not noticing that 'the female Gothic narrative is thus genuinely and profoundly novel', indeed, 'revolutionary' (138). Whereas previous feminist critics read the female Gothic and its representation of the female self as the record of patriarchal deformation, Williams sees it partly as the revenge of the Semiotic, and partly as a form of narrative self-help. Instead of reading the female Gothic as a means of diagnosing the ills of patriarchy, Williams believes that generations of female readers embraced the Gothic as means of regaining their bearings amidst the patriarchal ruins. This difference in emphasis is one aspect of Williams's originality. Another is her refusal to identify the Gothic with the novel. Her study usefully ranges across the genres, from poetry, to drama to fiction, and back again, and chronologically from Jacobean tragedy to *Dracula*.

Glen Cavaliero's *The Supernatural & English Fiction: From the Castle of Otranto to Hawksmoor* is a curiosity. Its blurb makes some rather ambitious claims: 'This book is the first to describe and discuss all the principal English writers who have handled the subject of the supernatural.' Given that it takes us from Walpole and Radcliffe, through Maturin, Mary Shelley, James Hogg, Bulwer-Lytton, the writers of the Victorian ghost-story, Kipling, Stoker, de La Mare, Henry James, before arriving at William Golding, Iris Murdoch and Muriel Spark – in other words, through more or less the same itinerary, but not as exhaustively, as that pursued by David Punter's *The Literature of Terror* – it is an outrageous claim, even for a blurb. We are also told that Cavaliero's book 'discusses the relevance of the supernatural . . . to contemporary literary theory and its ideological accompaniments'. The connection, we learn, is that there isn't one. 'To talk meaningfully about the supernatural calls for a basis of metaphysics; and that particular basis is usually either lacking or misunderstood, not to say disallowed for being irrelevant' (11). Contemporary literary theory is doing the misunderstanding and disallowing here. Cavaliero's basic argument is that whatever academic literary critics may say, readers read the supernatural because they wish to suspend their disbelief; writers write, and readers read, the supernatural because they believe in 'the mysterium', in the possibility of metaphysical indeterminacy. Given literary theory's short way with metaphysics, it can never understand the ground of supernatural writing, its purposes, conventions and pleasures. 'Failure to address the subject other than by interpreting it as displaced cultural, political, or sexual anxiety merely eludes the challenge, and thus the topicality, of supernaturalism. The end result is muddle' (14). Cavaliero's terms invoke the tradition of generic criticism inaugurated by Tzvetan Todorov' *The Fantastic* only to dismiss it as so much muddled endeavour. Cavaliero's treatment of the writers relevant here – Horace Walpole, Ann Radcliffe, Matthew Lewis and Charles Maturin – is perfunctory. In fact, it is reminiscent of early twentieth-century commentators of the Gothic, such as Jane Tompkins and Ernest Baker, only not so well informed.

Maggie Kilgour's title, *The Rise of the Gothic Novel*, is doubly misleading, in that her book is not about the *rise* of the Gothic novel, nor even much about the Gothic. Its real subject is that group of 1790s novels which came into being under the shadow cast by the Price–Burke 'revolution controversy'. The bare bones of her argument is that the Gothic novel started as a revolutionary form but turned reactionary with astonishing rapidity. At the same time, its florid excesses meant that after the 1790s it was only possible as parody or in a self-conscious form thematizing its own piecemeal monstrosity. In order to sustain this history, Kilgour has had to repress the story of the Gothic from Walpole to the mature Godwin. Indeed, her close discussion only really begins with *Caleb Williams* and Wollstonecraft's *Maria*, taken to exemplify revolutionary Gothic; she then continues with late Radcliffe (*Udolpho* and *The Italian*) and Lewis (*The Monk*), who represent reaction; and finally concludes by jumping 20 years to *Frankenstein*, where 'hideous progeny' conveniently allows Kilgour to tie the knot on her thesis: '*Frankenstein* is a central metaphor for the gothic genre as it thematises, and ultimately demonises, its own creation.' Kilgour's focus is somewhat foreshortened. In the post-Walpole interregnum, where do Sophia Lee, Charlotte Smith, Clara Reeve and the early Radcliffe fit in? Are they revolutionary or reactionary; or, indeed, are these the appropriate terms? And while it is true that critical attacks on the formulaic nature of the Gothic intensified in the late 1790s, it isn't the case that the genre collapsed, dispirited. The volume of production in the period 1800–20 continued unabated from its 1790s peak; and the flow of 'masterpieces' (insofar as the genre has them) remained a trickling constant (Dacre, Maturin, Hogg). Apart from the patchiness of its coverage there is another reason this book cannot be considered a history of the rise of the Gothic: it doesn't provide a coherent picture of that which was allegedly rising. Rather than a working definition of the Gothic we are given a generic soufflé which is first inflated with hot revolutionary air before suddenly collapsing in the reactionary backdraft. That said, there is much here to engage a reader prepared to drop expectations raised by the title, especially readers interested in Burke's influence. Kilgour's study really begins with Burke's role in politicizing the 'Gothic' and how that impinged upon the genre, until now a neglected topic. Burke restored the word's modish ring through his identification of chivalry as Britain's stabilizing, organic past. Radicals responded by agreeing that Britain's institutional past was indeed chivalric, Gothic and feudal. Beginning her study with Wollstonecraft and Godwin, where the ideological issues are clear, enables Kilgour to identify Burke's presence in Radcliffe and Lewis, where it is implicit and ghostly. By beginning with the politically conscious, Kilgour is able to disinter the genre's political unconscious in a more thorough way than previous studies, albeit within the narrow band 1794–99.

Burke's chivalrous defence of Marie Antoinette also figures centrally in Claudia Johnson's *Equivocal Beings: Politics, Gender, and Sentimentality in the 1790s: Wollstonecraft, Radcliffe, Burney, Austen*, one of the year's few works to encompass both 'novel' and 'romance' in its field of critical vision. Johnson's general aim, amply realized, is to counter two received ideas: that the 1790s women's novel is embarrassingly bad and that sensibility during this period was successfully stigmatized with Jacobinism. While she accepts that the 1790s produced a 'body of novels distinctive first and foremost for their egregious affectivity', this affectivity was the mark of their engagement with the turbulent politics of the decade, and not a sign of their alienation from it. Johnson's point of entry into her argument is Burke's stiff defence of his masculinity with regards to the protection he had extended to the French Queen. Burke was unperturbed by Radical accusations that his lachrymose depictions of outraged modesty exhibited foppish effeminacy. Johnson's argument here (extending a line first developed by J. G. A. Pocock) is that

Burke writes out of a conservative tradition which saw sentimentality, in general, and chivalry, in particular, as expressions of civic virtues historically rooted in the origins of polite society. Chivalry was not a feudal hangover, but a marker of advanced civilization. It signalled a revolution in manners indispensable to a modern, commercial society. Proper veneration and respect for women, the protection of the weak, and vigorous commerce were of a piece. False sentiment, such as Jacobinical sensibility, might be implicated in the horrors across the channel, but true sentiment was part and parcel of British progressive stability. Sentiment was therefore not universally proscribed during the 1790s reaction; on the contrary, the chivalrous version of it was infused with ideological value. Excessive displays of masculine sensibility (such as Burke's) reveal the extent to which feminine qualities had been subject to a process of 're-Masculinization'. In the scene of virtue, women were relegated to a passive, non-speaking role, while the male actor wept copiously, orated nobly, or showed other signs of sentimental virtue. Johnson argues that the narrative imaginations of her chosen writers work themselves in and around, in opposition to, and along the grain of, this equivocal 'nexus of politics, affectivity, and gender'.

The Female Thermometer: Eighteenth-Century Culture and the Invention of the Uncanny collects together many of Terry Castle's recent essays on the subject. Those interested in the prose of the Romantic period will be particularly pleased to see the inclusion of Castle's seminal essay on Radcliffe, 'The Spectralization of the Other in *The Mysteries of Udolpho*', together with her equally influential 'Phantasmagoria and the Metaphorics of Modern Reverie'. There is also a new essay, 'Spectral Politics: Apparition Belief and the Romantic Imagination'. The rest of the volume is mainly composed of eighteenth-century material. The collection is tied together by Castle's suggestion that 'the uncanny itself first "comes to light" – becomes a part of human experience – in that period known as the Enlightenment' (7). For Castle, the 'estranging of the real' is a marker of modernity, is in fact produced by modernity in various complex ways. Castle's essays set out to map the emergence of our modern interest in the spectral and phantasmal.

There were a number of major articles on the Gothic, the best being Edward Jacobs's superb 'Anonymous Signatures: Circulating Libraries, Conventionality, and the Production of Gothic Romances' (*ELH* 62.603–29). Jacobs's long, sophisticated, bibliographically and historically informed argument is too complex for me to rehearse here, but I would like to give something of its gist. 'The dominant view', says Jacobs, 'has been that circulating libraries vulgarised literature, by pandering fiction to women, servants, and other people who had previously been excluded from reading by the high cost of books or by literacy.' Although Jacobs ends up with a position not dissimilar to this, he tells a far more involved, and interesting story. In the first half of the eighteenth century, female writers significantly contributed to the generic fashioning of the 'realist novel', building up a material investment in its means of production. However, an unforeseen consequence of Walpole's newspaper war with Bolingbroke was to marginalize the literary culture of the female realist novel. Walpole's subsidies for the newspapers opposing *The Craftsman* gave them control of the presses; coincidentally, these same publishers produced Fielding and Richardson, thus redefining 'realism'. This take-over was discursively defended through the introduction of the 'Gothic romance', a fresh, stigmatizing term which rewrote the historical record: female writers produced giddy romances rather than sober novels. In order to make inroads into the late eighteenth-century novel market, circulating libraries began to publish cheap unknowns, who, among other things, resuscitated, by making new, the 'Gothic romance'. However, as these writers became known (Radcliffe is the paradigmatic case) they switched to the established publishers, generally for very large fees. The significance of Jacobs's article is not just that it tells a new and compelling story about the vicissitudes of the eighteenth-century female novelist; it is that it is supported by detailed research into the minutiae of lending, reading and publishing.

Emily Jane Cohen's 'Museums of the Mind: The Gothic and the Art of Memory' (*ELH* 62.883–905) is also an original attempt to rethink the Gothic. Cohen begins her essay with a paradox inherent in the Lockean foundations of sensibility. Empiricism may have endeavoured to impart to experience a steadying rationality, but one of its effects was to undermine the security of identity. For Locke, to perceive was to be; insensibility thereby threatened nullity. Cohen reads the Gothic as part of a larger cultural stay against ontological oblivion. The late eighteenth-century growth in tourism focused on the collection of curiosities and mementoes, souvenirs from the grand tour. In a secular age, the art of memory became increasingly important as a means of fixing recollection, and hence the self. The Gothic novel was in this respect a literary form of this new, secular art of memory, in which curious objects from the past, and/or other countries, were collected and stored, or aesthetically codified (as beautiful, picturesque or sublime). Hence the tendency of the Gothic novel – first really noticed by Terry Castle – to reify its concerns, turning experiences, or people, into objects or things, as if to fix them amidst the perceptual, ontological flux. Equally innovative is Mark Canuel's ' "Holy Hypocrisy" and the Government of Belief: Religion and Nationalism in the Gothic' (*SIR* 34.508–30). Canuel turns the usual view of Gothic anti-Catholicism upside down. Whereas most criticism stresses the British nationalism inherent in the Protestant attack on European Catholicism, Canuel argues that such Gothic anti-monasticism is in fact a coded, ideological expression of English disestablishmentarianism. Canuel equates anti-monasticism with attacks on a confessional society, and then, in an audacious move, links English support for the Established Church with confessional technologies, ones designed to coerce assent. Canuel's main exemplars are Burke and Bentham, the one championing established religion as the grounds of legality and nationhood, the other successfully opposing it. Overall, Canuel insists that the argument was a pervasive one throughout the late eighteenth century, leading up to 1828 and the repeal of the Test and Corporation Acts. Bentham may seem a surprising figure to find linked with anti-confessional technologies, given his association with the panopticon, but for Canuel the essential point is that for Bentham the panopticon was designed to exact punishment and not confessions. Its purpose was in fact entirely secular. Similarly, the novel's significance was that it signified literariness – with its inherent plurality of views – as opposed to religious dogma. In this respect, the novel was the antithesis of the 'catechism', or discourse in the service of doctrinal compulsion. So although the Gothic novel may cloak itself in stout Protestant anti-Catholicism, the real motivation of its practitioners was to attack, and so weaken, establishment discourse, with its investment in uniformity, and finally, conformity. Canuel quite rightly finds in Radcliffe a chief exemplar of middle-class dissent, the tracking of which produces a strong map of the ideological diversity of this ambiguous genre. In particular, he helpfully points out how the Gothic novel is a product of Dissenting culture engaged in a cloaked, inward debate with the Established Church.

Kim Ian Michasiw's 'Ann Radcliffe and the Terrors of Power' (*ECF* 6.iv.327–46) is a lively and challenging intervention in the debate about the cultural reproduction of relations of power, derived chiefly from the work of Foucault. Michasiw argues that 'Radcliffe represents the relations between the individual and the social order not in terms of a binary opposition of the individual and society but in terms of a tripartite opposition of the individual, society, and the state' (329). It is this that distinguishes her writing from the anti-social solipsism of her Romantic successors, and gives peculiar force to her investigations of terror as a mystified misapprehension of power in *The Mysteries of Udolpho* (Montoni's empty tyranny), and of horror as a more accurate measure of institutional power (Schedoni's deployment of church authority). There is a novel disregard for questions of gender in this analysis, but it is nevertheless a valuable, well-written exposition of Radcliffe's political interests in the two best known fictions, along with interesting commentary on the posthumously published, *Gaston de Blondeville*.

Elsewhere, in another of their welcome reprints, Athlone Press have brought out Coral Ann Howells's *Love, Mystery and Misery: Feeling in Gothic Fiction*, first published in 1978. Howells adds a short preface and a selected bibliography. There were three significant pieces of work on Matthew Lewis. Frederick S. Frank has provided a very useful new bibliography of *The Monk* just in time for the novel's bicentenary (*BB* 52.iii.241–60). Like all of Frank's bibliographies, it is thorough, and as close to completeness as one could reasonably wish. This one covers bibliographical and biographical sources; books on *The Monk*; articles and chapters; doctoral dissertations; editions; early reviews; plus a selection of early chapbook and shilling shocker versions. In 'Let's talk About Sex: Confessions and Vows in *The Monk*' (*ArAA* 20.ii.307–16), Michael Meyer reads Lewis's text as in keeping with Foucault's argument that far from repressing sexuality the late eighteenth century actively produced sex as discourse. '*The Monk* exemplifies Foucault's observation of the increasing discursivization of sexuality by transferring its confessions and vows from the religious into the private sphere'. Emma McEvoy's *The Monk*, for the World's Classics, keeps Howard Anderson's authoritative version of the first edition, but provides a new introduction and notes. McEvoy's preface doesn't essay a new interpretation of Lewis's text; it is, however, a very efficient and useful introduction, covering *The Monk*'s reception, its relationship to Radcliffe and the Gothic tradition in general, including German influences. McEvoy writes about *The Monk*'s themes in a lively style, while being shrewdly cognizant of the way Lewis's parody complicates and disrupts them.

Adriana Craciun ' "I hasten to be disembodied": Charlotte Dacre, the demon Lover, and Representations of the Body' (*ERR* 6.75–91) is largely focused on Dacre's poetry; however, her contextualizing focus on the representations of the body in the late Enlightenment and their connections with the Romantic imagination equally pertain to Dacre's novels. Anyone interested in Dacre's career as a novelist will want to consult this essay. I think

Craciun is essentially right in arguing that one of Dacre's main appeals is that her oeuvre consistently evades, and so questions, not just contemporaneous gender divisions, but those imposed on the period by recent commentators. As a woman writer, Dacre is neither a proper lady nor an unsexed 'blue', but something Byronically, and transgressively, in-between.

Frankenstein continues to be the main focus of the work done on Mary Shelley, although more of her other works are coming into view. There were two monographs this year. Tim Marshall begins *Murdering to Dissect* with a problem. He wants to argue that Shelley's text is imbricated in the grave-robbing controversies surrounding the Anatomy Act of 1832 and the Burke/Hare scandal of 1829–32. Indeed, he wants to go further and say that the issues raised by these events are allegorically inscribed in Shelley's text. The problem, of course, is that the first edition of *Frankenstein* dates from 1818, a year before John Abernethy first proposed that unclaimed paupers' bodies should serve science as anatomy fodder. Marshall finds his solution to this temporal dislocation in the theoretical models of representation provided by Bakhtin and Foucault, and in the quasi-sociological perspective of Elias Canetti's neglected *Crowds and Power* (Farrar, Straus and Giroux, 1984). Marshall's materials 'concern fables and realities of building people and destroying people, and above all the doctor/scientist as a figure of threat ... in the anatomy literature there is much slippage between the surgeon, the dissector, the murderer – and the writer and the artist' (12–13). That is to say, we are dealing with a discursive economy where ideas circulate along the troubled axes of power/knowledge (medical discourse) but also of money and class (its winners and losers). Historical events transpired in such a way as to reveal fully *Frankenstein*'s deep participation in the discursive economy of anatomy. In the end, Marshall's 'problem' is really the catalyst for his ingenious meditations on what made *Frankenstein*'s prolepses possible. Marshall takes us through the ins and outs of the Anatomy Act of 1832, its 'pre-history' in the 'medical gaze and popular culture' of the eighteenth century, the 'resurrectionist culture' of the early nineteenth, as well as through collateral representations of murder and dissection in De Quincey, Dickens and others. The other monograph of the year is Katherine Hill-Miller's *'My Hideous Progeny': Mary Shelley, William Godwin, and the Father–Daughter Relationship*, 'a study of the influence of William Godwin on his daughter' which explores 'Godwin's unsettling psychological legacy – and his generous intellectual gifts' to Mary Shelley. The book opens with a biography of Godwin and Shelley's father–daughter relationship, followed by chapters on *Frankenstein, Mathilda, Lodore* and *Falkner*.

The focus of Ellen Cronan Rose's 'Custody Battles: Reproducing Knowl-edge about *Frankenstein*' (*NLH* 26.809-32) is the way feminist criticism of *Frankenstein* has shadowed wider movements in the general culture. Whereas Ellen Moers grounded the text in Shelley's experience of parturition and mothering, subsequent feminist critics re-situated *Frankenstein* in the field of theory, where the problematic entry into the patriarchal Symbolic replaces the maternal body as the dominant origin of textual conflict. Just as feminist critics used French theory to repudiate Moers's autobiographical focus, so feminists at large moved from the ambivalence towards childbirth typical of Moers's generation to a brave new world in which technology – or theory – would set them free from biological destiny. When the technology of fertility began to seem dubious to the next generation of feminist scholars, attention shifted to patriarchal attempts to control feminine reproduction (including writing). Putting her finger to the wind, Rose senses that the recent even-handed focus of gender studies is beginning to produce readings that focus on *Frankenstein*'s concern with the destructive force of masculine ideology. I found Rose's reading of the cultural inflections of changing Frankenstein criticism both convincing and useful.

Frann Michel, in 'Lesbian Panic and Mary Shelley's *Frankenstein*' (*GLQ* 2.237–52), also takes issue with feminist interpretations based on French theory. For Michel, the central dynamic of *Frankenstein* has less to do with the ideological fall – out of insertion into the Symbolic order (an approach she sees as typified by Margaret Homans), and more with suppression of female same-sex desire. We are to understand the horrified responses of those gazing upon the monster as being essentially cognate with the response elicited by early nineteenth-century lesbian panic. Michel uses biographical and associated textual evidence linked to Shelley's desire to re-insert female homosexuality into the creative hinterland of the text, a presence actually absent in *Frankenstein*, but discernible in reactions to the monster. Indeed, for Michel, the monster comes to figure 'sapphic sexuality' itself. Much of Michel's critical ingenuity is devoted to showing how mainstream feminists, but also leading gay studies theorists, such as Eve Kosofsky Sedgwick, have elided this central textual dynamic, either by imposing a heterosexual agenda on the text, or by viewing it as a critique of male homophobia.

Alan Rauch, in 'The Monstrous Body of Knowledge in Mary Shelley's *Frankenstein*' (*SIR* 34.227–53), investigates Mary Shelley's concern with bad science, typified by secretiveness, egotism, grandiose ambition, a lack of social obligation, curiosity, or a sense of the need to communicate and share useful discoveries. The monster, in this respect, becomes the embodiment of Frankenstein's anti-social knowledge. Although Rauch contrasts Frankenstein with the progressive scientists and physicians of Mary's and Percy's acquaintance, such as William Lawrence, he does not identify Frankenstein with any particular or regressive school of Georgian science, but reads him as a generic or composite figure. Also on the scientific theme, Martin Willis, in '*Frankenstein* and the Soul', argues that *Frankenstein* closely represents current debates between Romantic and materialist conceptions of science, debates hinging on the issue of electricity as the vital, soul imparting spark (*EIC* 45.i.24–35). His conclusion is more or less the reverse of that taken by Marilyn Butler in her recent edition of the novel (*YWES* 75.413). Crudely, where Willis sees Shelley Romantically embracing electrical vitalism, Butler sees her as satirizing it. Butler's is by far the more cogent argument; it is also the more obviously informed, scientifically and historically. Brian Stableford's 'Frankenstein and the Origins of Science Fiction' (in *Anticipation: Essays on Early Science Fiction and its Precursors*, ed. David Seed) is a derivative, 'common sense' review of the novel's claims to pioneering status as a work of science fiction.

Stephen Behrendt's 'Mary Shelley, *Frankenstein*, and the Woman Writer's Fate' (in Paula R. Feldman and Theresa M. Kelley, eds, *Romantic Women Writers*) appears at the start to be another reading of the novel as transfiguration of the author's victim status as woman writer, but happily it branches off into less frequented fields, to look at the attempts of a range of female authors

– including Mary Tighe, Felicia Hemans as well as Shelley herself – to negotiate the material and ideological pitfalls of the literary marketplace. The presentation of this material is engaging and learned, but Behrendt nevertheless returns to the cliché that 'Frankenstein's Creature shares the situation of Romantic women, marginalized and spurned by a society to whose patriarchal schemata they fail to conform'. If the word-play in the title of Leila Silivana May's 'Sibling Revelry in Mary Shelley's *Frankenstein*' (*SEL* 35.670–85) can be forgiven, the reader will find a creditable examination of the sibling bond and 'sororal desire', in the mainstream feminist tradition. Not very adventurous, but May does justice to her proposition that '*Frankenstein* performs a major revision of a chief Romantic tenet: male narcissism is no longer valorized, but is monstrously punished'. Ellen J. Goldner in 'Monstrous Body, Tortured Soul: *Frankenstein* at the Juncture between Discourses' (in Lee Quinby, ed., *Genealogy and Literature*) reads Shelley's novel as a perfect allegory of Foucault's *Discipline and Punish*, with the Monster featuring as the 'old discourse of the marked and public body' while Frankenstein appears as the newly emergent 'figure of the romantic soul'. All very neat, and far too reverent towards the master-theory to be entirely convincing. There is an additional argument about the reception of the novel, which itself allegedly operated, in its nineteenth-century dissemination, as a 'soul-making' enterprise and instrument of internal discipline through effects of reading; while in the postmodern culture of today, *Frankenstein* permits a demystifying glimpse at the genealogy of our own configurations of 'power/knowledge'. The contents of 'The Corrected *Frankenstein*: Twelve Preferred Readings in the Last Draft' (*ELN* 33.i.23–35) by David Ketterer are pretty much summed up by the title: this is a review of errors of spelling, grammar or typography either derived from, or correctable on the basis of, Shelley's final draft of the novel. A few of the corrections have minor interpretative consequences, but by and large this is an article for editors of Shelley and true fanatics only. Ketterer's work of transcribing the Last Draft and Fair Copy fragments and collating them with the 1818 edition, will make possible an 'as-near-perfect-as-possible critical text of the 1818 edition'.

'Mary Shelley's *Valperga*: The Triumph of Euthanasia's Mind' (*ERR* 5.133–48) by William D. Brewer is a useful example of old-fashioned scholarship, which links Shelley's novels to other literary treatments of the theory of the 'ruling passion' by Godwin, Joanna Baillie and William Wordsworth, and takes the character of Euthanasia as an embodiment of the enlightenment ideals found in *Vindication of the Rights of Woman*. A final section ventures tentatively into a Freudian comparison for Euthanasia's exposition of the divided but balanced human mind, which 'goes beyond the simple theory of the ruling passions', but retains an ultimate faith in reason.

Frances Burney and Maria Edgeworth continue to attract critical interest. Miranda J. Burgess's 'Courting Ruin: The Economic Romances of Frances Burney' (*Novel* 28.ii.131– 54) is a pleasingly polemical article, which situates Burney within a field of debate on ethics and economics defined by Hume and Burke. Here, Burney figures as a social and economic conservative, and by no means as the outspoken feminist described in much recent criticism. Her novels 'reproduce and condemn the co-operation of conduct books and *laissez-faire* economics' (140), by illustrating the hapless collusion of the heroines with a relativist culture of credit. 'Goblin Laughter: Violent Comedy and the Condition of Women in Frances Burney and Jane Austen' by Audrey Bilger (*WS* 24.323–40) claims that 'women writers have produced violent comedy as a response and a challenge to oppressive conditions'. In demonstration, Bilger ranges over some familiar passages from Burney and, more interestingly, Jane Collier's *The Art of Ingeniously Tormenting* and Austen's juvenilia. The argument remains undeveloped: there is a failure to consider comedy as a literary genre or indeed as anything other than a direct response to the experience of gender oppression. Kathryn Kirkpatrick's 'Putting Down the Rebellion: Notes and Glosses on *Castle Rackrent*, 1800' (*Éire* 30.i.77–90) is a careful and rewarding examination of the textual genesis of the novel, with special attention to the glossary, antiquarian footnotes and the role of the 'Editor' in relation to the voice of the Irish Catholic narrator. The conclusion that Edgeworth's position as a woman writer allowed her to produce a sympathetically 'realist' representation of the colonized Irish is not particularly original, but the links between gender and colonial politics in her fiction are usefully indicated.

There were two articles on the wider topic of the woman novelist and revolution, both glancing across to Claudia Johnson's *Equivocal Beings*. In 'Women Novelists and the French Revolution Debate: Novelizing the Revolution / Revolutionizing the Novel' (*ECF* 6.iv.369–88), Gary Kelly signposts historical developments and locates a wide range of writers and their works with customary assurance. Equally characteristic is the absence of quotation from or detailed reference to primary texts: this is thought-provoking hypothesis, rather than critical demonstration. The article asks, 'Why did the novel, especially women's novels, become important in the Revolution debate?' (373), and sketches a reply in terms of the growing cultural authority of the private sphere and valorization of subjective experience. Rhonda Batchelor's 'The Rise and Fall of the Eighteenth Century's Authentic Feminine Voice' (*ECF* 6.iv.347–68) aims to show how 'cultural revolution' is reflected (the contested term is not inappropriate here) in Wollstonecraft's *The Wrongs of Woman*, Radcliffe's *The Italian*, Jane Porter's *The Scottish Chiefs* and Shelley's *Frankenstein*. Batchelor asserts that 'these novels reveal the taking up and taking over of the source and attributes of the authentic female self by male voices' (368). There is a considerable debt to Gary Kelly's model of gendered social change, but also a good deal of critical naiveté in complaints that female characters are reduced to a 'two-dimensional critical presence'.

Colonialism currently appears to be the preferred route for arriving at a critical apprehension of Sir Walter Scott's historical moment. In 'Colonial Space and the Colonisation of Time in Scott's *Waverley*' (*SIR* 34.155–87), Saree Makdisi investigates Scott's complex involvement in the colonial possession of Highlands space. Makdisi argues that the colonial project is not to transform the subjugated space but in a sense to evacuate it: 'it involves an appropriation and clearing-away of this space as a site in which modernity can then be planted by force' (187). On the one hand, Scott resisted this process through his collaboration with the reinvention of Highland culture, attributing to the Highlands distinct customs, culture, and a history it didn't actually have. But in reclaiming the otherness of the Highlands, Scott paradoxically assisted in the colonialization of Highlands space by occluding what was actually happening on the ground, thus facilitating modernity's work. James Buzard covers much the same territory (including, in a few instances, quotations) in

'Translation and Tourism: Scott's *Waverley* and the Rending of Culture' (*YJC* 8.ii.31–59). Buzard phrases Scott's ambiguous position somewhat differently. Buzard contrasts Macpherson's *Ossian* (translation without an author) with Scott's *Waverley* (translation without an original). The first amounts to literary fraud; the second to 'culture' (or, as we now say, to 'heritage'). In producing his picture of the Scottish Highlands, Scott partakes of the romance of an indigenous, unified culture. Whereas the foreign, imperial observer translates in order to traduce, Scott's work represents 'autoethnography'; Scott is part of the Scots 'Other that participates in its own representation'. Aware of the contemporaneous disappearance of Highland culture, Scott rescues it by 'translating' it from the past. This 'translated' Highland culture comes to stand for Scotland as a whole, at the expense of the Lowlands. Where Makdisi sees Scott easing the way for modernity in a Scottish context, Buzard sees him contributing to a British identity, where the Briton is defined as 'at once alien and English'. The Highlands, in this context, 'becomes the site of a *Scottish* cultural difference' (37). The double move here is that in sympathetically inventing a Highland past Scott only succeeds in creating a cultural difference that is immediately subsumed within the larger category of Britishness. Chris Ferns arrives at a similar position with regards to Scott's double attitude towards Scottishness and colonialism, but via a very different route. In 'Look Who's Talking: Walter Scott, Thomas Raddall, and the Voices of the Colonized' (*ArielE* 26.iv.49–67), Ferns suggests that Scott's belief in the historical triumph of an 'emergent capitalist order' created the confidence whereby the voices of the marginalized were allowed space, to the point of often upstaging 'those of both narrator and protagonist'. This inclusive dialogism is contrasted with the monologic narratives of the Canadian historical novelist Thomas Raddall, where a sense of cultural transformation isn't so secure. Christopher Johnson's 'Anti-Pugilism: Violence and Justice in Scott's "The Two Drovers" ' (*ScLJ* 22.46–60) is not as theorized as the other essays on Scott, but is equally concerned to draw out the historical context of Scott's representation of conflict between Highlanders and the English. Johnson convincingly shows that contemporary attitudes towards pugilism provide the context of the clash of cultural difference which forms the subject-matter of Scott's story, as well as the key to Scott's ambivalent nationalist feelings.

Thomas Love Peacock continues to attract scant attention; but if there isn't much quantity this year, there is certainly quality. James Mulvihill's 'Peacock's *Nightmare Abbey* and the "Shapes" of Imposture' (*SIR* 34.553–68) is a fascinating reading of the change of direction Peacock takes between *Melincourt* and *Nightmare Abbey*. Where *Melincourt* was 'a vehicle for ideology', *Nightmare Abbey* was 'the critique of a mentality'. Mulvihill has two key theses. The first is that 'Peacock's main strength as a satirist is his sensitivity to the transformative properties of ideology' (562). Whereas in *Melincourt* Peacock's characters to an extent believe in what they say, in *Nightmare Abbey* what they say is controlled by a mentality beyond their ken; the stories the characters tell have a transformative momentum beyond the content they want their narratives to impart. Mulvihill's second thesis is that this condition of universal imposture is in line with Jurgen Habermas's theory of the fallen public sphere, where staged display and phatic communication predominate; that is to say, where only imposture is possible.

Jurgen Habermas also makes an appearance in Jon Klancher's superb

'Godwin and the Republican Romance: Genre, Politics, and Contingency in Cultural History' (*MLQ* 56.ii.145– 65). Klancher's essay investigates the odd status and character of Godwin's essay, 'Of History and Romance', which went back into his bottom drawer, unfinished, in 1797, at the same moment that he published his exercise in polite letters, *The Enquirer*. To an extent, Klancher's essay is a political archaeology of what was involved in Godwin's apparent moment of uncertainty and revision. At its simplest, one could say that it registered Godwin's faltering confidence in the possibility of a 'public sphere'. Klancher's essay is far too involved, and subtle, to summarize here, but what will be of most interest to scholars of fiction of the Romantic period is Klancher's suggestion that Godwin's tentative elevation of romance over history amounts to the assertion of contingency against the rigid, developmental historiography of the Scottish Enlightenment. That is to say, romance allows one to imagine possible histories, and is therefore less prone to the teleological fictions of Scottish historiography. In particular, romance allows one to imagine a republican history. This conception of the radical possibilities of romance, although still-born in Godwin's essay, is nevertheless useful for thinking about the complex relationship between romance and novel during this period, and as such, along with Claudia Johnson's work, provides the most effective map for charting the points of connection between Austen, Shelley and the Gothic.

The year saw two essays on *Caleb Williams*. In ' "Magnetical Sympathy": Strategies of Power and Resistance in Godwin's *Caleb Williams*' (*Criticism* 37.ii.213– 32) Eric Daffron notes the disjunction between the novel and the 1798 edition of *Political Justice*. Both texts evince a concern with the limits of sympathy: on the one hand, sympathy is necessary in order to engender social passions and hence progress; but on the other it can lead to imitation, passivity and finally social stagnation. Where the philosophical work tends to take a restricted view of the possibility of employing sympathy as a mode of political resistance, the novel, in its more concrete imagining, foresees greater possibilities. In 'Constructive Treason and Godwin's Treasonous Constructions' (*Mosaic* 28.ii.43–62), Randa Helfield argues that in his pamphlet on the treason trials Godwin develops a view whereby legal truth is unrelated to its linguistic representation, whereas in *Caleb Williams* legal truth is revealed as a matter of linguistic construction. Gregory Maertz's 'Generic Fusion and Appropriation in Godwin's *St. Leon*' (*ERR* 5.214–29) investigates the sources of the generic diversity of Godwin's romance.

Books Reviewed

Ackroyd, Peter. *Blake*. Sinclair-Stevenson. pp. 399. £20. ISBN 1 85619 278 4.
Ashfield, Andrew, ed. *Romantic Women Poets 1770–1838*. ManUP. pp. 327. hb £35, pb £12.99. ISBN 0 7190 3788 3, 0 7190 3789 1.
Bainbridge, Simon. *Napoleon and English Romanticism*. Cambridge Studies in Romanticism 14. CUP. pp. xiv + 259. £35. ISBN 0 521 47336 5.
Ballaster, Ros. *Jane Austen: Sense and Sensibility*. Penguin. pp. 346. pb £2.50. ISBN 0 14 043425 9.
Barbauld, Anna Laetitia. *Eighteen Hundred and Eleven: A Poem 1812*. RevR. Woodstock. pp. 40. £25. ISBN 1 85477 176 0.

Barnes, Margaret G. *Twentieth Century Wordsworth*. Janus. pp. 61. pb £6.95. ISBN 1 85756 236 4.

Baron, Michael. *Language and Relationship in Wordsworth's Writing*. Longman Studies in 18th and 19th Century Literature. Longman. pp. xiii + 280. £40. ISBN 0 582 06194 6.

Beer, John, ed. *Questioning Romanticism*. JHUP. pp. xiv + 319. hb £40, pb £17.95. ISBN 0 8018 5052 5, 0 8018 5053 3.

Bentley, Jr, G. E. *Blake Books Supplement: A Bibliography of Publications and Discoveries about William Blake 1971–1992 being a Continuation of Blake Books (1977)*. Clarendon. pp. 789. $135. ISBN 0 19 812354 X.

Betz, Paul F. *Romantic Archaeologies: Comprising Some Images of the Age and Selected Women Writers*. Albin O. Kuhn Library and Gallery and Wordsworth Trust America. pp. 32. no details.

Bialostosky, Don H. and Lawrence D. Needham, eds. *Rhetorical Traditions and British Romantic Literature*. IndUP. £35. pp. vii + 312. ISBN 0 253 31180 2.

Blank, G. Kim. *Wordsworth and Feeling: The Poetry of an Adult Child*. AUP. pp. 270. £30. ISBN 0 8386 3600 4.

Butler, Marilyn, ed. *Jane Austen. Northanger Abbey*. Penguin. pp. 232. pb £1.99. ISBN 0 14 043413 5.

Cannon, Garland, and Kevin R. Brine. *Objects of Enquiry: The Life, Contributions, and Influences of Sir William Jones (1746–1794)*. NYUP. pp. 185. £32. ISBN 0 8147 1517 6.

Castle, Terry. *The Female Thermometer: Eighteenth Century Culture and the Invention of the Uncanny*. OUP. pp. 278. hb £27.50, pb £12.99. ISBN 0 19 508097 1, 0 19 508098 X.

Cavaliero, Glen. *The Supernatural & English Fiction: From The Castle of Otranto to Hawksmoor*. OUP. pp. 273. £18.99. ISBN 0 19 212607 5.

Claeys, Gregory, ed. *Political Writings of the 1790s: The French Revolution Debate*. 8 vols. P&C. pp. 3,600. £495. ISBN 1 85196 320 0.

——, ed. *The Politics of English Jacobinism: Writings of John Thelwall*. PSUP. pp. 608. hb £67.50, pb £19.95. ISBN 0 271 01347 8, 0 271 01348 6.

Clej, Alina. *A Genealogy of the Modern Self: Thomas De Quincey and the Intoxication of Writing*. StanfordUP. pp. xxiv + 348. £27.95. ISBN 0 8047 2393 1.

Davis, James P. *An Experimental Reading of Wordsworth's Prelude: The Poetics of Bimodal Consciousness*. SSELRR. Mellen. pp. 193. $89.95. ISBN 0 7734 1245 X.

Day, Aidan. *Romanticism*. The New Critical Idiom. Routledge. pp. xii + 217. pb £6.99. ISBN 0 415 08378 8.

Dörrbecker, D. W., ed. *William Blake: The Continental Prophecies*. William Blake's Illuminated Books. Vol 4. Tate Gallery and the William Blake Trust. pp. 367. £50. ISBN 1 85437 154 1.

Fay, Elizabeth A. *Becoming Wordsworthian: A Performative Aesthetic*. UMassP. pp. viii + 279. £31.50. ISBN 0 87023 960 0.

Feldman, Paula R. and Theresa M. Kelley, eds. *Romantic Women Writers*. UPNE. pp. viii + 326. hb £38.95, pb $19.95. ISBN 0 8745 1711 7, 0 8745 1724 9.

Ferguson, Moira. *Eighteenth Century Women Poets: Nation, Class, and Gender*. SUNYP Series in Feminist Criticism and Theory. SUNYP. pp. 164. £34.75. ISBN 0 7914 2512 6.

Franklin, Michael J. *Sir William Jones*. UWalesP. pp. 137. pb £4.95. ISBN 0 7083 1295 0.

——, ed. Sir William Jones. *Selected Poetical and Prose Works*. UWalesP. pp. xxx + 415. hb £45. ISBN 0 7083 1294 2.

Garside, P. D., ed. *James Hogg. The Stirling/South Carolina Research Edition of the Collected Works of James Hogg: A Queer Book*. EdinUP. pp. xxxvii + 278. £29.50. ISBN 0 7486 0506 1.

Gassenmeier, Michael, Katrin Kamolz and Kirsten Sarna, eds. *Romantic Visions and Revisions of a New World: The Relevance of Romanticism for Teaching and Studying English Literature*. Blaue Eule. pp. 175. n.p. ISBN 3 89206 688 4.

Griffin, Robert J. *Wordsworth's Pope: A Study in Literary Historiography*. Cambridge Studies in Romanticism 18. CUP. pp. xii + 190. £30. ISBN 0 521 48171 6.

Halsey, Alan. *A Skeleton Key to Death's Jest-Book*. The Thomas Lovell Beddoes Society (John Lovell Beddoes, 11 Laund Nook, Belper, Derbyshire DE56 1GY). pp. 40. pb £3. ISBN 0 9525063 1 9.

——, *The Text of Shelley's Death*. FSP. pp. 82. £25. ISBN 0 947960 04 X.

Hanley, Keith, assisted by David Barron. *An Annotated Critical Bibliography of William Wordsworth*. HW. pp. 329. £65. ISBN 0 13 355348 5.

Harding, Anthony John. *The Reception of Myth in English Romanticism*. UMissP. pp. xiv + 289. £35.95. ISBN 0 8262 1007 4.

Harrison, Gary. *Wordsworth's Vagrant Muse: Poetry, Poverty and Power*. WSUP. pp. 237. $34.95. ISBN 0 8143 2481 9.

Hemans, Felicia. *The Domestic Affections 1812*. RevR. Woodstock. pp. 188. £27.50. ISBN 1 85477 181 7.

Heppner, Christopher. *Reading Blake's Designs*. CUP. pp. 320. £45. ISBN 0 521 47381 0.

Hill-Miller, Katherine. *'My Hideous Progeny': Mary Shelley, William Godwin, and the Father–Daughter Relationship*. UDelP. AUP. £29.50. ISBN 0 87413 535 4.

Hogg, James. *William Blake's Recreation of Gnostic Myth: Resolving the Apparent Incongruities*. Mellen. pp. 155. n.p. ISBN 0 7734 4188 3.

Howells, Coral Ann. *Love. Mystery and Misery: Feeling in Gothic Fiction*. Athlone. pp. 199. £12.95. ISBN 0 4851211 5.

Jackson, H. J., and J. R. de J. Jackson. *Samuel Taylor Coleridge. The Collected Works of Samuel Taylor Coleridge, Volume 11: Shorter Works and Fragments*. Routledge and PrincetonUP. pp. xliv + 1762. £100. ISBN 0 415 03010 2.

Johnson, Claudia L. *Equivocal Beings: Politics, Gender, and Sentimentality in the 1790s: Wollstonecraft, Radcliffe, Burney, Austen*. UChicP. pp. 256. hb £27.50, pb £12.99. ISBN 0 226 40183 9, 0 226 40184 7.

Jones, Mark. *The 'Lucy Poems': A Case Study in Literary Knowledge*. UTorP. pp. xiv + 337. £35.75. ISBN 0 8020 0434 2.

Jordan, John O., and Robert L. Patten. *Literature in the Marketplace: Nineteenth Century British Publishing and Reading Practices*. CUP. pp. xiv + 338. £40. ISBN 0 521 45247 3.

Kaul, R. K. *Studies in William Jones: An Interpreter of Oriental Literature.* Indian Institute of Advanced Study. pp. 123. Rs 140. ISBN 8185952 213.

Kearns, Sheila M. *Coleridge, Wordsworth, and Romantic Autobiography: Reading Strategies of Self-Representation.* AUP. pp. 202. £26. ISBN 0 8386 3546 6.

Kilgour, Maggie. *The Rise of the Gothic Novel.* Routledge. pp. 280. pb £14.99. ISBN 0 415 08182 3.

Langan, Celeste. *Romantic Vagrancy: Wordsworth and the Simulation of Freedom.* Cambridge Studies in Romanticism 15. CUP. pp. x + 304. £35. ISBN 0 521 47507 4.

Le Faye, Deidre, ed. *Jane Austen's Letters.* Third edition. OUP. pp. xxviii + 643. hb £30, pb £14.99. ISBN 0 19 811764 7, 0 19 283297 2.

Lincoln, Andrew. *Spiritual History: A Reading of William Blake's Vala or The Four Zoas.* Clarendon. pp. 322. £40. ISBN 0 19 818314 3.

Looser, Devoney, ed. *Jane Austen and Discourses of Feminism.* St. Martin's. pp. 197. $39.95. ISBN 0 312 12367 1.

Low, Donald A. ed. *Byron: Selected Poetry and Prose.* Routledge English Texts. Routledge. pp. viii + 400. pb £10.99. ISBN 0 415 07317 0.

Marshall, Tim. *Murdering to Dissect: Grave Robbing, Frankenstein and the Anatomy Literature.* ManUP. pp. 354. hb £45, pb £15.99. ISBN 0 7190 4542 8, 0 7190 4543 6.

McEvoy, Emma, ed. *Matthew Lewis: The Monk.* OUP. pp. 456. pb £6.99. ISBN 0 19 282435 X.

Morton, Timothy. *Shelley and the Revolution in Taste.* CUP. pp. xiii + 298. £37.50. ISBN 0 521 47135 4.

Nattrass, Leonora. *William Cobbett: The Politics of Style.* Cambridge Studies in Romanticism 11. CUP. pp. 263. £37.50. ISBN 0 521 46036 0.

Newey, Vincent. *Centring the Self: Subjectivity, Society and Reading from Thomas Gray to Thomas Hardy.* Scolar Press. pp. xviii + 273. £42.50. ISBN 1 85928 151 6.

O'Donnell, Brennan. *The Passion of Meter: A Study of Wordsworth's Metrical Art.* KSUP. pp. xii + 290. £31.50. ISBN 0 87338 510 1.

Perkins, Mary Anne. *Coleridge's Philosophy: The Logos as Unifying Principle.* OUP (1994). pp. xii + 310. £30. ISBN 0 19 824075 9.

Pyle, Forest. *The Ideology of Imagination: Subject and Society in the Discourse of Romanticism.* StanfordUP. CUP. pp. 225. £30. ISBN 0 8047 1649 8.

Quinby, Lee, ed. *Genealogy and Literature.* UMinnP. hb £28, pb £13.95. ISBN 0 8166 2560 3, 0 8166 2561 1.

Roberts, Warren. *Jane Austen and the French Revolution.* Reprint. Athlone. (1979) pp. 224. pb £12.95. ISBN 0 485 12110 7.

Robinson, Eric, David Powell, and P. M. S. Dawson, eds. *John Clare. Northborough Sonnets.* Carcanet. pp. xxii + 136. pb £9.95. ISBN 1 85754 198 7.

Robinson, Jeffrey C. *Romantic Presences: Living Images from the Age of Wordsworth and Shelley.* Station Hill. pp. 214. £14.99. ISBN 0 88268 198 2.

Robinson, Mary. *Poems 1791.* RevR. Woodstock. pp. 260. £30. ISBN 1 85477 191 4.

Roe, Nicholas, ed. *John Keats. Selected Poems.* Everyman. pp. xxxii + 374. pb £6.99. ISBN 0 460 87549 3.

—, ed. *Keats and History*. CUP. pp. xviii + 320. £40. ISBN 0 521 44245 1.

Schneider, Matthew. *Original Ambivalence: Autobiography and Violence in Thomas De Quincey*. Lang. pp. 197. ISBN 0 8204 2632 6.

Seed, David, ed. *Anticipation: Essays on Early Science Fiction and its Precursors*. Liverpool Science Fiction Texts and Series 2. SyracuseUP. pp. 256. $42.50. ISBN 0 8156 2632 0.

Spacks, Patricia Meyer, ed. *Jane Austen. Persuasion*. NCE. Norton. pb £5.95. ISBN 0 393 96018 8.

Spiegelman, Willard. *Majestic Indolence: English Romantic Poetry and the Work of Art*. Clarendon. pp. xii + 221. £30. ISBN 0 19 509356 9.

Stocking, Marion Kingston, ed. *The Clairmont Correspondence: Letters of Claire Clairmont, Charles Clairmont and Fanny Imlay Godwin, Vol. I: 1808–1834*. JHUP. pp. lxxix + 704. £45. ISBN 0 8018 4633 1.

Tinkler-Villani, V., ed. *Exhibited by Candlelight: Sources and Developments in the Gothic Tradition*. Rodopi. pp. ix + 298. hb £56, pb £18. ISBN 90 5183 832 8, 90 5183 828 X.

Wallace, Tara Ghosal. *Jane Austen and Narrative Authority*. Macmillan. pp. 155. £40. ISBN 0 333 60727 9.

Webb, Timothy with George E. Donaldson, eds. *Percy Bysshe Shelley. Poems and Prose*. Everyman. pp. xxxv + 552. pb £6.99. ISBN 0 460 87449 7.

Wendling, Ronald C. *Coleridge's Progress to Christianity: Experience and Authority in Religious Faith*. AUP. pp. 266. £32. ISBN 0 8387 5312 4.

Whitehead, Frank. *George Crabbe: A Reappraisal*. AUP. pp. 243. £29.50. ISBN 0 945636 70 9.

Williams, Ann. *Art of Darknesss: A Poetics of Gothic*. UChicP. pp. 311. hb £31.25, pb £11.95. ISBN 0 226 89906 3, 0 226 89907 1.

Woof, Robert, and Stephen Hebron. *John Keats*. The Wordsworth Trust. pp. viii + 188. pb £14.95. ISBN 1 870787 15 3.

Wordsworth, Jonathan, ed. *William Wordsworth, The Prelude: The Four Texts (1798, 1799, 1805, 1850)*. Penguin Classics. Penguin. pp. lxvi + 667. pb £9.99. ISBN 0 14 043369 4.

Worrall, David, ed. *William Blake: The Urizen Books*. William Blake's Illuminated Books. Vol. 6. William Tate Gallery and the William Blake Trust. pp. 231. £39.50. ISBN 1 85437 155 X.

Wu, Duncan, ed. *Romanticism: A Critical Reader*. Blackwell. pp. xxvi + 462. pb £16.99. ISBN 0 631 19504 1.

—, *Wordsworth's Reading 1800–1815*. CUP. pp. xxix + 307. £40. ISBN 0 521 49674 8.

Wyatt, John. *Wordsworth and the Geologists*. Cambridge Studies in Romanticism 16. CUP. pp. xiv + 268. £35. ISBN 0 521 47259 8.

XIII

The Nineteenth Century: The Victorian Period

INGA BRYDEN, WILLIAM BAKER, KENNETH WOMACK, JUDE V. NIXON and VICTOR EMELJANOW

This chapter has four sections: 1. Cultural Studies and Prose; 2. The Novel; 3. Poetry; 4. Victorian Drama and Theatre. Section 1 is by Inga Bryden; section 2 is by William Baker and Kenneth Womack; section 3 is by Jude V. Nixon; and section 4 is by Victor Emeljanow.

1. Cultural Studies and Prose

(a) General
The year's work on Victorian culture and prose was dominated by the critical perception of texts as cultural products. 'Objects', ranging from the *Illustrated London News*, to valentines, to a personal commonplace book, were read for what they revealed about the dynamics of Victorian culture. Allied to this was a particular concentration on the production of texts, and on the interaction of word and image within texts; a close reading of 'linguistic-pictorial moments'. Another related concern was the relationship between texts and readers; the shaping of audience ideologies.

This year saw, predictably, a range of writing on the *fin de siècle*; attempts by cultural critics to carve out their territory in the race to make historical sense of the approaching millennium. Critics were particularly interested in the dynamics between gender and empire. *Cultural Politics at the 'Fin de Siècle'* (ed. Sally Ledger and Scott McCracken) is an accessible collection of essays which deals centrally with the relationships between our own cultural politics ('by which we mean the recognition that culture is never fixed or stable') and those of the late nineteenth century, characterized by cultural fragmentation. It calls for a sophisticated historical cultural criticism by which the dialectical relationship between past and present can be understood. The essays focus on the Woman Question and gender identities, the formation of subjectivities, the ideologies of imperialism, socialist politics and the development of mass culture. As the editors note, 'there is no false optimism' in the book. Terry Eagleton, in the opening chapter 'The Flight to the Real', argues for a return to the last *fin*'s dynamic amalgam of spirituality and materialism: otherwise, the nineties will remain a version of the previous *fin de siècle* 'shorn of its politics'. Regenia Gagnier's 'Is Market Society the *Fin* of History?' provides a thought-provoking conclusion. Gagnier discusses the interaction of economics and aesthetics in the late nineteenth century, in the context of a developing democratic market society. 'If we are prepared to say that Marxism is dead, and that Smith's sympathy and Mill's progressivism are discredited, are we also prepared to make the image of our future the stage of *Salomé* or the picture of Dorian Gray?'

Sally Ledger focuses on the ideology of eugenics and theories of degeneration in the late nineteenth century in 'In Darkest England: The Terror of Degeneration in *Fin-de-Siècle* Britain' (*L&H* 4.71–86). She argues that cultural anxieties about Britain's imperial decline were as much to do with the political pressures of groups – women, the working classes – at home as they were concerned with the state of British civilization abroad. In arguing for a 'postcolonial and class-inflected' feminist literary criticism ('blindspots' for current feminist critics of *fin de siècle* culture) Ledger proceeds to discuss the interrelations of eugenicist theory, feminism, imperialism and socialism. Eugenic discourses, appropriated by a variety of interest groups, were another form of social categorization; a categorization according to 'race'.

As this year's work shows, it is now being acknowledged that the relationship between imperialism and feminism was a complex one. Ledger points out in 'In Darkest England' that imperialism offered imaginative and actual possibilities for women at home. And eugenics were appropriated in the field of sexual choice for women. Yet in popular fiction and writing about the East End of London, anxiety about working-class women as reproductive beings is evident. Ledger concludes by discussing the relationship between Conrad's *Heart of Darkness* and 'urban slumland fiction' such as Margaret Harkness's *In Darkest London*.

Two chapters in *Late Imperial Culture* (ed. Román de la Campa, et al.) are concerned with late nineteenth-century texts and practices in the context of postcolonical discourses. ' "Getting to Know You": Travel, Gender, and the Politics of Representation in *Anna and the King of Siam* and *The King and I*' confronts the issue of how to read feminist texts that celebrate the liberation that travel allows, since in the colonial discourses of western women's travel, mobility symbolized 'the middle-class myth of self-determination'. Caren Kaplan discusses the interaction of colonial and postcolonial narratives in Anna Leonowens's travel memoirs (and the literary and filmic versions of them). David Glover's ' "Dark Enough fur Any Man": Bram Stoker's Sexual Ethnology and the Question of Irish Nationalism' aims to restore Stoker's writing to its specifically Irish origins and to an Anglo-Irish Gothic literary tradition. Glover discusses the instability of ethnic signifiers in *Dracula* and *The Snake's Pass* against the background of setbacks for the Home Rule movement.

In *Travel, Gender and Imperialism: Mary Kingsley and West Africa*, Alison Blunt gives an account of imperialism which draws on feminist and post-structuralist theories. Blunt initially sets out the contexts of her study: the history of western women and imperialism and the 'imperialist underpinnings' of nineteenth-century British geography. These overlapping contexts lead to a consideration of women's place within a historiography of geography. More particularly, Blunt is interested in the constitution of subjectivity within unpredictable discourses which alter across space and time. Thus, in focusing on Mary Kingsley, Blunt is concerned with the construction of travelling 'subjects' in general rather than in resurrecting a 'heroine' for feminism. Within the above contexts, Blunt examines the distinctive features of travel writing by nineteenth-century women, how these represented spatiality (in terms of gender for example) and how women travel writers were constructed in terms of difference. This is clearly written and includes a useful and interesting section on the metaphorical and material importance of travel and travel writing. At times, though, Blunt is rather too careful in insisting that she is paying attention to that familiar trio gender, race and class. The social and cultural crises surrounding sexuality and sex were particularly pronounced in the later nineteenth century in the context of, for example, the emergent New Woman Question. Alice Domurat Dreger's article 'Doubtful Sex: The Fate of the Hermaphrodite in Victorian Medicine' (*VS* 38.335–70) makes a useful contribution to the debate about how late Victorians (in this case medical men) 'read' signs of sex. There is a wealth of evidence concerning nineteenth-century cases of 'mistaken sex' and Dreger refers to numerous medical and social cases. This evidence suggests that, above all, the medical profession sought to keep 'sex' differences between men and women theoretically and practically distinct, despite examining a series of 'hermaphrodites' whose 'sexually ambiguous bodies' disrupted those very categories. Dreger also speculates on the significance of the predominantly male medical profession's insistence on categories of sexual difference in the face of social/sexual threats posed by feminism.

Contemplating our own *fin de siècle* necessitates reappraising the late Victorian period and raises questions to do with nostalgia. A group of this year's texts were concerned with how we read the Victorians and how the Victorians read past cultures. Theoretically sophisticated and thoroughly argued, Garrett Stewart's 'Film's Victorian Retrofit' (*VS* 38.153–98) offers a long overdue critique of the cultural significance of recent filmic interpretations of the Victorian period. The film medium (which is photographically based) at our *fin de siècle* contains a version of the Victorian period as a kind of nostalgic cultural fantasy rather than offering it as a social memory. Stewart moves beyond simply finding reasons for the self-conscious revival of the 'Victorian' in contemporary films, to think about 'the residual role of Victorian culture in the genre and technology of general film practice'. He analyses a series of scenes structured around 'photographic moments' in films such as *The Age of Innocence*, *The Piano*, *Howard's End* and *Bram Stoker's Dracula*. These 'moments' recall the history of photography (the media history of the films' own 'image system') whilst introducing questions about the representation of human presence. Drawing on sociological, technological and aesthetic theories, Stewart argues that in contemporary films about the Victorian period 'the nostalgic patina may attach to the rudiments of the medium itself, the lost charm of photography's original magic, rather than to the social world it represents'.

In ' "This Feminine Preserve": Historical Biographies by Victorian Women' (*VS* 38.371–93), Rohan Maitzen's main aim is to bring to critical notice historical biographies (mainly of female historical figures) by Victorian women. Maitzen argues that these numerous and popular works – by writers such as Agnes Strickland, Julia Kavanagh and Hannah Lawrance – should be considered as a distinct genre of Victorian women's writing. Of course, study of such writers has implications for the wider study of Victorian historiography and for current feminist revision of 'traditional' historical study. In writing memoirs or biographies (constructed as aptly 'feminine') the women 'historians' were distanced, and distanced themselves, from 'serious historians'. Maitzen argues that they forged an alternative historical discourse based on 'feminine' gossip, which emphasized social and personal detail and was directed towards a female audience. Yet here ideology and historiography meet. Women's history was part of social history, but it had to be recorded in ways deemed culturally appropriate for women writers. Both historically and ideologically, woman was positioned as having an oblique, pervasive, rather than an active, heroic effect.

'No other period of the past intruded on the Victorian present so discordantly as the seventeenth century' claims Timothy Lang in *The Victorians and the Stuart Heritage: Interpretations of a Discordant Past* where he discusses nineteenth-century historians' interpretations of the Stuart past. Lang is particularly interested in the cultural and religious meanings of the Cromwell cult in nineteenth-century Britain. For the Victorians the most pertinent question raised by the English Civil War concerned the 'role of Protestant Dissent in an officially Anglican society'. Looking at texts by Henry Hallam, Thomas Babington Macaulay, Thomas Carlyle and Samuel Rawson Gardiner, Lang shows that Victorian Britain witnessed a growing tendency to accommodate or domesticate Cromwell and the Puritans. Lang argues that this process was linked to the formation of a unifying national history whereby sectarian divisions (for example those affecting Dissenters) were taken away. Distinctively, Carlyle located a reverence for authority and order in Puritanism which was lacking in contemporary society. Puritanism represented true religiosity and faith in leadership. Lang also points out though that the Cromwellian past as imperial myth was bound to fail.

This year's work was to a degree concerned with Victorian social categorization; the processes by which the Victorians constructed 'others' and defined themselves. In 'A Working Distinction: Vagrants, Beggars, and the Laboring Poor in Mid-Victorian England' (*PSt* 18.74–104), Laura Sagolla Croley is concerned with how new conceptions of work and self-improvement took hold in mid-Victorian culture. Croley first focuses on social commentators' constructions of 'vagrancy' as a sub-cultural phenomenon of the late 1840s to the early 1860s. The term 'vagrancy' designated a new breed of 'criminal' wanderers. Croley draws on Foucault's theories of power relations to show that the commentators' textual constructions 'repressed' the lowest-of-the-low, but simultaneously 'produced' a more respectable group of working-class poor who, in turn, defined their own identities and social status against the beggars. The final section of the article examines selected autobiographical accounts of vagrants and the 'respectable' working poor, such as James Dawson Burn's *Autobiography of a Beggar Boy* (1855) and Josiah Basset's *Life of a Vagrant* (1850). These texts demonstrate, Croley argues, both the writers' self-consciousness of the social boundaries being constructed and their resistance to those boundaries.

Policing Gender, Class and Family: Britain, 1850–1940 is a well-documented study of child welfare institutions, or juvenile reformatories, in late nineteenth and early twentieth-century Scotland. Using this as a case study, Linda Mahood works within social science and feminist frameworks to evaluate the concept of the social. She aims to 'construct an aetiology of the social' by historically contextualizing the Scottish child-saving movement in early nineteenth-century social and political changes, and by arguing that the social is a material, a gendered and an ideological space. Mahood includes among her evidence material from interviews with former inhabitants of the welfare institutions. This information contributes to the conception of the social as an area of contestation.

In *Nobody's Angels: Middle-Class Women and Domestic Ideology in Victorian Culture*, Elizabeth Langland interprets fictional representations of middle- and working-class Victorian women. Texts are read as documents which expose the strategies by which the middle class policed others (working-class women for example) and defined itself. Literary texts are discussed in relation to class narratives of feminine business and household management and the book contains an interesting section on household management manuals.

This year's work on the cultural meanings of periodicals focused on the interaction between editor, journal and audience, whilst raising questions about the relationship of gender and genre. In 'Reviews of Tragedies in the Nineteenth-Century *Blackwood's*' (*VPR* 28.95–108) Dale Kramer discusses the variety of responses in *Blackwood's* to Greek tragedy – a touchstone for measuring contemporary dramatic and literary productions. Nearly half of the reviews/articles in *Blackwood's* between 1837 and 1901 dealing with a notion of the 'tragic' are by Margaret Oliphant and Elizabeth Hasell. Kramer focuses on two essays of the 1840s – Thomas De Quincey's 'Theory of Greek Tragedy' and Archibald Alison's 'The Greek and Romantic Drama'; on the distinctions between Oliphant's and Hasell's work; and finally on George Saintsbury's 'The Two Tragedies –A Note'. He shows that in this case-study, *Blackwood's* was not consistently reactionary in its views.

Solveig C. Robinson, in 'Editing *Belgravia*: M. E. Braddon's Defense of "Light Literature" ' (*VPR* 28.109–22), looks at Braddon's role as editor of *Belgravia: A London Magazine* – how it affected her literary identity and shaped the journal's critical profile. Robinson argues that in creating a critical forum appreciative of 'low' literature such as sensation fiction, Braddon altered the critical discourse surrounding such fictional forms. Moreover, as a successful sensation novelist Braddon constructed for herself a more respectable persona as editor and critic, whilst simultaneously validating the creative work she favoured.

David S. Nash's article 'Unfettered Investigation – the Secularist Press and the Creation of Audience in Victorian England' (*VPR* 28.123–35) is an interesting, focused discussion of the secularist press from the 1850s onwards. Nash contextualizes 'Secularism' and the papers it produced in both political and ideological terms. Through its press, mid-nineteenth-century secularism aligned itself with a libertarian tradition, whilst also paying homage to its earlier radical ideological roots. Nash details the ways in which the secularist papers adapted to shifting ideological positions within the movement. Ultimately, the British secularist press in the nineteenth century 'represented the apogee of liberal trust in the power of the written word to be instrumental in social and political change'.

Paul Thomas Murphy's study of nineteenth-century British working-class periodicals, *Toward a Working-Class Canon: Literary Criticism in British Working-Class Periodicals 1816–1858*, takes into account working-class voices and the views of the members of the Victorian middle class who spoke for the working class. It investigates the kinds of literature which had an impact on the formation of nineteenth-century personal and class reading histories. John M. Robson's *Marriage or Celibacy? The "Daily Telegraph" on a Victorian Dilemma* argues that the debate surrounding marriage, as represented in *The Daily Telegraph*, contributed to a focus in journalism on readers' participation. Peter W. Sinnema's 'Reading Nation and Class in the First Decade of the *Illustrated London News*' (*VPR* 28.136–52) is a theoretically informed series of close readings of 'various linguistic-pictorial moments', looking particularly at how the ideological categories 'nation' and 'class' interact and construct a reading audience. Sinnema sees the *ILN* as a cultural product – in the 1840s and early 1850s it was the 'site of complex new mediations between the art of wood engraving and the dissemination of news, and functions as a sort of self-contained, comprehensive textual phantasmagoria'. In each linguistic-pictorial instance, some sort of ideological position is being marketed. Sinnema offers convincing close readings, although the context of nineteenth-century cultural attitudes towards the interaction of word and image is not sufficiently acknowledged.

A group of the year's works dealt exclusively with the cultural and literary contributions of nineteenth-century women. *'Criminals, Idiots, Women, and Minors': Nineteenth-Century Writing by Women on Women* (ed. Susan Hamilton), is a useful anthology of writing by middle-class Victorian women printed in major reviews and journals of the Victorian press. It focuses on the connections between women's particular relation to the periodical press (for example, in the creation of a feminist press) and the significance for women of the Woman Question debate in the mainstream press. A concisely written introduction discusses women's role in the periodical press and addresses the question 'What then does it mean for a woman to write in the mainstream, respectable press on the Woman Question?'. The material in the anthology indicates the contradictory nature of Victorian feminism, ranging from pieces on sexual difference (Eliza Lynn Linton's essays) to those on the status of women's work (Harriet Martineau's 'Female Industry'), to those on the institution of marriage (Frances Power Cobbe's essays).

What Katy Read: Feminist Re-Readings of 'Classic' Stories for Girls by Shirley Foster and Judy Simons brings together feminist literary theory and fiction for 'girls' produced in the period 1850–1920. The eight texts discussed in this enjoyable and accessible book include Charlotte Yonge's *The Daisy Chain*, Louisa May Alcott's *Little Women*, Susan Coolidge's *What Katy Did* and Frances Hodgson Burnett's *The Secret Garden*. Like Kate Flint's study of the 'Woman Reader' (*YWES* 74.375) this book has implications for an understanding of nineteenth-century canonical literature and it addresses important questions about readership and acculturation. The focus here is on the 'prioritization of heroic femininity and the ideologies of girlhood that children's literature encodes'. A useful introduction discusses historical and critical contexts. It also highlights characteristics common to the selected texts (for example, that they reposition themselves in relation to the traditions of adult and juvenile literature) and discusses factors affecting theme and tone (for example, changing attitudes towards adolescence). Several of the texts discussed are based on the framework of a moral pilgrimage; others focus more on the psychological dimension of growing up.

This year a special issue of the *PULC* (57) was dedicated to Victorian women of letters, successful in their own day. Victorian literature is strongly represented in the Princeton University Libraries' Department of Rare Books and Special Collections. The article 'Telling Her Story: British Women of Letters of the Victorian Era' (*PULC* 57.147–62) by Peggy Meyer Sherry is a commentary on an exhibition of the Victorian holdings (specifically of women of letters) held at Princeton. Sherry summarizes the literary contribution of the women represented which includes Queen Victoria, Jean Ingelow, Ouida, Sarah Grand, Christina Rossetti and Dora Greenwell.

U. C. Knoepflmacher, in 'Male Patronage and Female Authorship: The Case of John Ruskin and Jean Ingelow' (*PULC* 57.13–46), looks in detail at Ruskin's letters to Ingelow, who gained popularity as a poet in late nineteenth-century Britain and America, but who disliked any circulation of details about her life. Knoepflmacher raises questions concerning the status of textual evidence in constructing a literary biography of a Victorian woman: it is suggested that a sense of Ingelow's significance is best obtained from the admiring and patronizing prose of Ruskin's letters to her. Furthermore, the Ruskin-Ingelow correspondence is notable for its demonstration of a relationship in which there is an avoidance of power conflict. Ruskin invests Ingelow with a segregated female 'purity' as a writer for children, and Ingelow did not subvert this male ideology.

'Dora Greenwell's Commonplace Book' (*PULC* 57.47–74), by Janet Gray, is an interesting reading of a particular object – in this case a personal compilation of songs and art – for what it tells us about Victorian culture. Gray aims to transform this commonplace book 'from junk into historical document', thereby revising academic conceptual frameworks which prioritize particular ways of interpreting cultural history. She discusses such an object first in the context of Greenwell's personal and social histories, then in terms of its contents. In the article's final section the commonplace book, and questions raised by it, are set in the context of social history informed by cultural theory. The book is 'both the product of a practice of collecting and a support for the practice of performing music'. Drawing on Susan Stewart's definitions of the terms souvenir and collection, Gray shows how the commonplace book is both shaped by and shapes the relationships between gender and performance.

'Glass House Visionary: Julia Margaret Cameron Among the Writers' (*PULC* 57.106–25) is a brief discussion of two books of Cameron's photographs which concern literary subjects (in two senses): *Lord Tennyson and His Friends* and a copy of volume one of *Idylls of the King and Other Poems*.

Anne Lundin examines the 'Greenaway Vogue' in the last decades of the nineteenth century in Britain and America (*PULC* 57.126–46). 'Kate Greenaway's Critical and Commercial Reception' usefully discusses the interaction of word and image in Greenaway's books, setting Greenaway's work in the context of developments in children's book publishing, and in book production generally. Greenaway's work 'remains a part of folk culture as well as a landmark in the history of children's bookmaking'. The remainder of the article discusses the critical reception of books included in the Princeton exhibition: *Mother Goose*, *An Apple Pie*, *The Pied Piper* and the *Almanacks*.

A significant number of this year's works approached Victorian culture through novelistic discourse, or explored ways of reading nineteenth-century fictions through an understanding of Victorian cultural discourses: public health, radical politics, medicine and so on. In 'The Moral of the Failed Bank: Professional Plots in the Victorian Money Market' (*VS* 38.199–226), Timothy L. Alborn focuses on the 'discursive reconstruction' of two bank failures in Victorian Britain: the crash of the Royal British Bank in 1855 and the failure of the City of Glasgow Bank in 1878. Alborn looks in particular at the changing contemporary response of bankers and financial journalists. Financial journalists, adopting the language used by popular novelists, saw the first failure as a symptom of wider commercial corruption. Mid-nineteenth-century novelists incorporated bank failures into narratives of more general social disintegration and depicted communal responsibility as located in the domestic home, not in the national institution. Indeed the banker in the 1850s was a 'father figure', protecting the money markets. In the context of increasing professionalization, bankers looked after their own and kept bank failures 'within their own ranks' rather than having recourse to novelistic plots or to the moral system of classical economics. By way of contrast, however, late nineteenth-century novels continued to depict finance as profoundly ambivalent.

In *Novel Possibilities: Fiction and the Formation of Early Victorian Culture*, Joseph W. Childers adopts an approach which draws on cultural materialism and poststructuralist notions of intertextuality. Childers sees the 'social-problem' novels of the 1840s as forming one public discourse among many shaping the culture of the period. Moreover, texts produced within the discourses of radical politics, public health and religion, were constituted by, and informed, the novels. That is, Childers sees the novels *Mary Barton*, *Coningsby* and *Alton Locke* (which are the three literary focal points of the book) as discursive and as 'problematic cultural artifacts'. The broader aim of the book is how to theorize cultural change. Non-literary texts studied include Robert Peel's 'Tamworth Manifesto', Thomas Babington Macaulay's essays and parliamentary speeches, memoirs and letters and a range of prose-writing from the popular press and specialist publications. In effect the novel, or novelistic discourse, is examined mainly in so far as it provided 'interpretative possibilities' for other contemporary ways of understanding culture. Parts of chapters four and five and a version of chapter six, all on Chadwick's Sanitation Report, appeared in last year's issues of *VS* and *PSt* (*YWES* 75.424–5).

Unstable Bodies: Victorian Representations of Sexuality and Maternity is a series of essays which, using literary, social and medical texts from the 1840s to the 1870s, investigate the cultural construction of 'womanhood' and female sexuality. Biomedical discourses concerning maternity and sexuality are analysed in their relationship to how, specifically, women's writing contributed to changing cultural perceptions of sexuality. Jill Matus amply demonstrates the contradictory nature of representations of sexuality in scientific and literary texts. The 'unstable bodies' of the title refer both to the bodies of biomedical and cultural discourses and to the 'representations themselves as an "unstable body" of discourse'. Illuminating discussions of novels such as *Mary Barton*, *Ruth*, *Lady Audley's Secret* and *Middlemarch* centre on specific cultural debates about sexuality and its representation: working-class sexuality, prostitution and infanticide.

Gender Roles and Sexuality in Victorian Literature (ed. Christopher Parker), has a misleading title, since some of its chapters do not deal with literary texts, whilst others are not concerned with sexuality. Rather, the interesting questions and issues raised within chapters are those relating to Victorian culture. It is not clear from the introduction what particular focus the book has, or what its methodology is, other than mention of 'the inter-action of literature and cultural history'. Neither are the terms gender and sexuality differentiated. None the less, under this umbrella title, individual chapters stand out on their own merits. Brian Maidment offers a thorough and interesting reading of the title pages of *The Family Economist* produced between 1848 and 1850. He analyses the ideological work of the title page (a combination of the 'visual, verbal, narrative and graphic') in a variety of contexts. There are sections on the 'cottage' magazine, the motto as a 'typographical and cultural event', and the narrative of cottage 'contentment'. Cynthia Dereli discusses gender issues in relation to the central period of the Crimean War, focusing on the public perception and portrayal (especially in poetry) of Florence Nightingale. The chapter also assesses the contribution of women to both the war and the body of poetry it produced. Several chapters look at *fin de siècle* writing: Lyn Pykett, for instance, reassesses Mona Caird's fiction in the light of the 'revisionary history of modernism'.

Barry Milligan's *Pleasures and Pains: Opium and the Orient in Nineteenth-Century British Culture* is a fascinating study of opium and the Orient as complex socio-cultural forces. Although literary criticism is fore-grounded, Milligan also draws on the disciplines of history, psychology and sociology. Milligan offers a 'series of local, detailed examinations of nineteenth-century English cultural products that figure perceptions of and responses to opium and the East'. These responses to the Orient, mingling fear and desire, were represented metaphorically by attitudes towards opium. Milligan demonstrates that cultural anxieties concerning both opium and the Orient were primarily to do with the transformability of national and individ-ual identities; anxieties about 'bilateral cultural exchange'. In this sense *Pleasures and Pains* challenges the notion of the dominant discourses of imperialism subjecting colonized 'others'. Milligan is interested in the merging of voices – in the 'corrosive effects the very possibility of [subjected] voices had upon the dominant discourses'. Indeed the late nineteenth-century 'opium den' narratives show the opium den as the melting-pot of English and Oriental cultural identities.

Critics this year were interested predominantly in the book as a cultural product and at least several works were concerned with the 'local conditions' of Victorian fiction, but more significantly, with the production process in its widest cultural sense. In lieu of an introduction, *Victorian Fiction: Writers, Publishers, Readers* has a preface in which John Sutherland briefly sets out his aims. Sutherland's mission is to encourage study of the 'local conditions' of Victorian fiction as a way of gauging 'Victorianness'. So the focus of *Victorian Fiction* is on factors relating to 'composition, publication, distribution, and consumption of novels'. Although Sutherland spends much of his time dis-cussing narrative strategies, he gets us to think about ways of approaching texts through an understanding of Victorian literary culture. This is apparent, for example, in the posing of the question 'how conscientious or careful was [Thackeray] in devising his fictions?'. An attention to close reading of the text becomes part of a discussion about serial publication, and fiction becomes evidence of contextual arguments such as those relating to the incarceration of relatives in asylums. The final chapter tackles the question of who was producing 'novels' in the Victorian period, with Sutherland asserting some (generalized) statements about 'novelists', taking into account gender and historical circumstance.

John Jordan and Robert Patten concede, in their introduction to *Literature in the Marketplace: Nineteenth-Century British Publishing and Reading Practices*, that they are dealing with a subject 'still in its formative phase'. The introduction provides a useful summary of different critical approaches to the history of British book publishing. Thus, the essays in this collection can be viewed as testing grounds for establishing the criteria upon which a study of nineteenth-century British publishing might be based. The opening essay by Simon Eliot discusses patterns of book production and factors affecting the marketplace, whereas other essays focus on how an individual author negotiated, and was constructed by, the production process. J. Hillis Miller offers a lively, interesting essay 'Sam Weller's Valentine'. Using the speech-act theories of de Man and Derrida, Hillis Miller investigates how 'promises' work as, among other things, commercial products. Valentines are historically contextualized and analysed as graphic and linguistic products in relation to the notion of performance.

The essays in *Literature in the Marketplace* focus on the 'effects of format', the dynamics of serial production, and the gendered nature of consumption. The editors make a plea for treating publishing history as 'hypertext'; a history which would take account of mediation, intangibles and the ambiguities of print culture.

This year saw valuable contributions towards the interdisciplinary study of Victorian culture, particularly concerning the relationship between literature and the visual arts. When Courbet designed the frontispiece for Champfleury's *Les Amis de le nature* (a collection of anecdotal statements about art and nature) he unusually drew upon a photograph of Champfleury by Paul Nadar. Heather McPherson, in 'Une "Allégorie Réelle": Courbet's 1859 Frontispiece For Champfleury's *Les Amis de le nature*' (*NCS* 9.31–54), interprets the complex, 'allegorical' frontispiece in relation to Champfleury's text and in the context of mid-century debates about Realism. McPherson sees the illustration as addressing the debate about artistic imagination versus direct observation, whilst it is also a Realist artifact documenting the artistic collaboration of Courbet and Champfleury. Ultimately, it 'speaks to the conflicted relationship between image and text and the signs that purportedly generate meaning, since semiotics is generally construed as anti-realist'.

Victorian Literature and the Victorian Visual Imagination (ed. Carol Christ and John Jordan), is a fascinating and readable collection of 15 essays which establishes the diversity and importance of nineteenth-century visual culture. It succeeds in demonstrating that the Victorians were preoccupied with both objective and subjective paradigms for perception. Furthermore, as the editors point out in the introduction, it explains how and why the Victorians were fascinated by the visible trace as evidence, both in empirical and legal senses. The essays discuss the public figure as (photographic) spectacle; the cultural activity of spectatorship and its relation to optical gadgetry; the links between writing and drawing, and photographic and literary representations of the city.

Lindsay Smith's focused and thorough *Victorian Photography, Painting and Poetry: The Enigma of Visibility in Ruskin, Morris and the Pre-Raphaelites* explores the ways in which Ruskin's art theory, Morris's early poetry (particularly *The Defence of Guenevere and Other Poems*), and Pre-Raphaelite painting represent the desire for a 'literality' of visual perception. Smith looks at the implications for 'seeing' raised by technical developments and the discourse of photography in order to assess how Ruskin and Morris, using medievalism, exploited those implications in radical terms. Both Ruskin and Morris 'engage in a critique of the apparent certainties of geometrical perspective as a ubiquitous visual model in western culture'. The Pre-Raphaelites also figure in Herbert Sussman's *Victorian Masculinities: Manhood and Masculine Poetics in Early Victorian Literature and Art*, alongside key figures such as Carlyle, Pater and Robert Browning. Sussman investigates the formation and inscription of various masculinities from the 1830s to the 1860s. The construction of versions of artistic manhood is examined in conjuction with the Carlylean masculine poetic formed for the industrial age (and later disrupted by a homosexual discourse). Drawing on work by Foucault and Theweleit, Sussman sees 'Victorian cultural products as inscriptions of varied male practices of the self'.

Women in the Victorian Art World (ed. Clarissa Campbell Orr) is based on events held in 1991 celebrating the centenary of the artist Barbara Leigh Smith Bodichon. It is an important addition to the ongoing feminist revision of art history. The nine essays, arranged into the sections 'Women, art and the public sphere', 'Culture, criticism and connoisseurship' and 'The making of the woman artist', allow us to assess what it meant to be a woman in the public world of Victorian art. They discuss, among other things, artistic sisterhoods, feminist politics, art education for women, the woman art critic, the woman collector and the woman consumer.

Mention must be made of *The Victorian Church: Architecture and Society* (ed. Chris Brooks and Andrew Saint): an important contribution to our understanding of Victorian religious debate and the role of churchbuilding within this. *The Victorian Church* discusses the social, economic, religious and cultural debates which impinged on the churchbuilding drive of the Anglican Establishment and the nonconformists. In return, 'the great building campaigns of the Victorian churches had a profound impact, not only on the lives and habits of churchgoers, but also on the economic, cultural and physical composition of the larger society'. There are chapters on the rural church, urban churchbuilding, nonconformity and restoration.

Unavailable for review were: Richard Aldrich, *School and Society in Victorian Britain: Joseph Payne and the New World of Education* (Garland); Joseph Carroll, *Evolution and Literary Theory* (UMissP); Robert Fitzgerald, *Rowntree and the Marketing Revolution, 1862–1969* (CUP); James Kincaid, *Annoying the Victorians* (Routledge); Roy Porter and Lesley Hall, *The Facts of Life: The Creation of Sexual Knowledge in Britain, 1650–1950* (YaleUP); Carolyn Steedman, *Strange Dislocations: Childhood and the Idea of Human Interiority 1780–1930* (Virago).

(b) Individual Authors
J. B. Bullen in *The Myth of the Renaissance in Nineteenth-Century Writing* explored at length the Victorians' construction of a particular past, or myth of

the past (*YWES* 75.430–1). Chapter seven of Bullen's text discusses the myth of the Renaissance in John Ruskin's writings, and the point is made that *Stones of Venice* is a 'romance' in which the city of Venice is feminized and eroticized. The notion of the feminized architectural Venice (which invokes a whole range of critical perspectives on the nineteenth-century city and urban experience) is developed by Bullen, with more of a biographical critical slant, in 'Ruskin, Venice, and the Construction of Femininity' (*RES* 46.502–20). Here Bullen focuses on *Stones of Venice* as offering both a multivalent myth and a personification of Venice. He is interested in investigating the relations between the author's (subjective) history and the history of the city; in 'the dialectic between outer and inner, between empirical history and subjective historiography'. Ruskin seems to exercise a 'compulsive feminization' of the city. Bullen argues that there are connections between Ruskin's 'general construction' of, and attitudes towards, femininity, and his distortions of history. Ruskin can be seen to be projecting his fears and desires onto an absent female/city; both his relationship with Effie Gray and his association with Venice are ultimately ruinous.

The timely *Ruskin and Environment: The Storm-Cloud of the Nineteenth Century* (ed. Michael Wheeler), is a varied and impressive collection of essays concerning Ruskin's writings and pronouncements on what we would now term environmental issues. In the conclusion, Terry Gifford argues that the key question which emerges from discussion of Ruskin's views on the natural and built environments is 'What key features of Ruskin's work have led to important attitude change in the past, and what key concepts appear to be useful in our environmental discourse today?'. This question is kept to the forefront of the eight essays which together address issues confronting the reader of Ruskin's late work: how can the observer and the observed, the subject and the object, or autobiography and documentary observation be separated? In a fascinating opening essay, 'The Discourse of Natural Beauty', Keith Hanley unpicks what the particular 'Ruskin's View' at Kirkby Lonsdale signified for Ruskin. The view eventually came to represent England's ruin by industrialization, and Ruskin's critique of the urban environment is the subject of the next two essays. Other essays range from the study of cartographic images and ideas in Ruskin's work, to Ruskin's involvement in specific areas of Victorian environmental debate: the preservation of the built environment (now 'cultural heritage'), the growth of the railways and the climate of ideas which led to the founding of the National Trust.

In the introduction to his biography of Thomas Carlyle, Simon Heffer claims 'without understanding Carlyle one cannot properly understand the Victorian era, and without understanding that era we cannot understand where, culturally, we have come from'. *Moral Desperado: A Life of Thomas Carlyle* aims on the one hand to 'rediscover' Carlyle for the twentieth century (although the process of reclamation has already started) and on the other to reinterpret Carlyle's writings as political (and social) texts. This is a thoughtful biography which assesses the complexities of Carlyle, and his influence on contemporary writers, with a sensitive distance. Heffer charts a story of critical neglect, ending with Carlyle's death, which he argues was largely due to Froude's biography of Carlyle.

Gregory Maertz, in 'The Eclipse of the Text in Carlyle's Critical Discourse' (*VN* 87.14–20), is concerned with Carlyle's role as mediator, translator and interpreter of German culture in nineteenth-century Britain. He focuses on Carlyle's forging of a 'hermeneutic criticism' underpinned by a biographical impulse which saw biography as a fusion of personality and literary style. The figure of Goethe and Carlyle's assessment of Goethe's cultural significance is crucial here. Carlyle's hermeneutic criticism, Maertz argues, was made 'in the image of Goethe's strong personality' and was partly influenced by Goethe's own writings on literature. Other writers, such as George Eliot and Matthew Arnold, tried to surrender to or resist 'the siren call of Goethe's personality'. Maertz even states that 'mediating Goethe emerges as one of the chief organizing principles in the cultural life of nineteenth-century Britain'. Yet he goes on to suggest that it was 'cultural outsiders' (in terms of gender, class, religious and national identities) who were largely responsible for the reception of German literature and thought in Victorian Britain. For those at the margins of dominant culture, sensitized to the politics involved in translating texts across cultures, 'mediating' German texts was a way of launching their own work, of forging literary careers.

A tension between science and poetry, as perceived within western culture, is often assumed and indeed simplified. George Levine explores this 'false antithesis' in a further addition to his study of Darwin's life and theories. 'Darwin and Pain: Why Science Made Shakespeare Nauseating' (*Raritan* 15.97–114) reveals that poetic and scientific narratives were inextricably intertwined in Darwin's experience: 'poetry was part of what made him a scientist and science could only work its antipoetic effects on him because he was steeped in poetry'. Later in life Darwin abandoned literature – Levine is interested in why this was. Although Darwin read poetry on his voyages the exotic places he visited showed him not a poeticized landscape, but the 'repellent truth'. Levine details in moving terms Darwin's reaction to the death of his second child, Annie, a death which further alienated Darwin from poetry's supposed comforts. Levine concludes that poetry in the end failed to offer the kind of 'humanly satisfying narratives' which Darwin rejected in natural theology.

2. The Novel

(a) General

As with previous years, this year is marked by splendid editions of correspondence. Ongoing editions of the letters of Dickens, Gissing and Charlotte Brontë are complemented by editions of the correspondence of Stevenson and George Henry Lewes. However, the nature of the recent critical, historical and biographical analyses regarding the Victorian novel remains similar to the commentary examined in recent surveys in the *YWES*. In addition to forays into feminism, deconstruction, new historicism and textual and bibliographical study, recent criticism of the nineteenth-century novel features philological, linguistic and postmodernist examinations, among a host of other critical pursuits. Additionally, the Victorian fictive canon continues to remain relatively stable, perennially including such predominant novelists as Dickens, Charlotte and Emily Brontë, George Eliot and Hardy. It is refreshing to see the great diversity of work on the Victorian novel, particularly on such major figures as Thackeray, Trollope, Mrs Gaskell, Stevenson and Gissing, in addition to welcome attention to the writings of Stoker, Wilde, Conan Doyle, Carroll and MacDonald, amongst others. Noteworthy are analyses of 'Empire', 'Colonialism', 'Art' and gender which draw upon the works of a host of significant writers, as well as works by Catherine Gore, Fanny Trollope, Sheridan Le Fanu and such neglected novelists as Olive Schreiner, George Meredith, Charles Reade, Mrs Oliphant and others.

Drawing upon a combination of discourse analysis, performance techniques, critical theory and creative writing, Rob Pope's *Textual Intervention: Critical and Creative Strategies for Literary Studies* discusses the current debates about cultural production and reproduction, as well as reconstruction and deconstruction. Pope features close textual readings of a wide range of texts from Shakespeare and the Victorian novel to modernist and Afro-Caribbean poetry. Using the works of such writers as Charles Dickens, Wilkie Collins and Robert Louis Stevenson, among others, Marty Roth attempts to map the genre of classic detective fiction in *Foul and Fair Play: Reading Genre in Classic Detective Fiction*. In addition to exploring the roles of detectives, criminals and crimes in such fictions, Roth discusses themes of exhibitionism, community, the convention of the solution and masculinity endemic to the genre. In *Somatic Fictions: Imagining Illness in Victorian Culture*, Athena Vrettos investigates the central role of psychosomatic illness as an imaginative construct in Victorian culture. Vrettos argues that illness shaped the terms upon which Victorians perceived relationships between body and mind, self and other and private and public. Using works by Charlotte Brontë, Elizabeth Gaskell, George Eliot, George Meredith, Bram Stoker and H. Rider Haggard, Vrettos examines the historical assumptions and patterns of belief that infused sickness and health with cultural import.

In *Subversive Discourse: The Cultural Production of Late Victorian Feminist Novels*, Rita S. Kranidis explores the often covert production of late Victorian feminist novels, arguing that the era's prevailing aesthetic ideologies functioned as a mechanism for containing and negating the progressive literary and social agendas of Victorian feminists. Kranidis also discusses the narrative and textual strategies articulated by Victorian feminists in order to publish their texts in the conservative literary marketplace of that era. Christopher Morash's *Writing the Irish Famine* examines literary representations of the Irish famine of the 1840s by such writers as William Carleton, Anthony Trollope, James Clarence Mangan, John Mitchel and Samuel Ferguson. Morash argues that the famine remains largely misunderstood by scholars, in addition to exploring the famine's historical interconnections with the postulation of a variety of histories, sermons and economic treatises that collectively construct a narrative of the famine's tremendous impact upon Irish history and culture of the nineteenth century. Morash draws upon recent insights in new historicist criticism in his exploration of the literary memorialization of the Irish famine. In *The Lion and the Cross: Early Christianity in Victorian Novels*, Royal W. Rhodes studies more than 130 religious novels of the Victorian period and offers a comprehensive account of the theological premise underlying nineteenth-century religious and historical thought. Rhodes argues that the early Christian novels of the Victorian era were employed by theological writers of the period in order to explore religious questions under the guise of antiquity. Rhodes affords attention to the works of such writers as Wilkie Collins, Walter Pater, John Henry Newman, Charles

Kingsley, Nicholas Cardinal Wiseman, Edward Bulwer-Lytton, Thomas Moore, John Mason Neale, Charlotte Yonge, Frederic Farrar and Marie Corelli, among others.

Herbert Sussman's *Victorian Masculinities: Manhood and Masculine Poetics in Early Victorian Literature and Art* examines the notions of manhood and masculinity as they developed in the early Victorian era, affording particular attention to their diverse representations in the novels and art of the period. Sussman also investigates manhood as an unstable equilibrium that simultaneously subverts and maintains patriarchal power. In *Melodramatic Tactics: Theatricalized Dissent in the English Marketplace, 1800–1885*, Elaine Hadley discusses melodrama as a theatrical genre, as well as a behavioral paradigm for nineteenth-century theatre, literature and society. Hadley argues that the melodramatic mode reaffirmed the familial, hierarchical and public grounds for ethical behaviour and identity that characterized eighteenth-century value systems for social exchange and organization. Hadley examines, for example, works by George Meredith and Charles Dickens in juxtaposition with a number of nineteenth-century social reforms. Lorraine Janzen Kooistra's *The Artist as Critic: Bitextuality in Fin-de-Siècle Illustrated Books* explores the role of pictures in the production of meaning in works by Oscar Wilde and Sir Arthur Conan Doyle, as well as such relatively unknown writers as Laurence Housman, Margaret Armour and Alice Sargant, among others. In addition to analysing the *fin-de-siècle* era's preoccupation with sex, knowledge and power, Kooistra argues that a theory of 'bitextuality' – the product of words and pictures – illuminates the illustrated books of the late Victorian era. Kooistra identifies the function of bitextuality in these works through her postulation of five models, including quotation, impression, parody, answering and cross-dressing.

In *Nineteenth-Century Literary Realism: Through the Looking Glass*, Katherine Kearns argues that realism functions as a literary mode committed to depict the imperilled ecological system of soul and society. Using works by Dickens, among others, Kearns discusses realism in terms of its inherently reformist agenda. Kearns further suggests that realism operates as a fundamentally disruptive mechanism for undermining the established norms of nineteenth-century narrative. Using a diversity of works that includes Elizabeth Gaskell's *Cousin Phillis*, John Boorman's film *Deliverance* and Thomas Hardy's *Jude the Obscure*, Linda Ruth Williams's *Critical Desire: Psychoanalysis and the Literary Subject* traces the history of psychoanalytic interpretations of literature. In addition to offering accounts of the development of Freudian analysis, Kleinian and Lacanian analysis, and the works of such figures as Winnicott and Laplanche, Williams also explores the nature of the recent shifts in psychoanalytic thought regarding culture and aesthetics. In *Walking the Victorian Streets: Women, Representation, and the City*, Deborah Epstein Nord traces instances of rambling in novels of the nineteenth century, particularly in the works of Charles Dickens and Elizabeth Gaskell. In addition to discussing the role of urban settings in the nineteenth-century novel, Nord examines the depiction of the 'new woman' of the Victorian era in these fictions, while also exploring the place of motherhood and feminism in these works. Additionally, Nord investigates the moral conditions inherent in the nineteenth-century novel, particularly regarding prostitution and gender roles.

In *Byron and the Victorians*, Andrew Elfenbein assesses Byron's influence upon such Victorian literary figures as Carlyle, Emily Brontë, Tennyson, Bulwer Lytton, Disraeli and Wilde. Elfenbein also analyses the manner in which the cultural institutions of the Victorian era functioned as a mediating mechanism between both the means of textual production and the historical interface between writers of divergent literary periods. In *Secret Texts: The Literature of Secret Societies*, Marie Mulvey Roberts and Hugh Ormsby-Lennon include a number of essays of interest to students of the Victorian novel, including Elizabeth Imlay's 'Freemasonry, the Brontës, and the Hidden Text of *Jane Eyre*' and Paul Rich's 'Kim and the Magic House: Freemasonry and Kipling'. In *Essays in Appreciation*, Christopher Ricks's latest collection of essays assembles his wide-ranging responses to literary works by a diversity of writers that includes Elizabeth Gaskell, George Eliot, Jane Austen and Charlotte Brontë, among others. Ricks provides commentary regarding such subjects as canon formation, the evolution of critical theory and the development of political criticism, among other subjects. The essays in Ricks's volume are based on lectures and previously published articles. Sally Ledger and Scott McCracken's *Cultural Politics at the Fin-de-Siècle* features essays exploring issues of race, class and gender in the historical and literary experience of the *fin-de-siècle*. Selections of relevance to the novel include Terry Eagleton's 'The Flight to the Real'; Ledger's 'The New Woman and the Crisis of Victorianism'; Laura Chrisman's 'Empire, "Race," and Feminism at the *Fin-de-Siècle*: The Work of George Egerton and Olive Schreiner'; Ed Cohen's 'The Double Lives of Man: Narration and Identification in Late Nineteenth-Century Representations of Ec-Centric Masculinities'; Anne Janowitz's '*The Pilgrims of Hope*: William Morris and the Dialectic of Romanticism'; Lynne Hapgood's 'Urban Utopias: Socialism, Religion, and the City, 1880 to 1900', Alexandra Warwick's 'Vampires and the Empire: Fears and Fictions of the 1890s'; Judith Halberstam's 'Technologies of Monstrosity: Bram Stoker's *Dracula*'; McCracken's 'Postmodernism, a *Chance* to Reread?'; and Regenia Gagnier's 'Is Market Society the fin of History?'.

In *The Historical Novel from Scott to Sabatini: Changing Attitudes Toward a Literary Genre*, Harold Orel surveys the genre of historical fiction in the works of a wide range of literary figures, as well as many neglected ones. Orel treats novels by Sir Walter Scott, Sir Walter Besant, Richard Doddridge Blackmore, Sir Arthur Quiller-Couch, Sir Arthur Conan Doyle, Stanley John Weyman, Anthony Hope, Sir Henry Rider Haggard and Rafael Sabatini. Orel discusses the relationship between research and imagination in the composition strategies of these novelists, while also assessing the significance of language and character in their works. Elizabeth Langland's *Nobody's Angels: Middle-Class Women and Domestic Ideology in Victorian Culture* explores the complex image of femininity in Victorian culture, affording particular attention to the notorious gender stereotype of the angel in the house. Drawing upon the theoretical insights of Foucault, Benjamin and Bourdieu, Langland examines works by such figures as Dickens, Gaskell, Oliphant and George Eliot. In addition to discussing the memoirs of Hannah Cullwick – a former domestic servant who married a middle-class man – Langland investigates the place of the middle-class female in the Victorian era, arguing that such women supported a rigid class system and set the stage for a feminist revolution. Ruth Y. Jenkins's *Reclaiming Myths of Power: Women Writers and the Victorian*

Spiritual Crisis investigates the response of Victorian women writers to the spiritual crisis of that era. Using the lives and works of such writers as George Eliot and Elizabeth Gaskell, Jenkins offers a close analysis of the relationship between spiritual crisis and the radical revision of women's social subjection in the novels of the Victorian era. Jenkins argues that such writers provided women readers with an ideological means for rejecting cultural roles, as well as with an alternative ethical agenda that embraces the needs of the individual. In *Novel Possibilities: Fiction and the Formation of Early Victorian Culture*, Joseph W. Childers investigates the role of the social-problem novel of the 1840s in the interpretation and shaping of the literature and culture of the early Victorian era. Childers focuses on novels by Benjamin Disraeli, Elizabeth Gaskell and Charles Kingsley, while also discussing the social and political treatises of Edwin Chadwick, Robert Peel and T. B. Macaulay. Childers draws upon a range of political memoirs, parliamentary speeches, historical essays and governmental reports in his analysis of the interconnections between the pre-Victorian novel and the political and social reforms of that era.

Deirdre David's stimulating *Rule Britannia: Women, Empire, and Victorian Writing* investigates the role of women in the literature of the colonial and imperial British nation, both as writers as well as the subjects of representation. In addition to discussing the parliamentary speeches of Thomas Macaulay and the private correspondence of Emily Eden, David traces the lives of Victorian women through close readings of novels by Charlotte Brontë, Charles Dickens, Wilkie Collins and H. Rider Haggard. David argues that in these works the historical and symbolic roles of Victorian women were linked to the British imperial enterprise abroad. In *Writing the Colonial Adventure: Race, Gender and Nation in Anglo-Australian Popular Fiction, 1875–1914*, Robert Dixon traces a series of popular late nineteenth-century texts that depicted Australia, Africa, India and the Pacific Islands as sites of imperial adventure. Using works by Sir Walter Scott, Robert Louis Stevenson, H. Rider Haggard, Rosa Praed and Louis Becke, Dixon examines the construction of empire, masculinity, race and nationalism in their texts. Dixon argues that the manner in which these texts range from such topics as imperialism, lost worlds, invasion and espionage underscores the nature of popular fiction during this era. Michael Ragussis's *Figures of Conversion: "The Jewish Question" and English National Identity* investigates the nineteenth-century phenomenon of Jewish conversion and its emergence as the subject of popular enthusiasm, public scandal, national debate and its occasional demonization as the 'English madness' by its critics. In addition to reading the historical narratives of English Jews from this era, Ragussis provides close examinations of novels by Disraeli, Trollope and Eliot, among others. Ragussis argues that these writers shared in the redefinition of English national identity through their attention to revising the nature of the tradition of the novel, the new science of ethnology and the rewriting of modern European history. Much may be learnt from essays in John O. Jordan and Robert L. Patten's excellent *Literature in the Marketplace: Nineteenth-Century British Publishing and Reading Practices*, which features a variety of essays that explore the artistic, historical and economic realities of the Victorian literary marketplace. Selections include Simon Eliot's 'Some Trends in British Book Production, 1800–1919'; Patten's 'Serialized Retrospection in *The*

Pickwick Papers'; Linda K. Hughes and Michael Lund's 'Textual/Sexual Pleasure and Serial Publication', which draws upon Mrs Gaskell's *North and South*, 'Lizzie Leigh' and *Cranford*, amongst other works; Kelly J. Mays's 'The Disease of Reading and Victorian Periodicals,' which focuses on the responses to periodicals by a changing reading public; Jonathan Rose's 'How Historians Study Reader Response: Or, What Did Jo Think of *Bleak House*?'; Gerard Curtis's 'Dickens in the Visual Market'; Catherine A. Judd's 'Male Pseudonyms and Female Authority in Victorian England'; Maura Ives's 'A Bibliographical Approach to Victorian Publishing', with its welcome focus on the physical format of Meredith's texts; and Elizabeth Morrison's 'Serial Fiction in Australian Colonial Newspapers', the final essay in this important collection, which affords attention to the neglected study of 'Colonial' editions.

Lavishly illustrated, Joseph A. Kestner's *Masculinities in Victorian Painting* examines the cultural construction of masculinity through an assessment of the male form in a variety of contexts, including social, historical, legal, literary, institutional, anthropological, educational, marital, imperial and aesthetic venues. Kestner includes images from a range of Victorian artists, including Leighton, Waterhouse, Burne-Jones, Alma-Tadema, Dicksee, Pettie, Watts, Woodville and Tuke, among others. Kestner identifies five paradigms of masculinity in his study: the classical hero, the gallant knight, the challenged paterfamilias, the valiant soldier and the male nude. He also draws upon twentieth-century conceptions of race, the male gaze, and male sexuality in his theoretical approach to Victorian representations of masculinity. In *Sisters: Relation and Rescue in Nineteenth-Century British Novels and Paintings*, Michael Cohen examines the 'grammar of sisterhood' in Victorian novels and paintings. Using works by Dickens, Collins, Meredith, Gaskell and Eliot, Cohen discusses such issues as twinning, rivalry, sexual difference and rescue between sisters. Lavishly illustrated, Cohen's volume also affords attention to such neglected novelists as Olive Schreiner, as well as numerous Victorian artists, including John Everett Millais and Augustus Egg, a friend of Dickens and Wilkie Collins. John Robert Reed's extensive monograph, *Dickens and Thackeray: Punishment and Forgiveness*, traces the attitudes towards punishment and forgiveness in the moral texts of the Victorian period. Using works by Dickens such as *Oliver Twist*, *Martin Chuzzlewit* and *Our Mutual Friend* and Thackeray's *Vanity Fair* and *The Virginians*, among others, Reed's learned work explores the roles of education and the judiciary in delivering punishment and forgiveness during the Victorian age. In *Victorian Fiction: Writers, Publishers, Readers*, another distinguished critic, John Sutherland, investigates the remarkable proliferation of the print culture during the Victorian era, a period in which more than 3,500 novelists produced more than 50,000 works. Sutherland traces the cultural, social and commercial factors that intersected in this era of vast literary output, affording special attention to the marketing and compositional strategies of such writers as Collins, Dickens, George Eliot, Thackeray, Trollope, Reade, Lytton and Mrs Humphrey Ward, among a host of others.

Sutherland's volume largely consists of revisions of previously published articles, as well as a useful appendix of plot summaries. Carol T. Christ and John O. Jordan's *Victorian Literature and the Victorian Visual Imagination* features a variety of essays regarding Victorian fiction, including Judith L.

Fisher's 'Image versus Text in the Illustrated Novels of William Makepeace Thackeray'; Linda M. Shires's, 'The Author as Spectacle and Commodity: Elizabeth Barrett Browning and Thomas Hardy'; and Audrey Jaffe's 'Spectacular Sympathy: Visuality and Ideology in Dickens's *A Christmas Carol*'.

In *The Supernatural and English Fiction: From* The Castle of Otranto *to* Hawksmoor, Glen Cavaliero addresses a wide range of practitioners of English supernatural fiction, including such writers as Sheridan Le Fanu and Rudyard Kipling, among a host of others. In an effort to discriminate the nature of the supernatural fiction as a genre, Cavaliero assesses its relationship with a number of other fictional forms, including the Gothic novel, the occultist romance, the ghost story, novels of paranormal psychology, nature and mysticism and works of allegory and fable. Drawing upon the recent insights of biographical and autobiographical theorists, the essays in John Batchelor's *The Art of Literary Biography* explore the abiding popularity of the genres of biography and autobiography, with particular emphasis upon Victorian letters. There is much of interest for students of the Victorian novel in Batchelor's volume. The selection of relevance is Catherine Peters's 'Secondary Lives: Biography in Context' (43–56), which not surprisingly offers a discussion of the composition of Peters's seminal Wilkie Collins biography. Using biographies, correspondence, demographic data and literally dozens of Victorian novels, Penny Kane's *Victorian Families in Fact and Fiction* demonstrates the manner in which the nineteenth-century novel reflects the practices and attitudes regarding the family. Kane provides close readings of texts by Dickens, Eliot, Gaskell, Hardy and Kipling in her study. Kane employs a variety of historical sources in her volume that offer readers useful insights into Victorian society and culture.

In *Dandies and Desert Saints: Styles of Victorian Masculinity*, James Eli Adams examines Victorian conceptions of masculinity, using Carlyle's vision of the 'hero as a man of letters'. Drawing upon texts by Charles Kingsley and Oscar Wilde, among others, Adams identifies the principal elements of the aesthetic hero – virility, martial strength and wealth. Adams argues that the discourse of masculinity impinges upon all aspects of Victorian culture, particularly regarding the foundations of its social structure. In *The Birth of Liberal Guilt in the English Novel: Charles Dickens to H. G. Wells*, Daniel Born traces the emergence of liberal guilt in the fictions of such writers as Dickens, Kipling and Gissing. Born argues that these writers attempted to purge their consciences through the composition of their works. In this manner, Born suggests, such authors sought to assuage the collective guilt of their respective cultures. In a special issue of *PULC* (57) scholars address the literary contributions of nineteenth-century female writers. Patricia H. Marks's 'Queen Victoria's Literary Ladies' (9–12) discusses the achievements of a variety of figures from the Brontës and Elizabeth Gaskell to George Eliot and Kate Greenaway, among others. 'Victorian women of letters,' Marks writes, 'could enjoy their fame without flaunting their anger or independence'. In 'Telling Her Story: British Women of Letters of the Victorian Era' (147–62), Peggy Meyer Sherry surveys the Princeton University Library's collection of Victorian literature by women. Sherry also discusses the library's exhibition on Victorian women of letters, entitled 'Telling Her Story: British Women of Letters of the Victorian Era', which features analyses of the lives and work of Charlotte Yonge, Dinah Maria Mulcok Craik and Margaret

Oliphant. The exhibition included portrait photographs, original letters and manuscripts, and early printed editions of books by women writers of the Victorian era.

In *Imperial Leather: Race, Gender, and Sexuality in the Colonial Contest*, Anne McClintock explores the cultural production of capitalism in England during the colonial era. Drawing upon texts by Olive Schreiner, H. Rider Haggard and Arthur Munby, among others, McClintock discusses the roles of race, gender and sexuality in the colonial enterprise. McClintock devotes particular attention to the dynamics of power and moral urgency in the fictions of the English colonial era. In *The Ruling Passion: British Colonial Allegory and the Paradox of Homosexual Desire*, Christopher Lane examines the interconnections between British colonialism and male homosexuality in a variety of works by Kipling and Wilde, among others. In addition to exploring the artistic dimensions of homosexuality in novels that impinge upon British imperialism, Lane discusses such issues as desire, warfare and mourning in the literature of this era. Lane also attempts to map the growing body of literary and historical work on same-sex representation.

In *The New Girl: Girls' Culture in England, 1880–1915*, Sally Mitchell attempts to revise our understanding of girlhood and the literature of girls in the late nineteenth century. In addition to drawing upon a variety of late Victorian texts in her study, Mitchell argues for connections between the act of reading and daydreaming and fantasy. Lavishly illustrated, Mitchell supplements her volume with an expansive bibliography regarding the literature of girls' culture in turn-of-the-century England. Employing the insights of feminist theory and cultural studies, Lynne Vallone's *Disciplines of Virtue: Girls' Culture in the Eighteenth and Nineteenth Centuries* examines depictions of girlhood in eighteenth- and nineteenth-century British and American texts and their representations as figures of adornment in need of refuge, rescue and reform. Through her analyses of children's and adult literature, conduct manuals and religious tracts, Vallone reveals the historical and social construction of girlhood in Britain and America. In *What Katy Read: Feminist Re-Readings of 'Classic' Stories for Girls*, Shirley Foster and Judy Simons discuss the genre of popular works of fiction written for girls. In addition to considering such subgenres as the domestic myth and the school story, Foster and Simons argue that such fictions remain a crucial element in most girls' formative literary experiences. Foster and Simons include close readings of a variety of texts by Susan Warner, Charlotte Yonge, Louisa May Alcott, Susan Coolidge, E. Nesbit, L. M. Montgomery, Frances Hodgson Burnett and Angela Brazil.

Drawing upon recent insights in critical theory, feminism and social history, Andrew H. Miller's *Novels Behind Glass: Commodity Culture and Victorian Narrative* discusses the ways in which the social world of Victorian culture was reduced to an exhibit for satisfying the economic appetites of others. Using works by Gaskell, Thackeray, Dickens, Eliot and Trollope, Miller examines such issues as the vagaries of desire, the rationalization of social life, the gendering of subjectivity, the power of nostalgia, and the fear of mortality. Miller argues that such writers provide readers with graphic and enduring images of the power of commodities as a means for impacting social experience. In *Centering the Self: Subjectivity, Society, and Reading from Thomas Gray to Thomas Hardy*, Vincent Newey investigates the themes of selfhood and subjectivity in various works including those by George Eliot and Thomas Hardy. In addition to illuminating the interrelations between texts and social, political and biographical contexts, Newey discusses the significance of reading in the process of creativity and interpretation. He argues that 'existentialism' provides readers and artists with a means for creating meaning in an impersonal and indifferent world.

Keeping the Victorian House: A Collection of Essays (ed. Vanessa D. Dickerson) features a number of essays regarding the depiction of the Victorian household, including Dickerson's introduction, 'Housekeeping and Housekept Angels'; Martin A. Danahay's 'Housekeeping and Hegemony in Dickens's *Bleak House*; Deborah Denenholz Morse's 'Stitching Repentance, Sewing Rebellion: Seamstresses and Fallen Women in Elizabeth Gaskell's Fiction'; Laura Fasick's 'God's House, Women's Place'; Julia M. Gergits's 'Women Artists at Home'; Eileen Connell's 'Playing House: Frances Hodgson Burnett's Victorian Fairy Tale'; Jessica Gerard's 'The Chatelaine: Women of the Victorian Landed Classes and the Country House'; Thad Logan's 'Decorating Domestic Space: MiddleClass Women and Victorian Interiors'; Francis L. Fennell and Monica A. Fennell's ' "Ladies – Loaf Givers": Food, Women, and Society in the Novels of Charlotte Brontë and George Eliot'; Maura Ives's 'Housework, Mill Work, Women's Work: The Functions of Cloth in Charlotte Brontë's *Shirley*'; and Lynn M. Alexander's 'Loss of the Domestic Idyll: Shop Workers in Victorian Fiction'. Finally, the *Collected Essays of John Goode* (ed. Charles Swann, intro. Terry Eagleton), commemorates the life and career of the esteemed Victorian literary critic John Goode, who died last year. Eagleton aptly describes Goode's early death as a 'catastrophe for criticism, and a grievous loss to his political comrades'. The collection includes Goode's critical musings on a variety of subjects, including the works of such figures as Thomas Hardy, George Eliot and George Gissing, among a host of others. This volume not only reminds us of the tremendous intellectual loss in Goode's unfortunate passing, but also of the remarkable gifts that he left behind.

(b) Individual Novelists
In *The Young Disraeli, 1804–1846*, Jane Ridley inaugurates her multi-volume study of the life and work of this major figure in English letters. Drawing upon recently published letters and Disraeli's often neglected early novels, Ridley offers a fresh and notably sympathetic look at the writer's youth and his early rise to fame with the publication of *Vivian Grey*. Ridley also affords attention to Disraeli's personal religious crisis, his radical politics and parliamentary tenure, and his later encounters with the Chartists and the Whigs. The volume concludes with a useful 'Chronology of Books and Pamphlets by Benjamin Disraeli'. In addition to featuring a foreword by Victoria Glendinning, Teresa Ransom's *Fanny Trollope: A Remarkable Life* provides an extensive biography of the mother of Anthony Trollope, who was a prolific travel writer and novelist in her own right. Drawing upon neglected archival material, Ransom examines Trollope's later fiction, in addition to her famed *Domestic Manners of the Americans* (1832). Ransom considers Trollope's influence upon her son. The book contains nicely produced photographs, and offers a useful introductory guide to Trollope's life and work. The life and work of Sheridan Le Fanu receive extensive attention in Gary William Crawford's *J. Sheridan Le*

Fanu: A Bio-Bibliography, which provides scholars with a wealth of information regarding this all too often neglected figure in nineteenth-century letters. In 'Elegies for the Regency: Catherine Gore's Dandy Novels' (*NCL* 50.189–209), Winifred Hughes surveys the contributions of Gore to the genre of silver fork or fashionable novels that were popular during the Regency era. In addition to discussing such novels by Gore as *Cecil; or, The Adventures of a Coxcomb* (1841) and *Cecil, a Peer* (1841), Hughes examines the novelist's satire of high society and her sympathetic, good-humoured depictions of the dandy in her fictions. Hughes also investigates the manner in which early Victorian critics and readers appear to have been unreceptive to a literary genre that satisfied audiences during the previous decade.

The year's work in Elizabeth Gaskell studies continues to proliferate. Drawing upon such works as *North and South* and *Cranford*, Robin B. Colby's *Some Appointed Work To Do: Women and Vocation in the Fiction of Elizabeth Gaskell* discusses the vocational diversity of women inherent in Elizabeth Gaskell's fictions. Colby argues that such a variety of female occupations allows Gaskell to present a community of self-sufficient women in her works who control property and participate in a burgeoning industrial society. In *Family and Society in the Works of Elizabeth Gaskell*, E. Holly Pike takes issue with the prevailing critical notion that Gaskell's comic novels – particularly *Sylvia's Lovers* – should be approached as a separate body of work from her social problem novels. Pike argues that these ostensibly disparate works in fact impinge upon the same theme regarding the proper constitution of society. In addition to providing a discussion of nineteenth-century notions about social structures and close readings of Gaskell's major works, Pike traces the shift in Gaskell's conception of the ideal structure of society and shows her development as a realist novelist. Terence Wright's *Elizabeth Gaskell, 'We Are Not Angels': Realism, Gender, Values* provides an analysis of the artistic and moral themes that motivated the composition of such novels as *Mary Barton, Wives and Daughters, Ruth* and *North and South*. Wright devotes special attention to the investigation of Gaskell's moral vision, particularly her beliefs regarding the interconnections between women, writing and the evolution of nineteenth-century history. Wright's volume offers convincing testimony regarding Gaskell's place among the most significant writers of her age. In ' "Manning the World": The Role of the Male Narrator in Elizabeth Gaskell's *Cousin Phillis*' (*VR* 21.129–44), Jeni Curtis examines the effect of Gaskell's male narrator upon the rhetoric of her narrative. Curtis suggests that the overt presence of masculinity underscores, at least in Gaskell's narrative ideology, the secondary place of women in nineteenth-century life. James Mulvihill's 'Economies of Living in Elizabeth Gaskell's *Cranford*' (*NCF* 50.337–56) discusses the narrative structure of Gaskell's novel, in addition to exploring the treatment of economic matters in the Victorian household. In 'The Education of Cousin Phillis' (*NCF* 50.27–50), Philip Rogers investigates the role of nineteenth-century women's education in Gaskell's powerful short story, while Leah Price's 'The Life of Charlotte Brontë and the Death of Miss Eyre' (*SEL* 35.757–68) examines Brontë's treatment in Gaskell's well-known biography of the novelist.

Following the publication last year of G. E. Sadler's edition of George MacDonald's correspondence, *Orts, the Newsletter of the George MacDonald Society* (36) features news and notes about the writer, including attention to the sale of his childhood home in Huntly, 'The Farm'. The newsletter also reports on the British Library's June exhibition this year of MacDonald's *Lilith* in their 'Manuscript of the Month' series. In addition to commenting upon an April symposium on *Lilith* at Cologne this year, *Orts* discusses the recent visit by John Docherty, the newsletter's secretary, to a Boston workshop on MacDonald's novel, *Adela Cathcart*. Docherty emphasized the novel's themes of storytelling as a means of therapy. The newsletter also reported the discovery of a MacDonald memorial in North Carolina, where the society intends to place a brass commemorative plate in the future. *Orts* features the complete text of Rachel Johnson's 'Pilgrims Revisited', her address to the George MacDonald Society on 13 October this year. Johnson devotes special emphasis to the influence of *The Pilgrim's Progress* upon MacDonald's fictions, in addition to discussing the thematic place of the pilgrimage in MacDonald's works. Mary Riso's 'Awakening in Fairy Land: The Journey of a Soul in George MacDonald's *The Golden Key*' (*Mythlore* 20.46–51) also explores the role of the journey in MacDonald's fictions. *George Borrow Bulletin* (9–10) provides Borrow scholars with a valuable resource for learning more about the novelist's life and work. In 'Borrow, the Palgraves and the Worships' (9.10–20), Angus Fraser comments upon the writer's relationship with two influential families, while Howard Godfrey's 'The Welsh Potosi Mine' (9.21–3) discusses the topographical details of Borrow's *Wild Wales*. In 'Borrow and the "Pallid Indoor Student"': A Proposed Encounter in June–July 1995' (9.24–27), David Mount argues for the canonical reconsideration of such works as *Lavengro* and *The Romany Rye*. Richard Shepheard's 'A Fallen Nobleman' (9.27–9) identifies the location of the skull of Robert the Bruce at Abbotsford and discusses its place in the narrative of *Lavengro*'s second chapter. Paul Watkins's 'A Borrovian Adventure on Staines Station' (9.30–32) narrates the author's first encounter with Borrow's fiction, while Angus Fraser's 'More Books from Borrow's Shelves' (10.16–25) investigates the dispersal of Borrow's private library and the current location of the novelist's more than 750 volumes. In 'Borrow House Restored' (10.26–30), Tony Fielder discusses his role in the restoration of Borrow's Norwich home, which he purchased with Ann Rostron last year. Richard Shepheard's 'The Case for the Crow Inn' (10.31–43) explores the geographical terrain of such novels as *Lavengro* and *The Romany Rye*, while David Chandler's 'Borrow and Hunter' (10.44–6) comments upon the writer's relationship with Joseph Hunter, a Bath minister. Finally, in 'Samuel Morton Peto and His Impact on East Anglia' (10. 47–9), Adrian Vaughan addresses Borrow's acquaintance with Samuel Morton Peto.

A rather thin year in Thackeray studies, although not without important works, including Micael M. Clarke's *Thackeray and Women*, which surveys the novelist's formative years and identifies the foundations of Thackeray's sympathy for and participation in the Victorian women's movement. Clarke provides close readings of Thackeray's major works, while also offering wide-ranging discussions of Victorian conceptions of gender and patriarchy. Clarke affords special attention to the novelist's behaviour after the onset of his wife's madness, when Thackeray began educating his daughters and following contemporary gender issues with particular diligence. In *Vanity-Fair: A Novel without a Hero* – published as part of Twayne's Masterwork Studies series – Edgar F. Harden's examination of Thackeray's novel provides readers with a broad overview of the historical, literary and critical environment that shaped the writer's life and work. In addition to exploring Thackeray's elaborate characterization strategies in the novel, Harden discusses the work's serialization and its impact upon *Vanity-Fair*'s cultural consumption. Harden also affords attention to the role of the narrator in the work, as well as to the novel's critical reception. *The Thackeray Newsletter* (42) features essays of interest to students of the novelist, including Sheldon Goldfarb's 'A New Thackeray Manuscript Found and a Long-Lost Friend: "The Opinions of One Fond of Liquor" and John Elton Mervyn Prower' (1–8). Goldfarb describes his discovery of a new Thackeray manuscript in Vancouver, British Columbia, in September 1993. Known as 'The Opinions of One Fond of Liquor', the manuscript also includes original pen-and-ink drawings by the novelist. Goldfarb locates the manuscript's composition to the early 1830s, during Thackeray's stay in Weimar, Germany. J. Russell Perkin's ' "Scripture only means a writing": Thackeray's Religious Opinions' (9–11) addresses the novelist's often neglected reputation as an intellectual. In addition to exploring the religious subtexts of Thackeray's narratives, Perkin discusses the writer's attention to his literary craft. In 'Thackeray and the *Wellesley Index*' (11–12), Robert A. Colby employs Harden's recent edition of Thackeray's correspondence in an effort to confirm the writer's authorship of two previously unattributed items. Donald Hawes's 'Thackeray: Some Notes and Queries' (12–13) reports on a number of pertinent developments in Thackeray study, including the BBC radio broadcast of *Barry Lyndon* in May and June this year. Hawes also comments on interconnections between Thackeray and the works of Mark Twain and Dorothy L. Sayers, among other writers. In ' "Proving a thing even while you contradict it": Fictions, Beliefs, and Legitimation in *The Memoirs of Barry Lyndon, Esq*' (*SNNTS* 27.493–514), Robert P. Fletcher comments upon the roles of sham and suspicion in Thackeray's early novel. As Fletcher concludes, 'Barry Lyndon's inconsistent fictional life ... dramatizes the potential unreliability of the fictions we ourselves live by' (509). Peter Shillingsburg's 'Editing Thackeray: A History' (*SNNTS* 27.363–74) discusses the editor's experiences while editing the works of Thackeray. Shillingsburg devotes particular attention to the creation of an electronic scholarly edition of Thackeray that would provide 'a medium with the dexterity, capacity, flexibility, and agility to incorporate multiple editorial intentions and readerly intentions' in a single edition (373).

Once again, the highlight of the year in Dickens is yet another volume in the great Pilgrim edition of the letters, this time encompassing the years 1856–8, which include the writing of the serialization of *Little Dorrit*; work with Wilkie Collins on *The Frozen Deep*; his relations with Ellen Ternan; and the editing of *Household Words* and *All the Year Round*, amongst a myriad of other activities. Once again, the edition is replete with the most detailed and helpful annotations. There are 11 appendices, an index of correspondents, and an index of names and places. Thick, but sturdily bound, *The Letters of Charles Dickens, Volume 8: 1856–1858* (ed. Graham Storey and Kathleen Tillotson), will be indispensable for students of Dickens. Published in a slip-cased and rather drably bound set of four volumes, Michael Hollington's *Charles Dickens: Critical Assessments* assembles the critical response to Dickens from 1870 through to the present. The volumes include a general introduction, as well as a chronology of Dickens's life, a chronological list of the criticism and a bibliography of the novelist's major works. Hollington's edition, with its expansive historical overview of the critical reaction to Dickens's works, will surely provide students of the novelist with an invaluable resource for years to come.

In *To Kill a Text: The Dialogic Fiction of Hugo, Dickens, and Zola*, Ilinca Zarifopol-Johnston addresses the interpretive possibilities of Bakhtin's dialogic criticism upon the works of Hugo, Dickens and Zola. Zarifopol-Johnston argues that Dickens and Hugo demonstrate Zola's conception of the novel as a 'graft' of one work upon another that produced hybrid mixtures of various genres and styles of representation. Drawing upon Harold Bloom's theory of the anxiety of influence, Zarifopol-Johnston employs Bakhtin's notions of dialogism and heteroglossia as a means for reading the narratives of works by Hugo, Dickens and Zola. The works of Dickens also receive attention in J. Hillis Miller's *Topographies*, which applies the insights of continental philosophy to the works of a host of other writers. In *Dickens, Violence, and the Modern State: Dreams of the Scaffold*, Jeremy Tambling provides a postmodern reading of the novelist's work through the critical perspectives of Freud, Marx, Lacan, Foucault, Kristeva and Nietzsche, among others. Tambling contends that Dickens's London world was infected by the manifold deficiencies of Victorian culture. In addition to referring to the writer's immense corpus as a single entity, Tambling argues that Dickens was constricted by the 'bourgeois, imperialist, nationalist' ideology of the Victorian era. Kevin McLaughlin's *Writing in Parts: Imitation and Exchange in Nineteenth-Century Literature* draws upon works by Marx, Balzac, Dickens, Adorno and Benjamin in his analysis of the mass commodification and imitation inherent in nineteenth-century Europe. McLaughlin traces the development of commercial culture in England and France through his study of the literary marketplace's mimetic disposition towards the commodification of culture during this era. McLaughlin devotes particular attention to Dickens's role in the rapidly developing literary marketplace of the Victorian era.

In *Imitation as Resistance: Appropriations of English Literature in Nineteenth-Century America*, Raoul Granqvist explores American responses to British literature during the nineteenth century, particularly to the works of Scott, Byron and Dickens. In addition to examining the manner in which American writers echo, parody and pay tribute to British texts, Granqvist discusses the ways that American culture attempted to free itself from Old World value systems and worldviews. Granqvist argues that American writers employed imitation as a means for seeking their ways out of years of dependence upon their British literary precursors. Martha C. Nussbaum's *Poetic Justice: The Literary Imagination and Public Life* employs Dickens's *Hard Times* as a means for testing her contention that ethical criticism provides a useful means for assessing the particularly human qualities of public and private modes of discourse. Nussbaum argues that texts such as Dickens's offer readers a range of interpersonal models of behaviour. Nussbaum further suggests that such works provide readers with an informed conception of public reasoning and remain essential to the humanistic study of literature and its capacity for enriching the lives of readers. Virginia L. Blum's *Hide and Seek: The Child between Psychoanalysis and Fiction* employs such Dickens novels as *Bleak House* and *Oliver Twist* in a study of the child as a vehicle for self-invention. Blum affords particular attention to the depiction of the mute child as an object of exploitation that serves adult needs. Using Dickens's narratives, Blum argues the child's historical invisibility both precedes and follows adult exploitation.

As always, *DQ* (12) provides students of the novelist with a number of useful essays and notes. Maura Spiegel's 'Managing Pain: Suffering and Reader Sympathy in *Bleak House*' (3–10) focuses on Adam Smith's notion of moderate expression as a key factor in Dickens's evocation of a sympathetic response in his novel. Spiegel argues that Dickens's characterization of Esther offers 'an exemplary model of a survivor of a current epidemic, to represent both the correct and most therapeutic management of suffering' (9). In 'Wolves within and without: Dickens's Transformation of "Little Red Riding Hood" in *Our Mutual Friend*' (12.11–17), Cynthia DeMarcus argues that allusions by Dickens to 'Little Red Riding Hood' enable him to 'express the terrors of the modern world and to plunge the reader into an exploration of his or her own dark unconscious' (11). DeMarcus also provides a brief survey of Dickens's appropriation of fairy tales and other magical narratives in a number of his novels, from *Dombey and Son* and *Hard Times* to *The Mystery of Edwin Drood* and *Our Mutual Friend*. Richard A. Currie's '*All the Year Round* and the State of Victorian Psychiatry' (18-25) argues that the essays in the periodical provided a critique of mid-nineteenth-century psychiatry through their attention to such issues as the physiognomy and the diagnosis of the insane. Currie writes that '*All the Year Round* insists upon the humane treatment of the insane'. Moreover, 'the periodical's discussion of physiognomy in both essay and novel finds flaws in Victorian psychiatry diagnosis that perhaps account for the dead end that Victorian psychiatry reaches at mid century' (22). In 'Defence Mechanisms in *Our Mutual Friend*' (45–59), James Roy King examines the roles of nineteenth-century greed and materialism as central themes in Dickens's novel. King argues that the defence mechanisms in *Our Mutual Friend* function as shields and buffers against the worst aspects of Victorian life. King notes that in Dickens's fictive world 'individuals who "go it alone" are destroyed or severely damaged, where mutuality is the rule, effective buffers come into play' (58). In ' "The Narrow Track of Blood": Detection and Storytelling in *Bleak House*' (*NCF* 50.147–67), Peter Thoms explores the significance of the nuances of detection and mystery that mark the latter chapters of Dickens's novel. Thoms argues that this habitual process of detection operates as an oppressive process of self-scrutiny in which the characters of *Bleak House* in effect police themselves in a collective effort to escape entrapment. Thoms suggests that these characters attempt to nourish their spiritual hunger by figuratively feeding upon the identities of others.

Mark M. Hennelly Jr's ' "Toy Wonders" in *Our Mutual Friend* (Part One)' (60–72) explores the roles of toys and play in Dickens's novel. Hennelly argues that the novel's 'play motifs, particularly of role-playing and of often disturbing toys, also qualify and accommodate these tropes to the harsher, more realistic demands of the contemporary existential wasteland' (61). In the second part of his essay (95-107), Hennelly continues his analysis of the roles of play signifiers in Dickens's narrative of *Our Mutual Friend*. Hennelly underscores the manner in which Dickens employs metaphors of play as a means for glorifying virtue in his novels. In ' "Gone Astray": Dickens as Journalist (Part One)' (108–22), Ella Kusnetz treats Dickens's work as a journalist. Using a psychoanalytic perspective, Kusnetz argues that Dickens's periodical publications reveal his abiding interest in the mysteries of the self. Ella Westland's 'Dickens and Critical Change: Critical Contexts' (123–34) traces the interpretation of Dickens throughout the poststructuralist era, with particular emphasis upon the variety of critical contexts which have treated Dickens's texts. Westland concludes with the hardly profound observation that 'whenever a Dickens critic picks up a pen in the study or communicates across continents by e-mail, history is being made' (131). Michael Swanton's 'A Readership (and Non-Readership) for *Martin Chuzzlewit*, 1843–44 (Part Two)' (161–71) maps the readership of Dickens's novel during the 1840s. Swanton devotes special attention to the serial publication of mid-nineteenth-century texts. Arthur P. Patterson's 'Sponging the Stone: Transformation in *A Christmas Carol*' (172–6) examines the notions of personal identity and transformation in Dickens's novel. Patterson argues that understanding the significance of the work requires readers to integrate the novel's psychological and spiritual messages. Patterson writes that 'the *Carol*'s conception of conversion involves a transformation of consciousness through living simulta-neously in the past, present, and future' (176). In 'Making Mother Suffer, and Other Fun in Dickens' (177–86), Natalie McKnight observes that 'Dickens beats, burns, scars, and strikes with paralysis and muteness numerous bitchy mothers and surrogate mothers in his novels' (177). McKnight argues that the manner in which Dickens's maternal characters suffer indicates the powerful and complex passions that inform the novelist's own conceptions of mothers. For this reason, McKnight explores Dickens's feelings towards his own mother, Elizabeth, who sent him to the blacking factory to work while his father languished in a debtors' prison.

In 'Family Connections: The Influence of the Crewe Family on *Bleak House*' (*Dickensian* 91.5–32), Gillian West addresses Dickens's acquaintance with the Crewes, while Paul Graham's 'The Bravo Murder: A Tenuous Dickensian Connection' (*Dickensian* 91.33–5) investigates the historical sources of Dickens's works. Margaret E. Conrow's 'Double "g" in Fictional Surnames' (*Dickensian* 91.85–93) examines the linguistic nature of Dickens's characters, while Shifra Hochberg's 'Madame Defarge and a Possible Car-lylean Source' (*Dickensian* 91.99–101) discusses the well-worn furrow of Thomas Carlyle upon Dickens. In 'Krook's Dyslexia' (*Dickensian* 91.102–6), N. M. Jacoby explores the behavioural depiction of Dickens's legendary figure of deceit. In '*The Dickensian* at 90: A Celebration of the First Three Editors, 1905–1968' (*Dickensian* 91.165–71), Michael Slater commemorates nearly a century of *Dickensian* scholarship with an illuminating review of the editors who shared in establishing the periodical's well-deserved scholarly promi-nence. Stephen Pulsford's 'The Aesthetic and the Closed Shop: The Ideology of the Aesthetic in Dickens's *Hard Times*' (*VR* 21.145–60) examines the political agenda of Dickens and its influence upon the composition of his novels. Pulsford takes particular issue with those critics who argue that Dickens was naive and confused regarding political issues. As Pulsford notes, 'The aesthetic in *Hard Times* registers and cultivates all the particularity of individuals' sufferings under institutional oppression' (157). In 'The Cup and the Lip and the Riddle of *Our Mutual Friend*' (*ELH* 62.955–78), Gregg A. Hecimovich discusses the place of riddles in Dickens's novel. In addition to describing *Our Mutual Friend* as a 'novel about surface and substance, disguised identity, linguistic conundrums', Hecimovich surveys the role of riddles, enigmas and word games throughout the history of serialized literature (955).

In ' "Playing at Leap-Frog with the Tombstones": The *Danse Macabre* Motif in Dickens' (*ELWIU* 23.227–43), Mark M. Hennelly Jr discusses the word games and comic inflections that mark Dickens's narratives. Hennelly treats such novels as *The Pickwick Papers*, *The Mystery of Edwin Drood*, *Martin Chuzzlewit* and *A Tale of Two Cities* in his essay. In *Dickens in Bedlam: Madness and Restraint in His Fiction*, David D. Oberhelman examines the novels and journalistic efforts of Dickens. Oberhelman also explores the treatment of mental illness and self-control in Dickens's texts. Dominic Rainsford's 'Flatness and Ethical Responsibility in *Little Dorrit*' (*VN* 88.11–17) identifies the ethical imperatives inherent in Dickens's narrative, while Joseph Bottum's 'The Gentleman's True Name: *David Copperfield* and the Philosophy of Naming' (*NCF* 49.435–55) explores the onomastic underpinnings in Dickens's novel. In 'Broken Mirror, Broken Words: Autobiography, Prosopopeia, and the Dead Mother in *Bleak House*' (*SNNTS* 27.42–62), Carolyn M. Dever investigates the treatment of self-representation in the novel. Dever also discusses images of mourning in *Bleak House*. James R. Simmons Jr's 'Scrooge, Falstaff, and the Rhetoric of Indigence' (*ELN* 32.43–6) offers a rhetorical study of Dickens's characterization strategies in *A Christmas Carol*. Simmons compares Dickens's Scrooge with Shakespeare's legendary characterization of Sir John Falstaff. In 'Managing the House in *Dombey and Son*: Dickens and the Uses' (*SP* 91.361–82), Andrew Elfenbein explores Dickens's use of analogy in his novel. Eric P. Levy's 'Dickens's Pathology of Time in *Hard Times*' (*PQ* 74.189–207) examines Dickens's treatment of time in his fictions, while in 'Invigilating *Our Mutual Friend*: Gender and the Legitimation of Professional Authority' (*Novel* 28.154–72), Cathy Shuman discusses the roles of gender and authority in the narrative structure of *Our Mutual Friend*. The substantial criticism that Dickens receives demonstrates the contemporary vitality of his work, although his less well-known works are certainly deserving of more critical attention. Once again, though, the highlight of the year's work in Dickens is the latest volume in Storey and Tillotson's edition of the novelist's correspondence.

Scholars continue to demonstrate Trollope's significant role in the evolution of the novel as a literary genre. Using recent insights in feminist, reader response and narratological criticism, Lynette Felber's *Gender and Genre in Novels Without End: The British Roman-Fleuve* attempts to map the role of genre in works of the British roman-fleuve literary tradition, a genre of novels denoted by their lengthy and multi-layered narratives. Felber features close readings of Anthony Trollope's Palliser novels. In addition to exploring the history, reception and narrative complexities of the *roman-fleuve* tradition, Felber examines the ways in which gender impinges upon the composition of the Palliser novels. It was only a matter of time before Lacan was brought to bear upon the works of Anthony Trollope. Drawing upon the insights of contemporary critical theory and psychology, Priscilla L. Walton's *Patriarchal Desire and Victorian Discourse: A Lacanian Reading of Anthony Trollope's Palliser Novels* explores the images of patriarchal desire and masculinist discourse in the Palliser novels of Anthony Trollope. In addition to linking feminist analysis with psychoanalytic theory, Walton examines Trollope's writings in terms of the implication of the hierarchical structures of Victorian culture. Using the six volumes of the Palliser novels, Walton focuses on the psychological portrayal of women in Trollope's texts. Jane Nardin's thoughtful *Trollope and Victorian Moral Philosophy* examines the role of the Stoic-Hebrew-Christian ethical tradition in the life and works of Trollope. Nardin affords particular attention to Trollope's defence of this moral-philosophical tradition through a series of novels written during the 1870s and 1880s. Nardin argues that in these novels Trollope rejected the belief in reason and innovation upon which most Victorian moral philosophy ultimately rests. In *Closer and Closer Apart: Jealousy in Literature*, Rosemary Lloyd examines the roles of jealousy and rivalry in the novels of Anthony Trollope. Lloyd argues that jealousy functions as a narrative construct that pertains to the negative and destructive sides of the emotion itself. Lloyd also contends that jealousy threatens to release a chaos that will ultimately subvert the norms of the society depicted in texts by writers such as Trollope. In ' "Something Both More and Less than Manliness": Gender and the Literary Reception of Anthony Trollope' (*VLC* 22.151–71), Nicola Thompson addresses the role of gender in the critical reception of Trollope's novels. In addition to arguing that Victorian critics considered gender in their assessment of Trollope's fictions, Thompson investigates the prevailing contention that Trollope wrote as an intensely masculine writer to a predominantly female circulating audience. 'Being a "Queen" of the Victorian circulating library was problematic for any writer when popular and high art began to diverge', Thompson observes, 'but particularly problematic if the author happened to be male' (167). In 'Rhetoric and Courtship in *Can You Forgive Her?*' (*ELH* 62.217– 35), Randall Craig discusses the rhetoric of courtship in Trollope's novel. William A. Cohen's often outrageous but stimulating 'Trollope's Trollop' (*Novel* 28.235–56) examines the treatment of sexuality in Victorian-era fiction. Amongst Cohen's suggestions are an extensive excursion into the ramifications of the word 'trollop' and Lizze Eustace's jewel box, which apparently has something to do with female genitalia! Certainly an article worth pursuing. David D. Oberhelman's 'Trollope's Insanity Defense: Narrative Alienation in *He Knew He Was Right*' (*SEL* 35.189–806) investigates Trollope's use of isolation and alienation in his novel's narrative structure.

The year's work in Charlotte Brontë studies is highlighted by a British Library edition of the novelist's *High Life in Verdopolis: A Story from the Glass Town Saga*. Introduced and edited by the fine Brontë scholar Christine Alexander, the volume is presented with facsimile illustrations from the manuscript with the novelist's own drawings. *The Letters of Charlotte Brontë: With a Selection of Letters by Families and Friends, Volume 1: Family and Friends* (ed. Margaret Smith), will surely provide students of the novelist with a valuable resource for decades to come. Smith's edition features more than 380 letters by the novelist to her close friend Ellen Nussey that will usefully supplement earlier editions of the writer's correspondence by T. J. Wise and John A. Symington, among others. In addition to a valuable and detailed introduction, 'The History of the Letters', which discusses the role of Mrs Gaskell, Ellen Nussey, Thomas Wemyss Reed, Horsfall Turner, C. K. Shorter and T. J. Wise, pays full tribute to 'the work to whom the edition is dedicated'. Smith concludes the volume with a valuable appendix, 'Reminiscences of Charlotte Brontë by a Schoolfellow'. J. A. V. Chapple and Margaret Smith's

'Charlotte Brontë and Elizabeth Gaskell in Society' (*BST* 21.161–7) provides a reception study of Brontë's work, with additional emphasis upon her relationship with Gaskell. In 'Dis-Membrance of Things Past: Re-Vision of Wordsworthian Retrospection in *Jane Eyre* and *Villette*' (*VLC* 22.73–102), Ruth D. Johnston argues that Charlotte Brontë revises Wordsworth discourse in her fictions. Johnston suggests that the Brontës create meaning in these novels by reducing the level of narration to introspection. Christine Alexander's ' "The Burning Clime": Charlotte Brontë and John Martin' (*NCF* 50.285–320) investigates the landscape imagery in Brontë's work, as well as her creative debt to John Martin. C. S. Wiesenthal's 'Anti-Bodies of Disease and Defense: Spirit-Body Relations in Nineteenth-Century Culture and Fiction' (*VLC* 22.187–220) traces the Victorian fascination with spirits and the material body in Charlotte Brontë's *Jane Eyre* and *Villette*. According to Wiesenthal, the Brontës 'cast each other into striking relief, managing to encompass between them the entire nineteenth-century dialectic of materialism and spiritualism, of empiricism and subjectivism, and of naturalism and supernaturalism as it has disclosed itself in the debates over the significance of apparitions' (195).

Mark M. Hennelly, Jr's ' "In a State Between": A Reading of Liminality in *Jane Eyre*' (*VLC* 22.103–28) traces modes of liminality in Brontë's novel. Hennelly draws upon the anthropological insights of Victor Turner in his study. J. Russell Perkin's 'Inhabiting *Wuthering Heights*: Jane Urquhart's Rewriting of Emily Brontë' (*VR* 21.115–28) discusses the contemporary novelist's reconfiguration of Brontë's novel in *Changing Heaven* (1990). In addition to addressing the metafictional nature of Urquhart's enterprise, Perkin argues that *Changing Heaven* parodies *Wuthering Heights* through the former novel's uneasy mixture of emotional intensity and ironic comedy. In 'Joseph's Currants: The Hermeneutic Challenge of *Wuthering Heights*' (*VLC* 22.267–85), James L. Hill surveys the radically divergent critical interpretations of Brontë's novel. Hill argues that Brontë's 'extremely sophisticated control of narrative places hermeneutic responsibility on the reader to an extent unprecedented in Victorian novels' (267). Edited by Christine Alexander, Branwell Brontë's *Branwell's Blackwood's Magazine: The Glass Town Magazine* was published by the Juvenilia Press, a series that combines scholarship with pedagogy as its central aim. Written when he was only 11, Brontë's first publication features illustrations by Rebecca Alexander. Finally, the lives and work of the Brontë family are commemorated in Christopher Gable and Gillian Barbara Lynne's ballet, *The Brontës*. Mary Clarke's '*The Brontës*: Northern Ballet Theatre's New Ballet' (*DanT* 85.754–55) provides details regarding the ballet's recent stage production.

This year was an eventful – although unusually uneven – year in George Eliot studies. In *Jerusalem Recovered: Victorian Intellectuals and the Birth of Modern Zionism*, Michael Polowetzky's somewhat derivative work provides an introductory overview of the influence of Jewish history and culture upon a wide range of influential men and women of the nineteenth century, including Benjamin Disraeli, George Eliot, Anthony Ashley-Cooper, Charles Warren and Laurence Oliphant, among others. Frederick R. Karl's biography, *George Eliot, Voice of a Century*, receives a good deal of unfavourable comment in the British and American academic and nonacademic press, although Peter Ackroyd praised it in *The Times* (3 August), where he commented on the novelist's enduring reputation despite her often enigmatic behaviour: 'her posthumous reputation has always been one of serene and triumphant intelligence ... she could often be exceedingly furtive and peculiar'; Ackroyd attributes the novelist's high-mindedness to her pursuit of 'fame and success with great determination' (32). Much light is shed upon George Eliot, her fiction and other literary activities, as well as other writers of serial fiction in William Baker's *The Letters of George Henry Lewes*. Of particular interest are the newly published letters to George Smith from the John Murray Archives regarding the founding and publishing of the *Cornhill*, the fiction in its pages and Lewes's role not only as editor but as reader of fiction submitted to the magazine. This collection assembles 499 new or newly transcribed letters by George Henry Lewes. Chronologically arranged and heavily annotated, these letters, when combined with those already published in Gordon S. Haight's *The George Eliot Letters*, present the reader with all of Lewes's known correspondence. These volumes – over 500 pages – will provide the student of the novel, of Lewes, of George Eliot and of Victorian literary and intellectual history with an indispensable research tool.

Ellen Zetzel Lambert's *The Face of Love: Feminism and the Beauty Question* examines the 'beauty myth' and argues that women should free themselves from over-arching concerns about their physical appearances. Lambert suggests that the fact that many women still feel compelled to attend to the beauty myth underscores one of the lacunae in the success of the modern feminist movement. In addition to examining the depiction of the beauty myth in such works as George Eliot's *Middlemarch*, Lambert also discusses Fanny Burney's narrative of the mastectomy that she underwent without anaesthesia in 1811. Ian MacKillop and Richard Storer's *F. R. Leavis: Essays and Documents* includes William Baker's 'Leavis as Reader of *Daniel Deronda*', an analysis of one of the most important twentieth-century critical voice's response to Eliot's novel. Baker examines marginalia in Leavis's copy of the Blackwood 1878, one-volume edition of *Daniel Deronda*. MacKillop and Storer's volume also features Storer's 'Leavis and 'Gwendolen Harleth,'' which treats the publication history of Leavis's attempt to truncate *Daniel Deronda* by publishing only the Gwendolen portions: too easy to be dismissed as 'a Leavisian folly' (47). In *Sexing the Mind: Nineteenth-Century Fictions of Hysteria*, Evelyne Ender examines scenes of hysteria in the fictions of George Sand, Gustave Flaubert, George Eliot and Henry James, while also exploring the writings of Sigmund Freud. Ender argues that these texts represent distinctive attempts to break loose from erotic, political and epistemological models of Victorian masculinity and femininity. Drawing upon conceptions of hysteria in various medical and literary texts, Ender discusses the interplay between writing, subjectivity and sexual identity in nineteenth-century fictions of male/female consciousness. Students of George Eliot should also note the publication of two new editions of her novels, Terence Cave's *Daniel Deronda*, published in the Penguin Classics series, and D. J. Enright's *The Impressions of Theophrastus Such*, published by Everyman. Cave's text is accompanied by useful explanatory notes and biographical and critical introductions. Enright's edition leaves much to be desired, including getting the title right! Edited by Juliet McMaster, George Eliot's *Edward Neville* was published as part of the Juvenilia Press series. Illustrated and annotated by McMaster, Eliot's volume is a fragment of a historical novel that she wrote at the age of 14 in a school notebook. Set in Chepstow Castle at the time of the English Civil War, Marian Evans's earliest known work shows the young equestrian hero in conflict with his sinister uncle, the regicide Henry Marten [see G. S. Haight's appendix to his great *George Eliot: A Biography* (1968)]. In ' "At Once Narrow and Promiscuous": Emily Davies, George Eliot, and *Middlemarch*' (*NCS* 9.1–30), Laura Green examines the influence of the reformer Emily Davies upon the narrative of Eliot's landmark novel. Arguing that the subject of education remains central to our understanding of *Middlemarch*, Green contends that Eliot's novel critiques education in both an intellectual as well as an institutional sense.

The *GEFR* includes a report, written by Caroline Levine and Mark Turner, of a conference held by the Center for English Studies at the University of London entitled 'Reviving *Romola*' (25.17–9). Also featured is the text of 'Mary Ann Did Not Go: Why George Eliot Stayed Away from Church', the title of the Twenty-Third George Eliot Memorial Lecture – 1994, delivered by Canon Michael Sadgrove, the Vice-Provost and Precentor of Coventry Cathedral (*GEFR* 26.24–9). Canon Sadgrove provides a sympathetic account and appraisal by a clergyman of the Church of England of one of the key events in George Eliot's life. Canon Sadgrove argues that her refusal to attend church 'cannot simply be described as a rejection of faith, for it was also the prelude to a new religious awareness'. He admits that her world view 'is not religious in the conventional sense' but generously ends his lecture with an assertion that 'our own vision of life would be the poorer without her' (29). William Baker and Donald Hawes reproduce and comment on four previously unpublished letters recently acquired by the British Library: one to Edward Lyulph Stanley (who was prominent in the field of public education) and three to Florence Hill, the younger sister of Gertrude, Charles Lee Lewes's wife (*GEFR* 26.30–4). In 'Thou Shalt Not Read: Maggie's Arrested Development in *The Mill on the Floss*' (*GEFR* 26.35–40), Karen E. Hottle surveys the difficulties and opposition Maggie encounters in her girlhood reading and argues that she is unable to develop ' "book learning", knowledge drawn from experience, and creative intelligence' (37). Graham Handley's 'Charles Christian Hennell and George Eliot: Human and Narrative Affinities' (*GEFR* 26.41–5) argues that Hennell had profound and wide-ranging effects on her analyses of the human condition, her sense of historical perspective and her narrative structure. When reading both writers, 'one is aware', Handley writes, 'of a presence, a personality, working and writing for good, for the enlightenment of mankind through the revealed truths of practical idealism and human interaction' (45).

The relationship between Positivism and George Eliot receives attention in Judith Siford's 'Dismal Loneliness: George Eliot, August Comte and "The Lifted Veil" ' (*GEFR* 25.46–52). Siford cites George Eliot copying passages in a notebook now in Nuneaton Library, Warwickshire, from Comte concerning the channelling of egoism into altruism by submission. Brenda McKay's 'Race and Myth: *The Spanish Gypsy*' (*GEFR* 25.53–60) examines George Eliot's 'longest excursus into poetry', arguing that its theme is an investigation of 'the different mythological traditions of man, particularly Classical traditions of the West and the Judaism of the Near East' (53). McKay concludes that the poem is more pessimistic and more sceptical than the novels, particularly *Daniel Deronda*. Linda K. Robertson's 'Horses and Hounds: The importance of Animals in *The Mill on the Floss*' (*GEFR* 25.61–3) catalogues the creatures that appear in Eliot's novel. Robertson argues that these animals assist readers in understanding Eliot's characters and their relationship to society. In 'Utopian Mentality in George Eliot's *Middlemarch* and in D. H. Lawrence's *The Rainbow*' (*UtopS* 6.30–39), Hans Ulrich Seeber argues that a sense of idealism and a utopian mentality reveals the ostensibly realist narrative of Eliot's novel. In addition to comparing Eliot's female protagonists with those of Lawrence's novel, Seeber surveys the utopian constructs that mark the narratives of *Middlemarch* and *The Rainbow*.

The September issue of *GEGHLS* (28–29) includes Margaret Soenser Breen's 'Silas Marner – George Eliot's Male Heroine' (1–15), which explores the role of gender and the use of a male pseudonym in Eliot's fictions, particularly *Silas Marner*. Breen concludes that 'Eliot's literary production tells us something of Victorian women writers' polemical relation to gender issues, particularly within the fictive worlds that they authored' (13). Keith A. Waddle's 'Mary Garth, the Wollstonecraftian Feminist of *Middlemarch*' (16–29) ascribes the feminist elements in Eliot's novel to the ideal woman in Mary Wollstonecraft's ideology of gender. Waddle writes that 'Eliot's feminism is the courage to see women and men as they are – and the grace to accept them anyway' (27). In a scholarly essay drawing upon George Eliot's notebooks, Lesley Gordon's 'George Eliot and Plutarch' (30–41) addresses the influence of Greek culture and tragedy upon Eliot's novels, particularly *Middlemarch* and *The Mill on the Floss*. Gordon argues that Plutarchian models are evident in the narrative structures of Eliot's fictions. Alain Barrat's 'G. H. Lewes, Goethe, and Science: From Romanticism to Positivism' (42–9) investigates the scientific influences upon the life and work of G. H. Lewes, with particular attention to the composition and publication of the *Life and Works of Goethe*. In 'G. H. Lewes, "Metamorphoses", and George Eliot' (50–6), Graham Handley argues that the writings of Lewes and Eliot were interactive. Handley concludes that the neglected 'Metamorphoses' is the 'literary analogue which registers that capacity for giving and sharing, confiding, exchanging, and, above all, inspiring each other in their metamorphosed lives' (56). P. D. Edwards's 'George Henry Lewes, George Eliot, and Edmund Yates' (57–66) publishes a Lewes-Yates letter now at the University of Queensland and remarks upon the relationship between Lewes, Eliot and Yates, while D. J. Trela's 'Margaret Oliphant and George Eliot: A Note on the Denial of Influence' (67–70) discusses the creative interaction between Oliphant and Eliot. Juliet McMaster's 'George Eliot's "Prentice Hand"' (71–3) explores the composition of Eliot's work of juvenilia, *Edward Neville* and discusses the Juvenilia Press series.

In ' "The Other Side of Silence": Matrimonial Conflict and the Divorce Court in George Eliot's Fiction' (*NCF* 50.322–36), Andrew Dowling argues that a Victorian legal reform has a possible bearing on George Eliot's presentation of marital dissension. Dowling discusses the ways in which silence can exert a disturbing or even malevolent influence in Eliot's portrayal of marital unhappiness and breakdowns, with particular emphasis upon the role of silence in *Middlemarch* and *Daniel Deronda*. Alain Barrat's 'Nostalgia and Reform in *Scenes of Clerical Life*' (*CVE* 41.47–57) examines the complexity of attitude revealed in Eliot's depiction of the provincial environment in her first works of fiction. Barrat argues that her criticisms of the provinces should not be seen as a comprehensive indictment, since she also implies that human nature is fundamentally good and that the potential for regeneration exists. Michael Schiefelbein's 'Crucifixes and Madonnas: George Eliot's Fascination with Catholicism in *Romola*' (*VN* 88.31–4) offers a carefully argued discussion of some basic emotional sympathies that Eliot evinces regarding Catholicism in the novel, despite her lack of a conventional Christian faith. Schiefelbein associates Romola's attitudes with George Eliot's own fears and longing for love. In 'George Eliot's *Romola* and Emerson's "The American Scholar" ' (*ELN* 32.70–75), Ernest Fontana discusses Eliot's meeting with Emerson on his second visit to England in the summer of 1848. Fontana argues that in 'The Blind Scholar and his Daughter' (Book 1, Ch. 5) 'there is a direct incorporation and creative application of Emerson's landmark 1837 lecture "The American Scholar" to the relationship between Romola and her father, the blind scholar Bardo de Bardi' (71). The 6 October 1995 issue of the *TLS* features a conversation between A. S. Byatt and Ignes Sôdrè on the place of Gwendolen Harleth in *Daniel Deronda*. Entitled 'The Dislikable Gwendolen: A Conversation between A. S. Byatt and Ignes Sôdrè' (19–20), the conversation explores Gwendolen's simultaneous existence as an angel and a demon, while also impinging upon her penchant for self-deceit.

In ' "Grammatical Fair Ones": Women, Men, and Attitudes to Language in the Novels of George Eliot' (*RES* 46.11–25), Lynda Mugglestone employs sociolinguistics in order to highlight cultural, moral and psychological issues. Mugglestone argues that 'perceptions of linguistic superiority' were 'especially associated with women in Eliot's moral world' (11). Mugglestone affords special attention to language in the narratives of *Felix Holt, the Radical* and *Middlemarch*. Rita Bode's 'Power and Submission in *Felix Holt, the Radical*' (*SEL* 35.769–88) argues that Esther's submission to Felix is only superficial. Bode concludes that 'if the vain, conceited Esther of the first scenes promises to be another Angel in the House by the novel's end, the impression is that it will be her own house in which she presides' (788). In 'Determined Heroines: George Eliot, Augusta Webster, and Closet Drama by Victorian Women' (*VP* 33.89–109), Susan Brown compares Augusta Webster's *A Woman Sold* with *The Spanish Gypsy*. Brown defines 'closet drama' as 'drama that either by intention or default, finds its performance in the minds of readers within their "closets" or private rooms' (89). Brown argues that dramatic form, which deprives the reader of explicit authorial guidance, enables specifically feminist questions to be seen as complex, thus problematizing the possibility of clear and simple responses. Brown concludes that in Victorian women's poetic drama women were depicted as 'at once heroic and socially constrained' (109). In 'Acting Naturally: Brontë, Lewes, and the Problem of Gender Performance' (*ELH* 62.409–42), Lynn M. Voskuil discusses the conflicting responses of Lewes and Charlotte Brontë to theatrical performances, especially to the acting of Rachel (the 'Vashti' of *Villette*). Voskuil argues that Lewes valued 'natural' acting, and emphasized its influence upon the audience.

In a major biography drawing upon the writer's correspondence and manuscripts, Elisabeth Jay's *Mrs. Oliphant: A Literary Life* discusses the prolific literary career of Oliphant in an era of male-dominated publishing. In addition to her explorations of Oliphant's themes regarding the family, religious orthodoxy and the role of women in Victorian society, Jay examines the way in which the writer perceived her own life and work. D. J. Trela's *Margaret*

Oliphant: Critical Essays on a Gentle Subversive assembles a variety of essays that assess the life and work of the hitherto largely ignored novelist from a diversity of perspectives. Selections include Trela's introduction, 'Discovering the Gentle Subversive'; John Stock Clarke's 'The Paradoxes of Oliphant's Reputation'; Margarete Rubik's 'The Subversion of Literary Cliches in Oliphant's Fiction'; Linda Peterson's 'The Female *Bildungsroman*: Tradition and Subversion in Oliphant's Fiction'; Esther Schor's 'The Haunted Interpreter in Oliphant's Supernatural Fiction'; Joanne Shattock's 'The Making of a Novelist: Oliphant and John Blackwood at Work on *The Perpetual Curate*'; Laurie Langbauer's 'Absolute Commonplaces: Oliphant's Theory of Autobiography'; Elisabeth Jay's 'Freed by Necessity, Trapped by the Market: The Editing of Oliphant's *Autobiography*'; Dale Kramer's 'The City That Binds: Oliphant's Theory of Domestic Tragedy'; and Merryn Williams's 'Feminist or Antifeminist?: Oliphant and the Woman Question'. In 'Mrs. Oliphant's Prodigal Son' (*N&Q* 42.201), Williams also provides biographical background regarding the novelist's relationship with her son, Cyril Francis Oliphant.

Wilkie Collins's critical reputation in the year's work continues to grow, as do writings on him. In *Wilkie Collins to the Forefront: Some Reassessments*, Nelson Smith and R. C. Terry assemble a diversity of responses to the life and work of Wilkie Collins. Smith and Terry's volume includes papers originally presented at the Wilkie Collins Centennial Conference held at the University of Victoria, British Columbia, from 29 September through 1 October last year. Uniformly excellent selections include Terry's ' "Myself in the Background and the Story in Front": Wilkie Collins As Others Knew Him'; Catherine Peters's ' "Invite No Dangerous Publicity": Some Independent Women and Their Effect on Wilkie Collins' Life and Writing'; William M. Clarke's 'A Teasing "Marital" Correspondence with a Twelve Year Old'; Sue Lonoff's 'Sex, Sense, and Nonsense: The Story of the Collins-Lear Friendship'; Christopher Kent's 'Probability, Reality, and Sensation in the Novels of Wilkie Collins'; John Sutherland's 'Wilkie Collins and the Origins of the Sensation Novel'; John R. Reed's 'The Stories of *The Moonstone*'; William M. Burgan's 'Masonic Symbolism in *The Moonstone* and *The Mystery of Edwin Drood*'; Ira B. Nadel's 'Wilkie Collins and His Illustrators'; Peter L. Caracciolo's 'Wilkie Collins and "The God Almighty of Novelists": The Example of Scott in *No Name* and *Armadale*'; Peter Thoms's 'Escaping the Plot: The Quest for Selfhood in *The Woman in White*'; Barbara Fass Leavy's 'Wilkie Collins' *The New Magdalen* and the Folklore of the Kind and the Unkind Girls'; Kathleen O'Fallon's 'Breaking the Laws About Ladies: Wilkie Collins's Questioning of Gender Roles'; Barbara T. Gates's 'Wilkie Collins' Suicides: "Truth As It Is in Nature" '; and C. S. Wiesenthal's 'From Charcot to Plato: The History of Hysteria in *Heart and Science*'.

In 'Pre-Raphaelite Paintings and Jungian Images in Wilkie Collins' *The Woman in White*' (*VN* 88.26–31), Sophia Andres traces the aesthetic and psychological terrain of Collins's novel. In 'Satan in the Hairbrush: *The Moonstone* and Literary Subversion' (*TWeb* 1.18–20), Sarah Clark surveys the critical reception of *The Moonstone* and the effect of serialization upon its popular success. In addition to arguing that the novel seems fragmented as a result of its serial publication, Clark ascribes *The Moonstone*'s initially poor critical reception to the cynicism that pervades Collins's narrative. Clark's essay appears in the first issue of a magazine devoted to crime and detective fiction. John Sutherland's Penguin Classics edition of Collins's *Armadale* (1866) should remain the definitive edition for a long time to come. In addition to a detailed introduction, there is a thorough note on the text and on the manuscript. Sutherland's notes contain details regarding textual revision and passages hitherto unpublished from the original manuscript. There is even an appendix on the dramatic versions of the novel. Sutherland's edition 'follows the first published version of *Armadale*, as published in the *Cornhill Magazine*, with the addition of the dedication, Collins's foreword, and the 'Appendix' (xxxii). Julian Thompson provides students of Collins with an edition of *The Complete Shorter Fiction*, which includes the editor's brief introduction assessing the strengths and weaknesses of Collins's development as a short story writer. In his 'Note on the Text' Thompson writes that 'I have tried to include all the fiction under novella length published by Collins in his lifetime. For this purpose the novella has been deemed to contain 30,000 words' (xiii). Excluded are some of Collins's contributions to the Christmas number of *Household Words* and *All the Year Round*, which 'do not seem ... to be sufficiently self-contained to merit reprinting' (xiii). Useful introductory notes preface each of the 49 stories featured in this excellent volume.

Lenora Ledwon's 'Veiled Women, the Law of Coverture, and Wilkie Collins' *The Woman in White*' (*VLC* 22.1–22) explores the place of women's bodies in nineteenth-century culture. Using Collins's novel, Ledwon argues that the veiled woman simultaneously haunts the legal system and the social order that endeavours to obscure and silence her. Ledwon praises 'Collins' sincere and sympathetic depiction of the plight of loss of feminine identity and his exposure of the legal fiction that is coverture' (20). Kenneth Millard's 'My Father's Will: Self-Determination and Mental Breakdown in *Basil, The Professor* and *The Ordeal of Richard Feverel*' (*English* 44.25–39) discusses the treatment of self-help and sexual repression in Collins's aesthetic. Millard also compares Collins's fictive depictions of mental illness with those in novels by Charlotte Brontë and George Meredith. In 'Sensational Sisters: Wilkie Collins' *The Woman in White*' (*PCP* 30.82-102), Leila Silvana May explores Collins's contributions to the genre of the sensation novel, while Michael Taylor's ' "In the name of Her Sacred Weakness": Romance, Destiny, and Woman's Revenge in Wilkie Collins' *The Woman in White*' (*UTQ* 64.289–304) investigates Collins's treatment of romantic love in his novel. Taylor also discusses Collins's depictions of destiny and revenge in *The Woman in White*.

In *Lewis Carroll: A Biography*, Morton N. Cohen offers a new investigation of the enigmatic author of *Alice's Adventures in Wonderland* and traces the writer's existence as an Oxford don and mathematician, as well as his private life as the author of children's books. Drawing upon previously unpublished family documents pertaining to Charles Lutwidge Dodgson, Cohen examines the evolution of the author's vivid and innovative imagination. Cohen also discusses Dodgson's paradoxical life as a proper Victorian, as well as his private penchant for young girls and the creation of wild, nonsensical literature. Jo Elwyn Jones and J. Francis Gladstone's *The Red King's Dream, or Lewis Carroll in Wonderland* examines the diaries of Lewis Carroll and his portraits of a variety of Victorian celebrities – including Faraday, Huxley, Tennyson and Ruskin – in an effort to unravel the author's critique of Victorian life and politics in the pages of his 'Alice' tales. In addition to arguing that Tweedledum and Tweedledee were inspired by the machinations of Tennyson's sons, Jones and Gladstone identify the inspirations for such characters as the White Rabbit, the mad Hatter and the Red King, among others. Carol Mavor's *Pleasures Taken: Performances of Sexuality and Loss in Victorian Photographs* explores the photographs of Carroll, as well as those of Julia Margaret Cameron and Hannah Cullwick. Amply illustrated, this volume provides a useful supplement to Carroll's fictions.

In *Harriet Martineau: The Poetics of Moralism*, Shelagh Hunter assesses the life and work of one of the Victorian era's most important pioneers in popular educational and mainstream journalism. Hunter argues that the Victorian concept of 'moral health' to which Martineau aspired empowered her pragmatic career marked by its adherence to social altruism. Hunter traces Martineau's ethical system to a Wordsworthian moral psychology that successfully united religion, politics and self-development into a moral framework that Martineau described as 'moral independence'. She thoroughly discusses Martineau's oeuvre, including her novels *Deerbrook* (1839) and *Five Years of Youth* (1831). Scholars interested in the works of Charles Kingsley should note the publication of a new edition of *The Water-Babies* in the World's Classics series. Edited with an introduction and notes by Brian Alderson, this new volume affords particular attention to detailing the novel's variants, its iconography and the full annotation of its many diverse references. The detective fiction of Sir Arthur Conan Doyle receives critical treatment in R. F. Fleissner's 'On the Pedigree of the Name of *Holmes*: Apropos of the First English Detective Work' (*Clues* 16.67–76). Fleissner examines the role of onomastics in Conan Doyle's characterization strategies. Harold Orel's 'Sherlock Holmes and His Creator: A Case of Mistaken Identity' (*CIQ* 31.169–78) investigates the biographical background of Conan Doyle's most famous creation, while Frances Wilson's 'A Case of Identity: Tracking Down Sherlock Holmes' (*WS* 12.29–46) traces Conan Doyle's character development of Holmes. In 'From Sherlock Holmes to Dr. Thorndyke: Arguments for the Morality of Science' (*Clues* 16.1–12), J. K. Van Dover compares the treatment of science in Conan Doyle's fictions with the scientific writings of Richard Austin Freeman.

Hardy studies continue to proliferate. Drawing upon a range of Hardy novels, Daniel R. Schwarz's *The Transformation of the English Novel, 1890–1930: Studies in Hardy, Conrad, Joyce, Lawrence, Forster, and Woolf* discusses the evolution of the English novel in the late nineteenth- and early twentieth-century novels of Hardy, Conrad, Joyce, Lawrence, Forster and Woolf. Schwarz affords particular attention to the experimental modes of narration, humanistic formalism, and textual construction inherent in the innovative novels of these writers, particularly Hardy. Using a variety of psychological insights, Robert Langbaum's *Thomas Hardy in Our Time* examines Hardy's prose and poetry in terms of the themes of the unconscious and sexuality endemic to his work. Langbaum discusses Hardy's poetry as a reaction against the emerging modernist verse, while also investigating Hardy's minimalization of sexuality in such works as *The Mayor of Casterbridge* and his last novel, *The Well-Beloved*. Drawing upon Hardy's correspondence, his autobiography and his immense canon of novels and verse, Timothy Hands's *Writers in Their Time: Thomas Hardy* attempts to situate the writer with the historical moment in which he lived. Hands discusses Hardy's response to the Romantic movement, as well as the contemporary critical response to Hardy's novels. Hands also traces Hardy's various philosophies on society and his knowledge of the contemporary arts of the Victorian era. In *The Decline of the Goddess: Nature, Culture, and Women in Thomas Hardy's Fiction*, Shirley A. Stave investigates the place of the goddess myth in Hardy's novels from *Jude the Obscure* to *The Return of the Native*. Stave argues that the evolution of the myth in Hardy's fiction underscores his evolving consciousness regarding the connections between patriarchy, Christianity, sexism and classism, among other issues. Stave suggests that Hardy's emphasis upon the goddess figure in his novels presages a later narrative world devoid of spiritual meaning. The year's work in Hardy studies is accented by Everyman's new edition of *Jude the Obscure*, edited and introduced by Timothy Hands. Using the manuscript of the 1912 Wessex edition of the novel, Hands supplements his text with a chronology and a map of the Wessex of Hardy's novels.

THY (21) provides students of the writer with several new selections of interest, including Trevor Hearl's 'Thomas Hardy at Florence in 1887' (5–7), which examines Hardy's Italian experiences in the late 1880s. In addition to discussing Hardy's reactions to Italy in *The Life*, Hearl addresses the writer's apparently moody recollections of Florence. Hearl also considers Hardy's newspaper accounts of his Italian journey. In ' "The race for money and good things": *Far from the Madding Crowd*' (8–30), John R. Doheny investigates Hardy's novel as a work of economic propaganda. Doheny argues that Hardy evinces distinctly modern economic views in the narrative of *Far from the Madding Crowd*. In addition to assessing the influence of John Stuart Mill's *On Liberty* on the novelist, Doheny examines the role of Hardy's nineteenth-century economic ideals upon his narrative. G. A. Schirmer's ' "A Woman Lost": Strategies of Irony in Hardy's Love Poetry' (31–51) discusses the role of the rural Wessex of Hardy's celebrated novels upon his later verse. Schirmer devotes special attention to investigating Hardy's conceptions of love in his poetry and in such novels as *A Pair of Blue Eyes*. Hardy, Schirmer argues, was 'committed to celebrating the power of love while at the same time never failing to recognize all that makes it imperfect and incomplete, and therefore, for Hardy, real' (48). Alma Evers's ' "Two Devotions, Two Thoughts, Two Hopes, and Two Blessings": Dualism as Theme and Patterning in *Two on a Tower*' (52–60) argues that Hardy's novel operates as a series of parallels, analogues, opposites, simple choices, pairings and divisions. Evers suggests that all of the many forms of duality in the novel can be read as metaphors for divided awareness and allegiance. Evers ultimately ascribes Hardy's narrative agenda to the 'equally basic concepts of the division of matter into the animate and inanimate' (58). Hardy's fictive explorations of sex-role reversal receive attention in Ellen Lew Sprechman's *Seeing Women as Men: Role Reversal in the Novels of Thomas Hardy*. Samir Elbarbary's 'The Male Bias of Language and Gender Hierarchy: Hardy's Bathsheba Everdene and His Vision of Feminine Reality Reconsidered' (*CVE* 41.59–79) discusses Hardy's creation of a female point-of-view in *Far from the Madding Crowd*. In addition to examining Hardy's treatment of sex roles in the novel, Elbarbary investigates the relationship between language and masculine discourse in the rhetoric of Hardy's narrative. Ailee Cho's 'Individuality of a "Relative Creature" ' (*JELL* 41.61–73) investigates the individualistic nature of Sue

Bridehead in *Jude the Obscure*, while Forest Ryle's 'Demands of History: Narrative Crisis in *Jude the Obscure*' (*NLH* 26.359–78) explores the roles of historical consciousness and community in the novel. In ' "Bees Up Flues" and "Chips in Porridge": Two Proverbial Sayings in Thomas Hardy's *The Return of the Native*' (*Proverbium* 12.315–22), J. B. Smith identifies Hardy's appropriation of proverbs in the narrative structure of *The Return of the Native*. Also of interest to Hardy scholars is Pamela Dalziel's 'Whose Mistress?: Thomas Hardy's Theatrical Collaboration' (*SB* 48.248–59), which explores the complex relationship between a 'printed ur-text, called *The Mistress of the Farm*' (249), and the dramatization of *Far from the Madding Crowd*. Dalziel draws attention to 'a complex revision process involving at least three hands, an intricately collaborative work with a far from automatic claim to inclusion in Hardy bibliographies' (259).

Bradford A. Booth and Ernest Mehew have assembled the final four volumes of the correspondence of Stevenson in *The Letters of Robert Louis Stevenson*, which detail the latter years of the novelist's life and work. In addition to underscoring the writer's tremendous impact upon Victorian letters, Booth and Mehew's edition traces Stevenson's existence from the 1880s through his death in 1894. Published with a spate of useful editorial matter, Booth and Mehew's landmark edition of the correspondence will provide students of Stevenson and of the late-Victorian period with an invaluable resource. In *Far-Fetched Facts: The Literature of Travel and the Idea of the South Seas*, Neil Rennie provides a history of travel literature from the classical era to early accounts of the New World and the South Seas. Using works by Montaigne, Bacon, Swift and Defoe, Rennie reads these texts in relation to fictional and nonfictional accounts by other travellers to the South Seas, including Melville and Stevenson, among others. Rennie devotes special attention to tracing the Western notion of the South Seas as it evolved from the lost paradise of Biblical and classical literature to the false paradise of modern-day tourism. In *Defoe in Edinburgh and Other Papers*, Paul H. Scott assembles a variety of essays that includes attention to Robert Louis Stevenson, among other figures. Scott highlights the cultural and historical interconnections between Scotland and its frequently obscured literary heritage. Scott also features essays on such subjects as the Scottish National Theatre, the Scottish National Galleries and Scottish broadcasting, among other topics. The work of Stevenson is also celebrated in Douglas Dunn's *Oxford Book of Scottish Short Stories*, a volume that includes some of the writer's short fiction. Students of Stevenson should note the publication of two editions of his work by EdinUP. Catherine Kerrigan's edition of *Weir of Hermiston* and Peter Hinchcliffe and Kerrigan's edition of Stevenson and Lloyd Osborne's *The Ebb-Tide: A Trio and a Quartette*. Both editions feature new introductions to Stevenson's works and a host of other useful ancillary matter. In 'Toward the Production of a Text: Time, Space, and *David Balfour*' (*SNNTS* 27.351–62), Barry Menikoff examines the prepublication history of Stevenson's novel. In addition to exploring the composition of Stevenson's work, Menikoff discusses the textual production and publication of the novel in 1893 by Cassell and Scribners, who published the novel in England as *Catriona*. Stephen D. Arata's 'The Sedulous Ape: Atavism, Professionalism, and Stevenson's *Jekyll and Hyde*' (*Criticism* 37.233–59) discusses the writer's treatment of atavism and professional issues in his landmark novel.

In *Visualization in Popular Fiction, 1860–1960*, Stuart Sillars investigates the significant yet often neglected tradition of English illustrated fiction in the nineteenth and twentieth centuries. Sillars provides close readings of a number of representative texts. Sillars draws upon Roland Barthes's theories of narratology in his analysis of the role of illustration in Edwardian fiction and magazines, as well as in later visual representations in comic strips and film. New editions of the works of William Alexander also mark the year's work in Victorian studies. Alexander's *My Uncle the Baillie* and *Johnny Gibb of Gushetneuk*, both edited by William Donaldson, provide readers with new introductions to the life and work of this neglected man of nineteenth-century letters. Students of George Egerton should note the publication of *Keynotes and Discords*, edited and introduced by Martha Vicinus, as part of Virago's Modern Classics series. Meredith is still largely neglected. In ' "The Cock of Lady Plume": Sexual Selection and *The Egoist*' (*NCF* 50.51–77), Jonathan Smith discusses the roles of natural selection and sexual attraction in George Meredith's work. Smith also traces the influence of Charles Darwin's *The Descent of Man* upon Meredith's creative aesthetic. Giselan Argyle's 'Meredith's "Readable Marriage": A Polyphony of Texts' (*ELWIU* 23.244–52) examines the role of the reader in the production of meaning in Meredith's last novel, *The Amazing Marriage*. Argyle demonstrates the ways in which Meredith integrates a variety of fictive sources from such works as *The Ordeal of Richard Feverel, One of Our Conquerors* and *Diana of the Crossways*. Argyle argues that Meredith's textual polyphony allows 'all the other texts to have their say, their great number and variety suggesting an open-ended process to which the reader can add' (252).

Richard Michael Kelly's *The Art of George du Maurier* provides readers with a richly illustrated and well-designed study that contains a detailed analysis of du Maurier's artistic and illustrative achievement. In addition to *Trilby* (1894), du Maurier illustrated innumerable works including novels by Henry James, Wilkie Collins, William Makepeace Thackeray and George Meredith. The volume contains an extensive essay on du Maurier's work, 'Illustrations from *Punch*', examples from his illustrations for the *Cornhill Magazine*, including his artwork for Elizabeth Gaskell's *Wives and Daughters* and his own *Trilby*. Kelly provides scholars with an important addition to the study of the Victorian novel. Oxford's Popular Fiction series offered a new edition of George du Maurier's *Trilby*, edited and introduced by Elaine Showalter. Showalter's edition features illustrations by the author, formerly a celebrated cartoonist for *Punch*. Oxford's Popular Fiction series also published Ouida's *Under Two Flags* (1867), edited with a new introduction by John Sutherland. The life and work of Ouida receives attention in Jane Jordan's 'Ouida: The Enigma of a Literary Identity' (*PULC* 57.75–105). Jordan addresses Ouida's role in the evolution of the sensation novel, while also discussing this much neglected writer's evolving place in academic study. Female practitioners of the sensation novel also receive attention in Randa Helfield's 'Poisonous Plots: Women Sensation Novelists and Murderesses of the Victorian Period' (*VR* 21.161–88). Helfield discusses the lives and works of such neglected Victorian writers as Madeleine Smith, Adelaide Bartlett and Mary Elizabeth Braddon, among others. Braddon's work also receives critical attention in Richard Nemesvari's 'Robert Audley's Secret: Male Homosocial Desire in *Lady Audley's Secret*' (*SNNTS* 27.515–28). Nemesvari surveys elements of homosexuality and forbidden desire in Braddon's novel, while also assessing their possible effects upon the novel's nineteenth-century audience. Nicola Thompson's ' "Virile" Creators versus "Twaddlers Tame and Soft": Gender and the Reception of Charles Reade's *It Is Never Too Late to Mend*' (*VIJ* 23.193–218) addresses the popular and critical reception of one of the Victorian era's most esteemed novels. Thompson argues that an understanding of the work of this often critically neglected figure provides scholars with a significant insight into the Victorian criteria for literary value and the place of gender in nineteenth-century culture.

Unlike Meredith or Reade studies, Gissing studies flower. *The Collected Letters of George Gissing, Volume 6: 1895–1897* and *Volume 7: 1897–1899* (eds. Paul F. Mattheisen, Arthur C. Young and Pierre Coustillas) offers scholars a vital research tool for understanding the final decade of Gissing's life. Using a diversity of sources, including newspapers, the author's memoirs, biographies and sales catalogues, the editors provide a valuable context for understanding this significant moment in the aesthetic shift between the Victorian age and the advent of modernism. Fully annotated, this important edition of Gissing's work should serve for years to come as a central resource to Gissing scholars and students of late Victorian culture. Of considerable interest in Volume 7 are Gissing's letters to Gabrielle Fleury, with whom he was passionately in love during these years. Again noteworthy is the extent and the breadth of annotation in these volumes, which contain very detailed introductions, as well as other miscellanea and corrigenda. Robert L. Selig's revised *George Gissing*, published in Twayne's English Authors series, provides readers with a guide to the wealth of Gissing materials currently available. In 'Realism, Sympathy, and Gissing's Fictions of Failure' (*VIJ* 23.27–50), Stephen D. Arata discusses the over-arching role of failure in Gissing's artistic mindset. In addition to arguing that Gissing viewed his works in terms of failure, Arata addresses Georg Lukacs's indictment of late-nineteenth-century fiction as an era of creative decay. Arata suggests that Gissing's 'fiction martyrs its gods without even the saving hope that such a sacrifice might become a ground for salvation and renewal' (43).

GissingJ (31) continues to provide students of the novelist with scholarship of the highest calibre. Bouwe Postmus's 'Mr. Harmsworth's Blue Pencil: "Simple Simon" Revisited' (1–9) traces the composition and publication of Gissing's short story, 'Simple Simon'. In addition to remarking upon the writer's relationship with his agent, William Morris Colles, Postmus discusses the themes of vegetarianism and hypocrisy that receive treatment in Gissing's satirical tale. Postmus reproduces the text of 'Simple Simon' at the conclusion of his article. John Simpson's 'T. W. Gissing and Algernon Gissing in the *QED*' (10–12) provides scholars with a listing of Gissing's various citations in the *Oxford English Dictionary*. In 'The Critical Response to Gissing in the *Chicago Tribune*' (12–24), Robert L. Selig and Pierre Coustillas survey the often unfavourable reviews of Gissing's novels in the *Tribune*. Selig and Coustillas partially reprint brief reviews of *Denzil Quarrier*, *Sleeping Fires* and *In the Year of Jubilee*, among other novels, in their article. Pierre Coustillas's 'The 1894 Booker Prize' (25–8) speculates upon the possible winners of the Booker Prize in 1894 had such an award existed. Coustillas assesses Gissing's chances of winning the prize on the strength of *In the Year of the Jubilee* against such literary luminaries as Kipling, Hope and Stevenson. A panel of contemporary judges ultimately chose George Moore's *Esther Waters* as winner of the mythical 1894 Booker Prize. In 'The Unclassed in *The Odd Women*' (1–15), Michael Cronin examines Gissing's novel as a document of late nineteenth-century life and the human condition. In addition to addressing the role of epiphanies in the work, Cronin discusses the fateful place of society as a force in Gissing's narrative. Cronin argues that Gissing's depictions of psychology and sexuality in *The Odd Women* provide his work with the trappings of modernity. Pierre Coustillas's 'An Uphill, Unrewarding Struggle: The Letters of Algernon Gissing to James B. Pinker' (15–34) investigates Algernon Gissing's acquaintance with Pinker and the difficulties experienced by Gissing's brother as he pursued a career in letters. Coustillas illustrates his essay with useful reproductions of their correspondence. Masahiko Yahata's 'Pathos and Patience: "The Light on the Tower" and "The Schoolmaster's Vision" ' (35–8) discusses the author's experiences while translating Gissing's short stories into Japanese. In addition to exploring the tremendous appeal of Gissing to Eastern readers, Yahata remarks upon the difficulties of translating Gissing's sense of pathos into the Japanese tongue. In 'You Have Not Dunne 'Til You Have Done: The Story of Gissing and B. B. Dunne' (31.1–18), Paul F. Mattheisen investigates the relationship between Gissing and Dunne, the popular New Mexico journalist of the early twentieth century. Emanuela Ettorre's ' "The Salt of the Earth" and the Ethics of Self-Denial' (31.19–30) comments upon the composition and publication of Gissing's short story. Bouwe Postmus's 'Clara Collet's Clairvoyance' (1–32) investigates the relationship between Gissing and Collet, one of the novelist's closest friends during the last years of his life. In 'Scattered Critical Responses to Gissing in Four Chicago Papers' (33–9), Robert L. Selig continues in his survey of the Chicago journalistic response to Gissing's novels. Selig reprints reviews of such Gissing novels as *The Odd Women*, *Denzil Quarrier*, *Veranilda* and *The Town Traveler*, among other works. In 'An Eerie Incident in Gissing's Life' (39–41), Pierre Coustillas discusses the tragic suicide of a German baron whom Gissing had encountered in February 1898. Coustillas elaborates upon the tremendous impact of the man's death upon Gissing, who, according to Coustillas's research, still felt the reverberations of the tragedy some 19 months later while visiting Switzerland in the company of Gabrielle Fleury.

In *The Thief of Reason: Oscar Wilde and Modern Ireland*, Richard Pine examines the life and work of Wilde in a predominantly Irish context. In addition to arguing that homosexuality and Irishness provide the writer with ways of thinking and seeing, Pine identifies Sheridan Le Fanu, Samuel Ferguson and Charles Maturin as significant influences upon Wilde's creative aesthetic. Pine's discussion of Wilde's work attributes the writer's enigmatic personality and deviance to his Irishness and his heritage of philosophy and criticism. Joy Melville's *Mother of Oscar: The Life of Jane Francesca Wilde* examines the life of Lady Wilde, the courageous and strong-minded mother of Oscar Wilde. In addition to discussing her marriage to surgeon, Dr William Wilde, Melville traces Lady Wilde's spirited defence of her husband in a libel case, as well as her fierce loyalty to her sons. Melville also devotes attention to Lady Wilde's early years, when she defied her family's pro-Union politics and wrote passionate tirades in verse and prose against the English domination of Ireland. Melville concludes her study with discussion of Lady Wilde's life in London with her famous son during the latter decades of the nineteenth century. The work of Bram Stoker receives attention in David Glover's ' "Our Enemy is not merely spiritual": Degeneration and Modernity in Bram Stoker's *Dracula*' (*VLC* 22.249–65). Glover argues that a number of boundaries are challenged in Stoker's novel, including the distance between male and female, animal and human, science and the occult and femininity and the 'New Woman', among others. Glover contends that such narrative distortions underscore the incipient modernity of *Dracula*. Pascale Krumm's 'Metamorphosis as Metaphor in Bram Stoker's *Dracula*' (88.5–11) examines the elements of transformation that undergird Stoker's narrative. In 'Fred Whishaw' (*ABM* 22.18–22), William H. P. Crewdson discusses the life and work of one of the most popular adventure writers of the 1890s. Well illustrated, Crewdson's article details Whishaw's phenomenal success as the author of such works as *The Romance of the Woods*, *Lost in African Jungles* and *Sons of Freedom*, among other novels. Crewdson concludes his essay with a useful 'Check-List of the First Editions of Fred Whishaw', which documents more than 70 volumes by the novelist.

Finally, W. J. Keith's *The Jefferies Canon: Notes on Essays Attributed to Richard Jefferies without Full Documentary Evidence* surveys the publication history of the more than 200 essays attributed to Jefferies in one instance or another since his death. In addition to confirming authorship for more than half of the writer's known publications, Keith's study provides students of Jefferies with a valuable research tool. Extensively cross-referenced, Keith's volume should assist readers in adequately addressing Jefferies's remarkable contributions to nineteenth-century literature and criticism. Donald Davie's *Essays in Dissent: Church, Chapel, and the Unitarian Conspiracy* collects his previously unpublished lectures on the Enlightenment era, as well as related pieces regarding such issues as literary figures as dissent and the life and work of Rudyard Kipling, among other subjects. Many of the selections were drawn from Davie's participation in the Clark Lectures (1976) and the Ward-Phillips Lectures (1980). Students of Kipling should note a selection of valuable essays in the *KJ* (69), including Bruce Shaw's 'The Wheel of Life versus the Great Game in Kipling's *Kim*' (12–21), which argues that Kipling's novel maintains a dramatic tension between two quests – the Great Game and the individual's search for enlightenment. In addition to observing that the search for enlightenment largely occurs in Tibetan Buddhist terms, Shaw explores the place of the Wheel of Life in Kipling's fictive world. Gillian Sheehan's 'Kipling and Medicine' (22–39) rehearses the novelist's encounters with the medical profession and the place of those experiences in his fictions. In 'Romance, the Sea, and the Open Road' (42–8), the late Fred Cherry comments upon the roles of romance and wanderlust in Kipling's aesthetic. 'The sense of romance [that] Kipling associated with the mystery, excitement, freedom, and lawlessness of life', Cherry writes, 'he transferred from India to the sea' (43). In addition to relegating attention to the writer's short stories in his study, Cherry addresses the senses of nostalgia and hope that pervade Kipling's narratives.

3. Poetry

If 1992 was 'the year of Tennyson', as the *YWES* reviewer proclaimed it, this year might well be the year of the anthology and the year of the woman in

Victorian literature and art. The year saw *Victorian Literature and the Victorian Visual Imagination* (ed. Carol T. Christ and John O. Jordan), an interdisciplinary collection of essays on literature and the visual arts. In it, Linda M. Shires's 'The Author as Spectacle and Commodity: Elizabeth Barrett Browning and Thomas Hardy' examines the ways authors in the hundred years between the publication of the first volume of poems by Elizabeth Barrett and the publication in the 1920s of Hardy's last volume of poetry sought to legitimize and commodify themselves as authors. Their attempt at authorial self-definition 'depended on being seen – seen at certain places, with certain people, and in particular outfits or poses'. The spotlight, Shires argues, shifted its focus from the essentialism of the poet's text to the material trappings of the author's life. Where earlier writers like Dickens and Tennyson 'couched self-dramatization in a rhetoric and stance of withdrawal', complicating self-identify, not so Carlyle and Wilde, who sought to make themselves, as well as their work, an active spectacle. Shires selects Barrett Browning and Hardy because she sees them concerned with consciously monitoring 'the performative nature of their careers' and experiencing 'alternating moments of attraction to spectacle and withdrawal from it'. In another essay, Miriam Bailin's 'Seeing Is Believing in *Enoch Arden*' argues that Tennyson privileges the visual ('things seen') over the auditory ('things heard'), setting up in the poem a rivalry between these two emotive experiences. But while the poem asserts the primacy of the visual over speech, the visual is often presented in the tradition of the Victorian picturesque, textual ornamentation, yielding precious little apprehension. *Enoch Arden* presents another, and more powerful, example of ekphrastic poetry, a rivalry or, better, an exchange between the bigamy of the visual and the verbal that structures many of Tennyson's 'idyllic miniatures'.

The year saw several valuable works on women, including an important anthology of *Victorian Women Poets* (ed. Angela Leighton and Margaret Reynolds) and a special autumn series of the *PULC* (57) devoted to British women authors and focusing on what might be called the crisis of identity, authorship and reception. While not all of these essays deal principally with Victorian poetry, they provide invaluable treatments of the cultural and literary milieu that help illuminate the poetry. Deirdre David's *Rule Britannia: Women, Empire and Victorian Writing* deals primarily with the Victorian novel, but instances places where some poems by Elizabeth Barrett Browning critique Empire and some by Tennyson (notably 'Maud', 'Locksley Hall' and 'The Palace of Art') decidedly Eurocentric, endorse British geopolitics and racialism. Deborah Epstein Nord's *Walking the Victorian Streets: Women, Representation, and the City* concerns itself with illegitimacy, played out in the profession of the Victorian street walker, women's sexuality and issues of disease, health, employment and the family. *Reclaiming Myths of Power: Women Writers and the Victorian Spiritual Crisis*, by Ruth Y. Jenkins, examines the ways Florence Nightingale, Charlotte Brontë, Gaskell and Eliot reclaim the image of women in the Judeo-Christian myth in order to 'depatriarchalize the language justifying their marginalization' within a patriarchal Victorian society. Of value to Victorian poetry is the way Jenkins's argument could be applied to such works as *Aurora Leigh* and 'Goblin Market', as well as challenging largely patriarchal poetic texts.

Important biographies of Elizabeth Barrett Browning and Christina Rossetti were also published, and Christine Alexander and Jane Sellars brought out *The Art of the Brontës*, filling an important literary gap in our consideration of this literary/artistic family. This is a rather substantial collection, with invaluable commentary, of the artistic production of all of the Brontës. The essays in the volume attempt to historicize their art and provide information on the artistic training (formal and informal) the Brontës received. This work contributes vastly to our understanding of the Brontës' art, novels and poetry. Not to be forgotten are the male poets of the period, with Tennyson and Hopkins garnering the most scholarly attention. This year Robert Langbaum published *Thomas Hardy in Our Time*; Helen Vendler's *The Breaking of Style: Hopkins, Heaney, Graham* and Eugene Hollahan's *Hopkins Against History* appeared. Mary Ellis Gibson's *Epic Reinvented: Ezra Pound and the Victorians* will be reviewed in *YWES* 77.

The Leighton anthology of women poets deals with poetry written from the 1820s to the 1920s, broadening our traditionally held understanding of the period to include a more 'ideological-aesthetic' temperament rather than mere historical periodization. Where possible, the anthology includes long poems to combat the prejudice long held that women poets either did not, or were unable to, write long works, contesting the specious claim that it takes balls to write epic. In addition to the more well-known poets in Elizabeth Barrett Browning and Christina Rossetti, the anthology includes the lesser known ones in L.E.L, Frances Kemble and the Brontë sisters, and re-acquaints us with Jane Wilde, Bessie Parkes and Michael Field, making this anthology a truly modern *Keepsake*. Such reclaimed voices lend a more comprehensive and, indeed, 'truthful' understanding of what is meant by Victorian.

The spring issue of *VP* (33) is devoted entirely to many of these rare voices. Edited by Linda K. Hughes, this special issue on 'Women Poets 1830–1894' evaluates ways of reading non-canonical poetry by women and attempts to situate the place of gender and women's poetry in a tradition still decidedly male. Kathleen Hickok's ' "Intimate Egoism": Reading and Evaluating Non-canonical Poetry by Women' (13–30) suggests that the way to approach non-canonical women's poetry is to read each new poem as though coming to it for the very first time, allowing its author a 'fair chance at an audience and a re-evaluation'. Using standard, first-order interpretive strategies, Hickok explicates four poems by Eliza Cook, Augusta Webster, Emily Pfeiffer and Louisa Bevington. These poems address such prevailing Victorian themes as the mother-daughter relationship, death, doubt and faith, science and equal education for women and women suffrage. Hickok warns readers of finding the texts they are looking for and at the same time to avoid an extremely politicized gendered approach, whereby the protest is rescued but the poem lost. ' "The fruitful feud of hers and his": Sameness, Difference, and Gender in Victorian Poetry' (149–68), by Dorothy Mermin, explores issues of a 'traditionally gendered system of poetic difference' central to Victorian women's poetry, and how these play out simultaneously in Victorian male poetry. One of the ways male as well as female poets do so is through the form of the dramatic monologue to 'counter and control the poetic objectification of women'. Characters in these male poetic texts, especially Tennyson's and Browning's, fight objectification and the structure of gender created by difference. Poets also contest the structures of gender difference by establishing an 'androgynous ideal', a hermaphroditic other, that co-opts and harmonizes both sexes as well as other ossified binary oppositions. In the case of much of Arnold's poetry, the goal is to escape the 'impasses of subjectivity', often through a loss or denial of sexuality.

On particular poets, Virginia Blain's 'Letitia Elizabeth Landon, Eliza Mary Hamilton, and the Genealogy of the Victorian Poetess' (VP 33.31–52) traces how the term 'poetess' in the work of Elizabeth Landon and Eliza Mary Hamilton assumes the connotation of moral reverence as well as ridicule in negotiating the larger question of accomplishment or fame. Heidi Johnson's ' "Matters That a Woman Rules": Marginalized Maternity in Jean Ingelow's A Story of Doom' (75–88) examines Ingelow's poem, 'A Story of Doom' (1867), which retells the story of Noah and Niloiya, insisting, as Mary Wollstonecraft had earlier argued, that in limiting women's full participation within culture and towards self-development, they are denied spiritual maturation and exercise of the Christian faith. Maternity to Ingelow, as Elizabeth Barrett Browning had theorized, is an inadequate source of spiritual potency. This imaginative and refreshing retelling of Milton reading Eve privileges Eve above Adam in the spiritual hierarchy, quite unlike the myth of the fallen woman that dominates Victorian literature. Still, like Wollstonecraft's, Ingelow's arguments for women suffrage, considering the times, are understandably muted.

Examining the obscure tradition of nineteenth-century closet drama, Susan Brown, in 'Determined Heroines: George Eliot, Augusta Webster, and Closet Drama by Victorian Women' (VP 33.89–109), looks to this lesser-known genre that blurs the lines between poetry and theatre. The texts of this genre – George Eliot's *Armgart* and Augusta Webster's *A Woman's Soul*, in particular – are 'indigenous precursors of *fin-de-siècle* and suffragist drama in England'. Both offer insights 'into a particular representational strategy explored by women poets for the representation of women', the politics of that agenda appearing largely social: domestic abuse, marital conflicts, the status of the fallen woman, disinheritance, suicide and the position of the female artist. Eliot's dramatic form, more so than her novels or lyric poems, 'is highlighted by importance of the diva as a figure for female achievement and emancipation'. Webster's closet drama, on the other hand, perhaps less ambivalent than Eliot's in deciding on its position within the feminist camp, served a similar purpose in exploring 'social questions in a form that did not lend itself to simplistic reduction'. In the end, closet dramas by Victorian women poets, says Brown, represent the middle-class woman as 'split subjects, divided against themselves in their conflicting desires and in the differences between their self-representations and the actions that are possible to them'. Unfortunately, Brown's essay does not show how these dramas relate to the relative inconspicuousness of the drama in the Victorian period and how that absence reflects, perhaps, Tennyson's epical lament that 'the good old times are dead'.

Two essays on Michael Field – Holly Laird's 'Contradictory Legacies: Michael Field and Feminist Restoration' (VP 33.111–28) and Yopie Prins's 'A Metaphorical Field: Katherine Bradley and Edith Cooper' (129–48) examine the diverse ways sexuality is played out in these two poets and what it means in the nineteenth century to write 'lesbian' or Sapphic. Laird examines this 'particularly unusual instance of ' "lesbian" co-authorship', donning a variety of masks so as not to 'enfeeble' creativity, concealing their (Bradley and Cooper) sexuality, and preserving their oneness against the prejudice of co-authorship. Bradley and Cooper saw themselves as more closely married than even the Brownings, arguing that the latter, in failing to quicken each other, failed to effect literary insemination. Yopi Prins finds in the love lyrics of *Long Ago* and in the poem 'Underneath the Bough' an attempt to contest legitimate ownership of the Sapphic signature through the transformation of Sappho's Lesbos into a lesbian topos. Travelling north of the English border, Florence S. Boos's 'Cauld Engle-Cheek: Working-Class Women Poets in Victorian Scotland' (53–74) finds in the works of Scottish women poets of the Victorian period – Jessie Russell, Ellen Johnston and Janet Thomson Hamilton – a poetry concerned with the problems of working-class women: problems with domestic violence, education, employment and living conditions. A number of non-proletarian women poets also sympathized with women's causes. Joanna Picken venerated the unmarried life, Agnes Stuart Mabon of Jedburgh supported labour unions and protested domestic abuse and Marion Bernstein criticized the unfairness of marriage laws to women.

Not included in this special issue of Victorian women poets, but important none the less to the period and culture, Margaret D. Stetz's ' "The mighty Mother cannot bring thee in" ': E. Nesbit in the Wilderness' (*VP* 33.221–32) examines the poetry of Edith Nesbit Bland (E. Nesbit), a late-Victorian poet who produced more than eight complete books of poetry. Admired by Swinburne and Symons, Nesbit was included in Alfred Miles's *Poets and Poetry of the Century* (1892) with the likes of Wilde, Hopkins, Kipling and Gosse. Her failure was an inability to mediate between her political narrative arguing reformation of the class system with her passionate desire for nature poetry, love lyrics and spiritual meditation. She could not find, so Stetz argues, a suitable model ('female forerunners') to assist her.

The autumn and winter issue of *VP* (33.iii–iv) is yet another special issue, devoted this time to the conjunction between word and image in Victorian literature and art. The volume is guest edited by Dianne Sachko Macleod, whose 'Intertextuality in Word and Image' (333–9) introduces the collection. Julie F. Codell's 'Painting Keats: Pre-Raphaelite Artists Between Social Transgressions and Painterly Conventions' (341–70) looks at the ways Keats's life and poetry influenced the PRB's attention to nature and employment of a symbolic and sensuous language 'to convey tensions between social demands represented by rich material settings and intense interior emotional states expressed through body language'. The paintings by Millais and Hunt become a major 'mid-Victorian construction of Keats'. Theirs is an attempt to capture in Keats the symbol that lies beyond mere iconography. 'Idylls of Real Life' (371–90), by Victoria C. Olsen, finds that Julia Cameron's photographic representation of scenes from Tennyson's *Idylls* 'complicates Victorian attempts to distinguish between the text and the image, the real and the ideal, the commodity and the art object'. Cameron believes that photography transcends mere verisimilitude, for it can capture external as well as internal states of beauty. Here, then, is the blending of the real and the ideal critics discover in Cameron's photographs, not the least of which are those based on Tennyson's *Idylls*. To declare her autonomy as artist and to present photography as its own authentic agency, Cameron uses Tennyson's signature for the poems and hers for the photographs. While Tennyson himself insisted on realistic representation of his poems, Cameron, wanting 'to free photography from its service to "realism" ' followed no such convention, an enterprise Tennyson in fact, rather surprisingly, applauded. Her photographs re-present in subtle but none the less recognizable ways the prevailing gendered roles and stereotypes of women in Victorian literature and art.

Included in the collection are Pamela Gerrish Nunn's 'Between Strong-Mindedness and Sentimentality: Women's Literary Painting' (*VP* 33.425–47), and Barbara Onslow's 'Deceiving Images, Revealing Images: The Portrait in Victorian Women's Writings' (*VP* 33.450–75). Nunn's essay, by its own admission, 'introduces women's literary painting as a rich but neglected area of Victorian art, and considers the use of literature in Victorian painting as a practice which the female artist shared with her male contemporary and in which she participated in ways both consistent with and distinct from her male contemporaries'. Nunn considers the ways these women artists, even in their very conscious policing of subjects, use art as 'a back door into the higher ranks of the genres'. She examines such famous pieces as Emma Sandys's *Viola*, Jane Bowkett's *Lucy Ashton at the Mermaidens' Fountain*, Emily Macirone's *Little Nelly showing the Monuments in Old Church*, Rebecca Solomon's *Behind the Curtain*, Sophie Anderson's *Elaine* and Sarah Setchell's *The Momentous Question*, perhaps the most popular early Victorian piece. These artists were convinced that literary painting would bring them more attention, notoriety and fame than portrait or landscape paintings. Tennyson and Dickens were especially fertile ground for such literary adaptations.

Onslow examines the different ways Victorian women novelists – Eliot, Oliphant, Gaskell, the Brontës and Mary Braddon, in particular – exploit 'the iconic value of portraiture' in their novels, often subverting its 'male meaning', whether to debunk posterity, sentimentality or male definitions of women's roles. Whether it was to emphasize truthfulness, the value of strength and inner rebellion, in which cases associations with Sappho and Cleopatra dominate, these novelists all attempt to re-inscribe the image of the woman in portraiture. 'Browning's Corpses' (391–401), by Carol T. Christ, looks at the nineteenth-century preoccupation with dead bodies (Tennyson's Lady, Hopkins's tall nun and the PRB's dead women) and especially at the way Browning 'frequently stages poems in the presence of a corpse'. This 'animation of corpses', Christ finds, 'is closely connected to his conception of the dramatic impulse and to the form of the dramatic monologue', a type of poetry that traffics in 'the habitation of corpses'. The poet's craft, unlike God's, is not generating new life, but 'resuscitation'; the poet is therefore 'the resurrectionist'.

A special autumn issue of the *PULC* (57.i) is devoted to what Patricia Marks has called 'Queen Victoria's Literary Ladies'. U. C. Knoepflmacher's 'Male Patronage and Female Authorship: The Case of John Ruskin and Jean Ingelow' (13–46) examines Ruskin's letters to Ingelow, finding in them a writer he admired and steadily patronized, however much Ingelow chose to remain within the 'calyx' of a domestic or familial sphere without transgressing the line Eliot, Gaskell and Barrett Browning, she felt, crossed. Ingelow, Knoepflmacher believes, became Ruskin's 'calming feminine *alter ego*'. He points to Ruskin's frequent citations of Ingelow's works, in particular 'Songs of Seven', his frequent meetings with her after 1867, and at least 13 letters to her, dating from 1867 to 1882, letters Knoepflmacher cites with extensive and valuable elucidation. Their literary relationship and personal friendship was one in which both writers profited equally, and their correspondence 'suggests an interaction that significantly differs from other instances of male Victorian patronage in its avoidance of a juggling for power'. Jane Gray's 'Dora Greenwell's Commonplace Book' (47–74) examines this miscellaneous text of 70 copied songs with words and music, illustrations and settings of poems dominated by Caroline Norton and Felicia Hemans. This portfolio is itself a narrative of Greenwell's social development, of a Tory who later switched political allegiance to support French and Spanish revolutionary adventurism. Both souvenir and scrapbook, Greenwell's commonplace book presents a quite gendered idea of artistic/musical performance – gender itself being performative – and explores the struggle in which women were engaged in an attempt to expand their intellectual space and attract an audience for their creative work.

'Ouida: The Enigma of a Literary Identity' (75–105), by Jane Jordan, examines the neglected Victorian novelist Marie Louise Rame. Important to readers of Victorian poetry are the prevailing gender, marital and social issues Ouida engages. Her novels, says Jordan, 'explore with candor the abused wife's "unlawful" action of denying her husband his conjugal rights, in the face of opposition from powerful male relatives, representatives of ecclesiastical and parliamentary authority'. Ouida's familiarity with nineteenth-century journals and journalists provide some startling links to familiar Victorians. Linda M. Shires's 'Glass House Visionary: Julia Margaret Cameron Among the Writers' analyses Cameron's paintings, familiar portraits of notable Victorians and her role in establishing the intellectual circle centred on the Isle of Wight. Although known for her stunning portraits of famous Victorians, notably Tennyson and Carlyle, her friendship with Thackeray's daughters and care of them after his death, Cameron, great-aunt of Virginia Woolf, is perhaps best remembered for her illustrations of Tennyson's *Idylls of the King and Other Poems*, illustrations 'important for studying the relationship among Victorian art forms', and important too in catching dynamic moments in which poetic details are 'subsumed to expression through pose and face'.

In 'Kate Greenaway's Critical and Commercial Reception' (*PULC* 57.126–46), Anne Lundin examines the wide circulation and broad appeal of Greenaway's *Under the Window: Pictures and Rhymes for Children*, attractive to Victorian children and adults alike. This work was pivotal in opening the commercial market and a new audience for children's books. Greenaway collaborated on a number of projects with the famous colourpainter Edmund Evans, whose entrepreneurial skills helped to popularize woodengravings, illustrations, children's books and juvenile literature. Reviewers applauded her 15 or so productions of almanacs, gift books and nursery rhymes, and saw in Greenaway an author who knew children and the child in adults. 'Telling Her Story: British Women of Letters of the Victorian Era' (147–62), by Peggy Meyer Sherry, is the narrative catalogue of Princeton's first exhibition of its impressive holdings in Victorian literature. It includes selections from Queen Victoria's mostly burned diary, Frances Milton Trollope's (mother to the novelist) important travelogue, *Domestic Manners of the Americans* (1832), works by three generations of Victorian women novelists, the women poets (Norton, Barrett Browning, Rossetti, Ingelow, Greenwell, Mathilde Blind, Amy Levy, Michael Field and Edith Cooper), children's authors and illustrations of children's books, and such non-literary feminists as Frances Cobbes, Emily Davies, Josephine Butler and Millicent Fawcett.

The poetry of Matthew Arnold went almost unnoticed but for William Baker's slight 'Matthew Arnold and The Eastern Question: An Unpublished Letter to George Howard' (*N&Q* 42.197–8). In this letter, Howard solicits sympathy for the Turks through an 'Eastern Question Association'. Arnold called the Turks 'odious', but declined involvement in any public demonstration, citing the need not to have his literary career hampered by political constraints. Elizabeth Barrett Browning, in contrast, attracted a great deal of attention. An edition of her poems was published: a useful Penguin edition of *Aurora Leigh and Other Poems* (ed. John Bolton and Julia Holloway), which includes 'The Cry of the Children', 'The Runaway Slave at Pilgrim's Point' and selections from *Prometheus Bound*. Marjorie Stone's fascinating biography, *Elizabeth Barrett Browning*, feminist in approach, seeks to reclaim Elizabeth Barrett Browning as a major poet of her day based on the remains of her works and her impact on other writers. Yet, as Stone shows, Barrett Browning has all but disappeared from mainstream Victorianism, because 'intersecting ideologies of gender and genre, sometimes compounded by the artificial barriers of historical periodization', have conspired to obscure or conceal Barrett Browning's poetical achievement in a range of poetical or literary models'. Based on the years leading up to her 1844 *Poems*, Stone presents Barrett Browning not as the legend or a vegetable (the familiar crypt analogy) awaiting discovery and invigoration by a man, an Isabella, a Mariana or a Porphyria, but as a first rate poet 'empowered by a matrix of other women writers', fighting ill health, and struggling to discover her poetic voice. To many contemporaries, 1844 *Poems* showed Barrett as a legitimate rival to Tennyson. Yet this 'Fugitive Angel' or dauntless black slave was 'erased, and replaced by the woman chiefly known as one man's daughter and another man's wife'. Stone culls an array of biographical evidence to show that, prior to her marriage, Elizabeth Barrett was every bit the poet and Victorian sage.

Chapter 2, 'Romantic Revisionism', examines the ambitious poetical works of Barrett Browning between 1820 and 1844, finding in them the Romantic influence of Wordsworth, Keats, Shelley and 'above all Byron'. But Barrett's version of Romanticism is as much masculine (manifesting revolutionary energy, power, the sublime) as it is feminine (concerned with treating female subjectivity and domesticity). Chapter 3 examines Barrett Browning's place in the ballad tradition, employing it only 'to circumvent the ideologies of passionless purity and self-sacrifice confining middle-class Victorian women'. She gives the Romantic ballad form a 'distinctively gynocentric focus', recognizing 'the sterility of the chivalric ideal of womanhood'. 'Juno's Cream' situates *Aurora Leigh* within the tradition of Romantic/Victorian sage discourse heretofore granted exclusively to male writers, notably Newman, Carlyle and Ruskin. *Aurora Leigh* enters into the sage tradition through 'its representation of a prophetic speaker, its pronounced Biblical allusions and typological patterning, its polemical sermonizing ... and its vision of a new social and spiritual order'. The final chapter of the biography, which would have presented a more convincing argument for Barrett Browning's centrality had it come earlier in Stone's commendable study, examines the critical reception of Barrett Browning's work between her death in 1861 and the second wave of feminism. The chapter identifies a number of 'broad cultural transformations' exclusive of gender (the Classical preferred to the Romantic, art for art's sake preferred to a social or political ['hysterical'] agenda, and the supplanting of Barrett Browning by Christina Rossetti) that 'contributed to the drastic decline in Barrett Browning's reputation within fifty years of her death'. In the 1930s, 1940s, and 1950s when the Victorian literary tradition was being formulated, *Aurora Leigh* could not be conceived by misogynistic constructivists as 'a work of transformative gynocentric sage discourse'. Invoking, only to revise, Bloom's revisionary taxonomies in her effort to reclaim Barrett Browning as a powerful presence in the great Victorian literary tradition, and bringing together a wide selection of reviews, Stone shows convincingly that the real erasure of Barrett Browning as a major poet was gender related, an end-of-the-century hostility to 'Women's Powers' in literature.

Only a handful of essays were published on Barrett Browning. Responding to earlier editors who did not recognize the reference to Camoes' 'minor poems' in a letter from Richard Home, George Monteiro's 'Camoes' "Minor Poems": A Reference in a Letter to Elizabeth Barrett Browning' (*N&Q* 42.189) identifies the 'minor poems', as opposed to his epic poem, *Os Lusíadas*, as a volume of his *lírica* which Barrett Browning read in English translation. Sharon Smudders, in 'Sincere Doubt, Doubtful Sincerity, and Sonnets from the Portuguese 37' (*ANQ* 8.iv.18–23), examines how Barrett Browning, in ways characteristically different from Spenser and Shakespeare, uses conceits of shipwreck and rescue to destabilize the conventional structure of the Petrarchan sonnet and to discover the reliability of sincerity and love in the problematic and shifting domain of doubt. In 'Elizabeth Barrett Browning and the Wordsworthian Sublime' (*EIC* 45.i.36–56), John Woolford sees Barrett Browning concerned with the Romantic idea of the 'double' and the 'sublime', peculiarly of a Wordsworthian kind. Barrett Browning appears principally interested in 'cross-gender doubling more often, as in *Aurora Leigh*, with the subject female and its male double. In the case of the sublime, imagined most often as male, Barrett Browning, Woolford notices, invokes it self-consciously in 'thought': to 'force the mind to view the mind', forcing, that is, the subject into submission – imagined forcible as penetration or rape. Fearing such invasion, she became attracted in the late 1830s to Wordsworth, whom she felt afforded 'a more hospitable model for a woman writer'. She even envisioned herself in the more safe domain as his child.

Michael Bright's *Robert Browning's Rondures Brave* examines the frequency with which Browning's poems end the way they begin, forming a circular or rondure pattern and affecting, as Bright simplistically concludes, 'a finished poem'. Ending a poem the way it begins does not, as Barbara Hernnstein Smith has convincingly argued, logically effect satisfactory closure, whether ideological, emotional or structural. More valuable to the circular conclusion is its function in re-establishing dramatically and thematically the poem's controlling idea. Bright illustrates the repetitive structure that dominates Browning's poetry, a structure meaningfully repetitive in the middle portions of poems. Bright sees Browning's poems following four patterns: the perfect round, in which a stated theme at the opening is developed in the middle portion of the essay and then restated in the conclusion; the less than perfect round, more spirical than circular, in which poems state the central idea at the opening, modify it, then conclude with a statement of the advanced idea; the even more dynamic group of poems, 'diametrical oppositions', which drastically alters the introductory idea, and concludes with an antithetical statement; and, finally, the most dramatic group of poems that achieves a double turn, the first altering the opening idea and the second restating or re-establishing it.

Browning saw sparse treatment in the journals. In one of two *Expl* articles, Nathan Cervo's 'Browning's "Bishop Bloughman's Apology"' (53.ii.87–9) believes that Browning assigns the name Sylvester to the Bishop because Saint Sylvester's Night in Italy is the same as New Year's Eve. In this Janus image, Browning, whose Sylvester is a portrait of Cardinal Wiseman, intends for England to look back to its Roman Catholic past and forward to a brighter future. Michael DiMassa's 'Browning's Christmas Eve lines 560–2' (53.iv.201– 4) associates Browning's ambivalent use of the hive image to the Dome of St Peter's and 'swarm to communicants'. In 'Personality in Robert Browning's Dramatic Monologues' (*EA* 48.ii.140–7), Earl G. Ingersoll explores readers' attraction to the personalities in Browning's 'My Last Duchess' and 'Fra Lippo Lippi' in spite of the serious moral problems with the characters in these monologues.

This year saw the publication of Robert Langbaum's *Thomas Hardy in Our Time*. Langbaum's goal, admittedly minimalist, is to present Hardy as an important precursor of modernism. His point is to 'see how far Hardy can be considered minor in a non-pejorative sense, since many minor poets (Hopkins an obvious example) have become classics'. To do so, Langbaum looks to Hardy's imagism, poetic development and the degree of his innovativeness. The dominant Victorian influence on Hardy is Browning (the dramatic monologue, love poems and elegiac poems for Emma), with lesser influence in Swinburne, especially his atheism, metre, novel ideas about sexuality and 'imagery of oblivion'. Langbaum's other chapters consider George Eliot's influence on Hardy, Hardy's influence on Lawrence, issues of sexuality and eroticism, and the various genres – pastoral, antipastoral, the near tragic, tragic, the dark comedic – represented in the novels. In these, as Langbaum shows, we find more than traces of the romantic influence of Wordsworth.

Attention to Hardy this year was mostly focused on the novels. Of the few essays on the poetry, Kerry McSweeney's 'Hardy's *Poems of 1912–13*: A Presence More than the Actual' (*VP* 33.191–220) situates these later poems in the context of Hardy having found two manuscripts among the personal effects of his dead wife. 'What I Think of My Husband' and 'Some Recollections' ('diabolic diaries', one critic has called them) give Emma's side of the relationship, with its hatred and abuse. Her literary remains transport Hardy nostalgically back to Atlantic Cornwall where the two met, courted and were married. 'The poetic expression of Hardy's inner life in the months between Emma's death and his return to Cornwall in March 1913', McSweeney writes, is detectable 'in his elegiac sequence, *Poems of 1912–13*'; some, like the poems 'The Going' and 'Your Last Drive', elegize Emma and admit Hardy's cruel treatment of her. Helped by Tennyson's *In Memoriam*, McSweeney reads these elegiac/love (necromantic) poems through Emma's writings and voice. Hardy has conjured her up for him to confess, to reminisce and to receive direction, as though she were 'an Unseen Power of great benevolence [that] directs my ways'. But such 'fond imaginings', as McSweeney calls Hardy's attempts to confront the fact of Emma's absence, 'can hardly have provided more than momentary consolation for the grieving poet'. Still, 'the creative achievement of *Poems of 1912–13* is, of itself, more than any single positive moment recorded in it, the principal recompense for the sudden loss that so undid the poet'. For all of her presumed unsociableness and gaudiness, Emma remains a 'woman much missed'.

In that same issue of the *VP* (33.295–8), Norman Vance's 'Hardy's "The Darkling Thrush"' and G. F. Watts's *Hope*' connects Hardy's wintry landscape 'Like strings of broken lyres' and the desired hope in the poem to Watts's painting *Hope* (1886). Watts's painting depicts a blindfolded maiden clutching a damaged lyre with broken strings etched against a dreary sky. Hardy knew Watts personally and was quite familiar with his paintings. Another essay on overt borrowings, 'Le Miroir Perdu: The Lady of Shalott de Tennyson et The Trumpet-Major de Thomas Hardy aux fils du texts' (*CahiersE* 42.55 66), by Pierre Subils, shows the intertextual reliance of Hardy's 'The Trumpet-Major and Robert His Brother' (1880) on the prominent romantic myth in the figure of Tennyson's Lady of Shalott. J. H. Stape's 'Thomas Hardy: An Uncollected Letter' (*N&Q* 42.204) reveals a letter omitted in Millgate's *The Collected Letters*. The letter from Hardy to Charles Longman, editor of *Longman's Magazine*, concerns publishing details of Hardy's essay on 'The Dorsetshire Labourer' requested by the magazine. Finally, Roy Neil Graves examines the bawdy sexual language used to describe the mating of ship and iceberg in 'The Convergence of the Twain' (*Expl* 53.ii.96–9).

Of the poets, Hopkins received the most attention this year. The year, however, revealed only one book-length publication on Hopkins. Eugene Hollahan's *Hopkins Against History* is founded on the thesis that Hopkins resists 'bordering'. An 'ontological prosodist' pursuing essences (inscapes), Hopkins, Hollahan argues, evades 'both the nightmare of history and certain ideological distortions of Victorian historiography'. Hopkins's accentual versification intended to challenge or counter the 'constraints of historical time' in order to 'body forth his own version of historical time'. Hollahan attempts to historicize Hopkins according to his own view of history, a view standing in antithetical relation to the Victorian period. In 'The Windhover', for instance, Hollahan pursues an 'Ariadne's thread' in Hopkins's dialectical exchanges with Henry Thomas Buckle and his popular multi-disciplinary *History of Civilization* (1857–1861) that establishes a tradition for lyrical assortments. 'The Windhover', says Hollahan, 'constitutes a critique of Buckle as embodying a liberal or skeptical Victorian consciousness'. Hopkins mentions Henry Wadsworth Longfellow only in his critique of some of Patmore's pieces, but that infrequency does not deter Hollahan from arguing that Hopkins's *The Wreck of the Deutschland* is an antithetical ('distress') reworking of Longfellow's 'The Wreck of the Hesperus', a copy of which the Hopkins family owned. Hollahan also discovers an 'abstruse' association between Hopkins's falcon and a sonnet on a falcon by the thirteenth-century Giacomo da Lentino with ties to a treatise on falconry by his sonneteering master, Frederick II, 'a historiographer against whom Hopkins would react'. As 'a means of escaping or erasing history', Hopkins also turned to music. Four interchapters survey the poems from Norman Mackenzie's Oxford edition (*YWES* 71.427) finding in most of them a decided avoidance of the terms 'crisis' and 'history'. While it does invoke Bloomian theories of anxiety, Hollahan's is more a study in confluence than influence. Literary borrowings, or so the theorists tell us, are most profound the more subtle, inconspicuous and unconscious they are. In becoming culturally diffusive, embedded, they become all the more pervasive. The speculative nature of Hollahan's assumptions unsettles those of us fettered to air-tight historical connections. Intriguing and tendentious as Hollahan's claims are, the study certainly challenges us to explore other and more remarkable ways of looking at Hopkins.

Still on the subject of influence, John Kerrigan's 'Writing Numbers: Keats, Hopkins and the History of Chance', from Nicholas Roe's *Keats and History*, looks to Keats and Hopkins as numbering authors, regularly employing numbers, and not just in the classical sense of metrical patterning, in their works. '[C]ompetent in and fascinated by the art of numbers', Hopkins, so Kerrigan argues, was obsessed with numerical patterns, a penchant (derived in part from his father and reflecting the atomism of the age) evident in Hopkins's journal entries, Mariolatry and in poems such as *The Wreck of the Deutschland*. Kerrigan also explores Hopkins venturing into statistics and its connection to free will, chance and divine sovereignty.

This year brought together a crop of essays on Hopkins. Four essays on Hopkins appeared in the French journal *QWERTY*, which will be reviewed in *YWES* 77. In 'Music Alone Survives: Collapsing Faith in Some Sonnets of G. M. Hopkins and Geoffrey Hill' (*CVE* 42.91–107), Christine Pagnoulle believes that Hill shares with Hopkins, whose verse affected in some way 'all twentieth-century poets', a 'passionate involvement in a spiritual quest'. Hill's sonnets, particularly the ones in *Tenebrae* (1978), Pagnoulle believes, owe a great deal to Hopkins, especially 'The Windhover', where, admittedly 'going against the grain of most Hopkins criticism', Pagnoulle finds an undermining of the very faith the poem seeks to proclaim – a faith torn, wavering and collapsing. In this same volume, Jacky Martin's 'Writing the Presence: Hopkins's "Spelt from the [sic] Sibyl's Leaves" as Mantic Pronouncement' (109–27) believes that in this poem Hopkins attempted to use words ('a specific type of diction') to get beyond the inadequacy of human discourse in order to explain or experience 'the numinous presence of the Divine'. One would have liked Martin to probe how the Divine numinous in the creation is handled in a poem like 'Sibyl's Leaves', clearly in the Victorian apocalyptic tradition. 'Heraclitean Fire' answers man's fate in the apocalypse, but not so clear is the future of nature in 'Spelt from Sibyl's Leaves'.

Hopkins's links to Newman, to the waning influence of the Oxford Movement, and to a Tractarian aesthetic continue to appeal to critics. Joseph J. Feeney, in 'My dearest Father: Some Unpublished Letters of Gerard Manley Hopkins' (*TLS* 4838.13–14) reveals four previously unpublished letters of Hopkins written between 1882 and 1888. Three of these letters are to fellow Jesuits who had written to congratulate Hopkins on taking his Final Vows, one of which, the letter of Revd Francis Goldie, concerns Hopkins's sonnet, 'In Honour of St Alphonsus Roderiguez'. The letter to Newman was written on 20 February 1888 at University College, Dublin, and sent to commemorate Newman's birthday (his eighty-eighth on 21 February), a practice Hopkins had consistently maintained for two decades. In the letter, Hopkins laments the condition of this Catholic university (which Newman founded) in the face of inadequate funding and divisive Irish politics. Rene Gallet's 'Hopkins et Newman' (*Etudes Newmaniennes* 11.201–17) will be reviewed in *YWES* 77, as will be Helen Vendler's *The Breaking of Style: Hopkins Heaney, Graham*. In 'Another Link Between Hopkins and Newman' *HQ* 22.43–50), Tom Zaniello considers Sister Maria Pia of the Visitation Order and sister-in-law of Hopkins's favourite Aunt Maria (his first drawing teacher) an intimate friend of Newman. Zaniello's goal is to recognize Hopkins's obscure familial ties to the Gibernes and Sievekings. He considers Sister Pia, also a talented artist and scholar in science and theology, a 'significant' Roman Catholic model for Hopkins's later conversion. Maria was a figure of great interest to Newman and his agnostic brother Francis, an interest approximating sexual attraction, or at least 'an unusual kind of triangle ... that could never be resolved'. Maria refused Frank's several marriage proposals, perhaps because of her demonstrable affection for John, her involvement in his literary work and Tractarian agenda and her financial and personal support for him during the Achilli scandal. Another friendship is explored in 'Spooner in America' (*N&Q* 42.196–7), in which Sjaak Zonneveld sketches a relationship between Hopkins and William Archibald Spooner, who advocated relief of the poor coming first from their family and then from private charities or the Poor Law.

In 'Hopkins and Job' (*VP* 33.283–93), James Finn Cotter finds in *The Wreck of the Deutschland* and the Hopkins's sonnets of desolation 'a number of phrases and lines that appear to allude, consciously and unconsciously, to the text of Job and to reflect Jobean imagery' (snowstorm, breakers, winnowing, harvesting, pottery) and themes (evil, suffering, terror, mortality, patience). These allusion and themes are absent in the poems of Hopkins's mid-career. The Jobean presence are efforts by Hopkins to find God's superintendence of a world seemingly beset by evil and suffering. 'For the Jesuit poet, God's answer to Job', says Cotter, 'was to become Job', for 'only in the Word made flesh' – the Incarnation – 'has the problem of pain been answered'. In a not all that novel connection, John Le Vay associates the Andromeda-Perseus story in Hopkins's 'Andromeda' to the Church and Christ (*Expl* 53.iii.156–8). Showing that the arrow of influence also points the other way, John Wareham, in his treatment of John Clare's 'The Awthorn' (*Expl* 53.iv.197–200), recognizes in Clare's aesthetic treatment of the hawthorn a 'particularity' that 'achieves an inscape of almost Hopkinsian precision'. Clare's nature landscape, like that in so many Hopkins poems, is also barbarous and unspoiled by humans. Francis L. Fennell's 'Familiar Hopkins: The Popular Use of His Poetry' (*HQ* 22.i–ii.31–41) illustrates the 'social' Hopkins, the Hopkins whose poetry extends beyond the academy to the larger society through the use of 'proof-texting' at once enriching and alchemic.

Aesthetic issues, negotiated in a variety of ways, continue to be the greatest concern to Hopkins critics. Maureen F. Moran's 'Manl(e)y Mortal Beauty: Hopkins as Tractarian Aesthete' (*HQ*.22.i–ii.3–29) focuses on Hopkins's attraction to physical beauty, especially male, a 'complex relation' that manifests ties to Hopkins's 'aesthetic and cultural milieu'. Although drawing from Jude V. Nixon's arguments for Hopkins's 'aesthetics of renunciation' (*Gerard Manley Hopkins and His Contemporaries* [1994]), Moran believes that such readings fall short of recognizing Hopkins's attempt to synthesize the binary aesthetic oppositions between physical beauty of the Hellenic variety proclaimed by Pater and Arnold and spiritual beauty of the Hebraic quality that aesthetic Tractarians like Newman and Keble pursued. The tradition in which this reconciling of beauty (the physical and the spiritual) falls is definitively

Tractarian, an aesthetic that also emphasizes absence and indirection. Moran's argument, however, fails to distinguish the temporariness Hopkins accords physical beauty from the permanence (the 'animated' instants) a Paterean aesthetic pursues. In ' "There lives the dearest freshness deep down things": Articulating the Distinctions Between Man and the Things of Nature' (*HQ* 22.iii–iv.53–77), Rebecca Boggs explores several of Hopkins's nature poems to insist on a volition present in humans but absent in nature, a volition that must be mastered by God if complete selfhood (a transformed self) is to be achieved. Ultimately, Hopkins's aesthetic, according to Boggs, is one founded in the natural world and not in the world of the human.

In that same issue of the *HQ* (79–87), Troy L. Thibodeaux's 'The Resistance of the Word: Hopkins's "(Carrion Comfort)" ' discovers tension, ambiguity, if not a fissure, between the Word and the verbal struggle to discover it, as between Hopkins's vocation as a priest and avocation as a poet. In much the same vein, George M. Johnson's ' "The Caged Skylark": A Psychobiographical Portrait of G. M. Hopkins' (*Biography* 18.ii.134–57) probes the depression, his 'world within' (of a bi-polar or manic-depressive kind) plaguing Hopkins throughout his life, and the ways poetry allowed him to manage those 'fits of sadness' by making him more aware of their existence and condition. Because Hopkins's dark sonnets are so personal, Johnson believes, we can find in them covert indicators of the poet's 'extremity of mind'. As plausible as some of this might be, the evidence is just not there to support Johnson's claims, hence the tendency on the part of Hopkins's biographers, Robert Martin and Norman White, otherwise open to an unapologetic examination of Hopkins, to remain cautious of such psychobiographical readings. While one could easily grant the 'stressors' in Hopkins's life and especially his periods of severe depression marked by despair, extreme guilt and intense feelings of unworthiness, it is another thing altogether to read 'The Caged Skylark' as a poem about Hopkins's moodswings. Still, Johnson's study raises a number of profound questions about Hopkins's mental state and poetic inception.

In 'Hopkins and the Pushed Peach' (*CritQ* 37.iii.43–60), Peter Swaab is convinced that 'Hopkins's culture and temperament', to say little of his familiarity with the homosexual apologists of his day, 'brought him to a self-conscious understanding of homosexual attraction ... constrained and contained' by his religious vocation. Swaab uses Hopkins's poem/fragment 'Dents', 'The Bugler's First Communion', the shipwreck elegies, and 'Epithalamion' to argue that Hopkins's Jesuit vocation 'may actually have worked to enable and not to repress the sensual forthrightness of his poetry'. Although granting a great deal to Hopkins's attraction to physical and especially manly beauty, Swaab believes that Hopkins's excessively sensuous and rapturous apprehension of the 'juice' and 'joy' of the season of spring finds its real fulfilment in its creator.

Housman, Patmore, Dante Gabriel Rossetti and Swinburne received scant attention in this year. In fact, the only Housman essay, Graham Nelson's 'Philip Larkin's "Love Again" and Auden's "A. E. Housman" ' (*N&Q* 42.219–20), is not even about Housman but about Auden's Housman. Nelson traces the Larkin line 'Something to do with violence' to Auden's 'Something to do with violence and the poor', a borrowing that might have to do with both poets' 'horror of inevitable lust'. Robert M. Polhemus's 'John Millais's Children: Faith and Erotics: The Woodman's Daughter', in *Victorian Literature and the Victorian Visual Imagination* (eds. Carol T. Christ and John O. Jordan), examines representations of children in the Pre-Raphaelite painter John Everett Millais. Patmore's 'The Woodman's Daughter' became the subject of Millais's own *The Woodman's Daughter* (1851) and inspired Edward Burne-Jones's famous *King Cophetua and the Beggar Maid* (1884). Patmore's most lightning-rod subject, his view of the Victorian woman as domestic and angel ('As long as they keep quiet by the fire / ... their angelic reach / Of virtue, chiefly used to sit and darn', as Aurora Leigh describes her), continues to draw much criticism. The relative silence on Patmore, however, should end with a forthcoming *VP* special issue commemorating the hundredth anniversary of Patmore's death. Whether this attention would be enough to revive interest in Patmore remains to be seen.

The single essay on Dante Gabriel Rossetti, Tirthankar Bose's 'The Blessed Damozel' (*Expl* 53.iii.151–2) finds yet a third voice supposedly distinct from the poet's and damozel's in the fourth stanza of the poem. There appears a distinct difference between the strong, assertive voice of the poet and the less-assured voice of the earthbound lover. The third voice is that of the omniscient poet-narrator whose very existence is a product (an alter ego) of Rossetti's earthbound lover, the controlling male consciousness in the poem. Rikky Rooksby's 'Swinburne's Revision of the "Prelude" to *Tristam of Lyonesse*' (*N&Q* 42.200–1) identifies the changes in the 'Prelude' between the 1871 and 1882 versions, a rare device for Swinburne who seldom emendates already published poems. The changes reflect greater sharpness of images, precision and conciseness.

Christina Rossetti received a fair amount of attention this year. The most significant is the publication of Jan Marsh's monumental biography, *Christina Rossetti: A Writer's Life*. Only six years ago, Katherine J. Mayberry's *Christina Rossetti and the Poetry of Discovery* (*YWES* 70.449) examined the poetry, trying not to be swayed unduly by the historical or biographical, the flaw, Mayberry claims, of so much critical work on Rossetti. Marsh's study, it seems to me, uses precisely the approach that Mayberry frowned upon, but her study avoids diminishing, obtruding or misreading either the life or the poetry. Marsh's splendid rendition of Rossetti's life as a writer, combining both the biographical and literary, reads more like the delightfully sublime fiction of a Joyce's *Portrait* or a Carlyle's *Sartor* than the dry, chronological, 'factual' stuff that we have come to expect from conventional biographical narrative. Invoking these two classics, the biography charts the life of a precocious young girl, whose bout of teenage melancholia and nervous breakdown, perhaps religiously or sexually (abuse) induced, manifested itself in sudden eruptions. The themes and images in Rossetti's writings are informed significantly by Puseyism and the Anglo-Catholicism of the Oxford Movement.

Part 2 covers the decade from 1850 to 1860, a time marked by Rossetti's poetic denouncement of worldly gains. A disappointed and heartbroken Rossetti sought refuge in poetry and religion, depression never far off. Her broken engagement (the second such) with James Collinson is reflected in her poems, especially *Maude*, the St Elizabeth of Hungary poems, and her manuscript book, *A Dirge*. The period also saw Rossetti taking up drawing lessons and the end of her formal connection with the Pre-Raphaelite Brotherhood, though not without invoking their memories in *The Lost Titian*. Her parting with the PRB and the demise of the *Germ* gave rise to new acquaint-ances, this time to a community of women (Sara Coleridge and Letitia Scott, among others). Their magazine, *The Bouquet from Marylebone Gardens*, created for Rossetti the persona of Calta, in the tradition of Lamb's Elia, whose satirical wit and prose opened a new channel for Rossetti's creative energies. Poems repudiating worldly desires ('commonly glossed as the desire for esteem') continued none the less. The period also saw poems depicting male demonization of women, at odds with the support from men Rossetti had historically received; however, as Marsh explains, Rossetti 'could hardly fail to mark the disparity between the sexes'. She also nerved herself to submit poems to *Blackwood's* and *Fraser's*, meeting with rejection from both organs. Part 2 concludes with Rossetti's work as a volunteer at St Mary Magdalene Penitentiary in Highgate, a recovery home for young prostitutes and the inspiration for her masterpiece 'Goblin Market'. This poem about temptation, resistance, fall and redemption also answers Pope's *The Rape of the Lock*.

Part 3, from 1861 to 1870, witnessed the growth of Rossetti's career and reputation, with 'Up-hill' and other pieces in the newly launched *Macmillan's Magazine*. It also saw the selection of pieces for her first volume of poetry, *Goblin Market and Other Poems* (1861). The period is marked by Rossetti's visit to France and, more important to her, Italy. While she still felt foreign in England, Italy was also 'strange, and not my mother'. Rossetti would again approach relationships, this time with Swinburne and Charles Cayley, declin-ing an offer of marriage from the latter. This period ended with Rossetti turning to a new genre in children's stories and nursery rhymes, including trying her hand at social commentary in the novella *Commonplace*. The final part of Marsh's biography covers the years 1871 to 1894, beginning with the deterioration of Rossetti's health and an illness difficult to diagnose. There was, however, only a slight decrease in her creative energies. No single theme emerged dominant during these last years, but for devotional writings. She also culled into one 'fattish' volume a new collection of *Goblin Market, the Prince's Progress and Other Poems* (1875), along with a third and final major collection, *Later Life and Other Poems* (1881). Rossetti refused to go quietly into that good night, protesting to the very end British imperialism and supporting a bill decrying the plight of youthful harlots. A career that began with 'Goblin Market' ended with the strongest of arguments for the protection and rights of women.

There were only a few essays on Rossetti. 'The Poetic Context of Christina Rossetti's "After Death" ' (*ES* 76.ii.143–55), by Catherine Maxwell, uses Rossetti's youthful sonnet to illustrate the poem's rich associations with Tennyson's and Millais's 'Mariana' and Browning's 'Porphyria's Lover'. More enriching is the poem's use of confessional tropes in the tradition of the dramatic monologue and its delighting in 'screening and disclosure, in suggest-ing cryptic and encrypted narrative detail'. While she relies on male precursors, Rossetti, Maxwell finds, adapts their scripts 'for her own pur-poses'. In a way, the voice in 'After Death', decidedly Rossetti's, is that not of 'a ghost, nor a phantom of the former self, but a purged or essentialised version of it'. Similarly, Joseph Bristow's ' "No Friend Like a Sister"?: Christina Rossetti's Female Kin' (*VP* 33.257–81) examines the importance of sisterhood to Rossetti, however much the concept to her is not entirely the ideal forum in which 'women's dependence might be realized'. Accepting as she has routinely done the reality, perhaps even the authority, of a male ecclesiastical priesthood makes ambivalent Rossetti's stance on women's suffrage. Still, she indicates that women's inability to break free from their own antagonisms derive from male centres of power. Even with reading 'Goblin Market' alongside her brother's poem 'Jenny', Christina Rossetti is convinced of the possibility of 'same-sex desire' between women. The person and image of Sappho feature prominently in Rossetti. Her catalogue of poems on sisterhood reveals that 'sisterhood rests on an enduring contradiction'. Ultimately, in Rossetti there is no friend like a sister, but there is potentially no enemy like one too.

Tennyson continues to attract much critical attention, but the year saw no single book-length study on him. Two essays appeared in *Sense and Transcendence: Essays in Honour of Herman Servotte* (ed. Ortwin de Graef). Joseph Sendry's '*In Memoriam* as Apocalypse' illustrates Tennyson's knowledge of the Bible and frequent use of apocalyptic allusions in structuring *In Memoriam*, most of them built around the third Christmas celebration. 'Besides heralding a new age', Sendry notices, 'the third Christmas is notable for its refusal to celebrate the traditional feast in the traditional way ... Hallam is transformed into a figure of social, ultimately cosmic, importance ... bringing order out of chaos'. Thus, the Hallam in CXXVII who smiles on universal disaster is a 'happy star'. Ortwin de Graef's 'Saint Sign: Tennyson on the Poet-Prophetic Condition' examines the evolutionary shift from Tennyson's 'Armageddon' to 'Timbuctoo', a shift from Hebrew prophet to Romantic poet marked by the suppression of the 'prophetic appeal' to 'divine inspiration' that ultimately gives way to 'the subjective power of the imagination'. De Graef also shows how Tennyson's 'St Lawrence' is the perfect affirmation of Christian faith. But Tennyson soon 'swerve[s] from this received figure of Christian fortitude' in composing a poem on the infamous Simeon of the Pillar, 'St. Simeon Stylites'. Again, as in the shift from 'Armageddon' to 'Timbuctoo', the shift is from the suggestively Christian orthodox to the Romantic insane, a gamble that shows Tennyson spending his 'creative energy on the poetical intricacies of volition, freedom, and determination'. All of his ironies, contradictions, hypocrisies, self-aggrandizement, saintliness and grace, tied up as they are in the image and person of Simeon, come together to define Tennyson's view of himself as poet in a postprophetic age. I was unable to review Marion Shaw's 'Elizabeth Gaskell, Tennyson and the Fatal Return: Sylvia's Lovers and Enoch Arden' (*GSJ* 9.43–54), as well as Robert Welsh's 'The Poet-Philosopher Confronts His Shadow: Tennyson's "Lucretius" ' (*JEP* 16.i–ii.121–33).

Shuli Barzilai's 'The Politics of Quotation in *To the Lighthouse*: Mrs. Woolf Resites Mr. Tennyson and Mr. Cowper' (*L&P* 41.iii.22–43) examines why, biographically and socioculturally, Mr Ramsay quotes from Tennyson's 'The Charge of the Light Brigade'. Barzilai assumes that 'a poetics of quotation ... also entails a politics of quotation'. Mr Ramsay, he contends, relies on Tennyson 'to indulge his own phantasies', finding the poem food to satiate his own aesthetic pleasures. Equally at work is Woolf's use of the poem to satirize both Mr Ramsay and Tennyson, citing but only to subvert the poem and with it British/Victorian heroism. Though supportive of Britain and salutary of its obedient troops, Tennyson was not altogether blind to his nation's blunders. In 'Descriptions of Darkness: Control and Self-Control in Tennyson's

Princess' (*VP* 33.233–55), Katherine Frank and Steve Dillon explore in the poem those 'feminine spaces' imagined by men as 'areas of darkness'. One of those dark areas is the way the narrative attempts to control women by defining them, establishing in so doing a tension or conflict in the poem with the desire by women to use language to describe themselves.

Finally, three essays on Tennyson appeared in the journal *CVE* (42). Ortwin de Graef's 'Laus Stupiditatis/Radical Overkill: Tennyson's Politics of Poetic Licence' (15–39) seeks to explore the complex poetics and to problematize the politics evident in Tennyson's writing, a 'purposively non-radical poetical politics' at once supportive of Britain's monarch and individual human freedom, and a politics tending often towards Enlightenment ideals and democratization. 'It is in response to this inner split that Tennyson's political poetry takes its particular shape'. William J. Gracie's 'Tennyson and His Queens: Guinevere, Mary, Victoria' (41–53) examines Tennyson's poems on historical/mythic British queens, believing that these poems reveal Tennyson's attitude towards the monarchy. That view is characteristically equivocal and shifting, charting the monarchy's fading light, noting problems with succession, but lamenting none the less public neglect of the monarch and investing it (the image of Victoria especially) with much symbolic value. G. John Stott, in 'The Horns of Elfland and the Inadequacy of Love' (67–74), finds Tennyson's Elfland as a place entirely 'other', 'an emblem of something transcending everyday reality'. That something, to Tennyson as well as to other Victorians (like Arnold), is nuptial bliss and the domestic sphere, both of them alternatives to nineteenth-century religious scepticism and doubt.

4. Victorian Drama and Theatre

This year has seen a welcome increase in the number of play texts easily available to illustrate the wealth of dramatic writing in the period. OUP's World Classics have released four volumes: Michael Booth's edition of *The Lights o' London and Other Victorian Plays*, Peter Raby's collection of Wilde plays *The Importance of Being Earnest and Other Plays*, a volume dedicated to the works of Pinero, *Trelawny of the 'Wells' and Other Plays* (ed. J. S. Bratton), and Peter Hollindale's edition of Barrie's plays *Peter Pan and Other Plays*. Although the Barrie volume falls outside the Victorian period, the plays do demonstrate one Victorian's attempt to fuse its values with a new and at times revolutionary perspective on playwriting. The Booth volume is a timely replacement for his earlier OUP paperback edition of *The Magistrate and Other Nineteenth-century Plays*, now long out of print. The present selection of plays reflects the spectrum of melodramatic taste from Fitzball's early *The Inchcape Bell* (1828) to Henry Arthur Jones's *The Middleman* (1889) as well as providing a glimpse of Victorian humour in Stirling Coyne's farce *Did You Ever Send Your Wife to Camberwell?* (1846) and G. H. Lewes's sardonic comedy about Victorian materialism, *The Game of Speculation* (1851). Perhaps the most exciting find of the collection is G. R. Sims's *The Lights o' London* (1881) which has never existed in any printed form and which was an astounding triumph for the actor Wilson Barrett. It is indeed a 'classic' of Victorian melodrama and deserves the accolades customarily bestowed on Jones's *The Silver King*. Pinero's reputation has been revived by recent productions of three of the four plays in Bratton's collection: *The Magistrate*, *The Second Mrs. Tanqueray* and *Trelawny of the 'Wells'* (one of the last stage performances of Sir Michael Hordern). *The Schoolmistress* on the other hand is less well known and Bratton has done us a real service in bringing it once more to our attention. It is a play in which young, resourceful people are central to the action and is likely therefore to appeal to young contemporary performers and theatre companies. It is as well a model of late Victorian farce. Perhaps one might have wished for the inclusion of a play like *The Profligate* or *The Benefit of the Doubt* or Pinero's subversive *The Freaks* written after World War I to illustrate Bratton's contention that Pinero's 'contribution to European theatre has yet to be fully recognized and measured' (xvii), but these will serve as an introduction to those not familiar with his work. Although none of James Barrie's Victorian plays: *Walker, London, The Professor's Love Story* or *The Little Minister* are represented in Hollindale's edition, he makes a convincing case for a re-evaluation of Barrie's place in the period 1902–20 with a selection from *The Admirable Crichton* (1902) to *Mary Rose* (1920). They show an idiosyncratic and often lonely Victorian exploring a world of fantasy which to him was far more actual than the often harsh reality which he lived through. The edition also illustrates Barrie's enigmatic and ambiguous personality. There have been recent editions of Wilde's plays but this one brings them together accessibly and usefully throws in *Salomé* as well. Raby's introduction is perhaps a little perfunctory. It would have been useful for example to have had more contextualization of the plays within late Victorian theatre: its forms and values especially those of Gilbertian burlesque. Indeed, this lack of context can also be felt in Hollindale's introduction to Barrie which focuses too narrowly on textual variants and critical constructions. Some sense of context, however, is provided by Raby's article ' "The Persons of the Play": some reflections on Wilde's choice of names in *The Importance of Being Earnest*' (*NCT* 23.i–ii. 67–75). Wilde had a particular ear for the resonance of names and Raby offers a further gloss on this sensitivity which enabled Wilde to lend social authority to his characters and to invite audiences to measure 'the fictional/factual tension' (68) implied by the names themselves. There has always been a magic about naming and Wilde's care about his 'persons' reflects both his Celtic belief in the efficacy and suggestiveness of names as well as his highly crafted awareness of their satirical potential.

There is nothing perfunctory about Joseph Donohue's extraordinary edition of *The Importance of Being Earnest* which he has edited (with the assistance of Ruth Berggren) and whose format he has as well designed. The book appears under the aegis of the Princess Grace Irish Library and its text is intended to approximate as closely as possible to that of the original production by George Alexander in 1895. This is the product of an exhaustive recension of available typescripts and printed editions as well as promptbooks. The edition also chronicles Alexander's intervention in reducing the original four act version to three, the changes in the text which accompanied this and the further emendations required for the play's later revivals in 1901–2. The edition is accompanied by detailed notes ranging from the very useful placing of clubs like the Albany or restaurants like Willis's within the cultural topography of West End London (accompanied by photographs and street maps) to the rather otiose detail of the exact meaning of an 'afternoon tea', and the difference between a 'sofa' and a 'couch'. There is also a wealth of detail ranging from studio production shots to the design of the original dresses and what a man about town might have seen at the Empire in 1895. This is obviously a labour of love which has occupied Donohue for nearly 30 years and shows his affection for the play and its context admirably. It is, however, an awkward book. Not only does its format (a 'landscape' printed A4 page) make it impossible to house on a library shelf but its absorption in the play's textual variants makes the occasion of the 'first production' curiously remote and difficult to place as a resource despite the plethora of visual and aetiological information. It may illustrate Society Drama but appears to offer little to assist a contemporary reader in an understanding of Wilde's perennial popularity.

In considering the late Victorian dramatic world of Pinero and Wilde or to provide a further comparison with the comedy of Lewes it is difficult to omit reference to the influence of T. W. Robertson, the playwright credited with the revival of English drama in the 1860s and who possessed the meticulous eye for the details of stage composition to which both Gilbert and Pinero were indebted. Daniel Barrett is a Robertsonian enthusiast and his book *T. W. Robertson and the Prince of Wales's Theatre* seeks to present a balanced account of Robertson's achievements whose reputation has oscillated between uncritical praise in his lifetime to equally uncritical disparagement in the twentieth century. In so doing he believes that by placing Robertson within the context of London's stage conditions in the 1860s the plays can better 'be seen as both product of and challenge to the theatrical, social, and political norms of the day' (2). Unfortunately, it is this aspect which is the least successful in a book which really does compel one to re-examine Robertson's plays on their own merits. Barrett's view of London theatre is geographically limited to the West End and his discussion of plays against which those of Robertson might be measured is confined to those of Tom Taylor with a glance at Dion Boucicault. Barrett's view of theatre audiences is also a myopic one which repeats the judgements both of contemporary middle class critics and those who have accepted these judgements as definitive. Thus contemporary audiences are described as 'intellectually flaccid' and 'indifferent to what they saw on stage' (8) in order to demonstrate the quantum leap performed by Robertson and the Bancroft management of the Prince of Wales's theatre in attracting an engaged and alert new audience. It is a particularly uncritical judgement. On the other hand, Barrett clearly positions Robertson at the crossroads, susceptible to the new influences of French plays and their performers, sympathetic to those English actors like the Wigans and Fanny Stirling who were seeking to demonstrate an awareness on stage of the existence of an actual world uncluttered by the accretions of stage convention, and looking for an opportunity to challenge conventionalized expectations with 'fresh character drawing' (25). Barrett shows the trajectory from Robertson's early success with *David Garrick* to his acknowledged masterpiece *Caste*. Indeed, his chapters on *Society* and *Caste* are particularly good. After the success of *Caste* Robertson's achievements seem to lessen and even the popular *School* was clouded by Robertson's own embarrassing deception about its origins. Despite Barrett's enthusiasm and his attempts to illustrate Robertson's unflagging inventiveness in either his later plays like *M. P.*, *Birth* and *War* or in his plays for managements other than at the Prince of Wales's, the argument is unconvincing. Robertson remains uniquely a man of his own time, fortunate to have a company at his disposal to realize some of his ambitions for the theatre but also constrained by their demands for a constant succession of vehicles which would highlight their abilities. Outside that company, Robertson's efforts were almost uniformly unsuccessful which inevitably begs the question about the exact nature of the Bancroft contribution to his reputation. About this aspect Barrett is disappointingly terse.

There is continuing interest in the roles played by women in Victorian society and women's understanding of the negotiations which they were required to perform to sustain a sense of personal integrity. That they were required to 'perform roles' is noted in Angela John's biography *Elizabeth Robins: Staging a Life 1862–1952*. The subtitle addresses a key element in any evaluation of a figure closely identified with Ibsen in the Victorian period and the women's suffrage movement in the Edwardian period as well as one who was a professional journalist, a friend of many of the leading artists and politicians from the 1880s to the 1940s, a successful novelist and author of the key dramatic suffrage play *Votes for Women* and withal a woman who consciously obscured her 'real' self by interposing a series of constructions between herself and those around her. Robins was a secretive person who embodied shifting personae throughout her life and staged these for her audience. Because she camouflaged herself and re-fashioned herself continuously, Robins invites evaluation through a strategy of biographical bricolage. Although Angela John avoids this post-modern approach, she does take into account the multiplicity of selfhood staged by Robins by structuring her biography as a series of 'stages' which acknowledge both Robins's innate theatricality as well as the staging posts in a long career which, though connected to each other on her journey through life, form discrete entities or facets in themselves.

Robins's connection with Victorian theatre commences as she assumes her first identity, that of 'Bessie Robins' which occupies the period from her birth in Louisville, Kentucky in 1862 to her arrival in England via Norway in 1888. Overcoming the parental disapproval of her intellectual father at her intention to become an actress, a dreaming girl 'full of romance and checked ambitions' (23), she left her Ohio home for New York and began her career with James O'Neill's Company in 1881. Touring in small parts and understudying she was exposed to the vicissitudes and frustrations of performers and especially male attitudes towards actresses. She met and married George Parks, an actor in the Boston Museum Company in 1885. Insecure, not especially talented, and incapable of managing the financial setbacks of touring, Parks committed suicide in 1886. This action was to affect Robins profoundly and she would investigate the nature of suicide and the right of individuals to take their own lives in a book which she would publish in 1898. In 1887 Robins went on her last American tour with Lawrence Barrett and Edwin Booth and, after returning to New York, went with Sara Bull the widow of 'the noted Norwegian violinist and nationalist Olé Bull' (45) to Norway, arriving finally in London in September 1888.

The second Robins identity is that of 'Lisa of the Blue Eyes' a sobriquet which emanated from her performance as the heroine in *The Sixth Commandment*, a version by Robert Buchanan of *Crime and Punishment*. It marks her theatrical identity in the period to 1902 when she gave her last professional performance. Robins's debut in London in 1889 was hardly an auspicious one and she already saw the need to develop her abilities as a journalist and fiction writer to supplement her stage income. Her exposure to Ibsen at a production of *A Doll's House* was decisive and influenced her to develop her awakening interest in Ibsen. She met William Archer and decided to go into joint management with fellow-American Marion Lea in a production of *Hedda Gabler* which opened in April 1891. By 1902 her involvement with Ibsen would include *John Gabriel Borkman, Little Eyolf* and *The Master Builder.* 'The experience of acting and producing Ibsen's plays and the reactions to her work helped to transform Elizabeth over time into a committed supporter of women's rights' (62). The experience would also help to formulate her support for 'the theatre of the future' by starting the New Century Theatre with Archer, Sutro and H. W. Massingham and proselytizing for Archer and Granville Barker's idea of a National Theatre. Beneath the mask of the successful performer, however, lay the ambiguous and often secretive world of Robins's relations with William Heinemann, Henry James, Beerbohm Tree and, pre-eminently, William Archer. He together with Florence Bell would provide the most influential friendships which Robins would treasure until their deaths in 1924 and 1930 respectively. With Archer she collaborated in Ibsen translations and he stood as a sounding board for her ideas and her writing. With Bell she shared her commitment to theatre and writing which found expression in their collaborative play *Alan's Wife* performed in 1893. But the Bells were opposed to the other great preoccupation of women's suffrage with which Robins became increasingly involved.

The third persona which overlaps the second is that of 'C. E. Raimond' under whose pseudonym Robins wrote *George Mandeville's Husband* (1894), her first published novel. John suggests that, in part, Robins's aim in her fiction was to replicate what Ibsen had done for drama. Her real purpose was, however more utilitarian: 'The prime motivation was economic' (102). Starting off as a need to supplement her theatrical earnings, writing became her committed profession which she would practise for the remainder of her life. Although she continued to try her hand at dramatic writing, it was her fiction – novels and short stories – which gained her recognition despite her insistence on the secrecy of her identity. They also provided a focus for her increasing commitment to feminism and her infuriation with the 'presumptions of the privileged' (115) which deeply permeates her writing.

'Elizabeth Robins', the fourth part of the biography suggests the emergence of an authentic voice. It is her voice in support of the women's suffrage movement in the Edwardian period which produced her best known novel *The Convert* and her influential play *Votes for Women* (1907) which she began writing in 1906 and was first performed during the last Court Theatre season under the Barker-Vedrenne management. The last part of John's biography 'From E. R. to Anonymous' implies a retreat into relative obscurity as age, illness and the deaths of her greatest friends all took their toll. Nevertheless, Robins continued her active interest not only in politics in the period 1918 to World War II but also in the theatre, following the career of Sybil Thorndike with particular affection. For all that, Robins began her retreat into a world of shadows where she was ultimately more comfortable.

Fanny Kemble, another icon of nineteenth-century feminism, is investigated in Alison Booth's 'From Miranda to Prospero: the works of Fanny

Kemble' (*VS* 38.227–54). Her long life from performer under her father's shadow to independent writer is recounted in terms of Kemble's lifelong admiration for Shakespeare's *The Tempest*. Throughout her career she, like Robins, 'staged' herself both to validate her actions to herself and in her voluminous writings, her self-conscious engagements with the social conflicts which faced her and her audiences in the theatre and as readers. Repeatedly she refers to these struggles through the metaphor of the play in her 'quest of a European woman for power' (228). In doing so she became a unique figure – a nineteenth-century woman writing her own life. But the life she recounts, as Booth suggests, is not necessarily a transparent one. Kemble 'artfully exploited, in her own life and writings, her talent for being "so many people"' (249) and retained to the end her performer's awareness of the power of suggestion and role-playing.

Both Robins and Kemble wound up on stage providentially as much as by design, the one to assert her independence, the other by accident of birth and familial connections. Both found themselves confronted by the gendered expectations of middle-class domesticity as well as the moral pigeon-holing of female performers. Equally, both were determined to exert their own ungendered individuality. In Lauren Chattman's 'Actresses at home and on stage: spectacular domesticity and the Victorian theatrical novel' (*Novel* 28.i.[1994].72–86) the binary opposition is shown at work in two theatrical novels, Geraldine Jewsbury's *The Half Sisters* and Wilkie Collins's *No Name*. Both engage with the ambiguities of 'staging' the feminine and the tensions inherent in female self-effacement on the one hand and self-display polarizing domestic norms of behaviour and the stage's demand for personal exposure. From a theatre historian's perspective, Jewsbury's is the more interesting although from a feminist one the thesis of *No Name* in which 'the combination of domestic self-effacement and theatrical self-display [which] not only supports but also threatens to subvert a middle-class ideology of gender' (85) may offer a more rewarding discourse.

Susan Brown's discussion 'Determined heroines: George Eliot, Augusta Webster, and closet drama by Victorian women' (*VP* 33.89–109) centres on two instances of plays which were published but remained unproduced: Eliot's *Armgart* (1871) and Webster's *A Woman Sold* (1882). Brown suggests convincingly that they offer considerable 'insight into a particular representational strategy exploited by women poets for the representation of women' (90). Both plays offer explorations of women at odds with their social contexts and especially the 'sexual script of marriage' (97). The dramatic form unmediated by performance seems to have liberated female writers to the extent that it allowed a direct voice or voices to be heard especially as they articulated the constraints imposed by the social contexts in which their protagonists found themselves. Brown differentiates such plays from the 'mental theatre' of the Romantics by their insistence on 'the relation between the self and the social world' (105).

Beerbohm Tree has always been enigmatic from a critical point of view. As a person he was warm, generous, feckless and with a scintillating sense of humour. His matinee seasons exposed new plays ranging from Ibsen to Grand Guignol and he would have been responsible for changing the direction of actor training in England by bringing Stanislavsky and the Moscow Art Theatre to London had not World War I happened. At the same time, critics constantly undervalued his Shakespearean productions, viewing them as the last vestige of Victorian upholstered staging methods inherited from Charles Kean. Brian Pearson reminds us that Tree was particularly sensitive to Shakespeare's visual imagery and describes his responsiveness to the aural and visual textures of *The Tempest* ('Beerbohm Tree's production of *The Tempest*, 1904', *NTQ* 44.xi.299–308). The dark potential of the play as realized by Tree certainly impressed critics like Wilson Knight and Pearson argues that we should place Tree's experimentation within a tradition of Shakespearean interpretation which starts with Gordon Craig and reaches down to Brook, Strehler and Peter Stein. It is a timely and profitable reminder.

In some respects, James Cassius Williamson can be regarded as the Australian version of Beerbohm Tree. Veronica Kelly's 'J. C. Williamson produces *Parsifal, or, the redemption of Kundry*: Wagnerism, religion and sexuality' (*TS* 15.161–81) describes the attempt by the astute theatre manager to capitalize on both the controversies surrounding Wagnerian mysticism and the prevailing international fascination with what David Mayer calls 'toga drama' identified principally with Wilson Barrett's *Sign of the Cross* and *Claudian*. Though the production took place in the Edwardian era its context is the late Victorian preoccupation with muscular Christianity. As well, as the sub-title of Kelly's article shows, the production sought 'to reconcile sexuality with godliness' (163) as the many photographs of Minna Tittel Brun in the role of Kundry attest. The production was immensely successful and invited comparisons with the Roman productions of Beerbohm Tree in its spectacular authenticity. It also stirred up a considerable religious debate especially since the play, written by an Anglican minister, featured a version of the Victorian 'fallen woman' who 'triumphs in a salvational temperance drama' (177).

Dale Kramer's essay 'Reviews of tragedies in the nineteenth-century *Blackwood's*' (*VPR* 28.ii.95–108) is predominantly concerned with the reviews not of actual performances but rather of publications of tragedies by authors like Arnold, Swinburne and William Morris. These reviews are moreover confined to those by Elizabeth Hassell and Margaret Oliphant who appear to have dominated the debate about tragedy, its Greek precedents and the search for dramatic models in *Blackwood's* from the 1860s to the 1890s. Much of the discussion seems to have centred around the significance of self-sacrifice and 'higher moral standards' within a nineteenth-century context and to this extent shows the pervasive influence of domestic values. Kramer believes that Oliphant was responsible for institutionalizing 'domestic tragedy' as a descriptive term.

The only essay relevant to the Victorian period in J. Ellen Gainor's compilation *Imperialism and Theatre: Essays on World Theatre, Drama and Performance* is Michael Hays's 'Representing empire: class, culture and the popular theatre in the nineteenth century'. The springboard for this discussion is Edward Said's analysis of colonial and imperialist moments in nineteenth-century literature which Hays relates to the specific moment of the production of Charles Reade's *It's Never Too Late to Mend* (1865) and what that reveals about cultural difference. On the one hand, melodrama chronicles internal social conflict and difference which forms 'part of the advent of the imperial metropolis' (135) while on the other, Hays appears to be seeking an engaged drama which should have promoted the 'development of an alternative critical analysis' (144) but lamentably did not and thus conspired to aid notions of national superiority and imperialism.

Dagmar Kift, however, argues that music hall was indeed a site of subversion and in her article 'The Unspeakable Events at the Glasgow music halls, 1875' (*NTQ* 43.xi.225–9) she focuses on a particular moment of confrontation in Glasgow between the forces of moral conservatism exemplified by John Burns, the principal of the Cunard Shipping Company, and the leisure habits of young white collar workers who attended music halls. Characteristically, the opposition concentrated on the demoralizing effects of scantily dressed female dancers upon young males who ought to be responsive to middle-class socialization. In the event, on this occasion there seemed to be little which could justifiably be done. The music hall was far too potent a force to brook moral interference even in a society where the kirk's power was a pervasive one. The article is part of Kift's ongoing interest in the social composition of music hall audiences and the opposition of moral activists to the nature of the entertainments being offered to the predominantly working-class and lower-middle-class patrons who supported the music hall in the period to the 1890s.

Elaine Hadley's contention that a melodramatic mode informs various manifestations of individual and collective resistance to dominant hegemonies is extensively explored in *Melodramatic Tactics: Theatricalized Dissent in the English Marketplace 1800–1885*. She defines this mode as 'familial narratives of dispersal and reunion, its emphatically visual renderings of bodily torture and criminal conduct, its atmospheric menace and providential plotting, its expressions of highly charged emotion and its tendency to personify ... good and evil'(3). She distances her historicist approach from Peter Brook's location of melodrama 'within the psyche of the individual' and applies her understanding of the melodramatic mode to an analysis of not only stage texts but to opposition to the New Poor Law of 1834, *Oliver Twist*, the writings of Caroline Norton, the speeches of Josephine Butler and George Meredith's novel *Diana of the Crossways*. For our purposes the relevant chapters occupy the early part of the book. Hadley's argument is that all facets of individual and social interaction were affected by the element of theatricality; indeed, that individual identity was a product of performance 'reinforced by theatricalized public exchanges of deferential feelings'. The nineteenth century inherited the hierarchic patterns of eighteenth-century social interaction and found them increasingly irrelevant. Melodrama preserved many of these values.

Hadley investigates the Old Price Riots at Covent Garden in 1809 somewhat differently from Marc Baer (*YWES* 73.470–1) who viewed them as providing an arena for political manoeuvring. Her analysis cogently demonstrates the appropriation of the auditorium as a site for spectacle and theatrical engagement in nineteenth-century theatre. In so doing she documents the ways in which melodramatic values inform the behaviour of the audiences relating the 'us and them', the patrician and proletarian oppositions manifest in the stridency of the O. P. rioters to the elitist strategies of Kemble and others. So far so good. Hadley's insistence on relating these elements of the theatre to the broader canvas of public and political theatricalization does indeed demonstrate the pervasiveness of ritualized behaviour more suitable perhaps to a socially cohesive eighteenth-century context and increasingly at odds with the fragmentation of nineteenth-century models of social and private behaviour. The difficulty lies in her insistence on equating such behaviour with 'melodrama', descriptions of which appear to be reductionist and simplistic. Moreover, many of her excursions into theatre history let alone her understanding of the state of theatrical scholarship are literary-based and outdated despite her familiarity with contemporary critical discourses which she brings to bear in support of her arguments. Melodrama is not, however, as simple-minded as she makes it out to be, nor is it an unchanging paradigm which can be imposed on all instances of nineteenth-century resistance. Hadley slides between melodrama and the melodramatic with journalistic imprecision. It is an imprecision which detracts from an otherwise thought-provoking study of the nature of the nineteenth-century 'gaze'. With the wisdom of hindsight it would have been better to retain the sub-title: the book would have retained its accuracy and precision. Patricia Dee Berry's *Theatrical London* and Terence M. Freeman's *Dramatic Representations of British Soldiers and Sailors 1660–1800* also appeared this year and contained material relevant to this section. Ellen Donkin's *Getting Into the Act: Women Playwrights in London 1776–1829* is reviewed in chapter XI above.

Books Reviewed

Adams, James Eli. *Dandies and Desert Saints: Styles of Victorian Masculinity*. CornUP. pp. 249. $39.95. ISBN 0 8014 3017 8.

Alderson, Brian. *Charles Kingsley. The Water Babies*. OUP. pp. xxxvi + 230. £4.99. ISBN 0 19 282238 1.

Alexander, Christine, ed. *Branwell's Blackwood's Magazine: The Glass Town Magazine*. Juvenilia. pp. xiv + 45. $7. ISBN 0 9698 2711 3.

——, ed. *Charlotte Brontë. High Life in Verdopolis: A Story from the Glass Town Saga*. British Library. pp. xxiii + 103. £12.95. ISBN 0 7123 0408 8.

——, and Jane Sellars, eds. *The Art of the Brontës*. CUP. pp. 484. hb $79.95. ISBN 0 521 43248 0.

Baker, William, ed. *The Letters of George Henry Lewes*. 2 vols. ELS. pp. 295 (vol. 1) + 280 (vol. 2). $32.50 (Canadian). ISBN 0 920604 80 3 (vol. 1), ISBN 0 920604 82 X (vol. 2).

Barrett, Daniel. *T. W. Robertson and the Prince of Wales's Theatre*. American University Studies, series XXVI, vol. 23. Lang. pp. xviii + 279. $49.95. ISBN 0 8204 2369 6.

Batchelor, John, ed. *The Art of Literary Biography*. Clarendon. pp. xii + 289. $29.95. ISBN 0 1981 8289 9.

Berry, Patricia Dee. *Theatrical London*. Sutton. pp. 158. pb £7.99. ISBN 0 7509 0942 0.

Blum, Virginia L. *Hide and Seek: The Child between Psychoanalysis and Fiction*. UIllP. pp. 299. $17.95. ISBN 0 252 06458 5.

Blunt, Alison. *Travel, Gender and Imperialism: Mary Kingsley and West Africa*. Guilford (1994). pp. 190. pb £16.99. ISBN 0 898 62546 7.

Bolton, John, and Julia Holloway, eds. *Elizabeth Barrett Browning: Aurora Leigh and Other Poems*. Penguin. pp. 517. pb $11.95. ISBN 0 140 43412 7.

Booth, Bradford A., and Ernest Mehew, eds. *The Letters of Robert Louis*

Stevenson, Volume 5: July 1884–August 1887. YaleUP. pp. 465. £29.95. ISBN 0 300 06190 0.

——, and ——, eds. *The Letters of Robert Louis Stevenson, Volume 6: August 1887–September 1890.* YaleUP. pp. 443. £29.95. ISBN 0 300 06191 0.

——, and ——, eds. *The Letters of Robert Louis Stevenson, Volume 7: September 1890–December 1892.* YaleUP. pp. 488. £29.95. ISBN 0 300 06213 3.

——, and ——, eds. *The Letters of Robert Louis Stevenson, Volume 8: January 1893–December 1894.* YaleUP. pp. 448. £29.95. ISBN 0 300 06214 1.

Booth, Michael, ed. *Edward Fitzball. The Lights o' London and Other Victorian Plays.* OUP. pp. 288. pb £6.99. ISBN 0 19 282736 7.

Born, Daniel. *The Birth of Liberal Guilt in the English Novel: Charles Dickens to H. G. Wells.* UNCP. pp. 213. $39.95. ISBN 0 8078 4544 2.

Bratton, Jacky S., ed. *Arthur W. Pinero. Trelawny of the 'Wells' and Other Plays.* OUP. pp. 352. pb £5.99. ISBN 0 19 282568 2.

Bright, Michael. *Robert Browning's Rondures Brave.* OhioUP. pp. 255. £32.95. ISBN 0 82141125 X.

Brooks, Chris, and Andrew Saint, eds. *The Victorian Church: Architecture and Society.* ManUP. pp. 228. hb £40, pb £16.99. ISBN 0 719 04019 1, 0 719 04020 5.

Cavaliero, Glen. *The Supernatural and English Fiction: From* The Castle of Otranto *to* Hawksmoor. OUP. pp. xiv + 273. $29.95. ISBN 0 1921 2607 5.

Cave, Terence, ed. *George Eliot. Daniel Deronda.* Penguin. pp. xl + 850. pb £2.99. ISBN 0 14 043427 5.

Childers, Joseph W. *Novel Possibilities: Fiction and the Formation of Early Victorian Culture.* UPennP. pp. 218. £31.50 ($32.95). ISBN 0 8122 3324 7.

Christ, Carol T., and John O. Jordan, eds. *Victorian Literature and the Victorian Visual Imagination.* UCalP. pp. xxix + 371. hb £50, pb £15.95. ISBN 0 520 08641 4, 0 520 20022 5.

Clarke, Micael M. *Thackeray and Women.* NIUP. pp. 235. $30. ISBN 0 87580 197 8.

Cohen, Michael. *Sisters: Relation and Rescue in Nineteenth Century British Novels and Paintings.* FDUP. AUP. pp. 187. $60. ISBN 0 8386 3555 5.

Cohen, Morton N. *Lewis Carroll: A Biography.* Knopf. pp. 577. $35. ISBN 0 679 42298 6.

Colby, Robin B. *Some Appointed Work To Do: Women and Vocation in the Fiction of Elizabeth Gaskell.* Greenwood. pp. xii + 120. $49.95. ISBN 0 3132 9373 2.

Crawford, Gary William. *J. Sheridan Le Fanu: A Bio-Bibliography.* Greenwood. pp. x + 155. $59.95. ISBN 0 3132 8515 2.

David, Deirdre. *Rule Britannia: Women, Empire, and Victorian Writing.* CornUP. pp. xiv + 234. $15.95. ISBN 0 8014 8277 1.

Davie, Donald. *Essays in Dissent: Church, Chapel, and the Unitarian Conspiracy.* Carcanet. pp. 264. $45. ISBN 1 8575 4123 5.

De Graef, Ortwin, ed. *Sense and Transcendence: Essays in Honour of Herman Servotte.* LeuvenUP. pp. 325. pb $87.50. ISBN 90 6186 667 7.

De La Campa, Román, Ann E. Kaplan, and Michael Sprinker, eds. *Late Imperial Culture.* Verso. pp. 226. hb £34.95, pb £12.95. ISBN 1 859 84950 4, 1 859 84050 7.

Dickerson, Vanessa D., ed. *Keeping the Victorian House: A Collection of Essays.* Garland. pp. xxxi + 476. $64. ISBN 0 8153 1575 9.

Dixon, Robert. *Writing the Colonial Adventure: Race, Gender and Nation in Anglo-Australian Popular Fiction, 1875–1914*. CUP. pp. x + 228. $59.95. ISBN 0 5214 8190 2.

Donaldson, William, ed. *William Alexander. Johnny Gibb of Gushetneuk.* Tuckwell. pp. xxiii + 312. £11.99. ISBN 1 89841 044 5.

——, ed. *William Alexander. My Uncle the Baillie.* Tuckwell. pp. vi + 217. £9.99. ISBN 1 898410 15 1.

Donkin, Ellen. *Getting into the Act: Women Playwrights in London 1776–1829.* Gender in Performance. Routledge. pp. xiii + 240. pb £13.99. ISBN 0 415 08250 1.

Donohue, Joseph, with Ruth Berggren, eds. *The Importance of Being Earnest.* The Princess Grace Irish Library 10. Smythe. pp. 376. £35. ISBN 0 86140 378 9.

Dunn, Douglas, ed. *Oxford Book of Scottish Short Stories.* OUP. pp. xxix + 476. $25. ISBN 0 1921 4235 6.

Elfenbein, Andrew. *Byron and the Victorians.* CUP. pp. xi + 285. $54.95. ISBN 0 5214 5452 2.

Ender, Evelyne. *Sexing the Mind: Nineteenth-Century Fictions of Hysteria.* CUP. pp. xi + 307. $17.95. ISBN 0 8014 8083 3.

Enright, D. J., ed. *George Eliot. The Impressions of Theophrastus Such.* Everyman. pp. xxviii + 176. £5.99. ISBN 0 460 87550 7.

Felber, Lynette. *Gender and Genre in Novels Without End: The British Roman-Fleuve.* UPFlor. pp. 205. $39.95. ISBN 0 8130 1402 6.

Foster, Shirley, and Judy Simons. *What Katy Read: Feminist Re-Readings of 'Classic' Stories for Girls.* Macmillan. pp. 223. hb £35, pb £11.99. ISBN 0 333 58253 5, 0 333 62673 7.

Freeman, Terence M. *Dramatic Representations of British Soldiers and Sailors 1660–1800: 'Britons Strike Home'.* Studies in British History 36. Mellen. pp. 351. £59.95. ISBN 0 7734 8928 2.

Gainor, J. Ellen, ed. *Imperialism and Theatre: Essays on World Theatre, Drama and Performance.* Routledge. pp. xvi + 264. hb £45, pb £12.99. ISBN 0 415 10640 0, 0 415 10641 9.

Granqvist, Raoul. *Imitation as Resistance: Appropriations of English Literature in Nineteenth-Century America.* AUP. pp. 305. $45. ISBN 0 838636 99 X.

Hadley, Elaine. *Melodramatic Tactics: Theatricalized Dissent in the English Marketplace 1800–1885*, StanfordUP. pp. viii + 303. £27.95. ISBN 0 8047 2403 2.

Hamilton, Susan, ed. *'Criminals, Idiots, Women, and Minors': Nineteenth-Century Writing by Women on Women.* Broadview. pp. 307. pb £11.95. ISBN 1 551 11056 3.

Hands, Timothy, ed. *Thomas Hardy. Jude the Obscure.* Everyman. pp. xxxviii + 423. pb £2.99. ISBN 0 460 87567 1.

——, *Writers in Their Time: Thomas Hardy.* Macmillan. pp. xiii + 209. $39.95. ISBN 0 33354 998 8.

Harden, Edgar F. *Vanity Fair: A Novel Without a Hero.* Twayne. pp. xv + 127. $23.95. ISBN 0 8057 4460 6.

Heffer, Simon. *Moral Desperado: A Life of Thomas Carlyle.* W&N. pp. 420. £20. ISBN 0 297 81564 4.

Illnchcliffe, Peter, and Catherine Kerrigan, eds. *Robert Louis Stevenson and Lloyd Osbourne. The Ebb Tide: A Trio and a Quartette.* EdinUP. pp. xxxii + 172. £10.95. ISBN 0 7486 6476 6.

Hollahan, Eugene. *Hopkins Against History.* CreightonUP. pp. 545. pb $17.95. ISBN 1 881 87113 4.

Hollindale, Peter, ed. *J. M. Barrie. Peter Pan and Other Plays.* Oxford Drama Library. OUP. pp. 384. £37.50. ISBN 0 19 812162 8.

Hollington, Michael, ed. *Charles Dickens: Critical Assessments.* 4 vols. Helm Information. pp. 864, 656, 848, and 720. $595. ISBN 1 873403 13 5 (set).

Hunter, Shelagh. *Harriet Martineau: The Poetics of Moralism.* Scolar. pp. xiv + 274. $68.95. ISBN 1 85928 135 4.

Jay, Elisabeth. *Mrs. Oliphant: A Literary Life.* OUP. pp. x + 355. $39.95. ISBN 0 1981 2875 4.

Jenkins, Ruth Y. *Reclaiming Myths of Power: Women Writers and the Victorian Spiritual Crisis.* BuckUP. AUP. pp. 200. $35. ISBN 0 8387 5278 0.

John, Angela V. *Elizabeth Robins: Staging a Life 1862– 1952.* Routledge. pp. xiv + 283. £25. ISBN 0 415 06112 1.

Jones, Jo Elwyn, and J. Francis Gladstone. *The Red King's Dream, or Lewis Carroll in Wonderland.* Cape. pp. 312. £10. ISBN 0 7126 7306 7.

Jordan, John O., and Robert L. Patten, eds. *Literature in the Marketplace: Nineteenth-Century British Publishing and Reading Practices.* CUP. pp. xiv + 338. £40 ($59.95). ISBN 0 5214 5247 3.

Kane, Penny. *Victorian Families in Fact and Fiction.* St. Martin's. pp. 172. $35. ISBN 0 312 12517 8.

Karl, Frederick R. *George Eliot, Voice of a Century: A Biography.* Norton. pp. xxi + 708. $30. ISBN 0 393 03785 1.

Kearns, Katherine. *Nineteenth-Century Literary Realism: Through the Looking Glass.* CUP. pp. x + 308. $54.95. ISBN 0 5214 9606 3.

Keith, W. J. *The Jefferies Canon: Notes on Essays Attributed to Richard Jefferies without Full Documentary Evidence.* Petton. pp. 40. £4.50. ISBN 0 9522813 0 7.

Kelly, Richard Michael. *The Art of George du Maurier.* Scolar. pp. 264. $99.95. ISBN 0 85967 977 2.

Kerrigan, Catherine, ed. *Robert Louis Stevenson. Weir of Hermiston.* EdinUP. pp. xxxvi + 178. £10.95. ISBN 0 7486 0473 1.

Kestner, Joseph A. *Masculinities in Victorian Painting.* Scolar. pp. 323. $69.95. ISBN 1 85928 108 7.

Kooistra, Lorraine Janzen. *The Artist as Critic: Bitextuality in Fin de Siècle Illustrated Books.* Scolar. pp. xiv + 304. $66.95. ISBN 1 85928 159 1.

Kranidis, Rita S. *Subversive Discourse: The Cultural Production of Late Victorian Feminist Novels.* St. Martin's. pp. xvi + 143. $39.95. ISBN 0 312 10739 0.

Lambert, Ellen Zetzel. *The Face of Love: Feminism and the Beauty Question.* Beacon. pp. xiii + 236. $24. ISBN 0 8070 6500 5.

Lane, Christopher. *The Ruling Passion: British Colonial Allegory and the Paradox of Homosexual Desire.* DukeUP. pp. 326. $49.95. ISBN 0 8223 1677 3.

Lang, Timothy. *The Victorians and the Stuart Heritage: Interpretations of a Discordant Past.* CUP. pp. 233. £30. ISBN 0 521 47464 7.

Langbaum, Robert. *Thomas Hardy in Our Time*. St. Martin's. pp. 256. hb $49.95, pb $29.95. ISBN 0 312 12200 4, 0 312 16409 2.

Langland, Elizabeth. *Nobody's Angels: Middle Class Women and Domestic Ideology in Victorian Culture*. CornUP. pp. x + 268. hb $39.50, pb $15.95. ISBN 0 801 4 3045 3, 0 801 48220 8.

Ledger, Sally, and Scott McCracken, eds. *Cultural Politics at the Fin de Siècle*. CUP. pp. 329. hb £37.50 ($59.95), pb £13.95. ISBN 0 521 44385 7, 0 521 48499 5.

Leighton, Angela, and Margaret Reynolds, eds. *Victorian Women Poets: An Anthology*. Blackwell. pp. 691. hb £60, pb £15.99. ISBN 0 631 17609 8, 0 631 17609 X.

Lloyd, Rosemary. *Closer and Closer Apart: Jealousy in Literature*. CornUP. pp. 205. $32.50. ISBN 0 8014 3151 4.

MacKillop, Ian, and Richard Storer, eds. *F. R. Leavis: Essays and Documents*. ShaP. pp. 300. £39.50. ISBN 1 85075 564 7.

Mahood, Linda. *Policing Gender, Class and Family: Britain, 1850–1940*. UCL. pp. 215. £35. ISBN 1 857 28188 8.

Marsh, Jan. *Christina Rossetti: A Writer's Life*. Viking/Penguin. pp. 634. ISBN 0 670 83517 X.

Mattheisen, Paul F., Arthur C. Young, and Pierre Coustillas, eds. *The Collected Letters of George Gissing, Volume 6: 1895–1897*. OhioUP. pp. xvi + 404. $70. ISBN 0 8214 1098 9.

——, ——, and ——, eds. *The Collected Letters of George Gissing, Volume 7: 1897–1899*. OhioUP. pp. lx + 438. $70. ISBN 0 8214 1123 3.

Matus, Jill L. *Unstable Bodies: Victorian Representations of Sexuality and Maternity*. ManUP. pp. 280. hb £40, pb £14.99. ISBN 0 719 04347 6, 0 719 04348 4.

Mavor, Carol. *Pleasures Taken: Performances of Sexuality and Loss in Victorian Photographs*. DukeUP. pp. xvi + 171. $47.95. ISBN 0 8223 1603 X.

McClintock, Anne. *Imperial Leather: Race, Gender, and Sexuality in the Colonial Contest*. Routledge. pp. 449. $55. ISBN 0 415 90889 2.

McLaughlin, Kevin. *Writing in Parts: Imitation and Exchange in Nineteenth Century Literature*. StanfordUP. pp. 200. $32.50. ISBN 0 8047 2411 3.

McMaster, Juliet, ed. *George Eliot. Edward Neville*. Juvenilia. pp. xvii + 30. pb $7. ISBN 0 9698271 4 8.

Melville, Joy. *Mother of Oscar: The Life of Jane Francesca Wilde*. Murray. pp. xi + 308. £39.50. ISBN 0 71955 102 1.

Miller, Andrew H. *Novels Behind Glass: Commodity Culture and Victorian Narrative*. CUP. pp. 232. $54.95. ISBN 0 521 47133 8.

Miller, J. Hillis. *Topographies*. StanfordUP. pp. xvi + 376. $49.50. ISBN 0 8047 2378 8.

Milligan, Barry. *Pleasures and Pains: Opium and the Orient in Nineteenth-Century British Culture*. UPVirginia. pp. 156. £23.50. ISBN 0 813 91571 6.

Mitchell, Sally. *The New Girl: Girls' Culture in England, 1880–1915*. ColUP. pp. 258. $17.50. ISBN 0 231 10247 X.

Morash, Christopher. *Writing the Irish Famine*. OUP. pp. 256. $45. ISBN 0 19 818279 1.

Murphy, Paul Thomas. *Toward a Working Class Canon: Literary Criticism in*

British Working-Class Periodicals 1816–1858. OhioUP. pp. 211. $39.50. ISBN 0 814 20654 9.

Nardin, Jane. *Trollope and Victorian Moral Philosophy.* OhioUP. pp. viii + 172. £32.95. ISBN 0 8214 1139 X.

Newey, Vincent. *Centering the Self: Subjectivity, Society, and Reading from Thomas Gray to Thomas Hardy.* Scolar. pp. 291. $69.95. ISBN 1 85928 151 6.

Nord, Deborah Epstein. *Walking the Victorian Streets: Women, Representation, and the City.* CornUP. pp. xiii + 270. $39.95. ISBN 0 8014 8291 7.

Nussbaum, Martha C. *Poetic Justice: The Literary Imagination and Public Life.* Beacon. pp. xix + 143. $20. ISBN 0 8070 4108 4.

Oberhelman, David D. *Dickens in Bedlam: Madness and Restraint in His Fiction.* YorkP. pp. 48. $15.95 (Canadian). ISBN 0 919966 96 9.

Orel, Harold. *The Historical Novel from Scott to Sabatini: Changing Attitudes Toward a Literary Genre.* St. Martin's. pp. vii + 189. $49.95. ISBN 0 312 12473 2.

Orr, Clarissa Campbell, ed. *Women in the Victorian Art World.* ManUP. pp. 208. pb £14.99. ISBN 0 719 04123 6.

Parker, Christopher, ed. *Gender Roles and Sexuality in Victorian Literature.* Scolar. pp. 194. £40. ISBN 1 85928 146 X.

Pike, E. Holly. *Family and Society in the Works of Elizabeth Gaskell.* Lang. pp. viii + 165. $37.95. ISBN 0 8204 2241 X.

Pine, Richard. *The Thief of Reason: Oscar Wilde and Modern Ireland.* St. Martin's. pp. 478. $35. ISBN 0 312 15813 0.

Polowetzky, Michael. *Jerusalem Recovered: Victorian Intellectuals and the Birth of Modern Zionism.* Greenwood. pp. 176. $49.95. ISBN 0 275 95213 4.

Pope, Rob. *Textual Intervention: Critical and Creative Strategies for Literary Studies.* Routledge. pp. 350. $59.95. ISBN 0 415 05436 2.

Raby, Peter, ed. *The Importance of Being Earnest and Other Plays.* OUP. pp. 400. pb £4.99. ISBN 0 19 282246 2.

Ragussis, Michael. *Figures of Conversion: 'The Jewish Question' and English National Identity.* DukeUP. pp. xi + 340. $16.95. ISBN 0 8223 1570 X.

Ransom, Teresa. *Fanny Trollope: A Remarkable Life.* Sutton. pp. xviii + 236. £9.99. ISBN 0 7509 1269 3.

Reed, John Robert. *Dickens and Thackeray: Punishment and Forgiveness.* OhioUP. pp. xvi + 505. $65.50. ISBN 0 8214 1117 9.

Rennie, Neil. *Far Fetched Facts: The Literature of Travel and the Idea of the South Seas.* OUP. pp. 352. $55. ISBN 0 19 811975 5.

Rhodes, Royal W. *The Lion and the Cross: Early Christianity in Victorian Novels.* OSUP. pp. x + 400. $49.50. ISBN 0 8142 0648 4.

Ricks, Christopher. *Essays in Appreciation.* OUP. pp. 304. $24.95. ISBN 0 19 818344 5.

Ridley, Jane. *The Young Disraeli, 1804–1846.* Sinclair-Stevenson. pp. x + 406. £20. ISBN 1 85619 250 4.

Roberts, Marie Mulvey, and Hugh Ormsby-Lennon, eds. *Secret Texts: The Literature of Secret Societies.* AMS. pp. 349. $55. ISBN 0 404 64251 9.

Robson, John M. *Marriage or Celibacy? The 'Daily Telegraph' on a Victorian Dilemma.* UTorP. pp. 365. £39. ISBN 0 802 07798 6.

Roe, Nicholas, ed. *Keats and History*. CUP. pp. 328. $65. ISBN 0 521 44245 1.

Roth, Marty. *Foul and Fair Play: Reading Genre in Classic Detective Fiction*. UGeoP. pp. 312. $45. ISBN 0 8203 1622 9.

Schwarz, Daniel R. *The Transformation of the English Novel, 1890–1930: Studies in Hardy, Conrad, Joyce, Lawrence, Forster, and Woolf*. 2nd edn. St. Martin's. pp. x + 336. $17.95. ISBN 0 312 12283 7.

Scott, Paul H. *Defoe in Edinburgh and Other Papers*. Tuckwell. pp. 252. £12.99. ISBN 1 8984 1039 9.

Selig, Robert L. *George Gissing*. Rev. edn. Twayne. pp. xiv + 156. $22.95. ISBN 0 7734 9485 5.

Showalter, Elaine, ed. *George Du Maurier. Trilby*. OUP. pp. xxv + 291. £4.99. ISBN 0 19 282323 X.

Sillars, Stuart. *Visualization in Popular Fiction, 1860–1960*. Routledge. pp. x + 191. £40. ISBN 0 4151 1914 6.

Smith, Lindsay. *Victorian Photography, Painting and Poetry: The Enigma of Visibility in Ruskin, Morris and the Pre-Raphaelites*. CUP. pp. 245. £30. ISBN 0 521 47288 1.

Smith, Margaret, ed. *The Letters of Charlotte Brontë: With a Selection of Letters by Families and Friends, Volume 1: Family and Friends*. OUP. pp. 627. $90. ISBN 0 19 818597 9.

Smith, Nelson, and R. C. Terry, eds. *Wilkie Collins to the Forefront: Some Reassessments*. AMS. pp. xiv + 273. $55. ISBN 0 404 64351 5.

Sprechman, Ellen Lew. *Seeing Women as Men: Role Reversal in the Novels of Thomas Hardy*. UPA. pp. xi + 137. $29.95. ISBN 0 8191 9863 3.

Stave, Shirley A. *The Decline of the Goddess: Nature, Culture, and Women in Thomas Hardy's Fiction*. Greenwood. pp. 184. $49.95. ISBN 0 313 29566 2.

Stone, Marjorie. *Elizabeth Barrett Browning*. Women's Writers. St. Martin's. pp. 254. $24.95. ISBN 0 312 12201 1.

Storey, Graham, and Kathleen Tillotson, eds. *The Letters of Charles Dickens, Volume 8: 1856–1858*. Clarendon. pp. xxviii + 807. £150. ISBN 0 19 812662 X.

Sussman, Herbert. *Victorian Masculinities: Manhood and Masculine Poetics in Early Victorian Literature and Art*. CUP. pp. xii + 227. £30 ($49.95). ISBN 0 521 46571 0.

Sutherland, John, ed. *Ouida. Under Two Flags*. OUP. pp. xxi + 528. pb £5.99. ISBN 0 19 282328 0.

——, *Victorian Fiction: Writers, Publishers, Readers*. Macmillan. pp. x + 191. hb £35, pb 12.99. ISBN 0 333 63286 9, 0 333 64422 0.

——, ed. *Wilkie Collins. Armadale*. Penguin. pp. xxxvi + 715. £6.99. ISBN 0 14 043411 9.

Swann, Charles, ed., intro. Terry Eagleton. *Collected Essays of John Goode*. KeeleUP. pp. xvi + 491. £45. ISBN 1 85331 068 9.

Tambling, Jeremy. *Dickens, Violence, and the Modern State: Dreams of the Scaffold*. Macmillan. pp. 237. $49.95. ISBN 0 312 12684 0.

Thompson, Julian, ed. *Wilkie Coillins. The Complete Shorter Fiction*. C&G. pp. xvi + 925. $34.95. ISBN 0 7867 0134 X.

Trela, D. J., ed. *Margaret Oliphant: Critical Essays on a Gentle Subversive*. SusquehannaUP. pp. 199. $33.50. ISBN 0 945636 72 5.

Vallone, Lynne. *Disciplines of Virtue: Girls' Culture in the Eighteenth and Nineteenth Centuries*. YaleUP. pp. x + 230. $25. ISBN 0 300 06172 2.

Vendler, Helen. *The Breaking of Style: Hopkins, Heaney, Graham*. Richard Ellman Lectures in Modern Literature. pp. 144. £19.95. ISBN 0 674 08120 X.

Vicinus, Martha, ed. *George Egerton. Keynotes and Discords*. Virago. pp. xix + 253. pb £8.99. ISBN 0 86068 293 5.

Vrettos, Athena. *Somatic Fictions: Imagining Illness in Victorian Culture*. StanfordUP. pp. xii + 240. $34.50. ISBN 0 8047 2424 5.

Walton, Priscilla L. *Patriarchal Desire and Victorian Discourse: A Lacanian Reading of Anthony Trollope's Palliser Novels*. UTorP. pp. viii + 180. $45. ISBN 0 8020 5987 2.

Wheeler, Michael, ed. *Ruskin and Environment: The Storm-Cloud of the Nineteenth Century*. ManUP. pp. 202. £40. ISBN 0 719 04377 8.

Williams, Linda Ruth. *Critical Desire: Psychoanalysis and the Literary Subject*. Arnold. pp. 224. $59.50. ISBN 0 340 64557 1.

Wright, Terence. *Elizabeth Gaskell, 'We Are Not Angels': Realism, Gender, Values*. St. Martin's. pp. 220. $49.95. ISBN 0 312 12649 2.

Zarifopol-Johnston, Ilinca. *To Kill a Text: The Dialogic Fiction of Hugo, Dickens, and Zola*. AUP. pp. 264. $39.50. ISBN 0 87413 539 7.

XIV

The Twentieth Century

JULIAN COWLEY, MACDONALD DALY, RICHARD STORER,
FIONA BECKET, JAGO MORRISON, STUART SILLARS, DAVID
HERD and PETER WOMACK

This chapter has the following sections: 1. Fiction; 2. Poetry; 3. Drama. Section 1(a) is by Julian Cowley; section 1(b) is by Macdonald Daly, Richard Storer and Fiona Becket; section 1(c) is by Jago Morrison; section 2(a) is by Stuart Sillars; section 2(b) is by David Herd; and section 3 is by Peter Womack.

1. Fiction

(a) General Studies
Sally Ledger and Scott McCracken have edited *Cultural Politics at the Fin de Siècle*, aiming to rescue the period from the 'backwater status in literary and cultural criticism' it receives when viewed as a transitional phase, but also to identify aspects of its significance for our sense of the ending of the current century. The book's relevance to twentieth-century literary studies is signalled in the opening words of the initial essay, where Terry Eagleton announces, 'The *fin de siècle* arrived early this century', and then elaborates a parallel with the 'structure of feeling' that characterized the English 1960s. This is reinforced in Regenia Gagnier's concluding 'Is market society the *fin* of history?', where Francis Fukuyama's economic analysis is counterpointed with nineteenth-century theories. These essays frame an informative and purposeful collection of pieces whose concerns radiate from the 1890s. So McCracken offers 'Postmodernism, a *Chance* to reread?', interrogating the usefulness of the concept, postmodernism, when looking at texts such as Conrad's novel (published in 1913; begun in 1898), 'rooted in the cultural politics of the *fin de siècle*'. Particularly noteworthy is Marcia Ian's 'Henry James and the spectacle of loss: psychoanalytic metaphysics', a study (using *What Maisie Knew* and the 1910 essay 'Is There a Life After Death?') of 'the crisis of interiority' in James's work and in *fin de siècle* writing more generally.

In *The Wilde Century: Oscar Wilde, Effeminacy and the Queer Movement* Alan Sinfield followed the lack of consistent historical congruence between homosexuality and recognized signs of effeminacy. Joseph Bristow, in *Effeminate England*, proceeds from this disclosed divergence to expose tensions arising from the currency of those signs in relation to gay identity traced through the lives and letters of Wilde, Forster, Ronald Firbank, Jocelyn

Brooke, J. R. Ackerley, Quentin Crisp and Alan Hollinghurst. The exposition is a lucid consolidation rather than a substantial extension of Sinfield's thesis. Bristow concludes with an assertive flourish that 'the hetero/homo binary is nothing less than a theoretical sham that has devastating effects on separating men from one another'.

Lynette Felber, in *Gender and Genre in Novels Without End*, offers the 'first theoretical study of the *roman-fleuve* as a genre', with particular reference to Trollope's Palliser novels, Dorothy Richardson's *Pilgrimage*, and Anthony Powell's *A Dance to the Music of Time*. The 'gender' element hinges on her contention that the sequence novel has an affinity with an *écriture féminine*. Felber's reading of Cixous and Irigaray assumes that the gendering of narrative is a strategic metaphorical process, so she is bold enough to argue that Trollope, in certain ways, anticipates *écriture féminine*. The case made for Richardson as a precursor of contemporary feminist theorists is perhaps more readily assimilated. Powell is presented as mediating between structure and flow, between realism and postmodernism, in many ways closer to Trollope than Proust. Yet the Victorian novelist is declared 'a precursor for modernist experiments with narrative'. There is much here that readers may contest, but Felber's exploratory mapping of a genre is worthy of attention.

Beginning with the assertion that 'We are born into stories', Linda Ruth Williams proceeds to explore the interconnection and interdependence of psychoanalysis and literature (with occasional and fruitful forays into film). *Critical Desire* is a lively introduction to basic concepts in psychoanalytic theory, presenting a series of illuminating and pertinent readings, and containing a helpful range of references to signal encounters between the disciplines. Williams takes Poe's work as 'a touchstone for shifts in psychoanalytic criticism throughout this century', and surveys those shifts, with Lacan at their heart, treated here with refreshing clarity. She then looks at Angela Carter 'as the writer of literature's unconscious', focusing on fantasy as a 'realm within which cultural categories and psychoanalytic formulations explicitly collide and collaborate'. The chapter makes constructive use of Winnicott and Klein. Other chapters use less obvious literary sources: Margaret Oliphant's *Autobiography* (1899) is read with the Wolf Man case-study. Williams uses *Jude the Obscure* to generate her concluding overview of trends linking 'Psychoanalysis and the Literary Subject'.

To entitle a book, *The Gender of Modernity* is boldly to run the risk posed by handling overfamiliar concepts. Rita Felski has run that risk with expert skill, producing an important study which succeeds in its aim 'to unravel the complexities of modernity's relationship to femininity through an analysis of its varied and competing representations'. Her project combines cultural theory with cultural history, seeking 'to establish points of connection between the texts of the past and the feminist politics of the present'. In popular romance (she pays special attention to the sentimentality of Marie Corelli), Felski unearths 'a foundational trope within the modern itself': that of 'nostalgic yearning for an indeterminate "elsewhere"'. She uses Georg Simmel to explore constructions of the archetypal female; ranges through the aesthetics and erotics of consumption; investigates the avant-garde challenge to masculinity posed by Wilde, Huysmans and Sacher-Masoch, and 'the links between sexual perversion and the aestheticization of identity' as exemplified by Rachilde; and she makes 'an excavation of the philosophies of history evident in the speeches and tracts of first-wave feminists'. Altogether this is an impressive reading in the history of femininity and modernity, executed with rare control and intellectual poise.

Bonnie Kime Scott acted as general editor for a major anthology, *The Gender of Modernism* (1990). Now she has written a two-volume study under the heading, *Refiguring Modernism*. The refiguring begins with her selection of Virginia Woolf, Rebecca West and Djuna Barnes 'as central representatives of modernist writing, where typically a cluster of male figures have stood'. The figure of the web (taken primarily from Woolf) is then traced to attachments radiating from Scott's three elected centres, producing a figure for conceptualizing modernist literary history, alternative to the masculinist 'scaffold'. Volume 1 is entitled 'The Women of 1928', a deliberate counter to Wyndham Lewis's denomination of 'The Men of 1914'. Woolf, West and Barnes are initially approached through an account of relationships within their immediate families. Then, Scott moves to 'more remote and imaginary supports' derived from Edwardian 'uncles', such as Bennett and Wells, before passing to the 'midwives of modernism', who include Violet Hunt, May Sinclair, Katherine Mansfield and Dorothy Richardson. Scott argues convincingly against Elaine Showalter's charge that West and Woolf were modernist in aesthetics to the exclusion of activist engagement. The next part of this volume locates the trio in a broader 'contemporary female network', where the personal is complemented by the overtly political. We are reminded that 1928 was the year votes were extended to British women, as well as the year in which censorship of *The Well of Loneliness* became a matter for debate. In the lively middle section of the first volume, Scott addresses directly those 'men of 1914' (Joyce, Pound, Wyndham Lewis and Eliot) to disclose 'their limited usefulness as attachments for women writers'. She is at her most obviously polemical here, highlighting facets of the male writers that are customarily concealed. The figure of the web continues to underpin Volume 2, 'Postmodern Feminist Readings of Woolf, West, and Barnes', where Scott traces, in a series of close readings, each writer's negotiation with 'modernist questions of enduring importance to postmodern readers'. Woolf is read as 'the woman writer in process', resisting the lure of mastery over language; Barnes in light of her attachment to tapestries, reverberating through her explorations of cultural impositions upon nature; and West is recuperated from her conventional status as ancillary to Wells, to be shown 'writing in an experimental range and blend of genres'. The book concludes with '1939 and the Ends of Modernism', where the responses of all three to the realities of fascism in Europe are clarified in terms of their own development, and of changing historical perspectives.

James J. Sosnoski initially conceived the book which has become *Modern Skeletons in Postmodern Closets* as a theory of literary criticism. The fruit of his research is offered as 'a cultural studies alternative', and much of his work here is dedicated to destabilizing understanding of literary critical practices and institutions as a coherent and logical discipline. Addressing fellow critics, he argues that 'continuing to give ourselves a disciplinary formation constrains what we do and commits us to institutional evaluations that put us at a serious disadvantage'. His case is that many critics who consider themselves postmodern, actually work within assumptions and horizons that are grounded in a previous phase of cultural history, 'the modern'. Sosnoski's postmodernity is a period characterized by information technology, and an electronic revolution which is transforming academic institutions into virtual universities. He outlines and advocates 'a figural mode of understanding' as appropriate to postmodern literary study, or 'Professing Literature in 2001'. Varying interpretations of Joyce's 'Araby' provide a test case for his argument; the theoretical tenets of Cleanth Brooks are contrasted with those of Paul de Man; but the main authority cited here is Gerald Graff, and his critique of institutional structures and procedures. Much in Sosnoski's account is contentious, but he offers in this book a theoretical arena for consideration of practical problems that confront many engaged in teaching literature today.

The Postmodern Arts is an introductory reader (ed. Nigel Wheale), which starts from the truism that 'modernism and postmodernism are now the two most comprehensive and influential terms applied to twentieth-century culture'. Wheale then asserts that 'cultural production ... is exceptionally vigorous and diverse at the moment'. This volume is presented in support of that affirmation, and also to clarify the distinction between those dominant terms, under four headings: Popular Culture; Architecture and the Visual Arts; Literature; and Documentary Film. Predictably, an array of delimiting qualifications are needed, as Wheale charts his chosen vectors through the field. Still, this is intelligent mapping, sensitive to the possibilities for further exploration by students and teachers of contemporary cultural theory and practice. The literature section comprises Wheale himself on John Ashbery, and Gayatri Chakravorty Spivak's 'Reading *The Satanic Verses*', previously available in her *Outside the Teaching Machine* (*YWES* 74.684). Wheale identifies 'weak postmodernism' as acceptance of 'groundlessness as a reason to act out of pure relativism and nihilism'. Unsympathetic readers might find this tendency exemplified in Nicholas Royle's *After Derrida*. 'After', we are told, signals 'later in time than', 'in the manner of', and 'going in search of' Royle's intellectual hero. His Derrida is primarily ludic, and, commencing with an appraisal of the relationship of deconstruction and new historicism, Royle (unsurprisingly) places emphasis on the element of surprise in reading. He celebrates the weird and the comic in the Derridean oeuvre. A lengthy chapter brings telepathy to bear on the Bacon-Shakespeare controversy. The book concludes with 'On not reading: Derrida and Beckett', the argument drawing 'an appropriate spectrality and passivity' from the latter's demise. Royle assures us: 'Beckett and Derrida: their laughter is almost indistinguishable'.

Ihab Hassan now seems to feel uncomfortable with common perception of his role in introducing 'postmodernism' into Anglo-American critical discourse. *Rumors of Change* gathers essays written over five decades as testimony to a far broader achievement. Hassan respects 'wit, style and civility', and those qualities are amply evident here, along with incisive intelligence and rare erudition. He is following his own changes, but the capacity of these essays to enlighten and stimulate is consistently high. Of particular relevance are: 'The Antihero in Modern British and American Fiction' (1959); 'Joyce, Beckett, and the Postmodern Imagination' (1975); and 'Motion and Mischief: Contemporary British Travel Writing' (1989).

In his 1984 essay 'Timely Pleasures', Hassan considered the nature of pleasure. Marginalization of aesthetic pleasure in contemporary intellectual debate is the concern of Wendy Steiner's book *The Scandal of Pleasure*.

Steiner makes the case for liberal and pluralist values, with sustained eloquence, as she ranges across varied terrain where extremist or fundamentalist
intolerance has threatened freedom of expression in recent years. She probes
the tensions and contradictions raised by controversies surrounding pornography, political correctness, Robert Mapplethorpe's photography and Salman
Rushdie's fiction, before looking at Anthony Blunt, Martin Heidegger and
Paul de Man, as exemplars of ostensible duplicity between intellectual affiliation and political behaviour. Whether or not one agrees with Steiner's
diagnosis of crisis in the humanities today, this is a considerable work of
cultural analysis, crucially concerned with the function of personal taste in acts
of criticism, as well as appreciation.

   Color Codes is an unusual book: a 'suite of essays' as its author, Charles A.
Riley II, terms it. Displaying a distinctly modernist bias, Riley explores
theories of colour in the work of philosophers (notably Wittgenstein, but
Spengler, Adorno, Barthes and Derrida are amongst others considered),
painters (from Monet to Charles Clough), architects (Le Corbusier, Michael
Graves, James Stirling), composers (especially Schoenberg and Messiaen),
psychologists (mainly Jung) and writers. The latter are an idiosyncratic
grouping: Gide, Proust, Joyce, Trakl, H. D., Wallace Stevens, John Hollander,
Thomas Pynchon and A. S. Byatt. The principle of selection is to trace a
lineage of literary thinking, identified by Wendy Steiner in her *Colors of
Rhetoric* (1982), of authors grappling with colour 'as a perceptual conceptual
problem'. Riley is most at ease, and writes with most authority on painting; the
discussion of literature is disappointingly brief at barely 50 pages. None the
less, if approached as a series of interconnected probes, rather than an attempt
at a coherent theory, the essays constitute an informative and thought-
provoking addition to the literature of interart analysis.

   Evans Lansing Smith has written 'An Archetypal Poetics of Modernism'
entitled *Ricorso and Revelation*. His four archetypes (labyrinth, Great Goddess, alchemical transformation and Apocalypse) are considered not only as
thematic components of modernist literature, but as models for the creative
process. All are considered as elemental forms of the mind, but also in relation
to contemporary activity in such fields as archaeology and anthropology.
Smith examines the 'mythical method' as mediation between the particular
and the universal, and appropriately to that project, he divides each of the
chapters dealing with his archetypes into subsections that address the work of
a particular author. Predictably, Joyce and Lawrence loom large; as do
Thomas Mann and T. S. Eliot. The result is a rather static, descriptive work,
aiming to reveal a pattern through specific instances, rather than through
extended abstraction of more theoretical concerns. Much of what the book
discloses is familiar, and Smith is arguably at his most interesting when
touching, all too briefly, upon interart comparison with the work of such
painters as Picasso, Kandinsky and Klee.

   The emergence of literary modernism in terms of 'sites of imaginary space'
is examined by Dee Reynolds in *Symbolist Aesthetics and Early Abstract Art*.
Reynolds draws her primary materials from Rimbaud and Mallarmé, Kandinsky and Mondrian, with chapters devoted to close readings of each. Her
larger aim is the reinstatement of imagination as a central concept in the
criticism of literature and of the visual arts. Her particular reference is to 'the
reception of semantically disruptive poems and paintings', but she provides a

broader basis for interart analysis of modernist texts. Kant, Baudelaire and C. S. Peirce are amongst the authorities deployed in the process of producing a cogent case with regard to 'the particular emphasis at the end of the last century and the beginning of this one on transforming perception of the artistic medium through its interaction with the imagination of the receiver'.

In *Boredom*, Patricia Meyer Spacks essays 'the literary history of a state of mind'. She announces that 'the critical act derives from a commitment to pay attention to a text', and she follows that rubric faithfully, showing herself to be an attentive and shrewd reader. But encountering broad assertions about shifting perceptions of what it means to be bored, one might reasonably expect more cultural historical evidence than this approach tends to furnish. In addition, such a project inevitably raises serious questions regarding criteria for selection of texts representative for various phases of the history. Spacks is strongest in her treatment of the eighteenth century, less satisfactory as she approaches the present day. The penultimate chapter considers modernism in relation to boredom considered as an ethical issue. Her decision to begin this consideration with George Eliot's *Daniel Deronda* arguably generates more uneasiness about the classification than its inclusion warrants. Proceeding to *The Portrait of a Lady* does not really assist clarification. Cursory treatment of T. S. Eliot and of Evelyn Waugh leads to suggestive, but regrettably brief readings of Lawrence's *Women in Love* and of writings by Gertrude Stein. The concluding survey of the postmodern inclines to the anecdotal and the journalistic. After looking at Donald Barthelme, Spacks touches on A. S. Byatt and Julian Barnes before dwelling a little longer on Anita Brookner. Beckett's absence is rather disarming. As a study of the cultural constructions of boredom and of interest this book has important implications, but there are evident limitations to its observations on twentieth-century experience of these states.

Altered Conditions is not a work of literary criticism, but an historicist study of medical discourse as narrative, which raises important issues for the analysis of storytelling in general. Julia Epstein presents fascinating accounts of hermaphroditism, of fetal deformities, and of AIDS as perceived through explanatory narratives, or what Oliver Sacks calls 'clinical tales', and as realized 'in the production of embodied stories in the law, in social ideologies, and in human experience'. The approach is by now familiar, and Michel Foucault, Hayden White and Stephen Greenblatt are among the theoretical touchstones cited, but this volume is a lucid and stimulating exposition.

Alternative Identities is subtitled 'The Self in Literature, History, Theory'. Its editor, Linda Marie Brooks, explains in a prefatory essay that the collection is intended 'to address the question of the individual agent in current gender-, racial-, ethnic- and culturally-based models of selfhood'. She acknowledges that the volume sidesteps 'the internal inconsistencies' of identity politics, seeking rather to establish 'a notion of personal identity as evolving and multifaceted'. In practice, poststructuralist positions are delineated within a broadly multicultural perspective. Brooks's editing is to be commended for its imposition of a framework within which diverse and stimulating essays are effectively orchestrated. The investigations range from vernacular writing in twelfth-century France to contemporary American pop songs. 'The Self in Literature' is addressed explicitly in R. Baxter Miller's 'The Rewritten Self in African American Autobiography', and in Margaret

Dickie's 'The Maternal Gaze: Women Modernists and Poetic Authority' (which looks at H.D., Marianne Moore, and Gertrude Stein), but the collection is a useful resource for literary study beyond overt engagement with literary texts.

Literature Against Philosophy, Plato to Derrida is a title that may deter potential readers, suspecting further dry rehearsal of a familiar polemic against theory. In fact, Mark Edmundson has written a fine, subtle study of what, following Arthur Danto, he calls 'the philosophical disenfranchisement of art'. Edmundson's focus is on poetry, but his argument extends to literature in general, and its capacity to contribute 'visions of enlarged future possibility'. Exuberance and energy characterize his notion of the positive, and this he finds in Harold Bloom at his best. Edmundson evaluates current theoretical orthodoxies – de Man, Lacan, Derrida, Foucault and Bloom all receive measured attention. The twist in the tail comes with the suggestion that anxiety of influence is a concept more applicable to academic criticism than to literary work. This is a lucid, valuable book that aims to counter the aridity of criticism which diminishes literature in order to affirm itself.

Belief that 'literary studies can no longer ignore the ethical without yielding up a once central part of its intellectual responsibility and constituency to other disciplines' is the platform from which David Parker proceeds in *Ethics, Theory and the Novel*. The book is 'a reconceived defence of the "literary canon" (understood as ever-developing and multi-vocal)', taking it to be 'theory's resistant Other'. Parker's declared intention to keep 'close concrete touch with literary texts' will surely cause poststructuralist hackles to rise, but this is no merely clumsy or naïve rearguard action; it is a serious study furnishing necessary grist for the mill of intelligent debate. Parker begins with extended consideration of the ramifications of Martha Nussbaum's observation that literary theory has tended to privilege ontology, semantics and epistemology to the exclusion of moral philosophy. Discussion of the nature of evaluative discourse precedes detailed readings of *Middlemarch*, *Anna Karenina* and three novels by Lawrence (*The White Peacock, Women in Love, Lady Chatterley's Lover*). Parker's readings retain 'working concepts of subjectivity, personhood and moral agency', and in the process raise important questions about literature as the mode of a particular kind of moral thinking which is now engaging the attention of notable moral philosophers.

Peter Uwe Hohendahl's *Prismatic Thought* is an admirably lucid study of Theodor Adorno. Hohendahl locates the critical theorist in relation to various currents of poststructuralism, clarifies his complex response to American culture and, valuably, foregrounds Adorno's contribution to literary criticism. The latter is concentrated on modernism, notably in essays on Proust, Mann and Kafka, and Hohendahl explores Adorno's ambivalent attitude towards the avant-garde. His critical exposition of Adorno's readings of mass culture is designed to redress their simplistic and misleading representation in certain recent accounts. Overall this book is a splendid resumé from which readers may turn or return to Adorno's challenging and important work.

Titanic Light continues Ortwin de Graef's survey of Paul de Man's work. *Serenity in Crisis* (UNebP, 1993) examined the years 1939 to 1960; this sequel looks at the following decade, examining the nature of de Man's 'postromanticism'. De Graef's readings are rigorous and sophisticated, and are directed to readers with considerable preliminary insight into de Man's writing. The project confirms de Man's status as a major figure informing contemporary literary criticism, and the style of this book's composition is itself testimony to his legacy.

Evelyn Waugh famously stressed that the artist 'must be reactionary'; it was imperative, he argued, 'to stand out against the tenor of the age'. The *New Criterion* has, since 1982, enshrined such opposition as the critic's crucial role, and in *Against the Grain*, Hilton Kramer and Roger Kimball offer a selection of essays designed to resist postmodern levelling of evaluative hierarchies, and what they regard as a left-wing assault on culture (Stalin recurs as *bête noire* here). Assembled in one volume the prevailing tone becomes oppressive, and tends to appear merely ill-tempered. Among the more worthwhile review essays are John Gross on Max Beerbohm, Brooke Allen on Shaw and David Fromkin on T. E. Lawrence.

The invaluable Guy Davenport contributes to *Against the Grain* a brief piece on Gertrude Stein. He also provides a highlight of *Teaching Literature*, Judy Kravis's collection of interviews. Other contributors include Hermione Lee, Gabriel Josipovici and Howard Barker, as well as eminent Americans (Ron Padgett, Anne Waldman, Kenneth Koch, Edmund White). The orientation and teaching situations of the interviewees vary considerably (academic study, creative writing, in universities, in prisons), but the responses are generally characterized by resignation to the fact that students rarely read with the commitment their teachers desire, and by their own demonstrable passion for literature, and for the occasional but real rewards that spring from classroom discussions. The book will be found resonant by all who have shared in that process.

The Western Canon is Harold Bloom's broadside against 'the neo-Feminists, pseudo-Marxists, and Francophile reductionists who make up our current School of resentment'. It is also his account of the transmission of aesthetic value in Western literary history. The canonical author 'startles the common reader at each fresh encounter'; strength and strangeness are the qualities Bloom extols. Insistently provocative and immensely erudite, the book is both a celebration of aesthetic achievement and a jeremiad for academic study of literature. Following Joyce in borrowing from Vico, Bloom identifies the twentieth century as the Chaotic Age, an anxious coda to the Aristocratic and Democratic Ages, anticipating the imminent return of Theocratic certainties. Nietzsche is a recurrent authority for his judgements; Bloom's nine representative modern authors are Freud, Proust, Joyce, Kafka, Woolf, Neruda, Beckett, Borges and Fernando Pessoa.

Beth Carole Rosenberg has combined Bakhtin's dialogism with Bloom's argument for the anxiety of influence in her concise study of the Common Reader as conceived by Dr Johnson, mediated by Leslie Stephen, and developed in the essays and the fiction of Virginia Woolf. *Virginia Woolf and Samuel Johnson: Common Readers* is a closely focused discussion that links those authors in ways to challenge the dominance of readings locating Woolf at the heart of efforts to represent psychological reality, widely regarded as 'the signature of the modern British novel'. Whether or not one endorses the notion of 'influence' found here, the connection with Johnson presents a version of literary history that has quite dramatic implications for current mapping of the modernist canon, and Rosenberg's distillation of the argument lends it undeniable weight.

Woolf, awake at 4 a.m., tormented by the cool reception granted *The Years*, compared to its detriment to *Daughters and Sons*, is among the many memorable moments to be discovered in *Ivy*, which brings together in one volume *Ivy When Young* (1974) and *Secrets of a Woman's Heart* (1984), the two parts of Hilary Spurling's splendid biography of I. Compton-Burnett. Its publication is an important event both because it sets a standard for literary biography, and because of its subtle, biographically based readings of the novels. The book is worthy testimony to one of the major oeuvres in twentieth-century British literature.

A very different kind of biography, grounded in deconstructionist practices, emerges from Louis Kaplan's *Laszlo Moholy-Nagy: Biographical Writings*. Taking Derrida's insights into the effect of the signature as a starting-point for his exploration of the significance of the Constructivist, Kaplan draws additional weight from recognition that 'both abstract art and theories of language in the twentieth century have problematized the representation of the (biographical) object of study and the claim of immediate, direct, and easy accessing of the referent'. Moholy-Nagy then becomes a singularly suitable object, and Kaplan's subtle, generally restrained probes yield thought-provoking observations on the formation of artistic identity and the complex relationships within modernism of creativity, technique and authorship.

That matrix is to be met in another mode in *Sursum Corda!*, the first volume of Malcolm Lowry's collected letters. Sherrill E. Grace has exercised immense care in compiling letters from 1926 to 1946 which demonstrate the author's perennial devotion to wordplay. This highly allusive correspondence indicates his total immersion in literature. There is emphatic illustration here of Lowry's passion and tenacity, and his numerous letters to Conrad Aiken are singular documents of a fertile mind at play. Beyond this the volume reflects obstacles and frustrations faced by an ambitious author encountering the realities of modern publishing. The centrepiece of the collection is Lowry's famous letter of January 1946 to Jonathan Cape, which Grace rightly identifies as 'one of the most extraordinary literary letters ever written, ... an apologia and explication of great eloquence and depth'. This *tour de force* is, like the other letters in the volume, appropriately annotated by the editor.

Fred Inglis makes it clear that his *Raymond Williams* is a biography infused by the warmth of admiration, reflecting personal affection felt for this Father of the academic Left. The effect of reading his account, however, is a curious one of diminution. It emerges that Williams's crucial quality was an implacable self-assurance, that his great strength was enshrined in his person, his ability to contain difficult social situations, and to pass beyond enmity to some kind of mutual understanding. Flaws in his writing, in terms of style, method and range of knowledge are brought to view, and Williams comes across as a teacher who neglected his students, and a husband who dominated his wife and kept his home in thrall to his work. Inglis's Williams becomes, by an accident of birth, an incarnation of permission for socialist academics, a working-class touchstone for theoreticians of literary and cultural studies. His origins encapsulated, in Inglis's infelicitous phrase, 'the open, hospitable politics of the signal box'. Yet 'the ideal was only real when he wrote'. So, Inglis takes exception to Terry Eagleton's memorial tribute to Williams as a 'centred and rooted' man, delivered to an audience derisive of 'the very notion of a "centred self" '.

Inglis stresses Williams's lack of commitment to feminist values, but his legacy is at times evident in '*Ladies, Please Don't Smash the Windows*', a book developed from Maroula Joannou's Cambridge doctoral thesis, an origin perceptible mainly in a (useful) 30-page bibliography. Joannou is covering ground that has grown familiar, but in a measured and persuasive way, examining 'crucial interstices' of gender and class. Vera Brittain is reconsidered as a professed feminist and socialist, whose *Testament of Youth* is 'incompatible with the egalitarian and democratic impulses underwriting both political philosophies'; Leonora Eyles is brought to light as a contrasting socialist feminist; fiction by Flora Mayor, and Sylvia Townsend Warner, amongst others, is read for the ideological implications of literary characterization of the spinster; *Orlando* is considered against *The Well of Loneliness* as a representation of lesbian relationships; feminism and femininity are explored through texts by Elizabeth Bowen, Rosamond Lehmann and Rebecca West; and Woolf's *Three Guineas* is reviewed alongside Katherine Burdekin's anti-Fascist novel, *Swastika Night*. This worthwhile volume would have benefited from more efficient proofreading.

In *Hearts Undefeated*, Jenny Hartley has collected fragments recording the responses of women writers to experiences of the Second World War. As is often the case with Virago anthologies, the selection is well made, and has appropriate cumulative effect, but the framing commentary is regrettably slight. Sources are fully documented, however, and there is a short supporting bibliography. Among the writers are Jan Struther, Vita Sackville-West, Vera Brittain, Sylvia Townsend Warner and Barbara Cartland. Although Hartley is properly self-conscious about the middle-class bias of the contributions, that is to some extent redressed by the range of experiences recorded.

Adam Piette's *Imagination at War* addresses British culture's guilt 'about its own isolation from the real horrors of the war between 1939 and 1945'. More generally, it seeks to uncover 'the inside story of the war', its impact upon 'the private imagination'. Texts he examines include Keith Douglas's *From Alamein to Zem Zem*, Elizabeth Bowen's *The Heat of the Day*, James Hanley's *No Directions*, Mervyn Peake's *Titus Groan* and Henry Green's *Caught*. A chapter is devoted to Evelyn Waugh, another to Alun Lewis, another to positions taken on the writing of propaganda. The concluding two chapters are readings of poetry. Altogether this is a substantial and common-sensical study, which falls short of its aim to dispel 'nostalgia, glorification, and fond reflection', but offers thought-provoking readings of texts that merit wider attention.

Hugh Cecil's *Flower of Battle* is less a study of fiction generated by experiences of the First World War, than an account of the circumstances from which certain British writers produced such fiction. As a skilled historian, Cecil avoids large claims and generalities, and builds a picture through judicious selection and telling contrast. There are broad divisions within the book, examining both pessimistic and positive views of the war, and pondering 'the gulf between combatants and non-combatants'. He sidesteps literary critical judgements in order to configure the well-known (such as Richard Aldington, R. H. Mottram and Herbert Read) and the neglected (including Ronald Gurner, Richard Blaker and 'Peter Deane') in illustration of a range of individual experiences and of written responses.

Ariela Halkin has assumed an ingenious approach to analysing British taste between the World Wars. In *The Enemy Reviewed*, she gauges interest in German literature during this period, measured by the number of translations, and by their reception in reviews and their popularity with the reading public. In broad terms her argument is that the displacement of French by German as the most widely translated foreign works between 1918 and 1939 constitutes a set of 'veiled revelations', disclosing British cultural anxieties. Paying particular attention to the discourse of critical reception, she delineates a multifaceted image of Germany constructed by a nation nervous about its own cultural identity in the modern world.

Halkin cites Arnold Bennett in 1928 declaring the English historical novel to be 'comatose', and advocating German models. Harold Orel, in the coda to his *The Historical Novel from Scott to Sabatini*, concurs that 'not a single one of the important novelists born after 1880 – those who came to dominate the market in the 1920s – thought it worth their while to write historical romances'. Orel's study is predominantly concerned, then, with nineteenth-century fiction, or rather with the writers of such fiction, as the chapters tend towards literary biography. His concern is 'to define the direction in which the writing of fictions about the past moved' from Scott's example, through a phase of didacticism, to resurgence with Stevenson, and on to decline with the arrival of the twentieth century, Rafael Sabatini's popularity prefacing a lull until the Second World War. The book is a solid, rather old-fashioned survey that defiantly offers no 'critical thesis'.

Telling Histories is a collection of essays (ed. Susana Onega), which proceeds primarily along lines defined by Linda Hutcheon's category of 'historiographic metafiction', exploring issues of 'narrativizing history' and 'historicizing literature'. The collection is divided into two parts, the first entitled 'The End of the Classical Period', the second 'The Postmodernist Era'. Part 1 is predominantly concerned with nineteenth-century texts, but concludes with an essay by Felicity Hand on John Masters's *Nightrunners of Bengal* (1951) and M. M. Kaye's *Shadow of the Moon* (1957), both novels about the Indian Mutiny of 1857. Part 2 begins with essays on Salman Rushdie's *Midnight's Children* and on William Golding's *Rites of Passage*, and ends with consideration of American novelist David Bradley. Between lies the heart of the volume with contributions on Angela Carter, Jeanette Winterson and Margaret Drabble. All the essays here are worthwhile, but the case presents itself that a more exclusive focus upon contemporary women writers might have made for a more coherent volume.

Amy J. Elias's 'Defining Spatial History in Postmodern Historical Novels' is a very brief essay making a stark distinction between 'traditional' and 'postmodernist' approaches to writing historical fiction. The latter is defined in terms of Umberto Eco's notion of the open work, and Joseph Frank's concept of spatial form. Cursory attention is paid to fiction by Julian Barnes, Peter Ackroyd and D. M. Thomas, alongside numerous American writers, but the thesis remains underdeveloped. The essay is to be found in *Narrative Turns and Minor Genres in Postmodernism* (ed. Theo D'haen and Hans Bertens). The majority of contributions here address American literature, with notable essays by Allen Thiher (on the critic Jerome Klinkowitz), by Carl Malmgren (on Donald Barthelme and on Paul Auster), and by David Seed (on Philip K. Dick).

David Seed has taken from H. G. Wells the title for a collection of essays,

Anticipations. The contributors identify signal moments in the history of a genre which has increasingly asserted its importance during the twentieth century. As Edward James points out, in 'Science Fiction by Gaslight', the modern label has granted 'a spurious kind of unity' to 'a collection of disparate sub-genres, with differing literary histories and characteristics'. *Anticipations* is a partial mapping of these sub-genres, suggesting rather than exhausting lines of enquiry. Stephen R. L. Clark boldly makes the case for Kipling as a precursor of science fiction in 'Alien Dreams'. Patrick Parrinder contributes an essay to *Anticipations* on 'The Thames Valley Catastrophe', as envisaged by writers from Mary Shelley to Wells. In *Shadows of the Future*, another volume in the LiverUP series of Science Fiction studies, Parrinder writes with customary authority on 'Wells, Science Fiction and Prophecy'. This is an admirably concise and clearly delineated study that is 'offered as a contribution to an unwritten history of modernity and its cultural discourse', on the basis that it reviews the significance of Wells as a cultural presence within the history of the early twentieth century, amid the science of the time and with the emergence of science fiction as a genre. Parrinder is particularly concerned with 'how Wells developed and explored the literary potential of prophecy', as an inheritor of 'the Shelleyan ideal of the poet as hierophant'. The second half of the book looks at the impact of Wells upon George Orwell and Yevgeny Zamyatin, and at his more widespread legacy.

'I suppose I began life as a Wellsian. Now I'm more a Huxleyan', declares Brian Aldiss in *The Detached Retina*. The pieces here are collected from diverse sources, with some new ones among them. There are observations on Wells, and on Huxley, on Mary Shelley, Orwell's *Nineteen Eighty-Four*, Olaf Stapledon, Kingsley Amis, Anna Kavan, on several American Science Fiction writers and on the state of the genre. Aldiss announces at the beginning that these are not academic essays; rather, they are informed appreciations by a major practitioner, alert to trends and developments in writing and criticism in this field.

Aldiss is taken as an exemplary writer of modern science fiction by Damien Broderick, in *Reading by Starlight*. His exemplar of the postmodern is the American novelist, Samuel Delaney, whose work is addressed in some detail in the second part of the book. The first part poses salient questions about evaluation of literary quality in consideration of science fiction; it investigates possibilities for and limitations of generic classification; and it explores kinds of critical approach which might most appropriately serve analysis of this writing. The main thrust of the study, which refers to a wide range of British and American novelists, is to affirm that science fiction texts, in their language, their tropes, and their narrative structures, may be especially well-suited to address the epistemic changes faced by postmodern cultures.

Broderick concludes with a quotation from his introduction to a 1985 collection of Australian speculative fiction entitled *Strange Attractors*. The same title has been borrowed from mathematics by Harriet Hawkins, for her study of literary texts in the light of chaos theory, as articulated by scientists such as Benoit Mandelbrot and David Ruelle. Pursuing metaphorical parallels between science and art can prove treacherous, but Hawkins treads warily, and produces suggestive rather than doctrinaire readings, ultimately concerned to show that contemporary scientific theorists are confirming literature's persistent 'mythical and metaphorical representations of the deterministically chaotic ways of the world'. Hawkins has elected to use texts by Shakespeare and Milton as her primary materials amid a wide range of cultural reference, including Wells's *The Island of Dr Moreau*, Rider Haggard's *She* and Karen Blixen's *Out of Africa*.

In a year that demonstrates lively and substantial interest in science fiction, a collection of essays by Joanna Russ stands out as among the most incisive works of criticism. *To Write Like a Woman* is in two sections: the first aims to clarify the nature of science fiction writing and its concerns, and (like Damien Broderick's book) makes convincing arguments for its legitimacy as the object of serious study; the second assembles essays which take a more overtly feminist angle on women writers and their work (including Mary Shelley, Willa Cather and Charlotte Perkins Gilman). The entire volume is characterized by intelligent and informed political analyses, made from the point of view of a lesbian feminist novelist. Their critical weight is not diminished by the fact that (as Sarah Lefanu notes in her introduction) their style is informal and lucid, sensible and elegant.

Modes of the Fantastic assembles 25 papers from the 12th International Conference on the Fantastic in the Arts, held in 1991, in Florida. As Rob Latham points out in his introduction, an underlying assumption of most is that fantasy is intrinsically subversive. Brian Aldiss, the conference's 'permanent special guest', contributes a brief meditation on the distinction between fantasy and science fiction, identifying the former as more characteristically British than American. Brian Attebery makes explicit 'The Politics of Fantasy', translating Tolkien's Middle-Earth into actual political equivalents, in a discussion that extends to the Rushdie controversy. In another essay, Margaret Elphinstone writes on contemporary feminist fantasy by Scottish women, looking at Janice Galloway and Sian Hayton, Emma Tennant, Naomi Mitchison and Muriel Spark. Overall, this is a buoyant and varied collection, with numerous stimulating contributions, some of which make use of unexpected sources. Pierrette Frickey provides an illuminating piece on Louis Aragon, Nicole Bufford-O'Shea writes on Boris Vian, and Bernadette Bosky contributes 'Occult Fantasies/Occult Fact', on the work of Charles Williams. Williams is amongst the writers considered by Joe Sanders in ' "My God, No!"': The Varieties of Christian Horror Fiction', in *Contours of the Fantastic* (ed. Michele K. Langford), which collects papers from the 1987 Conference. That volume also includes, notably, Mickey Pearlman's 'The Element of the Fantastic and the Artist Figure in the Novels of Muriel Spark'. This earlier collection (1990) is less impressive, but is none the less a worthwhile volume from a useful series.

In *Words Still Count with Me*, Herbert Mitgang presents 'a chronicle of literary conversations'. His introduction proffers advice on how to conduct interviews with writers, drawing on his own extensive experience as a journalist. The book does not contain interviews as such, but brief narratives of encounters with an array of literary celebrities. These include Americans (e.g. Carl Sandburg, Norman Mailer, Susan Sontag, Ralph Ellison and Alice Walker), Europeans (e.g. Italo Calvino, Leonardo Sciascia, Samuel Beckett and Czeslaw Milosz), and British writers (Anthony Burgess, Rebecca West, Frank Swinnerton, Stephen Spender, Christopher Isherwood, William Golding, Eric Ambler and J. B. Priestley). These are 'impressionistic pieces', entertaining rather than illuminating, and despite Mitgang's claims they do little to reveal the creative lives of their subjects.

Swinnerton and Priestley, scarcely fashionable figures, also furnish material for *Writing Englishness*, Judy Giles and Tim Middleton's anthology illustrating dominant perceptions of national identity during the period 1900–50. Producing a representative selection raises obvious problems, and the editors have played safe in their choice, but to the end of providing a sourcebook for students, the volume serves that end well. Forster, Lawrence, Ford, Wyndham Lewis, Orwell and Woolf are included here, along with Jan Struther, Edward Thomas and Daphne du Maurier, amongst others, and documents from politicians such as Churchill and H. V. Morton. The practical aim is foregrounded in a chronology, a bibliography and a series of suggestions for classroom activities.

The canonic texts of twentieth-century Scottish literature are almost exclusively by male authors; that is the assumption from which Christopher Whyte's collection, *Gendering the Nation*, sets out to explore parallels between 'the politics of nation and the politics of gender'. Most of the essays deal with fiction written since the First World War. Two approaches are adopted: engagement with non-canonical texts, and 'unprecedented readings' of the canonical. Berthold Schoene attacks homophobia and misogyny in novels by Alan Sharp; Whyte himself offers a harsh evaluation of Neil Gunn. More constructive readings are granted Naomi Mitchison, Catherine Carswell, Nan Shepherd, Willa Muir, Christine Gow, Ellen Galford, Iona McGregor and Sian Hayton. In addition, two essays address gender issues in Scottish drama, and the collection concludes with an exuberant performance by Edwin Morgan, 'A Scottish Trawl'. Overall, this is a collection with an evident mission, and partly because it discloses some relatively neglected writing, partly because of the purposeful clarity of the contributions, it succeeds in ways that comparable collections often do not.

Michael J. Meyer has assembled a diversity of essays under the heading, *Literature and the Grotesque*. His brief introduction offers no definition or conceptual framework, although it does endorse the suggestion that the grotesque has become 'typical for our age'. The essays deal mainly with American writing (from Jack London to Harry Crews), and with drama (Pirandello, Beckett, Peter Shaffer), without chronological or other evident principle for their sequence. Kelly Anspaugh contributes a lively essay, ' "Jean qui rit" and "Jean qui pleure": James Joyce, Wyndham Lewis and the High Modern Grotesque', asserting Joyce's alignment with Rabelais as Horatian satirists, and of Lewis with Swift as followers of Juvenal.

Anspaugh cites Flann O'Brien as 'one of Joyce's most extraordinary Irish epigones'. M. Keith Booker has traced O'Brien's satirical orientation in *Flann O'Brien, Bakhtin, and Menippean Satire*. As well as providing a helpful introduction to Bakhtin's concept of the 'menippea', Booker locates O'Brien's work in relation to the more prominent members of the triumvirate that has dominated twentieth-century Irish fiction: Joyce and Beckett. The most concentrated comparison comes in a chapter that addresses the posited futility of epistemological inquiry. Other chapters look at O'Brien's major fictional works individually, while a concluding chapter essays a more ambitious placing of O'Brien amongst twentieth-century writers, ranging from Kafka to Garcia Márquez and Mikhail Bulgakov.

Keith Hopper's *Flann O'Brien: A Portrait of the Artist as a Young*

Post-modernist also reads the novelist in the light of Bakhtin, as part of a declared Formalist approach. In fact, Hopper's methodology is far less coherent in application than this suggests, and the deployment of theoretical models (including a kind of feminism) at times seems a little callow when compared to Booker's analysis. Despite the title there is little attempt to identify a post-modern context, beyond iteration of Ihab Hassan's now well-worn set of criteria. Hopper asserts that Beckett and Nabokov are the two authors whose work most closely resembles O'Brien's, and inevitably there is comparison with Sterne and with Joyce. This is a book to be read for local insights rather than systematic placement of O'Brien's fiction.

Forging in the Smithy (ed. Joep Leerssen, A. H. van der Weel, and Bart Westerweel), assumes strikingly diverse angles upon the relationship of national identity to representation in Anglo-Irish literary history. Ranging from Edmund Spenser to contemporary socialist drama, the volume can scarcely be expected to deliver a consistent thesis, and is intended rather to 'illustrate the possibilities open to a proper historical understanding of Anglo-Irish literature'. Establishing what is 'proper', James Murphy writes on 'Rosa Mulholland, W. P. Ryan and Irish Catholic Fiction at the Time of the Anglo-Irish Revival'. The other essay to address twentieth-century fiction here is Richard Wall's scholarly 'Politics and Language in Anglo-Irish Literature', referring primarily to Joyce, unpacking a number of rare or obscure idiomatic usages.

Declan Kiberd's *Inventing Ireland* is a long book, elaborating the interaction of Irish and English identity formation, by means of a sketchy, yet pointed, historical survey of Ireland this century, and a series of studies of major figures in the modern Irish canon. Kiberd's approach is unequivocally to read Irish writing as post-colonial, and occasional analogies with the writing of Salman Rushdie, V. S. Naipaul and Gabriel García Márquez are offered. But the book is clearly intended for a general readership, rather than for specialists in the field, and aside from sporadic references to Frantz Fanon, there is little in the way of overt theoretical grounding. This is a readable and coherent account, although some of Kiberd's assertions will meet with resistance from readers who choose to read Joyce, Beckett and Flann O'Brien in a more orthodox modernist context. For example, to claim Leopold Bloom as an adept of 'oral culture', serves the book's argument well, but ignores Joyce's insistence on the Hebraic entwined with the Hellenic within literate culture.

'In the absence of a revolutionary aesthetic, it is the great reactionaries who stand askew to a degraded present, invoking spiritual values whose political implications are occasionally odious, but whose artistic depth and intricacy resonate far beyond the workaday decencies of an E. M. Forster'. This characteristically pungent evaluation of literary modernism, is taken from Terry Eagleton's collection of 'Studies in Irish Culture', *Heathcliff and the Great Hunger*. The book will, of course, be read for the expert way in which Eagleton brings 'to bear on Ireland the language of contemporary cultural theory', while disclosing 'the current repressions and evasions' of the latter. Wilde and Shaw figure in the final chapter, but it is Joyce who looms through the latter half of the book, the avant-garde exception within Ireland's 'peculiarly mandarin modernism in which, by and large, the archaic triumphs over the contemporary'. Eagleton's assertion that twentieth-century intellectual life has been dominated by exiles and émigrés is one means by which he expands the frame of relevance for his readings beyond the immediate concern for the stories Ireland has been able to recount of itself.

Malcolm Bradbury's *Dangerous Pilgrimages* is a substantial work of cultural history, well-suited for a general readership, yet with the occasional diverting detail to please a more specialized reader. The book is subtitled 'Trans-Atlantic Mythologies and the Novel', although it is novelists rather than their works who receive Bradbury's attention, the focus being squarely on literary lives, with passing references to texts they generated. The mythologies are the familiar ones; the majority of writers discussed are American. In the twentieth-century section of the book, D. H. Lawrence's evaluation of American literature is addressed, Joyce is glimpsed in Parisian exile, Malcolm Lowry is followed on his self-destructive travels, and Evelyn Waugh is seen at loggerheads with Edmund Wilson. Bradbury's own *Stepping Westward* receives brief mention, before he moves on to consider Jonathan Raban and other practitioners of the postmodern period. The trans-Atlantic traffic is largely one-way, and the book contains few real surprises, yet it is a highly readable summary of Bradbury's version of literary relations between the Old World and the New.

Specifically a study of Conrad, Christopher GoGwilt's *The Invention of the West* has aspirations beyond the customary range of single-author scholarship. GoGwilt initially defines his study against Said's *Orientalism*, arguing that 'the idea of the West' emerged at the turn of this century, within a matrix of imperialist expansion and democratic crisis. He reads Conrad as exemplary of his argument that the shift from European to Western identity necessarily entailed a political construct masquerading as cultural and historical reality. In other words, 'the West' has been a strategy to recuperate historical continuity beyond 'the worldwide shattering of cultural traditions', of which literary modernism is one notable offshoot. The book's epilogue, 'A Brief Genealogy of the West', suggests the need for a further study, amplifying and clarifying more general aspects of GoGwilt's case; as it is, this is a notable addition to Conrad studies, and a stimulating inquiry into the intellectual history of the period.

Theo D'haen and José Lanters have edited *Troubled Histories, Troubled Fictions*, assembling papers on twentieth-century Anglo-Irish prose given at a conference headed 'The Literature of Politics, The Politics of Literature'. That rubric is observed with most urgency in Margaret Scanlan's 'An Acceptable Level of Violence: Women, Fiction, and Northern Ireland'. Other pieces discuss the writings of Julia O'Faolain; 'The Political *Bildungsroman*' realized by William Trevor, Brian Moore, John Banville and Jennifer Johnson; Eimar O'Duffy's satires; Molly Keane's variations on the Gothic; Elizabeth Bowen's *The Last September*; and James Stephens, presented as the 'literary twin' of James Joyce. Over half of the volume is given over to Joyce himself, notably Bruce Stewart's substantial 'Joyce at Tara'. Michael Brian mines etymology in 'Ivy Day in the Committee Room'; Martin Croghan considers female sexuality in *Ulysses*; and S. J. Boyd muses on Joyce as pornographer.

Boyd's essay concludes with an assertion 'that the methods of deconstruction "can lead only to disaster in the real-life practices of the law" '. Parallels to the debate between Jacques Derrida and Hans-Georg Gadamer, enacted on the field of jurisprudence by Stanley Fish, Owen Fiss and Ronald Dworkin are delineated by Ian Ward in the brief third chapter of *Law and Literature*.

The volume sets out to outline 'possibilities and perspectives' on 'law and literature', perceived as a 'movement', rather than a mere interdisciplinary conjunction. Ward's preliminary synoptic overview predictably identifies two complementary strands: scrutiny of literary texts by students of law, and application of literary critical techniques to legal texts. In fact, Ward is primarily concerned in this book with what lawyers might learn from encounters with literature, and it is likely that literary specialists will gain little from his discussions of Barthes and Foucault on authorship; feminist criticism; constitutional thought in Shakespeare's histories; jurisprudence in children's literature; or Kafka and Camus as (inevitable) touchstones for law and literature scholarship. Chapters on the Czech novelist Ivan Klima, and on Umberto Eco's *Name of the Rose*, might prove more rewarding.

P. D. James, in her preface to *The Letters of Dorothy L. Sayers*, sets out cases made by Sayers's supporters and detractors. Barbara Reynolds is unequivocally of the former camp, and she has selected and edited this volume, covering the period 1899–1936, with appropriate dedication. C. S. Lewis regarded Sayers as one of the century's finest letter-writers, and there is much here to support his view, from the animated letters of a schoolgirl, through moving responses to turbulent personal relationships, to the professional correspondence of the writer. Reynolds has appended the subtitle, 'The Making of a Detective Novelist', and the volume offers numerous insights into Sayers's literary practices, her approach to research, her views on precursors and contemporaries in detective fiction and her dealings with publishing institutions.

Marty Roth's prodigious ability to hold in prose suspension a startling array of ostensibly diverse texts, makes reading *Foul and Fair Play* a singular experience. The result is a stimulating immersion, although at times the mass of allusion threatens to overwhelm, as Roth ranges through 138 fictions, quoting 'lavishly', aspiring through induction, rather than deduction, to delineate the genre of classic detective fiction as 'variations on a tight set of conventions'. Beginning with summary of the lines drawn up by dismissive critics and by apologists, he proceeds to orchestrate details so that fictions from Poe to the 1960s can be read as if a single story. He acknowledges Todorov as a point of departure, but Roth does no more than suggest the skeleton supporting the flesh derived from Arthur Conan Doyle, Agatha Christie, Ian Fleming, Margery Allingham, John Dickson Carr, John Buchan, Eric Ambler and Dorothy Sayers, along with other British and American writers. Roth's insistence that this is an intrinsically masculine form of popular fiction will doubtless fuel debate.

The French novelist Georges Perec wrote of his interest in the detective novel as 'a game between an author and a reader'. This is cited in *Playtexts*, where Warren Motte examines the importance of the ludic in contemporary literature in a series of case-studies, including Perec, Italo Calvino and Umberto Eco. Vladimir Nabokov and Harry Mathews are the writers in English Motte addresses, which suggests neglect amongst British writers of the various modes of literary play. A useful introduction evaluates the contribution to discussion of the ludic of such theorists as Johan Huizinga, Roger Caillois and Jacques Ehrmann.

The Oulipo, founded by Raymond Queneau and François Le Lionnais in 1960, is the most significant group of writers devoted to exploration of ludic possibilities in literary composition. *Oulipo Laboratory* has been assembled by Atlas Press with customary care for accuracy in translation and high quality of presentation. Readers seriously concerned with European literary history in the twentieth century owe a real debt to this small publishing house, navigating the backwaters of the avant-garde, and bringing to light documents without which our understanding remains partial. This anthology collects theoretical statements, such as Italo Calvino's exposition of the compositional procedures that generated *If on a Winter's Night a Traveller*, and exemplary pieces such as Claude Berge's Oulipean tale of detection, 'Who Killed the Duke of Densmore?'. It is uniformly fascinating.

An earlier group of writers inviting the attention of readers concerned with twentieth-century literary history is identified in Martyn Cornick's *The Nouvelle Revue Française under Jean Paulhan, 1925–1940*. In addition to Paulhan's own work, the study examines Gide and Julien Benda, in particular, within the cultural history of the period. Cornick clarifies the engagement of this notable literary review with political issues in Europe between the world wars, and identifies Paulhan as 'arguably the century's most influential cultural impresario'.

In *The Time of Theory*, Patrick Ffrench sets out 'to rescue *Tel Quel* from the largely pejorative images of it in the English-speaking academic world'. So, while necessarily addressing the theoretical context constituted by such luminaries as Althusser, Lacan, Barthes, Foucault, Kristeva and Derrida, the emphasis in Ffrench's study falls on that review's presentation of 'a coherent and consistent theory of literature'. Philippe Sollers is the central figure, and *Tel Quel*'s engagement with earlier writers, and notably with Joyce, is carefully traced. By dividing and sub-dividing chapters, Ffrench manages to follow the various contributory strands without entangling them, and produces a welcome history of this significant arena for theorizing literary practices between 1960 and 1983.

Deborah L. Madsen has compiled *Postmodernism*, a bibliography that begins with a collection of essays published under that heading in 1926 by Bernard Iddings Bell. Madsen ventures across all disciplines 'from anthropology to zoology', but omits publications that do not have 'postmodernism' in their bibliographical title. Entries are arranged chronologically, which provides enlightening documentation of the currency gained by the term and its usage across various fields of enquiry. Madsen has aimed for comprehensiveness, but invites readers to inform her of omissions. She provides both a subject index and an author index to make this a most useful resource.

It is apposite to mention here that Susan Stewart's *Crimes of Writing* (1991) is now available in a paperback edition. Subtitled 'Problems in the Containment of Representation', Stewart explains: 'These essays examine the notions of authorship, authoring, authenticity, and authority within [the] history of exchanges between subjectivity and language'. The volume confirms Stewart as one of the most considerable cultural analysts and literary theorists currently at work. A striking combination of erudition and insight characterizes her readings, which include engagements with the rights of authors in seventeenth-century Europe, the eighteenth-century forger and inveterate imposter George Psalmanazar, the appropriation of folkloric genres to literary tradition, and the conjunctions of incest, travel and art in Hawthorne's *The Marble Faun*, before moving on to contemporary issues arising from practices of graffiti and pornography. A 'Coda' discusses J. G. Ballard's *Crash*, drawing on Lacan to propose 'the alterity of the Real'.

Mack Smith's *Literary Realism and the Ekphrastic Tradition* is an earnest and rigorous study of realism as 'a mode of literary change'. Smith examines the representation of works of art, their description and discussion, within five works of narrative fiction, in order to trace shifts in definition of that mode over centuries. Joyce's *Ulysses* and Pynchon's *Gravity's Rainbow* are his exemplary texts for analysing the revision of realism in the twentieth century. Studies of *Don Quixote*, *Emma* and *Anna Karenina*, precede them. At the heart of Smith's reading of *Ulysses*, lies his understanding that Joyce's 'representational technique reflects a shift in the modernist paradigm from a scientistic early modernism, as seen in Wittgenstein's atomistic theory of correspondence, to the coherentism of late modernism, as seen in the later Wittgenstein's theory of reality's social and linguistic construction'. This is an ambitious book, critically lucid and frequently insightful.

Stephen Bury's *Artists' Books* is a selective bibliography of the book as work of art during the years 1963 to this year. Sterne, Joyce and Michel Butor are acknowledged as novelists who have worked in adjacent areas, and who have provided inspiration, but Bury is specifically concerned with books made by workers in the visual arts. In prefatory essays he suggests a poetics of the artist's book, traceable from Blake through Mallarmé, Futurism, Dada, Surrealism and Fluxus. The inventiveness evidenced here will be of interest to readers considering the history of the book, and options available after *Finnegans Wake*. A serious criticism to be levelled at this well-produced volume is that the identity of illustrations is not always readily apparent, due to inadequate labelling.

In *Money, Language, and Thought* (1982), Marc Shell produced a singularly invigorating work of literary theory. Now, in *Art and Money*, he has written a handsomely illustrated complementary volume. Issues of representation and exchange, of reproduction and forgery arising from analysis of money as a cultural phenomenon are here considered in relationships with visual art, from Christian iconographic tradition to the work of contemporary artists such as Les Levine and Joseph Beuys. Admirers of Shell's earlier work will find much of interest here.

(b) Individual Authors: 1900–1945

The Conrad who interests Christopher GoGwilt, in *The Invention of the West: Joseph Conrad and the Double-Mapping of Europe and Empire*, is 'the Conrad who consistently sustains an ambivalent rhetorical position towards the larger cultural, historical, and political realities his fiction seeks to represent'. In particular, the idea of the West is at stake here. GoGwilt argues that in Conrad's narratives the 'crisis of modernity' is not 'a crisis of Western culture' but 'a crisis that produces, in reaction, the idea of Western culture'. His study proceeds to examine Conrad's fiction in relation to this general argument about the 'historicity' of the term 'the West'. He admits that 'these terms are not rigorously theorized, but are rather attempts to link literary analysis with debates on intellectual history'. After a fascinating introductory chapter on Conrad's rhetorical invention of the west, GoGwilt pursues extended discussions of 'Karain: A Memory', *Lord Jim*, *A Personal Record*, *Heart of Darkness*, *Under Western Eyes*, *The Secret Agent* and *Nostromo*. This excellent study is capped with a Raymond Williams-inspired genealogy of the keyword 'the West'. It is one of the finer books on Conrad to have appeared in recent years.

Ralph E. Matlaw, in 'Dostoevskii and Conrad's Political Novels', in *Dostoevskii and Britain* (ed. W. J. Leatherbarrow), provides convincing evidence for us to suspect that Conrad's expressed 'hatred' of Dostoevskii ('he is too Russian for me') disguises the 'patent similarity' of his books to Dostoevskii's. However, he also argues that recognition of the relationship needs to be more than gestural acknowledgment, and wishes to elaborate this critical commonplace with more extended analysis. It is therefore something of a pity that he should allow his comparative discussion of *Under Western Eyes* and *Crime and Punishment* to be diluted by a brief concluding excursion into the potential similarities of *The Secret Agent* and *The Devils*.

In 'Twirling Moustaches and Equestrian Statuary: Polish Semiotics in Conrad's *Nostromo*' (*Mosaic* 28.iii.31–56), Jean M. Szczypien juxtaposes a number of paintings by Polish artists in which the wearing of a moustache is a patriotic emblem (and discourses in which the *twirling* of the moustache 'portends something ominous', usually reluctance or resentment) with the facial hair sported, and sported with, by Charles Gould and Nostromo. She then brings in Polish statuary to explain the imagery of Gould as a figure on the 'Horse of Stone ... at the entrance of the Alameda'. As the shifts of attention suggest, the article is something of a farrago of miscellaneous connections, but it is an engaging and entertaining one.

Obe Martin Skilleås writes on 'Restraint in the Darkness' (*ES* 76.52–63). What he means by 'restraint' is nothing theorized, but the quotidian senses of personal ethical and official social moderation and repression. Kurtz, of course, works in an environment in which neither can be sustained. The narrative, however, practises linguistic and stylistic restraint by refusing to tell all. Thus restraint and its lack are both demonstrated. Con Coroneos also has a stab at probing the darkness produced by the narrative's reticence in 'The Cult of *Heart of Darkness*' (*EIC* 45.1–23). Contrasting two views of art – one which sees it as that which 'repairs damaged experience' and another which views art as itself internally flawed and contradictory – Coroneos asks us to consider their potential compatibility, and sees *Heart of Darkness* as 'an exemplary instance of the interplay of suspicion and redemption'. The discussion that follows relates the aura-like qualities of Conrad's writing *in general* with the thinking of, among others, Benjamin, Freud, Wittgenstein and Marx. But it doesn't offer the analysis of *Heart of Darkness* which it promises.

Alissa Hamilton examines 'The Construction and Deconstruction of National Identities Through Language in the Narratives of Ngugi wa Thiong'o's *A Grain of Wheat* and Joseph Conrad's *Under Western Eyes*' (*ALC* 8.137–51): 'Conrad and Ngugi both embark, in gripping their pens, on the colonial enterprise destined to direct them into the heart of a land containing the seeds of contamination. While the journey of the one ends in paralysing infection, the journey of the other ends in a mobilizing injection with the seeds of contamination.' Conrad is the former. Another comparativist, Bart Westerweel, explores *She* as a precursor of *Heart of Darkness* in ' "An Immense Snake Uncoiled": H. Rider Haggard's Heart of Darkness and Imperial Gothic', one of the contributions to *Exhibited by Candlelight: Sources and*

Developments in the Gothic Tradition (ed. Valleria Tinkler-Villani, Peter Davidson and Jane Stevenson).

Priscilla L. Walton writes on ' "This vague feeling of their difference": Race, Gender, and the Originary Impetus in Conrad's *Almayer's Folly*' (*ArielE* 26.ii.95–108). The 'originary impetus' is the desire (by Conrad and his characters) to return to their beginnings. Walton feels that in *Almayer's Folly* 'the precedent ... assumes an inordinate importance', that the text 'overtly privileges that which has gone before', particularly in that Almayer seeks a return to Europe, Mrs Almayer to pre-colonial Sambir, and their daughter Nina to her Malay roots. As well as emphasizing the desirability of seeking one's origins, the novel also signifies its inevitable failure.

Tony Tanner does something rather unique in 'Paper Boats and Casual Cradles' (*CritQ* 37.1.42–56), the text of a lecture in a series in which senior critics were asked 'to re-read an early piece of criticism which they had written, and to consider the difference between the critical assumptions underlying or motivating the early piece and their current critical position or orientation'. Tanner's chosen text is his 'earliest critical effort – a short monograph on Conrad's *Lord Jim*'. Surprisingly, he discovers that there is little that he would want to change, that the early Tanner was perhaps more 'on the ball' than the later. Much of what follows is autobiographical. If Tanner wouldn't change much, he would 'undoubtedly say more on certain topics'. But none of these topics disrupts the bourgeois humanist cast of thought which Tanner is consciously proud of espousing. The lecture is more of a paean to that than to Conrad.

Revel K. Wilson offers 'Ivan Turgenev's *Rudin* and Joseph Conrad's *Heart of Darkness*: A Parallel Interpretation' (*CLS* 32.26–41). Essentially, this is a routine summary of similarities in plot, character and thematic concern: 'Both Turgenev and Conrad looked to reason, light, and duty, to define what is best in humanity. As potential bearers of light, Rudin and Kurtz both appeal to those common mortals who in an atheistic age crave spiritual and moral authority.' Brian W. Shaffer explores 'the connection between a "criminal class of revolutionists" and the consumers of illicit pornography' in ' "The Commerce of Shady Wares": Politics and Pornography in Conrad's *The Secret Agent*' (*ELH* 62.443–66). In making this connection, Conrad was both representing and playing on 'late-Victorian England's pervasive twin-anxieties over uncontrolled sex and politics'. But he was also, Shaffer suggests, lampooning those anxieties – an ingenious but arguable reading which does have the merit of compounding this novel's already legendary status as an exemplar of irony and paradox. Mahmad K. Kharbutli wants to know 'why is the journey back to man's primitive existence, or to the unconscious, so significant to Marlow on the personal level?' in 'Marlow's "Victory" in Conrad's *Heart of Darkness*' (*FMLS* 31.289–97). In an article which ought to be commended for its brevity, his answer is that it allows him to overcome his complexes.

In 'Defining Frames: The Prefaces of Henry James and Joseph Conrad' (*HJR* 16.66–92), Vivienne Rundle stresses contrasts rather than confluences: James's prefatory frames are 'authoritarian', whereas 'Conrad's prefaces are designed to encourage the reader's participation in the narrative system'; unlike James, 'Conrad appears hesitant to theorize ever about his own novels'. This essay won a competition co-sponsored by the Henry James Society and the Joseph Conrad Society, and one can see why: it is a piece of major scholarship. S. W. Reid, looking aslant at the possibilities for Conrad scholars in the digital age, welcomes the prospects but argues that a book-centred scholarly culture needs to be retained, in 'Conrad in Print and on Disk' (*SNNTS* 27.375–86). Anthony J. Cascardi wonders 'What has Conrad to say to philosophy that it does not already know?', and vice versa, in 'Ethics and Aesthetics in Joseph Conrad' (*WHR* 27.iii.17–35). In what is essentially an assessment of Fredric Jameson's reading of Conrad, his essay takes in *Lord Jim*, *The Nigger of the 'Narcissus'* and, in passing, *Heart of Darkness*. Marja Warehime's 'Exploring Connections and Rediscovering Difference: *Gide au Congo*' (*FR* 68.457–65) is only tangentially about Conrad.

Michael Squires looks at 'D H Lawrence's Narrators, Sources of Knowledge, and the Problem of Coherence' (*Criticism* 37.469–91). The awkwardness of the title is matched by the difficulty of Squires's chosen range of reference: *The White Peacock*, *Sons and Lovers*, *The Rainbow*, *Women in Love* and *Lady Chatterley's Lover* are all cited and quoted in an article whose main body is only 20 pages long. The argument is that the 'complex fragmentation' of Lawrence's prose can be understood by attention to his use of fictional narrators. Squires examines particular passages from the texts noted above in great detail, actually offering 'recast' versions of each which eliminate disruptions in textual coherence. Such an exercise may appeal to those using Lawrence to teach about language: Squires is much less modest, in his final paragraph, about the importance of his method.

Mosaic (28) has been extraordinarily keen on Lawrence this year. There are no less than three articles on him in as many issues. James C. Cowan continues his fascinating exploration of Lawrence's sex life and views on sexuality in 'Lawrence, Freud and Masturbation' (i.69–98). This is done with the usual *élan* that Cowan has shown on previous occasions. He studies Lawrence's frequent comments on and condemnations of masturbation in parallel with the very similar views of Freud and other early psychoanalytic theorists. He then tries something much more difficult, namely to 'discuss Lawrence's own masturbatory experiences and fantasies'. The main sources are the (two versions of the) poem 'Virgin Youth' and a number of miscellaneous passages in other poems and some of the fiction. But it is impossible to 'reconstruct' anything adequately biographical from such sources, although Cowan does his best. In 'The Thermodynamics of Gender: Lawrence, Science and Sexism' (ii.83–108), Michael Wutz considers Lawrence's interest in science and technology. As usual in such discussions, the extent and profundity of a writer's connection with the body of knowledge which interests the critic is grossly exaggerated. Who would have guessed that 'the protocols and theorems of thermodynamics . . . operate as organizational models in Lawrence's world', or that 'these principles become a paradigm for his management of gender relationships', and that 'thermodynamic principles function in concentrated form in one of Lawrence's most famous stories, "Odour of Chrysanthemums" '? Needless to say, Lawrence was not conscious of these connections: the science of heat was simply so 'deeply embedded in the cultural imagination of late Victorian England' that Wutz feels quite happy that it must also have been deeply embedded in D. H. Lawrence's. If one accepts this logic, the article will be invaluable. Isobel M. Findlay, in 'Word-perfect but Deed-demented: Canon Formation, Deconstruction, and the Challenge of D. H. Lawrence' (iii.57–81) wants critics to 're-read Lawrence for themselves' rather than the mediated Lawrence that comes to us via Eliot and Leavis. But what about the Lawrence mediated by Isobel M. Findlay – one whose literary criticism can rather smoothly be aligned with a revolutionary but para-doxically establishment deconstruction? Shouldn't critics be just as suspicious of that in deciding to 're-read Lawrence for themselves'?

The comparativists have also been out in force around Lawrence this year. Robert Gingher draws a number of biographical and textual comparisons between Ezra Pound and Lawrence in 'Pound/Lawrence: A Revaluation' (*Paideuma* 24.ii–iii.149–62). His bottom line is that, as well as sharing acquaintances, they both wanted to 'make it new'. There is a brief compar-ative discussion of Lawrence's 'Bavarian Gentians' with Pound's fourth canto. For George A. Panichas, it is a 'vision of evil' that Lawrence has in common with Dostoevskii, in 'F M Dostoevskii and D H Lawrence: Their Vision of Evil' (in W. J. Leatherbarrow, ed., *Dostoevskii and Britain*). This is essentially a series of observations on the confluences between Loerke in *Women in Love* and Svidrigailov in *Crime and Punishment* and between Gerald Crich and Rodion Raskol'nikov in the same two novels respectively. Panichas's easy acceptance of 'evil' as a valid concept in literary discussion prepares us for his positively religious conclusion: the two authors' 'brave refusal to surrender to those forces that would destroy creative life is a source of the greatness of their art, and it lends to their search and prophetic vision a quality of heroism that carries with it the seeds of hope and redemption'. George J. Zytaruk is thankfully more down to earth in his contribution to a book in the same series, *Tolstoi and Britain* (ed. W. Gareth Jones). 'D. H. Lawrence's *The Rainbow* and Leo Tolstoy's *Anna Karenina*: An Instance of Literary "Clinamen"' views *The Rainbow* as a 'swerve' (*clinamen*) from *Anna Karenina*. Lawrence, in a Harold Bloom-like way, is seen as inevitably 'misreading' Tolstoi to produce Ursula as 'a correction and extension of Anna'. Meanwhile, Calvin Bedient thinks 'Robinson Jeffers and D. H. Lawrence came spinning out of the same cultural waterspout' in that, for both, 'physics and theories of evolution on the one hand, and disgust with historical humanity on the other ... led to a religion of the inhuman universe' ('Robinson Jeffers, D H Lawrence, and the Erotic Sublime', in William B. Thesing (ed.), *Robinson Jeffers and a Galaxy of Writers: Essays in Honor of William H Nolte*). In terms of specific texts, the focus is mainly on Jeffers's 'Roan Stallion' *vis-à-vis* Lawrence's *St Mawr*, with Jeffers's 'Cawdor', 'The Inhumanist' and 'The Women at Point Sur' thrown into the pot along with Lawrence's 'The Woman Who Rode Away' and 'The Man Who Died'.

The most notable and original book of the year in Lawrence studies was *Editing D. H. Lawrence: New Versions of a Modern Author* (ed. Charles L. Ross and Dennis Jackson). At first glance this looks like an extended apology for the Cambridge Edition of the Works and Letters of D. H. Lawrence: ten of its contributors are directly involved in that project. Some of the essays are, regrettably, just that: Helen Baron clearly thinks the CUP edition of *Sons and Lovers* which she jointly prepared should render 'interred' the 'eighty-year-old tradition of reprinting a botched, censored, and butchered text'. The emotiveness of the language here suggests that her contribution, 'Some Theoretical Issues Raised by Editing *Sons and Lovers*', is more a cry of defensiveness against some of the reviews that edition received than the theoretical reflection its title promises (for a version of the 'butchered' text, see the Oxford World Classics edition, edited – or not edited – by David Trotter, and published this year). But thankfully, even within the Cambridge coterie, there are more liberal voices. John Worthen's 'Facts in Fiction: With a Short Argument About Authorial Intention' is a convincing critique of G. Thomas Tanselle's influential theory of editorial practice, valuably stressing that 'editorial methods, while often claiming an origin in editorial principles, are in my experience as likely to be based on strategies as on principles'. What Worthen means, in particular, is that the intended market for a particular edition is likely to influence the methods its editor uses. He might have added, of course, that methods are sometimes deployed *to create* a market (arguably the case with the CUP *Sons and Lovers*, for example). The volume as a whole, then, is much more plural than its domination by CUP editors would suggest. Those who are not CUP editors – particularly one of the editors of the volume itself – are sometimes heavily critical of Cambridge's pretensions and hubris. The book even contains its own meta-reflection, William E. Cain's 'Commentary on *Editing D. H. Lawrence: New Versions of a Modern Author*'. The volume is that rare creature: one that lives up to its claim to establish a dialogue between practice and theory.

Macdonald Daly's 'Lawrence, Leavis and the Left' (*DUJ* 87.343–56) charts Lawrence's changing fate at the hands of English socialist critics in the 1930s, explaining the changes and shifts in their evaluations of Lawrence as the product of an attempt to balance two countervailing forces, namely indigenous British cultural traditions and the demands of Soviet cultural policy in this period.

A matter of little moment is covered in Stephen Derry's 'D. H. Lawrence, "Future Men", and *The War of the Worlds*' (*N&Q* 42.208–9), which sets the record straight on the source of a reference made in a letter of 1913, and instructs the editors of the Cambridge edition to rewrite their explanatory note. Those who consider it valuable to publish on this sort of thing could easily have a piece in every issue of *N&Q* from now until Doomsday: the Cambridge edition is inevitably full of such negligible errors. A more interesting connection of Wells and Lawrence is John Worthen's 'Orts and Slarts: Two Biographical Pieces on D. H. Lawrence' (*RES* 46.25–40), in which he issues two supplements to his biography of Lawrence's early years. The first concerns a correspondence between Louie Burrows and Wells soon after the publication of his novel *The Bulpington of Blup* in 1932. Burrows assumed that Theodore Bulpington, the main character, was modelled on Lawrence. She had no basis for doing so. Wells's side of the correspondence is missing, other than his terse note on Burrows's embarrassed reply once he had informed her of her mistake: '*File*. This lady is a mythomaniac.' Worthen briefly re-reads the novel and comments on how the correspondence demonstrates that Burrows was still obsessed with Lawrence more than 20 years after their abortive engagement. The second half of Worthen's article answers at considerable length a telling question inadequately considered in his biography: 'Why on earth did Lawrence send his old friend Jessie Chambers – the original of his fictional creation of Miriam Leivers – the page-proofs of *Sons and Lovers* in March 1913, two months before the book was published?'

Steven Venturino's 'Translating Tibet's Cultural Dispersion: Solzhenitsyn, Paine, and Orwell in Dharamsala' (*Diaspora* 4.153–80) explains how differently *Animal Farm* and *Nineteen Eighty-Four* are (or can be) read within the frames of Tibetan politics and culture and attempts to explain how this might inform translation theory.

Michael Patrick Gillespie's 'The Legacy of 1914: Pound, Lewis, Eliot, and the Composition of *Finnegans Wake*' (*Paideuma* 24.2/3.131–48) points out that Joyce's novel acknowledges 'the formative impact of Pound, Eliot and Lewis as literary figures and, obliquely, as influences and models', but apart from telling us that Joyce 'held Wyndham Lewis in high esteem' it has remarkably little to say about the putative relationship [M.D.].

In his foreword to Vincent J. Cheng's *Joyce, Race and Empire*, Derek Attridge claims that it is the first book on Joyce devoted to 'exploring the role of art within the struggle against national and racial oppression'. There have actually been numerous books and articles on Joyce's oppositional politics in recent years, so if this hyperbolic claim is true at all, it can only be in the limited sense that previous studies have foregrounded discourses of gender or class rather than race (although Enda Duffy went over some of this ground in *The Subaltern Ulysses* [*YWES* 75.511–12]). Cheng himself is rather more circumspect and admits that he is just one of a number of scholars who have begun to revise the 'High Modernist acceptance of an apolitical Joyce'. This ritual dethronement of the 'apolitical Joyce' is becoming rather unconvincing as a way of inaugurating new contextual studies of his work. Cheng's study, in particular, turns Joyce into such an exemplary critic of colonial ideology that it raises questions about what it means to be 'political' at all. *Joyce, Race and Empire* is divided into three main sections, on *Dubliners*, *Ulysses* and *Finnegans Wake*, in each of which Cheng very carefully and methodically combines detailed reading of the text with historical research and the insights of such writers as Edward Said and Frantz Fanon. As a textbook, rather than a pioneering 'first' book, it is very sound. But it always moves towards the same conclusion: Joyce analyses and exposes the workings of 'binary enmity' and recommends (particularly in the person of Bloom) internationalism and the acceptance of 'heterogeneous multiplicities'. In this way, ironically, by ensuring that Joyce always emerges as the transcendent critic of any and every oppressive discourse, Cheng also ensures that he actually remains a fundamentally 'apolitical' figure.

A more genuinely ground-breaking work, in this respect and many others, is Joseph Valente's *James Joyce and the Problem of Justice: Negotiating Sexual and Colonial Difference*. Valente does not waste time setting up a dummy 'apolitical Joyce'. He recognizes the deeper paradox that binary structures may be involved in a critique of the law as well as in its enforcement and sees Joyce's texts as struggling towards justice rather than easily prescribing it. His book is an extended contribution to discussion of the relevance of literature to jurisprudence and ethical issues. According to Valente, 'the problem of justice finds its proper home in literary writing' and he sets out to explore, through readings of selected texts, the way in which 'the liberal imperative to justice . . . acts as a shaping force in Joyce's representational and counter-representational strategies'. This alone would probably make for an interesting and original study. But Valente has greatly added to its value by selecting texts which highlight what he calls 'the underdiscovered Joyce': his three central chapters focus on 'A Mother' from *Dubliners*, *Giacomo Joyce* and *Exiles*, and are highly instructive and illuminating on each. This approach ensures that the book amply repays the considerable attention it demands;

which is just as well, because it must be said that Valente's writing is extremely difficult to follow at times, and it does sometimes seem that the difficulty of the prose is in excess of the difficulty of the concepts themselves. But there are some wonderful touches elsewhere, and the scholarship and insight are of a very high order throughout.

Joseph Valente also has an essay, 'The Novel and the Police (Gazette)' (*Novel* 29.8–18), in a special issue of *Novel* on 'Joyce and the Police'. Here he homes in on the reference to the *Police Gazette* in 'Cyclops' and shows how it 'serves to explore, one might say expose, the underlying affective dynamic of tabloid journalism, which has become an increasingly pervasive and powerful discourse in western culture to the present day'. Other essays in the same issue, which originated in a conference on 'Joyce and Modern Culture', include Kimberly J. Devlin on 'Bloom and the Police: Regulatory Vision and Visions in *Ulysses*' (*Novel* 29.45–62), and a response to Devlin and Valente by Jennifer Levine, 'Rounding up the Usual Suspects' (*Novel* 29.100– 13). As the issue title suggests, all the essays are concerned in one way or another with the dynamics of cultural history at work in Joyce's texts. History, particularly Irish history, is a rather more problematic affair for Thomas C. Hofheinz in his *Joyce and the Invention of Irish History: Finnegans Wake in Context*. Hofheinz's preoccupation is with the *Wake* as a meditation on historiography, and as such his study is an extension of work begun by James Fairhall and Robert Spoo in their recent books on the earlier fiction. But Hofheinz is much less comfortable than his predecessors with theoretically determined frameworks for the analysis of narrative and context, and takes particular issue with materialist or collectivist approaches to Joyce, preferring to emphasize the uncertainties of individual consciousness: 'Joyce depicts narration as a compulsive, essential, but inadequate expression of human desire ... people who tell stories to and/or about themselves communicate not only their attempted masteries of life and time, but also the anxieties they feel as their stories' light flickers uncertainly against encroaching darkness.' There is some interesting documentary detail in later chapters, relating the *Wake* to different aspects of Irish historiography, and also reconsidering Joyce's use of Vico. But a flickering and uncertain light is not the best kind for reading by, and it is questionable whether this difficult book, about a still more difficult book, will prove (as Hofheinz says he hopes it will) 'widely useful to readers of many backgrounds'.

Finnegans Wake has come in for an unusually large share of this year's work on Joyce. Hofheinz's interest in the reader is echoed in James Cahalan's ' "Dear Reader" and "Drear Writer": Joyce's Direct Addresses to His Readers in *Finnegans Wake*' (*TCL* 41.306–18), in which Cahalan notes that although Joyce never addresses his readers directly in any of his other works, he does so repeatedly in *Finnegans Wake*, in a manner that may be designed to evoke the innovations of eighteenth-century novelists. Readers who struggled with Sheldon Brivic's last book, *The Veil of Signs: Joyce, Lacan and Perception* (UIIlP, 1991) may wonder at the subtitle of his latest, *Joyce's Waking Women: An Introduction to Finnegans Wake*. In fact Brivic's idiosyncratic style works well in this context, and the book can be recommended as a helpful textbook, easy to read and with plenty of cross-references to other Joyce scholarship. Brivic does not pretend to offer a comprehensive overview of the text. His interest is in feminism in the *Wake*, particularly as articulated through ALP, and there is an interesting chapter on ALP's association with images of Africa. Brivic's way of embracing feminism may, however, be problematic for some readers. Danis Rose makes an important contribution to the study of the way *Finnegans Wake* was put together in *The Textual Diaries of James Joyce*. The 'diaries' he refers to are the notebooks that Joyce filled with lists of words and phrases from his reading and that he later used as the basic quarry for his 'Work in Progress'. The notebooks were purchased and catalogued by the University of Buffalo, and have been available since 1978, in photo-replicate form, as part of *The James Joyce Archive*. Rose now provides a new annotated catalogue of this material, fully cross-referenced to the Buffalo catalogue but designed to supersede it, based on his reconstruction of the order in which Joyce used the notebooks and including a number of non-extant notebooks, the existence and probable contents of which he has been able to infer from other documents. Rose's mastery of his material, not just the notebooks themselves but the translation of their contents into the drafts and final text of *Finnegans Wake*, is awe-inspiring, and his enthusiasm for his task is engaging. As a result, what might have been a fairly arid exercise in obscure textual scholarship (the catalogue after all is only relevant to users of *The James Joyce Archive*) becomes a rather compelling read. The book works at several different levels, combining editorial apparatus with biographical narrative and exegesis of particular passages from the *Wake* (or *wake* as Rose always types it) and providing several useful appendices, including a list of all Joyce's addresses between 1922 and 1941. Rose represents the 'genetic' approach to *Finnegans Wake*, the theoretical implications of which are explored in more detail in the essays collected in *Probes: Genetic Studies in Joyce* (ed. David Hayman and Sam Slote). A further contribution to this project is provided by Inge Landuyt and Geert Lernout in 'Joyce's Sources: *Les grands fleuves historiques*' (*JJA* 99–138), which suggests a new secondary source for some of Joyce's more erudite references in *Finnegans Wake*. In 'The Complexity of *Finnegans Wake*' (*JJA* 79–98), Thomas Jackson Rice reflects on the gap between this kind of 'local' study of particular elements in Joyce's text and more 'global' explanations of the work as a whole. The gap can be filled, he suggests, by an awareness of the 'emergent sciences of complexity' which can 'provide the external frame of reference that may support an ultimate solution of the *Finnegans Wake* "problem"', making a local and a global grasp of the *Wake* possible in terms of the nature, function, and significance of complication *per se*'.

Scientific awareness is productively applied to *Ulysses* by Stephen Whittaker and Francis X. Jordan in 'The Three Whistles and the Aesthetic of Mediation: Modern Physics and Platonic Metaphysics in Joyce's *Ulysses*' (*JJQ* 33.27–47). Whittaker and Jordan take as their starting-point this question: how, in 'Telemachus', does Mulligan contrive to whistle from the Martello Tower at just the right moment to get two answering whistles from the departing mailboat a mile away? The answer does not lie in coincidence but in the artful manipulation of Newtonian physics: Mulligan relies on being able to *see* the steam whistle being blown several seconds before the sound of it reaches the tower. Whittaker and Jordan then compare the way these two signals arrive at different times to the way information is mediated in different stages in the narrative (we are told about the whistles before we are told about the mailboat) and go on to develop the concept of an 'aesthetic of mediation' at work in *Ulysses*. The general concept is not as illuminating as the initial explanation, but the article also makes some interesting connections between Bloom, Odysseus and Socrates, via Plato's myth of reincarnation at the end of *The Republic*. Metaphysics is all very well, but as the narrator of 'Eumaeus' observes, it is 'the money question' that is really 'at the back of everything'. This is one of many cues for Mark Osteen's major new work, *The Economy of Ulysses: Making Both Ends Meet*, which offers a comprehensive reading of the novel in terms of economics: economic activity, economic metaphors, economies of style, even Joyce's way of 'repaying' people who had offended him by making fun of them as figures in the narrative. Osteen starts by noting a tension in Joyce's own life between extravagance and reserve, reflected in his writing in 'the oscillation between an economy of verbal excess and expenditure and an equally strong impulse towards control'. Osteen then proceeds to work his way through the whole novel, following up every detail that can possibly be related to his theme. The first reference to the money-lender Reuben J. Dodd in 'Hades', for example, produces four pages of very informative and interesting discussion of his relation to the real Dodd (John Joyce's creditor) and his significance in the novel, which in turn leads on to more interesting notes on Bloom, florins, drowned and saved men, and other recurring images. This is an ingenious book, amazingly rich in detail and insight. Other work on *Ulysses* this year includes Mark Gaipa, 'Culture, Anarchy, and the Politics of Modernist Style in Joyce's "Oxen of the Sun" ' (*MFS* 41.195–217), which interprets 'Oxen of the Sun' in terms of Matthew Arnold and 'the politics of national acculturation'; and Mark A. Wollaeger, 'Stephen/Joyce, Joyce/Haacke: Modernism and the Social Function of Art' (*ELH* 62.691–707), a thought-provoking discussion, focusing on a passage from 'Wandering Rocks', of the difficulties inherent in any attempt to 'recover and redeploy the avant-garde energies of Joyce's texts'. Johanna X. K. Garvey's 'City Limits: Reading Gender and Urban Space in *Ulysses*' (*TCL* 41.108–23) is an interesting but fairly brief survey of male appropriation of urban space in Joyce's Dublin, which probes the ambiguity of Joyce's attitudes to gender division and exclusion. Jay Clayton also analyses Joyce's representation of the city in 'Londublin: Dickens's London in Joyce's Dublin' (*Novel* 28.327–40). Still on *Ulysses*, Dennis Vanderspek's 'A Note on the Paradisiacal Era' (*N&Q* 42.211–12) suggests that a late addition to the proofs of 'Circe' can be traced to Joyce's irritation at Ezra Pound's announcement of 'the Pound era'.

More archival research on Joyce and Pound, and on many other subjects, is presented in a special issue of *JJQ* (32), 'Out of the Archives'. Robert Spoo presents a selection of 'Unpublished Letters of Ezra Pound to James, Nora, and Stanislaus Joyce' (533–81); and in 'Ezra Pound's Censorship of *Ulysses*' (583–95) Paul Vanderham analyses Pound's reasons for deleting certain passages from 'Calypso' before it was published in *The Little Review*. In 'Fascism and Silence: The Coded History of Amalia Popper' (*JJQ* 501–22), Vicki Mahaffey provides more information about the life of the woman who was identified by Richard Ellmann as the subject (or rather object) of *Giacomo Joyce*, and who also seems to have served as another model for Molly Bloom. Amalia Popper later published Italian translations of five stories from *Dubliners* and Mahaffey speculates about the coded message she may have been sending to Joyce through the stories she chose. Her article also includes an English version of Popper's short biographical sketch of Joyce, published with the *Dubliners* translations in 1935, which is of particular interest because it seems that Joyce himself may have ghost-written it. Joyce's editorial control over other early accounts of his life and work by his friends is further documented by Hugh Witemeyer in 'He Gave the Name: Herbert Gorman's Rectifications of *James Joyce: His First Forty Years*' (522–32).

After so many studies which position Joyce as transcendent hero, it is quite refreshing to find deprecatory references to him as 'this poor man' and 'this duplicitous man' in Kathleen Ferris's *James Joyce and the Burden of Disease*. Ferris's study, which is mainly biographical in its frame of reference, although it includes much sophisticated handling of textual detail, is a contribution to the ongoing revision of Richard Ellmann's classic account of Joyce's life. Ellmann's Joyce was a secular humanist who outgrew his Catholic background: Ferris begins by inviting readers to set aside this familiar construction and consider her 'very different representation of the artist as a guilt-ridden, diseased, deracinated Catholic who repented his sins, and whose works form an allegory of his life'. The disease in question is syphilis, and Ferris assembles a quite impressive array of evidence, literary and medical, to argue that Joyce contracted this disease in his early twenties and that he then went on to infect not only his family but also (by way of confession) his two main characters, Stephen and Bloom, who betray various symptoms in *Ulysses*. The theory extends to some ingenious readings of *Finnegans Wake*: all the references to tea, for example, and to the letter T in *The Book of Kells*, are interpreted as allusions to *T.pallidum*, the spirochete which causes syphilis. It is a stimulating read, but there are several problems with Ferris's approach. She is adept at uncovering possible allusions to disease in Joyce's writing, but does not allow for the possibility that Joyce as literary artist may have had other reasons for putting them there besides confession. There is also the problem that, as a hypothesis about Joyce's medical history, Ferris's argument is dependent on medical evidence which few readers will be qualified to evaluate. The idea that Joyce had syphilis has been debated before, and it seems unlikely that *James Joyce and the Burden of Disease* can or will settle the matter. But any future biographer of Joyce will certainly have to address Ferris's contribution to this issue and in the meantime she has provided an interesting alternative perspective on Joyce's writings. The same kind of judgement is invited by Martha Fodaski Black's overlong *Shaw and Joyce: 'The Last Word in Stolentelling'*, which sets out a detailed case for George Bernard Shaw's 'relevance and presence in Joyce's fiction as a precursor'. Black finds 'shards of Shaw' in all the major works, including *Exiles* and *Stephen Hero*, and traces parallels and connections between the lives of the two writers. *Shaw and Joyce* inevitably invites comparison with Grace Eckley's *The Steadfast Finnegans Wake* (*YWES* 75.515–16) which attempted to establish that W. T. Stead, Shaw's adversary in *The Quintessence of Ibsenism*, was the key 'presence' for Joyce. Black's argument is rather less restrictive in scope and probably more convincing than Eckley's. Her review of Eckley (*JJQ* 32.441–6) can be read as a companion-piece to this book (though the existing 445 pages will probably be more than enough for most readers).

Without any of the controversy surrounding his earlier critical edition of *Ulysses*, Hans Walter Gabler has brought out companion critical editions of *Dubliners* and *A Portrait of the Artist as a Young Man*. I was not able to obtain review copies of these editions, which were published by Garland in 1993, but they are discussed in detail by Laurie Teal in *ELT* 38.186–94. CUP also included *Dubliners* (ed. Andrew Goodwyn), in their 'Cambridge Literature' series, designed primarily for use in schools and colleges. Goodwyn provides some interesting teaching resource material, which could usefully be adapted to undergraduate work, but fails to point out that the text he is using seems to be the uncorrected 1914 first edition, complete with non-Joycean quotation marks and various other disfigurements (Gabriel has to 'get out' rather than 'set out' on his journey westward in 'The Dead', for example). This text has turned up in several cheap editions since it came out of UK 50-year copyright in 1992, but a European Union directive this year should have had the effect of consigning it back into copyright for a longer term. On this complicated issue of copyright, which seems increasingly fraught with tension for Joyce studies, there are two helpful statements in *JJQ* (32 [1994].155 and 33.13–16). Carol Loeb Shloss also discusses the legal and moral issues involved in confrontations between Joyce scholars and the Joyce Estate in 'Joyce's Will' (*Novel* 29.114–27).

This year saw the welcome reappearance of *JJB*, the last issue of which was dated 1992. This Leeds-based broadsheet does not publish substantial scholarly articles, but it is a useful source of information, reviews and shorter discussion pieces such as Michael Mason's 'Which *Ulysses*?' (*JJB* 42.1), a survey of the ten different editions that have become available since 1992. More substantial in one way, much less so in another, *HJS* made its debut in cyberspace this year. Besides articles such as Lawrence James's 'Phoenix ex Machina: Joyce's Solicitation of Hypertext' and Donald Theall's 'Beyond the Orality/Literacy Dichotomy: James Joyce and the Pre-History of Cyberspace', the first 'issue' includes a useful catalogue of films and videos (including adaptations) relevant to the study of Joyce, and a list of other Joyce-related hypertext projects. Donald Theall preaches the gospel of hypertext and the 'post-mass-mediated age of telematics' with irritating complacency in *Beyond the Word: Reconstructing Sense in the Joyce Era of Technology, Culture and Communication*. This is not so much a book *about* Joyce as one in which he makes a special guest appearance in each chapter, often in quite interesting company – Orson Welles, Marshall McLuhan, *Star Trek*. Theall sees Joyce as an avant-garde communication theorist whose project, particularly in *Finnegans Wake*, was 'providing a new role for the poetry of language in a world where traditional conceptions of the book would wither away'. There is not much sense of the 'poetry of language' in the way Theall presents his case. But it cannot be denied that by making Joyce central to his argument about the future of all communication systems he has opened up a new field for the discussion of Joyce's continued relevance and avant-garde potential.

Two veteran captains of the 'Joyce Industry', Fritz Senn and Zack Bowen, had collections of their essays published this year. The essays in the Bowen volume, *Bloom's Old Sweet Song: Essays on Joyce and Music*, span over a quarter of a century of research on Joyce and music, but most are recent and post-date Bowen's previous book on this topic, *Musical Allusions in the Works of James Joyce*. The essays in the Senn collection, *Inductive Scrutinies: Focus on Joyce* (ed. Christine O'Neill), are mostly concerned with *Ulysses* and *Finnegans Wake*. Almost all the essays in both books have been published before. But *Inductive Scrutinies* includes an interview with Senn, and a bibliography of his writings since his previous collection in 1984.

As its title suggests, *James Joyce A–Z: An Encyclopaedic Guide to His Life and Work* (ed. A. Nicholas Fargnoli and Michael Patrick Gillespie), is a large-format reference book, designed mainly for non-specialist readers of Joyce. The range of topics covered, in over 800 entries and seven appendices, is commendable. One can find information here on most of the significant figures in Joyce's life and even quite minor characters in his fiction; there are entries for individual poems, essays and reviews in *Critical Writings*, stories in *Dubliners* and episodes in *Ulysses* and *Finnegans Wake*; the coverage also extends to important concepts and developments in Joyce scholarship and there are separate entries for some 20 eminent Joyceans, including Senn and Bowen. The glaring misprint on the back cover ('Stand *by* me now and ever in good stead'?) is not reassuring. It is also a pity there are no maps to accompany the geographical entries. But it is impossible for a book of this kind to satisfy all the demands that might be made of it, and on the whole the editors are to be congratulated for their sensible and accurate provision. Established Joyce scholars will probably have little use for this book (though they may be interested to see whether they are in it) but for those who are less familiar with the infrastructure of Joyce studies it should be a very useful source of basic information and elementary guidance.

Everyman have made a significant contribution to the study of H. G. Wells by publishing new editions of a dozen or more titles, in a format that includes introductory essay, explanatory notes, plot summary, critical history and a chronology of Wells's life and times. Taken together, all this material constitutes a substantial body of new work on Wells. The titles have been distributed to different editors in an intriguing way, implying several different audiences for Wells: some have gone to eminent science-fiction writers, some to freelance Wells enthusiasts, and some to academics. The academic editors seem to have done the best job: Macdonald Daly's edition of *The Invisible Man*, in particular, is very thoroughly annotated and contains an interesting analysis of the 'contrived scientificity' of Wells's treatment of invisibility. Where Wells features in other work published this year it is mostly by association with other authors. John Worthen's '*The Bulpington of Blup*: A Biographical Sidelight' (*RES* 181.26–32) tells how Louie Burrows misinterpreted Wells's 1932 novel *The Bulpington of Blup* as a portrait of her ex-fiancé, D. H. Lawrence, and wrote to Wells to thank him for his sensitive treatment of their relationship. Wells denied the identification and privately dismissed Burrows as a 'mythomaniac', but Worthen more sympathetically traces the parallels that Burrows would have responded to, and suggests that the novel serves as a useful reminder of 'the forces acting upon middle-class and lower-middle-class young people in the decade before the First World War'. A reference to Wells in one of Lawrence's own letters is traced to its source by Stephen Derry in 'D. H. Lawrence, "Future Men" and *The War of the Worlds*' (*N&Q* 42.208–9). It is worth noting that there are over 40 letters from H. G. Wells to George Bernard Shaw, many of them previously unpublished, in *Bernard Shaw and H. G. Wells* (ed. J. Percy Smith), the latest selection from Shaw's correspondence. Patrick Parrinder's *Shadows of the Future: H. G. Wells, Science Fiction and Prophecy* is reviewed in Section 1(a) of this chapter.

The Huxley centenary bore substantial fruit this year in *Now More Than*

Ever: Proceedings of the Aldous Huxley Centenary Symposium Munster 1994, a collection of 21 essays, edited by Bernfried Nugel. The essays are divided into six sections: Biography; Society and Politics; Religion; Philosophy; 'Genre and Beyond'; and 'Huxley's Critique of Pure Utopian Thought'. As this suggests, interest in Huxley extends across a range of different disciplines. Literary interests are represented in several sections: Peter Firchow discusses Huxley's use of Laforgue in 'Huxley, Eliot and the Origins of Poetic Modernism'; and Hans J. Rindisbacher examines the trope of 'olfactory perception' in *Brave New World* in 'Sweet Scents and Stench: Traces of Post/Modernism in Aldous Huxley's *Brave New World*'. Sally A. Paulsell argues that visual perception was peculiarly significant for Huxley in 'Color and Light: Huxley's Pathway to Spiritual Reality' (*TCL* 41.81–107) [R.S.].

This year as last, critics of Woolf seem to have been interested in, and exercised by, biography and the subject. It is fitting then, that this year should see the publication of the Shakespeare Head Press Edition of Woolf's own biography of *Roger Fry* (ed. Diane F. Gillespie), the product of an immense tension in Woolf between the impressionistic and the factual, written during the build up to the Second World War which turned her thoughts increasingly to Fry's views on 'civilisation'. Gillespie's introduction to the volume is thorough and well documented, focusing on Woolf's anxieties as both professional biographer and far from impartial friend of her subject. Her worries at the thought of the project before she undertook it, and as she gathered the copious material from Fry's family, friends and acquaintances, are recorded, as are Woolf's accounts of Fry's relationships with men and women, and her downplaying, in the book, of the relationship between Fry and Vanessa Bell. Such important relationships are examined briefly by Gillespie in the light both of Woolf's own squeamishness when it came to certain details, and of the pressure on her from Fry's family to be discreet. Gillespie also details the revisions and augmentations which Woolf made to the text at quite late stages, basing this edition on a comparison between the first English edition and a typescript version held in the United States. Omissions in the first American edition which are the result of pressure on Woolf from interested parties at the time, are replaced, although none of these changes are significant enough to alter the substance of the book for a new generation of readers. The edition includes the unacknowledged 'technical appreciation' of Fry's work, written by Vanessa Bell and Duncan Grant, and Woolf's *Woman's Leader* review of Fry's *Vision and Design*. By presenting the many responses to the work (by Woolf's contemporaries and by her later critics) Gillespie allows her reader to revisit the idea of biography, to ask questions about its form and function, as well as about the biographer who has, it can be said, more acknowledged cultural importance than her subject.

Helen Wussow demonstrates a related interest in biography in 'Virginia Woolf and the Problematic Nature of the Photographic Image' (*TCL* 40.1–14). Here, Wussow provides an interesting examination of Woolf's play with the idea of proliferating meanings through the visual image and its relation to the text which frames it, in particular her use of photographic images as part of her challenge to the centred, delimited subject of biography. She traces a way into Woolf's critique of the form of biography and examines the 'specular subject' of Woolfian biography, with particular reference to *Orlando* and *Roger Fry*, and includes a comparison of biographers' versions of

Woolf (principally Quentin Bell and Louise DeSalvo: Hermione Lee's biography was published too late for Wussow) through the manipulation and agency of the photographic image. *To The Lighthouse* is the principal point of reference in two other articles on Woolf in the same issue of this journal. William R. Handley, in 'The Housemaid and the Kitchen Table: Incorporating the Frame in *To The Lighthouse*' (15–41), plays fruitfully with an idea of frames and framing in *To The Lighthouse* (informed by Derrida's meditation on the *passe partout* of *The Truth in Painting*), by means of a critique of the novel's emphasis on aesthetic and socio-political judgements. In an accomplished essay it is shown how the domestic and the political are framed each by the other, giving rise to the other within the complex economy of ideas represented by *To The Lighthouse*. Handley succeeds, through close reading, in creating useful links between the details of psychoanalytic and philosophical meditations and the speech, thoughts and actions of Woolf's characters, particularly Lily Briscoe and Mr Ramsay, who polarize the artistic and the philosophical, a polarization that is implicitly dismantled by the use of Heidegger as a starting point. Laura Doyle's ' "These Emotions of the Body": Intercorporeal Narrative in *To The Lighthouse*' (42–71), is an interesting analysis of the phenomenological character of Woolf's narratives. Doyle's opening strategy is to align Woolf in the first instance with the later Merleau-Ponty, in particular emphasizing the significance of the relation of speech-body-world in the thought of both. Woolf is represented as 'politicizing' Merleau-Ponty's position by showing that 'the speech of intercorporeality' is far from neutral, and through her presentation of the narrative interplay of public and private spheres, for instance, exposes the patriarchal heterosexism that restricts Mrs Ramsay's 'intercorporeal mode of being' even while the figure of the mother is located at the centre.

Clare Hanson, in *Virginia Woolf*, locates *To The Lighthouse* as a pivotal text within the oeuvre because it identifies a shift in Woolf's exploration of gender towards a position where masculinity and femininity are examined as culturally constructed, subject to revision and renegotiation. In a book which deals with the novels and the longer discursive writing through meticulous attention to textual details, Hanson repositions Woolf within recent feminist readings of her work, emphasizing recognized parallels with Cixous and Irigaray, but altering the perception that their common ground is unchanging from the early to the later work. The later work is represented as moving towards a 'post-individual', 'post-humanist' vision of the future which is developed in *Between the Acts*, and which problematizes received notions of the construction of the subject and, ultimately (through meditations on history and art), meaning.

George M. Johnson's ' "The Spirit of the Age": Virginia Woolf's Response to Second Wave Psychology' (*TCL* 40.139–64), is introduced as the winner of the *TCL* Andrew J. Kappel Prize in Literary Criticism. The essay examines the intellectual contexts, actually confined to Cambridge, in which Woolf encountered 'modern' psychology, and traces pre-Freud notions of repression and social control in *The Voyage Out* and *Night and Day*. Pages of close reading result in Johnson asserting the derivative nature of Woolf's versions of the aetiology and significance of dream, and the relation between memory and instinctive behaviour, by underlining a debt to 'second wave' psychologists, specifically Henri Bergson and James Sully, via Nietzsche and Pater. What is perceived as a related Woolfian interest in the uncanny is laid at the door of her acquaintance with members of the Society for Psychical Research. Johnson subsequently maps Woolf's representations of 'interiors' onto end-of-century models available to her through her masculine acquaintances.

Johnson's essay is printed alongside two other articles on Woolf. The first of these is by Anne Fernald who, in '*A Room of One's Own*, Personal Criticism and the Essay' (*TCL* 40.165–89), examines the complex relation of literary criticism and autobiography, addressing the strengths and weaknesses of contemporary examples (by Jane Tompkins, Jane Gallop and Elizabeth Abel), alongside the insertion of the self in Woolf's discursive writing, particularly in *A Room of One's Own*. Woolf's responsiveness as a reader, rather than a tendency to legislate in cultural and intellectual contexts (she is contrasted with T. S. Eliot as critic), is underlined, in an argument which returns to questions of authority and, eventually, to Woolf's subtle use of interruption and 'distraction' as a means of making the point about (patriarchy's) power and woman's relation to thought. Next, Caroline Webb, in 'Listing to the Right: Authority and Inheritance in *Orlando* and *Ulysses*' (*TCL* 40.190–204), aligns Woolf's sketch of 'The Jessamy Brides' in her diary for March 1927 with Stephen Dedalus's 'A Pisgah Sight of Palestine', indeed, contrasts Woolf with Joyce essentially to confirm Woolf's marginal relation to a literary tradition inherited by Joyce. Woolf's writing practice in *Orlando*, particularly the preface, is seen as addressing related questions of 'linguistic and literary authority' as Joyce's serious word-play in *Ulysses*. The preface is read as a 'masque' foregrounding the complex play on authority and identity in *Orlando* itself as 'biography'.

Lucio Ruotolo, in 'Bernard Malamud's Rediscovery of Women: The Impact of Virginia Woolf' (*TCL* 40.329–41), examines the significance of Woolf's writing to Bernard Malamud, employing as a starting place Malamud's sense of his inability to write women and women's experience. This is a relatively undeveloped comparative study that initially aligns Malamud's 'In Kew Gardens' and 'Alma Redeemed' with Woolf's early sketches. Justification for the comparison is largely Malamud's enthusiasm for Woolf, and on the whole moments of interpretation, principally of episodes from *Dubin's Lives*, are interlaced with observations from Woolf biography. Not, strictly speaking, a comparative study, Kelly Anspaugh's 'Blasting the Bombardier: Another Look at Lewis, Joyce and Woolf' (*TCL* 40.365–78), is written entirely to contradict Bonnie Kime Scott's position on Wyndham Lewis as a modernist and critic of his modernist peers in her article 'Jellyfish and Treacle: Lewis, Joyce, Gender and Modernism' in Morris Beja and Shari Benstock, eds, *Coping with Joyce: Essays from the Copenhagen Symposium* [OSUO, 1989]). The sometimes facetious tone of the essay speaks to a collection of barely disguised agendas, and the conclusion reached is that Joyce needs saving, 'not *for* feminism, but *from* feminism – or, more precisely, from biographically phallacious feminist readings'. The views of Woolf and Lewis on *Ulysses* are contrasted. In the same issue but in a very different vein, Christy L. Burns, in 'Re-Dressing Feminist Identities: Tensions Between Essential and Constructed Selves in Virginia Woolf's *Orlando*' (*TCL* 40.342–64), suggests that Woolf engineers a 'parodic displacement' of essentialist positions on the subject, charted through *Orlando*. The novel, it is argued, anticipates contemporary debates which polarize essentialist and anti-essentialist positions: 'The crucial question of Woolf's novel becomes that of subjectivity, but subjectivity as it is embroiled in the problematics of historical change and sexuality.' Burns rehearses Woolf's continuation of the debate on identity in *A Room of One's Own*, engaging in the close reading of both it and *Orlando*.

Adam Parkes, in 'Lesbianism, History, and Censorship: *The Well of Loneliness* and the SUPPRESSED RANDINESS of Virginia Woolf's *Orlando*' (*TCL* 40.434–60), begins by distancing himself from Jane Marcus and Shari Benstock in their assertions of Woolf's solidarity with Radclyffe Hall during the trial of *The Well of Loneliness* for obscenity. In his analysis of contemporary responses to Hall's text, Parkes shows how notions of 'proper' reading were marshalled in the official view, and censure, of the book. He further emphasizes Hall's anti-feminist position and her stated support of various masculine medical/sexological discourses which aligned lesbianism and deviancy, making the focus Hall's reinforcement of heterosexism. In its ludic treatment of desire and identity, in contrast to Hall's perceived polemicism, *Orlando* is seen as 'dramatizing the problems of censorship in relation to "sapphism" ', which nourishes the debate on external agencies constructing the subject. In *Orlando*, Woolf is seen to anticipate Judith Butler's account of gender as performance, largely by calling into question the assumptions underpinning Hall's construction of lesbian identity in *The Well of Loneliness*.

Also with a concentration on Woolf and her contemporaries, Brian W. Shaffer's 'Civilization in Bloomsbury: Woolf's *Mrs Dalloway* and Bell's "Theory of Civilization" ' (*JML* 19.73–87) aligns Woolf and Clive Bell, presenting Bell's views on 'civilization' as expressed in *On British Freedom* and *Civilization* as part of the 'extratextual contexts' of Woolf's fiction, particularly *Mrs Dalloway*. The main emphasis is given to Bell's élitist discourses on class which Woolf is represented as challenging, even while she is identified as endorsing other aspects of Bell's 'philosophy'. Shaffer's conclusion repeats Raymond Williams's views on the value of 'individualism' for Woolf and her immediate friends, and, on the whole, he confirms existing views of Woolf on class and 'civilization', rather than carving out a new position. His principal interest stays with the notion of a strong identification with Bell, on the part of Woolf, which is ultimately subjected to a rigorous critique in the novels which are apparently motivated by an interest in, and anxiety concerning, 'civilization'.

Ellen Tremper is also interested in the notion of identification, both in terms of ideas and figures. In ' "The Earth of our Earliest Life": Mr Carmichael in *To The Lighthouse*' (*JML* 19.163–71), she takes issue with John Ferguson's essay, 'A Sea Change: Thomas De Quincey and Mr Carmichael in *To The Lighthouse*' (*JML* [1987]14.45–63; *YWES* 68.521), in particular with his 'misidentification' of De Quincey as the basis of *To The Lighthouse*'s Mr Carmichael. This she regards as irresponsible, not only because it is based, she demonstrates, on weak textual criticism, but also, primarily, because Ferguson uses it to reinforce the idea of 'madness' as the basis of Woolf's creativity. Ferguson's reasons for identifying De Quincey as the source for Carmichael are given, and subjected to considerable critical pressure. Tremper's impatience with his conclusion is justified by her own identification of a mathematician, Mr Wolstenholme, a visitor to the Stephens's house during Woolf's childhood, as the basis for Carmichael, which she does by careful reference to Quentin Bell's biography and to Woolf's 'A Sketch of the Past'. This identification, she suggests, neither upsets the crucial relationship in the novel between Lily Briscoe and Mr Ramsay, nor returns to a discredited thesis of 'madness' as the motivation for Woolf's literary production.

Patricia Kenig Curd, in 'Aristotelian Visions of Moral Character in Virginia Woolf's *Mrs Dalloway*' (*ELN* 33.40–57), reads *Mrs Dalloway* alongside certain of Aristotle's claims from the *Poetics* (read by Woolf) and the *Nichomachean Ethics* (not read by Woolf), to argue for the Aristotelian basis of moral character presentation in that novel. The suggestion that Woolf's work constitutes a feminist response to, or appropriation of, Aristotle, is barely developed, and the article in fact becomes a further representation of the characters of Clarissa Dalloway, Septimus Warren Smith and Richard Dalloway. Concentrating on the same novel, Jacob Littleton, in '*Mrs Dalloway*: Portrait of the Artist as a Middle-Aged Woman' (*TCL* 41.36–53), represents Clarissa Dalloway as a type of modernist artist, whose social gatherings can be viewed as happenings, or examples of 'event-art', which serve to destabilize certain traditional structures both of the culture and art. Clarissa, whose re-creation of experience is presented as a creative act of memory, is viewed as a controlling figure who subverts while she conforms. The analysis emerges out of an examination of Woolf's representation of public and private spheres within the novel and on the relationship between collective experience and individual existence. In this context the emotional parallels between Clarissa and Septimus are once again played out. The article is perhaps weakest where it attempts to deal with questions of 'Being' in *Mrs Dalloway* without staking out the philosophical territory to sustain the whole (no reference, strangely, is made to statements of collective identity, or community, in *Moments of Being*). The language used to establish the reading suggests a Sartrean parallel which is not fully, or confidently, developed in the given debate around 'Being', memory and forgetting. Donna K. Reed's 'Merging Voices: *Mrs Dalloway* and *No Place on Earth*' (*CL* 47.118–35) explores the parallels between *Mrs Dalloway* and Christa Wolf's novel *No Place on Earth* in terms of narrative style and their structural similarities, which are given their aesthetic and ideological significance. The article covers some of the same ground as Jacob Littleton's '*Mrs Dalloway*: Portrait of the Artist as a Middle-Aged Woman' in its emphasis on community feeling relieving individual isolation, acknowledging, as one would expect, the different social and political contexts in which Woolf and Wolf write. The emphasis is on intimacies of communication as 'communion' set up between the woman writer and reader, part of the general theme of erased boundaries and the interpersonal 'narration of consciousness', building on a thesis of the 'utopian' potentialities of genuine communication which is achievable between individuals but which is 'no place'. Within the novels women's voices achieve 'subjective authenticity' which characterizes the 'feminist utopia' which would yet include the spectrum of dispossessed, disenfranchised individuals. Woolf and Wolf both recognize, it is suggested, how conventional situations, mores and conditioning (the conventions that order the quasi-informal social gathering, for instance) provide a language in which unconventional statements may be made: this is the positive duplicity both writers enjoy and explore. Genuine communion occurs, both novelists assert, despite the rigid imposition of given social and political structures.

Following a very different trajectory, Diana L. Swanson, ' "My boldness terrifies me": Sexual Abuse and Female Subjectivity in *The Voyage Out*' (*TCL* 41.284–309), offers a reading of Woolf's first novel which refers almost exclusively to Louise DeSalvo's readings of Woolf's early experiences and their influence on her later writing offered in *Virginia Woolf: The Impact of Childhood Sexual Abuse on her Life and Work* (WP, 1989), and *Virginia Woolf's First Voyage: A Novel in the Making* (Macmillan, 1980). In contexts which are extremely diagnostic, blurring the boundary between Rachel Vinrace and Woolf herself, Woolf's writing practice is linked with degrees of self-censorship combined with the desire to tell, leading to an examination of *The Voyage Out* as an 'hysterical' text, arising out of the 'nameless atrocities' which, it is assumed, define the father–daughter relationship in both histories. This is ushered in by an assessment of critical responsibility as the sensitive decoding of messages distributed in the text, within an examination of Woolf's motives in covering her tracks in this 'writing cure'. Swanson is writing so much in the domain of DeSalvo that a question has to be asked about what she adds to the general premiss, within a recently explored thesis. The birth of Woolf as a subject, it is suggested, is written into her constant revisions of *The Voyage Out*, which also enacts her anxieties about intimate self-revelation. The challenge that defines Rachel Vinrace is to read the signs of personal and social repression more clearly than she is able to, where a successful act of interpretation would deliver her from the oppressive structures of patriarchy and give rise to her as a subject rather than an object of desire. Within the overall argument the article does not problematize the notion of the subject, and avoids questions of the performative completely.

In 'Reinventing Grief Work: Virginia Woolf's Feminist Representations of Mourning in *Mrs Dalloway* and *To The Lighthouse*' (*TCL* 41.310–27), Susan Bennett Smith examines the construction of women within Victorian mourning practices (where periods of isolation and the wearing of black are in imitation of death), and analyses attitudes to mourning in *Mrs Dalloway* and *To The Lighthouse* as signs of Woolf's critique of gendered assumptions about surviving the dead. *To The Lighthouse* 'offers a defeminized and demedicalized model for grief practices' where grief is productively 'worked out' through different kinds of labour (the work of painting, of journeying, of holding a boat steady), in contrast to *Mrs Dalloway* where Septimus Smith represents in his grief for Evans a feminized madness that has no outlet but in suicide.

Julie Kane, in 'Varieties of Mystical Experience in the Writings of Virginia Woolf' (*TCL* 41.328–49), sets out to provide contexts for what she perceives to be an arrested interest in Woolf in mysticism. References in Woolf's autobiography to 'moments of being' are recast as 'mystical experiences', and in the major fiction any number of references to 'vision' and the self are read with an emphasis on the literalness of the narratives so that such episodes in *Mrs Dalloway*, *To The Lighthouse* and *The Waves* are refigured as transcendental in the mystical sense. The narrative of *The Waves* in particular is seen as representing out-of-body experience, while *Orlando* is a fable of reincarnation: all debate on the self is at this level. The diagnostic impulse in this article manifests itself most clearly where extracts from Woolf's diaries referring to vision and sickness are represented as astral vision or the mystical visionary, buoyed up by a reminder that Clarissa Dalloway believes in ghosts. The several allusions to Hindu myth-systems and philosophies in Woolf's fiction are represented as identical with a highly personal interest in mysticism, which may be debatable. Kane argues that this interest was latent in Woolf, only gaining expression in her mature fiction as she overcame the behaviourism, and scepticism, of her husband and father, helped along by a productive encounter with Yeats. Fear in Woolf of the uncanny, a word not used by Kane, is eventually associated with a fear of her own mental illness, and the link between artistic creativity and madness is once again made, without any sense of this link itself being problematic.

Writing on Forster this year includes Mary Lago's *E. M. Forster: A Literary Life*. Not writing as a biographer specifically, but focusing on his writing career, Lago draws on the contexts that she perceives to have informed the production of Forster's novels, short fiction and radio broadcasts. In her commentary on *A Passage to India*, Lago, unlike Sara Suleri Goodyear (see below) who shows Forster problematizing 'intimacy' in a context of cross-cultural homoeroticism, represents the friendship between Fielding and Aziz as significant because of the possibility of cross-cultural 'symmetry' it represents (alongside the axes of possibility represented by the relationships of Aziz and Adela Quested, and Aziz and Godbole). She follows through the arrest of this possibility in contexts which are used to confirm Forster's reportage of the British in India as accurate in its assessment of colonial prejudices and mythologies. Lago describes Aziz's destiny not in terms of his shift into nationalism, but leaves him as a strangely unpoliticized figure who is, by the end of the book, 'more focused in his opinions, more cautious in friendship'. The book's 'real theme' is 'the search for the everlasting Friend', a judgement which threatens to paper over the more subtle analyses of multiculturalism within the novel. Consistently, Forster is represented as having an intuitive understanding of the main currents in Indian culture, demonstrable in 'the Indian novel', an assumption which is never really subjected to critical pressure, but which determines the level of critical commentary. After an introductory account of the social and cultural contexts which give rise to Forster, *A Room with a View*, *Where Angels Fear to Tread*, *The Longest Journey* and *Howards End* are dealt with as 'The Suburban Novels' in a chapter which offers synopses rather than analysis. The final chapter presents the short fiction as a testing ground where Forster develops the themes underpinning *Maurice*, with the focus on the composition and publication histories, and the reception of the novel, in a sketchily drawn account of British parliament's attempts to legislate on 'morality'. A chapter on Forster's long broadcasting career with the BBC touches on his relationships with significant contemporaries like Orwell, H. G. Wells and Benjamin Britten, and outlines his commitment to the educational values of broadcasting, concluding with a description of his career with the Third Programme. True to its editorial brief, and useful on detail, Lago's book nevertheless maintains a distance from contemporary analyses of, for instance, multiculturalism and the novel, class and sexuality which do usefully motivate critiques of Forster's work.

Audrey P. Lavin, in *Aspects of the Novelist: E. M. Forster's Pattern and Rhythm*, has written a book which might best be classified as an enthusiastic appreciation of the novelist, but one that barely suggests the critical and intellectual contexts of the 1990s. Her stated aim is to read Forster from within Forster, indeed, to apply 'the critical apparatus of pattern and rhythm supplied by E. M. Forster himself' to *A Room with a View, Where Angels Fear to Tread, The Longest Journey* and *Howards End*. Possibly the convenience of this grouping could have been adhered to less, and more rigorous analyses offered of the sidelined texts: *A Passage to India* and *Maurice*, for instance, hardly get critical treatment, yet occasional asides underline their relevance to the general argument. This relatively brief book seeks to remind readers about the internal complexity of Forster's narratives: form is presented as the 'rhetorical underpinning' of Forster's own liberal philosophy. Consequently, there is much in this book about 'journeys' and 'windows', and a language of symbols, but little that is really satisfying about questions of value or values in Forster.

New Casebooks: *E. M. Forster* (ed. Jeremy Tambling), comprises essays from a variety of sources, each accompanied by a detailed synopsis written by the editor, who also introduces the volume. Twelve essays, culled from around ten years of criticism starting in 1983, have been chosen to demonstrate the effectiveness of bringing recently established critical perspectives to bear on Forster, and include Benita Parry's 'The Politics of Representation in *A Passage to India*' alongside 'Forster's Imperial Erotic' by Sara Suleri Good-year, who departs from Parry's analysis and examines the sexualization of the racial body in *A Passage to India*, via the homoeroticism written into the friendship of Fielding and Aziz, and the continuous deferral of their cross-cultural intimacy. James Buzard's 'Forster's Trespasses: Tourism and Cultural Politics' examines Forster's use of tourism in Italy and India as the basis of a debate on 'authenticity', and the devolving of the plot onto the body as the site where otherness and desire are inscribed. Rae H. Stoll, ' "Aphrodite with a Janus Face": Language, Desire and History in *The Longest Journey*', offers a psychoanalytical critique focusing on the de-centred subject of *The Longest Journey*, a novel that is also addressed in Carola M. Kaplan's 'Absent Father, Passive Son: The Dilemma of Rickie Elliot in *The Longest Journey*', which examines its narrative as enacting a kind of subterfuge against its stated intentions. Peter J. Hutchings's 'A Disconnected View: Forster, Modernity and Film' is the only essay written specifically for the volume, and considers the reclaiming of Forster in film to increasingly reactionary positions, against the critical drift of his aesthetic. Hutchings examines the versions of Englishness projected in the films as an aspect of the heritage industry particularly as it developed in the 1980s and continued in the 1990s. The issues of vision and modernity mediated through tourism are underpinned by an undeveloped Heideggerian perspective. The volume as a whole works as an edited collection, the editorial choices and decisions having been skilfully made. Certain directed themes (Englishness, modernism, gender, race and empire) guide the shape and style of the book.

Quite apart from Virginia Woolf's *Roger Fry*, this year has seen the publication of some interesting critical editions by other authors. Martin Stannard has meticulously edited Ford Madox Ford's *The Good Soldier*, conscientiously reconstructing an 'unreliable' text, and representing the compositional and textual histories of the novel with the attention to detail with which we are now familiar in the NCE series. Additional material includes contemporary American and British reviews from the mainstream press, and a number of essays, including work by Ford on literary impressionism, with Joseph Conrad, Henry James and Ford forming a creative triangle. Seventeen critical assessments of *The Good Soldier* by, among others, Samuel Hynes, Frank Kermode and Michael Levenson, are usefully introduced by Richard Aldington's 'Homage to Ford Madox Ford'. Another critical edition published this year is Djuna Barnes's *Nightwood* (ed. Cheryl J. Plumb). The rationale for editorial choices is clearly given, and the difficulties of editorial responsibility are rehearsed. Based on the 'three original typescripts' the editorial influence of T. S. Eliot, Frank Morley and Emily Coleman is minimized, except where Barnes tacitly, if not explicitly, accepted alterations that persisted between editions [F.B.].

(c) Individual Authors: Post-1945
This year sees the release of two significant general studies of post-1945 fiction, reflecting a divergence of critical strategy which is visible more widely in the field as a whole.

The project of Patricia Waugh's *Harvest of the Sixties*, firstly, is to construct an authoritative literary history for the period 1960–90, and in so doing to mount a defence of literature as 'an important corrective to the increasing tendency of Western liberal cultures to be blind to the necessity for establishing an ethical foundation for politics which defines needs and conceives of equality in more than purely material terms'. Accordingly, Waugh's study opens with a pair of chapters setting out political and cultural contexts, including 'swing', 1960s counter-culture, the breakdown of consensus politics in the 1970s and the impact of the Thatcher revolution in the 1980s, which together form a backdrop for the reading of Larkin's poetry of disillusionment, Amis's critique of consumerism, and the decline of contemporary fiction criticism during this period. If, to readers more accustomed to Waugh's postmodernist engagements, this sounds like a meta-narrative approach to literature/culture/society, it is. Certainly, Waugh's disclaimer that 'any deistic perspective upon events' would be impossible does not substantially mitigate the overarching impression of textual reading being subordinated to historical factuality. This apparently regressive use of history, which facilitates judgements such as that of Islamic fundamentalism as 'still medieval', then, arguably feels the lack of further theoretical justification. Later chapters examine the response of writers to the 'moral and spiritual vacuum' at the heart of late modernity, the contestation of rationality/rationalization and imagination, and the multifaceted renegotiation of nation and national identity in this period, with women's fiction oddly appended as a section in the concluding chapter covering various 'post-consensus fictions'. This last textual arrangement is perhaps particularly surprising in that the cultural and geographical inclusiveness of Waugh's book as a whole is impressive. The book will clearly be of use to students looking for a reliable, if traditionally framed, overview of literary and cultural change in 1960–90.

Andrzej Gasiorek's *Post-War British Fiction: Realism and After* is arranged far more clearly around specific author studies and close textual analysis. Unlike Waugh's book, Gasiorek does not set out to offer a survey of fiction for the period he addresses, but rather to make specific literary readings in terms of the conflict between Realism and Experimentalism, and significantly within that to argue that 'the impulse to represent a changing social world with the greatest possible fidelity remains central' to the project of much of the fiction of recent decades. He is concerned through this strategy nevertheless to show a diversity rather than a homogeneity of fictional writing in this period. An initial chapter centres on an analysis of Realism, followed in chapter 2 by an introduction to and discussion of the late modernism of Ivy Compton-Burnett and Henry Green. Gasiorek then proceeds to a close reading of V. S. Naipaul and George Lamming, in which Naipaul's inscription of the Caribbean and Africa is identified as reductive and orientalist. Whilst Naipaul's popularity in Britain can therefore be attributed to the absence of ideological challenge in his work, Lamming's fictions for Gasiorek can be read as far more radically transformative of the language and history of colonialism. Having explored the ideological contrasts available in British Caribbean writing, Gasiorek proceeds to the uneasy negotiations of Socialism, Realism and Experimentalism in Doris Lessing and John Berger, with a further examination of the themes of Liberalism and Social Democracy in relation to Angus Wilson and John Fowles. Fowles, in particular, is identified here as showing a lesser attachment to Socialism than often suggested, but rather 'a greater affinity with an Arnoldian Paternalism'. Moving to 'Feminist Critical Fictions', and a final chapter on 'Postmodernism and the Problem of History' Gasiorek prefaces his critical remarks with brief but helpful introductions to salient debates within feminism and postmodernism, before focusing again in detail on the work of Angela Carter, Sara Maitland, Graham Swift, Julian Barnes and Salman Rushdie. Nevertheless, despite frequent gestures towards theoretically engaged analysis, the over-riding sense in Gasiorek's study is of the imperative of user-friendly literary 'coverage' emerging as the shaping force over broader thematic and theoretical exploration.

Continuing the generalized analysis of late twentieth-century fiction, the text of Peter Widdowson's inaugural professorial lecture at the University of Brighton is published in CS (7.i.3–17) as 'Newstories: Fiction, History and the Modern World'. It is both a defence of the need to study and/or teach literature and a(nother) reiteration of the notion of literature as production which emerges within a network of discourses and practices rather than in a flash of genius/greatness/transcendent insight. Widdowson locates contemporary fiction within a somewhat 'pop' postmodernist discussion of history, but ends up justifying it via the orthodox Cultural Materialist route of envisaging literature as privileged access to a contemporary structure of feeling, as well as to the possibilities for its contestation.

On a similar theme, Del Ivan Janik's 'No End of History: Evidence From the Contemporary English Novel' (TCL 41.160–89) explores the fictions of A. S. Byatt, Peter Ackroyd, Julian Barnes, Kazuo Ishiguro and Graham Swift to demonstrate that the postmodernist proclamation of the 'End of History' provides no check to the continued affirmation of history as a mode of knowing in contemporary English fiction. If this critical line seems rather trite at first glance, this impression is only confirmed by closer acquaintance with Janik's argument, which is that these novelists explore histories as cultural constructs/myths and are interested in the processes through which such constructs/myths operate in private and public spheres.

Barry Lewis's article 'The Death of the Postmodernist Novel and Other Stories' (English 44.97–109) explores the postmodernism/fiction axis from a slightly different direction, by running through the results of a 1991 survey by Raymond Federman on leading writers' and critics' views in that year on the 'Death of Postmodernism'. Towards the end of the essay even the 'Death of the Novel' is hauled in to add interest to what is less an examination of debates around the postmodern than an idiot's guide to a few salient themes which, in this year, unfortunately seems as tired as its references to Monty Python. Kelly A. Marsh's 'The Neo-Sensation Novel: A Contemporary Genre in the Victorian Tradition' (*PQ* 74.99–123), meanwhile, offers little more in the way of insight, reading novels by Graham Swift, Margaret Drabble, A. S. Byatt, Jane Smiley and Richard Powers as a new genre in the image of the Victorian sensation novel. Marsh takes us through the generic features of that tradition, such as the use of shocking material and the characteristic interest in crime, to produce the startling revelation that various contemporary fictions work via a pastiche of nineteenth-century Realist conventions. In doing so, she argues not entirely convincingly that the 'neo-sensation novel' represents a refutation of postmodernist and poststructuralist thinking by articulating 'the conviction that truth exists'.

In critical work devoted to single authors, Iris Murdoch has perhaps received most sustained critical attention during the year. David J. Gordon's *Iris Murdoch's Fables of Unselfing*, for example, an expansion to book length of his similarly titled essay of 1990 (*TCL* 36.115–36), represents a tightly argued if traditional treatment of Murdoch's fictional output. Gordon examines the writer with conventional solemnity in terms of theme, literary influence and the author's imaginative and philosophical development from the 1950s onwards. In a clear indication of its theoretical orientation, one of the central stated aims of this study lies in 'attempting an overall evaluation of her work and its bid for permanence'. Thus whilst Gordon does indeed include engagements with such thinkers as Freud and Sartre, Murdoch's relationship with the values and principles of Humanism are a far greater concern. His argument is, not altogether surprisingly, that Murdoch should not herself be identified as a Humanist but rather as a 'puritan', and he foregrounds *Under the Net* as an articulation of the 'visionary aspiration' which needs to be read through Murdoch's work, and which in itself clearly forms a position on the processes of writing and reading:

> Why should life be made endurable? I know that nothing consoles and nothing justifies except a story – but that doesn't stop all stories from being lies. Only the greatest men can speak and still be truthful. Any artist knows this obscurely; he knows that a theory is death, and that all expression is weighted with theory. Only the strongest can rise against that weight. For most of us, for almost all of us, truth can be attained, if at all, only in silence. It is in silence that the human spirit touches the divine.

In the light of considerable detailed analysis of Murdoch's texts throughout his study the conclusion at which Gordon arrives is then a disappointingly anachronistic affair concerning the comparison of Murdoch to various representatives of the 'Great Tradition,' with Gordon meditating finally that it would be 'pleasant' to think that she might find a place within this tradition.

In a comparable vein, Peter J. Conradi's 'Iris Murdoch and Dostoevskii' (in W. J. Leatherbarrow, ed., *Dostoevskii and Britain*) traces the role of Dostoevskii as a 'kindly midwife' alongside Shakespeare, Tolstoi, Proust and James in the birth of Murdoch's fiction. The essay also includes a pair of short and low-brow responses from Iris Murdoch and John Bayley on the paper's original presentation at the Free University of Amsterdam's 1986 Murdoch symposium. Despite one or two eyebrow-raising references to sado-masochism, Conradi's discussion again remains decidedly conservative in tone and method, a study of literary influence between two canonized writers, which is divided neatly into 'beliefs or vision' and 'form or technique'. Conradi's range of insights on Murdoch are perhaps limited partly by the overall project of Leatherbarrow's collection, within which the function of his essay is most importantly to show, via Murdoch, that Dostoevskii can 'feel "modern" to us in ways that even the great Dickens does not'.

More incisively, Thomas Jackson Rice's 'Death and Love in Iris Murdoch's *The Time of the Angels*' (*Crit* 36.130–44) seeks to redress what Rice sees as the lack of critical attention paid to metaphysical exploration in Murdoch's tenth and perhaps most densely philosophical novel, ably contrasting its intellectual strategies with Murdoch's academic philosophical texts of the same period, and in particular *The Sovereignty of Good*. *The Time of the Angels* thus emerges in Rice's reading as a characteristic exploration by Murdoch of the space between psychoanalytic insight and the possibility of moral value in a post-theistic world.

The collection *Lawrence Durrell: Comprehending the Whole* (ed. Julius Rowan Raper et al.) also emerges this year as a product of the 1988 International Lawrence Durrell Society conference, with the stated aim of showing not only the range of Durrell's own work but also the variety of critical approaches enabled by his writing. To some extent this is successful, including readings from the Liberal Humanist to the Derridean, and from the Roman-ticist to the Jungian, but at the same time the collection is often over-apologetic in tone, with a number of the contributions showing a sig-nificant lack of critical ambition. A more adequate bibliography and introduction would also have been useful additions. Critical coverage of Durrell is divided fairly effectively into four sections, beginning with his early writings and including what biographer Ian MacNiven helpfully notes Durrell referred to as 'the shit novel' *Panic Spring*, as well as *Pied Piper of Lovers* and *The Black Book*. Shelley Cox's essay on the Durrell collection at Southern Illinois University offers a useful inventory for Durrell completists of the 9.5 cubic feet of material archived there. The function of the second section is to offer new readings of Durrell's most familiar work, especially the *Alexandria Quartet*, in relation to Shelley, Derrida, *The Sacred Wood* and finally in Bynum's essay 'The Artist as Shaman' a reading of Durrell as a 'tribal seer' who, fulfilling the collection's title, can indeed 'comprehend the whole'. Section three or 'Hidden Durrell' moves on from the familiar oeuvre to offer some very short contributions examining the writer's dramatic, poetic and comic work, including the *Antrobus* series and, viewed with a grammarian's eye, *The Ikons*. Lastly, 'Final Durrell' examines the later fiction. Here Leo-nard Orr attempts to critically revamp *Tunc* by comparison of themes and technique with Pynchon, whilst Julius Raper (psychoanalytic and alchemic influences) and Melody Enscore (gnostic and templar imagery) explore the *Avignon Quintet*. Finally, Paul Lorenz completes the hermeneutic exercise by reading the *Quintet* as an extension of the post-Einsteinean/Heisenbergian meditation begun in Durrell's *Alexandria Quartet*, concluding with the opti-mistic observation that: 'We have the ability to tap the essence of the cosmos, to use that power to evolve ourselves into a new form of the species, at least in spirit.'

William Golding receives some re-evaluation in a pair of articles published in *CS* 7. Kevin McCarron's '*Darkness Visible* and *The Dunciad*' (44–50), first, re-examines the orthodox interpretation of *Darkness Visible* in terms of the personification and polarization of good and evil in the opposition of the novel's two main characters. He does this by realigning the primary 'source' of Golding's title from Milton's *Paradise Lost* to Pope's *Dunciad*, and thereby increasing the interpretive significance of entropy in the novel. Coming from a quite different critical direction, secondly, Stefan Hawlin's 'The Savages in the Forest: Decolonising William Golding' (125–35) convincingly reads *Lord of the Flies* through the discourses of British imperialism in the 1950s. Hawlin traces Golding's chauvinism, Eurocentrism and complicity with hierarchical notions of 'savagery/civilization' in an attempt to mirror Chinua Achebe's critical operation on *Heart of Darkness* in *Hopes and Impediments* (Heinemann, 1988). The essay represents a refreshingly under-awed treatment of Golding, and concludes by arguing for the inclusion of Anglo-African writing in English curricula to provide a counterweight to the imperialist canon.

The divergence of critical strategy apparent here is also mirrored in the reading of Anita Brookner. For Deborah Bowen in 'Preserving Appearances: Photography and the Postmodern Realism of Anita Brookner' (*Mosaic* 28.123–48) the task is to rescue Brookner from her reputation for inch-of-ivory literary conservatism, by arguing that the Realist conventions which novels like *Hotel du Lac* appear to articulate are in fact the target of a rigorous deconstruction in Brookner's work. What her novels reveal, it seems, is on the one hand a postmodern world of simulacra and on the other hand a profoundly modernist sense of loss over the erasure of Realism's sense of reference and absolute value. It is Brookner's profound moral sense, meanwhile, which provides the motivation for producing the narrative stability which can provide solace in the face of a destabilized world. Ann Fisher-Wirth's far more persuasive reading of the novelist in 'Hunger Art: The Novels of Anita Brookner' (*TCL* 41.1– 15), however, is much less optimistically framed. For Fisher-Wirth the problem of Brookner's conservatism is not one for which re-reading is a solution: 'How can she offer *that*, I ask myself again and again, as an image of life, of womanhood?' Her article works skilfully through the litany of women's humiliation and betrayal that is Brookner's oeuvre, significantly identifying the writer's 'answer' to American Feminism as the suggestion in *Dolly* that confident, forceful women just as much as her more usually reticent heroines 'find their truth in limitation, their passion in despair'.

In Glenwood Irons's collection *Feminism in Women's Detective Fiction* it is a rather different range of femininities which become the subject of analysis. The aim of this book is to correct dominant assumptions about the detective as an expression of masculinity operating outside the bounds of sexual conventionality. Demonstrating very effectively the heterogeneity of women's detective fiction, the collection seeks to go further in identifying the female sleuth as 'a "reflection and valuable barometer" of a culture which is finally, in its popular fiction, beginning to grapple with the aspirations and the constraints of women who ... unwrite the existing idea of Woman in order to challenge it and make a brand-new game'. Divided into explorations of British and modern American fiction, Irons's selection begins with early woman detectives before moving to the exploration of Dorothy L. Sayers and P. D. James (Sue Ellen Campbell and Nicola Nixon) and subsequently to contemporary women detectives such as Lynda La Plante's *Prime Suspect* protagonist Jane Tennison and Clarice Starling in Jonathan Demme's film *The Silence of the Lambs*, both identified by Sandra Tomc as examples of the 'new feminist mysteries'. The second section, focusing on American women detectives, is also impressive for its range of engagement, including in particular discussions by Jeanne Roberts and Susan Leonardi of the analogy between the epistemological concerns of the detective and those of academic scholarship, and explorations of the complex interplay between notions of sexual transgression, lesbianism and domesticity within the framework of detective fiction by Rebecca Pope and Kathleen Gregory Klein.

Examining a connected set of issues but on more well trodden critical ground, Ellen F. Shields's essay 'Hysteria, Sexual Assault, and the Military: The Trial of Émile de la Roncière and *The French Lieutenant's Woman*' (*Mosaic* 28.iii.83–108) reads John Fowles's novel in relation to the infamous 1831 trial of de la Roncière for the attempted rape of Marie de Morell. Shields explores the explicit parallel between this case read as a constellation of shifting narrative scenarios and Fowles's handling of the sexual history of Sarah Woodruff *vis-à-vis* Charles and Varguennes. This critical strategy then enables her to read against the grain of Fowles's novel to identify its complicity with misogynist discourses around 'hysteria'.

Returning to another well-read text, Beth A. Boehm's essay 'Feminist Metafiction and Androcentric Reading Strategies: Angela Carter's Reconstructed Reader in *Nights at the Circus*' (*Crit* 37.1.35–49) examines high-profile 'mis-readings' of Carter's novel in the *New York Times* and *Times Literary Supplement*. Unfortunately, Boehm draws on Peter Rabinowitz for a rather problematic definition of 'mis-readings' as 'failures to employ the interpretive strategies the author has imagined to be available to the reader', clearly at a fairly short distance from banal authorial intention. By exploring these 'mis-readings' she hopes to correct the masculinist bias in current canons of postmodernist fiction. Boehm's attention to the novel's use of parody, allusion and metafictional play, as well as her efforts to explore the literary implications of Carter's feminist commitment do certainly lead to more interesting and effective readings of *Nights at the Circus* than those managed by the reviewers she discusses – and without any obvious need for reliance on the idea/implication of 'correct reading' which hovers around her discussion.

Martin Amis is another writer to come in for significant critical reading during the year, with the publication of James Diedrick's *Understanding Martin Amis* in particular. In line with the rest of the UCSP's *Understanding Contemporary British Literature* series, Diedrick's study has significant pedagogical as well as critical aims, and as such is accessible and largely inoffensive, including an extensive and useful bibliography. Diedrick's strategy is to foreground Amis's privileged, bourgeois and patriarchal affinities, beginning by examining the author's problematic relationship with his father, with socialism and with feminism, and moving on to explore the satirical and parodic techniques deployed by Amis in his characteristically experimental attempts to fictionalize the postmodern condition. Subsequent chapters deal with Amis's first three novels, with *Other People*, with *Money*, with *Einstein's*

Monsters, *London Fields*, *Time's Arrow* and, finally, with *The Information*, with a style of treatment that remains consistently engaging and analytical. Diedrick also includes one chapter in his book examining Amis's journalistic and non-fictional writing, in which a modernist and self-satisfied notion of literary value is clearly illustrated, but at the same time also a clear sense of the daring and incisiveness of much of Amis's critical writing. This material is not simply presented as a bolt-on extra to the reading of Amis's fiction but as essential to its understanding, or, as Diedrick says 'a useful corrective to the reader who would confuse the narrators of his novels with their creator'. In this sense particularly the volume will clearly be useful to students unsure how to deal critically with Amis's frequently misogynistic and pretentious narrators.

This particular aspect of Amis's fiction is further explored in Brian Finney's essay 'Narrative and Narrated Homicides in Martin Amis's *Other People* and *London Fields*' (*Crit* 37.i.3–15). Finney analyses the notion of the implicit violence of authorial control, by tracing the self-consciously capricious narrative voice used in these two novels. For reasons that are not entirely clear, Finney seems particularly impressed by Amis's technique of defamiliarization through the theme of memory loss, arguing that the novel works effectively to involve us as readers in complicity with its exploitation and violence. There are also attempts to lend Amis literary credibility by comparison in the use of metaphysical interruption to Cervantes and Shakespeare, and theoretical credibility by reference to Baudrillard and postmodernist theory.

Metafictional strategies are again the focus in Julian Gitzen's article 'A. S. Byatt's Self-Mirroring Art' (*Crit* 36.ii.83–95), which analyses experimentation in Byatt's novels, and provides some useful close readings of 'writerly' and 'painterly' technique, allegory and allusion in *The Virgin in the Garden*, *Still Life* and *Possession* in turn. Gitzen's general tone in discussing Byatt is notable for its reverence, tempered only by a slightly embarrassed afterthought in which reference is made to her novels' self-conscious academicism. No such privilege is accorded to Ian McEwan by Paul Edwards, however, in 'Time, Romanticism, Modernism and Moderation in Ian McEwan's *The Child in Time*' (*English* 44.41–55). Edwards's article again includes some subtle textual and intertextual analysis, examining the complex treatment of childhood in the novel, but without any lack of questioning alongside that of McEwan's narrative strategies. Thus Edwards is able to point to the slightly heavy handed invocation of new scientific theories (familiar from McEwan's earlier oratorio *Or Shall We Die?*) and uses references to thinkers such as Henri Bergson to make McEwan's treatment of non-linear time seem rather dated. Politically, Edwards accuses McEwan's novel of an ultimate quietism in the face of the Thatcherism it sets itself up to critique, inasmuch as the closure the novel offers centres on notions of fertility and timeless continuance, values more closely associated with metaphysical than political engagement.

2. Poetry

(a) Poetry: 1900–1950

As in previous years, the compilation of this section has been much aided by the assistance of the library staffs of the University of the Incarnate Word and Trinity University, San Antonio. It has, however, been hampered by the continuing and self-defeating reluctance of so many publishers to supply review copies.

Burton Hatlen's 'The Imagist Poetics of H.D.'s *Sea Garden*' (*Paideuma* 24.ii–iii.107–30) suggests that Imagism offers more possibilities than is generally agreed, and that H.D. later built on rather than rejected it. Her work is revolutionary in stressing the otherness of the object, refusing to see it as part of the consciousness, presenting in *Sea Garden* sharply focused, 'hard edged' and vibrantly energetic objects. H.D.'s Imagism is thus clearly different from the 'Impressionistic' tendency of much Imagist poetry – that of J. G. Fletcher or F. S. Flint, for example. The major event in H.D. scholarship was Caroline Zilboorg's volume, *Richard Aldington and H.D.: The Later Years in Letters*. Such is the hold of literary periodization that we tend to think of these figures as existing only in the years before and after the First World War, as recorded in Zilboorg's earlier *Richard Aldington and H.D.: The Early Years in Letters*. They cover the period of H.D.'s journeying, emotional as well as geographical, set against the relative fixity of Aldington: as well as revealing tantalizing hints about the writings of each, they offer a view of literary life that is enlightening in its stress on the need simply to keep going, keep writing – in the case of Aldington, on Ezra Pound's pre-1914 typewriter. This volume will lack the resonances of Zilboorg's earlier collection, yet it is a book of surprising delights as well as sadnesses.

Robert Gingher's 'Pound/Lawrence: A Re-evaluation' (*Paideuma* 24.ii–iii.149–62) is primarily concerned with the novels, but does mention in passing the likenesses between 'Bavarian gentians' and the fourth *Canto* to show the shared concern with 'transcendent mystery', the quest for the other and 'the sacredness of the present moment'. The same journal contains a fascinating, if more general, illustrated article on Modernist aesthetics, Melita Schaum's 'The Grammar of the Visual: Alvin Langdon Coburn, Ezra Pound, and the Eastern Aesthetic in Early Modernist Photography and Poetry' (*Paideuma* 24.ii–iii.79–106).

Simon Featherstone's *War Poetry: An Introductory Reader* is part of Routledge's *Critical Readers in Theory and Practice* series, which attempt to balance 'basic texts and detailed, introductory exposition'. It is a tall order to cover this topic in a volume of 280 pages, especially when an attempt is made to offset the dominance of the English officer poets and introduce new material, mainly in a section of First World War poems from the Ilkeston Pioneer and Ilkeston Advertiser and some Scottish poems from the 1940s. There are poems by Owen, Rosenberg, Gurney, H.D. and a passage from *In Parenthesis*, but no Sassoon or Blunden: the later war is represented by Herbert Read, Sorley MacLean, Hamish Henderson, Keith Douglas, Terence Tiller and G. S. Fraser. One can always cavil about what is included and excluded, but here the publisher's aim to cover both texts and theory seems to fail simply because of the lack of material presented. The dearth of women poets is especially to be regretted: the introduction's claims that much of the women's poetry does not demonstrate the change of style and sensibility found in the men's, and that women's experience was 'domestic and personal, and so detached from the "real war"' seem dismissive of a major aspect of the female voice and also over-selective in its view of what constitutes 'reality'. There is a great body of women's poetry and prose that deserves far wider readership, as Catherine Reilly has shown – Eleanor Farjeon and Alice

Corbin are two of many who have important things to say, and in terms of sheer popularity and exposure the voice of Jessie Pope cannot be ignored. And, as far as a 'real war' concerned with suffering and anguish goes, Enid Bagnold's *A Diary Without Dates* is both shocking and compassionate. The introductory chapters attempt to discuss war and British society, politics, popular culture, gender and ideas of Englishness and masculinity, all in 100 pages. References, too, are limited: it is churlish of me to mention the omission of my own *Art and Survival in First World War Britain* (Macmillan, 1987) from the works cited, but valid to regret several other gaps, such as John Carey's *The Intellectuals and the Masses* (Macmillan, 1993), and recent work by Douglas Kerr and Elizabeth Marsland. Overall, the idea behind the book is strong, but its extent – probably demanded by the publishers in response to practical considerations – means that it does not achieve fulfilment. Undergraduates are still better off with one or two of the well-known anthologies supplemented by a range of critical readings and some personal research into the popular writings, which are easy enough to find in any collection of contemporary newspapers and periodicals.

Several short articles discussed the writing of First World War poets. Bernard Schweiger's 'Blunden's "Two Voices" ' and "Preparations for Victory" ' (*Expl* 53.iv.226–30) shows the poet's exploration of the senses. Multiple ambiguities of speaking and hearing in the first poem ensure that sound suggests only death, even when at its most naturally beautiful. The second poem does much the same for the visual sense – there is no retreat from war in visual beauty. Both poems, however, overcome the fragmentation of war by using it structurally, thus 'restoring a sense of wholeness'. 'The Great Gatsby and Edward Thomas's "Rain" ', by W. L. Godshalk (*ELN* 32.iv.75–8), suggests that the line 'Blessed are the dead that the rain falls on' overheard by Nick Carraway was misremembered from Thomas's poem. This suggests an unlikely, though not impossible, path of influence, although it is sad that Godshalk has to quote the whole poem because 'it is not well known'. Patrick Campbell's 'Sassoon's "Blighters" ' (*Expl* 53.iii.170–1) offers a reading of the poem to clarify the Blighters/Blighty/Blight overlap and the fantasy elision of Bapaume and the Music-Hall as yet another dimension of the well-known schism between home and the front. Christopher Lane's 'In Defense of the Realm: Sassoon's Memoirs' (*Raritan* 14.i.89–108) argues against the elegiac myth of First World War poetry as it is constructed by the British in Sassoon and other poets, arguing instead that the poets moved from support to criticism of the war. The article does not even live up to the promise of this level of conventionality and, when it refers to the poetry of 'Owens' then it is clear that it does not deserve serious attention. Much more satisfactory is D. Haden's article on 'Owen's "Page Eglantine" ' (*Expl* 53.iii.172–3). This is an ingenious and complex reading of the poem as 'a brilliantly "queer" crossword puzzle' in which Owen hints at the identity of Page Eglantine as a young boy with whom the poet was romantically linked – the 'Mon petit ami en Scarborough' mentioned in a letter to Leslie Gunston. In the circle of homosexual writers with whom Owen corresponded, this would have been instantly recognizable, and presumably quickly decoded. The article is of value not only for what it says, but because it suggests that conflicting levels of meaning, conflicts and games were part of Owen's writing – a key pointer to a deeper and more complete reading of his poetry.

'Emerging Views of Byzantium, 1850–1930: Germs of the Modern and Its Paradoxes' by Jane Spirit (*ELT* 38.ii.157–67) surveys views of Byzantium brought by Victorian travellers into art and literature, seeing its influence in Roger Fry and T. E. Hulme and its concrete, or rather red-brick, symbol in Westminster Cathedral. All of this is seen as a prelude to Yeats's poem, with its stress on an aesthetic community of both energy and collapse, a key duality of Modernism in its impossibility of achievement. A more specific textual source is suggested by Edward Larrissey in 'Yeats's "Sailing to Byzantium" and Scott's *Count Robert of Paris*' (*N&Q* 42.210–11). This finds a possible source of the 'golden bird' in Scott's novel. Sterner stuff is Malcolm Bull's 'Yeats's "Rough Beast": Sphinx or Manticore?' (*N&Q* 42.209–10). The beast shares features described by Edward Topsell in 1607 or, more recently, by Flaubert in *La tentation de Saint Antoine*, which Yeats read in the translation of Rene Francis. This implies that the 'rough beast', the savage manticore, is bringing with it a second massacre of the innocents. Nathan Cervo sees things differently in 'Yeats's "The Second Coming" ' (*Expl* 53.iii.161–3). He links the 'rough beast' through a chain involving the Balfour declaration in favour of a Jewish nation, Marcionite Christology, The Golden Dawn and Yeats's poem 'Demoin Est Deus Inversus', with the 'man of lawlessness of Thessalonians', the 'transcendental ideal of the Self' that will replace our present culture. Doubtless, in Yeats's Blakean world, both can be true.

Eliot as usual much preoccupied critics this year. Some are concerned with episodes from his life, Adam Piette, for one, exploring 'Eliot's Breakdown and Dr. Vittoz' (*ELN* 33.i.35–9). The most interesting part of this study of the relations between the poet and pre-Freudian analyst is the assertion that Eliot's concern for the undissociated sensibility came from Vittoz's idea of the destructiveness of a 'dissociation of the conscious and unconscious centres'. Others explored specific textual sources. Carlos Campo writes on 'Identifying the "Lazarus" in Eliot's The Love Song of J. Alfred Prufrock' (*ELN* 32.[1994].i.66–70), stressing that it is the one in Luke's gospel, not John's, that is intended. Luke's Lazarus has his existence after death described, in the manner of the passage from the *Inferno* that Eliot uses as epigram. This Lazarus is a beggar desiring to be richly fed, as is Prufrock; the phrase 'from the dead' appears in both Eliot and Luke's gospel, but not John's; and the character fits the 'tone and imagery' of the poem much more completely. 'Eliot's "The Love Song of J. Alfred Prufrock" ' by Christopher Krogstad and James D. Alexander (*Expl* 53.i.53–4) finds the poem's 'you and me' and earlier similar references echoes of 'Some little talk awhile of ME and THEE' in *Omar Khayyam* XXXII. The speaker in Fitzgerald is engaging in erotic love, while Prufrock will never do so, thus providing an ironic contrast in the intertextual reference. Textual sources are also the subject of Sukhbir Singh in 'Shakespeare's "Dolphin" in Eliot's Drawing Room: *The Waste Land*, II, Line 96'. This suggests a contrast between Belladonna and her partner and Antony and Cleopatra in Eliot's ironic reference to Shakespeare's cupids, mermaids and dolphins: Shakespeare's are real and dynamic, Eliot's are carved and sterile.

'Eliot's "Journey of the Magi" and Black Identity' by Robert F. Fleissner (*ELN* 32.ii.65–71) finds elements of black culture in the poem, the result of Eliot's study of anthropology at Harvard, and his study of *Othello*. This leads to the suggestion that the speaker in the poem is himself black, showing Eliot to be not quite as ethnically biased as has been suggested – an intriguing thought, although I'm not sure that reading *Othello* indicates submersion in black culture. Susan Wanlass writes on 'An Easy Commerce: Specific Similarities Between the Writings of T. S. Eliot and F. Scott Fitzgerald' (*ELN* 32.3.58–68). This begins by discussing the writers' mutual respect and the closeness of Eliot's poetry to prose, continuing to list shared phrases and sentences, especially those with images of water, in their work. After an extended comparison of *Tender is the Night* with 'The Waste Land' and 'The Dry Salvages', Wanlass suggests that, while Fitzgerald's novel is not necessarily a source or influence, the texts reveal 'a strong literary connection between the two writers'.

Longer studies focused on Eliot's religious and meditative poems. Marylu Hill's 'Learning to Sit Still: The Confrontation of Human Language and Divine Silence in "Ash Wednesday"' (*YER* 13.iii–iv.85–8) engages with the problem of whether poetry is 'mere noise' or 'a conductor to silence', suggesting that the complexity of 'Ash Wednesday' reveals the difficulty of 'naming the divine', revealing the spiritual truth in the moments of silence on the way to the 'sitting still' achieved at the poem's end. The conflict thus aroused between poetics and contemplation is only finally resolved in the *Four Quartets*. Eric Wilson's 'On the Way to the Still Point: Eliot's *Four Quartets* and Martin Heidegger' (*YER* 13.iii–iv.56–62) did not start well: my copy of the journal lacked page 56, and page 57 began with a reference to 'a phenomena', and for a moment I thought that this marked the final triumph of aporia and silence. Things got better, though: Wilson argues that Heidegger's translation of Heraclitus is much closer than others to Eliot's ideas, in particular his 'still point', which resembles Heidegger's Being and Heraclitus's *logos*. The former's *Ereignis* and the Greek *aletheia* on which it rests resemble Eliot's 'way of the mystic', the 'negative way'. Reading the *Quartets* through Heidegger in this way reveals it as 'more temporal, projective and capable of dealing with tension' than is generally supposed. Starting from the passage in 'Burnt Norton' that refers to William Harvey's discovery of circulation, John Gordon, in 'T. S. Eliot's Hand and Heart' (*ELH* 62.979–1000), sees 'The Waste Land' and *Four Quartets* as an opposition between head and heart cast as brain and blood, modern anxiety and older nobility. Gordon chronicles the historical influences of medical research on body images and goes on to discuss the neuropathology of Eliot's earlier poems in the context of literature that stresses the brain over the body, written by rationalists who are, as Eliot says in *The Rock*, 'Betrayed in the mazes of your ingenuities'. By contrast, the brain is reinvigorated by 'fringe experience' in the *Quartets* – fringe because on the margins of intellectual perception and analysis – in which the body is rediscovered in a return to the politics and culture of Harvey's age. If this seems largely to restate a view of Eliot's movement, it does so in terms that are vivid, enlarging and more suggestive than a good deal of fashionable body-criticism.

Three essays explore facets of the poet's aesthetic and language across the breadth of his work. Loretta Johnson, in 'Citizenship and Solitude: T. S. Eliot's "Metoikos" Figure or "Resident Alien"' (*YER* 13.iii–iv.71–7) explores the idea of the 'alien guest' in the poet's life and writing, drawing together the early and later pseudonyms with the notion of exile and exclusion that can be seen as a key motif throughout his work. 'T. S. Eliot's Puritan

Language: "A Calvinistic Heritage and a Puritanical Temperament" ' (*YER* 13.iii–iv.78–84) by Dal-Yong Kim is an important extension of our grasp of Eliot's moral and linguistic outlook. Kim stresses the influence on Eliot of New England Puritanism, especially the concept from the opening of John's gospel of the sanctity of the Word as 'God's self-disclosure'. This is done by relating the poetry to Cotton Mather, Edward Taylor and Jonathan Edwards, Puritan writers seen as the basis of Eliot's vision of 'the sense of the uprooted modern age'. This allows the poet to use language to explore the relation of human beings to God, largely through explaining what it lacks. Possibly the densest and most suggestive essay of the year is Joseph D. Lewandowski's 'T. S. Eliot and the Impossibility of "Immediate Experience" ' (*YER* 13.iii–iv.49–55). This pursues the hermeneutics of Eliot's dissertation on F. H. Bradley to suggest 'an Eliotic theory of interpretation' and show how this might illumine temporality in *Four Quartets*. In the complex equation between matter and mind, language and object, 'The grand dialectic continually turns', leaving experience indefinable and incomplete so that, in Eliot's words, 'no view is original or ultimate'. Lewandowski concludes that Eliot has three principles: linguistic signs 'mean' only in their difference from other signs; signs can only be read in specific discourses; and experiential knowledge is the effort to interpret signs in contexts. This last implies a constant shifting and dividing – which is exactly that of the musical motion of *Four Quartets*, which seek to unite the temporal and the spatial, the sign and the discourse, in an experience that is constantly fluid. This is a valuable essay, not least since it provides one of the most cogent short summaries of Eliot's thesis on Bradley.

Eliot's prose criticism also came under scrutiny. Paul Kreller's 'Definitions of Classicism and Romanticism: Argumentative Strategies in the Eliot–Murry Debate (1923–1927)' (*YER* 13.iii–iv.63–70) first surveys the exchange and then examines it in the light of Chaim Perelman's ideas of definition in argument. The article usefully summarizes and clarifies the positions of each and the methods they adopt in advancing them. David Bradshaw unearths 'Eleven reviews by T. S. Eliot, hitherto unnoted, from the *Times Literary Supplement*: A Conspectus' (*N&Q* 42.212–15). This he does by using the News International Archive in London to identify Eliot as reviewer. Bradshaw quotes briefly from the reviews of F. L. Lucas's edition of John Webster, Julian Benda's *La trahison des clercs*, and other books on Dante, Elizabethan drama, Augustan political theory and the early novel. This is of interest not only in the new idea of Eliot that it reveals, but in making known the vast possibilities of similar discoveries now that the cherished anonymity of the *TLS* has been unlocked. Using the same source, Sumanyu Satpathy's 'Eliot and J. W. N. Sullivan' (*N&Q* 42.216) identifies the original reviewer of 'The Waste Land' as not Harold Child, as claimed by Valerie Eliot in her letters, but J. W. N. Sullivan. The article goes on to suggest that Sullivan, a friend of Eliot and Aldous Huxley and a regular contributor to *The Times*, was invaluable to Eliot in helping him grasp contemporary scientific developments and Thomist philosophy. Keith Crook's 'A Lost T. S. Eliot Review Recovered' (*YER* 13.iii–iv.89–92), which discusses a review of books on the history, economy and industry of India, is a republication of the article in *YER* 12.ii. with a slight, but significant, correction of a passage printed incorrectly. It is good to see that there is still honour among publishers.

Andrew J. Kappel looks at Eliot as editor in 'Presenting Miss Moore, Modernist: T. S. Eliot's Edition of Marianne Moore's *Selected Poems*' (*JML* 19.129–50). He begins with a chronicle of the stages of Eliot's relationship with Moore's work, leading up to his 1934 edition of the *Selected Poems*, and then moves on to discuss the order of the poems in it. Central is Eliot's decision to put the complex writings of 1932–4 at the start of the volume, before poems taken from the earlier *Observations*. This privileges 'the dynamic of observer and observed embodied in a descriptive poetic', with all its attendant Modernist epistemological difficulties. As a result of this, the confrontation of the problem of order in the syllabic poems, which Kappel sees as Moore's 'unique contribution' to this key problem of Modernism is partly obscured. Yet if in doing this Eliot slightly distorted Moore's poetic nature, his introduction to the volume does much to clarify it, and his work as editor is thus vindicated. Other Modernist relationships are analysed in Michael Patrick Gillespie's 'The Legacy of 1914: Pound, Lewis, Eliot and the Composition of *Finnegans Wake*' (*Paideuma* 24.ii–iii.131–47). Joyce's links with the other 'men of 1914' are exposed in revealing the 'double displacement' of Joyce's work as both Modernist and postmodernist. The article's primary interest will be to those studying Joyce's generative processes, but the idea that the links clarify the critical response to *Finnegans Wake*, seeing the critic as the central consciousness, is of value in a larger historical sense.

Rainer Emig's *Modernism in Poetry: Motivations, Structures and Limits* seeks to explain 'what goes on in poems that make them modernist' in terms of the interchange between internal 'self' and external reality. This is done in separate sections looking at Hopkins, Yeats, Eliot and Pound, with additional chapters on Modernist poetry as 'a Universal Compensation Strategy', its relations with psychoanalysis and language philosophy, and one which looks at poetry in terms of an economic equation between text, reality and symbol in the pre-Modern and the Modern age. If the density of this makes Emig's conclusion, that 'The truth of modernist poems lies in their continual failure', sound contorted and tricksy, this is not a proper reflection of the book: its secure foundation in contemporary theory is matched by a subtle self-awareness, and a stress that this is only one way of seeing. Aimed at general students of twentieth-century literature, the book advances some genuinely original ideas which make it both more, and less, than the introductory study it presents itself as.

Modernism with a slightly different focus is explored by Mark Perrino in *The Poetics of Mockery: Wyndham Lewis's The Apes of God and the Popularization of Modernism*. This is properly concerned with Lewis's novel and will be of use primarily in this regard, but it is of interest in the way in which Lewis's compound embrace and satire of the mannerisms of Modernist art and artist is seen as both popularizing and satirizing a certain view of the Modernist. This in turn helps to inform our reading of later Modernist poetry by giving us something of the popular horizon against which it was seen. Of similarly tangential relation to English poetry of this period is *Poetic Process* by W. G. Kudszus, a study of the writing processes of Georg Trakl with sidelights on Heidegger, Jung and Joyce.

Auden's poetry was the subject of four articles this year. David Mason, in 'The *Civitas* of Sound: Auden's *Paul Bunyan* and *New Year Letter*' (*JML* 19.115–28) seeks to rehabilitate the somewhat neglected opera that Auden wrote with Benjamin Britten in 1941 by comparing its structure and ideas, especially its concern with knowledge and the nature of art, with the better-known poem with which it is almost contemporary. Both texts emerge as powerful, spontaneous and unsettling, in an article that should do much to expand the Auden canon. 'Auden's [Hearing of Harvests Rotting in the Valleys]' (*Expl* 53.i.57–8) finds in the geographical features of the poem an opposition of the scenery around the Malvern town of Colwell, where Auden was teaching at the time, and the 'islands' of Greece where Isherwood was staying. The poem's 'sorrow' thus reflects Auden's mental state, caught between the two extremes of personal response to external events. The two remaining articles revolve between similar polarities, while looking in greater detail at the origins and directions of the poetry. The first is Jeffrey Donaldson's 'The Company Poets Keep: Allusion, Echo and the Question of Who is Listening in W. H. Auden and James Merrill' (*ConL* 36.35–57). This explores Auden's use in 'Letter to Lord Byron' of the earlier poet as a 'synechdochic figure for an ideal public readership', lamenting the loss of audience for the contemporary poet. Yet because he knows who Lord Byron is, Auden is constantly being ironic in the effort to communicate, and at the same time address the whole situation of the letter-writer. This is then contrasted with the intertextuality of James Merrill, in *Sandover*, and its direct address to Auden himself. Auden's allusions declare his social concern but also comment on the difficulty of finding an audience: Merrill focuses on a company that lets him talk. Much more inclusive and suggestive is an article by Richard Bozorth, ' "But who would get it"': Auden and the Codes of Poetry and Desire' (*ELH* 62.709–27). This aims to show how Auden's use of codes to address 'the structures of knowing and unknowing that comprise the closet' reference to Spender's novel *The Temple*, drafted in 1929, reveal the extent to which Auden's landscapes must be seen in terms of a 'new country . . . of sexual and discursive liberation'. The private world of Mortmere, the Auden group's imaginary nation, is revealed as enduring a war against homosexuality as well as being peopled with spies. Poems such as 'The Secret Agent' stand revealed as inversions of romantic lyric that taunt us with their gay significance, 'preserving it but flaunting its closetedness', a particular version of Barthes' textual pleasure. This is an important essay in the study of Auden and his circle, and also a key work in allowing us to read gay texts with a fuller, if still occluded, vision. Another landscape, and a perhaps related audience, are the concerns of Jonathan Bolton in ' "The Historian with his Spade"': Landscape and Historical Continuity in the Poetry of Bernard Spencer' (*JML* 19.273–87). Starting from the standpoint of Said's *Orientalism*, this traces the path by which Spencer's poetry moves from fine observation to a transcendence of his English roots 'to merge with his surroundings' yet paradoxically fulfil the aim of the Auden generation to relate the personal and the public. That he does this by meeting 'his audience in a common landscape' is evidence of how far he has travelled from his English origins.

A different sort of thirties landscape is presented in *Women's Poetry of the 1930s: A Critical Anthology* edited by Jane Dowson. This is a ground-breaking new anthology in that it makes available material buried too long by tacit acceptance of publication circumstances. So much women's poetry appeared in little magazines unavailable to all but the most determined researcher that up to now we have known only a handful of names – Anne Ridler, Laura

Riding and perhaps E. J. Scovell. Dowson is eclectic in choice, embracing both the aristocratic Lilian Bowes Lyon and the communist Valentine Ackland, and presenting a stylistic range that includes Stevie Smith alongside Vita Sackville-West and Winifred Holtby. Each writer's poems are prefaced by a list of works, biography and further reading; in the cases of Laura (Riding) Jackson and Kathleen Raine we get no further, since each refused to have her work reproduced in a 'segregated anthology'. That in itself should be enough to raise a whole forest of issues for the undergraduate readers at whom the anthology is aimed. The only qualification I make to an otherwise enthusiastic welcome to this redefinition of the period's poetry is that the anthology doesn't go far enough, with less than 200 pages covering 17 poets, with an additional four poems reprinted from *The Listener* and five from *Time and Tide*. A volume the size of one of the Oxford anthologies is needed, and soon: these are voices we need to hear.

It is pleasing to see an increasing amount of serious attention being given to the work of David Jones, especially when it regards him as a serious contributor to Modernist innovation. The three major articles which appeared this year do this by discussing the problem of structure in the longer Modernist text as it is engaged with in his writing. Patrick Deane, in 'David Jones, T. S. Eliot and the Modernist Unfinished' (*Renascence* 47.ii.75–88), locates Jones's use of fragmentation more firmly within the tradition of drama and dramatic monologue than within that of mythic utterance. In this, the 'invocation of a recognizable structure' displaces its actuality while maintaining the premise of its achievement. Yet, because of their length, the works after *The Anathemata* have an 'intractable fragmentariness', as Jones refused to take the two paths chosen by Eliot – verse drama and the tight stylistic variation of the *Quartets*. The premise of 'David Jones's *The Deluge*: Engraving the Structure of the Modern Long Poem' (*JML* 19.5–30) by Thomas Dilworth is that the definitive form of the non-narrative long poem of the modern age is established by Jones in his engravings to the Chester *Play of the Deluge* (1927). In following an arch form, in which each image reflects its counter around a central 'hinge', Jones constructs the form he is to use in a verbal equivalent in *In Parenthesis* and *Anathemata*. There is some very convincing writing about the images, and it is good to see them reproduced. Finally, Tom Goldpaugh writes 'On the Traverse of the Wall: The Last Long Poem of David Jones' (*JML* 19.31–53). This is a lengthy and detailed account of the long manuscript, called by Jones 'the Roman poem', which was the writer's main concern between 1941 and 1945 and which formed part of *The Roman Quarry* and *The Sleeping Lord*. It is a thorough and suggestive study, exploring in particular the use that Jones makes of such diverse sources as Tacitus and Spengler, and it is valuable as much for its extensive quotation as for its discussion of the formal, moral and intellectual difficulties the writer faced in composition. Pending the publication of the material in the National Library of Wales, including the lovely manuscript, with drawings, of *In Parenthesis*, this is the nearest most of us will get to the text of Jones's last long poem. Separately, the articles assist our understanding of the texts each discusses: together, they remind us of Jones's central place in the structure and experience of Modernism.

A Reader's Guide to Dylan Thomas has been re-issued in paperback. When it first appeared, in 1962, Margaret Willy said that it 'offers a detailed elucidation of the complexities of style and imagery which can so easily daunt the newcomer to Thomas's writing' (*YWES* 44.311). Thirty-five years later, the direct discussion of structure and meaning reads as a model of New Critical analysis: the individual must decide whether this is a valuable aid to readers not waving but drowning, or a voice from an ancestral discipline.

(b) Poetry: Post-1950

With the award of the Nobel prize for literature, and with the much trumpeted publication, as *The Redress of Poetry*, of the lectures he gave while Professor of Poetry at Oxford, there can be no doubt that this was Seamus Heaney's year. It was too late, of course, for most (though not all) publishers and periodicals to react to Heaney's triumph. However, the year's work on post-1950 poetry does perhaps help us to understand why that triumph occurred. Heaney received sustained critical consideration in all formats this year, the weight of which amounts to the kind of critical mass that propels a writer to the highest honour. More significantly, Heaney's thinking – and thinking about Heaney – was at the centre of a rich discussion of Irish poetry. One way or another, so the criticism shows, his linguistic and poetic decisions, and the magisterial manner in which he articulates those decisions, inflect upon the thinking of most Irish and Northern Irish poets and their commentators. With the IRA cease-fire the eyes of the world were on the island, and so the culture, of Ireland. Heaney, like Yeats before him, is clearly at the centre of that culture.

The issue of centrality, in its various guises, was to the fore in the year's criticism. Irish poetry has unquestionably benefited from an attention to the literary margins born of post-colonial discourse. The centre was England, or more precisely London, of course. That centre, the criticism shows, has not held. This is a positive development in many respects. This year close attention was paid to writing in Scotland and Gaelic, and in Wales and Welsh, with those bodies of literature seeming the stronger for it. English poetry fared less well from this shift from the centre. Positively, considerable attention was paid this year to a number of marginalized poets: Basil Bunting, Charles Tomlinson, J. H. Prynne and Peter Redgrove, to name but four. What equally emerges from the criticism, however, is that the crucial *topos* of place, which, without unifying, certainly lends coherence to writings about Irish, Scottish and Welsh writing, can no longer operate with comparable force in discussions of English poetry. There is, in other words, a post-colonial anxiety about pursuing the theme of Englishness. The net effect is that while debates about the poetry of the so-called margins are centred, discussion of English poetry is increasingly fragmented. Judging by this year's work, then, English poetry is in serious need of a critical discourse which, without attempting a false unification, can find a way of dealing with, say, both Larkin and Prynne.

Heaney introduces the ten lectures which make up *The Redress of Poetry* by quoting Frost's poem 'Directive', which closes with the injunction to 'Drink and be whole again beyond confusion'. This making 'whole again beyond confusion' constitutes, for Heaney, poetry's obligation, its redress. The poet, then, who would most be the poet, should offer 'more than just a printout of the given circumstances of [their] time and place'. Rather, 'The truly creative writer, by interposing his or her perception and expression, will transfigure the conditions thereby achieving what I have been calling the "redress of poetry"'. The question arising is what kind of criticism is produced by a poet whose practice involves 'interposing his or her perception and expression'. Two of Heaney's lectures fall within the remit of this essay: 'Dylan the Durable? On Dylan Thomas', and 'Joy or Night: Last Things in the Poetry of W. B. Yeats and Philip Larkin'. Heaney has finely crafted observations to make about each of the poets concerned. He communicates a highly nuanced sense of the way the shape of the poets' lives affect the shape of their poems, while his readings find details of artistry which immediately seem clinching even though one hadn't noticed them before. Ultimately, however, one feels that these lectures are most valuable for the way they define the shape of the poet's own mind. Thomas is presented as a warning of the dangers of overemphasizing the plasticity of language, of overrating 'the lyre's ability to stay or reverse the course of nature'. We learn about Thomas, then, in this lecture, but we also observe Heaney finding the limits of the redressing sensibility. Similarly, Larkin stands at the other end of Heaney's argument for redress – as a poet who concentrated too much on things as they were. He has finely insightful, and appreciative things to say about 'Aubade'. Again, though, Larkin appears not in the wholeness of his own performance, but rather as he enters Heaney's field of vision, and as he marks one edge of that vision so we are only offered a glimpse of his practice. Heaney's criticism, like Eliot's, is useful not least as it envisions the context in which his own poetry should be read.

John Wilson Foster's *The Achievement of Seamus Heaney* was the first book to take account of Heaney's 'Nobel Laureateship' (the fact that the Lilliput press got the work out in the year of the award being itself no mean achievement). Foster has two objects in writing his monograph. First, he wants to chart the evolution of the tropes and metaphors, what he calls the 'mythography', that have structured Heaney's career so far. Moving from *Death of a Naturalist* to *Seeing Things*, he traces the movement from physicality to absence, the process by which 'poetry's proper element is no longer seen as earth (or sea) but as air'. This is hardly a ground-breaking insight, but the shift is articulated smoothly and through a series of skilful readings. Foster's second object is to honour Heaney, to whom he is grateful for his articulation of Ulster's sensibility. The personal note this implies manifests itself in various ways. Foster has been reviewing Heaney for years, and frequently draws on those reviews here. This strategy works quite well, both confirming Foster's authority to judge, and providing an index of the way Heaney has established himself as a representative voice. In other respects, however, the personal note intrudes on the critical act. Thus Foster is rather quick to defend Heaney's political stance. He suggests in the introduction that 'poetry has been Heaney's conscience, preventing blatant partisanship or propaganda, keeping him in the political no man's land as fidelity to poetry dictates'. As a position this is clearly sustainable, but one would wish that it had been more comprehensively argued. The further side-effect of Foster's personal investment, as this quotation indicates, is that in his analyses he sometimes finds it rather difficult to step outside Heaney's own seductive metaphors, the result being an exposition which rather too often participates in the mythographical process it intends to describe.

Richard Tillinghast's article 'Seamus Heaney's "Middle Voice" ' (*NewC* 14.iv.77–80) also takes the award of the Nobel Prize as its occasion. Placing Heaney by setting his work among prevailing Irish poetic strategies, Heaney,

Tillinghast suggests, is right to resist the nomination British, but is equally right to resist the 'cultural parochialism' he finds in 'nativism' (the most extreme example of which, he claims, is poetry in Irish). Heaney's achievement is thus to mediate between the resources of Irish culture and the English language, hence the 'middle voice' of the title. He is 'not a product of the Northern Irish conflict', rather 'his is a sensibility that seeks to assuage . . . and to heal'. No doubt this is what Heaney seeks. The tougher question of whether, in any real sense, he manages the task, goes unanswered because unasked. Tillinghast, like Foster, tends to view the cultural politics of Northern Ireland from the perspective with which Heaney provides him.

One kind of measure of Heaney's achievement is that he is the only poet from the archipelago of Britain and Ireland to figure in Helen Vendler's collection of essays, *Soul Says: On Recent Poetry*. Indeed, Vendler devotes three essays to Heaney (more than to any other poet save her current favourite, Jorie Graham), the most exacting of which is 'A Wounded Man Falling Towards Me: Seamus Heaney's *The Government of the Tongue*'. Vendler finds the essays constantly instructive, both as they present 'the darts and feints of Heaney's mind', and as they constitute 'bravura pieces of characterisation, the best in recent memory'. Probing the implications of Heaney's discussion of poetry and totalitarianism, she concludes, sternly, that he does not sufficiently address the possibility that for all that art will sometimes necessarily oppose ideology, so equally 'it can work happily within a civic or ecclesiastical ideological consensus'. It is the absence of this possibility in Heaney's thinking that causes him, she suggests, to misconstrue Herbert. She is much happier with Heaney's discussion of Anglo-American poets (Auden, Lowell and Plath), approving his suggestion that these artists achieved because they undertook the arduous aesthetic work of individuating themselves. Heaney's emphasis on work and works allows Vendler to jab at those (Marxists and Deconstructionists) who insist on reducing verbal art to texts. At this point the writing descends into polemic. For the most part, however, Vendler provides a fine nuancing of Heaney's already nuanced observations.

Introducing the compendious anthology of essays *Poetry in Contemporary Irish Literature* (the second in the Smythe series Studies in Contemporary Irish Literature) the editor, Michael Kenneally, observes that, 'taken together, the essays are intended to lay the foundation for a solid critical introduction to contemporary Irish poetry'. On balance the volume achieves this objective, though the quality is distinctly uneven, and not all the 24 essays earn their place. Heaney is prominent, of course, but not overbearingly so, and the sum value of the book is the vitalizing diversity it finds in the Irish poetry scene. Of the three essays which centre on Heaney, Robert Tracy's 'Into an Irish Free State: Heaney, Sweeney and Clearing Away' is the least necessary. Like Foster, Tracy pursues the metaphorical shift – from digging to flying – that constitutes Heaney's career. His account, however, is laboured, and though shorter, feels considerably longer than Foster's, which stands as the better of the year's introductory treatments. The images of Heaney presented by Stan Smith and Peter McDonald are decidedly more challenging, not least to one another. Smith's 'The Language of Displacement in Contemporary Irish Poetry' aims to provide an overview of the way twentieth-century Irish poets have responded to their post-colonial situation. Neatly combining

Heaney's critical discourse with his own, Smith suggests that the challenge for Irish writers is how to handle the 'pre-occupied' language in which they find themselves working. Yeats's strategy was to delineate a series of oppositions, thereby demarcating a Celtic identity and a distinctive Irish-English. The problem with this stance, Smith observes, is that it preserves the colonial relationship, Irishness in all its forms being judged against the gold standard of Englishness. This problem outlined, Smith presents a series of younger writers who move beyond the Yeatsian opposition by unsettling, in a post-structural manner, both of the rhetorics involved. The post-Yeatsian account Smith provides of McGuckian (her eccentric procedures responding to the gravity of his utterance) is the best thing here. The suggestion that Heaney, on whom Smith dwells at length, has 'like the jocoserious Joyce ... taken refuge in the comedy of justified margins' is rather less compelling. Overall, though, Smith's is the best of this volume's general discussions.

The Heaney presented in Peter McDonald's strong and important essay on the poet's criticism is anything but post-structuralist. McDonald's concern is with Heaney's tendency to root the authority of his critical judgement in his identity as a poet. The problem, as he sees it, is that the authority of the poet rests on a relation with his or her culture which for Heaney is necessarily mysterious. The poet's critical pronouncements are thus legitimized by a mysterious authority which is, by its nature, beyond argument. McDonald's serious concern, then, is that Heaney's critical judgements have a tendency to go unargued.

In the main, those essays in this volume which attempt the overview struggle to avoid superficiality. An exception is Caoimhín Mac Giolla Léith's consideration of 'Contemporary Poetry in Irish', in which he presents a number of responses to the central problem in Irish language poetry, the problem of 'Béarlachas' (Englishness). Starting with the Irish-language revival of the 1950s, Léith demonstrates the way its major poets all focus on the need to articulate the often anxious relationship between the Modern (which is so often Anglo) and the Gaelic inheritance. The most effective contemporary response to the problem is shown to be the work of Nuala Ní Dhomnaill's relaxed, acquisitive, heterogeneous approach to discourse, the result of which is a genuinely contemporary Irish language poetry unencumbered by fears of Englishness. A differing view of Ní Dhomnaill's work is presented by Deborah McWilliams Consalvo in 'The Lingual Ideal in the Poetry of Nuala Ní Dhomnaill' (*Éire* 30.148–57).

The majority of the essays in Kenneally's volume are case-studies of individual poets or groups, and the most significant of these are Edna Longley's 'Derek Mahon: Extreme Religion of Art', Clair Wills's 'Voices from the Nursery: Medbh McGuckian's Plantation' and Bernard O'Donoghue's ' "The Half-Said Thing to Them is Dearest": Paul Muldoon'. Longley's argument is that for all its post-Yeatsian transcendental yearning Mahon's poetry is by no means guilty of evading history. The weak version of her argument is that his poetry is historicized in part by virtue of his acute awareness of the tradition in which he writes. Her stronger defence is that Mahon's lyric yearning for the utopian should be construed not as an evasion, but as a responsible reaction to history; a claim she grounds in Benjamin's notion of messianic time. Clair Wills's essay is less fluent than Longley's, but then her subject, Medbh McGuckian, for all the fluidity of her line, is much less tractable than Mahon. The strength of Wills's account is that it attempts not only to explicate McGuckian's writing, but to communicate its value. Wills makes the poetry available through considerations of the function of the female body in Irish poetry, and of the European aspect of McGuckian's writing. There is no single argumentative thread holding the discussion together, but this is because we are still learning the McGuckian language, a language which feels more familiar for the attention Wills has paid it. Finally, the book concludes on a high, if immaculately understated, note, with Bernard O'Donoghue's discussion of Paul Muldoon. Approving 'the creation of this anti-dogmatic world, which is the preserve of Muldoon' (and his telling contribution to Northern Irish poetics), O'Donoghue's essay is itself intelligently 'anti-dogmatic'. Settling on the development of Muldoon's (Keatsian) strategies for living in uncertainties as his uncomplicated theme, O'Donoghue's relaxed prose allows him to modulate smoothly between theoretical and political registers, between close readings and biographical comment. The result is an essay which students of Muldoon will want to mine for its insights. Fenella Copplestone offers a slightly more sceptical account of Muldoon's achievement in 'Paul Muldoon and the Exploding Sestina' (*PNR* 22.ii.33– 6).

A number of the contributions to *Poetry in Contemporary Irish Literature*, which, reading between the lines, seems to have been some time in the making, are already reprinted elsewhere. One such is Gerald Dawe's essay on Thomas Kinsella, which also appeared this year in his book *Against Piety: Essays in Irish Poetry*. Kinsella is clearly important to Dawe, opening as he does with Kinsella's observation, made to the MLA in 1966, that 'for the present – especially in the present – it seems that every writer has to make the imaginative grasp at identity for himself; and if he can find no means in his inheritance to suit him, he will have to start from scratch'. In his attitude both to tradition and to audience, Kinsella stands at the opposite pole, in contemporary Irish poetry, from Heaney. He thus provides Dawe with a point of reference from which to offer an alternative, Modernist map of the post-war period. Dawe's opening essay amounts to a strongly sceptical revisiting of the value of literary tradition in Ireland. Caught up as it is in the vocabulary of 'influence', 'roots', 'place' and 'identity', Irish poetry tends to invest too heavily in its traditions, and so tends to become caught in the abundant meanings that tradition supplies. The clear advantage of drawing on such conventional meanings is that they guarantee the poet's relationship with his audience. The corresponding danger is that 'the present is swept aside ... and with it the complex relationship of the self with the world it inhabits is trivialized'. Dawe's argument can be heard straining at times, particularly in his second chapter, and his mapping is unstable (he is uncertain, for instance, in which camp to place Tom Paulin), but his book, which proceeds to offer a series of case-studies, affords an important alternative route through the contemporary Irish scene.

Kinsella himself weighed into the debate this year with *The Dual Tradition: An Essay on Poetry and Politics in Ireland*. This is a contentious, insightful but curiously fragmented work. Possibly the fragmented style reflects hasty composition. Equally, it could be strategic, a Modernist device of sorts, meant to register a fractured post-colonial sensibility, or to break up conventional wisdom. Kinsella's theme is the fragmentation of Irish literature, the fragmentation which comes of the fact that it is written in two languages, and which results in the dual tradition of his title. The key choice facing the contemporary poet, he suggests, rests on the question of audience: on whether 'to address the work toward a responsive primary audience, but away from the facts of experience, or, like Joyce or Yeats in his later poetry, toward a primary audience sharing the facts of experience intimately with the writer – an audience that may not exist, an ideal audience'. The subsequent discussions of Austin Clarke, Patrick Kavanagh and Samuel Beckett don't quite live up to this clear-headed polarization of the issue facing contemporary poets, but each is worth consideration. Kinsella's final chapter is a marvellously angry polemic on the 'Politics of the Dual Tradition'. His central complaint here is against the idea of 'Northern poetry'. Given, he suggests, that in a postcolonial situation, questions of definition are all important, then the idea of an Ulster Renaissance, which does not bear, so he argues at length, either literary historical or geographical scrutiny, serves only to 'add a literary argument to arguments' for an 'Ulster naturally separated within Ireland'. Less composed than Dawe's book, Kinsella's is more likely to ruffle feathers.

Perhaps confirming Kinsella's standing as the major alternative to Heaney in contemporary Irish poetry, this year saw the publication of the first full-length treatment of his work: Thomas H. Jackson's *The Whole Matter: The Poetic Evolution of Thomas Kinsella*. Within the overarching claim (that Kinsella is 'the most important and compendious Irish poet since Yeats') Jackson has two precise claims to defend. The first is that 'the ideal (and reality) of wholeness lies at the core of his poetry'. And the second is that some time in the mid-1960s Kinsella embarked on a 15-year pursuit 'of the depth he came to realise his art demanded', a process from which he emerged 'not as a strong simple self but as a consciousness more or less continuous with what it speaks of'. To establish the first claim, Jackson develops the helpful idea of 'isomorphism', a term which aims to elucidate the way Kinsella traces structural similarities between people, events, consciousness and things. The process of deepening is charted by a series of relentlessly dense close readings, which draw heavily on Jackson's knowledge of the Jungian psychology and Modernist (especially Poundian) poetics which informed Kinsella's self-transformation. Jackson's book is not for the faint-hearted, but with patience it comes to compel a serious attention, and manages, finally, to make the story of Kinsella's evolution seem a matter of considerable importance.

Finally, in this section of the review, the Irish poetry special issue of *SoR* (31) is a quite monumental slab: 416 pages of poems, translations, interviews and essays, with contributions from all sides of the Irish literati. Introducing the collection, the editors James Olney and Dave Smith confidently assert that 'the Irish poetry scene shows more activity and excitement than almost any other today', a confidence borne out by the diverse mix of Irish language and Irish-English poetry they include. The essays are of a more consistent standard than those in Kenneally's book (one suspects tougher editing) but three in particular stand out: Maire Mhac an tSaoi's 'Writing in Modern Irish – A Benign Anachronism?', Peter Sirr's ' "How Things Begin to Happen": Notes on Eiléan Ní Chuilleanain and Medbh McGuckian' and Eavan Boland's 'Writing the Political Poem in Ireland' (*SoR* 31.424-31,450-67,485-98). tSaoi sets out to answer the question 'Why write in Irish?' – a pertinent question given that the audience is very small, almost coterminous with a head-count of writers. The essay proceeds to provide a panoramic view of present-day writing in Irish, while paying particular attention to Nuala Ní Dhomnaill. Dhomnaill, she suggests, shows 'a mindless capacity for evil and illusion, which we have forgotten how to handle, but which the folk mind has not'. tSaoi concludes in stirring fashion, her answer to her question being that, 'we write in Irish, not only because of the magnificent resources of the language, but because we seek to preserve the essential habitat of our country's soul'.

Peter Sirr, like Dawe, opens by lamenting what he takes to be the conservatism of Irish poetry, citing as proof the fact that Kinsella has been effectively marginalized because he has neglected the 'comforting', and 'primarily lyric', norms of the Irish poem. In Ní Chulleanain and McGuckian he finds two poets who have risked relinquishing control of their language. (To retain control, as Sirr sees it, being to reach 'only part-way down the well'.) His essay wisely resists the temptation to force links between the two poets. Rather, each half is a patient registering of strategies and devices, with each discussion advancing our understanding of these difficult poets.

Eavan Boland's poetry is given useful consideration in 'The Extraordinary Within the Ordinary: The Poetry of Eavan Boland and Nuala Ní Dhomnaill' (*SoAR* 60.ii.31–46). Boland's own contribution to *SoR* special issue is quite the most arresting essay I encountered in this year's work in English studies: a manifestly significant piece of writing. Her central object is to challenge the assumption that public poetry is necessarily political poetry. The political poem, she contends, in a most clear-headed statement of the matter, cannot be written 'with truth and effect unless the self who writes that poem ... is seen to be in a radical relation to the ratio of power to powerlessness with which the political poem is concerned'. Given the place that female iconography has had in Irish poetry, and especially public Irish poetry – she refers to 'the nationalization of the feminine, the feminization of the national' – she concludes that women are almost uniquely placed to write the Irish political poem. Strong as it is, the algebra of Boland's argument cannot catch its force. Suffice to say that given that in poets as different as Heaney and Kinsella we encounter precisely the kind of 'feminization' she identifies, Boland's essay is essential reading.

On the assumption that it is sometimes good to see ourselves as others see us, a consideration of the year's work in studies of British literatures does well to start with Keith Tuma's review essay, 'Who Needs Neo-Augustanism? On British Poetry' (*ConL* 36.718–36): a discussion of the issues arising from Patrick Deane's *At Home in Time: Forms of Neo-Augustanism in Modern English Poetry* and Robert Hampson and Peter Barry's *New British Poetries: The Scope of the Possible*. After a brief survey of the divisions disfiguring American poetry, Tuma moves swiftly to the opinion that 'things could be worse. Or so the British poetry scene seems to suggest, from this distance at least.' Tuma is sympathetic to the poetries presented in Hampson and Barry's book. He is dismayed, however, by the intensity of the polemics dividing 'mainstream' and 'alternative' writing. Neither, he suggests, is a sustainable category: 'mainstream' designating Davie and Tomlinson as well as Larkin, 'alternative' (as represented by Hampson and Barry) pointing to such divergent ideas about identity as Peter Middleton's and Fred D'Aguiar's. Tuma is resistant to the idiom of Neo-Augustanism ('maturity', 'civility'), but is equally persuaded that 'caricatures' of the mainstream 'are finally self-defeating in perpetuating hatred on all sides'. British poetry, he concludes, is falsely stratified.

Tuma's conclusions are harsh, but the thrust of his essay seems unavoidable. Thus, while there is a discourse in Irish criticism which can mediate both Heaney and Kinsella, Larkin and Prynne would seem to occupy different universes. In answer to Tuma's leading question, however, nobody, judging from the year's criticism, really wants 'Neo-Augustanism'. Even Andrew Swarbrick's *Out of Reach: The Poetry of Philip Larkin* is written in the conviction that Larkin's poetry is 'more adventurous and challenging than we are used to recognising', thus rebutting 'the old charges of genteel parochialism and the new charges of ideological incorrectness'. In attempting this rendering, Swarbrick is knowingly going against the grain of Larkin's public presentation of himself. The whole point of the book, however, is to emphasize the constructed character of that public self. Swarbrick's argument starts with an unpicking of Larkin's claim that in 1946 he deserted Yeats and converted to Hardy. Making good use of his Oxford poems to make his case, Swarbrick endeavours to show that Yeatsian yearnings went much deeper with Larkin than he could bring himself to admit, and having done so proceeds to locate their shaping force at every stage of his subsequent career. That career, Swarbrick argues, was constructed on Larkin's sense that he had failed both to achieve his high poetic ambitions, and as a novelist. His response was to develop a curmudgeonly, Hardyesque public persona, which served both to conceal his aspirations, and to permit a sublime self-forgetting. Swarbrick's readings are unforced and one is persuaded that, for all his anxious resisting of the impulse, Larkin was more motivated than commentators have allowed by the desire to get beyond the frame of the poem, and to articulate that which is beyond reach. Less persuasive, because altogether forced, is Swarbrick's use of theory. He several times claims that Larkin is Bakhtinian, though his quotations come from David Lodge, not Bakhtin himself, and whatever else he may be Larkin is surely not carnivalesque. Equally, his attempt to turn Larkin's persona into an instance of the postmodern performative self seems an ill-judged attempt to win readers troubled by Larkin's gender politics by suggesting affinities with Judith Butler. Swarbrick persuades, then, that Larkin desired that which is out of reach, but over-reaches in his forays into theory.

A deft and instructive use of theory, on the other hand, is just one of the virtues of *Nearly Too Much: The Poetry of J. H. Prynne* by N. H. Reeve and Richard Kerridge. Fully aware of the danger of taming the poetry (and so hoping to recommend it in its more radical state) the authors' object here is to 'mediate between the radicalism of Prynne's poetry – its sheer range of vocabulary and reference – and the more familiar ways of organizing discourse'. Remarkably, given the inherent difficulty of this project, Reeve and Kerridge succeed, collaborating to produce an introduction to Prynne that any serious student of contemporary British poetry will want to consult. The book is divided into four long-ish chapters. The first considers the difficulties posed the reader by a series of devices which seem to alienate – notably a rapid shifting of scale. The second considers Prynne's relation to lyricism. The third presents the poetry alongside the theoretical findings of Bakhtin, Kristeva, Lyotard and Habermas. The fourth stages an extended reading of 'The Oval Window'. The book works because Reeve and Kerridge have managed to develop a critical discourse which is intimate with Prynne's procedures, but far enough from the poetry's way of speaking to locate it. This discourse consists of: an innovative handling of literary history – showing, for instance, how Prynne develops lines of thinking which originate with George Eliot; a fluent but not undemanding use of theory; and a remarkably patient style of close reading. Still, one would quibble with the caricatures of Larkin and Heaney (though not of Armitage). More importantly, however, Reeve and Kerridge persuade that Prynne is as significant as anybody in his treatment of the question 'what is poetry for?', and the abiding image that emerges from this excellent book is not of an avant-garde elitist, but of a strangely public poet.

Terry Gifford's stated object in *Green Voices: Understanding Contemporary Nature Poetry* is to explore how 'through the elaboration and questioning of notions of nature in contemporary poetry the human species is learning, still, how to live on the earth now'. The book is marred by its introduction and conclusion, the former lacking the suppleness to present – as it aims to – 'a theoretical framework for discussions of nature poetry', the latter succumbing to superficiality in a brisk survey of a plurality of contemporary nature poetries, when a deepening of the argument was necessary. Sandwiched between, however, is a highly controlled history of the pastoral in post-war British and Irish poetry. Gifford tours far and wide in gathering the poets necessary for his argument. Norman Nicholson, George Mackay Brown, John Montague and R. S. Thomas are taken to present 'some versions of pastoral'. Patrick Kavanagh's 'The Great Hunger' constitutes an anti-pastoral manoeuvre. Sorley Maclean, Heaney and Hughes are each shown to offer a post-pastoral nature poetry, a green poetry as Gifford wants to call it. The idea of the local is important throughout Gifford's study, his agreeable contention being that strong contemporary nature poetry enables a community to understand more deeply its relation with its place. Proceeding from this premise, Gifford's immaculately researched chapter on Maclean is probably the most impressive discussion here. This book's strength, then, is the detailed attention it pays to given locales. Inevitably, perhaps, its attempts to universalize its thinking about the local seem ungainly by comparison.

Poetry in the British Isles: Non-Metropolitan Perspectives (ed. Hans-Werner Ludwig and Lothar Fietz), has a similarly local focus. The editors aim to foreground 'poetry written in the indigenous territorial languages of the British Isles', and to explore 'poetry's relation to place, and its role in the self-definition of communities as the monolithic ideologies of the nation-state fragment'. The book opens with a rather unfortunate rant by Christopher Harvie (' "My country will not yield you any sanctuary": A polemic by way of preface'), Harvie firing off against 'a metropolitan elite drowsily but profitably talking to itself, its hefty volumes resting, perhaps even read, on the coffee-tables of the south-east'. Quite how the likes of Iain Sinclair and Denise Riley fit into this image of literary London is not made clear. Thereafter, the book divides into three sections: establishing a historical perspective on the topos of place in British poetry; surveying the range of poetry being written in Ireland, Scotland, Wales and non-metropolitan England; and offering case-studies of individual poets identified with a particular place, such as Tomlinson and Harrison. The freshest pieces here are those written on or from a Welsh perspective. M. Wynn Thomas's 'Prints of Wales: Contemporary Welsh poetry in English', asks whether it is possible 'to write about an increasingly Anglicized life in Wales without writing an Anglophone (or frankly English) poetry'. His provisional answer is that it is possible to locate an 'oppositional spirit', 'a feeling that Wales is some place other than England' in the writing of such 1980s poets as Robert Minhinnick, Tony Curtis, Gwyn A. Williams and John Davies. These poets, he suggests, articulate a 'new freedom', neither feeling constrained to identify Wales as an entirely separate cultural entity, nor pointing their proverbial television aerials across the Mendip Hills. These writers of the 'new freedom' have learned, Thomas suggests, from the supple strategies of, among others, the Aberystwyth-based poet Jeremy Hooker, and Hooker's supple and subtle thinking is certainly evident in his ' "The centre cannot hold": Place in Modern English Poetry'. Hooker considers the important but ambivalent relation English poetry has had to place in modern times. He makes a broad distinction between poets such as Kipling and Newbolt, for whom the idea of 'home' colluded with imperial designs, and the likes of Edward Thomas and David Jones, for whom speaking in defence of place constitutes a defence of all peripheral places against all imperial centres. The essay pursues the second tradition through Bunting, Fisher, Hughes and Davie and goes some way to making a sustainable critical discourse out of non-hegemonic ideas of Englishness. Finally, Gareth Alban Davies's 'The Multi-Screen Cinema: Poetry in Welsh 1950–1990' is an informative introduction to the field. Following a detailed history of the re-emergence of the Welsh language in the 1950s, and charting the changes in the technologies of publishing and broadcasting which made it possible, Davies details three kinds of Welsh language poet: 'y bardd gwlad' or 'country poet', deriving from the bardic tradition; the Eistedfodd poet; and the Modern poet. This last, Davies suggests – and Waldo Williams is the major example – is the product of the collapse of the rural economy and the drift to the towns, thereby identifying an intriguing little contra-flow in this centrifugal book.

For a less exacting consideration of the question of Englishness than Hooker's, one could consider John Whitehead's *Hardy to Larkin: Seven English Poets*. Whitehead finds in his poets – the other five being Hopkins, Kipling, Housman, Thomas and Owen – a 'common appeal in their Englishness'. His essays were not written in 'pursuance of any preconceived theory about poetry' but rather to 'encourage in [readers] the habit of teasing out of each line precisely what it was the poet had in mind'. One can hardly object to this intention, but one feels that a book on this subject would have done well to consider Donald Davie on *Thomas Hardy and British Poetry* (Routledge, 1973).

Two English poets who have never received the attention their achievements deserve were given the special-issue treatment this year, with a *Charles Tomlinson: International Issue* of *Agenda*, guest edited by Richard Swigg, and *Sharp Study and Long Toil: Basil Bunting Special Issue*, published under the Durham University Special Supplement imprint, and edited by Richard Caddel. Introducing the Tomlinson volume, William Cookson echoes Hooker's formulation with the suggestion that 'while always rested in place, [Tomlinson's] work resists provincialism in all its forms; it is international in the best sense'. And developing this thought in the second editorial, Richard Swigg observes that Tomlinson's 'voyaging out has also been a means of coming home: a sharpening and deepening of his native sensibility'. It is this transaction the issue sets out to explore.

Hugh Kenner's contribution to this group analysis of Tomlinson, 'Pebble-Strewn Speech', shows him to be on characteristically good and helpful form

(*Agenda* 33.ii.32–43). His subject is meter, and his intention is to show how Tomlinson's poetry moves with 'staccato accuracy'. Tomlinson's art, he demonstrates, is an art of stress and emphasis, a salient art. Quoting generously, he provides a topography of Tomlinson's writing, so allowing the reader to see how the poetry itself maps its scenes. It is exemplary criticism by an old master – colloquial, erudite and deft. Kenner concludes by despairing that the British literati 'would rather bow toward a Larkin collection than savour "A Peopled Landscape" or "The Shaft" '. Michael Schmidt is similarly dismayed, but having pondered the question of Tomlinson's neglect long and hard, feels he can offer explanations (*Agenda* 33.ii.44–5). Tomlinson's essays, he suggests, generously focus on their subjects rather than 'deliberately create a context for his poems'. Tomlinson has never, Schmidt points out, rested on a single genre, and seldom repeats himself. Finally, where Larkin has characteristic imagery, Tomlinson 'almost invariably has very specific images in mind'. He is, Schmidt observes, 'by instinct a particularist' and so 'there are no easy endings, few rhetorical lift-offs'. Such poems, he observes, 'require rare readers'.

Several contributions treat Tomlinson's internationalism directly, discussing his relations with other literatures either in terms of translations or poetic friendships. The most interesting of these discussions is Eduardo Zuccato's 'The Unsubjective South: Tomlinson's Italy' (*Agenda* 33.ii.98–108). Zuccato opens with an expert consideration of the artistic reasoning behind Tomlinson's decision to translate the Italian poets Piccolo, Ungaretti, Guido, Gozzaro and Bertolucci. Zuccato's real interest, however, lies in Tomlinson's suggestion that Italian light made him a poet. The detailed answer Zuccato proposes is that the poet 'saw in Mediterranean light a quality he also found in a part of Italian art. The transition seems to have been from light in nature to the clarity of artistic forms and from both to his own poetry, which tries to recreate them'. This combines nicely with his suggestion that Italy and America seem to constitute the extremes of Tomlinson's mental geography, and that 'their combination has often been essential to his poetry'. It is, after all, perhaps only a short hop from the clarity of Tuscan light to the clarity of Williams's New England.

Richard Caddell's *Sharp Study and Long Toil* brings together a fine mix of Bunting resources, including Bunting's ' "Thumps" and "Wyatt": Two Lectures on Prosody', 'Three Essays' ('Mr. Ezra Pound', 'Butler', 'Observations on Left-Wing Papers') and his 'Shakespeare's Sonnets Edited'. There are poems in his honour from Roy Fisher, Catherine Walsh, Susan Howe, Robert Creeley, George Evans and Tomlinson. Of the essays the most useful of those referring to Bunting's postwar poetry are Peter Quatermain's 'Parataxis in Basil Bunting and Louis Zukofsky', the late Eric Mottram's 'Basil Bunting: Human Framework and Nature', and Joseph Vicary's 'Desire and Disgust in the Poetry of Basil Bunting' (*DUJ.* [1995]. 54–70,71–82,163–72).

Quatermain opens with a good explanation and defence of the paratactical procedure, a procedure which, he suggests, in its pure form, empowers the reader by refusing to impose an order on materials. Bunting, he contends, does not practise parataxis in its purest form, because as a regionalist, and as an advocate of regional dialects, he would object to readings which did not endeavour to weigh the specific local force of a term. Zukofsky, on the other hand, would be much more inclined to permit readings grounded in lexical mistakes, given his inclination always to collaborate with his reader. The meat of Quatermain's argument lies in his expert tracing of the manuscript histories of both 'Briggflatts' and 'A'. He gets inside the procedures of both poets, and is thus able to speak with confidence about their kinds of empowerment. He does not, however, ponder the question of how the reader is supposed to proceed who encounters these texts without access to the preparatory manuscripts.

Eric Mottram's article is itself a kind of parataxis. It can read like a jumble of insights, but the jumble is deliberate. His theme (or rather anti-theme) is Bunting's 'ways of coming to terms with experiences ... with a minimal pre-existent authoritarian principle'. He wants to show how Bunting's writings 'are not returned to a hub centre, exemplifying that kind of need for coherence through pre-conceived systemic frame'. This is a difficult position to make sound impressive. It can amount to saying that the poet had no vision. The power of the position lies in the resistance it makes to authority. Mottram's way of indicating this power is, in effect, to accumulate a catalogue of the various authority figures to whom Bunting's modernist predecessors and contemporaries (from Pound to Zukofsky) succumbed. Only a critic of real erudition could carry this kind of exercise off convincingly. Mottram was such a critic, and the force of Bunting's resistance is made clear.

The starting point for Joseph Vicary's essay on 'Desire and Disgust' in Bunting is the coprophagy (excrement-eating) scene in the first part of the third movement of 'Briggflatts'. The point of this bracing opening is to introduce the argument that for all Bunting's distaste for abstractions, the poem does have thematic content, with 'shame, disgust, guilt and betrayal', together forming one of the central topics of the poem. Boldly offering a simple summary of the poem, Vicary suggests that it is 'to do with how much squalor has to be gone through before beauty can finally be achieved and celebrated'. Disgust does prove to be a good point of entry into Bunting's imagination, enabling Vicary to mount a detailed re-reading of his major work which finds its affinities with those other Modernist anatomists of disgust, Eliot and Pound.

Stefan Hawlin's 'Bunting's Northumbrian Tongue: Against the Monument of the Centre' (*YES* 25.103–13) is an erudite and forceful consideration of Bunting's commitment to the local. Hawlin moves smoothly from the question of Bunting's dialect to what he takes to be the central theme of the poetry, which is transience. Bunting aims, Hawlin suggests, 'to destroy uniformity ... and give men a chance to live and vary without interference'. He stakes this claim on a reading of 'At Briggflatts Meeting House', a poem which he shows to take issue with both Horace and Pound, and in which Bunting 'places himself against the power of the centre'.

Several of the year's occasional articles on individual poets merit a mention. In 'Singing the Real: The Later Poetry of Peter Redgrove' (*English* 44.139–62), Paul Bentley offers a reading of Redgrove rooted in Lacanian and Kristevan theory. W.S. Milne's 'An Essay on W. S. Graham' (*Agenda* 33.ii.81–8) endeavours to substantiate Edwin Morgan's claim that Graham 'is one of the most distinctive and distinguished voices in Scottish Poetry'. C. K. Stead explores Craig Raine's relation to Modernism in 'Craig Raine and History' (*LMag* 34.xi–xii.84–92). Discussing Geoffrey Hill, Colin Thompson shows an appropriately acute ear for etymologies and allusions in 'The Resonances of

Words: Lope de Vega and Geoffrey Hill' (*MLR* 90.i.55–70), while Ranjana Sidhanta explores the effects, or otherwise, of displacement on the poetry of 'Sujata Bhatt' (*PNR* 21.vii.44–7).

Finally, and unfortunately, the reader has to be warned against *Taking Stock: A First Study of the Poetry of U. A. Fanthorpe* by Eddie Wainwright. Referring to the poet as 'UAF' throughout, distinguishing her from those feminists he 'has dubbed the Piranha School', and making a virtue of the fact that he 'made no study of any reviews and articles which [Fanthorpe's] work has stimulated', Wainwright's truest observation is perhaps that 'the views expressed, whether about particular poems' concerns or about points of detail ... are just mine and have no special authority ... '. Badly written and poorly conceived, this book can hardly be recommended to the A-Level students at whom it is opportunistically targeted.

3. Drama

The academic study of drama, and especially of modern drama, is in a rather complicated state, as 'theatre studies', drawing on such non-literary intellectual sources as cultural history and performance theory, extends its autonomy *vis-à-vis* literary criticism, yet without abandoning its interest in dramatic scripts. The work reviewed here is consequently a rich generic mish-mash, which I have not attempted to categorize, merely putting the items into a rough chronological order of topic.

Angela V. John, *Elizabeth Robins: Staging A Life, 1862–1952* offers useful context for the study of the activist end of the 'new drama' of the early century. Robins was one of the strong, politically aware actresses who came to the fore in the 1890s through playing Ibsen on the English stage; in 1907 her play *Votes for Women* was staged by Granville Barker. The script has been available in a modern edition for some time, and the complicated web of literary, theatrical and political relationships out of which it came is well charted here. On the cover, it is hailed as 'a new form – biography as social history'. This is a great exaggeration: the form is that of a conventional biography, which naturally embraces a certain amount of social history when the subject has social commitments as diverse as this one: a friend of, and in some cases collaborator with, William Archer, James, Masefield and Shaw, she was clearly where things were happening in the drama of those years, besides the significant things which she made happen herself. The result is not critical or analytic, but it is informative.

There is more solid work on the Barker era in Rudolf Weiss's article 'John Galsworthy's *Strife*: Striving for Balance or the Audience as Jury' (*TRI* 20.7–18). This is unpretentious literary history: revisions to the script, relevant correspondence, press cuttings. It usefully and effectively documents what Galsworthy was trying to do with this intelligent if 'minor' play.

The study of pre-First World War drama has also been enhanced by two collections of plays from OUP. *The Playboy of the Western World and Other Plays* (ed. Ann Saddlemyer) is the affordable offspring of the same scholar's standard edition of Synge (1968). It contains all Synge's plays except *When the Moon Has Set*, together with prefaces, first-night casts, and glosses for the mere English reader (in the case of *Playboy* these are Synge's own, neatly borrowed from his letters to his German translator). There is also an exemplary introduction. The volume is a model of what this kind of edition should be, and will perhaps, despite its title, help to bring the 'other plays' out from the long shadow of *Playboy*. The other Oxford collection, *Peter Pan and Other Plays*, edited by Peter Hollindale, is rather odder, I suppose because of the oddity of the dramatist, J. M. Barrie. The other plays here are *The Admirable Crichton*, *What Every Woman Knows*, *Mary Rose* and *When Wendy Grew Up*, which is not so much a play as an alternative ending to *Peter Pan*, used as such in the RSC's reputation-saving revival. *Peter Pan* is very much at the centre of the selection: it is more amply annotated than the others, the complicated evolution of the text between the première in 1904 and the eventual publication in 1928 is expertly though not, of course, comprehensively traced, and the other plays have been chosen at least partly to complement it (which makes the omission of *Dear Brutus* rather puzzling). The commentary combines biographical information and uncertainly pitched explanation with a sort of running advocacy, the editor anxiously pointing up the skill and unsentimentality of the writing, as if, understandably, he cannot quite trust us to accept Barrie as a 'World's Classic'.

Two short articles cast interesting lights on Irish drama between the wars. Masaru Sekine, 'Noh and Yeats: A Theoretical Analysis' (*ArielE* 26.135–50), draws on the writings of the fifteenth-century master Ze-Ami to enquire how far Yeats's *Four Plays For Dancers* are, and are not, Noh. The comparison emphasizes how modernist Yeats's archaism is, cultivating division and aporia where his classical Japanese models tend towards unification on the basis of religious truth. That is interesting, but the value of the exercise is limited by its confining itself to the written dramatic forms: the topic cries out for a consideration of performance as well. Shaun Richards, ' "Suffocated in the Green Flag": The Drama of Teresa Deevy and 1930s Ireland' (*L&H* 4.65–80), looks at the two plays Deevy wrote for the Abbey in its De Valeran doldrums, not exactly defending their timid and closed dramaturgy, but placing it in an intelligible political and cultural context. I am not familiar with Deevy's work, but this study does not make her look like a major acquisition for that lost female dramatic canon whose recovery is by no means complete yet.

The rest of this survey concerns work on the second half of the century, at and after the canonical dramatic revolution of the mid-1950s. Two books reflect, in interestingly different ways, on that legendary watershed. Stephen Lacey, *British Realist Theatre: The New Wave in its Context 1956–1965*, is directly devoted to the 'moment of anger'. This phenomenon was identified before it was well over in John Russell Taylor's *Anger and After*, and the ground thus staked out has been pretty well tilled since by general surveys, monographs on the individual playwrights, and books about the principal institutions involved. It is not immediately clear what this new study has to add. Certainly it is not an essay in revisionism. Lacey's canon, dominated by Osborne and Wesker, is even more restricted than Taylor's was: the invisible writers of the decade – Henry Livings, David Rudkin, N. F. Simpson, John Whiting – remain firmly invisible here, and geographically the book is unshakably centred on Sloane Square and, to a lesser extent, Stratford East. What it rather seeks to do is to situate the familiar story in a moment of cultural history: if there is less about plays and theatres here than in earlier accounts, there is more about the sociology of an emergent youth culture, about the break-up of a 'post-war' consensus, and about the formation of the political culture around CND and the beginnings of *New Left Review*. This all makes for a useful textbook, but it is an approach which yields surprisingly little critical distance – perhaps because the concepts with which it is constructed are essentially those which were developed at the time by Raymond Williams and Stuart Hall: in other words, the book is itself a late (and epigonal) instance of the configuration it seeks to name.

Charles Duff, *The Lost Summer: The Heyday of the West End Theatre*, approaches the 'moment of anger' in a more roundabout fashion. It is a biography of Frith Banbury, actor (1930–47) and then director (1947–89) in just that posh and complacent West End over which the New Wave supposedly broke. Duff is uncritical to the point of identification, not only championing Banbury's work but also reproducing in his own writing the camp and gossipy manner of the circle he describes. His argument is that Royal Court mythology has produced a retrospective caricature of the 1950s mainstream, and led to unfair dismissal of such writers as Wynyard Browne, Rodney Ackland and Robert Bolt; this is a tenable case, but the discriminations which would be needed to make it get lost in the mélange of gushing tribute and backstage anecdote. The interest of the book lies rather in its evocation of a period: I learned a good deal about the structure of the post-war theatrical hegemony of H. M. Tennent Ltd, and also about the strange, prim lawlessness of an establishment whose respectability was at once rigid and precarious because so many of its key players were actively gay. The book lacks almost all of Lacey's academic virtues – if anything, it is marked by a deliberate anti-academic animus. But what it does do, mostly on the basis of letters and personal conversations, is to present a very specific configuration of theatre, sex and money – that is, it relates an episode in the *cultural* history of drama more illuminatingly than many books which brandish the word on their title pages. It is also more fun to read.

The same historical transition looms large in a curious project about Harold Hobson, consisting of two books, both by Dominic Shellard: *Harold Hobson: Witness and Judge – The Theatre Criticism of Harold Hobson*, and *Harold Hobson: The Complete Catalogue 1922–1988*. Hobson started reviewing drama in the early 1930s, and wrote his last notice in 1983. For much of that time (1947–76) he was principal drama critic of the *Sunday Times*. The first of these books is a critical biography, the second a comprehensive list of his writings. The latter has a kind of potential usefulness, in that it constitutes, as it were at one remove, an index of London openings during the period of Hobson's career. But, on reflection, the one remove is disabling: the list is almost complete but not quite (Hobson occasionally missed things), and the referencing is very sparse, usually supplying only the titles and authors of plays, with nothing about directors, casts or managements, which makes the information on revivals, especially, very uncommunicative. There are also some inaccuracies – forgivably, given the large amount of unconnected detail. The work is in fact an ideal reference tool only for someone who is making a detailed study of Hobson himself, and since Shellard has just done that (in the other volume), it is hard to imagine a reason for doing it again. The biography makes what case it can for Hobson's significance: it portrays him as a valuable corrective to the historical authority of his more glamorous opposite number on the *Observer*, Kenneth Tynan; it rightly points to his early and contentious

support for Beckett and Pinter; and it stresses the value of his knowledgeable
love of French theatre at a time when English drama was particularly provincial. It also offers a modest apologia for his personal obsessions (on certain
subjects, such as William Douglas Home, Edwige Feuillère and Francis
Warner, Hobson could not be relied upon to retain his sense of proportion).
All these strengths and weaknesses were seized upon and discussed by readers
of the posh Sundays at the time, but Shellard does not demonstrate that they
possess the abiding importance which this grandiose treatment implies. When
he embarks on a close reading of Hobson's review of *The Birthday Party* as if
it was a lyric poem, the evanescent object buckles under the weight of the
interpretation. Shellard, and Keele, might have done better with an anthology.

Of the Royal Court's 1950s discoveries, the most securely canonized today
is Pinter. Susan Hollis Merritt, *Pinter in Play: Critical Strategies and the Plays
of Harold Pinter*, was first published in 1990 and now appears in paperback
with brief updating additions. Merritt, who is the Bibliographical Editor of
Pinter Review, provides at once a study and a symptom of the institutional
emergence of a Pinter 'critical community'. I have not had an opportunity to
examine the year's issue of the *Review* itself.

Javed Malick, *Towards a Theater of the Oppressed: The Dramaturgy of John
Arden*, is an old-fashioned piece of work in several ways. Despite its title, its
true genre is the literary criticism of drama: it passes over Arden and D'Arcy's
community work and experimental extravaganzas in order to concentrate on
their scripts for the established theatre, and pays surprisingly little attention to
the circumstances of performance even of these. It discusses nothing after *The
Island of the Mighty* in 1972, regarding that date as the end of Arden's
relations with the professional theatre; I am not sure whether this means that
Malick imagines 7:84 to have been an amateur company. The effect is that
although it praises Arden's polemics against authorial ideology, the book
operates in practice entirely inside it, confining itself to the exposition of
authorial intention and to those plays whose forms and conditions make such
an approach reasonable. Within these severe limitations, the criticism is that
of an unreconstructed theatre Marxist: the main chapters characterize
Arden's dramaturgy as epic, transindividual, and ludic, in relentless contrast
with bourgeois realism, which appears as monolithically ahistorical, individualist and illusionist. A final chapter discovers that the true hero of *The
Island of the Mighty* is the people. The curious result is a description of Arden
which can identify no significant difference between him and Brecht. It is
refreshing to read a critic for whom left politics are about oppression and
resistance rather than identity and representation; all the same, there has to be
something missing here.

Bourgeois realism is also the villain of Steven Berkoff's *Meditations on
Metamorphosis*, an expanded rehearsal diary of Berkoff's 1992 Tokyo production, the tenth and last, of his legendary Kafka adaptation. His loathing for
what he calls naturalism is absolute, but its grounds are not political ones;
rather, it is based on his romantic faith in the mechanical and expressive
potential of the body. For him, releasing that potential is what theatre is for,
and to restrict the performer to the constrained and commonplace gestures of
everyday life is an act of treachery. His key term of approval in the theatre is
'energy', and it is interesting that what he writes about really well here, besides

the rehearsal process itself, is his own physical states – feeling loose, or focused, or blocked and out of sorts. What he does not do well is travel writing: the shopping-and-sushi aspect of the book is tiresome. But it is still a valuable document: Berkoff is that rare creature, an English practitioner who is not a pragmatist, but has a considered doctrine of theatre which informs whatever he does. It is always worth knowing what he thinks is going on.

Arden now seems to have turned into a novelist, and Berkoff's play-writing is almost incidental to his work as an exponent and director of performance. The dedicated professional playwrights of that generation are represented in Duncan Wu, *Six Contemporary Dramatists: Bennett, Potter, Gray, Brenton, Hare, Ayckbourn*. This rather directionless book looks suspiciously like an eight-week university lecture series printed out. No rationale is offered either for the implicit definition of contemporary drama as the exclusive preserve of middle-aged white males or, even granting that, for the selection of this particular half-dozen. The book shows no interest in dramatic form, let alone theatrical practice (it moves from stage to television to prose fiction with no sense of crossing generic frontiers); and it breathes a political atmosphere which is almost as complete a vacuum – 'Thatcherism' appears as a common determinant of the dramatists' development in the 1980s, but only as an unanalysed outbreak of selfish materialism and/or a crisis in the funding of drama. What there is left to write about is what the individual writers are 'saying', and in the absence of any material issues that inevitably comes down to insubstantial questions such as whether one is an optimist or a pessimist, or whether there are any moral absolutes. Incidentally, I requested this book for review in mid-1996, to be told that it was already out of print: it seems to be the victim, in more ways than one, of publisher's absent-mindedness.

Perhaps the largest absence in Wu's mini-canon is Edward Bond; two short articles remind us that this volcano is by no means extinct yet. Hilde Klein, 'Edward Bond: An Interview' (*MD* 38.408–15) is actually archive material: Klein fails to date the conversation she transcribes, but internal evidence suggests 1984–5. Bond was apparently on form that day, and allowed himself to be provoked by Klein's rather innocent questions into a series of vicious moral paradoxes – lively marginalia to Bond's now weighty body of critical writing. Cassandra Fusco, ' "The Wretched of the Earth": The Ethics of Political Violence and its Ministers of Sacrifice in Edward Bond's *Jackets*' (*EA* 48.296–305), has, despite its title, nothing to do with Fanon: its most definite subject is Bond's dissenting relationship with the metaphysics of tragedy.

Susanne Bach, 'Extending Ancient Myths: Freud, Fromm, and the Plays of Peter Shaffer' (*CML* 15.345–56), regards Shaffer as an un-dissenting tragedist. The Sophocles to whom she connects him, however, comes mediated by a sort of Freudian humanism which makes the stories into mythic negotiations of psychoanalytic themes. It more or less works.

Joe Winston, 'Re-Casting the Phaedra Syndrome: Myth and Morality in Timberlake Wertenbaker's *The Love of the Nightingale*' (*MD* 38.510–9), is in similar territory, but on much more forthrightly feminist terms, arguing that by juxtaposing her principal story (Philomele and Tereus) with a gender-reversed mirror (Hippolytos and Phaedra), Wertenbaker contests the 'phallocratic authority' of the ancient myths. Not extending but re-casting.

There is still more dialogue with classical antiquity in W. B. Worthen, 'Homeless Words: Field Day and the Politics of Translation' (*MD* 38.22–41).

The plays in question are *The Riot Act, Translations* and *The Cure at Troy*. Since two of these are reasonably 'faithful' translations, and the other includes a kind of idyll of peasant Hellenism, Worthen questions whether Field Day are not here declaring a quasi-neoclassicist faith in the ancient text as true-for-all-time; he concludes that they are not because the language of all three writers, the divisive energy of their staged Irish-English, opens up the possibility of 'interrogating', rather than just accepting, the authority of the old plays.

This is to bring to contemporary Irish drama a rather too well-formed sense of what one would like it to be doing; the same can be said of Jochen Achilles, ' "Homesick for Abroad": The Transition from National to Cultural Identity in Contemporary Irish Drama' (*MD* 38.435–49). Here, fairly programmatically, 'national' is bad (unity, closure, archaism) and 'cultural' is good (diversity, forward-looking acceptance of otherness). The readings, on this basis, of Brian Friel's *Making History* and Sebastian Barry's *Prayers of Sherkin* are quite convincing, but there is an uneasy sense of postcolonial risk-taking shading into a blander discourse which might be called eurocriticism.

Still with the rich contemporary Irish scene, Helen Losek, 'Watching Over Frank McGuinness's Stereotypes' (*MD* 38.348–61) is a plain expository essay on a single play, *Someone Who'll Watch Over Me*.

'English Studies' of new Irish drama are of course increasingly influenced by the categories of postcolonial theory. Tom Maguire, 'When the Cutting Edge Cuts Both Ways: Contemporary Scottish Drama' (*MD* 38.87–96), is a theoretical attempt to read the context of Scottish political theatre – essentially the ventures associated with John McGrath – as another postcolonial variant. The result is less useful than Maguire's earlier and more circumstantial work on the fate of 7:84 in *TRI* 17 (1992).

Keir Elam, 'Tempo's Sickle: Rapping, Zapping, Toasting and Trekking through History in Black British Drama' (*YES* 25.173–98), is an altogether more substantial essay in postcolonial reading. Its postmodish title refers to the range of black Englishes staged in the 30 years between Erroll John's *Moon on a Rainbow Shawl* in 1958 and the chosen terminus of the survey, *Blood Sweat and Fears* by Maria Oshodi, staged in 1988. (Elam writes informatively and persuasively in praise of the latter.) The issue of how to speak is so central to black English dramaturgy, politically and artistically, that Elam's tight focus on language is not at all limiting. Fairly ignorant in this field myself, I found this the most exciting article I have read this year.

On another disciplinary boundary, Elaine Aston, *An Introduction to Feminism and Theatre*, introduces itself as an attempt to explain 'how and why feminism has been important to theatre studies'. This sounds at first like a dispiritingly intra-academic question, but it turns out to be much broader than that. Just as theatre studies in general is concerned to dismantle the barrier between text and performance, so Aston undermines, through working contacts and shared political goals, the barrier between theatre studies and theatre practice. The book ends by considering Liz Lochhead's Mary Shelley play *Blood and Ice* and April de Angelis's *Breathless*, an exercise in Gothic and hysteria – that is, plays whose themes are explicitly those of feminist literary scholarship. Here the writers of textbooks are not so much the practitioners' critics as their colleagues in a common project. This solidarity makes for a welcome political specificity, but it does risk producing a convenient caricature of the opposition: it seems as if outside explicitly feminist theatre there is nothing but a male 'mainstream' whose uniformity is never disturbed by the numerous women who work in it. As Aston's own earlier work shows, she is well aware that the situation of women (and of feminists) in the theatre offers more possibilities than that; but this book, perhaps for the sake of 'introductory' clarity, comes close to offering a bare choice between separateness and incorporation. The resulting tone of political urgency has the effect of rendering artistic judgements inadmissible: the pressing question about a show is whether it is, so to speak, one of ours, not whether it works. In a pendant to the book, 'Daniels in the Lion's Den: Sarah Daniels and the British Backlash' (*TJ* 47.393–403), Aston surveys reviews of Daniels's plays and attributes the bad ones – and by extension the relative neglect of Daniels by theatres which might perform her more – to male hostility to her sexual politics. What if a reviewer was *genuinely* bored?

A similar lack of 'outsideness' is felt in Graham Woodruff, ' "Nice Girls": The Vic Gives a Voice to Women of the Working Class' (*NTQ* 42.109–27), which is a straightforwardly partisan account of Peter Cheeseman's eleventh documentary show, which was performed in 1993, and celebrated a group of women who occupied a pit threatened with closure earlier the same year. The account of the process and the show is informative, but reads as if both Woodruff and Cheeseman had learned nothing and forgotten nothing since 1979.

Finally, it is worth noting an article rather like this one: David Ian Rabey's 'Review of Playtexts Published in Britain, 1994' (*TRI* 20.277–81). Actual plays are outside my remit here, but studying and teaching contemporary drama clearly depends first of all on what scripts are in print: Rabey's little survey, inevitably personal and admittedly superficial, is a useful guide.

Books Reviewed

Aldiss, Brian W. *The Detached Retina: Aspects of SF and Fantasy*. LiverUP. pp. 224. hb £25.00. pb £11.75. ISBN 0 85323 289 X, 0 85323 299 7.

Aston, Elaine. *An Introduction to Feminism and Theatre*. Routledge. pp. 166. hb £35, pb £10.99. ISBN 0 415 08768 6, 0 415 08769 4.

Berkoff, Steven. *Meditations on Metamorphosis*. Faber. pp. 142. pb £8.99. ISBN 0 571 17629 1.

Black, Martha Fodaski. *Shaw and Joyce: 'The Last Word in Stolentelling'*. Florida James Joyce series. UFlorP. pp. 445. £44.95. ISBN 0 813 01328 3.

Bloom, Harold. *The Western Canon: The Books and School of the Ages*. Macmillan. pp. 578. pb £10.00. ISBN 0 333 63952 9.

Booker, M. Keith. *Flann O'Brien, Bakhtin, and Menippean Satire*. SyracuseUP. pp. 163. £27.95. ISBN 0 8156 2665 7.

Bowen, Zack. *Bloom's Old Sweet Song*. Florida James Joyce series. UFlorP. pp. 151. £31.50. ISBN 0 813 01327 5.

Bradbury, Malcolm. *Dangerous Pilgrimages: Trans-Atlantic Mythologies and the Novel*. S&W. pp. 515. hb £30. pb £15.00. ISBN 0 436 20328 6, 0 436 20330 8.

Bristow, Joseph. *Effeminate England: Homoerotic Writing After 1885*. OpenUP. pp. 193. pb £13.99. ISBN 0 335 09665 4.

Brivic, Sheldon. *Joyce's Waking Women: An Introduction to Finnegans Wake.* UWiscP. pp. 162. hb £39.95, pb £15.95. ISBN 0 299 14800 9, 0 299 14804 1.

Broderick, Damien. *Reading by Starlight: Postmodern Science Fiction.* Routledge. pp. 197. hb £37.50, pb £12.99. ISBN 0 415 09788 6, 0 415 09789 4.

Brooks, Linda Marie, ed. *Alternative Identities: The Self in Literature, History, Theory.* Garland. pp. 327. $55.00. ISBN 0 8153 1721 2.

Bury, Stephen. *Artists' Books: The Book as a Work of Art, 1963–1995.* Scolar. pp. 207. £65. ISBN 1 85928 163 X.

Cecil, Hugh. *The Flower of Battle: British Fiction of the First World War.* S&W. pp. 415. £25. ISBN 0 436 20290 5.

Cheng, Vincent J. *Joyce, Race and Empire.* Cultural Margins. CUP. pp. 329. pb £12.95. ISBN 0 521 47859 6.

Cornick, Martyn. *The Nouvelle Revue Française under Jean Paulhan, 1925–1940.* Rodopi. pp. 224. pb Hfl. 65. ISBN 90 5183 797 6.

D'haen, Theo, and Hans Bertens, eds. *Narrative Turns and Minor Genres in Postmodernism.* Rodopi. pp. 317. pb $33. ISBN 90 5183 850 6.

D'haen, Theo, and José Lanters, eds. *Troubled Histories, Troubled Fictions: Twentieth-Century Anglo-Irish Prose.* Rodopi. pp. 174. pb Hfl. 35. ISBN 90 5183 781 X.

Daly, Macdonald, ed. *H. G. Wells. The Invisible Man: A Grotesque Romance.* Dent. Everyman. pp. 182. pb £4.99. ISBN 0 460 87628 7.

Dawe, Gerald. *Against Piety: Essays in Irish Poetry.* Lagan Press. pp.193. ISBN 1 87368775 3.

de Graef, Ortwin. *Titanic Light: Paul de Man's Post-Romanticism 1960–1969.* UNebP. pp. 289. £32.95. ISBN 0 8032 1695 5.

Deane, Patrick. *At Home in Time: Forms of Neo-Augustanism in Modern English Poetry.* McG-QUP (1994) pp. 266. £25. ISBN 07735 1215 2.

Diedrick, James. *Understanding Martin Amis.* USCP. pp. 207. £32.95. ISBN 1 57003 058 8.

Dowson, Jane, ed. *Women's Poetry of the 1930s: A Critical Anthology.* Routledge. pp. 248. £40. ISBN 0 415 13095 6.

Duff, Charles. *The Lost Summer: The Heyday of the West End Theatre.* NHB. pp. 272. pb £12.99. ISBN 1 85459 209 2.

Eagleton, Terry. *Heathcliff and the Great Hunger.* Verso. pp. 355. £19.95. ISBN 1 85984 932 6.

Edmundson, Mark. *Literature Against Philosophy, Plato to Derrida: A Defence of Poetry.* CUP. pp. 242. hb £35.00, pb £12.95. ISBN 0 521 41093 2, 0 521 48532 0.

Emig, Rainer. *Modernism in Poetry: Motivations, Structures, and Limits.* Studies in Twentieth Century Literature. Longman. pp. 280. £37. ISBN 0 582 23919 2.

Epstein, Julia. *Altered Conditions: Disease, Medicine, and Storytelling.* Routledge. pp. 275. pb £14.99. ISBN 0 415 90718 7.

Fargnoli, A. Nicholas, and Michael Patrick Gillespie, eds. *James Joyce A–Z: An Encyclopaedic Guide to his Life and Work.* Bloomsbury. pp. 304. £25. ISBN 0 747 52409 2.

Featherstone, Simon. *War Poetry: An Introductory Reader.* Critical Readers in Theory and Practice. Routledge. pp. 256. £40. ISBN 0 415 07750 8.

Felber, Lynette. *Gender and Genre in Novels Without End.* UPFlor. pp. 205. £31.95. ISBN 0 8130 1402 6.

Felski, Rita. *The Gender of Modernity*. HarvardUP. pp. 247. hb £21.95, pb £10.50. ISBN 0 674 34193 7, 0 674 34194 5.

Ferris, Kathleen. *James Joyce and the Burden of Disease*. UPKen. pp. 182. $24.95. ISBN 0 813 1893 X.

Ffrench, Patrick. *The Time of Theory: A History of Tel Quel (1960–1983)*. Clarendon. pp. 306. £37.50. ISBN 0 19 815897 1.

Foster, John Wilson. *The Achievement of Seamus Heaney*. Lilliput. pp. 60. pb £4.99. ISBN 1 87467571 6.

Gasiorek, Andrzej. *Post-War British Fiction: Realism and After*. Arnold. pp. 202. £12.99. ISBN 0 340 57215 9.

Gifford, Terry. *Green Voices: Understanding Contemporary Nature Poetry*. ManUP. pp. 198. pb £12.99. ISBN 0 7190 4346 8.

Giles, Judy, and Tim Middleton, eds. *Writing Englishness, 1900–1950: An Introductory Sourcebook*. Routledge. pp. 285. hb £40, pb £13.99. ISBN 0 415 11441 1, 0 415 11442 X.

Gillespie, Diane F., ed. *Virginia Woolf. Roger Fry*. Blackwell. pp. 389. £55. ISBN 0 631 17727 2.

GoGwilt, Christopher. *The Invention of the West: Joseph Conrad and the Double-Mapping of Europe and Empire*. StanfordUP. pp. 280. £25. ISBN 0 8047 2401 6.

Goodwyn, Andrew, ed. *Dubliners*. Cambridge Literature series. CUP. pp. 240. pb £3.85. ISBN 0 521 48544 4.

Gordon, David J. *Iris Murdoch's Fables of Unselfing*. UMissP. pp. 199. £31.95. ISBN 0 8262 1028 7.

Grace, Sherrill E., ed. *Sursum Corda!: The Collected Letters of Malcolm Lowry. Volume One: 1926–1946*. Cape. pp. 690. £35. ISBN 0 224 03290 9.

Halkin, Ariela. *The Enemy Reviewed: German Popular Literature Through British Eyes Between the Two World Wars*. Praeger. pp. 211. £43.95. ISBN 0 275 95101 4.

Hampson, Robert, and Peter Barry. *New British Poetries: The Scope of the Possible*. ManUP. pp. 247. £12.95. ISBN 0 7190 4692 0.

Hanson, Clare. *Virginia Woolf*. Macmillan Women Writers. Macmillan (1994) pp. 216. pb £11.50. ISBN 0 333 45157 0.

Hartley, Jenny, ed. *Hearts Undefeated: Women's Writing of the Second World War*. Virago. pp. 302. pb £9.99. ISBN 1 86049 201 0.

Hassan, Ihab. *Rumors of Change: Essays of Five Decades*. UAlaP. pp. 261. hb £39.95, pb £19.95. ISBN 0 8173 0802 4, 0 8173 0830 X.

Hawkins, Harriet. *Strange Attractors: Literature, Culture and Chaos Theory*. PH/HW. pp.180. pb £11.95. ISBN 0 13 355355 8.

Hayman, David, and Sam Slote, eds. *Probes: Genetic Studies in Joyce*. European Joyce Studies. Rodopi. pp. 286. hb $80, pb $27. ISBN 9 051 83860 3, 9 051 83860 3.

Heaney, Seamus. *The Redress of Poetry: Oxford Lectures*. Faber. pp. 213. pb £8.99. ISBN 0 571 17537 6.

Hofheinz, Thomas C. *Joyce and the Invention of Irish History: Finnegans Wake In Context*. CUP. pp. 200. £32.50. ISBN 0 521 47114 1.

Hohendahl, Peter Uwe. *Prismatic Thought: Theodor W. Adorno*. UNebP. pp. 287. £32.95. ISBN 0 8032 2378 1.

Hollindale, Peter, ed. *J. M. Barrie. Peter Pan and Other Plays*. OUP. pp. 338. pb £6.99. ISBN 0 19 282572 0.

Hopper, Keith. *Flann O'Brien: A Portrait of the Artist as a Young Post-modernist.* CorkUP. pp. 292. hb £25.00, pb £14.95. ISBN 1 85918 041 8, 1 85918 042 6.

Inglis, Fred. *Raymond Williams.* Routledge. pp. 333. £19.99. ISBN 0 415 08960 3.

Irons, Glenwood, ed. *Feminism in Women's Detective Fiction.* UTorP. pp. 192. hb £32.50, pb £12.95. ISBN 0 8020 0519 5, 0 8020 6954 1.

Jackson, Thomas H. *The Whole Matter: The Poetic Evolution of Thomas Kinsella.* SyracuseUP. pp. 165. hb $39.95, pb $17.95. ISBN 0 8156 2659 2, 0 8156 2660 6.

Joannou, Maroula. *'Ladies, Please Don't Smash These Windows': Women's Writing, Feminist Consciousness and Social Change 1918–38.* Berg. pp. 236. pb £14.95. ISBN 1 85973 022 1.

John, Angela V. *Elizabeth Robins: Staging A Life, 1862–1952.* Routledge. pp. 283. £27.50. ISBN 0 415 06112 1.

Jones, W. Gareth, ed. *Tolstoi and Britain.* Berg Anglo/Russian Affinities. Berg. pp. 303. £39.95. ISBN 1 85973 028 0.

Kaplan, Louis. *Laszlo Moholy-Nagy: Biographical Writings.* DukeUP. pp. 232. pb £14.95. ISBN 0 8223 1592 0.

Kenneally, Michael, ed. *Poetry in Contemporary Irish Literature.* Smythe. pp. 462. ISBN 0 8614 0310 X.

Kiberd, Declan. *Inventing Ireland: The Literature of the Modern Nation.* Cape. pp. 719. £20. ISBN 9 780224 041973.

Kinsella, Thomas. *The Dual Tradition: An Essay on Poetry and Politics in Ireland.* Carcanet. pp. 129. pb £9.95. ISBN 1 85754182 0.

Kramer, Hilton, and Roger Kimball, eds. *Against the Grain:* The New Criterion *on Art and Intellect at the End of the Twentieth Century.* Dee. pp. 463. £30.99. ISBN 1 56663 069 X.

Kravis, Judy, ed. *Teaching Literature: Writers and Teachers Talking.* CorkUP. pp. 275. hb £22, pb £12.95. ISBN 1 85918 025 6, 1 85918 026 4.

Lacey, Stephen. *British Realist Theatre: The New Wave in its Context 1956–1965.* Routledge. pp. 206. hb £40, pb £12.99. ISBN 0 415 07782 6, 0 415 12311 9.

Lago, Mary. *E. M. Forster: A Literary Life.* Macmillan Literary Lives. Macmillan. pp. 170. hb £40, pb £9.99. ISBN 0333 57723 X, ISBN 0 333 60956 5.

Langford, Michele K., ed. *Contours of the Fantastic: Selected Essays from the Eighth International Conference on the Fantastic in the Arts.* Greenwood (1990) pp. 232. £49.50. ISBN 0 313 26647 6.

Latham, Robert A., and Robert A. Collins, eds. *Modes of the Fantastic: Selected Essays from the Twelfth International Conference on the Fantastic in the Arts.* Greenwood. pp. 234. £62.50. ISBN 0 313 29585 7.

Lavin, Audrey P. *Aspects of the Novelist: E. M. Forster's Pattern and Rhythm.* American University Studies. Lang. pp. 155. $35.95. ISBN 0 8204 1966 4.

Leatherbarrow, W. J., ed. *Dostoevskii and Britain.* Berg Anglo/Russian Affinities. Berg. pp. 310. £44.95. ISBN 0 85496 784 2.

Ledger, Sally, and Scott McCracken, eds. *Cultural Politics at the Fin de Siècle.* CUP. pp. 329. hb £37.50, pb £13.95. ISBN 0 521 443857, 0 521 48499 5.

Leerssen, Joep, A. H. van der Weel, and Bart Westerweel, eds. *Forging in the Smithy: National Identity and Representation in Anglo-Irish Literary History.* Rodopi. pp. 249. pb Hfl. 40. ISBN 90 5183 751 8.

Ludwig, Hans-Werner, and Lothar Fritz, eds. *Poetry in the British Isles: Non-Metropolitan Perspectives*. UWalesP. pp. 319. pb £14.95. ISBN 0 7083 1266 7.

Madsen, Deborah. *Postmodernism: A Bibliography, 1926–1994*. Rodopi. pp. 622. Hfl. 300. ISBN 905 183 887 5.

Malick, Javed. *Towards a Theater of the Oppressed: The Dramaturgy of John Arden*. UMichP. pp. 224. £31.60. ISBN 0 472 10597 6.

Merritt, Susan Hollis. *Pinter in Play: Critical Strategies and the Plays of Harold Pinter*. DukeUP. pp. 343. pb £16.95. ISBN 0 8223 1674 9.

Meyer, Michael J., ed. *Literature and the Grotesque*. Rodopi. pp.195. pb Hfl. 60. ISBN 90 5183 793 3.

Mitgang, Herbert. *Words Still Count with Me: A Chronicle of Literary Conversations*. Norton. pp. 320. pb £18.95. ISBN 0 393 03880 7.

Motte, Warren. *Playtexts: Ludics in Contemporary Literature*. UNebP. pp. 233. £29.50. ISBN 0 8032 3181 4.

Nugel, Bernfried, ed. *Now More Than Ever: Proceedings of the Aldous Huxley Centenary Symposium Munster 1994*. Lang. pp. 379. £40. ISBN 3 631 47917 4.

Onega, Susana, ed. *Telling Histories: Narrativizing History, Historicizing Literature*. Rodopi. pp. 208. pb $40. ISBN 90 5183 754 2.

Orel, Harold. *The Historical Novel from Scott to Sabatini: Changing Attitudes toward a Literary Genre, 1814–1920*. Macmillan. pp. 189. £35. ISBN 0 333 607 627.

Osteen, Mark. *The Economy of Ulysses: Making Both Ends Meet*. SyracuseUP. pp. 488. hb £44.95, pb £16.50. ISBN 0 8156 2653 3, 0 8156 2661 4.

Parker, David. *Ethics, Theory and the Novel*. CUP (1994). pp. 218. £35. ISBN 0 521 45283 X.

Parrinder, Patrick. *Shadows of the Future: H. G. Wells, Science Fiction and Prophecy*. LiverUP. pp. 170. hb £25, pb £14.95. ISBN 0 85323 439 6, 0 85323 449 3.

Perrino, Mark. *The Poetics of Mockery: Wyndham Lewis's The Apes of God and the Popularization of Modernism*. MHRA Texts & Dissertations. Maney. pp. 170. £25. ISBN 0 901285 52 4.

Piette, Adam. *Imagination at War: British Fiction and Poetry 1939–1945*. Macmillan. pp. 341. pb £12. ISBN 0 333 64468 9.

Plumb, Cheryl J., ed. *Djuna Barnes. Nightwood: The Original Version and Related Drafts*. pp. 319. Dalkey. ISBN 1 564 78080 5.

Queneau, Raymond, *inter alia*. *Oulipo Laboratory: Texts from the Bibliothèque Oulipienne*. Atlas. pb £7.99. ISBN 0 947757 89 9.

Raper, Julius Rowan, Melody L. Enscore, and Paige Matthey Bynum, eds. *Lawrence Durrell: Comprehending the Whole*. UMissP. pp. 193. £31.95. ISBN 0 8262 0982 3.

Reeve, N. H., and Richard Kerridge. *Nearly Too Much: The Poetry of J. H. Prynne*. LiverUP. pp. 196. pb £11.99. ISBN 0 8532 3850 2.

Reynolds, Barbara, ed. *The Letters of Dorothy L. Sayers, 1899–1936: The Making of a Detective Novelist*. H&S. pp. 421. £25. ISBN 0 340 53623 3.

Reynolds, Dee. *Symbolist Aesthetics and Early Abstract Art: Sites of Imaginary Space*. CUP. pp. 290. £40. ISBN 0 521 42102 0.

Riley II, Charles A. *Color Codes: Modern Theories of Color in Philosophy,*

Painting and Architecture, Literature, Music, and Psychology. UPNewE. pp. 351. £28.95. ISBN 0 87451 671 4.

Rose, Danis. *The Textual Diaries of James Joyce.* Lilliput. pp. 198. £20. ISBN 1 874 67558 9.

Rosenberg, Beth Carole. *Virginia Woolf and Samuel Johnson: Common Readers.* St Martin's. pp. 144. £28. ISBN 0 333 62090 9.

Ross, Charles L., and Dennis Jackson, eds. *Editing D. H. Lawrence: New Versions of a Modern Author.* Editorial Theory & Literary Criticism. UMichP. pp. 258. £38. ISBN 0 472 10612 0.

Roth, Marty. *Foul and Fair Play: Reading Genre in Classic Detective Fiction.* UGeoP. pp. 284. £39.95. ISBN 0 8203 1622 9.

Royle, Nicholas. *After Derrida.* ManUP. pp. 178. hb £35.00, pb £12.99. ISBN 0 7190 4378 6, 0 7190 4379 4.

Russ, Joanna. *To Write Like a Woman.* IUP. pp. 181. pb £9.99. ISBN 0 253 20983 8.

Saddlemyer, Ann, ed. *J. M. Synge. The Playboy of the Western World and Other Plays.* OUP. pp. 213. hb £30, pb £5.99. ISBN 0 19 812155 5, 0 19 282611 5.

Scott, Bonnie Kime. *Refiguring Modernism, Volume 1: The Women of 1928.* IUP. pp. 318. hb £31.50, pb £14.99. ISBN 0 253 32936 1, 0 253 20995 1.

——. *Refiguring Modernism, Volume 2: Postmodern Feminist Readings of Woolf, West, and Barnes.* IUP. pp. 217. hb £27.50, pb £12.50. ISBN 0 253 32937 X, 0 253 21002 X.

Seed, David, ed. *Anticipations: Essays on Early Science Fiction and its Precursors.* LiverUP. pp. 225. hb £27.50, pb £12.25. ISBN 0 85323 348 9, 0 85323 418 3.

Senn, Fritz. *Inductive Scrutinies: Focus on Joyce* (ed. Christine O'Neill). Lilliput. pp. 252. £25. ISBN 1 874 67533 3.

Shell, Marc. *Art and Money.* UChicP. pp. 213. £27.95. ISBN 0 226 75213 5.

Shellard, Dominic. *Harold Hobson: The Complete Catalogue 1922–1988.* KeeleUP. pp. 316. £50. ISBN 1 85331 155 3.

——. *Harold Hobson: Witness and Judge – The Theatre Criticism of Harold Hobson.* KeeleUP. pp. 255. £20. ISBN 1 85331 154 5.

Sinfield, Alan. *The Wilde Century: Oscar Wilde, Effeminacy and the Queer Movement.* Cassell (1994). pp. 216. ISBN 0 304 32903 7.

Smith, Evans Lansing. *Ricorso and Revelation: An Archetypal Poetics of Modernism.* Camden House. pp. 194. £33.50. ISBN 1 57113 066 7.

Smith, J. Percy. *Selected Correspondence of Bernard Shaw: Bernard Shaw and H. G. Wells.* UTorP. pp. 242. £25.95. ISBN 0 802 03001 7.

Smith, Mack. *Literary Realism and the Ekphrastic Tradition.* PSUP. pp. 269. £31.50. ISBN 0 271 01329 X.

Sosnoski, James J. *Modern Skeletons in Postmodern Closets: A Cultural Studies Alternative.* UPVirginia. pp. 247. pb £15.95. ISBN 0 8139 1621 6.

Spacks, Patricia Meyer. *Boredom: The Literary History of a State of Mind.* UChicP. pp. 290. £19.95. ISBN 0 226 76853.

Spurling, Hilary. *Ivy: The Life of I. Compton-Burnett.* Richard Cohen. pp. 621. £30. ISBN 1 86066 069 X.

Stannard, Martin, ed. *Ford Madox Ford. The Good Soldier.* NCE. Norton. pp. 401. pb £6.95. ISBN 0 393 96634 8.

Steiner, Wendy. *The Scandal of Pleasure: Art in an Age of Fundamentalism.* UChicP. pp. 251. £19.95. ISBN 0 226 77223 3.

Stewart, Susan. *Crimes of Writing: Problems in the Containment of Representation.* DukeUP (1994) pp. 353. pb £15.95. ISBN 0 8223 1545 9.

Swarbrick, Andrew. *Out of Reach: The Poetry of Philip Larkin.* Macmillan. pp. 202. pb £10.99. ISBN 0 333 59660 9.

Tambling, Jeremy, ed. *E. M. Forster.* New Casebooks. Macmillan. pp. 236. hb £37.50, pb £11.50. ISBN 0 333 60129 7, 0 333 60130 0.

Theall, Donald. *Beyond the Word: Reconstructing Sense in the Joyce Era of Technology, Culture and Communication.* Theory/Culture. UTorP. pp. 328. £39. ISBN 0 802 00630 2.

Thesing, William B., ed. *Robinson Jeffers and a Galaxy of Writers: Essays in Honor of William H. Nolte.* USCP. pp. 218. £28.50. ISBN 1 570030 43 X.

Tinkler-Villani, Valleria, Peter Davidson, and Jane Stevenson, eds. *Exhibited by Candlelight: Sources and Developments in the Gothic Tradition.* Rodopi. pp. 298. hb £56, pb £18. ISBN 90 5183 832 8, 90 5183 828 X.

Trotter, David, ed. *D. H. Lawrence. Sons and Lovers.* OUP. WC. pp. 484. pb £5.99. ISBN 0 19 283107 0.

Valente, Joseph. *James Joyce and the Problem of Justice: Negotiating Sexual and Colonial Difference.* CUP. pp. 282. £35. ISBN 0 521 47369 1.

Vendler, Helen. *Soul Says: On Recent Poetry.* HarvardUP. pp. 266. £16.95. ISBN 0 6748 2146 7.

Wainwright, Eddie. *Taking Stock: A First Study of the Poetry of U. A. Fanthorpe.* Peterloo Poets. pp. 88. pb £6.95. ISBN 1 8714 7147 8.

Ward, Ian. *Law and Literature: Possibilities and Perspectives.* CUP. pp. 264. £32.50. ISBN 0 521 47474 4.

Waugh, Patricia. *Harvest of the Sixties: English Literature and its Background 1960–1990.* OUP. pp. 240. pb £7.99. ISBN 0 19 289226 6.

Wheale, Nigel, ed. *The Postmodern Arts: An Introductory Reader.* Routledge. pp. 295. hb £35, pb £12.99. ISBN 0 415 07776 1, 0 415 12611 8.

Whitehead, John. *Hardy to Larkin: Seven English Poets.* Hearthstone. pp. 246. £25. ISBN 0 9520 4712 8.

Whyte, Christopher, ed. *Gendering the Nation: Studies in Modern Scottish Literature.* EdinUP. pp. 235. pb £12.95. ISBN 0 7486 0619 X.

Williams, Linda Ruth. *Critical Desire: Psychoanalysis and the Literary Subject.* Arnold. pp. 212. £35. ISBN 0 340 64557 1.

Wu, Duncan. *Six Contemporary Dramatists: Bennett, Potter, Gray, Brenton, Hare, Ayckbourn.* Macmillan. pp. 172. hb £40, pb £10.99. ISBN 0 333 61368 6, 0 333 67068 X.

Zilboorg, Caroline C. *Richard Aldington and H. D.: The Later Years in Letters.* ManUP. pp. 271. £40. ISBN 0 7190 4570 3.

XV

American Literature to 1900

HENRY CLARIDGE, KEVIN McCARRON and JANET BEER

This chapter has four sections: 1. General; 2. American Literature to 1830; 3. American Literature 1830 to 1865; 4. American Literature 1865 to 1900. Sections 1 and 2 are by Henry Claridge, section 3 is by Kevin McCarron and section 4 is by Janet Beer.

1. General

Current bibliographical listings for the field and the period continue to be available quarterly in *AL* and annually in *MLAIB*. *AmLS* for 1993, under the editorship of Gary Scharnhorst, sees the restoration of chapters on 'Drama', 'Poetry: 1900 to the 1940s' and 'Poetry: The 1940s to the Present', though it is to be regretted that, as a result of illness, Martha Nell Smith was unable to contribute her chapter on 'Whitman and Dickinson'; she hopes to cover two years of the relevant scholarship in *AmLS* for 1994. There is little point in my adding anything to my encomiums of previous years: suffice it to say that *AmLS* remains the natural point of departure for those who want to keep abreast of the criticism and scholarship of American literature.

A new edition of James D. Hart's *The Oxford Companion to American Literature* is welcome. Many readers will have found this an indispensable reference guide. It is now over half a century old and this latest, sixth edition, has been entirely reset. At his death in 1990, James D. Hart had prepared a further 77 entries and Phillip W. Leininger, the new editor, has added 104 of his own, 'seeking the dynamic balance between past and contemporary literature that James D. Hart always sought to maintain'. The entries are characteristically brief but informed and while the keen eye can always detect omissions the compendiousness of this guide is to be admired. The Chronological Index at the end 'tracks' literary history alongside social history from 1577 to the late summer of last year. Another bibliographic and reference tool worthy of note is Michel Fabre's *The French Critical Reception of African-American Literature: From the Beginnings to 1970*. This is an annotated bibliography of criticism of African-American literature printed in French. As Fabre notes in his introduction, there are lacunae (notably the reviews of Frank Yerby's novels) but scholars in the field will still find this an immensely useful, though expensive, resource. Items are entered year by year and each is afforded a thorough annotation. The volume is well indexed and Fabre has also provided a useful bibliography of French translations of African-American texts. Also worthy of note is the *Bibliographic Guide to Black Studies, 1994* which covers New York Public Library holdings for African-American writers.

Haskell Springer's *America and the Sea: A Literary History* is a multi-author volume, the 'first to explore exclusively the presence of the sea in American writing'. Fifteen essays, among them a general introduction by the editor, explore the 'written presence' of the Atlantic Ocean, the Pacific Ocean and the Gulf of Mexico in a wide variety of American writings, and the inland seas of the Great Lakes are also afforded their own chapter. The contributors are, broadly speaking, concerned with the ways in which the sea has challenged the imaginations of the poet and the novelist but many essays find occasion for consideration of more theoretical matters, notably the 'gendering' of the sea in poetry and fiction and the psychological and symbolic language that writing about the sea so frequently elicits. Springer's introduction offers an extensive overview of the book's theme and an annotated portfolio of American seascape art opens up interesting areas of art-historical enquiry. The appended primary and secondary bibliographies are an immensely useful research resource. The whole is to be highly recommended. (I shall deal with the chapters devoted to the Colonial and Federal eras and James Fenimore Cooper below.)

Using what he calls the 'perspectives of cultural change and the processes of acculturalization' Raoul Granqvist in *Imitation as Resistance: Appropriations of English Literature in Nineteenth-Century America* addresses a heterogeneous body of materials that offer American responses to British literature. His study centres on those English (and Scottish) writers most frequently appropriated by American writers – Shakespeare, Milton, Scott, Byron, Dickens and Tennyson – but he also ventures down less familiar avenues. One of these is his chapter on 'elocutionary handbooks' ('British Writers in American Elocutionary/Literary Textbooks') where he shows how English writers such as Shakespeare, Milton and Dickens serviced both rhetorical and elocutionary skills and moralistic and nationalistic ends. Often, he points out, 'the prestige attached to a particular textbook was linked with its enrollment in the national campaign for an improved all-American school system', and the textbook 'was defined as an instructive and ethical component in the project to instill into the young citizens of the country a sense of the binding value of traditions'. His penultimate chapter on 'British Writers on the American Stage' concerns itself largely with dramatic adaptations of Byron, Scott and Dickens in the American theatre, arguing that 'American culture-formation employed "imitation" ... to achieve its ends'. Granqvist looks at Scott's *Marmion*, *The Lady of the Lake* and *Guy Mannering*, at Byron's *Mazeppa* and Dickens's *The Cricket on the Hearth* and *The Old Curiosity Shop* showing how high art was frequently recast into the more popular forms of melodrama, burlesque, vaudeville and circus. We have had a good deal of commentary on this aspect of nineteenth-century popular entertainment before (see, for example, Lawrence Levine's *Highbrow/Lowbrow: The Emergence of Cultural Hierarchy in America* [*YWES* 69.553]) but Granqvist's emphases on 'cultural encounters' and the ideological 'negotiations' involved in literary appropriation cast a good deal of new light on these materials. His book, it might be added, is very well documented and the bibliography alone is a valuable resource. Those with interests in British-American literary relations in the nineteenth century should track this down.

2. American Literature to 1830

Daniel A. Cohen's *Pillars of Salt, Monuments of Grace: New England Crime Literature and the Origins of American Popular Culture, 1674–1860* (1993) takes as its point of departure the unambiguous observation that 'Crime and punishment were sources of endless fascination for readers of colonial and early national New England'. He shows how 'a rich popular literature' dealing with the complex social realities of crime and punishment emerged in early modern England and how, in turn, this was transplanted to the American colonies. In effect, criminal knowledge became a 'thriving industry', notably in antebellum Boston, and 'authors, reporters, and publishers produced a seemingly endless stream of accounts of illicit sexuality and criminal violence because large numbers of people, most likely old and young, male and female, urban and rural, middle-class and working-class, were willing to pay for the privilege of reading them'. Cohen is not oblivious of the ways in which these interests are echoed in the popular reading of the present day and in his conclusion he suggests that 'the defining characteristics of modern crime coverage can be traced back to our earlier literature', though he notes that while we have lost 'the spiritual gumption to proudly hang a saint ... our cultural landscape is still littered with pillars of salt'. In his desire to give his research the feel of the contemporary there is a tendency to collapse historical distinctions and to read materials shaped by different social and political 'print cultures' along what one might call the same continuum. But it would be churlish to find fault with this impressive book: the standard of research is exemplary, the exposition is intelligent and the writing is lucid and cogent; it comes, moreover, with numerous black and white illustrations (many of them annotated) that add much to his compelling narrative. Relatedly, Christopher W. Jones's 'Praying Upon Truth: *The Memoirs of Stephen Burroughs*' (*EAL* 30.32–50) – an essay with some interesting black and white illustrations – looks at Burroughs' memoirs as an example of the 'criminal-confession genre', seeing them as a form of picaresque narrative of post-Revolutionary America that seeks to subvert the dominant social ideals of the time. Also in *EAL* (30.88–91) the reader will find an exchange of correspondence between Cohen and Daniel E. Williams in which Cohen replies to Williams's review of his study.

John E. Smith's 'Puritanism and Enlightenment: Edwards and Franklin' in *Knowledge and Belief in America: Enlightenment Traditions and Modern Religious Thought* (ed. William M. Shea and Peter A. Huff), attempts to understand how the two 'outlooks' (not a terribly felicitous word in this context) of Puritanism and Enlightenment thinking 'stand in relation to each other'. Jonathan Edwards and Benjamin Franklin are taken as representative figures and their philosophical contributions to American thought are briskly, and rather clumsily, summarized. What interests Smith, above all, is their collective legacy and here he argues that 'both Edwards and Franklin, regardless of their differences, were similar in their *seriousness* about life and the entire gamut of human concerns', so much so that their importance for Smith is very much bound up with the challenges they offer to modernist and postmodernist moralities, notably what he calls the 'frivolousness' of post-modernists who betray a 'reluctance to express strong convictions about what is worth living for ... ' and 'make light of those who do hold such convictions'. I share some of Smith's concerns about the ethos of postmodernism, but this is a disappointing essay in what is otherwise a good collection: Smith says little that we don't already know about Edwards and Franklin and his attempt to make sense of the persistence of their ideas lacks any coherent sense of the shape of American intellectual history. There is a more informed view of Edwards in Mark A. Noll's 'The Rise and Long Life of the Protestant Enlightenment in America' in this collection of essays.

Donald P. Wharton contributes two essays to *America and the Sea* (ed. Haskell Springer), one on 'The Colonial Era', the other on 'The Revolutionary and Federal Periods'. In the former he notes that 'the sea literature of the colonial period is almost entirely a sea-deliverance literature'. Few writers, he continues, intellectualize their maritime experience 'and there is little deliberate aesthetic contemplation of the natural beauty or power of the sea'. He considers a number of new world writings here, notably Bradford's *Of Plimouth Plantation*, Mather's *Magnalia Christi Americana* and Richard Steere's *Monumental Memorial of Marine Mercy*, reading them in the light of invocation of images 'inherited from centuries-old dreams of Novus Mundi and the Terrestrial Paradise', arguing that the Puritans 'saw the ocean crossing as a regenerating, converting experience that made sacred what was otherwise secular space'. In his essay on the revolutionary and federal periods he notes how attitudes to the sea changed, largely as a consequence of the growth of maritime technology and commerce, but also as a result of scientific advances. By the outbreak of the Revolution, 'the providential sea-deliverance narrative of a century earlier no longer existed'. In some of Freneau's poetry he detects imagery of the sea that is 'essentially patriotic and nationalistic' while in fiction from the same period (for example, James Ellison's *American Captive* and Susanna Rowson's *Slave of Algiers*) a similar celebration of American naval power is at work. Wharton's essay concludes at that point at which a 'new age in American sea literature' begins in the early fiction of James Fenimore Cooper. Both the novels of Ellison and Rowson have Barbary settings and in 'The Barbary Captivity Narrative in Early America' (*EAL* 30.95–120) Paul Baepler usefully surveys narratives of white slavery in Africa, suggesting that they 'give us a rare glimpse of how the British and early Americans imagined Africans and both justified and questioned institution-alized slavery in this country'.

Turning to article literature on the early writers. Eileen Razzari, Elrod's ' "Mouth Put in the Dust": Personal Authority and Biblical Resonance in Anne Bradstreet's Grief Poems' and Carol R. Mehler's 'Anne Bradstreet's House Fire: The Careless Maid and Careful God' (*SPAS* 5.35–62; 63– 71) were not seen. In *'The Countesse of Lincolne's Nurserie* as Inspiration for Anne Bradstreet' (*N&Q* 42.364–6), Virginia Brackett suggests a 'sociopolitical influence' on Bradstreet in Elizabeth Knevet Clinton's text of 1622 which 'while its breast-feeding theme likely impressed Bradstreet, so surely must have the fact that it was written by a female, a rarity among published works in the seventeenth century'. William J. Scheick explores the related treatments of women and witchcraft in Cotton Mather and Bradstreet in 'Authority and Witchery: Cotton Mather's *Ornaments* and Mary English's Acrostic' (*ArQ* 51.1–32), an essay that is characteristically informed and cogent. I have not seen Theresa Freda Nicolay's *Gender Roles, Literary Authority, and Three American Women Writers: Anne Dudley Bradstreet, Mercy Otis Warren, Margaret Fuller Ossoli* (Lang). *SPAS* 5 has two articles on Edward Taylor this year: Gregory T. Carvey's 'To Fill Christ's Coach: The Poet and Pastor in Edward Taylor's *God's Determinations*' (73–93) and Christy Friend's ' "My Case is Bad. Lord, Be My Advocate": The Use of Classical Rhetoric in Edward Taylor's Meditation 1.39' (105–24). A number of articles were published about Mary Rowlandson: Rebecca Blevins Faery, 'Mary Rowlandson (1637–1711)' (*Legacy* 12.ii.121–22); Deborah J. Dietrich, 'Mary Rowlandson's Great Declension' (*WS* 24.427–39); and Jules Zanger's 'Mary Rowlandson's Captivity Narrative as Confessional Literature: "After Such Knowledge, What Forgiveness" ' (*AmStScan* 27.ii.142–52).

I have not seen Joseph A. Conforti's *Jonathan Edwards, Religious Tradition, and American Literature* (UNCP) and John Smith's, Harry S. Stout's and Kenneth P. Minkema's edition of *A Jonathan Edwards Reader* (YaleUP). In 'Beyond the Romance Theory of American Vision: Beauty and the Qualified Will in Edwards, Jefferson and Audubon' (*AmLH* 7.381–414), Elisa New intelligently addresses some of the philosophical issues raised by the way in which 'the eye undergoes the experience of seeing, an experience that abrogates the priority of either subject or object', in Edwards's *Freedom of the Will*, Jefferson's 'Query IV' and Audubon's *The Birds of America*. It is Edwards's notion of the qualified will, she argues, that 'gives beauty such a prominent role in his thought' and it is in the experience of nature that 'he finds the key to understanding God's grace in the spectacle of a dense and vividly cohering earth, carapaced by gravity, gathered into itself, held up by nothing but God's inclination'. Frank Shuffleton's 'Presenting Jefferson' (*EAL* 30.275–85) reviews three recent books on Jefferson: Jay Fliegelman's *Declaring Independence: Jefferson, Natural Language, and the Culture of Performance* (*YWES* 74.530–1); Kenneth Lockridge's *On the Sources of Patriarchal Rage: The Commonplace Books of William Byrd and Thomas Jefferson and the Gendering of Power in the Eighteenth Century* (NYUP, 1993); and Peter S. Onuf's edition of *Jeffersonian Legacies* (UPVirginia, 1993). He argues that Jefferson's reputation has 'been an index to the shifting concerns of an often troubled nation' and where 35 years ago scholarly efforts were 'dominated by desires to celebrate Jefferson as a pattern for democratic possibilities', now the 'celebratory tones are muted by writers conscious of national failures to establish the principles of equality and liberty that Jefferson once supposedly stood for'.

Narrative in colonial America is explored in Susan Stabile's '*A Circumstantial Account:* Or, *The Rake's Design*: Robert Bolling's Epistolary Novel' (*AL* 67.1– 22) where she reads this obscure work, written as a retrospective diary, in the light of its use of an extravagant, but by eighteenth-century standards, conventional 'rake-figure' whose 'amorous and aggressive passions' co-exist alongside a Hobbesian and philosophical intelligence, while Grantland S. Rice, also in *AL*, considers a more familiar work, Hugh Henry Brackenridge's *Modern Chivalry* in '*Modern Chivalry* and the Resistance to

Textual Authority' (*AL* 67.257–81) reading this largely satirical text for its 'commentary on the struggle of the writer in American culture' and suggesting that the novel's lack of success created an 'alienated author' who 'clung tenaciously to the ideal of an educated republic ... but who witnessed the failure of his efforts to surmount the conventionalizing power of a print culture industry and the hegemonic ideology of his readership'. One essay on Susanna Rowson has appeared, Christopher Castiglia's 'Susanna Rowson's *Reuben and Rachel*: Captivity, Colonization, and the Domestication of Columbus' in Sharon Harris's *Redefining the Political Novel: American Women Writers, 1797–1901* (OUP) which was not available for review.

Work on poetry is largely confined to Philip Freneau, Phillis Wheatley and Joel Barlow. In 'Philip Freneau, poete et journaliste, ou la lutte contre l'oubli' (*EA* 48.12–24) Robert Sayre discusses Freneau's journalism (notably for periodicals such as the *Philadelphia Freeman's Journal* and the *National Gazette*, the latter founded and edited by him at Thomas Jefferson's urging) in the light of his fierce anti-British and strongly pro-American sentiments. Gilbert L. Gigliotti in 'Off a "Strange, Uncoasted Strand": Navigating the Ship of State through Freneau's *Hurricane*' (*CML* 15.357–66) returns us to the maritime concerns of Donald P. Wharton (see above) in his reading of Freneau's poem of 1785 and its imagery of the new nation seeking for a 'new Columbus' to 'take the helm' of state. Carla Willard's 'Wheatley's Turns of Praise: Heroic Entrapment and the Paradox of Revolution' (*AL* 67.233– 56), seeks to ironize Wheatley's 'acquisition' of her admirers (among them the Earl of Dartmouth and the Countess of Huntingdon) and asks 'why, although her themes were literally revolutionary, she did not use the searing satire and biting irony that marked most social criticism of her time', the answer given being one that sees the confusion in the reader for the fact that readers 'mistake Wheatley's critical praise for pure glorification is indicative, in part, of the confusion of the poem's ideal heroes with the actual men of the poet's colonial world'. I have not seen Karla F. C. Holloway's 'The Body Politic' in (ed. Michael Monn and Cathy N. Davidson) *Subjects and Citizens: Nation, Race, and Gender from Oronooko to Anita Hill* (DukeUP). The vexed and seemingly intractable debate about the nature of the American epic resurfaces in Ralph Bauer's 'Colonial Discourse and Early American Literary History: Ercilla, The Inca Garcilaso, and Joel Barlow's Conception of a New World Epic' (*EAL* 30.203–32) where Bauer considers the significance of the heroic mock epic 'American Antiquities', written by the Connecticut Wits (Joel Barlow, Lemuel Hopkins, David Humphreys and John Trumbull), which appeared in the pages of the *New Haven Gazette* and the *Connecticut Magazine* between 1786 and 1787; his essay is particularly concerned with Barlow's epic poetry and he suggests that it is 'essential to reread him in the context of colonial and countercolonial discourse about America in an hemispheric perspective', rather than simply though his indebtedness to English Augustanism (and here he takes issue with the readings of William Dowling in *Poetry and Ideology in Revolutionary Connecticut* [*YWES* 71.543]), developing this by opening up parallels between Barlow's conception of the epic and the writings of Alonso Ercilla y Zuniga in *La Araucana* and el Inca Garcilaso de la Vega in *The Royal Commentaries of the Incas, and General History of Peru*.

John Trumbull's literary career and its relationship to the rapid expansion of Connecticut printing and publishing is intelligently discussed in Christopher Grasso's 'Print, Poetry, and Politics: John Trumbull and the Transformation of Public Discourse in Revolutionary America' (*EAL* 30.5–31) where Grasso sees Trumbull's work as the product of a 'skillful writer' adopting 'rhetorical strategies and new modes of print in an effort to cultivate a new, politicized reading public'; his essay is noteworthy for its commentary on Trumbull's *M'Fingal*. Relatedly, 'The Scribblings of a Plain Man and the Temerity of a Woman: Gender and Genre in Judith Sargent Murray's *The Gleaner*' (*EAL* 30.12–44) by Kirstin Wilcox analyses how through its 'heteroglossic layering of voice and form' *The Gleaner* makes the public sphere of print 'a place in which the early American woman's reverence for herself could be written and read', and, like Grasso, Wilcox seeks to enlarge our understanding of the different kinds of 'literary authority circulating in the eighteenth century'.

Two essays on Charles Brockden Brown have appeared this year, both in *EAL*. Elizabeth Jane Wall Hinds writes on *Edgar Huntly* in 'Charles Brockden Brown's Revenge Tragedy: *Edgar Huntly* and the Uses of Property' (*EAL* 30.51–70) where she argues that 'the novel's revenge elements both establish the basis for Edgar's actions and enter the current debate about economic policy and practice, a discussion registering the shift in power, during the American 1790s, from a landed to an entrepreneurial class', so much so that with its signifying properties '*Edgar Huntly* places in the foreground the literal and psychological value of property as the source of revenge in a culture undergoing the shock of economic transformation'. In 'Charles Brockden Brown's Earliest Letter' (*EAL* 30.71–77), John R. Holmes prints Brown's verse letter of 8 June 1788 to his brother (titled 'Epistle the First') with a contextual commentary that establishes 'Brown's twin emphases on American commerce and freedom' and his invocation of political heroes from the American revolution.

A rather thin year for James Fenimore Cooper scholarship. Hugh Egan's 'Cooper and His Contemporaries' in *America and the Sea: A Literary History* (ed. Haskell Springer) notes the paradox that the ' "sea novel" can be seen as a contradiction in terms, for those very elements that make a novel seaworthy work against its being a novel at all – at least one in the British tradition with which Cooper was familiar'. He sees Cooper's sea as, in some ways, analogous with the image of the forest in other American works, 'a trackless area of possibility on which a nation traces its own history', and, like the forest, it is a region of 'spontaneous violence' where the sea is often the enemy itself. His essay is of general nature and there is little in the way of detailed readings of Cooper's sea fiction but he opens up interesting areas of comparative enquiry with contemporaries such as Irving, Poe, Melville and Thoreau, and it is well worth consulting. James D. Wallace in 'Race and Captivity in Cooper's *The Wept of Wish-ton-Wish*' (*AmLH* 7.189–209) argues that the novel is not about 'the horrors of miscegenation but the glories of amalgamation', Cooper's attitudes to intermarriage being shaped not by the racist attitudes that surfaced in the United States after the Civil War but by a discourse that lacks 'any elements of genetics or any other science of race' where the fact of captivity merges the 'generative power' of two races; his essay is a useful contribution to our understanding of Cooper's attitudes towards racial differences.

This year saw the appearence of a number of items of a general nature on critical, scholarly and pedagogical issues in the study of early American literature. 'The Round Table: New Directions in Early American Studies' in *EAL* (30.145–87) brings together five papers from the Modern Language Association of America conference of December of last year in which Carla Mulford, Thomas W. Krise, Arnold Krupat, Sharon M. Harris and Anthony Kemp contribute to the continuing debate about ' "new" directions' in the field: the essays by Krise and Krupat address issues of hybrid identity in Jamaican and Native American texts respectively, Krise reading Robert Robertson's *The Speech of Mr John Talbot Campo-Bell* (1736) as a work that resorts 'to appropriating and ventriloquizing a representative member of a group already appropriated in the most heinous fashion', while Sharon M. Harris puts forward a case for a 'materialist feminist perspective' on early American historical narratives written by both men and women, and Anthony Kemp briefly discusses reformation radicalism and 'attacks' on the structure of time in texts such as Bradford's *Of Plimouth Plantation* and Edward Johnson's *Wonder-Working Providence*. Two review essays are also worthy of note in this context: in 'Troping America' (*EAL* 30.188–95), Kathryn Zabelle Derounian-Stodola reviews William C. Spengemann's *A New World of Words: Redefining Early American Literature* (YaleUP, 1994) alongside essays by Norman S. Grabo, Philip F. Gura and Annette Kolodny in the light of the questions they raise about the 'status' of early American texts, and Lucy Maddox's 'Representing America' (*AmLH* 7.141–50) considers five recent books, among them Thomas Gustafson's *Representative Words: Politics, Literature, and the American Language* (*YWES* 73.550) and K. P. Van Anglen's *The New England Millenium: Literary Reception and Cultural Authority in the Early Republic* (UNCP, 1994) as studies that problematize the notions of 'America' and 'American' whilst simultaneously raising issues about historiography and history, and language and ideology.

3. American Literature 1830 to 1865

The year was dominated by the publication of *The Cambridge History of American Literature, Volume Two: Prose Writing 1820–1865* (ed. Sacvan Bercovitch). At almost 900 pages this is actually four books with an all too brief introduction by Bercovitch, in which he refers to the vitality of American literary criticism over the last 30 years and the influence of, among other cross-disciplinary modes of investigation, gender studies, ethnic studies and popular-culture studies. Bercovitch notes that for a new generation of American critics and scholars, American literary history is no longer the history of a certain, agreed-upon historical perspective on American writing. He notes that the quests for certainty and agreement continue, as they must, but they proceed now within a climate of critical decentralization – of controversy, competition, and, at best, dialogue among different frames of explanation. He goes on to assert, or to warn: 'the term "American" is neither a narrative premise in these volumes nor an objective background. Quite the reverse: it is the complex subject of a series of literary-historical inquiries'. All four of the authors in this book consider 'America' in this theoretically sophisticated manner.

Michael Davitt Bell, in 'Conditions of Literary Vocation', evaluates the profession of writing during the period and, as might be expected, he focuses more intently upon historical circumstance and economic force than he does on considerations of individual authorial genius. His account of the 'legitimizing' of non-utilitarian writing, its eventual presence as a market commodity, is linked to such events as the Copyright Law of 1790 and the opening of the Eire Canal in the 1820s, and he is highly informative on the role played by magazines, noting, for example, that such magazines as *Graham's* and *Godey's*, with circulations of 40,000 to 50,000 reached a far broader public than Irving and Cooper could have dreamed of only two decades earlier. The most influential writers of the period are usefully contextualized and students, in particular, will find the sections on Cooper and Irving essential reading, while more advanced readers are more likely to profit from Bell's appraisal of less well-known writers, such as W. G. Sims, James K. Paulding and John P. Kennedy. In the chapter entitled 'Women's Fiction and the Literary Marketplace in the 1850s' Bell analyses the crucial role played by F. O. Matthiessen in constructing an American canon. He queries Matthiessen's exclusive list and writes that given most readers were women, as were the most successful writers: 'to suppress a large body of popular literature in order to assert the "stature" of five male writers is to suppress what may be *the* crucial fact about American literature in the 1850s'. This is well said and surely indisputable. This section is extremely informative on a large number of women writers and their work, offering economical plot summaries and intelligent readings. Bell writes particularly well on the links between American gothic and the nineteenth-century domestic novel, suggesting that the haunted house of American gothic fiction and the home of the domestic novel are in effect doubles, or mirror images, of one another; in both, the symbolic inner space is suffused with feminine influences. Other topics covered in this chapter include drama, sensationalist literature, humour, and the New York literary wars.

In 'The Literature of Expansion and Race', Eric J. Sundquist begins by discussing the historical fact of national expansion before focusing on the 1848 Gold Rush and its attendant literature. He writes, somewhat tautologously: 'In the best writing about California in the 1850s, however, gold was not a rigid symbol but a metaphor evocative of the apparent triumph of American Destiny.' Sundquist does not confine himself to imaginative literature, however, and offers economical summaries and analysis of geographical, historical, economic and political texts. He writes particularly well on Native Americans and there is a particularly interesting appraisal of the influential painter and writer George Caitlin, in which he suggests that the record Caitlin left in *Letters and Notes on the Manners, Customs, and Conditions of the North American Indians* (1841) makes his trip among the most significant Euro-American imperial explorations of the century. Sundquist's readings of Native American texts are sympathetic and illuminating and he notes that their oral literature is inherently tribal and communal, inspired by and focused on links across generations and geographically diverse communities rather than on aesthetic distinction or individual self-expression. He is equally interesting on writing about Native Americans and his appraisal of the Pocahontas myth is especially provocative. He devotes considerable space to 'Captivity Narratives' and he writes of the genre: 'As a literature organized along psychogeographical boundaries that justified Euro-American advance while also revealing deep anxieties about it, the captivity narratives were often sensational, even incredible, at the same time that they posed as factual accounts of life beyond the frontier'. Sundquist links captivity narratives with slave narratives and his evaluation of the latter genre is illuminated by periodic cross-referencing to historical events in Haiti and Cuba. He writes as well on slave songs and chants as he does on Native American songs and he concludes with a section on Frederick Douglass, in which he views his celebrated *Autobiography* as one achievement among many: 'His many volumes of speeches and editorial writings constitute probably the most complete social and political record left by any one individual of the struggle for black freedom in the nineteenth century.'

Barbara L. Packer, in 'The Transcendentalists', begins with an account of Unitarianism and notes that the first sign of the trouble that would be labelled 'Transcendentalism' came with an attack on two fronts: the philosophy of John Locke and on the educational system at Harvard. Coleridge and Carlyle feature prominently in the opening sections, as do American writers such as Alcott, Very, Peabody and Fuller. Packer consistently links her appraisals of seminal figures with the politics of the time, and she lays considerable stress upon the role played by money in underwriting Transcendentalist experimentation, writing particularly well on legacies and the wealth of the Huidekoper family. Although her evaluations of Thoreau, Emerson and Fuller are comprehensive and perceptive, it is the depiction of the remarkable Orestes Brownson which is even more engaging. She wittily writes: ' "Men like to make an effort," Orestes Brownson asserted in one of his early essays for the *Christian Examiner*. The proposition may not be true of the human race as a whole, but it certainly is true of the man who advanced it.' She gives considerable space to Brownson's review of Emerson's 'Divinity School Address', quoting passages which are still striking for their fiercely moral pragmatism. Utopian communities, real and fictional, are assessed and Packer provides a sympathetic and comprehensive overview of the life and work of Margaret Fuller, which contains a sketch of Fuller's visit to Sing Sing prison in 1844. She closes her section with Thoreau and offers brilliant readings of both *Walden* and 'Autumnal Tints'.

In 'Narrative Forms', Jonathan Arac divides narratives into four categories: national narrative (1820s–1830s), local narratives (1830s), personal narratives (1840s), and literary narratives (1850s), and then evaluates each of these categories in some detail. 'Establishing National Narratives' focuses on George Bancroft, Toqueville, and Cooper, of whose work Arac writes with particular insight: 'Cooper's work troubles modern readers because it is not realistic in its technique, but it is emphatically referential in its substance.' Poe and Hawthorne dominate the second section and Arac's ability to recognize similarities in discourses is an especially enjoyable feature of this section. He notes, for example, that Hawthorne was a Massachusetts writer not by virtue of his employing Yankee vernacular diction, but by his historical resurrection of the colonial past. Like the other contributors, Arac consistently emphasizes the political and economic issues that contribute to a literary career, noting that Poe's career depended on a primary fact of modern American life: the growth of cities. In 'Personal Narratives' he begins with evaluations of Parkman's *Oregon Trail* and Dana's *Two Years Before The Mast*, but the section is dominated by Melville's early work. In 'Local Narratives', Hawthorne and Melville's later work is central to Arac's discussion, and he offers brief, illuminating readings of each of their important texts.

William E. Lenz, in *The Poetics of the Antarctic: A Study in Nineteenth-Century American Cultural Perceptions*, argues that American hopes for confirming identity come to be focused on an unlikely goal, the discovery of the illusive Antarctic continent. The editor, Benjamin F. Fisher, writes in his preface: 'The commercial, scientific, visionary, and adventurous implications of Antarctic voyaging, which often overlap, are clearly established by Lenz, who relates them to the developing American nationalism in the eighteenth and nineteenth centuries.' Lenz writes well on Cooper and Dana, but examines in particular detail James Palmer's long poem *Thelia: A Tale of the Antarctic* (1843), later revised and expanded into *Antarctic Mariner's Song* (1868). The book is engaging and well written and while, at times, Lenz's thesis is perhaps too vigorously promoted, the formidable scholarship is extremely persuasive; particularly bold is his decision to list several pages of titles of travel and exploration narratives in the body of his own text, rather than relegate them to endnotes – the overwhelming ubiquity of these books supports Lenz's argument in a manner that is almost dramatic. Adam Sweeting, in ' "A Very Pleasant Patriarchal Life": Professional Authors and Amateur Architects in the Hudson Valley, 1835–1870' (*JAMS* 29.33–53), discusses writers' homes and, more specifically, the public interest in such homes. Interest in such residences, Sweeting suggests, was partly fuelled by the cult of domesticity: 'the broad cultural programme which helped direct the nation's moral and aesthetic energies toward the home'. Sweeting's argument that the literary community of the time built houses as if they were architectural manifestations of literary issues is supported by detailed reference to the homes of Irving, Nathaniel Parker Willis and Donald Grant Mitchell, all of whom built or renovated an old-looking house in the Hudson Valley or southern New England. Jonathan A. Cook, in ' "Prodigious Poop": Comic Context and Psychological Subtext in Irving's *Knickerbocker History'* (*NCL* 49.483–512), suggests of the *Knickerbocker History* that it is an ironic expression of nostalgia for a lost world of childhood and Dutch colonial history, growing out of a unique blend of biographical and historical imagination. He writes: 'Irving facetiously yet nostalgically reworked the archetypal myth of America as a new world in which human nature might be restored to a prelapsarian state of innocence – the myth surviving despite (or because of) its repeated disconfirmation.'

The subtitle of Lloyd Rohler's *Ralph Waldo Emerson: Preacher and Lecturer* clearly indicates the focus of his book. Throughout, Rohler confronts the notion of Emerson as a poor speaker and there are numerous contemporary accounts of Emerson's great gifts as an orator. The early portion of the book assesses Emerson's career as a preacher with Rohler noting that Emerson wrote 171 sermons and preached 885 times, and in an appropriate organic metaphor Rohler stresses the crucial importance of Emerson's early years, saying of his sermons: 'Although they may never take the place of the great essays or lectures, they are more than the seedbed of Emerson's inspiration. If they are not the full flower of his sunny days, they are at least the root and stalk of his ideas.' Rohler is not only, or even primarily, interested in Emerson's ideas, however, and he provides close textual analysis of many of Emerson's lectures, evaluating the use of imagery, structure and rhetoric. He provides particularly detailed appraisals of 'The American Scholar' and 'The Divinity School Address', noting that Emerson wrote well on ceremonial occasions and that precisely because ceremonial writing is stylized writing Emerson's training in the pulpit was very effective training in the use of metaphor. Rohler never separates Emerson's achievements from larger social forces but includes sufficient quotation from his lectures to remind us just how singularly provocative a speaker Emerson was at his best.

Similarly, *Emerson's Literary Criticism* (ed. Eric W. Carlson), invites us to remember Emerson's qualities as a critic. The book is divided into five chapters: 'Art as Experience', 'The Creative Process', 'The Art of Rhetoric', 'Toward a More Critical Perspective', and 'Writers and Books', the last chapter itself subdivided into four sections. Throughout the book, Carlson prefaces each one of Emerson's essays with a concise and helpful summary of its contents; for example, he writes of 'Intellect', in the second section: 'It represents his major definition of experiential realization as an organic process, with a fine sense of the stages of incubation and intimation-illumination, or the interplay of receptivity and revelation.' It is a clever strategy to present some of Emerson's letters as literary criticism, for they contain some of his most memorable observations, as when he writes to Carlyle about Whitman and refers to the poet's 'terrible eyes and buffalo strength'. Emerson's ideas are contextualized historically and politically throughout the book and Carlson writes particularly well on Emerson's intellectual influences.

Despite his title: *Mythic Archetypes in Ralph Waldo Emerson: A Blakean Reading*, Richard R. O'Keefe stresses that his book is not a source study. Rather, he argues, that while Emerson was not a systematic thinker he is a consistent poet, and poetic devices, modes and tropes appear in his work in the form of archetype and myth. The book consists of a series of very detailed readings of important Emerson texts and O'Keefe's detached manner is entirely appropriate to this form of analysis: 'If one reviews the apparent discords in "Circles" ... one may detect a very interesting phenomenon.' O'Keefe considers Emerson's images with the help of analogous Blakean models and persuasively argues that Emerson is a literary artist: 'not a minor (or confused) philosopher, but a major (and consistent) poet'.

Robert Milder, in *Reimagining Thoreau*, acknowledges an interest in reconstituted authorial criticism and he firmly contextualizes Thoreau within three specific periods: 1837–49, 1845–54, and 1854–62, each of which constitutes a separate section of the book. Milder is scrupulous in maintaining a debate with Thoreau's earlier critics while his own observations are shrewd and comprehensible: 'The effect of making nature fill the place of human intimacy is a confusion about its ethical character that complicates Thoreau's entire relationship to it.' He pays considerable attention to Thoreau's *Journals* and concludes this excellent book with a close reading of 'Wild Apples', in the course of which he suggests that the essay differs from Walden primarily in that it shows Thoreau's new willingness to put forward his tropes as tropes, harvesting them for their metaphoric yield without ascribing an inherent significance to objects.

The Cambridge Companion to Henry David Thoreau (ed. Joel Myerson) contains 14 essays which cover all aspects of Thoreau's work, including his contemporary and posthumous reputation. Although never stated, many of the contributors to this volume also have an interest in 'reconstituted authorial criticism'. Linck C. Johnson, for example, writes in his appraisal of *A Week on the Concord and Merrimack Rivers*: 'The loss of his brother not only prompted Thoreau to begin to plan a book about their 1839 voyage, it also profoundly influenced the form and contents of *A Week.*' There are many fine essays in the book, including Robert Sattelmayer's 'Thoreau and Emerson', Steven Fink's 'Thoreau and his audience' and Ronald Wesley Hoag's 'Thoreau's later natural history writings', but perhaps the most provocative is Elizabeth Hall Witherell's 'Thoreau as poet'. In some ways this is a misleading title, as she asserts early in her essay: 'Thoreau's poetry is for the most part unremarkable in its subject and its form, and it suffers in comparison with even the quotidian prose of the journal.' Her real interest is in analysing the poems in the context of Thoreau's literary ambitions, which she does extremely well, but her analysis always incorporates other works of Thoreau into it, and so is never really an evaluation of Thoreau 'as poet'. Nevertheless, along with Richard J. Schneider's *'Walden'*, it is possibly the most interesting of all the essays in this very useful book. Schneider writes well on Thoreau and economics, and notes that for Thoreau spirit is found in Nature, not through it. He further notes that *Walden* proceeds in dialogic pairs of chapters on contrasting topics and he writes vividly of Walden pond: 'In reflecting the shoreline also, the pond reveals new views to the alert observer and provides an art gallery of nature's masterpieces.'

Jonathan Elmer begins *Reading at the Social Limit: Affect, Mass Culture, and Edgar Allan Poe* by noting that the distinction between high and low culture is anachronistic when considering antebellum culture. Elmer makes a compelling case for reading Poe as an author who was highly engaged with mass culture, noting that Poe's career is marked by alternate solicitations and repudiations of mass popularity, both a desire for merger with the general taste and an equally intense compulsion to distinguish himself from it. He notes that Poe's ostensibly psychological tales and poems, in their very focus on representational and psychic division attending the individual – and despite their frequent lack of reference to contemporary conditions – are in fact profoundly responsive to social reality. The book contains an extensive section on plagiarism and an interesting assessment of epigraphs. Elmer writes well on sentimental fiction and suggests that the emergence of horror out of sentimental fiction has a complex history to which Poe is a primary contributor. His chapter on the 'Confessional Tales' is excellent; he observes that these tales exhibit compulsively an unnerving sociability in even the most antisocial characters: 'the tales are finally about an elusive social exigency demanding communication in the face of that communication's doubtfulness, undecipherability, or futility'. Laurence Frank, in ' "The Murders in the Rue Morgue": Edgar Allan Poe's Evolutionary Reverie' (*NCL* 50.168–88), notes that this story appeared in 1841, when a resurgent evangelicism and a conservative natural theology were confronted by a positivist science that was to have its nineteenth-century culmination in Darwin's *Origin of Species*. He then constructs a compelling argument which depicts Dupin as a creature of history who must reconstruct the past even as he comes upon the contingency of certain events. The story becomes 'a harrowing vision, centred upon the presence of the Ourang-Outang, with its seemingly motiveless frenzy, introducing the terror of a history secularized and devoid of design'. The autumn edition of *SAF* has a special section devoted to Poe and in the first of the essays: 'Poe's "Diddling" and the Depression: Notes on the Source of Swindling' (*SAF* 23.195–201), Terence Whalen offers a source study of Poe's satire on swindling 'Diddling Considered as One of the Exact Sciences'. Whalen notes that articles pertinent to Poe's essays appeared in the *Corsair*, the *United States Magazine* and the *Democratic Review*, but he also makes a larger case for historicism, arguing that it should strive to 'reconstruct the frame of reference by using individual sources to reconstruct the general context of signification'. In 'Lifting the Lid on Poe's "The Oblong Box"' (*SAF* 23.203–14), Bonnie Shannon McMullen argues that in 'The Oblong Box' (1843) self-referentiality, and social or political statement were, for Poe, part of the same exercise and that in this story Poe seems to be asserting that all art is a copy of something that has come before, 'although the copying process may, to sensitive nostrils, smell'. William Crisman, in 'Poe's Dupin as Professional: The Dupin Stories as Serial Text' (*SAF* 23.215–229), follows the Dupin stories in their self-conscious sequence from 'The Murders in the Rue Morgue', through 'The Mystery of Marie Roget', to 'The Purloined Letter' to show the development of an increasing professionalism and a commensurate interest in renumeration for ratiocination.

Each section of Claudia Durst Johnson's *Understanding The Scarlet Letter: A Student Casebook to Issues, Sources, and Historical Documents* is followed by a series of tasks for the student, and within its own clearly defined context this is a very useful book. Although the book is dominated by a naive belief that 'total comprehension' of a text is possible: 'Having done a literary analysis of *The Scarlet Letter*, the reader who wants to master the novel should then look at the Puritan world in which it is set.' Johnson writes informatively on Puritanism and remains consistently true to her announced intention of contextualizing *The Scarlet Letter*. She concludes by analysing the sit-com *Murphy Brown* and also considers the implications of the Jimmy Swaggart scandal in an attempt to make some of Hawthorne's novel's principal issues relevant to a younger readership. In his preface to *The Province of Piety: Moral History in Hawthorne's Early Tales*, first published in 1984 and now reprinted in paperback, Michael Colacurcio writes that his book 'looks steadily to the "before" of the Hawthorne text; and, within that domain, to the remote religious more methodically than to the proximate political prediction of Hawthorne's early tales'. Colacurcio notes that Henry James's observation that 'sin' is an imported characteristic in Hawthorne's fiction poses a remarkably long-lived theoretical question in Hawthorne studies. Although Colacurcio notes that he cannot indulge in the academic luxury of a review of classic Hawthorne criticism, he comes close to it and his book offers a comprehensive, at times overwhelming, survey of 'classic Hawthorne criticism'. Essentially, he rejects both James's claim that Hawthorne used sin for aesthetic effect, and Melville's suggestion that Hawthorne took very seriously Puritan notions of Sin and Damnation. For Colacurcio, Hawthorne is, primarily, an historian. As might be expected in a book of nearly 700 pages, Colarcurcio offers a series of extremely detailed readings of Hawthorne's early stories, with particular emphasis on 'Roger Malvin's Burial' and 'Young Goodman Brown'. He links 'Lady Eleanore's Mantle' with the smallpox epidemic of the 1720s, by pointing out that for the Puritans the disease was clearly caused by rampant pride. He writes especially well on Puritanism and suggests that Hawthorne's interest in his own Puritan ancestors may have derived from a recognition that the history of the Puritan Mind can be regarded as a sequence of attempts to get the ideas of community and depravity into satisfactory relation. In ' "The Artist of the Beautiful": Crossing the Transcendental Divide in Hawthorne's Fiction' (*NCL* 50.78–96), Frederick Newberry links 'The Artist of the Beautiful' with 'Drowne's Wooden Image', and he uses the work of Wolfgang Iser, Nelson Goodman and Kendall L. Walton to argue that in 'The Artist of the Beautiful' no less than in 'Drowne's Wooden Image' Hawthorne leads us through a narrative up to a threshold where the text invites us to enter a new realm unlimited in possibilities. Both a transcendental moment and place, this new realm appears every bit as real as the external reality it critiques and upon which it referentially depends for its differences and point of departure. Matthew Gartner, in '*The Scarlet Letter* and the Book of Esther: Scriptural Letter and Narrative Life' (*SAF* 23.131–51), suggests that Hester Prynne is named after the biblical Queen Esther and he interweaves extracts from the Book of Esther with *The Scarlet Letter* to construct a very convincing case under a sequence of headings such as 'Haman and Chillingworth', and 'Religious Dissent'. Gartner notes that the Book of Esther is the only book of the Hebrew Bible not to include the word God, while *The Scarlet Letter* also has as its centre a peculiar verbal lacuna, the absence of the letter A, and this lacuna can be seen as contributing to a literature of secrecy and hiddenness, coded signs, veiled clues and cryptic meanings. Richard Kopley, in 'Hawthorne's Transplanting and Transposing "The Tell-Tale Heart" ' (*SAF* 23.231–241), suggests that even as Hawthorne may have rebuilt 'The Fall of the House of Usher' for *The House of the Seven Gables*, he may have transplanted 'The Tell-Tale Heart' into *The Scarlet Letter*. Kopley argues that the 'Evil Eye' at the centre of Poe's story has its equivalent in 'God's Eye' which he sees as being at the centre of *The Scarlet Letter*. He points out that Hawthorne's novel has affinities with the providence tradition, in which two symmetrical halves of a literary work, symbolizing the Old Testament and the New Testament, frame a significant midpoint occurring under the hot noonday sun, an image taken to represent Christ come in judgement. The scaffolding of the plot of *The Scarlet Letter*, he notes, comprises three scenes involving characters standing on the town scaffold, and each of these scenes features Christ, as the noonday sun, rendering judgement.

In 'Julian Hawthorne and the "Scandal" of Margaret Fuller' (*AmLH* 7.210-33), Thomas R. Mitchell argues that when in 1844 Julian Hawthorne published his father's infamous 1858 notebook entry analysing Fuller's marriage and her character he intentionally provoked a literary scandal that he hoped would realign and strengthen his father's position in literary history even as he destroyed Fuller's. Mitchell offers a highly detailed account of the controversy and debate and persuasively argues that the issue is not only of considerable interest in itself, but is instructive as a dramatic exposure of the usually unarticulated, often unconscious, politics which lie behind the making and unmaking of literary reputations and national canons. Will and Mimosa Stephenson, in 'Oxymoron in *The Marble Faun*' (*NHR* 21.1–13), suggest that in this novel, for the first time in Hawthorne's fiction, oxymoron becomes a dominant rhetorical device. They construct their argument around the novel's most celebrated paradox: The Fortunate Fall, but they assess numerous others in the course of a highly persuasive argument. In the same issue, Benjamin

Goluboff, in ' "A Virtuoso's Collection": Hawthorne, History, and the Wandering Jew' (14– 25), considers the legacy of the Wandering Jew and Hawthorne's re-working of it in 'A Virtuoso's Collection', while in ' "Tracing the Original Design": The Hawthornes in Rappaccini's Garden' (26–35), Julie E. Hall offers an interesting source study of 'Rappaccini's Daughter', suggesting of the story that Sophie Hawthorne serves as one model for Beatrice Rappaccini's fanciful nature, spiritual purity, childlike innocence and isolated life.

Nancy Fredericks, in *Melville's Art of Democracy*, seeks to identify and analyse various theoretical possibilities represented in Melville's work that bear on the relationship between democratic values and artistic critical practice. Some readers may not be particularly impressed by Fredericks's claim that Melville's class consciousness, his hostility towards the upper classes and his valorization of the lower, has escaped the attention of all but a few Melville scholars. Noting that H. Bruce Franklin attributes this critical neglect to the class-induced blindness of the academy, Fredericks lists her own credentials for writing about class: 'My own class consciousness has been shaped by a working class family and years in the work force before putting myself through college. This experience has sensitized me to Melville's critique of the American class system's inequalities and injustices.' However, this is a very good book and actually far less centred on class than its opening might suggest. She writes particularly well on the Kantian sublime and notes that Ahab seems to think that by driving the harpoon into Moby Dick he can pierce through the phenomenological realm into the noumenal. She compares and contrasts *Moby-Dick* and *Pierre*, suggesting that while the former is a critique of fanaticism, the latter is a critique of enthusiasm. She concludes by suggesting that *Pierre* is not Melville's failed attempt at tragedy, as is commonly supposed, but instead shares melodrama's concerns with the injustices of the class structure. William V. Spanos, in *The Errant Art of Moby-Dick: The Canon, the Cold War, and the Struggle for American Studies*, combines Heideggerian ontology with a sociopolitical perspective derived primarily from Foucault to construct a largely persuasive argument that the traditional identification of *Moby-Dick* as a "Romance" renders it complicitous in the discourse of the Cold War. This is not an easy book to read as Spanos's prose style makes few concessions: 'To put Melville's project positively, this criticism overlooks that ontological decenteredness of *Moby-Dick* which, in resisting the hegemonic discourse of the "American Renaissance" (the transcendentalist-inspired discourse of "self-reliance"), also resists appropriation by both the *essentialist* hegemonic discourse of Modernist humanism (the elitist, class-determined discourse of "high culture") and of the Cold War.' Spanos can also be bullish: 'It is true, of course, that Melville's matter in *Moby-Dick* is the narrative of the American Adam.' Equally, it is not true, but overall this is a very impressive book. Spanos writes well on generic and philosophical issues, suggesting both that Melville over-determines the 'tragic' in *Moby-Dick* to expose the discourse of tragic vision and that Ishmael is characterized by his destructive interrogation of naming and his emergent ontological willingness to remain in uncertainties without trying to objectify them. *Herman Melville: The Contemporary Reviews* (ed. Brian Higgins and Hershel Parker) was among the most enjoyable books received this year. The editors stress how important reviews were to Melville, and the lengthy and interesting introduction links Melville's career to every tranche of reviews. Each of Melville's works receives approximately the same amount of space and, a consistent feature of this excellent series, there is a check-list of additional reviews at the end of each chapter. The editors make a strong case for the importance of 'Review Studies', quoting Kevin Hays and Hershel Parker: 'reviews constitute the best possible evidence for reader-response study – for learning how the class of professional reviewers actually responded to and talked about literary works'. This book contains a lukewarm review of *Typee* by Margaret Fuller, an enthusiastic review of *Omoo* by Whitman, and a highly imaginative response to *Mardi* by Evert A. Duyckinck. Perhaps the most interesting section is the one devoted to *Pierre*. Although there are considerably more favourable contemporary reviews than might be expected, the hostile reviews are remarkably aggressive. George Peck, for example, begins his review emphatically: 'A bad book! Affected in dialect, unnatural in conception, repulsive in plot, and inartistic in construction. Such is Mr Melville's worst and latest book.' However, Peck has a good eye for Melville's excesses and he writes with wit; his review is a remarkable document in its own right. Robert L. Gale's *A Herman Melville Encyclopedia* is precisely that; a brisk, no-nonsense informational work. All the entries in the book are usefully cross-referenced, while all of Melville's titles and characters have separate entries, so that Bartleby, for example, is listed first as a character and then as 'Bartleby', a story. Every one of Melville's characters, no matter how small their role, is duly acknowledged: 'Coffin, Sal. In *Moby-Dick*, she is Peter Coffin's wife. The Coffins have two sons, Sam and Johnny', and the book is extremely informative on Melville's immediate family. There are other interesting entries as well; under Income, for example, Gale notes that Melville earned $228 per year from his writing during the years 1851–66. This thoroughly researched book is easy to use and will surely become a valuable research tool. Brian Cosgrave, the editor of *Literature and the Supernatural*, also contributes 'Reading the Signs in *Moby Dick*: Ahab's Perverse Religious Quest' to the book. He focuses on hermeneutics: either the world is all-meaning, or it is a blank, a void. Ishmael, as Cosgrave sees him, is a sceptic as to the possibility of 'knowledge' but Ahab is engaged in a profoundly religious quest: he embodies an archaic desire to know the sacred, 'even if it be the case that he defies the *numinosum tremendum*' and can only know it through that act of defiance. Cosgrave persuasively argues that in the character of Ahab both the real hermeneutic drive and the genuine theological quest are perverted by a vindictive need to avenge himself on an ultimate power who is himself seen as vindictive and unjust. Richard V. McLamore, in 'Narrative Self-Justification: Melville and Amosa Delano' (*SAF* 23.35–53), examines Delano's *Narrative* and, essentially, notes the various ways in which Melville refashions it in his own 'Benito Cereno'. McLamore suggests that Melville's representation of the greed and insecurity underlying his personification of American benevolence mocks both the voice of Delano's *Narrative* and the lawyerly narrator Melville develops in his own fiction. He concludes this excellent article by noting that 'Benito Cereno' represents not Delano's point-of-view or consciousness, but that of someone purporting to explain or justify it.

The Cambridge Companion to Walt Whitman (ed. Ezra Greenspan) is an extremely accessible collection, divided into ten chapters, all of which are informative and well written. In 'Fratricide and Brotherly Love: Whitman and the Civil War', M. Wynn Thomas uses Whitman's letters to great effect, arguing that they lay bare one of the deepest compulsions behind Whitman's wartime activities; his passionate determination to record the achievements and sufferings of the 'unknown' soldier and to restore to those soldiers at least a trace of that personal identity that had almost been obliterated by the new techniques of mass warfare. Ezra Greenspan himself contributes a more-interesting-than-it-sounds essay on Whitman's use of the present participle, and Ed Folsom's 'Appearing in Print: Illustrations of the Self in *Leaves of Grass*' contains some reproductions of engravings of Whitman which Folsom illuminatingly places against several of Frederick Douglass. Folsom also edits *Walt Whitman: The Centennial Essays*, the proceedings of a conference which opened on 26 March 1992, 100 years to the day after Whitman's death. The book has 20 chapters and is divided into four sections: 'The Biographical Whitman', 'The Texts', 'The Culture' and 'The Influence'. In the first section, Joel Myerson considers the value of applying bibliography to biography while Gay Wilson Allen looks at the contemporary state of Whitman biography, Jerome Loving looks specifically at the Binns biography and Vivian R. Pollak considers Whitman after the Civil War. In the second section there are interesting papers on 'Whitman's Reading', 'Discourse Markers in *Leaves of Grass*', 'Whitman's Physical Eloquence' and 'Whitman and the Visionary Experience'. The third section features essays on Whitman's relationship to labour, homosexuality and politics while in the final section James R. Miller, in 'Whitman's Multitudinous Poetic Progeny: Particular and Puzzling Instances', is impressively comprehensive in his claims for Whitman's poetic influence. Overall, the book avoids the common fault of collections of conference papers and speaks outward to its readers, rather than inward to its contributors. Martin Klammer, in *Whitman, Slavery, and the Emergence of 'Leaves of Grass'*, suggests that Whitman's thinking about African Americans and slavery is essential to the poetry of the 1855 *Leaves of Grass*. He offers a very impressive reading of 'Blood Money', noting that Whitman portrays the slave as a second Christ and suggesting that this is the first expression of Whitman the poet's egalitarian sympathy. Klammer is at his most impressive when he merges his considerable knowledge of the historical background of this period with analysis of the poems. His reading of 'Pictures' argues that the poem's power derives from a tension between Whitman's conventional racist perceptions and an attempt to transcend those perceptions. He notes that 'Pictures' is the first work of Whitman's to anticipate the long line, the catalogue style and the fluid, associative movement of the poems in *Leaves of Grass*. Klammer is even-handed in his appraisal of both Whitman and the poem, noting that he was inextricably embedded in the racism of his culture even as he may have been seeking to liberate himself from it.

Julia Stern, in 'Excavating Genre in *Our Nig*' (*AL* 67.439–66), argues that in *Our Nig* Harriet Wilson interrogates the idealization of maternity in nineteenth-century American culture. Stern suggests that while the novel's sentimental frame attempts to function as a structure of containment, it cannot quite suppress, and indeed it underscores, the gothic protest seething beneath the narrative's surface. Stern argues that in *Our Nig* the affective associations with which American culture coded its domestic and civic space undergo a fascinating reversal: 'Wilson privileges the public sphere as an arena of safety and freedom, in contrast to the private, which is figured as a gothic realm of violence and mortal danger.'

The Civil War Diary of Clara Solomon: Growing Up in New Orleans, 1861–1862 (ed. Elliott Ashkenazi) was another of the year's most enjoyable books. Written by a 16-year-old Jewish girl living in New Orleans during the early years of the Civil War, this previously unpublished diary is both a remarkable historical document and a fascinating account of a young girl's growing comprehension of the horror of war. She writes of her initial enthusiasm for the Southern cause, then her doubts as the death toll increases, and finally her despair as New Orleans is occupied by Northern troops. Running throughout the book is the subtext of her self-conscious attempts to 'become' a writer. There are numerous comic moments: 'Light has just spread her mantle o'er the darkened earth, and I am writing, scarcely able to trace the lines', and yet as the diary progresses she writes with vivacity and imagination: 'The morning is *growling* & I would almost venture to assert that the long-expected rain will visit us today.' *From the Cannon's Mouth: The Civil War Letters of General Alpheus S. Williams*, edited by Milo M. Quaife, is a superbly edited collection of letters, primarily written to Williams's daughters. Williams was 51 when war broke out and he was commissioned brigadier general of volunteers in the Army of the Potomac. His account of the battle of Antietam is powerfully written and it is instructive to compare his account of Bull Run with Clara Solomon's. Both writers can be unwittingly comic, and Williams writes of the Union occupation of Winchester: 'My reputation for kindness and leniency has preceded me.' Williams takes a professional soldier's interest in slavery – virtually none, and he is far more concerned with the iniquitous system of promotion in the Union Army. His account of the burial of war dead at Rosacea is an unusual blend of detachment and compassion and is quite characteristic of this professional soldier and amateur author: 'It is interesting to see how tenderly and solemnly they gather together their dead comrades in some chosen spot, and with what sorrowful countenances they lay them in their last resting place. There is much that is beautiful as well as sad in these bloody events.'

4. American Literature 1865 to 1900

In *The American Literary History Reader*, Gordon Hutner collects some of the most outstanding essays from five years of the Journal *ALH*. This is an invaluable resource, bringing together, as it does, Lauren Berlant on Hawthorne, Richard Brodhead on the 'Veiled Lady', Nina Baym on early American history, Myra Jehlen on Mark Twain, Henry Louis Gates Jr on 'the Culture of Criticism' and Betsy Erkkila on Emily Dickinson – amongst others. No library should be without this book.

Carla L. Peterson, in *"Doers of the Word": African-American Women Speakers and Writers in the North (1830–1880)*, makes manifest the significance of black women activists – namely Sojourner Truth, Maria Stewart, Jarena Lee, Nancy Prince, Mary Ann Shadd Cary, Frances Ellen Watkins Harper, Sarah Parker Remond, Harriet A. Jacobs, Harriet E. Wilson and Charlotte Forten – in the 'racial uplift efforts in the North from the antebellum era through Reconstruction'. Peterson brings an inter-disciplinary approach, briefly acknowledging Foucault as a model, to an analysis of the cultural productions of these women in fiction, in religious evangelism, public speaking, in autobiography and in accounts of travel. She provides an explanation of the necessity for the women to locate themselves in 'a state of liminality' outside the social structure, turning to writing or public speaking 'in reaction to, and in tension with, their exclusion from black national institutions'. Peterson is particularly compelling on the 'shift from autobiography to novel, from first- to third-person narration' and exegeticizes that shift through discussion of *Our Nig* and *Incidents in the Life of a Slave Girl*, linking the tradition of the tragic mulatta with that of the seduction novel on the way to a rejection of sentimentality by writers concerned to demonstrate 'the inadequacy of love and sympathy as mechanisms to correct social evil in a world of racial hostility'. John Ernest also discusses Jacobs, Harper and Wilson, in addition to William Wells Brown, Martin R. Delany and Frederick Douglass in his *Resistance and Reformation: Nineteenth Century African-American Literature*, a study which 'presents six case studies in literary activism, six attempts to construct understanding of Christian mystery capable of opening new vistas of human history, six writers who challenge their readers' reliance on the undervalued and misapplied tools of a culture devoted to dangerously deceptive notions of human order and progress'. Ernest looks in detail at *Clotel* and *Our Nig* as texts resistant to generic categorization and makes that which he projects as Wilson's insistence that the text is to be read within the 'racial, gender, and economic matrix of secular history, as distinct from "sacred" literary history' the foundation-stone of his discussion of the text. In his chapter on Frederick Douglass, Brown examines the shift between the successive narratives as being from 'a clear economy of selfhood to the expanding economy of an ungovernable public identity' and sees Harper similarly engaged in the struggle to construct a narrative – in *Iola Leroy* – which can accommodate the exigencies of an increasingly 'incoherent world … without losing the simplicity and coherence needed to provide practical and moral instruction'. Harriet Wilson is the subject of an essay by Julia Stern, 'Excavating Genre in *Our Nig*' (*AL* 67.iii.439–66), which examines the relationship between sentimental and gothic literary forms to unpick conventional wisdom about the representation of motherhood in nineteenth-century texts; as Stern says, for Wilson, 'the maternal is always already implicated in and tainted by patriarchal structures of power'.

Priscilla Wald's book, *Constituting Americans: Cultural Anxiety and Narrative Form*, considers the work of five writers – Frederick Douglass, Herman Melville, Harriet Wilson, W. E. B. Du Bois and Gertrude Stein – and, like Ernest, she is concerned to critique the ways and means through which writers explore 'National narratives'. Wald examines the writings of her subjects in relation to 'official stories' – 'narratives that surface in the rhetoric of nationalist movements and initiatives – legal, political, and literary' so that, for example, Douglass's autobiographies are read in the context of the Supreme Court cases of *Cherokee Nation v. Georgia* (1831), *Scott v. Sanford* (1857) and the speeches of Abraham Lincoln. In an engaging and rich discussion of Melville's *Pierre* and Harriet Wilson's *Our Nig*, Wald examines the texts in contiguity to illustrate the distinct terms of their individual engagement with the kind of literary nationalism advocated by the 'Young Americans' at the *Democratic Review*. Whilst *Pierre*, in Wald's reading,

'directly addresses the literary nationalist program of Young America ...
[dooming] the would-be author to plagiarism and ... self-destruction', *Our
Nig* demonstrates allegorically the struggle to find 'representation within a
national narrative'. Wald's combinations of texts and writers are always
arresting and she consults a range of voices – Anzia Yezierska, Jacob Riis
William James, James Weldon Johnson among them – in her chapters on Du
Bois and Stein. Russ Castronovo is in neighbouring territory to Wald's in his
study, *Fathering the Nation: American Genealogies of Slavery and Freedom*,
which is also concerned with narratives of 'America', his self-declared intention being 'to read and dismantle the architecture of national narrative' by
bringing together as representative works of 'cultural criticism' texts like
Lincoln's Gettysburg Address, Melville's *Moby Dick* and Douglass's 'The
Heroic Slave'. Castronovo argues that pre-war writers in both North and
South articulated nation through genealogy, utilizing 'family metaphors to
allegorize the nation' but he also seeks to use genealogy himself as a means to
'uncover the disjunctions in the patriarchal imagining of the nation'. This
approach enables him to explore the tensions and inconsistencies inherent in
the attempt to construct a monolithic national identity, not only within the
work of those excluded from the patrilineal line of descent, but also in early
biographies of George Washington or works by Melville like 'The Bell
Tower', read as a story which 'acts against the body politic and records the
genealogy of sin that the American populace sought to deny through specious
historical constructions'. Robert O. Stephens's account of *The Family Saga in
the South: Generations and Destinies*, opens with Andrew Lytle's definition of
the particular nature of the family as ' *"the* institution of Southern life" ' and,
having once enumerated the generic features of the saga, the rest of this study
is absorbed by the rehearsal of the plots of a number of different texts which
demonstrate it to be 'a prototypal story with clearly recognised marking points
and expectations'. The defining features of the genre – as derived from the
Book of Genesis – are outlined in the opening chapter and Stephens then
proceeds to parade their manifestations in a range of Southern literary texts.
The work of the first author discussed, George Washington Cable, is capable
of yielding most interest when considered in generic terms and Stephens
examines the literary antecedents of his 1879 novel, *The Grandissimes*, in
order to make a case for the uniquely Southern nature of the opportunity
which presented itself to the writer: to take up the family story and make it
their own. He also includes some useful observations on the practice of their
craft by the novelists he chooses to discuss, Caroline Gordon, Allen Tate,
William Faulkner and Eudora Welty among them, and delineates the writing
of the otherwise forgotten T. S. Stribling as consolidating the work Cable had
begun; a separate chapter is devoted to 'The Black Family Saga in the South'
and the conditions of its coming of age in the mid-twentieth century are given
brief outline by Stephens in the context of work by Margaret Walker, Alex
Haley, Ernest Gaines and Toni Morrison.

   Periodical Literature in Nineteenth-Century America (ed. Kenneth M. Price
and Susan Belasco Smith) provides a timely resource for the growing number
of scholars interested in periodical literature. The editors introduce the
volume and contribute individual essays; Belasco Smith illuminates the contingencies of the serial publication of *Uncle Tom's Cabin* and Price examines
the conditions of Charles Chesnutt's relationship with *The Atlantic Monthly*,

and particularly with that most reactionary of editors, Thomas Bailey Aldrich. David S. Reynolds contributes a very readable essay on Walt Whitman's work in journalism, his role as publisher of sensation fiction and his own early efforts in that and other popular genres, Larry J. Reynolds discusses the making of *Woman in the Nineteenth Century* and Paula Bennett looks at women's poetry in Victorian periodicals. Other contributors write on Emily Dickinson, Fanny Fern, Herman Melville, Edmund Quincy and Ambrose Bierce. This is a wide-ranging collection which offers more than an introduction to the area, providing a cultural context as well as a demonstration of the heterogeneity of the periodical genre and the opportunities which were offered to the writer as a result of the broadness of the magazine audience. Another study substantially concerned with the genre of the periodical is Patricia Okker's *Our Sister Editors: Sarah J. Hale and the Tradition of Nineteenth-Century American Women Editors*. Hale edited *Godey's Lady's Book*, the most popular periodical of its day in the United States, between 1837 and 1877, but she was also an extremely prolific writer, producing poetry, fiction and history as well as reference books on housekeeping, all of which Okker considers. She begins, however, by marking Hale not as exceptional in her work as editor but as one among many women editors – over 600 in fact – and she includes, as an appendix, a list of these women, their journals or newspapers and the extent of their editorial power and duration of office. Okker describes Hale's early vacillations between 'an Enlightenment emphasis on women's intellectual equality with men and a Victorian belief in women's moral difference from men' but shows how Hale soon moved into separatist mode, focusing on more and more specialized audiences and converting to a 'woman-centered Victorian ideology', made evident in her own writing as well as in her editing. This is an interesting and informative study of Hale, her *Lady's Book*, her contemporaries and the different ideological positions that could be adopted by women editors.

In *American Women Short Story Writers: A Collection of Critical Essays* (ed. Julie Brown) there are chapters on Lydia Maria Child, Rose Terry Cooke, Elizabeth Stoddard and Louisa May Alcott although the majority of the essays are concerned with twentieth-century writers. Brown's introduction provides a brief survey of short story genre criticism, pointing to the deficit of attention paid to women short story writers in particular and highlighting aspects of such writing which are in need of development and discussion. Bruce Mills, in 'Literary Excellence and Social Reform: Lydia Maria Child's Ultraisms for the 1840s', offers Child's fiction as reflecting aesthetic as well as didactic ambitions, whereas Sherry Lee Linkon, in her 'Fiction as Political Discourse: Rose Terry Cooke's Antisuffrage Short Stories', considers Cooke's short fiction as the most important weapon in her armoury 'in the fight against women's rights' but also as the site of a conflicted and problematic ideology. Timothy Morris throws light into a dark corner in his examination of Elizabeth Stoddard as a precursor of modernism; in particular he focuses on the destabilizing and complicating effects which Stoddard's use of the unreliable narrator has on the possibilities of the short story, whilst Gail K. Smith reorientates our reading of Alcott's sensation fiction into a regendering of the ' "confidence man" ' story. The paired volumes, *The Oxford Book of Women's Writing in the United States* and *The Oxford Companion to Women's Writing in the United States* (both ed. Linda Wagner-Martin and Cathy N.

Davidson), do not need much explication beyond their titles. The former is organized on both generic and thematic lines and is thus inclusive of both private and public writing, of geographical and ethnic diversity – from the seventeenth century to the present day – and communicates a provocative sense of the profusion of possible material from unpredictable as well as predictable sources. The organization of the collection places the much anthologized alongside the obscure, the speech alongside the play, 'Recipes' nestle next to 'Erotica', and intriguing pieces can be followed up through the companion volume which provides additional bibliographical as well as biographical material. Published in paperback this year is another, more tightly focused, anthology, *American Women Regionalists: 1850–1910* (ed. Judith Fetterley and Marjorie Pryse). The editors begin by establishing what 'a regionalist women's tradition in American literature' might look like: demonstrating genealogies of influence, for example, tracing a line from Stowe through Jewett to Cather and demarcating the contours of regionalism as practised by a rich variety of women writers. The introduction is fluent and persuasive in its delineation of the generic properties of the regional and the introductory notes and bibliography dedicated to each author are full and useful. Kate Chopin is one of the writers included by Fetterley and Pryse and, along with Edith Wharton, Chopin also features in *The Cambridge Companion to American Realism and Naturalism*. Donald Pizer, the editor, enumerates his principles of organization in the introduction and part of the success of the volume as a whole can be found in its opening statement of purpose: 'The controlling strategy of this book ... is that of dialectic'. The book is organized into three sections: 'Historical Contexts', 'Contemporary Critical Issues' and 'Case Studies', the latter featuring specific texts by Twain, Crane, Norris, Howells, James, Dreiser, Chopin, Wharton, London, Sinclair, du Bois and Johnson. Blanche H. Gelfant reinvigorates Sister Carrie in a dynamic comparison with Tim O'Brien's 1990 story, 'Sweetheart of the Song Tra Bong'; John Crowley brings Howells and James into complex and complicating dialogue, scrutinizing 'their earlier readings of one another for signs of a formative rhetoric of realism', and the pervasive and enduring influence of Howells the critic in the taxonomy of realism and naturalism is evidenced in J. C. Levenson's discussion of Crane and Norris in relation to the elder novelist's response to their writing. All the author specific essays are notable and are well-served by Louis J. Budd on 'The American Background', Richard Lehan on 'The European Background', Michael Anesko on 'Recent Critical Approaches' and Elizabeth Ammons, capacious as ever, on 'Expanding the Canon of American Realism'.

There is currently a proliferation of well-edited collections of previously inaccessible material by women writers and some of the single-author collections are a particularly welcome addition to books in print. Madeleine Stern follows her outstanding record of reclamation of Louisa May Alcott's writing with the volume, *Louisa May Alcott Unmasked: Collected Thrillers*. This is a vastly entertaining collection of fiction with an introduction which details the detective work carried out by the editor and her partner, Leona Rostenberg, in tracking down the stories published anonymously or pseudonymously by Alcott, as well as discussion of genre and key themes. (For further discussion, see p. 647 below.) Jean Pfaelzer edits and introduces an invaluable collection of fiction and non-fiction in *A Rebecca Harding Davis Reader* in which

Harding's life and works are placed in context. Pfaelzer considers Harding's relationship with the editorial establishment, especially with James Fields at the *Atlantic Monthly* and interweaves details of her personal life with an account of her writing career; the volume contains a useful cross-section of stories and essays.

In an uncharacteristically quiet year in Dickinson scholarship, *Emily Dickinson's Fascicles: Method and Meaning* by Dorothy Huff Oberhaus is an intense, detailed reading of the fortieth fascicle, as assembled by R. W. Franklin. Oberhaus reads the fortieth fascicle as 'a three-part meditation addressing in turn the three powers of the mind: first, sight and memory; then, understanding; and finally, will'. She goes on to examine, in minute detail, the poems, their place in the organization of the larger organization of the fascicle and the structural relationship of the whole to the Bible.

Having featured as subject in a considerable number of the texts devoted to the study of multiple authors, Frederick Douglass is one of the subjects in a collection which largely concentrates on twentieth-century African-American writers: *The City in African-American Literature* (ed. Yoshinobu Hakutani and Robert Butler). It is the latter who writes on 'The City as Liberating Space in *Life and Times of Frederick Douglass*', positioning Douglass in opposition to the mainstream American writers of the period and their use of pastoral as representing 'physically liberating and morally good' space. Douglass, as Butler demonstrates, inverts notions of the rural as idyll and his successive autobiographies are seen to testify so conclusively to the powers of release located in urban experience that, Butler concludes, a challenge to 'the modernist premise embedded in much canonical American literature that the self must always be at odds with the social, political, and cultural realities of urban life' is issued.

Theodore Dreiser: Beyond Naturalism (ed. Miriam Gogol) contains a number of interesting essays on *Sister Carrie* amongst which Irene Gammel on 'Sexualizing the Female Body: Dreiser, Feminism and Foucault' is of particular note. Gammel ranges between the novel and Dreiser's sketches, *A Gallery of Women* (1929), and the autobiography of his early years, *Dawn* (1931) in order to build a persuasive argument about the dynamics of Dreiser's affirmation of masculine sexuality as it works alongside his refutation of gender bias, an argument which invokes not only Foucault but de Beauvoir and Freud in its construction. Scott Zaluda looks at 'The Secrets of Fraternity: Men and Friendship in *Sister Carrie*', pursuing references made to the Order of the Elks through the text; Leonard Cassuto considers 'Lacanian Equivocation' in three Dreiser novels and 'A Heideggerian Perspective' on *Sister Carrie* is offered by Paul A. Orlov. Two other essays on the novel do useful cultural work; in M. H. Dunlop's 'Carrie's Library: Reading the Boundaries Between Popular and Serious Fiction' the presence of the works of particular writers in the text is understood to permit Dreiser's 'characters to express subtleties of self-disgust that their situations and communicative abilities would not otherwise allow them', and, in James Livingston's '*Sister Carrie*'s Absent Causes', the question of Dreiser's location of 'a realist style within the apparently archaic form of romance' is addressed.

Carol Farley Kessler, critic of the Utopian, has again turned her attention to Charlotte Perkins Gilman in her *Charlotte Perkins Gilman: Her Progress Toward Utopia with Selected Writings*. This book, which includes ten short stories and four extracts from novels by Gilman as well as critical discussion of the writer's Utopian vision, collects together all the apparatus necessary to gain an overview both of Gilman's writing in the genre and the 'cultural work' that she expected her fiction to do. Kessler begins by placing the use of the Utopian in the context of Gilman's unswerving commitment to social activism, emphasizing the opportunities for didacticism offered by the genre which were fully exploited by Gilman, before moving onto a 'Biographical Exploration' which acts as a useful introduction to the personal and professional conditions under which Gilman laboured. Kessler provides extracts from Gilman's juvenilia and also from her essays, one of which, 'Coming Changes in Literature', includes Gilman's formulation of 'six new areas of subject matter' for the story teller. This list alone would be enough to make this volume fascinating reading, especially when placed up against the stories and extracts, but there are all sorts of treasures here, most particularly the thoroughness of Farley Kessler's bibliographical enterprise. The historian Mary Hill also revisits Gilman's life story in her volume, *A Journey from Within: The Love Letters of Charlotte Perkins Gilman, 1897–1900*, which collects together the letters written to her second husband, Houghton, in the years immediately prior to their marriage. Hill introduces what she sees as the foundations of Gilman's theories of gender inequality before describing the personal struggle between commitment to the continuation of her work as social theorist, writer and lecturer and the pull towards the conventional idea of marriage as constituting, as Gilman critiques it in one of her letters, 'A long life of beautiful service and devotion, given wholly to [the husband's] interests'. Hill describes the conflicting emotions generated by Gilman's adherence to her principles – 'Work first - love next' – and particularly the seeming 'contradictions and confusions' of Gilman's struggle to find a voice which would express her emotions whilst allowing her to maintain her hard-won and much contested professional autonomy. Hill does not attempt to explain or rationalize the inconsistencies in Gilman's means of expression here but she does provide a context and an intelligent and lucid commentary on letters which chart the period which was not only a centrally important one in Gilman's personal life but also the time in which she was writing the book which stands at the pinnacle of her achievement, *Women and Economics*. Henry B. Wonham in his essay, 'Writing Realism, Policing Consciousness: Howells and the Black Body' (*AL* 67.701–24) considers a number of Howells's novels and other writings in order to examine the effects of his characteristic 'effacement of African American subjectivity'; for instance, Howells describes the effect of Paul Laurence Dunbar's poetry as 'white thinking and white feeling in a black man', and, more generally, 'makes the fictional black body a vehicle for representing emotional and psychological states that his fully individualized white characters can entertain only at the price of severe moral censure'.

Nancy Bentley's study, *The Ethnography of Manners: Hawthorne, James, Wharton*, is concerned to re-orient our understanding of the novels of Hawthorne, James and Wharton within a cultural nexus of interdependent disciplines and discourses designed to display the writers' 'enhanced authority over a bounded sphere of culture, an aesthetic and intellectual "ownership" of manners intended to surpass coarser forms of cultural possession'. The texts which inform her literary as well as cultural critique are a range of works by Bronislaw Malinowski, Marcel Mauss, Thorstein Veblen and Emile Durkheim, as well as E. B. Tylor's *Primitive Culture*, Matthew Arnold's *Culture and Anarchy* and Charlotte Perkins Gilman's *Women and Economics* amongst others. Bentley's introductory chapter familiarizes us with the pleasures to be gained from the intersections of genre, many of which are illustrated through James's 1901 novel, *The Sacred Fount*, read as a scientific romance which is poised in an ambiguity designed to incorporate both decadence of style and of subject. The individual texts which then form the chief locations for Bentley's exhaustive negotiations between literary and cultural criticisms are Hawthorne's *The Marble Faun*, where the discussion focuses on anxieties surrounding postbellum reconceptualizations of race in the culture, James's *The Spoils of Poynton*, viewed through property and exchange media, and Wharton's *The Custom of the Country*, considered in the context of the anthropology of womanhood where Undine Spragg's divorces are seen to 'signify only a surface temporizing within an emerging modern polyandry'. It is perhaps in discussion of James, however, that Bentley's thesis comes most incisively to life as she anatomizes forms of violence in the Jamesian text, comparing the writing in *The Golden Bowl*, in a glancing reference which leaves one wishing for more, to the tone of 'lurid composure that characterizes ethnographies'. Her analysis of *The Spoils of Poynton* is capacious, allusive and enlightening, drawing the widest possible anthropological range of reference around the text in order to illustrate the means by which James estranges both aesthetics and manners in the construction of 'the war of property'.

Critics of Henry James's life and works have been out in force this year, with a large number of journal articles as well as book-length studies appearing. The Norton edition of *The Portrait of a Lady*, reissued for the first time since 1975, reproduces the New York edition of 1908 but includes in a textual appendix all the substantial changes made to the first edition of 1880–1 arranged so as to facilitate comparisons between the two. The editor, Robert D. Bamberg, also includes three essays on the revision of the novel; the one new to this volume – Nina Baym's 'Revision and Thematic Change in *The Portrait of a Lady*'– concentrates specifically on the means by which Isabel Archer is transformed into a heroine 'with the acute, subtle consciousness required for a late James work', but finds much to regret in the loss of the freshness of the first version. The two most recent pieces included in the edition are William Veeder's 'The Portrait of a Lack' and Millicent Bell's 'Isabel Archer and the Affronting of Plot', the first reading the novel in conjunction with James's autobiography as dramatizing 'James's precarious but tenacious sense of himself', and the second demonstrating Isabel to be the 'victim rather than the perpetrator of "plot" ' – in all senses of the word – yet also resistant to the conclusiveness of plot with Isabel's renunciation of the 'temptation to terminate her own story'. James's *The Turn of the Screw* is added to the Bedford Books' 'Case Studies in Contemporary Criticism' series here edited by Peter G. Beidler who provides a clear introduction and explanatory notes as well as a critical history which offers fictional influences as well as case histories and culminates in a survey of interpretations of the death of Miles from 1934 to 1994. Among the varieties of criticism, the reader-response essay here is by Wayne C. Booth who advises a 'constantly revising state' as the condition in which to approach reading and re-reading the text; the deconstructionist perspective is provided by Shoshana Felman whose reading – via Lacan – alerts us to the 'grasp', both intellectual and physical, with which James begins and ends his tale; the psychoanalytic approach is taken by Stanley Renner who extends discussion of the text into the cultural; and the feminist case is argued by Priscilla Walton who foregrounds 'the ways in which James is able to write from a feminine perspective and still retain the authority of his maleness, while he concomitantly draws upon the governess's feminine lack of authority for the complexity of his text'. In 'Travel Writing and the Metropolis: James, London, and *English Hours*' (*AL* 67.201–32), Brigitte Bailey charts James's movement towards an urban aesthetic through the deliberate organization of the essays in *English Hours* to reflect the aim of 'developing ways of seeing the modern imperial city': a lucid account of the 'elite spectator becoming conscious of the ways in which his privileged gaze enacts empire'. Jonathan Freedman is also concerned with cultural contexts and discusses 'The Poetics of Cultural Decline: Degeneracy, Assimilation, and the Jew in James's *The Golden Bowl*' (*AmLH* 7.477–99), in focusing on 'the strange admixture of centrality and marginality accorded to the figure of the Jew and the echoes between that combination and the novel's drama of racial decline and renewal' – a drama which is taking place at a time of 'ideological reformulation', as Freedman has it, in the dominant Anglo-American order. Caroline Field Levander in 'Bawdy Talk: The Politics of Women's Public Speech in *The Lecturess* and *The Bostonians*' (*AL* 67.467–85), provides an account of the 'political interests structuring the associations between women's speech and sexual identity' in the nineteenth century by comparing the strategies employed by Sarah J. Hale and Henry James in order to 'critique prevailing assessments of women's relation to language'. A study of *Henry James* by Kenneth Graham works sensibly and inclusively through the life and works. Graham does not venture very far into the realms of the 'obscure hurt' nor does he enter the contested territory of James's sexuality but prefers instead to concentrate his efforts on introducing the familiar cultural conditions of James's work – both European and American – using and acknowledging Leon Edel as his major source of material and inspiration. The texts under discussion here are examined by context, theme and close reading and Graham pays consistent attention to the development of James's prose style, always concerned to characterize 'general traits' belonging to each phase of his writing. The names which appear and reappear in this account of James's life and works are those of his contemporaries – colleagues, family and friends – not the names of those critics who have elaborated and complicated readings of James over the past decade, although a selection of the latter appears in the bibliography. The book is a capacious, if a little safe, account of the life and works and provides, as it should, a fluently written and confident introduction to the subject. Carol Holly, however, in her *Intensely Family: The Inheritance of Family Shame and the Autobiographies of Henry James* seeks to penetrate beyond the exordia in order to reveal the obfuscating effects of Percy Lubbock's editing of the letters and Leon Edel's 'partial and idealized' James. To illuminate both the autobiographical act and the autobiographer, Holly begins with an account of Henry James Sr – both as child and parent – and questions of unresolved inter-generational conflict as they were passed on and weighed, in turn, upon Henry Jr and his siblings. Taking shame-based family psychology to interrogate the experience of both familial and professional failure, Holly looks in detail at *A Small Boy and Others* and contiguous correspondence, mapping the delicate territory of James clan reactions to the 'Family Book' and especially the painful negotiations with James's nephew Harry. Holly does not claim that the Jamesian autobiographical act had the power to heal or resolve but that it did, at least, create 'new reasons and fresh opportunities for him to re-fortify his emotional defenses' in relation to that less complicated audience, the paying public. Holly is also one of the contributors to David McWhirter's *Henry James: New York Edition: The Construction of Authorship*, where she is joined in the exploration of shame by Eve Kosofsky Sedgwick, whose take on the subject – 'James, then, in the prefaces is using reparenting or "reissue" as a strategy for dramatizing and integrating shame' – moves us far beyond the family drama into the 'intestinal drama' of the prefaces (or as I repeatedly find myself typing, orefaces) and the 'queer performativity' of James's erotically charged lexicon. The volume has contributions from many of the scholars who are dominant in recent James criticism and the editor of the volume draws attention to the felicity – for those concerned with contemporary theory – of working with the Jamesian text: 'Recent James criticism – a virtual encyclopedia of the pluralistic universe of contemporary literary theory – has found in the novelist's work a ready vehicle for current debates about canonicity, intentionality, authority, intertextuality, and literary value.' The contributors to the volume scrutinize the New York Edition from all angles but most are claimed by the editor as participating in a project which offers a Foucauldian demystification of 'The Master' in order to problematize the authority of the Edition. From Ross Posnock's assault on the 'Aura' of Henry James to Martha Banta's consideration of 'The Excluded Seven' and their capacity to demonstrate 'a practice of omission and an aesthetics of refusal that yielded positive gain' the volume is exhaustive in its interrogation of the prefaces, the illustrations, the processes of revision and the transatlantic reception of the Edition as well as providing a full and authoritative bibliography.

Tony Tanner, in *Henry James and the Art of Non-Fiction*, takes an apparently limited brief – the transformations wrought by James upon the genres of travel writing, criticism and autobiography – but his investigations and observations reverberate 'beneath and behind' the non-fiction into all corners of James's writing in this elegantly written and indispensable book. In the case of the travel writing, Tanner describes how James effects the depopulation of the scenes in which he describes the 'accommodated haunter', as James characterizes himself, eliminating all other possible presences at the scene by celebrating the absent, as in the submerged Dunwich, where 'All the grossness of its positive life is now at the bottom of the German Ocean . . .'. Tanner finds likeness across cultures in the characteristic Jamesian mode of recording the impressions given by the historic site: 'the generalized response'; but he also finds difference, most crucially in the bathetic ease of access to the American interior. As Tanner so felicitously expresses it: 'James wants to *want* to penetrate; but he also wants to be prevented *from* penetrating. For James, art was engendered precisely in the precious space between desire and prevention.' In his discussion of James's literary criticism – in particular that which focuses on the sacred quartet: George Eliot, Turgenev, Balzac and Flaubert – Tanner offers us the following schema: 'James the novelist uses American conscience in English society in books written in emulation of the French' even whilst convincing the reader that James refuted categorization and any fixed notion of what 'legitimate material for the novelist' might be. Tanner's celebration of his subject's generic perversities culminates in consideration of 'James as the writer of autobiography that will have nothing to do with chronology or conventional sequence' but nevertheless an autobiography within which it is possible to descry the great themes of the fiction. Sheila Teahan's *The Rhetorical Logic of Henry James* reads seven of James's novels through the re-designation of the 'center of consciousness' as a rhetorical device which must culminate in self-destruction; she sees such literal or figurative annihilation as dramatizations of 'the undoing or dismantling of the central consciousness as both phenomenological structure and formal device'. Teahan chooses texts which exemplify the pattern she identifies, ranging between *Roderick Hudson* and *The Golden Bowl* and bringing the too often dismissed early works under the same close deconstructive eye that is trained on the later novels. Alongside discussion of the individual novels she offers substantiation for her argument from the prefaces and other theoretical writings in order to contend that 'rhetorical and cultural criticism ... are or should be complementary rather than antithetical'. This is a densely argued and tightly focused study which offers close readings of the novels which are subject to Teahan's formula; her analysis of *The Wings of the Dove*, in particular, is compelling on 'the novel's own strategy of hanging fire on the edge of the unspeakable'. In ' "I Trust You Will Detect My Intention": The Strange Case of *Watch and Ward*' (*JAmS* 29.365–78), Lindsey Traub describes James's conscious use of the work of his contemporaries in the exercising of the 'guardian-who-marries-his-ward theme'; Traub shows James ironizing and refuting the standard execution of such a plot although, as she warns, 'His attempt at resolution, the marriage of Nora and Robert on new terms of self-knowledge and equality, appears to have confronted him with contradictions which even revision could not circumvent'. Donald Weber's essay also takes a comparative approach: 'Outsiders and Greenhorns: Christopher Newman in the Old World, David Levinsky in the New' (*AL* 67.725–45), and likens the two characters in their bewilderment when confronted with, respectively, Europe and America, in order to highlight the discourses of 'open and closed societies, of tolerant and intolerant cultures, of incorporation and expulsion, of shame and self-hatred – that form crucial matrices for understanding both James's novel and later American ethnic expression'. *The Henry James Review* features many of the critics who have been active elsewhere and the three numbers of *HJR* 16 contain essays which are, in the main, brief and cogent; the contributors range widely throughout the works and even into the garden at Lamb House. *HJR* 16.iii is a special 'Race Forum' and includes essays by Sara Blair, Ross Posnock, Walter Benn Michaels and Leland S. Person who writes engagingly on gender indeterminacy in the South by linking *The Bostonians* with Frederick Douglass's *Narrative* of 1845.

In an eventful year for Mark Twain studies the writer is outed, his attitude on race continues to be debated, he is found risible and is inscribed as a notable blasphemer. Gerald Graff and James Phelan have edited *Adventures of Huckleberry Finn*, introducing the text and context, a collection of illustrations from the 1885 edition, and an assembly of Twain critics organized so as to appear to be engaged in lively debate. The editors divide the critical essays into three sets of controversies: the first, 'The Controversy over the Ending: Did Mark Twain Sell Jim Down the River', includes the old guard, T. S. Eliot, Lionel Trilling, and Leo Marx as well as James M. Cox and Richard Hill, whilst the second, 'The Controversy over Race: Does *Huckleberry Finn* Combat or Reinforce Racist Attitudes?', features an overview by Justin Kaplan of one hundred years – 1884–1984 – of critical and cultural reactions to the novel, as well as a collection of other contributions whose authors are ranged on one side of the debate or the other and variously present biographical, close reading, historical and reader response investigations of the text. The third section, 'The Controversy over Gender and Sexuality: Are Twain's Sexual Politics Progressive, Regressive, or Beside the Point?' needs no further explication and features Nancy Walker and Myra Jehlen in dialogue as well as Leslie Fiedler and Christopher Looby. *The Cambridge Companion to Mark Twain* (ed. Forrest G. Robinson) is also very much in the same territory as the above collection but the majority of the essays here are new and examine *Connecticut Yankee* and the travel writing in addition to *Huckleberry Finn*. The majority of the articles, however, are thematic and the collection opens entertainingly with Louis J. Budd on 'Mark Twain as American Icon' and continues with Shelley Fisher Fishkin on 'Mark Twain and Women', an interrogation of the received wisdom of 'those who felt women were bad for Twain and those who felt Twain was bad for women'. Myra Jehlen is back in the thick of the controversy with 'Banned in Concord: *Adventures of Huckleberry Finn* and Classic American Literature' and Eric Lott on 'Mr Clemens and Jim Crow: Twain, Race, and Blackface' adds much to the argument in his analysis of *Pudd'nhead Wilson*, concluding 'Blackface furnished Twain's very language of race, a language riddled with ambiguities Twain did not so much illuminate as reiterate'. Along with the 'Case Study' this collection should be available to all students of Twain for its compact and lucid presentation of some of the central critical issues. 'Mark Twain and Homosexuality' is the subject of an essay by Andrew J. Hoffman (*AL* 67.23–49) which seeks, in a faux-modest manner – 'I see room for doubt' – to explode the foundations upon which Twain biographical scholarship is based by making a claim that the author had a series of homosexual affairs before his marriage and at least one after it. Hoffman lards his text with expressions of reasonable doubt but in his description of Twain's associates and milieu – especially the 'gender-role confusion' amongst the 'Bohemians' of late nineteenth-century San Francisco and Nevada – and of his relationships with women, the essay throws down a gauntlet to challenge 'traditional conceptions of a literary icon'. In *Mark Twain on the Loose: A Comic Writer and the American Self*, Bruce Michelson shows himself more than willing to treat Twain's comic writing with a good deal of solemnity, providing a definition 'heavily pruned, almost primordial: humor as a subversion of seriousness', chief weapon in 'Mark Twain's unrestricted war against seriousness'. Michelson begins by offering Twain's Petrified Man, his Whittier birthday speech and the various incarnations of the jumping frog as the means to gauge the 'depth and courage of his insurrections', moving on to detailed consideration of the travel books in his second chapter, 'Fool's Paradise' before plunging into 'The Quarrel with Romance'. In this long chapter, Michelson is insistent on a reading of Huck in the extended company of Tom Sawyer and in so doing releases a multiplicity of Hucks before engaging with *A Connecticut Yankee in King Arthur's Court* as a book whose 'targets expand to encompass any system or thesis that threatens liberty or ultimate fluidity of being, everything that might conceal the truth about the self *from* the self'. The anarchic refusnik who Michelson celebrates is also on display in *The Bible According to Mark Twain: Writings on Heaven, Eden and the Flood* (ed. Howard G. Baetzhold and Joseph B. McCullough), which features the writing of four decades, some of which is previously unpublished. The editors provide introductory material for each text and most of the anthologized material is taken from the original manuscript, or typescript in the case of dictated work. There are multiple pleasures here including Adam's diary account of his lighting out from the Garden in order to escape the attentions of 'the new creature with the long hair' who can 'shed water out of its face' and the often lyrical, much less sardonic 'Eve's Diary', described as Twain's 'moving eulogy to his wife Livy', recently dead.

Millicent Bell begins her *Cambridge Companion to Edith Wharton*, with a survey of the contemporary reviews of Wharton's major novels and moves through critical assessments of the novelist's work between the 1930s and the revival led by R. W. B. Lewis and Cynthia Griffin Wolff in the late 1970s. The essays that follow treat, in the main, the most well-known of Wharton's work but two of the most welcome pieces in the *Companion* concern her first, most critically neglected novel, *The Valley of Decision*; the final word is given to Wharton's friend and mentor in the Italian subject, Vernon Lee, with the first republication of her 1903 critique of the novel. It is hard to recall a more coherent and compelling reading of *The Age of Innocence* than that offered by Pamela Knights in her 'Forms of Disembodiment: The Social Subject in *The Age of Innocence*'. She positions the novel in the context of 'contemporary debates about the social basis of consciousness' and places Newland Archer's old-fashioned anthropology up against 'the more sophisticated ethnological eye of the novel as a whole'. Nancy Bentley's essay on ' "Hunting for the Real": Wharton and the Science of Manners' is complementary to Knights's work in taking the scientific discourse of *The Age of Innocence* and applying it to the question of the constitution of the novel of manners, whilst a different ideological and critical direction is signalled by reference to social Darwinism in Wharton's work in Elizabeth Ammons's essay: 'Edith Wharton and the Issue of Race'. Ammons reads selectively in order to redefine the fiction 'within a multicultural U.S. literary-historical context'. The essay by Maureen Howard, 'The Bachelor and the Baby: *The House of Mirth*', offers a very different version of Simon Rosedale to Ammons' 'invading Jew', as the 'closest thing to a sympathetic male in the novel', whilst Elaine Showalter, noting the 'reflex anti-Semitism' of Wharton's old New Yorkers in *The Custom of the Country*, relocates – to good effect – Elmer Moffat and Undine Spragg in the Trump Tower. Gloria Erlich, rehearsing the same thesis as in her book, *The Sexual Education of Edith Wharton* (1992), that Wharton's fiction is reducible in thematic terms to the personal effects upon the author of 'divided mothering' (p. 98), demonstrates here, unfortunately, only the limitations of such an approach.

Dale M. Bauer's study of Wharton's later fiction in *Edith Wharton's Brave New Politics* begins with *Summer* and progresses, still in a sweat, to 'Roman Fever', taking in *The Mother's Recompense, Twilight Sleep, The Children, Hudson River Bracketed* and *The Gods Arrive* along the way. Bauer's use of ' "cultural dialogics", a theory of her late fictions that suggests how her writing configured the mass culture around her as another "voice" in the representation of an orchestrated, and carefully controlled, dialogue' refutes the oft-repeated charge that by the mid-1920s Wharton no longer understood anything about American popular culture. The novels of the twenties, according to Bauer, actually 'offer a vision of the interrelation of intimate and inner life with the political ambiguities of mass culture', an approach which yields significant results and particular rewards in her reading of *Twilight Sleep* and *The Children* which she places in the context of theories of motherhood current at the time. Bauer puts 'Roman Fever' to work as a story exemplifying Wharton's horror at the growth of fascism in Europe, wrapping the story round with a multitude of interpretative possibilities which centre on 'The Law of the Father and Racial Purity' and uses insights provided by a variety of social theorists. This is a provocative and worthwhile study of the later fiction which, if overstated at times, usefully redresses the deficit in attention paid to Wharton's later work.

Kathy A. Fedorko, in *Gender and the Gothic in the Fiction of Edith Wharton*, illuminates the furthest reaches of the writer's literary imagination, reading a range of short stories and six of her novels through gothic convention in order to 'explore the tension between feminine and masculine ways of knowing and being', exegeticizing androgyny as well as 'gender tension' within Wharton's work. Fedorko organizes her discussion chronologically and developmentally; she divides Wharton's writing life into four periods and takes a body of short stories and one or two novels as representative of her work in the Gothic text in each phase. Her readings are informed by feminist archetypal theory as well as female gothic which makes for full and detailed reading of the texts under consideration and Fedorko is particularly stimulating in her chapter 'Reclaiming the Feminine' where *Summer* is juxtaposed with *The Age of Innocence* – the latter seen as a text which revises the 'Gothic paradigm' – which then modulates into a discussion of 'The Young Gentlemen', 'Miss Mary Pask' and 'Bewitched'. The book concludes with a discussion of Wharton's last completed story, 'All Souls', which Fedorko uses to illustrate the distance travelled between the gendered conflicts of the early texts and the final version of gothic communicated here by an androgynous narrator with literary leanings: 'by using a narrator of unidentified gender who possesses characteristics of both genders, Wharton provides a fitting culmination to her evolving development of the fe/male self who acknowledges the frightened self within yet is able to comfort and accept that self'. Fedorko's project is very successfully executed; she maintains a nicely judged balance of theory and close critical analysis in order to prosecute her thesis.

In Carol J. Singley's book *Edith Wharton: Matters of Mind and Spirit*, the work of Edith Wharton is contextualized in the larger traditions of American philosophical and religious thought, doing justice along the way to the broad intellectual scope of her writing. In charting Wharton's intellectual debts, Singley endows her subject with a coherence, a structural principle with which to approach a reading of the fiction as a whole and her analysis of Wharton's reading, in particular the enduring influence of those whom Wharton termed her 'Awakeners', produces a good many new insights into the novels and stories discussed here. Singley illuminates Wharton's conscious use of the work of philosophers, natural scientists and biblical texts in her fiction and autobiographical writings, and yet withal, keeps alive our sense of the lightness of touch with which these engagements with the intellectual debates of her age feature in Wharton's fiction and other writings. Carol Singley discusses both obscure and well-known Wharton texts but brings fresh insights to them and also provides future scholars with new avenues of research to pursue. The evidence substantiating the effect of Wharton's huge and ecumenical intelligence is brought together, made sense of and renewed by Singley's work. The woman Paul Bourget described as an 'intellectual tomboy' whose 'energy of culture' both fascinated and alienated him is well served here because of, and not as in the past, in spite of, her scholarship. Singley describes Wharton as one of the ' "tourists of the supernatural", whose agnosticism and hard-edged positivism prevented her surrender to historical nostalgia or simple belief, yet whose spiritual longings sustained the search for immutable values', and in this study the authentication of the influence of such diverse figures as St Augustine, Jonathan Edwards, Charles Darwin, Henry Coppée and George Santayana in Wharton's life and works illuminates both the context and content of her creative endeavour.

Sarah Bird Wright has edited a collection of Wharton's travel writings, *Edith Wharton Abroad: Selected Travel Writings, 1888–1920*, which includes extracts from all Wharton's most important books, including the recently discovered 'The Cruise of the Vanadis', the first known piece of travel writing by Edith Wharton. Wright contextualizes each extract and draws attention to the abiding concerns which fuelled and underpinned Wharton's wander-lust and the familiar terms of her aesthetic engagement with the art, architecture and scenery of the lands she visited. Wharton was a well-informed traveller who had distinct and well-defined tastes and Wright chooses well among the range of Wharton's work to give a broad picture of her tastes, her boldness, her aesthetic values and, above all else, her skill as communicator of the exotic.

Books Reviewed

Ashkenazi, Elliott, ed. *The Civil War Diary of Clara Solomon: Growing Up in New Orleans, 1861–1862*. LSUP. pp. 458. £32.95. ISBN 0 8071 1968 7.

Baetzhold, Howard G., and Joseph B. McCullough, eds. *The Bible According to Mark Twain: Writings on Heaven, Eden and the Flood*. UGeoP. pp. 384. £26.95 ($29.95). ISBN 0 8203 1650 4.

Bamberg, Robert D., ed. *Henry James: The Portrait of a Lady*. 2nd edn. NCE. Norton. pb £7.95. ISBN 0 393 96646 1.

Bauer, Dale M. *Edith Wharton's Brave New Politics*. UWiscP. hb £49.50, pb £15.95. ISBN 0 299 14420 8, 0 299 14424 0.

Beidler, Peter G. *The Turn of the Screw. A Case Study in Contemporary Criticism*. St. Martin's. pp. 320. pb $8.65. ISBN 0 312 53341 1.

Bell, Millicent. *The Cambridge Companion to Edith Wharton*. CUP. pp. 240. pb £12.95. ISBN 0 521 48513 4.

Bentley, Nancy. *The Ethnography of Manners: Hawthorne, James, Wharton*. Cambridge Studies in American Literature and Culture 90. CUP. £37.50. ISBN 0 521 46190 1.

Bercovitch, Sacvan, ed. *The Cambridge History of American Literature, Volume Two: Prose Writing 1820–1865*. CUP. pp. 887. £55. ISBN 0 521 30106 8.

Bibliographic Guide to Black Studies. Hall. pp. v + 395. $39.95. ISBN 0 7838 2164 6.

Brown, Julie, ed. *American Women Short Story Writers: A Collection of Critical Essays*. Wellesley Studies in Critical Theory Vol. 8. Garland. pp. 400. $64. ISBN 0 8153 1338 1.

Carlson, Eric, ed. *Emerson's Literary Criticism*. UNebP. pp. 252. pb £9.50. ISBN 0 8032 6728 2.

Castronovo, Russ. *Fathering the Nation: American Genealogies of Slavery and Freedom*. UCalP. pp. 287. £25. ISBN 0 520 08901 4.

Cohen, Daniel A. *Pillars of Salt, Monuments of Grace: New England Crime Literature and the Origins of American Popular Culture, 1674–1860*. OUP. 1993. pp. xi + 350. £30. ISBN 0 19 507584 6.

Colacurcio, Michael J. *The Province of Piety: Moral History in Hawthorne's Early Tales*. DukeUP. pp. 670. £20.95. ISBN 0 8223 1572 6.

Cosgrave, Brian, ed. *Literature and the Supernatural*. ColUP. pp. 176. £25. ISBN 1 85607 143 X.

Elmer, Jonathan. *Reading at the Social Limit: Affect, Mass Culture, and Edgar Allan Poe*. StanfordUP. pp. 259. £25. ISBN 0 8047 2541 1.

Ernest, John. *Resistance and Reformation in Nineteenth Century African-American Literature*. UPMissip. pp. 352. hb $45, pb $17.95. ISBN 0 87805 816 8, 0 87805 817 6.

Fabre, Michel, ed. *The French Critical Reception of African-American Literature from the Beginnings to 1970: An Annotated Bibliography*. Greenwood. pp. xv + 310. £59.95. ISBN 0 313 25368 4.

Fedorko, Kathy A. *Gender and the Gothic in the Fiction of Edith Wharton*. UAlaP. pp. 224. £31.50. ISBN 0 8173 0788 5.

Fetterley, Judith, and Marjorie Pryse. *American Women Regionalists: 1850–1910. A Norton Anthology*. Norton. pp. 627. £14.95. ISBN 0 393 31363 8.

Folsom, Ed, ed. *Walt Whitman: The Centennial Essays*. UIowaP. pp. 262. £15.95. ISBN 0 87745 462 0.

Fredericks, Nancy. *Melville's Art of Democracy*. UGeoP. £35. ISBN 0 8203 1682 2.

Gale, Robert L. *A Herman Melville Encyclopedia*. Greenwood. pp. 537. £71.95. ISBN 0 313 29011 3.

Gogol, Miriam, ed. *Theodore Dreiser: Beyond Naturalism*. NYUP. pp. 320. hb £36, pb £15.25. ISBN 0 8147 3073 6, 0 8147 3074 4.

Graff, Gerald, and James Phelan, ed. *Mark Twain: The Adventures of Huckleberry Finn: A Case Study in Critical Controversy*. St. Martin's. pp. 528. $39.95. ISBN 0 312 12261 6.

Graham, Kenneth. *Henry James: A Literary Life*. Macmillan Literary Lives. Macmillan. pp. 226. hb £35, pb £9.99. ISBN 0 333 43354 8, 0 333 43355 6.

Granqvist, Raol. *Imitation as Resistance: Appropriations of English Literature in Nineteenth-Century America*. AUP. pp. 305. £34.50. ISBN 0 8386 3669 X.

Greenspan, Ezra, ed. *The Cambridge Companion to Walt Whitman*. CUP. pp. 234. hb £35, pb £12.95. ISBN 0 521 443431, 0 521 44807 7.

Hakutani, Yoshinobu, and Robert Butler, eds. *The City in African-American Literature*. FDUP. AUP. pp. 234. £29.50. ISBN 0 8386 3565 2.

Hart, James D., and Phillip W. Leininger, eds. *The Oxford Companion to American Literature*. OUP. pp. ix + 779. £35. ISBN 0 19 506548 4.

Higgins, Brian, and Hershel Parker, eds. *Herman Melville: The Contemporary*

Reviews. American Critical Archives. CUP. pp. 480. £70. ISBN 0 521 41423 7.

Hill, Mary A., ed. *A Journey from Within: The Love Letters of Charlotte Perkins Gilman, 1897–1900.* BuckUP. AUP. pp. 432. £38. ISBN 0 8387 5293 4.

Holly, Carol. *Intensely Family: The Inheritance of Family Shame and the Autobiographies of Henry James.* UWiscP. pp. 224. hb £45, pb £21.50. ISBN 0 299 14720 7, 0 299 14724 X.

Hutner, Gordon, ed. *The American Literary History Reader.* OUP. pp. 432. £17.50. ISBN 0 19 509504 9.

Johnson, Claudia Durst. *Understanding The Scarlet Letter: A Student Casebook to Issues, Sources, and Historical Documents.* Literature in Context. Greenwood. pp. 229. £28.95. ISBN 0 313 29328 7.

Kessler, Carol Farley. *Charlotte Perkins Gilman: Her Progress Toward Utopia, with Selected Writings.* Liverpool Science Fiction Texts and Studies 5. LiverUP (1994). pp. 288. hb £27.50. pb £15. ISBN 0 85323 489 2, 0 85323 499 X.

Klammer, Martin. *Whitman, Slavery, and the Emergence of 'Leaves of Grass'.* UPennP. pp.176. £32.50. ISBN 0 271 01315 X.

Lenz, William E. *The Poetics of the Antarctic: A Study in Nineteenth-Century American Cultural Perceptions.* Garland. £37.50. pp. 248. ISBN 0 8153 1473 6.

McWhirter, David, ed. *Henry James: New York Edition: The Construction of Authorship.* StanfordUP. £27.95. ISBN 0 8047 2564 0.

Michelson, Bruce. *Mark Twain on the Loose: A Comic Writer and the American Self.* UMassP. hb £42.50, pb £16.50. ISBN 0 87023 966 X, 0 87023 967.

Milder, Robert. *Reimagining Thoreau.* Cambridge Studies in American Literature. CUP. pp. 237. £35. ISBN 0 521 46149 9.

Myerson, Joel, ed. *The Cambridge Companion to Henry David Thoreau.* CUP. pp. 224. pb £13. ISBN 0 521 44037 8.

Oberhaus, Dorothy Huff. *Emily Dickinson's Fascicles: Method and Meaning.* PSUP. £35.95. ISBN 0 271 01337 0.

O'Keefe, Richard. *Mythic Archetypes in Ralph Waldo Emerson: A Blakean Reading.* KSUP. pp. 228. £30. ISBN 0 87338 518 7.

Okker, Patricia. *Our Sister Editors: Sarah J. Hale and the Tradition of 19th-century American Women Editors.* UGeoP. pp. 280. $40. ISBN 0 8203 1686 5.

Peterson, Carla L. *"Doers of the Word": African-American Women Speakers and Writers in the North (1830–1880).* OUP. pp. 284. $35. ISBN 0 19 508519 1.

Pfaelzer, Jean, ed. *A Rebecca Harding Davis Reader: "Life in the Iron Mills"; Selected Fiction and Essays.* UPittP. pp. 640. pb $9.95. ISBN 0 8229 5569 5.

Pizer, Donald, ed. *The Cambridge Companion to American Realism and Naturalism: From Howells to London.* CUP. pp. 320. hb £35, pb £12.95. ISBN 0 521 43300 2, 0 521 43876 4.

Price, Kenneth M., and Susan Belasco Smith, eds. *Periodical Literature in Nineteenth-Century America.* UPVirginia. pp. 292. $45. ISBN 0 8139 1630 5.

Quaife, Milo. *From the Canon's Mouth: The Civil War Letters of General Alpheus S. Williams*. UNebP. pp. 406. £13.95. ISBN 0 8032 9777 7.

Robinson, Forrest G., ed. *The Cambridge Companion to Mark Twain*. CUP. pp. 288. hb £35. pb £11.95. ISBN 0 521 44036 X, 0 521 44593 0.

Rohler, Lloyd. *Ralph Waldo Emerson: Preacher and Lecturer*. Greenwood. pp. 197. £47.95. ISBN 0 313 26328 0.

Shea, William M., and Peter A. Huff, eds. *Knowledge and Belief in America: Enlightenment Traditions and Modern Religious Thought*. CUP. pp. ix + 360. £35. ISBN 0 521 55011 4.

Singley, Carol J. *Edith Wharton: Matters of Mind and Spirit*. CUP. £35. $49.95. ISBN 0 521 47235 0.

Spanos, William. *The Errant Art of Moby-Dick: The Canon, the Cold War, and the Struggle for American Studies*. DukeUP. pp. 374. £22. ISBN 0 8223 1599 8.

Springer, Haskell, ed. *America and the Sea: A Literary History*. UGeoP. pp. xi + 414. £31.95. ISBN 0 8203 1651 2.

Stephens, Robert O. *The Family Saga in the South: Generations and Destinies*. LSUP. $30. ISBN 0 8071 1988 1.

Stern, Madeleine. *Louisa May Alcott Unmasked: Collected Thrillers*. NortheasternU. pb £23.50. ISBN 1 55553 226 8.

Tanner, Tony. *Henry James and the Art of Non-Fiction*. UGeoP. pp. 112. $22.50. ISBN 0 8203 1689 X.

Teahan, Sheila. *The Rhetorical Logic of Henry James*. LSUP. pp. 184. $30. ISBN 0 8071 2005 7.

Wagner-Martin, Linda, and Cathy Davidson, eds. *The Oxford Book of Women's Writing in the United States*. OUP. pp. 672. £20. ISBN 0 19 508706 2.

——, and ——, eds. *The Oxford Companion to Women's Writing in the United States*. OUP. pp. 1,021. £35. ISBN 0 19 506608 1.

Wald, Priscilla. *Constituting Americans: Cultural Anxiety and Narrative Form*. DukeUP. pp. 368. hb $56.95, pb $17.95. ISBN 0 8223 1550 5, 0 8223 1547 5.

Wright, Sarah Bird. *Edith Wharton Abroad: Selected Travel Writings, 1888–1920*. Hale. pp. 368. £15.99. ISBN 0 312 12417 7.

XVI

American Literature: The Twentieth Century

LIONEL KELLY, PAT RIGHELATO, HENRY CLARIDGE,
DEBORAH PARSONS, STEVEN PRICE and CHRISTINE
MACLEOD

This chapter has four sections: 1. Poetry; 2. Fiction 1900–1945; 3. Drama; 4. Black American Literature. Section 1 is by Lionel Kelly and Pat Righelato; section 2 is by Henry Claridge and Deborah Parsons; section 3 is by Steven Price; and section 4 is by Christine MacLeod. This year there is no section on 'Fiction since 1945'. YWES 77 will review material in this area for 1995–6.

1. Poetry

(a) General

Timothy Bahti's *Ends of the Lyric: Direction and Consequence in Western Poetry* begins by reviewing theories of lyric and lyric closure, quoting with approval Helen Vendler's emphasis: 'a lyric is a role offered to a reader'. Poets selected for detailed discussion include Shakespeare, Coleridge, Keats, Wallace Stevens and Paul Celan. Bahti's general emphasis is upon the tropological prominence of chiasmus in the lyric practice of these writers; he argues that their poems 'begin and end, but by their end they have inverted the end into its opposite, a nonend'. Chapter 7, on Wallace Stevens, undertakes a linguistic analysis of 'The Snow Man', 'The Man on the Dump' and 'A Clear Day and No Memories'. Readers need to be up to coping with phrases such as 'to read the loss of the sight and site of reading, to read reading reading itself away', but there are rewards: Bahti is alert to the paradox of Stevens as a poet whose work 'seems to exude a sense of completion and achievement' but which escapes back into its own process of making.

American Poetry: The Modernist Ideal (ed. Clive Bloom and Brian Docherty) is a collection of essays tracing the search for 'authenticity in voice and form' as the central quest of American modernist poetry following its inheritance from Whitman, and somewhat oddly, Edgar Allan Poe. Dickinson is a generally neglected figure in this collection, though her impact on H.D. in the 1920s is noted. Within the frame of an over-worked distinction between the formalist and experimental traditions this collection attends in principal to the experimental line with essays on H.D., Pound, Williams, Rexroth, e.e. cummings, Objectivism, Frank O'Hara, Charles Olson, Allen Ginsberg, Ed Dorn and Robert Creeley, though there are also essays on Wallace Stevens,

Marianne Moore and Denise Levertov, so that the programme of this book is not entirely convincing and one has the sense that inclusions and exclusions were not entirely governed by the editors. However, there are some valuable essays by notable scholars such as Ian F. A. Bell on Pound, Gregory Woods on Hart Crane and Geoff Ward on Ed Dorn. I particularly enjoyed Richard Bradbury's account of Objectivism, the best I have read, and Pat Righelato's brief account of the enabling consciousness in Stevens.

Albert Cook's voluminous writings on world poetry are difficult to keep track of both in the particular concerns of each of his books and the extraordinary reach of his familiarity with poetry in many languages, ancient and modern. This tracking is made more difficult by Cook's persistent desire to work in terms of universals which will be true in time and place wherever his focus alights, like those old-fashioned 'eternal verities'. In his most recent book *The Reach of Poetry*, for example, a chapter on 'The Stance of the Modern Poet' refers to Georg Trakl, Rilke, Baudelaire, Valéry, Mallarmé, Laforgue, Eliot, Heraclitus, Homer and Stevens in the first three pages before he has really established the terms of his debate, which seems to be about the modern poet's self-consciousness of performance beyond the parameters of reflexivity into what are here called 'meta-statements', an unwieldy term by which Cook really means wisdom and vision, terms which relate to Cook's desire to find the spiritual everywhere inherent in modern poetry.

In *The Modern Voice in American Poetry* William Doreski defines the literary voice as 'one that speaks in any of the modes of poetic diction, tone, and pronominal usage readily available and common in a given era. This voice would be one a reader in that era would readily associate with poetry or verse.' This unexceptional definition assumes a common poetic voice in the era of the 'modern', yet Doreski is actually more interested in the differences between the poetic voices of this century as he works from Frost, Stevens, Williams, Moore, Eliot, Pound and Lowell through to a final chapter on contemporary poets. For example, Williams and Moore are contrasted in their use of the 'Colloquial Style', and Eliot and Pound through their 'Voicing of Difference' in a 'Political Discourse'. Doreski makes an eclectic use of contemporary theory throughout, and his interest in the rhetorical strategies of his chosen poets illuminates their relationship to allegory, symbol and myth. In a strong chapter on Lowell he disputes Harold Bloom's denial of the 'trope of vulnerability', and in 'Meditation and Impersonality in Contemporary Poetry' sees a line from Lowell to the 'new dynamic' of John Ashbery, Louise Glück and Robert Pinsky which is said to derive from the tension in their work 'between impersonality and the fiction of self-revelation'. This is an intelligent and rewarding study.

Rainer Emig's *Modernism in Poetry: Motivations, Structures and Limits*, attempts to answer some troublesome questions in this theoretically sophisticated study of the vocabulary and strategies of modernist poetry. One question he regards as crucial – 'what is it that makes a work a modernist one?'. Emig distinguishes between 'modernist', 'modernity' and the 'avant-garde' as a basis for delineating the characteristics of modernist poetics, and situates the modernist text as located somewhere between the Enlightenment concept of modernity and the 'radical gestures of the avante-garde' with their singular focus on art. He opens with a reading of Hopkins who, it is argued, approaches Saussure in his understanding of the unreliability of the sign, yet seeks to overcome the sign's arbitrariness in a struggle religious in its motives, and reads Hopkins's endeavour to 'bridge the gap between reality and language' as endemic to the aesthetics of modernist poetry. This is followed by an account of Yeats's search for a solution through symbolism, the resource to metaphor and metonymy in Eliot, and the uses of myth in Pound. Later chapters take a psychoanalytic, economic and philosophic route in this attempt to delineate the nature of modernist poetry.

The writers discussed in Frederick Garber's *Repositionings: Readings of Contemporary Poetry, Photography, and Performance Art* include Gerald Stern, Jerome Rothenberg, David Antin, Carolee Schneemann and Steve McCaffery. Garber's attention to the concept of the self explored by these writers is read in conjunction with the work of some contemporary photographers and performance artists and poets where issues of subjectivity and genre are 'repositioned'. Garber traces these developments back to Dada, the movement which 'was to bring performance to the forefront' through the paradox of an intensely held immediacy 'and the undoing of immediacy' conditions which anticipate postmodern configurings of the instability of the self in relation to history and aesthetics. This is an illuminating interdisciplinary account of the passions and desires involved in a variety of different negotiations of contemporary selfness.

Literary canonization is a fact of life we mostly comply with however much we might challenge it in particulars. Alan Golding's *From Outlaw to Classic: Canons in American Poetry* seeks to analyse the 'contingencies of value' inherent in canon formation and to locate 'how such contingencies work at particular sites and moments of practice' in the context of American poetry. His study of the effects of institutional education in canon formation illustrates the role of those powerful critical voices whose hierarchical determinations affect the structure of syllabi and the anthologies we work with and sets these voices against those 'outlaws' beyond the academy, the contributors to and editors of little magazines whose products nurture the climate of experiment and innovation by which the canon is, eventually, modified using Cid Corman's *Origins* as a case history. Golding then turns to the Language poets and their relationship of 'complicitous resistence' to the academy. If in present-day representations of modern American poetry the exclusions of ethnic and women's voices from the canon is now less glaring, the conflict between 'classic' and 'popular' culture remains at the heart of our anxieties about canon formation and the exercise of our power over what other people should read. Golding's contribution to the debate about the canon is scholarly and unusual in his attention to poetry.

Alan Holder's *Rethinking Meter\A New Approach to the Verse Line* opens with a tirade against the tyranny of a 'foot'-based concept of metre in the discourse of prosody and the criticism of poetry: once over this Holder offers an alternative method of prosodic practice which privileges the unit of the verse line and works by phrasal analysis, and, in his final chapter, turns to intonation to 'offer a preliminary sketch of how that element of speech might be incorporated into our prosody'. Holder's endeavour is to formulate a prosodic theory which can apply equally to formal and free verse, a requirement all the more necessary in these times when free verse is the dominant mode in American poetry, as is evident in the recent attention to the 'New Formalism' and those poets who work in traditional metrics. The history of the case for and against a foot-based metrics goes back in this century at least to Frost and his insistence on the poet's mastery in this and includes Williams's formulation of the 'variable foot', a system of measure which has long bedevilled commentary on him. Holder's abrasive denunciation of this system is as thorough as his advocacy of 'phrasalism' is persuasive, and it is a pleasure to follow his arguments through his phrasal readings of particular poems especially in the reading of pitch and intonation in Stevens's 'Sunday Morning' in the final chapter. Those of us who make our living teaching poetry have much to learn from Holder's book, though I expect it will upset the specialists in prosodics.

Why is it that writers remain wedded to the notebook in the age of the computer laptop? This is a question posed by Charles Simic in his preface to *The Poet's Notebook*, a collection of notebook entries from the work of 26 contemporary poets including Simic himself and the late lamented James Merrill. Simic's most serious answer to his own question is that notebooks 'are an invitation to write in a certain way. They demand from us absolute conciseness, an aesthetic of modesty', this last a nicely Bishop-like phrase. This collection is edited by Stephen Kuusisto, Deborah Tall and David Weiss, with entries from the notebooks of Rita Dove, Joy Harjo, X. J. Kennedy, J. D. McClatchy, Heather McHugh, William Stafford and others. Rita Dove's notebook gives us bits of poems, a posh epigrammatic view of the idea of suffering as 'the supreme token of seriousness' from Susan Sontag, a telling comment on Thomas Hardy as the first of the poets 'so numerous now, who are suspicious of writing well', and the kind of self-admonitory entry most of us will have made at some point in time – 'You must learn French'. The James Merrill entries include self-deprecating ironies such as the recall of a blond youth in a tank top who comes up to him after a reading at Dartmouth and boldly asks 'Who *are* you? Are you American? What sort of English are you speaking?' And I especially enjoy these two Merrill entries – 'The gods of rock and tree, their masses celebrated by Cézanne' and 'Alpine valleys, meadows around Barbizon – genre painters virtually Hindu in their worship of the cow'. The privileged view this anthology gives of the intimacies of the poet's mobile workplace is endlessly fascinating.

Becoming Canonical in American Poetry by Timothy Morris is a study of the history and dynamics of audience reception and a critique of the poetics of presence in relation to Whitman, Dickinson, Marianne Moore and Elizabeth Bishop. Morris argues that both Moore and Bishop were 'forced into an ancillary category' in that William Carlos Williams's strategy of containment was to present Moore as the perfect miniaturist and purifier of language, whereas Bishop's peers praised her for her descriptive powers, a category which placed her outside 'the larger Whitmanic functions of authorial presence': the effect in both cases was diminishment and their early canonical status now seems second class. Thus Marianne Moore has become 'the American Adam's fussy spinster sister' and the dialogic quality of her writing has been downgraded. Morris focuses on the discontinuities of Bishop's work and her 'mutable national identity', arguing that her poetry is an opportunity to 'let the tradition of presence go', to abandon the attempt to construct heroic American identities in the process of canonization. This witty, thought-provoking addition to reception studies emphasizes the role of readers in constructing the dialogic performances of American poetry.

In a graceful introduction to *Playing It By Ear*, a selection of his literary essays and reviews, William H. Pritchard tells of the casual onset of his work as a journeyman-reviewer, an occupation he has run in tandem with his academic career over the past 30-odd years becoming in the process widely respected for the vigour and frankness of his writing. These qualities are much in evidence in his damning account of E. C. Lathem's corrupt edition of *The Poetry of Robert Frost* (1969), and in a nicely ironic dumping on Stephen Spender (too ample a target, perhaps), and less successfully in a challenge to 'The Hermeneutical Mafia'. Yet I think Pritchard is at his best when showing us what he admires in the work of a poet, as in the longish essay on Philip Larkin reprinted from *Raritan* (6.iv.[1987].62–86), and the surprising tribute to Kingsley Amis as a poet. Amongst the many qualities Pritchard admires in Larkin is his mastery of formal verse, and it is therefore surprising that Pritchard cannot see the same qualities in John Ashbery who is, predictably enough, challenged for his want of specific referents, but less plausibly rebuked for his enormous productivity which might have been usefully checked, according to Pritchard, if Ashbery had been willing to work more with 'rhyme and traditional stanza' forms. For a reviewer of poetry and books about poetry whose career spans that of Ashbery's, this is a curiously ill-informed reading of one whose intimacy with the long traditions of European and American poetry and the varieties of verse forms is everywhere apparent.

Jerome Rothenberg and Pierre Joris give us the first volume – itself a massive 800-page compilation – of their anthology *Poems for the Millennium*, this covering 'From Fin-de-Siècle to Negritude', the term coined by the poet Aimé Césaire in 1939 and thereafter used to define the Caribbean repudiation of colonial models of literature and the visual arts. This is a big bold anthology which has as its ambitious programme the response of poets and painters to the post-Enlightenment situation of the human, specifically the tension between romantic radicalism and its insistence on the 'rights' of man against the growth of modern nation-states and their institutionalized power structures. It therefore opens with a section called 'Forerunners', nineteenth-century radical voices whose work has proved so instigatory in this century, from William Blake through Baudelaire, Whitman and others to Stéphane Mallarmé. Thereafter the principles of selection are international in character and emphasize explorations in language and form, the 'intersections' between poetry and art, Surrealism and its engagement with dream and vision, the return to poetry as a performative kind, aural and visual experiments in the typographical presentation of art and poetry, ethnopoetics, and the ever mobile relationship between the ideologies of art and politics. The real pleasure of this anthology is to be found in its international inclusiveness, so that the versions of modernism it implicity exhibits are mediated through the iconoclastic interventions of Cubism, Dada, Futurism, Surrealism, Abstractionism and so on. All this provides for a splendidly eclectic gathering of voices where familiar figures such as Yeats, Rilke and Stevens share these pages with Akhmatova, Montale, Lorca, Neruda, Kusano Shimpei and others, a rich gallery of exhibits. The editors' call on ethnic voices is equally expansive, giving not mere representativeness but the occasions where Eurocentric art is confronted by the challenges of writings from other cultures and languages. The sense of the millennial invoked by the title relates to the history of much that has made our human consciousness what it is over the past 200 years, and provides therefore an appropriate sense of summation as we near the end of this troubled century.

In *Erotic Reckonings: Mastery and Apprenticeship in the Work of Poets and Lovers*, Thomas Simmons investigates the mentor–apprenticeship relationship between three pairs of poets, Ezra Pound and H.D., Yvor Winters and Janet Lewis, and Louise Bogan and Theodore Roethke. Simmons is interested in the 'erotic tension' inherent in the relationship between mentor and apprentice as it impinges upon the conflict between the mentor's 'allegiance to a tradition and allegiance to the personhood of the apprentice', which is a delicate way of expressing the difficulties to be faced in undertaking this creative-erotic role of teacher-lover, even where the relationship is sexually unconsummated, as with Pound and H.D., minimally sustained between Roethke and Bogan, or developed through marriage in the case of Winters and Lewis. It is a little odd at this stage in time to encounter a version of Pound and H.D. in these terms, given the contemporary status of H.D. as an independent modernist, but Simmons's versions of the other pairs is more rewarding, especially his reading of the late influence of Bogan on Roethke. This intelligent and scrupulously courteous study of difficult relationships is highly recommended.

Rafael Pérez-Torres's study of *Movements in Chicano Poetry\Against Myths, Against Margins* begins with a modest denial that this book attempts to sketch the landscape of contemporary Chicano poetry, but it none the less provides an illuminating view of that landscape to the outsider. Torres's way of working is to situate his reading of this poetry within the traditions of Chicano culture and through the discourses of postcoloniality and postmodernism so that this is as much a work of cultural history as literary history in his analysis of the conditions of production of this 'marginal' literature. This is clearly a major study, essential reading for Americanists of all persuasions.

Helen Vendler's *The Given and the Made: Recent American Poets*, based on the 1993 T. S. Eliot Memorial Lectures at the University of Kent, comprises 'Robert Lowell and History', 'John Berryman: Freudian Cartoons', 'Rita Dove: Identity Markers', 'Jorie Graham: The Nameless and the Material'. In pursuance of her topic, 'the possibilities for lyric in America after the Second World War', Vendler identifies an inescapable existential '*donnee* which the poet could not avoid treating' and considers how 'he or she found symbolic equivalents for it'. Thus, in one phase, Lowell's sense of public history becomes informed by the free associations of the psychiatric couch, by minor characters such as 'The night attendant, a B.U. sophomore', whereas Berryman's 'Freudian vaudeville' enacts the dialectic of white and black America. Dove 'composes both with and against racial identity'; out of the given of Graham's trilinguism is made an art more 'diaphanous' than that of any other of her contemporaries. The distinction of these essays, as always with Vendler, lies in the readiness to assist with pertinent information, to select winningly for detailed analysis as in the schema of 'Aircraft' from Dove's *Thomas and Beulah*, to trace nuances of language with minute discrimination as in the analysis of Berryman's 'Henry-dialect', and to give the reader the opportunity to become 'the true speaker of the lyric'. No more could be said of any critic.

This year Vendler also published *Soul Says: On Recent Poetry*, a collection of 21 essays including ten of her reviews from *The New Yorker* and three from *The New York Review of Books*. American poets discussed include John Ashbery, Gary Snyder, Dave Smith, Rita Dove, Adrienne Rich, Jorie Graham, James Schuyler, A. R. Ammons, Frank Bidart, Louise Glück and James Merrill. Assessments range from the down-to-earth comparison of Graham and Rich to the attuned meditation on Ashbery's *Flow Chart*. There is help for weary examination question-setters, too, in the thought-provoking one-liners: 'for all her stylistic appearance of realism, then, Rich is a moral allegorist'. A version of the concluding essay, 'Fin-de siècle Poetry: Jorie Graham', also appears in *Fins de Siècle* (ed. Elaine Scarry). Vendler suggests that Graham, 'screen-mobile rather than painting-static', preoccupied with history, is the authentic mode of being ' "deep into the lateness now" '. Once again, Vendler has written eloquently and persuasively on the lyric voice. To quote her own words: 'It is through poets such as those I reflect on here that the coming centuries will be able to know, as Stevens put it, "what we felt at what we saw".'

(b) Individual Authors

Susan M. Schultz, editor of *The Tribe of John: Ashbery and Contemporary Poetry*, surveying the development of the Ashbery industry, argues that he has not yet been situated in 'our time' and declares that the aim of her contributors is to focus on 'Ashbery's work as context more than on his work as text'. The four accomplished and experienced critics who comprise the first section, 'New Readings', Jonathan Morse, Charles Altieri, Fred Moramarco and Bonnie Costello, do not, happily, avoid texts but press for a lyric potentiality and romantic configurations beyond postmodern indeterminacy. The essays in the second and third sections consider either Ashbery's influence on individual poets (in some cases, the writer of the essay) or his broader cultural impingement. John Ernest compares Ashbery with William Bronk, James McCorkle links him with Ann Lauterbach, and John Shoptaw's massively serious essay, 'The Music of Construction', analyses the relational structures, the polyphonic dimensions of Ashbery and Charles Bernstein's experiments in form (a Bernstein essay poem stands as an Afterword to the collection). Stephen Paul Miller periodizes 'Self Portrait in a Convex Mirror' by an analogy with Watergate, and Andrew Ross contextualizes *The Tennis Court Oath*. John Koethe's essay, 'The Absence of a Noble Presence', remains provocatively central: he argues that the Ashbery influence has constituted the generic contemporary poem characterized by acquiescence in indeterminacy, a conception of poetry antithetical to Ashbery's fundamental impulse to portray 'subjectivity's contestation of its objective setting in a world which has no place for it'. The perspectives of scholars and poet-critics in this collection engage in stimulating and sophisticated debate. Articles on Ashbery this year include Joshua Clover's 'In the Act: John Ashbery's *And the Stars Were Shining*' (*IowaR* 25.i.177–82); Catherine Imbriglio's ' "Our Days Put on Such Reticence": The Rhetoric of the Closet in John Ashbery's *Some Trees*' (*ConL* 36.249–88); Jody Norton's ' "Whispers Out of Time": The Syntax of Being in the Poetry of John Ashbery' (*TCL* 41.281–305); and Bin Ramke's 'How French Is It? Recent Translations and Poems by John Ashbery' (*DQ* 29.118–24).

Whilst Ambrose Bierce is represented in anthologies of classic American short stories, it is less customary to think of him as a poet, but this year sees a selection of his *Poems* (ed. M. E. Grenander). That Bierce took himself seriously in this medium is evident from his gathering of his poems for the 1909–12 12-volume edition of his *Collected Works*, and the poems and essays in this selection are taken from this source, with the addition of some few uncollected poems. Grenander makes claims for the complexity of Bierce's theory of poetry though these seem rather exaggerated on the evidence of his essays on 'Poetry and Verse' and 'Thought and Feeling'. None the less, it is good to have this handsomely presented selection of a neglected area of his writing, and there is a special nugget of interest in the letters reprinted herein about Bierce's response to being sent a copy of Pound's 'The Ballad of the Goodly Fere' by Homer Pound, and his capable defence of this early example of Pound's work.

A special issue of the *WSJour* on Stevens and Elizabeth Bishop, reviewed below, contains most of the journal articles on Bishop this year. In addition, there is James Longenbach on 'Elizabeth Bishop's Social Conscience' (*ELH* 62.467–86), Jeffrey Powers-Beck's ' "Time to Plant Tears": Elizabeth Bishop's Seminary of Tears' (*SoAR*, 60.iv.69–87) on Bishop and George Herbert, Judith P. Saunders on ' "Large Bad Picture" and "The Rime of the Ancient Mariner": A Note on Elizabeth Bishop's Modernist Aesthetics' (*ANQ* 8.iii.17–22), and Thomas Travisano's 'The Elizabeth Bishop Phenomena' (*NLH* 26.iv.903–30) on the history of Bishop's reputation.

Alan Williamson writes on Hart Crane's 'The Broken Tower' in 'A Valediction on Difficulty' (*APR* 24.v.51–5); the Fall issue of *RCF* (ed. Douglas Gunn) was devoted to Robert Creeley's fiction but includes an interview by Bruce Comens with Creeley (15.iii.82–94), and Charles Bernstein on the poetry in 'Creeley's Eye and the Fiction of the Self' (137–40).

Publications on H.D. include Raffaella Baccolini's *Tradition Identity Desire: Revisionist Strategies in H.D.'s Late Poetry* (University of Bologna), not seen for review, and the Spring–Fall issue of *Sagetrieb* devoted to her with contributions by Robert G. Babcock on H.D., Pound, translations and the Greek Anthology (14.i–ii.202–16), Susan Stanford Friedman on the discovery of a draft manuscript of 'Helen' (7–11), Eileen Gregory on H.D.'s working notebooks for *Helen in Egypt* (83–109), George Hart on memory and forgetting in *Helen in Egypt* (161–77), and two pieces on *Trilogy*, Scott Boehnen on war and the language of fantasy (179–200) and Lawrence H. McCauley on her use of pun in the *Trilogy*. Charlotte Mandel has an essay on *Helen in Egypt* and *The Sleeping Beauty* (*CIRev* 9.i–ii.155–9), and Burton Hatlen writes on H.D.'s imagist poetics in *Sea Garden* (*Paideuma* 24.ii–iii.107–30). Grace Cavalieri conducts an interview with Rita Dove (*APR* 24.ii.11–15), and Emily Walker Cook writes on gender roles and gender symbolism in Dove's *Thomas and Beulah* (*CLAJ* 38.iii.322–30).

Work on Robert Frost includes *His 'Incalculable Influence on Others': Essays on Robert Frost in Our Time* (ed. Earl J. Wilcox) which includes contributions by Dorothy Judd Hall on Frost, Wilbur and William Jay Smith; Peter Stitt on Frost and James Wright; Jonathan N. Barron on Frost, Rita Dove, Richard Wilbur and some sources in Wordsworthian Romanticism; Pamela Davis on Frost and Theodore Roethke; and a view of the treatment of rural life in Frost and Wendell Berry by Edward Ingerbretsen. Journal articles include William Logan on 'The Other Other Frost' (*NewC* 13.x.21–34), Scott Romine's 'Frost on Frost: Marginalia from Lynda Moore's Copies of His Poetry' (*ANQ* 8.iv.35–8), and a study of Frost and George Herbert by James Boyd White (*GHJ* 18.i–ii.59–80). Ann Shifrer writes on 'Iconoclasm in the Poetry of Jorie Graham' (*CLQ* 31.ii.142–53), whilst the relationship between quilting and writing is discussed by Craig Douglas Dworkin in 'Penelope Reworking the Twill: Patchwork, Writing, and Lyn Hejinian's *My Life*' (*ConL* 36.i.58– 81).

Robinson Jeffers: Dimensions of a Poet is edited by one of the stalwarts of Jeffers scholarship, Robert Brophy, and here gives us a gathering of new essays by those who share his enthusiasm for the Californian recluse: Alex Vardamis, Robert Zaller, Terry Beers, Tim Hunt, David J. Rothman and others. Vardamis provides a survey of Jeffers's critical reputation whilst Zaller returns to the theory of Inhumanism and a version of the dialectic between Hegelian and Nietzschean ideas of history. Beers investigates 'Thurso's Landing' for a view of its narrative unity, and Hunt looks at issues of narrative and consciousness in 'Roan Stallion'. Rothman writes on Jeffers's prosody which he argues is neither traditional nor free, but carefully 'inscribed' as though worked in stone, and commends us to become familiar with Jeffers's technical resources if we are to read him accurately. Kirk Glaser reads the domestic conditions of Jeffers's pastorals, and Alan Soldofsky looks at the dialogue between Jeffers and Czeslaw Milosz. This collection reprints an excerpt from William Everson's *The Excesses of God: Robinson Jeffers as a Religious Figure* (*YWES* 69.601), and includes a panel discussion from the American Literature Association conference of 1993 on 'Jeffers and the "Female Archetype" '.

Robinson Jeffers and a Galaxy of Writers: Essays in Honor of William H. Nolte (cd. William B. Thesing) features a number of notable critics of American poetry not normally associated with the Jeffers industry – Charles Altieri, Terence Diggory, Calvin Bedient and Albert Gelpi. The intention of this collection is to establish his importance for other poets such as Robert Frost and Gary Snyder, to place his environmental and ecological interests alongside those of W. S. Merwin, Robert Hass and James Dickey, and to situate his relationship to modernism through comparisons with Lawrence, Yeats and Eliot. The unintentional effect is to suggest that Jeffers needs this credit by association as it were, a way of pushing him into the forefront which he cannot make on his own. An alternative strategy is to propose that Jeffers held apart from mainstream modernism because he could read its inadequacies, and by this route he is seen to anticipate postmodernism. This does not seem a helpful strategy, and the best of the essays in this collection are those which detail Jeffers's value for later poets, such as Patrick Murphy's account of Jeffers and Gary Snyder.

An enthusiastic view of Galway Kinnell comes from Karen Maceira in 'Galway Kinnell: A Voice to Lead Us' (*HC* 32.iv.1–15); and Ann Lauterbach is discussed by Garrett Kalleberg in 'A Form of Duration' (*DQ* 29.iv.98–109): Lauterbach is the subject of Charles Altieri's contribution to the special issue of the *WSJour* on Stevens and Bishop, discussed below.

It is to be hoped that *Robert Lowell and the Sublime* marks a revival in Lowell studies. Henry Hart contends that the early religious, the autobiographical and the political phases of Lowell's career are linked by a

Promethean sense of struggle, that this is, as Randall Jarrell commented, 'one story', an allegorical pattern of battle and quest rooted in the poet's Oedipal relationship with his father and his restless search for a lofty poetics. Hart's research has turned up a good deal about Lowell's early interest in the sublime and he is insightful about the 'phantasmal battlefield', the ongoing psychomachia energizing the political tiltings: 'politics which he didn't know beans about ... he wrote about anyway', to quote one of Lowell's friends, John Thompson. Hart argues that the poems of 'battle and progress were his strongest' and he provides sublime readings of the famous ones, tracing the 'furious denunciations and guilty identifications' of this Ahab/Ishmael going on Caligula. Only age, lithium, Caroline Blackwood's mansion in Ireland, and the postmodern, seem to have slackened the allegory. The well-sustained thesis of this book disregards the confessional perspective and manoeuvres Lowell into the traditional canon in relation to Whitman, Emerson and Stevens; the effect, curiously, is more of an addition to those 'Melodramas of Beset Manhood' which Nina Baym registered, than of a visionary company.

Articles on Lowell include Hilene Flanzbaum on 'Surviving the Marketplace: Robert Lowell and the Sixties' (*NEQ* 68.44–57), Farhad B. Idris on the problematics of family relations in Lowell in ' "When the Clubbed Flintlock Broke My Father's Brain": Oedipal Lowell and the Father' (*ArkR* 4.i.95–117), and Hong-pil Lee on 'Beyond Modernist Poetics: Self-Expression and Its Peculiarity in Life Studies' (*JELL* 41.i.3–23). Commentary on the life and work of James Merrill, from a panel discussion at Washington University in November last year, appears in *SWR*, where the participants include Steven Meyer, Helen Vendler, Rachel Hadasm, Richard Kenney and Steven Yenser (80.ii–iii.159–85), accompanied by Steven Yenser's account of Merrill's achievement in the same issue (186–204). Merrill's *The Changing Light at Sandover* is called on by Jeffrey Donaldson in 'The Company Poets Keep: Allusion, Echo, and the Question of Who is Listening in W. H. Auden and James Merrill' (*ConL* 36.35–57).

Marianne Moore and the Visual Arts: Prismatic Color by Linda Leavell is an excellent study drawing on unpublished archival material to reveal the acuity of Moore's participation in the aesthetic cross-currents of New York. Leavell shows that Moore chose a modernism interactive with the visual arts and that the arts and crafts ideology of her upbringing gave her a democratic openness, a readiness to respond to the modern primitivism of the tapestries of Marguerite Zorach, to the idealism of Stieglitz and to the 'consistent rigor of selection' which she admired in the work of Joseph Cornell. She bought her own copy of the expensive Blue Rider almanac in 1916, responding to its spirituality and to its eclecticism. Leavell is perceptive in relating Moore's experiments in spatial form to the challenges of analytic and synthetic cubism: Moore is 'looking with the painters'. She also argues that Moore's assemblage techniques are oblique portraits indicative of her relish for enigmatic disguise and that her interest in 'transcendent geometry', her images of shelter and protection are analogous to those of Gaston Bachelard. Very convincingly, Leavell shows that the enigma of the assemblages of the long poems such as 'An Octopus' resists canonical expertise and subverts the totalizing powers of form. This elegantly written, scrupulously researched, beautifully judged book, entirely worthy of its subject, consolidates Marianne Moore's position at the centre of American modernism.

Cristanne Miller's *Marianne Moore: Questions of Authority* is one of the best studies of Moore in recent years. Central to this timely account is Miller's argument about Moore's relationship to the concept of poetic authority in which masculine notions of the authority of an 'author' are jettisoned in favour of Moore's negotiation of an interactive role as a reader and listener to her own poems. Miller argues that this egalitarian practice is developed from Moore's belief in 'a communally focused authority' that refuses the 'ego-centric and essentialist assertions of a subjective self while also avoiding the self-erasure which is their opposite and double'. Moore is seen as a questioning agent in her own work who 'inscribes herself in her verse without making herself its subject or assuming she can control (or has originated) its full meaning'. The sources of that 'communally focused authority' are to be found in Moore's active engagement with the political and cultural conditions of her time, and through the importance of her family life. Miller's researches into these areas and their significance for Moore's poetry are extensive and original, as is her account of Moore's complex response to gender issues in relation to the feminism of her time, and to the equally complicated area of Moore's handling of the difficulties of racial equality. In her close reading of the poems, Miller draws on aspects of J. L. Austin's speech-act theory to support her view of Moore's poetic strategies of authorship in which her aesthetic of 'correspondence, conversation, and exchange' establishes an interactive equality of relations between writer and reader to displace the dynamics of power relations Austin reads as conventionally inherent in speech acts. This is an important study of Moore and of the politics of authorship in the age of high modernism.

Robin G. Schulze's admirable *The Web of Friendship: Marianne Moore and Wallace Stevens* is a fascinating record based on archival research of their poetic conversation from the post-First World War years until Stevens's death in 1955. Following the lead of James Longenbach and Alan Filreis, Schulze explores how the two poets were shaped by 'the actual world', especially in the Depression years when both faced ideological pressure to write socially committed poetry. Rejecting Bloomian influence theory and Gilbert and Gubar's gender-essentialist model of poetic relations, Schulze finds their relationship supportive, yet not static. Moore's early response in her review, 'Well Moused Lion', to the brutality and exoticism of *Harmonium* gave way to a detailed recasting of her 'animiles' in which the Stevensian frigate bird emphasizing 'vision rather than service' is an emblem of Moore's own desire in this period to become less effacing: the jerboa (Moore's nickname for herself was 'Rat') sought 'levity with strength', the qualities of the Frigate-pelican. Stevens, in turn, felt that in 'The Steeple-Jack' Moore was able to 'hybridize' her romanticism by 'association with the actual'. By their ésprit, their self-possession, their tensile provisionality, they recognized each other as romantic and kindred spirits: it was Moore who asked Stevens to place 'Final Soliloquy of the Interior Paramour' at the end of his *Selected Poems*. This is an excellent and heartening book, scholarly yet unpretentious and inward with the poetry.

An extensive study of Gary Snyder's nature poetry and his ecological commitments is Won-chung Kim, 'Making Love with Nature: Gary Snyder's Ecological Vision' (*JELL* 41.649–72). Harry Thomas publishes 'A Conversation with Robert Pinsky' (*TriQ* 92.21–37): Jacqueline Shea Murphy writes on violence and the human body in Plath in 'This Holocaust I Walk In' (*BuR* 39.i.104–17), and Patricia Hampl contributes 'The Smile of Accomplishment: Sylvia Plath's Ambition' (*IowaR* 25.i.1–29).

Armageddon politics and the threat of nuclear annihilation of the human race seems an unlikely context for a study of the contiguities and differences between three twentieth-century poets, in this case Pound, Williams and Zukofsky, yet these are the terms Bruce Comens sets for himself in *Apocalypse and After: Modern Strategy and Postmodern Tactics in Pound, Williams, and Zukofsky*. Comens's argument is that an awareness of the threat of universal extinction through nuclear war informs the shift from modern to postmodern poetics, expressed in terms of apocalyptic and post-apocalyptic tendencies, specified here as a critical distinction between strategy and tactics, where strategy is allied to modernism and tactics to postmodernism. While the distinction between strategy and tactics may be germane to military theorists, it seems more than a little stretched in this application, despite the intelligence Comens brings to his commentaries on these three poets. If tactics is a significantly postmodern term, which I doubt, it is further evidence that anything can be adduced as a condition of the postmodern, a term in itself so elusive as to defy categorization in a way which makes sense in considering poets like these three, addicted as they were to the possibilities of the long poem, an addiction implicit with a belief that there would be someone around to read them.

There will be considerable sympathy with Michael Coyle's attempt to read Pound primarily as a cultural critic, rather than a poet and literary critic interested in broad cultural issues, and Pound's central engagement with history, economics and politics in the *Cantos* goes a long way towards justifying Coyle's practice in his study *Ezra Pound, Popular Genres, and the Discourse of Culture*. The difficulty here is in the phrase 'Popular Genres', for Pound was nothing if not violently antagonistic to all notions of popular cultural forms, as in his early denial of the value of cinema as a cultural medium, his general disinterest in prose fiction, other than that by the 'masters' he was prepared to acknowledge, Flaubert, James and Joyce, and his aversion to what we would now call 'classical music', once separated from its role as an accompaniment to the human voice, a separation Pound persistently lamented. A good deal of Coyle's argument for the 'multicultural' practice of the *Cantos* is organized contra Eliot, who is seen as narrowly literary in his concerns, surely a misreading of Eliot's socio-religious preoccupations from the mid-thirties onwards. In addition, Coyle's focus on those areas of the *Cantos* where he argues that this broad multicultural programme can be found dwells on 'The Adams Cantos', the 'Rock Drill Cantos' and 'Thrones', sections of the poem only marginally less rebarbative to populist notions of the literary and the cultural than the 'Chinese History Cantos'. This bold study is not without interest but the concept of populism, cultural or other, seems desperately inappropriate to a study of Pound, whose embrace of the peasant and the commoner is always briefly performed in moments of lyric intensity in other places in the *Cantos* than those Coyle dwells on.

Modernism's aestheticizing of the political and politicizing of the aesthetic is examined through the case of Pound in Mary Ellis Gibson's *Epic Reinvented: Ezra Pound and the Victorians*. She reads Pound's Victorian inheritance as rooted in the shared belief of Carlyle, Ruskin and Morris in the connections between the health of art and the health of society, paying special attention to Pound's debt to Browning, a forerunner who like his successor 'was as much a picker of historical bones as a prophet'. For these Victorian predecessors 'the belief in historical order or aesthetic unity was countered by the skepticism and the ironies of existential historicism', conditions which affect Pound's attempt at a 'postromantic epic' where the questions of art and social order 'led directly to the problem of Pound's politics'. Gibson offers her reading of this influence not as a 'Bloomian family romance' but as a scrutiny of Pound's cultural situation and his ambition to make a case for poetry in the modern world and she reads him through two dominant metaphors, 'the poet as pedagogue or canon builder and the poet as ragpicker'. Her early chapters address genre, history and form in *The Cantos*, and she then moves to a critique of the contemporary controversy that links modernism, fascism and poststructuralist theory as she challenges the tendency to celebrate *The Cantos* as a metonymic epic. Gibson works by metaphor rather than metonymy, as in her illuminating image of the Renaissance *condottiere* Sigismundo Malatesta 'horsed' on a 'bronzed pedestal' facing a sculpted Aphrodite on her 'pedestal at Terracina looking at him with blind marble eyes', an image which makes concrete her view of the conflict at the heart of Pound's created world 'caught between violence and love, between power and art'. I think no better account of Pound and the Victorians exists.

An exposition of Pound's fiscal theories, *The Gold Thread\Ezra Pound's Principles of Good Government & Sound Money* by Robert Luongo argues for the clarity of Pound's vision of the relationship between monetary policy and good government: the animus in this short study, as in the *Cantos*, is directed at those national and international financial cartels who exploit usurious interest rates for their own benefit against the common good of the people. This is a passionately reverential view of Pound, rancorous towards those of his critics who deny the unity of the *Cantos* and the wisdom of his economic and social theories. This is an elegantly produced small press publication available in Britain from Portobello Books, London. Michael Alexander and James McGonigal have edited a collection of essays, *Sons of Ezra: British Poets and Ezra Pound* (Rodopi), not seen for review, which includes essays by notable British Poundians along with Michael Alexander, William Cookson, Donald Davie and Peter Russell, and the poets Douglas Dunn, Roy Fisher and Charles Tomlinson. The same publishers have issued Peter Davidson's *Ezra Pound and Roman Poetry: A Preliminary Survey*. In addition, Daniel Tiffany's *Radio Corpse: Imagism and the Cryptaesthetic of Ezra Pound* appeared from HarvardUP.

Journal articles on Pound include Robert von Hallberg's expansive study 'Libertarian Imagism' (*Modernism/Modernity* 2.ii.63–79) which disputes the consensus view notably formulated by Donald Davie of the 'clear and unbroken' development from imagism in poetry to fascism in politics. Against this, Hallberg asks whether Imagism 'was not libertarian or antisocialist rather than protofascist in its political significance', a question he pursues through Pound's engagement with Dora Marsden and *The New Freewoman* – later *The Egoist*, and the 'antistatist' politics of their mutual interests. The Fall/Winter issue of *Paideuma* includes Melita Schaum's discussion of the relationship between Pound and the American photographer Alvin Langdon Coburn (24.i–ii.79–106), for whom Pound wrote an introduction to his one-man exhibition in London in 1917, and who encouraged Coburn to try his hand at abstract photography through his invention of the 'Vortoscope', a triangulation of mirrors through which Coburn took his images: this short-lived experiment did produce some stunning portraits of Pound, where face, beard and posture are all clearly identifiable within the disfracted planes of the photograph. Larry D. Griffin gives a reading of the sources in *Noh* drama of Pound's 'Fourth Canto' (*CCTEP* 55.84–94), and Peter Nicholls also turns to the impact of *Noh* on Pound in 'An Experiment with Time: Ezra Pound and the Example of Japanese *Noh*' (*MLR* 90.1–13).

Articles on Adrienne Rich include Peter Erickson's 'Singing America: From Walt Whitman to Adrienne Rich' (*KR* 17.103–19), Jeanne Perreault's ' "Signified by Pain": Adrienne Rich's Body Tracks' (*ABSt* 10.ii.87–103), Colette Peters on ' "Whatever Happens, This is": Lesbian Speech–Act Theory and Adrienne Rich's "Twenty-One Love Poems" ' (*ESC* 21.189–205), and Jeffrey A. Walker on 'Remapping Freudian America: Adrienne Rich and the Adult Son' (*NDQ* 63.iii.76–93). Cary Nelson and Jefferson Hendricks continue their recovery of the work of Edwin Rolfe with a paperback selection of his poems, *Edwin Rolfe: Trees Became Torches: Selected Poems* (UIllP).

There have been two books on Stevens designed to introduce him to the novice reader, Frank Kermode's intellectually elegant study of 1960 in the British 'Writers and Critics' series and Robert Rehder's *The Poetry of Wallace Stevens* of 1988. To this list we must now add Janet McCann's *Wallace Stevens Revisited: The Celestial Possible*, published under Twayne's imprint and designed for the uninstructed reader. The virtue of McCann's account is in her clearly stated conviction that Stevens's work undergoes a variety of developments which move inexorably towards his late conversion to Roman Catholicism: but this creates a prohibitive difficulty for those who do not share her belief that the trajectory of Stevens's work leads to this affirmation of conventional faith at the end of his life, and raises the question whether such a book should be recommended to beginners. This aspect of McCann's study would matter less if she had not allowed it to affect her reading of particular poems where she finds signs of this latent religiosity few specialist readers of Stevens would concur with. This apart, McCann's book will certainly help the uninitiated reader through the complexities of the poems, and many readers will be grateful for her agile descriptions of his individual collections.

In view of Wallace Stevens's essay 'The Noble Rider and the Sound of Words', it is perhaps surprising that it has taken so long for someone to centre on the implied significance of sound as a crucial aspect of the construction of his poetry. This is Anca Rosu's subject in her innovative study *The Metaphysics of Sound in Wallace Stevens*, where she is committed to the view that Stevens uses sound in his poems as an alternative source of meaning to the logocentric epistemology inscribed in the traditions of Western philosophy. Rosu argues her case from two perspectives, one philosophical, the other practical, though these are inevitably connected. She challenges the orthodoxy of Stevens's Heideggerian inflections and centres him in the American pragmatist tradition on the basis of the importance of William James and George Santayana to the philosophical climate inherited by Stevens in his Harvard years, and submits a good many of the poems to very close analysis for their sonic effects as a way of uncovering his play with meaning against conventional notions of the representativeness of language. This is an engaging study, instructive in the way it illuminates the devices of repetition, choricism and the extensive deployment of aural registers in the poems, yet irritating in the way Rosu repeatedly drifts away from her central concerns, and she is sometimes excessively complicated and demanding in the minute particulars of her reading of individual poems, as in the prolonged account of 'The Comedian as the Letter C', which merits a chapter to itself. But this is an absorbing study, fit to delight and vex Stevens's readers.

The editor of the *WSJour*, John N. Serio, with B. J. Leggett, has gathered a set of essays by many of the current leading Stevens scholars under the title *Teaching Wallace Stevens: Practical Essays*. This collection is a pedagogical demonstration of how to teach Stevens from a wide variety of critical perspectives; its 24 original essays include: Jacqueline Vaught Brogan on the playful and the 'display of theory'; Joseph Carroll on Stevens as a late Romantic; Eleanor Cook on intellect and spontaneity; Margaret Dickie on teaching Stevens within the frame of New Criticism; Charles Doyle on Stevens and the relations between poetry and painting; George S. Lensing on the poet's prosody; A. Walton Litz on Stevens and his modernist peers; Alison Reike on the devices of estrangement; Anca Rosu on sound imagery and metaphysics in Stevens; Robin Gail Schulze on Stevens and Marianne Moore; Lisa M. Steinman on Stevens and Williams; and Helen Vendler on teaching the commonly anthologized poems. A further study of Stevens appeared this year which we have not had for review, Theodore Sampson's *Beyond Music: The Poetics of Wallace Stevens* (B. Giannicos & Co, Athens, Greece).

Joseph Harrington writes on 'Wallace Stevens and the Poetics of National Insurance' (*AL* 67.95–114) where he disputes the eighties' view that alleges Stevens's indifference to political issues and circumstances, and the more recent endeavours of James Longenbach and others to read his vagueness on these matters as a conscious stand for imaginative freedom. Harrington argues that neither of these approaches will do and provides a version of Stevens as a political liberal protective of the ancient rights to privacy and property, and argues that this position provides ways of reading the modernist view of the relationship of literature to political discourse. Excluding the contributions to *WSJour*, other journal articles on Stevens include Anne Stevenson's 'The Way You Say the World Is What You Get' (*MQR* 34.55–73) and Rob Wilson's 'Meditation as Symbolic Action: Wallace Stevens and Christian Interiority' (*Poetica* 42.105–22).

The Spring issue of *WSJour* (19.i) opens with an interesting, elegantly written essay, ' "The Lawyer in the Poet": Stevens' Use of Legal Terminology' (3–18), by an attorney-at-law, Elizabeth Rosen, which considers the legal resonance of terms such as *res* and *transcript* and the concept of supreme fiction as a version of legal fiction in allowing 'the law to speak poetically'. Richard A. Kaye's ' "Intangible Arrows": Stevens, St. Sebastian, and the Search for the Real' (19–35) discusses the evocation of the saint in 'Holiday in Reality' in relation to pictorial iconography. A cognitive version of the sublime with some postmodern slippage is proposed in Paul Endo's 'Stevens and the Two Sublimes': the sublime affect occurs between the 'emergent' (36–50) that is the instant 'flick' of self-conception, and the 'dialectical' more critical recognition of its powers. Thomas F. Bertonneau, in a very lengthy essay, proposes 'The Idea of Order at Key West' as an anthropological meditation on immolation rituals (51–70). David M. Linebarger reads 'The

Comedian as the Letter C' as an attempt to create an analogy to Stravinsky's ballet, *Petrushka* (1911) (71–87). Apart from the first essay, the contributors, rather like Crispin, seem assailed by the 'torment of fastidious thought'.

The Fall issue of *WSJour* is a special on 'Stevens and Elizabeth Bishop' with a very distinguished list of contributors. Margaret Dickie, in her introduction, notes how the collection shifts the emphasis from the Stevens Bloom imagined to a Stevens keenly attached to the actual world. She emphasizes, too, how much is to be gained in understanding twentieth-century poetry by following through a line of development from Stevens to Bishop and onward to Lauterbach, Jordan, Strand and Ashbery. George S. Lensing argues that Bishop learned the value of precise observation from Stevens; Celeste Goodridge focuses on the Florida poems as an analogue for Bishop's own psychic complexity. Albert Gelpi sets Stevens, the high modernist, against the postmodernist Bishop closer to Ashbery, whereas Thomas Gardner, in contrast, argues that the more humanist Bishop and the more language-orientated Ashbery offer different routes out of Stevens. Barbara Page's urbane 'Elizabeth Bishop and Postmodernism' places Bishop on the cusp of the postmodern. In 'Narrative Secrets, Lyric Openings', Bonnie Costello shows how Stevens evolves and subverts narrative in his anecdote poems, whereas Bishop in 'The Prodigal' 'suspends the narrative logic of its original'. Charles Altieri argues that Bishop's style is analogical, whereas Stevens's more dialectical mode is developed by Ann Lauterbach. Alicia Ostriker, responding to Vernon Shetley's *After the Death of Poetry* (see *YWES* 75.599), relates Bishop's erotic subtexts to the poetry of Sharon Olds: however, Stevens 'does not sail in ... the main channel of erotic poetic discourse'. Jacqueline Vaught Brogan, the Guest Editor, writes on the 1945 Cummington Press edition of *Esthétique du Mal* (four of the illustrations are reproduced) and links Stevens's war poetry to that of Bishop, Rich and Jordan. Thomas Travisano, in a genial essay on the affinities of the two poets, draws attention to their contemporaneity, noting that 'The Imaginary Iceberg', published in the April/June 1935 issue of *Directions*, actually preceded 'The Poems of Our Climate' (1938). This is a very harmonious and gracious collection which deserves a larger circulation; in its context, Stevens's comment, 'I know Miss Bishop's work. She lives in Key West', seems, indeed, 'enough'.

Work on the poetry of Robert Penn Warren includes a book we have not had for review, Robert S. Keppelman's *Robert Penn Warren's Modernist Spirituality* (UMissP), and three articles in the Winter issue of *MissQ* (48.i), Mark D. Miller's 'Faith in Good Works: The Salvation of Robert Penn Warren' (57–71); James A. Perkins on 'Racism and the Personal Past in Robert Penn Warren' (73–81); and Paul Randolph Runyon's 'Repeating the "Implacable Moonstone" in *Thirty-six Poems*' (39–56). Also published this year was Rodney Stenning Edgecombe's *A Reader's Guide to the Poetry of Richard Wilbur* (UAlaP).

It seems almost inevitable that in the years soon after the completion of A. Walton Litz and Christopher MacGowan's extensive labours on their edition of *William Carlos Williams: The Collected Poems* (*YWES* 68.631–2) followed by *Paterson* (*YWES* 73.609), someone would come along to privilege the earliest collections, the *Collected Poems 1921–31* published in 1934, and *The Complete Collected Poems 1906–1938*, of 1938. This is Robert J. Cirasa's endeavour in *The Lost Works of William Carlos Williams*, where he argues that the earliest two collections were unified into 'lyrical sequences' in Williams's search to add 'profundity' to his corpus, and thus to rescue his work from the general critical view that he was no more than a 'miniaturist', as Kenneth Burke put it, the 'master of the glimpse ... the minute fixating of a mood, an horizon, a contrast'. Cirasa contends that the constructive organization of lyrical sequentiality in the early collections was significantly dispersed in Williams's later attempts to collect his work to the detriment of his reputation, an argument tested here by close scrutiny of all the collections prior to MacGowan's.

In *The Revolution in the Visual Arts and the Poetry of William Carlos Williams*, Peter Halter adds significantly to the corpus of studies on Williams's long and fertile response to the the art of painting. Halter argues that there is a correspondence between Williams's experimental poetics and the disruptions of conventional linear perspective and the fracturing of mimetic representations in Cubism and the other early twentieth-century forms of abstract art. This study therefore has much to show us of Williams's generative response to the Armory Show of 1913 and of his friendship with certain American painters including Charles Demuth, to whom Williams dedicated *Spring and All*, Charles Sheeler, Marsden Harley and Alred Stieglitz whose '291' gallery on Fifth Avenue was a meeting ground for the young avant-garde of the day, a show-place for the best contemporary photographers, and a site where drawings and sculptures by Brancusi, Matisse, Picasso and others could be seen. Halter provides a well-documented reading of Williams's early poems inspired by particular paintings and shows how Williams sought to encourage an interactive relationship between reader and poem on the basis of the dynamic visual aesthetics he found in the innovative techniques of contemporary visual art.

A revisionary version of the significance of Williams's familial inheritance is given in Julio Marzan's *The Spanish American Roots of William Carlos Williams*, an extensive study of the poet's Caribbean background mediated through his mother Elena, and his father, whose native Englishness was displaced, according to Marzan, by the Puerto Rican intellectual and literary culture habitual to him through his life in the islands. This is the fullest account we have yet had of the influence of Spanish American mores on Williams's writing and his image of himself as a poet committed to particularly American ideas of place and occasion, part of whose creative resources were deliberately concealed by the poet himself, a concealment colluded with by many of his critics who have regularly distanced these matters to the sidelines, or reduced them to the psychobiographical distinction between 'Bill' and 'Carlos' in the poet's make-up. Marzan's book makes a substantial case for reconfiguring the importance of Williams's 'ethnic' inheritance. Two other studies published this year were not received for review, T. Hugh Crawford's *Modernism, Medicine, & William Carlos Williams* (UOklaP), and Maurice Daniel's *The Writings of William Carlos Williams: Publicity for the Self* (UMissP).

The Spring issue of *WCWR* opens with an acute analysis of Williams's improvisational method in *Spring and All* by John Palatella in 'But if it Ends The Start is Begun: *Spring and All*, Americanism, and Postwar Apocalypse' (1–21) where Williams's 'idealization of relations' in the equation of the female body with nature is seen as historically contingent upon the literary and political conditions out of which the improvisations of *Spring and All* were made. Jessica Levine's 'Spatial Rhythm and Poetic Invention in William Carlos Williams's "Sunday in the Park" ' (23–31) takes this moment from the second book of *Paterson* to argue that his invention of the triadic stanza and the 'variable foot' is 'rooted in a conception of space, both external and internal or biological, that is constantly moving in a rhythmic fashion'. Thomas F. Bertonneau takes an anthropoetic approach to *Paterson* in 'The Sign of Knowledge in Our Time: Violence, Man, and Language in *Paterson*, Book 1' (33–51) to argue that the revelatory origin of the poem is ethical in kind, concerned with 'the relation of violence to language, and of language to a redemption from violence' as the community seeks to protect its conditions from the human urge to violence that always threatens its existence. In the Fall issue, Lorna J. Smedman's 'Skeleton in the Closet: Williams's Debt to Gertrude Stein' (21–35) traces the history of the significant effect Stein had on Williams, most especially in his understanding of her 'accomplishment in getting words back clean, clean of symbolic and associational baggage'. Elizabeth Gregory in 'Figures of Williams's Modernist Ambivalence: Poetic Lineage and Lesbians in *Paterson*' (37–58) gives an assured reading of Williams's ambivalent relativism in relation to the spectres of creative originality and authority and locates this ambivalence in his handling of gender in *Paterson*, 'particularly in relation to his choice of poetic heirs'.

The central feature of writing on Zukofsky is Marjorie Perloff's ' "Barbed-Wire Entanglements": The "New American Poetry," 1930–1932' (*Modernism/Modernity* 2.i.145–75), a brilliant account of the impact of the 'Objectivist' number of Poetry of February 1931, guest-edited by Zukofsky, and the little magazine *Pagany* (1930–32), named by its editor Richard Johns in homage to William Carlos Williams's *A Voyage to Pagany*. Through an analysis of some contributions by Williams, Zukofsky and Stein to *Pagany* Perloff instructs on the complexities of the aesthetic and political alignments of the literary avant-garde in the early 1930s.

2. Fiction 1900–1945

The implication of the concepts of 'space' and 'place' on narrative has become an increasingly popular subject of critical interest, to which Diane Dufva Quantic's comparative study of the literature and cultural geography of the Great Plains in *The Nature of the Place* is an original and valuable contribution. Quantic focuses on the effect of place on perspective, arguing that natural features of landscape have psychologically significant effects because they determine how far and what one can see. Studying myths of settlement in Great Plains fiction, particularly the homesteaders' unrealized ideal that the mid-Western desert plains could be cultivated as the Edenic garden of the industrializing East, she compares the unfamiliar land itself with the mythic preconceptions of the settlers and analyses the community that evolved from this combination. The flatlands of the stark and empty plains posed a particular problem of response for settlers, as they bore no reference to any previously known and remembered landscape. They were a blank 'space' that needed to be created as a 'place' by the settlement of the plains pioneers. To support her argument for a common mythic framework and collective sociocultural experience of the region of the plains and prairies, Quantic offers stimulating and sensitive readings encompassing a quite phenomenal variety of texts, in both fictional and autobiographical genres, by both male and female writers, and from the earliest days of settlement to the present day. Although focusing on the writings of Willa Cather, O. E. Rølvaag, Margaret Laurence, Wright Morris and Laura Ingalls Wilder, she never loses sight of the position of these writers within their historical context, arguing that they write within conceptual frameworks in which different myths compete for dominance, in tension with each other and thus undercutting any one definitive history of the Great Plains. Taking what is ultimately a position of socio-geographic determinism, *The Nature of the Place* assesses the interrelation of the meanings of space and place, of place and society, and of place and language, to suggest that soil, climate and landscape influence the character and quality of life on the plains. Great Plains fiction illustrates the function of space and place in the formation of language, and manifests the transformation of a people by a landscape and the emotional response it evokes rather than vice versa.

Madeleine B. Stern continues the unveiling of the secret literary life of Louisa May Alcott with three new collections: *The Feminist Alcott, Louisa May Alcott Unmasked: Collected Thrillers* and (with Joel Myerson and Daniel Shealy) *The Selected Letters of Louisa M. Alcott*. The first is a selection of four of Alcott's thrillers, in which conventional gender roles are upturned and passionate, violent and powerful heroines triumphantly gain power over male protagonists. Three of these women resemble the femme fatale rather than the feminist, however. 'Pauline's Passion and Punishment', which won a hundred dollars as a prize story for *Frank Leslie's Illustrated Newspaper*, was Alcott's first success as a sensation writer and tells of the powerful desire for revenge in a deserted woman and the life of punishment that results from her destructiveness. The protagonist of 'V.V.: or, Plots and Counterplots' is a mercenary, manipulating and murderous femme fatale who yet escapes final punishment for her actions through suicide. In 'Behind a Mask: or, A Woman's Power', the protagonist Jean Muir combines feminism and deceit, defying the social conventions that would label her a spinster and capturing a lord as her prize only by disguising herself as a conventionally meek and youthful governess. 'Taming a Tartar' is perhaps the most overtly feminist of the tales, in which an independent and self-assertive young teacher struggles for and wins sexual mastery in her relationship with a chauvinistic Russian prince. *Louisa May Alcott Unmasked* includes all four stories and is a far more comprehensive example of the variety of tone within her sensation fiction, containing all of her anonymous and pseudonymous published work. Registering Alcott's persistent feminist concerns, taken as a whole they also illustrate her versatility in tailoring her writing to particular publications and audiences, whether the rather lurid sensationalism of the *Illustrated Paper* or the more conventional romanticism of Frank Leslie's other publication, the *Lady's Magazine*. Particularly noteworthy are 'A Marble Woman: or, The Mysterious Model', a reworking of the Pygmalian/Galatea myth, and 'A Whisper in the Dark', in which a young girl's mind is manipulated almost to the point of insanity. Stern's informative introduction describes her discovery of Alcott's secret authorial persona and offers brief and provocative commentaries on several stories from which more extensive studies of Alcott's oeuvre will surely emanate. *The Selected Letters* span almost half a century, from

Alcott's childhood to her death, and are filled with information on her development as a professional woman and writer. From the letters of her twenties, in which she describes the excitement of her life in Boston, the beginning of her tutoring and writing and her growing fanaticism for the theatre, to those of her later years as a successful novelist and feminist campaigner, Alcott's relationship with her family, her publishers, her public and her art itself are extensively recorded. Alcott's fame as a writer of children's literature was only one aspect of her literary identity, and Stern's discovery of her thrillers has illuminated the other. Her letters, however, express the writer herself in what Stern describes as 'a full-length portrait', indispensable to any study of Alcott's work. In addition to these collections is Elizabeth Lennox Keyser's *Whispers in the Dark*, a welcome extended critical study of Alcott's fiction that covers the range of her literary interests. Organized in two parts, which cover respectively the periods up to and after the publication of *Little Women*, Keyser's analysis focuses on the March family trilogy, the social novel *Work* and the sensation stories 'A Whisper in the Dark', 'A Marble Woman: or, The Mysterious Model' and 'Behind a Mask: or, A Woman's Power' to illustrate the various outlets of Alcott's socio-political concerns. Paying particular attention to the intertextuality and self-reflexivity of Alcott's writings, Keyser argues that she both employed and resisted nineteenth-century gender ideology in her depictions of female experience [D.P].

There are four books on Willa Cather to consider this year and there might be an understandable temptation to conclude that Cather studies are in a particularly healthy state; the quality of the criticism is, however, distinctly uneven. Gary Brienzo's *Willa Cather's Transforming Vision: New France and the American Northeast* explores the importance of the 'American Northeast and the adjacent New France' in her fiction, largely through an extended analysis of *Shadows on the Rock*, though his concluding chapter looks at 'four major later works', *Obscure Destinies*, *Lucy Gayheart*, *Sapphira and the Slave Girl* and the posthumously published *The Old Beauty and Others*. His brief study attempts to locate and understand the 'symbolic significance' of these regions in her fiction and to show how pivotal *Shadows on the Rock* is to her 'growing need of order to make life potentially beautiful and significant' and to an understanding of 'how that artistic ordering could be explained in terms of a domesticity that encompasses diverse social classes and both secular and clerical forces'. His criticism is not of a very sophisticated nature – much of it is descriptive rather than analytical – and the narrowness of his concerns means that his book is of rather limited use for the student of Cather, but we should welcome anything that contributes to the discussion of her later fiction. Evelyn Helmick Hively's *Sacred Fire: Willa Cather's Novel Cycle* is an exercise in myth criticism, postulating, as one aspect of its methodology, 'a cyclical design' that begins with *O Pioneers!* and ends with *Shadows on the Rock* and which 'traces a rise, maturity, and fall of the American West'. Hively is eager to contextualize Cather's fiction in the light of its influences and affinities, with historians, philosophers and mythographers: she reads *O Pioneers!* for its 'primitive attitudes to the natural world and the rituals of the Great Mother', *One of Ours* for its reworking of the Parsifal legend (Claude Wheeler as 'mortal fool'), and in *Death Comes for the Archbishop*, the protagonists, 'although they are Roman Catholic priests, can easily be translated in terms of comparative mythology as the Twin Heroes of Navajo myth who follow the holy trail'. The other novels discussed by Hively are *The Song of the Lark*, *My Antonia*, *A Lost Lady*, *The Professor's House* and *My Mortal Enemy*, key texts in any critical account of Cather's achievement and thus making this study rather more useful to the student than that of Brienzo, though it has to be said that the readings are frequently laboured and formulaic. In *Redefining the American Dream: The Novels of Willa Cather*, Sally Peltier Harvey addresses a theme more conventionally analysed in novelists such as Fitzgerald and Dreiser, namely the myth of success and its relationship to the pervasive, but ill-defined, notion of the American Dream. Cather, she suggests, attempts some accommodation with 'the Dream' instead of an abandonment of it, seeking to refashion it 'without the "ugly crest of materialism" stamped on it'. Success is construed as a matter of individual fulfilment and social progress rather than the acquisition of wealth or status, thus *O Pioneers!* and *My Antonia* celebrate heroines 'who creatively shape and courageously realize their own dreams' outside the conventional terms of material reward'. Such a reading makes Cather's fiction, in the final analysis, optimistic, for Harvey sees her as a writer whose 'vision of America never ceased to recognize an imperfect but evolving dream of personal fulfilment'. Finally, Joseph R. Urgo's *Willa Cather and the Myth of American Migration* is a book that has elicited a good deal of interest among Cather scholars. Urgo sees 'the dialectic between migration and settlement' as an 'informing aspect of New World history' and chides other scholars for failing to recognize that 'the central theme, the overarching myth, the single experience, that defines American culture at its core is migration: unrelenting, incessant, and psychic mobility across spatial, historical, and imaginative planes of existence'. Cather, he suggests, felt neither 'alienated nor detached by displacement but in fact marked intellectual bounty by her own spatial mobility' and thus her work becomes 'a comprehensive resource for the demarcation of an empire of migration in U.S. culture'. In his reading *The Professor's House*, for example, becomes a novel in which Cather asks 'whether the ideas and images that we have packed up to carry with us, our spiritual resources, possess the vitality to ensure our continued well-being within the context of continuous transit, of tremendous change and migration', while *Lucy Gayheart* 'suggests that Lucy's significance is not in her death but in her flight, in the refusal to allow material circumstances to dictate the imagination'. The interpretations here are considerably more informed, and, indeed, subtle, than those in the works on which I have commented above and Urgo is well versed in the recent debates about nation and empire (though, rather perplexingly, he says little about the debates that were contemporaneous with Cather's writing, for example Randolph Bourne's observations on the character and development of a 'trans-national America'), but he seems somewhat insensitive to the anxieties Cather's fiction expresses about the inevitable decline of traditional, inherited cultures, and the ahistorical progressivism he finds in her fiction will not be apparent to every reader. This remains, however, the most important book on Cather to be covered this year.

Rita Barnard's *The Great Depression and the Culture of Abundance: Kenneth Fearing, Nathanael West, and Mass Culture in the 1930s* is at one and the same time an essay in literary criticism and a contribution to what one might call the sociopolitical and economic study of modern American culture, particularly popular culture. In this latter respect it has affinities with Lawrence W. Levine's *Highbrow/Lowbrow: The Emergence of Cultural Hierarchy in America* (*YWES* 69.553) and Andrew Ross's *No Respect: Intellectuals and Popular Culture* (Routledge [1989]) and Barnard draws, to some extent, on the methodologies of both. Adorno and Benjamin also inform her study, notably in her sense that Benjamin's work 'negotiates a space between, on the one hand, his sympathies for the avant-gardist practices of Brecht and the Surrealists, plus his genuine interest in the possibilities of the new media, and, on the other hand, the gloomier more mandarin cultural politics advocated by his friend Adorno (and justified by the dismal political developments around him)'. Fearing and West emerge from her study as writers who were 'deeply troubled by the cultural and political situation in which they lived', but never retreated into a defensive cultural elitism, and both were simultaneously producers and consumers, 'assembly-line writers' during a period 'when the culture industry was standardizing its products and consolidating itself as a vast oligopoly'. Barnard's contextual and theoretical opening chapter is followed by two substantial sections, the first devoted to Fearing, the second to West, that make up the rest of her study and, as a consequence, her discussion of the two writers is detailed and spacious, though, one would have to say, it is frequently uncritical (she suggests, for example, that Fearing's 'Saturday Night' shows the influence of Eliot's 'Rhapsody on a Windy Night' but a comparison of the two poems only serves to confirm how much more measured, and economical, is Eliot's achievement). Her reading of West emphasizes the degree to which, for all 'his disdain for mass culture', his fiction 'refuses to celebrate high culture as a repository of value and recognizes that a critique of the times must take a cue from the commercial language of the times', a statement that challenges us, but finally can't persuade us, to think of West as more a writer of his age than, say, Steinbeck or Thomas Wolfe. But for all my sense that Barnard's materials don't justify her conclusions this remains an important book about a decade in American culture that is all too frequently neglected or naively construed through its proletarian and quasi-Marxist sentiments; above all it shouldn't be ignored by those interested in Fearing and West.

The seemingly exponential growth of the criticism of William Faulkner shows little sign of abating and four books have come to my attention this year, three of them from last year. Richard Gray's *The Life of William Faulkner: A Critical Biography* is 'an attempt to understand Faulkner's novels in terms of his life, his place and his times'. As a biography Gray's book has little to add to what we already know from biographers such as Joseph L. Blotner and Frederick R. Karl, and both Blotner and Karl are more informative about the day-to-day details of Faulkner's life. But Gray is not to be judged in this way: his book, we might say, is a more 'inward' kind of biography in which what he calls 'the old ineradicable rhythm ... the fundamental passions and obsessions that fired writer and culture into life' occupies the centre ground. Gray is especially attentive to modernist 'constructions' of Faulkner, notably to Bakhtinian ideas of voice and polyphony (he is very good on the affinities between Faulkner and Dostoevsky, though he says nothing about the obvious affinities between Conrad and Faulkner which can be similarly construed) and he suggests that if we are ever to understand him properly, we need to situate him 'among the voices that circled and inhabited him ... to perceive his private life as a part of the public life of a particular locality and moment in history'. His introductory chapter, 'Fictions of History: An Approach to Faulkner' is a sensitive and finely nuanced account of how Faulkner can be read through a Bakhtinian methodology which insists that 'the voice or word of the character is not subordinated to the voice or word of the author', so much so that there is 'no privileging of the author: each character, realized in terms of speech, is allowed the fundamental right of being active and apart – in Faulkner's own special terms, his privacy'. This approach – an, at times, intricate negotiation of the inner and outer worlds of Faulkner's novels – informs Gray's readings of the individual novels which he treats in chronological sequence, taking us from *Soldier's Pay* to *The Reivers* and attending, where appropriate, to the shorter fiction, though not exhaustively (Gray tends to discuss the short stories where they impinge on, or contribute to, the novels, thus there is no discussion of 'Spotted Horses', arguably one of the greatest comic works in American literature, beyond its reappearance as 'The Peasants' in *The Hamlet*). Gray is frequently over-generous to the rhetorical excesses of Faulkner's prose (how often, when reading him, we want to listen to his characters speak, and thus listen to his wonderful notation of dialect, idiom and the vernacular, rather than listen to him talking *about* them) but this study contains much impressive criticism, as those who have read Gray on Faulkner and other Southern writers before will, no doubt, expect, and I surmise it will quickly come to be seen as one of the very best of recent books on Faulkner. *Light in August* will occupy a central position in any list of Faulkner's greatest fictional achievements and Hugh Ruppersburg's *Reading Faulkner: 'Light in August', Glossary and Commentary* is 'an explication of the world and the text of *Light in August*' which attempts to 'explain, identify, and comment on any aspect or detail of the novel that a reader might conceivably find unfamiliar or difficult'. The annotations are thorough and frequently critically suggestive and this book will be of considerable use, particularly for the undergraduate reader.

Recent criticism of Faulkner has been much exercised by questions of race, gender and class and Diane Roberts's *Faulkner and Southern Womanhood* is a significant contribution to current thinking about these issues. What particularly recommends it is its clarity and accessibility, for even when Roberts is addressing questions of an intractably theoretical kind she writes with admirable perspicuity. She identifies six familiar representations of womanhood in Faulkner's fiction – the Confederate woman, the mammy, the tragic mulatta, the new belle, the spinster and the mother. These 'creations', as she calls them, are culturally and historically specific and, as she says of the 'mammy-figure', she is interested in not only Faulkner's 'creation of her but how his fictive employments of her relate to the web of tensions and possibilities in southern culture'. This is a matter of challenging 'unexamined stereotypes' (for example those of Leslie Fiedler in *Love and Death in the American Novel* [Doubleday (1992)]) for Faulkner's fictions are 'too complex, too contradictory, and too much the product of troubled times in southern culture' for these stereotypes to carry much authority, especially since his female characters 'are so disruptive in a text that a reductive approach cannot tell the whole story'. There is, however, something wrong with a book that interrogates stereotypes by inventing stereotypes, and we should be careful, after all, not to impugn 'typicality' in imaginative literature as if it were, necessarily, a weakness. Roberts's 'confederate woman' is 'a woman in crisis' who during the Civil War 'recreated herself to accommodate, even valorize hardship'; her prototypes occur in Sir Walter Scott, Byron and Mary Chesnut, and she rematerializes as Granny Millard and Drusilla Hawk in *The Unvanquished* and Judith Sutpen in *Absalom, Absalom!* The 'mammy' is a less problematic, arguably less complex figure: she evolves from the 'politics of Aunt Jemima', is the 'super-mammy' of *Gone with the Wind*, takes corporeal form in Caroline Barr, Faulkner's real-life 'Mammy' to whom *Go Down, Moses* is dedicated, and fictional form in Louvinia in *The Unvanquished* and, of course, Dilsey Gibson in *The Sound and the Fury*. Both the 'confederate woman' and the 'mammy' are constructions of class and ideology, for both serve the hegemony of the existing class structure which provides each with a sense of identity, even though the identities are those of servant and master. It might seem unkind to say that this is conventional stuff nicely wrapped up in an elegant style and a scholarly bearing, but the intelligent undergraduate, uncluttered by the apparatus of archival research, could probably come to similar conclusions from a close reading of Faulkner's texts. All novelists make fiction 'out of a time and a place' – they have little in the way of an alternative – and what Roberts has done, the cynical reader might say, is simply give these 'situations' a scholarly specificity, something done, though admittedly in a different way, in Richard Gray's book. Faulkner, she concludes, questions the stereotypes and thus can be appropriated to a progressive oulook on the South, though such a position sits uneasily alongside some of Faulkner's public pronouncements about the 'burden of Southern history'. But her research is solid, if selective (why, for example, is the importance of religion to Faulkner's world so sedulously ignored?) and her critical readings are often perceptive and challenging, so much so that her study deserves a wide readership. Deborah Clarke's *Robbing the Mother: Women in Faulkner* (UPMissip [1994]) is in a similar vein but has not yet been received for review.

The Cambridge Companion to William Faulkner (ed. Philip M. Weinstein), draws together nine new essays on Faulkner (plus Weinstein's introduction), divided into two sections, 'The Texts in the World' and 'The World in the Texts'. Many of the contributors will be well known to scholars of Faulkner: Andre Bleikasten, John Matthews, Richard C. Moreland, Carolyn Porter, Warwick Wadlington and Judith Bryant Wittenberg are numbered among them. The essays are broadly theoretical in character and address many of those issues that figure largely in contemporary debate about him, notably his place in discussions of modernism and postmodernism, his relationships with European and Latin American fiction (in respect of the latter Ramon Saldivar explores his affinities with the Chicano novelist Americao Paredes in 'Looking for a Master Plan: Faulkner, Paredes, and the Colonial and Postcolonial Subject'), and his contributions to the vexed questions of race and gender. The essays are uneven in quality – those of Richard C. Moreland on 'Faulkner and Modernism' and Warwick Wadlington's 'Conclusion: The Stakes of Reading Faulkner – Discerning Reading' are meandering and inconclusive – and one would hesitate to send the undergraduate reader to this collection for an introduction to Faulkner's work, but the more advanced reader will, no doubt, find something of interest here. The volume comes with a brief chronology of Faulkner's life and a good selected bibliography under 'Works Cited'. Donald M. Kartiganer's and Ann J. Abadie's edition of the papers from the 1991

Faulkner conference in Oxford, Mississippi, *Faulkner and Psychology/Faulkner and Yoknapatawpha, 1991* (UPMissip[1994]), has yet to be received for review. [H.C.]

Turning to articles on Faulkner. Particularly stimulating essays on William Faulkner (ed. Minrose C. Gwin) make up the *MissQ* Special Issue (48.iii). In 'Benjy, the Reader, and Death: At the Fence in *The Sound and the Fury*' (407–20), Arthur A. Brown parallels Walter Benjamin's theories of reading with Faulkner's practice, and argues that Faulkner aligns the reader with his narrators, who suspend Caddy's mortal death through their narrative rereading of it. Judith Bryant Wittenberg's 'Temple Drake and *La parole pleine*' (421–41) is an intertextual analysis of *Requiem for a Nun* and Lacan's 'Function and field of speech and language in psychoanalysis', and analyses Temple Drake's confessions concerning her actions eight years previously (the subject of *Sanctuary*) as a psychoanalytic 'talking cure'. Wittenberg suggests that the value of the experience is questionable, however, as although Drake gains emotional benefit from facing the past through her narrative, her present language becomes fragmented and faltering as she faces the intimidation of her coercive male questioners.

The current critical vogue for relating literature to studies of the 'poetics' of space and place is represented in two articles. In the provocative 'Faulkner's Real Estate: Land and Literary Speculation in *The Hamlet*' (443–57), Joseph Urgo parallels Flem Snopes's development of the property value of the Old Frenchman place with Faulkner's development of the literary value of North Mississippi in the creation of Yoknapatawpha. Both perform 'real estate speculation', transforming and adding value to a landscape by a process of ordering, mapping and cultivating it, in which waste land becomes valuable property when accorded a narrative of ownership. Urgo's argument is a fresh and perceptive study of the spatial rather than historical significance of the geography of Yoknapatawpha, and stresses the importance for Faulkner himself of property as a visible referent of success, manifest in the 'landed-capitalist aesthetics' embodied in *The Hamlet*. It is worth reading Urgo's essay alongside Louise Westling's equally excellent 'Women, Landscape, and the Legacy of Gilgamesh in *Absalom, Absalom!* and *Go Down, Moses*' (501–21), which describes Faulkner as continuing the traditional equation of women and landscape that originates from the Neolithic Sumerian legend in which Gilgamesh opposes and destroys the vital power and habitat of the goddess Inanna. Westling's fascinating essay focuses on Faulkner's representation of the white man's appropriation of the New World, in which the landscape prompts the same reaction as Inanna does in the legend and presents an aspect that is primeval and threatening to the male, who must devastate it in order to assert his own identity. Incidentally, 'Culture-Wars/Gender-Scars: Faulkner's South vs. America' (*JAmC* 18.33–41), by William E. H. Meyer Jr, is a more conventional study of the metaphor of the ' "civil war" of the sexes', describing the Southern woman as iconized as representative of various versions of the ante-bellum myth (the matriarch, virgin, heroine or whore) from which the Southern male ego is severed.

In 'Something New and Hard and Bright: Faulkner, Ideology, and the Construction of Modernism' in *MissQ* 48 (459–79), James M. Mellard analyses the role of Robert Penn Warren and George Lukács in the construction of modernism, arguing that aesthetic ideologies are generally defined in retrospect rather than by preliminary manifestos and that therefore it is the critic rather than the practitioner who is most self-aware of writing within them. In Mellard's example, the creation of the modernist aesthetic involves not only Faulkner, who renders a new perspective, but also Warren, who recognizes that this perspective *is* new, and Lukács, who defines and labels it. David Newman, in ' "The vehicle itself is unaware": New Criticism on the Limits of Reading Faulkner' (481–99) continues the focus on critical practice by disputing the view that New Criticism is apolitical in its assertion of the autonomy of literature, arguing that the intention of its proponents was to preserve the connection of art and society that they believed would dissolve in the sociologizing of literature. According to Newman, critics such as Allen Tate and Cleanth Brooks were involved in a political critical practice of texts even if not concerned with the political implications of subject-matter. The issue also contains a useful bibliography on 'Faulkner and Gender', which offers a selection of articles and books from 1982 to 1994, accompanied by brief but informative abstracts, and covers the spectrum of theoretical approaches to the issue of gender.

Belief-systems and how they structure textual aesthetics was another focus of interest this year, one notable study being William E. H. Meyer Jr's 'Faulkner's Aural Evangelism' (*CLAJ* 39.104–15), which discusses the role of Faulkner's preacher's rhetoric in transforming traditional formalist aesthetics and religion into an aural aesthetic style, informed by an evangelical folk-religion of the Deep South. Interesting in relation is the focus on Calvinism and its significance for racial issues in 'Racial Predestination: The Elect and the Damned in *Light in August*' (*ELN* 33.62–9) by Peter Hays. Nietzschean nihilism is the alternative framework for Faulkner's oeuvre offered by Marco Abel in 'One Goal is Still Lacking: The Influence of Friedrich Nietzsche's Philosophy on William Faulkner's *The Sound and the Fury*' (*SoAR* 60.35–52). Abel points to the preoccupation with loss of order common to the styles and thematics of both writers and, endorsed by a commendably perceptive reading of Nietzsche's philosophy, persuasively argues that the dominant structural and narrative tone of *The Sound and the Fury* is one of nihilism, the paradoxical nature of which Faulkner attempts to resolve through a belief in human tenacity and endurance. This faith in human nature's indefatigability in the face of chaos is perhaps also manifest in his passion for Cervantes's novel *Don Quixote*. Montserrat Ginés's stimulating 'Don Quixote in Yoknapatawpha: Faulkner's Champions of Dreams' (*SLJ* 27.23–42) describes Faulkner's construction of Yoknapatawpha and his characters' idealism as an escape into a Quixotic world of mythic honour but also social estrangement. An additional essay of interest is Scott DeShong's 'Toward an Ethics of Reading Faulkner's *Sanctuary*' (*JNT* 25.238–57), which employs Levinasian ethics to suggest in postmodernist fashion that the Faulkner text portrays humanity from a broadly empathic ethical stance rather than a traditionally deterministic one.

The Spring issue of *NDQ* 62 is largely devoted to innovative critical approaches to Ernest Hemingway. Notable is William Braasch Watson's 'Investigating Hemingway: The Scene' (11–40), in which Watson describes how the desire for substantiating evidence to support his theoretical study of two visits by Hemingway to a guerrilla outfit in Alfambra during the Spanish Civil War, led to his own journey to the village and consequently a heightened understanding of both Hemingway's actual experiences and the workmanship by which he transformed these into art. Erik Nakjavani, in 'On Autobiography and Multiple Personality: The Case of Morley Callaghan Remembering Ernest Hemingway' (55–82), focuses on Callaghan's memoir *That Summer in Paris* to investigate the nature of auto/biography, particularly in terms of the omitive and additive aspects of remembrance, and then points to the inadequacies of conventional biography and the difficulty of interpreting recollected 'facts' concerning the infamously mythogenic Hemingway. Two essays concentrate on Hemingway's views on art and aesthetics. 'Hemingway's Old Lady and the Aesthetics of *Pundonor*', by Donald Junkins (195–204), is a brief but excellent study of *Death in the Afternoon* as an aesthetic treatise in which Hemingway defines the standards and values of art in terms of those of the bullfight. James Plath's 'Fishing for Tension: The Dynamics of Hemingway's "Big Two-Hearted River" ' (159–65) describes Hemingway's literary translation of the painterly technique of Cézanne, notably in an evocation of tension and movement through a juxtaposition of separate, angled and opposing spatial planes. Other interesting contributions include Paul Smith's 'Stein's Remarks, Hemingway's Literature' (95–102) on the tale of Hemingway's apprenticeship to Gertrude Stein, Paul Strong's ' "You Know Me, Don't You?": Role Reversal in the Nick Adams Stories' (132–9), which examines Hemingway's narrative strategy of repeated yet reversed scenes, and Lloyd Halliburton's 'Hemingway's Use of *Máquina* in *For Whom the Bell Tolls*' (183–92), addressing the question of Hemingway's fluency in and subtle use of the Spanish language. Finally, Robert Gajdusek's suggestive 'Sacrifice and Redemption: The Meaning of the Boy/Son and Man/Father Dialectic in the Work of Ernest Hemingway' (166–80) reveals a pattern of son/father relationships in the Hemingway canon in which young men frequently usurp the status of manhood from lost or failing father figures, yet are then necessarily sacrificed to allow for the latter's re-empowerment. He argues that this is an attempt to resolve an anxiety over the failure of the patriarchal role model in the modern Western world.

Hemingway's connection with Hollywood has been topical this year. Leonard J. Leff recounts the interesting history of the progress of *The Sun Also Rises* from page to screen in 'The Sun Almost Rises: Hemingway and the Hollywood Marketplace of Depression America' (*ArQ* 51.45–67), and convincingly connects the cautious response to the novel by production companies to the crisis of masculinity arising in the Depression era. Considered and rejected by Hollywood from 1926, the novel was finally filmed by Twentieth Century-Fox in 1957. Hemingway's box-office appeal improved dramatically in later years and the rights to *For Whom the Bell Tolls* were bought by Paramount in 1940 for the record-breaking sum of $100,000. Hemingway's full correspondence to agent Donald Friede regarding the film adaptation is published for the first time in Peter Carroll's 'Ernest Hemingway, Screenwriter: New Letters on *For Whom the Bell Tolls*' (*AR* 53.261–83), and give evidence of Hemingway's concern at the loss of aesthetic and political nuance in the ineptly written script and his consequent involvement in the final reconstruction of the novel.

Hemingway has traditionally sported a hypermasculine cultural image, yet attention has been drawn in recent years, by Mark Spilka among others, to a preoccupation with the instability of gender roles in his fiction. In 'Performance Art: Jake Barnes and "Masculine" Signification in *The Sun Also Rises*' (*AL* 67.77–94), Ira Elliot defines androgyny and homosexuality as performative categories and examines the consequently ambiguous gender position of the wounded and sexually impotent Jake Barnes. Of other essays on Hemingway, Dennis Ryan's 'Dating Hemingway's Early Style/Parsing Gertrude Stein's Modernism' (*JAmS* 29.229–40) is a useful and thorough survey of interest in Stein's contribution to Hemingway's literary style that commends the more recent and long overdue acknowledgement of her influence. In 'Observations on Hemingway, Suggestiveness, and the Modern Short Story' (*MQ* 32.11–26), Robert Paul Lamb assesses the stylistic, structural and descriptive demands of the short story genre, and argues that Hemingway successfully follows the aesthetic principles of earlier masters such as Maupassant and Chekhov, evoking actions, character and emotion in a compressed narrative space through the use of suggestive language and a selectivity of focus. Psychoanalytic theory is represented by Pamela A. Boker's 'Negotiating the Heroic Paternal Ideal: Historical Fiction as Transference in Hemingway's *For Whom the Bell Tolls*' (*L&P* 41.85– 112), which describes the novel as a uniquely successful attempt by Hemingway to resolve the ego-ideal crisis and construct a psychologically coherent masculine identity. Finally, 'Consuming Hemingway: "The Snows of Kilimanjaro" in the Postmodern Classroom' (*JNT* 25.23–46) is a refreshing study in which L. Bush reveals both her belief in and scruples about the value of contemporary cultural criticism. Drawing on her own experience of teaching Hemingway, she warns that theory should be used to provoke questions about his writing rather than simply re-package the cultural myth of the author into a new consumable or answer.

There were only a few essays on F. Scott Fitzgerald this year. Susan Wanlass compares Fitzgerald and T. S. Eliot as writers of the climate of the Lost Generation in 'An Easy Commerce: Specific Similarities Between the Writings of T. S. Eliot and F. Scott Fitzgerald' (*ELN* 32.58–69). In a more innovative study, 'The Political F. Scott Fitzgerald: Liberal Illusion and Disillusion in *This Side of Paradise* and *The Beautiful and the Damned*' (*ASInt* 33.60–70), Craig Monk counters the general critical opinion that Fitzgerald's early fiction is largely apolitical, arguing that his portrayals of US society are informed by the political turmoil of the post-war years and the Republican ascendancy over the internationalist idealism of the Democrats. Monk notes an increasing liberal disillusionment in Fitzgerald's first two novels as the altruistic ideals of international reform were unrealized and narcissistic interests of personal gain took precedence. Charles R. Hearn's 'F. Scott Fitzgerald and the Popular Magazine Formula story of the Twenties' (*JAmC* 18.33–40) informatively assesses Fitzgerald's lucrative writing for the mass audience, suggesting that, despite conforming to the popular rags-to-riches formula, he manipulated this code to hint at the tensions and tragedies within it that were the concerns of his novels.

Zelda Fitzgerald attracted belated attention in Simone Weil Davis's fascinating and informative essay ' "The Burden of Reflecting": Effort and Desire in Zelda Fitzgerald's *Save Me the Waltz*' (*MLQ* 56.327–61). In *Save Me the Waltz*, Fitzgerald portrays the rich extravagance and subsequent ennui of 1920s America as it directly affected women. Weil Davis successfully counters the reductionist identification of the schizophrenic discourse with the writer's psychological imbalance, arguing that Fitzgerald's text is a perceptive analysis of the role of commodity culture in the construction of a pervasive female identity, and the way in which this identity becomes a means by which women can manifest control over their physicality. [D.P.]

3. Drama

(a) General

Walter J. Meserve's *An Outline History of American Drama*, the second edition of which has now been published, is not a critical analysis but a compact, practical handbook which provides a chronological survey of the field from its beginnings to the present. Each of the six chapters is framed by an overview and summary of a period, with a concluding selective bibliography; within the chapters, a system of headings and subheadings indicates significant theatrical developments, trends, playwrights and plays. The account of the plays is predominantly descriptive, but Meserve goes some way towards placing the drama in relation to social and political contexts and to the material conditions of theatre production, including the development of dramatic criticism. Students will find this user-friendly text helpful as a preparatory tool for further study, as Meserve conveniently exposes the skeleton of a conventional narrative history of American drama.

Darwin T. Turner's introduction to the second edition of his *Black Drama in America: An Anthology* is on the short side, but contextualizes an interesting and unpredictable selection of plays. Darwin includes Willis Richardson's *The Chip Woman's Fortune*, Langston Hughes's *Emperor of Tahiti*, Theodore Ward's *Our Lan'*, Owen Dodson's *Bayou Legend*, Louis Peterson's *Take a Giant Step*, Alice Childress's *Trouble in Mind*, Ed Bullins's *In the Wine Time*, Charlie L. Russell's *Five on the Black Hand Side*, Amiri Baraka's *Great Goodness of Life (A Coon Show)*, George Houston Bass's *Black Masque*, Charles H. Fuller Jr's *A Soldier's Play*, August Wilson's *Ma Rainey's Black Bottom*, J. e Franklin's *Miss Honey's Young'uns*, and Pearl Cleage's *Flyin' West*. The omission of *Dutchman* is perhaps surprising, but may be justified on the grounds that it is more readily available than *Great Goodness of Life*; the exclusion of Lorraine Hansberry, Adrienne Kennedy and Ntozake Shange, however, gives a somewhat distorted picture of drama by women in this period. Nevertheless, with supplementation this book could form the basis for an undergraduate course or further independent study.

American Theatre: A Chronicle of Comedy and Drama, 1914–1930 is the second volume in Gerald Bordman's massive project of providing a narrative survey of every major Broadway production, and as many as possible of those played at the smaller houses which eventually became 'off-Broadway'. Aiming at comprehensive coverage rather than close critical analysis, Bordman nevertheless gives a fairly detailed account of many of the productions, and summarizes the opinions of contemporary reviewers. Collectively, Bordman's series will provide an invaluable narrative chronology of mainstream theatre in New York.

Regional and experimental playwrights are well represented in two complementary reference works published by Greenwood. *American Playwrights, 1880–1945: A Research and Production Sourcebook* (ed. William W.

Demastes) is the companion volume to *American Playwrights Since 1945: A Guide to Scholarship, Criticism, and Performance* (ed. Philip C. Kolin [*YWES* 70.674]). Kolin's collection includes entries on 40 dramatists, the career of each of whom is considered under the following headings: achievements and reputation; primary bibliography; production history; secondary sources (bibliographies, biographies, dramatic and non-dramatic influences, general studies, and analyses of individual plays); future research opportunities; and a checklist of secondary sources. Demastes provides entries on a further 40 playwrights and includes similar material, although it is differently arranged. Taken together, the Greenwood volumes constitute an invaluable reference source on the American drama of this century. They will be the first port of call for information on such lesser-known figures as Clyde Fitch, Abram Hill, Percy Wallace MacKaye, Augustus Thomas, Charles Gordone and Preston Jones, while the material on the major dramatists is concisely presented and soundly evaluated. Many of the contributors are scholars of international renown; the entries are of a uniformly high standard; and although of necessity the bibliographies are not absolutely comprehensive, and the price is restrictive, the editors have succeeded in presenting a remarkable range of information in a very convenient format.

Greenwood has also published *Theatrical Directors: A Biographical Dictionary* (ed. John W. Frick and Stephen M. Vallillo), which contains around 300 'biographical sketches'. The dictionary includes entries on both living directors and others who, the editors explain in a pleasing euphemism, 'are no longer working'. The title is slightly misleading, since the preface adds the qualification that the emphasis has been placed on 'those whose work has significantly influenced American theatre'. The matter is further confused by the claim that the book aims to include other directors 'if their work has had a major impact upon the theatre of their homeland'. These principles of selection appear uncertain, and give a rather blurred picture of national theatres: there is no room for Terence Gray, Terry Hands, Elijah Moshinsky or Steven Berkoff, for instance, among British-based directors. A one-volume reference work of this sort can make no attempt to be exhaustive, of course; and although niggles about selection are compounded by the brevity of the entries, this is offset by the elegantly analytical and evaluative prose and the inclusion of excellent and extensive bibliographies.

Clive Bloom's short introduction to *American Drama*, which he has edited for Macmillan's *Insights* series, argues for the 'primary authenticity' of American drama, which in its totality he figures as a drama of 'legitimacy' and 'sin' in its development of both the 'isolated and paranoid' serious play and the 'optimistic and buoyant' musical. That only the former is considered in the following essays is indicative of the book's major weakness. On the one hand, there are no major contextualizing accounts of such important areas as the musical, pre-twentieth century drama, or the Federal Theatre Project; Charlotte Canning's account of contemporary feminist theatre has space to consider only five plays; and aside from A. Robert Lee's essay on Imamu Amiri Baraka, which provides a superb account of the political and theatrical context of radical black American drama of the 1960s, African-American theatre is badly under-represented. On the other hand, the book is not really adequate as a collection of pieces on the canonical figures either: Edward Albee and August Wilson, for example, are serious omissions, while Adrienne

Kennedy and Ntozake Shange receive only minimal attention. Some of the essays provide descriptive and evaluative introductions: Barbara Ozieblo on Susan Glaspell; Chris Banfield on the short, later plays of Arthur Miller; Darryll Grantley on Marsha Norman. Others, such as Mark Tully's discussion of Tennessee Williams's work as expressions of the dramatist's sexuality, or Michael J. Hayes's study of Sam Shepard as a writer whose use of language and music provide an experience analogous to that of a rock concert or religious ceremony, also take a broadly familiar line, although one that is often inflected in unusual ways. Others are more ambitious. The late Eric Mottram provides a wide-ranging study of how Eugene O'Neill's dramatizations of creativity and self come into conflict with deterministic social, mythic and psychological structures. Michael Woolf resists the common tendency to regard Clifford Odets as a writer of proletarian agit-prop dramas in the 1930s whose talent was destroyed by Hollywood, and examines his work in the contexts of Jewish-American literature, American Romanticism and the Depression. In comparable vein, Michael Woolf describes Neil Simon's plays as 'comedies of urban disorder', locating their nostalgic impulse and treatment of family relations within the context of Jewish-American literature and experience. Edward J. Esche argues that David Mamet writes 'contemporary problem play[s] along Shakespearean lines', which lead the audience into recognizing their complicity in making erroneous moral choices about the action.

Yvonne Shafer's superbly presented and meticulously documented study of 35 *American Women Playwrights, 1900–1950* represents one of the year's major contributions to scholarship in the field of American drama. Although the book is far from schematic, Shafer generally gives a biographical sketch of the dramatist, followed by a chronological survey of the plays, including plot summaries and contemporary critical reception. The work of many of these writers, for example Rachel Crothers, Susan Glaspell, Lillian Hellman, Gertrude Stein and Carson McCullers, is already fairly well known; but with others, such as Zona Gale, Alice Gerstenberg and Sophie Treadwell, it is revealing to have the small number of plays which have received recent critical attention placed in a wider context. Shafer demolishes the myth that there was little dramatic writing produced by American women during this period, and in the process brings to light a number of obscure playwrights such as Josephine Preston Peabody and Cornelia Otis Skinner. She pays detailed attention to the huge variations in the material and social conditions under which these plays came to be written. In some cases the playwrights were already independently wealthy or developed successful careers, but many African-American writers, for example, were obliged to produce their work in conditions of poverty. Hence Shafer's particular interest not only in such diverse figures as Georgia Douglas Johnson, May Miller and Zora Neale Hurston, but in the different forms of communal and institutional theatre available to women of different backgrounds. Shafer's book is an outstanding introduction to a subject of increasing critical attention; for excellent supplementary material, see the aforementioned Greenwood volumes edited by Kolin and Demastes.

Paul Sporn's *Against Itself: The Federal Theater and Writers' Projects in the Midwest* is a Marxist-humanist 'worm's eye view' of the social, political and aesthetic repercussions of the New Deal's WPA programme in a region whose 'industrial isolationism . . . acted to reinforce rather than transform the dynamics of shared experiences and exclusionary traditions'. The Midwest is, for Sporn, 'a crucible of American culture', 'more provincial and industrial, more highly ethnic and working class in population – and therefore more reflective of the mosaic that constitutes the backbone of American culture – than are the more distinguished cosmopolitan centers'. That diversity is explored here in separate chapters detailing the dialectical relationships between the federal arts programmes and the Polish, Finnish, Yiddish and African-American cultures of the region. There is little close analysis of the drama and writing which came out of the programmes, since Sporn is appropriately more concerned to analyse the politics of the programmes themselves. There are, however, detailed sections on the series of regional guides and the studies of folklore and black culture, supported by extensive archival research, in which Sporn draws attention to the distorting effects of the centralized control of the projects and of the researchers' lack of expertise. The broader aim of the book is to examine the politics of arts funding in America and the effects of liberal cultural interventions within an essentially *laissez-faire* economy, and Sporn highlights the continuing relevance of the New Deal experiments to the contemporary debate. At times the book is heavy going, but this is almost inevitable given its massively detailed analysis of the structural problems of different forms of artistic funding.

Sporn's work provides a valuable historical context within which to view the current controversies surrounding the reactionary stance taken in recent years by the National Endowment for the Arts. The crisis has been particularly acute for performing artists, and informs most of the critical work currently being published in this area. A second concern of this work is to examine the implications of distinctions between drama and performance art. These two problems underlie many of the essays in *Acting Out: Feminist Performances* (ed. Lynda Hart and Peggy Phelan). In her introduction, Hart expresses 'the desire to displace the dominance of text-based work in theater studies, to value the ephemerality of performance', and notes that 'most of the performance texts under discussion in this collection do not have the status of "plays" '. The essays following the twin introductions (Phelan's is a wide-ranging, Derridean meditation on the political and gender implications of reproducibility and citation in relation to performance art) are divided into three sections. The first explores the 'Politics of Identities', and illustrates the resistance of feminist subjectivities to reductive categorizations. Sandra Richards discusses Anna Deavere Smith's dialogic performances of the words of her tape-recorded interviewees. The work of another prominent artist, Holly Hughes (one of the 'NEA Four'), is placed by Kate Davy in the context of the aforementioned funding controversies. Yvonne Yarbro-Bejarano shows how in *Shadow of a Man*, Cherrie Moraga problematizes any notion of a unified Chicana identity. Jill Dolan's 'Desire Cloaked in a Trenchcoat' is a revised version of a previously published essay on the gaze, while in the final piece in this section, Lynda Hart provides further theoretical support for one of its consistent themes, the instability of identities, by arguing that lesbian desire is a politically charged question of identifications.

Four of the six chapters in 'Performing Histories', the second section of *Acting Out*, are devoted to feminist theatre companies: Janelle Reinelt on the Monstrous Regiment, Joyce Devlin on the Siren Theatre, Julie Malnig and

Judy C. Rosenthal on the Women's Experimental Theatre and Vivian M. Patraka on Split Britches. Most of these essays focus to a greater or lesser extent on the politics of funding, as does C. Carr's interview with another of the 'NEA Four', Karen Finlay. A previously published essay by Carr on an early Finlay performance is also reprinted here. The more theoretically based third section of *Acting Out* is a diverse collection of essays, each of which considers the problem in performance art of 'The Reproduction of Visibility'. Some of these essays again focus on specific performers or groups, often mingled with an emphasis on more overtly autobiographical significances for performer or critic: Rebecca Schneider on Spiderwoman Theatre; Raewyn Whyte on Robbie McCauley; Lynda Hill on Zora Neale Hurston. Two of the essays discuss aspects of the work of women at the forefront of popular culture: Philip Auslander on the rage at misogyny which underlies the comedy of Roseanne Barr, and Amy Robinson on the multiple identities of Madonna. The section also contains three wide-ranging theoretical contributions: by Hilary Harris, who reconsiders distinctions between sex and gender in the context of lesbian performance; by Elin Diamond, in a revised version of an essay which considers performances by several artists in providing a basically familiar deconstruction of notions of the origin; and by Peggy Phelan, whose 'White Men and Pregnancy' focuses explicitly on this section's concern with questions of reproduction and visibility.

Phelan and Hart have also contributed 'Queerer Than Thou', a dialogic meditation on and celebration of the work of Deb Margolin, to a special issue of *TJ* (47.ii.269–82) devoted to gay and lesbian 'queeries'. The collaborative nature of the essay connects it to ' "Preaching to the Converted" ' (169–88), by David Román and another of the 'NEA Four', Tim Miller, a piece which draws much of its inspiration from Miller's experiences on stage. The title phrase is intended 'first, as a descriptive which names the potential affinities between the two terms of its locution – preacher/congregation, performer/audience; second . . . as a descriptive for community-based, and often community-specific, lesbian and gay theatre and performance'. Kate Davy's 'Outing Whiteness' (189–205) grapples with the problem of how the dynamic of the WOW (Women's One World) Café in New York has inhibited the involvement of African-American women. For essays in this issue on the plays of Tony Kushner and Tennessee Williams, see under individual dramatists, below.

The most entertaining book I received this year was John Tytell's *The Living Theatre: Art, Exile, and Outrage*. Although it gives detailed accounts of the circumstances surrounding all of the Living Theatre's productions, this is not the place to look for detailed critical or performance analyses. Instead, Tytell has written a racy biography of Julian Beck and Judith Malina, in a popular style, which goes into graphic detail about such matters as what Malina's sexual partners were like in bed. This is the kind of book which in other circles would be described as 'unputdownable', but it is also an academically significant study, since it traces in extraordinary detail the relationships between a hugely disparate range of artists and writers congregating in and around New York from the 1940s onwards, including James Agee, Eric Bentley, Allen Ginsberg, Paul Goodman, Robert Motherwell, Jackson Pollock, Tennessee Williams, William Carlos Williams and many others. Similar stories of these circles have been told many times before, of course, but rarely in such a readable and gossipy style. There is a short but excellent overview of the 'intermedia' work of one of the most important and central figures in Tytell's book in Natalie Crohn Schmitt's ' "So Many Things Can Go Together": The Theatricality of John Cage' (*NTQ* 11.72–8).

Amy S. Green's *The Revisionist Stage: American Directors Reinvent the Classics* examines in detail some examples of American directorial 'rewrightings', from the 1960s onwards, of 'classic' plays: of the Greek and Roman theatre (by Andrei Serban, Richard Schechner and Lee Breuer); of Shakespeare (Joseph Papp, Robert Woodruff, JoAnne Akalaitis and Breuer); of Molière (Serban, Garland Wright, Richard Foreman, Liviu Ciulei and Lucian Pintilié); and of a Mozart trilogy, by Peter Sellars. As one would expect, the primary value of Green's book lies in the detail in which she has researched, documented, reconstructed and evaluated these productions, all of which, of course, represent radical transformations of their source material. On broader questions, however, she is less sure-footed. Although her central claim is that 'this essential contradiction between a familiar, well-established text and its all-new theatrical idiom ... marks contemporary classic revival as the unique product of our specific theatrical, cultural, and historical milieu', her survey of precedents in Europe and America suggests that the difference is of degree rather than kind. Similarly, while the account of each production is fresh and lively, the book lacks sharpness in defining theoretical developments during the last 30 years: the possible distinctions between 1980s' performance and 1960s' notions of authenticity are more fully explored in Philip Auslander's *Presence and Resistance* (*YWES* 75.672–3), and although Green frequently mentions Artaud and Derrida, she seems unaware of the latter's essay on the former, which precisely anticipates and articulates this crucial problem of authenticity. Indeed, in view of Green's judicious evaluation of contemporary performance reviews, it is surprising that she often prefers instead to foreground contemporary theory, of which she appears both ill-informed and dismissive. She recommends reading secondhand accounts written in 'plain English', which would account for some of the more obvious lapses, such as a serious misrepresentation of Saussure, as well as the casual idiom which repeatedly creeps into the text, of which 'Papp's 90-minute *Hamlet* was, in current critical lingo, a deconstruction' is but one example.

In each of the six chapters of her *Anglo-American Interplay in Recent Drama*, Ruby Cohn finds a basis for pairing an English and an American dramatist: Alan Ayckbourn and Neil Simon, Edward Bond and Sam Shepard, Harold Pinter and David Mamet, Maria Irene Fornes and Caryl Churchill, David Hare and David Rabe, Christopher Hampton and Richard Nelson. Some of these connections appear natural, others arbitrary; but it is striking how frequently Cohn either inadvertently emphasizes the tenuousness of the comparison (a play of Hampton's is considered alongside one of Nelson's on the grounds that 'both dramas set characters outside of their native lands and both are steeped in literature'; Shepard and Bond have both written plays with the word 'fool' in the title), or indeed concedes the extent of the dissimilarity: even with an obvious pairing, she admits that 'the works of Pinter and Mamet do not bend readily to larger comparisons of theme and structure'. Worryingly, she often notices points of contact arising 'coincidentally' or 'fortuitously'. The problem is that Cohn's introduction, blithely 'ignoring theory' and supplying instead a 'scattershot of historical dates', and the absence of any concluding remarks, condemn the book to a series of disconnected points and random comparisons, with no basis for deciding which might be significant, and why. Previously, Cohn has contributed much to the critical understanding of modern drama, and this book displays once again the range of her reading and theatre-going, but one wonders whether in this case her very pre-eminence has contributed to a slipshod effort.

June Schlueter's *Dramatic Closure: Reading the End* is at once more and less extensive in ambition than its title might suggest. In a series of short, excellently written chapters amounting to well under 150 pages, Schlueter covers a remarkable range of material, exploring the various ways in which awareness of closure shapes a reading of such matters as dialogue, character and genre in a diverse selection of plays including *King Lear, A Streetcar Named Desire* and Arthur Miller's *The Ride Down Mount Morgan*, alongside less extensive discussion of many additional works. Methodologically, Schlueter aims to explore closure 'within both a traditional Aristotelian paradigm and contemporary reader-response theory'. In practice, the project is underpinned by the theoretical writings of Hans-Robert Jauss and, particularly, Wolfgang Iser, and herein lies the limitation of Schlueter's approach. Although she mentions the 'ideological concerns' of genre and notes the importance of 'such categories as race, ethnicity, gender, and class' in determining spectatorial response, she spends very little time on ideology and does not take note of the many Marxist critiques of Iser and Jauss, providing instead a number of textual analyses which appear to posit a relatively autonomous reader. Similarly, her appropriation of post-structuralism, for example in borrowing Barthes's distinction between the 'readerly' and the 'writerly' text, evades its radical ideological implications. However, as a survey of liberal forms of reader-response theory and their possible applications to traditional categories of dramatic discussion, *Dramatic Closure* comes strongly recommended.

(b) Individual Dramatists

In *Staging Depth: Eugene O'Neill and the Politics of Psychological Discourse*, Joel Pfister creates a version of O'Neill which departs significantly from those of earlier studies. He argues that O'Neill's depth is 'staged', an effect of style and the materiality of production and, more interestingly, of the influence of pop psychology on the development of the middle-class American family. In this way, Pfister distances himself from the more narrowly biographical emphases of so many discussions of this playwright, and without devaluing the creative achievement focuses instead on how the structure of O'Neill's New England Irish Catholic family, and his domestic dramas, were shaped by the political and ideological imperatives of the cult of domesticity and forms of psychology popularized in America from the turn of the century onwards. This productive use of history, bolstered by extensive archival research, both contextualizes O'Neill within those ideologies of interiority and individualization amenable to the professional-managerial class, and allows for the recuperation of some contemporary, radical, left-wing critiques of his work. Pfister posits a kind of postmodern O'Neill, whose 'tendencies to produce and to demystify a modern psychological self are in fact contrary, in a state of conflict and tension'. *Staging Depth* is an excellent book, wide-ranging, deeply knowledgeable, and critically informed, and should take its place alongside the work of Louis Sheaffer, Virginia Floyd and Travis Bogard as one of the indispensable studies of O'Neill.

AmDram 4.ii, 'Re-Visioning the '30s', is a special issue containing essays on five dramatists. In *'Between Two Worlds*: Elmer Rice Chairs the Thirties Debate' (1–16), Barry Witham brings biographical evidence in support of his argument that this disregarded play reflects the Comintern's attempts to instruct 'the American Communist Party to moderate its anti-capitalist stance in favor of a more balanced view that could achieve the Popular Front'. Gabriel Miller has written the first account of 'Clifford Odets's and Elia Kazan's "Mother's Day" ' (17–35), only the title of which was previously known to scholars. In his account of the three extant drafts of this abortive fragment, Miller indicates its connections to earlier and later works by Odets, and concludes that the authors were right to abandon it. In attempting to account for the contradictions between Susan Glaspell's early feminist plays and her apparent subordination to men later in her career, Marcia A. Noe, in 'Reconfiguring the Subject/Recuperating Realism' (36–54), finds the answer in the motif of the unconventional but unseen woman in her plays, who allows Glaspell to 'reconcile [her] feminine and feminist impulses', paves the way for more radical characters in the later Provincetown plays, and articulates Glaspell's own position in relation to the Provincetown Players. There is a nod towards feminism in David K. Sauer's oddly titled 'George S. Kaufman's Exploitation of Women (Characters): Dramaturgy and Feminism' (55–80), but the essay takes an essentially conventional view of dramatic character-ization and authorial development by focusing on the representation of women in his first five plays. In 'A Fictitious Injustice: The Politics of Conversation in Maxwell Anderson's *Gods of the Lightning*' (81–96), Jennifer Jones concludes that this dramatization of the trial of Sacco and Vanzetti is far from radical or subversive. Another of Anderson's plays of the 1930s, *High Tor*, is the subject of Tony Speranza's 'Renegotiating the Frontier of Amer-ican Manhood' (*AmDram* 5.i.16–35), which similarly finds the playwright occupying the middle ground, here by reconciling, in the 'comradely ideal' of marriage, the older traditions of the virile frontier pioneer with the contempo-rary demands of corporate capitalism.

Alice Griffin's *Understanding Tennessee Williams* is aimed squarely at a general readership, although some undergraduates may find it useful for its straightforward representation of what were until recently the most familiar general lines along which this playwright's work tended to be viewed. An introductory chapter contains a biographical sketch, a brief general discussion of characters and themes, and a very hasty overview of those plays deemed insufficiently significant to merit substantial attention. These include all the plays produced after *The Night of the Iguana*, and Griffin's failure to provide any sense of the recent critical revaluations of some of the later work is the major weakness of her book. In each of the nine remaining chapters she provides a reasonably detailed analysis of one of the better-known plays, at a level which will be helpful to those coming to Williams for the first time.

The first thing one should stress about George W. Crandell's *Tennessee Williams: A Descriptive Bibliography* is that it deals with the primary works only, in nine sections. The chapter on separate publications takes up well over half the book and contains illustrations of dust jackets and title and copyright pages, in the course of a chronological listing of all printings of English editions, and details of first productions. The remaining sections are as follows: 'first-appearance contributions to books, pamphlets, and occasional publications'; 'first appearances in magazines and newspapers', with a separate section on 'interviews and articles quoting Williams'; three short sections on music (texts of Williams's lyrics set to music by others), 'blurbs' written by Williams as advertising copy for works by other authors, and sound recordings of Williams's readings and interviews; a 50-page section on translations, arranged by language; and two pages of compiler's notes on miscellaneous rumoured or known publications not listed elsewhere. The second point that requires emphasis is that Crandell's book is essentially a bibliographical description: it gives precise information about typography, bindings and so forth, but merely lists the presence of textual variants in different editions without, except on rare occasions, specifying what these variants are. Although much of the enormous amount of information in this bibliography is fascinating, there is little here which will aid in the analysis of the plays themselves, and even ardent Williams scholars are likely to be deterred by the prohibitive cost. The book is so specialized, in fact, that one questions whether it is even an appropriate purchase for any but the largest university libraries, since almost everyone will find Drewey Wayne Gunn's *Tennessee Williams: A Bibliography* (*YWES* 73.625) more useful.

It is impossible in a few sentences to do justice to Lyle Leverich's monumental *Tom: The Unknown Tennessee Williams*, which focuses on the playwright's life up to the premiere of *The Glass Menagerie* (a second volume, *Tenn: The Timeless World of Tennessee Williams* is due to appear in 1998). Williams selected Leverich as his authorized biographer, and consequently Leverich has been able to draw on his own interviews and, more importantly, on a substantial body of previously unreleased material. His research provides us with substantially different accounts of Williams's relationships with his tormented sister Rose and with his parents, especially his father. Leverich's treatment of the parents is symptomatic of his tendency to read Williams in terms of dualisms (the Tom/Tenn distinction is another, the fascinating account of his early bisexuality a third), which makes for a well-structured narrative but leads to some repetitiveness and distortion, somewhat exaggerated by Leverich's serviceable but unexciting style. These minor reservations about the overall organization of the book should not, however, detract from the significance of the wealth of detail or the important re-readings of some hitherto relatively obscure aspects of Williams's formative years. Leverich's work comfortably supersedes earlier accounts, and will become the standard biography.

The tendency to read Williams's plays as coded autobiography is exemplified in '*Cat on a Hot Tin Roof*: The Uneasy Marriage of Success and Idealism' (*MD* 38.324–35), in which Marian Price argues that the revisions to this play ensured both commercial success and Williams's artistic survival. By contrast, in 'Self-Consuming Artifacts: Power, Performance and the Body in Tennessee Williams's *Suddenly Last Summer*' (*MD* 38.336–47), Andrew Sofer shows that the investigation of Sebastian Venable, the absent protagonist, produces not a stable referent but a self-consumption which paradoxically generates a proliferation of discourses. This play has been the subject of a number of re-readings in recent years; Sofer's account is one of the best, and shares a number of tropes and interpretive strategies with Robert F. Gross's 'Consuming Hart: Sublimity and Gay Poetics in *Suddenly Last Summer*' (*TJ* 47.229–51). Gross argues that the play represents Williams's 'recasting of Edmund Burke's concept of the Sublime, with all its heterosexual male assumptions, within a gay subjectivity' which recognizes that 'if the pleasure of the Beautiful requires the power of feeling completely in control, the pleasure of the Sublime is to be had in surrendering to a masculine power other than one's own'. Gross traces the workings of the Sublime in two plot-triangles, in each of which Sebastian is the site of a struggle between other characters, and in a meta-triangle, 'a very personal charting of Williams's own creativity, situated between the poetics of the Mother and an alternative gay poetics'.

Anne Fleche published two articles on Williams, each of which focuses on rhetorical tropes. 'When a Door is a Jar, or Out in the Theatre: Tennessee Williams and Queer Space' (*TJ* 47.253–67) is a wide-ranging study both of Williams and of queer theories of the closet, and concentrates on 'the inside/outside distinction, perhaps *the* overriding trope in gay and lesbian criticism and theory'; while Fleche's 'The Space of Madness and Desire' (*MD* 38.496–509) suggests that neither realism nor expressionism fully closes the gaps produced by desire and the rhetorical modes of representation in *Streetcar*.

MissQ 48.iv. is a special issue on Williams (ed. Philip C. Kolin), which includes poems and recollections by acquaintances, as well as examples of 'Tennessee Williams's Graphic Art', with accompanying discussion by William Plumley (789–805). There are several interviews: three by Patricia Grierson (with Eudora Welty, Margaret Walker Alexander and James Whitehead); one by Robert Bray with the Dakin Williams; and another, by Harry W. McCrew, with composer Luigi Zaninelli, who discusses Alex North's music for cinema adaptations.

The critical essays range from the insignificant to the magnificent. Focusing on the presentation of an 'undifferentiated and androgynous ideal' in a work of juvenilia, Francesca M. Hitchcock's 'Tennessee Williams's "Vengeance of Nitocris"' (595–608) argues that elements of this story endorse the playwright's suggestion that it may be seen as 'the keynote for most of the work that has followed'. In 'Tennessee Williams's St. Louis Blues' (609–25), Allean Hale provides detailed biographical information to support her assertion that this city is the 'actual locale' of many of the plays and characters, and 'was the catalyst that transformed him into a writer'. The unfamiliarity of this argument rather gives the lie to Kimball King's strange assertion in 'Tennessee Williams: A Southern Writer' (627–47) that 'surprisingly little has been said about his debt to Southern literary conventions or his regional bias'. King's essay unsurprisingly has little difficulty in countering this view, but provides a worthwhile overview of Williams's Southern precursors and some detailed arguments for Williams as a writer of the 'deep' South. Thomas P. Adler's 'Culture, Power, and the (En)Gendering of Community' (649–65) argues that Williams associates patriarchy with racism, and art with revolution. Adler's sharp and engaging political reading, and his view that power is gendered, gains strongest support from *Cat*. In contrast, Colby H. Kullman's desultory 'Rule by Power' (667–76) presents the non-argument that what Kullman calls the 'Big Daddyism' in Williams's plays is comparable to the world-view of *Nineteen Eighty-Four* and *Catch-22*. Much more significant is 'The Stork and the Reaper, the Madonna and the Stud' (677–700), in which Joan Wylie Hall traces the surprising recurrence and importance of procreation and mothering in the plays, themes which should now be seen to have major relevance for studies of sexuality in Williams's work, a representative example of which is contained here in Mark Royden Winchell's 'Come Back to the Locker Room Agin, Brick Honey!' (701–12), a post-Fiedlerian study of homosexuality in *Cat*.

Philip C. Kolin, who has previously written on many different performances of *Streetcar*, adds to the list by contributing a piece on 'The Japanese Premiere of *A Streetcar Named Desire*' (713–33), but the two most remarkable essays in the collection are more theoretical studies of performance. Taking three classic Broadway productions as examples, John Gronbeck-Tedesco's 'Ambiguity and Performance in the Plays of Tennessee Williams' (735–49) argues that the style of performance recalls the Renaissance style of Mannerism in the visual arts, creating the impression of complex psychology and 'conflicting cultural forces' by the positioning and torque of the actors' bodies in relation to one another. In 'Gaze and Resistance in the Plays of Tennessee Williams' (751–61), John Timpane argues that the gaze, for Williams, is essentially masochistic, and encompasses four areas: ' "place" as a construction of the imagination, a metaphor for the chaotic determination of identity; people as subjects rather than selves; humanity as a single group composed of infinite, resistant versions, any of them potential objects of desire; and the "Southern" as a metaphor for a kind of conflicted identity'. Due to their subject and theoretical density these essays must be read in their entirety; they are arguably the finest studies yet of Williams's plays in performance, while Gronbeck-Tedesco's piece in particular represents an important intervention within the field of performance studies as a whole.

Brenda Murphy's *Miller: Death of a Salesman* appears in Cambridge's Plays in Production series, and provides an in-depth study of carefully selected productions on stage and in other media. The extensive chronology, index and bibliography aside, more than one third of the book, some 69 pages, is devoted to the first Broadway production of 1949. Murphy is the ideal guide, having previously explored the working relationship of director Elia Kazan and designer Jo Mielziner in her excellent *Tennessee Williams and Elia Kazan: A Collaboration in the Theatre* (*YWES* 73.625). Inevitably, much of the material is familiar from the memoirs of Miller, Kazan and Mielziner, and Murphy's account also follows a sequence (composition, the assembling of the production team, the design process, music, directing, revisions, rehearsals and critical reception) closely foreshadowed as recently as last year in a chapter on *Salesman* in Andrew B. Harris's *Broadway Theatre* (*YWES* 75.668–9). No matter: Murphy's lucid distillation of a wealth of material, including much from unpublished sources, along with several reproductions of Mielziner's designs, makes this the definitive study. Her detailed explanation of how the production team overcame endemic problems in text and staging justifies the emphasis on this first production, and the comparatively cursory overview, in just 56 pages, of other productions is therefore less incongruous than might appear at first sight. Both stage and television versions of the 1985 production featuring Dustin Hoffman are considered at some length, since Hoffman's interpretation differed markedly from Lee J. Cobb's original. Also included is a lengthy and especially valuable account of a more elusive, landmark 1966 television version, featuring Cobb and adapted by Miller and director Alex Segal. Throughout, Murphy presents the material in her characteristically scholarly yet accessible style, to provide both a fine stage history and an important critical introduction to the play.

Gerald Weales has unearthed ten of at least 17 radio scripts by Miller which were broadcast, often as wartime propaganda, between 1939 and 1946, and describes them in a fine scholarly article, 'Arthur Miller Takes the Air' (*AmDram* 5.i.1–15). Weales notes Miller's distaste for the medium, and considers the scripts to be rather weak apprentice pieces. The same issue contains an interview with Miller by Steven R. Centola ('The Last Yankee', *AmDram* 5.i.78–98), in which Miller suggests that the impact of film and television on actors has contributed to the decline of the theatre; attributes the absence of modern tragedy to the contemporary tendency to feel not directly but ironically; and discusses *The Ride Down Mount Morgan*, *Broken Glass* and *The Last Yankee* in some detail. An earlier work is the subject of Stephen Marino's 'Arthur Miller's "Weight of Truth" in *The Crucible*' (*MD* 38.488–95), which traces the associations of the words 'weight' and 'weighty' in this play, but ultimately the discussion is rather insubstantial. However, Bernard Rosenthal's superb *Salem Story: Reading the Witch Trials of 1692* will be of major interest to *Crucible* scholars. Rosenthal provides both a fresh exposition of the events of the trials, and a critique of the ideological imperatives behind the myths which have subsequently formed around them. Rosenthal concludes that explanation of the events of 1692 requires the detection of neither witchcraft nor hysteria: instead, the behaviour of the accused was a rational, if desperate, attempt to save themselves from the gallows by following and contributing to the logical narrative which developed during the proceedings in court. Rosenthal's account allows us to see *The Crucible*, first, as contributing to the mass hysteria explanation; and, secondly, as one expression of the contradictions implicit in many recent retellings of the story. On the one hand, '[t]he myth of Salem as something that cannot happen again, because the age of "witchcraft" has passed, ironically reassures us of our safety from random irrationality by the state even as we evoke Salem to label acts of persecution'; on the other, we are confronted with 'the paradox of rational explanations intertwined with a vocabulary that, intentionally or not, implicitly affirms the victims of the trials as witches'.

In 'Albee's Martha' (*AmDram* 5.i.51–70), Bonnie Blumenthal Finkelstein sees *Who's Afraid of Virginia Woolf?* as 'social criticism' which draws attention to the limited opportunities open to women in 1962. Finkelstein suggests that Martha fears Virginia Woolf because she represents madness, but also because her creativity and ability to play the leading role in her own life contrast with Martha's barren and dependent existence.

For some years, Sam Shepard's work has been subjected to a number of re-readings closely informed by developments in post-1960s literary and dramatic theory. The first part of Laura J. Graham's *Sam Shepard: Theme, Image and the Director* offers, by contrast, a study grounded in the concerns of traditional literary interpretation: the relations between author and work; the establishment of continuities between earlier and later texts; an interest in character and theme; a study of much of the canon as expressing 'the tragic nature of the human condition'; the exploration of myth via such authorities as Frazer, Jung and Campbell. This solid, but familiar and unexciting, study provides the platform for the second, much more interesting half of the book. Here, Graham places more emphasis on visual and aural texture; explores the theoretical and practical questions raised in acting and staging the text; and describes her own experiences of directing some of the works. Shepard's presentation of women is discussed in an appendix, again in rather traditional terms of dualism and myth. Overall, this book is a good example of one strand of Shepard criticism, which sees his work as expressing an American Romanticism refracted through 'a late 20th century version of existentialism'; but the postmodernist directions in his writing are addressed only by implication.

A related approach to this dramatist is followed by James H. McTeague in *Playwrights and Acting: Acting Methodologies for Brecht, Ionesco, Pinter, and Shepard*. Not surprisingly, McTeague sees these four playwrights as rebels against the conventions of realism and naturalism and their plays as problematizing the Stanislavskian system of acting, the methods of which are outlined in an opening chapter. He then approaches the work of each of the four dramatists, using their own comments upon acting, and those of some of the actors and directors with whom they have been associated, to outline the acting methods appropriate to each. In consequence, the chapters tend to consist of a large number of lengthy quotations joined together by McTeague's commentary. This is an unambitious book, but it is useful as a kind of handbook to questions raised in the process of transposition from text to stage. Interestingly, the focus on acting leads both Graham and McTeague to posit much closer affinities between the earlier and later works of Shepard than are commonly accepted.

Israel Horovitz: A Collection of Critical Essays is the first book-length study of this playwright, whose works to date have received greater attention in France than in Anglophone countries. The book is edited by Leslie Kane, who has also supplied an introduction, an interview with Horovitz, and an essay on *The Widow's Blind Date*, which traces the development of the play through a number of versions. The concern with violence in this essay recurs in a number of contributions, most extensively in William Demastes's keynote discussion of the 'national cycles of violence' in the playwright's work; Robert Skloot's analysis of ethnicity; and John Watkins's and Andrew Elfenbein's exploration of 'Violence and Homosexual Subtexts in Israel Horovitz'. Thomas F. Connolly provides an informed account of the playwright's adopted home in 'The Place, The Thing: Israel Horovitz's Gloucester Milieu', and argues that the threat of obsolescence hanging over the town gives the Gloucester plays a universal and historical significance. Several critics trace some of the more significant literary influences, including Robert Combs on O'Neill, Robert Scanlan on Beckett and Dennis A. Klein on 'The Influence of Aeschylus's *Oresteia* on Israel Horovitz's *Alfred Trilogy*'. Other essays focusing on specific works include Liliane Kerjan's discussion of *The Quannapowitt Quartet*, Martin J. Jacobi's perceptive analysis of *Mackerel*, Steven H. Gale's 'Israel Horovitz's *Strong-Man's Weak Child/Strong-Men*: From Stage Play to Screenplay', and two feminist critiques of the playwright: Susan C. Haedicke's 'Portraits of Wo(Men) in Israel Horovitz's *North Shore Fish* and *Park Your Car in Harvard Yard*', which argues that his female characters remain trapped within the 'male-derived narrative' of which they are a part, and Ann C. Hall's 'Machismo in Massachusetts: Israel Horovitz's Unpublished Screenplays *The Deuce* and *Strong-Men*'. Like Haedicke, Hall considers that women are objectified by the narrative structure of these works, in this case because of their reliance on the formulae of the Hollywood screenplay, although Hall does suggest that there is a more complex critique of masculine behaviour in Horovitz's work. Taken together, the essays in this collection make a strong case for Horovitz as a major, and underrated, contemporary American playwright.

In 'The Politics of Gender, Language and Hierarchy in David Mamet's *Oleanna*' (*JAS* 29.190–213), Christine MacLeod convincingly argues that the power struggle between John and Carol is a question of institutional status: gender becomes a tactical weapon, and if Carol's conduct is 'demonstrably unfair', this actually exposes the workings of patriarchy, whose 'operations and assumptions only become truly visible when seen in an unfamiliar light'. Verna Foster takes a related view of the same play in 'Sex, Power, and Pedagogy in Mamet's *Oleanna* and Ionesco's *The Lesson*' (*AmDram* 5.i.36–50). Foster astutely uses the comparison with Ionesco's play to argue that the realism of *Oleanna* is only superficial, although the argument of the essay actually affirms the realism by maintaining what appears to be the logical contradiction that *Oleanna* is 'an allegory of higher education'.

Philip Middleton Williams's *A Comfortable House: Lanford Wilson, Marshall W. Mason and the Circle Repertory Theatre* might accurately be described as a documentary, rather than a critical book. Following a journalistic account of the development of the collaboration between playwright Wilson and director Mason, Middleton provides three chapters on the Talley plays. The 1978 play *5th of July*, and the revisions which led to its transformation into *Fifth of July* in 1980, are discussed at length, but the chapters on *Talley's Folly* and *Talley and Son* are very brief, although Williams does helpfully give some account of an earlier version of the latter called *A Tale Told*. To a great extent, Williams allows Wilson and Mason, and some of those who have worked with them, to tell the story. For the most part the chapters are constructed from very lengthy quotations and textual extracts, connected by an uncritical commentary which probably amounts to considerably less than 50 per cent of the text, even discounting the six interviews transcribed at the end of the book. *A Comfortable House* nevertheless has its value, of course, as a book which attempts to efface the signs of authorship in presenting the views of its subjects.

Neal A. Lester's *Ntozake Shange: A Critical Study of the Plays* is the first book-length study of this playwright, and a fine introduction to her work. Separate chapters on *for colored girls who have considered suicide/when the rainbow is enuf*, *spell no. 7*, *a photograph: lovers in motion*, *boogie woogie landscapes* and *From Okra to Greens* manage the formidable achievement of providing illuminating close readings of works which are consistently irreducible to the purely verbal or textual. These detailed studies are given sharper focus by the many illuminating comparisons and sources Lester provides in describing Shange's general style: for example, he notes that her experiments in form and syntax were influenced by Amiri Baraka, and observes that the characteristic air of celebration and unity in her work may be contrasted with Adrienne Kennedy's note of despair and fragmentation. Lester's account of the African-American sources of Shange's distinctive form, the 'choreopoem', is particularly valuable, and provides important contexts for the discussion of her resistance to patriarchal and Eurocentric theatre. He discusses fully the important and controversial questions surrounding Shange's representation of African-American men, although the implications of her remarks concerning 'the potential threat of violence any female might feel in the presence of any male' in 'patriarchy's universally oppressive system' are perhaps still more radical than Lester concedes.

In 'Audience, Utopia, and a Queer Sort of Materialism' (*TJ* 47.207–27), David Savran links the presentation of politics, history and utopia in Tony Kushner's *Angels in America* to Kushner's reading of Walter Benjamin and to the ideology of Mormonism. Savran accounts for the play's popularity by arguing that, for all its ambivalence and even its apparent radicalism, it finally 'assures the (liberal) theatre-going public that a kind of liberal pluralism remains the best hope for change'.

Four books have recently appeared on August Wilson, of which *May All Your Fences Have Gates*, a collection of new essays (ed. Alan Nadel), is the most substantial. John Timpane, in 'Filling the Time', sees African-American history in Foucauldian terms of radical disjuncture. Characters such as Ma Rainey or Troy Maxson sacrifice themselves to bring such changes into being, yet to survive after the event they are compelled to deceive themselves in ways which contradict the audience's retrospective knowledge, thereby setting up a tension between 'excluded' and 'empowered' readings of history. A more radical approach to history is proposed in Alan Nadel's fascinating 'Boundaries, Logistics, and Identity: The Property of Metaphor in *Fences* and Joe Turner's *Come and Gone*', which reads the inversions of the literal and the figurative in Wilson's plays in the context of racial law in antebellum America: the existence of the Mason-Dixon line, for example, required black Americans to privilege the figurative over the literal if one was 'to consider oneself human'. Michael Morales retains some more familiar distinctions between the literal and the metaphoric in relating Wilson's treatment of history to forms of African ritual. Anne Fleche's argument in 'The History Lesson' that the presentation of African-American experience exists in a present, ironic relation to a more stable referent, that 'of a dominant (white) history', begs a number of questions, most starkly illuminated by Mark William Rocha's account of 'American History as "Loud Talking" in *Two Trains Running*'. Rocha notes that speeches addressed to a second character may really be addressed to a third party, the (often white) audience, whose shortcomings are thereby revealed.

In Wilson's plays, music is frequently a medium of history, and it is no surprise to find essays in this collection on jazz (a lengthy contribution by Craig Werner) and blues (Sandra Adell's discussion of *Ma Rainey's Black Bottom*, which contains the interesting but surely questionable suggestion that Nietzsche's views on Wagner are equally applicable to the blues). Less frequently remarked is the influence of visual art on Wilson's work, but his acknowledged indebtedness to the paintings of Romare Bearden is the subject of a detailed study by Joan Fishman, who relates the work of both to traditions of African performance. Also reprinted here is Wilson's own 'I Want a Black Director', a short piece concerning the controversy which has scuppered the filming of *Fences*, followed by a lengthy and only partially convincing response by Michael Awkward.

Contrary views of Wilson's presentation of women are offered by Sandra G. Shannon (the compiler of the volume's lightly annotated bibliography), who feels that the playwright is 'coming to grips with the depth and diversity of African American womanhood' despite noting that most of his female characters occupy the position of 'nurturer', and Harry J. Elam, for whom 'the choices that these women make are conservative ones that reaffirm the traditional patriarchal order'. Missy Dehn Kubitschek's focus on the figure of the shaman offers a surprisingly different view. For her, the shared rituals of male and female shamans in the plays demonstrate the preferability of an African-American notion of 'overlapping spheres' to a Eurocentric notion of 'separate spheres'.

Inevitably, some of the material in Nadel's book is repeated in different form in *August Wilson: A Casebook* (ed. Marilyn Elkins). Mark William Rocha, in another fine essay, outlines the profound influence on Wilson of the 'four B's': Romare Bearden, Imamu Amiri Baraka, Jorge Luis Borges and the Blues, and considers that a knowledge of these influences is essential to a decoding of the unique sign-system informing Wilson's work. By contrast, Joanne Gordon's discussion of Wilson and Athol Fugard fails to establish the centrality of the relationship, while Eileen Crawford's essay on the blues in *Ma Rainey* should be read alongside Sandra Adell's in the Nadel collection.

Several of the *Casebook* essays complement the aforementioned studies of Wilson's Afrocentricity. Trudier Harris's account of 'August Wilson's Folk Traditions', which focuses on *Joe Turner's Come and Gone*, adds to Kubitschek's study of shamanism, while providing additional perspectives on the blues. Similarly, Patricia Gantt's account of the 'Ghosts from "Down There": The Southernness of August Wilson' places the mythological and metaphysical present-ness of the Southern past within the context of Southern folklore and the memory of slavery.

Pamela Jean Monaco offers a less expansive reading of Wilson as a playwright whose work marks a shift in African-American drama from the political activism of the 1960s and 1970s towards family-based drama. More interestingly, Gunilla Theander Kester argues that the dialectic of body and history in Wilson's work situates it within a specifically 'African American postmodernism', resulting in part from the need to supplement a history which is either largely unknown or negotiated in silence. Kim Marra's lengthy essay on gender suffers by comparison to the corresponding pieces in Nadel's collection: she, also, notes the tendency towards stereotyping, but the possibility of a dialectic or developing critique is prohibited by her monolithic representations of 'the sexist values of white supremacist capitalist patriarchy'. Nadel includes few accounts of dramaturgy in his book, but the balance is redressed to some extent in the *Casebook* by the inclusion of Joan Fishman's scholarly account of the progress of *Fences* through five drafts, Sandra G. Shannon's discussion of the central creative collaboration between Wilson and director Lloyd Richards, and interviews with both Wilson and Richards by Richard Pettengill.

The two essay collections make redundant most of Kim Pereira's slim *August Wilson and the African-American Odyssey*. His account of 'the themes of separation, migration, and reunion', 'cultural identity and self-affirmation' and the 'fight for survival' lacks the historical rigour and theoretical sophistication of most of the aforementioned accounts, as does his emphasis on the centrality of music. The discussions of *Ma Rainey*, *Fences*, *Joe Turner* and *The Piano Lesson* are competent enough, but marred by an outdated and rather naïve presentation of characters and themes, a weakness compounded by Pereira's novelistic tendency to retell the stories of the characters' lives in the past tense. Of much greater interest is Sandra D. Shannon's *The Dramatic Vision of August Wilson*. Like Pereira, Shannon devotes a chapter to each of the major plays, but in her case these include *Two Trains Running* as well as the most substantial account available of the unpublished *Jitney!* Shannon's primary emphasis is biographical: she notes both the personal experiences that contribute to each of the major plays, and the development of Wilson's method and style as his career progresses. Although Shannon is less explicitly theoretical in her historiography than many of the contributors to Nadel's book, she provides a detailed historical context for the themes of slavery, migration, African and Southern roots, and economic racism which permeate the works. This is a most readable and illuminating study of Wilson, and the most straightforwardly helpful general introduction to the playwright. The *Casebook* may be recommended as an important supplement to *May All Your Fences Have Gates*, which contains the more significant analyses of Wilson's central concern with the revisioning of African-American history.

4. Black American Literature

Since African-American poetry and drama continue to be covered under the relevant genre headings in Sections 1 and 3 of the present chapter, this new section focuses primarily on fiction and on the general debates surrounding black literary expression. The survey is in two parts: (a) general studies, arranged alphabetically by author/editor; and (b) studies of individual writers.

(a) General
If frequency of reference is anything to go by, W. E. B. Du Bois's famous passage about the 'double-consciousness' of African-Americans must surely be regarded as the *locus classicus* of contemporary scholarship on black literature. Aptly, therefore, Sandra Adell's *Double Consciousness/Double Bind: Theoretical Issues in Twentieth Century Black Literature* heads my list for review. The book offers a robust enquiry, not just into Du Boisian ideas but, more generally, into the way his concept of the divided self, grounded as it is in European metaphysics, may be seen to prefigure the 'double bind' that characterizes recent African-American critical practice. Henry Louis Gates Jr and Houston Baker notwithstanding, Adell believes that attempts to promulgate 'black-specific' theories of writing are necessarily misconceived. Neither the former's vernacular model of 'signifyin(g)' nor the latter's 'blues matrix', she argues, can escape methodological reliance on Western critical paradigms. Paradoxically, therefore, 'the more the black theorist writes in the interest of blackness, the greater his Eurocentrism reveals itself to be'. The paradox as such does not bother Adell. Rather, her concern is with a disciplinary crisis arising from reluctance to acknowledge an essential corollary: that 'to identify itself, the Same needs the Other'. Specifically targeting Gates, Baker and certain doctrinaire tendencies in recent black feminist discourse, Adell's later chapters dissect the intellectual inconsistencies of an exclusivist approach to the African-American literary enterprise. The result is a spirited and searching critique, with important implications for the contemporary theoretical debate.

Like Adell, Michael Awkward is not afraid to be controversial. Like Adell too, he is profoundly engaged with issues of literary theory, and firmly opposed to the 'protectionist critical maneuvers' that have marked some recent varieties of Afrocentric and feminist practice. In *Negotiating Difference: Race, Gender, and the Politics of Positionality*, Awkward sets out to challenge critical paradigms based on 'the authority of experience'. Interpretive competence *vis-à-vis* counter-hegemonic texts, he argues, does not depend on one's racial or sexual credentials. Acutely aware, however, of his own precarious location 'somewhere on the borders of black feminist criticism', he does not pretend that reading across the boundaries of biological or cultural difference is easy. The insidious danger, always, is that such forays may function merely to reinscribe and consolidate hegemonic power. So how *can* male scholars engage adequately with women's texts and contexts? By the same token, how can white scholars validly address themselves to black literature? In Part 1 of the book, Awkward moves expertly through these overlapping minefields, and anyone even remotely committed to the risks (and rewards) of critical boundary-crossing would do well to be guided by him. Part 2 puts theory into lively practice, with investigations of cultural phenomena from Spike Lee and Mike Tyson to August Wilson's *Fences* and Toni Morrison's *Song of Solomon*. The latter discussion, reprinted from *Callaloo* 13 (*YWES* 71.643), is an outstanding piece, fully alert to Morrison's subtle reappraisal of the traditional epic quest. If this is 'black male feminism' in action, we need more.

Whether manifest as autobiography, *Bildungsroman* or quest narrative, one of the most familiar patterns in black literature is that of personal growth and development directed towards the creation of a 'whole self'. In *Conversions and Visions in the Writings of African-American Women*, Kimberly Rae Connor proposes a 'hitherto unexplored way' of reading this pattern. Works as historically and formally disparate as *The Narrative of Sojourner Truth*, Zora Neale Hurston's *Their Eyes Were Watching God* and Paule Marshall's *Praisesong for the Widow*, she argues, can best be understood as 'dramas of conversion' within a distinctive tradition of black female spirituality. The autobiographies of Harriet Jacobs and Rebecca Jackson, together with Morrison's *Sula* and Alice Walker's *The Color Purple*, complete the tally of texts considered. Connor is well versed in the scholarship surrounding the origins and qualities of African-American religious sensibility, and knowledgeable about ways in which the experience of conversion has been interpreted. Particularly germane are theologian Hans Mol's view of life in faith as a 'sacralization of identity' and William James's concept of conversion as the psychological process of unifying a divided self. Combining these ideas with recent feminist redefinitions of the sacred, Connor presents her case for reading black women's narrative acts of self-discovery and self-affirmation as, in essence, religious acts. If occasionally the 'principle of conversion' is stretched too thinly (to cover, for instance, a mere 'disposition toward change and seeking' in *Sula*), elsewhere it points to some important intersections between literary and religious accounts of identity formation.

For many black Americans, Countee Cullen's still-resonant question 'What is Africa to me?' is far from rhetorical, and, as Robert Eliot Fox shrewdly observes, 'neither "nothing" nor "everything" are acceptable replies'. Having lived and worked in Africa for seven years, Fox is perhaps in a better position than most to explore both the ruptures and the cross-cultural continuities of the black Atlantic experience. This, in general terms, is his aim in *Masters of the Drum: Black Lit/Oratures Across the Continuum*. The book is a miscellany of essays and interviews, old work and new, loosely centred on a sense of the common 'beats' (or what he elsewhere calls the 'deep song') to which African and black diasporan cultures respond. Despite the obvious dangers of postulating a version of 'natural rhythm' as the basis of a black aesthetic, Fox does not, in practice, overplay romantic notions of racial unity. Indeed, one of the best essays is an explicit and judicious assessment of some of the divisive issues that have surfaced in African-American literature and criticism since the 1960s. From subsequent pieces, however – for example on the work of Caribbean women writers, the Somali novelist Nuruddin Farah, and the Nigerian critic Chidi Amuta – it becomes clear how many of black America's 'internal' theoretical debates do have wider intra-racial dimensions. The problematics of cultural nationalism, the relationship between writing and the oral tradition, the responsibilities of criticism, and the place of theory itself, are fundamental concerns which can only benefit from being studied, as Fox suggests, across the continuum.

One of the critical highlights of the year was Farah Griffin's *'Who Set You Flowin'?' The African-American Migration Narrative*, which proposes and develops with real interdisciplinary flair an important perspective on twentieth-century black cultural expression. The thesis is that out of the African-American experience of mass northward migration there has emerged, across a variety of art forms, an identifiable set of images and narrative conventions amounting to a distinctive genre. Griffin's evidence, drawn from a scintillating array of fiction, poetry, painting, photography, journalism, blues and rap lyrics, demonstrates that although the migration narrative shares with nineteenth-century slave autobiographies the notion of 'ascent' from South to North, it is distinguished by its focus on the urban landscape, by its greater ambivalence about what was left behind and by its structural orientation around certain 'pivotal moments' of departure, arrival, conflict and appraisal. In separate chapters devoted to each of these 'moments', the discussion identifies how literary, visual and musical narratives have represented the migrants' trajectory. Some 12 writers are addressed in the study, including Jean Toomer, Richard Wright, Ann Petry, James Baldwin, Gloria Naylor and Toni Morrison. Despite the breadth of coverage, however, Griffin's individual readings also go deep, and her cross-reference to the tropes and iconography of migration in other expressive media is confident and unfailingly apt. Set Wright's *Uncle Tom's Children* alongside a Jacob Lawrence painting and Billie Holliday's rendition of 'Strange Fruit', for example, and the insights sparkle.

The City in African-American Literature, edited by Yoshinobu Hakutani and Robert Butler, consists of 16 new essays by various hands, on topics ranging from Frederick Douglass's autobiographies to Samuel Delany's science fiction cityscapes. It is a curiously incoherent and curate's-eggish collection. Some contributors focus on literary history, documenting the biographical evidence of a particular writer's urban experience. Some are concerned with textual analysis, with fictional *representations* of the city. And some, inexcusably, appear to think that biography and fiction are the same thing. Further confusions stem from the editors' introduction. Given the inevitable association of rural life with slavery and Southern peonage, they argue, the idealizing pastoral impulse has had little currency in African-American culture, and writers have turned instead to the city for positive images of liberation, opportunity and renewal. Hence, in summary, 'the main tradition of black literature has been persistently pro-urban in vision'. What 'main tradition' is this, I wonder? How do such claims correlate with the nightmare world of Wright's Bigger Thomas, or with the grim urban pathologies of Ann Petry, Willard Motley, John A. Williams, Amiri Baraka, Gloria Naylor? The fact that the collection actually covers work by all these writers merely underlines the dubious value of the editorial thesis. None the less, one must be grateful for sterling contributions from Donald Gibson on the Harlem Renaissance city, Fred Standley on Baldwin's New York, Larry Andrews on Petry and Michael Lynch on Naylor.

Two studies of the black *Bildungsroman* as a distinctive genre appeared this year. The first, Gunilla Kester's *Writing the Subject: 'Bildung' and the African-American Text*, is a densely argued and theoretically demanding study, heavy going at times. Kester has a firm grasp of the genre, though, and her meticulous attention to the ideological assumptions and narrative strategies of its European antecedents enables her to mount a credible case for the culturally specific features of the black American tradition. Notions of 'doubling' are central to the discussion, and are developed well beyond the obligatory genuflection to Du Bois's idea of the 'twoness' of African-American subjectivity. Distinguishing between the *dialectic* subject of the classic *Bildungsroman*, the *dialogic* subject of modernist European versions, and the *double* subject of her African-American texts, Kester suggests that the latter, from Douglass onwards, have of necessity pursued both an individual and a representative identity, and, in what amounts to a postmodernist reformulation of the genre, have called into question the very concept of progress towards a coherent and unified self. Aspects of the thesis are argued in relation to five main texts: predictably, Ralph Ellison's *Invisible Man* and Morrison's *The Bluest Eye*, and further off the beaten track, Gayl Jones's *Eva's Man*, Charles Johnson's *Oxherding Tale* and Sherley Anne Williams's *Dessa Rose*.

Related in theme, but suffering somewhat by comparison, is Geta LeSeur's *Ten is the Age of Darkness: The Black Bildungsroman*. This is a content-oriented survey of childhood and maturation as presented in the fiction of black writers in the United States and the West Indies. Eliding most of the formal differences between her selected texts, LeSeur's American chapters cover *Invisible Man* and *The Bluest Eye* again, together with Baldwin's *Go Tell It on the Mountain*, the fictionalized autobiographies of Langston Hughes and Richard Wright, and works by Gwendolyn Brooks, Paule Marshall and Ntozake Shange. Some tentative cross-cultural observations emerge – for instance, that the Caribbean authors appear to be more celebratory of the 'lost domain' of childhood, and less geared to social protest, than their African-American counterparts. However, the largely narrative approach militates against real depth of analysis. The discovery that stories of female initiation 'are very different from the boys' stories discussed ... mainly because of gender differences' scarcely qualifies as a critical breakthrough. Another problem is that LeSeur's cursory and untheorized delineation of the European *Bildungsroman* provides insufficient basis for her assertion that the genre has been pressured and indeed re-formed by the specific racial legacies of slavery and colonialism. Still, the general reader wishing to explore a variety of childhood experiences in fiction of the African diaspora will find the book an approachable introduction.

Under the title *The Changing Same: Black Women's Literature, Criticism, and Theory*, Deborah McDowell has put together a number of her essays from the past decade, including an early benchmark piece 'New Directions for Black Feminist Criticism' and individual readings of Emma Dunham Kelley, Frances Harper, Jessie Fauset, Nella Larsen, Morrison, Walker and Sherley Anne Williams. Much of the material has been previously published elsewhere. For example, two influential articles responding to the furore over alleged 'anti-male bias' in contemporary black women's writing have appeared, respectively, in the agenda-setting symposium *Afro-American Literary Study in the 1990s* (UChicP, 1989) and in Cheryl Wall's edited collection *Changing Our Own Words* (*YWES* 71.631). However, for all its scattered and occasional origins, the volume has a coherence which is more than the mere sum of its parts. The juxtaposition of essays spotlights three defining moments in the history of fiction by African-American women (the 1890s, the Harlem Renaissance, and the resurgent creativity of the 1970s and 1980s), and draws attention to recurring issues in the conceptualization of a black female literary tradition. At the same time, McDowell is keenly alert to questions of critical method and theory, and, through interpolated commentary and critique of her own earlier work, she is able to map out some of the shifting emphases of a still-evolving black feminist discourse.

Strictly speaking, a review of Richard Merelman's *Representing Black Culture* might seem beyond the remit of this essay. The author is a professor of political science, and almost the only direct reference he makes to African-American literature is a single sentence yoking Spike Lee with August Wilson and 'countless black writers from Ralph Ellison to Toni Morrison'. However, Merelman's analysis of the role of black culture in American race relations, and the critical perspectives to be derived from his discussion, strike me as simply too valuable to pass without notice. The book's subject is the dynamics of cultural projection – that is, the ways in which dominant and subordinate social groups represent themselves and attempt to shape how they are perceived by others in their society. Such projection takes four basic forms, functioning to promote either cultural syncretism, hegemony, polarization or counterhegemony. To Merelman's eternal credit, he turns these usually graceless abstractions into elegant, practical and penetrating instruments of enquiry. Through lucid and patient example, ranging from case-studies on the teaching of black history to the incidence and affective outcome of subordinate group imagery in television news coverage, we are shown how the various forms of black cultural projection actually work (or fail to do so), and are invited to consider how the results bear on the future of racial politics in the United States. The insights are compelling, the analytical framework is readily transferable to the criticism of black literature, and the book deserves to be widely read.

James Robert Saunders's *The Wayward Preacher in the Literature of African-American Women* is predicated on the view that the Christian church within the black community, for all its achievements of leadership and inspiration, has also functioned to legitimate and perpetuate the subordination of women. Accordingly, the argument goes, writers such as Larsen, Hurston, Marshall, Naylor and Terry McMillan have mounted a critique of the institution by exposing the fallibility of its traditional figurehead, the black preacher. There is plenty of potential here, both in the idea and the material selected, but Saunders diffuses and for pages at a stretch almost abandons his point in enthusiastic pursuit of inconsequential comparisons. What, one wonders, does a discussion of Sinclair Lewis's Carol Kennicot, Faulkner's Thomas Sutpen, or even the philandering televangelist Jimmy Swaggart, reveal about a black female perspective on abuses of power in the African-American pastorate? To be fair, the frame of reference is not always so peculiar. Contemporary testimony from disenchanted followers of Father Divine in the 1920s and 1930s is usefully adduced to reinforce Paule Marshall's fictional portrayal of the cult leader Father Peace in *Brown Girl, Brownstones*, and a worthwhile chapter on Naylor annotates her novels from *The Women of Brewster Place* to *Mama Day* in terms of their movement towards an alternative and self-affirming spirituality mediated through women. The project as a whole, however, required a steadier focus and a more disciplined methodology.

Cheryl Wall's *Women of the Harlem Renaissance* is a rewarding discussion, which usefully combines social and cultural history with illuminating biography and detailed literary criticism. Wall undertakes to redress the masculinist imbalance which typically – from Alain Locke's promotional claims for the 'New Negro' in 1925 to Nathan Huggins's landmark study of 1973 – has tended to obscure, when it has not actively disparaged, the significant contribution made by black women to the literary energies of the Harlem Renaissance. The central figures in her thesis, inevitably, are Fauset, Larsen and Hurston, but their lives and achievements are both clarified and contextualized in relation to a substantial network of lesser-known female contemporaries, and the overall focus on the participation of women compels a serious rethinking of many of the easy generalizations which have previously served to define the period. Whilst avoiding tendentious claims for her subjects, Wall gives courteous, historically informed attention to the constraints and cultural agendas which shaped their writing, and teases out their varying perspectives on the struggle for racial and sexual identity. Particularly stimulating is her extended cross-reference to other women artists. For example, contemporary public discourse about Josephine Baker is seen to reverberate in the European experience of Larsen's Helga Crane in *Quicksand*, while 'blueswomen' such as Bessie Smith, uncircumscribed by an alien aesthetic tradition, are credited with a freedom and vernacular exuberance which Wall contrasts sharply with the more decorous output of their literary sisters.

In *Identity, Family and Folklore in African-American Literature*, Lee Alfred Wright looks at representations of personal and family identity in a handful of well-known works of black fiction. Originally, I suspect, the project was conceived as a direct comparison of Alice Walker and Toni Morrison. Four of the five main chapters are devoted, respectively, to *Meridian*, *The Color Purple*, *The Bluest Eye* and *Sula*, and what interests Wright is the way these texts interrogate traditional concepts of motherhood and explore the legacies of abuse and/or abandonment in black families. Consideration is given to the strengths and limitations of the folk heritage as a source of behavioural models, and a historical dimension is supplied by brief readings of three earlier texts: William Wells Brown's *Clotel*, Harriet Jacobs's *Incidents in the Life* and Charles Chesnutt's *The Conjure Woman*. There may be a few raised eyebrows at the vagaries of typography – for instance, at the characterization of Plum in *Sula* as 'a heroine addict' (*sic*) – but otherwise the discussion is largely unsurprising, an accessible regrouping of familiar ideas rather than a signpost to new ones.

I have left until last the most general of all this year's 'General' titles: *The Schomburg Center Guide to Black Literature* (ed. Roger Valade). Fascinating, frustrating, and deeply flawed, this hefty A–Z reference book is optimistically advertised as 'a comprehensive resource to consult for in-depth information' on authors, works, characters, themes and critical theories relevant to American and international black literature from the eighteenth century to the present. As if this agenda were not large enough, the rubric 'relevant to black literature' is then interpreted so loosely as to cover political figures, historians, journalists, screenwriters, television presenters and indeed virtually any public person of African descent who has ever got into print. Hence, the biographical summaries include entries for Arthur Ashe, Bill Cosby, Winnie Mandela, Kwame Nkrumah and Sidney Poitier; quite the weirdest, undoubtedly, is for a Jamaican image consultant, Grace Ciee, whose claim to literary fame, apparently, rests on such publications as *Radiant Women of Color: Embrace, Enhance and Enjoy the Beauty of Your Natural Coloring*. Plot synopses are given for approximately 460 major works, and characters within these works also have cross-referenced entries (e.g. 'Beloved. Character in *Beloved*'). Additionally, there are brief explanatory essays on general topics such as Apartheid, the Black Aesthetic, Pan-Africanism, the Trickster Tale and the Underground Railroad. The text is attractively laid out and, beyond question, contains a wealth of useful information. By no stretch of the imagination, though, is the *Guide* either 'comprehensive' or 'in-depth'. Even unsystematic browsing reveals errors, omissions and anomalies on a scale to infuriate the specialist and render the material unreliable and often unhelpful to the general reader. Woe betide anyone enquiring about Marita Bonner, for instance: she does not appear in the index, and only sheer luck will discover her lurking behind her married name, Occomy. An entry on the Ivory Coast writer Bernard Dadie wrongly identifies Chinua Achebe and Wole Soyinka as belonging to 'a group of noted African authors writing in French'; the index conflates two entirely different Jesse Jacksons; two different publication dates are given for Ishmael Reed's *Japanese By Spring*; and in an entry on the blues, Audre Lorde unaccountably becomes male. Of course a carping critic can always find fault with both the detail and the coverage in this kind of supposedly encyclopaedic project. However, while it might (just) be possible to concede the omission of Jess Mowry as a judgement call, the failure to include Harriet Jacobs and *Incidents in the Life of A Slave Girl* is, quite simply, inexcusable.

Another major irritation is the inadequacy of the 'Further Reading' suggestions which, more often than not, merely serve as self-referential advertisements for previous Gale publications. Symptomatically, a biographical entry on the critic Arnold Rampersad rightly credits him with 'the definitive biography' on Langston Hughes; yet the entry on Hughes himself ignores this definitive source and directs us instead to six Gale reference books. It is disappointing that, under the auspices of the prestigious Schomburg Center for Research in Black Culture, a more scholarly production was not forthcoming. The book may have its uses in a school library, but it is certainly not the 'one-stop authoritative guide' it claims to be.

(b) Individual Authors

In a strong and well-diversified issue of *CollL* (22.iii) devoted to 'Race and Politics: The Experience of African-American Literature', Pierre Walker writes on 'Racial Protest, Identity, Words and Form in Maya Angelou's *I Know Why the Caged Bird Sings*' (91–108). A chapter in Sandra Adell's book (see General section above) draws on the same Angelou text, together with Richard Wright's *Black Boy*, to construct a Lacanian account of black autobiographical acts as 'a process of self/other creation'.

Relative to the size of his oeuvre, work on James Baldwin seems to have slowed to a trickle this year. There are two essays in the Hakutani and Butler collection (see above), and, in *CEA*, a discussion of 'James Baldwin, *Giovanni's Room*, and the Biblical Myth of David' (57.41–58) by R. J. Frontain. Ernest Champion's *Mr Baldwin, I Presume* (UPA) has not been received for review.

By contrast, critical interest in David Bradley – or more precisely, in the second of his two novels to date – seems to be on the increase. Matthew Wilson's 'The African-American Historian' (*AAR* 29.97–107) and W. Lawrence Hogue's 'Problematizing History' (*CLAJ* 38.441–60) both focus on *The Chaneysville Incident* and on the protagonist's search for a historical method capable of reconstructing his personal and racial past. Wilson thinks the truth of that past is accessible through 'rejection of Western assumptions about history' and intuitive entry into 'an African concept of time'. Hogue, however, argues that the protagonist develops a postmodern attitude and agenda; his search, therefore, is less for the 'truth' of history than for an imaginative projection – a narrative of what *could* have happened – which will legitimate and make coherent his present experience. The gender dimensions of the quest are explored by Cathy Brigham in 'Identity, Masculinity and Desire in David Bradley's Fiction' (*ConL* 36.289–316), where the earlier novel *South Street* is included in a thesis about women as narrative catalysts in Bradley's 'reinvention' of male identity. *The Chaneysville Incident* also features in a comparative essay by Helen Lock (*CollL* 22.iii.109–20) which, under the title 'Building Up From Fragments', examines how Bradley, Paule Marshall and Toni Morrison seek to represent and validate the processes of memory as they operate in an oral culture.

Black America's two leading practitioners of science fiction, Octavia Butler and Samuel Delany, are known and admired within the SF community, but not widely discussed by critics outside that enclave. A pity, because the way in which generic conventions may be inflected to engage with distinctively ethnic concerns is well worth attention. Cathy Peppers demonstrates this in 'Dialogic Origins and Alien Identities in Butler's *Xenogenesis*' (*SFS* 22.47–62), where she argues that the Butler trilogy destabilizes traditional discourses of origin in order to propose new ways of imagining racial and gender identity. Reaching out to genre-shy newcomers, Burton Raffel's enthusiasm for Butler's stylistic power and 'driven, insightful intelligence' is conveyed in a panoramic and proselytizing survey 'Genre to the Rear, Race and Gender to the Fore: The

Novels of Octavia Butler' (*LitR* 38.454–61). A discussion of Delany's work occupies almost one third of Damien Broderick's *Reading By Starlight: Postmodern Science Fiction*, but the emphasis here is heavily genre-specific. Broderick writes on the Neveryona sequence, *The Einstein Intersection* and, in some detail, on *Stars in My Pocket*, but his primary interest is in Delany as a 'semiotic-cum-poststructural theorist concerned with creating an adequate SF analytics'.

The European provenance of Du Bois's philosophical ideas is explored in the early chapters of Sandra Adell's *Double Consciousness/Double Bind* (see above). Shamoon Zamir's full-length study *Dark Voices: W. E. B. Du Bois and American Thought, 1888–1903* provides a scholarly account of that period when Du Bois's engagement (and dissatisfaction) with certain traditions of American philosophical and social thought can be seen to take shape. The first section deals with archival materials and other writings from the Harvard years through to the turn of the century, and includes discussion of a previously unpublished satirical sketch, 'A Vacation Unique'. The second section provides a meticulous reading of *The Souls of Black Folk* in its entirety. Quite apart from its intrinsic interest – and such sustained attention to the organic literary structure of the text is rare enough – Zamir's analysis also reveals the gap between Du Boisian thought and some of the contemporary ideologies it has inappropriately been made to serve. The famous passage on 'double-consciousness', he argues, must be understood not as an all-purpose, transhistorically true summation of homogenous African-American psychology, but as a limited, class-specific description of the 'Talented Tenth' in intellectual crisis following the failure of Reconstruction. Moreover, Du Bois's complex examination of the Sorrow Songs offers a sociology of folk culture that carefully avoids the primitivist 'nostalgias of collectivity' to which more recent proponents of black exceptionalism have fallen prey. Also worth mentioning in this context is Ross Posnock's essay 'The Distinction of Du Bois: Aesthetics, Pragmatism, Politics' (*ALH* 7.500–24), which thoughtfully explores and resolves the seeming contradiction between Du Bois's democratic socialism and his allegedly elitist emphasis on aesthetic experience.

Ralph Ellison's death last year has not yet prompted the kind of full-scale critical retrospective that might have been anticipated. Already in press when Ellison died, however, was Jerry Watts's important study *Heroism and the Black Intellectual: Ralph Ellison, Politics, and Afro-American Intellectual Life*, and despite the now-anachronistic present tenses of the discussion, its probing assessment of Ellison's career and cultural significance will, I suspect, serve as a touchstone for continuing scholarship. As the title suggests, Watts's priorities are not directly literary-critical. He is a political scientist concerned with the way black America's intelligentsia has perceived its social function and negotiated the often contradictory demands of personal creativity and political engagement. From this perspective Ellison's embattled mandarin stance, defined by Watts as 'heroic individualism' and seen by others as ivory tower elitism, makes for an ideal case-study. Drawing on the biographical record and the essays of *Shadow and Act* and *Going to the Territory*, Watts defines and appraises Ellison's intellectual style through comparisons with the more socially oriented strategies adopted by Wright, Hughes and Baldwin. Ultimately, though respectful of Ellison's 'heroism' in pursuit of artistic excellence, Watts is disturbed by and at times scathingly critical of both the bases and the consequences of such apolitical 'hyperindividuality'. Exercised like Harold Cruse and Du Bois before him by the responsibilities of the African-American intellectual enterprise, Watts reconfigures for the nineties the perennial question of whether and how best the black writer can or should serve the needs of the broader ethnic community.

The Spring issue of *Callaloo* (18) has a special section on 'Remembering Ralph Ellison', which prints two of his short stories and, for the rest, consists mainly of tributes and personal reminiscences that say more about the man than about his writing. John F. Callahan's warmly appreciative 'Frequencies of Memory' (298–309) is an expanded version of a eulogy delivered at Ellison's funeral. An oddly self-absorbed piece by Steve Cannon entitled 'Reminiscin' in C' (288–97) is revealing evidence of how some younger black writers contrived to marginalize Ellison and persuade themselves that his hard-won vision was 'not a framework in which to talk about these times'. Keneth Kinnamon's 'Ellison in Urbana' (273–9) contextualizes and reprints a 1967 interview conducted for the University of Illinois student newspaper, and Nathan A. Scott revises a previously published critical essay on 'Ellison's Vision of Communitas' (310–18). In 'The World as Possibility: The Significance of Freud's *Totem and Taboo* in Ellison's *Invisible Man*' (*L&P* 41.1–18), Caffilene Allen reaches sensible conclusions about the novel, even if some of the parallels drawn between clinical theory and fictional action seem a bit strained. Unavailable for review was *Cultural Contexts for 'Invisible Man'* (St Martin's/Macmillan), edited by Eric J. Sundquist.

'One of the best books I've ever published was the book by Leon Forrest.' The verdict is Toni Morrison's, in interview with Cecil Brown (see below), and although the book in question is unspecified – *There is a Tree More Ancient than Eden*, probably – one would think that with such praise, from such a source, Forrest's work should command a wider audience than it does. Those seeking more information on the author will get an engaging impression of his distinctive voice and vision from 'The Yeast of Chaos: An Interview with Leon Forrest', by Molly McQuade (*ChiR* 41.ii–iii.43–51).

Ernest J. Gaines's first novel appeared in 1964. Since then he has published a collection of short stories and five more novels, including *The Autobiography of Miss Jane Pittman* (1971), the superb *A Gathering of Old Men* (1984), and, most recently, *A Lesson Before Dying* (1993). Despite this substantial body of work, however, critical recognition has been slow in coming. Perhaps the 'regionalist' label is to blame: Gaines's quiet care for rural southern lives seems remote from the more flamboyantly contested urban experience depicted in work by his contemporaries. Perhaps, too, his deceptively straightforward style masks the vigorous intelligence of his novels. In any event, Herman Beavers's book *Wrestling Angels Into Song: The Fiction of Ernest Gaines and James Alan McPherson* deserves credit for its attempt to redirect attention to Gaines's considerable achievement. Less successfully, the study also addresses the short stories of McPherson and, further, seeks through extensive comparison to posit and explore a 'literary triad' consisting of Gaines, McPherson and their precursor Ralph Ellison. What the three have in common, Beavers says, is a desire to understand their American identity in terms larger than those afforded by race. Some striking insights emerge, especially on the Ellison/Gaines axis, but overall I found both the conceptual apparatus and the style of expression rather cumbersome. However, if many of Beavers's best ideas are inchoate rather than fully realized, it merely confirms his own view that there is 'still ... much to do with these authors'. Philip Auger picks up the baton in 'A Lesson About Manhood: Appropriating "The Word" in Ernest Gaines's *A Lesson Before Dying*' (*SLJ* 27.74–85). Holding with Bakhtin that 'one must take the word and make it one's own', Auger shows how the discursive formations of white supremacy that surround the novel's condemned prisoner must be (and are) subverted before he can go to the electric chair 'like a man'. An earlier novel, *Of Love and Dust*, is explored by H. Nigel Thomas in his comparative essay 'The Bad Nigger Figure in Selected Works of Richard Wright, William Melvin Kelley and Ernest Gaines' (*CLAJ* 39.143–64). Also published this year, but not seen, was *Conversations with Ernest Gaines*, ed. John Lowe (UMP).

In 'The Griot from Tennessee: The Saga of Alex Haley's *Roots*' (*CritQ* 37.ii.46–62), Helen Taylor deftly relates the so-called 'black *Gone With the Wind*' to the generic codes of the plantation epic. Haley's claims to factual authenticity may now be severely tarnished, but Taylor finds that this in no way diminishes the power his text draws from its taproot in the mythologized master-narrative of Southern history.

Eighteen years in the writing, Carolivia Herron's prodigiously allusive, myth-laden and multivocal *Thereafter Johnnie* (1991) is a demanding novel whose tragic vision has been compared (by Carlos Fuentes, no less) to Faulkner's. As yet, however, few critics have ventured to engage with the work, so it is worth reporting Brenda Daly's 'Whose Daughter is Johnnie?' (*Callaloo* 18.472–91), a brave attempt to sort out the intricacies of Herron's 'revisionary mythmaking' in relation to the father/daughter incest theme.

Conversations with Chester Himes (UMP), edited by Michel Fabre and Robert Skinner, was published this year but has not been received for review. In 'From the Far Side of the Urban Frontier' (*CollL* 22.iii.68–90), Robert Crooks offers an excellent comparative study of Himes and Walter Mosley, appraising their use of the detective genre to represent and enact varieties of subcultural resistance, and concluding that the formal experimentation of Himes's Harlem novels 'possesses a more radical potential than anything in Mosley's writing to date'.

Langston Hughes: The Man, His Art and His Continuing Influence (ed. C. James Trotman), is a collection of papers from the May 1992 conference held at Lincoln University, Pennsylvania, to mark the twenty-fifth anniversary of Hughes's death. With genial authority, Arnold Rampersad's keynote address maps the broad contours of Hughes's creative versatility and his lifelong immersion in black cultural life. Subsequent essays pick out individual features of the terrain, decently alternating between familiar paths and specialist by-ways. Two contributors focus on the achievement of the 'Simple' stories; two deal with examples of short fiction from *The Ways of White Folks*; and two (including Cheryl Wall with her customary contextual verve) move outwards from the novel *Not Without Laughter* to explore Hughes's representation of the blueswoman. Other topics include the intersection of poetry, blues and gospel in Hughes's writing, and the friendship between Hughes and Gwendolyn Bennett. Three further essays document some of Hughes's collaborative ventures: Trotman writes about the libretto produced for the 1949 opera *Troubled Island*; Thadious Davis analyses *Sweet Flypaper of Life*, pointing to the interaction between Hughes's text and Roy DeCarava's photography; and

Bruce Kellner gives a fascinating account of the lyrics and blues fragments Hughes provided for Carl Van Vechten when the latter was forced to excise copyrighted material from the original version of *Nigger Heaven*. Donna Harper, one of the volume's contributors, also published a full-length study this year entitled *Not So Simple: The 'Simple' Stories by Langston Hughes* (UMissP), but I have not yet seen it.

Christopher De Santis, editor of *Langston Hughes and the 'Chicago Defender': Essays on Race, Politics, and Culture*, has collected and arranged over 100 of the weekly columns Hughes wrote for Chicago's leading black newspaper between 1942 and 1962. From memories of the Scottsboro boys to the murder of Emmett Till, from early hopes of Soviet Communism to the grim climate of McCarthyism, from the wartime segregation of Red Cross blood banks to the opening salvos of the Civil Rights Movement, the journalism touches on many salient aspects of a turbulent and transitional era. The material itself, therefore, is of undeniable value, extending our knowledge of Hughes's interests and ideas, and frequently intersecting with the characteristic voice of his poetry and fiction. I have reservations, though, about the editorial method. De Santis claims he has tried to present Hughes's columns 'as they originally appeared', but in practice his decision to group the pieces thematically violates the most basic aspect of their original appearance: the chronology. This has several unfortunate consequences. It distorts the calculated variety of Hughes's week-by-week topics, thus denying us a sense of his evolving relationship with his readers; it makes consecutive entries appear carelessly repetitive, whereas in fact they may be separated by anything up to three years; and it also creates some bewildering discontinuities. The provision of access to these fugitive writings is welcome, but the collection as a whole, I think, would have benefited from less intrusive editorial shaping. Michael Thurston fills in some significant gaps with 'Black Christ, Red Flag: Langston Hughes on Scottsboro' (*CollL* 22.iii. 30–49), an essay which elucidates the range of political positions that emerge from an intertextual analysis of Hughes's Scottsboro-era writings.

Freed from the requirements of embattled proselytizing, scholarship on Zora Neale Hurston looks set to enter a new phase. The major campaigns have been successful, the rescue mission is accomplished, and Hurston's position in the American literary pantheon is now secure enough for critics to start refining their perspectives on her achievement. John Lowe's *Jump at the Sun: Zora Neale Hurston's Cosmic Comedy* is the first study to focus in depth on comedy as a structuring principle in Hurston's novels and short stories. Drawing on Bakhtin's theory of the 'carnivalization of language' along with insights from anthropology and psychology, Lowe asks us to see past the comic surfaces, past the exuberant play of vernacular speech, to the cultural 'work' performed by folk humour: its role in healthy ego formation, its contribution to group solidarity, its deflationary and subversive potential. His approach cogently establishes a number of recurring patterns in the fiction, such that even the 'untypical' and often-marginalized *Seraph on the Suwanee* is drawn into productive relation with the rest of Hurston's writing. Also striking is his analysis of a sustained dialectic between 'freedom's joy' and 'freedom's law' in *Their Eyes Were Watching God* and *Moses, Man of the Mountain*. By and large the study succeeds in conveying a sense of coherence and continuity, not only across the oeuvre but also between the poles of human and holy, between Hurston's earthy comic realism and what Lowe perceives as the 'cosmic' dimensions of her imagination.

In *Every Tub Must Sit on Its Own Bottom*, Deborah Plant focuses on Hurston's political and philosophical ideas. The study begins by rebutting traditional accounts of Hurston as a naïve, compromised and ultimately lightweight thinker. To the contrary, Plant argues, Hurston's 'ideology of individualism' was a serious and sophisticated amalgam of the self-help doctrines of Booker T. Washington, the anthropological insights of Franz Boas and Ruth Benedict, and the philosophy of Spinoza and Nietzsche. Each of these intellectual influences is carefully analysed and related to the characteristic stances of Hurston's life and writings, thereby clarifying her disputes with the literati of the Harlem Renaissance and doing much to account for the apparently reactionary temper of her autobiography *Dust Tracks*. The thesis also underpins a vigorous reading of *Moses*, seen here as the fullest expression of Hurston's Nietzschean scorn for 'slave morality' and her belief in the self-reliant individual's will-to-power. Plant then turns to more recent critical accounts which, she claims, have equally misrepresented Hurston by hailing her as a spokeswoman for feminist ideals. Curiously, in view of a repeated insistence on her subject's 'empowering legacy', Plant detects little evidence of feminism in the sexual and colour politics of Hurston's fiction. Indeed, we are told, 'her texts, in essence, reinscribe and celebrate patriarchy' and, moreover, reveal a 'repressed enthralment' with white standards of beauty. In the present climate, Plant's findings verge on heresy, but there is enough substance in the argument to compel attention, and the very willingness to vex such questions is a sure sign of health in Hurston studies.

Work in the journals includes two stimulating essays on Hurston's best-known novel. In 'Should Their Eyes Have Been Watching God? Hurston's Use of Religious Experience and Gothic Horror' (*AAR* 29.17–25), Erik Curren disturbs conventional pieties about black folk culture, arguing that Tea Cake et al. in the Everglades section are presented as victims of a '*negative* folk belief' which, infected by the master/slave dialectic, has fostered a superstitious dependence on hierarchical authority. Carla Kaplan's 'The Erotics of Talk: "That Oldest Human Longing" in *Their Eyes Were Watching God*' (*AL* 67.115–42) may also unsettle some orthodoxies. The novel, Kaplan suggests, rewrites sexual desire as the desire to tell one's story; hence it is not Tea Cake but the patient listener Pheoby who, as 'bee' to the protagonist's narrative 'blossom', ultimately provides the erotic fulfilment Janie seeks.

Charles Johnson's brilliant and controversial *Middle Passage* won the National Book Award in 1990, but since then, apart from Ashraf Rushdy's article, 'The Phenomenology of the Allmuseri' (*AAR* 26[1992].373–94), the critical silence on the novel has been almost palpable. This year's clutch of three essays must therefore count as something of a breakthrough, even if one of them, S. X. Goudie's ' "Leavin' a Mark on the Wor(l)d": Marksmen and Marked Men in *Middle Passage*' (*AAR* 29.109–22), is perhaps too enmeshed in its own Derridean convolutions to explicate much of the text for other readers. Daniel Scott's 'Interrogating Identity: Appropriation and Transformation in *Middle Passage*' (*AAR* 29.645–55) is also a difficult piece, but worth wrestling with. Reading the novel's title as a trope for Johnson's attack on structures of dualistic thought, Scott says that the narrative opens up a 'middle space' of hybridity, ambivalence and indeterminacy, where identity can be reconfigured to encompass 'all that dichotomy denies'. Celestin Walby's approach in 'The African Sacrificial Kingship Ritual and Johnson's *Middle Passage*' (*AAR* 29.657–69) is myth-oriented, linking the fictional Allmuseri's notion of intersubjectivity to recurrent traditions of self-sacrifice, death and resurrection in Bambara, Dogon and Egyptian religious beliefs. James Coleman discusses an earlier and (to my mind) equally distinguished novel in 'Charles Johnson's Quest for Black Freedom in *Oxherding Tale*' (*AAR* 29.631–44). In Coleman's analysis, this novel's defiantly multicultural and multiracial intertextuality reflects Johnson's effort to free African-American writing from what he regards as the stereotyped and limiting aesthetic modes prescribed by the dominant black textual tradition.

Published this year but not available for review was Sondra K. Wilson's two-volume edition of *The Selected Writings of James Weldon Johnson* (OUP). Volume I covers the *New York Age* editorials (1914–23), and Volume II consists of Social, Political and Literary Essays. Johnson's 1912 novel *The Autobiography of an Ex-Colored Man* is the subject of an essay by Neil Brooks, 'On Becoming an Ex-Man: Postmodern Irony and the Extinguishing of Certainties' (*CollL* 22.iii.17–29), which shows how the quandary of 'passing' in the novel anticipates structures of alienation now considered to be characteristic of postmodernism.

Gayl Jones's work has never fitted comfortably into homogenizing accounts of African-American women's writing. All the more reason, therefore, to welcome two powerfully argued essays which both acknowledge and value her difference. In 'Gayl Jones and the Matrilineal Metaphor of Tradition' (*Signs* 20.245–67), Madhu Dubey reads *Corregidora* and the long poem *Song for Anninho* as implicit critiques of recent feminist discourse on matrilineage. *Contra* Alice Walker's model of black women 'in search of [their] mothers' gardens', these texts suggest that a preoccupation with maternal tradition may obstruct rather than assist the emergence of the daughter's voice. Carol Davison's essay ' "Love 'em and Lynch 'em": The Castration Motif in Gayl Jones's *Eva's Man*' (*AAR* 29.393–410) is as unusual and compelling as the novel it deals with. Approaching her theme through Bakhtinian notions of carnival and grotesque, Davison explicates Eva's gruesome attack on her lover as a 'redemptive ritual' whereby she achieves temporary liberation from the phallocentric order.

Two major beneficiaries of revisionist work being done on the Harlem Renaissance are Nella Larsen and Jessie Fauset. Extended consideration of their individual achievements appears in both McDowell and Wall (see above), and I note – though I have not seen – the following full-length studies: *The Politics of Color in the Fiction of Jessie Fauset and Nella Larsen* (UPVirginia) by Jacqueline McLendon and Thadious Davis's *Nella Larsen: Novelist of the Harlem Renaissance* (LSUP, 1994). *CLAJ* (39.165–78) has an essay by Bettye Williams on 'Nella Larsen: Early Twentieth-Century Novelist of Afrocentric Feminist Thought'. Claudia Tate's essay 'Desire and Death in *Quicksand*, by Nella Larsen' (*ALH* 7.234–60) is a zealously Lacanian attempt to uncover what she believes is the text's (and Helga Crane's) 'repressed and prohibited desire for the lost paternal object', and issues of portraiture and identity in *Quicksand* are discussed by Pamela Barnett in ' "My Picture of You Is, After All, the True Helga Crane" ' (*Signs* 20.575–600). In 'Veils of the Law: Race and Sexuality in Nella Larsen's *Passing*' (*CollL* 22.iii.50–67), Corinne Blackmer reads Larsen's second novel in relation to the Supreme Court's infamous ruling in *Plessy v. Ferguson*, and offers a thought-provoking analysis of the way recent legal reasoning on homosexuality is producing a contemporary discourse analogous to that which governed race in Larsen's time.

Paule Marshall has been described by Alice Walker as a writer 'unequalled in intelligence, vision, craft, by anyone of her generation'. While the claim may seem a large one, Walker is by no means alone in the belief that Marshall's work deserves more sustained critical attention than it has hitherto received. This year saw a step in the right direction with the publication of two studies, both of which claim to be the first book-length treatment of their subject. In *The Fiction of Paule Marshall*, Dorothy Denniston offers a straightforward and informative introduction, approaching the four novels and a clutch of shorter stories in chronological order so as to posit an emerging design that imaginatively reverses the Middle Passage and shows black people in transit from the New World back towards Africa. Much is made of Marshall's own cultural positioning as the American-born daughter of Barbadian immigrants, and of her consequent sensitivity to issues of identity formation as well as to the differences and 'hidden continuities' between various diasporan communities. Central to her artistic agenda, we are told, is a desire to affirm the ancestral source of these 'hidden continuities'. Hence, both in the orality of its narrative technique and in its content, her fiction stresses the importance of reclaiming and reconnecting with 'a core African value system'. Inevitably, Joyce Pettis's *Toward Wholeness in Paule Marshall's Fiction* covers much of the same ground. Though she takes a topical rather than a chronological approach to the material, Pettis is similarly preoccupied with the idea of 'the journey back', with the need for peoples of the black diaspora to embrace their African cultural origins in order to heal the psychic damage inflicted by life in the West. The scholarship is slightly more ambitious than Denniston's, more willing to articulate comparisons that help to place Marshall in a tradition of black women's writing, and more up-to-date in its bibliography. Both books, however, exhibit the characteristic flaws of romantic Afrocentricity, including a tendency to reinscribe the very stereotypes of cultural difference which shaped the polarizing rhetoric of white racism in the first place. Constantly invoking essentialist notions of a traditional, untainted and recoverable 'African sensibility', constantly opposing these to the alien and alienating values of the West, both books reduce Marshall's finely judged intercultural negotiations to a simple matter of rejecting western influence and opting for 'wholeness' through identification with Africa. Yet Marshall herself is never this schematic. As Michael Awkward points out in *Negotiating Difference*, even at Avey Johnson's 'blackest moment' in *Praisesong for the Widow* (that is, at the triumphant moment when the protagonist most fully embraces the meaning and responsibility of her Ibo heritage), she still sees and defines her task of cultural witness as that of a latter-day Ancient Mariner. The Coleridgean reference is not incidental: it signals a greater alertness to the contemporary realities and creative possibilities of cultural hybridity than either Denniston or Pettis wants to acknowledge. Geta LeSeur is also lured by the temptations of binary thinking, but in 'The Monster Machine and the White Mausoleum: Paule Marshall's Metaphors for Western Materialism' (*CLAJ* 39.49–61), a more limited focus on recurrent patterns of imagery keeps the editorializing impulse in check.

Predictably, Toni Morrison continues to receive more critical interest and attention than any other contemporary black writer. A short and reasonably accessible overview is Linden Peach's *Toni Morrison*, which has a chapter on each of the novels, traces connections between them, and contextualizes the material in terms of relevant aspects of the author's biography and issues in recent African-American criticism. Defining his perspectives 'under the general label of post-structuralist', Peach none the less insists that Morrison's fiction cannot be understood within the parameters of Euro-American literary criticism alone. Instead, he stresses the way in which African-American concerns and a distinctively black ontology inform the work, creating (he believes) 'narrative possibilities not previously realized in fiction'. This part of the thesis, unfortunately, is weakened by overstatement. It is certainly true that Morrison's oeuvre is 'not easily approached through reading habits developed in relation to the realist novel', but one can only wonder where Peach has been for the past 20 years if he really believes that challenges to realism, disruptions of linearity, multi-voiced narrative and a resistance to closure are innovative strategies arising from a uniquely African-American perspective.

CulS (9.ii) is a special issue devoted to 'Toni Morrison and the Curriculum'. It features essays of both critical and pedagogical interest, including David Bleich on 'Toni Morrison and the Indivisibility of Language' (256–69), Robin Small-McCarthy on 'The Jazz Aesthetic in Toni Morrison's Novels' (293–300) and Joyce Middleton on 'Confronting the "Master Narrative": The Privilege of Orality in *The Bluest Eye*' (301–17). An overview of Morrison's engagement with postcolonial issues of identity, essence, marginalization and 'otherness' is provided in 'Necessary Narratives: Toni Morrison and Literary Identities' (*WSIF* 18.585–94), by Mary Madden. Cecil Brown's 'Interview with Toni Morrison' (*MR* 36.455–73) is poorly edited, inaccurate in details and at times distinctly edgy in tone, but it probes intra-group issues – for instance, the allegedly preferential treatment accorded to black women in the literary market place – with an immediacy and emotional candour often lacking in Morrison's more smoothly scripted public performances.

Substantial commentary on individual novels appears in several of the books reviewed in the 'General' section above: particularly worth noting are Griffin (on *Song of Solomon* and *Jazz*), and Connor and McDowell (both on *Sula*). Acolytes of feminist archetypal criticism may also enjoy Michele Pessoni's pursuit of the Great Mother in ' "She was laughing at their God": Discovering the Goddess Within in *Sula*' (*AAR* 29.439–51). *Tar Baby*, the least discussed of the novels, features as part of Karin Luisa Badt's comparative enquiry into the discourse of maternal desire in 'The Roots of the Body in Toni Morrison' (*AAR* 29.567–77).

A welcome addition to CUP's useful 'American Novel' series is *New Essays on 'Song of Solomon'* (ed. Valerie Smith). While the brief of the series is to provide introductory critical guides 'specifically designed for undergraduates', the range and sophistication of the interpretive strategies deployed in this instance suggest that the putative undergraduates must be uncommonly bright ones. Valerie Smith's opening essay does an excellent job of outlining general issues in the reading of black literature, and locates Morrison's work intelligently in relation to debates about the construction of race and gender in American culture. The remaining four essays, in one way or another, all deal with what one contributor calls 'the politics of literacy'. Joyce Middleton's 'From Orality to Literacy' looks at the textual strategies that privilege the oral tradition over written constructions of knowledge. Marilyn S. Mobley writes on 'Call and Response', pointing out that dialogism, as theorized by Bakhtin, is indigenous to African-American expressive culture and central to *Song of Solomon*'s multivocal effects. Wahneema Lubiano sees the novel's post-modernism as specifically structured by the subversive dynamics of black America's vernacular tradition of signifying. Marianne Hirsch's contribution, 'Knowing Their Names', seems to me an unusually constructive application of psychoanalytic theory to the novel's exploration of paternity and masculinity, permitting a finely nuanced reading of the metaphor of flight both as heroic transcendence and anti-heroic evasion. Her reading also dovetails nicely with Michael Awkward's excellent 'male feminist' account of *Song of Solomon* in his *Negotiating Difference* (see above). Periodical work on the novel includes another psychoanalytic study, 'Through the Maze of the Oedipal: Milkman's Search for Self' (*L&P* 41.52–84), by Eleanor Branch, and two essays in *AAR*: Richard Heyman writes on 'Universalization and Its Discontents: Morrison's *Song of Solomon* – A (W)hol(e)y Black Text' (29.381–92), and a troop-rallying piece by Bertram Ashe entitled ' "Why Don't He Like My Hair?": Constructing African-American Standards of Beauty' (29.579–92) compares Morrison's Hagar and Pilate with Hurston's Janie Crawford in order to explore the battleground of 'black hairstyle politics'.

Caroline Rody's essay on 'Toni Morrison's *Beloved*: History, Rememory, and a "Clamor for a Kiss" ' (*ALH* 7.92–119) posits 'structures of historio-graphic desire' beneath the novel's haunted negotiations with the African-American past, while Carl Malmgren's briefer but refreshingly direct 'Mixed Genres and the Logic of Slavery' (*Crit* 36.96–106) looks at central issues of form and meaning in *Beloved* and finds the idea of 'possession', in various senses, to be the unifying motif of the novel. Lynda Koolish's 'Fictive Strategies and Cinematic Representations in *Beloved*: Postcolonial Theory/Postcolonial Text' (*AAR* 29.421–38) is misleadingly titled: the novel's post-coloniality is neither theorized nor in fact even mentioned beyond the opening paragraph. The discussion does, however, make interesting use of filmic vocabulary – freeze frame, jump cut, 'relational editing', reverse shot, etc.– to pinpoint the visual qualities of Morrison's narrative technique. Also relevant here are two essays in *ConL* 36. William Handley writes on 'The House a Ghost Built: Allegory, "Nommo", and the Ethics of Reading in *Beloved*' (676–701), and an absorbing argument from Kristin Boudreau, 'Pain and the Unmaking of Self in Toni Morrison's *Beloved*' (447–65), identifies and explores the novel's critique of those romantic and blues-based traditions that valorize suffering. In 'Utopia Unlimited: Post-Sixties and Postmodern American Fiction' (*MFS* 41.75–97), Marianne DeKoven compares *Beloved* with E. L. Doctorow's *The Waterworks*, seeing in both novels an implicit resonance between the post-utopian moment of their historical setting and the post-modern failures of idealism at the time they were written.

Jazz, for some reason, often seems to tempt academic critics into an obscurantist mode better calculated to put readers *off* the novel than to communicate and clarify its exhilarating richness. Congratulations, therefore, to Philip Page for 'Traces of Derrida in Toni Morrison's *Jazz*' (*AAR* 29.55–66). Not only does Page make the concept of *différance* seem comprehensible and actually relevant to one's experience of reading (a rare achievement in itself); he also illuminates the text both in detail and as a whole with an enthralling account of Morrison's 'play' between the binaries of presence and absence. In ' "A Music Seeking Its Words": Double-Timing and Double-Consciousness in Toni Morrison's *Jazz*' (*Callaloo* 18.451–71), Richard Hardack's argument that the novel 'uses fragmentation to resituate the improvisational against the inevitable' is a meaty one, but the proportion of accompanying gristle is high. Anyone brave enough to approach *Jazz* via a 'woman-centered use of metonymy and synecdoche' should consult Jocelyn Chadwick-Joshua's essay in the Hakutani and Butler collection.

In May this year Walter Mosley participated in the '90s Fictions' event co-sponsored by *CritQ* and Serpent's Tail at the University of Sussex. A transcript of his (brief) talk, together with a new short story 'Equal Opportunity', appear in the special Winter issue of *CritQ* (37.iv.113–28). The first three of Mosley's Easy Rawlins mysteries are thoughtfully discussed in Robert Crooks's essay 'From the Far Side of the Urban Frontier: The Detective Fiction of Chester Himes and Walter Mosley' (*CollL* 22.iii. 68–90).

As noted in the General section, there are worthwhile chapters on Gloria Naylor's fiction in the Hakutani and Butler collection, and in Saunders. In the journals, Stephanie Tingley writes on *Linden Hills* in 'A "Ring of Pale Women": Willa Nedeed as Feminist Archivist and Historian' (*CEA* 57.59–67), focusing on the last of the Nedeed wives as she retrieves and reconstructs the stories of her predecessors. Gary Storhoff uses Jungian archetypes to clarify the mysterious resolution of *Mama Day* in ' "The Only Voice is Your Own": Gloria Naylor's Revision of *The Tempest*' (*AAR* 29.35–45). Less successful is Maxine Montgomery's 'Authority, Multivocality and the New World Order in *Bailey's Cafe*' (*AAR* 29.27–33), which, despite its imposing title, does little more than recapitulate the novel's search for ways to redeem women's stories of pain.

I note that Ishmael Reed is one of five writers discussed by Richard Walsh in *Novel Arguments: Reading Innovative American Fiction* (CUP), but the book has not been received for review. Nor has *Conversations with Ishmael Reed* (UMP), edited by Bruce Dick and Amritjit Singh. Robert Fox (see General section) reprints a 1984 essay on the 'semiotics of neo-hoodoo' in Reed, which cheerfully encompasses the Yoruba pantheon, Derrida, cowrie shell divination, and James Joyce's black eye-patch. Fox, like Reed himself, is patently a devotee of 'the ludic mode, which insists on ... keeping ideas in play', but as he admits, 'obscurity is always a danger when the dance of the mind is underway': less agile readers should consider themselves fore-warned.

'Toomer does not impress me as one who knows his Georgia.' So wrote Du Bois in 1923 on publication of Jean Toomer's *Cane*, and critics still lean towards 'mythic' readings of the book that downplay the regional specificity of its southern backdrop. Barbara Foley, however, has done detailed research in local archives, and her findings, presented in 'Jean Toomer's Sparta' (*AL* 67.747–75), establish beyond reasonable doubt both the direct and the satiri-cally veiled historical verisimilitude that shaped Sparta, Georgia, into *Cane*'s fictional town of Sempter.

No book-length studies of Alice Walker or Richard Wright were received this year. In the journals, Alyson Buckman writes on 'The Body as a Site of

Colonization: Alice Walker's *Possessing the Secret of Joy*' (*JAmC* 18.ii.89–94), and *AAR* 29 has an intelligent and well-substantiated essay by Linda Selzer on 'Race and Domesticity in *The Color Purple*' (67–82), which effectively counters the familiar charge that Walker's 'restricted focus' on Celie's private and domestic sphere erases the wider institutional and political aspects of race and class. Aside from three biographically oriented essays of variable quality in Hakutani and Butler (above), the year's work on Wright, so far as I can discover, is limited to Eugene Miller's 'Richard Wright, Community, and the French Connection' (*TCL* 41.265–80), and two articles in *CLAJ*. Miller's project is to demonstrate how the fiction of Henri Barbusse provided 'structural, tonal, and imagistic grist ... to the mill of Wright's imagination'. In *CLAJ* (39.420–40), Laurel Gardner recycles, as if new-minted, a series of well-worn observations on the narrative and ideological trajectory from Big Boy to Bigger Thomas in 'The Progression of Meaning in the Images of Violence in *Uncle Tom's Children* and *Native Son*'. The same two texts feature in 'The Bad Nigger Figure in Selected Works of Richard Wright, William Melvin Kelley and Ernest Gaines' (*CLAJ* 39.143–64), by H. Nigel Thomas, but here the comparative approach to literary variants on the folkloric antihero provides some useful new ways of thinking about Wright's fictional protagonists.

Books Reviewed

Adell, Sandra. *Double Consciousness/Double Bind: Theoretical Issues in Twentieth Century Black Literature.* UIllP (1994). pp. 172. $25.95. ISBN 0 252 02109 6.

Awkward, Michael. *Negotiating Difference: Race, Gender, and the Politics of Positionality.* UChicP. pp. 235. hb $42.50, pb $14.95. ISBN 0 226 03300 7, 0 226 03301 5.

Bahti, Timothy. *Ends of the Lyric: Direction and Consequence in Western Poetry.* JHUP. pp. viii + 288. pb £13. ISBN 0 8018 5193 9.

Barnard, Rita. *The Great Depression and the Culture of Abundance: Kenneth Fearing, Nathanael West, and Mass Culture in the 1930s.* Cambridge Studies in American Literature and Culture. CUP. pp. viii + 271. £35. ISBN 0 521 45034 9.

Beavers, Herman. *Wrestling Angels Into Song: The Fictions of Ernest J. Gaines and James Alan McPherson.* UPennP. pp. 304. £32.95. ISBN 0 8122 3150 3.

Bloom, Clive, ed. *American Drama.* Macmillan Insights series. Macmillan. pp. 196. £13.99. ISBN 0 333 53287 2.

——, and Brian Docherty, eds. *American Poetry: The Modernist Ideal.* Macmillan. Insights series. Macmillan. pp. ix + 274. £40. ISBN 0 333 53288.

Bordman, Gerald. *American Theatre: A Chronicle of Comedy and Drama, 1914–1930.* OUP. pp. 446. £35. ISBN 0 19 509078 0.

Brienzo, Gary. *Willa Cather's Transforming Vision: New France and the American Northeast.* AUP (1994). pp. 120. £22.50. ISBN 0 945636 66 0.

Broderick, Damien. *Reading By Starlight: Postmodern Science Fiction.* Routledge. pp. 224. hb £40, pb £12.99. ISBN 0 415 09788 6, 0 415 09789 4.

Brophy, Robert, ed. *Robinson Jeffers. Dimensions of a Poet.* FordUP. pp. xvii + 24. hb $27, pb $16.95. ISBN 0 8232 1566 0, 0 8232 1565 2.

Cirasa, Robert J. *The Lost Works of William Carlos Williams: The Volumes of Collected Poetry as Lyrical Sequences*. FDUP. AUP. pp. 342. £38. ISBN 0 8386 3576 8.

Cohn, Ruby. *Anglo-American Interplay in Recent Drama*. CUP. pp. 190. £27.95 ($39.95). ISBN 0 521 47267 9.

Comens, Bruce. *Apocalypse and After: Modern Strategy and Postmodern Tactics in Pound, Williams, and Zukofsky*. UAlaP. pp. xiv + 218. pb £21.50 ($23.95). ISBN 0 8173 0732 X.

Connor, Kimberly Rae. *Conversions and Visions in the Writings of African-American Women*. UTennP (1994). pp. 317. hb $34, pb $18. ISBN 0 87049 818 5, 0 87049 908 4.

Cook, Albert. *The Reach of Poetry*. PurdueUP. pp. xi + 335. pb $14.95. ISBN 1 55755 069 6.

Coyle, Michael. *Ezra Pound, Popular Genres, and the Discourse of Culture*. PSUP. pp. x + 256. £33.95 ($37.50). ISBN 0 271 01421 0.

Crandell, George W. *Tennessee Williams: A Descriptive Bibliography*. Pittsburgh Series in Bibliography. UPittP. pp. 673. $195. ISBN 0 8229 3769 7.

Demastes, William W., ed. *American Playwrights, 1880–1945: A Research and Production Sourcebook*. Greenwood. pp. 494. £75. ISBN 0 313 28638 8.

Denniston, Dorothy Hamer. *The Fiction of Paule Marshall: Reconstructions of History, Culture and Gender*. UTennP. pp. 187. hb $32, pb $15. ISBN 0 87049 838 X, 0 87049 839 8.

De Santis, Christopher C., ed. *Langston Hughes and the 'Chicago Defender': Essays on Race, Politics, and Culture 1942–62*. UIllP. pp. 261. hb $35.95, pb $14.95. ISBN 0 252 02105 3, 0 252 06474 7.

Doreski, William. *The Modern Voice in American Poetry*. UPFlor. pp. xviii + 179. $39.95. ISBN 0 8130 1362 3.

Elkins, Marilyn, ed. *August Wilson: A Casebook*. Casebooks on Modern Dramatists. Garland (1994). pp. 228. $42. ISBN 0 8153 0922 8.

Emig, Rainer. *Modernism in Poetry: Motivations, Structures and Limits*. Longman. Studies in 20th Century Literature. Longman. pp. xii + 270. hb £36, pb £13.99. ISBN 0 582 23919 2, 0 582 23920 6.

Fox, Robert Elliot. *Masters of the Drum: Black Lit/Oratures Across the Continuum*. Greenwood. pp. 180. £39.95. ISBN 0 313 29296 5.

Frick, John W., and Stephen M. Vallillo, eds. *Theatrical Directors: A Biographical Dictionary*. Greenwood. pp. 567. $95. ISBN 0 313 27478 9.

Garber, Frederick. *Repositionings: Readings of Contemporary Poetry, Photography, and Performance Art*. PSUP. pp. 244. pb $17.95. ISBN 0 271 01409 1.

Gibson, Mary Ellis. *Epic Reinvented: Ezra Pound and the Victorians*. CornUP. pp. xvii + 240. £29.50. ISBN 0 8014 3133 6.

Golding, Alan. *From Outlaw to Classic: Canons in American Poetry*. UWiscP. pp. xvii + 243. hb £49.65, pb £17.95. ISBN 0 299 14600 6, 0 299 14604 9.

Graham, Laura J. *Sam Shepard: Theme, Image and the Director*. American University Studies. Lang. pp. 332. $58.95. ISBN 0 8204 2121 9.

Gray, Richard. *The Life of William Faulkner: A Critical Biography*. Blackwell Critical Lives. Blackwell (1994). pp. xvi + 448. £19.99. ISBN 0 631 16415 4.

Green, Amy S. *The Revisionist Stage: American Directors Reinvent the Classics*. Cambridge Studies in American Theatre and Drama. CUP. pp. 226. £32.50. ISBN 0 521 45343 7.

Grenander, M. E. *Poems of Ambrose Bierce*. UNebP. pp. xliv + 202. £32.95. ISBN 0 8032 1246 1.

Griffin, Alice. *Understanding Tennessee Williams*. Understanding Contemporary American Literature. USCP. pp. 266. $34.95. ISBN 1 57003 017 0.

Griffin, Farah Jasmine. *'Who Set You Flowin'?' The African American Migration Narrative*. OUPAm. pp. 232. hb £27.50, pb £14.50. ISBN 0 19 508896 4, 0 19 508897 2.

Hakutani, Yoshinobu, and Robert Butler, eds. *The City in African-American Literature*. FDUP. AUP. pp. 265. £29.50. ISBN 0 8386 3565 2.

Halter, Peter. *The Revolution in the Visual Arts and the Poetry of William Carlos Williams*. CUP (1994). pp. xii + 270. £37.50 ($59.95). ISBN 0 521 43130 1.

Hart, Henry. *Robert Lowell and the Sublime*. SyracuseUP. pp. xxx + 168. £31.50. ISBN 0 8156 2610 X.

Hart, Lynda, and Peggy Phelan, eds. *Acting Out: Feminist Performances*. UMichP (1993). hb $49.50, pb $18.95. ISBN 0 472 09479 3, 0 472 06479 7.

Harvey, Sally Peltier. *Redefining the American Dream: The Novels of Willa Cather*. AUP. pp. 190. £26.50. ISBN 0 8386 3557 1.

Hively, Evelyn Helmick. *Sacred Fire: Willa Cather's Novel Cycle*. UPA (1994). pp. 197. pp. 212. ISBN 0 8191 9481 6.

Holder, Alan. *Rethinking Meter\A New Approach to the Verse Line*. AUP. pp. 298. £32.50. ISBN 0 8387 5292 6.

Kane, Leslie, ed. *Israel Horovitz: A Collection of Critical Essays*. Contributions in Drama and Theatre Studies 55. Greenwood (1994). pp. 221. £49.50. ISBN 0 313 29147 0.

Kester, Gunilla Theander. *Writing the Subject: 'Bildung' and the African American Text*. Lang. pp. 178. $52.95. ISBN 0 8204 2332 7.

Keyser, Elizabeth Lennox. *Whispers in the Dark: The Fiction of Louisa May Alcott*. UTennP. pp. 288. pb $17. ISBN 0 87049 906 8.

Kuusisto, Stephen, Deborah Tall, and David Weiss, eds. *The Poet's Notebook. Excerpts from the Notebooks of 26 American Poets*. Norton. pp. xiv + 306. $25. ISBN 0 393 03866 1.

Leavell, Linda. *Marianne Moore and the Visual Arts: Prismatic Color*. LSUP. pp. xiii + 237. £23.95. ISBN 0 8071 1986 5.

LeSeur, Geta. *Ten is the Age of Darkness: The Black Bildungsroman*. UMissP. pp. 233. £31.50. ISBN 0 8262 1911 2.

Lester, Neal A. *Ntozake Shange: A Critical Study of the Plays*. Garland. pp. 321. $49. ISBN 0 8153 0314 9.

Leverich, Lyle. *Tom: The Unknown Tennessee Williams*. Crown. pp. 644. $35. ISBN 0 517 70225 8.

Levi, Jan Heller, ed. *A Muriel Rukeyser Reader*. Norton. pp. xii + 320. pb £11.50. ISBN 0 393 31323 9.

Lowe, John. *Jump at the Sun: Zora Neale Hurston's Cosmic Comedy*. UIllP (1994). pp. 373. $34.95. ISBN 0 252 02110 X.

Luongo, Robert. *The Gold Thread\Ezra Pound's Principles of Good Government & Sound Money*. Strangers Press. pp. v + 130. £12. ISBN 0 9631722 4 7.

Marzan, Julio. *The Spanish American Roots of William Carlos Williams*. UTexP (1994). pp. xiii + 288. $30. ISBN 0 2927 1143 3.

McCann, Janet. *Wallace Stevens Revisited: The Celestial Possible*. Twayne. pp. 162. $29.95. ISBN 0 8057 7644 3.

McDowell, Deborah E. *The Changing Same: Black Women's Literature, Criticism, and Theory*. IndUP. pp. 222. hb £27.50, pb £11.99. ISBN 0 253 33629 5, 0 253 20926 9.

McTeague, James H. *Playwrights and Acting: Acting Methodologies for Brecht, Ionesco, Pinter, and Shepard*. Contributions in Drama and Theatre Studies 59. Greenwood (1994). pp. 176. £39.95. ISBN 0 313 28975 1.

Merelman, Richard M. *Representing Black Culture: Racial Conflict and Cultural Politics in the United States*. Routledge. pp. 330. hb £40, pb £12.99. ISBN 0 415 91074 9, 0 415 91075 7.

Meserve, Walter J. *An Outline History of American Drama*. 2nd edn. Feedback. pp. 408. $19.95. ISBN 0 937657 18 2.

Miller, Cristanne. *Marianne Moore: Questions of Authority*. CUP. pp. xiv + 303. £25.50 ($35). ISBN 0 674 54862 0.

Morris, Timothy. *Becoming Canonical in American Poetry*. UIllP. pp. xviii + 173. pb $12.95. ISBN 0 252 06428 3.

Murphy, Brenda. *Miller: Death of a Salesman*. Plays in Production. CUP. pp. 246. hb £32.50, pb £11.95. ISBN 0 521 43451 3, 0 521 47865 0.

Myerson, Joel, Daniel Shealy, and Madeleine B. Stern, eds. *The Selected Letters of Louisa May Alcott*. UGeoP. pp. 352. pb $19.95. ISBN 0 8203 1740 3.

Nadel, Alan, ed. *May All Your Fences Have Gates: Essays on the Drama of August Wilson*. UIowaP (1994). pp. 270. hb $34.95, pb $15.95. ISBN 0 87745 428 0, 0 87745 439 6.

Peach, Linden. *Toni Morrison*. Macmillan. pp. 148. hb £35, pb £10.25. ISBN 0 333 62243 X, 0 333 62244 8.

Pereira, Kim. *August Wilson and the African-American Odyssey*. UIllP. pp. 123. hb $29.95, pb $12.95. ISBN 0 252 012371 1, 0 252 06429 1.

Pérez-Torres, Rafael. *Movements in Chicano Poetry\Against Myths, Against Margins*. Cambridge Studies in American Literature and Culture. CUP. pp. xii + 332. hb £40 ($59.95), pb £13.95 ($17.95). ISBN 0 521 47019 6, 0 521 47803 0.

Pettis, Joyce. *Toward Wholeness in Paule Marshall's Fiction*. UPVirginia. pp. 173. $29.50. ISBN 0 8139 1614 3.

Pfister, Joel. *Staging Depth: Eugene O'Neill and the Politics of Psychological Discourse*. Cultural Studies of the United States. UNCP. pp. 327. hb $45, pb $17.95. ISBN 0 8078 2186 1, 0 8078 4496 9.

Plant, Deborah G. *Every Tub Must Sit on Its Own Bottom: The Philosophy and Politics of Zora Neale Hurston*. UIllP. pp. 214. $25.95. ISBN 0 252 02183 5.

Pritchard, William H. *Playing It By Ear. Literary Essays and Reviews*. UMassP. pp. xii + 270. hb $45, pb $16.95. ISBN 0 87023 947 3, 0 87023 948 1.

Quantic, Diane Dufva. *The Nature of the Place: A Study of Great Plains Fiction*. UNebP. pp. 203. hb $25. ISBN 0 8032 3800 2.

Roberts, Diane. *Faulkner and Southern Womanhood*. UGeoP (1994). pp. xv + 246. pb £13.95. ISBN 0 8203 1741 1.

Rosenthal, Bernard. *Salem Story: Reading the Witch Trials of 1692*. Cambridge Studies in American Literature and Culture. CUP (1994). pp. 286. hb £35, pb £13.95. ISBN 0 521 44061 0, 0 521 55820 4.

Rosu, Anca. *The Metaphysics of Sound in Wallace Stevens*. UAlaP. pp. xv + 180. $39.95. ISBN 0 8173 0797 4.

Rothenberg, Jerome, and Pierre Joris, eds. *Poems for the Millennium. The University of California Book of Modern and Postmodern Poetry*. UCalP. pp. xxviii + 811. pb $24.95. ISBN 0 520 07227 8.

Ruppersburg, Hugh. *Reading Faulkner: 'Light in August', Glossary and Commentary*. UMP (1994). pp. xiv + 324. pb £19.50. ISBN 0 87805 732 3.

Saunders, James Robert. *The Wayward Preacher in the Literature of African-American Women*. McFarland. pp. 169. $27.50. ISBN 0 7864 0060 9.

Scarry, Elaine, ed. *Fins de Siècle: English Poetry in 1590, 1690, 1790, 1890, 1990*. JHUP. pp. xiii + 142. hb £32, pb £11.50. ISBN 0 801 84928 4, 0 801 84929 2.

Schlueter, June. *Dramatic Closure: Reading the End*. FDUP. pp. 144. £23. ISBN 0 8386 3583 0.

Schultz, Susan M., ed. *The Tribe of John: Ashbery and Contemporary Poetry*. UAlaP. pp. xiii + 280. $28.95. ISBN 0 8173 0767 2.

Schulze, Robin G. *The Web of Friendship: Marianne Moore and Wallace Stevens*. UMichP. pp. x + 252. $42.50. ISBN 0 472 10578 7.

Serio, John N., and B. J. Leggett. *Teaching Wallace Stevens: Practical Essays*. Tennessee Studies in Literature, Vol. 35. UTennP. pp. xii + 328. $32.98. ISBN 0 87049 817 7.

Shafer, Yvonne. *American Women Playwrights 1900–1950*. Lang. pp. 546. $34.95. ISBN 0 8204 2142 1.

Shannon, Sandra G. *The Dramatic Vision of August Wilson*. Howard. pp. 254. hb $38, pb $17.95. ISBN 0 88258 069 8, 0 88258 070 1.

Simmons, Thomas. *Erotic Reckonings: Mastery and Apprenticeship in the Work of Poets and Lovers*. UIllP (1994). pp. xiii. + 227. $27.50. ISBN 0 252 02120 7.

Smith, Valerie, ed. *New Essays on 'Song of Solomon'*. CUP. pp. 120. hb £22.95, pb £9.95. ISBN 0 521 45440 9, 0 521 45604 5.

Sporn, Paul. *Against Itself: The Federal Theater and Writers' Projects in the Midwest*. Wayne. pp. 373. £19.95. ISBN 0 8143 2590 4.

Stern, Madeleine B., ed. *Louisa May Alcott Unmasked*. NortheasternU. pp. 754. £52.50. ISBN 1 55553 226 8.

——, *The Feminist Alcott: Stories of a Woman's Power*. NortheasternU. hb £38, pb £13.95. ISBN 1 55553 265 9, 1 55553 266 7.

Thesing, William B., ed. *Robinson Jeffers and a Galaxy of Writers: Essays in Honor of William H. Nolte*. USCP. pp. xvi + 218. $29.95. ISBN 1 57003 043 X.

Trotman, C. James, ed. *Langston Hughes: The Man, His Art, and His Continuing Influence*. Garland. pp. 178. $27. ISBN 0 8153 1763.

Turner, Darwin T. *Black Drama in America: An Anthology*. 2nd edn. Howard. pp. 736. $34.95. ISBN 0 88258 062 0.

Tytell, John. *The Living Theatre: Art, Exile, and Outrage*. Grove. pp. 434. $30. ISBN 0 8021 1558 6.

Urgo, Joseph R. *Willa Cather and the Myth of American Migration*. UIllP. pp. 209. pb £14.95. ISBN 0 252 06481 X.

Valade, Roger M., ed. *The Schomburg Center Guide to Black Literature from the Eighteenth Century to the Present*. Gale. pp. 550. £60. ISBN 0 7876 0289 2.

Vendler, Helen. *The Given and the Made: Recent American Poets*. Faber. pp. xii + 137. pb £7.99. ISBN 0 571 17078 1.

——. *Soul Says: On Recent Poetry*. Belknap. pp. viii + 266. pb £9.50. ISBN 0 674 82147 5.

Wall, Cheryl A. *Women of the Harlem Renaissance*. IndUP. pp. 246. hb £23.50, pb £11.99. ISBN 0 253 32908 6, 0 253 20980 3.

Watts, Jerry Gafio. *Heroism and the Black Intellectual: Ralph Ellison, Politics, and Afro-American Intellectual Life*. UNCP (1994) pp. 156. hb $34.95, pb $14.95. ISBN 0 8078 2164 0, 0 8078 4477 2.

Weinstein, Philip M., ed. *The Cambridge Companion to William Faulkner*. CUP. pp. xxi + 236. pb £11.95. ISBN 0 521 42167 5.

Wilcox, Earl J. *His 'Incalculable Influence on Others': Essays on Robert Frost in Our Time*. UVict (1994). pp. 108. ISBN 0 920604 78 1.

Williams, Philip Middleton. *A Comfortable House: Lanford Wilson, Marshall W. Mason and the Circle Repertory Theatre*. McFarland (1993). pp. 211. $32.50. ISBN 0 89950 836 7.

Wright, Lee Alfred. *Identity, Family, and Folklore in African-American Literature*. Garland. pp. 153. $43. ISBN 0 8153 1864 2.

Zamir, Shamoon. *Dark Voices: W. E .B. Du Bois and American Thought, 1888–1903*. UChicP. pp. 307. hb £39.95, pb £12.75. ISBN 0 226 97852 4, 0 226 97853 2.

XVII

New Literatures in English

FEMI ABODUNRIN, BRIAN KIERNAN, HELEN HEWSON, EVA-MARIE KRÖLLER, PAULA BURNETT, PHILLIP LANGRAN and CAROLE DURIX

This chapter has six sections: 1. Africa, by Femi Abodunrin; 2. Australia, by Brian Kiernan and Helen Hewson; 3. Canada, by Eva-Marie Kröller; 4. The Caribbean, by Paula Burnett; 5. India, by Phillip Langran; 6. New Zealand and the South Pacific, by Carole Durix.

1. Africa

(a) General
This year *JCL* included 'Addenda to Chris Dunton's "A Bibliographic Listing of Nigerian plays in English, 1956–1992"', additions and corrections by Bernth Lindfors (30.i.97–103), as well as Dunton's own 'Supplementary Listing of Nigerian Plays in English' (30.i.105–6). Special issues of journals included *Commonwealth* on 'Women and Representation in the New Literatures in English'; *ArielE* (26.i and iii) on 'Postcolonialism and its Discontents'; *RAL* (26.i) on 'New Voices in African Literature', with an introduction by Edna Aizenberg; *RAL* (26.ii) on 'Flora Nwapa' (ed. Chikwenye Okonjo Ogunyemi and Marie Umeh); *RAL* (26.iii) on 'African Cinema' (ed. Kenneth Harrow) and *CW* (7.ii) on 'Orality in Southern African Literary Studies'.

Karin Barber's 'African-Language Literature and Postcolonial Criticism' (*RAL* 26.iv.3–30) and Fredric Michelman's 'French and British Colonial Language Policies: A Comparative View of Their Impact on African Literature' (*RAL* 26.iv.216–25) bring into sharp perspective the challenges faced by both the writers and critics of African literature in our era. According to Michelman, although they resulted in rather different colonial language policies, the underlying philosophies of the two dichotomous colonial powers, the French and the British, were equally 'based on convictions of cultural superiority'. Michelman contends further that it is only when one turns to the vast and flourishing literatures from Africa in English and French, that 'the impact of the respective colonial legacies [which] may be somewhat less obvious but nonetheless real' become quite significant. For Michelman, Chinua Achebe's well-known attempt to 'extend the frontier of English so as to accommodate African thought pattern' is ample evidence of the 'stretching' of the European language that has occurred in anglophone authors such as

Gabriel Okara or Ken Saro-Wiwa, 'or with the less "conscious" liberties that Amos Tutuola or the "Onitsha Market Literature" have taken with the Queen's English'. Juxtaposing Achebe's *Arrow of God* with Laye's *L'enfant Noir*, Gabriel Okara's *The Voice* with Chiekh Hamidou Kane's *L'aventure Ambigüe*, one of Michelman's primary conclusions is that while the passages he quotes from the texts written in French might be very beautiful, they adhere strictly to the French classical literary tradition: the English of *The Voice*, on the other hand, 'has been molded to reflect the imagery and syntax of the author's native Ijaw'. However, Barber's essay, with its emphasis on the 'evolutionist' tendencies of postcolonial criticism (or criticism that tends to construct a simplistic cultural divide whenever it is required to compare and contrast African-language literature with its counterpart flourishing in English and French), contends that the elliptic nature of postcolonial criticism arises out of the fact that it is the relationship with English that defines the postcolonial condition – not just for the highly educated elite or for anglophone writers but for entire populations – 'for "the postcolonial subject" in general: the whole of the colonial world [...] all natives, male and female'. After a vigorous engagement with all the *sine qua non* of this ill-defined (postcolonial) condition, the remainder of what Abiola Irele describes as Barber's valuable contribution to the on-going debate focuses on the likely effects of this amorphous relationship on 'African-Language Discourses', ways and means of 'dissolving the dichotomous paradigm', and a lucid account of what she calls 'the colonial scene of literary production in Yoruba'.

Michelman's and Barber's contributions to the all-important issue of language supply an essential context to all the other critical issues bestriding African literature in our era: 'Women and Representation', to which *Commonwealth* devotes a special edition, is one such issue, a second being what *RAL*, in another special issue, describes as 'New Voices in African Literature'. In his introduction to the volume *Essays on African Writing: Contemporary Literature 2*, Abdulrazak Gurnah contextualizes these two seemingly unrelated critical issues by highlighting what he calls 'the representation of patriarchal structure as unproblematic', in a reading of the work following that of the first 'generation' of post-independence African writers whose writing was the subject of the previous volume. In the same vein, introducing *RAL*'s special issue on 'Flora Nwapa', Chikwenye Okonjo Ogunyemi's 'The Invalid, Dea(r)th, and the Author: The Case of Flora Nwapa, aka Professor (Mrs.) Flora Nwanzuruahu Nwakuche' (*RAL* 26.ii.1–16), chronicles the critical issues at stake as 'the invalidation of the African woman as novelist, the birth of a certain type of theory, as well as the dearth of scholarship on African Women's writing [...] petty warfare that kill her as author'. For Ogunyemi, as the frenetic scramble for the African theoretical space continues, and as one theoretical model replaces another 'which is already there in the original', these petty warfare assume amazing transformations, 'from the international scene to an African, gender-specific concern about Barthes's Author: what happens where there is no reader, or the writer is practically her only reader?'.

Introducing *The Pressures of the Text: Orality, Texts and the Telling of Tales*, Stewart Brown also locates a paradigmatic opening in Barthes's ironic subversion of the notion of the 'pleasures of the text'. The conferees at the University of Birmingham's world-famous Centre of West African Studies where the first drafts of these essays were presented in May 1993, according to Brown, were asked to deliberate (in a pun on Barthes's irony) on, among other things, whether 'the pressures of the text are political and sociological rather than literary, related to changes in gender roles or the incursion of new technologies like video or the word processor?'. Perhaps more importantly, Brown's subtitle to the volume interrogates the interaction, or the lack of one, between three seemingly disparate elements: 'Orality, Texts and the Telling of Tales'. The subtitle is extrapolated from the postcolonial conundrum in a bid to locate the problematic quantum: 'is the *pressure* rather in the widespread notion of an hierarchical or competitive relationship between written texts and oral performance in which text signifies modernity and orality "tradition", or where education is understood in terms of mastery of certain texts and orality equated with illiteracy [...]?'. Karin Barber (who contributes another characteristically lucid essay entitled 'Literacy, Improvisation, and the Public in Yorùbá Popular Theatre' to the volume edited by Brown), provides critical elucidation of the vexed issue of a postcolonial relationship constructed on the shaky grounds that she describes as 'evolutionist territory' in her essay discussed above: 'the suggestion is that [anglophone, the world of literature] *evolved out of* indigenous folklore [Yorùbá, the world of orature] with [Yorùbá-English; oral-written] as an intermediate stage' [italics in the original], to cite just one of Barber's trenchant examples.

Still on theory, *ArielE*'s special issue on 'Postcolonialism and its Discontents' (26.i) chronicles what one of the contributors, Deepika Bahri, has termed 'the ambiguities and dissonances that plague "postcoloniality" '. Elucidating what one of the three editors of *ArielE*'s special issue, Stephen Slemon, describes as a 'conceptually dis/contented [...] suitcase blown open on the baggage belt', in 'Once More With Feeling: What Is Postcolonialism?' (51–82), Bahri observes that even the most conventional definitions of postcolonialism as, for example, that which has been preceded by colonization, or the *American Heritage Dictionary*'s definition of the postcolonial phenomenon as 'of, relating to, or being the time following the establishment of independence in a colony', are not 'empty of ideological content or the power to encapsulate and transfix a "thing" simply by naming it'. Martina Michel's 'Positioning the Subject: Locating Postcolonial Studies' (83–99) highlights yet more reasons why defining the literature of the diverse areas now traditionally described as postcolonial is considered increasingly problematic: these reasons range from crucial issues of hierarchical relationships that exist between ethnic groups within the so-called settler colonies in New Zealand, Australia or those between black and white writers in South Africa, to gender relations. Michel also observes that 'the third major reservation that has been formulated against the use of the label "postcolonial" is its alleged complicity in what is often loosely referred to as the postmodern'. Not surprisingly, this alleged complicity between the postcolonial and the postmodern has, in the delineation of M. Keith Booker's 'African Literature and the World System: Dystopian Fiction, Collective Experience, and the Postcolonial Condition' (*RAL* 26.iv.58–75), led African literature along the path of its Western counterpart to a decidedly dystopian turn in the twentieth century. African writers of dystopian fiction, according to Booker, 'face special complications in their attempt to explore new cultural identities within a quintessential bourgeois form that seems inherently inimical to the utopian imagination'.

Tejumola Olaniyan's *Scars of Conquest/Masks of Resistance: The Invention of Cultural Identities in African, African-American and Caribbean Drama* is a book-length study confronting head-on the alleged complicity between what is loosely referred to as the postcolonial and the postmodern. Arun Mukherjee's equally trenchant observation, cited in Martina Michel's essay, also becomes one of the yardsticks by which the authenticity of studies like Olaniyan's could be measured. According to Mukherjee:

> The postcolonial theorist's generalisations about 'all' 'postcolonial people' suggest that Third Worldism and/or nationalism bind the people of these societies in conflictless brotherhood, that the inequalities of caste and class do not exist in these societies and that their literary works are only about 'resisting' or 'subverting' the colonizer's discourses.

Starting from the increasingly problematic and slippery terrain of what he calls 'the historic issue of black–white encounter in general and the impact of Euro-American cultural hegemony on black cultural identity in particular', Olaniyan avers that 'the evident cross-continental, cross-cultural bent' readily observable in his study is meant *not* to propose a sameness of black cultures across space or time, or so much to affirm an identity of 'race' as simultaneously – and perhaps more importantly – to underscore, as Ellison puts it, an 'identity of passion'. Side-tracking none of the three critical issues highlighted in Martina Michel's essay above, Olaniyan elucidates what he has also described as the post-Afrocentric cultural space inhabited by the work of the three playwrights, Wole Soyinka, Derek Walcott and Amiri Baraka, 'who also happen to be leading playwrights in their respective regions'. A critique of their work, according to Olaniyan, 'proceeds through a detailed consideration of the feminist artist Ntozake Shange, who is also engaged in the same struggle but in ways that interrogate, extend and re-vision the work of the other three'. Consequently, the charges of implying a conflictless brotherhood, or side-tracking inequalities of caste and class, are also recontextualized through Olaniyan's critical appropriation of Michel Pecheux's tripartite schematic outline of a dominated subject's relationship to the dominating discourse. Via this formulation, Olaniyan recognizes three dominant attitudes bestriding what Ogunyemi described *inter alia* as 'the frenetic scramble for the African theoretical space': '(1) the "good subject" who "consents" to domination, (2) the rebellious "bad subject" who "counteridentifies" with the discourse of domination, and (3) the subject who "disidentifies" with the existing structures of domination and gestures at their "transformation-displacement" or "overthrow-rearrangement" '. Olaniyan locates the four dramatists studied at what he calls 'the interface between counter-identification and disidentification'.

David Kerr's *African Popular Theatre: From Precolonial Times to the Present Day* is another book-length study focusing on the relatively understudied but wide-ranging varieties of African popular theatre. A daunting task, by Kerr's own admission, but one driven by the need to provide a general introduction to this important genre in the African literary experience. Again, the issue of conflictless synthesis, or what is termed the 'safety valve' theory of African theatre elevated to the level of philosophical equivocation by African intellectuals in the 1930s and 1940s, constitutes Kerr's primary starting point. Retaining the static view of African history but praising it in contrast to the dynamic, often creative, but ultimately destructive sterility of European culture, Kerr argues that 'the notion of a communal, sharing, pre-colonial society has found a theoretical equivalent in an aesthetic emphasis on African theatre's anonymous, participatory qualities'. Kerr's dialectical framework has helped to group together popular theatre forms, including, among others, the *Okumpa* masked plays among Nigeria's Afikpo people and the Yoruba *Egungun/Alarinjo/Apidan* theatre, according to the dialectic of their historical moments. Such a dialectical grouping of different popular theatre forms problematizes the relationship of the different popular theatre practitioners to their societies and audiences, thus 'allowing a society to maintain cultural continuity through licensed criticism'. Kerr also points to 'the fierce resistance to imperialism which pre-colonial African popular theatre forms made when colonialism was imposed in the late nineteenth century [which] can only be explained by the existence of a popular theatre tradition of resistance to dominant ideologies before European imperialism'. In 12 chapters, Kerr traces the numerous transformations of that tradition of resistance from the pre-colonial, through the colonial to the neo-colonial present.

Finally, introducing *RAL*'s special issue on 'African Cinema', Kenneth Harrow's 'Shooting Forward' (*RAL* 26.iii.1–5) describes an art form which 'like African literature itself [...] has had to struggle against great odds to come into existence, and it still finds its existence to be a precarious one'. From the complacency of the African academia to excruciating lack of funds, according to Harrow, 'it is hard to imagine any other aspect of culture so controlled by neo-colonial forces as is African film – a control extended in many ways by the expansion of television in Africa'. Stephen A. Zacks's 'The Theoretical Construction of African Cinema' (*RAL* 26.iii.6 17), and the collaborative piece entitled 'Towards a Theory of Orality in African Cinema' (18–35) by Keyan G. Tomaselli, Arnold Shepperson and Maureen Eke, are just two out of the essays; review essays; interviews with leading African film makers such as Sembéne Ousmane of Senegal, Flora Gomes of Guinea-Bissau and Ghana's Kwaw Ansah; and reviews chronicling, according to the editor of the volume, ways and means through 'which the African artist has struggled not only to "write back" but also to "shoot forward" '.

(b) West Africa

Increasingly, critical attention is beginning to focus pre-eminently on what *Commonwealth* describes as 'Women and Representation in the New Literatures in English', and what Abdulrazak Gurnah has termed the work which followed that of the first 'generation' of post-independence African writers. Introducing *RAL*'s special issue on 'New Voices in African Literature', Edna Aizenberg observes that 'a writer, a text, or genre only becomes "new" in relation to something else', and sees the 'new' as always aiming 'at liberation – the freedom of women from patriarchal bonds, of African nations from political corruption, of language from dead weight and outmoded norms'. However, regional variances, according to Aizenberg, demonstrate the complexity and at times the contradictions of 'newness'. To cite just one cogent example: while new African Portuguese-language poets have worked away from their precursors' poetry of commitment towards more experimental forms, their English-language counterparts, on the other hand, have shunned the formalism of their elders and embraced, in Aizenberg's view, 'meaning and engagement'.

Stewart Brown's 'Daring the Beast: Contemporary Nigerian Poetry' (in Gurnah, ed. *Essays on African Writing*); Aderemi Bamikunle's 'The Development of Niyi Osundare's Poetry: A Survey of Themes and Technique' (*RAL* 26.iv.121–37); Tijan Sallah's 'The Eagle's Vision: The Poetry of Tanure Ojaide' (*RAL* 26.i.20–9); Ode S. Ogede's 'Billets of Prose: Ojaide's *Labyrinths of the Delta*' (*CE&S* 17.ii.102–10); and to a large extent Tanure Ojaide's own 'New Trends in Modern African Poetry' (*RAL* 26.i.4–19) are some of the choice essays focusing on the peculiar characteristics of 'newness' or what Edna Aizenberg describes as 'the old-new tug between "form" and "content" ' within the poetic genre alone, in the West African region.

For Stewart Brown, privileging 'content' over 'form' – as the works of many of Nigeria's contemporary poets, with their blunt 'messages from the front', have shown – does not work 'insofar as we equate poetry with subtlety and linguistic cunning'. Brown's essay is an uncompromising overview of the rather bleak contemporary poetic scene in Nigeria, a landscape which is symptomatic of that 'alter-native' aesthetic from which the poets have seemingly derived the licence to foreground content over form, to value accessibility above linguistic or imagistic subtlety and prefer 'statement' over 'song'; all of which, according to Brown, connote an abdication of poetic craft for the clichéd language of protest. However, the second half of Brown's essay is also devoted to a critical evaluation of two contemporary Nigerian poets whose works are exceptions to the prevalent rule of artless predictability: these are Odia Ofeimun and Niyi Osundare. Brown describes Ofeimun as being effectively the founder of the 'alter-native' tradition, even though his poems are uncompromising and he remains 'concerned with both form and the power of wit and startling imagery as poetry's most effective agents'. But, if Ofeimun is the voice of the harlequin, the goad, the wit puncturing the pomposities of Nigeria's rulers with his ironic barbs and bells, then Niyi Osundare is the high priest of the 'alter-native' vision. Surveying themes and technique in Osundare's poetry, Aderemi Bamikunle's essay buttresses the majority of Brown's critical findings, and his affirmation of the poetic authenticity of Osundare's work. Concerned with vivid exposition of the various forms of social malaise, Osundare's poetry, according to Bamikunle, 'is not doctrinaire and not riddled with revolutionary jargon, but the point of view reflects familiar revolutionary views as the powers of the peasantry as the most revolutionary class in the society'. But as Biodun Jeyifo has cautioned in his 1987 introduction to the second edition of Osundare's *Songs of the Marketplace*, both Brown and Bamikunle are quick *not* to give the impression of perfection, of a definitive arrival in the poetic trajectory of Niyi Osundare. Definitely, as Jeyifo warns, 'the "errors of rendering" [Okigbo's wry self-criticism] are all there'.

'Billets of Prose' is the phrase Ode S. Ogede employs in describing the poetry of Tanure Ojaide, another contemporary Nigerian poet whose work has received substantial approval in the Commonwealth. *Labyrinths of the Delta* is Ojaide's second volume and it is here that Ogede evaluates Ojaide's poetic manifesto, starting from the relatively well-known attempt by the poet to shun the obscurantist tendencies of his precursors. The poem which succinctly encapsulates the magnitude of Ojaide's exasperation by the obscurantism of his predecessors in *Labyrinths*, according to Ogede, is 'A Bottle in the Pit'; but in the poem, 'he [Ojaide] wrongly nails "obscurity" down to a shallowness on the part of the artist and says it asserts the lack of matter in whatever message a writer who is guilty of it wishes to impart'. One of Ogede's primary conclusions, most especially at the level of ideological and technical predisposition, is that 'Ojaide the good sympathiser whose aspiration like all liberals, is to secure the freedom of individuals to pursue their own interests freely, expresses deeply liberal sensibilities, despite his avowed radical postures'. Tijan M. Sallah's 'The Eagle's Vision: The Poetry of Tanure Ojaide' is more conciliatory, and asserts that 'overall Ojaide's artistry can be surmised as pivoting around the themes of protestation against political and economic tyranny'. Sallah also quotes Ojaide's description of the abiding attribute of his poetry (in a 1989 essay published in *Geneve-Afrique*) as ' "unpoetic" in the old way because he [Ojaide] employs the syntax of prose'. However, it is Ojaide's overview and description of 'newness' in his essay 'New Trends in Modern African Poetry' that is most revealing of the source of his artistic inspiration. In the old–new tug between 'form' and 'content', Ojaide locates two major sources of critical and creative disquiet: the elitism of his precursors, and what he describes as the intellectual tastes of the time, created and promoted by those he calls European Africanist critics such as Ulli Beier and Gerald Moore. Furthermore, according to Ojaide: 'From the style of Okigbo, Soyinka and Clark, among others of their generation, it seems they consciously wanted to prove themselves as fine poets and impress outsiders. As if form was an end in itself, there was over-emphasis on form at the expense of meaning.'

The complexity and contradictions of 'newness' also bestride the novelistic genre. Olatubosun Ogunsanwo's 'Intertextuality and Post-Colonial Literature in Ben Okri's *The Famished Road*' (*RAL* 26.i.40–52); John C. Hawley's 'Ben Okri's Spirit-Child: *Abiku* Migration and Postmodernity' (*RAL* 26.i.30–9); Ato Quayson's 'Orality-(Theory)-Textuality: Tutuola, Okri and the Relationship of Literary Practice to Oral Traditions' (in Brown, ed., *The Pressures of the Text*) as well as Quayson's 'Esoteric Webwork as Nervous System: Reading the Fantastic in Ben Okri's Writing' (in Gurnah, ed., *Essays on African Writing*) have all attempted in their individual and collective manners to trace an organic link between 'the old' and 'the new'. Virtually all of these critics have tried to trace in Okri's writing what the African-American critic, Henry Louis Gates Jr, has since described as a situation of 'tertiary formal revision, by which authors revise at least two antecedent texts, often taken from different generations or periods within the tradition', in terms of Okri's relation to his novelistic precursors in technique and thematic predisposition.

According to Ogunsanwo, Okri, through his creative efforts in *The Famished Road*, 'has truly sought to achieve a decolonization of colonial education, which, Appiah says, "produced a generation immersed in the literature of the colonizers, a literature that often reflected and transmitted the imperialist vision", and imperialist technique'. John Hawley sees Okri as having 'an aesthetic, rather than overtly political or psychological aim' in his writing. Okri's lukewarm response of 'I accept them', when asked how he relates to the older generation of Nigerian writers, is enough of a pointer for Hawley to surmise that 'his [Okri's] agenda for fiction is not what he imagines theirs to have been'. Ato Quayson's rigorously theorized contribution to the novelistic oeuvre of Okri – concerned as it is with the intersection between anthropology and literary theory in a bid to contextualize a discussion of the works of Amos Tutuola and Ben Okri and the relationship they establish with traditional oral sources – makes the important observation that 'in Okri's work there seems to be a constant displacement of the concepts operative in Tutuola's work, so as to display a range of applications that extend to embrace ideological and aesthetic concerns of a different status from Tutuola's'. According to Quayson, two things result from Okri's deployment of certain concepts from the traditional resource base: in deploying some of the concepts operative in Tutuola's narratives, Okri shows a certain rich ambivalence towards the traditional resource base. On the one hand, there is a fascination for its potential for generating multiple focuses, but on the other hand, there is an acute sense of its inadequacy in addressing the pressures of an aesthetic facing the exigencies of a postcolonial reality that is cosmopolitan, in-between and riddled by multiple identities.

Besides Katherine Fishburn's book-length study *Cross-Cultural Conversations: Reading Buchi Emecheta*, and *RAL*'s special issue (26.ii) on the work of the late Flora Nwapa (ed. Chikwenye Okonjo Ogunyemi and Marie Umeh), other critical engagements with the work of the older genera-tion of West African novelists are C. L. Innes's 'Conspicuous Consumption: Corruption and the Body Politic in the Writing of Ayi Kwei Armah and Ama Ata Aidoo' (in Gurnah, ed., *Essays on African Writing*), focusing on 'the responses of two contemporaneous Ghanaian writers [...] to the later years of Nkrumah's regime and Nkrumah's political manifesto'; P. J. Whyte's 'Symbolical Patterns in Ayi Kwei Armah's *The Beautyful Ones Are Not Yet Born*' (*CE&S* 17.ii.93–101), examining the related issue of the nature of the symbolical pattern in a novel which has been considered a piece of propa-ganda directed at the Nkrumah regime; Okwute J. Abah's 'The Mbari Tradition in *Anthills of the Savanah*' (*FAB* 7.vii.99–107), which demonstrates how the Mbari principle is the aesthetic basis upon which Achebe constructed *Anthills*; Kwame Ayivor's 'Africa's Golden Age Deflated: A Reading of Yambo Ouologuem's Bound to Violence' (*ESA* 37.ii.37–62), which sets out to debunk the widely held hypothesis that Ouologuem's magnum opus is designed to deflate Africa's image and the African Golden Age; and Ranu Samantrai's 'Caught at the Confluence of History: Ama Ata Aidoo's Neces-sary Nationalism' (*RAL* 26.ii.140–57), which sees Aidoo's acclaimed novel as 'an example of how a non-racialist, non-foundational African identity might lead to Pan-African solidarity'. Augustine C. Okere's 'Art, Mimesis, Mythog-raphy and Social Relevance: An Essay of Wole Soyinka's *Season of Anomy*' (*Ufahamu* 23.ii.35–46) contextualizes the ethnic disturbances, hostilities, mur-ders and pogroms making up the Nigerian experience in 1966 which is believed to have inspired the novel; and the ways and manner in which a web of relationships between actors in the tragic drama, and between them and events both past and present, are clearly discernible.

Fishburn's book-length study of the fictional work of Buchi Emecheta plunges into 'the current conversation that is focused more generally on issues of cross-cultural understanding'. Without concerning herself much with the ongoing intellectual project of theorizing an African approach to African literature, à la Chinweizu et al., Fishburn describes one of the primary concerns of the book as an attempt to rebut 'much of the [white] Western feminist criticism that has been generated on Buchi Emecheta and her fiction', and constantly reminds the reader that her quarrel is not with Afrocentric readings but white feminist ones. Fishburn sees it as imperative for all Western readers (and most particularly feminist readers) to ask themselves whether they are so beholden to their liberal humanist (or liberal feminist) tradition that they close themselves off from the newness and strangeness of feminist/ womanist African novels. Above all, many readers would welcome Fishburn's rigorously theorized attempt to avoid a false universalism, and her advocacy of a politically grounded interpretive approach that challenges, rather than reinscribes, the discourses of Western critical 'truth'.

Similarly, Flora Nwapa's compelling novelistic oeuvre – which, according to Marie Umeh, resists the canonical politics of erasure and leads the author to distance 'herself from the term "feminist" in order to describe her ideological position in global letters' – has received much deserved critical attention in the special issue of RAL (26.ii). Besides Chikwenye Okonjo Ogunyemi's lucid introduction (see above) 'The Invalid, Dea(r)th, and the Author: The Case of Flora Nwapa, aka Professor (Mrs.) Flora Nwanzuruahu Nwakuche' (which examines, among other paradigmatic manoeuvres in Nwapa's writing, how through 'deconstructing the works of her male contemporaries, Nwapa carved a feminine space out of this cultural imaginary with her novels'), other choice essays in the volume include Sabine Jell-Bahlsen's 'The Concept of Mammy-water in Flora Nwapa's novels' (30–41); Chimalum Nwankwo's 'The Igbo Word Flora Nwapa's Craft' (42–52); Brenda F. Berrain's 'The Reinvention of Woman Through Conversations and Humour in Flora Nwapa's One Is Enough' (53–67) and the extremely useful 'Bibliography: Flora Nwapa (1931–1993)'. Ama Ata Aidoo's lyrical tribute entitled 'These Days III – A Letter to Flora Nwapa' (17–21) supplies creative affirmation to Ogunyemi's critical summation that it is definitely not ' "apocalypse Now": "Sweet" Flora has died; long live the other, Author Flora Nwapa'.

J. O. J. Nwachukwu-Agbada's 'The Dramatic Works of Tess Onwueme' (CE&S 17.ii.30–5), Muyiwa Awodiya's The Drama of Femi Osofisan: A Critical Perspective, and James Gibbs's Talking With Papers – Wole Soyinka at the University of Leeds 1954 to 1958: The Making of a Playwright provide the dwindling critical coverage, compared to that of the novelistic and poetic genres, on the work of major West African playwrights writing in English. Nwachukwu-Agbada's contribution makes the point with the observation that since 'the eighties saw the rise of far more poets and novelists than dramatists', it is probably logical to assume that the most social of literary genres has suffered a commensurate decrease in criticism for the same reason. However, Muyiwa Awodiya, a director and producer of several of Femi Osofisan's plays, appears to match Nwachukwu-Agbada's description of the dying species of 'a Nigerian critic still writing from home', since it is now a commonplace fact that a substantial number of influential Nigerian critics have left the country due to the current down-turn of the economy. In a concise preface to Awodiya's book-length study, Olu Obafemi, himself a major Nigerian playwright and critic, observes that Awodiya's effort, in spite of the hard times, 'is even more remarkable when one realizes that apart from Wole Soyinka, no other

Nigerian dramatist has enjoyed such a full-length, painstakingly researched, critical study of this magnitude by a Nigerian scholar'. In eleven chapters, Awodiya places before us a wealth of information on Osofisan's writing; critical elucidation on Osofisan's 21 published plays to date is provided via the circuitous but rewarding contexts of the universe of the plays, the influence of oral tradition and Ósofisan's well-known but contentious creative attempts to demystify the interpretation of the Yoruba/Orunmila's divination process. Form and technique, as well as matters of aesthetics and language, among others, are also contextualized, while the depth of the research confirms Awodiya's assertion that Osofisan is indeed Nigeria's leading playwright of the generation immediately following that of Wole Soyinka. Finally, in contrast to the old–new tug between form and content readily observable in West African poetry, or the setting up of individual aesthetics in the case of the novel, Nwachukwu-Agbada observes how Tess Onwueme's 'mythic imagination which avoids the pitfalls of anthropological description places her on par with Wole Soyinka, J. P. Clark and Femi Osofisan, her obvious models'.

James Gibbs's 48-page monograph engages in a critical monologue of a different sort, focusing on the easily talismanic and mythic years of Soyinka's sojourn to 'the Athens of the North of England' roughly from October 1954 to May 1958, where, according to Gibbs, 'Africanist critics' claim Soyinka was 'infected with Anglo-Modernist mannerisms'. However, sifting through what he calls 'a variety of sources' including contemporary Leeds publications, archival material, Soyinka's work and interviews with him, Gibbs asserts that it was during the busy Leeds years that Soyinka acquired both the assurance to describe his profession in November 1959, shortly before he returned to Nigeria, as 'Writer free-lance'; and what Baroka in *The Lion and the Jewel* calls 'The habit of talking with papers', which helped him to become a writer. In 'The Two-Faced Ogun: Postcolonial Intellectuals and the Positioning of Wole Soyinka' (*EinA* 22.ii.44–69), Brenda Cooper examines, in theoretical terms, the vexed question of the African writer's position on the postcolonial map, and applies views and opinions gained from this theoretical exploration to a critical analysis of developments in Soyinka's writing. Critical inquiry into the evolution of Soyinka's writing from a position bordering on cosmopolitanism to a decolonizing nationalist position, Cooper suggests, might commence with analysis of an early play, *The Road*, and could then move on to the highly publicized debate between Soyinka and the troika, Chinweizu et al., 'which established Soyinka's reputation as a cosmopolitan'. One of Cooper's primary conclusions is that, the acrimony of their exchange notwithstanding, even though he retains his insistence on the fundamental reality of modern life, 'paradoxically, Soyinka has become more pure than the purists, more ethnic than the neo-tarzanists'.

(c) East and Central Africa

Eldred Ibibiem Green's critical survey of 'Early East African Prose in English: Beginnings, Influences and "Encouragements" ' (*CE&S* 17.ii.82–92) examines the constituent sites of East African prose fiction in English to the 1970s. Concerned with issues of critical and creative 'influences, encouragements', and related themes, Green observes that although some critics have argued that Elspeth Huxley's and Karen Blixen's works on Kenya, for example, can be said to belong to 'English "Colonial" Literature', and Denmark respectively, 'there is also the fact that Huxley and Blixen both precede, and have links with Ngugi, who started by challenging their presentations. By reacting to them he [Ngugi] was helping to build a tradition.' Transcending paradigmatic moments even before the emergence of Blixen and Huxley, Green's essay traces East African writing in English back to its roots in literacy in the medium of the Roman alphabet and Christian missionary activity: a survey of vernacular literature in East Africa, according to Green, 'reveals that a great deal of early writing was done in Uganda particularly in Buganda where the first Christian missionaries arrived in 1877'.

Along similar retrospective lines, Cristiana Pugliese has followed her critical commentary 'The Organic Vernacular Intellectual in Kenya: Gakaara wa Wanjau' (*RAL* 24[1993].iv.177–87) with a book-length study on the 'Author, Publisher and Gikuyu Nationalist' under the title *The Life and Writings of Gakaara wa Wanjau*. According to Pugliese, Wanjau is not just the major writer in Gikuyu, and certainly the most prolific Kenyan author, but also probably a unique case in Africa of an author and publisher in an African language whose activity has never ceased in the last 50 years. Besides the uniqueness of Wanjau's writing as an example of highly independent literary production, from the very beginning of his career as a writer, 'he has published his own books and since the early sixties has also printed them with his own press'. Pugliese traces one of the earliest influences on the author to his being the son of a minister of the Church of Scotland, who belonged to the Christianized and educated Gikuyu elite and sent him to the exclusive Alliance High School. Like Ngugi wa Thiong'o's famous remonstration with 'the colonial educational system as making English the prerequisite for upward movement [...] the official vehicle and the major formula to colonial elitedom', cited in Green's essay, according to Pugliese, although Wanjau never abandoned political and historical writing completely, from the mid-sixties he concentrated on writing short narratives, or 'stories' as he calls them, 'to teach proper behaviour and Gikuyu customs' to the younger generations, who were leaving their villages to live in town, and were abandoning a traditional code of morality to follow the new modes of behaviour created by urbanization.

The year under review also, possibly, represents the highest point of recognition for the writing of Gakaara wa Wanjau's younger 'successor' and Gikuyu/Kenyan compatriot, the irrepressible Ngugi wa Thiong'o. According to Charles Cantalupo, editor of *The World of Ngugi wa Thiong'o*, and *Ngugi wa Thiong'o: Texts and Contexts*, the latter volume alone contains 20 essays selected from over seven times that number presented at a conference of the same name. The gathering was large and diverse, including over 200 scholars from Africa, Asia, Europe, Canada, the Caribbean and the United States, all reading their work on or related to Ngugi. 'The liberty and authority embodied in the work of Ngugi wa Thiong'o', Cantalupo postulates, form the primary basis for these collections of essays, interviews and poetry, corroborating further Cantalupo's trenchant observation in the earlier volume, *The World of Ngugi wa Thiong'o*, that 'with the tragic exception of Kenya, since his exile in 1982, the eloquence of Ngugi's novels, essays and plays has rung out and echoed in nearly all the geographical and intellectual centres in the world of arts and letters'. Reiterating a postcolonial context for 'this tragic exception of Kenya' from the world-wide reception of Ngugi's work, Oliver

Lovesey's 'Chained Letters: African Prison Diaries and National Allegory' (*RAL* 26.iv.31–43) examines the allegorical connotations implicit in the prison diaries of African writers imprisoned by leaders in postcolonial Africa. Detained in Kenya between December 1977 to December 1978 after the enormous success of his Gikuyu dramas, Ngugi, in *Detained*, calls these leaders:

> 'Africa's tin gods' – whose suspicion of artistic expression articulated what Ngugi, following Frantz Fanon, defined as one of colonialism's most debilitating consequences: the colonization of the mind, or Gramsci's 'subalternity': '[L]ike their colonial counterparts, they had become mortally afraid of the slightest manifestation of a people's culture ... '.

Similarly, Jeannine DeLombard's 'Mzee's New Clothes: Neocolonial Detention as a Spectacle of Invisibility' (in Cantalupo, ed., *Text and Contexts*) recognizes the allegorical manifestations implicit in the author's role as witness and the corresponding responsibility to testify, but sees detention as 'the state-imposed absence of the individual from society'. The ironies and paradoxes which the state-imposed absence of the writer has bred are also recognized in Annie Gagiani's 'Blixen, Ngugi: Recounting Kenya' (in Cantalupo, ed., *Text and Contexts*): 'At a stage when he had long taken his well-known decision to write in Gikuyu, Ngugi said of his earlier choice of English as a medium that it "had already marked [him] as a writer in exile". Ironically, his Gikuyu writings propelled him into physical exile.' In 'Natio, Nation and Postcoloniality: The Example of Ngugi' (in Cantalupo, ed., *Texts and Contexts*), Wole Ogundele's primary focus is on the vexed issue of language; he sees the language issue *vis-à-vis* the ideology-laden choice of switching between Gikuyu and English, for example, as the quintessential litmus test of (postcolonial) critical theory itself. In theoretical terms, language symbolizes the insistence of another 'alter-native' and precolonial polity, the community or *Natio*, on questioning the political rationale of the nation state. According to Ogundele, now that Ngugi 'writes in Gikuyu, the language of that *natio*, he has fully disclosed that antagonism between *natio* and state that is half-obscured but ever present in the earlier novels'. Modhumita Roy's 'Writers and Politics/Writers in Politics: Ngugi and the Language Question' (in Cantalupo, ed., *Texts and Contexts*) also problematizes the issue of language, revealing it as the over-arching tendency of Third World intellectuals to prioritize 'the question of audience and purpose of cultural production [which] is not academic but one that is posed as a practical, often a tactical problem with far-reaching political implications'. Reiterating an earlier paradigm of the language question, F. Odun Balogun's 'Ngugi's *Matigari* and the Refiguration of the Novel as Genre' (in Cantalupo, ed., *World of Ngugi*) describes 'Ngugi's historic decision to abandon English for his native Gikuyu and Kiswahili as his primary language for writing [...] as the most significant achievement of Obi Wali's school of language discourse in African literature'.

Before postulating the thesis that a major crisis exists in what he describes as the tendency of African cultural and intellectual discourse to succumb to a wholesale disillusionment, Neil Lazarus's 'Return to the People: Ngugi wa

Thiong'o and the Crisis of Postcolonial African Intellectualism' (in Canta-lupo, ed., *World of Ngugi*) establishes first Ngugi's best-known critical credentials, referring only indirectly to his achievements as a novelist and champion of African language literatures. According to Lazarus, 'for more than fifteen years now – most notably in his influential book, *Decolonizing the Mind: The Politics of Language in African Literature* (1986) – Ngugi has been calling for African Literature to be written in African languages', in order to transcend 'the "neo-colonial [...] relationship to Euro-America" that struc-tures contemporary African social existence on the levels of politics and economics'. At a period when many African writers, whose work constitutes the co-text to Ngugi's compulsive oeuvre, merely echoed that bourgeois nationalist discourse which Frantz Fanon had criticized in *The Wretched of the Earth* as falsely maintaining its identity with 'the innermost hope of the people', and were intellectually cocooned in the belief that the substance of their progressivism does not stand in need of verification at the hands of 'the people', Ngugi, according to Lazarus, 'moved to take up a revolutionary position on the place of the writer in postcolonial society'.

The unflattering cost of taking up such 'a revolutionary position' is the subject of Henry Chakava's 'Publishing Ngugi: The Challenge, the Risk and the Reward' (in Cantalupo, ed., *Texts and Contexts*). From the well-informed and articulate perspective of a publisher who has been involved with the publication of Ngugi's work since 1972, Chakava describes publishing Ngugi as 'a pleasurable and enriching experience', albeit one that is fraught with its challenge, its risk and its reward. Besides the danger of economic annihilation by the postcolonial state and its agents, according to Chakava: 'I began to receive threatening death calls from anonymous callers, first through our switchboard and later through my private line and house.' Simon Gikandi's suggestive 'Moments of Melancholy: Ngugi and the Discourse of Emotions' (in Cantalupo, ed., *World of Ngugi*) structures Chakava's state-imposed absence of the writer/publisher from society into historical and critical terms, seeing it as 'the discourse of emotions in Ngugi's work [which] seems to be the primary condition for recovering a history foreclosed from the self by the culture of empire and neo-colonialism'. However, the culture of empire and neo-colonialism, according to Gitahi Gititi's 'Recuperating a "Disappearing" Art Form: Resonances of "Gicaandi" in Ngugi's *Devil on the Cross*' (in Cantalupo, ed., *World of Ngugi*), as well as Alamin Mazrui's and Lupenga Mphande's 'Orality and the Literature of Combat: The Legacy of Fanon' (in Cantalupo, ed., *World of Ngugi*) can never be understood or put in its proper historical context without a rigorous engagement with Ngugi's affirmation that ' "it is impossible to understand what informs African writing, partic-ularly novels by Africans" [...] without reading Fanon's *The Wretched of the Earth*, among other books'.

Both *The World of Ngugi wa Thiong'o* and *Ngugi wa Thiong'o: Texts and Contexts*, represent, first and foremost, a well-deserved recognition for Ngu-gi's novels, essays and plays – the eloquence of which, according to Cantalupo, has rung out and echoed in nearly all the geographical and intellectual centres in the world of art and letters. Many writers have contributed poignant creative pieces to the two volumes (Kamau Brathwaite, Sam Mbure, Gitahi Gititi, Amiri Baraka, Ezenwa-Ohaeto, Charles Cantalupo and Frank Chipa-sula); among them is the African American poet Sonia Sanchez, who echoes

Cantalupo's critical recognition of the hallmark of Ngugi's works as 'the liberty and authority' they embody in saying that the best homage that can be paid to such a compulsive oeuvre is to:

> Organize. Unite. Come together for a world peace.
> for our children and if we do
>   it'll get better, in twi words
>   EBE YIYE, EBE YIYE ...

Finally, in a 1993 interview entitled 'Moving the Centre: An Interview by Charles Cantalupo' (in Cantalupo, ed., *World of Ngugi*), Ngugi reiterates one, among many others, of his own overarching paradigms and the ultimate goal of his lifelong struggle:

> Particularly just before his death, Martin Luther King was talking about moving the democratic centre from its prison in the estab- lishment to creative locations among the people [...] There is still a structural imbalance between the West and the rest of us, so to speak. This imbalance is basically economic, but it is also political, and it has cultural implications. So, moving the centre, in an international situation, is really a movement toward correcting this structural imbalance.

The 'Ears and Eyes' of the neo-colonial state are also under close and intense scrutiny in Mpalive-Hangson Msiska's 'Geopolitics: Subterraneanity and Subversion in Malawian Poetry' (in Gurnah, ed., *Essays on African Writing*). Jack Mapanje, Frank Chipasula and Steve Chimombo are Malawi's leading poets whose works constitute the object of critical focus in Msiska's essay; they are comparable to Renaissance poets who had to develop an elaborate language of circumspection 'largely as a result of the political and cultural circumstances under which they worked'. According to Msiska, notwithstanding historical and cultural differences between the two traditions (the Renaissance and the Malawian), at least in their deployment of the resources and facilities of language, the writings of Mapanje, Chipasula and Chimombo approximate what Msiska describes as 'Malawian poetry during the regime of President Banda, which similarly constitutes itself as a poetic of ideological concealment'. Both Mapanje and Chimombo have ransacked Malawian creation myths, and while Chimombo employs an elaborate geo- logical structure, Mapanje's approach to myth is both 'colloquial and critical'. Largely because most of Chipasula's verse was written in exile, it is less constrained in its criticism of the Malawian regime than the poetry of Chi- mombo and Mapanje, produced inside the country. However, with the trauma of the years of repression under President Banda gradually receding, replaced by a more democratic regime which, according to Msiska, 'so far has shown an exceptional capacity for tolerance and criticism', the enduring legacy of that era of repression remains the 'aesthetics of concealment' which it bred. Msiska suggests that the post-Banda Malawian poet could retain the metaphorical density of myth and folklore, but the use of allegory, among other creative devices, must 'defamiliarise reality convincingly enough for our perception of the [new] political situation being described to be enriched'. Similarly,

Anthony Nazombe's 'The Role of Myth in the Poetry of Steve Chimombo' (in Emmanuel Ngara, ed., *New Writing From Southern Africa*), examines, in all its social, cultural and political ramifications, the traditional contents of Chimombo's poetry, comprising: (i) the myth of Napolo, a subterranean snake believed to be responsible for landslides and floods; (ii) the myth of M'bona, a martyred pre-colonial prophet and rainmaker; (iii) the creation myth of Kaphirintiwa; and (iv) the Chameleon and Lizard story about the origin of death. According to Nazombe, there are three basic creative uses to which Chimombo puts myth: the cyclical view of history derived from the Napolo and M'bona myths 'enables the poet to cover a wide range of themes, both local and universal', and observations and conclusions drawn from the premises of these wide-ranging themes assist in defining the role of the writer in his society, while the last major role to which Chimombo puts myth is closely related to what Nazombe describes as the quest motif – the all-important theme of identity. The proverbial 'errors of rendering', however, exist in Chimombo's poetic oeuvre, and according to Nazombe, in this particular instance, it resembles the point Sean Lucy makes in relation to Eliot's poetry which is also relevant to Chimombo: 'we have here a poetry "unified by a developing personality, which at the same time is traditional in the fullest sense"'.

(d) Southern Africa

Walter Ehmeir's 'Publishing South African Literature in English in the 1960s' (*RAL* 26.i.111–31) identifies censorship as the central factor by which the politics of South Africa intruded directly and apparently into the sphere of literature: 'in the 1960s, the government created legal means for controlling publications that were more comprehensive and stringent than any previous laws, and applied censorship more thoroughly and resolutely than before'. The policy of apartheid introduced after 1948 led to the adoption of the advancement of Afrikaans as a literary language and African-language literature for the limited purposes of Bantu education. According to Ehmeir, English language publishing was the first casualty of the policies of the apartheid state, and 'the situation was particularly bad for black authors who wanted to publish books'.

In order to articulate the peculiar Southern African variety of 'newness', the volume of essays *New Writing from Southern Africa* (ed. Emmanuel Ngara) focuses on 'Authors who have become prominent since 1980'. As Edna Aizenberg has reminded us, 'a writer, a text, or genre only becomes "new" in relation to something else', and in describing the sociocultural and political factors that inform 'newness' in the Southern African context, Ngara observes that it is the end of apartheid which has heralded a new era in Southern Africa with South Africa once again becoming part and parcel of the political, economic and cultural life of the continent. The most debilitating effect of decades of colonialism and racial strife is the suppression of a rich literary tradition which the history of the region and its diverse cultural heritage could have given birth to long before now, and with eminent justification Ngara refers to the essays contained in this volume as 'some indication of the wealth of the region'. Since the demise of what Ngara describes as the aberration of apartheid, young writers such as Njabulo Ndebele, Tsitsi Dangarembga and Dikolbe wa Mogale have made a mark on the literary scene, while some authors whose works had previously seen the light of day, such as André Brink and Breyten Breytenbach, rose to new heights. Thus 'newness' in the Southern African context is not synonymous with the age of the writer, but with the more paradigmatic sense in which the 'rebirth' of South Africa has become an 'opportune moment for examining the literary wealth of Southern Africa'. In 'Voyaging Toward Freedom: New Voices From South Africa' (*RAL* 26.i.61–74), Julie Phelps Dietche ranks, among others, Ellen Kuzwayo, writing in her late sixties, among 'New Voices', describing her as speaking 'with a voice made strong by time and experience, telling of her struggles as a teacher, a social worker, and a regional secretary of the YWCA to help her people'.

Godfrey Merintjes's 'A Chain of African Voices: The Prose Oeuvre of André Brink' (in Ngara, ed., *New Writing*), Louise Viljoen's 'Reading and Writing Breytenbach's *Return to Paradise* from Within and Without' (*CW* 7.i.1–17) and Judith Lütge Coullie's 'The Difference of Masks: Breytenbach's *The True Confessions of an Albino Terrorist*' (in Ngara, ed., *New Writing*) are focused on two writers who have been writing for the past four-and-a-half decades, but whose works have not been known to the generality of readers of African literature. While Merintjes's essay sets out to demonstrate the manner in which a chain of African voices is generated in the narrative process at work in the prose oeuvre of André Brink as a whole, Coullie's contribution examines Breytenbach's *True Confessions* within the context of South African autobiographies written in English in the last 44 years, and Viljoen surveys differences in the reception of the 'triptych' *Return to Paradise* (1993) by Afrikaans- and English-speaking reviewers in South Africa and abroad, and suggests that 'it [the text] may deserve a particular kind of reader and a new way of looking at the process of reading'. Within the ramifying parameters of what Duncan Brown has described (while introducing *Current Writing*'s special issue on 'Orality in Southern African Literary Studies' (7.ii)) as 'central themes of what has become the South African national narrative: colonial dispossession and resistance; indigenous belief and Christianity; rural–urban migrations; tradition versus modernity; ethnicity and nationalism; ownership of the land; black subjugation and assertion; as well as industrialisation and labour organisation', the critical issues examined in the writing of Brink and Breytenbach by Merintjes, Coullie and Louise Viljoen, among other critics focusing on their work, centre mostly on the first in Brown's suggestive categorization – colonial possession and resistance. Besides the issue of Southern Africa's cultural diversity, Ngara also cites the following as justification for the inclusion of essays on Brink and Breytenbach in a collection focused on 'New Writing from Southern Africa':

> the need to show that the struggle against oppression and racial injustice in the creative arts was not confined to black authors and to the more well-known English language white writers such as Nadine Gordimer and Alan Paton as even Afrikaans language artists found it necessary to grapple with the aberration of apartheid.

However, Tony Morphet's review article on Peter Alexander's 1994 *Alan Paton: A Biography*, entitled 'Courteous Confused: The Paton Biography' (*CW* 7.i.117–24); Robert Cancel's 'Nadine Gordimer Meets Ngugi wa

Thiong'o: Text into film in "Oral History" ' (*RAL* 26.iii.36–48); Dominic Head's 'Gordimer's *None to Accompany Me*: Revisionism and Interregnum' (*RAL* 26.iv.46–57); Rose Pettersson's book-length study *Nadine Gordimer's One Story of a State Apart*; and Karen Lazar's review article, ' "The Passing Away of the Old Regime": Change, "Truth" and Sexuality in Gordimer's *None to Accompany Me*' (*CW* 7.i.104–16), among others, all demonstrate that critical interest in the more well-known English language writers, far from waning, is revisiting the constituent sites of the authors' paradigmatic starting points. Dominic Head suggests that there is perhaps no better place to commence such a retrospective critical inquiry than the premises of Gordimer's famously titled essay of 1959, 'Where do Whites Fit in?', which began with a pessimistic answer to its own question: 'nowhere' – a view which has been subjected to revision repeatedly in Gordimer's writing. But Tony Morphet's review article sees the moment of historical impasse as that which predates Gordimer's 1959 essay; bringing it back to 1948 – the time of resistance to direct tyranny – Morphet argues that it was Alan Paton's *Cry, the Beloved Country* which 'took the liberal vocabulary out of the smooth, temporising and duplicitous mouths of South Africa's social and business elite and couched it in terms which could be used without shame by Chief Luthuli's ANC'. Karen Lazar's review of *None to Accompany Me* is equally critical of Paton's (1948) refurbishment of South Africa's liberal vocabulary and Gordimer's (1959) seemingly more radical remonstration with the ever-present threat of political and historical impasse: in the 1994 novel, according to Lazar, 'Gordimer is again considering her vision of the place of whites within South Africa's future. The image seems to suggest that whites will take their place in South Africa's future under the leadership of those blacks who are empowered and only with their sanction.' Focusing on the film version of the short story 'Oral History', Robert Cancel observes how the film 'takes Gordimer's understated, nuanced story and overlays it with a powerful African liberation theme'. Examining Gordimer's long journey out of what she calls the 'white laager', Rose Pettersson reminds us that South Africa is no longer a state apart, and that it is the tyranny of 'place' which has always exerted a special influence on the way Gordimer tells her one story.

Dan Wylie's rigorously theorized essays 'Shaka and the Myths of Paradise' (*EinA* 22.i.19–47) and 'The Selves in the Other: The Shaka Poems of D. J. Darlow and F. T. Prince' (*CW* 7.i.70–87) encapsulate an 'aphrodisiac' type of discourse, and one in which both blacks and whites participate. Examining what has for centuries constituted an essential element in European thinking about alien peoples, one of Wylie's primary conclusions is that 'the language used to invoke the variants of paradise in Shakan literature has not been mere elaboration, but the symptom of a network of culture-bound approaches to the alien'. In the same vein, Ian E. Glenn's 'The Wreck of the *Grosvenor* and the Making of South African Literature' (*EinA* 22.ii.1–18) describes the Pondoland Coast incident of 4 August 1782, in which the *Grosvenor* – an East Indiaman – was wrecked, as the beginning of South African literature in English: 'the shipwreck stands at the source of an English South Africa culture facing an indigenous culture and a pre-existing European culture, in spite of the misgivings it has about the latter. The history of English South Africa writing during the next two centuries is in large measure the consequence of that choice.' A contemporary consequence of that paradigmatic 'choice' is latent in Richard Peck's 'The Mystery of McClure's Trekkersburg Mysteries: Text and Non-Reception in South Africa' (*EinA* 22.i.49–71) which examines the mystery surrounding why James McClure's detective novels set in 'Trekkersburg' (Pietermaritzburg) are not better received in South Africa. Elaborating on Ian Glenn's advocacy of a sociology of literature that would embrace and enliven the sense of what, why and when literature tells us what it does about people and society, Peck uses the novels of 'Progressive' mystery writer McClure, and their reception, as a lens through which to see aspects of the 'lived ideology' of English-speaking white South Africa. Rob Gayland's ' "A Man is a Man Because of Other Men": The "Lesane" Stories of Es'kia Mphahlele' (*EinA* 22.i.72–90) is also concerned with the critical issue of 'text and non-reception', and in this case the largely neglected 'Lesane' stories of Mphahlele published in Drum magazine between December 1956 and April 1957. In striking similarity to Richard Peck's observation that especially in white settler areas of eastern, central and southern Africa, a century-long tradition of adventure writing reveals an ideology of imperialism, racism and apartheid far more extreme than that espoused by the official publications of the state, albeit with only few exceptions to the usual conservatism of their genre, unlike those blacks who 'take the easy way out: just remain elite', the 'Lesane' stories deal with ordinary hopes and fears and with recurring human situations – with what Ndebele refers to as 'the essential drama in the lives of ordinary people'.

Lokangaka Losambe's 'History and Tradition in the Reconstitution of Black South African Subjectivity: Njabulo Ndebele's Fiction' (in Ngara, ed., *New Writing*), Liz Gunner's 'Remaking the Warrior? The Role of Orality in the Liberation Struggle and in Post-Apartheid South Africa' (*Commonwealth* 17.ii.19–30), Colin Gardner's 'The Poetry of Dikobe wa Mogale' (in Ngara, ed., *New Writing*), Deborah James's 'Oral Performance of Northern Transvaal Migrant Women' (*CW* 7.ii.97–116), Duncan Brown's 'South African Oral Performance Poetry of the 1980s: Mzwakhe Mbuli and Alfred Qabula' (in Ngara, ed., *New Writing*) and 'Orality and Christianity: The Hymns of Isaiah Shembe and the Church of the Nazarites' (*CW* 7.ii.69–95) all situate us in the postcolonial, post-apartheid era. In Losambe's words, what demarcates the writing of the contemporary era from the creative concerns of its precursor is that 'it analyses various issues affecting the oppressed as they subtly strive to assert their subjectivity in the face of all odds created by apartheid'. History and tradition are important restorative factors at the forefront of Ndebele's creative evocation of the lives of the oppressed. According to Losambe, through a detailed description of 'ordinary' lives as manifested, for example, 'in the relationship between human beings and nature, Ndebele provides an important framework within which one can effectively read the entire South African history and appreciate its restorative potential for both the oppressed and the oppressors'. In (re)situating the poetry of remembrance or South Africa's oral poetry within the paradigmatic contexts of nation and culture, Liz Gunner problematizes further the orality versus literacy debate in South Africa, and concedes that while praise poetry can, in a sense, be atavistic, 'it can at the same time make itself part of the present and the "modernity" of national culture'. Similarly, problematizing an integral aspect of one of the numerous trappings of insipid 'modernity', Duncan Brown observes how the messianic evangelist Isaiah Shembe's attempts to revitalize Zulu society through the maintenance and revival of social customs and mores were rejected by the mission churches. Reading Dikobe wa Mogale's poem 'Crucifixion', Colin Gardner highlights a basic paradox in the orality/modernity, tradition/Christianity debate: 'in so far as the oppressed are associated with Christ (as they often are in Dikobe's poems), the persecutors accept communion from Christ even as they crucify him'. According to Deborah James, the irresolvable debate about the relationship between the text and context continues to straddle what James has termed as aesthetic anthropological theories' scepticism as to whether 'expressive culture does much more than mask or provide momentary alleviation for the uncertain conditions of people's existence'.

Liz Gunner's equally poignant observation of 'the contradictions in the status of women – where they exist emblazoned as central emblems of the nation but are consigned to its margins in its actual operations'– has to a large extent informed the following: Pauline Ada Uwakweh's 'Debunking Patriarchy: The Liberational Quality of Voicing in Tsitsi Dangarembga's *Nervous Conditions*' (*RAL* 26.i.75–84), Supriya Nair's 'Melancholic Women: The Intellectual Hysteric(s) in *Nervous Conditions*' (*RAL* 26.ii.130–9), Anthony Chennells's 'Authorizing Women, Women's Authoring: Tsitsi Dangarembga's *Nervous Conditions*' (in Ngara, ed., *New Writing*), Rosemary Gray's ' "Unnatural Daughters": Postmodernism and Tsitsi Dangarembga's *Nervous Conditions*' (*CE&S* 17.ii.1–7) and Derek Wright's ' "More than Just a Plateful of Food": Regurgitating Colonialism in Tsitsi Dangarembga's *Nervous Conditions*' (*CE&S* 17.ii.8–18). Uwakweh's observation about the male-dominated Zimbabwean literary arena matches Abdulrazak Gurnah's editorial comment in *Essays on African Writing: Contemporary Literature 2* that 'the predominance of writers who were men' has for so long been reflected in the presentation of patriarchal structures as unproblematic. According to Uwakweh, it is the self-referential nature of the autobiographical mode adopted by Dangarembga as a literary strategy that marks her attainment of voice in the Zimbabwean male-dominated literary arena. 'Women as central emblems of the nation' is also the primary focus of Supriya Nair's essay, and it is the melancholic condition of postcolonial intellectuals – totalized and masculinized in much fiction – which, according to Nair, has overshadowed 'the conflicted issue of women and colonial education': 'one version of this history is summoned in Tsitsi Dangarembga's *Nervous Conditions*, a title which "signifies" upon the absent bodies in Fanon's analysis of colonized natives'. According to Anthony Chennells, 'if Africa's problems are located in Europe, the continent is absolved from any necessity to look critically at its own institutions', 'black peculiarity' of class, sexuality, gender, age, ethnicity, economics and political consciousness can only remain embedded in a meta-narrative, and it is precisely because *Nervous Conditions* is a novel concerned with women's narratives that 'it constitutes other and different dialectical processes than those put in motion by Europe's initiatives and Africa's responses'. Situating *Nervous Conditions* in a postmodern context, Rosemary Gray reads the novel's archetypal carnival along Bakhtian lines 'as the feast of becoming, change and renewal' that 'was hostile to all that was immortalized and completed'; this theoretical construct, according to Gray, enables the young protagonist, Tambudzai – at the tender age of seven – the much needed opportunity to avail herself of an education customarily the preserve of male (black) children in Africa. The enigmatic Libyan leader Muammar Gaddafi once claimed that the cumulative effect of freeing the oppressed is that 'the Ozone layer, which is disintegrating because of the body odour of the rich and the tyrants, will heal': locating Dangarembga's novel in a long line of African fictions that have dwelt on bodily functions to do with eating, Derek Wright describes Dangarembga's narrative strategy as one rigorously applied through an intricate network of connections, between education and consumption, skilfully using eating as the governing metaphor for Africa's consumption – nutritional, cultural, educational – of second-hand imitative Western values, a process which removes the book's heroine ever further from her African family, language and self.

However, the colonial Rhodesia of the 1960s and the liberation war years which form the setting of Dangarembga's novel have also been the object of creative allegorization by other Zimbabwean writers, and the following are some of the works focusing on them: Caroline Rooney's 'Re-Possessions: Inheritance and Independence in Chenjerai Hove's Bones and Tsitsi Dangarembga's *Nervous Conditions*' (in Gurnah, ed., *Essays on African Writing*), R. Zhuwarara's 'Gender and Liberation: Chenjerai Hove's *Bones*' (in Ngara, ed., *New Writing*), Rosemary Moyana's 'Literature and Liberation ... the Second Phase: Shimmer Chinodya's *Harvest of Thorns*', Solomon M. Mutswairo's 'The Poetry of Musaemura Zimunya' (all in Ngara, ed., *New Writing*) and Abdulrazak Gurnah's ' "The Mid-point of the Scream": The Writing of Dambudzo Marechera' (in Gurnah, ed., *Essays on African Writing*). In Hove's *Bones*, according to Rooney, there is a deadlock between two necessities, and 'the deadlock is not some simple opposition'; 'there is a law of the father and the state or father-state, a law of men in two senses'. Hove's handling of the theme of the deadlock between these two necessities has produced a hypnotic text, in its rhythms, syntax, rhetoric and its suspensions of decidable meanings. The clash in outlook and sensibility between the heroine Marita and two of her female disciples, according to Zhuwarara, has earned *Bones* the distinction of being one of the first novels in Zimbabwean literature to focus on African reaction to colonialism from the point of view of gender. While Shimmer Chinodya's *Harvest of Thorns* and the poetry of Musaemura Zimunya are described by Rosemary Moyana and Solomon M. Mutswairo as designed to register 'the pains and joys of national rebirth' as well as 'convey sentiments about home – and experience in colonial Rhodesia', respectively, Hove, according to Caroline Rooney, 'tends to be characterized by those who read Zimbabwean literature as the caring true son, whereas his "brother" writer, Dambudzo Marechera, is characterised as the uncaring, truant son'. The middle-ground between Hove and Dambudzo in creative terms, however, is Tsitsi Dangarembga, whose *Nervous Conditions* can be situated between *Bones* and *The House of Hunger*, for example. In his critical commentaries on the controversial but compulsive oeuvre of Marechera, Abdulrazak Gurnah's engaging contribution responds to many of the social, cultural and political upheavals surrounding the emergence of Marechera as a writer who has been described as 'the spokesman for the disenchantment of a generation'. Describing Marechera's writing as both an account of alienation and a celebration of alienated writing, all Marechera's writing, according to Gurnah, 'from *The House of Hunger* to *The Black Insider*, contests the possibility of writing' – but the quintessential difference remains that Marechera's writing also possesses a historical specificity which takes it beyond alienated outrage: 'the joyless and fragmented township in which the "brutalised humanity" of black Rhodesia live, had come about via "capitalists [...] imperialists [...] and bloody whites" '.

Russell G. Hamilton's 'The Audacious Young Poets of Angola and Mozambique' (*RAL* 26.i.85–96), Michael Chapman's 'Making a Literature: The Case of Namibia' (*EinA* 22.ii.19–28) and Kenneth Birch's 'The Birch Family: An Introduction to the White Antecedents of the Late Bessie Amelia Head' (*EinA* 22.i.1–18) are critical responses to the complex, but compelling, set of social, political, cultural and aesthetic factors which has ushered in a contemporary period of literary activities in the other Southern African states of Angola, Mozambique, Namibia and Botswana, respectively. In Angola, for example, Paula Tavares's 'erotico-tropicalist poetry' epitomizes what Hamilton has described as the kind of experimentation that, in the 1980s and beyond, many of the post-independence poets – who possess the legacy of such imposing poets as Augustinho Neto and Aires de Almeida Santos – have carried to levels of what can only be called audaciousness. Concerned with creative and critical issues such as language – not only with words as poetry's raw material, but also with the real and imagined tension between Portuguese and Bantu languages of Angola and Mozambique – these young poets, according to Hamilton, have many of the same concerns that preoccupied their predecessors: 'related to this concern is the preoccupation with identity (individual, ethnic, macro-ethnic, cultural and national, to mention the most salient) and, concomitantly, alienation from primordial sources (real and imagined) and from inevitably elusive forms of authenticity'. Similarly, Michael Chapman's contextualization of 'The Wild South-West of Colonial Imagination' – with a majority of Bantu-speaking Ovambo, several other Bantu African groups including the Herero, and settled whites of German and Afrikaans extraction – aggregates the sociocultural and political background to the attempts of Africa's most recently independent country, Namibia, to find answers to the all-important question of 'Namibianness'. Literary-political debate, according to Chapman, 'has begun to turn attention to the questions of what might qualify the writer as Namibian – birth or commitment? – and whether commitment in a functioning democracy should continue to operate as a euphemism for SWAPO affiliation'. While he urges every prospective inquirer not to ignore its potential for reconstruction, Chapman's open-ended approach to the question of Namibianness also recognizes the challenges for literature in post-independence Namibia's racial/ethnic melting-pot; 'challenges which in the future may become more testing from the perspective of civil as distinct from national consciousness now that SWAPO – as a result of its massive electoral victory in 1994 – has the right to alter the Namibian constitution'.

(e) North Africa
According to Marie-Thérèse Abdel-Messih's 'Identity Text History: The Concept of Inter/Nationalization in African Fiction' (*RAL* 26.iv.163–71), whenever a disjunction occurs in the microcosm, it is often a picture of the disintegration in the macrocosm, and it is only the disjunctive text which renders the condition effectively. Like the Egyptian writer, Son'-Allah Ibrahim, whose novel *Zhat* Abdel-Messih compares and contrasts with Ayi Kwei

Armah's *Why Are We So Blest?*, Assia Djebar and Tahar Ben Jelloun are both from North Africa – Algeria and Morocco respectively. While Abdel-Messih perceives the work of Armah and Ibrahim as conveying a global loss of identity which needs to be restored by restructuring history, Abdulrazak Gurnah describes the writing of Djebar and Jelloun as addressing issues which are central to their cultures, and 'justifies' the inclusion of essays on these two writers in the volume *Essays on African Writing* by citing the need 'to bring them to the attention of readers of African writing'. Perhaps more importantly, Gurnah also observes:

> Their work [Djebar's and Jelloun's] deserves to be better known and the fact that it isn't reflects the implicit sub-heading for 'African literature' as writing from south of the Sahara, though their relative neglect is also just as much to do with the ambivalent cultural affiliations of North African societies.

Belinda Jack's 'Strategies of Transgression in the Writing of Assia Djebar' and Lucy Stone Mcneece's 'Tahar Ben Jelloun's Post-Modern Folly?: The Writer Through the Looking Glass' (in Gurnah, ed., *Essays on African Writing*) complement Abdel-Messih's essay in articulating the ambivalent cultural affiliations of North African societies, on the one hand, and what Abdel-Messih describes as the themes of fictionalizing, identity formation and historical textualization readily observable in most of these works, on the other.

If the absence of a linear plot in Ibrahim's *Zhat* is marked by a discontinuity in its events, it also projects a fictionalized narrative by which the author plays the role of both reader and author. Zhat, the protagonist, and her husband, Abdel-Meguid, are two commoners who have to survive the norms of a postcolonial society, a situation in which consumption and deception constantly replace labour and solidarity: 'obscurantism replaces enlightenment, leading to the loss of the self and disjunction in social relations'. The historical and fictional narratives, which, according to Abdel-Messih, are presented in alternating chapters, are symbolized and metaphorized further by Zhat's quixotic quest which evolves along three phases in her life, marked by three historical decades in postcolonial Egypt: the 1960s, the 1970s and the 1980s. The ambivalent cultural affiliation of North African societies notwithstanding, therefore, the illusion involved in the implicit sub-heading of 'African Literature' as writing from the south of the Sahara has been fragmented by the narrative strategies of Armah and Ibrahim. While in the fictionalized narrative, 'even Zhat's fossilised colleagues refuse to admit her into their circle until she is able to conform to their socio-religious norms'; in the historical narrative, 'the environment of conspiracy is instigated by the collaboration between mass media and money makers, foreign companies and high officials, American aid and economic inflation, ex-ministers and booming investment companies, prostitution and Arab statesmen, the Gulf states and the USA' – a situation of cross-linkage between author and reader, the history of the self and that of the nation, the national and the international.

Language, however, 'is part of a complete set of relationships between corporeal confinement and freedom encountered in multiple guises', and in the writing of Assia Djebar, Belinda Jack identifies strategies of transgression in a situation which 'speech itself is already the assuming of a position in a society which denies it to women'. The exposed body, forbidden sexual, and often violent, encounters and illegitimacy of various kinds, are some of the factors identified by Jack as areas of conflict. These antitheses are associated with space (open and closed), the female body (veiled and masked), with language in the French sense of *langue* ('tongue' – French and Arabic), and language in the sense of *langage* ('linguistic system' – written and oral); and it is Djebar's sensitive handling of these themes which, according to Jack, has earned her texts 'privileged status as touchstones within the growing corpus of Francophone texts written by North African women'.

Denounced by Algerian critics, Djebar (like her North African counterpart, the Moroccan writer Tahar Ben Jelloun), according to Mcneece, 'naturally invites criticism from those who conceive of national and cultural identity in linguistic terms'. With respect to Ben Jelloun, Mcneece also suggests that we look to the literary effects and questions of 'textuality' that have been identified with postmodern culture. Ben Jelloun's constant 'play' with his readers – setting them on a hermeneutical quest that becomes a kind of 'reader's progress', and tendency progressively to alter the reader's habits of interpreting literary language as he shifts their position in respect to the narrative – has earned Ben Jelloun, most especially among Moroccans impatient with his postmodernist experimentations (or folly?), the accusation of writing to please European readers, offering them an exotic and distorted vision of Moroccan culture. For Mcneece, however, other ways of 'reading' the principle of uncertainty and ambiguity typical of Ben Jelloun's characters ought not be discountenanced: for, 'it is only possible that he (Ben Jelloun) is speaking simultaneously in several codes to readers on both sides of the Mediterranean about their common misconceptions'.

2. Australia

(a) General

While the last two years' essays for this section recorded a decline in the publication of literary scholarship and criticism, at least as these have been traditionally understood, this year saw some welcome developments. For the first time, the Association for the Study of Australian Literature published its conference papers: *Proceedings of the Sixteenth Annual Conference 1994*. In the past, papers delivered at the conference have appeared as essays in a number of journals; but diminishing outlets for such contributions – as the traditional literary magazines shifted from literary criticism to cultural theorizing, and to the interview with an author rather than an essay on the work – have encouraged the Association to take this welcome step. The 33 papers collected in the *Proceedings* comprehend, and often conflate, a wide range of interests from the scholarly to the theoretical, across the genres and the historical span of writing in Australia. Elizabeth Jolley, Patrick White and Barbara Hanrahan each attracted two papers; there was a panel on war writing; and interests in landscape, gender, Aboriginality and ethnicity were prominent. As ASAL is the body most representative of scholars of Australian literature, the reassurance these *Proceedings* offer is that more, and more varied, research is taking place than has been represented by publication in recent years.The proceedings of the inaugural conference of the Religion, Literature and the Arts Project last year, sponsored by the School of Studies in Religion, University of Sydney, the Department of Literature and Languages, Australian Catholic University and the Institute of Theology and the Arts, Sydney, include papers both general and specific on religious themes and concerns in local literature, as also do this year's proceedings. Noel Rowe's observation in this year's volume, that theologians reading Patrick White use their theology to read his fiction, but they do not allow his fiction to read their theology, could readily be extended to most of the contributions that touch on literature.

As noted in the essays for the two preceding years, much effort has been expended of late on deconstructing the myths of Empire, Nation-Building, and other grand Anglo-Celtic patriarchal narratives. This year was notable for the increase in the number of thoroughly researched, 'full dress' biographies, another development that will continue next year. Is it, with the once grand narratives commanding only incredulity, that there is now properly no history, only biography (as Emerson observed long ago)? Literary subjects among this year's crop of biographies are Henry Kendall, 'Steele Rudd' and Louis Esson. These will be noted in the appropriate section below (though it is worth observing here, among the welcome developments, that the Esson is published by CUP, which has recently and rapidly built up an impressive list of substantial literary and cultural-historical studies). The subject of Laurie Hergenhan's *No Casual Traveller: Hartley Grattan and Australia*, however, straddles the genre divisions below. Grattan, an American freelance, commented widely on Australia from the publication of his *Australian Literature* (1929) to his two-volume history *The Southwest Pacific* (1963). A friend of the Palmers and other Australian writers, he was also responsible for the American edition of Furphy's *Such is Life* (1948). Hergenhan's meticulously researched life gives this previously shadowy commentator on Australian culture substance, and details his interactions with (and influence upon) the then small band of home-grown proponents of a national literature. Also a valuable addition to cultural history in the same period is Brian Kennedy's *A Passion to Oppose: John Anderson, Philosopher*. While Anderson, Professor of Philosophy at the University of Sydney in the period 1927–58, is a less shadowy figure than Grattan, the influence of his ideas, including aesthetics, on generations of students (many of whom became writers), has been rather elusively in the background of much commentary about Australian intellectual, and specifically literary, culture. Kennedy's biography valuably details much that has often been taken for granted in previous discussions.

A further volume of ASAL conference proceedings, more literary titles from CUP, and more literary biographies await next year's survey. As also do books on a controversy that surfaces in a number of journal articles this year: 'the Demidenko Affair'. Last year the judges of the country's most prestigious prize for fiction, the Miles Franklin Award, ruled that novels by Peter Carey, Elizabeth Jolley and Frank Moorhouse were ineligible under the terms of the bequest (for a discussion of this decision see Paul Washington, ' "Nation" and Australian Cultural Studies: The Case of the Miles Franklin Award', *NLR* 28/29.129–39). This year the judges bestowed it upon Helen Demidenko, a 23-year-old of claimed Ukrainian descent, for *The Hand That Signed the Paper*, a novel set primarily in the Ukraine during the Second World War which details the collaboration of the narrator's family in Nazi genocide. No sooner had questions about the novel's literary merit and claimed anti-Semitism been raised, than it was revealed that 'Demidenko' was in fact Helen Darville, daughter of English immigrants. The media became fascinated by issues dear to theorists: the relations of authors to text, of fiction to history, and of texts to other texts (as Darville was also accused of plagiarism). Articles which appeared this year include Robert Manne's 'The Strange Case of Helen Demidenko' (*Quadrant* 319.21-8) which considers the novel anti-Semitic; Morag Fraser's 'The Begetting of Violence' in *Meanjin* (54.419–29), Anne Waldren Neumann's 'The Rationalizing of Violence, the Incitement of Violence' (*Meanjin* 54.613–25) and Kathy Laster's 'Crime and Punishment' (*Meanjin* 54.626–39); Serge Liberman's 'On Helen Demidenko's *The Hand that Signed the Paper*' (*Southerly* 55.iii.161–74), William Schaffer's 'The Book that Evaded the Question' (*Southerly* 55.iii.175–84) and Peter Kirkpatrick's 'Moral Authoritarianism and *The Hand that Signed the Paper*' (*Southerly* 55.iv.155–65); *Overland* editor John McLaren and contributors also engaged more summarily with some of the issues (141.29–39).

Supporting the observation made in previous essays that, while outlets for traditional literary criticism have diminished, much valuable scholarship is emerging from multi-disciplinary centres, are two books from prominent feminist cultural historians in departments of Women's Studies: Susan Sheridan's *Along the Faultlines: Sex, Race and Nation in Australian Women's Writing 1880s–1930s* and Kay Schaffer's *In the Wake of First Contact: The Eliza Fraser Stories*. Sheridan distances herself from the contemporary myth (noted in last year's essay) that Australian women writers in the past were silenced outsiders, which she considers a construction of 1970s' feminists. Instead, she sees the women who wrote over the half century she examines as having participated in the discourses constituting sex, race and nation. The faultlines she discerns occur where these signifying codes meet, clash and implicate women writers in the patriarchal discourse. *Along the Faultlines* includes and extends articles Sheridan has published over the past decade or more. The first three chapters in Part I, 'The Sexual Politics of Romantic Fiction', reprint discussions of Ada Cambridge, Barbara Baynton and other female colonial romancers; to these are added a discussion of the literary and sexual politics of women's fiction in the 1930s, taking account of more recent scholarship, and a ground-breaking chapter on 'The Romance of Experience' in the early twentieth century. Part II, 'Feminist Journalism and the Politics of Nationhood', adds to the previously published 'Louisa Lawson, Miles Franklin and Feminist Writing' two closely researched chapters on feminism and socialism. Part III contains, in addition to an already published chapter on Aborigines in colonial women's writing, chapters on their representation in the writings of Mary Gilmore and K. S. Prichard, and another on women addressing the nation which discusses how a number of significant Australian women novelists addressed themselves to 'the nation and thereby hijacked nationalist discourse'. As this might suggest, Sheridan observes not only subversion of the patriarchal discourse but also degrees of complicity with it, and 'ambivalence' is a recurrent term in her independently critical, theoretically sophisticated and rigorously researched new version of feminist literary history. In her preface to *In the Wake of First Contact: The Eliza Fraser Stories*, Kay Schaffer recounts how she began investigating the historical basis for

Patrick White's *A Fringe of Leaves*, only to end up years later with a 260-page study of the culture of colonialism and its contemporary effects. Her deconstructive pursuit of representations of her legendary subject range from Fraser's own time to the present and through texts as various as (to mention only the better known) Sidney Nolan's paintings, a long poem by Michael Ondaatje, a play by Gabriel Josopovici and a novel by Andre Brink. Schaffer sees White's novel as the most complex version of all the Eliza Fraser narratives, but by the time she grants it a chapter it can seem only 'a new version of an old and increasingly vulnerable white man's mythology'.

Constructing Gender: Feminism in Literary Studies (ed. Hilary Fraser and R. S. White) contains 16 essays ranging from medieval literature to the present. Three are on Australian subjects: Ian Saunders in ' "The Most Difficult Love": Expectation and Gender in Barnard Eldershaw's *Tomorrow and Tomorrow and Tomorrow*' finds that this novel disappoints current feminist expectations. Amanda Nettlbeck writes on 'The Ambivalence of Women's Experience in Elizabeth Jolley's *My Father's Moon* and *Cabin Fever*', but her effort must seem to have been overtaken by the appearance of the final volume of Jolley's trilogy; and Susan Midalia discusses 'Art for Woman's Sake: Kate Grenville's *Lillian's Story* as Female *Bildungsroman*'.

Speaking Positions: Aboriginality, Gender and Ethnicity in Australian Cultural Studies (ed. Penny van Toorn and David English) contains Kay Ferres's discussion of sex, race and gender in Rosa Praed's autobiography, Gerhard Fischer on Mudrooroo's adaptation of Heiner Müller's *Der Auftrag* and Wenche Ommundsen's 'Writing as Migration: Brian Castro, Multiculturalism and the Politics of Identity' which, while focused on Castro's fiction and essays, is of considerably wider interest because it rehearses, lucidly and independently, the issues of literary multiculturalism currently being debated. Annette Robyn Corkhill's *The Immigrant Experience in Australian Literature*, intended as a teaching resource, provides generous quotation from, and biographical notes on, writers included in her *Australian Writing: Ethnic Writers 1945–1991* (*YWES* 75.710). The obverse of multiculturalism is the subject of Ouyang Yu's 'The Chinese in the *Bulletin* Eyes, 1888–1901' (*Southerly* 55.ii.130–43) which draws together some, mainly familiar, examples of that nationalistic period's racism which appals so many commentators today.

An international conference on 'National Biographies and National Identity: A Critical Approach to Theory and Editorial Practice' was held at the National Library of Australia, and Patricia Grimshaw's paper 'Female Lives and the Tradition of Nation-Making', reprinted in the Library's journal *Voices* (5.iii.30–44), 'provides a reinterpretation of colonial women's history influenced by post-colonial critiques of white women's writing on coloured women'. Drawing on radical writers, who yet had somewhat limited sympathies (Louisa Ann Meredith, Katie Langloh Parker, Bessie Harrison and Louisa Lawson), Grimshaw also 'calls for consideration of race and gender in the construction of "nation" '. Journal entries from Meredith, Ellen Clacy and Ann Henning inform Emma Curtin's 'Gentility Afloat: Gentlewomen's Diaries and the Voyage to Australia, 1830–80' (*AHS* 26.civ.634–52), which reveals the considerable role women played 'in the transference of gentility to the colonies'. In *Absences*, the text of a wide-ranging lecture filled with fresh detail, Peter Pierce revisits colonial laments over the lack of ivied ruins etc. to consider the construction of history in writing and painting, and to draw attention to some notable absences, chiefly of Aborigines and convicts. Routledge's *The Post-Colonial Studies Reader* contains a dozen contributions by Australians, including those of its editors, Bill Ashcroft, Gareth Griffiths and Helen Tiffin.

Serial bibliographies remain the same as in recent years: the monthly and annually cumulated *Australian National Bibliography*, Thorpe's bi-monthly *Guide to New Australian Books*, the annual *ALS* bibliography of studies in Australian literature, the *JCL* bibliography for Australia and New Guinea, and *Antipodes'* annual bibliography of Australian literature and criticism published in North America. Other general bibliographical aids published during the year are the first volume of Stuart Lee's *Southerly Index*, which covers 1939–61; Ewa Gajer's *Australian Women Short Story Writers: A Selective Bibliography*, which omits stories included in collections and stories for children; and Horst Priessnitz's *German Poetry in Australia 1830–1992: A Checklist of Literary Translations, Adaptations and Comments by Australian Authors*. Juliet Flesch's *Love Brought to Book* is a bio-bibliography of twentieth-century Australian writers of romance. Given the interest in colonial women's romance in recent years, it seems extraordinary that contemporary writers of romance have been so overlooked. As Marion Lennox points out in one of the forewords to *Love Brought to Book*, Harlequin Mills and Boon titles have been translated into 26 languages and are available in more than 100 international markets. Twenty-seven Australian authors sold one million books through Mills and Boon between 1984 and 1994, the best-known of them being Joyce Dingwell and Emma Darcy; even so, Flesch has clearly experienced difficulty in gathering basic biographical and bibliographical information on these internationally most popular of Australia's writers.

(b) Fiction and Autobiography

Mulini Press, which specializes in reprints of nineteenth-century literature, was very active this year, issuing Mary Vidal's *Tales for the Bush* (1845) with an informative and thoughtful introduction by Susan Lever; *Tasma's Diaries: The Diaries of Jessie Couvreur*, edited by Patricia Clark (whose biography of Tasma was noted last year); Robert Dingley's *The Land of the Golden Fleece*, a thoroughly edited collection of articles on Australia and New Zealand by the London *Daily Telegraph's* celebrated travel writer and coiner of the phrase 'Marvellous Melbourne', George Augustus Sala; and *Cowand: The Veteran's Grant* (1859) by the first native-born woman novelist, Louisa Atkinson, edited by Elizabeth Lawson. For UNSW Press's Colonial Texts series Rosemary Foxton has edited Catherine Martin's *The Silent Sea* (1892), set in South Australia. This is its first republication since it originally appeared as a serial in various Australian newspapers, a three-decker in London and a paperback in New York, and the text Foxton has expertly collated from these different versions is accompanied by 80 pages of apparatus.

Today, Rosa Praed (1851–1935) is among the best-known of Anglo-Australian women writers of romance. Attempts to 'recuperate' her reputation have taken place over a long period, however. When working on his biography of Praed, *In Mortal Bondage* (1948), Colin Roderick persuaded her heirs to deposit her papers in the John Oxley Library, Brisbane, and Chris

Tiffin prepared a general checklist of them in 1967. Now, with Lynette Baer, Tiffin has compiled *The Praed Papers: A Listing and Index* which will greatly assist future researchers with its exemplary descriptive notes on individual items and its indexes of proper names and titles. Also exemplary is John Barnes and Lois Hoffman's *Bushman and Bookworm: Letters of Joseph Furphy*, a selection of 250 letters. With its introduction, annotations, biographical notes, index of correspondents, checklist and general index, it is a model of scholarly editing rarely seen in Australia. It is also, through its judicious selection, a delight to read – bringing together much that is familiar to devout Furphians from Miles Franklin's rambling attempt at biography (1944) and fragmented quotation from those who had consulted the correspondence in libraries. It is no criticism to say that this is a considerably belated book of a kind that in another publishing culture we might have expected to have had much earlier when its appearance would have constituted an event; sadly, with the disparagement of stereotyped radical nationalists now prevailing, it passed all but unnoticed. Once the Lawson-Furphy tradition was advanced (but also disputed) as *the* Australian tradition; now nativist interpretations of earlier literary history are an embarrassment. It is a relief, therefore, to find Adrian Mitchell offering fresh and subtle observations on the texts rather than his own ideological discomfits in *The Short Stories of Henry Lawson*. This is in OUPAus's Horizon series for senior secondary students and undergraduates, and Mitchell discusses the most frequently prescribed and anthologized stories by this now frequently demonized icon of the radical nationalist patriarchy. (Unfortunately, OUPAus has announced the cessation of this imprint.)

Even more enduringly popular than Lawson's stories of rural life have been those of his *Bulletin* contemporary Arthur H. Davis ('Steele Rudd'), yet, in comparison with Lawson, Davis is all but an anonymous author. The title of Richard Fotheringham's *In Search of 'Steele Rudd': Author of the Classic Dad and Dave Stories* suggests how Davis's reputation has been all but completely eclipsed by that of his pseudonym. While Fotheringham's exhaustive researches into Davis's ancestry, selection life in Queensland, A. G. Stephens's considerable role in creating and promoting 'Steele Rudd', Davis's own entrepreneurship and his characters' eventual escape from his control to become public property on stage, screen and radio are presented chronologically, this is less a biography of Davis, who remains elusive, than a fascinating account of the continual reconstruction and marketing of a myth.

In *Writing the Colonial Adventure: Race, Gender, and Nation in Anglo-Australian Popular Fiction, 1875–1914* (another of the new CUP titles), Robert Dixon decodes ideologically a branch of fiction contemporaneous with but very different from Furphy's, Lawson's or Davis's on the one hand, or Rosa Praed's on the other: the 'rattling yarns' of male adventure. Dixon argues that these, influenced by Scott, Rider Haggard and R. L. Stevenson, 'were participating in an imperial endeavour to make Australia, Asia and the Islands appropriate sites of adventure for English people'. His subtitle announces the same interests in ideology as Sheridan's *Along the Faultlines*, and he acknowledges the contribution she has made to raising consciousness of these cultural formations. But he reverses the now usual assumption that romance was the province of Victorian and Edwardian women writers and readers by claiming that for metropolitan 'New Imperialists' and Australian federationists alike, 'realism and decadence were disturbingly feminine'. While this, surely too sweeping, generalization is merely asserted, the instances Dixon analyses (without attempting to argue that ripping yarns were great literature) allow him persuasively to expose deep uncertainties at the heart of masculinist, imperialist ideology. *Writing the Colonial Adventure* lends a provocative new twist to the continuing reappraisals of colonial romances, which have gendered them as female, and it will no doubt prove stimulating, though it is curiously repetitious in sections (some of which have appeared previously as articles).

Philip Mead in 'Death and Home-work: The Origins of Narrative in *The Fortunes of Richard Mahony*' (*ALS* 17.ii.115–34) presents a 'psycho-rhetorical' reading of this now little-read trilogy that breathes new life into it, by showing that the writing, which in the age of New Criticism was assumed to be flatly unimaginative, is richly ironic and responsive to contemporary interests. Some of these interests are picked up by Catherine Pratt in 'Fictions of Envelopment - Henry Handel Richardson's *The Getting of Wisdom*' (*Antipodes* 9.i.3–9). Pratt argues that this autobiographical novel 'not only explores the constraint of the female body and mind but also the constraint of narrative', so that when it is read 'in the context of its own literary self-consciousness and against *Myself When Young*, two forms of narrative come into focus – the popular romance and the *Bildungsroman*'. Donna Coate, in 'Lesbia Harford's Homefront Warrior and Women's World War I Writing' (*ALS* 17.i.19–28), generously summarizes the posthumously published novel *The Invaluable Mystery* (Penguin, 1987) to claim that this is the only wartime text to provide a view of the working-class woman at home, and contrasts it with works by Ethel Turner, Mary Grant Bruce and other women writers of the period, who portrayed the male as the dominant heroic character and the females as 'suspended in holding patterns, waiting' for their husbands, sweethearts and brothers to return.

The most famous collaboration in Australian literary history was that of Marjorie Barnard and Flora Eldershaw, who over 20 years co-authored five novels and many stories, three histories, a pioneering volume of literary criticism and numerous articles and lectures. Selecting from their disparate voluminous writings for *M. Barnard Eldershaw* in UQP's Australian Authors series must have confronted Maryanne Dever with an even more impossible task than usually confronts editors of such anthologies. Instead of offering extracts from their more familiar works (e.g. *A House Is Built*), Dever has reprinted for the first time in its entirety their novel *Plaque with Laurel* (1937), a lightly satirical presentation of then contemporary local literary culture which centres on a conference in Canberra. This fills most of the volume, and is complemented by a stringent selection of essays, reviews and correspondence which widens the context to suggest the central role Barnard and Eldershaw played in the development and promotion of local writing through the 1930s into the 1950s, a role authoritatively outlined in Dever's informative introduction. Related to this is Patrick Buckridge's analysis of a preoccupation with the idea of ' "Greatness" and Australian Literature in the 1930s and 1940s: Novels by Dark and Barnard Eldershaw' (*ALS* 17.i.29–37) which reveals their 'anxious' response to a perceived absence of cultural authority and tradition. Other articles reappraising novels of this period are Brenton Doecke's 'Challenging History Making: Realism, Revolution and Utopia in

The Timeless Land' (ALS 17.i.49–57), which draws attention to the way in which Dark presented history as 'a field of contestation rather than pretending to describe things as they really were'; Cath Ellis's 'A Tragic Convergence: A Reading of Katharine Susannah Prichard's *Coonardoo' (Westerly* 40.ii.63–71), which sees this novel symbolically extending the conflict between white and Aboriginal traditions beyond the characters and events; and Lydia Wevers's 'Terra Australis: Landscape as Medium in *Capricornia* and *Poor Fellow My Country' (ALS* 17.i.38–48), which argues that, while the role of the white man in these novels suggests 'a white appropriation of the black landscape and its powers', Herbert also incorporates the Aboriginals' sense of the power and meaning of their land.

Patrick White's fiction continues to attract exegetes, each with a key to unlock its mysteries. For David Coad, in 'Intertextuality in Patrick White's *The Solid Mandala' (CE&S* 17.111–16), it is Jung's *Psychology and Alchemy*, together with this novel's epigraphs from Eluard, Meister Eckhart and Dostoyevsky. For Cleo Lloyd Da Silva, in 'Separation and Individuation in *The Aunt's Story' (Kunapipi* 17.ii.42–51), 'the Object Relations theories of Margaret Mahler, Melanie Klein and others offer some psychological explanations for Theodora Goodman's mental confusion'. For Michael Giffin, in 'Between Athens, Jerusalem, and Stonehenge: The Christian Imagination in the Novels of Patrick White' (*C&L* 32[1994].ii.167–88), it is not White's critique of Christianity, as many have argued, but his critique of 'the pre-existing matrix of mythical hermeneutics essentially Primitive, Semitic, and Hellenic into which the Christian revelation of God in Christ was born'. For Noel Macainsh, in 'Patrick White's *Voss* – the Irony', in Volker Wolf (ed.), *Lesen und Schreiben: Literatur-Kritik-Germanistik*, a Festschrift for Manfred Jurgensen, the key is the mode of narration. Appropriately for this novel, he draws on a historical range of German understandings of irony. While his conclusion might leave the reader uncertain whether *Voss* can 'say' anything other than that its author is ironic, it is a welcome change to find this complicated *literary* issue of White's irony engaged with informedly. Also literary in its focus, this time on modernist literary techniques, is Lee Spinks's 'Austerities and Epiphanies: A Note on Fantasy and Repression in Patrick White's "Five-Twenty" ' (*Westerly* 40.i.39–44).

Peter Pierce's *Australian Melodramas: Thomas Keneally's Fiction* appears in UQP's Studies in Australian Literature series. Pierce was quoted in the 1993 essay lamenting the lack of local critical generosity towards Keneally and other internationally and commercially successful authors; he also contributed the chapter on literary history to *The Penguin New Literary History of Australia* (1988), in which he presented the time-honoured conflicts between different versions of that history as melodrama. His study of the prolific Keneally eschews the conventional chronological survey from his early novels, which excited expectations that he might be the next Patrick White, to those that made him an international best-seller. Instead, Pierce approaches his subject through his critical reception, and turns the tables on Keneally's detractors by claiming that the melodrama they deplore in his fiction is not only Keneally's great strength but is also a characteristic of the Australian literary imagination. Pierce structures his argument by comparing early and later novels which have common concerns (convicts, Aborigines, Antarctica, War, the Irish), positing an underlying thematic coherence in Keneally's writings over 30 years. His argument, especially about melodrama, and how it might reveal the national temper, is not always easy to follow; but it is a calculatedly provocative reappraisal aimed as much at the assumptions of Keneally's critics as at the works themselves, and future writers on this novelist will not be able to ignore it. A response has already come from one of the critics Pierce singles out, Imre Salusinszky. In 'Thomas Keneally: My Part in His Downfall' (*Quadrant* 320.23–6), Salusinssky renews his attack on the poor (or non-existent) editing of Keneally's prose, and finishes by pronouncing him 'without a doubt, one of the two or three most over-rated writers in the world today'.

Amanda Nettlbeck's *Reading David Malouf*, in OUPAus's Horizon Studies in Literature series, discusses in relation to *Johnno, An Imaginary Life, Fly Away Peter* and *The Great World* 'the recurring themes ... of mapping language, and the construction of identity' which Nettlbeck and others pursued in *Provisional Maps* (*YWES* 75.717). While many contributors to that volume threatened to bury Malouf's fiction under a mass of theory, Lee Spinks in 'Allegory, Space, Colonialism: *Remembering Babylon* and the production of Colonial History' (*ALS* 17.ii.166–74) writes lucidly and illuminatingly on the fiction's engagement with the metaphors, images, divisions and projections of colonialism, and on how Malouf represents the 'other' without speaking 'for' it. As is so often the case with Patrick White's characters, Malouf's are in search of the secret in-dwelling self, according to Genevieve Laigle in 'Approaching Prayer, Knowledge, One Another: David Malouf's *Remembering Babylon*' (*CE&S* 18.i.78–9), in which she identifies those who discover and nurture this other world, and are supported by perceptive companions who understand that being open to epiphanic revelations may often lead one to seemingly darker places.

The fiction of Elizabeth Jolley and Peter Carey continues to attract attention. Likening the moral judgements we make in life to a form of literary criticism, Jennifer Livett in 'Two Answers to Every Question: Elizabeth Jolley's Fiction, Ethics and Criticism' (*ALS* 17.i.10–18) explores the ethical haze which develops when writer betrays reader, or when the categories of 'real life' and fiction are confused. In 'Marian Engel's *Bear* and Elizabeth Jolley's *The Well*' (*ArielE* 26.ii.65–91), Gerry Turcotte compares the Gothic elements in both novels; and in 'Contesting the "One Law – the One Sublimating Transcendent Guarantor"': Elizabeth Jolley's *The Well* and *Sugar Mother*' (*SPAN* 40.54–71), Doreen D'Cruz maintains that the well is 'not simply the narrative site for the marginalization of female homosocial relations by phallic heterosexuality but is the site of contest between two sorts of lesbianism – phallic lesbianism and feminine lesbianism'. The interest shown in Carey this year is similarly diverse. David Callahan in 'Whose History is the Fat Man's?: Peter Carey's *The Fat Man in History*' (*SPAN* 40.34–54) finds the stories in this first collection of central importance to the direction taken by contemporary Australian writing because 'they articulate contemporary issues and anxieties in Australia during the 1970s [...] with the fantastic symbolic energies of writers like Kafka and Borges'. Employing three modes of narrative temporality – historical, postmodern and allegorical – Carolyn Bliss examines 'Time and Timelessness in Peter Carey's Fiction – The Best of Both Worlds' (*Antipodes* 9.ii.97–105) and discovers 'that an early fondness for the allegorical gives partial way to a characteristically Carey medley of the historical and postmodern, but resurges in the latest novels so that he juggles both time and timelessness in *The Unusual Life of Tristran Smith*'. Ruth Brown's 'English Heritage and Australian Culture: The Church and Literature of England' in *Oscar and Lucinda* (*ALS* 17.ii.135–48) spells out some of the grand imperial narratives parodied in this novel; and on another tangent altogether is Barbara Bode's 'Angels and Devils – Child Sexual Abuse in Peter Carey's *The Tax Inspector*' (*Antipodes* 9.ii.97–105).

Is Thea Astley's most recent novel, *Coda*, a brilliant satire on old age, or on the way in which old age is regarded, or could it be a satire on life itself? Considering these questions, Robert L. Ross in 'Reaching Towards the Centre' (*WorldI* 2.316–21) finds Astley's eccentric characters, all participants in the mythology long associated with Australia's interior, caught up in an unconventional spiritual quest for the unattainable. Ross, a prominent American critic of postcolonial literatures in English, also contributes ' "The Poetry of Revolution" in Thea Astley's *Beachmasters*' to *Nationalism vs. Internationalism: (Inter)National Dimensions of Literatures in English*, edited by Wolfgang Zach and Ken L. Goodwin. Ross particularly draws attention to the ways in which Astley in the novel presents Christianity as complicit with imperialism. Tracing through Astley's novels how far the church has moved from the centre of her imagination, Elaine Lindsay in 'Reading Thea Astley – From Catholicism to Post-Christian Feminism' (*Antipodes* 9.ii.119–22) finds that many of her characters discover God 'outside of Christian practice': in 'the goodness of nature, the exercise of charity, and the primacy of love'. Shirley Hazzard, on the other hand, is seen by Russell McDougall in 'Beyond Humanism? The Black Drop of Shirley Hazzard's *The Transit of Venus*' (*JCL* 30.ii.119–33) as writing an 'allegory of the death of humanism'.

Gerald Murnane's fiction is increasingly attracting critical attention. In *ArielE* (26.ii.25–39), Sue Gillett's 'Gerald Murnane's *The Plains*: A Convenient Source of Metaphors' details how the novel's mythic quality is achieved through lack of specificity, of landscape and the historical past, and an inversion of the mythologies of exploration and pioneering to privilege the intellectual rather than the practical man; 'but this inversion still takes place within the parameters of male concerns'. *Southerly* 55.iii has a focus on Murnane: Dominique Hecq contributes 'The Inescapable Plain of Trespass: On Translating *The Plains*' (63–72). Don Anderson, in ' "A Terrible Denudation": Gerald Murnane's *Emerald Blue*' (73–83), invokes Henry James's famous litany of all that was lacking in Hawthorne's America to consider a similar cultural 'denudation' in Murnane's settings, but finds Murnane seeking an aesthetic and ethical 'compensation' for this through the structures of his prose. Nicholas Birns in a reflective general essay, 'Indefinite Desires: Love and the Search for Truth in the Fiction of Gerald Murnane' (48–62), finds that his subject is 'by far, the most Petrarchan writer of the twentieth century'. Birns, an American who instinctively relates Australian writing to wider contexts, is a stimulating essayist and his 'Frank Moorhouse's *Grand Days* and Post-Colonial Idealism' (*Westerly* 40.i.67–71) is the first sustained consideration of this otherwise critically overlooked major novel. While Moorhouse's reputation is primarily that of a satirist, Birns finds *Grand Days* permeated with an idealism that he attributes to the author as well as his protagonist, an idealism he sees as inherently Australian and a counter to modernist and postmodernist, including postcolonial, cultural pessimism. Like Moorhouse's,

Helen Garner's writing is widely admired but has received little sustained discussion. This year it is the subject of two articles informed by French feminist theory: Philippa Kelly's 'Transgressive Spaces: Helen Garner's *Cosmo Cosmolino*' (*Westerly* 40.i.19–25) and Eleanor Hogan's 'Borderline Bodies: Women and Households in Helen Garner's *Other People's Children* and *Cosmo Cosmolino*' (*NLitsR* 30.69–82), which draws on Kristeva's 'borderline cases' to argue that in these fictions 'a kind of homology exists between the body of the feminist woman and the body of the collective household'. French critic Xavier Pons writes again (see *YWES* 74) on Beverley Farmer's fiction in 'Dramatising the Self' (*ALS* 17.ii.141–8), appreciating the 'exquisite sensuousness' her writing can achieve.

In 'Odysseus Unbound/Singing with the Sirens: Liminality and Stasis in Glenda Adams's *Dancing on Coral*' (*NLitsR* 28/29.55–64), Karen Brooks sets this novel in a tradition of the female *Bildungsroman* which includes Richardson and Stead, and which projects 'the literary struggle between the monologic voice of the Old world and the multiplicitous voices of the New'. The gender-based marginalization of Janette Turner Hospital's characters is the focus of Kate Temby's examination of 'Gender, Power and Postmodernism in *The Last Magician*' (*Westerly* 40.iii.47–55), while Lynn Jacobs's 'Ancestral Furies: The Fiction of Beth Yahp, Ding Xiaoqui and Alex Miller' (*NLitsR* 28/29.153–64) examines 'the frictions between answering to one's ancestors or celebrating individual choice' in recently published novels by these writers, finding in them expressions of 'transnational consciousness'. Consideration of such consciousness, and of postmodern practices, have been closely related in Brian Castro's reception. Surveying his fiction in ' "Things Are Cast Adrift" ' (*ALS* 17.ii.149–56), and noting its increasing self-referentiality, Peter Pierce regretfully reaches the conclusion that 'many of Castro's self-referential games have been long enough in the literary playground, and that he would be better advised to write novels, rather than to write about writing them'. Not seen is 'After Castro, Post Multiculturalism?' in *Rubicon* (ii.54–61) by Wenche Ommundsen, whose essay on Castro and multiculturalism in *Speaking Positions* was noted in the General section.

Sally Morgan's autobiographical *My Place* has created considerable critical discussion, being 'unique in the totality of Australian written and oral story [...] and offering an illuminating version of Australian history for all white Australians' according to Rhonda Ozturk in 'Sally Morgan's Discovery of True Identity and Black History from Minimal Family Lore' (*AuFolk* 10.61–78). Subhash Jaireth draws on Bakhtin in his analysis of how Morgan has created herself as subject in 'The "I" in Sally Morgan's *My Place*: Writing of a Monologised Self' (*Westerly* 40.iii.69–78), and again in 'Who Speaks for Whom?: Mikhail Bakhtin and the Idea of Chronotopic Nature of Speaking and Listening' (*Imago* 7.iii.78–83). In responding to 'the central question of "speaking and writing" i.e. who can speak for whom' raised by Jaireth, Jo Robertson presents a theoretical paper on 'the politics of enunciation' based on the reception of *My Place*; and considers whether 'the experience of being colonized is essential for writing about colonial and post-colonial situations' (84–92). In *SoRA*, similar issues of 'positionality' (as it has become referred to overnight) are engaged with by Annabel Cooper in 'Talking About My Place/ My Place: Feminism, Criticism and the Other's Autobiography' (2.140–53), and by Penny van Toorn writing on 'Mudrooroo and the Power of the Post:

Alternative Inscriptions of Aboriginalist Discourse in a Post Aboriginalist Age' (2.121–39). Despite the paralysing uncertainties of 'positionality', Pauline McMillan manages to provide a sympathetic account of the work of a prominent Aboriginal writer and activist in 'Kevin Gilbert and Living Black' (*JAS* 45.1–14).

The continuing reception of *My Place* exemplifies how recent criticism has challenged many of the assumptions traditionally associated with the recording of personal history. Laurie Hergenhan's 'Open Access? Geoffrey Dutton's *Out in the Open* and Contemporary Autobiography' (*Imago* 7.iii.54–65) insightfully discusses its immediate subject in relation to the experimentation and pluralism found in many Australian personal histories since the 1960s. Drusilla Modjeska's *Poppy* is just such an instance of such experimentation, and pluralism, according to Leslie Hopkins in 'Reading Poppy' (*Island* 64.52–5), which sees Modjeska moving beyond a wide range of binaries, including the masculine/feminine dichotomy. David McCooey's 'Australian Autobiographies of Childhood: Beginning and Myth' in *Southerly* (55.i.132–45) is a chapter from his study of modern Australian autobiography, published by CUP, which will be reviewed next year. Kerry Kilner's *Playing the Past: Three Plays by Australian Women* was also published this year.

(c) Poetry

Michael Ackland's authoritative *Henry Kendall: The Man and the Myths* is an exhaustively researched biography which is at its best in locating his subject's verse within the contexts, local and English, of his times. Ackland, who has recovered many of Kendall's 'lost' contributions to journals, provides a good sense of the different literary cultures his subject was involved in, and imaginatively interprets his verse in relation both to the events of his life and to the poetic influences to which he was responding. While it integrates chronologically much that will make it an invaluable resource for future scholars, it might not break sufficiently often into sustained biographical narrative to hold the interest of more general readers.

The three 1994 Townsville lectures, given by Dennis Haskell and published as *Australian Poetic Satire*, range widely and stimulatingly over the full historical span as he considers the relationships of satire to parody and irony. He begins with a well-informed consideration of satire in general and its transformations since Barron Field's 'Kangaroo'. The second lecture is on Kenneth Slessor as satirist, which Haskell is well qualified to deliver as he, with Geoffrey Dutton, edited Slessor's *Collected Poems* (noted last year). In the third lecture, Haskell engages with feminist theory to discuss insightfully some contemporary Australian women satirists. Showing the full historical span of women's poetry is one of the intentions Susan Lever announces in her introduction to *The Oxford Book of Australian Women's Verse*. Like Sheridan in *Along the Faultlines*, Lever is at pains to correct a misapprehension that arose among 'second-wave' feminists during the 1970s, who 'often assumed they were the first generation of women to speak out'. Lever's first selection dates from 1838 and from there she proceeds to illustrate how 'at every stage in Australia's history women poets have been published and respected by their contemporaries'.

Geoff Page's *A Reader's Guide to Contemporary Australian Poetry* provides brief biographical notes and short essays (many drawn from reviews he has published over the years) on 100 poets active during the past 30 years. While he acknowledges in his introduction that many will be unhappy (either way?) with his arbitrary figure of 100, his eclecticism and non-partisanship make this a useful reference guide not only for his observations on the work of individuals but also on movements, trends and influences. Two of the remaining titles in OUPAus's Australian Writers series appeared this year (others will be reviewed next year). With a play on the title of one of her subject's critical works, Jennifer Strauss in *Judith Wright* suggests her study could be subtitled 'Preoccupations in the Poetry of Judith Wright' and she is most insightful in reading closely poems that span Wright's long career and, simultaneously, setting them within the developing pattern of Wright's concerns with family, regional history and, even, 'nation' (the latest term to be placed under erasure). Unabashedly allowing the repressed author to return, Strauss argues persuasively and illuminatingly that Wright's deepening involvements with ecology and Aboriginal reconciliation led to a change in her conception of the relationship between the natural world and the poetic imagination. In *Kenneth Slessor*, Adrian Caesar resurrects his author to press questions he feels have been evaded by preceding commentators: how truly a modernist was Slessor, how readily can the poet be separated from the journalistic hack and why did he abandon poetry? Caesar's consciously provocative and closely interwoven answers involve both fresh readings of familiar poems and re-contextualizations of them in terms of Slessor's aesthetic and political preferences.

Coinciding this year with the appearance of *Dorothy Hewett: Collected Poems*, edited by William Grono, is *Dorothy Hewett: Selected Critical Essays* edited by Bruce Bennett. Lawrence Bourke's 'Dorothy's Reception in the Land of Oz: Hewett Among the Critics' concludes the collection, but provides a good starting point for locating the other contributors' points of departure. Analysing Hewett's critical reception over the decades, Bourke shrewdly discerns that many of the old concerns have refashioned themselves, parading now in deconstructionist garb. Bennett opens the collection with some observations on the depiction of place in her writings in varied genres. John McLaren, in 'Dorothy Hewett and the Left', discusses her work thematically as well as biographically. Jennifer Strauss writes on Hewett's continual engagement with myth and fairytale, Stephen Knight on '*Bobbin Up* and the Working Class Novel' and Peter Fitzpatrick on her significant place in contemporary Australian drama. Barbara Holloway's 'Negative and Positive: Dorothy Hewett in Visual Images' illustrates how photographs continually recycled in the media have served as capsules of meaning within contemporary constructions of 'Literature', 'sexuality' and 'woman/artiste'. This interest is extended by Lyn McCredden in 'Imaging Dorothy Hewett' which discusses the visual texts with which Hewett surrounds her poems. 'In Seeking Woman: Dorothy Hewett's Shifting Genres', Susan Lever considers the intractable problems of representing female experience within literary genres which conventionally mask women. Jenny Digby's 'Representations of Female Identity in the Poetry of Dorothy Hewett' is a shorter version of her *Southerly* (54[1993].ii) article noted last year. David Brooks in 'The Wheel, the Mirror and the Tower: Desire in the Writings of Dorothy Hewett' discerningly discusses imagery which recurs not only in Hewett's writing but also in that of contemporaries, male as well as female. Bill Dunstone in ' "Dreams . . .

Visions ... Spells ... Stories": Representation and Identity in *Bon-bons and Roses for Dolly'* discusses the intertextuality of cinema and theatre within this play; and Harry Garlick in ' "In the Bio-Box": The Use of Hollywood Myth in Some Early Dorothy Hewett Plays' extends this interest. In all, it is a strong collection that should stimulate reconsideration of this long-controversial writer. Marvin Gilman's 'Lines of Intersection: The Two Dorothys and Marxism' (*NLitsR* 28/29[1994/1995].23–32) adds another dimension with his examination of an interrelatedness which exists between Hewett and Dorothy Livesay of Canada.

Noel Macainsh's 'Romance and Tale: A Duadic Principle in Brennan's *Poems 1913'* (*AUMLA* 83.54–67) explores Christopher Brennan's attraction to Novalis's idea 'that it is solely through poetry one can come to know the unity between the spirit and Nature that characterizes the Golden Age'. Macainsh supports this with references (marked by Brennan in his copy) to *Novalis Schriften*, and to *Die Christenheit oder Europa*. Otherwise, articles in journals have concentrated on modern, and especially contemporary, poets. In 'Body-Landguage [*sic*]: Linguistic Inhabitation of Land in the Poetry of Judith Wright and Oodgeroo of the Tribe Noonuccal' (*Kunapipi* 17.ii.5–14), Anne Collette introduces the concept of 'landsculpt' – which she claims as a new mode for inducing a sense of 'belonging built on the acknowledgement of aboriginal inheritance and a land/body indivisibility that might also be ours, given time', and which may yet produce a poetry linking land, body and word. A close reading of early and later examples of Rosemary Dobson's poetry has provided evidence for Marie-Louise Ayres of a poetic which draws together many threads, and at times returns to rework some previously used 'to weave a rich epistemological fabric'. Her ' "The Folds of Unseen Linen": The Fabric of Rosemary Dobson's Poetry' (*ALS* 17.i.3–9) foregrounds these important characteristics which may have been obscured by critical focus on the linear development in her writing. David McCooey in ' "Looking into the Land-scape": The Elegiac Art of Rosemary Dobson' (*Westerly* 40.ii.15– 25) provides a sensitive and perceptive analysis of the elegiac form, particularly as found in the later poems. Similarly, this critic is drawn to the pastoral and elegiac aspects in the poetry of Vivian Smith, describing him in 'Still Life: Art and Nature in Vivian Smith's Poetry' (*Westerly* 17.ii.157–65) as a postcolonial exile writing 'the kind of pastoral which has little faith in Arcadia as being more than a transitory state'. McCooey's work highlights the way in which 'the pastoral imagination has to continually re-illuminate its natural surroundings' and this is consonant with the conclusion to Gary Catalano's assessment, 'Vivian Smith' (*Quadrant* 322.57–60), that 'from first to last his poetry is marked by a consistent and compelling radiance'.

There is a welcome resurgence of the critical essay, particularly on contemporary poetry, in this year's *Southerly*. In the first issue, Martin Duwell's ' "Having Been Someone Like Myself": The Early Poetry of Bruce Beaver' (55.i.23–39) identifies Beaver's distinct 'signature' in his first three collections, but also paths not pursued subsequently; and Nicolette Stasko in 'The Love Poetry of Bruce Beaver' (40–51) traces the development of this subject through all his work, indicating the influence of Rilke. The last issue contains Peter Alexander's ' "Vital Organs with Strings Attached": The Poetry of Rhyll McMaster' (55.iv.14– 20); Billy Marshall-Stoneking's 'π: An Appreciation' (40– 53), Roula Tsokalidou's 'P. O.: The Poet Who Cracked the Code'

(54–65) and Ivor Indyk's '*24 Hours*', a review essay on this poet's latest book (66–72); David McCooey's ' "Secret Truths": The Poetry of Kevin Hart' (109–21); Joy Wallace's ' "In the game I make of sense": The Poetry of Hazel Smith' (136–46); and John Hawke's 'Robert Gray and the Vitalist Tradition' (96–105).

(d) Drama

The major reference work this year, not only for drama studies, is the *Companion to Theatre in Australia*, edited by the late Philip Parsons (with Victoria Chance) and published by Currency Press (co-founded by Parsons), the major publisher of local playtexts and studies of the theatre. It is the first in a projected three-volume series – the others being a Companion to Music and Dance in Australia and a Companion to Film, Radio and Television. The *Companion to Theatre* which, as the preface declares, is 'about theatre in Australia, not Australian theatre' alone, includes circus, mime, puppetry and music theatre and attempts to cover 'every major development and every major figure in theatre in Australia, from earliest colonial times to the present'. This preface is unusual in pointing to gaps in the entries because of the research remaining to be done on, for example, important localities or ethnic theatres. The result, which draws on the expertise of a large team of researchers, is, however, splendid: there are entries for theatre companies, venues, playwrights, plays, producers, directors, actors and reviewers. There are also topic or survey entries; for example, 'Playwrights and the Screen', 'Repertoire', 'Melodrama' and 'Research and Scholarship' – the last extending for 11 columns and including the locations of the major collections of manuscripts and archives. Further reading lists are provided at the end of individual entries, which are attributed to the contributors. While there are no cross-heads, cross-reference is elaborate through the use of small capitals in the text of entries and the provision of an index. This *Companion* is handsomely produced and lavishly illustrated, and the consistently high quality of the editing compares very favourably with that in the second edition of *The Oxford Companion to Australian Literature* (*YWES* 75.704–5) and at 703 similarly formatted pages it has not been a significantly lighter undertaking.

Also from Currency is a revised and updated edition of Dennis Carroll's *Australian Contemporary Drama*, first published by Lang (1985). While Carroll disavows any intention of offering a history, his chronologically arranged chapters on representative playwrights – from Louis Esson, Vance Palmer, Katherine Susannah Prichard, and the beginnings of modern Australian drama before the First World War, through to Jack Davis, the leading Aboriginal playwright, and the present – in fact constitute an admirable *critical* history of twentieth-century Australian drama. The work of each playwright is closely analysed stylistically (with that of Douglas Stewart and David Williamson receiving a chapter each), yet it is also contextualized within the patterns of development, theatrical and social, that Carroll perceives, with the overriding pattern being that of the continual transformation of ambivalent Australianist myths which lend the drama its national character. Over half the book is devoted to the period from the beginnings of the New Wave at the end of the 1960s to the present; and Carroll displays exemplary skill in bringing the internal history of local drama (which was interacting with international influences) into focus with the external history of the political, economic and cultural changes to which the dramatists, directly or indirectly, individually as well as collectively, were responding.

Peter Fitzpatrick's *Pioneer Players: The Lives of Louis and Hilda Esson* provides the fullest account yet of those central figures and events with which Carroll begins his history of modern Australian drama. As a biography, Fitzpatrick's surpasses the others reviewed this year by providing, as well as much valuable information for specialists, the pleasures of a compellingly told, if sad, story. His narrative has the old-fashioned novelistic virtues of fully fleshed-out characters and strongly evoked settings and events, combined with a confident authorial view that is both sympathetic and critical. While this full and finely detailed dual biography is anything but muck-raking, it dispels the myth, propagated by Louis himself, that his talents were too advanced for the philistine culture he was fated to endure. Reference has already been made to Richard Fotheringham's biography of Arthur H. Davis, the author of the Dad and Dave stories. A condensed exploration of the involvement of Davis, Bailey, Beaumont Smith and Ken Hall is provided in 'The Plays of "Steele Rudd" ' (ADS 26.81–100) in which Fotheringham also discusses the influence on local writers of an American bucolic comedy imported by J. C. Williamson, *In Mizzoura*.

In a special issue of *ADS*, entitled 'Women Making Theatre For Social Change', Susan Pfisterer's 'Cultural Anxiety and the "New Woman" Playwright' (27.143–50) unearths an Australian example of this genre by Sydney playwright, Mrs E. S. Haviland: *On Wheels*, a three-act comedy set in 1896. As well as being about two daughters who reject their Victorian upbringing, desire a useful education and financial independence, and temporarily scorn love and marriage, Pfisterer claims it can be read as an early example of a lesbian and transsexual drama. *AuFS* (10.xxi.143–50) is also a special issue, devoted to the proceedings of the Third International Women Playwrights' Conference. The difficulties women playwrights have faced in the past formed one topic; discussion also centred on the role of the Australian New Theatre in producing such plays as Betty Roland's *The Touch of Silk* (1928), *Vote No! An Anti-Conscription Play* (1938); Nancy Wills's *Christmas Bridge* (1950), Mona Brand's *Here Under Heaven* (1948), and Oriel Gray's *The Torrents*, which shared first prize with Lawler's *Summer of the Seventeenth Doll* in the Playwrights' Advisory Board competition of last year. The *Doll* is itself the subject of an invigoratingly fresh reconsideration by Kerryn Goldsworthy in *Southerly* (55.i.89–105). Her playful title, 'Is It a Boy or a Girl?: Gendering the Seventeenth Doll', suggests how she avoids heavy-handedness in bringing contemporary theoretical awareness to bear on this now classic text (which has just been cast into an opera).

Although still comparatively few in number, studies of drama and theatre have been particularly strong this year. To a large extent, this strong showing could be attributed to the coincidental publication of a number of long-maturing projects; but over recent years this area of scholarship has been sustaining itself at a level, of quantity and quality, unimaginable before the establishment of drama or theatre-studies departments in universities around the country. Together with the other developments mentioned above, this augurs well for the future of scholarly and critical literary studies in general.

3. Canada

(a) General
Some writers embody the spirit of their times more poignantly than others, and good biographers know how to evoke such defining contexts. Foremost among the life-writing this year are books on two key figures of the 1960s, the heyday of Canadian cultural production: Rosemary Sullivan's award-winning *Shadow Maker: The Life of Gwendolyn MacEwen* and James Hoffman's *The Ecstasy of Resistance: A Biography of George Ryga.* Sullivan's narrative constructs a compassionate, if sometimes overly hypothetical, story from the incomplete and contradictory data of MacEwen's troubled life, which included an insane mother, an alcoholic father, some disastrous relationships (including one with Milton Acorn, whose supporters have since felt compelled to correct Sullivan's depiction of his and MacEwen's brief marriage), great poverty and finally death by alcoholism. As is common in life-writing, Sullivan's discussion of MacEwen's writing is subordinated to biographical priorities and not much more than adequate, but MacEwen's prodigious talents and remarkable charisma are chronicled with admiration and respect. The book excels in its depiction of 1960s' coffee-house culture in Toronto (with a brief excursion to Jane Rule's house on the West Coast) and thus provides an important complement to Douglas Fetherling's memoir *Travels by Night* and to Ira B. Nadel's recent biography of Leonard Cohen (*YWES* 75.724). George Ryga's cultural roots are very different from MacEwen's, and his name is associated with places in western Canada (Edmonton, Summerland, Vancouver), but there are still a number of remarkable similarities between the two writers. In writing *The Ecstasy of Resistance,* James Hoffman sought to broaden the picture of Ryga's accomplishments in Canadian literature and to see him as more than the author of a 'Canadian classic', namely *The Ecstasy of Rita Joe.* Hoffman takes great care to establish Ryga's Ukrainian ancestry and the lingering influence of its passionate nationalism (the book received a grant from the Department of Canadian Heritage), both of which – so Hoffman argues – predisposed Ryga towards the patriotic lyricisms of cultures in similar situations, Scotland among them. Hoffman describes Ryga's travels in Europe, his obsession with the poetry of Robert Burns and his early political commitment. Brilliantly gifted like MacEwen, Ryga also drew on ancient traditions to ground his work. As a Marxist, however, he insisted on historic specificity, while MacEwen tended to endow her subjects with a mythic aura, even when her material was historic, as in her treatment of the ill-fated Franklin expedition and of T. E. Lawrence's life-story. If Sullivan persuasively evokes the cultural ambience of 1960s' Toronto, Hoffman is very good at documenting the nationalist rhetoric of the centennial decade which, while creating a culture on jingoistic steroids, still provided a paradoxically nurturing framework for achievements like *The Ecstasy of Rita Joe.* In both books, the photographs chosen to illustrate the text poignantly trace the all-too-rapid decline of two immensely gifted individuals. Other biographies published by ECW this year include J. R. Miller's *Big Bear (Mistahimusqua)* and *Irving Layton: God's Recording Angel*, by Francis Mansbridge, while the late Robertson Davies's work undergoes a theological reading in Dave Little's *Catching the Wind in a Net: The Religious Vision of Robertson Davies.*
Margaret Atwood's Clarendon Lectures, *Strange Things: The Malevolent*

North in Canadian Literature, although intermittently amusing, are a generally disappointing series of plot-summaries with clichéd conclusions. Notwithstanding Atwood's disclaimer that she is a writer and not an academic, both the occasion and the subject (newly topical, as numerous recent 'Northern' narratives testify) would have deserved more careful thought. As it is, we have somewhat superficial explorations of four 'Northern' themes, focusing, respectively, on the Franklin expeditions, the Grey Owl phenomenon of white men 'gone native', the Wendigo myth and its close association with cannibalism and the presence of women in an environment that Atwood describes as a metaphorical extension of the vampiric females of Black Romanticism. In the last chapter in particular, Atwood appears to suffer a relapse into the selectivity of *Survival* where only those texts were included that confirmed the book's controversial thesis. *Various Atwoods: Essays on the Later Poems, Short Fiction, and Novels* (ed. Lorraine M. York) makes for an apt companion piece to *Strange Things*, especially in Sherrill Grace's discussion of the myths surrounding the Franklin expeditions. Grace focuses on the 1987 CBC special 'Frozen in Time' covering the exhumation of three of Franklin's crew from their permafrost graves, and on Atwood's fictional response to the TV feature in 'The Age of Lead'. The shrewd linkages proposed by Lorraine York between Atwood's own iconic public persona and her insistence on debunking such personae in her work are also instructive. Other essays feature Diana Brydon on *Bodily Harm*, Glenn Willmott on *The Handmaid's Tale* (novel and film), Molly Hite on *Cat's Eye*, Coral Ann Howells on *Wilderness Tips* and Shannon Henger on *The Robber Bride*; while Linda Wagner-Martin, Hilda Hollis and Patricia Merivale explore poetry and prose poems.

The general soul-searching about the profession of English continues. *English Studies in Canada: Then and Now*, ed. Heather Murray, is a special issue of *UTQ* (64.iii). Mercifully free of the woolly ideological speculations that sometimes posture as investigations into university mandate and pedagogy these days, this volume contains essays by Anna Sonser on women's education, in 'Literary Ladies and *The Calliopean*: English Studies at the Burlington Ladies' Academy (1846–1851)' (368–80) and by Henry Hubert on the teaching of composition at Canadian universities ('Babel After the Fall: The Place of Writing in English', 381–97). There are also two case-studies, of the University of British Columbia and the University of Saskatchewan respectively, by Margery Fee ('Puck's Green England and the Professor of English', 398–416) and L. M. Findlay ('Prairie Jacobin: Carlyle, King and Saskatchewan English', 417–30), as well as edited versions, with introductions, of speeches by James de Mille, W. M. Tweedie and James Cappon. A charming autobiographical piece by William Blissett on 'A Lifetime in English Studies' is not made any less entertaining by the author's slightly dotty suggestions for the teaching of poetry (354–67). A temporary slip into self-congratulatory prose about the achievements of the University of Saskatchewan's Department of English notwithstanding, all of the essays offer rich historical research, astute analysis and clear parallels with the present, the latter sometimes delivered with a passion that displays the author's faith in, and commitment to, her profession. This volume contributes much to our knowledge of the university's role in nation-building, but it is equally good at documenting the human ambitions and insecurities that determine the daily business of academia.

Several of the contributions in *Cultural Studies in Canada*, eds. Faye Pickren, Linda Hutcheon, Stephen Pender – also a special issue of the *UTQ* (64.iv) – dovetail with the discussions in *English Studies in Canada*. Particularly noteworthy are Jo-Ann Wallace's illustration, in 'English Studies versus the Humanities?', of retrenchment politics at the University of Alberta, where interdisciplinarity has been co-opted by administrative expediency (506–13), and Jody Berland's very fine discussion in 'Marginal Notes on Cultural Studies in Canada' of the documents and tropes encapsulating typical preoccupations in Canadian cultural studies. Beginning with an analysis of government papers such as the Massey and Applebaum-Hébert Reports, Berland proceeds to the study of communication and nationhood in Harold Innis, Marshall McLuhan, George Grant, Arthur Kroker and Margaret Atwood before concluding, rather apocalyptically, that '[w]ithout a myth of common identity, without security of government support, without desire to be elsewhere, and perhaps (or is this fear of precipitous change our dispositional legacy) without a conceivable future, Canada's culture(s) turns to face itself' (514–25).

(b) Fiction
Imagining Culture: New World Narrative and the Writing of Canada by Margaret E. Turner is an odd sort of book. Focusing on the work of John Richardson, F. P. Grove, Sheila Watson, Robert Kroetsch and Jane Urquhart, it presents perfectly good but also unoriginal readings of their books. Turner's contention that 'to point up the way in which an entire hemisphere and its cultural products have been constructed is to point up the discursive nature of the new world' may be a mouthful but it hardly describes her much more modest project of giving four highly canonical writers and one somewhat less so (all of European descent) yet another critical spin. The topic would have required a much more extensive confrontation with the literature of the Americas to fulfil its ambitious claim. As it is, this is an articulate but also somewhat outdated doctoral dissertation.

James Doyle's *The Fin de Siècle Spirit: Walter Blackburn Harte and the American/Canadian Literary Milieu of the 1890s* chronicles one writer's largely unsuccessful efforts to establish a North American version of decadence (or 'euphuism' as Doyle calls it) and to negotiate the uneven literary markets in Canada and the United States while doing so. Some aspects of Harte's milieu and several of his associates are fascinating: Harte married a sister of Edith Eaton (Sui Sin Far) and Winnifred Eaton (also known as Onoto Watanna), both of whom have begun to attract considerable attention as early Eurasian commentators on Asians in North America. Grace Harte too was a remarkable woman who, after her husband's early death, became a successful Chicago lawyer. It is unfortunate that Doyle appears to have carved up his various forays into the Harte-Eaton milieu into discrete articles, notes, and this book. While all together might have produced a picture of remarkable sociological and historical complexity, individually their interest is too modest to support Doyle's exaggerated claim that Harte's story 'effectively epitomizes the creative experience of the fin de siècle' and, paraphrasing Phyllis Grosskurth, even 'epitomize[s] the experience of creative humanity as a whole'.

As usual, discussions of Atwood's work are found in several different contexts. *The Handmaid's Tale* occurs a few times in *Out of this World:*

Canadian Science Fiction and Fantasy Literature, the companion volume to an exhibition at the National Library of Canada (ed. Andrea Paradis). Although an odd mix between traditional scholarship and SF cultism, the book points out useful historical genealogies, sketches differences between American and Canadian science fiction, and points up the Utopian dimensions of well-established cultural tropes like Canada's obsession with the North. Thus *Out of this World* inadvertently provides a complement to Atwood's Clarendon lectures. One of the few classics of Canadian science fiction is James De Mille's *A Strange Manuscript Found in a Copper Cylinder*. *CanL* 145 contains no fewer than four essays on the novel, including Linda Lamont-Stewart's 'Rescued by Postmodernism: The Escalating Value of James de Mille's *A Strange Manuscript* ... ' (21–36), Gwendolyn Guth's 'Reading Frames of Reference: The Satire of Exegesis in James de Mille's *A Strange Manuscript* ... ' (39–59), Flavio Multineddu's 'A Tendentious Game with an Uncanny Riddle: *Strange Manuscript* ... ' (62–81) and Stephen Milnes's 'Colonialist Discourse, Lord Featherstone's Yawn and the Significance of the Denouement in *A Strange Manuscript* ... ' (84–106). All are preoccupied with the generic classification of the book, most argue that the novel acquires new interest as a postmodern text *avant la lettre* and one, Milnes, suggests that De Mille was a postcolonial critic, also before his time. Carole Gerson takes a similar position to Milnes's in her essay in the special issue of *ECW* (56) on 'A Contrapuntal Reading of *A Strange Manuscript* ... ' (224–35). With the exception of John Thurston's 'Remember, My Dear Friend: Ideology and Genre in Upper Canadian Travel Writing' on Canadian travel and settlement narratives (183–97), all papers in the section entitled 'postcolonial reading strategies' are preoccupied with fiction: in addition to Gerson's essay, there are Robert Fleming's 'Supplementing Self, A Postcolonial Quest[ion], for [of] National Essence and Indigenous Form' on Catharine Parr Traill's *Canadian Crusoes* (198–223), Ajay Heble on Ondaatje's *In the Skin of The Lion* (236–54) and Dee Horne on Thomas King's *Green Grass, Running Water* (255–73). One of the virtues (and ironies) of this volume is the way in which the individual contributions enter into dialogue with each other, sometimes deliberately, and sometimes accidentally. Thus Diana Brydon, editor of the volume, eschews the polite conventions of edited collections by sharply taking issue with contributors with whose views she disagrees (1–19). In particular, she scolds Sylvia Söderlind for casting aspersion on 'the value of theorizing margins, arguably one of postcolonialism's energizing terms'. Söderlind's essay, which may well be the most energetic and courageous piece in the book, presents an anatomy of what has become a very clichéd term indeed and by implication targets a critical vocabulary which is every bit as sterile and self-serving as the ones it purports to replace (96–109). Söderlind also finds herself under attack in Arun Mukherjee's essay on racial minority women, Mukherjee's objection that, in her book *Margin/Alias*, Söderlind uncritically applied 'the terms "colonized" and "postcolonial" ' to a small selection of 'white male Canadian and Québécois writers' is well taken (and could equally well be raised against Turner's *Imagining Culture* reviewed above). In addition to generating debate herself and encouraging it among her contributors, Brydon has also done well in including work with broad historical sweep, such as Heather Murray's essay on 'English Studies in Canada and the Case of Postcolonial Culture' (51–77) and Chris Gittings's 'Canada and Scotland:

Conceptualizing "Postcolonial" Spaces' (135–61). The claim, in the introduction, that this collection offers 'a fundamental rethinking' of earlier approaches to postcoloniality and Canadian literature is too ambitious (there is some sophomoric work in this volume, and some contributions are reprints), but this is a well-conceived collection nevertheless.

(c) Drama and Poetry
Contemporary Issues in Canadian Drama, ed. Per Brask, includes a broad range of essays that take stock and offer new perspectives. Particularly commendable are Chris Johnson's observations on canon formation in Canadian drama, a piece which is both well researched and differentiated in its argument. Agnes Grant's discussion of Native drama offers a new, if somewhat contradictory, Native response to George Ryga's *The Ecstasy of Rita Joe*, while other contributors present perspectives on various ethnic and regional aspects of the drama. *SCL* (20.ii) features six papers on Canadian drama. The essays are strong because they are concerned with questions of technical performance as much as with academic considerations. Particularly fine are the papers analysing gender construction on stage. These not only pay detailed attention to the physicality of drama, but also insist on the changing psychological and societal dynamics brought to bear on each new performance. Celeste Derksen's 'Masculinity and the *mise en scene: The "Collected Works of Billy the Kid"*' raises an important question when she queries the role of the spectator 'in male homoerotic narratives' (22–33). Marta Dvorak discusses female stand-up comedy, with illuminating asides to Québec theatre where the comic monologue is a tradition of long and politically influential standing ('Carnivalesque Comedians', 57–65).

Phyllis Webb's *Nothing But Brushstrokes: Selected Prose* assembles a number of occasional pieces on subjects ranging from Proust to Canadian unity. Perhaps the most interesting among these, for readers of Webb's poetry, are her reflections on the poetic line and on 'Poetry and Psychobiography'. A selection of photo-collages with an accompanying essay are also included.

Among the sparse publications on poetry, Adam Carter's 'How Struggle Roots Itself in Ritual: A Marxist Reading of the Poetry of Patrick Lane' (1–21) on Pat Lane in *ECW* (55) stands out. Working with a Marxist framework (and numerous references to Walter Benjamin), Carter revisits the vexed question of formalist versus expressive poetry with particular reference to poetry motivated by social concerns, looks at the lyric (much maligned as a form preoccupied with personal expression, hence also prone to self-indulgence), and re-evaluates allegory as more germane to political content than symbol. This volume of *ECW* also features 'The Incurable Beauty of the Earth', an interview, by Graham Barron, with Roo Borson (230–9). Besides the standard questions about the poet's formative influences (Robert Binghurst and Michael Yates receive special mention), the interview makes clear once again how much of a gap exists between writers and academics.

4. The Caribbean

(a) General

It is pleasing to record the fiftieth anniversary issue of an historic journal, the Guyanese literary magazine *Kyk-Over-Al* (46/47), the only one of the early Caribbean magazines – *Bim* in Barbados, *Focus* in Jamaica and the *Beacon* in Trinidad were the others – to be still in fairly regular publication. Its founding editor A. J. Seymour, whose mantle Ian McDonald has assumed, lives on in this edition; it has reprints of the first edition's editorial, one of his poems, and his account of the first 28 issues, published in 1956, as well as a new commemorative piece from his widow, Elma Seymour, recording her husband's dedication of the editorship to McDonald: 'to Ian as my son, I leave this in your hands to carry on for future generations'. It is easy when faced with longevity to take it for granted. In reality, the publication of a literary magazine sustained for 50 years throughout the vicissitudes of any Caribbean history, let alone Guyana's, is little short of a miracle, and bears moving testament to the vision, conviction and tenacity of those who made it happen. Unlike its mostly slimmer forebears, the fiftieth anniversary issue offers over 300 pages of good things: poems from Guyanese poets such as Fred D'Aguiar, Michael Gilkes, Ian McDonald and Sasenarine Persaud, as well as other Caribbean poets such as Cecil Gray and John Figueroa (Stewart Brown goes down here as Jamaican, which will no doubt please him). There are stories from Guyanese names more familiar some years ago, like Cy Grant, as well as from rising stars such as Pauline Melville, although regrettably some famous Guyanese names such as Wilson Harris, John Agard and Grace Nichols are not contributors. A pan-Caribbean flavour is a welcome feature of the collection, however, with contributions from Edward Baugh, Ken Ramchand, John Wickham and the late Andrew Salkey alongside those of Guyanese academics such as Frank Birbalsingh and Mark McWatt. The latter is marked here as the recipient of the 1994 Guyana Prize for Poetry for *The Language of El Dorado*. Important in critical terms are Birbalsingh's interview with a fine, deplorably neglected poet, Martin Carter; Salkey's memorial to Selvon; and, among others, Keith Henry's appreciation of Austin Clarke, Birbalsingh's of Edgar Mittelholzer and Philip Nanton's of John Figueroa. There is also a lively review section. In addition, the visual arts are not neglected: the volume is illustrated by drawings from the Rain Forest Series by Martin Jordan; and Anne Walmsley, well known for her work on the Guyanese painter Aubrey Williams, interviews a painter of the next generation, George Simon. This special edition deserves to reach a wide readership; all those with an interest in Caribbean writing, and all those struggling to keep small magazines afloat, will find it uplifting.

Likely to become a classic of its kind, Ashcroft, Griffiths and Tiffin's *The Post-Colonial Studies Reader* follows the success of their critical handbook *The Empire Writes Back* with an anthology of non-fiction texts ranging from the high imperialism of Macaulay's infamous 'Minute on Indian Education' to the latest from postcolonial critics worldwide. This exceptionally well-chosen and wide-ranging selection includes classics like Fanon, but also a lot of extracts on theoretical issues from writers who have devoted their lives to fiction: Achebe, Ngugi, Rao, Walcott, to name a few. The Caribbean is well represented. As well as a passage from Fanon, there are others from George

Lamming, Wilson Harris, Walcott (a snippet from the essay 'The Muse of History'), Jamaica Kincaid and Stuart Hall, as well as three excerpts from Brathwaite: from *The History of the Voice*, his scholarly history *The Development of Creole Society in Jamaica 1778–1820* and the essay 'Jazz and the West Indian Novel' (available in full in the collection of Brathwaite essays, *Roots*, which the University of Michigan reprinted in 1993). In addition, specifically Caribbean topics are covered in the sections from Peter Hulme, Gayatri Chakravorty Spivak and Michael Dash. It is a reminder of how central to postcolonial theorizing the Caribbean experience is. The referencing makes it easy for those who want to pursue ideas from an excerpted passage by consulting the full, original version to do so. Another virtue is that the selection is predominantly from critics who have personal histories in the former colonies, which lends authority to the collection. The division of the material into 14 themed parts, each provided with a short introduction, makes this a clear and practical volume which will be of great help to students. The contents are not too difficult to be accessible to a wide range of readers but are rich in ideas, and although most are abbreviated, the passages have been carefully chosen to stand interestingly on their own. Academic handbooks don't come better than this. The volume is a stimulating example of how a potentially routine task can be brilliantly performed.

Bruce King has brought his 1979 survey up to date in the revised and expanded second edition of *West Indian Literature*. Sixteen rightly respected contributors supply a chapter each, while King reserves the (completely rewritten) introduction and the (brought up to date) chapter on Naipaul to himself. The book is divided into two halves in ways which beg some questions – but then it is never easy to structure a survey such as this to render it ideally useful. In the first part the first seven chapters are historic, concluding with a new one from Laurence Breiner on the 1980s – the first half of the 1990s seems to be unnecessarily neglected – followed by loosely generic new chapters on 'Contemporary women writers' and 'West Indian writing in Canada', by Renu Juneja and Victor Ramraj respectively. These are conceptually the weakest parts of the volume in that they inevitably raise questions about other possibilities: why not West Indian writing in Britain, for instance, or the USA? Why not an overall geographical or nationalist structure? And the chapter on women writers exposes the masculinist choices to come in the second half in which, once again, only Jean Rhys is selected to stand on an equal footing with the main men. The second part uses an author-based approach, offering chapters on Rhys, Mittelholzer, Harris, Selvon, Lamming, Walcott, Brathwaite, Naipaul, Lovelace and Rhone, the last two being new additions. It is difficult to avoid the question 'Why Mittelholzer?' – and perhaps 'Why Rhone?' – when other important writers, some of them dramatists, such as Dennis Scott, are excluded. That said, the essays are generally informative, perceptive and well written. In the main they pull off deftly the difficult task of introducing a writer to readers to whom the work is new at the same time as offering something of value to those very familiar with it. This volume can be confidently recommended to experts and starting students alike.

Usefully reprinted, particularly for the latter, is L. Emilie Adams's *Understanding Jamaican Patois*, an aid for non-Caribbean readers who have difficulties with literature using the Jamaican vernacular. It provides a clear and well-illustrated introduction to contemporary usage, including a glossary.

Sensitive to linguistics without being inaccessible to the non-linguist, it demonstrates how a popular orientation does not have to be unscholarly. Cassidy's work is frequently acknowledged, but this is something different, not for specialists but a practical guide to Jamaican as a language in its own right.

Dorothy Lane uses Shakespeare's *Tempest* as the 'master' text from which to give an intertextual reading of selected works from Caribbean (and New Zealand) literature. Surprisingly perhaps, George Lamming features only marginally in *The Island as Site of Resistance*, the focus for the Caribbean falling instead on Jean Rhys, Phyllis Allfrey, John Hearne and Derek Walcott. While it is refreshing to see close attention to some currently neglected writers such as Allfrey and Hearne, the absence of a close reading of Lamming does signify, because the project has large ambitions, suggesting that the two literatures examined are paradigms for anticolonial writing. Building on Diana Loxley's *Problematic Shores: The Literature of Islands* (St Martin's, 1991) (on the nineteenth-century fashion for island fictions), Lane moves the study of island discourse on to its counter-discourse in twentieth-century postcolonial fiction. At the end she acknowledges Antonio Benitez-Rojo's *The Repeating Island: The Caribbean and the Postmodern Perspective* (*YWES* 74.653–4). This probably came out too late to have much bearing on Lane's book, which is a pity as its depth, although explored from a different theoretical angle, could have added to the later study. This is not meant as a major criticism of Lane's work, however; it is intelligent and interesting within the objectives and strategies it sets itself. The drift of her argument is that some attempts to counter the imperialist island discourse (such as Rhys's *Wide Sargasso Sea* and Allfrey's *The Orchid House*) are 'finally unable to escape the replication of colonialist paradigms'; that others (instanced by Hearne's *Land of the Living* and *The Sure Salvation*) 'interrogate further the very notion of island as isolated and simplified space' and construct 'a space that resists colonisation', an 'Africa' within the island; and that postcolonial dramas (here Walcott's *Pantomime* and Allen Curnow's 'The Axe') succeed through their polyphony in modelling 'the island's integrity rather than its peripherality to and dependence upon the imperial centre'.

Lane's attention to the discursive production of space shows awareness of others' work in the field, and suggests a new, if rather strained, figure, that of a 'postcolonial continent of islands', which would be 'eternally dynamic, hybrid, and with a focus upon "play" rather than overseeing'. The imperialist trope of the controlling gaze, here punningly linking the one who 'oversees' with the one from 'overseas', is successfully subverted, she argues, less by direct inversion which risks 'overturning the structures of authority but simultaneously reproducing them', than by its dissolution in multiplicity, an ongoing 'continental self-discovery'. Lane's concluding of her argument in readings of plays emerges as a discursive response to genre: drama, she suggests, is a key site for successful counter-discourse because it is necessarily multivoiced. There are lacunae in this study – the preoccupation with the Prospero position is somehow not adequately answered by the thesis that a notional Miranda–Caliban liaison counters it; its perception that psychoanalytic criticism and the postcolonial are incompatible is a limitation, and it fails to address adequately either Ariel or Sycorax (the latter being an important figure to Brathwaite in recent work, for example) – but what it does do it does persuasively. Its focus on textuality produces some thoughtful analysis, and for its opening chapters alone, on 'The Figure of the Island in Colonial Discourse' and 'Rehearsing the Master Plot: Shakespeare's *The Tempest*', the book merits a place on the shelves of anyone seriously interested in the postcolonial perspective.

The next work also has an antipodean connection. Although not principally a literary study, Glenn Jordan and Chris Weedon's *Cultural Politics: Class, Gender, Race and the Postmodern World* engages energetically with the cultural debates – particularly those in the field of the visual arts – which are central to the postcolonial critique. Its main case-study is on Aboriginal writing, but Caribbean topics are also featured. Metropolitan responses to the work of Aubrey Williams, the Guyanese painter, are exposed for their neocolonialism; their refusal to admit him to the unqualified category of 'artist' is here viewed as covertly racist. Under a heading of black feminist fiction, Joan Riley's work comes in for analysis alongside that of Vernella Fuller, a Jamaican-descended British writer. Their writing is seen as exposing the effects of white racism and as refusing essentialist representations of black people. In demonstrating how the 'ethnic' label is used to marginalize artists, the book calls for 'genuine multiculturalism' based on a repudiation of hierarchies, with all cultures deemed equal and a pedagogy to suit: 'Caribbean literature would be taught as an integral part of English literature – Derek Walcott alongside Shakespeare, Edward Braithwaite [*sic*] alongside Chaucer, Joan Riley alongside Virginia Woolf.' While other names than Riley's might be more apt a parallel to Woolf, the point sought is clear and persuasive – although the book's damning analysis of the ethnocentric construction of primitivism on which cultural hegemonies still ride makes this seem a rather pious hope. There are some irritating stylistic devices here – the constant subtitling for instance – but the work overall is closely argued and perceptive, particularly about the way the establishment is still fuelled by the racism it purports to deny.

Edward Said's perception that the geographic is a principal dimension of postcolonial representations acquires an unexpected resonance in *Writing Across Worlds: Literature and Migration* (ed. Russell King, John Connell and Paul White) in that its essays are chiefly by geographers. Paul White's introduction describes a discipline with an oblique interest in literature – rather surprisingly he defines it as 'generally aimed at uncovering empirical worlds of experience interpreted through literature taken as a secondary source' – but he also identifies a growing engagement 'with literature for its own sake'. Interestingly, to the literary reader there is relatively little sense of distance, although the footnotes reveal a rather different academic base from that of the lit. crit. discipline. The assembly, in one volume, of articles on worldwide literatures in many languages is also unfamiliar. There are different presentational conventions too: formally prefacing each chapter with an introduction and ending with a titled conclusion might not be a bad habit for lit-critturs to imitate. The critical content on Caribbean topics here is sharp and useful. Claire Alexander's ' "Rivers to cross": Exile and Transformation in the Caribbean Migration Novels of George Lamming' situates Lamming against the ideas of Bhabha and Gilroy as well as Walcott and the Anansi tradition. She contrasts the structural devices of linearity and circularity to produce a reading of the novels as creating 'imaginative space in which nation and nationhood, identity and belonging, are narrated, interrogated and transformed', and concludes that Lamming shows migration as a process of 'becoming'. The book also offers an article on the French Caribbean by Robert Aldrich, and a short section on Naipaul in a piece on South Asian British fiction, a neglected category, by Suresht Renjen Bald. It is easy to miss relevant aspects of interdisciplinary studies. This volume is a timely reminder of how permeable the boundaries between some of the disciplines now are, which has to be good news.

The invisibility, to most anglophone readers, of the francophone Caribbean is a deplorable legacy of cultural centrisms. The text of Césaire's address given in Italy in 1962, 'Y a-t-il une civilisation africaine?', is now usefully reprinted in French (*Caribana* 4.15–25), but it is the availability in English of the literature itself and of critical studies which is the vital aid to greater cross-cultural awareness, to which this journal has already made a signal contribution. A new translation, in a bilingual edition, by Mireille Rosello, of Césaire's seminal *Notebook of a Return to my Native Land* (a modernist prose-poem written in the late 1940s and of huge impact on the whole of subsequent Caribbean literature and black politics) plugs the gap left by the long out-of-print Penguin edition. In addition, Debra Anderson's study making connections between French Caribbean and American literature provides a useful introduction to critical theorizations emanating from Martinique for English-speaking readers, as well as for those with a particular interest in the francophone world. Since the text of *Decolonizing the Text: Glissantian Readings in Caribbean and African-American Literatures* is in English, it is a pity that quotations in French are not accompanied by translations, as non-French-speaking readers will find themselves marginalized. Likewise, the absence of a general index makes the book less readily useful than it otherwise might have been. Nevertheless, Anderson in tracing the lineage of *négritude-antillanité-creolité* maps out an important Caribbean cultural history which resonates beyond linguistic boundaries. Her project is to fold the creole poetics, marked out by Bernabé, Chamoiseau and Confiant against the position of Edouard Glissant in the *Éloge de la Créolité*, back into Glissant's concept of the *poétique de la relation*. She does so not only by devoting chapters to the *négritude/antillanité* and *antillanité/créolité* developments, but by positing some unfamiliar connections: for instance, Chamoiseau's dependence on Toni Morrison as literary foremother. Faulkner's *Go Down, Moses* is also brought into the case for an 'intertextual *métissage*' (a term which translates as 'creolization' or 'miscegenation', 'mixing'). While the links with Faulkner and Morrison have a certain arbitrariness which works against the tight relation Anderson posits, it remains refreshing to see such intercultural affinities suggested. Glissant, with whom Anderson studied, is less well known among the anglophone community (including the Caribbean one) than he ought to be. The book lives up to its Glissantian title in stimulating ways. How many English-language-based critics with an interest in the Caribbean region, for instance, are as familiar with Glissant's *Caribbean Discourse*, translated in 1989 for the UPVirginia by J. Michael Dash (who has done more than most to help francophone Caribbean literature become visible in English), as they are with fellow-Martinican Fanon's writings? This book is an invaluable guide to Glissant's thought, as well as an exposer of revealing details such as the significant alteration of *Caribbean Discourse*'s layout in the English version, or Glissant's approach to 'roots': he develops Deleuze and Guattari's testing counter-sign 'rhizome' into a trope of *créolité*, the rhizome demonstrating the versatility and multiplicity which help to ensure survival.

The *JCL* annual bibliographical volume again has no section on the Caribbean, but this is the last of the lean years: listings for the region for this year are to be found in *JCL* 31. For an update of the Naipaul bibliography see below.

(b) Fiction

Another work with a French angle but which also addresses anglophone writing is Francoise Lionnet's *Postcolonial Representations: Women, Literature and Identity*. Although not restricted to the Caribbean it does devote a good proportion of its space to Caribbean women writers. Maryse Condé and Myriam Warner-Vieyra form part of the book's case for *Logiques metisses*, a phrase borrowed from Jean-Loup Amselle's controversial book on black identities, but the first chapter is on Michelle Cliff's *Abeng*. Lionnet examines the novel from the point of view of genre as well as language and history, arguing that it modifies autobiographical discursive practice, 'challenging us, its readers, to become multicultural subjects as well'. The conclusion is that Cliff articulates 'a form of multivalent subjectivity capable of resisting shifting networks of power' – a now familiar position in identity politics, perhaps, but one which is here usefully articulated against a specifically French theoretical base, and which by virtue of the diversity of texts it gathers to its gaze refreshingly practices what it preaches. Lionnet's work strikes as fresh and interesting.

Cliff also comes in for attention from Thomas Cartelli, this time for her 1987 novel *No Telephone to Heaven*. In 'After *The Tempest*: Shakespeare, Postcoloniality and Michelle Cliff's New, New World Miranda' (*ConI*. 36.i.82–102), Cartelli looks at the myth of Shakespeare (including the Merchant-Ivory film *Shakespeare Wallah* of 1965) and situates the novel as one of the intertextual fictions 'writing back' to *The Tempest* – a reading somewhat against the grain as the Shakespeare is only a 'residual presence', as he acknowledges, while Brontë's *Jane Eyre* and Rhys's *Wide Sargasso Sea* are invoked more conspicuously as intertexts. The focus is wrenched rather awkwardly onto the Miranda figure. Cartelli asserts that Cliff sets up for her character Clare 'an associative identification with Caliban', but then proceeds arrogantly to claim that the writer 'fails to remark that [...] it is Miranda' who is most germane to the book and to herself – more so than Caliban or Ariel. With a nod in the direction of Sylvia Wynter's essay 'Beyond Miranda's Meanings: Un/silencing the "Demonic Ground" of Caliban's "Woman"', which concludes Carole Boyce Davies's and Elaine Savory Fido's *Out of the Kumbla* (*YWES* 71.742, 748), Cartelli postulates finally that, with her mixed-race Clare, Cliff produces 'a thoroughly creolized and womanized novel in which the new, New World Miranda effectively replaces both Prospero and Caliban as an agent of self-determination and cultural change'. This thesis is argued to trouble Nixon's case (*CritI* 13.557–78) that the postcolonial usefulness of *The Tempest* as reference point waned after the 1970s, because it shows Miranda alive and well in a 1987 text, but Cartelli's reading of Cliff is unconvincing, and, should we so wish, Nixon can more readily be countered by other texts – not least, Marina Warner's *Indigo*.

An equally interesting but newer writer is Pauline Melville, whose 1990 short stories tracing the connections lived between Guyana and Britain have attracted attention. In 'Mathematical Limbs and Other Eventualities: Trans-locations of the Body in Pauline Melville's *Shape-Shifter*' (*NLitsR* 30.47–67), Elaine Savory focuses on the surreal story 'The Girl With The Celestial Limb' as trope for a penetrating discussion of Melville's poetics of the postcolonial body: 'the shape of identity is constantly changing'. Like Melville, 'a native daughter of the Caribbean who is also Miranda's child, but who chooses to position herself within Caribbean, not European discourse', the stories are about people who 'live in multiple bodies, accents, and images and destabilize what might be termed reality, but always from a Caribbean point of view', and thereby 'transform, among other things, feminism and postmodernism'. 'Decolonising Bodies' is the theme for this issue of this increasingly important Australian journal, which also has an essay on Naipaul. In 'V. S. Naipaul, *The Enigma of Arrival* and the Unbearable Body' (*NLitsR* 30.97–112), Christine Crowle gives a sensitive reading of the narrator's 'anxiety about his body', arguing that this surfaces in sexual motifs of castration, mutilation and disease which 'can be read as the body's somatic refusal of a particular identity', but that this refusal is also a resistance to the colonial discourses of race and gender, resulting in a profoundly ironic meaning for 'arrival'.

Another woman writer who tends to attract critical attention, though not often for the text in question, is Jamaica Kincaid, whose *A Small Place* provides the site for Alison Donnell to test some concerns about the unfolding debates around the postcolonial. In ' "She ties her tongue": The Problem of Cultural Paralysis in Postcolonial Criticism' (*ArielE* 26.i.101–16), she identi-fies defensively what she sees as the hijacking of the emerging postcolonial discipline, usefully engaged in unsettling orthodoxies, by factions wanting to fix it according to 'an entrenched cultural protocol'. The big question is, she says, 'who is allowed to speak'. The defensive tone is explained: questions of insider/outsider and the authority to speak are personal, as, like many critics working in the field, Donnell is an outsider to the region whose literature she anatomizes. She clearly feels the need to claim as much authority to speak as the next critic – perhaps she has been under attack in some quarters for what is perceived as a neo-colonial appropriation. Her terminology moves on to reading – 'questions concerning the right to read are highly charged' – which pinpoints how absurd the controversy is. Criticism is of course only a 'reading', and anybody can read. The identity of the critic should surely be irrelevant: what matters is whether a critical text has anything illuminating to say about a literary text. Insiders will have a different angle on their culture's texts from that of outsiders, often a more perceptive one, but both are in principle valid and can be mutually enlightening. Donnell goes on to enlist Kincaid's text to her cause. She calls it 'a complex work of ventriloquism' which finally refuses to privilege one voice over another, but 'bids for a thorough consideration of how all groups might now ethically and effectively respond to each other'. The fierce polemic of *A Small Place* does finish with an even-handed fairness, but in the spirit of the abused taking her case to law. Donnell is mistaken if she thinks Kincaid is letting the 'you' she addresses off the hook. Donnell overstates her case, missing the residual 'J'accuse', about which Kincaid has elsewhere been quite clear. Outsiders should beware of playing down insiders' legitimate anger.

Two studies address the problematic of the Caribbean father resulting from the social dislocations and psychological trauma imposed by slavery and imperialism. Mary Donnelly invokes Jameson, Fanon and Freud in her reading of George Lamming, 'Mother Country, Father Country: *In The Castle Of My Skin* and Oedipal Structures of Colonialism' (*ArielE* 26.iv.7–20), which augurs well. Labelling Barbados the protagonist G's 'Mother Country', she traces the *Bildungsroman* from his beginning in parturition via the symbolic birthing waters of the novel's opening; but then construes G's colonial education as a benign process leading to 'a coherent identity', its 'Oedipal dynamic' enabling him to make the necessary passage from absorption in the 'Mother' to patriarchal maturity – identifying with the 'Father Country', Britain. This is one of the more absurd results of schematic sub-Freudian reading; it traduces Lamming's painstakingly angry anatomizing of the self-alienation which that colonial acculturation entailed.

Bénédicte Ledent also uses the family as trope to address Caryl Phillips's third novel, 'bolder and more subversive' than the first two. In ' "Overlapping Territories, Intertwined Histories": Cross-Culturality in Caryl Phillips's *Crossing the River*' (*JCL* 30.i.55–62), Ledent traces the search for the absent father to the history of slavery. In the novel the family 'is primarily a site of fracture', but 'such fractures mean that surrogate ties, very often of a cross-cultural and ambiguous kind, are woven to replace the genuine ones'. Using Paul Gilroy's term, Ledent argues that the novel's 'loose and puzzle-like image of the family is [...] a metaphor for the black Atlantic', with the African diaspora conspicuously 'open and catholic'. Phillips here 'challenges cultural essentialism, ethnic purity and political correctness' and 'refutes the idea of a return to the African homeland'. Although there may be a new tone to his writing, Phillips's forte is still the use of binary structures to deliver a narrative underpinned by a fine fury. Since all three novelists, Kincaid, Lamming and Phillips, are identified with a militant cultural politics, it is something of a shock to see them all given recuperative 'outsiderly' readings, calculated to put a different spin on their perceived stances – a sign, perhaps, of where Donnell's defensiveness is coming from. But if these provocative critiques return us to the texts to check them out, they will have done the best service any criticism can perform, after all.

It is some comfort that Sam Selvon saw the publication of two books exclusively on his work before his death. Last year's *JWIL* (6.ii) is dedicated to his memory. Elsewhere, Michael Thorpe pays tribute to him in a short memorial (*WLT* 69.i.86–8) as a 'humane and liberal figure' who thought in world literature terms rather than in those of combative race politics. He concludes by citing Selvon's 1979 judgement: 'We have had a great deal of that. We want to rise above that.' Now *Kunapipi* has brought out a special edition (17.i) to honour him, also published as a book, *Tiger's Triumph: Celebrating Sam Selvon*. Edited by Susheila Nasta and Anna Rutherford, it prints a number of examples of his work, including a poem from 1949, an important but undated interview with Reed Dasenbrock and Feroza Jussawalla, as well as some critical essays and a lot of memorial tributes: from Ismith Khan, Austin Clarke, Wilson Harris, Henry Swanzy, Jessica Huntley, Victor Ramraj, Anne Walmsley and Louis James. There are also creative responses: an extract, dedicated to Selvon, from David Dabydeen's latest novel *The Counting House*, a narrative from Kenneth Ramchand depicting creatively Selvon's last days, and a poem from Cecil Gray. A select critical bibliography would have made a useful addition to the volume. As it is, it provides in a footnote a small-print list of Selvon's main publications, and a reference to the full bibliography (now becoming out of date) in the volume on Selvon edited by Nasta and Ramchand in 1989. There are four extended critical essays, by Roydon Salick, Helen Tiffin, Grace Eche Okereke and the editor, Susheila Nasta, which between them cover the London and Trinidad novels. It is a pity that Selvon's drama is not addressed, however. Tiffin's piece on the 'Moses' trilogy is particularly perceptive, and Nasta, as one has come to expect, writes on the London novels with acumen and affection. She concludes her foreword to the volume with an exposition of its title: as well as creating a literary 'Tiger' he 'was also a special kind of Tiger himself, a tiger whose voice has risen from the language of the island and triumphed in stretching that language across the mouth of the world'. Selvon's example, in using his people's language not just in dialogue but as the narrative voice, has shaped a generation of writers since the 1950s, as Dabydeen and others acknowledge, and will go on leading the way. The volume makes it abundantly clear how much Selvon, as a person, was loved.

Another journal special edition dedicated to a single writer is the fine collection on Wilson Harris in *Callaloo* (18.i). As well as an extract from Harris's latest work, *Jonestown*, it offers an impressive range of substantial critical essays, some from established leaders in the field of Harris criticism, such as Hena Maes-Jelinek, Jean-Pierre Durix, Paul Sharrad and Alan Riach, alongside others from the less well known. Michael Gilkes's name is regrettably not among them. This is altogether a more substantial volume than the Selvon one, not only, perhaps, because the Selvon memorial tributes tend to be brief, but because the nature of Harris's work is very different in tone and scale. Somehow it seems to evoke subtle and thoughtful responses, richly textured rather than snappy, like Harris's prose. As well as 11 critical studies covering a wide range of Harris's novels (including two on *The Palace of the Peacock*), the volume offers two interviews, with Vera Kutzinski and Charles Rowell, a review of the collection of Harris lectures, *The Radical Imagination* (*YWES* 74.663) and a six-page select bibliography by Krishna Ray Lewis, all interspersed with a series of black and white photographs of Harris at different stages of his life – one from 1948 with Jan Carew – and some of book-jacket designs. This Harris special should, like the Selvon one, be treated as a book, and be put high on the list of library acquisitions in the field. If such special journal editions were indexed in the way a scholarly book is, they would be even more useful.

One of the most striking essays on Harris remains, however, T. J. Cribb's revaluation of the connection between his fiction and his early years as a surveyor. From research into the Guyanese government archive, Cribb discovered that the crew names in Harris's first extraordinary novel, *Palace of the Peacock*, are nearly all drawn from life. In 'T. W. Harris – Sworn Surveyor' (*JCL* 29.i.33–46) he scans the history of mapping Guyana in which the name Schomburgh is prominent, and reveals that the young Harris in his early work as a hydrographic surveyor on the rivers of the Amazon rainforest – the Harris of the 1948 snapshot – was indeed accompanied by people who bore those now familiar names, Carroll, Vigilance, De Souza, Schomburgk. He uses this as the basis for a penetrating new reading: the surveying documents 'supply an important corrective on the one hand to those commentaries which treat the writing solely at a conceptual and intellectual level, and on the other hand to those doubters who cannot make the act of faith necessary to overcome the difficulty of the writing and who consequently suspect it as esoteric and elitist. The surveying records show that the writing has a solid base in experience and a moral and political responsibility to it in the profoundest senses of those words.' Anyone planning another anthology of critical essays on Harris should be sure to reprint this excellent article, based on the kind of original primary research many critics seem to have forgotten.

Another substantial volume takes forward the evaluation of the long life's work of C. L. R. James. Selwyn Cudjoe and William Cain edit *C. L. R. James: His Intellectual Legacies*, a fat volume which springs some surprises, including tributes from British politician Michael Foot and Derek Walcott – the text of the latter's address (chiefly about *Beyond a Boundary*, on cricket as symbol, which for Walcott 'celebrates grace') is followed by a passage from *Omeros* and the transcript of a question session. Although much of the volume is concerned less with literature than with politics, there is a section headed 'The Literary Dimension' which offers a stimulating essay by Selwyn Cudjoe on James's love letters (even!), one by Cedric Robinson on C. L. R. and the 'World System' (which has a good deal to say on his Melville critique), while William Cain also addresses his reading of *Moby-Dick* alongside that of *Othello*. The organization of the book is puzzling, however, as it offers the most 'literary' chapters elsewhere, including two essays on his novel *Minty Alley* and one on the play *Toussaint L'Ouverture* – not to mention two on his history *The Black Jacobins*, often praised for the quality of its writing. Careful indexing, however, makes the anomalies of the structure less inhibiting to the majority of users, who are unlikely to read from cover to cover.

The award to V. S. Naipaul of the first David Cohen Prize for a lifetime's achievement in British literature is marked by *Wasafiri* (21.5–6) with a rare interview with him, conducted by Alastair Niven, followed by the text of his acceptance speech and a photograph. The interview will be of interest to all students of the enigma of the Naipaul phenomenon. He expounds his philosophy of mutability, which puts a burden of innovation on the writer, who 'has to find new ways of capturing the reality'. Naipaul clearly has no problem about using concepts like reality and truth, but these are never simple terms. A certain elegiac ring to his self-narration lends poignancy to his firmness: 'I am very glad I had the courage to follow difficult instincts about the truth', and 'I have never done a single thing which I have not wanted to do' – and not a lot of us can say that. He is, he says, 'more serene' now, though less vigorous, but still fascinated by the world. Long may he remain so. Jeremy Poynting in a short survey article, 'From Shipwreck to Odyssey: One Hundred Years of Indo-Caribbean Writing', in the same issue, traces the literature's story from a century back, when 'there are odes to Queen Victoria, but no Indian lives', to the present, in which writers such as Naipaul and the two Dabydeens 'attempt to stage an art out of the "intercreolising" relationship between old and new selves' – a serviceable phrase.

Two new Naipaul studies are jostling for position in a well-supplied market. Fawzia Mustafa's *V. S. Naipaul* is a rival to Bruce King's slim survey of the work, inevitably if temporarily having the edge in being more up to date. It covers the whole extensive oeuvre chronologically through its six chapters, with frequent subheads and without separating fiction and non-fiction or the geography of settings. The structure is based, she says, on 'the belief that [...] the development of Naipaul's work is basically linear'. There is an appealing common sense to this, but inevitably with this railroading approach the danger is that some of the books flash by like stations from an express train. Wisely the more recent work is given proportionately more of the space. Mustafa identifies the Amerindian themes in *A Way in the World* as a new focus, though one not without antecedents. She suggests it 'can serve as a measure of Naipaul's current attitude towards the world he has spent his life discovering' – a phrase which is typical of Mustafa's tendency just to miss saying anything really striking or memorable in her cautious, hedged-about presentation. She rejects the view of Naipaul as 'irredeemable', noting that he embodies a paradox of postcolonial literature, 'the disjunction between the materiality of language and the materiality of history'. As she observes, his skill as craftsman 'lends his views of the world credence and acceptance among his advocates' – which is a subtler point than it seems. Typical of her tendency to waste the energy of an interesting thought in mealy-mouthed expression is her suggestion that it is 'not coincidental [...] that Naipaul's writing should function as one of the illustrative sites of critics' efforts to theorize, and problematize, the discourse of colonialism and the construction of the colonial subject'. By contrast, her quotation from Irving Howe's 1992 epilogue to the reprint of his 1947 book, *Politics and the Novel*, leaps off the page. Howe calls himself an 'uneasy admirer', uneasy because of Naipaul's 'surplus of disgust and paucity of tenderness', but an admirer because of his 'strict refusal of romantic moonshine'. Naipaul at 60, to Howe, is 'a writer beleaguered by his own truths, unable to push past them', but he suggests 'we ought simply to be content that in his austere and brilliant style he holds fast to the bitterness before his eyes'. If only we could all write like that. None the less Mustafa's book is carefully researched and useful, and deserves to sit alongside King's on library (and private) shelves, though it is unlikely to displace it.

The next on the lengthening shelf of critical monographs on Naipaul is Judith Levy's *V. S. Naipaul: Displacement and Autobiography*. Unlike Mustafa's compendious survey it selects five texts for a Lacanian study, analysing the writing as an extended narrative of self. The early period is represented by *A House for Mr Biswas*, the middle period by *The Overcrowded Barracoon* and *In a Free State* and the later period by *Finding the Centre* and *The Enigma of Arrival*. A full chapter is dedicated to each, but Levy acknowledges that by selecting five texts from an oeuvre four times as big she cannot lay claim to an exhaustive or definitive evaluation. None the less her study does attempt to narrate Naipaul's development as a writer in terms which are clearly intended to hold good for the work as a whole. The overarching figure of the quest for selfhood is traced through the five books spanning a lifetime's work in a stimulating way. Levy is careful to define her relationship to theoretical positions, and to defend her autobiographical readings in judicious terms. She interprets Mr Biswas's life story as a classic Oedipal configuration and gives it the Lacanian spin: 'the father must be killed not only to allow entrance into the symbolic order but also because the only possible symbolic order available under the political and cultural conditions of the time is not congruent with the father's speech; it is alien and foreign-English culture and language. The father's heritage, the lost and dislocated Hindu civilization, is repudiated.' Levy's basic proposition – that Naipaul moves from a dissociated self, as recorded in *Biswas*, to the successful integration of selfhood in *Enigma* – is fine up to a point: where it falls down is in its inability to accommodate the fact that Naipaul senior was a writer in English – always already! It also underplays the very real triumph of Mr Biswas – his heroic success in securing identity through culture, place and family – and fails to address the active creolization of Hindu tradition which the Tulsis are shown to be devising. Levy needs the simplistic antithesis between Hindu tradition, associated with the father, and Caribbeanness, located in the writer-self, for her argument to work. Unfortunately, the reality of the books, not to mention the reality of Caribbean lives, of which Naipaul's is one and his father's another, is more complex, traversed by multiple crossings and mutual involutions between diverse cultures and histories. That said, Levy's book remains thought-provoking, with a lot of perceptive close comment which Naipaul readers will find returns them to the books from a new angle. She concludes that Naipaul finally succeeds in constructing his own myth of origin 'in a uniquely executed autobiographical mode', but her preoccupation with whether or not this should be labelled postmodern is essentially trivial.

Kelvin Jarvis usefully brings his scholarly 1989 bibliography on Naipaul (for Scarecrow) up to date (*ArielE* 26.iv.71–85). The listings cover the period from the earlier volume's cut-off date 1987, to last year, a period during which Naipaul has published three new books and more than 18 substantial pieces, not counting lectures and acceptance speeches. Jarvis divides the material under six headings, the first on the primary material, the second on other bibliographical listings, the third on critical monographs, the fourth on critical articles of a general nature, the fifth on reviews and critical studies of single works and the sixth on doctoral theses. It is tempting to be picky: why does the primary list include the South Bank Show television interview of 1987 but not the equally important 'Face To Face' interview of last year, for instance? But this is an invaluable aide to Naipaul scholarship. It is a salutary reminder of his gathering status that in the monographs section as many as 16 books are listed as published since 1987 (although two of these are published in 1995, Levy's and Mustafa's, technically outside the years specified) – a scale of serious attention which few writers alive today can match.

Another entry for Jarvis's next stage of Naipaul bibliography is Abdollah Zahiri's 'Enlightenment Myopia: A Critique of V. S. Naipaul's *Among the Believers*' (*NLitsR* 28/9.165–75). As the bibliography confirms, this is one of the least commented on of Naipaul's works – one which I happen to know he himself is currently 'rewriting', in the manner in which *A Way in the World* revisits the topics of *The Loss of El Dorado*. It seems that many critics, less fearless than Naipaul himself, are wary of tackling what is regarded as a volatile subject. Zahiri historicizes Naipaul's research visit to Iran in 1979 which gave him his Iranian material for the book, and using Foucault's figure of the panopticon, an architectural surveillance design, finds Naipaul's response to the Iranian revolution Orientalist, betraying his Western education and outlook. From Zahiri's Islamic perspective, Naipaul simply 'refuses to read the huge fundamentalist potential to decentre the "logic" of development and innovation', preferring 'to represent as "factional" the believers of whom he can no longer be a part'. Was he ever a part of that belief system, one is tempted to ask. To collapse Islam into Hinduism – or religion in general – in the context of this book seems distinctly odd.

Naipaul and Rhys come in for some sparklingly refreshing critique from Judie Newman in *The Ballistic Bard: Postcolonial Fictions*. The figure for the title is borrowed from J. G. Farrell's book *The Siege of Krishnapur*, a satiric undermining of the ramparts of the raj (retrospectively, in 1973) which has the electrometal heads of British writers used as cannonballs. The novels addressed are chosen for their resistance to colonial discourse through intertextuality. As Newman's truism has it, 'Intertextuality can be revolutionary'. Intertextuality, however, is not interpreted in a narrowly literary sense. There is a stimulating cultural-studies dimension to this work, in which a telling deconstruction of the Ralph Lauren phenomenon, for example, is as glowing a find as an erudite but sharp discussion of chaos theory. The critiques constantly spring surprises by their approach and the connections they suggest, but their inventiveness is unfailingly brilliant. Newman discusses the relationship between *Wide Sargasso Sea* and *Jane Eyre*, for instance, through the discourse of zombification, evident not only in the popular culture of the Caribbean but in Hollywood films. The title for her Rhys chapter is 'I walked with a zombie: Jean Rhys, Wide Sargasso Sea', using the title of a 1943 film described by its producer as 'Jane Eyre in the tropics'. Spirit thievery emerges as a figure for the cultural appropriations of empire, displacing subjectivities, as well as for the complex meanings of intertextuality, and the strategies of counter-discourse. Reading *Wide Sargasso Sea* from the perspective of zombification produces at the same time new contours from a much-trodden text, and Arawak myth enables Newman to salvage the openness of Rhys's ending, thereby revealing the hegemony implicit in some critics' insistence on a deterministic reading controlled by *Jane Eyre*.

Newman's chapter on Naipaul's *Guerillas* begins by pinpointing the odd phenomenon 'that so many people have been prepared to write lengthy, detailed and scholarly books about a writer whom they appear to deplore'; it has long been 'open season on Naipaul'. Newman enters the lists as a formidable champion for Naipaul, giving the most perceptive reading of his work seen for a long time. Here is a critic, one feels, whose awareness of textual strategy comes close to that of the writer. Her gender critique is persuasive: she looks at the representation of Jane, for instance, in the text's whole mapping of gender, and instead of applying the anti-feminist label many have slapped on the book she understands how Jane is intended to be seen as 'a mimic woman, continually performing her gender'. Drawing on Erving Goffman's ideas of the performative (adapted later by Bhabha) she identifies the bisexuality of Jimmy as Naipaul's 'careful strategy to avoid gender as foundation' – a destabilizer of the binaries which underpin dangerously simplistic ideas. Peronism is one ideology to which Newman relates the novel: her chapter title is ' "Don't cry for me Argentina" – Jane Eyre as Evita Peron; V. S. Naipaul, *Guerrillas*', and she here adduces not just the familiar Brontë connection but also Naipaul's essay 'The Return of Eva Peron'. In typically trenchant form she concludes that Naipaul's strategy in the novel is 'to write against his reader's own dependence, to refuse to allow us an "authority" outside the text, which will frame events and tell us what is going on. Dispassionately, pessimistically, the novel considers the possibilities for action in its imaginary island, and discounts them. The fundamental achievement of the novel remains to maintain the sense of a world entirely at sea, a shifting chaos without form, foundation or future.' Newman penetrates the subtleties at the heart of all the works she addresses (including novels by Coetzee, Mukherjee, Desai, Jhabvala, Emecheta and Gordimer) with wit and wisdom. She is as much at home with the Gothic and with Tarzan as with the latest postcolonial thinking – and indeed she begins with an apologia for her use of the term postcolonial, problematic as it is. *The Ballistic Bard* is dedicated to her son who was born in its midst: we (and he) will no doubt have the good fortune to hear more of Judie Newman.

Austin Clarke looks out from the cover of Stella Algoo-Baksh's biography, grey-haired, academic, with a rigorous gaze. It is clear that he is a literary figure of substance, achieved by a lifetime's self-dedication to writing. Yet reading the process whereby such an image is realized is a moving and humbling experience. Algoo-Baksh's biography unfolds stage by stage a life, a micro-history which mirrors the macrohistory. Born in Barbados in 1934, Clarke began with what he has defined as a triple disadvantage: he was black, poor and illegitimate. At every stage the biography reveals the negatives waiting to defeat the aspirations of such a child and such a youth, however talented. The biography tells of a colonial upbringing and education in tension: an education promoting self-alienation but an upbringing supporting self-worth. The book tells the story of Clarke's tussling with those tensions, to the point where his 'resentments are focused to serve his art, rather than his art the resentments' (142). Ultimately, it argues, the life demonstrates that 'the black man can carve a place for himself in a white society without "accommodating" to it, without sacrificing his self-respect and his own unique identity' (196). Algoo-Baksh writes straightforwardly but with a sensitivity to the heroism of achievement. She is good on the way the individual story maps the wider history of a generation of colonial migrants. The fiction is contextualized against the personal, historicized in contemporary concerns and the unfolding story of both West Indian and Canadian literature. Although it does not offer extended critical analysis of the work, the limited bio-criticism is illuminating, and the bibliography provides useful access to primary and secondary material, including reviews (although broadcast material referred to in the text would have extended it helpfully). Clarke is one of those substantial writers who has received relatively little critical attention as yet. Algoo-Baksh's book, thorough and well-researched, and sensitive to the underlying story of black identity politics, is a welcome step in the right direction.

David Dabydeen's novel *The Intended* is given a reading in *Contemporary Writing and National Identity*, edited by Tracey Hill and William Hughes. David Ellis places the novel in the context of Dabydeen's biography and his ongoing concern to expose the centrality of the black experience within Britishness. The text is located against its Conradian intertext as a story of the narrator's intellectual and physical journey up the Thames to Oxford, rather than up the Congo: neatly summed up as a 'stripping of personal authenticity in search of the polite savagery of the Oxbridge voice'. Ellis challenges Benita Parry over the discourse of Thatcherite materialism which beckons the youths; he sees it not as in popular opposition to the Oxbridge elitism, but rather as another facet of the assimilating master culture.

Although Chris Tiffin and Alan Lawson's *De-scribing Empire* (*YWES* 75.453, 707, 711, 729) engages chiefly with antipodean texts, it includes two chapters on Caribbean fiction. Paul Sharrad gives an intertextual reading of

Caryl Phillips's *Cambridge* against Dickens's *Oliver Twist*. The latter is used as a paradigm of the colonial text which 'obscures and silences Empire by covering it over with inscription', while the former allows 'the unspeakable a place in which to speak, uncovering gaps in discourse and revealing hidden dialogue and intercourse'. But the almost Brechtian anti-romantic distance Phillips establishes, Sharrad argues, opens his text to the risk of being read 'as merely a literary historical reconstruction'. Phillips's work in some ways lends itself by its repeated dialectical structures to discursive analysis. There is room for further such thoughtful and perceptive critiques. In the same volume, Sue Thomas reads the feminism of Jean Rhys's important story 'Let Them Call It Jazz', first published in 1962, against the history of the suffragettes, who like the story's protagonist often had experience of Holloway Prison. Illustrations of suffragette iconography help situate the argument. The attempt to incorporate a reading of 'the Caribbean picaresque' and to respond to what Thomas calls the 'cross-racial voice' results in the study finally losing focus, but the initial intertextual proposition is illuminating: that Rhys reinflects generic narratives of suffragette modernity at the historic point of second-wave British feminism.

Sue Thomas provides another important contribution to Rhys scholarship in 'Jean Rhys, "grilled sole", and an Experience of "mental seduction"' (*NLitsR* 28/9.65–84). This is the first substantial critique of one of Rhys's notebooks in the University of Tulsa archive which gives an account of the sexual advances made to her at the age of 14 by an English plantation owner, a Mr Howard. Thomas's psycho-sexual interpretation of the autobiographical piece locates its traumatizing effect against Rhys's dysfunctional family situation and her anomalous legal status in relation to sexual acts as a 14-year-old girl in 1905 in the Windward Islands, where the age of consent had not been raised as it had been in Britain. The 'sole', which Rhys recalls interrupting Howard's verbal seduction to ask for, Thomas reads as a Freudian jokework for 'soul' – recording a 'desire to be souled in his story and to have the fate of the "sinner" (by the standards of her religious upbringing) articulated in it'. Thomas is alive to the pathos of Rhys's situation while keeping a firm hold on the rigours required to theorize such an experience. Her account, based on primary research like Cribb's essay, adds another revealing chapter to the sad biography which led to Rhys's work.

(c) Poetry

Kamau Brathwaite's work has at last begun to receive the international recognition it has long deserved. Not only has a handsome special edition of *WLT* (68.iv) marked the award of the Neustadt Prize last year, but now Seren Books has brought out a fine collection of specially commissioned essays (ed. Stewart Brown). *The Art of Kamau Brathwaite* does not produce the sense that important issues are being condensed to little more than headlines. Yet the volume makes room for words from Brathwaite himself in that it begins with an interview with Nathaniel Mackey and concludes by reprinting his meditative prose/poem, 'Metaphors of Underdevelopment: a Proem for Hernan Cortez', written in the early 1980s and hitherto available only in journals. These frame 11 critical essays on all aspects of Brathwaite's work. As the introduction points out, this is 'the first full length study of his work as a whole, attempting to relate the various facets of his activity one to another'. The volume's impressive bibliography is a reminder that there are now more than a score of poetry (and 'proem') publications, two volumes of plays, eight books of cultural criticism, five of history, not to mention many volumes edited, and innumerable essays – an oeuvre which has generated ten pages of secondary bibliography. Brathwaite's contribution to the unfolding of a contemporary Caribbean culture has been immense – seminal and widely disseminated – and he has been loved and respected by many of those who have been unable to shed a sense of ambivalence about Walcott. The first six essays are thematic, dealing with Brathwaite in relation to language, Africa, jazz, his cultural criticism, the pan-Caribbean dimension and the Caribbean Artists Movement (CAM). The second half of the book consists of five essays examining specific works in historical order. The list of contributors is a distinguished one. Some of the writers are well-established critics in the field, such as Gordon Rohlehr (who wrote the 1981 monograph on Brathwaite, *Pathfinder*, and here links *The Arrivants* to *X/Self*), Anne Walmsley (whose fine book on CAM is here reprised) and Louis James (here writing on jazz). Others, like Brathwaite himself, combine the roles of poet and critic, such as Mervyn Morris. Younger critics such as Glyne Griffith demonstrate fresh talent: he examines Brathwaite as cultural critic with an elegant perspicacity. The talents Brown has assembled here have risen to a demanding task with imagination and vision. Between them they have created a book which should prove influential as an enabler of Brathwaite studies, and one which is long overdue.

The celebratory edition of *WLT* devoted to Brathwaite is of equivalent importance. Non-subscribing libraries should purchase this as a one-off, as well as the Brown-edited volume. There is some overlap of themes – each for instance has an essay on Brathwaite's relationship to jazz – and of contributors – Nathaniel Mackey, Elaine Savory, Anne Walmsley and Gordon Rohlehr are to be found in both – but there are no repeats as such, and each volume creates its own map of the rich and extensive work. Unlike the book, the *WLT* edition is extensively illustrated with black-and-white photographs, not only related to the Neustadt award but portraying Brathwaite's life through family pictures. The personal is foregrounded by the inclusion of a memoir from his sister, a tribute from Ngugi (to whose family Brathwaite owes his name 'Kamau'), and a sensitive account from Anne Walmsley of his grief at the death of Doris, his wife, in relation to *Zea Mexican Diary* which it inspired. The volume opens with the text of Brathwaite's address/performance given to acknowledge the Neustadt award, which makes a good introduction to his work for newcomers. Thirteen full critical essays conclude, appropriately, with Rohlehr's brilliant reading of Brathwaite's *DreamStories* (1994). This is a fine clutch of seminal studies, covering both individual works and trilogies, and particular dimensions of the work, several of them from fellow creative writers. Graeme Rigby addresses what for some readers has been a problematic development, the concrete poetry of his page-presentation with its thorny unpredictability. He gives a perceptive account of Brathwaite's originality in disrupting typographic norms with the resources of new technologies – a strategy which has conspicuously revolutionized critical discourse, too, for example in Brathwaite's tussle with Peter Hulme over Jean Rhys (*Wasafiri* 22.69–78, in reply to 20.5–11). For Joan Dayan he is simply 'the most remarkable poet writing in English today' – an assertion which the quality of these two publications powerfully supports.

Joan Dayan is also the author of an impressive monograph on the history of a dimension of Caribbean spirituality – the angle from which she approaches Brathwaite too – which although not directly about the anglophone Caribbean should be required reading for all serious students of the history of the region's culture. Her *Haiti, History and the Gods* is divided into three sections: 'Rituals of History', 'Fictions of Haiti' and a bifurcated third part in which 'Last Days of Sainte-Dominique' is followed by 'Gothic Americas', a powerful indictment which traces the horrors de Sade depicts to the historical actuality of slavery in the Antilles. As she says, 'The landscape of Haiti is filled not only with spirits of the dead seeking rest and recognition but with other corporeal spirits who recall the terrors of slavery and the monstrous, institutionalized magic of turning humans into pieces of prized and sexualized matter.' Early discourses of race, gender and spirituality – particularly of *vodou* – are traced through to the folk culture, but also to the literature of the twentieth century. The main focus, however, is on the evidence in pre-twentieth century writings and records, many of which have not been critiqued or quoted in English before. The book is full of fascinating information about such spiritual figures as Legba, Baron Samedi, Danbala and Ezili, and includes black-and-white illustrations of *vévés* and folk sculpture. Although most texts referred to are francophone, some writers in English feature in the discussion – among the moderns, Derek Walcott and Jamaica Kincaid, for example. The generation of belief and ritual as resistance to a cruel history makes for grim but inspiring reading. This is primarily a history, as its tabulated 'Chronology' (relating Haiti and the USA to France from 1492 to 1915) suggests. But it is also a cultural history of importance to the whole Caribbean region, and to the whole Black Atlantic, giving testimony to an enduring, courageous humanity, surviving the most extreme of abuses.

As well as being a novelist, David Dabydeen is a fine poet whose work, like that of his compatriot Fred D'Aguiar, has moved from a staging of Guyanese orality to a music which is closer to standard language – a change which some readers have regretted. Mark McWatt takes another look at Dabydeen's first work in 'His True True Face: Masking and Revelation in David Dabydeen's *Slave Song*' (*Kunapipi* 17.ii.22–9). Regarding the book as having the 'same complex intellectual playfulness, though towards a different end' as Pope's *Dunciad*, he examines the different discourses which it deploys: the poems in Indo-Guyanese Creole, impenetrable to outsiders, accompanied by translations and explanations, as well as illustrations. Dabydeen's commentary makes us uneasy, he says: 'the poet deliberately puts on this mask and grins at us from behind it' – but quite which is the 'true true' face and which the mask remains open to question. For McWatt, Dabydeen is 'conducting an elaborate post-colonial critique of traditional notions of the integrity of the text': the strategy 'calls into question the whole enterprise of literary criticism when applied across racial and socioeconomic divides such as those highlighted in this work'. This is an important and unsettling insight which deserves reflection. McWatt goes on to give an alternative account of the multivocal approach as a sign of a young poet's 'natural diffidence'. Practicality is certainly relevant: if the poems were to reach an audience they needed explication. McWatt takes the point on, however, to identify the apparatus perceptively as necessary 'simply to contain and manage the enormous energy of the poetic voice from the Indian villages of Guyana – a voice hardly heard before'. The voice carries a kind of 'dread', which McWatt glosses as 'accumulated animosity' and 'the desperate need for an audience'. McWatt captures something profound in these tense phrases.

Many Caribbean poets are also prose writers or dramatists. Two interviews – with writers who began as poets but have since turned to prose and achieved the success which is perhaps more elusive for poetry – help to elucidate the desires and conflicts involved. One is David Dabydeen, who is interviewed by Chelva Kanaganayakam in *Configurations of Exile: South Asian Writers and Their World*. He boldly holds Dabydeen's poetry to be 'as significant' as that of Brathwaite and Walcott, no small claim, although if we compare them at equivalent ages the comparison may not seem so extravagant. Dabydeen tells how his 'instinct is for poetry', and how he is 'much happier with *Turner* than with the two novels'. Novelists, he says, 'tend to write travel writing between novels. I think poets write novels between poems.' Having just finished his third novel, with a 'Naipaulian' protagonist, he talks about literary affiliations, and about the language choices he has made for different projects: the first two novels with their different styles – *The Intended* 'consciously untidy and Creole', *Disappearance* 'very engineered' in a 'conscious nod' to Naipaul, 'a beautiful engineer of prose'. He speaks also of his love for medieval alliterative verse, pre-colonial and 'innocent': 'You almost begin to love England when you read medieval literature.' Like Walcott he recognizes the epic quality of the sea, the great leveller, with its lack of memory and its 'enormous power [...] to deny nationalistic and imperialistic efforts'. Asked if the poetic becomes political he answers emphatically, 'Of course it does. It becomes a weapon against all form of tyranny because the sea resists all enclosures.' *Turner* he acknowledges as ending with the sea 'an empty Eden', but he looks to the language for redemption: 'I would hope the music of the poem offers some element of hope, even though the theme is bleak.'

Fans of Olive Senior's finely crafted work will find Wolfgang Binder's interview (*CE&S* 18.i.106–14) illuminating. Senior places her recent work in the context of her early life and her beginnings as a writer. She talks about Jamaica and Canada, about gods and Caribbean women, and about a *magnum opus* in progress: an encyclopedia of Jamaican folklore. As a writer of both poetry and fiction she explains how the success of *Summer Lightning*, a collection of stories, kept her away from poetry until a year spent in many places, with no real home, drove her back to it 'because poetry is something you can carry around in a little notebook and work on as you find the time'. Her latest volume of poetry, *Gardening in the Tropics*, is talked about in some detail. It is easy to forget how tenuous is the survival of poetry in the teeth of the novel's big business – and how tenacious has been the commitment of Brathwaite and Walcott in sticking to it.

A woman poet from an earlier generation is Alison Donnell's subject in 'Contradictory (W)omens? – Gender Consciousness in the Poetry of Una Marson' (*Kunapipi* 17.iii.43–58). She surveys Marson criticism to date – sparse and hostile, apart from Erika Smilowitz – and goes on to give her own reading. Looking at the sonnet's 'eurocentrically gendered system of signification', Donnell considers Marson's use of the genre as 'crucially different [...] by inverting the gender roles'. Using 'In Vain' as her example she argues that although it is an 'ambivalent representation of woman as slave', it 'explores but does not endorse the surrender of self'. Similarly, Marson's satire on Kipling's 'If' (the texts are included in the article), Donnell argues, uses patriarchal language to explore and explode 'the mythologies constructed to support racism and sexism'. This is useful criticism. For all its complicity in historic discourses Marson's work does indeed show a subversive irony which is more original than she is often given credit for. What is more, unlike most poets, she can make you laugh out loud.

The best essay on Walcott for a long time is 'The Anarchist's Mirror: Walcott's *Omeros* and the Epic Tradition' (*CE&S* 17.ii.67–81) from David Hoegberg. He is one of the few to understand the radicalism of this great work, and the particular way it situates itself within the Western tradition originating in Homer in order to act subversively against it. Walcott scholarship has tended to ascribe to him a patrician and assimilationist stance, but Hoegberg draws trenchant parallels with Fanon and Kropotkin to demonstrate how much such readings miss.

Two books are partly devoted to reprints of critical essays on Walcott. The reductionist tendency of the metropolitan critical establishment is only too evident in the new volume in Macmillan's New Casebook series. Under the title of *Postcolonial Literatures* – these are apparently regarded as modest enough to be addressed in one volume, and the terminology deemed unproblematic – it reprints essays on four writers, each of whom by rights demands a Casebook to him/herself: Achebe, Ngugi, Desai and Walcott. It is a title which teachers will need to hold up to students as an example of the old problem, rather than a move towards a solution. Walcott's gallon is squeezed into the half-pint pot of four essays (one more, at least, than Ngugi and Desai who only get a parsimonious three). Macmillan has a fine reputation in publishing in the postcolonial field, its current programme of Caribbean monographs being particularly outstanding – although its refusal to list them in its main literature catalogue is both infuriating and stupid – so it is a pity that the editors, Michael Parker and Roger Starkey, were not persuaded that their project would betray an irredeemably centrist attitude to its subject, all the more conspicuously in a Casebook list which is increasingly being geared less to whole oeuvres than to single works of what clearly remains 'the canon'. Still, I suppose it remains true that you have to start somewhere. The essays here collected on Walcott were originally printed in *ArielE*, *CE&S*, *JCL* and *SoR* between 1986 and 1991. Some attempt is made to suggest the range of Walcott's oeuvre in that his poetry, drama and non-fiction are represented, but inevitably the choice of four is as frustrating as it is narrow. Clement Wyke's perceptive study of the verse collection *The Fortunate Traveller* is usefully reprinted (although it betrays the weakness of ducking extended analysis of the complex title poem), as is Daizal Samad's 'Cultural Imperatives in Walcott's *Dream on Monkey Mountain*', which gives a perceptive reading of this important and controversial play. Sidney Burris reviews *Omeros* in 'An Empire of Poetry', relating it to Walcott's theatre and to Joyce. Although he finds the epic poem 'sprawling', he demonstrates a fine sensitivity to its subtle strategies. Alongside these it is depressing to see a quarter of the precious space devoted to a widely available, ill-founded, hostile critique, Elaine Savory [Fido]'s essay now retitled 'Value Judgements on Art and the Question of Macho Attitudes: The Case of Derek Walcott', which raises feminist objections to gender representations in some of the early work. The myth of Walcott as misogynist, which sorts ill even with the early work and is completely out of tune with the more recent works, is regrettably given another lease of life in this publication, which is likely to shape attitudes in an educational context where readers have limited direct experience of the writer's work, and therefore limited opportunities to test the opinions being retailed to them.

Michael Parker is also behind a reiteration of the same tired charge of sexism in his article 'Derek Walcott: Voicing Whose Identity?' in *Contemporary Writing and National Identity* (ed. Tracey Hill and William Hughes). Once again, early work provides the main ammunition for a shallow reading, including a fatally unaware analysis of *Dream on Monkey Mountain*. Conspicuous misprints such as '*Dream of Monkey Mountain*' and the misquotation of Joyce's intention to forge the uncreated 'consciousness' of his race – which should read 'conscience' – do not help to inspire confidence. Parker begins by taking heteroglossia as his topic but seems to confuse it with intertextuality. Fortunately, Walcott's reputation does not depend on such misprision.

Although superficially a similar type of book, Donald Herdeck's *Three Dynamite Authors* does not lay itself open to similar strictures. This at least has a coherent overall rationale in that it selects for reprinted critical coverage three Nobel Prize winners (hence the explosives joke in the title – Nobel made his fortune out of dynamite), and is significantly different in that it selects from its own pre-existing titles. TCP already publishes the equivalent of Casebooks in its Critical Perspectives series, one devoted entirely to each of the authors now commemorated specifically as Nobel winners: Derek Walcott, Naguib Mahfouz and Wole Soyinka. The new anthology thus functions as a lead to the pre-existing publications which already mark how seriously the publisher takes these writers, unlike the embarrassing Casebook. Herdeck's volume leads with Walcott as the newest Nobel winner of the three (in 1992, while Mahfouz and Soyinka won in 1988 and 1986 respectively). His short introduction asks 'what "vitamins" possibly lacking in the experience of the Western reader can be found in this new work from the "vast-abroad" world other than England, France, America, etc.?' He defends the situating of a writer's work culturally and historically in preference to tossing it into 'the Roman arena of "world literature" [...] unarmed, almost culturally naked', which is 'cruel at worst and arrogant at best'. He defines the task of introducing a non-Western writer's product to 'our Euro-North American neighbors', the first job being to 'select the impact works – those which can do the most "damage" to cultural fascism in the quickest time', the second 'to provide the nexus of the work', and the third, 'to identify the value or intrinsic interest of the work for us, the "outsiders" '. Although Herdeck's five-page presentation is less academic and sophisticated than Parker and Starkey's 30-page introduction to their volume, it captures something vital which the others miss. Herdeck represents Walcott, however, only by two pieces from Robert D. Hamner: his general introduction to TCP's *Critical Perspectives* volume which he edited, and his introduction to *Another Life*. Although the first piece has the merit of functioning like an extended encyclopedia entry to sketch in the broad outlines of the life and work – a service which is lacking from the Casebook – the short and rather superficial study of *Another Life* does not really meet the volume's need for some kind of in-depth critique, and whether it is that poem which best meets Herdeck's criterion of doing the most damage to 'cultural fascism' is open to question. Perhaps the most immediately useful of Walcott's texts from that point of view is his Nobel speech, *The Antilles, Fragments of Epic Memory*, issued in book form but also reprinted in its entirety twice in 1993 in *WLT* (67.ii.260–7) and in *S. E. Asia Writes Back! The Scoob Pacifica Anthology no. 1* (302–17) edited by Ike Ong. From Herdeck's point of view, however, selection from work in which his press already held copyright was probably a commercial imperative. It is a reminder that poetry, of all literary forms, is the one where the pernicious operations of the market remain most damaging.

(d) Drama
Norman Rae furnishes a useful introduction to the work of Trevor Rhone in Bruce King's *West Indian Literature*, as mentioned above, situating it against biographical information. Rhone studied drama at the Rose Bruford school in Britain and returned to Jamaica to devote himself to theatre. He has written not only popular plays, fuelled in Rae's view by 'finely-targeted satire', but screenplays. Rae relates how he wrote the film *The Harder They Come* with Perry Henzell and adapted his own stage play *Smile Orange* for the screen.

Two other collections mentioned above include essays which bring a theatrical angle to bear on a writer not known as a dramatist. In the journal devoted to Brathwaite (*WLT* 68.iv.741–6), Abena Busia in 'Long Memory and Survival: Dramatizing the *Arrivants* trilogy' narrates the challenge of producing at Rutgers University last year a staged reading/performance for four musicians, four actors and a dancer, of selections from the Brathwaite trilogy, 'interrupted by the voice of Grace Nichols's *long memoried woman*'. In the collection dedicated to studies of Wilson Harris (*Callaloo* 18.i), Al Creighton uses Harris's early drama 'Canje (The River of Ocean)', published as part of his first collection of poems *Eternity to Season* in 1954, as a way into a more recent fiction. The essay 'The Metaphor of the Theater in *The Four Banks of the River of Space*' (*Callaloo* 18.i.71–82) includes sections on theatre and carnival, and covers Harris's use of masks, in an illuminating discussion.

The growing international response to Walcott's work is evident in the expansion of translations. *Ti Jean e i suoi Fratelli*, translated by Annuska Palme Sanavio, was staged by Elettra Produzioni under the direction of Sylvano Bussotti at the Istituto del Dramma Popolare di San Miniato in July 1993. Cristina Scaglia gives a short review of the production in 'The Teatro Nazionale of Milan goes Caribbean with the Complicity of Derek Walcott's *Ti-Jean*' (*Caribana* 4.35–41). The illustrations are particularly interesting, showing a Walcott watercolour sketch 'Ti-Jean's Family' as well as production photographs, and drawings by Bussotti, who designed the production as well as directing it. Adelphi Edizione of Milan published in 1992 a bilingual edition of selected poetry by Walcott under the title *Mappa Del Nuovo Mondo*, translated by Barbara Bianchi, Gilberto Forti and Roberto Mussapi and prefaced by a translation of Brodsky's essay 'The Sound of the Sea'. In 1993, it followed this with a volume placing the *Ti-Jean* translation alongside a translation by Fernanda Steele of *Dream on Monkey Mountain* as *Sogno sul Monte della Scimmia*.

Walcott's play *Pantomime* features in the work by Dorothy Lane, and there is an essay by Daizal Samad on *Dream on Monkey Mountain* in the Macmillan New Casebook (ed. Parker and Starkey) discussed above. It is Bruce King's book on Walcott's theatre, however, which steals the limelight. Burdened with a mouthful of a title, *Derek Walcott and West Indian Drama: 'Not Only a Playwright But a Company': The Trinidad Theatre Workshop 1959–1993*, this is a work of cultural history as important as Gordon Rohlehr's study of calypso (*YWES* 71.740–1) or Anne Walmsley's history of the Caribbean Artists' Movement (*YWES* 74.652–3). It will be invaluable to students of Walcott and of West Indian theatre, as it traces the intricate story of Walcott's obstinate pursuit of a vision of a national theatre, despite besetting odds. The narrative is divided into three sections: 'Roots' (1948–65), 'The Great Years' (1966–76) and 'Separation and Reconciliation' (1977–93) which charts the story since Walcott has been predominantly based in the USA. A wealth of hitherto unavailable data about Walcott's decades of devotion to the theatre informs this fascinating book, which touches on New York and other places as well as the Caribbean. As well as production details, it gives extensive information on some unpublished and unperformed plays. Eight pages of black-and-white plates, welcome though they are, make the reader long for many more. A useful bibliography includes sections on recordings and unsigned journalism. A ten-page chronology of the Trinidad Theatre Workshop's productions gives eloquent testimony to the achievement of this company, essentially amateur in commercial terms but unmistakably professional at the level of its art.

An oppositional though unstated relationship to Walcott's drama seems to inform an unpublished, strongly visual play *Danse* produced in Trinidad in 1991, which is the subject of an interview by Pietro Dandrea with its creator and director Lesley-Ann Wells (*Caribana* 4.27–34). Wells adapted a symbolic feminist story written by her sister, which has three sisters (an inversion perhaps of the *Ti-Jean* structure) taking revenge against the man who has made one of them pregnant. She tells how she was attacked for sexism in Trinidad – 'a very male oriented society' – but her response is clear: 'if for once there is one play showing a woman's point of view with the man just brought on the stage to be killed, what is wrong with that?' Some feminist readings of *Dream on Monkey Mountain*, in which the symbolic figure of a woman is killed, come to mind. Wells denies being influenced by other writers or directors, but it seems that in this play she may be mounting a conscious challenge to Walcott.

The interview is once again a reminder of how important it is that journals should record something of theatre productions. They are intrinsically ephemeral but no less an important part of the unfolding of a literature and culture, and so few play-texts get published that if we do not record reviews and interviews of this sort (outside the equally ephemeral local newspaper review), subsequent histories of theatre in our time will be even more impossible and imperfect. Bruce King was able to sit at the feet of Walcott and others to research his book – and Walcott's work is relatively well documented. Later scholars of theatre will have only the paper record. King concludes his study with a plea that Walcott – whether regarded, he suggests, as the Shakespeare of our time or simply the Webster – should be filmed in action as a director for posterity. As he says, the near non-existence of any screen record of his productions is a scandal of our time.

5. India

(a) General, Poetry and Drama

Shyamala A. Narayan's annual review and bibliography of work published in the previous year ('India' [*JCL* 30.iii.35–70]) is as readable and thorough as ever. Her perspective on creative and critical writing offers a refreshing contrast to some western metropolitan orthodoxies. Rushdie's collection of short stories, *East, West*, is given a lukewarm reception, not least for his use in one story of a ' "Peter Sellers" type of English', and elsewhere her discussion of fiction is characteristically concerned with issues of authenticity. Assumptions that Indian drama in English is virtually moribund are challenged; Mahesh Dattani's *Final Solution and Other Plays* is singled out as the most important book of last year, establishing him as 'the leading Indian English dramatist'. The controversy surrounding the Sahitya Akademi Award for G. N. Devy's *After Amnesia* (1993) is interestingly outlined, with Narayan supporting those Indian critics who argue that Devy fails to offer a clearly defined, viable alternative to the 'Orientalist' Sanskrit tradition which he sees as so damaging to Indian critical thought. The review also covers poetry, autobiography and travel writing, and the bibliography supplies an extensive list of texts, many of which are only published in India, as well as useful details of Indian literary journals.

The foreword to a special issue of *Wasafiri*, entitled 'India, South Asia and the Diaspora' (21.i), urges the reader to 'celebrate the diversity [and] the variegated topography' of this relatively neglected field, suggesting that the literatures of the Indian diaspora have been somewhat overshadowed by the critical attention given to African-American and Afro-Caribbean literary diasporas. As a guide and an initial resource for readers this issue ably fulfils the aim of introducing a variety of contemporary writing from the subcontinent and beyond. The critical pieces include discussion of the short story in India, recent Parsi fiction and Indian cinema, together with concise regional surveys of writing from Canada, Britain, South East Asia and the South Pacific, the Caribbean, Pakistan, Sri Lanka and Bangladesh, all of which supply useful bibliographical information. There are also interviews with Vikram Seth and V. S. Naipaul, a generous selection of poetry, and some review articles.

Elleke Boehmer's *Colonial and Postcolonial Literature* is an ambitious and cogent attempt 'to expand some of the discrete observations of postcolonial theory into a longer *durée*: a narrative about the writing that accompanied empire, and the writing that came to supplant it'. In the process, Boehmer demystifies many of the terms and concerns of recent theory, and supplies useful textual references and analysis. Her approach makes stimulating use of Indian texts and contexts, drawing on a substantial body of work from the period of the Raj (including Bankim Chandra Chatterjee's Bengali novels and Kipling's fiction) through to the postmodernist narratives of the last decade. The scope of the study obviously precludes sustained, detailed analysis of Indian matters, but the sub-continent repeatedly figures in the discussion. The part played by Rabindranath Tagore, Raja Rao and Mulk Raj Anand in breaking 'the monopoly on imperial writing' is emphasized, as is the importance of writers of the diaspora such as Amitav Ghosh, Salman Rushdie, Vikram Seth and Bharati Mukherjee in developing the migrant literature so much admired and analysed by influential metropolitan critics. There is also a consideration of the nature of 'mimicry' in the early work of R. K. Narayan and V. S. Naipaul, suggesting that these novelists share a common approach of 'subversion by imitation', avoiding 'the stance of overt repudiation' of British culture and imperialism. Some of Narayan's later novels, together with the work of Rao and Rushdie, are mentioned in a brief discussion of the hybrid fictional forms emerging from the use of indigenous structures and symbols. Other writers who feature, albeit briefly, in Boehmer's narrative include Anita Desai, Kamala Das, Nayantara Sahgal, Shashi Tharoor and Upamanyu Chatterjee. In all, this is an illuminating study of the connections and disjunctures between a wide range of writing, and Boehmer's clear, expositionary approach should be especially welcome in teaching contexts.

Despite the editors' insistence in their introduction that they are 'not interested in establishing a canon of theories or theorists', *The Post-Colonial Studies Reader* (ed. Ashcroft, Griffiths and Tiffin), is likely to be extremely influential in the teaching of postcolonial theory. The opening section of this extensive collection of extracts and short pieces highlights the intensity of recent debates in the field, as pieces by Gayatri Chakravorty Spivak and Homi K. Bhabha are followed by Benita Parry's critique of their positions, 'Problems in Current Theories of Colonial Discourse'. The scope of the volume, however, is far wider than this initial impression might suggest. The section on language usefully reprints Raja Rao's introduction to *Kanthapura* ('Language and Spirit'), and includes Braj B. Kachru's 'The Alchemy of English', and there is an interesting section on education, featuring Gauri Viswanathan's 'The Beginnings of English Literary Studies in British India' and Thomas Macaulay's 'Minute on Indian Education'. There is also an extract from Dipesh Chakrabarty's 'Postcoloniality and the Artifice of History: Who Speaks for "Indian" Pasts?', which investigates the subalternity of the academic discourse of 'Indian history', with some reference to the work of Salman Rushdie and Nirad C. Chaudhuri. The volume offers a good indication of the variety of approaches and sources available in the field of postcolonial studies and, in its coverage of material relating to India, it brings together some very useful pieces.

Probal Dasgupta's *The Otherness of English: India's Auntie Tongue Syndrome* (1993) offers a challenging sociolinguistic 'interpretation of the presence of the English language in India', arguing that English remains a 'technical' rather than a 'human' language on the sub-continent. In the present context this is especially provocative, since it leads Dasgupta to question both creative and academic work in the field of Indian literature in English, stating that 'post-modern India's English, in contrast to classical India's Sanskrit, has been a failure as far as independent creative expression is concerned'. Perhaps even more controversial is the statement that the 'Indian English writer is able to scale genuinely creative peaks only as an expatriate, living in (or in ever-attentive contact with) an English-speaking country and attached, as a migrant, to its community, in the manner of Joseph Conrad'. Meanwhile, the academy should focus its efforts on the appropriately technical task of translation and renarration, which is seen as having produced valuable results, and should relegate the analysis of Indian-English writing to an ancillary position. Given the already lively debate about the future of English studies in

India, this intervention can be expected to produce some interesting responses from critics and authors.

Nayantara Sahgal's 'The Myth Reincarnated' (*JCL* 30.i.23–28) gives a novelist's response to the continuing power of the west in mapping and therefore controlling the world, noting how the political settings of her novels are part of a specifically Indian experience of colonial and neo-colonial domination: 'Because we had no political voice, I found it especially satisfying to express myself politically and to speak a political idiom that was rootedly Indian, yet modern in its twentieth century legacy.' Suranjan Ganguly's 'Poetry into Prose: The Rewriting of Oudh in Satyajit Ray's *The Chess Players*' (*JCL* 30.ii.17–24), whilst making brief reference to the Munshi Premchand short story that is the source of Ray's 1977 film, is chiefly concerned with analysing the ways in which the filmic text dramatizes an Indian encounter with a radically different culture. It suggests something of the power of the film in conveying the contrast between the prosaic, utilitarian nature of Victorian imperialism in India and the poetic, aesthetic values of Oudh, just prior to its annexation by the British in 1856. Ganguly also makes interesting use of the problematic issues of translating/rewriting culture raised by Ray's juxtaposition of mutually exclusive discourses. In 'Amitav Ghosh's *In An Antique Land*: The Ethnographer-Historian and the Limits of Irony' (*JCL* 30.ii.45–55), Javed Majeed details Ghosh's use of a dual narrative to contrast 'the fluidity of the medieval world' with 'the inflexibility of modern boundaries'. Ghosh builds on his anthropological studies in an Egyptian village and his research into medieval manuscripts to depict the modern village as bearing traces of a bucolic past, and his 'composite genre' of literary, ethnographic and historical discourses seems well suited to a text that memorializes a flexibility that is felt to be increasingly threatened. However, Majeed finds Ghosh's treatment of irony to be problematic and in contradiction to the book's apparent distaste for the 'modern'. The way in which 'the author's own authoritative persona is continually reaffirmed rather than subverted' suggests evidence of a collusion with 'the exclusive identities of modernity' in a text that offers only a 'reconstruction of a synthetic medieval past' and ultimately revolves around a preoccupation with the author's own exclusive identity. Florence D'Souza-Deleury's 'To Be or not to Be in Prafulla Mohanti's Writings' (*CE&S* 18.i.4–12) focuses on Mohanti's autobiographical works, exploring themes of belonging and the tensions between tradition and modernity in the work of a writer resident in England but with a strong sense that rural Orissa is 'home'.

Given that fiction tends to dominate the criticism of Indian writing in English, it is gratifying to find a full-length study devoted to poetry. Sudesh Mishra's *Preparing Faces: Modernism and Indian Poetry in English* is a perceptive study which offers a detailed contextualization of post-Independence poetry in relation to the themes and techniques of modernism. Identifying Nissim Ezekiel as the pioneering figure in the 1950s' revolt against what Syd Harrex has memorably termed the 'Bumblebee Romantics' of the period of the Raj, Mishra draws attention to the ways in which the modernist programme of rejection and revolt has become a key feature of recent poetry. Paradoxically, modernist notions of a 'radical departure' had, by the 1980s, become the defining characteristics of a new Indian poetic 'tradition'. Taking ten poets from the new canon of Indian poetry, Mishra examines the extent to which they reflect the dominance of an Anglo-American modernist ideology. Individual chapters on each poet offer penetrating analyses of their central concerns; for example, Ezekiel's treatment of the city, Arvind Krishna Mehrotra's use of surrealism, Arun Kolatkar's interest in the quest motif and A. K. Ramanujan's use of personae. Other poets who are seen to belong to the broader trend include Keki N. Daruwalla, R. Parthasarathy and Adil Jussawalla. The thesis is convincingly argued, demonstrating that these writers might be seen to fit into what is essentially a neo-colonialist paradigm of western influence, whilst allowing for the assertion that three of the chosen poets (Gieve Patel, Jayanta Mahapatra and Kamala Das) 'write from outside the matrix of modernism', circumventing 'the modernist tendency to dehumanize literature; in fact, they participate in its rehumanization'.

Anthologists of Indian poetry in English have been more than simply instrumental in terms of canon-formation; they have largely dictated the terms under which debates about the work have been conducted. The preface to Makarand Paranjape's recent collection, *Indian Poetry in English* (1993), highlights their 'disproportionate importance and influence', stating that 'From the very beginning of its systematic study, anthologies have played a crucial role in deciding how this literature is to be interpreted', before reviewing the practice of previous anthologists. Paranjape chooses to steer a middle course between an uncritical and all-inclusive approach and the tendency to limit the selection to a handful of chiefly modernist post-Independence poets. The result is an interesting and wide ranging selection that spans over 150 years of poetry, from Henry Derozio's early nineteenth-century poems to the work of contemporary poets such as Vikram Seth and Imtiaz Dharker, whilst 'placing figures like Tagore and Aurobindo at the centre of the anthology' and restoring a number of poets who have suffered undue neglect. The introduction offers a useful survey of the history of the field, with observations on such topics as periodization, scope and origins.

(b) Fiction

Judie Newman's *The Ballistic Bard: Postcolonial Fictions* examines a varied selection of contemporary texts by African, Indian and Caribbean writers in relation to issues of intertextuality. The starting point is 'the relation between postcolonial literature and its predecessors', as suggested by the title's reference to J. G. Farrell's *The Siege of Krishnapur*, where connections are made between British military and cultural domination of India in the nineteenth century. Newman makes interesting use of the contrasting ways in which Anita Desai and Ruth Prawer Jhabvala appropriate and rewrite Forster's *A Passage to India*, in *Baumgartner's Bombay* and *Heat and Dust*. The practice of reading 'new' literatures in relation to canonical texts to highlight their simultaneous imbrication with and resistance to metropolitan discourses has produced some fruitful discussion in recent years, and this study makes a valuable contribution to that project, but it is also concerned with a far wider range of reference, allowing Newman to argue that these texts are far from simply dependent on the centre, and doomed to rework the canon. She highlights ways in which her chosen novelists also engage with politics and history through a process of 'writing across' to each other, and through intertextual strategies that connect with extra-literary discourses. Hence, Bharati Mukherjee is seen to respond directly to V. S. Naipaul's work; in a chapter on *Jasmine* the principles of chaos theory that underpin the narrative are explored to demonstrate that Mukherjee's vision is of a generative disorder, in contrast to Naipaul's entropic vision. There is also a brief consideration of the relationship between Upamanyu Chatterjee's *English, August: An Indian Story* and Jhabvala's *Heat and Dust*, followed by a more detailed discussion of the latter's use of different discourses of sati. This is an adventurous, stimulating and closely argued study, framed by a pleasing awareness of the somewhat precarious position of the postcolonial theorist and novelist in resisting a collusive role with neo-colonialist discourses.

Postcolonial Literatures: Achebe, Ngugi, Desai, Walcott (ed. Michael Parker and Roger Starkey), usefully collects three recent journal articles on Anita Desai. The editors' informing principle 'is that postcolonial literatures are interpretative discourses, reshaping the languages whence they arise, disclosing to former colonising cultures redefinitions of centralising literary, cultural and political histories'. Judie Newman's 'History and Letters: Anita Desai's *Baumgartner's Bombay*' (originally published in *WLWE* and appearing in a modified form as one of the chapters in *The Ballistic Bard*) highlights the intertextual use of literary and historical discourses in Desai's construction of an Indo-European world. In '*Fire on the Mountain* – a Rite of Exit', Bettina L. Knapp explores the Hindu context to inform an interesting psychoanalytical study of Desai's use of traditional Indian symbols. Finally, Harveen Sachdeva Mann's ' "Going in the Opposite Direction": Feminine Recusancy in Anita Desai's *Voices in the City*' takes issue with apolitical and universalist readings of Desai's second novel, asserting that it 'can be regarded as a significant discourse on modern Indian feminism'.

Indian-English Fiction 1980–1990: An Assessment (1994) is a collection of 18 essays originally given as papers at a University of Bombay seminar in 1991. The editors, Nilufer E. Bharucha and Vilas Sarang, suggest that the 1980s saw Indian fiction in English 'liberated from the colonial yoke' and becoming 'an integral part of the Indian environment', with a substantial indigenous readership and a legitimate role in Indian literature. This is chiefly because it 'displays a sense of social consciousness, is concerned with Indian sociopolitical realities and is authentically Indian'. The majority of contributors subscribe to this view, although it is to the editors' credit that they include a dissenting voice in the collection, reminding us that debates about the role of English in India are also an integral part of the academic environment. G. N. Devy, one of the more outspoken advocates of indigenous language writing and criticism, offers a challenging overview that suggests the need for a reconstitution of the field to include works in translation, together with a more scrupulous historicization and analysis of dominant concerns across this proposed range of work. The bulk of the volume is, however, devoted to interesting detailed analysis of specific writers, themes and groupings. The range is impressively wide, and the individual contributions maintain a high standard. Work published by older writers during the decade is considered alongside the work of the many new novelists to emerge, with single author studies of Salman Rushdie, Shashi Deshpande, Rohinton Mistry, Bharati Mukherjee, Amitav Ghosh, Nayantara Sahgal, Anita Desai, Raja Rao and R. K. Narayan. The importance of women writers is stressed, as is the major contribution made by novelists from the Parsi community. There are also pieces that address the specific concerns of the many expatriate writers that are claimed by the field, and some useful essays on the urban experience, autobiographical aspects and novels of the Partition. Other writers who receive fairly detailed attention include Upamanyu Chatterjee, Shashi Tharoor, Firdaus Kanga and Bapsi Sidhwa.

Fawzia Afzal-Khan's *Cultural Imperialism and the Indo-English Novel: Genre and Ideology in R. K. Narayan, Anita Desai, Kamala Markandaya, and Salman Rushdie* (1993) builds interestingly on the work of Edward Said, developing the argument that all of the chosen writers resist, albeit in strikingly different ways, 'colonialist and Orientalist literary strategies of containment'. Genre, particularly the combining of mythic and realistic modes, is seen to play an important ideological role in this process; Narayan's earlier novels achieve a balance between myth and realism that reconciles traditional Indian values with modernity in the face of the colonialist fragmentation of Indian culture, whilst Desai's work shows an aesthetic attraction to the mythic mode but a moral identification with critical and social realism. Markandaya's refusal to reconcile myth and realism in her work suggests a programme designed to exemplify the fragmentation and confusion of the postcolonial situation, whilst Rushdie's work takes this a stage further by debunking both modes in a liberating strategy that rejects essentialist notions of Third World societies. Afzal-Khan analyses a good range of primary texts, and the scope of the study is extended by some interesting comparative discussion of writers (notably V. S. Naipaul and Ruth Prawer Jhabvala) who are seen to accept 'contained' images of otherness.

With the trend towards comparative study and the global perspective inherent in much postcolonial theory, book-length studies of single authors are becoming somewhat rare, especially in western publishing circles. Michel Pousse's *R. K. Narayan: A Painter of Modern India* offers a detailed analysis of Narayan's work, simultaneously locating his fiction in a specifically Indian context whilst asserting that his 'vision of man, socially and religiously integrated is that of the European humanists. It abolishes all distinctions between race and caste, all notions of East and West.' There are some interesting insights into individual works, but on the whole this is a rather unfocused work which is further marred by a large number of typographical errors.

The flood of articles on Salman Rushdie continues unabated, with work of variable quality being produced. Aron R. Aji's ' "All Names Mean Something": Salman Rushdie's "Haroun" and the Legacy of Islam' (*ConL* 36.i.103–29) eschews a 'topical'/biographical approach to *Haroun and the Sea of Stories* in favour of a reading that sheds light on the story's complex range of reference to Islamic religious and cultural traditions. A less focused discussion of the same text is offered in Suchismita Sen's 'Memory, Language, and Society in Salman Rushdie's *Haroun and the Sea of Stories*' (*ConL* 36.iv.654–75), which looks at 'the process of sending messages through stories', particularly through Rushdie's 'use of the South Asian variety of English' to depict a lost world that is felt to be especially resonant for an Indian readership. 'The Story Teller Silenced: A Study of Rushdie's *Haroun and the Sea of Stories*' by Latha Rangachari and Evangelini Manickam (*LCrit* 30.iv.15–24) offers a concise examination of Rushdie's central concern with the role of the storyteller. In ' "Fusions, Translations, Conjoinings": Cultural Transformation in Salman Rushdie's Work' (*WLWE* 34.ii.27–37), Rufus Cook sees Rushdie as 'a properly self-reflexive postmodernist' who incorporates a distrust of objective truth or value into the style and structure of his fiction, stressing the partial, constructed nature of narrative and memory. The flexible, commodious style of Rushdie's work especially suits his thematic concern with cultural transformation and hybridity. Neil Ten Kortenaar's ' *Midnight's Children* and the Allegory of History' (*ArielE* 26.ii.41–62) is also concerned with Rushdie's interest in exposing fictionality, specifically in relation to the history of the Indian nation. *Midnight's Children* 'is a meditation on the textuality of history and, in particular, of that official history that constitutes the nation'. The article builds to an interesting conclusion; having exploded the unitary, stable identity of the nation, Rushdie invites a 'sceptical, provisional faith' in a secular India imagined by Nehru, rather than the Gandhian or transcendental vision of India. In 'In the Name of the Nation: Salman Rushdie's *Shame*' (*CE&S* 18.i.48–55), Cynthia Carey Abrioux identifies a double agenda in Rushdie's 'semi-fictional representation of Pakistan': 'within the deconstructive resistance to neo-colonialism is embedded the positive reinscription or coding of an ancient but dynamic culture'.

Other articles on Rushdie testify to his emergence as a key figure for postcolonial theorists, since his work acts as a springboard for broader discussion of topics such as hybridity, migrancy and the relationship between postcolonialism and postmodernism. In 'Postcolonial Differend: Diasporic Narratives of Salman Rushdie' (*ArielE* 26.iii.7–45), Vijay Mishra focuses on the Indian-Pakistani diaspora in Britain with particular reference to *The Satanic Verses*, which is viewed as '*the* text about migration, about the varieties of religious, sexual, and social filiations of the diaspora'. Employing Lyotard's notion of the differend, and examining the novel in relation to aesthetic, religious and political discourses, Mishra comes to the conclusion that 'In the case of the Rushdie Affair, compromise or justice is not possible because the grounds of the arguments are incommensurable'. This suggests a basis for diasporic theory as concerned with the inconclusive. Revathi Krishnaswamy's 'Mythologies of Migrancy: Postcolonialism, Postmodernism and the Politics of (Dis)location' (*ArielE* 26.i.125–46) directly addresses Rushdie's elevated status in the metropolitan academy, due to his position as a migrant, and the novelist's own claims for the superior vision emerging from the 'migrant sensibility'. The collusion of Rushdie and his admirers in indulging in 'self-legitimizing mythologies and self-aggrandizing manoeuvres' which privilege immigrant writers may obscure 'alternative strategies for change' in the field of postcolonial studies.

Saros Cowasjee's *Studies in Indian and Anglo-Indian Fiction* (1993) collects together a number of pieces originally given as conference papers between 1975 and 1990, and previously published in periodicals, books and conference proceedings. Nearly half of the collection is devoted to discussions of British writers on India. The remaining essays give considerable attention to the work of Mulk Raj Anand, but there is also discussion of Manohar Malgonkar, R. K. Narayan and Khushwant Singh.

In addition to the continuing fascination with Rushdie, journal articles have this year examined something of the variety of Indian fiction in English. Chitra Sankaran's 'Misogyny in Raja Rao's *The Chessmaster and His Moves*' (*JCL* 30.i.87–95) is a carefully argued, complex analysis of the religious and philosophical concepts informing Rao's novel. The quest of the protagonist-narrator, Siva, for self-realization is seen to involve distinctly misogynistic elements, but Sankaran, whilst acknowledging the existence of such a strand within Hinduism, warns against a reductive interpretation of what she sees as a diverse complex of systems united by 'the conviction that the ultimate goal of life is to break free of the fetters of mundane existence'. Siva's manipulation of Hindu scriptural tenets to justify his actions is to be read as a self-deceptive and self-defeating activity. *WLWE* features an interview with Sashi Deshpande by Romita Choudhury (34.ii.15–26) which offers some useful insights into her themes and techniques. Nilufer E. Bharucha's ' "When Old Tracks are Lost"': Rohinton Mistry's Fiction as Diasporic Discourse' (*JCL* 30.ii.57–64) gives a clear and concise sociohistorical contextualization of the Parsi community detailed in Mistry's work, and a brief analysis of the themes of some of his short stories and his first novel. Bharucha suggests that the marginal status of Parsis inspires a discourse which 'challenges and resists the totalization of the dominant culture within India itself'. In 'Gita Mehta's *A River Sutra*: An Analysis' (*LCrit* 30.iii.27–56), E. Galle offers an extensive commentary on a novel that interweaves a multitude of 'Indian beliefs, doctrines and preoccupations', including, of course, Hinduism, but also drawing on elements of Islam and animism, for example, to suggest 'a reinterpretation of Indian traditions'.

The value of the comparative method, particularly in relation to the relatively neglected area of Indian writing in translation, is apparent in Anand Patil's 'Colonial and Post/Neo-colonial Discourse in Two Goan Novels: A Fanonian Study' (*ArielE* 26.iv.87–112). Analysing Francisco Louis Gomes's nineteenth-century Portuguese language novel, *Os Brahamanes*, and Lambert Mascarenhas's *Sorrowing Lies My Land*, written in English and published in this year, in relation to Frantz Fanon's three phase theory of literary development, Patil convincingly demonstrates how the earlier work suffers from its confinement within a Eurocentric discourse, whilst the later novel 'exemplifies Fanon's phase of violence and resistance'. Finally, the work of the Bengali writer Mahasweta Devi has for some time been championed by Gayatri Chakravorty Spivak. In *Imaginary Maps: Three Stories by Mahasweta Devi*, Spivak offers her own translation of fiction characteristically concerned with the contemporary life of the indigenous tribes of India. The volume also includes a transcript of a conversation with the author and a preface and afterword by the translator.

6. New Zealand and the South Pacific

1. New Zealand

(a) General Studies
John Thomson's introduction to his New Zealand 1994 bibliography (*JCL* 30.iii.109–31) provides a personal evaluation of literary production during that year. Among the well-established writers' publications, he chooses Karl Stead's *The Singing Whakapapa* which he sees as an effort to placate the New Zealand public after the ostentatious Eurocentric broils in which this author has recently been involved. Maurice Gee's *Crime Story* is, for Thomson, 'unassumingly accomplished' while Witi Ihimaera's best-seller *Bulibasha* is

very entertaining but perhaps lacks depth. Thomson feels that there is a new willingness to publish the novella form, but judges *Fooling* by Marilyn Duckworth, *Pomare* by Elizabeth Knox and *State Ward* by Alan Duff proficient though not inspiring. Although it was feared that less independence in the publishing world would lead to fewer poetry collections, Thomson notes an impressive list for 1994. He selects three major books for mention: Kevin Ireland's *Skinning a Fish*, Lauris Edmond's *Scenes from a Small City* and Cilla McQueen's *Crik'ey*. The comparatively small output of established poets has left space for newcomers of varied inspirations such as Michele Leggott, Bernadette Hall, Lynda Earle and Chris Orman. Contradicting the general belief that women poets tended to be silenced by male editors in the 1930s and 1940s, Thomson indicates that Eileen Duggan was perhaps the country's most popular poet between 1920 and 1950; the re-publication of *Selected Poems* from her work and the poems of Mary Stanley in *Starveling Year* is proof that these women's writing has outrun such male ostracism. In the world of the theatre, Thomson finds the greatest vitality and growth in those plays that are by and about Maori, by and about women and those that deal with historical and documentary material. Special mention is made of Hone Kouka's *Tangata Toa* (*The Warrior People*) which is a transposed version of Ibsen's *The Vikings at Helgeland*. The violent clashes that occur are 'successfully channelled through a variety of ceremonial occasions, formal speeches and declaimed poetry' some of which is in Maori (translations provided in the text).

Landfall 188 is devoted to the theme 'Auto/Biographies' and includes an illuminating account by Lauris Edmond of the scenes behind the production of an autobiography and the problems that arise when the actors in the author's life are still alive. In 'Only Connect: The Making of an Autobiography' (*Landfall* 188.247–54) Edmond underlines the initial fears, the fascination with her journey of discovery of her own identity and the process of placing her development within the wider context of the 1970s and 1980s feminist movement. She gives a vibrant account of the rules by which she felt she had to abide, and the technical tricks she elaborated in order to integrate her subsequent reactions to particular events in her life into her narration. Finally, she concludes that the techniques of writing an autobiography run more closely parallel with those of a novelist than she had ever suspected before undertaking the task. As a consequence, the 'subject' of her writing gradually became a distanced 'her' rather than a personal 'me'.

In his introduction to *Opening the Book: New Essays on New Zealand Writing* (9–31) Mark Williams traces the evolution of New Zealand literature and culture. He maintains that women and Maori continue to struggle against male and Pakeha bias but that their contribution to New Zealand literature is now well established. He comments on the waning interest in nationalism and realism in literature, on the taste for theory among critics and on the necessity for 'an acceptance of ambivalence, a cultivation of the art of seeing merit in oppositions in order to make workable and liveable syntheses'. But here Williams foresees two parallel obstacles in current cultural circles: in an attempt to avoid provincialism critics may embrace cosmopolitan literary and critical discourse, thereby overlooking that which distinguishes New Zealand from the rest of the world; while those who concentrate solely on local production may fail to notice the wider context in which much of the local literary output must be situated.

Margaret Mahy's 'A Fantastic Tale' (ed. Williams and Leggott, *Opening the Book*) is a fascinating personal response to the presence of magic realism in New Zealand fiction. She believes that fantasy leads the reader away from everyday reality while magic realism returns them to it by illustrating the deformations of the outward perception of life. Margaret Mahy, as New Zealand's best-known writer of fiction for children, discusses this phenomenon in the context of Borges and Tolkien, illustrating her argument from the works of Patricia Grace, Fiona Farrell and Elizabeth Knox. She concludes that 'Magic realism can, through its inventions and exaggerations, allow the reader to make connections with the visionary astonishments of everyday life'.

In her very fine analysis ' "History" in the New Zealand Novel and Film Today' (ed. Williams and Leggott, *Opening the Book*) Anne Maxwell, who takes *The Piano* and Ian Wedde's *Symmes Hole* as evidence, finds that the most compelling rewritings of New Zealand history are currently to be found in film and in fiction, rather than in history or anthropology. She bases her demonstration on the concepts fashioned by Jameson, De Certeau and Foucault. Maxwell reasons that Wedde's version aims to be subversive by illustrating the colonial bias of many historical accounts while Campion's film highlights the intolerance that New Zealand society displays in face of individuals who 'dare to be different'. Yet this critic believes that the public will continue to prefer historical accounts as theorized by De Certeau, with which they can associate their personal experience.

The absence of note references in 'Some Maori Versions of Pastoral' (in Bennett and Haskell, eds, *Myths, Heroes and Anti-Heroes*) is to be deplored, and the Eurocentric analysis of what Ken Arvidson's article names the 'pastoral' in Maori literature is redolent of colonial attitudes. By reducing Maori writing to romance, fable and tradition, Arvidson fails to accept the Other as an equal. When he accuses the Maori of exclusion because Pakehas figure rarely in their writings one is tempted to reply 'why should they?'.

New Zealand Literature Today (ed. R. K. Dhawan and Walter Tonetto) is a collection of introductory essays, in many cases simplistic, that are long outdated before being published in this edition. This is particularly true of the essays on Janet Frame, Katherine Mansfield and Frank Sargeson. Indeed, even the more profound analyses are re-publications of work produced many years ago whose bibliographical references should have been acknowledged by the present editors.

How to be Nowhere is a selection of Ian Wedde's various articles on literature and art that have been published over the years. These illustrate how Wedde looks at a work of art or reads a book, rather than provide information about the work of art itself. Reading Sargeson, Wedde recognizes the 'moral' though unmoralistic quality of his writing achievement, noting the 'alertness' of being able to convey experience in an apparently unordered sequence. The critical articles also cover writers such as Maurice Duggan and Russell Haley. This is an eclectic collection of articles which has little coherence in itself except as an insight into the way Wedde works – a series of oblique approaches and repetitions which the reader may appreciate as a performance in itself without actually perceiving any logical end to the argumentation.

When Lynne Alice was asked to edit *Beginning with Ourselves: Responses to Religion in Aotearoa*, she became aware of a number of fundamental questions to which answers were necessary. Her article ' "Unlearning Our Privilege As Our Loss": Postcolonial Writing and Textual Production' (*WSJ* 9.i.26–46) is a very interesting exploration into postcolonial writing and criticism in which this critic attempts to clarify her cultural politics. Faced with the indigenous English of Maori oral accounts, Alice questions the Eurocentric concept of 'meaning' since she recognizes that the manner of expression defies accepted literary pacts while engaging both reader and writer in a common effort of piecing together a range of possible meanings. Alice continues her questioning by challenging the term 'postcolonial' itself, believing it reflects the hegemony of the imperialists. Less convincingly, she draws parallels between this 'postcolonial' situation and some of the problems that feminists are endeavouring to combat. She is, however, quite right to raise the problem of publishing ethnic voices and respecting their individual 'varying narrative forms' and 'hybridised English'. Neither condescension nor appropriation by undue editing are solutions; for this critic, an acknowledgement of 'the potential richness of contributions from the multiplicity of differently located voices' is the only acceptable approach for the would-be editor.

In his article 'Who is the Colonist? Writing in New Zealand and the South Pacific' (*WLT* 68.iii.488–92), Murray S. Martin gives a detailed historical analysis of the various patterns of colonization in the South Pacific, claiming that the Polynesians have always been adaptable and that this perhaps reflects 'the nature of oral as opposed to written traditions'. At each modification of their history they seem to have taken stock of the situation to envisage how to incorporate the new tradition into their own. This has not always occurred without friction but Martin sees, in the New Zealand context, an example of two or more populations developing in parallel and interacting in order to express their own New Zealandness. Signs include the Pakeha's distancing himself from the mother country, the re-creation of myths, the re-writing of history, the adaptation of European forms to Maori needs and the consolidation of the position of women writers. For Martin, Pacific writing is the coalescing of traditions to provide the reader with new and enriching insights.

(b) Fiction
In 'Pakeha, Maori, and Alan: The Political and Literary Exclusion of Alan Duff' (*SPAN* 40.72–80), Danielle Brown traces the modification of the attitudes of both Maori and Pakeha critics to the writing of Alan Duff. Although both groups hailed it favourably initially, recognizing its political correctness from the Maori point of view or its original power by literary criteria, Brown currently discerns a certain reserve from both communities that may derive from the binary racial politics of New Zealand. Brown argues that it is perhaps precisely this ambivalence that requires questioning since it excludes those who have integrated both cultures into a form of hybridity which satisfies neither community.

In an interview entitled 'The Book, the Film, the Interview' (*Meanjin* 54.i.6–13), Christina Thompson gives Alan Duff enough 'space' for the reader to appreciate his personality. Duff describes the dual nature of his upbringing – his father's scientific interests and his mother's involvement with the Maori community and its inherent strife and violence. Duff claims to have instigated a certain maturing process within Maori circles and feels that they should take more responsibility for their own advancement, believing that the obstacles that prevent Maori from gaining education stem more from socio-economic conditions than from ethnic origins. Duff is in the process of setting up a film company which will privilege the employment of Maoris willing to live up to Duff's ideals of a work ethic. After the arguments over the film rights of 'Once Were Warriors' he fully intends to come out even with this next film.

Suzette Henke examines the way in which Keri Hulme's writing has been influenced by other literary works in 'Keri Hulme's *the bone people* and *Te Kaihau*: Postmodern Heteroglossia and Pre-textual Play' (ed. Dhawan and Tonetto, *New Zealand Literature Today*). Henke believes that Hulme's work is closer to the epics of Shakespeare, Dante, Rabelais or Joyce than to the sparse writing of Hemingway or Mailer with whom she has been compared. She sees the use of the self-reflexive double spiral narrative structure described by Webby as a metaphor for a future multicultural heritage in which the best elements of Maori, Pakeha and European traditions are combined.

In 'Constructing the Female Hero: Keri Hulme's *the bone people*' (ed. Bruce Bennett and Dennis Haskell, *Myths, Heroes and Anti-Heroes*), Suzette Henke claims that this author has at last evacuated the 'gender-laden, gender-limited expectation in an attempt to define a female protagonist who offers [...] a serious model of contemporary heroism'. For Henke, Kerewin is proud, dauntless and aloof; at the end of this novel she has prevailed and through the medium of a mysterious Maori oral history she has redefined her place and status within a male-dominated white world.

For Anna Smith who explores the different 'love' relationships in *the bone people* in 'Keri Hulme and "Love's Wounded Beings" ' (ed. Williams and Leggott, *Opening the Book*) this novel 'locates the sublime in the renaissance of Maori culture'. This is symbolized by the spiral-shaped marae where former antagonistic situations are resolved; yet she states that the 'ideal love object' is unrepresentable. For this critic, *the bone people* 'bears witness to the speech of wounded beings longing for love who discover a measure of contentment in the prospect of a collective, if evanescent, future'.

Antoinette Holm in ' " ... of indeterminate sex": Escaping Androgeny in Keri Hulme's *the bone people*' (*NLitsR* 30.83–96) examines the discussion on gender codes, transvestites and androgyny that both the author and the protagonist of *the bone people* has provoked in literary circles. Holm posits that the reactions stem from a 'cross-dressing' from female to male in three sectors: physical or bodily cross-dressing, the transvestism of social space and ethnic and racial transvestism. Holm also argues that the triangular existence of Kerewin, Joe and Simon challenges the male/female or Maori/Pakeha divide and echoes the tripartite existence of Te Kore, Te Po and Te Aomarama that govern Maori culture. She concludes: 'Of primary importance here is the way in which a reading in terms of androgeny obscures transgression and depoliticises the novel. By offering a reading of Kerewin as a crossdresser I have, I hope, eluded the containment of sexual, racial and spatial dualisms and realised the transgressive transvestite space.'

Paul Sharrad's 'A Rhetoric of Sentiment: Thoughts on Maori Writing with Reference to the Short Stories of Witi Ihimaera' (ed. Dhawan and Tonetto, *New Zealand Literature Today*) is a republication of work produced some years ago. Sharrad argues that the minority writer's dilemma is to express the sentiment of otherness with regard to the colonizer and yet utilize the literary tools of the same colonizer in order to publicize his creation.

Jane McRae's 'Patricia Grace and Complete Communication' (ed. Williams and Leggott, *Opening the Book*) was initally published in *Australian and New Zealand Studies in Canada* 10 in December 1993 (*YWES* 74.692–3).

Patrick L. West's 'The Lacanian Real and Janet Frame's *Living in the Maniototo*' (ed. Dhawan and Tonetto, *New Zealand Literature Today*) draws on the work of Kristeva in his discussion of the Real. For West, *Living on the Maniototo* effectively attempts to ' "write the Real" in the precise terms of New Zealand's post-colonial placement'. Alison Lambert's 'The Memory Flower, the Gravity Star, and the Real World: Janet Frame's *The Carpathians*' (ed. Dhawan and Tonetto, *New Zealand Literature Today*) argues that Frame's principal preoccupation in this novel is with the marginalized. The critic, however, discerns an underlying authorial ideology which is critical of the current social materialistic values of money and progress and advocates other aims that are based less on material advancement and more on the priceless treasure of memory which can only be expressed through language. In 'Postmodernist Strategies in Janet Frame's *Scented Gardens for the Blind*' (ed. Dhawan and Tonetto, *New Zealand Literature Today*), Valerie Sutherland posits that Frame's thesis that 'a definable transcendental truth exists which is not recoverable by humanity through normative behaviours or language' puts into doubt such a linguistic truth. She does, however, believe that this novel through its use of form and its content reaffirms the fundamental role of language in the human consciousness and in so doing can be considered as a postmodernist novel even though it predates postmodernist critical theory.

Susan Ash's 'Scandalously In-Different? Janet Frame, Postmodernism and Gender' (ed. Williams and Leggott, *Opening the Book*) attempts to answer the question: does Janet Frame engage with the postmodernist challenge to liberal humanism's assumption about truth, order and the unified subject, and how does gender figure in these challenges?

In his thematic article, 'Fantasy and Flight in the Novels of Maurice Gee (ed. Dhawan and Tonetto, *New Zealand Literature Today*) Som Prakash examines the recurrent appearance of the character of the literary recluse in Gee's novels. This critic sees this as a reluctance to accept reality and the present which consequently renders the acceptation of self impossible.

Chris Price's 'The Childish Empire and the Empire of Children: Colonial and Alternative Dominions in Robin Hyde's *Check to Your King* and *Wednesday's Children*' (ed. Williams and Leggott, *Opening the Book*) examines the way in which colonialism is depicted in these two works. Rejecting the individualism and materialism of the empire-builders, Hyde was always interested in those who were perforce isolated outside the mainstream of history. Women and children were often her subjects of choice, together with those at ease in natural surroundings. Thus, according to Price, 'Hyde foreshadowed the sometimes uneasy alliances between the feminists, environmental and indigenous rights movements that emerged during the 1960s and 1970s'.

Katherine Mansfield: In from the Margin (ed. Roger Robinson) contains 12 diverse essays selected from a vast number of contributions to two centennial conferences: 'Life, Text and Context' held at the Newberry Library in Chicago and 'The Katherine Mansfield Centennial Conference' at Victoria University,

Wellington in 1988. Robinson's general introduction brings the different articles together to form a well-balanced overview. Vincent O'Sullivan in 'Finding the Pattern, Solving the Problem: Katherine Mansfield the New Zealand European' examines the effects of the First World War on this writer's life and her complex relationships between the old and new worlds. Cherry Hankin in 'Katherine Mansfield and the Cult of Childhood' and Ruth Parkin-Gounelas in 'Katherine Mansfield Reading Other Women: The Personality of the Text' deal with Mansfield's treatment of the child and her relations with other women. In 'Katherine Mansfield and the Honourable Dorothy Brett: A Correspondence of Artists' Gardner McFall gives an account of her extensive manuscript research and evaluates the advantages of creative friendship between artists. The examination of Mansfield's moments of 'epiphany' in the light of her statements about painting, cinema and music is the subject of Sarah Sandley who, in her article 'The Middle of the Note: Katherine Mansfield's "Glimpses" ', also analyses Mansfield's responsiveness to the developments in Modernism. Sandley goes on to note the innovative technique this writer employed to translate such theories into a form of literature which was to last over the century. W. H. New's 'Reading "The Escape" ', Perry Meisel's 'What the Reader Knows; or, The French One' and Alex Calder's 'My Katherine Mansfield' are close texual studies of individual stories – 'Je ne parle pas français', 'Bliss', and 'A Married Man's Story' – that remain valid today. 'The Escape', which has been neglected, is given a more important role, placing it at the centre of Modernist fictional texts. The three biographical contributions, 'The French Connection: Francis Carco' by Christiane Mortelier, 'The French Connection: Bandol' by Jacqueline Bardolph and Gillian Boddy's ' "Finding the Treasure", Coming Home: Katherine Mansfield in 1921–1922' offer other views on this author who has been described as 'a New Zealand magazine writer wandering sick around Europe'. Viewing Mansfield's life from France, Mortelier translates the correspondence with Carco providing a new context for the study of 'An Indiscreet Journey' and 'Je ne parle pas français'. Bardolph shows how experiences at Bandol were transformed into essential elements of the story 'Sun and Moon'. Boddy studies the 'pattern' that may be perceived in Mansfield's last search for an artistic and emotional home for the New Zealand European. Finally, James Moore's 'Katherine Mansfield and Gurdjieff's Sacred Dance' traces this writer's last weeks in Fontainebleau, highlighting the themes of womanhood, relationship to European culture, her search for home and spirituality. Moore postulates that her choice to end her life in a fringe sect constitutes her last foray 'into the margin'.

In ' "Bliss" and Why Ignorance Won't Do: The Use of Criticism and Theory in Current Reading Practices' (ed. Williams and Leggott, *Opening the Book*), Mary Paul provides three parallel readings of 'Bliss': the first sees the text as the tale of a hysteric, the second is inspired by feminism while the third sets out to be modernist and historicist. This critic subsequently argues that different readings correspond to various modes and fashions which correspond to the time of reading.

Lydia Wevers explores exhaustively the importance of the sense of place in Katherine Mansfield's works as seen through her fiction and journals in ' "The Sod Under My Feet": Katherine Mansfield' (ed. Williams and Leggott, *Opening the Book*). The fact that the New Zealand landscapes in this author's stories are re-imagined, since she was writing in Europe, helps to adapt the surroundings more closely to the concerns which agitated her – the landscapes are 'of and for the imagination, the imagined nation turning loss into the language of metaphor, the metaphoricity of a signifying space whose quality of transience [. . .] speaks with historical, cultural and personal resonance'. Thus the social order in many of her New Zealand stories appears patriarchal, and although the physical environment is ever present, the Maori remain invisible beyond the confines of reality and fiction. Mansfield's New Zealand is distinctly conservative, colonial and somewhat materialistic, yet it never appears simplistic, for her art lies in the subtle variations and nuances of the individual. By regularly affirming their presence and values, the story-characters confirm the very existence of their adopted country, establish Eurocentric ways and beliefs and, in so doing, build the basis of a new nation in the antipodes.

Kai Jensen's 'Frank at Last' (ed. Williams and Leggott, *Opening the Book*) celebrates the fact that Frank Sargeson can now be acknowledged as a homosexual writer whose writings were underpinned by sexual references that critics to date had carefully ignored. Jensen believes that a complete re-reading of this famous author is required so as to put the true nature of his work into perspective. He concludes that Sargeson's repressed sexuality of the 1930s and 1940s lent tension to his narrations which later and more explicit works lacked.

To date there has been no significant review of Shadbolt's works and yet this writer has had a noteworthy literary production. *Ending the Silences: Critical Essays on the Works of Maurice Shadbolt*, competently edited by Ralph J. Crane, is therefore a very welcome contribution to literary criticism. Lawrence Jones, in a very well informed and thoroughly researched article, 'Out of the Rut and into the Swamp: The Paradoxical Progress of Maurice Shadbolt' provides an overview of Shadbolt's career as a novelist. In the first phase (1955–64), this writer attempted to move New Zealand fiction 'out of the rut' of the 1930s into which he thought Sargeson had put it. Jones places the young writer clearly in the context of the writers' quarrels in New Zealand at the time. Shadbolt seems to have borne the brunt of the barbs of the Auckland writers. The second stage from 1965 to 1977, according to Jones, culminates in *Strangers and Journeys* and is completed by *A Touch of Clay* and *Danger Zone*. During this period, the author's interest in present issues comes into conflict with his obvious liking for the past history of the country. In what Jones calls his third phase, this 'history' is given full importance. In her pertinent article 'Realist or Romantic: The Theme of Entrapment in Maurice Shadbolt's Short Stories', Cherry Hankin deals with the concern Shadbolt displayed in his writing for the young men and women struggling to locate themselves in the post-war years. This was not very well received by the 'Landfall coterie', who, according to Hankin, still believed that Frank Sargeson was the only possible model. Because his stories are never purely romantic, this critic believes that the inextricable intertwining of romanticism and realism can make their resolution problematic. Janet Wilson's 'Mythological Selves: Women in Shadbolt's Early Works' focuses on the marginalized women who inhabit the predominantly male world of his short fiction and early novels. The stereotyping of these women breaks down, Wilson claims, when Shadbolt describes women from such proximity that they appear elusive and ambiguous. McEldowney, 'Pushing it: *A Touch of Clay* and *Danger Zone*', highlights the unevenness of Shadbolt's early work but argues that it contains essential elements that were to be developed in later works where his strong points are a vigorous story-line and a larger sense of moral ambiguity. For Alan Riach, 'The Gothic Search: Maurice Shadbolt and *The Lovelock Version*' , *The Lovelock Version* represents the best of this writer's fiction for it presents a complex weave of stories and characters. This critic compares the novel with Sargeson's 'The Making of a New Zealander': the book is a quest during which Shadbolt sets out to populate historical New Zealand with characters and stories, fantastic visions and comedy. Ralph J. Crane's examination of Shadbolt's use of mediocre heroes within the context of his historical trilogy to direct the reader's gaze and encourage it to coincide with his own in 'Windows onto History: "Mediocre Heroes" in Maurice Shadbolt's New Zealand Wars Trilogy' illustrates how such characters act as vehicles in which many of the author's sensibilities can be conveyed within the novel. In a complementary discussion, Ken Arvidson focuses on 'The Waikato Chapters of *Season of the Jew*: Some Annotations'. In his comparison between fictional and real facts, Arvidson shows Shadbolt's meticulous attention to historicity.

(c) Poetry
Lawrence Bourke's 'New Zealand Poetry: What's New, What's Contemporary?' (ed. Dhawan and Tonetto, *New Zealand Literature Today*) is a discussion about the terms 'new' and 'contemporary' with reference to poetry collections as cultural markers. Bourke highlights the necessary selection and hierarchization in any such collection and questions whether 'contemporary' necessarily implies the total exclusion of previous poetry since the work discussed inevitably depends on previous productions. Once again, one may regret that the origin of the article is not supplied in this collection of essays, particularly as it refers to a 'forth-coming 1992 edition'! Alan Riach's 'New Zealand Poetry from "Then" till "Now": "Wordsworth's Last Stand!" ' (ed. Dhawan and Tonetto, *New Zealand Literature Today*) is a chronological overview of white New Zealand poetry from the mid-nineteenth century to the present day and illustrates how the poetry is 'marginal to or dependent on' mainstream English traditions, particularly with regard to Modernism and Romanticism.

This year's *Journal of New Zealand Literature* (*JNZL* 13) is wholly devoted to recording the highlights of the 'James Baxter: Poet and Prophet' conference that took place in Dunedin in August last year. The contributions varied between personal and anecdotal encounters with the poet and academic analyses of his philosophical attitudes to life as illustrated through the autobiographical material and his fictional and poetic corpus. In their diversity the articles throw new light on this mythical figure of New Zealand letters.

Bill Manhire's keynote address, 'Stranger at the Ranchslider' (*JNZL* 13.11–22) informally explores the ways in which Baxter created his own existential myth and endeavours to imagine the innumerable contradictory reactions that Baxter himself would have had about such a gathering as the present conference.

In the initial biographical section, Wilhelmina J. Drummund attempts to define the principal traits of this writer through the observations of his contemporaries in 'Insights into James K. Baxter's Personality and the New

Zealand Environment: 1950s to 1970s' (*JNZL* 13.23–38), while Tara Hawes in '"A Tribesman Cut off from his Tribe": Baxter and the Family' (*JNZL* 13.39–46) underscores the links that Baxter made between his life and writings and the role of the poet in New Zealand society at the different stages of his existence. Janet Wilson's approach in 'Archie, Millicent and James: The Baxter Autobiographies' (*JNZL* 13.47–64) investigates the family influences that bore on the man and the poet as revealed through the various autobiographies and memoirs of the Baxter family. Having defined autobiography as a means of constructing a subject's subjectivity, Wilson identifies in particular the lack of communication between mother and son and his empathy with his father which inexorably led to an unresolved Oedipal complex. She suggests that further studies into 'the way that family discourses intersect to contribute to his fictional and non-fictional self representations as man and poet' could throw interesting light on the complex personality of Baxter.

The literary section of the volume begins with Lawrence Jones's 'The Mythology of Place: James K. Baxter's Otago Worlds' (*JNZL* 13.65–96). This article graphically identifies the three Otago worlds that pervade the poet's work. They act as 'a mythic backdrop against which his (Baxter's) mythologized life, the central subject of his poetry, is acted out'. In 'One Baxter: A Study of James K. Baxter's Ballads' (*JNZL* 13.103–8), Sebastien Brook argues that the two aspects of the poet's character are able to co-exist in the ballads since this poetic form is traditionally rooted in the day-to-day lives of common people where the sacred and the profane combine to express the opinions of 'a populist poet'. Using the theories of Jung which define the relationship of 'self' and 'Self', Keith Russell examines the modification of selfhood and its relation to death in 'Kenosis In Baxter's "Pig Island Letters"' (*JNZL* 13.109–20).

Danielle Brown's 'James K. Baxter: The Identification of the "Poet" and the Authority of the "Prophet" (*JNZL* 13.133–42) is a fascinating contribution even if the parallel references to Maning's *Old New Zealand: A Tale of the Good Old Times by a Pakeha Maori* are rather strained, thereby upsetting the unity of the article. Brown explores Baxter's dual identification with the spiritual values of Christianity and the Maori community through the figure of the 'prophet'; she observes that this poet assumed the role of 'prophet' for himself as the 'poet', thus upholding the very power structures that he set out to undermine. This critic argues that while Baxter was a forerunner in drawing Pakeha and Maori cultures together, his speaking as 'prophet' on behalf of the Maori endowed him with a privileged position. Postcolonial theory has since overridden Baxter's stance so in spite of losing his status of 'prophet' his poetry still remains a challenge for current critics. William Broughton also believes that Baxter's preoccupations in the 1960s remain very contemporary. '"Troubled by his own Absurdity?" An Examination of Some of the Last Sonnets of Baxter' (*JNZL* 13.143–56) highlights the ongoing tension between celebration and melancholy and analyses how the seemingly light-hearted anecdotal material is used to express in-depth religious statements. Broughton concludes that the poet found it difficult to reconcile his own faith and the human condition of inevitable mortality. In his desire for self-abnegation Baxter was confronted by language. As a poet he could create poems but these contradicted the virtue of 'silence' as the supreme form of self-abnegation. The dilemma of 'his own absurdity' proved to be the inspirational font for Baxter's devotional poetry.

After a brief overview of the theories of Freud and more importantly Jung, Kai Jensen examines the symbolic in Baxter's poetry. In his article 'The Drunkard and the Hag: James K. Baxter's Use of Jung' (*JNZL* 13.211–34) he claims that Baxter was immersed in the ideas of Jung from the mid-1940s onward and that these theories 'have left their mark everywhere on the poems and plays'.

The following section of this volume deals with the interrelationship that other intellectuals have enjoyed with James Baxter both before and after his death. Peter Simpson in his highly interesting article 'Candles in a Dark Room: James K. Baxter and Colin McCahon' (*JNZL* 13.157–88) describes the striking parallels and interaction in the work of these two artists. Both incorporated (self) mythologizing fictions into their creations; both alluded to light and dark – McCahon in his 'A Candle in a Dark Room' and Baxter in his depiction of the poet as a 'light-giving force' – both were fascinated by religious imagery and texts and their contrast with the secular; and finally, both became influenced by international preoccupations as they matured and yet continued to 'fuse Maori and Christian elements' in their work. Riemke Ensing extends these lines of thought by illustrating Baxter's approach to life through a selection of painters' works in 'Images of Baxter (Poet and Prophet): The Resurrection' (*JNZL* 13.189–210). This critic posits that these painters have been so influenced by Baxter that their pictural creations continue to 'resurrect' and 'incarnate' the poet visually today.

Elizabeth Isichei's 'James K. Baxter: Religious Sensibility and a Changing Church' (*JNZL* 13.235–56), Ricard Matthews's 'James K. Baxter and Kopua' (*JNZL* 13.257–66) and Russell Phillips's 'James K. Baxter: A Dialogue with his Later Theological and Philosophical Thought in the Context of Aotearoa/ New Zealand' (*JNZL* 13.267–84) each deal with Baxter's contradictions and philosophical attitudes to and within the Roman Catholic Church.

This memorable volume of *JNZL* concludes with William Broughton's introduction to a witness account of Baxter's death, followed by 'Vonney Allan's Account of James K. Baxter's Death' (*JNZL* 13.285–90).

Besides providing an interesting viewpoint on much of Baxter's life and works, Alan Riach's 'James K. Baxter and the Dialect of the Tribe' (ed. Williams and Leggott, *Opening the Book*) examines the poet's fondness for his 'tribal' roots – his Scottish ancestors, the Roman Catholic religion and the Maori. This article was initially published in *NLitsR* 20 in 1990.

'Sacrifice and Signification in the Poetry of Allen Curnow' (ed. Williams and Leggott, *Opening the Book*) was first published in *Interstices* 2 in 1992. For Alex Calder, 'the poet who tries to write the unwriteable [never reaches] the pure referent but either a sacrifice made in its place or [...] the thing itself figured as an abject referent [...]. This is the hieroglyph of a kind of proto-writing that promises to join a thing and its name much as, in the pre-Oedipal space of abjection, mother and child are inextricably fused and joined.'

In a detailed analysis of Curnow's corpus, Stuart Murray in 'Writing an Island's Story: The 1930s Poetry of Allen Curnow' (*JCL* 30.ii.25–43) percep-tively explores both the role played by this writer in the definition of nationhood in the emerging literature of the 1930s, and the poetical sources which inspired his own poetry. Murray discerns contradictions between Cur-now's critical prescriptions on what the literary canon should be and the innate scepticism of his early poetry, between a fidelity to local phenomena

and the linguistic craft of the poet. Comparing Curnow with other poets such
as MacDiarmid, Yeats, Pound or Olsen, who also addressed nationalism(s),
this critic appreciates his 'constant refusal to allow the stereotypes of convention to simplify the complexities of New Zealand's spatial and temporal
location'. He recognizes the vitality of the editor who, while seeking to
privilege a 'New Zealand' voice, never allowed himself to be influenced by the
'location' of the material rather than its intrinsic excellence.

John Newton regrets that Bill Manhire continues to be under-read in 'The
Old Man's Example: Manhire in the Seventies' (ed. Williams and Leggott,
Opening the Book). He then presents a detailed analysis of *The Elaboration*
(1972), *How to Take off Your Clothes at the Picnic* (1977) and *Good Looks*
(1982) with the aim of encouraging reluctant readers to take the plunge.

Alan Brunton gives a very personal impression of recent poetry in New
Zealand in 'Holding the Line: Contested Contexts in Recent Verse' (ed.
Williams and Leggott, *Opening the Book*). For a critique of Michele Leggott's
'Opening the Archive: Robin Hyde, Eileen Duggan and the Persistence of
Record' (ed. Williams and Leggott, *Opening the Book*) which first appeared in
Hecate 20.ii in 1994 see *YWES* 75.760.

(d) Drama and Theatre

Joanne Thompkins's interesting survey of recent New Zealand drama, 'Re-
Playing and Dis-Playing the Nation: New Zealand Drama' (Williams and
Leggott, *Opening the Book*, 294–306), emphasizes the theatre's productive
'dis-association from the traditional definition of nationhood proffered by
politicians'. In this context, where the Maori advocate a return to the roots,
their theatre production as represented by Riwia Brown's *Roimata* and Hone
Kouka's *Mauri Tu* is surprising in its defence of co-habitation between Maori
and Pakeha. The appropriation or disappropriation of land immediately
becomes a major issue in this context. The Waitangi Land Tribunal highlighted the various versions that the history of a struggle can inspire;
Tompkins cites Rore Hapipi's *Death of the Land*, in which several Maori are
involved in the sale of land, and two re-writings of history: *ANZAC* by John
Broughton and *Once on Chunuk Bair* by Maurice Shadbolt. Feminism has
also proved very popular: Renée's plays encourage women to independence
and everyone to egalitarian attitudes. Finally, Tompkins addresses the phenomena of silence and language in the theatre which vary from mime and
dance to the music-hall tradition, from community events to the monologues
of social outcasts. Tompkins believes that 'theatre acts as a significant and
signifying location for [...] cultural debates'.

Arguments based on Mikhail Bakhtin's *Rabelais and His World* inform
Farrell Cleary's article 'Baxter's Plays: The Search for Life before Death'
(*JNZL* 13.121–32) which explores the two aspects of death that troubled
Baxter: namely, the physical death of the body and the death of the soul which
could undermine a man's life before his end.

John Davidson compares and contrasts J. K. Baxter's last play, *The
Temptations of Oedipus*, with Sophocles' *Oedipus at Colonus* on which it was
modelled, in 'James K. Baxter at Colonus' (*AUMLA* 83.43–54). Both plays were
the artists' final works. Baxter's fascination with the theme of 'incest' laid him
open to accusations of glossing over its more serious implications. According to
this critic, this play shows Baxter as an idealist whose only final victory in life was

his own death. Davidson rather tenuously concludes by quoting McNaughton when he states that while Baxter's 'dramatic impulses were basically sound, his sense of theatre was tentative and underdeveloped' in this play.

Interesting new light is thrown on the creation of a writer generally known only for his fiction by Philip Mann's contribution, 'Maurice Shadbolt The Dramatist: On the Dramaturgy of *Once on Chunuk Bair*' (ed. Crane, *Ending the Silences*). For Mann this play is a postcolonial work which confronts the moment when New Zealand came of age and realized its own identity as distinct from that of the imperial power.

Kevin Ireland's intimate contribution, 'Saying Boo' (ed. Crane, *Ending the Silences*), on *One of Ben's*, focuses on the intentions behind the book. Ireland has long been a close friend of Maurice Shadbolt's. *One of Ben's* is described as a wonderfully stimulating dramatic invention, the work of a self-conscious magician, full of ironical stunts, clever illusions and tricks and is essentially a personal testimony.

Brigid Shadbolt's most welcome select primary and secondary bibliography 'The Fiction of Maurice Shadbolt: A Selected Checklist, 1956–1994' (ed. Crane, *Ending the Silences*) shows that there has been a persistent interest in his work in New Zealand and overseas.

2. The South Pacific

In 'Pacific Island Literature' (*Manoa* 5.i.47–49), Vilsoni Hereniko defines three groups of literary publication: the international in English, the local in English and the local in the mother tongue. Obviously these overlap, particularly in the case of bilingual writers such as Joseph Veramu (Fiji) and Kauraka Kauraka (Cook Islands). Hereniko deplores the difficulty of obtaining books in the region and the fact that much literary criticism in the area is Eurocentric. He makes a plea for a more postcolonial approach to South Pacific literatures.

Using the counter-discourse theories of Homi Bhabha, Abdul JanMohammed and Helen Tiffin in ' "Reluctant Flame": Some Examples of Counter-Discourse in Solomon Islands' Fiction' (*SPAN* 40.10–17), Regis Jo'se Stella examines the writing of John Sauana, Rexford Orotaloa and Anne Kengalu. Stella concludes that the use of indigenous languages in these texts together with the strategy of code-switching without explanation underline the burden that imperialism has imposed on colonized cultures; and advocates the necessity for a plurality of ideologies in the postcolonial world.

'An Interview with Albert Wendt: Following in her Footsteps' (*Manoa* 5.i.51–7) is an abridged text of an interview made for the TV series 'Spectrum Hawai'. Vilsoni Hereniko skilfully leads Wendt to explain the influence of oral tales on his work, emphasizing the individual nature of each story told and his personal satisfaction with a tale well-told. For Wendt, writing is a lonely occupation and a literary work must never be taken as an anthropological thesis. He has modified his attitude to individualistic aims and now pleads for the mutual respect and unity of individuals within the extended family. Wendt continues to work for the decolonization of the arts. He will continue to do so despite his fear that postcolonial independence may degenerate into corruption. For him, writing is political in that it wields immense power.

Briar Wood's account of his conversation with Konai Thaman, 'An Ongoing Attempt at Synthesis: An Interview with Konai Thaman' (*SPAN* 40.1–9) explores the breadth of her poetry between 1974 and 1993. This well-travelled Tongan poet absorbs the ambience of other countries but remains faithful to the traditional themes of her homeland. She emphasizes her special relationship with nature, the alienating aspects of her colonial education and the importance of orality in her poetry.

Vilsoni Hereniko talks to the playwright John Kneubuhl in 'An Interview with John A. Kneubuhl: Comic Theatre of Samoa' (*Manoa* 5.i.99–105). Here Kneubuhl emphasizes that his duty is to be theatrical through the artificial medium of a play. He explains his adherence to 'fale aitu' which in Samoa is the house of spirits used for the performance of comedic sketches. These were of value formerly as a social control and their educative function was and is enhanced by the use of humour. Kneubuhl adds: 'fale aitu is not an aesthetic experience but a psycho-social experience. It tends more towards politics than art.'

Books Reviewed

Ackland, Michael. *Henry Kendall: The Man and the Myths*. Miegunyah-MelbourneUP. pp. 351. A$49.95. ISBN 0 522 84650 5.

Adams, L. Emilie. *Understanding Jamaican Patois: An Introduction to Afro-Jamaican Grammar. With a Childhood Tale by Llewellyn 'Dude' Adams*. Kingston (1991) reprint. pp. 109. np. ISBN 625 976 035 9, 1885642 03 2.

Afzal-Khan, Fawzia. *Cultural Imperialism and the Indo-English Novel: Genre and Ideology in R. K. Narayan, Anita Desai, Kamala Markandaya, and Salman Rushdie*. PSUP (1993). pp. 194. hb £31.50, pb £15.50. ISBN 0 271 00912 8, 0 271 01013 4.

Algoo-Baksh, Stella. *Austin C. Clarke: A Biography*. Barbados, Jamaica, Trinidad: University of the West Indies Press ECW (1994). pp. 234. pb £18.95. ISBN 976 640 0091 (UWI), 1 55022 218 X.

Anderson, Debra. *Decolonizing the Text: Glissantian Readings in Caribbean and African-American Literatures*. Francophone Cultures and Literatures 1. Lang. pp. 118. $46.95. ISBN 0 8204 2521 4.

Ashcroft, Bill, Gareth Griffiths, and Helen Tiffin, eds. *The Post-Colonial Studies Reader*. Routledge. pp. 526. hb £40.00, pb £14.99. ISBN 0 415 09621 9, 0 415 09622 7.

Association for the Study of Australian Literature. *Proceedings of the Sixteenth Annual Conference, 1994*. pp. 213. ISBN 0 646 23668 7.

Atwood, Margaret. *Strange Things: The Malevolent North in Canadian Literature*. Clarendon. pp.134. £15. ISBN 0 19 811976 3.

Awodiya, Muyiwa P. *The Drama of Femi Osofisan: A Critical Perspective*. Kraft. hb Nigerian Naira 1000, pb 750. ISBN 978 2081 59 0, 978 2081 58 2.

Barnes, John, and Lois Hoffman, eds. *Bushman and Bookworm: Letters of Joseph Furphy*. OUP. pp. 295. A$44.95. ISBN 0 195 53799 8.

Bennett, Bruce, ed. *Dorothy Hewett: Selected Critical Essays*. Fremantle. pp. 294. pb A$19.95. ISBN 1 863 68113 2.

Bennett, Bruce, and Dennis Haskell, eds. *Myths, Heroes and Anti-Heroes: Essays on the Literature and Culture of the Asia Pacific Region*. CSAL (1992) pp. 217. A$19.95. ISBN 0 86422 221 1.

Bharucha, Nilufer E., and Vilas Sarang, eds. *Indian-English Fiction 1980–1990: An Assessment*. New World Literature Series Vol. 77. B. R. Publishing Corporation (1994). pp. 242. Rs.200. ISBN 81 7018 775 3.

Boehmer, Elleke. *Colonial and Postcolonial Literature*. OUP. pp. 304. pb £7.99. ISBN 0 19 289232 0.

Brask, Per, ed. *Contemporary Issues in Canadian Drama*. Blizzard Publ. pp. 249. £17.50. ISBN 0 921368 51 8.

Brown, Stewart, ed. *The Art of Kamau Brathwaite*. Seren Books. pp. 275. pb £9.95. ISBN 1 85411 092 6, 1 85411 127 2.

——, ed. *The Pressures of the Text: Orality, Texts and the Telling of Tales*. Birmingham University African Studies Series No. 4. Birmingham. pp. 145. pb £6. ISBN 0 7044 1557 7.

Caesar, Adrian. *Kenneth Slessor*. OUP. pp. 127. pb $18.95. ISBN 0 19 553421 2.

Cantalupo, Charles, ed. *Ngugi wa Thiong'o: Texts and Contexts*. AWP. $19.95. ISBN 0 86543 444 1.

——, ed. *The World of Ngugi wa Thiong'o*. AWP. hb $49.95, pb $16.95. ISBN 0 86543 458 1, 0 86543 459 X.

Carroll, Dennis. *Australian Contemporary Drama*. Currency (1985, rev. edn). pp. 436. pb A$35. ISBN 0 868 19366 6.

Césaire, Aime. *Notebook of a Return to my Native Land*. Trans. Mireille Rosello with Annie Pritchard. Bloodaxe. pp. 160. pb £8.95. ISBN 1 85224 184 5.

Clarke, Patricia, ed. *Tasma's Diaries, The Diaries of Jessie Couvreur with another by her young sister Edith Huybers*. Mulini. pp. 152. pb A$29.95. ISBN 0 949 91059 7.

Corkhill, Annette R. *The Immigrant Experience in Australian Literature*. Academia. pp. 184. pb A$25. ISBN 0 95696 687 7.

Cowasjee, Saros. *Studies in Indian and Anglo-Indian Fiction*. Indus-HC (1993). pp. 178. pb £14.99. ISBN 81 7223 072 9.

Crane, Ralph J., ed. *Ending the Silences: Critical Essays on the Works of Maurice Shadbolt*. HMB. pp. 170. pb NZ$ 24.95. ISBN 0 340 58839 X.

Cudjoe, Selwyn, and William Cain, eds. *C. L. R. James: His Intellectual Legacies*. UMassP. pp. 476. hb £49.95, pb £17.95. ISBN 0 87023 906 6, 0 87023 907 4.

Dasgupta, Probal. *The Otherness of English: India's Auntie Tongue Syndrome*. Sage (1993). pp. 228. Rs. 235. ISBN 0 8039 9456 7.

Dayan, Joan. *Haiti, History and the Gods*. UCalP. pp. 339. £28. ISBN 0 520 08900 6.

Dever, Maryanne. *M. Barnard Eldershaw: 'Plaque with Laurel', Essays, Reviews and Correspondence*. UQP. pp. 283. pb A$19.95. ISBN 0 7022 2724 2.

Dhawan, R. K., and Walter Tonetto, eds. *New Zealand Literature Today*. ISCS. Rs. 250. ISBN 81 85218 69 2.

Dingley, Robert, ed. *George Augustus Sala. The Land of the Golden Fleece*. Mulini. pp. 242. hb A$35, pb A$20. ISBN 0 949 91056 2.

Dixon, Robert. *Writing the Colonial Adventure: Race, Gender and Nation in*

Anglo-Australian Popular Fiction, 1875–1914. CUP. pp. 228. pb A$29.95. ISBN 0 521 48439 1.

Doyle, James. *The Fin de Siècle Spirit: Walter Blackburn Harte and the American/Canadian Literary Milieu of the 1890s.* ECW. pb $15.95. ISBN 1 55022 232 5.

During, Simon. *Patrick White.* OUP. pp. 106. pb A$18.95. ISBN 0 195 53497 2.

Fishburn, Katherine. *Cross-Cultural Conversations: Reading Buchi Emecheta.* Contributions to the Study of World Literature. Greenwood. pp. 224. £53.95. ISBN 0 313 29589 1.

Fitzpatrick, Peter. *Pioneer Players: The Lives of Louis and Hilda Esson.* CUP. pp. 395. hb A$90, pb A$29.95. ISBN 0 521 45010 1, 0 521 45644 4.

Flesch, Juliet, comp. *Love Brought to Book. A Bio-Bibliography of 20th Century Australian Romance Novels.* NCAS. pp. 43. pb A$19.95. ISBN 0 732 60602 0.

Fotheringham, Richard. *In Search of 'Steele Rudd': Author of Classic Dad and Dave Stories.* UQP. pp. 227. A$49.95. ISBN 0 7022 2875 3.

Foxton, Rosemary, ed. *Catherine Martin. The Silent Sea.* Colonial Texts Series. UNSW. pp. 573. pb A$35.95. ISBN 0 868 40373 3.

Fraser, Hilary, and R. S. White, eds. *Constructing Gender: Feminism in Literary Studies.* UWAP (1994). pp. 30. pb A$24.95. ISBN 1 875 56034 3.

Gajer, Ewa, comp. *Australian Women Short Story Writers: A Selective Bibliography.* CALLS. pp. 127. pb A$20. ISBN 1 863 89259 1.

Gibbs, James. *Talking with Paper: Wole Soyinka at the University of Leeds 1954 to 1958: The Making of a Playwright.* Nolishment. pb £2.99. ISBN 1 89999 003 8.

Griffith, Michael, and James Tulip, eds. *Religion, Literature and the Arts.* Australian International Conference Proceedings 1995. AustCU/USydP. pp. 362. pb A$20. ISBN 0 949 23316 1.

Griffith, Michael, and Ross Keating, eds. *Religion, Literature, and the Arts.* Australian International Conference Proceedings 1994. AustCU/USydP. pp. 465. pb A$20. ISBN 1 863 65150 0.

Grono, William, ed. *Dorothy Hewett: Collected Poems 1940–1995.* Fremantle. pp. 416. pb A$19.95. ISBN 1 86368 114 0.

Gurnah, Abdulrazak. *Essays on African Writing: Contemporary Literature 2.* Heinemann. pp. 184. pb £12.99. ISBN 0 435 91763 3.

Haskell, Dennis. *Australian Poetic Satire.* The 1994 Colin Roderick Lectures. FALS. pp. 67. pb A$10.50. ISBN 0 864 43539 8.

Herdeck, Donald, ed. *Three Dynamite Authors.* TCP. pp. 132. hb $24, pb $16. ISBN 0 89410 773 9, 0 89410 774 7.

Hergenhan, Laurie. *No Casual Traveller: Hartley Grattan and Australia.* UQP. pp. 306. pb A$34.95. ISBN 0 702 22753 6.

Hill, Tracey, and William Hughes, eds. *Contemporary Writing and National Identity.* Sulis. pp. 168. £13.95. ISBN 0 9526856 0 4.

Hoffman, James. *The Ecstasy of Resistance: A Biography of George Ryga.* ECW. pp. 350. pb £18.95 ($19.95). ISBN 1 55022 246 5.

Jordan, Glenn, and Chris Weedon. *Cultural Politics: Class, Gender, Race and the Postmodern World.* Blackwell. pp. 624. pb £13.99. ISBN 0 631 16228 3.

Kanaganayakam, Chelva. *Configurations of Exile: South Asian Writers and Their World.* TSAR. pp. 160. $15.95. ISBN 0 920661 67 5.

Kennedy, Brian. *A Passion to Oppose: John Anderson, Philosopher.* MelbourneUP. pp. 272. £28.50 (A$49.95). ISBN 0 522 84683 1.

Kerr, David. *African Popular Theatre: From Precolonial Times to the Present Day.* Studies in African Literature. Heinemann. pp. 278. hb £35, pb £11.95. ISBN 0 85255 534 2, 0 85255 533 4.

Kilner, Kerry, ed. *Playing the Past: Three Plays by Australian Women.* Currency/NCAS. pp. 54. pb A$14.95. ISBN 0 868 19449 2.

King, Bruce. *Derek Walcott and West Indian Drama: 'Not Only a Playwright But a Company': The Trinidad Theatre Workshop 1959–1993.* OUP. pp. 350. hb £25, pb £14.99. ISBN 0 19 818258 9, 0 19 818464 6.

——, ed. *West Indian Literature.* 2nd edn. Macmillan. pp. 248. pb £9.95. ISBN 0 333 59463 0.

King, Russell, John Connell, and Paul White, eds. *Writing Across Worlds: Literature and Migration.* Routledge. pp. 304. hb £45, pb £14.99. ISBN 0 415 10529, 0 415 10530 7.

Krauth, Nigel, and Robyn Sheahan. *Paradise to Paranoia.* New Queensland Writing. UQP. pp. 284. pb $A19.95. ISBN 0 702 22785 4.

Lane, Dorothy. *The Island as Site of Resistance: An Examination of Caribbean and New Zealand Texts.* Studies of World Literature in English 6. Lang. pp. 181. $45.95. ISBN 0 8204 2642 3.

Lawson, Elizabeth, ed. *Cowand: The Veteran's Grant.* Mulini. pp. 110. pb A$25. ISBN 0 949 91046 5.

Lee, Stuart, comp. *Southerly Index,* Vol. 1. EA-USydP. pp. 200. pb $A25. ISBN 0 909 75526 4.

Lever, Susan, ed. *The Oxford Book of Australian Women's Verse.* OUP. pp. 259. pb A$24.95. ISBN 0 19 553505 7.

Levy, Judith. *V. S. Naipaul: Displacement and Autobiography.* Garland. pp. 151. £17.50. ISBN 0 8153 1468 X.

Lionnet, Francoise. *Postcolonial Representations: Women, Literature and Identity.* CornUP. pp. 198. $32.50. ISBN 0 8014 2984 6, 0 8014 8180 5.

Little, Dave. *Catching the Wind in a Net: The Religious Vision of Robertson Davies.* ECW. pp. 210. $20. ISBN 1 55022 264 3.

Mansbridge, Francis. *Irving Layton: God's Recording Angel.* ECW. pp. 150. pb $14.95. ISBN 1 55022 216 3.

Miller, J. R. *Big Bear (Mistahimusqua).* ECW. pp. 133. $14.95. ISBN 1 55022 272 4.

Mishra, Sudesh. *Preparing Faces: Modernism and Indian Poetry in English.* CRNLE. pp. 401. np. ISBN 0 7258 0578 1.

Mitchell, Adrian. *The Short Stories of Henry Lawson.* SUP/OUP. pp. 57. pb A$9.95. ISBN 0 424 00203 5.

Mustafa, Fawzia. *V. S. Naipaul.* CUP. pp. 255. pb £12.95. ISBN 0 521 40378 2, 0 521 48359 X.

Nasta, Susheila, and Anna Rutherford, eds. *Tiger's Triumph: Celebrating Sam Selvon.* Dangaroo. pp. 150. £6.95. ISBN 1 871049 23 7.

Nettlbeck, Amanda. *Reading David Malouf.* OUP. pp. 68. pb $9.95. ISBN 0 424 00204 3.

Newman, Judie. *The Ballistic Bard: Postcolonial Fictions.* Arnold. pp. 202. £35. pb £12.99. ISBN 0 340 53914 3, 0 340 53915 1.

Ngara, Emmanuel, ed. *New Writing From Southern Africa*. Currey. pp. 320. hb £35, pb £12.95. ISBN 0 85255 537 7, 0 435 08971 4.

Olaniyan, Tejumola. *Scars of Conquest/Masks of Resistance: The Invention of Cultural Identities in African, African-American and Caribbean Drama*. OUP. hb £35, pb £12.99. ISBN 0 19 509405 0, 0 19 509406 9.

Page, Geoff. *A Reader's Guide to Contemporary Australian Poetry*. UQP. pp. 345. pb $16.95. ISBN 0 702 22700 5.

Paradis, Andrea. *Out of this World: Canadian Science Fiction and Fantasy Literature*. Quarry-NLC. pp. 264. pb £18.95. ISBN 1 55082 150 4.

Paranjape, Makarand, ed. *Indian Poetry in English*. Macmillan (1993). pp. 253. Rs. 90. ISBN 0 333 92211 5.

Parker, Michael, and Roger Starkey, eds. *Postcolonial Literatures: Achebe, Ngugi, Desai, Walcott*. New Casebooks Series. Macmillan. pp. 288. hb £37.50, pb £10.99. ISBN 0 333 60801 1, 0 333 60802 X.

Parsons, Philip, and Victoria Chance, eds. *Companion to Theatre in Australia*. Currency/cup. pp. 704. hb A$95. ISBN 0 868 19357 7, 0 521 34528 6.

Pettersson, Rose. *Nadine Gordimer's One Story of a State Apart*. AUU. pp. 227. pb £16.50. ISBN 91 554 3437 1.

Pierce, Peter. *Absences*. CALLS. pp. 19. pb A$5. ISBN 1 8638 9084 X.

——, *Australian Melodramas: Thomas Keneally's Fiction*. UQP. pp. 202. pb A$14.95. ISBN 0 702 22813 3.

Pousse, Michel. *R. K. Narayan: A Painter of Modern India*. Studies of World Literature in English Vol. 4. Lang. pp. 211. £32.00. ISBN 0 8204 2768 3.

Priessnitz, Horst. *German Poetry in Australia 1830–1992: A Checklist of Literary Translations, Adaptations and Comments by Australian Authors*, ed. Sally Batten and Terence O'Neill. CBTS. pp. 75. pb A$15, A$20 overseas. ISBN 0 732 60893 7.

Pugliese, Cristiana. *The Life and Writings of Gakaara wa Wanjau*. African Studies 37. Bayreuth. DM39. ISBN 3 927510 35 1, ISSN 0178 0034.

Robinson, Roger, ed. *Katherine Mansfield: In from the Margin*. LSUP. pp. 209. £25.95. ISBN 0 8071 1865 6.

Schaffer, Kay. *In The Wake of First Contact: The Eliza Fraser Stories*. CUP. pp. 320. hb A$90, pb A$35. ISBN 0 521 45010 1, 0 521 49920 8.

Sheridan, Susan. *Along the Faultlines: Sex, Race and Nation in Australian Women's Writing 1880s–1930s*. A&UA. pp. 188. pb A$24.95. ISBN 1 863 73867 3.

Spivak, Gayatri Chakravorty. *Imaginary Maps: Three Stories by Mahasweta Devi*. Routledge. pp. 213. hb £35, pb £12.99. ISBN 0 415 90462 5, 0 415 90463 3.

Strauss, Jennifer. *Judith Wright*. OUP. pp. 115. pb A$19.95. ISBN 0 19 553278 3.

Sullivan, Rosemary. *Shadow Maker: The Life of Gwendolyn MacEwen*. HC. ISBN 0 00 255406 2.

Tiffin, Chris, and Alan Lawson, eds. *De-scribing Empire: Postcolonialism and Textuality*. Routledge (1994) pp. 254. pb £12.99. ISBN 0 415 10546 3, 0 415 10547 1.

Tiffin, Chris, and Lynette Baer, comps. *The Praed Papers: A Listing and Index*. LBQ. pp. 146. pb A$23.95. ISBN 0 724 25852 3.

Turner, Margaret E. *Imagining Culture: New World Narrative and the Writing of Canada*. McG-QUP. pp. 136. pb £11.95. ISBN 0 7735 1361 2.

van Toorn, Penny, and David English, eds. *Speaking Positions: Aboriginality, Gender and Ethnicity in Australian Cultural Studies*. VUT, Melb. pp. 221. pb A$22.95. ISBN 1 862 72461 X.

Vidal, Mary Theresa. *Tales for the Bush*. Intr. Susan Lever. Mulini. pp. 152. hb A$60, pb A$29.95. ISBN 0 9499 1045 7, 0 868 400 28 9.

Webb, Phyllis. *Nothing But Brushstrokes: Selected Prose*. NeWest. pp.200. pb $17.95. ISBN 0 920897 89 4.

Wedde, Ian. *How to be Nowhere*. VictUP. pp. 320. pb NZ$49.95. ISBN 0 86473 249 X.

Williams, Mark, and Michele Leggott, eds. *Opening the Book: New Essays on New Zealand Writing*. AucklandUP. pp. 335. pb NZ$39.95. ISBN 1 86940 115 8.

Wolf, Volker, ed. *Lesen und Schreiben: Literatur-Kritik-Germanistik: Festschrift fur Manfred Jurgensen*. Francke. pp. 337. DM120. ISBN 3 772 02149 2.

York, Lorraine M., ed. *Various Atwoods: Essays on the Later Poems, Short Fiction, and Novels*. Anansi (1994). pp. 224. pb £12.95. ISBN 0 88784 548 7.

Zach, Wolfgang, and Ken L. Goodwin, eds. *Nationalism vs. Internationalism: (Inter)National Dimensions of Literatures in English*. Stauffenburg. pp. 577. ISBN 3 860 57310 1.

XVIII

Bibliography and Textual Criticism

WILLIAM BAKER and KENNETH WOMACK

This chapter has three sections: 1. General Scholarship for 1993; 2. General Scholarship for 1994; 3. General Scholarship for 1995.

This retrospective essay of scholarship published between 1993 and this year inaugurates our annual survey of bibliography and textual criticism for *YWES*. These years were marked by a growing interest in monographs devoted to editorial theory and the history of the book, as well as the creation of serial bibliographies concerned with the works of individual authors. In addition to discussing the publication of books and articles regarding analytical and descriptive bibliography during this period, our survey will draw our readers' attention to the presence of valuable enumerative bibliographies in various works of scholarship devoted to literary and critical study. Finally, our review examines the publication of materials of interest to students of antiquarianism, various aspects of librarianship and book collecting.

1. General Scholarship for 1993

The year's work in bibliography and textual criticism for 1993 is most significantly marked by the publication of G. Thomas Tanselle's *The Life and Work of Fredson Bowers*. Tanselle's volume assesses the achievements and influence of the late, renowned bibliographer, Fredson Bowers, from his early years in New Haven, Connecticut, his work as editor of *Studies in Bibliography* and his accomplishments as author of such works as *Principles of Bibliographical Description*. With a foreword by David L. Vander Meulen, Tanselle's volume concludes with Martin C. Battestin's 'Fredson Thayer Bowers: A Checklist and Chronology'. A number of books and periodicals published in 1993 address various aspects of editorial theory, itself surely one of Bowers's most important scholarly legacies. W. Speed Hill's *New Ways of Looking at Old Texts: Papers of the Renaissance English Text Society, 1985–1991* documents the papers of the RETS from 1985 through 1991 in an effort to trace the evolution of contemporary approaches to the theory and practice of transcription, as well as the role of new historicism in editing early Renaissance manuscripts. Selections include Hill's introduction, 'Editing Non-dramatic Texts of the English Renaissance: A Field Guide with Illustrations'; Hill's 'The Theory and Practice of Transcription'; Gordon Kipling's

'*The Receyt of the Ladie Kateryne* and the Practice of Editorial Transcription'; A. R. Braunmuller's 'Accounting for Absence: The Transcription of Space'; John Pitcher's 'Editing Daniel'; Richard Proudfoot's 'Richard Johnson's *Tom a' Lincoln* Dramatized: A Jacobean Play in British Library MS. Add. 61745'; Elizabeth H. Hageman's '*Did* Shakespeare Have Any Sisters? Editing Texts by Englishwomen of the Renaissance and Reformation'; Elizabeth McCutcheon's 'Life and Letters: Editing the Writing of Margaret Roper'; Frances Teague's 'Provenance and Propaganda as Editorial Stumbling Blocks'; Josephine A. Roberts's 'Lady Mary Wroth's *Urania*: A Response to Jacobean Censorship'; Peter Beal's 'Notions in Garrison: The Seventeenth-Century Commonplace Book'; Bernhard F. Scholz's 'From Illustrated Epigram to Emblem: The Canonization of a Typographical Arrangement'; Arthur F. Marotti's 'Malleable and Fixed Texts: Manuscript and Printed Miscellanies and the Transmission of Lyric Poetry in the English Renaissance'; John Jowett's 'Jonson's Authorization of Type in *Sejanus* and Other Early Quartos'; Gary Spear's 'Reading Before the Lines: Typography, Iconography, and the Author in Milton's 1645 Frontispiece'; Thomas L. Berger's 'The New Historicism and the Editing of English Renaissance Texts'; Margreta de Grazia's 'What Is a Work? What Is a Document?'; Marotti's 'Manuscript, Print, and the English Renaissance Lyric'; Braunmuller's 'Work, Document, and Miscellany: A Response to Professors de Grazia and Marotti'; Sara Jayne Steen's 'Behind the Arras: Editing Renaissance Women's Letters'; Jean Klene's 'Recreating the Letters of Lady Anne Southwell'; James Fitzmaurice's 'Some Problems in Editing Margaret Cavendish'; John W. Velz's 'Giving Voices to the Silent: Editing the Private Writings of Women'; Steven W. May's 'Manuscript Circulation at the Elizabethan Court'; Edward Doughtie's 'John Ramsey's Manuscript as a Personal and Family Document'; and Ernest W. Sullivan II's 'The Renaissance Manuscript Verse Miscellany: Private Party, Private Text'.

Volume 6 of *Text*, edited by D. C. Greetham and W. Speed Hill, offers a variety of new essays regarding the study of bibliography and textual criticism. Selections include James Thorpe's 'Presidential Address: Reflections on Our Craft'; Fredson Bowers's 'Why Apparatus?'; Jo Ann Boydston's 'Standard for Scholarly Editing: The CEAA and the CSE'; Richard Knowles's 'Variorum Commentary'; Donald H. Reiman's 'Public and Private in the Study of Manuscripts'; James Willis's 'The Science of Blunders: Confessions of a Textual Critic'; James L. W. West III's 'Fair Copy, Authorial Intention, and Versioning'; a special panel on 'The Politics of Editing' featuring the insights of Hill, Mary-Jo Kline, Joel Myerson, David J. Nordloh and Reiman; Karl D. Uitti and Gina Greco's 'Computerization, Canonicity, and the Old French Scribe: The Twelfth and Thirteenth Centuries'; Ralph Hanna III's 'Annotating *Piers Plowman*'; John H. Fisher's 'Historical and Methodological Considerations for Adopting "Best Text" or "Usus Scribendi" for Textual Criticism of Chaucer's Poems'; Maria Grazia Pernis's 'Fifteenth-Century Patrons and the Scipio-Caesar Controversy'; John W. Velz's 'From Authorization to Authorship, Orality to Literature: The Case of Medieval and Renaissance Drama'; Betty Bennet's 'The Editor of Letters as Critic: A Denial of Blameless Neutrality'; Alan C. Dooley's 'Varieties of Textual Change in the Victorian Era'; C. Deirdre Phelps's 'The Edition as Art Form: Social and Authorial Readings of William Cullen Bryant's *Poems*'; Ronald

Schuchard's 'Yeats's Letters, Eliot's Lectures: Toward a New Form of Annotation'; Christopher Z. Hobson's 'Richard Wright's Communisms: Textual Variance, Intentionality, and Socialization in Wright's *American Hunger* and *I Tried to Be a Communist*'; and John Antush's 'Editing the Bi-Lingual Text at Cross-Cultural Purposes'. In *An Early London Printing House at Work: Studies in Bowyer Ledgers – With a Supplement to the Bowyer V. Ornament Stock (1973), an Appendix on the Bowyer–Emonson Partnership, and 'Bowyer's Paper Stock Ledger,' by Herbert Davis*, Keith Maslen provides a seminal study of the eighteenth-century London book trade focusing on the father and son printing firm, William Bowyer. Maslen explores a range of interesting topics, including the printshop's paper stock and their ledgers, the printing of *Robinson Crusoe*, early editions of Voltaire printed in London, new editions of Pope's *Essay on Man*, point-holes as bibliographical evidence, the printing of the votes of the House of Commons, the activities of William Strahan and Bowyer's chapel rules. The volume also includes Maslen's important review of D. F. McKenzie's *The Cambridge University Press, 1696–1712* (CUP, 1996).

AEB (7) – the periodical in which a dramatically modified form of the present survey originally appeared – features a number of essays devoted to the study of bibliography and textual criticism, including Marcia Lusk Maxwell's 'The Anglo-Norman Prose *Brut*: A List of Extant Manuscripts and Their Location'; Joseph A. Dane's 'The Presumed Influence of Skeat's *Student's Chaucer* on Manly and Rickert's *Text of the Canterbury Tales*'; Scott C. Pope's 'A New Manuscript Transcription of John Dryden's Translation of Virgil's *Third Georgic*'; T. H. Howard-Hill's 'The Institutionalization of Bibliography'; Gary A. Stringer's 'Breaking the Bibliographical Code in Seventeenth-Century Manuscripts and Printed Editions of (Mainly) Donne's English Epigrams'; Joseph L. Laurenti's 'Eight Unique Incunabula in the University of Illinois Library'; and Bernice W. Kliman's *'The Three-Text Hamlet*: A Response'. *Library* (15) contains Esther Potter's 'The London Bookbinding Trade: From Craft to Industry'; Paul F. Gehl's 'Watermark Evidence for the Competitive Practices of Antonio Miscomini'; and Martin Bodhardt's 'Partial Duplicate Setting: Means of Rationalization or Complicating Factor in Textual Transmission?' Kenneth Womack's 'Assessing the Rhetoric of Performance Criticism in Three Variant Soviet Texts of *King Lear*' (*YCGL* 41) explores the intersections between literary translation and editorial theory during the Soviet era through analysis of Boris Pasternak's 1949 Russian translation of *King Lear*. In *Black Riders: The Visible Language of Modernism*, Jerome J. McGann continues his ongoing project for merging literary and textual criticism through his analyses of the bibliographical dimensions of poetry. In addition to examining the symbolic and physical nature of literary texts, McGann discusses such printing-house luminaries as the Kelmscott Press, the Bodley Head and Yeats's Cuala Press, among others. He also devotes attention to typography and its role in our understanding of literary works.

PBSA (87) features a variety of studies of interest to textual critics, including Thomas O. Calhoun and Thomas L. Gravell's 'Paper and Printing in Ben Jonson's *Sejanus*'; Joseph A. Dane's 'The Notions of Text and Variant in the Prologue to Chaucer's *Legend of Good Women*'; David McKitterick's 'Old Faces and New Acquaintances'; Hans Walter Gabler's 'What *Ulysses*

Requires'; Geoffrey M. Sill's 'The Authorship of *An Impartial History of Michael Servetus*'; Harold Love's 'But Did Rochester Really Write *Sodom?*'; Mary Beth Winn's 'Vérard's Hours of 8 February 1489/90'; Nancy A. Mace's 'The History of the Grammar Patent, 1547–1620'; Philip M. Teigen's 'Concurrent Printing of the Gutenberg Bible and Proton Milliprobe Analysis of Its Ink'; John Jowett's 'Johannes Factotum: Henry Chettle and "Green's Groatsworth of Wit" '; and Claudia A. Limbert and John H. O'Neill's 'Composite Authorship: Katharine Philips and an Antimarital Satire'. George Bornstein and Ralph G. Williams's *Palimpsest: Editorial Theory in the Humanities* features several noteworthy essays, including D. C. Greetham's 'Editorial and Critical Theory: From Modernism to Postmodernism'; Peter L. Shillingsburg's 'Polymorphic, Polysemic, Protean, Reliable, Electronic Texts'; Williams's 'I Shall Be Spoken: Textual Boundaries, Authors, and Intent'; Betty T. Bennett's 'Feminism and Editing Mary Wollstonecraft Shelley: The Editor And?/Or? the Text'; James E. G. Zetzel's 'Religion, Rhetoric, and Editorial Technique: Reconstructing the Classics'; Gary Taylor's 'The Renaissance and the End of Editing'; Jerome J. McGann's 'The Case of *The Ambassadors* and the Textual Condition'; Bornstein's 'What Is the Text of a Poem by Yeats?'; Hans Walter Gabler's 'On Textual Criticism and Editing: The Case of Joyce's *Ulysses*'; David Noel Freedman's 'Editing the Editors: Translation and Elucidation of the Text of the Bible'; Kathleen Weil-Garris Brandt's 'The Grime of the Centuries Is a Pigment of the Imagination: Michelangelo's Sistine Ceiling'; Barbara Oberg's 'Benjamin Franklin's Correspondence: Whose Intent? What Text? I Don't Know's the Author'; Philip Gossett's 'Translations and Adaptations of Operatic Texts'; and Clayborne Carson's 'Editing Martin Luther King, Jr.: Political and Scholarly Issues'.

1993 also saw the publication of a variety of valuable studies of publishing history and librarianship. Evelyn B. Tribble's *Margins and Marginality: The Printed Page in Early Modern England* traces the interstices between marginal apparatus, authority and authorship, and argues that marginal commentary and text fuse together to form a page's inscribed identity. In this manner, Tribble reveals the ways in which book production altered profoundly the relations among readers, writers and cultural authority during the early modern era. In her study of marginalia, for example, Tribble demonstrates that pages were latent battlegrounds for ideological clashes regarding issues of political, religious, social and literary authority. Sidney F. Huttner and Elizabeth Stege's *A Register of Artists, Engravers, Booksellers, Bookbinders, Printers, and Publishers in New York City, 1821–42* offers a listing of the names of individuals and firms associated with the publication of the graphic arts in New York City between 1821 and 1842. Intended as a supplementary volume to George L. McKay's *Register* for the period from 1633 to 1820, Huttner and Stege's compilation records the history of the print trade in New York and the individuals that motivated its evolution during the early nineteenth century. In addition to its register denoting the city's sizeable print trade during that era, the edition includes two notable appendices: 'The Runners Vade Mecum (1842)' and 'Remarks on the Vade Mecum (1835)'. Huttner and Stege supplement their volume with an 'Index of Occupations'. Robin Myers and Michael Harris's *Serials and Their Readers, 1620–1914* features a number of informative contributions, including Stephen Bending's 'Bibliography of English Fiction, 1770–1830'; Joanne Shattock's 'Serials in the

Cambridge Bibliography of English Literature'; Rosamond McGuinness's 'Computer Register of Musical Data in the London Newspapers, 1660–1800'; Michael Frearson's 'The Distribution and Readership of London Corantos in the 1620s'; Caroline Nelson's 'American Readership of Early British Serials'; J. A. Downie's 'Periodicals and Politics in the Reign of Queen Anne'; Jeremy Black's 'Politicisation and the Press in Hanoverian England'; Laurel Brake's ' "The Trepidation of the Spheres": The Serial and the Book in the Nineteenth Century'; James Raven's 'Serial Advertisement in Eighteenth-Century Britain and England'; Bill Bell's 'Fiction in the Marketplace: Towards a Study of the Victorian Serial'; and Aled Jones's 'Constructing the Readership in Nineteenth-Century Wales'.

In *The Battle of the Frogs and Fairford's Flies: Miracles and the Pulp Press During the English Revolution*, Jerome Friedman addresses the manner in which ordinary people responded to the violent political and social ramifications of the English revolution through a close study of more than 500 newsbooks and pulp publications produced from 1640 to 1660. In addition to investigating why so many seventeenth-century bestsellers considered issues of witches, apparitions and divine curses, Friedman examines the publication history of the popular astrological and prophetic literature during the revolution. The volume concludes with a valuable, although unannotated, listing of the pamphlets cited in Friedman's study. Compiled as a tribute to University of Illinois Emeritus Professor of Germanic Languages and Literatures Henri Stegemeier, Thomas McGeary and N. Frederick Nash's *Emblem Books at the University of Illinois: A Bibliographic Catalogue* surveys the significant collection of emblem books housed in the archives of the Rare Book and Special Collections Library at the University of Illinois at Urbana-Champaign. Part 1, compiled by McGeary, lists 601 original editions of emblem books and related items published before 1800, while Part 2, compiled by Nash, includes a checklist of the 408 emblem books in reprint, facsimile, or microform editions. In addition to the inclusion of iconologies, books of hieroglyphics, emblematized fables, Dance of Death books, and fête books, McGeary and Nash's volume features books whose title pages purport them to contain emblems, despite their questionable inclusion of such fixtures. In *A Skeptic Among Scholars: August Frugé on University Publishing*, the renowned academic publisher August Frugé discusses his role in the formative years of the University of California Press, while also assessing its transformation into one of the largest intellectual publishing houses in America. Frugé remarks on the establishment of the first university paperback list in 1956, while also addressing his dealings with learned authors and troublesome university officers. Frugé affords particular attention to the manner in which he assembled the staff of the University of California Press, especially regarding such figures as Ward Ritchie, Adrian Wilson and John Goetz, individuals responsible for the Press's reputation for product quality. The volume concludes with the supplementary 'Addenda: Alternative Views', which includes Hugh Kenner's 'God, Swahili, Bandicoots, and Euphoria' and James H. Clark's 'Publishing *The Plan of St. Gall*'.

In *Scribal Publication in Seventeenth-Century England*, Harold Love explores the publication through handwritten copies of a number of English writers and composers after the establishment of the printing press. While censorship accounts for many of the instances of this practice, scribal publication also facilitated the publication of texts that required only small numbers, as well as satisfying the desires of authors wishing to avoid literally 'the stigma of print'. Love's study also examines the manuscript trade's role in the evolution of authorship and its place within the communication of ideas. Drawing upon his experience as editor of the manuscripts of Shelley and Byron, Donald H. Reiman's *The Study of Modern Manuscripts: Public, Confidential, and Private* addresses the fundamental editorial issue of textual authority and its role in the editing of postmedieval manuscripts. In addition to providing discussion of the manuscript traditions of the Renaissance, the Enlightenment, and Romantic periods, Reiman traces the historical developments of three manuscript types – the 'private', or personal; the 'confidential', or corporate; and the 'public'. Reiman also explores the controversies over the relative authority of manuscripts and first editions in cases involving the texts of Shelley and Wordsworth. In *The Mushroom Jungle: A History of Postwar Paperback Publishing*, Steve Holland offers a well illustrated history of British paperback publishing that flourished in the years following the end of the Second World War and collapsed in the late 1950s. Many publishing houses sprung up, briefly blossomed and disappeared. Bibliographically, many of these publications have sunk without trace (beyond Whitaker's or the British Museum Catalogue). Holland's volume provides an account of some of them, although he only describes the tip of the iceberg. The fascinating artwork is reflected in the reproduction of somewhat garish covers featuring women in various states of undress. Holland presents 'the story of the mushroom publishers, a story that spans the ten years of post-war Britain when rationing and regulation dictated our lives in ways that can barely be conceived by those who did not live through it'. Holland's is the first record of these activities, and hopefully not the last.

Preservations of Electronic Formats and Electronic Formats for Preservation, edited by Janice Mohlhenrich, features a host of essays that investigate electronic publishing formats and their application in the disciplines of library science and textual criticism. Selections include Anne R. Kenney's 'The Role of Technology in the Preservation of Research Library Materials'; Michael B. Pate's 'The Marquette Electronic Archive'; Fynnette L. Eaton's 'The National Archives and Electronic Records for Preservation'; Basil Manns's 'The Electronic Document Image Preservation Format'; Mark Arps's 'CD-ROM: Archival Considerations'; Don Willis's 'The Resolution Factor in Preserving Page-Based Materials'; and Mohlhenrich's conclusion. The volume also features two appendices: Karen L. Hanus's useful 'Annotated Bibliography on Electronic Preservation' and Tom Hall's glossary. Charles Scribner Jr's *In the Web of Ideas: The Education of a Publisher* offers memoirs of America's 'golden age' of publishing and his publishing house's role within it, while also including anecdotes about his relations with Ernest Hemingway, Sir Winston Churchill, S. S. Van Dine, C. P. Snow, Alan Paton and Albert Einstein, among a host of others. Scribner also features two appendices, 'Columns for Malcolm' and 'A Family Tradition'. Gary Taylor and John Jowett's *Shakespeare Reshaped, 1606–1623* addresses the agents and institutions that affected play texts, including legislated expurgation, theatrical innovation, and posthumous adaptation. Using Shakespearean texts from *King John* and *The Merry Wives of Windsor* to *King Lear* and *Measure for Measure*, Taylor and Jowett offer a new textual model for understanding the transformation of Renaissance plays from the mind of the playwright, to the stage, and ultimately, to the page. The volume concludes with a number of useful appendices that establish date and authorship for the plays featured in Taylor and Jowett's study.

Dedicated to the esteemed academic librarian, Reuben Musiker, the essays in *A World Too Wide: Essays on Libraries and Other Themes in Honour of Reuben Musiker* (ed. Joseph Sherman), include G. R. Bozzoli's foreword; B. K. Murray's 'A Great Job Greatly Done'; Phillip V. Tobias's 'Avant Propos: A Tribute to Reuben Musiker'; Oscar Norwich's 'The Friends of the Library'; A. S. C. Hopper's 'Academic Library Management in South Africa in the 1980s: A Selective Analysis of the Literature'; Peter Lor's 'The South African "System of Libraries and Information"': A Polite and Playful Critique of Report [D]ated 02-109 (91/03)'; Seth Manaka's 'The Future of Libraries in South Africa'; Christopher Merrett's 'Human Rights, Information, and Libraries in South Africa: A Radical Perspective'; Don Schauder's 'A Gentle Transformation: Information Technology and University Library Management in the Nineties'; Karl Tober's 'Libraries, Librarians, and Education'; Heather M. Edwards's 'By Accident or Design? Is the University Library Functional?'; Dawn E. Evenden's 'The Johannesberg Public Library: A Personal View of Some of the Events of the Last Fifteen Years'; Clare M. Walker's 'SLIS Turns Forty: Highlights from Four Decades, 1947–1987'; Ellison Kahn's 'Who Was Uriah Heep's "Mr. Tidd?"'; And the Romance of a Law Library'; Jacqueline A. Kalley's 'Bibliography: The Cornerstone of Scholarship'; A. K. Scholes's 'Information Science, Knowledge, and Communication: Some Reflections and Projections'; Adriaan Donker's 'The South African Publishing Scene'; Miles Blackwell's 'In Possession of Truth'; Moore Crossey's 'A Note on Southern African Political Ephemera at Yale'; Anna M. Cunningham's 'Reflections on a Career as an Archivist'; Douglas Varley's 'Random Reflections on the Future of the Book'; Sherman's 'Towards a "Proper" Library, or Six Thousand Books in Search of a Home'; Marcus Arkin's 'The Case for an Economics Component in Jewish Studies'; Bernard Steinberg's 'Jewish Education at the Crossroads: Some Reflections'; Patricia E. Scott's 'Discovering British Culture Transformation in Grahamstown, 1820–1922'; Asher Dubb's 'Medical Philately: The Doctor as Writer; The Writer as Doctor'; Beth Strachan's 'Values and Intentions: Some Observations on Africana Activities at the University of the Witwatersrand'; Frank R. Bradlow's 'A Lifetime in Africana'; Walter Mony's 'From Bearable Lightness to Appalling Popularity'; Robin Walton's 'A Seventeenth-Century Opera – or Musical'; and Ve Falk's 'A Follower Finds a Leader'. The volume concludes with a biography and bibliography devoted to Musiker.

The year's work in bibliography for 1993 witnessed the publication of a number and variety of useful reference guides and enumerative bibliographies worthy of attention. In the second edition of his popular *Literary Research Guide: A Guide to Reference Sources for the Study of Literatures in English and Related Topics*, James L. Harner offers a revised, annotated bibliographic guide to reference sources for the study of British, Irish, American and Canadian literatures, as well as other literatures in English. Harner also evaluates significant bibliographies, abstracts, databases, indexes, catalogues, surveys, dictionaries and handbooks, while also including useful annotations regarding related works and reviews. *BB* (50) continues to provide its readership with valuable, specialized listings regarding individual authors and themes. The latest volume includes Pamela Pasak Sawallis's 'Daisy Ashford: A Preliminary Checklist'; Donna L. Potts's 'Howard Nemerov: An Annotated Bibliography of Secondary Sources'; Patrick J. Stevens's 'Connolly, Pearse, Rebellion: A Bibliographical Note on the Holdings of the Irish Collection at Northwestern University'; Steve Fasano's 'Allen Ginsberg: An Annotated Bibliography, 1977–1990'; James McShane's 'The Norman Question: Relations between Russia and Scandinavia During the Middle Ages'; Lori A. Strauss's 'The Novelistic Portrayal of the Advertising Business and Its Practitioners, 1900–1990'; Jack W. C. Hagstrom and Joshua Odell's 'Emendations to Thom Gunn: A Bibliography, 1940–1978 (Part IV)'; Jeffrey Meyers's 'V. S. Naipaul: Essays, Stories, Reviews, and Interviews, 1948–1992'; John S. Spencer and Mary O'Neill's 'Josephine Humphreys'; Cathe Giffuni's 'Catherine Drinker Bowen: A Bibliography'; and Kathleen Sisak's 'Publishing Prizes in American History'.

Edwin T. Arnold and Dianne C. Luce's *Perspectives on Cormac McCarthy* concludes with 'Cormac McCarthy: A Bibliography,' an annotated listing of primary works, reviews, interviews and other writings by and about McCarthy. Similarly, Robert Harvey and Mark S. Roberts's edition of Jean-François Lyotard's *Toward the Postmodern* concludes with a useful and comprehensive enumerative bibliography of writings by and about Lyotard. Susan Lowenberg's *C. S. Lewis: A Reference Guide, 1972–1988* updates J. R. Christopher and J. K. Ostling's *C. S. Lewis: An Annotated Checklist of Writings about Him and His Works* (1974), and includes listings for the American publication of books, essays, chapters, articles and dissertations written about Lewis and his work between July 1972 and December 1988. Thoroughly annotated, Lowenberg supplements her study with an introductory essay to Lewis and his work, as well as a list of journals that concentrate on the writings of Lewis and his circle. Lowenberg divides the volume into three principal sections: 'Introduction: C. S. Lewis – His Life and Work', 'Writings by C. S. Lewis' and 'Writings about C. S. Lewis, 1972–1988'.

Emmanuel S. Nelson's *Writers of the Indian Diaspora: A Bio-Bibliographical Critical Sourcebook* includes a selected bibliography of scholarship by and about the writers of the Indian diaspora. In *A Reader's Guide to The Private Eye Novel*, Gary Warren Niebuhr offers mystery enthusiasts more than 1,000 annotated entries on titles by 90 authors writing in the genre, including works by figures from Dashiell Hammett and Raymond Chandler to Sue Grafton and Robert B. Parker. Each entry includes detailed cross-reference listings and notes on characters, settings and time periods. Don Lee Fred Nilsen's *Humor Scholarship: A Research Bibliography* traces humour through a variety of different venues and disciplines, including humour and its relation to the individual, the media and ethnicity. Nilsen also includes listings for the humour of personal interactions, national styles of humour, language play and rhetorical devices, humour and the fine arts and humour theory and epistemology. Nilsen supplements his bibliography with an appendix of 'Humor Resources', which lists journals, magazines, publishers, newsletters, organizations and newspapers devoted to humour and humour scholarship. Divided into two principal sections – 'Spencer's Writings' and 'Writings on Spencer' – Robert G. Perrin's *Herbert Spencer: A Primary and Secondary Bibliography* traces the publication history and critical reception of the author's work, including references for his correspondence, books and articles. Perrin also includes the wealth of biographical, philosophical psychological, and biological scholarship, among other disciplines, devoted to Spencer. The volume concludes with a chronological table that details Spencer's biographical and literary life.

Donald Pizer's *The Theory and Practice of American Literary Naturalism: Selected Essays and Reviews* contains 'A Selected Bibliography of American Literary Naturalism', while Jane Atteridge Rose's *Rebecca Harding Davis* concludes with a selected annotated bibliography of works by and about Davis. Written as a companion to the collected papers and correspondence of James Boswell, Marion S. Pottle, Claude Colleer Abbott and Frederick A. Pottle's *Catalogue of the Papers of James Boswell at Yale University* features listings for the journals, manuscripts and correspondence of Boswell acquired by Yale University in 1949. The catalogue also includes listings for non-manuscript material, financial papers and legal documents. In *The Eighteenth Century: The Intellectual and Cultural Context of English Literature, 1700–1789*, James Sambrook supplements his study with a selection of general bibliographies, as well as notes on relevant eighteenth-century English authors, including Addison, Pope, Defoe and Swift, among a host of others. A companion volume to Lawrence J. Shifreen's *Henry Miller: A Bibliography of Secondary Sources* (1979), Shifreen and Roger Jackson's *Henry Miller: A Bibliography of Primary Sources* catalogues more than 2,000 books, essays, pamphlets, recordings and translations, ranging from familiar works like *Tropic of Capricorn* and *Black Spring* to obscure pieces such as 'Chief Grumps' and 'A Philistine in Arcady'. Separated into six sections – books, pamphlets and broadsides; contributions to books; articles and water colour reproductions; translations; audio recordings; and video recordings – the bibliography documents the author's enormous textual corpus, while including useful and informative textual notes on many of the entries as well.

Richard Studings's catalogue of *Shakespeare in American Painting: A Catalogue from the Late Eighteenth Century to the Present* contains over 980 entries and listings for 372 artists, including such figures as Benjamin West, Mather Brown, Washington Allston, Lilly Martin Spencer, William Page and Edwin Austin Abbey, among others. Desmond Taylor and Philip E. Hager's *The Novels of World War II: An Annotated Bibliography* – a sequel to their 1981 text, *The Novels of World War I: An Annotated Bibliography* – assembles listings for the more than 3,000 novels about the war published since 1938. The novels included in Taylor and Hager's annotated survey employ the Second World War as a substantial part of their plot or background, and – because of the enormity of the Second World War fictional corpus – only novels in English or translated into English were included in their study. In *D. H. Lawrence: A Study of the Short Fiction*, Weldon Thornton includes excerpts from Lawrence's essays, reviews, miscellaneous writings and letters. Additionally, Thornton supplements his study with a partially annotated bibliography of scholarship regarding Lawrence's short stories and novellas. Gavin Wallace and Randall Stevenson's *The Scottish Novel since the Seventies* concludes with Alison Lumsden's unannotated, enumerative listing of 'The Scottish Novel since 1970: A Bibliography', while Eileen Watts's 'Annotated Bibliography of Malamud Studies, 1991–1992' (*Bernard Malamud Newsletter* (3)) features sections on articles, chapters, essays, interviews and dissertations written between 1991 and 1992, and devoted to the exegesis of Bernard Malamud's work. Kayla McKinney Wiggins's *Modern Verse Drama in English: An Annotated Bibliography* includes annotated entries relating to verse drama by some 230 modern playwrights of a variety of nationalities published since 1935. More than 550 verse plays and adaptations are featured in this comprehensive study – enduring testimony to the place of verse drama in the twentieth-century theatre. Alphabetically arranged by author, each entry includes full bibliographic and production information. The volume concludes with useful title and subject indexes. Michael Groden and Martin Kreiswirth's *The Johns Hopkins Guide to Literary Theory and Criticism* features 226 alphabetically arranged entries devoted to elucidating literary and critical terminology, providing biographical data regarding influential theorists, and isolating significant critical texts and genres within the contemporary theoretical debate. Groden and Kreiswirth supplement their entries with valuable primary and secondary bibliographies of scholarship.

Part of the Pittsburgh Series in Bibliography, Joel Myerson's *Walt Whitman: A Descriptive Bibliography* features nine chapters devoted to cataloguing and describing Whitman's corpus – 'Separate Publications', 'Collected Editions', 'Miscellaneous Collections', 'First Book and Pamphlet Appearances', 'First-Appearance Contributions to Magazines and Newspapers', 'Proof Copies, Circulars, and Broadsides', 'Reprinted Material in Books and Pamphlets', 'Separate Publication of Individual Poems and Prose Works' and 'Compiler's Notes'. Myerson also provides an appendix devoted to 'Principal Works about Whitman', and an index to the poems in *Leaves of Grass*. In *A Reader's Companion to the Fiction of Willa Cather* (ed. Marilyn Arnold and Debra Lynn Thornton), John March provides readers with a valuable resource to the life and work of Willa Cather, including detailed references to her entire canon of fiction and including such works as *O Pioneers!* and *My Ántonia*, among others. March supplements his study with a valuable primary and secondary bibliographical apparatus. In addition to including 796 annotated entries in his volume devoted to assessing the major published scholarship regarding Matthew Arnold, Clinton Machann's *The Essential Matthew Arnold: An Annotated Bibliography of Major Modern Studies* contains nine chapters – 'Bibliographies, Concordances, and Biographical Studies'; 'Editions'; 'Letters'; 'Biography'; 'General Studies'; 'Sources and Formative Influences'; 'Critical Reception, Reputation, and Influence'; 'Poetry'; 'Prose'; and 'Special Topics'. Machann also includes a useful introductory essay detailing the evolution of Arnold criticism during the twentieth century, with particular emphasis upon the shifting nature of Arnold's literary reputation during recent decades. David W. Madden's *Understanding Paul West* concludes with a primary and annotated secondary bibliography of works by and about West.

In *Encyclopedia of Contemporary Literary Theory: Approaches, Scholars, Terms*, Irena R. Makaryk assembles essays and terminological explanations from more than 170 scholars writing upon a wide range of disciplines – from philosophy, anthropology and linguistics to political economy, sociology and women's studies. Compiled in an effort to historicize the recent revolution in literary studies, Makaryk's edition also features a useful selection of bibliographies valuable for literary historians, teachers and students alike. The successor to the 1985 bibliography *Annals of English Verse, 1770–1835: A*

Preliminary Survey of the Volumes Published, J. R. de J. Jackson's *Romantic Poetry by Women: A Bibliography, 1770–1835* features listings of works by female Romantic poets. Each entry includes a detailed bibliographical description, and Jackson supplements his edition with a useful appendix of female pseudonyms from the Romantic era. Casper LeRoy Jordan's *A Bibliographical Guide to African-American Women Writers* offers an alphabetical listing of African-American women writers, as well as valuable biographical data on each literary figure. Jordan concludes the edition with listings of anthologies and general works by African-American women writers, as well as a supplement, 'Additional Writers and Sources, 1988–1991'. Geoffrey R. Kain's *R. K. Narayan: Contemporary Critical Perspectives* is supplemented with a Narayan biographical chronology and an unannotated primary and secondary bibliography devoted to the study of Narayan. Similarly, Douglas Keesey's *Don DeLillo* includes a selected enumerative bibliography of DeLillo's primary works, as well as an annotated bibliography of writings about DeLillo.

In his *Index to American Short Story Award Collections, 1970–1990*, Thomas E. Kennedy features listings for many of the major American short story award collections published during the previous two decades. Each entry includes a chronological index with story contents, an author index and a title index, and Kennedy divides his study into two primary sections, 'Anthologies' and 'Series of Single-Author Collections'. The award editions described in Kennedy's volume include the Pushcart Prize (1976–90), the American Fiction Award (1987–90), the Associated Writing Programs Short Fiction Award (1978–90), the Drue Heinz Literature Prize (1981–90), the Flannery O'Connor Award (1983–90), the University of Illinois Short Fiction Series (1975–90) and the Iowa School of Letters Award (1970–90). David A. Kent and D. R. Ewen's *Romantic Parodies, 1797–1831* concludes with a selected bibliography of critical scholarship regarding the history and nature of parody, while Elizabeth Evans's *Anne Tyler* contains an enumerative primary and annotated secondary bibliography of works by and about Tyler. Stephen Haven's *The Poetry of W. D. Snodgrass: Everything Human* contains Kathleen Snodgrass and Chard de Niord's enumerative and descriptive listing, 'W. D. Snodgrass Bibliography', which includes entries for Snodgrass's extensively reviewed poetic corpus. Likewise, Leslie Hill's *Marguerite Duras: Apocalyptic Desires* features an extensive bibliography of Duras's published work. Daniel Mark Fogel's *A Companion to Henry James Studies* concludes with two useful appendices: 'An Annotated Chronology of Henry James's Principal Publications in Book Form' and 'Landmarks of Henry James Criticism'. In *Modern Mystery, Fantasy, and Science Fiction Writers*, Bruce Cassiday provides listings for nearly 80 mystery, fantasy and science fiction writers. Each entry includes information useful for additional study of each writer, including data regarding each figure's biographical and literary life, as well as pertinent bibliographical details.

A supplement to *The Poems of Emily Dickinson: An Annotated Guide to Commentary Published in English, 1890–1977*, Joseph Duchac's *The Poems of Emily Dickinson: An Annotated Guide to Commentary Published in English, 1978–1989* assembles a number of critical works that explore Dickinson's work as both a woman and an American poet. Arranged alphabetically by the poems' first lines in the tradition of Thomas N. Johnson, Duchac's bibliography features a number of items published by Japanese scholars, thus reflecting two intensive decades of Dickinson criticism published in a nation with its own fervent Emily Dickinson Society. In addition to the inclusion of a useful 'Guide to Commentary', Duchac's annotations trace the critical reception of each Dickinson poem from 1978 to 1989. In *Contemporary Canadian and U.S. Women of Letters: An Annotated Bibliography*, Thomas M. F. Gerry assesses the achievements of a unique group of women writers – women of letters who have written poetry and fiction in addition to their work in literary criticism and theory – and annotates their critical and theoretical work in an effort to acknowledge their feminist strategies for transgressing traditional boundaries. In addition to primary entries on such figures as Sandra M. Gilbert, Jane Rule and Nicole Brossard, Gerry includes supplementary entries devoted to the works of Margaret Atwood, Joan Didion, Alice Walker and Eudora Welty. Usefully cross-referenced and extensively indexed, Gerry organizes his volume alphabetically, with chronological listings and critical commentaries for each writer.

2. General Scholarship for 1994

The year's work in bibliography and textual criticism for 1994 is accented by new editions of two seminal texts by the distinguished twentieth-century bibliographers Fredson Bowers and R. B. McKerrow. Originally published in December 1949, the reissue of Bowers's *Principles of Bibliographical Description* provides a comprehensive manual for the description of books as physical objects and includes a new introduction by G. Thomas Tanselle. Still the central authority of descriptive bibliography, Bowers's volume remains a landmark in the history of textual scholarship. Originally published in 1927, McKerrow's *An Introduction to Bibliography for Literary Students* contains an excellent and extensive new introduction by David McKitterick. In his important study, McKerrow explores the manner in which books are printed and distributed to the public, while also assessing the history of printed books in the era of the hand press. Drawing upon the recent interest in hypertext and hypermedia, Steven J. DeRose and David G. Durand's *Making Hypermedia Work: A User's Guide to HyTime* is of particular interest to bibliographers and other students of electronic text. DeRose and Durand's volume offers an overview of the HyTime international standard for hypertext and its usefulness for managers of electronic documentation, hypermedia and other related products. In addition to the inclusion of several appendices, a glossary and a bibliography, DeRose and Durand's volume provides readers with access to a wide range of multimedia documents and a variety of information types. The authors also feature templates for a host of prefabricated information structures.

Volume 7 of *Text* (ed. D. C. Greetham and W. Speed Hill), includes Paul Eggert's 'Document and Text: The "Life" of the Literary Work and the Capacities of Editing'; Joseph Grigely's 'Textual Criticism and the Arts: The Problem of Textual Space'; C. Deirdre Phelps's 'The Edition as Art Form in Textual and Interpretive Criticism'; Peter M. W. Robinson's 'Collation, Textual Criticism, Publication, and the Computer'; Jerome J. McGann's 'The Complete Writings and Pictures of Dante Gabriel Rossetti: A Hypermedia

Research Archive'; Derek Pearsall's 'Theory and Practice in Middle English Editing'; Ronald Broude's 'Establishing Texts in Quasi-Improvisatory Traditions'; Joseph A. Dane's 'The Lure of Oral Theory in Medieval Criticism: From Edited "Text" to Critical "Work" '; Mary-Jo Arn's 'On Punctuating Medieval Literary Texts'; Murray McGillivray's 'Towards a Post-Critical Edition: Theory, Hypertext, and the Presentation of Middle English Works'; Daniel W. Mosser's 'Reading and Editing the *Canterbury Tales*: Past, Present, and Future (?)'; Elaine E. Whitaker's 'A Collaboration of Readers: Categorization of the Annotations in Copies of Caxton's *Royal Book*'; Ted-Larry Pebworth's 'Manuscript Transmission and the Selection of Copy-Text in Renaissance Coterie Poetry'; Bradley Rubidge's 'Tristan Tzara Edits Sonnet 138: "When loue of truth sweares that she is made" '; Karen T. Bjelland's 'The Cultural Value of Analytical Bibliography and Textual Criticism: The Case of *Troilus and Cressida*'; Ernest W. Sullivan II's '*1633* Vndone'; Gerald MacLean's 'Literacy, Class, and Gender in Restoration England'; Beth Lau's 'Editing Keats's Marginalia'; Heather Bryant Jordan's '*Ara Vos Prec*: A Rescued Volume'; Lawrence Rainey's 'The Letters and the Spirit: Pound's Correspondence and the Concept of Modernism'; Ronald Bush's ' "Unstill, Ever Turning": The Composition of Ezra Pound's *Drafts & Fragments*'; David Leon Higdon and Mark C. Harper's 'Auden "Abandons" a Poem: Problems with Eclectic Texts'; and Tim Hunt's 'Double the Axe, Double the Fun: Is There a Final Version of Jeffers's *The Double Axe*?'

Published by the University of Iowa Center for the Book, the inaugural issue of *Counter* (1) provides readers with information about the Center's educational and creative missions. Selections include 'There Is No Way to Read Shakespeare without Reading a Book: An Interview with Max Thomas'; 'Papermaking Goes Electronic with Production of Video Tape Series'; and 'Apprentice Bridget O'Malley to Take Up Residence at Minnesota Center for Book Arts'. A special issue of *LCUT* (25) features the papers delivered at 'The State and Fate of Publishing: A *Flair* Symposium'. Selections include Thomas F. Staley's introduction; Robert Berdahl's welcome address; Fleur Cowles's opening remarks; Simon Jenkins's 'The Future of Culture: A Keynote Address'; Virginia Postrel's 'The Age of the Editor'; Robert Wallace's 'Magazines and Audiences'; Lawrence Wright's 'Countering Paranoia'; Cheryl Hurley's 'The Library of America'; M. Stuart Lynn's 'Disintermediation in the Digital Age'; Jerome S. Rubin's 'News in the Future'; David Bartlett's 'Cherish the Wealth ... Beware the Censors'; Joseph J. Esposito's 'The Ghost of Publishing Future'; Donald Lamm's 'Two Decades of Publishing: The 1920s and 1980s'; Anita Desai's 'Publishers, Agents, and Agendas'; Shelby Hearon's 'Fiction and the Sense of Order'; Bruce Hunter's 'Change and Improvement in Publishing'; and Carlos Fuentes's summary address.

Hyper/Text/Theory, edited by George P. Landow, includes essays devoted to exploring the role of new information technology and the manner in which it impinges upon the continuing evolution of the literary critical project. Selections include Landow's 'What's a Critic To Do?: Critical Theory in the Age of Hypertext'; Espen J. Arseth's 'Nonlinearity and Literary Theory'; Gunnar Liestøl's 'Wittgenstein, Genette, and the Reader's Narrative in Hypertext'; Mireille Rosello's 'The Screener's Maps: Michel de Certeau's "Wandersmänner" and Paul Auster's Hypertextual Detective'; J. Yellowlees Douglas's ' "How Do I Stop This Thing?": Closure and Indeterminacy in

Interactive Narratives'; Terence Harpold's conclusions on nonlinearity; Charles Ess's 'The Political Computer: Hypertext, Democracy, and Habermas'; Martin E. Rosenberg's 'Physics and Hypertext: Liberation and Complicity in Art and Pedagogy'; Stuart Moulthrop's 'Rhizzome and Resistance: Hypertext and the Dreams of a New Culture'; David Kolb's 'Socrates in the Labyrinth'; and Gregory L. Ulmer's 'The Miranda Warnings: An Experiment in Hyperrhetoric'. In *The Editing of Old English*, Fred C. Robinson explores the problems of transforming Old English texts into modern printed editions. He considers the implications of such an editorial enterprise for the interpretation of these texts, the understanding of their linguistic properties, the relevance of their punctuation to their study and the authority of their creators. Robinson concludes with editions of three Old English texts in an effort to demonstrate the problems associated with transforming them into modern English texts. Kenneth Womack's ' "B as in Byron": Addressing the Need for a Standardized System of Russian Transliteration in the Humanities' (*EdN* [13]) explores the dilemma of divergent Russian transliteration systems on the creation of enumerative bibliographies in the humanities.

PULC (56) features a variety of essays devoted to the study of bibliography, textual criticism and the institution's special collections. Selections include Mark Argetsinger's 'Harmony Discovered: P. J. Conkwright in the Tradition of Classical Typography'; 'A Portfolio of P. J. Conkwright's Designs Printed by The Stinehour Press'; Conkwright's 'Types and Time'; Conkwright's 'A History of American Printing since 1850'; 'A Portfolio of P. J. Conkwright's Designs Printed by Hull Printing Company'; 'Designed by P. J. Conkwright: Books Selected for the A.I.G.A.'s Fifty Books of the Year'; and Dale Roylance's 'From Will Bradley to P. J. Conkwright: Twentieth-Century Typography in the Princeton Graphic Arts Collection'. *PULC* 55 offers a special issue in honour of William H. Scheide (ed. William P. Stoneman), and includes Harold T. Shapiro's 'A Tribute to William H. Scheide'; Stoneman's ' "The Same Purposeful Instinct": Essays in Honor of William H. Scheide'; G. Thomas Tanselle's 'William H. Scheide as Seen from the Grolier Club'; Adelaide Bennett's 'The Scheide Psalter-Hours'; Edith W. Kirsh's 'The Scheide Gradual, Bernardino de Capris, and Manuscript Painting in Novara'; Don C. Skemer's 'In Defense of Ancient Libraries: Shrewsbury Abbey and the English Constitutional Crisis of 1297'; Guiseppe Avarucci and Ugo Paoli's 'The Monastery of San Vittore delle Chiuse: Preliminary Notes for a History'; Carl T. Berkhout's 'The Parkerian Legacy of a Scheide Manuscript: William of Malmesbury's *Gesta Regum Anglorum*'; Paul Needham's 'Aldus Manutius's Paper Stocks: The Evidence of Two Uncut Books'; Janet Ing Freeman's 'Anton Koberger's First Books: Paper Stocks and Sequence of Printing'; and Stoneman's 'Georg Sparsgüt, Rubricator'.

In addition to extensive reviews of a bibliographical nature, *AEB* (8) includes A. S. G. Edwards's 'John Davy Hayward: A List of His Published Writings, 1924–1964'; Arthur P. Young's 'Pre-Gutenberg Culture, Mutable Texts, and the Digital Tollway: A Management Perspective'; Joseph R. McElrath Jr's 'Charles W. Chestnutt's Library'; and Margaret Jane Kidnie's 'Printer's Copy Underlying the Four Editions of Philip Stubbes's *Anatomie of Abuses*'. *ABM* (21) contains Robin de Beaumont's 'Collector's Progress'; Mark Arman's 'Margaret Pole, Bookseller'; Charlotte Franklin's 'Contemporary Binding Exhibitions'; George Sims's 'A Life in Catalogues, Part III';

Michael Dawson's 'Tom Jackson – Bibliophile, Bonviveur, and Bonhomme'; Edward Ripley-Duggan's 'New York Book Fair'; Colin Hynson's 'Russian Avant-Garde Books, 1912–1934'; Paul Minet's 'June Book Fairs'; Hynson's 'Cambridgeshire Bookshops'; Michael Dawson's 'Philip Smith – A Binder Unbounded'; and George Sims's 'A Life in Catalogues, Part IV'.

BC (43) features Stuart Morrison's 'Records of a Bibliophile: The Catalogues of Consul Joseph Smith and Some Aspects of His Collecting'; Roger W. Peattie's 'Frank W. Burgess: Bookseller and Book Cover Artist'; Richard Landon's 'The Stillman Drake Galileo Collection'; Mirjam M. Foot's 'English and Foreign Bookbindings 66'; Robert Alan Shaddy's 'A World of Sentimental Attachments: The Cult of Collecting, 1890–1938'; Eugene D. LeMire's 'William Morris in America: A Publishing History from Archives'; James E. Crimmins's 'From an "Ultra-Democrat" to an "Ultra-Aristocrat": Bentham Tracts in the Adams Collection at Quincy, Massachusetts'; John Morris's 'English and Foreign Bookbindings 67'; Gwyn Walters's 'The Library of Thomas Burgess (1756–1837)'; Richard Pankhurst's 'The Manuscript Binding of Merca, Somalia'; W. Thomas Taylor's 'The Making of Audubon's "Salvator": The Royal Octavo Edition of *The Birds of America*'; Anthony James West's 'In Search of Missing Copies of the Shakespeare First Folio'; R. J. Goulden's 'English and Foreign Bookbindings 68'; Saul Jarcho's 'The Medical Imprints of Giambattista Bodoni'; Colin Franklin's 'Print and Design in Eighteenth-Century Editions of Shakespeare'; Guy de la Bédoyère's 'John Evelyn's Library Catalogue'; Roger L. Brooks's 'Matthew Arnold's "Then comes the whistling clown" '; and David Pearson's 'English and Foreign Bookbindings 69'.

Library (16) contains David Pearson's 'English Centrepiece Bookbindings, 1560–1640'; Oliver Pickering's 'Henry Hall of Hereford's Poetical Tributes to Henry Purcell'; Lishi Kwasitsu's 'Printing in Victoria, Australia, 1850–1900'; Peter Davison's 'Orwell: Balancing the Books'; Warwick Gould's 'W. B. Yeats and the Resurrection of the Author'; P. J. P. Goldberg's 'Lay Book Ownership in Late Medieval York: The Evidence of Wills'; Stephen Tabor's 'Additions to STC'; and Dennis E. Rhodes's 'Lelio Capilupi and the "Centones ex Vergilio" '. A special issue of *Library Trends* on 'Libraries and the Internet: Education, Practice, and Policy' (ed. Thomas D. Walker) features a number of valuable essays. Selections include: Walker's introduction, Charles R. McClure's 'User-Based Data Collection Techniques and Strategies for Evaluating Networked Information Services'; Tschera Harkness Connell and Carl Franklin's 'The Internet: Educational Issues'; Constance Wittig and Dietmar Wolfram's 'A Survey of Networking Education in North American Library Schools'; Diane K. Kovacs, Barbara F. Schloman and Julie A. McDaniel's 'A Model for Planning and Providing Reference Services Using Internet Resources'; Yuan Zhou's 'From Smart Guesser to Smart Navigator: Changes in Collection Development for Research Libraries in a Network Environment'; Judith J. Senkevitch and Dietmar Wolfram's 'Equalizing Access to Electronic Networked Resources: A Model for Rural Libraries in the United States'; Susan Hockey's 'Evaluating Electronic Texts in the Humanities'; and Ann Peterson Bishop's 'The Role of Computer Networks in Aerospace Engineering'. *PBSA* (88) contains W. B. Coley's 'Did Fielding Write the *Rat*?'; Mary D. Shepherd's 'Forrest's Curious Old Play'; Karen T. Bjelland's 'Variants as Epistemological Shifts'; Robert H. Hirst's 'Editing Mark Twain';

Michael F. Suarez, S.J.'s 'Dodsley's "Collection of Poems" and the Ghost of Pope'; and Robert D. Armstrong's ' "The Work Must Be Performed Elsewhere": The Printing of Montana's Laws and Legislative Journals, 1866–1881'.

Volume 47 of *SB* (ed. David L. Vander Meulen), features a wide range of scholarly articles on bibliography and textual criticism. Selections include G. Thomas Tanselle's 'Editing without a Copy-Text'; Paul Needham's 'Allan H. Stevenson and the Bibliographical Use of Paper'; Paul Eggert's 'Editing Paintings/Conserving Literature: The Nature of the "Work" '; Joel Fredell's 'Decorated Initials in the Lincoln Thornton Manuscript'; William McClellan's 'The Transcription of the "Clerk's Tale" in MS HM 140: Interpreting Textual Effects'; G. E. Bentley Jr's 'Images of the Word: Separately Published English Bible Illustrations, 1539–1830'; Ann R. Meyer's 'Shakespeare's Art and the Texts of *King Lear*'; James A. Riddell's 'The Concluding Pages of the Jonson Folio of 1616'; O M Brack Jr's 'Samuel Johnson and the Preface to Abbé Prévost's *Memoirs of a Man of Quality*'; Emily Lorraine de Montluzin's 'Attributions of Authorship in the *Gentleman's Magazine*, 1809–26: A Supplement to Kuist'; Nicholas A. Joukovsky's 'Thomas Love Peacock's Manuscript "Poems" of 1804'; Arthur Sherbo's 'Last Gleanings from *The Critic*: Clemens, Whitman, Hardy, Thackeray, and Others'; Sherbo's 'Shaw's Forgotten Lecture (and Other Matters Shavian)'; Louis J. Oldani's 'Dreiser's "*Genius*" in the Making: Composition and Revision'; and Nancy Yanoshak's 'Watermarks and the Dating of Old Russian Manuscripts: The Case of *Poslanie Mnogoslovnoe*'.

The year's work regarding the history of the book continues to grow at a remarkable pace. In *William Shakespeare and John Fletcher: Cardenio, or, The Second Maiden's Tragedy*, Charles Hamilton addresses the authentication of the composition by Shakespeare and John Fletcher, a fellow dramatist of the King's Men, of *Cardenio*, a play that met with censorship in October 1611 and was last performed before King James I's court during the Christmas season of 1612–13. Registered in 1653 as a play penned by Shakespeare and Fletcher, *Cardenio* languished for years under the censor's title, *The Second Maiden's Tragedy*, until it was rediscovered by Hamilton, a world-renowned paleographer. Jonathan Hope's *The Authorship of Shakespeare's Plays* gathers sociohistorical linguistic evidence regarding a rapid shift in English grammar during the late sixteenth and early seventeenth centuries in an effort to determine the authorship of Renaissance play texts. Hope devotes particular attention to the works of Shakespeare, his collaborations with Fletcher and Middleton, and the apocryphal plays. Hope features close analysis of *Henry VIII, The Two Noble Kinsmen, Macbeth, Pericles* and *Sir Thomas More*. Drawing upon a selection of graphs that offer his statistical data in a comprehensible fashion, Hope provides strong evidence that might yet confirm *Edward III* as a viable candidate for inclusion in Shakespeare's canon. Drawing upon a computer-assisted analysis of parallel texts of the plays, Kathleen O. Irace's *Reforming the 'Bad' Quartos: Performance and Provenance of Six Shakespearean First Editions* evaluates the six 'bad' quartos as viable theatrical scripts in their own right and attempts to solve the mystery of their origins. In addition to featuring close readings of the first printed editions of *Hamlet, Henry V, Romeo and Juliet, The Merry Wives of Windsor* and *I and II Henry VI*, Irace examines alternatives in plot structure, characterization and staging in the six play texts. A selection of appendices features tables that outline omissions and other differences between the quarto and folio versions of the plays.

In *Textual Bodies: Modernism, Postmodernism, and Print*, Michael Kaufmann offers a textual study of the unusual physical appearance of modernist novels, including special attention to their unique typography, pagination and binding. Drawing upon such texts as Faulkner's *As I Lay Dying*, Stein's *Tender Buttons*, Joyce's *Finnegans Wake* and Gass's *Willie Masters's Lonesome Wife*, Kaufmann explores the ways in which these writers appropriate the printed nature of their works as part of their fictions. *Crisis in Editing: Texts of the English Renaissance*, edited by Randall McLeod, features papers delivered at the Twenty-Fourth Annual Conference on Editorial Problems at the University of Toronto in November 1988. Selections include Nicolas Barker's 'Manuscript into Print'; Gary Taylor's 'The Rhetorics of Reaction'; Random Cloud's 'FIAT ƒLUX'; Jonathan Goldberg's ' "What? in a names that which we call a Rose": The Desired Texts of *Romeo and Juliet*'; Antony Hammond's 'The Noisy Comma: Searching for the Signal in Renaissance Dramatic Texts'; and Stephen Orgel's 'Acting Scripts, Performing Texts'. *Late-Medieval Religious Texts and Their Transmission: Essays in Honour of A. I. Doyle* (ed. A. J. Minnis) contains essays originally presented at the Sixth York Manuscripts Conference at the University of York in July 1991. Selections include: Bella Millett's '*Mouvance* and the Medieval Author: Re-Editing *Ancrene Wisse*'; O. S. Pickering's 'The Outspoken *South English Legendary* Poet'; Jocelyn Wogan-Browne's 'The Apple's Message: Some Post-Conquest Hagiographic Accounts of Textual Transmission'; Thomas G. Duncan's 'Two Middle English Penitential Lyrics: Sound and Scansion'; Sue Powell's 'The Transmission and Circulation of *The Lay Folk's Catechism*'; Ralph Hanna III's ' "Meddling with Makings" and Will's Work'; Vincent Gillespie's 'Thy Will Be Done: *Piers Plowman* and the *Pater Noster*'; Anne Hudson's 'Aspects of the "Publication" of Wyclif's Latin Sermons'; Alan J. Fletcher's 'A Hive of Industry or a Hornets' Nest?: MS Sidney Sussex 74 and Its Scribes'; A. S. G. Edwards's 'The Transmission and Audience of Osbern Bokenham's *Legendys of Hooly Wummen*'; and John J. Thompson's 'Another Look at the Religious Texts in Lincoln, Cathedral Library, MS 91'.

In *Print Culture in Renaissance Italy: The Editor and the Vernacular Text, 1470–1600*, Brian Richardson explores the editor's role in the production of Italian texts of Dante, Petrarch, Boccaccio, Ariosto and Castiglione, among others. In addition to featuring close analyses of the works of individual editors and their methodologies, Richardson examines the growth of importance of editorial functions during this era, as well as the relationship between editors and printers during the late fourteenth and fifteenth centuries. Richardson also analyses the role of editors in the standardization of the Italian language and the transmission of vernacular texts between 1470 and 1600. The essays in *A Millennium of the Book: Production, Design, and Illustration in Manuscript and Print, 900–1900*, edited by Robin Myers and Michael Harris, trace the history of the book as a physical artifact. Selections include Linda Nix's 'Early Medieval Book Design in England: The Influence of Manuscript Design on the Transmission of Texts'; Margaret M. Smith's 'The Design Relationship between the Manuscript and the Incunable'; Nicolas Barker's 'The Aldine Italic'; Nicholas Pickwood's 'Onward and

Downward: How Binders Coped with the Printing Press before 1800'; David Alexander's ' "Alone worth treble the price": Illustrations in Eighteenth-Century English Magazines'; Michael Twyman's 'The Emergence of the Graphic Book in the Nineteenth Century'; and George Mandl's 'Paper Chase: A Millennium in the Production and Use of Paper'. *Bookbindings and Other Bibliophily: Essays in Honour of Anthony Hobson* (ed. Dennis E. Rhodes) collects a wide array of essays that address bookbinding and other bibliographical issues. Selections include: Frederick B. Adams's foreword; Nicolas Barker's 'Anthony Robert Alwyn Hobson'; Manfred von Arnim's 'Grolier Bindings in the Otto Schäfer Library'; Giles Barber's 'From Baroque to Neoclassicism: French Eighteenth-Century Bindings at Oxford'; Elly Cockx-Indestege's 'On the History of Bookbinding in the Low Countries: A Glimpse of Prosper Verheyden and His Correspondents, c.1900–1947'; Georges Colin's 'Marques de libraires et d'éditeurs dorées sur des reliures'; Mirjam M. Foot's ' "Un grand Duc, immortel à la posterité": Some Bindings for Anne de Montmorency'; Lotte Hellinga's 'Peter Schoeffer and the Book-Trade in Mainz: Evidence for the Organization'; Bent Juel-Jensen's 'Three Ethiopic Bindings'; Piccarda Quilici's 'Legature del Piccolpasso e legature Viscontee nella Biblioteca Ambrosiana di Milano'; Rhodes's 'Some English, Scottish, Welsh, and Irish Book-Collectors in Italy, 1465–1800'; David J. Shaw's 'Books Belonging to William Warham, Archdeacon of Canterbury, c.1504–1532'; Jan Storm van Leeuwen's 'Some Observations on Dutch Publishers' Bindings Up Till 1800'; Jeanne Veyrin-Forrer's 'Notes sur Thomas Mahieu'; and a 'Bibliography of A. R. A. Hobson (to the End of July 1993)'.

W. David Sloan and Julie Hedgepeth Williams's *The Early American Press, 1690–1873* investigates the development of the early American press, particularly in Boston and Philadelphia, and addresses the role of the press during the American Revolution. In addition to chapters that address the expansion of the Colonial press during the early 1700s and the Stamp Act Crisis in the mid-1760s, Sloan and Williams conclude their study with a bibliographical essay of materials related to the development of the early American press. Originally published in 1907 by David McNeely Stauffer, the reprint of *American Engravers upon Copper and Steel* includes biographical sketches and a checklist of works by more than 700 engravers. This edition includes Mantle Fielding's 1917 supplement to Stauffer's checklist, as well as Thomas Hovey Gage's 1920 addition of an Artist's index to Stauffer's original text. Richard F. Whalen's *Shakespeare: Who Was He? – The Oxford Challenge to the Bard of Avon* summarizes the competing arguments in the authorship controversy regarding the identity of the author of the plays attributed to William Shakespeare. In addition to exploring the cases of Shakespeare and Edward de Vere, the seventeenth Earl of Oxford, Whalen discusses the candidacies of Bacon and Marlowe, among others. Whalen subscribes to the theory that the Earl of Oxford composed the plays because of the interconnections he discovers between the life of de Vere and the works of Shakespeare, particularly *Hamlet*. Whalen concludes his study with an expansive annotated bibliography devoted to the controversy.

Edited by John Rowe Townsend, *John Newbery and His Books: Trade and Plumb-Cake for Ever, Huzza!* features essays that explore the life and work of John Newbery, the eighteenth-century bookseller whose name graces the award – the John Newbery Medal – presented yearly since 1922 to the most distinguished American children's book of the year. Selections include Townsend's 'A Man of Parts'; Samuel Johnson's 'Jack Whirler'; Charles Welsh's 'A Bookseller of the Last Century'; George Colman's 'Mr. and Mrs. Folio at Oxford'; a listing of 'Mr. Newbery's Little Books'; an essay attributed to Newbery, 'Tommy Trip and His Dog Jouler'; and Townsend's appendices on 'Earlier Newberys', 'The *Reading Mercury*', 'The Newbery Books in America' and 'The Inheritors'. Townsend concludes this volume with a complete listing of Newbery Medal winners from 1922 to the present. Jack Stillinger's *Coleridge and Textual Instability: The Multiple Versions of the Major Poems* establishes and catalogues the appearances of numerous, divergent editions of Coleridge's most well-known poems, including items from *The Eolian Harp*, *The Rime of the Ancient Mariner* and *Christabel*. Stillinger also assesses the manner in which the existence of these texts calls into question the nature of Coleridge's canon, the editorial treatment of the poet's work and the ways in which multiple versions of his poems affect the interpretation of his verse as a unified – or disunified – body of work. Originally published in German as *Mittelalterliche Studien: Ausgewählte Aufsätze zur Schriftkunde und Literaturgeschichte*, Bernard Bischoff's *Manuscripts and Libraries in the Age of Charlemagne* features some of the renowned scholar's most outstanding work in the field of medieval paleography. Translated by Michael M. Gorman, the seven essays by Bischoff included in this edition investigate the manuscript evidence and the role of books in the transmission of culture from the sixth to the late eighth century, as well as exploring the court libraries of Charlemagne and Louis the Pious. Bischoff also addresses the principal writing centres and libraries associated with monastic and cathedral schools.

The essays in *For the Good of the Order: Essays in Honor of Edward G. Holley* (ed. Delmus E. Williams, John M. Budd, Robert E. Martin, Barbara Moran and Fred Roper), commemorate the achievements of Edward G. Holley, the distinguished librarian and Chairman of the Board of OCLC, Inc. Selections include: Williams's preface; James V. Carmichael Jr's 'Richer for His Honesty: A Personal Memoir of Edward Gailon Holley'; William Friday's 'The Future of the American Research University'; Haynes McMullen's 'The Founding of Libraries in American Colleges and Professional Schools before 1876'; Moran's 'What Lies Ahead for Academic Libraries?: Steps on the Way to the Virtual Library'; Irene B. Hoadley's 'Somewhere over the Rainbow: Organizational Patterns in Academic Libraries'; Robert E. Molyneux's 'More Hortatory Than Factual: Fremont Rider's Exponential Growth Hypothesis and the Context of Exponentialism'; David Kaser's 'Andrew Carnegie and the Black College Libraries'; Donald G. Davis Jr and John Mark Tucker's 'Change and Tradition in Land-Grant University Libraries'; Williams's 'The Urban University and Its Library'; Charles D. Churchwell's 'Diversity and Democracy in Higher Education'; Budd's 'Scholarly Communication and Libraries: Contemporary and Future'; Donald E. Riggs's 'Academic Library Literature'; Phyllis Dain's 'The Old Scholarship and the New: Reflections on the Historic Role of Libraries'; Wayne Wiegand's 'Catalog of "A.L.A." Library (1893): Origins of a Genre'; Robert N. Broadus's 'Theories of Collection Development in the Early Years of the Graduate Library School at University of Chicago'; John Richardson Jr's 'The State of Library and Information Science Education'; John N. Olsgaard and Roper's 'Future Directions for Programs of Library and Information Science Education';

K. Wayne Smith's 'OCLC: Past and Future'; E. Jens Holley's 'Edward G. Holley: A Select Bibliography'; and Carmichael's 'An Edward Gailon Holley Chronology'.

The essays in *Writers, Books, and Trade: An Eighteenth-Century English Miscellany for William B. Todd* (ed. O M Brack, Jr) address the history of the English book trade in the eighteenth century, while also providing a historical context for the writing, printing, publishing and distribution of books during that era. Selections include: James Raven's 'Selling One's Life: James Lackington, Eighteenth-Century Booksellers, and the Design of Autobiography'; C. J. Mitchell's 'Women in the Eighteenth-Century Book Trade'; Patricia Hernlund's 'Mid-Century Bankruptcy in Bookselling'; Beverly Schneller's 'Using Newspaper Advertisements to Study the Book Trade: A Year in the Life of Mary Cooper'; K. I. D. Maslen's 'Slaves or Freemen?: The Case of William Boyer, Father and Son, Printers of London, 1699–1777'; Jan Fergus and Ruth Portner's 'Provincial Subscribers to the *Monthly* and *Critical Reviews*, and Their Book Purchasing'; B. J. McMullin's 'Further Observations on the Incidence and Interpretation of Press Figures'; G. Thomas Tanselle's 'Press Figures in America: The Shop of Thomas Dobson'; David L. Vander Meulen's 'Unauthorized Editions of Pope's *Dunciad*, 1728–1747'; Hugh Amory's 'Master Arthur and the Boys: Author, Editor, and Compositor in Fielding's *Amelia*'; Brack's 'Tobias Smollett Puffs His Histories'; Nicholas Barker's 'William Strahan and Laurence Sterne'; John Horden's 'John Freeth: The Birmingham Poet'; Betty Rizzo's 'Bonnell Thornton, Reviewer: Evolution of a Technique'; J. D. Fleeman's 'Johnson's Shakespeare (1765): The Progress of a Subscription'; Donald D. Eddy's '*A Bibliography of John Brown*: A Supplement'; and Thomas R. Adams's 'Mount and Page Imprints, 1684–1800'. *Victorian Periodicals and Victorian Society*, edited by J. Don Vann and Rosemary T. VanArsdel, assembles essays that discuss the relationships between Victorian periodicals and professional occupations, the arts, commerce and popular culture. Selections include: Richard A. Cosgrove on 'Law'; M. Jeanne Peterson on 'Medicine'; Ruth Richardson and Robert Thorne on 'Architecture'; Albert Tucker on the 'Military'; William H. Brock on 'Science'; Leanne Langley on 'Music'; Patricia Anderson on 'Illustration'; Robert A. Colby on 'Authorship and the Book Trade'; Jane W. Stedman on the 'Theatre'; John E. C. Palmer and Harold W. Paar on 'Transport'; David J. Moss and Chris Hosgood on the 'Financial and Trade Press'; Terence Nevett on 'Advertising'; Bernard A. Cook on 'Agriculture'; Olwen C. Niessen on 'Temperance'; Vann on 'Comic Periodicals'; and Tony Mason on 'Sport'. The volume concludes with two appendices – Jonathan Rose's 'Worker's Journals' and VanArsdel and John S. North's 'Student Journals'.

Using the fourteenth-century text of *Libro de buen amor* as his editorial exemplar, John Dagenais's *The Ethics of Reading in Manuscript Culture: Glossing the Libro de buen amor* argues that the traditional philological practice of reducing manuscript evidence to a single critical edition founded upon problematic notions of 'authorial intention' and 'coherent texts' ultimately distorts the true nature of the medieval text. Dagenais maintains that such textual practices inevitably suppress the physical qualities of the manuscript – from its glosses, marginal notes, and pointing hands to its incidental scribblings, scribal errors and lost leaves. *The Cultures of Collecting*, edited by John Elsner and Roger Cardinal, contains essays devoted to investigating the primary human compulsion to accumulate, classify and arrange the objects of the collector's fancy. In addition to Elsner and Cardinal's introduction, the selections include: Jean Baudrillard's 'The System of Collecting'; Robert Opie's ' "Unless you do these crazy things . . . ": An Interview with Robert Opie'; John Windsor's 'Identity Parades'; Cardinal's 'Collecting and Collage-Making: The Case of Kurt Schwitters'; Mieke Bal's 'Telling Objects: A Narrative Perspective on Collecting'; Nicholas Thomas's 'Licensed Curiosity: Cook's Pacific Voyages'; Thomas DaCosta Kaufmann's 'From Treasury to Museum: The Collections of the Austrian Habsburgs'; Elsner's 'A Collector's Model of Desire: The House and Museum of Sir John Soane'; Anthony Alan Shelton's 'Cabinets of Transgression: Renaissance Collections and the Incorporation of the New World'; Susan Stewart's 'Death and Life, in that Order, in the Works of Charles Willson Peale'; John Forrester's ' "Mille e tre": Freud and Collecting'; and Naomi Schor's 'Collecting Paris'. In *The University of Colorado Library and Its Makers, 1876–1972*, Ellsworth Mason addresses the evolution of the library at the University of Colorado at Boulder from its earliest nineteenth-century origins until its emergence as a major research institution during the 1970s. The volume concludes with biographical appendices that discuss 'The Makers' of the university's library, including the library's first benefactor, Charles G. Buckingham, as well as the library's influential leader, Ralph Eugene Ellsworth.

1994 also witnessed the publication of a host of useful enumerative bibliographies. *BB* (51) includes Allan Metz's 'Assessments of President Bill Clinton's First 100 Days: An Annotated Bibliography'; John A. Drobnicki, Carol R. Goldman, Trina R. Knight and Johanna V. Thomas's 'Holocaust-Denial Literature: A Bibliography'; Evelyn Leasher's 'Ladies' Library Associations in Michigan: A Bibliography'; Christopher E. M. Pearson's 'A Selective Bibliography of Works of Le Corbusier Published in the 1980s'; James R. Bennett and Jason B. King's 'United States Literature and the Acquisitive Society, Background and Criticism: A Third Bibliography'; Kenneth Womack's 'Martin Donisthorpe Armstrong (1882–1974): A Primary and Secondary Bibliography'; Jack W. C. Hagstrom and Joshua Odell's 'Emendations to Thom Gunn: A Bibliography, 1940–1978 (Part V)'; Bill Morgan's 'Lawrence Ferlinghetti: An Updated Bibliography, 1980–1993'; David Pardue's 'Alternative Approaches to Contemporary Mayan Cultures: An Annotated Bibliography'; Ann Vreeland Watkins's 'Rachel Hadas, Poet and Essayist: A Bibliography, 1965–1993'; James Bense's 'Thomas Berger: Primary and Secondary Works'; Dawn Evans Radford's 'Annie Dillard: A Bibliographical Survey'; Janell Pierce's 'Tattoos: A Bibliography'; David Bradshaw's 'A New Bibliography of Aldous Huxley's Work and Its Reception, 1912–1937'; Lavonda Kay Broadnax's 'The Literature of Imhotep: Who Is This Ancient Black Egyptian, and Why Is So Little Known about Him?'; Peter Chobanian's 'Sidney Hillman: A Bibliography'; Ann Peterson's 'A Secondary Bibliography of George Crabbe, 1975–1989'; Steven E. Smith's 'Index to the *Poetry Book Society Bulletin*'; and Samuel Ben-Gad's 'Robert Bresson: A Bibliography of Works by and about Him, 1981–1993'.

Paul K. Alkon's *Science Fiction before 1900: Imagination Discovers Technology* concludes with a bibliographic essay that surveys recent developments in the field of science fiction criticism, while James S. Baumlin and Tita French Baumlin's *Ethos: New Essays in Rhetorical and Critical Theory* includes the unannotated listing, 'A Selected Bibliography of Modern Research on *Ethos*'. In addition to providing scholars and book collectors with valuable, annotated listings for a number of rare books, Bernice E. Gallagher's *Illinois Women Novelists in the Nineteenth Century: An Analysis and Annotated Bibliography* historicizes a selected group of novels written by Illinois women writers between 1854 and 1893. Including entries by Illinois writers from Mary Hartwell Catherwood and Hattie Tyng Griswold to Clara Louis Root Burnham and Celia Parker Woolley, Gallagher offers analysis of each volume and discusses its significance within the larger context of American literary and publishing history. The novels in Gallagher's study were originally chosen for inclusion in a collection of work by women that was exhibited in the 1893 World's Columbian Exposition in Chicago. The volume concludes with an extensive bibliography of work by the authors featured in Gallagher's study. Ian Hamilton's *The Oxford Companion to Twentieth-Century Poetry in English* includes individual entries for a diversity of poets writing in English during this century. Each entry includes a selection of personal data pertinent to each figure's biographical and literary life, as well as useful bibliographical information regarding each author's principal literary accomplishments. In *Herman Wouk*, Laurence W. Mazzeno provides readers with a comprehensive annotated bibliography of materials by and about Wouk.

Written as a complete reference work to Cather's short fiction, Sheryl L. Meyering's *A Reader's Guide to the Short Stories of Willa Cather* features entries for each of Cather's more than 60 stories. Each story entry includes the story's publication history, the circumstances of its composition, its connections with other works by Cather, its critical reception and a bibliography. Wolfgang Mieder and Stewart A. Kingsbury's *A Dictionary of Wellerisms* assembles more than 1,500 wellerisms drawn from an initial collection of more than 150,000 wellerisms now housed in the archives of the University of Missouri at Columbia. Each entry is indexed alphabetically and includes listings of variants and useful bibliographical information. In *Eudora Welty: A Bibliography of Her Work*, Noel Polk establishes the history of the writing, editing, publishing and printing of each of Welty's volumes in this expansive bibliography. Divided into two primary sections – 'Books' and 'Shorter Works' – Polk's volume details each entry's casing, colour, size, paper type, binding, format and dust-jacket, while also exploring Welty's contributions to journals, her juvenilia, book reviews, dust-jacket blurbs and photographic work. Polk's bibliography concludes with an appendix, 'A Eudora Welty Publishing Log', which lists chronologically items from the bibliography that reveal the strong interconnections between all aspects of Welty's career. John R. Roberts's *New Perspectives on the Seventeenth-Century English Religious Lyric* contains an unannotated listing of 'The Seventeenth-Century English Religious Lyric: A Selective Bibliography of Modern Criticism, 1952–1990', which selectively enumerates modern critical studies of religious lyricists of the late sixteenth and seventeenth centuries.

In *The Romance of Real Life: Charles Brockden Brown and the Origins of American Culture*, Steven Watts offers an important bibliographical essay devoted to recent developments in Brown criticism. Arranged alphabetically by author, Alan R. Weiner and Speans Means's *Literary Criticism Index* attempts to provide a primary research tool for students and scholars alike.

Extensively annotated, the updated *Literary Criticism Index* features entries on a number of significant authors and titles in the burgeoning field of literary criticism. *ShS 46* is *Shakespeare and Sexuality*, edited by Stanley Wells, and features three entries of particular interest to students of bibliography and textual criticism: Peter Holland's 'Shakespeare Performances in England, 1992'; 'Professional Shakespeare Productions in the British Isles, January–December 1991', compiled by Niky Rathbone; and 'The Year's Contributions to Shakespeare Studies,' which includes sections on 'Critical Studies', 'Shakespeare's Life, Times, and Stage' and 'Editions and Textual Studies', compiled by David Lindley, Martin Wiggins and H. R. Woodhuysen, respectively. Orphia Jane Allen's *Barbara Pym: Writing a Life* contains an enumerative 'Barbara Pym Bibliography: A Comprehensive Listing of Primary and Secondary Published Materials'. Originally published in 1975, Maurice Annenberg's *Type Foundries of America and Their Catalogs* offers a bibliography of American type specimen books, as well as historical accounts of each foundry, a list of its specimen books with size and number of pages and a variety of other historical and typographical information. Updated by printing historian Stephen O. Saxe, Annenberg's text includes new appendices, an introduction and a biographical sketch of Annenberg. This new edition includes listings for 72 additional type specimen books and particular attention to the discovery of a new type foundry that belonged to Abraham Riggs of New York City. Also featured are complete type specimen holdings of the New York City Public Library, the Smithsonian Institution and Saxe's personal collection. In *Native Americans in Fiction: A Guide to 765 Books for Librarians and Teachers, K-9*, Vicki Anderson's expansive bibliography affords students and librarians alike with annotations for 765 fictional titles representing the works of 115 different tribes. Ranging in date from 1960 to 1993, the books included in Anderson's study offer a diversity of cultural perspectives, including particular emphasis upon the daily lives and social value systems of Native Americans and their remarkable contributions to the evolution and development of the United States.

In *The New Men's Studies: A Selected and Annotated Interdisciplinary Bibliography*, Eugene R. August provides listings devoted to articles and monographs that pertain to the growing scholarly and popular interest in men's studies. Annotated and cross-referenced, August's bibliography addresses a host of subjects and their interrelations with masculinity, including anthropology, sociology, autobiography, biography, pornography, psychology and health-related topics. August includes chapters on humour, men's rights, the patriarchy, sexuality, sexual harassment and spirituality. Extensively indexed and cross-referenced, Erica Bauermeister's *500 Great Books by Women: A Reader's Guide* features listings for 500 notable works by female authors. Bauermeister devotes particular attention to delineating each work by its theme and genre, and includes chapters on such subjects as ethics, friendship, heritage, identity, power, violence, adversity and imagined worlds, among other subjects. Bauermeister offers seven indexes that provide readers access to the volumes in her study by title, author, date, genre, region and country, ethnicity and lesbian and gay texts. Eugene Benson and L. W. Conolly's immense *Encyclopedia of Post-Colonial Literatures in English* offers more than 1,600 biographical and critical entries regarding literary works and writers from more than 50 countries and mandated territories.

Alphabetically arranged into three major divisions – including national entries, major subject or genre entries, and a variety of broad literary overviews – Benson and Conolly's volume offers a valuable reference work that explores the effect of the colonial and post-colonial experience. Roger Jackson and William E. Ashley's *Henry Miller: A Bibliography of Primary Sources, Volume 2* updates Jackson and Laurence J. Shifreen's earlier volume with the addition of hundreds of new textual variants, several useful appendices and thousands of entries devoted to Miller's immense published corpus.

In *Dystopian Literature: A Theory and Research Guide*, M. Keith Booker offers an expansive vision of dystopian literature from its earliest origins in works such as Sir Thomas More's *Utopia* through its modern incarnations in works by Anthony Burgess, Vassily Aksyonov, George Orwell and Yevgeny Zamyatin, among a diversity of other practitioners of the genre. Booker divides his reference guide into five sections: 'A Guide to Selected Modern Cultural Criticism with Relevance to Dystopian Literature'; 'A Guide to Selected Utopian Fictions'; 'A Guide to Dystopian Fictions'; 'A Guide to Selected Dystopian Drama'; and 'A Guide to Selected Dystopian Films'. Jack DeBellis's *John Updike: A Bibliography, 1967–1993* includes listings of John Updike's books, plays, short fiction, poetry, articles and essays, reviews, interviews, letters and manuscripts, translations and graphics and reading. DeBellis also affords attention to secondary works about Updike, including general commentary, criticism of individual works, dissertations and theses and parodies and caricatures. DeBellis includes two appendices, 'Translations of Updike's Work' and 'Periodicals in Which Updike Has Published'. Designed for designers, typesetters, editors, proofreaders and related professionals, Richard Eckersley's *Glossary of Typesetting Terms* attempts to define the language of typesetting in terms of the present technology within a historical context. Eckersley affords special attention to the creation of typographical standards and traditionally accepted principles of typesetting. A selection of eight appendices address such subjects as 'The Parts of a Letter'; 'The Parts of a Book'; 'Type Styles'; 'Coding a Manuscript and Writing Specifications'; 'Elements of House Style'; 'Tables'; 'Accents, Diacritics, and Special Characters'; and 'Proofreaders' Marks'.

The publication of Robert N. Essick's *William Blake at the Huntington: An Introduction to the William Blake Collection in the Henry E. Huntington Library and Art Gallery, San Marino, California* commemorates the seventy-fifth anniversary of the founding in 1919 of the Henry E. Huntington Library and Art Gallery in San Marino, California. Essick discusses the Huntington's vast collection of Blake's manuscripts, illustrated books, illuminated volumes and individual works of art. Essick includes 'A Note on Blake's Illuminated Books' and a lavish selection of 'Plates and Commentaries'. R. A. Gekoski and P. A. Grogan's *William Golding: A Bibliography, 1934–1993* features seven sections: 'Books and Pamphlets'; 'Contributions to Books'; 'Contributions to Periodicals and Newspapers'; 'Broadcasts'; 'Translations'; 'Criticism'; and 'Reviews of Books, Plays, and Broadcasts'. This is *the* definitive Golding bibliography, splendidly executed with details and information in fecundity. It is an appropriate monument to an unageing intellect. John R. Greenfield's *Dictionary of British Literary Characters, Volume II: Twentieth-Century Novels* surveys 686 novels and more than 10,000 literary characters. Greenfield includes novelists who published the bulk of their work after 1900 and features some novels from the contemporary era, while offering useful information about each character's occupation, family relations, relations with other characters, class and gender roles, as well as that character's contribution to the novel's overall plots and themes. In *A Companion to The Crying of Lot 49*, J. Kerry Grant includes a valuable, annotated bibliographical survey of the secondary scholarship devoted to Pynchon's important postmodernist novel.

Elizabeth Harrison's *Andrew M. Greeley: An Annotated Bibliography* includes attention to the writer's books, contributions to books and periodicals, newspaper columns, film and book reviews, unpublished papers and theses, newsletters and miscellanea. In addition to featuring attention to the critical response to Greeley, Harrison includes appendices that address such subjects as American Catholicism; catechisms, meditations and prayers; education; ethnicity; the Irish; the priesthood; the religious imagination; social and political commentary; the sociology of religion; and youth ministry. In this updated second edition of the 1991 edition of *A Glossary of Contemporary Literary Theory*, Jeremy Hawthorn adds more than 50 new entries to his lexicon devoted to contemporary literary theory. In addition to his inclusion of an expanded new bibliography, Hawthorn features entries that allow the reader to gain the context for each term as well as its origin and development within the parlance of critical theory. In *John Steinbeck: Dissertation Abstracts and Research Opportunities*, Tetsumaro Hayashi and Beverly K. Simpson provide updated listings of dissertations devoted to the study of John Steinbeck from 1946 to 1993. Hayashi and Simpson supplement their volume with extensive indices to their collection of dissertation abstracts. Jean-Pierre V. M. Hérubel's *Annales Historiography and Theory: A Selective and Annotated Bibliography* includes critical entries that investigate the ways in which historical research and scholarship have been transformed by Annales approaches to writing about the past. In addition to a chapter on the history and evolution of the Annales, Hérubel features listings for 'Historiography and Theory' and 'Major Historians and Representative Scholarship'. In *Milton's Sonnets: An Annotated Bibliography, 1900–1992*, Edward Jones surveys the critical response to Milton's sonnets during the twentieth century. In addition to featuring chapters on general criticism of the sonnets, the Italian sonnets, and translations of Milton's sonnets, Jones includes a close analysis of the criticism devoted to the English sonnets during the twentieth century. Extensively indexed, Jones's study annotates more than 500 items of criticism devoted to Milton's sonnets.

In *The First Woman in the Republic: A Cultural Biography of Lydia Maria Child*, Carolyn L. Karcher concludes her study with a valuable and detailed listing of the 'Works of Lydia Maria Child', while Alvin A. Lee and Robert D. Denham's *The Legacy of Northrop Frye* provides a useful appendix of 'Northrop Frye's Books'. Rosemary M. Canfield Reisman and Christopher J. Canfield's *Contemporary Southern Women Fiction Writers: An Annotated Bibliography* features expansive annotated entries for critical works devoted to the study of women writers and the Southern literary tradition. In addition to providing annotations for the wide range of scholarship concerning such figures as Sallie Bingham, Lee Smith, Alice Walker, Alice Adams, Gail Godwin, Bobbie Ann Mason, Anne Tyler and Vicki Covington, among a host of others, Reisman and Canfield afford particular attention to assessing the shape and nature of the critical response to the literary achievements of contemporary Southern women writers. Liana Sakelliou-Schultz's *Feminist Criticism of American Women Poets: An Annotated Bibliography, 1975–1993* surveys the wide range of feminist critical scholarship regarding American women poets during the previous two decades. In addition to her exhaustive inclusion of both primary and secondary materials relating to a variety of American women poets, Sakelliou-Schultz affords special attention to the diversity of practical and theoretical feminist books, articles and dissertations on this subject published between 1975 and 1993. Munir Sendich's *Boris Pasternak: A Reference Guide* documents the recent revolution in Pasternak study that produced more than 300 scholarly articles and monographs during the 1980s. Sendich surveys the scholarship devoted to Pasternak from the publication of his early verse in volumes such as *My Sister, Life* (1922) and his autobiographical account, *A Safe Conduct* (1931), to his celebrated Russian translations of Shakespeare during the 1940s, and, finally, through the international controversy that followed the publication of *Doctor Zhivago* in Italy in 1957. Sendich annotates 1,049 works of criticism, as well as Pasternak's more than 500 publications from 1913 to 1990, including annotations for his essays, reviews, notes, commentaries, published lectures, correspondence, introductions, afterwords and various literary translations. In *Wallace Stevens: An Annotated Bibliography*, John N. Serio offers a chronological, annotated listing of criticism devoted to the works of Wallace Stevens published between 1916 and 1990. Extensively indexed, Serio's volume addresses more than a thousand items in the critical response to Stevens's vast poetic output. Finally, Carl Spadoni and Judith Donnelly's *A Bibliography of McClelland and Stewart Imprints, 1909–1985* surveys the monographs and other materials published by the McClelland and Stewart publishing company between 1909 and 1985. In addition to listing all of the imprint's publications of fiction, poetry, drama, biography, history, textbooks and nonfiction, Spadoni and Donnelly address the works that McClelland and Stewart imported from the United States and England before the Second World War.

3. General Scholarship for 1995

The year's work in bibliography and textual criticism features a variety of new theoretical approaches to editorial theory and literary study. *AEB* (9) contains Anthony James West's 'The Number and Distribution of Shakespeare First Folios 1902 and 1995' and Alexis Weedon's 'An Analysis of the Cost of Book Production in Nineteenth-Century Britain'. *ABM* (22) includes Colin Hynson's 'ABA Book Fair (Chelsea)'; Michael Dawson's 'A Bookworm at the Golden Gate'; Barry McKay's 'Book Collectors Weekend'; Pamela K. Harer's 'Dumpy Books for Children'; Mike Duckworth's 'The Book Garden'; Graham Hudson's 'With Wrappers, Complete'; Frank Herrmann's 'Maldon's Treasure – The Library of Thomas Plume'; Mike Duckworth's 'A New Look at Bookbinding'; Michael Dawson's 'Adventures in the Polar Book Trade'; Steve Hare's 'A Penguin First'; Roger Heavens's 'The Graham Watson Collection'; Martin Edward Earl's 'From Incunabula to the Internet'; Barry McKay's 'Annual Seminar on the History of the Provincial Book Trade, 1995';

Brian North Lee's 'The Bookplate Society'; Karl Showler's 'A Century of "Beebooks" in Translation' (Part I); Steven E. Smith's 'Books, Crooks, and Antiquarian Flatfoots'; David Pearson's 'The Bibliographical Society'; S. K. Speirs's 'Sixteenth-Century Books'; Karl Showler's 'A Century of "Bee-books" in Translation' (Part II); Pat Garrett's 'The Children's Books History Society'; and Michael Taylor's 'The Miss Margaret Sidney Davies Complete Collection of Special Gregynog Bindings'.

BC (44) contains Arthur Freeman and Janet Ing Freeman's ' "The Resort of the Illustrious Obscure"': Hazlitt, Rackets, and the Coronation'; Mary Hobbs's 'Books in Crisis at Barchester'; James S. Dearden's 'The Library Edition of the Works of John Ruskin'; Thomas Bean's 'Richard Ford and *Gatherings from Spain*'; John Morris's 'English and Foreign Bookbindings 70'; Theodore Hofmann, Joan Winterkorn, Frances Harris, and Hilton Kelliher's 'John Evelyn's Archive at the British Library'; Nicolas Barker's 'The Sale of the Evelyn Library, 1977–1978'; and Michael Hunter's 'The British Library and the Library of John Evelyn: With a Checklist of the Evelyn Books in the British Library's Holdings'; David Bruce's 'The Publishing History of "The Three Bears" '; Simon Franklin's 'How High Is a Bible?'; Robert A. Shaddy and John Neal Hoover's 'William Keeney Bixby: Portrait of a Bibliophile 31'; David Stoker's 'John Norgate: The Autobiography of a Seventeenth-Century Stationer and Bookbinder'; David Pearson's 'English and Foreign Bookbindings 71'; Ronald Mansbridge's 'J. P. Morgan and I: Book Collectors'; and Van Akin Burd's 'Frederick James Sharp, 1880–1957: Portrait of a Bibliophile 32'. A special issue of *LCUT* (26) surveys 'Alfred A. and Blanche W. Knopf, Publishers' in the collection of the Harry Ransom Humanities Research Center. In addition to featuring chapters investigating the origins of the Knopf collection at the University of Texas at Austin, this issue features attention to such issues as the role of the bookseller, apprenticeship, book design and the 'Knopf Dynasty', among other subjects. *Library* (17) contains Peter Davison's 'Bibliography: Teaching, Research, and Publication'; Robert Clare's 'The Theory of Authorial Revision between Quarto and Folio Texts of *King Lear*'; Anthony James West's 'Provisional New Census of the Shakespeare First Folio'; David Stoker's ' "Innumerable Letters of Good Consequence in History": The Discovery and First Publication of the Paston Letters'; Joseph A. Dane's 'On "Correctness": A Note on Some Press Variants in Thynne's 1532 Edition of Chaucer'; Nicholas Packwood's 'The Interpretation of Bookbinding Structure'; Peter Lindenbaum's 'Authors and Publishers in the Late Seventeenth Century'; and a bibliographical note, 'Two Early Gifts of the First Folio'. *RALS* (21) contains Michael Reynolds's 'Prospects for the Study of Ernest Hemingway'; Hershel Parker's 'Biography and Responsible Uses of the Imagination: Three Episodes from Melville's Homecoming in 1844'; Michael Guemple's 'A Case for the Appleton *Red Badge of Courage*'; Hilbert H. Campbell's 'Sherwood Anderson and Thomas Wolfe'; and Robert B. Jones's 'Jean Toomer: An Annotated Checklist of Criticism, 1923–1993'.

A special issue of *Library Trends* (44) on 'The Library and Undergraduate Education' includes Thomas G. McFadden and Theodore J. Hostetler's introduction; Barbara MacAdam's 'Sustaining the Culture of the Book: The Role of Enrichment Reading and Critical Thinking in the Undergraduate Curriculum'; Peter V. Deekle's 'Books, Reading, and Undergraduate Education'; Hannalore B. Rader's 'Information Literacy and the Undergraduate Curriculum'; Susan Griswold Blandy and Patricia O'Brien Libutti's 'As the Cursor Blinks: Electronic Scholarship and Undergraduates in the Library'; Judith M. Pask and Carl E. Snow's 'Undergraduate Instruction and the Internet'; Virginia M. Tiefel's 'Library User Education: Examining Its Past, Projecting Its Future'; Larry Hardesty's 'Faculty Culture and Bibliographic Instruction: An Exploratory Analysis'; Michael O. Engle's 'Forty-Five Years after Lamont: The University Undergraduate Library in the 1990s'; Steve Gowler's 'The Habit of Seeking: Liberal Education and the Library at Berea College'; Ellen Meltzer, Patricia Davitt Maughan, Thomas K. Fry's 'Undergraduate in Focus: Can Student Input Lead to New Directions in Planning Undergraduate Library Services?'; David F. Kohl's 'As Time Goes By . . .: Revisiting Fundamentals'; Evan Ira Farber's 'Plus ça Change . . . '; and Taylor E. Hubbard's 'Bibliographic Instruction and Postmodern Pedagogy'.

PBSA (89) contains Marcus A. McCorison's 'Thomas Green Fessenden, 1771–1837: Not in *BAL*'; Edward Jacobs's 'A Previously Unremarked Circulating Library: John Roson and the Role of Circulating-Library Proprietors as Publishers in Eighteenth-Century Britain'; Robert A. Wilson's 'Richard Wilbur and *Candide*'; Stephen Weissman's 'BSA Annual Address: What Use Is Bibliography?'; P. J. Klemp's ' "Betwixt the Hammer and the Anvill": Lancelot Andrews's Revision Techniques in the Manuscript of His 1620 Easter Sermon'; Edward Jacobs and Antonia Forster's ' "Lost Books" and Publishing History: Two Annotated Lists of Imprints for the Fiction Titles Listed in the Circulating Library Catalogs of Thomas Lowndes (1766) and M. Heavisides (1790), of Which No Known Copies Survive'; Ian MacPhail and Marjorie Sutton's 'A Bibliography of the Natural History Works Printed at New Harmony, Indiana, 1827–1843'; Jay A. Gertzmann's 'A Trap for Young Bookleggers: The First American Printings of Frank Harris's *My Life*, Volumes Three and Four (1927)'; Roger E. Stoddard's 'Book Catalogues and Life: A Preliminary Witness'; Giles Mandelbrote's 'A New Edition of *The Distribution of Books by Catalogue*: Problems and Prospects'; Richard Landon's 'The Antiquarian Book Trade in Britain, 1695–1830: The Use of Auction and Booksellers' Catalogues'; Lenore Coral's 'Towards the Bibliography of British Book Auction Catalogues, 1801–1900'; Karen Nipps's 'PACSCL's Auction and Dealer Catalogue Project'; Gabriel Austin's 'Catalogues of French Booksales: A Handlist'; Christian Coppens's 'A Census of Printers' and Booksellers' Catalogues up to 1600'; Henri Schiller's 'From Homer to Shakespeare: The Henri Schiller Collection, Its Objectives, and Its Manuscript File'; Eric Holzenberg's 'Book Catalogue Collections in Selected American Libraries'; and Roland Folter's 'An Annotated Checklist of Catalogue Literature'.

Volume 48 of *SB* (ed. David L. Vander Meulen) includes David Fairer's 'J. D. Fleeman: A Memoir'; Fairer's 'The Publications of J. D. Fleeman'; James McLaverty's 'Pope in the Private and Public Spheres: Annotations in the Second Earl of Oxford's Volume of Folio Poems, 1731–1736'; O M Brack Jr's 'Samuel Johnson and the Translations of Jean Pierre de Crousaz's *Examen* and *Commentaire*'; Keith Malsen's 'Dr. Hoadly's "Poems Set to Music by Dr. Greene" '; Hugh Amory's 'Virtual Readers: The Subscribers to Fielding's *Miscellanies* (1743)'; James E. Tierney's 'Eighteenth-Century Authors and the Abuse of the Franking System'; Gwin J. Kolb and Robert

DeMaria Jr's 'The Preliminaries to Dr. Johnson's *Dictionary*: Authorial Revisions and the Establishment of the Texts'; Anne McDermott's 'Textual Transformations: *The Memoirs of Martinus Scriblerus* in Johnson's *Dictionary*'; Donald D. Eddy's 'Richard Hurd's Editions of Horace and the Bowyer Ledgers'; Donald W. Nichol's 'From the Bishop of Gloucester to Lord Hailes: The Correspondence of William Warburton and David Dalrymple'; Thomas F. Bonnell's 'Patchwork and Piracy: John Bell's "Connected System of Biography" and the Use of Johnson's *Prefaces*'; Ann Bowden and William B. Todd's 'Scott's Commentary on *The Journal of a Tour to the Hebrides with Samuel Johnson*'; Pamela Dalziel's 'Whose *Mistress*?: Thomas Hardy's Theatrical Collaboration'; B. J. McMullin's 'Signing by the Page'; G. Thomas Tanselle's 'Printing History and Other History'; and Ralph Hanna III's 'With an O (Yorks.) or an I (Salop.)?: The Middle English Lyrics of British Library Additional 45896'.

As with previous surveys of the year's work in bibliography and textual criticism, the history of the book continues to receive special attention. In *John Dee: The Politics of Reading and Writing in the English Renaissance*, William H. Sherman reassesses the career and cultural background of John Dee, an eccentric Elizabethan philosopher and bibliophile. In addition to contextualizing Dee in terms of his participation in the academic, courtly and commercial circles of his era, Sherman discusses Dee's life and work at the massive library and museum at Mortlake, a precursor to modern 'think tanks' where Dee interacted with many of the period's most influential intellectuals and politicians. In *Victorian Fiction: Writers, Publishers, Readers*, John Sutherland investigates the remarkable proliferation of the print culture during the Victorian era, a period in which more than 3,500 novelists produced more than 50,000 works. Sutherland traces the cultural, social and commercial factors that intersected in this era of vast literary output, affording special attention to the marketing and compositional strategies of such writers as Collins, Dickens, George Eliot, Thackeray, Trollope, Reade, Lytton and Mrs Humphrey Ward, among a host of others. Frank J. Piehl's *The Caxton Club: Celebrating a Century of the Book in Chicago* traces the history of the Caxton Club as conceived by members of the organization's Centennial Committee. In addition to featuring discussion regarding the founding of the club in the early 1890s, Piehl examines the evolution of the Caxton Club from the early twentieth century through prohibition, the Depression, the Second World War and the present. Piehl includes appendices that feature biographies of prominent members of the Caxton Club, as well as listings of the organization's presidents and its honorary members. Robin Myers and Michael Harris's *A Genius for Letters: Booksellers and Bookselling from the Sixteenth to the Twentieth Century* features a number of essays of interest to students of bibliography and textual criticism. Selections include Anthony Hobson's 'Booksellers and Bookbinders'; Luigi Balsamo's 'Dealing across Frontiers: Italian Bookselling in the Eighteenth Century'; Germaine Greer's 'Honest Sam. Briscoe'; Giles Mandelbrote's 'From the Ware-House to the Counting-House: Booksellers and Bookshops in Late Seventeenth-Century London'; Christopher Edwards's 'Antiquarian Bookselling in Britain in 1725: The Nature of the Evidence'; James Tierney's 'Book Advertisements in Mid Eighteenth-Century Newspapers: The Example of Robert Dodsley'; William Zachs's ' "An Illiterate Fellow of a Bookseller": John Murray and His

Authors, 1768–1793'; Simon Eliot's 'Bookselling by the Back Door: Circulating Libraries, Booksellers, and Book Clubs, 1870–1966'; and Bill Bell's 'The Secret History of Smith and Elder: *The Publishers' Circular* as a Source for Publishing History'. In *Manuscript, Print, and the English Renaissance Lyric*, Arthur F. Marotti historicizes the print culture of the English Renaissance lyric verse, affording particular emphasis to sixteenth- and seventeenth-century issues regarding the places of women, politics and society in the publishing world of that era. Marotti features specific analysis of the treatment of obscenity and political scandal in the English Renaissance print culture, while also discussing verse anthologies as physical objects and mapping the notion of authorship during the Renaissance. Peter Martin's *Edmond Malone, Shakespearean Scholar: A Literary Biography* explores the life and work of Edward Malone, one of the most significant early editors of Shakespeare's works, the first historian of early English drama, the biographer of Shakespeare and Dryden, and the relentless investigator of literary fraud and forgery. Martin affords particular attention to an analysis of Malone's late eighteenth-century circle of artists, intellectuals and politicians, including such figures as Samuel Johnson, Edmund Burke, Sir Joshua Reynolds, Sarah Siddons and James Boswell. Lavishly illustrated, Norma Levarie's *The Art and History of Books* traces the history of book design from its earliest origins to the present. Levarie examines the history of fine book design with special attention to the patronage, improving technology, religious and social change and the global state of the arts. In addition to the inclusion of 176 facsimile pages from a host of fine books, Levarie's volume offers full bibliographical descriptions for both illustrated and unillustrated books. In yet another chapter in the saga of the notorious nineteenth-century pamphlet forger, Roger C. Lewis's *Thomas James Wise and the Trial Book Fallacy* examines the piracy by Wise and others of 'trial books', usually genuine proofsheets that pirates marketed as rare, privately printed first editions. Lewis examines Wise's piracy of proofsheets belonging to Alfred and Frederick Tennyson, Dante Gabriel Rossetti, Robert Louis Stevenson, Joseph Conrad and George Bernard Shaw. Nicholas A. Basbanes's *A Gentle Madness: Bibliophiles, Bibliomanes, and the Eternal Passion for Books* provides students of antiquarianism and book collecting with an insightful analysis of 'bibliomania', which the author defines as 'the passion for books which is not a modern phenomenon but reaches back at least 2,200 years ago to Alexandria'. Basbanes endeavours 'to show that however bizarre and zealous collectors have been through the ages, so much of what we know about history, literature, and culture would be lost forever if not for the passion and dedication of these driven souls', i.e., bibliomaniaés.

The year's work in enumerative bibliography is spearheaded by the contents of *BB* (52), which includes José Ramón Díaz-Fernàndez's 'Thomas Kyd: A Bibliography, 1966–1992'; R. Malcolm Hogg's 'Magna Carta, 1215: Guidance to the Meaning of Its Clauses'; Yael Herbsman's 'Women in Israel: A Bibliography, 1980–1991 (Part I)'; James R. Bennett's 'Bigotry in U.S. Literature, Film, and Video: Background and Criticism'; Robert Singerman's 'Jewish Translation History: A Bibliography of Bibliographies and Research (Part II)'; John C. Fredriksen's 'The Japanese Experience in World War II: A Bibliography of the Translated Accounts'; Jane Addison's 'Christina Rossetti Studies, 1974–1991: A Checklist and Synthesis'; David G. Hale's 'Interviews from the Brockport Writers Forum III: 1990–1994'; Reginald Clarke's 'Ebakih Teret Awralign: A Select Bibliography of African Creative Writing'; Patricia A. Ward's 'Madame Guyon in America: An Annotated Bibliography'; Janelle Wilcox's 'The Reception and Reappraisal of Gayl Jones's Novels: An Annotated Bibliography of Reviews and Criticism'; Paul Cairney's 'Writings about Zora Neale Hurston's *Their Eyes Were Watching God*: 1987–1993'; Robert Singerman's 'Jewish Translation History: A Bibliography of Bibliographies and Research (Part III)'; Yael Herbsman's 'Women in Israel: A Bibliography, 1980–1991 (Part II)'; Frank G. Hulse and Susan Marshall Richard's 'Frida Kahlo: A Selected Bibliography'; Roy A. Ziegler and Ruth S. Ziegler's 'The National Film Registry: A Videography'; José María Martínez Domingo's 'An Updated Bibliography of *Azul* ... and *Cantos de Vida y Esperanza*'; Allan Metz's 'Reviews of President Bill Clinton's First Two Years and Second Year in Office: An Annotated Bibliography'; James M. Hutchisson's 'Sinclair Lewis Manuscript Collections: A Descriptive Survey'; Frederick S. Frank's 'M. G. Lewis's *The Monk* after Two Hundred Years, 1796–1996: A Bicentenary Bibliography'; Megan S. Farrell's 'Jim Jarmusch: American Film *Auteur*'; Fred J. Hay's 'African-American Anthropology: A Bibliography of Bibliographies'; Devon White's 'Contemporary Criticism of Five Early American Sentimental Novels, 1970–1994: An Annotated Bibliography'; Andrew L. Erdman's 'Mary Coyle Chase: A Bibliography of Critical and Biographical Sources'; Ray Louis Kamoo's 'Ancient and Modern Chaldean History'; and Sam McBride's 'C. S. Lewis's *A Preface to Paradise Lost*, the Milton Controversy, and Lewis Scholarship'.

Arthur Asa Berger's *Cultural Criticism: A Primer of Key Concepts* features a bibliography devoted to cultural criticism that traces the emergence of the genre and its interconnections with Marxist criticism, semiotics, psychoanalysis and sociology, among other disciplines. In *Shakespeare: A Study and Research Guide*, David Moore Bergeron and Geraldo U. de Sousa's revised third edition of their 1975 reference volume, the compilers feature hundreds of new entries devoted to the collection of Shakespearean criticism and scholarship. In addition to providing their readers with new chapters delineating film and television productions of Shakespearean works, Bergeron and de Sousa offer chapters regarding a variety of critical genres from gender studies and textual criticism through new historical and postmodern approaches to Shakespeare. In addition to providing scholars and students alike with entries for hundreds of critical terms, Joseph Childers and Gary Hentzi's *The Columbia Dictionary of Modern Literary and Cultural Criticism* traces the evolution of critical theory through its detailed examinations of such disciplines as psychoanalytic criticism, deconstruction and film theory, among a host of others. Each entry features analysis of the place of its subject in the theatre of contemporary critical theory, while also providing readers with a useful bibliography of supplementary sources. In *Tennessee Williams: A Descriptive Bibliography*, George W. Crandell offers a chronological descriptive listing of Tennessee Williams's works, including a full bibliography of his separate publications; his contributions to books, pamphlets and occasional publications; his publications in magazines and newspapers; and interviews and articles that quote him. Crandell also includes listings of titles by Williams set to music; dust-jacket blurbs; sound recordings of him reading from his works; and translations of his work, including plays, poetry and essays by Williams. Gary William Crawford's *J. Sheridan Le Fanu: A Bio-Bibliography* explores the life and work of J. Sheridan Le Fanu and offers a chronology and biographical introduction. Crawford's primary bibliography includes attention to Le Fanu's contributions to magazines and anthologies, his books and his manuscripts. The secondary bibliography includes a research overview, as well as books, essays, general studies, introductions, articles, reviews and dissertations regarding Le Fanu's texts. An appendix lists films and plays based on Le Fanu's works. Robert William Croft's *Anne Tyler: A Bio-Bibliography* assesses the rich narratives of Anne Tyler's fictions, offering biographical and critical assessments of her fictions. Croft also features extensive chapters devoted to surveying the primary and secondary sources by and about Tyler. Elisabeth Weber's edition of Jacques Derrida's *Points: Interviews, 1974–1994* concludes with an unannotated 'Bibliography of Other Interviews with Jacques Derrida', while Margaret M. Dunn and Ann R. Morris's *The Composite Novel: The Short Story Cycle in Transition* contains a 'Survey of Scholarship: A Bibliographic Essay' and 'An Annotated List of Selected Composite Novels'. In *The Romantic Movement: A Selective and Critical Bibliography for 1994*, David V. Erdman draws upon a variety of on-line sources in this exhaustive, annotated listing of scholarship devoted to the literature of the Romantic era published during 1994. In *The CCCC Bibliography of Composition and Rhetoric, 1993*, Gail E. Hawisher and Cynthia L. Selfe compile an annual classified listing of scholarship on written English and its teaching. The bibliography cites nearly 2,000 titles, as well as a list of more than 100 contributing bibliographers. The volume features Erika Lindemann's 'Guidelines for the *CCCC Bibliography*'. M. Paul Holsinger's *The Ways of War – The Era of World War II in Children's and Young Adult Fiction: An Annotated Bibliography* offers expansive listings of works of children's and young adult fiction published between 1939 and 1945. Holsinger's bibliography of juvenile fiction is cross-referenced by geographical settings and military organizations, among other subjects. He concludes his study with an appendix, 'Children's and Young Adult Fiction About World War II (Published in Great Britain or Australia But Never Republished in the United States of America)'.

Amelia Howe Kritzer concludes her anthology of *Plays by Early American Women, 1775–1850* with a listing of 'Women Dramatists in the United States before 1900'. Steven Mailloux's *Rhetoric, Sophistry, Pragmatism* contains three selected bibliographies: 'Rhetoric and Recent Critical Theory'; 'Reinterpretations of the Greek Sophists'; and 'Developments in the Pragmatist Tradition'. In *Reading Hemingway: The Facts in the Fictions*, Miriam B. Mandel provides entries that attempt to account for the characters, animals, and cultural constructs that mark the fictional terrain of Hemingway's novels, from *The Torrents of Spring* and *The Sun Also Rises* to *The Old Man and the Sea* and *The Garden of Eden*. In addition to the valuable system of cross-referencing that undergirds her guide, Mandel offers useful secondary critical bibliographies for each of the Hemingway novels included in her study. In addition to offering an introductory discussion regarding the organization of their checklist and bibliography of works by and about James A. Michener, F. X. Roberts and C. D. Rhine's *James A. Michener: A Checklist of His Works, with a Selected, Annotated Bibliography* is divided into three principal sections. 'James A. Michener: A Checklist' includes books, book sections, stories and articles written by Michener, while 'James A. Michener: A Selected, Annotated Bibliography' includes listings of books, book sections and articles about him. The final section, 'James A. Michener: Selected Reviews' includes book reviews of Michener's works. Mary Suzanne Schriber's *Telling Travels: Selected Writings by Nineteenth-Century American Women Abroad* concludes with a useful selected bibliography devoted to the critical scholarship regarding American female travel writing. Finally, the late Warren S. Walker's *Twentieth-Century Short Story Explication* includes nearly 5,000 entries for nearly 700 short story writers. In addition to drawing explications from the Middle East, Australia, Africa, the Philippines, Europe and the Orient, Walker's volume features short story explications from Latin American and Spanish literature. The study concludes with two appendices, 'A Checklist of Books Used' and 'A Checklist of Journals Used'.

Books Reviewed

Alkon, Paul K. *Science Fiction before 1900: Imagination Discovers Technology.* Twayne (1994). pp. 200. $22.95. ISBN 0 8057 0952 5.

Allen, Orphia Jane. *Barbara Pym: Writing a Life.* Scarecrow (1994). pp. 261. $35. ISBN 0 8108 2875 8.

Anderson, Vicki. *Native Americans in Fiction: A Guide to 765 books for Librarians and Teachers, K-9.* McFarland (1994). pp. 180. $31.50. ISBN 0 89950 907 X.

Annenberg, Maurice. *Type Foundries of America and Their Catalogs.* Oak Knoll (1994). pp. 304. $49.95. ISBN 1 884718 06 X.

Arnold, Edwin T., and Dianne C. Luce, eds. *Perspectives on Cormac McCarthy.* UMP (1993). pp. 192. $30. ISBN 0 87805 654 8.

August, Eugene R. *The New Men's Studies: A Selected and Annotated Interdisciplinary Bibliography.* Libraries Unlimited, IN, USA (1994). pp. 440. $47.50. ISBN 1 56308 084 2.

Basbanes, Nicholas A. *A Gentle Madness: Bibliophiles, Bibliomanes, and the Eternal Passion for Books.* Holt. pp. 638. $35. ISBN 0 8050 3653 9.

Bauermeister, Erica. *500 Great Books by Women: A Reader's Guide.* Viking (1994). pp. 400. $12.95. ISBN 0 14 017590 3.

Baumlin, James S., and Tita French Baumlin, eds. *Ethos: New Essays in Rhetorical and Critical Theory.* (SMUP) (1994) pp. 408. $34.95. ISBN 0 87074 344 9.

Benson, Eugene, and L. W. Conolly. *Encyclopedia of Post-Colonial Literatures in English.* Routledge (1994). pp. 1,874. $199.95. ISBN 0 415 05199 1.

Berger, Arthur Asa. *Cultural Criticism: A Primer of Key Concepts.* Sage. pp. 220. $37. ISBN 0 8039 5733 5.

Bergeron, David Moore, and Geraldo U. de Sousa. *Shakespeare: A Study and Research Guide.* UKanP. pp. 208. $12.95. ISBN 0 7006 0693 9.

Bischoff, Bernhard. *Manuscripts and Libraries in the Age of Charlemagne,* trans. Michael M. Gorman. CUP (1994). pp. 224. $65. ISBN 0 521 38346 3.

Booker, M. Keith. *Dystopian Literature: A Theory and Research Guide.* Greenwood (1994). pp. 424. $79.50. ISBN 0 313 29115 2.

Bornstein, George, and Ralph G. Williams, eds. *Palimpsest: Editorial Theory in the Humanities.* UMichP (1993). pp. 318. $45. ISBN 0 472 10371 7.

Bowers, Fredson. *Principles of Bibliographical Description.* 1949. Oak Knoll (1994). pp. 536. $29.95. ISBN 1 884718 00 0.

Brack, O M Jr. *Writers, Books, and Trade: An Eighteenth-Century English Miscellany for William B. Todd.* AMS (1994). pp. 412. $57.50. ISBN 0 404 63519 9.

Cassiday, Bruce, ed. *Modern Mystery, Fantasy, and Science Fiction Writers.* Continuum (1993). pp. 544. $75. ISBN 0 8264 0573 8.

Childers, Joseph, and Gary Hentzi, eds. *The Columbia Dictionary of Modern Literary and Cultural Criticism.* ColUP. pp. 362. $49.50. ISBN 0 231 07242 2.

Crandell, George W. *Tennessee Williams: A Descriptive Bibliography.* UPittP. pp. 704. $195. ISBN 0 8229 3769 7.

Crawford, Gary William. *J. Sheridan Le Fanu: A Bio-Bibliography.* Greenwood. pp. 168. $59.95. ISBN 0 313 28515 2.

Croft, Robert William. *Anne Tyler: A Bio-Bibliography.* Greenwood. pp. 192. $45. ISBN 0 313 28952 2.

Dagenais, John. *The Ethics of Reading in Manuscript Culture: Glossing the Libro de buen amor.* PrincetonUP (1994). pp. 304. $45. ISBN 0 691 03246 7.

DeBellis, Jack. *John Updike: A Bibliography, 1967–1993.* Greenwood (1994). pp. 335. $65. ISBN 0 313 28861 5.

DeRose, Steven J., and David G. Durand. *Making Hypermedia Work: A User's Guide to HyTime.* Kluwer (1994). pp. 408. $68. ISBN 0 7923 9432 1.

Duchac, Joseph. *The Poems of Emily Dickinson: An Annotated Guide to Commentary Published in English, 1978–1989.* Hall (1993). pp. 525. $60. ISBN 0 8161 7352 4.

Dunn, Margaret M., and Ann R. Morris. *The Composite Novel: The Short Story Cycle in Transition.* Twayne. pp. 232. $23.95. ISBN 0 8057 0966 5.

Eckersley, Richard. *Glossary of Typesetting Terms.* UChicP (1994). pp. 182. $20. ISBN 0 226 18371 8.

Elsner, John, and Roger Cardinal, eds. *The Cultures of Collecting.* Reaktion (1994). pp. 320. $39.95. ISBN 0 674 17992 7.

Erdman, David V., ed. *The Romantic Movement: A Selective and Critical Bibliography for 1994.* Locust Hill. pp. 424. $60. ISBN 0 933951 65 5.

Essick, Robert N. *William Blake at the Huntington: An Introduction to the William Blake Collection in the Henry E. Huntington Library and Art Gallery, San Marino, California.* Abrams (1994). pp. 160. $29.95. ISBN 0 8109 2589 3.

Evans, Elizabeth. *Anne Tyler.* Twayne (1993). pp. 192. $21.95. ISBN 0 8057 3985 8.

Fogel, Daniel Mark, ed. *A Companion to Henry James Studies.* Greenwood (1993). pp. 568. $85. ISBN 0 313 25792 2.

Friedman, Jerome. *The Battle of the Frogs and Fairford's Flies: Miracles and the Pulp Press During the English Revolution.* St. Martin's (1993). pp. 320. $45. ISBN 0 312 09125 7.

Frugé, August. *A Skeptic Among Scholars: August Frugé on University Publishing.* UCalP (1993). pp. 365. $40. ISBN 0 520 07733 4.

Gallagher, Bernice E. *Illinois Women Novelists in the Nineteenth Century: An Analysis and Annotated Bibliography.* UIllP (1994). pp. 200. $39.95. ISBN 0 252 02065 0.

Gekoski, R. A., and P. A. Grogan. *William Golding: A Bibliography, 1934–1993.* Deutsch (1994). pp. 158. $65. ISBN 0 233 98611 1.

Gerry, Thomas M. F. *Contemporary Canadian and U.S. Women of Letters: An Annotated Bibliography.* Garland (1993). pp. 312. $49. ISBN 0 8240 6989 7.

Grant, J. Kerry. *A Companion to The Crying of Lot 49.* UGeoP (1994). pp. 176. $25. ISBN 0 8203 1635 0.

Greenfield, John R., ed. *Dictionary of British Literary Characters, Volume II: Twentieth-Century Novels.* Manly (1994). pp. 592. $65. ISBN 0 8160 2180 5.

Greetham, D. C., and W. Speed Hill, eds. *Text: Transactions of the Society for Textual Scholarship.* Vol. 6. AMS (1993). pp. 546. $54.50. ISBN 0 404 62556 8.

——, and ——, eds. *Text: Transactions of the Society for Textual Scholarship.* Vol. 7. UMichP (1994). pp. 568. $59.50. ISBN 0 472 10615 5.

Groden, Michael, and Martin Kreiswirth, eds. *The Johns Hopkins Guide to Literary Theory and Criticism.* JHUP (1993). pp. 775. $65. ISBN 0 8018 4560 0.

Hamilton, Charles. *William Shakespeare and John Fletcher: Cardenio, or, The Second Maiden's Tragedy.* Glenbridge (1994). pp. 275. $27.95. ISBN 0 944435 24 6.

Hamilton, Ian, ed. *The Oxford Companion to Twentieth Century Poetry in English.* OUP (1994). pp. 624. $39.95. ISBN 0 19 866147 9.

Harner, James L. *Literary Research Guide: A Guide to Reference Sources for the Study of Literatures in English and Related Topics.* 2nd edn. MLA (1993). pp. 766. $45. ISBN 0 87352 559 0.

Harrison, Elizabeth. *Andrew M. Greeley: An Annotated Bibliography.* Scarecrow (1994). pp. 389. $49.50. ISBN 0 8108 2931 2.

Harvey, Robert, and Mark S. Roberts. Lyotard, Jean François. *Toward the Postmodern.* Humanities (1993). pp. 280. $17.50. ISBN 0 391 03890 7.

Haven, Stephen, ed. *The Poetry of W. D. Snodgrass: Everything Human.* UMichP (1993). pp. 268. $15.95. ISBN 0 918644 47 X.

Hawisher, Gail E., and Cynthia L. Selfe, eds. *The CCCC Bibliography of Composition and Rhetoric, 1993.* SIUP. pp. 272. $49.95. ISBN 0 8093 1993 4.

Hawthorn, Jeremy. *A Glossary of Contemporary Literary Theory.* 2nd edn. Arnold (1994). pp. 320. $49.95. ISBN 0 340 60185 X.

Hayashi, Tetsumaro, and Beverly K. Simpson. *John Steinbeck: Dissertation Abstracts and Research Opportunities.* Scarecrow (1994). pp. 194. $29.95. ISBN 0 8108 2940 1.

Hérubel, Jean-Pierre V. M. *Annales Historiography and Theory: A Selective and Annotated Bibliography.* Greenwood (1994). pp. 192. $65. ISBN 0 313 29125 X.

Hill, Leslie. *Marguerite Duras: Apocalyptic Desires.* Routledge (1993). pp. 224. $55. ISBN 0 415 05047 2.

Hill, W. Speed, ed. *New Ways of Looking at Old Texts: Papers of the Renaissance*. English Text Society, 1985–1991. CMERS (1993). pp. 319. $25. ISBN 0 8669 8153 5.

Holland, Steve. *The Mushroom Jungle: A History of Postwar Paperback Publishing*. Borgo (1993). pp. 196. $35. ISBN 0 8095 6013 5.

Holsinger, M. Paul. *The Ways of War – The Era of World War II in Children's and Young Adult Fiction: An Annotated Bibliography*. Scarecrow. pp. 487. $29.95. ISBN 0 8108 2925 X.

Hope, Jonathan. *The Authorship of Shakespeare's Plays*. CUP (1994). pp. 208. $52.95. ISBN 0 521 41737 6.

Huttner, Sidney F., and Elizabeth Stege. *A Register of Artists, Engravers, Booksellers, Bookbinders, Printers, and Publishers in New York City, 1821–42*. BSA (1993). pp. 299. $50. ISBN 0 914930 15 X.

Irace, Kathleen O. *Reforming the 'Bad' Quartos: Performance and Provenance of Six Shakespearean First Editions*. UDelP (1994). pp. 232. $37.50. ISBN 0 87413 471 4.

Jackson, J. R. dc J. *Romantic Poetry by Women: A Bibliography, 1770–1835*. OUP (1993). pp. 484. $59.95. ISBN 0 19 811239 4.

Jackson, Roger, and William E. Ashley. *Henry Miller: A Bibliography of Primary Sources, Volume 2*. Roger Jackson (1994). pp. 526. $45. ISBN 0 9634136 6 X.

Jones, Edward. *Milton's Sonnets: An Annotated Bibliography, 1900–1992*. CMERS (1994). pp. 147. $20. ISBN 0 86698 127 6.

Jordan, Casper LeRoy. *A Bibliographical Guide to African-American Women Writers*. Greenwood (1993). pp. 416. $65. ISBN 0 313 27633 1.

Kain, Geoffrey R., ed. *R. K. Narayan: Contemporary Critical Perspectives*. MichSUP (1993). pp. 200. $27.95. ISBN 0 87013 330 6.

Karcher, Carolyn L. *The First Woman in the Republic: A Cultural Biography of Lydia Maria Child*. DukeUP (1994). pp. 928. $37.95. ISBN 0 8223 1485 1.

Kaufmann, Michael. *Textual Bodies: Modernism, Postmodernism, and Print*. BuckUP. AUP (1994). pp. 140. $29.50. ISBN 0 8387 5260 8.

Keesey, Douglas. *Don DeLillo*. Twayne (1993). pp. 256. $29.95. ISBN 0 8057 4009 0.

Kennedy, Thomas E. *Index to American Short Story Award Collections, 1970–1990*. Hall (1993). pp. 136. $45. ISBN 0 8161 1819 1.

Kent, David A., and D. R. Ewen, eds. *Romantic Parodies, 1797–1831*. AUP (1993). pp. 416. $59.50. ISBN 0 8386 3458 3.

Kritzer, Amelia Howe, ed. *Plays by Early American Women, 1775–1850*. UMichP. pp. 444. $39.50. ISBN 0 472 09598 6.

Landow, George P., ed. *Hyper/Text/Theory*. JHUP (1994). pp. 377. $48.50. ISBN 0 8018 4837 7.

Lee, Alvin A., and Robert D. Denham, eds. *The Legacy of Northrop Frye*. UTorP (1994). pp. 354. $55. ISBN 0 8020 0632 9.

Levarie, Norma. *The Art and History of Books*. Oak Knoll. pp. 328. $45. ISBN 1 884718 02 7.

Lewis, Roger C. *Thomas James Wise and the Trial Book Fallacy*. Scolar. pp. 260. $76.95. ISBN 1 85928 036 6.

Liuzza, R. M., ed. *The Old English Version of the Gospels: Volume I, Text and Introduction*. OUP (1994). pp. 280. $49.95. ISBN 0 19 722306 0.

Love, Harold. *Scribal Publication in Seventeenth-Century England.* Clarendon (1993). pp. 392. $65. ISBN 0 19 811219 X.

Lowenberg, Susan. *C. S. Lewis: A Reference Guide, 1972–1988.* Hall (1993). pp. 320. $60. ISBN 0 8161 1846 9.

Machann, Clinton. *The Essential Matthew Arnold: An Annotated Bibliography of Major Modern Studies.* Hall (1993). pp. 177. $55. ISBN 0 8161 9087 9.

Madden, David W. *Understanding Paul West.* USCP (1993). pp. 183. $29.95. ISBN 0 87249 886 7.

Mailloux, Steven, ed. *Rhetoric, Sophistry, Pragmatism.* CUP. pp. 290. $54.95. ISBN 0 521 46780 2.

Makaryk, Irena R., ed. *Encyclopedia of Contemporary Literary Theory: Approaches, Scholars, Terms.* UTorP (1993). pp. 576. $150. ISBN 0 8020 5914 7.

Mandel, Miriam B. *Reading Hemingway: The Facts in the Fictions.* Scarecrow. pp. 609. $72.50. ISBN 0 8108 2870 7.

March, John. *A Reader's Companion to the Fiction of Willa Cather.* Ed. Marilyn Arnold and Debra Lynn Thornton. Greenwood (1993). pp. 846. $99.50. ISBN 0 313 28767 8.

Marotti, Arthur F. *Manuscript, Print, and the English Renaissance Lyric.* CornUP. pp. 336. $45. ISBN 0 8014 2291 4.

Martin, Peter. *Edmond Malone, Shakespearean Scholar: A Literary Biography.* CUP. pp. 320. $52.95. ISBN 0 521 46030 1.

Maslen, Keith. *An Early London Printing House at Work: Studies in Bowyer Ledgers – With a Supplement to the Bowyer V. Ornament Stock (1973), an Appendix on the Bowyer-Emonson Partnership, and 'Bowyer's Paper Stock Ledger,' by Herbert Davis.* BSA (1993). pp. 256. $50. ISBN 0 914930 16 8.

Mason, Ellsworth. *The University of Colorado Library and Its Makers, 1876–1972.* UPColorado (1994). pp. 401. $42.50. ISBN 0 8108 2685 2.

Mazzeno, Laurence W. *Herman Wouk.* Twayne (1994). pp. 160. $23.95. ISBN 0 8057 3982 3.

McGann, Jerome J. *Black Riders: The Visible Language of Modernism.* PrincetonUP (1993). pp. 196. $35. ISBN 0 691 06985 9.

McGeary, Thomas, and N. Frederick Nash. *Emblem Books at the University of Illinois: A Bibliographic Catalogue.* Hall (1993). pp. 363. $45. ISBN 0 8161 0533 2.

McKerrow, Ronald B. *An Introduction to Bibliography for Literary Students.* 1927. Oak Knoll (1994). pp. 400. $29.95. ISBN 1 884718 01 9.

McLeod, Randall, ed. *Crisis in Editing: Texts of the English Renaissance.* AMS (1994). pp. 306. $49.50. ISBN 0 404 63674 8.

Meyering, Sheryl L. *A Reader's Guide to the Short Stories of Willa Cather.* Hall (1994). pp. 304. $65. ISBN 0 8161 1834 5.

Mieder, Wolfgang, and Stewart A. Kingsbury, eds. *A Dictionary of Wellerisms.* OUP (1994). pp. 208. $24.95. ISBN 0 19 508318 0.

Minnis, A. J., ed. *Late Medieval Religious Texts and Their Transmission: Essays in Honour of A. I. Doyle.* Brewer (1994). pp. 208. $63. ISBN 0 85991 386 4.

Mohlhenrich, Janice, ed. *Preservations of Electronic Formats and Electronic Formats for Preservation.* Highsmith (1993). pp. 128. $25. ISBN 0 917846 17 6.

Myers, Robin, and Michael Harris, eds. *A Genius for Letters: Booksellers and Bookselling from the Sixteenth to the Twentieth Century.* Oak Knoll. pp. 188. $30. ISBN 1 884718 16 7.

——, and ——, eds. *A Millennium of the Book: Production, Design, and Illustration in Manuscript and Print, 900–1900.* Oak Knoll (1994). pp. 192. $30. ISBN 1 884718 07 8.

——, and ——, eds. *Serials and Their Readers, 1620–1914.* Oak Knoll (1993). pp. 192. $30. ISBN 0 938768 48 4.

Myerson, Joel. *Walt Whitman: A Descriptive Bibliography.* UPittP (1993). pp. 1128. $250. ISBN 0 8229 3739 5.

Nelson, Emmanuel S., ed. *Writers of the Indian Diaspora: A Bio-Bibliographical Critical Sourcebook.* Greenwood (1993). pp. 504. $89.50. ISBN 0 313 27904 7.

Niebuhr, Gary Warren. *A Reader's Guide to The Private Eye Novel.* Hall (1993). pp. 323. $50. ISBN 0 8161 1802 7.

Nilsen, Don Lee Fred. *Humor Scholarship: A Research Bibliography.* Greenwood (1993). pp. 416. $65. ISBN 0 313 28441 5.

Perrin, Robert G. *Herbert Spencer: A Primary and Secondary Bibliography.* Garland (1993). pp. 1,024. $150. ISBN 0 8240 4597 1.

Piehl, Frank J. *The Caxton Club: Celebrating a Century of the Book in Chicago.* Oak Knoll. pp. 224. $75. ISBN 0 940550 09 1.

Pizer, Donald. *The Theory and Practice of American Literary Naturalism: Selected Essays and Reviews.* SIUP (1993). pp. 272. $34.95. ISBN 0 8093 1847 4.

Polk, Noel. *Eudora Welty: A Bibliography of Her Work.* UMissP (1994). pp. 450. $65. ISBN 0 87805 566 5.

Pottle, Marion S., Claude Colleer Abbott, and Frederick A. Pottle. *Catalogue of the Papers of James Boswell at Yale University.* EdinUP (1993). pp. 1,440. $275. ISBN 0 300 05410 6.

Reiman, Donald H. *The Study of Modern Manuscripts: Public, Confidential, and Private.* JHUP (1993). pp. 224. $29.95. ISBN 0 8018 4590 4.

Reisman, Rosemary M. Canfield, and Christopher J. Canfield. *Contemporary Southern Women Fiction Writers: An Annotated Bibliography.* Scarecrow (1994). pp. 237. $32.50. ISBN 0 8108 2832 4.

Rhodes, Dennis E., ed. *Bookbindings and Other Bibliophily: Essays in Honour of Anthony Hobson.* Oak Knoll (1994). pp. 368. $125. ISBN 88 85033 26 1.

Richardson, Brian. *Print Culture in Renaissance Italy: The Editor and the Vernacular Text, 1470–1600.* CUP (1994). pp. 256. $57.95. ISBN 0 521 42032 6.

Roberts, F. X., and C. D. Rhine. *James A. Michener: A Checklist of His Works, with a Selected, Annotated Bibliography.* Greenwood. pp. 152. $49.95. ISBN 0 313 29453 4.

Roberts, John R. *New Perspectives on the Seventeenth-Century English Religious Lyric.* UMissP (1994). pp. 336. $47.50. ISBN 0 8262 0909 2.

Robinson, Fred C. *The Editing of Old English.* Blackwell (1994). pp. 320. $62.95. ISBN 1 55786 438 1.

Rose, Jane Atteridge. *Rebecca Harding Davis.* Twayne (1993). pp. 216. $22.95. ISBN 0 8057 3958 0.

Sakelliou-Schultz, Liana. *Feminist Criticism of American Women Poets: An*

Annotated Bibliography, 1975–1993. Garland (1994). pp. 384. $54. ISBN 0 8240 7084 4.

Sambrook, James. *The Eighteenth Century: The Intellectual and Cultural Context of English Literature, 1700–1789*. 2nd edn. Longman (1993). pp. 290. $29.95. ISBN 0 582 21926 4.

Schriber, Mary Suzanne, ed. *Telling Travels: Selected Writings by Nineteenth-Century American Women Abroad*. NIUP. pp. 336. $35. ISBN 0 87580 195 1.

Scribner Jr, Charles. *In the Web of Ideas: The Education of a Publisher*. Scribner (1993). pp. 240. $22.95. ISBN 0 684 14591 7.

Sendich, Munir. *Boris Pasternak: A Reference Guide*. Hall (1994). pp. 376. $50. ISBN 0 8161 8992 7.

Serio, John N. *Wallace Stevens: An Annotated Bibliography*. UPittP (1994). pp. 456. $100. ISBN 0 8229 3836 7.

Sherman, Joseph, ed. *A World Too Wide: Essays on Libraries and Other Themes in Honour of Reuben Musiker*. University of the Witwatersrand Library (1993). pp. 375. $39.95. ISBN 1 868 38057 2.

Sherman, William H. *John Dee: The Politics of Reading and Writing in the English Renaissance*. UMassP. pp. 312. $35. ISBN 0 87023 940 6.

Shifreen, Lawrence J., and Roger Jackson. *Henry Miller: A Bibliography of Primary Sources*. Roger Jackson (1993). pp. 1,022. $95. ISBN 0 9634 1360 0.

Sloan, W. David, and Julie Hedgepeth Williams. *The Early American Press, 1690–1873*. Greenwood (1994). pp. 248. $59.95. ISBN 0 313 27525 4.

Spadoni, Carl, and Judith Donnelly. *A Bibliography of McClelland and Stewart Imprints, 1909–1985*. ECW (1994). pp. 862. $65. ISBN 1 5502 2171 X.

Stauffer, David McNeely, Mantle Fielding, and Thomas Hovey Gage. *American Engravers upon Copper and Steel*. Oak Knoll (1994). pp. 1,520. $175. ISBN 0 938768 47 6.

Stillinger, Jack. *Coleridge and Textual Instability: The Multiple Versions of the Major Poems*. OUP (1994). pp. 288. $49.95. ISBN 0 19 508583 3.

Studing, Richard. *Shakespeare in American Painting: A Catalogue from the Late Eighteenth Century to the Present*. AUP (1993). pp. 192. $65. ISBN 0 8386 3408 7.

Sutherland, John. *Victorian Fiction: Writers, Publishers, Readers*. Macmillan. pp. 191. $49.95. ISBN 0 312 12614 4.

Tanselle, G. Thomas. *The Life and Work of Fredson Bowers*. Bibliographical Society of the University of Virginia (1993). pp. 200. $25. ISBN 1 883631 00 9.

Taylor, Desmond, and Philip E. Hager. *The Novels of World War II: An Annotated Bibliography*. Garland (1993). pp. 920. $145. ISBN 0 8240 5684 1.

Taylor, Gary, and John Jowett. *Shakespeare Reshaped, 1606–1623*. OUP (1993). pp. 333. $54.95. ISBN 0 19 812256 X.

Thornton, Weldon. *D. H. Lawrence: A Study of the Short Fiction*. Twayne (1993). pp. 174. $23.95. ISBN 0 8057 0862 6.

Townsend, John Rowe, ed. *John Newbery and His Books: Trade and Plumb-Cake for Ever, Huzza!*. Scarecrow (1994). pp. 194. $25. ISBN 0 8108 2950 9.

Tribble, Evelyn B. *Margins and Marginality: The Printed Page in Early Modern England*. UPVirginia (1993). pp. 224. $35. ISBN 0 8139 1472 8.

Vander Meulen, David L., ed. *Studies in Bibliography*. Vol. 47. UPVirginia (1994). pp. 268. $35. ISBN 0 8139 1523 6.

——, ed. *Studies in Bibliography*. Vol. 48. UPVirginia. pp. 300. $35. ISBN 0 8139 1617 8.

Vann, J. Don, and Rosemary T. VanArsdel, eds. *Victorian Periodicals and Victorian Society*. UTorP (1994). pp. 416. $125. ISBN 0 8020 0522 5.

Walker, Warren S. *Twentieth-Century Short Story Explication*. Shoe String. pp. 366. $49.50. ISBN 0 208 02340 2.

Wallace, Gavin, and Randall Stevenson, eds. *The Scottish Novel since the Seventies*. EdinUP (1993). pp. 282. $24.50. ISBN 0 7486 0415 4.

Watts, Steven. *The Romance of Real Life: Charles Brockden Brown and the Origins of American Culture*. JHUP (1994). pp. 246. $35.95. ISBN 0 8018 4686 8.

Weber, Elisabeth, ed. Jacques Derrida. *Points: Interviews, 1974–1994*. StanfordUP. pp. 499. $55. ISBN 0 8047 2395 8.

Weiner, Alan R., and Spencer Means. *Literary Criticism Index*. 2nd edn. Scarecrow (1994). pp. 580. $62.50. ISBN 0 8108 2665 8.

Wells, Stanley, ed. *Shakespeare Survey 46: Shakespeare and Sexuality*. CUP (1994). pp. 220. $69.95. ISBN 0 521 45027 6.

Whalen, Richard F. *Shakespeare: Who Was He? – The Oxford Challenge to the Bard of Avon*. Praeger (1994). pp. 208. $19.95. ISBN 0 275 94850 1.

Wiggins, Kayla McKinney. *Modern Verse Drama in English: An Annotated Bibliography*. Greenwood (1993). pp. 184. $59.95. ISBN 0 313 28929 8.

Williams, Delmus E., John M. Budd, Robert E. Martin, Barbara Moran, and Fred Roper, eds. *For the Good of the Order: Essays in Honor of Edward G. Holley*. JAI (1994). pp. 370. $73.25. ISBN 1 55938 752 1.

Index I. Critics

Authors such as A. S. Byatt and Anita Desai, who are both authors of criticism and subjects of discussion, are listed in whichever index is appropriate for each reference.

Index II. Authors and Subjects Treated

Notes

1 Material which has not been seen by contributors is not indexed.
2 Authors such as A. S. Byatt and Anita Desai, who are both authors of criticism and subjects of discussion, are listed in whichever index is appropriate for each reference.
3 Author entries have subdivisions listed in the following order:

> (a) author's relationship with other authors;
> (b) author's relationship with other subjects;
> (c) author's characteristics;
> (d) author's works (listed alphabetically).

4 A page reference in **bold** represents the main entry for that particular subject.